法医损伤病理学

迈克尔·J·史克朗姆
加拿大安大略省伦敦市健康科学中心与
西安大略大学病理学系

大卫·A·拉姆齐
加拿大安大略省伦敦市健康科学中心与
西安大略大学临床神经病理学系

陈忆九　黄平　主译
司法鉴定科学研究院

上海科学技术文献出版社
Shanghai Scientific and Technological Literature Press

主 译
陈忆九　黄　平

译 者
（以姓氏笔画为序）

于笑天（司法鉴定科学研究院）	王金明（司法鉴定科学研究院）
王　磊（苏州市公安局）	邓恺飞（司法鉴定科学研究院）
田志岭（司法鉴定科学研究院）	刘宁国（司法鉴定科学研究院）
托　娅（上海健康医学院）	孙　杰（司法鉴定科学研究院）
吕叶辉（上海健康医学院）	杨明真（司法鉴定科学研究院）
李正东（司法鉴定科学研究院）	李成志（浙江大学）
邹冬华（司法鉴定科学研究院）	张　吉（司法鉴定科学研究院）
张建华（司法鉴定科学研究院）	张　慧（司法鉴定科学研究院）
陈　敏（司法鉴定科学研究院）	邵　煜（复旦大学）
林汉成（复旦大学）	秦志强（司法鉴定科学研究院）
钱　辉（司法鉴定科学研究院）	董贺文（司法鉴定科学研究院）
简俊祺（绍兴文理学院）	黎世莹（司法鉴定科学研究院）

译者序

面对涉及损伤的死亡案件，法医对死亡原因的判断离不开对损伤成伤机制、致伤物推断、损伤时间推断等的研究。即使死亡原因显而易见，也决不能忽视对成伤机制的具体分析，以免先入为主而得出差之毫厘谬以千里的结论。相信对成伤机制理清头绪之时，死亡原因也随之迎刃而解。

而纵观法医损伤病理学的发展历程，其主要建立在大量的案例实践基础之上，可以说是一门典型的经验性学科。因此，快速掌握各类损伤的特点对从事法医病理学专业的相关人员极为重要。如今虽不乏法医病理学相关专著，但针对法医损伤病理学研究的权威书籍寥寥无几。Michael J. Shkrum 和 David A. Ramsay 两位法医学专家合著的《法医损伤病理学》一书，可谓该领域的权威著作。该书着眼大局、着手细节，几乎覆盖了所有法医损伤死亡案件的内容，并给予了系统性阐述，为法医在从事损伤案件尸检时提供了有效的实践指导。值得一提的是，本书旁征博引，每一章节，甚至每一句话均有综述、案例报道等文献资料支撑，并配以案件现场、尸体解剖、组织病理学切片等高清照片，有助于读者对损伤有更为直观、系统的认识。因此，本书的中文译本具有极高的科学价值和现实需求。

本书的翻译和出版离不开团队的通力合作。每一章节均由富有经验的法医病理及医学英语专业学者参与翻译和校对，力求做到信、达、雅。希望这一历时近三年的译本能让广大学者对法医损伤病理学有更为深入的了解，从而胸有成竹地解决各类损伤案件。一言以蔽之，相信本书能成为各位案头的工具书，时翻时新，常翻常新，读后能深刻体会编者对待科学严谨求实的态度。

本书的出版得到了国家重点研发计划"司法鉴定创新技术研究与应用示范"项目（2016YFC0800700）、国家自然科学基金（81722027）的大力支持，本书出版得到了司法鉴定科学研究院（司法部司法鉴定重点实验室、上海市法医学重点实验室）的资助，并有幸与原著者 Michael J. Shkrum 博士和 David A. Ramsay 博士结下深厚友谊，再次表示衷心感谢。

陈忆九　黄平
2020 年 10 月

译者介绍

陈忆九

研究员，主任法医师，法医病理学专家，博士研究生导师，享受国务院特殊津贴。

1984年上海医科大学毕业后留校在法医学系工作，1990年获医学硕士学位。1997年起在司法鉴定科学研究院从事鉴定与研究工作。兼任上海市司法鉴定协会法医病理专业主任委员、中国法医学会法医病理专业委员会副主任委员、上海市人身伤害专家委员会委员、全国刑事技术标准化技术委员会法医检验分技术委员会副主任委员、中国实验室国家认可委专门委员会委员。主持科技部、国家自然科学基金、省（部）级科研项目10余项，发表学术论文90余篇，主编、主审专著5部，参编专著10部。2009年被司法部授予首届全国司法鉴定先进个人称号。

黄 平

研究员，主任法医师，法医病理学专家，硕士研究生导师。

2008年西安交通大学获法医学博士学位，2007年赴美国约翰霍普金斯大学交流学习，2009年起在司法鉴定科学研究院从事法医病理学的科学研究与鉴定工作。Forensic Imaging、Forensic Science International Synergy杂志国际编委。兼任上海市医学会医疗事故技术鉴定专家，国家自然科学基金优秀青年项目获得者。主持或参与多项国家和上海市项目。在国内外学术刊物上发表论文50余篇，主编专著1部，参编专著3部。2013年获上海市青年岗位能手称号，2016年获上海市科技进步二等奖。

序

当得知本书将成为一本权威的教科书,以供中国法医病理学者和鉴定人使用时,我们倍感荣幸。这一成就离不开司法鉴定科学研究院和上海科学技术文献出版社的通力合作。在此,我们对陈忆九教授和黄平博士及其翻译团队的不懈努力表示由衷感谢。

撰写本书的初衷是为了描述常见的法医学损伤"征象"或特征,并提供导致这些特征的常见及不常见原因的详细展示,这从章节标题可见一斑。本书每章内容不仅来自我们的实践经验,还基于经广泛同行评议的文献知识。这种通过定期回溯医学文献加以补充的循证方法,在日常实践中持续为我们的专家意见提供支撑,特别是对具有鉴定难度的或看似匪夷所思的案件。在探讨或调查涉及损伤的死亡案件时,均需采用此方法。为了正确解释尸检时观察到的所有损伤成因,需在死亡情况、死后时间间隔、医疗干预、疾病以及其他发现的基础上对法医学死因调查和尸体解剖的各个步骤进行客观、确定性的评估。

法医病理学实践离不开终身学习以积累经验。随着知识日新月异的发展,传统观念必将面临挑战。我们希望本书能激发读者在法医病理学探索之旅中开辟出新的道路。

万克尔·J·史克朗姆,医学博士(Michael J. Shkrum, MD)
大卫·A·拉母齐,全科医学博士(David A. Ramsay, MB ChB)

Preface

We are honoured that our textbook – "Forensic Pathology of Trauma: Common Problems for the Pathologist" – will be an authoritative textbook for learners and practitioners of forensic pathology in the People's Republic of China. This is a great achievement that could only have reached fruition through collaboration with the Academy of Forensic Science and the publisher, the Shanghai Scientific and Technology Literature Press. We extend our thanks to the dedicated efforts of the Professor Yijiu Chen and Dr. Ping Huang and their translation team.

When we wrote this book, our aim was to " ⋯ describe common medicolegal 'syndromes' or trauma patterns, which are exemplified by the chapter titles, and to provide comprehensive coverage of both common and uncommon causes of these patterns." The topics in each chapter were based on not only our experience but also the knowledge in the extensive peer-reviewed literature provided in each chapter. This evidence-based approach continues to support our expert opinions in our daily practices, supplemented by regular review of the medical literature, especially for challenging or puzzling cases.

This approach is required in any discussion or investigation of a fatality in which there has been physical trauma. An objective, but critical, evaluation during each step of a medicolegal death investigation and autopsy of a death due to injury is required in order that the significance of any observed trauma is correctly interpreted in the context of the circumstances of the death, postmortem interval, medical interventions, disease and other findings arising from the postmortem examination.

The practice of forensic pathology is a life-long learning experience. Traditional concepts are meant to be challenged and even changed by the evolution of new knowledge. We hope that this textbook will inspire its readers to blaze new paths in their journey in the field of forensic pathology.

Michael J. Shkrum, MD
David A. Ramsay, MB ChB

前　言

　　法医病理学主要任务是通过收集和分析与尸体有关的证据来分析死亡原因。对死亡原因的充分认识有助于法医进一步明确死亡方式，并给司法人员在执法过程中提供必要的法庭证据。对于死亡原因和死亡方式鉴定，不同司法调查机构有着不同的职责，包括向家属解释死亡原因、降低同类型的死亡发生率、拘捕与死亡相关的犯罪嫌疑人。

　　法医最重要、最常见的任务是调查死因不明的案件。然而，死亡原因较易明确，大多数由于损伤引起（损伤是指那些对机体产生伤害的暴力性因素）。《法医损伤病理学》旨在为法医在损伤案件的尸检中提供有价值的建议和信息，并为损伤案件的尸检提供分析思路。通常法医在实践中重点关注的问题是死亡原因，而忽视了损伤的重要性，本书的初衷是让法医在实践中除了明确死亡原因外，还要在尸检中更加关注损伤本身，避免出现认识和判断上的错误，同时应解决以下问题：①死者个体身份识别；②死亡时间推断；③致命伤环境重建；④致伤工具推断；⑤引起和掩饰损伤的因素分析等。

　　本书将在不同章节中详细描述实践中各类损伤的典型特征，同时对各类损伤的原因做出详尽的分析和解释，并提供了大量现场和损伤照片。然而由于篇幅有限，本书难以覆盖涉及损伤的全部内容，但本书提供的大量信息足以让法医在实践中充分地了解和认识损伤，在工作中能得心应手地处理各类损伤案件，避免出现判断性错误。

　　《法医损伤病理学》一书不仅有助于从事一般医学解剖的病理学医生对损伤的理解和认识，而且也会为那些期望从事法医事业的人带来极大的帮助。

万克尔·J·史克朗姆，医学博士
大卫·A·拉母齐，全科医学学士
钱辉　王金明　译

致 谢

诚挚感谢为此书付出过巨大努力和无私奉献的人。加拿大伦敦市健康科学中心病理学系 Lisa Noseworthy 和 Paula Miller 担任本书的编委会秘书，西安大略大学病理学系 Kris Milne 负责损伤照片的收集和整理，西安大略大学病理学系原毕业生 Kris Milne 从事本书的文字整理工作，伦敦市健康科学中心图书馆管理员 Linda Crosby 和 Wendy Tippin 为本书参考文献进行了大量的检索工作。本书也分别得到了安大略省首席法医官 Barry McLellan 博士、安大略省西北和西南地区地方法医官 David Legge 和 Thomas Wilson 博士的实践与理论支持。感谢那些从事死亡案件调查工作的法医和现场调查员为本书所做的艰辛工作；感谢加拿大安大略省汉密尔顿市法医中心 David King、Chitra Rao 博士及加拿大安大略省多伦多市法医中心 Michael Pollanen 博士为本书提供了大量的损伤照片；感谢伦敦市健康科学中心病理学系主任 Bertha Garcia 博士对本书的帮助、关心和支持；尤其要感谢在伦敦市和南安大略省与我们一同从事多年法医工作的同事们，感谢他们极大的耐心和无私的奉献精神。

——Michael J. Shkrum, David A. Ramsay

诚挚地感谢加拿大安大略省伦敦市的两任前首席法医官 Marvin Smout 和 Douglas Mills 博士，正是他们培养了我对法医病理学产生极大的兴趣；感谢北卡罗莱纳州前任首席法医官 Page Hudson 博士和现任首席法医官 John Butts 博士长期以来对我孜孜不倦的教导；感谢西安大略大学工程科学系多学科事故研究团队的 Kevin McClafferty、Paul Tiessen 以及 Robert Green 和 Edwin Nowak 博士，是他们让我更加深入地认识和理解交通事故损伤；感谢加拿大道路安全及车辆管理局碰撞调查研究所主任 Alan German 博士为本书提供了丰富的交通安全信息资料。

——Michael J. Shkrum

感谢我的同事 L. C. Ang 博士长期以来对我从事法医神经病理学工作的支持和帮助，感谢 J. Keith 博士为本书神经病理学照片给予了极其建设性的建议。感谢我的秘书 Lynn James 多年来精心细致的协助。还要感谢 J. Z. Young 教授和 M. R. Matthews 博士，他们教会我去思考和坚持；感谢 D. I. Graham 教授让我走进神经病理学的殿堂；感谢 I. D. Melville 博士，正是他们的人格魅力一直激励我至今。

——David A. Ramsay

目 录

序 ········ iii
前言 ········ v
致谢 ········ vii

第 *1* 章
系统性尸体检验——风险管理 ········ 1

第 *2* 章
死后尸体变化——"绝佳的伪装者" ········ 24

第 *3* 章
窒息 ········ 66

第 *4* 章
温度损伤 ········ 187

第 *5* 章
水中尸体 ········ 255

第 *6* 章
穿透性损伤——近距离火器创 ········ 307

第 *7* 章
穿透性损伤——锐器损伤 ········ 371

第 *8* 章
钝器损伤——包括航空器、火车和机动车辆损伤 ········ 421

第 *9* 章
颅脑损伤及脊柱损伤 ········ 551

第 *10* 章
神经源性猝死 ········ 637

第1章
系统性尸体检验——风险管理

概述

　　尸体检验是法医学死因调查的基础。尸体检验能否解决案件涉及的有关死亡原因、个体识别、损伤方式等诸多问题,取决于法医能否系统掌握尸体检验的程序与方法。系统性尸体检验是法医工作的必要环节,包括案情收集、尸表检验、尸体解剖及提取合适的人体组织样本供进一步辅助检测。法医最终出具准确的尸体检验报告应反映其在尸体检验过程中关注的各个方面,并阐明最重要的问题——死亡原因。法医在尸体检验过程中须注意各个环节的潜在风险,因为任何一个风险因素都会影响法医学调查的最终结果。

　　关键词: 法医病理学; 尸体检验; 风险管理

1 导言

　　法医是接受过系统医学培训和教育的尸体检验专家(1),能从尸体检验中获取有效的证据信息,并应用这些信息来解决法医学问题。法医在尸体检验的基础上,结合其他调查结果综合分析后得出鉴定意见,并有义务确保鉴定意见正确合理、有据可依,从而对死者家属和社会负责(1-5)。

　　尸体检验的关键是明确死因,这需要法医对死亡案件进行调查并提供鉴定意见(2,6,7)。尸体检验(需获得死者家属或法律的授权同意)不仅需要明确死因,还需要研究疾病的发生发展过程,对临床诊断的准确性和治疗的有效性进行评价,同时研究临床治疗与病理学改变之间的关系,用于医务人员教育和医学研究(2,6,8-14)。总之,法医学尸体检验必须解决五个"w"(表1-1)(15)。

　　法医病理学是一门研究疾病如何导致猝死、外部暴力因素如何引起致命性损伤的学科(4)。尸体检验能提高死因鉴定和死因统计的准确度(2,12,14,22,26-28)。研究表明,至少10%的死者存在与死亡相关的疾病,如果能在生前发现这些疾病并通过治疗手段进行干预,就可能提高患者的生存概率(6,14,29-33)。

尸体检验是法医学死因调查的重要组成部分。法医须经过相关培训、经验积累来应对死因调查过程中出现的各种问题(13,34)。为保持高水平的法医学调查能力,法医须参加同行能力评议、自我评估和继续教育培训(33)。专业能力指通过系统尸体检验完成鉴定并做出准确意见的能力,是鉴定质量的保证(1,6,35)。对损伤案件中出现的各类问题,法医须对损伤的病理学变化有全面、系统的认识(36)。Hirsch指出"部分法医认为损伤的病理学变化很简单,存在这样的观念是由于没有见过损伤的病理学改变,或对损伤的病理学变化没有深入思考"(36)。

表1-1 尸体检验的授权和五个"W"

	临床尸体检验	法医学尸体检验
授权(13,16-21)	通常需要死者家属或法定代理人同意	由法律强制规定 由司法管辖范围所决定——验尸官、法医或其他法律授权人员
"Why?"——死亡原因	主要关注点	主要关注点
"Under what circumstances?"——死亡方式(2,6,8,13,22)	自然死亡,如因疾病或衰老而死亡	死亡原因有助于判断死亡方式 **正常死亡** • 因疾病引起的猝死 • 任何一种可以导致死亡但未被医生诊断出的疾病 **意外死亡** • 未预料到的、非故意的行为所造成的死亡 **自杀** • 蓄意对自己施加暴力造成的死亡 **他杀** • 蓄意谋害他人导致死亡 **不确定类型** • 用于确定死亡方式的信息不充分或不完整(如死亡事件存在冲突的因素、仅存骨骼残骸)
"Where?"——现场(2,10,23)	医院 其他健康护理机构 家(很少见;接受姑息治疗的慢性病患者可能死于家中,但需要确保死亡环境中无可疑之处)	任何地点 可能不止一个现场——死者被发现的地点、死者实际受伤或死亡的地点、死者最后被看到活动的地点

续表

	临床尸体检验	法医学尸体检验
"Who?"——个体识别(2, 13, 20, 24, 25)	通常死者身份明确 尸体检验前需要确认 • 医院的标示腕带(手腕、脚踝) • 标示牌(运尸袋、脚趾) • 通过审查医院病历可知	对医疗服务机构中死亡的案件进行调查时,个体识别同临床尸体检验 **推断死者身份的方法** • 肉眼观察 • 通过衣物和随身物品辨认 • 通过环境信息辨认(如封闭公寓中的独居者) • 通过身体特征辨认(年龄、人种、性别、体重) **确证死者身份的方法**——对具有独特性的个体生前/死后信息进行同一认定 • 指纹 • 牙科学检查 • 影像学检查 • 特殊的身体特征(如纹身、瘢痕、手术瘢痕、畸形等皮肤特征) • DNA
"When?"——死亡时间(见第 2 章)	参考临床宣告的死亡时间 由目击者提供准确的死亡时间(如在心肺复苏过程中)	由可信的目击证人提供准确的死亡时间 没有目击证人在场的死亡:通过死后尸体的变化推断死亡时间(尸僵、尸斑、尸温、尸体腐败情况可辅助推断死亡时间)

2 系统性尸体检验

在鉴定实践中,法医并非独自工作,需要与侦查人员进行充分的讨论与交流(13)。系统性尸体检验要求有效整合调查过程中所获取的各种信息(图 1-1)(4)。通过系统性尸体检验可获得关于死亡原因、死亡机制、死亡方式的正确结论(13, 22, 37)。偏离侦查操作标准的行为,无论有意为之还是无心之举,都会增加法医学死因调查失败的风险。死因调查的周期同样取决于案情背景,例如,在对身份不明的遗骸进行死因调查时,调查周期可能会相当漫长。

3 尸体检验中的心理学

对于非正常死亡的案件,利用心理学可辅助确定死者的死亡方式(37-43)。这种方法特别适用于怀疑自杀但缺乏现场调查证据的案件。通过询问死者的家人、朋友、同事、医生和其他相关人士,调查者可深入了解死者临死前的心理状态和行为,从而分析其自杀原因(参阅第 3 章标题 14 [44])。

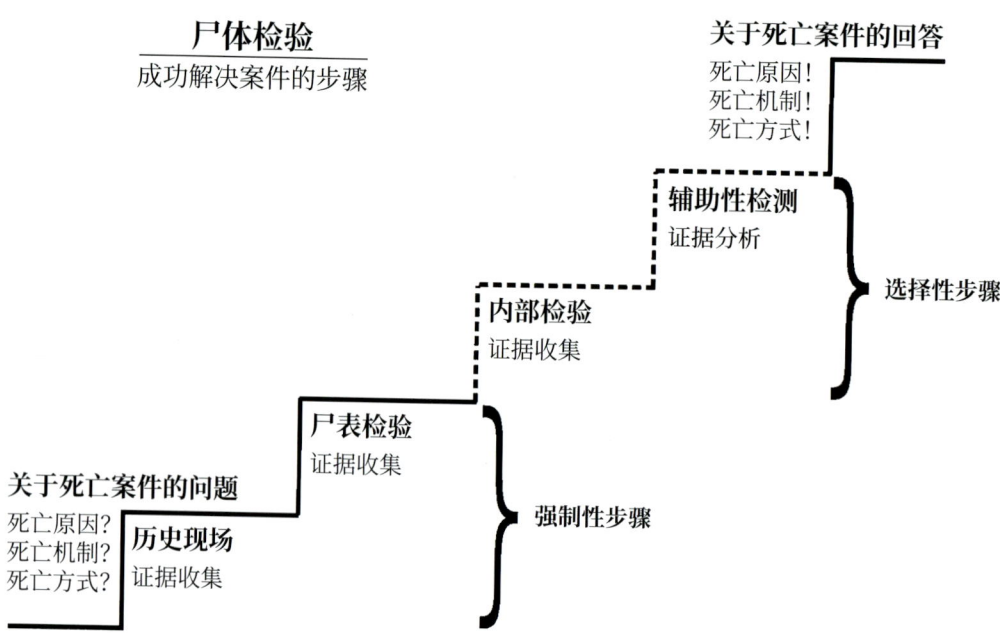

图 1-1 尸体检验：完成法医学死因调查所必须的调查步骤

4 现场("地点")

4.1 死亡现场

如果法医不在死亡现场开展尸体检验工作,会导致死亡调查存在潜在风险(15,23)。法医有时不需要或不能参与现场调查,因此现场调查员(侦查员、警察、消防员等)就需要在尸体检验之前将所获得的关于死亡现场和证人证言的资料以各种方式(图表、照片、视频和数码影像等)提交给法医(13,23)。

如果法医被要求进行现场勘查,法医需要记录死亡地点、现场人员和到达现场的时间。在现场调查中,法医需要将注意力集中在检查尸体上,还需要对与损伤、死因相关的现场环境(如地面上的血迹、药物、医疗用具等)进行检验。调查员通过询问死者家属和目击证人来获得死者信息(如医疗情况、精神状态、家庭成员和工作经历等)。如果死者生前在医院接受过治疗,病史材料对死因鉴定就尤为重要了,法医可以通过函件的方式要求医院提供病史材料。值得注意的是,任何抢救工作都可能造成人为损伤(参阅第3章标题2.6;第8章标题6.2)。死者的初始位置和观察到的死后变化需要被及时记录(13)。应注意不能过早地移动尸体。因为如果在现场过早或不恰当地移动尸体,将破坏调查结果间的关联性,如死后尸体变化受到影响会干扰死亡时间推断的准确性、现场证据收集不全会导致无法准确判断死者的个人财物和衣着完整性,以及造成死后人为现象的发生等。在现场调查过程中,法医要对在转运

第1章 | 系统性尸体检验——风险管理

过程中可能遗失的微量物证(如头发、纤维)进行采样,对能证明死者身份的信息进行搜寻,对死者的损伤进行总体评估(13,23)。对可疑的死亡案例,需用密封的运尸袋保护尸体,直到被送至尸体检验中心进行详细检查。

4.2 医院治疗

非暴力性死因可以是暴力性案件中患者的直接死因(如外伤入院的患者因肺动脉栓塞形成而死亡,肺动脉栓塞是外伤的并发症)。先前的暴力事件引起一系列病理生理改变,最终导致患者死亡(如患者因多发伤入院,治疗过程中采用固定体位,导致静脉血液高凝和淤滞;参阅标题11[20,22])。

对于外伤入院的患者,因非暴力性死亡原因导致的迟发性死亡案件,法医需要认识以下情况:

- 临床医生可能会忽略死亡案件中存在的法律问题,因此针对这类案件必须通知法医进行调查。
- 对外伤入院的患者在治疗过程中因并发症(直接死亡原因)而死亡的案例,需要鉴别该并发症是由治疗行为还是由自身疾病所引起(36)。

对于外伤引起的迟发性死亡案件,特别是在重症监护病房治疗过程中死亡的案例,法医在尸体检验之前需全面、充分、细致地审查病历,否则会影响死因鉴定结果,既无法准确解释临床问题,也无法满足法医学调查需求。法医在整理和审查病历时需要足够的耐心,不能遗失任何记录。法医需要有能力认识和理解外伤引发的各类并发症。

4.3 重症监护过程中出现的并发症

成人呼吸窘迫综合征(adult respiratory distress syndrome, ARDS)是一种以渐进式呼吸衰竭为主要临床表现的疾病,常在异常刺激后数小时内发病(45),典型表现为低氧血症(需要机械通气)、肺顺应性下降、无法通过心衰解释的双侧胸片改变(46)。外伤可以通过触发炎症反应的方式单独引起ARDS,也可以协同其他危险因素(如休克)引起ARDS。

弥漫性肺泡损伤(diffuse alveolar damage, DAD)是一种肺非特异性病理反应,可见于肺炎、误吸、败血症、休克、创伤、脂肪栓塞、烧伤、溺水(参阅第3章标题3.4;第4章标题5.2和表4-1;第5章标题4.4;第8章标题12.1[46])。在弥漫性肺泡损伤进展的过程中,炎症细胞介质会损伤肺泡上皮细胞和肺细胞。疾病在一周内进入渗出性阶段,尸体检验表现为肺体积增大和实变,呈红色水肿样改变(45);镜下见肺泡内纤维蛋白膜沉积(透明膜形成),肺间质可见以单核细胞为主的炎症细胞浸润,小血管内可见纤维素性血栓。发病一周后,疾病进入增生性阶段,Ⅱ型肺泡上皮细胞增生,肺间质和肺泡间隔中成纤维细胞增生。疾病向肺间质纤维化进展,最终可形成蜂窝肺。

全身炎症反应综合征(systemic inflammatory response syndrome, SIRS)是

一种以体温升高或降低、心率加快、呼吸急促、白细胞计数升高或降低、出现类似脓毒血症为主要临床表现的疾病(47,48)。各种感染或非感染因素、组织缺血性疾病(如感染、外伤、烧伤)可激活全身免疫反应,从而导致 SIRS。在血液循环中可检测到各类炎症介质,如 C 反应蛋白(49)。

SIRS 可继发多器官功能衰竭(multi-organ failure, MOF)/多器官功能障碍综合征(multiple organ dysfunction syndrome, MODS)/多器官功能衰竭综合征。多发伤患者常常可以通过治疗从休克状态中恢复,但几天或几周后会发展成多器官功能衰竭(50,51)。有研究表明,超过 60% 的迟发性创伤死亡案例中存在 MOF(52)。有学说认为,MOF 的发病机制可能是内源性肠道菌或其产物从缺血的肠管进入血液循环,从而导致了脓毒血症,所以临床治疗过程中出现血培养阳性的结果并不是器官衰竭的原因,而是器官衰竭的结果(51,53)。尽管死者生前出现脓毒血症,尸体检验过程中也可能无法发现相应的感染灶(53)。与临床治疗过程中的血液培养相比,死后血培养提供的信息有限(54)。血液标本污染或濒死期菌血症都可能导致血液培养出现假阳性结果,假阳性概率随死后时间的延长而升高(54)。

当患者凝血指标和血小板计数正常却出现 Frank 出血时(指粪便中带血,与消化道出血形成的柏油样便相反,Frank 出血可能由痔疮或肛裂引起),说明患者的失血已经通过外科手段得到治疗。弥散性血管内凝血(disseminated intravascular coagulation, DIC)指各种有创或无创原因引起的血管内皮或组织损伤,从而导致凝血系统被激活的病理过程(55)。血小板和凝血因子的减少会导致患者出现出血倾向。在皮肤穿刺点、手术切口和手术区域有血液渗出,全身出现皮肤瘀斑/紫癜,内部器官(如脑、肾、胃肠道、肺)出现点状出血上述现象均提示患者存在凝血障碍。因为全身微循环中出现血小板-纤维蛋白血栓,所以全身多器官内可同时出现缺血性改变。应用肝素和纤溶治疗可消除血栓,所以光镜下可能无法观察到血栓。

大量输血可能导致患者出现凝血功能障碍(56,57)。由于浓缩红细胞中无活性血小板,也会使某些凝血因子(如凝血因子Ⅴ、Ⅷ)明显减少。当输入红细胞和血小板时,血液被稀释,同样会导致患者凝血功能下降。当患者失血时,组织间液从细胞间质向血管内转移,凝血因子被进一步稀释,从而影响凝血功能。当静脉快速输入未回温的血液和静脉输液时治疗过程或麻醉使患者活动减少均会加快患者热量的散失,当患者体温过低时,凝血相关酶的活性也会降低,从而加剧凝血功能障碍。组织缺血所引起的酸中毒和输入库存过久的血也会进一步降低血小板活性、加剧凝血功能障碍。

5 个体识别("他是谁?")

准确识别未知个体或人体组织的必要性如下:
- 通知家人处理财产、进行保险索赔。

- 完善官方个人档案（如死亡证明、警方记录）。
- 询问/讯问潜在的目击者和与死者相关的人员。
- 是刑事和民事法律程序的一部分(6, 25)。

个体识别错误可能导致以下后果：
- 在错误的个体上进行未授权的尸体检验。
- 对误认死者的家庭造成精神损害，引起相应行政处理的延迟。
- 浪费前期调查资源。
- 影响相关法律进程。

不完整、不准确或误导性信息可造成个体识别错误。该问题通常发生在大型尸体检验中心，由于法医处理案件过于匆忙，误读尸体识别标签，从而导致个体识别错误。

可通过让熟悉死者的人直接观察辨认死者以实现个体识别，该方法只能用于推断死者身份，但在大多数案件中已可以满足个体识别的要求。在死亡现场或尸体检验中心都可对尸体进行观察和辨认(6, 13)。如果已在死亡现场完成了个体识别，需提交给法医相关的个体识别信息（如识别腕带等）。如果没有个体识别信息，法医在尸体检验之前应要求现场调查员再次观察、辨认尸体，并确定死者身份。如果让家属对死者进行重复辨认，会增加其精神负担。尸体运送服务机构有时可以帮助确定死者身份。如果死者生前在医院接受过治疗，则可通过医疗机构的识别腕带确定死者身份。

与死亡现场的环境和性质相比，停尸房具有更好的照明、通风和安全性，因此更适合在此进行尸体辨认工作。尸体辨认工作需要在独立的房间中进行，这样可以保护辨认者的隐私，同时不影响停尸房的正常工作。辨认工作可在尸体检验之前或之后进行。尸体检验人员需做好准备，并清洁整理尸体的颜面部，如清洁血迹和组织碎片(58)。对颜面部严重受损的尸体需进行面部重建。在清洁和重建死者面部之前，法医需准确记录任何可能引发变化的因素。对腐败、炭化或大面积创伤的死者，法医需评估死者面部是否能够被辨认。辨认尸体时，如果严重外伤导致死者面部难以被家属接受时，法医可在尸体面部覆盖毛巾。

通过死者面部照片辨别死者身份是代替直接观察辨认的一种方法。在这种情况下，需要以合适的角度对死者面部进行拍照，这样可减小因死者面部损伤使家属产生负面情绪(25)。辨认者需在合适的人员陪同下进行尸体辨认。尸体辨认过程需要尸体检验中心的工作人员、医院护士、社会工作者、牧师、警察和法医共同参与。即使尸体被妥善保存，辨认者依然会感到压力，观察时的情感会影响判断，且尸体通常没有表情，从而导致辨认者无法作出准确的判断。辨认者的抗拒情绪和主观预设会使尸体辨认更加复杂。在极少数情况下，辨认者会出于欺诈目的故意错认尸体（如隐瞒犯罪、保险欺诈）。不以辨认为目的的尸体查看（如情感、习俗、宗教行为）更适合在殡通过辨认死者的衣着和随身物品确认死者身份是另一种推断方法。死者的衣着可能具有独特性，准确描述死者的衣着可帮助最后看到死者生前活动的家属辨认其身份。故意放置或替换随身物品可能会误导个体识别。衣物和随身物品可能在现场就被移除或变动(25)。在现场或尸体检验中心对尸体进行个体识别时，应对死者钱包中的物品和随身佩戴的珠宝进行记录，在移交警察和殡仪馆时需清点确认这些贵重物品，以规避因物品被盗或遗失而引起的法律风险。法医需要在尸体检验报告中记录死者衣着和随身物品。

需要进行个体同一认定的情形如下：
- 没有人可直接观察、辨认出死者身份。
- 通过推断的方法(辨认尸体、衣着和随身物品、环境)所获得的结果不明确。
- 因为尸体腐败、炭化、白骨化或严重外伤，导致无法使用推断方法进行个体识别。

个体同一认定是通过比较死者生前记录和死后尸体检验发现的证据来而得出结论(表1-1)，需要使用多种来源的信息(如警方的指纹记录和失踪人口报告、牙科记录、医院或其他医疗机构的记录、影像学照片、实验室记录和样本、就业及服役记录)。

6 尸表检验

观察、记录和分析体表损伤是法医最重要的基本功(13)。相对于临床尸体检验，法医学尸体检验更关注体表损伤(13)。不准确或不完整地记录体表损伤会给法医的鉴定工作带来巨大风险(15)。

很多法医专注于尸体内部器官检验而忽视体表损伤检查，这样往往无法准确解释致命伤是如何产生的，即成伤机制。皮肤损伤对死因有重要的提示作用。在大多数案件中，皮肤损伤没有显著的病理生理学意义，但可提示丰富的侦查信息，如推断致伤物、判断损伤是否为致命伤。如外伤患者曾入院治疗，法医需审查所有医疗记录。任何治疗和诊断手段、心肺复苏操作都能改变原有损伤或产生新的体表或内部损伤(参阅第3章标题2.6；第8章标题6.2)。仔细审查医院病史材料可帮助法医详细描述体表损伤。临床医疗行为，特别是治疗严重外伤者，能提示致命伤。皮肤损伤经常被忽视，医疗人员常常没有足够的法医学经验来分析、辨认体表损伤(如火器伤；参阅第6章标题17)。法医需注重细节，任何看似微不足道的损伤都可能有重要的法医学意义，不注重细节会影响法医在死因调查和司法程序中的可信度。

有效记录损伤要使用各种方法。叙述性描述往往内容过长，描述损伤不够连贯，相应的记录也会难以理解。人体结构图可反映文字描述内容(图片优于文字描述[59])，使用人体结构图记录损伤可反映人体损伤的整体特征，特别是能突出损伤程度。人体结构图有助于对尸体检验照片进行解释，在诉讼程序中可代替照片作为展示性证据，以避免照片过于"真实"而刺激陪审员(20,59)。尸体检验照片可帮助现

第 1 章 │ 系统性尸体检验——风险管理

场调查员、其他专家和法官理解案件的调查结果(2,20,59)。尽管照片不是法医学报告的一部分，但作为一种直观记录可帮助起草法医学报告(20,59)。照片不能代替细致、准确的报告。法医要亲自或指导他人拍摄高质量的尸体检验照片，同时需保证照片能准确反映尸体检验过程中发现的结果(20,59)。对于犯罪案件，照片需作为证据体现在尸体检验报告中。

6.1 尸表检验中的摄影，可用于案件诉讼和教学

- 如果存在相关行政和法律规定，法医可能在患者死亡前(如在重症监护室中)就被要求对损伤进行检验，这种情况下需有警方陪同并拍照。
- 患者因外伤入院治疗并死亡，警方在经授权的调查过程中会拍摄外伤随时间变化的一系列照片，从而协助法医进行鉴定。
- 某些案件中(如可疑死亡、谋杀、工业事故)，法医要审查警方提供的现场图片(照片、数字图像、影像)。
- 当尸体被封存时，法医需对冰柜门和装尸袋上的封条进行拍照。
- 当照片被用于教学或其他展示时，要遮盖尸体的面部和外阴部。
- 对尸体面部进行拍摄时，要拍摄面部原始状态和清洁后状态，用于损伤记录和个体识别(参阅标题 5)。
- 对照片背景中不需要的细节部分可适当裁剪(如血迹、手套、工具、解剖台上的反光)。
- 对尸体的衣着进行整体拍摄。
- 脱去尸体上各层衣物后再次对尸体进行整体拍摄，在脱衣过程中应避免破坏衣物，要记录衣物上的破损和外来异物(13)。
- 应对损伤与相应位置的衣物破损进行对比(13)。
- 对被水或血液浸染的衣物，需干燥后再次检验。
- 对尸体进行全身拍摄时，需拍摄尸体正面和背面，记录抢救和其他医疗操作留下的痕迹(59)。
- 应特别关注某些检验结果——异物、具有辩识性的个体特征及损伤(59)。
- 对损伤的原始状态和清洁后状态都要拍照，以确保不遗漏特征性痕迹(如血迹分布)(59)。
- 阴性结果同样需要记录(如双手无损伤)(59)。在完成手部检验后再采集指纹。
- 近距离拍摄特写照片时，需放置比例尺并标注解剖号。
- 比例尺方向要与损伤方向一致(比例尺应位于损伤下方)，特别是在拍摄近距离特写时(59)。
- 在拍摄近距离特写照片时应包含明确的解剖学标志，如果拍摄范围内缺乏相应的解剖学标志，则需拍摄整体照片。

- 如果法医和警方分别拍摄了照片，需要进行刑事诉讼的案件则需按目录和顺序整理照片。
- 个人拍摄的解剖照片同样可以作为证据使用。

6.2 仅限尸表检验的尸体检验

死者家属可能会反对尸体解剖，仅允许法医进行尸表检验，但法医学死因调查不是一个妥协的过程（参阅标题7和参考文献8,13,19和60-62）。法医在收集到足够案件资料的基础上，可以仅进行尸表检验（63）。这种检验方式只限于某些特定案件（如自缢、严重外伤）。有研究表明，大部分外伤死亡的案件中，急救部门在抢救过程中就已将该损伤评估为致命伤。这个阶段中误诊与临床过程无关（64）。尽管缺乏住院患者内部器官损伤的解剖结果（14,62,65），但详细的临床病史材料（如交通事故中的受害者）和临床检查结果（如实验室检查、放射学检查）可提供足够的信息以作出死因鉴定。如果死因不够明确，就必须进行尸体解剖（66）。某些原本考虑为正常死亡的案件经过解剖后会发现是非正常死亡（67-71）。文献中报道过很多类似情况（63,67,69,70）。有研究评价了利用病史和尸表检验结果作出死因和死亡方式鉴定的准确性，并用尸体解剖进行了验证（63,67,68）。其中，对于大部分非正常死亡和交通事故案件，基于病史和尸表检验作出的死因是准确的（63）。然而，在约三分之一的死亡案件中，尸体解剖和单纯尸表检验的结论不一致（63,68）。另有研究表明，单纯尸表检验无法诊断某些特定的损伤（如颅骨骨折）（67）。确定死亡与损伤间的因果关系在刑事侦查、工伤赔偿案件、保险索赔中十分重要（37,72）。

有研究曾报道利用影像学检查方法检验尸体并确定死因，包括外伤死亡的案件（24,60,73）。死后影像学检查可有效帮助检验损伤（参阅第5章标题14.8；第6章标题16；第6章标题9），但使用复杂的影像学技术也有缺点，如成本较高、需要设备和影像学专家辅助诊断等。

7. 内部检验

对临床治疗中死亡且不需要法医学死因调查的案件，在大多数司法管辖范围内，法医只有在死者家属或代理人授权下才能进行尸体检验（10,18,60,62,82）。死者家属或主治医师可提出对尸体进行检验（包括内部检验）的委托。除非直接与死者家属接触，通常法医需要通过医护人员（一般是主治医师）来获取死者家属对进行尸体检验的知情同意（2,8,10,12,21）。负责与死者家属沟通的临床医务人员要了解死者家属的想法，让他们清楚尸体检验的价值并理解尸体检验的制度与流程（2,30）。医院会向死者直系亲属提供信息以帮助他们理解尸体检验的流程（2）。

临床获得许可的尸体检验的数量正逐年下降。在美国，从1972年到1992年，医院死亡案例中获得许可的尸体检验的百分比已低于10%（6）。导致医源性尸体检验比例下降部分因素有：

- 医院死亡案件无须通过尸体检验获得死亡证明(6,30,83)。
- 诊断性检查手段降低了尸体检验需求(2,6,30,84)。
- 病理医生由于种种原因对尸体检验存有矛盾情绪[如认为尸体检验对职业的收入、晋升和教育价值无益;反感尸体检验;担心感染;有病理学层面无挑战性;无临床价值;独立于其他临床部门等(1,6,14,30,83)]。
- 有一种观点认为死者家属的情绪会阻碍法医获得解剖许可(9,14,21,85)。
- 死者家属可能对解剖有负面认识[认为死者已经"饱受折磨"(14)]。
- 其他家属也可能反对解剖(83)。
- 主治医师与家属间对尸体检验的意义缺乏交流。
- 医科大学关于法医学的教育在减少,这意味着将来接受过法医学培训的专业人士会减少(1,2,6,8,9,12,14,21)。

尸体检验除了具有科学和教育的价值外,还可帮助死者家属从丧亲之痛中恢复过来(2,58,85,86),了解死因可以抚慰死者家属的情绪。确定死者生前的医疗行为是否合理可以减轻家属的怀疑和内疚(1,9,14,85,87)。

一项为期20年的研究表明,美国总体死亡人数中需要进行法医学尸体检验的比例稳定在5%(6)。法定义务决定某些死亡案件必须对死者进行尸体检验,其中大部分非正常死亡的案件需要对死者进行尸体检验(60,62)。在法医学死因调查期间,法医有对死者暂时的专有权,直到尸体被交还家属(16,21,88)。如果需对死者进行尸体检验,病理科医生可担任法医工作或协助法医尸检(8,13)。司法管辖范围的性质决定了哪些案件必须对死者进行尸体检验(如谋杀案件)。临床尸体检验中遇到的问题也同样存在于法医鉴定案件中(62)。病理科医生往往需要通过法医告知死者家属尸体检验的意义和必要性。尽管在法律层面,刑事案件中法医可对尸体进行强制性检查,但法医仍有义务向死者家属解释尸体检验的本质和必要性(62)。有研究表明,如果死者死因不明或案件存疑,同时不存在人寿保险理赔争议时,在阐明尸体检验的必要性后,死者的直系亲属会更愿意接受法医学尸体检验(12,58,83)。

7.1 受限的尸体检验

在临床上,死者家属为确定死因可授权尸体检验,包括检查所有体腔、解剖所有器官、保留组织和体液用于显微镜检查和其他用于病理学诊断的试验(2,14)。家属可要求尸体检验仅限于某些器官和体腔。

在法医学实践中,能够实施系统性尸体检验是最为理想的,但系统性尸体检验会被限制或调整。鉴定工作繁重、专业人员与辅助人员数量不足限制了尸体检验的完整性(20)。从其他国家运回的尸体身上可能只有切口,而没有进一步解剖(89)。为满足宗教要求,尸体检验需遵循某些特定步骤[如东正犹太教要求原位检查器官并返还尸体的体液(60)]。法医学尸体检验可能被要求及时返还尸体,尤其会受到来自殡仪馆的压力,所以尸体检验可能只限于确定死亡原因,而且必须及时完成报告。然而，受限制的尸体检验会导致某些与损伤有关的调查结果被忽视（如未诊断出脑部肿瘤引发的机动车碰撞事故），或者无法回答其他与损伤无关的问题（90）。

内镜检查作为一种尸体检验技术已经开始被应用（91,92）。穿刺检查（如对脑池进行穿刺以排除蛛网膜下腔出血）已经应用于尸体检验中，但是需排除出血不是人为操作引起（60）。

7.2 器官获取

由于严重外伤入院治疗的患者，其家属可能会被建议捐献患者器官，家属会因为替逝去的亲人做了有价值的事情而倍感安慰（93）。法医学死因调查优先于器官捐献，尤其是怀疑存在犯罪行为的案件（94）。尽管死者家属会对法医施加压力，要求尽快开展器官移植，但是器官捐献需要以不影响收集案件证据（如毒物分析样）、记录和解释损伤、确定死亡原因为前提（95）。警方、法医、医务人员和器官移植团队之间需要进行充分的沟通与交流（94,99）。单独性损伤（如头部外伤）可允许器官捐献和局部解剖同时进行。影像学检查和其他检查（如超声心动图）可以排除其他损伤。除了进行尸体检验，法医在去除角膜前应检查眼睛，为器官移植提供意见，并检验不用于移植的器官（95）。如果器官获取过程中法医不在手术室内，外科医生需要确认任何被移除的器官均不存在损伤（94）。

7.3 器官保留

在通过尸体解剖提取人体组织与器官后，最终的尸体检验报告以肉眼大体检查和尸表检查（如严重创伤）作为鉴定依据。某些案件组织器官的样本不需要进行甲醛固定和显微镜检查。但是，对于一些可能需要进行法律诉讼程序的案件，死者的器官和标本均会被固定保存，用于后期的回顾性审查。

基于不同的司法制度，家属拥有对死者尸体的处理权（如埋葬）（16,17,88,93,100）。对英国布里斯托尔案（1991—1995年，在布里斯托尔皇家学院医院接受心脏手术的30—35名儿童由于医院护理和管理不当而死亡）调查表明，父母对于保留孩子的器官表示不满，这促使皇家学院的病理医生重新评估临床尸体检验和法医学尸体检验中的器官保留政策（17,21,101）。相似的问题同样发生在澳大利亚（2）。在其他司法制度体系中，也有很多公众人士和专业人员意识到这一问题。

皇家学院的病理医生提出了关于器官保留的指南：
- 器官保留必须是合法的，例如，器官保留不能违反法律或习俗。
- 器官保留的原因必须合理、合规，在法律和临床实践中是正当的。

临床尸体检验需要至少一位死者家属知情同意，并授权法医保留器官，用于诊断、教学和研究（2,7,18,101）。虽然法医学尸体检验根据案件性质可进行强制性尸体检验（2,21），但对于这两种类型的尸体检验，在器官保留方面都存在限制（14）。保留器官是为了明确死因，而且希望能够被死者家属接受（7,103）。回顾某些案件，保留器官有时不能帮助法医确定死亡原因 [如检验脑组织未发现解剖学上的死亡原因

第 1 章 │ 系统性尸体检验——风险管理

时(101,104)〕。如果死者家属能意识到尸体检验的重要性,则更能接受尸体检验(8)。医生在查房或教学中使用尸体组织和解剖照片时更需要谨慎(21)。家属对科学研究持有各种看法,也许有些家属并不反对以诊断为目的合理使用人体组织器官(12,14),但是进行教学、科学研究时必须取得伦理许可(2)。某些研究需要使用一些常规解剖不会提取的器官(如脊柱),这时需要获得家属的特殊许可(21)。将组织器官用于教学和科学研究等任何超出死因调查范围时都需要经过法医学上级主管(如首席验尸官、首席法医)和死者家属的同意。

- 有相关指南提出,除非尸体检验程序是由法律直接规定的,否则在保持诊断准确性的基础上可满足死者家属的需求(7)。

不同意保留组织和器官可能导致尸体检验不完整(7,21)。法医在这种情况下可以拒绝检验尸体(103)。解剖中如果发现意外结果,法医应有保留尸体组织器官的选择权(7)。满足死者家属的需求意味着给尸体检验工作增加管理负担(21)。

- 皇家学院的病理医生还建议,如果尸体检验由法律直接规定,在可能且可行的情况下,尸体检验之前,死者家属应该被充分告知尸体检验的过程和目的(7)。

病理医生应当告知法医具体器官的保留情况(2,7,21,103),该信息也同样要告知死者家属(17)。家属可能会对某些器官(如大脑)赋予象征性的、宗教或文化意义,且该器官可能并不需要用于制作组织切片后进行显微镜观察(2,8–11,14,17,19,21,83,101,106,107)。但在很多外伤案件中,需保留脑组织来确定死亡原因(7,17,103)。

案件中可能会出现关于组织销毁方法和器官保留时间的问题(7)。家属可能要求将器官放回死者体内或要求殡仪馆对器官单独举办葬礼;然而,如果某个器官与损伤和死亡原因有关,该器官则应保留至相关法律问题得到解决或案件判决后。

8 检查

8.1 显微镜检查

对组织进行显微镜检查是法医最常用的手段(7)。不是所有法医学尸体检验都需要进行显微镜检查,而且这个尺度是模糊的,取决于法医的谨慎程度和案件性质(6,13,20,35)。选择性取材,而不是对所有器官进行常规取材,可缩短案件处理时间(11,14,108)。在某些外伤案件中,缺少显微镜检查就无法明确死亡原因(如外伤性轴索损伤)。根据死亡情况,甲醛固定的组织只能保留有限的时间,之后需被处理掉。组织切片和蜡块作为病历的一部分可被存档(7,21)。如果诉讼程序中提出要求,其他法医可通过检查组织切片来确认或修改最初的检验结果(6,21,103)。

8.2 其他标本

识别和收集证据是法医学鉴定的重要环节,是与临床尸体检验的重要区别之处(6,13,20)。在某些案件中(如怀疑药物或毒物摄入过量),当尸体检验没有阳性发现,又缺乏大体肉眼所见或组织病理学改变时,毒物分析可帮助明确死亡原因。收集毒物分析样本(通常是血液和尿液)时,为了保证证据的延续性,样品管和容器需要被密封。密封标签上应注明死者姓名、案件编号、日期、密封时间和样本类型,参与尸体检验的法医和警察需要在上面签名。如果受害人在医院存活一段时间后死亡,体内乙醇(酒精)或其他药物已被代谢,则对尸体样本进行毒物分析也就没有意义了(109)。如果在死者入院时就采集血液样本则应对该血样进行毒物分析。法医或专业人员(病理专家、警察)需要通知实验室保存这些样本。在这种情况下,医院需要有一个跟踪系统来确保证据的延续性(13,35)。如果不需要进一步分析,这些样本就可被储存起来。

在外伤案件中被手术切除的标本,法医同样需要对其进行检验。

9 尸体检验的观摩者

临床尸体检验的目的之一是教学,各类医务人员和实习生都会参与其中。法医学尸体检验同样具有教学意义,但因为保密条款,特别是在刑事侦查案件中,参与此类尸体检验的人员会受到限制(105)。

10 临床尸体检验结果和报告的发布

在临床尸体检验完毕后,病理医生可能会与主治医生交流并提供初步的尸体检验结果("临时解剖诊断")。临床医生会将这些结果告知死者家属。在显微镜检查和其他检验结束后,病理医生会出具最终尸体检验报告,通常会交给家庭医生和主治医生。报告复印件会被存入医院病案中,在适当授权下,供其他医生和家属使用。在完整的法医学尸体检验结束后,病理医生会将尸体检验结果告知法医。在这个阶段,任何关于死因的结论都不全面,要等待进一步检验(15,22)。如果法医和家属认为不存在医疗事故,病理医生可与死者的临床治疗小组讨论死因问题。

尸体检验报告作为保密文件,只能发送给法医或其他法律规定的当事人。由于司法体制不同,报告分发也有所不同(13)。如果刑事案件尚未判决,家属获取检验结果的请求可能会被推迟。法医需要就尸体检验报告与死者家属直接交流(110)。这份报告同样可以被各种机构和其他专家查看(110)。外伤患者的死因报告在送达医院病案室(可被临床医生查看)之前需要经法医确认。死者家属希望尽早获得尸体检验报告(110)。对于院内死亡案例,美国病理学会推荐在30天内完成常规案件的尸体检验报告,90天内完成复杂案件的尸体检验报告(111)。如果家属和其他有关当事人提出要求,法医需要加快完成报告。拖延完成报告不但会影响家属的情绪,还会延误各种经济和法律程序(如保险索赔、刑事诉讼程序)。

尸体检验报告的格式可以多样,但某些内容是固定的(34,111),除死者的姓名和检案编号外,尸体检验报告还需记录执行尸体检验的解剖医生、助手和其他参与人员。

组织尸体检验的法医同样需要被记录。还需记录的信息有尸体检验的地点和案件开始的日期。接下来是尸表检验,包括个体识别的方法和对死者衣着的记录。对于院内死亡案件,对死后变化(尸僵、皮肤发绀、尸体腐败)的记录更加重要。近期的治疗措施也要加以详细记录。内部检查需要对器官进行系统的检验。法医学尸体检验报告需要有尸表和内部损伤的描述,损伤记录要连贯,不能分散,这样才便于阅读。使用参考图表有助于理解观察到的损伤。任何收集的证据和照片都要记录,特别是怀疑存在犯罪行为的死亡案件。组织切片和摄影照片更具客观性,有助于案件的回顾审查,特别是刑事案件。

11 死亡原因:"底线"

因自然疾病而死亡的案件,其个体的尸体检验会提供很多病理学诊断。尽管对于这类案件,尸体检验报告并不一定要求明确死亡原因,但是需记录尸体检验过程中的异常发现并提供信息(解剖学诊断)给主治医生,以帮助医生向家属解释患者的死因。病理医生有责任提供尸体检验信息,以帮助法医准确判断死亡原因和方式。

Adelson 对死亡原因做出以下定义:"引起一系列短期或长期生理紊乱,并最终导致死亡的损伤、疾病或两者的结合"(112)。如果损伤或疾病迅速导致死亡并且没有后遗症或并发症,这一类损伤或疾病就是直接死因(112,113)。如果损伤或疾病出现并发症(如肺炎),则并发症为直接死因,而与并发症有直接因果关系的最初因素称为根本死因(参阅标题4.2;参考文献112,113)。如果患者存活了一段时间,临床医生可能会忽视与死亡相关的损伤,病理医生在审阅医院病案时需注意这个问题并与法医联系。

在大多数损伤案件中,死亡原因的确定都较为容易[如机动车碰撞所致的严重颅脑损伤(104,113-117)]。在死者发生损伤后仍存活一段时间的案件中,死亡原因则可能是多因素的(114),任何一个因素对个体死亡都有"贡献"(113,116)。某些条件或疾病可促进死亡发展,影响疾病进程,但与直接死因并不直接相关。这些"重要的"因素可能影响死亡原因[如死亡原因:硬脑膜下出血;重要的因素:急性乙醇中毒、糖尿病(113)]。

根据现场和死亡环境调查可以解释尸体检验中发现的潜在死亡原因(115,116)。法医和其他调查人员会提供外伤死亡案件的案情资料,然而这些资料可能来源于不可靠的证人证词,而且会发生变动(116)。

在多数案件中,通过系统性尸体检验就可得出死亡原因、死亡机制和死亡方式(图1-1)。在某些损伤案件中,死亡原因无法确定(没有解剖学上的死亡原因)。尸体腐败可影响对软组织损伤的检验(参阅第2章;参考文献115)。调查信息不全、对调查结果判断错误和不完整的尸体检验都可能导致无法确定死亡原因(114)。在个别损伤案件中,即使通过系统性尸体检验也无法确定解剖学上的死亡原因(参阅第

8 章标题 6.4.3；参考文献 118）。

邹冬华　孙杰　译

参考文献

1. Pellegrino, E. D. The autopsy. Some ethical reflections on the obligations of pathologists, hospitals, families, and society. Arch. Pathol. Lab. Med. 120:739–742, 1996.
2. Royal College of Pathologists of Australasia. Policy Statement: Autopsies and the use of tissue removed from autopsies 1993 (revised 2002). Available at: www.rcpa.edu.au/applications/DocumentLibraryManager2/upload/Complants%20Handling.pdf. Last accessed: May 15, 2006.
3. Richards, S. J. Confidentiality and the medical report. Med. Sci. Law 25:96–102, 1985.
4. Wright, R. K., Tate, L. G. Forensic pathology. Last stronghold of the autopsy. Am. J. Forensic Med. Pathol. 1:57–60, 1980.
5. Rose, E. F. Pathology reports and autopsy protocols: confidentiality, privilege, and accessibility. Am. J. Clin. Pathol. 57:144–155, 1972.
6. Burton, E. C., McPhee, S. J. Autopsy overview. In: Collins, K. A., Hutchins, G. M., eds. Autopsy Performance and Reporting. College of American Pathologists, Northfield, IL, pp. 3–12, 2002.
7. Royal College of Pathologists. Guidelines for the retention of tissues and organs at post-mortem examination. 2000.
8. Lynch, M. J. The autopsy: legal and ethical principles. Pathology 34:67–70, 2002.
9. Brown, H. G. Perceptions of the autopsy: views from the lay public and program proposals. Hum. Pathol. 21:154–158, 1990.
10. Svendsen, E., Hill, R. B. Autopsy legislation and practice in various countries. Arch. Pathol. Lab. Med. 111:846–850, 1987.
11. Roberts, W. C. The autopsy: its decline and a suggestion for its revival. N. Engl. J. Med. 299:332–338, 1978.
12. Sanner, M. A. In perspective of the declining autopsy rate. Attitudes of the public. Arch. Pathol. Lab. Med. 118:878–883, 1994.
13. Randall, B. B., Fierro, M. F., Froede, R. C. Practice guideline for forensic pathology. Members of the Forensic Pathology Committee, College of American Pathologists. Arch. Pathol. Lab. Med. 122:1056–1064, 1998.
14. Royal College of Pathologists. The autopsy and audit. 1991. Available at www.rcpath.org/resources/pdf/AUTOPSYANDAUDIT.pdf. Last accessed: May 15, 2006.
15. Moritz, A. R. Classical mistakes in forensic pathology (Am. J. Clin. Pathol., 1956). Am. J.

Forensic Med. Pathol. 2:299–308, 1981.

16. Matthews, P. Whose body ? People as property. Curr. Leg. Probl. 36:193–239, 1983.
17. Brazier, M. Human tissue retention. Med. Leg. J. 72:39–52, 2004.
18. Skegg, P. D. The use of corpses for medical education and research: the legal requirements. Med. Sci. Law 31:345–354, 1991.
19. Schmidt, S. Consent for autopsies. JAMA 250:1161–1164, 1983.
20. Butts, J. D. Postmortem examination: A statement of principles of the medicolegal autopsy. In: Fierro, M. F., ed. CAP Handbook for Postmortem Examination of Unidentified Remains. Developing Identification of Well–Preserved, Decomposed, Burned and Skeletel Remains. College of American Pathologists, Northfield, IL, pp. 11–46, 1998.
21. Royal College of Pathologists. Human bodies, human choices: response from the Royal College of Pathologists. 2002. Available at www.rcpath.org/resources/pdf/human–bodies.human–choices.college–response.pdf. Last accessed: May 15, 2006.
22. Hanzlick, R. L. Medical certification of death and cause–of–death statements. In: Froede, R. C., ed. Handbook of Forensic Pathology., College of American Pathologists, Northfield, IL pp. 31–48, 2003.
23. Ernst, M. F. Medicolegal death investigation and forensic procedures. In: Froede, R. C., ed. Handbook of Forensic Pathology. College of American Pathologists, Northfield, IL, pp. 1–10, 2003.
24. Schmidt, G., Kallieris, D. Use of radiographs in the forensic autopsy. Forensic Sci. Int. 19:263–270, 1982.
25. Fierro, M. F. Identification. In: Froede, R. C., ed. Handbook of Forensic Pathology. Northfield, IL, College of American Pathologists, pp. 49–60, 2003.
26. Wagner, B. M. Mortality statistics without autopsies: wonderland revisited. Hum. Pathol. 18:875–876, 1987.
27. Cameron, H. M., McGoogan, E. A prospective study of 1152 hospital autopsies: I. Inaccuracies in death certification. J. Pathol. 133:273–283, 1981.
28. Kircher, T., Nelson, J., Burdo, H. The autopsy as a measure of accuracy of the death certificate. N. Engl. J. Med. 313:1263–1269, 1985.
29. Combes, A., Mokhtari, M., Couvelard, A., et al. Clinical and autopsy diagnoses in the intensive care unit: a prospective study. Arch. Intern. Med. 164:389–392, 2004.
30. McPhee, S. J., Bottles, K. Autopsy: moribund art or vital science? Am. J. Med. 78:107–113, 1985.
31. Goldman, L. Diagnostic advances v the value of the autopsy. 1912–1980. Arch. Pathol. Lab. Med. 108:501–505, 1984.

32. Goldman, L., Sayson, R., Robbins, S., Cohn, L. H., Bettmann, M., Weisberg, M. The value of the autopsy in three medical eras. N. Engl. J. Med. 308:1000–1005, 1983.
33. Sens, M. A., Fierro, M. F. Quality assessment and improvement in autopsy pathology. In: Nakhleh, R. E., Fitzgibbons, P. L., eds. Quality Improvement Manual in Anatomic Pathology. College of American Pathologists, Northfield, IL, pp. 97–111, 2002.
34. Burke, M. P., Opeskin, K. Audit in forensic pathology. Am. J. Forensic Med. Pathol. 21:230–236, 2000.
35. Froede, R. C., Graham, M. A. The medicolegal autopsy: format and quality assurance. In: Froede, R.C., ed. Handbook of Forensic Pathology. College of American Pathologists, Northfield, IL, pp. 11–22, 2003.
36. Hirsch, C. S. Forensic pathology and the autopsy. Arch. Pathol. Lab. Med. 108:484–489, 1984.
37. Curphey, T. J. Role of the forensic pathologist in the medicolegal certification of modes of death. J. Forensic. Sci. 13:163–176, 1968.
38. Weinberger, L. E., Sreenivasan, S., Gross, E. A., Markowitz, E., Gross, B. H. Psychological factors in the determination of suicide in self-inflicted gunshot head wounds. J. Forensic. Sci. 45:815–819, 2000.
39. Ritchie, E. C., Gelles, M. G. Psychological autopsies: the current Department of Defense effort to standardize training and quality assurance. J. Forensic. Sci. 47:1370–1372, 2002.
40. Diller, J. The psychological autopsy in equivocal deaths. Perspect. Psychiatr. Care 17:156–161, 1979.
41. Litman, R. E. 500 psychological autopsies. J. Forensic. Sci. 34:638–646, 1989.
42. Jobes, D. A., Berman, A. L., Josselson, A. R. The impact of psychological autopsies on medical examiners' determination of manner of death. J. Forensic. Sci. 31:177–189, 1986.
43. Danto, B. L., Streed, T. Death investigation after the destruction of evidence. J. Forensic. Sci. 39:863–870, 1994.
44. Jobes, D. A., Casey, J. O., Berman, A. L., Wright, D. G. Empirical criteria for the determination of suicide manner of death. J. Forensic. Sci. 36:244–256, 1991.
45. Travis, W. D., Beasley, M. B. The respiratory system. In: Rubin, E., Gorstein, F., Rubin, R., Schwarting, R., Strayer, D., eds. Rubin's Pathology—Clinicopathologic Foundations of Medicine. Lippincott; Williams and Wilkins, Baltimore, MD, pp. 583–658, 2005.
46. Garber, B. G., Hebert, P. C., Yelle, J. D., Hodder, R. V., McGowan, J. Adult respiratory distress syndrome: a systemic overview of incidence and risk factors. Crit. Care Med. 24:687–695, 1996.

47. Levy, M. M., Fink, M. P., Marshall, J. C., et al. 2001 SCCM/ESICM/ACCP/ATS/SIS International Sepsis Definitions Conference. Intensive Care Med. 29:530–538, 2003.
48. Boyd, O., Newman, P. Systemic inflammatory response. In: Webb, A. R., Shapiro, M. J., Singer, M., Suter, P. M., eds. Oxford Textbook of Critical Care. Oxford University Press, New York, pp. 918–920, 1999.
49. Foex, B. A. Systemic responses to trauma. Br. Med. Bull. 55:726–743, 1999.
50. Johnson, D., Mayers, I. Multiple organ dysfunction syndrome: a narrative review. Can. J. Anaesth. 48:502–509, 2001.
51. Bion, J. F. Multiple organ failure—pathophysiology. In: Webb, A. R., Shapiro, M. J., Singer, M., Suter, P. M., eds. Oxford Textbook of Critical Care. Oxford University Press, New York, pp. 923–926, 1999.
52. Sauaia, A., Moore, F. A., Moore, E. E., et al. Epidemiology of trauma deaths: a reassessment. J. Trauma 38:185–193, 1995.
53. Deitch, E. A. Gut failure: its role in the multiple organ failure syndrome. In: Deitch, E. A., ed. Multiple Organ Failure—Pathophysiology and Basic Concepts of Therapy. Thieme Medical Publishers, New York, pp. 40–59, 1990.
54. Wilson, S. J., Wilson, M. L., Reller, L. B. Diagnostic utility of postmortem blood cultures. Arch. Pathol. Lab. Med. 117:986–988, 1993.
55. Schwarting, R., Kocher, W. D., McKenzie, S., Alomari, M. Hematopathology. In: Rubin, E., Gorstein, F., Rubin, R., Schwarting, R., Strayer, D., eds. Rubin's Pathology—Clinicopathologic Foundations of Medicine., Lippincott; Williams and Wilkins, Baltimore, MD, pp. 1018–1123, 2005.
56. Armand, R., Hess, J. R. Treating coagulopathy in trauma patients. Transfus. Med. Rev. 17:223–231, 2003.
57. Phillips, T. F., Soulier, G., Wilson, R. F. Outcome of massive transfusion exceeding two blood volumes in trauma and emergency surgery. J. Trauma 27:903–910, 1987.
58. Plattner, T., Scheurer, E., Zollinger, U. The response of relatives to medicolegal investigations and forensic autopsy. Am. J. Forensic Med. Pathol. 23:345–348, 2002.
59. Davis, D. Forensic photography. In: Froede, R. C., ed. Handbook of Forensic Pathology. College of American Pathologists, Northfield, IL, pp. 459–464, 2003.
60. Mittleman, R. E., Davis, J. H., Kasztl, W., Graves, W. M., Jr. Practical approach to investigative ethics and religious objections to the autopsy. J. Forensic. Sci. 37:824–829, 1992.
61. Orlowski, J. P., Vinicky, J. K. Conflicting cultural attitudes about autopsies. J. Clin. Ethics 4:195–197, 1993.

62. Rho, Y. M. Medical examiner's authority: challenges to perform autopsies. N.Y. State J. Med. 81:1687–1688, 1981.
63. Vanatta, P. R., Petty, C. S. Limitations of the forensic external examination in determining the cause and manner of death. Hum. Pathol. 18:170–174, 1987.
64. Seow, E., Lau, G. Who dies at A&E? The role of forensic pathology in the audit of mortality in an emergency medicine department. Forensic Sci. Int. 82:201–210, 1996.
65. Albrektsen, S. B., Thomsen, J. L. Detection of injuries in traumatic deaths. The significance of medico–legal autopsy. Forensic Sci. Int. 42:135–143, 1989.
66. Clark, M. A. The value of the hospital autopsy. Is it worth the cost? Am. J. Forensic Med. Pathol. 2:231–237, 1981.
67. Virkkunen, M., Penttila, A., Tenhu, M., et al. Comparative study on the underlying cause and mode of death established prior to and after medicolegal autopsy. Forensic Sci. 5:73–79, 1975.
68. Nashelsky, M. B., Lawrence, C. H. Accuracy of cause of death determination without forensic autopsy examination. Am. J. Forensic Med. Pathol. 24:313–319, 2003.
69. Asnaes, S. Mortality statistics and autopsy: reliability of estimation of the mode of death in Copenhagen and a rural district of Sealand, Denmark. Forensic Sci. Int. 14:177–180, 1979.
70. Marshall, T. K. The value of the necropsy in ascertaining the true cause of a non–criminal death. J. Forensic. Sci. 15:28–33, 1970.
71. Asnaes, S., Paaske, F. Uncertainty of determining mode of death in medicolegal material without autopsy—a systematic autopsy study. Forensic Sci. Int. 15:3–17, 1980.
72. Asnaes, S. The importance of medico–legal autopsies. An analysis of the complex problems regarding damages. Forensic Sci. Int. 23:123–127, 1983.
73. Bisset, R. A., Thomas, N. B., Turnbull, I. W., Lee, S. Postmortem examinations using magnetic resonance imaging: four year review of a working service. BMJ 324:1423–1424, 2002.
74. Thali, M. J., Yen, K., Plattner, T., et al. Charred body: virtual autopsy with multi–slice computed tomography and magnetic resonance imaging. J. Forensic. Sci. 47:1326–1331, 2002.
75. Thali, M. J., Yen, K., Schweitzer, W., et al. Virtopsy, a new imaging horizon in forensic pathology: virtual autopsy by postmortem multislice computed tomography (MSCT) and magnetic resonance imaging (MRI)—a feasibility study. J. Forensic. Sci. 48:386–403, 2003.
76. Brookes, J. A., Hall–Craggs, M. A., Sams, V. R., Lees, W. R. Non–invasive perinatal

necropsy by magnetic resonance imaging. Lancet 348:1139–1141, 1996.

77. Thali, M. J., Schweitzer, W., Yen, K., et al. New horizons in forensic radiology: the 60–second digital autopsy–full–body examination of a gunshot victim by multislice computed tomography. Am. J. Forensic Med. Pathol. 24:22–27, 2003.

78. Aghayev, E., Thali, M., Jackowski, C., et al. Virtopsy—fatal motor vehicle accident with head injury. J. Forensic. Sci. 49:809–813, 2004.

79. Thali, M. J., Braun, M., Buck, U., et al. Virtopsy—scientific documentation, reconstruction and animation in forensic: individual and real 3D data based geo–metric approach including optical body/object surface and radiological CT/MRI scanning. J. Forensic. Sci. 50:428–442, 2005.

80. Yen, K., Vock, P., Tiefenthaler, B., et al. Virtopsy: forensic traumatology of the subcutaneous fatty tissue; multislice computed tomography (MSCT) and magnetic resonance imaging (MRI) as diagnostic tools. J. Forensic. Sci. 49:799–806, 2004.

81. Bolliger, S., Thali, M., Jackowski, C., Aghayev, E., Dirnhofer, R., Sonnenschein, M. Postmortem non–invasive virtual autopsy: death by hanging in a car. J. Forensic. Sci. 50:455–460, 2005.

82. Skegg, P. D. Criminal liability for the unauthorized use of corpses for medical education and research. Med. Sci. Law 32:51–54, 1992.

83. McPhee, S. J., Bottles, K., Lo, B., Saika, G., Crommie, D. To redeem them from death. Reactions of family members to autopsy. Am. J. Med. 80:665–671, 1986.

84. Anderson, R. E., Hill, R. B. The current status of the autopsy in academic medical centers in the United States. Am. J. Clin. Pathol. 92: S31–S37, 1989.

85. McManus, B. M., Wood, S. M. The autopsy. Simple thoughts about the public needs and how to address them. Am. J. Clin. Pathol. 106: S11–S14, 1996.

86. Forrest, G. C., Standish, E., Baum, J. D. Support after perinatal death: a study of support and counselling after perinatal bereavement. Br. Med. J. (Clin. Res. Ed.) 285:1475–1479, 1982.

87. Hirsch, C. S. Talking to the family after an autopsy. Arch. Pathol. Lab. Med. 108:513–514, 1984.

88. Skegg, P. D. Medical uses of corpses and the "no property" rule. Med. Sci. Law 32:311–318, 1992.

89. Lowe, J. W. A post–mortem examination was not done through a large autopsy incision. Med. Sci. Law 37:78, 1997.

90. Moar, J. J. Renal adenocarcinoma with tumour thrombi in the inferior vena cava and right atrium in a pedestrian motor vehicle accident fatality: case report and medicolegal

implications. Forensic Sci. Int. 95:183−192, 1998.

91. Avrahami, R., Watemberg, S., Daniels−Philips, E., Kahana, T,. Hiss, J. Endoscopic autopsy. Am. J. Forensic Med. Pathol. 16:147−150, 1995.

92. Taff, M. L., Boglioli, L. R. Endoscopy is not autopsy. Am. J. Forensic Med. Pathol. 17:86−88, 1996.

93. Perper, J. A. Ethical, religious, and legal considerations to the transplantation of human organs. J. Forensic. Sci. 15:1−13, 1970.

94. Davis, J. H., Wright, R. K. Influence of the medical examiner on cadaver organ procurement. J. Forensic. Sci. 22:824−826, 1977.

95. Jaynes, C. L., Springer, J. W. Decreasing the organ donor shortage by increasing communication between coroners, medical examiners and organ procurement organizations. Am. J. Forensic Med. Pathol. 15:156−159, 1994.

96. Sturner, W. Q. Can baby organs be donated in all forensic cases? Proposed guidelines for organ donation from infants under medical examiner jurisdiction. Am. J. Forensic Med. Pathol. 16:215−218, 1995.

97. Shafer, T. J., Schkade, L. L., Evans, R. W., O'Connor, K. J., Reitsma, W. Vital role of medical examiners and coroners in organ transplantation. Am. J. Transplant 4:160−168, 2004.

98. Shafer, T. J., Schkade, L. L., Siminoff, L. A., Mahoney, T. A. Ethical analysis of organ recovery denials by medical examiners, coroners, and justices of the peace. J. Transpl. Coord. 9:232−249, 1999.

99. Kramer, J. L. Decreasing the organ donor shortage. Am. J. Forensic Med. Pathol. 16:257−260, 1995.

100. Samuels, A. Whose body is it anyway? Med. Sci. Law 39:285−286, 1999.

101. Mason, K., Laurie, G. Consent or property? Dealing with the body and its parts in the shadow of Bristol and Alder Hey. Mod. Law Rev. 64:710−729, 2001.

102. Hudson, M. Rights of possession in human corpses. J. Clin. Pathol. 50:90−91, 1997.

103. Royal College of Pathologists. Guidance for retention of brain and spinal cord following post−mortem examination and where criminal proceedings are in prospect. 2002. Available at www.rcpath.org/resources/pdf/GUIDELINESBRAIN−ARNedited.pdf. Last accessed: May 15, 2006.

104. Patel F. Ancillary autopsy—forensic histopathology and toxicology. Med. Sci. Law 35:25−30, 1995.

105. Roberts, L. W., Nolte, K. B., Warner, T. D., McCarty, T., Rosenbaum, L. S., Zumwalt, R. Perceptions of the ethical acceptability of using medical examiner autopsies for research

and education: a survey of forensic pathologists. Arch. Pathol. Lab. Med. 124:1485–1495, 2000.
106. Boglioli, L. R., Taff, M. L. Religious objection to autopsy. An ethical dilemma for medical examiners. Am. J. Forensic Med. Pathol. 11:1–8, 1990.
107. Pellegrino, E. D. Moral and religious concerns about the autopsy. In: Collins, K. A., Hutchins, G. M., eds. Autopsy performance and reporting. College of American Pathologists, Northfield, IL, pp. 27–38, 2003.
108. Rosai, J. The posthumous analysis (PHA). An alternative to the conventional autopsy. Am. J. Clin. Pathol. 106: S15–S17, 1996.
109. Koskinen, P. J., Nuutinen, H. M., Laaksonen, H., et al. Importance of storing emergency serum samples for uncovering murder with insulin. Forensic Sci. Int. 105:61–66, 1999.
110. Adelson, L. The forensic pathologist. "Family physician" to the bereaved. JAMA 237:1585–1588, 1977.
111. Hutchins, G. M., Berman, J. J., Moore, G. W., Hanzlick, R. L., Collins, K. A. Autopsy reporting. In: Collins, K. A., Hutchins, G. M., eds. Autopsy Performance and Reporting. College of American Pathologists, Northfield, IL, pp. 265–274, 2003.
112. Adelson, L. The Pathology of Homicide. Charles C. Thomas, Springfield, IL, 1974.
113. Petty, C. S. Multiple causes of death. The viewpoint of a forensic pathologist. J. Forensic. Sci. 10:167–178, 1965.
114. Perper, J. A., Wecht, C. H. Medicolegal problems in determining cause of death in motor vehicle accidents. Leg. Med. Annu. 19–25, 1975.
115. Cordner, S. M. Deciding the cause of death after necropsy. Lancet 341:1458–1460, 1993.
116. Pollanen, M. S. Deciding the cause of death after autopsy—revisited. J. Clin. Forensic Med. 12:113–121, 2005.
117. Gee, D. J. Reaching conclusions in forensic pathology. Med. Sci. Law 35:12–16, 1995.
118. Bohrod, M. G. The meaning of "cause of death." J. Forensic. Sci. 8:15–21, 1963.

第2章
死后尸体变化——"绝佳的伪装者"

概述

人在死后尸体会发生降解,从而产生一系列变化。尽管会受到各种干扰因素的影响,但观察某些尸体变化依然是确定死亡时间最常用的方法。法医需要分辨死后尸体变化和人为改变,而尸体变化会影响损伤或产生类似损伤样改变。

关键词: 死后变化;尸僵;尸体保存;昆虫学

1 导言

法医参与调查的案件通常缺乏目击证人,且尸体常在死后一段时间才被发现。因此,法医会面临死后尸体变化和病理学检验结果被掩盖的情况,这些死后变化会影响法医对死亡原因的准确判断。同时,死后变化可能导致在解剖学层面不能查出死因死后变化还可产生类似损伤样的改变,从而误导案件调查方向。

某些尸体变化被认为在死后以恒定的速率发生(速率参数),因此,根据死后尸体变化规律可推断死亡时间。文学和影视作品在一定程度上夸大了死亡时间推断的准确性,实际上回顾分析过去50年的法医学教科书,可发现依据各种死后尸体变化的演变过程推断出的死亡时间并不精确,法医对死亡时间的判断依然只能估算(1–8)。法医在调查或审判过程中会被要求确定死亡时间,然而法医在判断死亡时间时依然面临着巨大的困难。

对从现场运回后再进行尸体解剖的案例,尸体检验过程中发现的死后变化会受到各种因素的干扰,如对尸体的处理、尸体被保存在停尸间冰柜中等,这些干扰因素会增加死亡时间推断的误差。现场是进行尸体检验并记录死后变化的最佳环境。

尸僵、尸斑、尸温变化、尸体腐败和胃排空都是典型的死后变化,且在死后会逐渐演变,这也是法医解剖的主要观察内容。其他检测参数,如玻璃体液中的钾离子浓度,会受到各种因素的影响(如生前浓度、两眼之间可能存在的浓度差异、肾功能的影响；参考文献9-17）。利用生物标志物来推断死后时间已经超出了正常法医病理实践的范围（18）。对各种观察结果进行综合分析可以提高死亡时间推断的准确性（19）。

2 尸僵

尸僵是由于个体死亡后三磷酸腺苷（ATP）减少，导致肌动球蛋白代谢停止，引起肌肉收缩的一种死后变化（20）。

2.1 平滑肌的参与

立毛肌（毛囊的平滑肌）的收缩表现为鸡皮样改变（图2-1）

- 意义
  ○ 死后暴露在低温环境中。

精囊（平滑肌）的收缩（4）

- 意义
  ○ 精囊收缩导致阴茎头部有微量精液排出，提示死者生前可能存在性行为（图2-2）。

虹膜的睫状肌在尸僵过程中会改变瞳孔大小。正常瞳孔直径在0.2-0.9厘米（平均为0.4-0.5厘米，或者约0.25英寸）。瞳孔不是一直呈圆形的，两侧瞳孔能相对独立地改变，从而表现出不同大小（图2-3）。

- 意义
  ○ 瞳孔的大小与死因无关，不同的瞳孔直径并不意味着头部损伤。

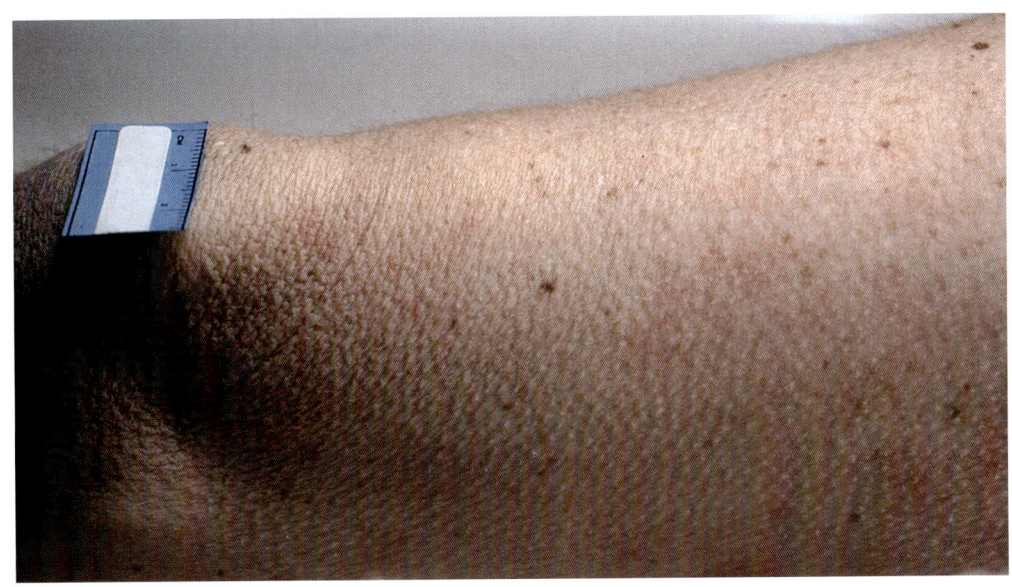

图2-1 尸体暴露于低温环境造成的皮肤鸡皮样改变。

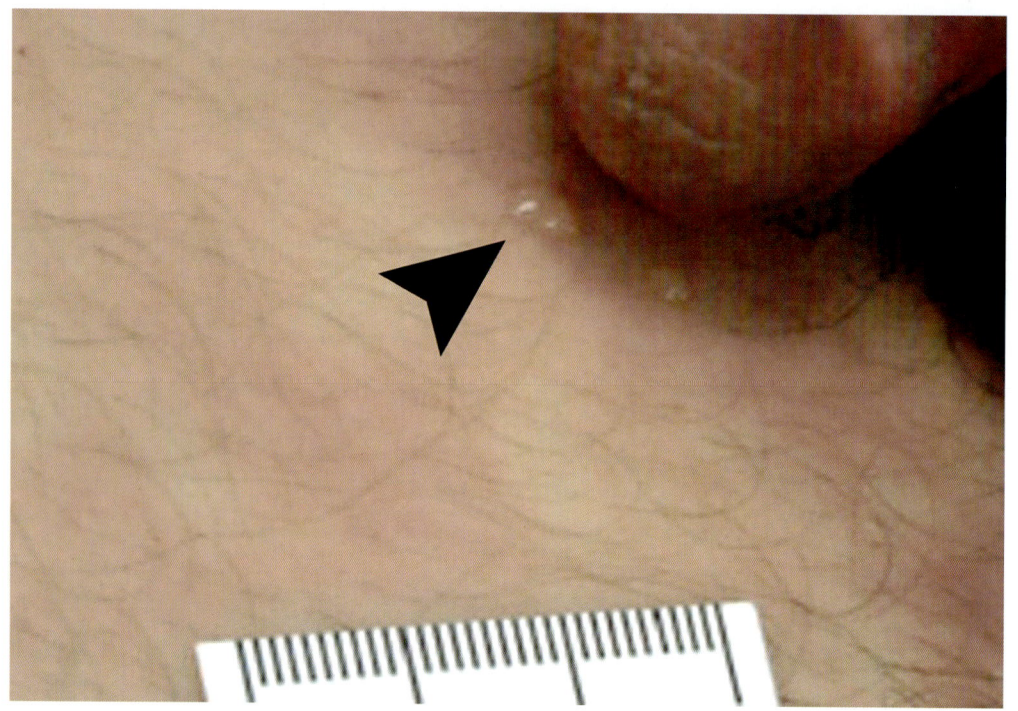

图 2-2　由于死后精囊收缩导致精液附着在大腿内部（三角箭头）。

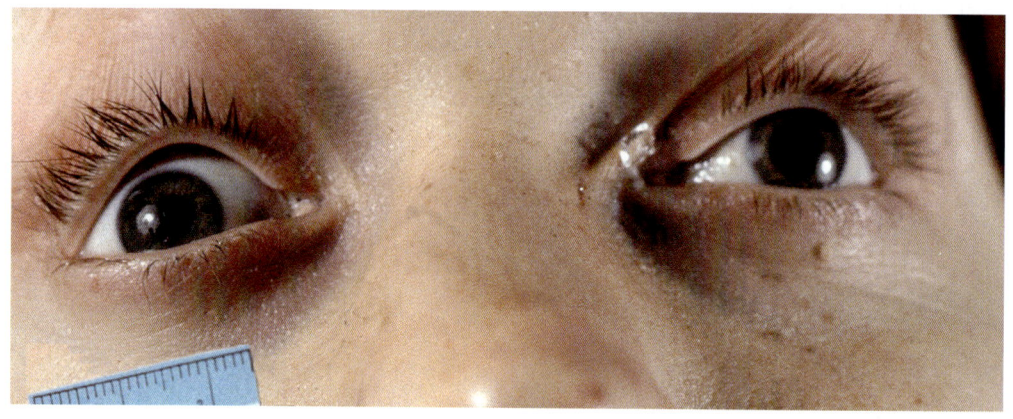

图 2-3　死后出现瞳孔直径不对称。

如果左心室心肌收缩，左心室壁会增厚，左心室腔中的血液含量就会减少。
- 意义
  ◦ 左心室壁肥厚明显。

2.2 骨骼肌的参与

骨骼肌的参与会引起关节僵硬，按以下顺序发展：
- 初始阶段肌肉会松弛（尸体痉挛例外）
  ◦ 在死后早期阶段，人体内储存的 ATP 可保证肌肉和关节松弛。这个阶段持续 0.5—7 小时[平均为 3±2 小时（7）]。
- 发生与发展
  - 人体所有肌肉同时开始形成尸僵，但小肌群的尸僵形成更快（20）。尸僵形成的速度不一定是恒定或匀速的（1,8）。尸僵开始形成于下颌关节，逐渐发展至上肢，然后至下肢。尸僵遵守 Nysten 规则（Nysten's law）：首先从咀嚼肌开始，然后是脸部、颈部、躯干和手臂，最后是腿部和脚部肌肉（7, 21）。用相关方法对关节进行检验以评估尸僵程度（如通过打开口腔来评估颞下颌关节，评估肘关节和踝关节的屈曲和伸展），可以将其分为没有尸僵、部分尸僵和完全尸僵。尸僵发展到全身所有关节需要 2—20 小时[平均为 8±1 小时（7）]。仰卧位的尸体会表现出轻微的肘关节和膝关节屈曲。尸僵会持续 24—96 小时（平均为 57±14 小时[7]）。
- 尸僵的消除（第 2 次松弛）
  - 尸僵的缓解和消除是由于肌动球蛋白连锁出现变性与分解。尸僵缓解和消除的顺序与发生的顺序相同。时间范围为 24—192 小时[平均为 76±32 小时（7）]。

以下各类内源性和外源性因素会影响尸僵的发展（22,23）：

（1）温度：尸体或环境温度升高会使尸僵发生变早，缓解速度加快（24）。尸僵发生变早是由于 ATP 的新陈代谢增快，尸僵缓解加快是由于肌动球蛋白连锁的快速变性所致。各种条件下的体温升高（如败血症、使用可卡因等）会加快尸僵发生，寒冷环境会使尸僵持续数天（25）。

（2）肌肉发达程度和体型：肌肉发达的死者尸僵出现得迟、程度强（3,26），尸僵缓解时间会延长（26）。老人、体弱者和婴幼儿的尸僵发生快、强度低、持续时间短。消瘦和肥胖死者可能不发生尸僵（1）。

尸僵从小肌群发展至大肌群可以用肌肉发达程度作为解释（21）。假设尸僵是一种生理化学过程并在所有肌肉同时开始发生，那么尸僵在小肌群中出现得更为迅速（如咀嚼肌）。动物研究表明咀嚼肌中 ATP 的下降速度明显快于大肌群（20,27）。尸僵发展的顺序同样可以通过关节周围的红、白肌纤维的比例来解释（21,27）。红肌纤维发生尸僵的速率明显快于白肌纤维（21）。人体的咀嚼肌比下肢肌群（如腓肠肌；参考文献 21）拥有更高比例的红肌纤维。

（3）生前肌肉收缩：死亡前的肌肉活动（如运动、癫痫）会促进尸僵（1）。尸体痉挛（死后抽搐、全身僵硬）是一种迅速发展的尸僵，通常出现于死亡过程中剧烈收缩的肌肉（图 2-4；参考文献 1）。尸体痉挛通常在死者非常兴奋和紧张的情况下发生。
- 意义
  - 在尸僵发生前，尸体可以被摆放成任意体位。
  - 一旦尸僵形成，尸体体位不会再随位置改变而变化（图 2-5）。

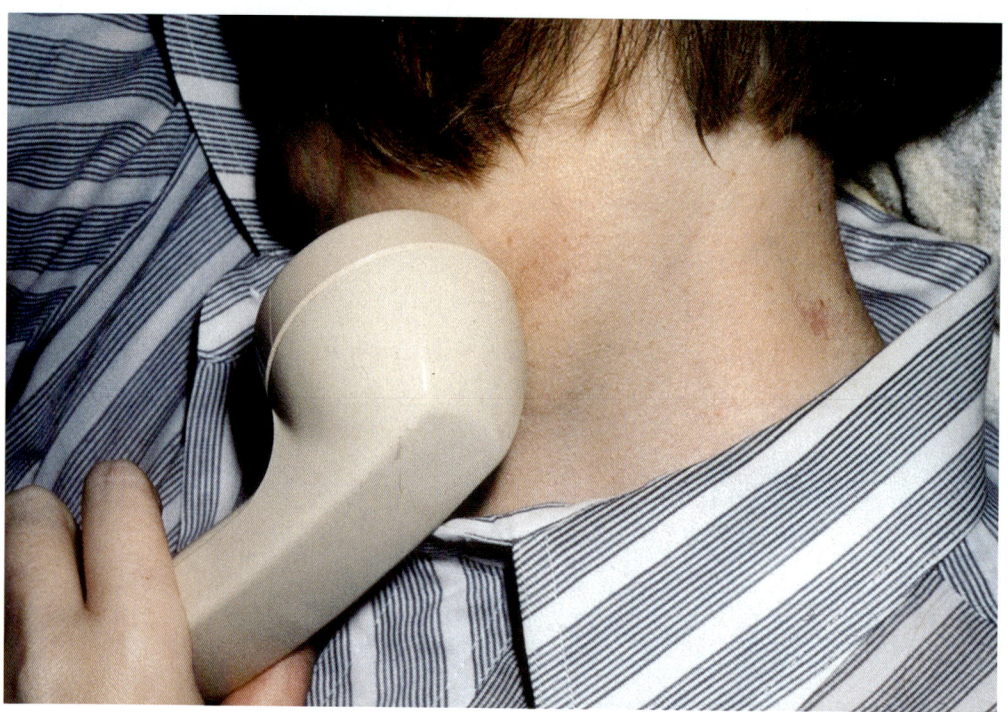

图2-4 尸体痉挛。猝死的死者手抓着电话。

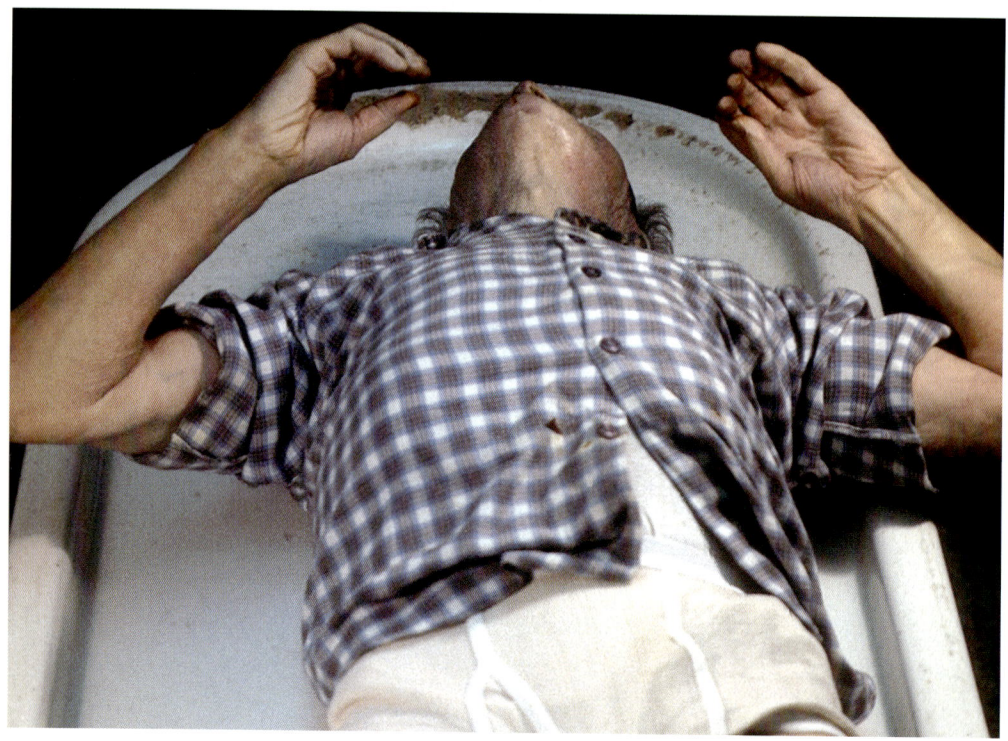

图2-5 男性死者被发现坐在厨房的桌子上,身体向前倚靠在手臂上,死者已从现场转移至解剖台。

- 利用尸僵推断死亡时间存在误差，因为有很多干扰因素可影响尸僵形成，仅用尸僵来推断死亡时间不够准确（28）。
- 对尸体的操作可破坏尸僵。如果尸僵已达到最大程度，尸僵被破坏后不会再形成。如果尸僵还未完全形成，破坏尸僵后，一些特定的关节会重新形成较小程度的尸僵（2—8 小时内 [7]）。暴力破坏尸僵可导致肌肉断裂、已有病理改变的长骨骨折（如骨质疏松、转移肿瘤；图 2-6）。人为的移动在尸体检验前各阶段都可能发生，包括在现场搬运和转移尸体，以及去除死者衣物时（如脱去尸体裤子会减弱腿部尸僵的程度）。有时需要破坏上肢的尸

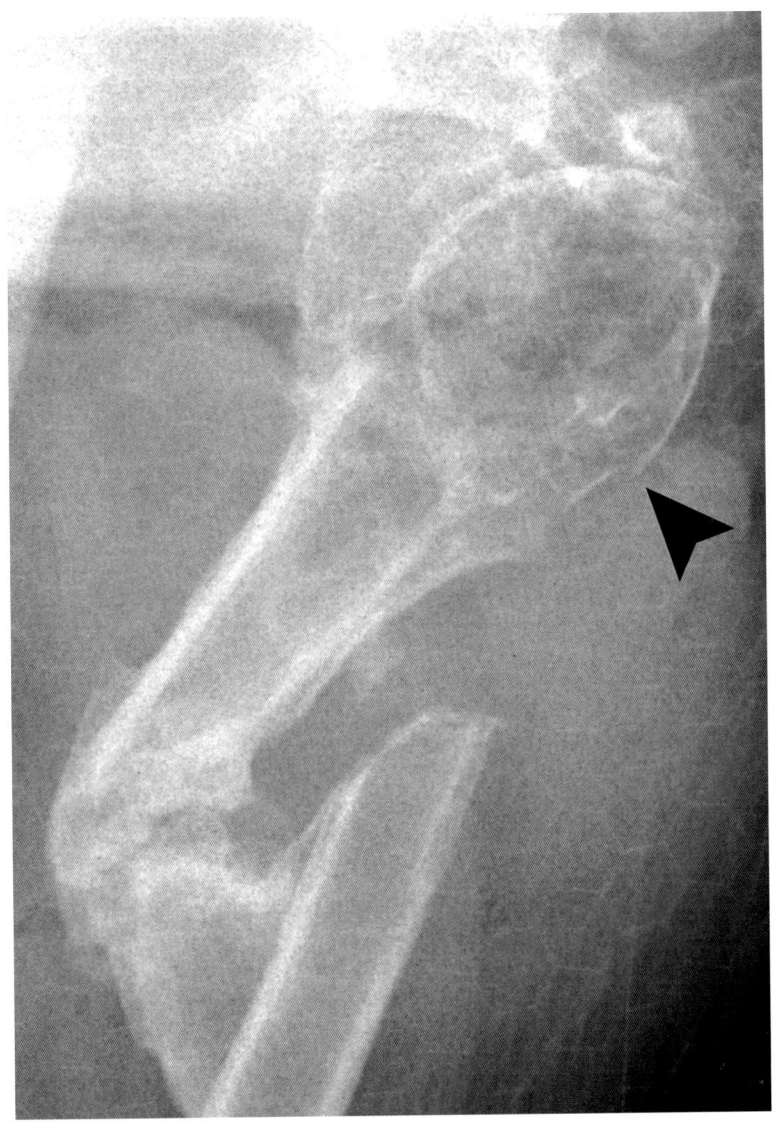

图 2-6 对原本存在上肢骨折的尸体进行暴力破坏尸僵时，引起肱骨头骨折（三角箭头）（加拿大安大略省伦敦市伦敦健康科学中心 E. Tweedie 博士供图）。

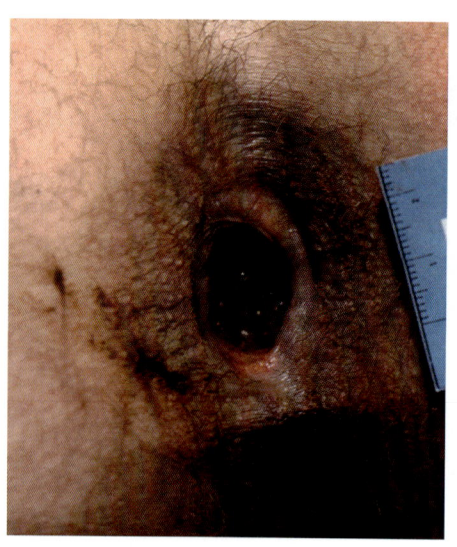

图 2-7 随着尸僵的消除,肌肉会松弛,从而导致肛门扩张。

图 2-8 电击死。男子拿着高压电线的手臂的屈肌显著收缩(美国北卡罗来纳州教堂山市法医局供图)。

僵来确保尸体躯干部有合适的解剖切口,有时还要破坏尸僵来暴露身体的特定区域(如死者肘窝处静脉注射药物留下的针眼)。

- 初次尸体检验,死者口腔难以打开,可以等下颌关节的尸僵消除后再检验口腔内部的损伤。
- 随着尸僵的消除,骨盆底部的肌肉也会松弛,从而导致阴道和肛门扩张,这种变化会使法医怀疑死者生前被性侵(图 2-7)。
- 尸僵的快速形成与某些特定的死因有关,这些死因与肌肉过强或异常收缩有关(如电击死、马钱子碱中毒、强直性肌肉营养不良;图 2-8)。
- 尸体在死后快速形成尸僵可以让尸体保持死亡当时的体位。

3 尸斑(皮肤发绀,死后血液坠积,死后瘀斑)

死后体内血液停止流动,血液会坠积在毛细血管和静脉中,从而导致未受压处的皮肤颜色发生变化(图 2-9)。长期患病和循环衰竭晚期的患者身上也可以观察到轻微的血液坠积(4)。尸体表面未受压处可以观察到斑块样尸斑(大小为 1—3 厘米或者 0.5—1 英寸),这是由于尸僵过程中肌肉收缩将静脉内的血液挤向皮肤表面所致(4)。尸斑的一系列变化如下所述:

- 发生与发展:人体死后 20 分钟至 4 小时开始出现尸斑(2,7),经过 3—16 小时,尸斑可以达到最大程度(7)。在尸斑"固定期",尸斑不会随尸体体位变化而转移(时间范围为 6—12 小时)。死后 2—6 小时可以发生尸斑的完全转移,4—24 小时可以发生尸斑的不完全转移(即尸斑会残留在原有位置,同时在新

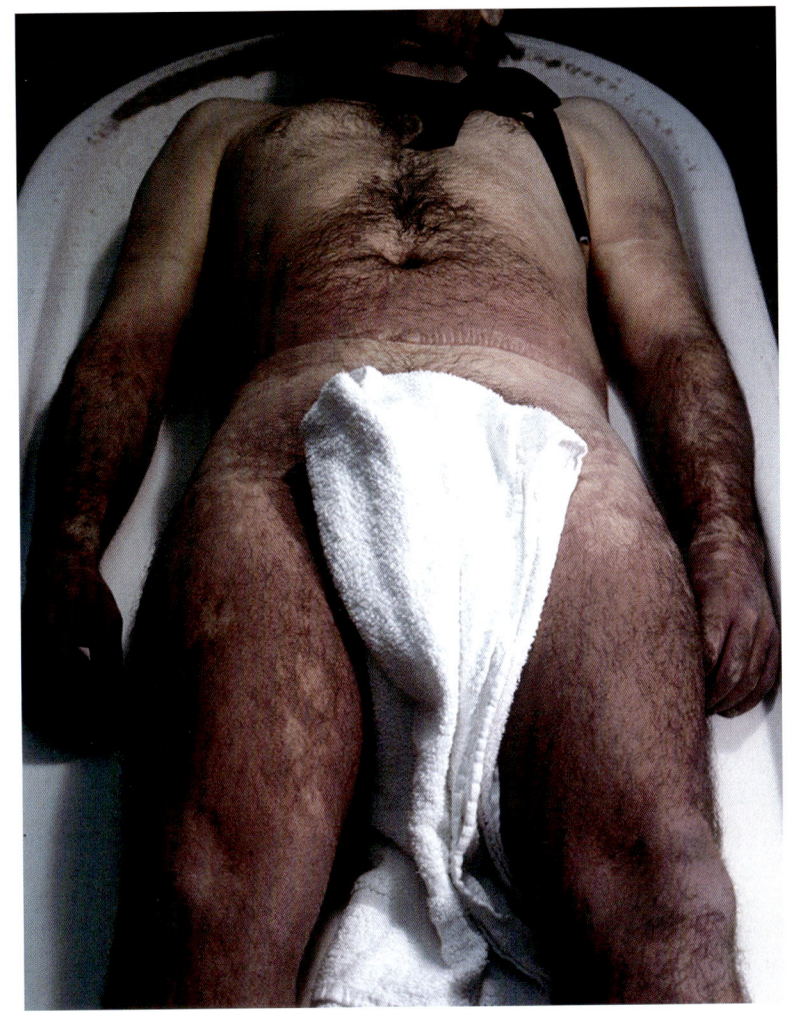

图 2-9 自缢身亡。尸体悬吊一定时间后,尸斑主要存在于手臂和腿部的低下部位。

的位置重新形成)(7)。尸斑固定期可以持续到死后 3 天(7, 29, 30)。死后 1—20 小时的尸斑可能出现指压褪色现象(7, 31)。

目前已提出多种机制来解释尸斑固定期。有机制认为,血液开始是液体,随后逐渐凝集,从而出现尸斑固定期,但死后凝血的发生和出现的时间是不固定的。也有机制认为是由于血管渗漏,血液弥散进入软组织从而出现尸斑的固定,但是在非固定期的尸斑中也能观察到这一现象,而且血液渗漏在固定期尸斑中也并非一直存在(1, 30)。血液不能从充盈的毛细血管中转移出来是因为相邻的血管压力很高(4)。还有一种机制提出,尸斑不褪色(固定期尸斑)是由于血管中血浆渗出导致血液进一步浓缩和红细胞聚集所致(30, 32)。

- 尸斑的消退:尸斑会持续存在,直到尸体腐败。
- 意义

- 通过评估尸斑程度可推断死亡时间。
- 在死亡现场发现尸体的非低下部位存在尸斑时，特别是固定期的尸斑，提示尸体的位置发生了变动(1)。

3.1 分布与"受力点"

尸体受压区域的皮肤颜色会保持正常，从而与尸斑之间产生界线。如果死者呈仰卧位，可以在枕部头皮、背部中间、臀部、大腿后侧、小腿和足跟处观察到"受力点"（图2-10）。如果死者呈俯卧位，则压力主要作用于额部、鼻子、面颊（如果头部发生转动）、下颌、胸部、下腹部和大腿前侧。受力点同样可以出现在狭窄或局部受压的区域（如穿着紧身衣物时，图2-10）。在仰卧位个体中，喉部会向脊柱方向压迫食管，从而在食管产生环形带状黏膜苍白样改变(4)。

- 意义
  - 颈部尸斑中出现不规则的苍白区域，提示死者颈部可能存在外力压迫（如扼死）。但这一提示有时难以成立，因为要出现这种情况需在尸斑形成过程中持续施加压力。
  - 颈部皮肤出现横向苍白带，提示在尸斑形成过程中存在缚线压迫，围绕颈部和面部捆扎或绑定气管插管可以形成这个现象（参阅第3章图3-20）。同样，突出的皮肤皱褶也可因挤压形成条状的中间皱褶（参阅第3章图3-20）。
  - 如果尸体的某个部位长时间接触某些特殊平面或物体，那么尸斑也会呈现物体接触面的形状。这一现象可以用来分析死亡现场和环境（图2-11）。

3.2 褪色

尸斑主要呈红色或蓝紫色，取决于血氧浓度。如果尸体处于寒冷状态，尸斑还会呈现鲜红色（图2-10）。这会与某些中毒死亡的情况相混淆［如一氧化碳中毒(33)］。深色皮肤的死者的尸斑不容易被识别。腐败会使尸斑颜色变为棕色或绿色。相关组织和器官可出现淤血或出血（仰卧位：肺后侧、腹膜后腔包括肾；俯卧位：前侧器官，如心和肠管）。

- 意义
  - 尸斑在某些个体中发展缓慢，如贫血、严重失血或器官移植术后。
  - 尸体面部明显发绀处也可能是尸斑。在肥胖个体中，当尸体心脏的水平位置高于头部水平位置时也会出现尸斑。
  - 不同的尸斑颜色可以与某些特定的中毒死亡相联系(1)：
      红色——一氧化碳（参阅第3章标题3.9；图2-12）、氟乙酸、氰化物；
      绿色——硫化氢（腐败过程中可以产生）；
      棕色——高铁血红蛋白血症（如摄入硝酸盐；图2-13）；
      深紫色——丙烷(34)。

第 2 章 ｜ 死后尸体变化——"绝佳的伪装者"

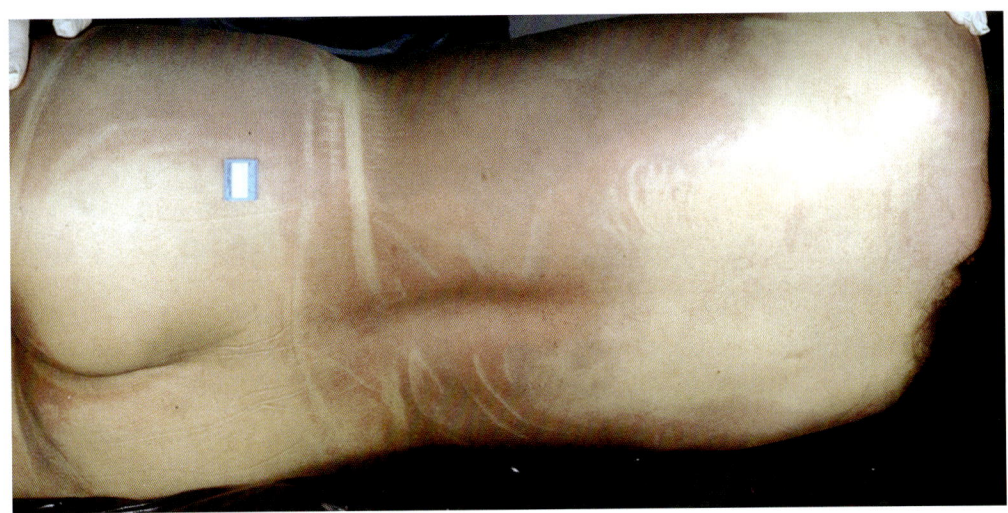

图 2-10 死者被发现处于仰卧位，尸斑出现在尸体背部，上背部和臀部出现典型的受力位置（皮肤苍白）。值得注意的是，腰部存在皮带和衬衣压迫所引起的皮肤苍白色条带。冷藏尸体会使尸斑在一定程度上更加鲜艳。

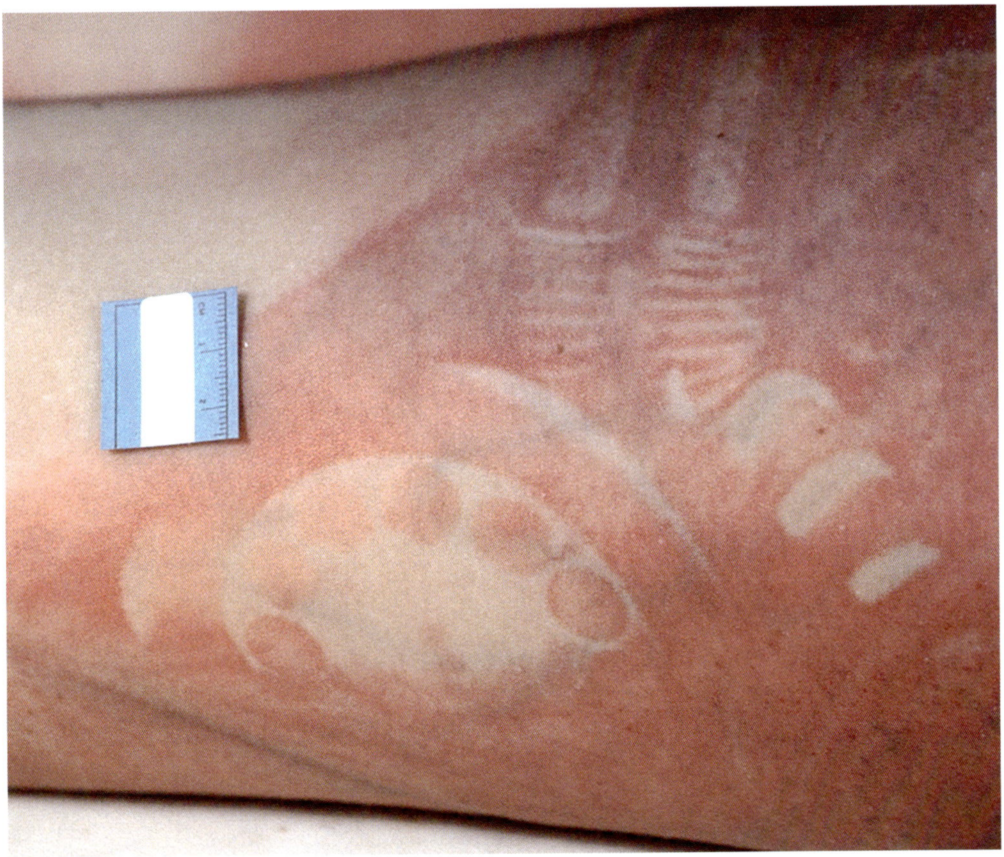

图 2-11 死者被发现时大腿压在电话上，在尸斑区域可以看到电话表盘和延长电线的印痕。

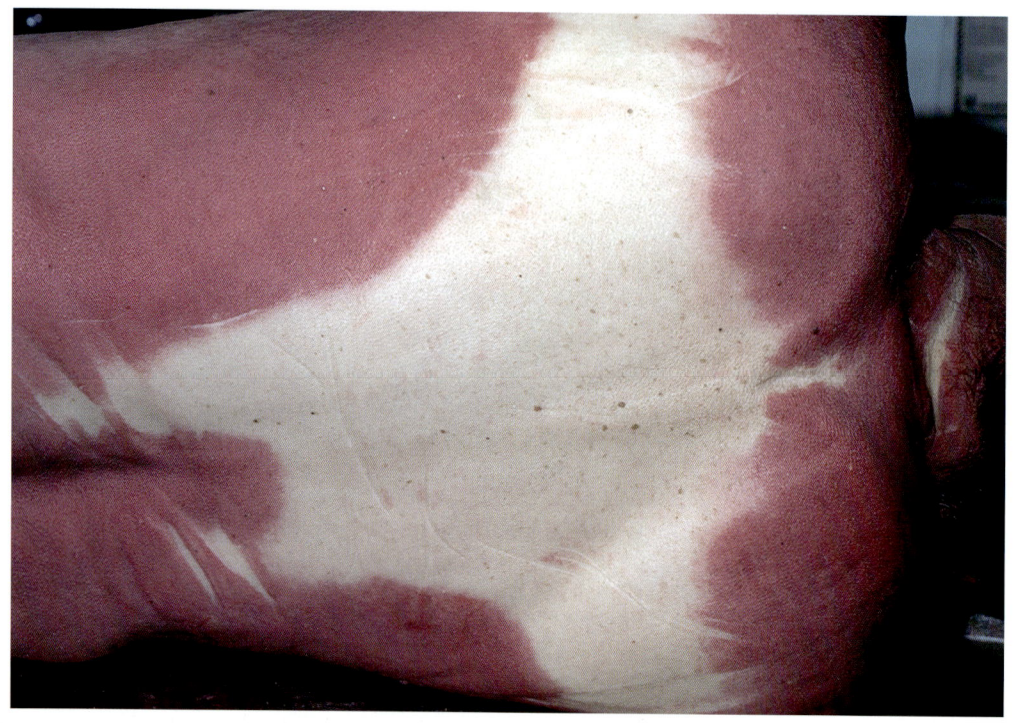

图 2-12 背部鲜红色尸斑。一氧化碳中毒。

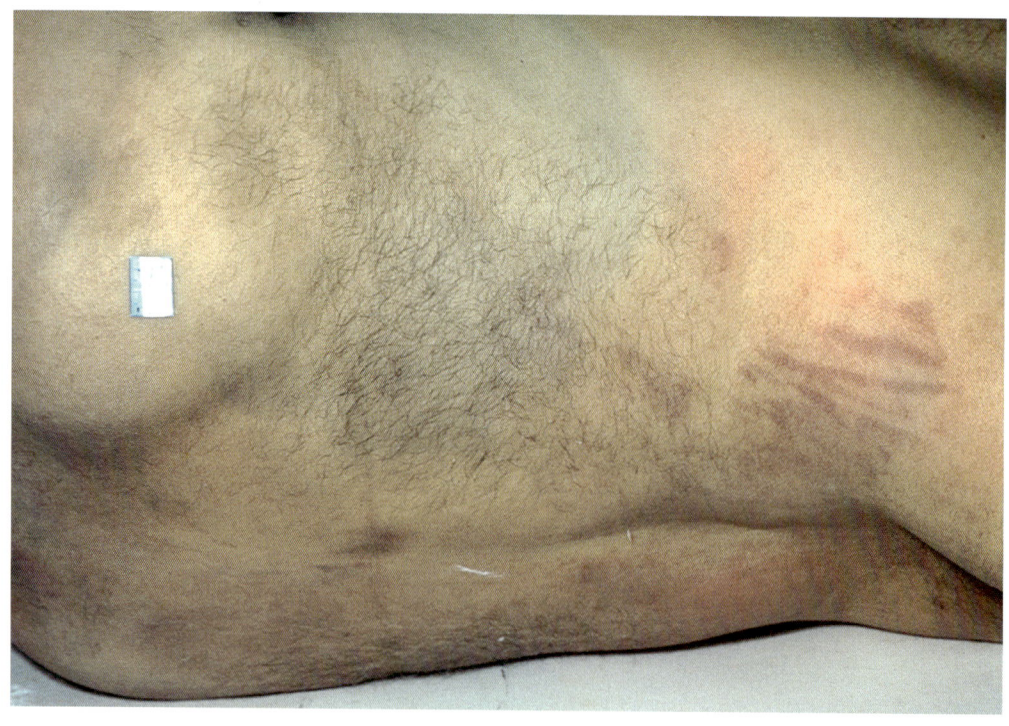

图 2-13 背部棕色尸斑。亚硝酸盐中毒引起的高铁血红蛋白血症。

- 在初次尸表检验中,尸斑会影响对挫伤的观察(图2-14)。在尸体检验过程中改变尸体位置会使尸斑从挫伤区域转移,从而可以更好地显现挫伤。可疑挫伤区域可以在尸体检验结束后再检查,因为尸体检验结束后血液将从尸体内排空,尸斑的程度会相应减弱。对冷冻尸体解剖后在次日再次检验时可以发现尸斑呈鲜红色但程度减弱,从而可以与暗红色的挫伤加以区分(图2-14)。
- 尸斑会与生前损伤相混淆。散在分布的皮肤红棕色变提示挫伤。如果该区域的尸斑处于非固定期,通过指压褪色的方法有助于鉴别尸斑和挫伤。同样,切开尸斑区域可看到血液从血管内渗出,而在挫伤区域,血液已渗入软组织中。

3.3 死后出血

死后血液淤积会导致血管破裂,引起死后出血。尸体体位引起的压力升高、早期尸体腐败和外伤都会引起死后出血。毛细血管破裂表现为皮肤瘀斑(Tardieu 斑)。皮肤瘀斑的出现被认为是尸体腐败的预兆,但在尸体被悬吊的案件中,皮肤瘀斑在死后2—4小时后就会出现(6)。较大的血管(小静脉)破裂可导致紫色瘀斑或较大的瘀斑。死后皮肤出血主要分布在尸斑区域,在其他区域则不会形成死后出血(图2-15)。

- 意义
  - 死后出血(瘀斑、紫斑/淤血或"假性挫伤"、外出血)会与生前的真实损伤相混淆(参阅第8章标题3.1,图2-16)。
  - 切开生前损伤可看到血液持续性渗出。切开死后损伤(如皮肤擦伤、撕裂伤)可见组织红染,这种组织红染与生前出血的生活反应相仿(35,36)。

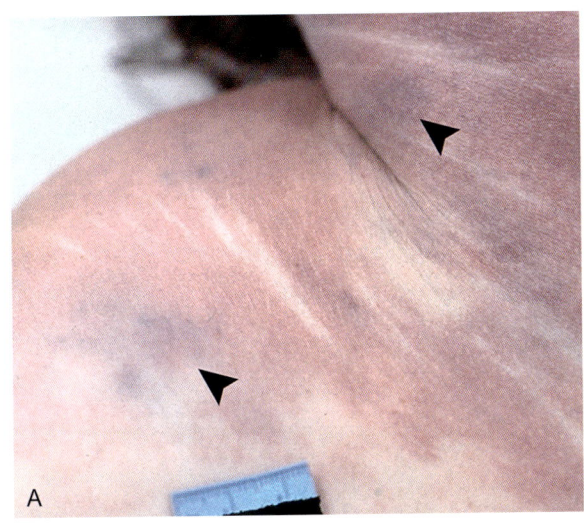
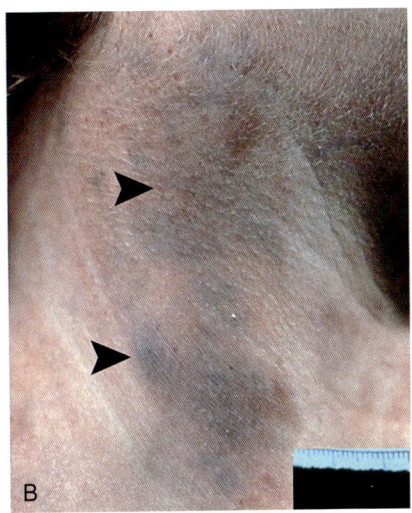

图2-14 被他人用手臂扼死的女性尸体。(A)颈部侧面在尸斑区域出现线性皮肤灰白区域,主要由颈部皮肤皱褶引起。模糊的擦伤(三角箭头)。(B)尸体解剖后次日再次对尸体进行检验。颈部侧面的尸斑程度减弱,从而使挫伤(三角箭头)得以更好地显现。

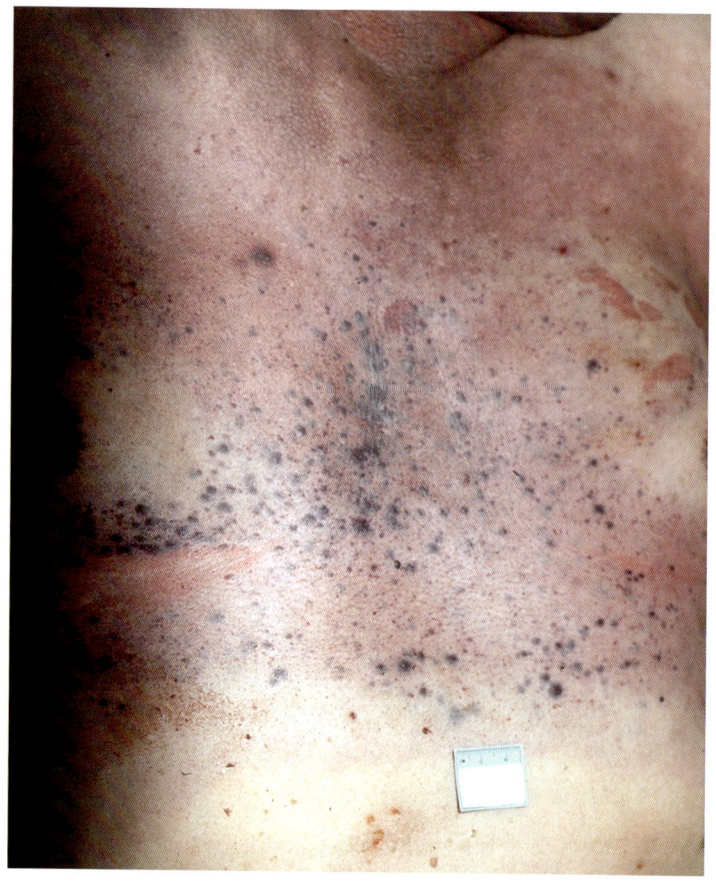

图 2-15 俯卧位的尸体。胸部尸斑中有许多皮肤出血点,而在腹部非尸斑区域就无此类皮肤出血点。

- 死亡后大量出血来自血管[如主动脉出血进入胸腔,失血量可达 100—1 300 毫升,平均 450 毫升(37)],如瞬间致命的脑干损伤案件,尸体检验见外伤性主动脉破裂所致的胸腔积血,提示出血可能是死后形成(37)。
- 显微镜观察无法区分早期生前挫伤的外渗血液和死后出血。
- 人体疏松结缔组织(如脸部、颈部)处的内、外部死后出血的发展更为快速(参阅第 5 章图 5-5)。

死后也会发生鼻腔出血(3)。"假性皮肤挫伤"往往较小,然而有案例报告显示,当尸体头部朝下时,面部会形成假性皮肤挫伤且持续存在(38)。眼眶周围血肿,即黑眼圈,可由外力直接导致,也可由头皮损伤的血液浸润或眶板骨折所引起的血液浸润(39)导致。黑眼圈可在遭受致命伤害时形成(39),也可在死后被观察到(参阅标题 11)。角膜移植手术也可引起眶周出血而形成黑眼圈(图 2-17;参考文献 39)。死后头部外伤也可引起眶周血肿,且尸斑会增强眶周血肿的程度(39)。与大面积双侧眼睑出血相比,由于缺乏损伤证据,单侧眼睑小面积皮肤血肿未必是生前损伤所致

第 2 章 | 死后尸体变化——"绝佳的伪装者"

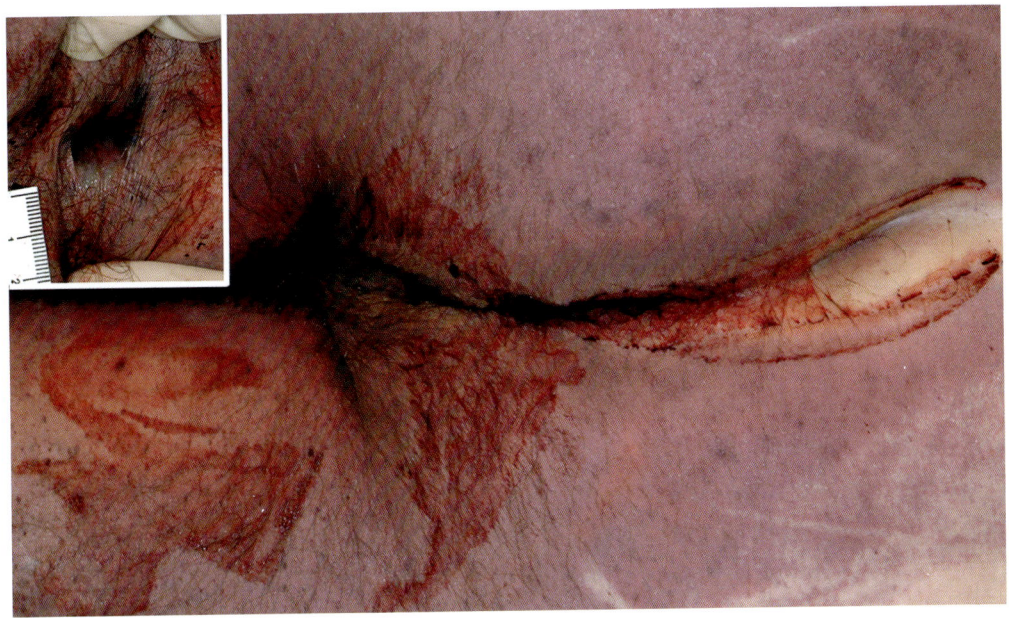

图 2-16 自缢身亡。死者生前用电线绑住双腿（参阅第 3 章，图 3-11）。下肢尸斑显著，且双腿后侧出现了皮肤点状出血。肛周会出现"出血"，但未检见肛门皮肤损伤痕迹（小图），同时可观察到黏膜血管淤血。

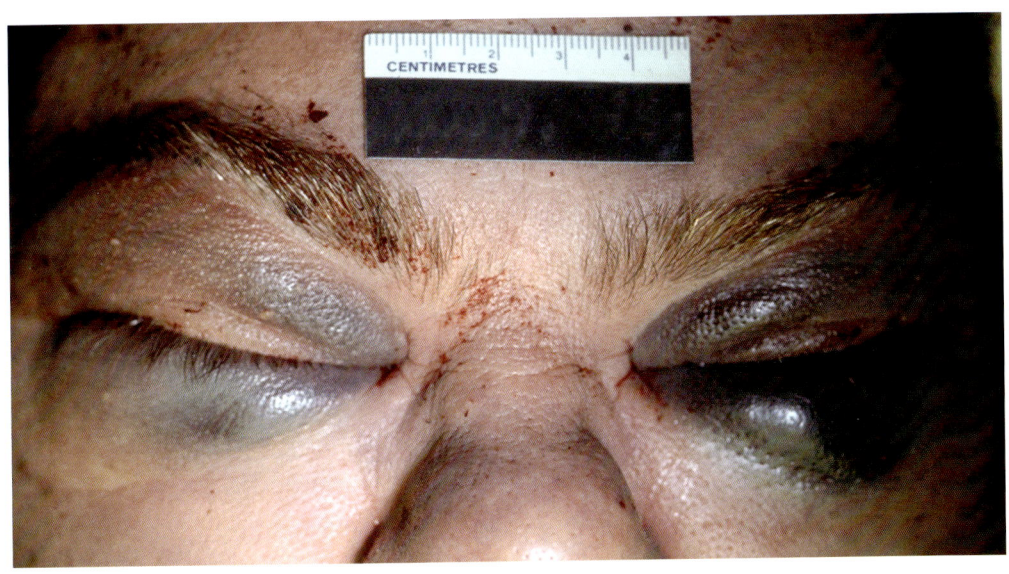

图 2-17 黑眼圈。肥胖的心肌病猝死者，眼睛用于器官捐献（加拿大安大略省哈密尔顿市法医病理办公室 D. King 博士供图）。

(39)。死后皮肤点状出血、结膜和巩膜融合性出血，是颈部受压导致窒息的证据（图 2-18 和图 2-19；参考文献 40-42）。对于该类案件性质的确定，需要通过细致的颈部解剖并结合死亡现场勘察综合判断。

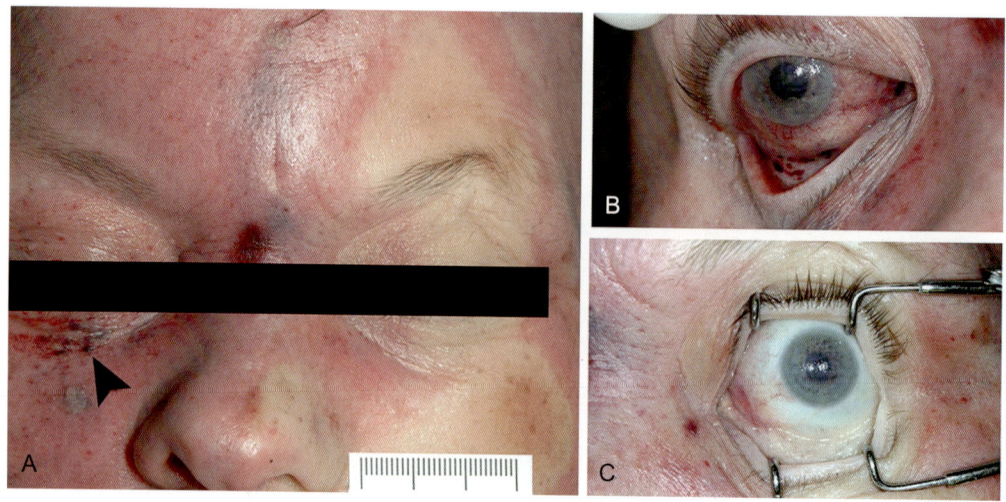

图 2-18 死后眼眶皮肤点状出血，由头朝下俯卧体位引起。(A)面部左侧与地板接触未形成尸斑。右眼睑下方的点状皮肤出血(三角箭头)。(B)右下眼睑结膜点状出血。(C)左眼结膜未见出血点。

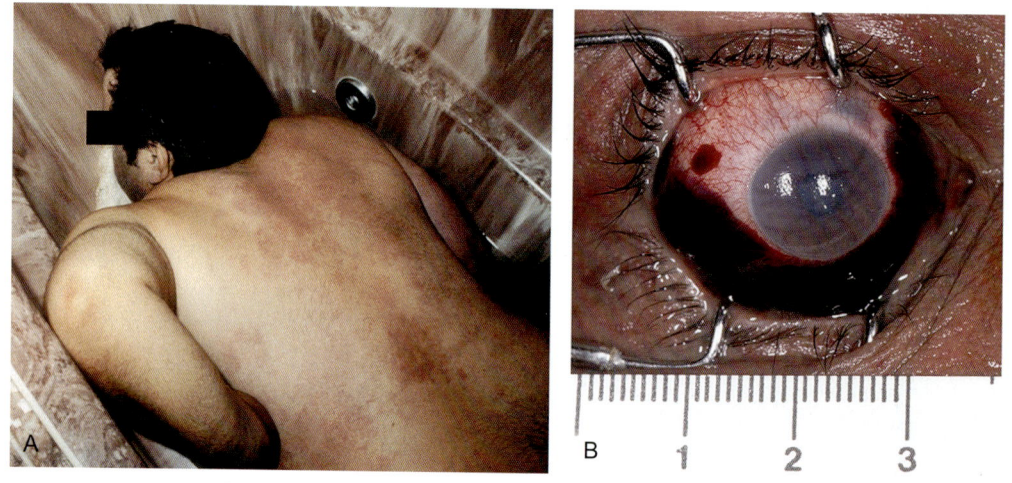

图 2-19 死后眼眶出血。(A)死者被发现趴在浴缸中。(B)严重尸斑引起眼睛死后出血。

颞肌和帽状腱膜的死后出血与尸体的头面部位置相关，这种死后出血与钝性损伤出血比较相似(参阅第 3 章图 3-2；参考文献 40)。在溺死案件中，尸体头部向下的体位被认为是颈部软组织出血的诱发因素(6)，且颈部软组织出血较为广泛(图 2-20；参考文献 43)。颈部前、中、后均可检见局灶性出血，这一现象一定程度上是由血液坠积引起[参阅第 5 章标题 10.6(43)]。颈部出血未必由溺死所致，俯卧位或头部向下的体位均可使尸体出现颈部死后出血现象(参阅第 3 章标题 1.4；第 5 章标题 12)。在尸体臀部处于高位时这种出血现象更明显。

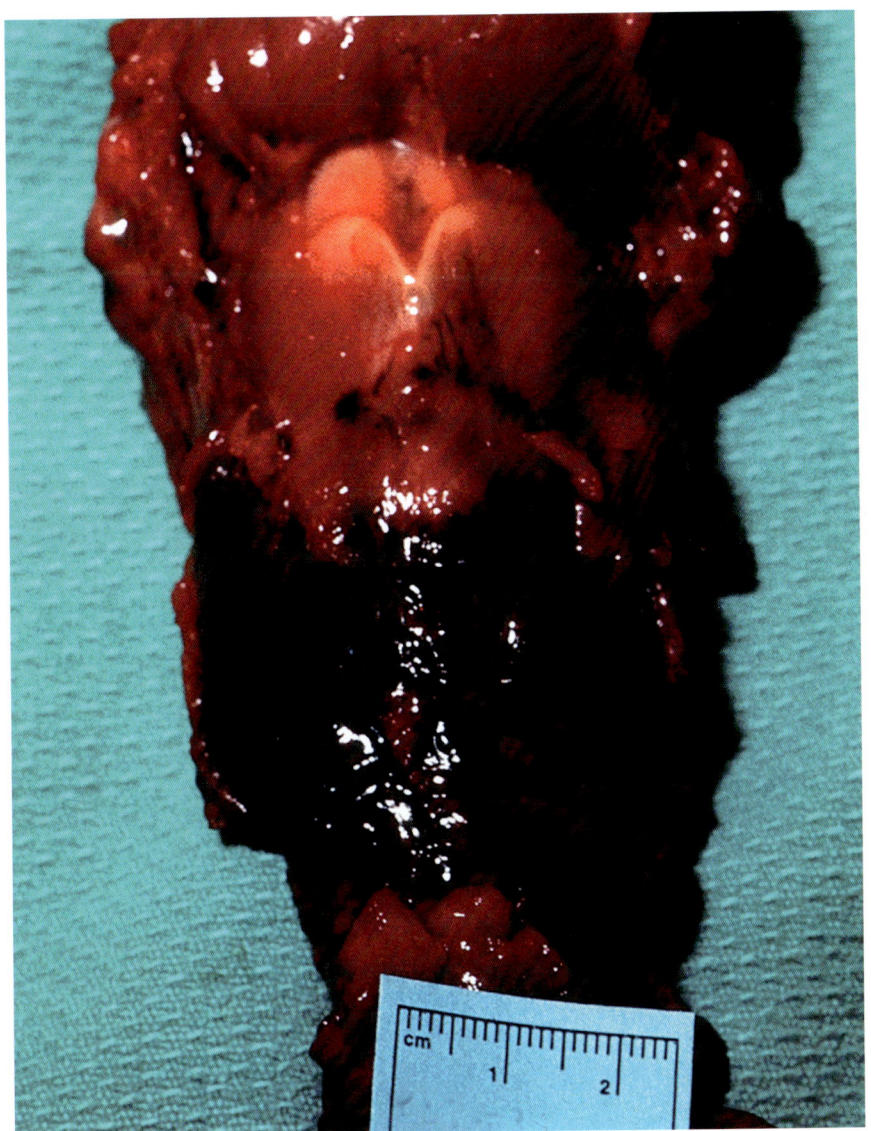

图 2-20 俯卧位尸体颈部前侧软组织广泛出血。舌骨 – 喉部未发现骨折。

4 尸冷

尸体的热量散失有以下四种机制,而且取决于死亡现场与环境。

- 水分蒸发:湿度和降水会影响水分从皮肤和衣物上蒸发。
- 热辐射:作为影响因素,随着尸体的冷却而逐渐减弱(如太阳照射在尸体上,住宅内开启的散热系统)。
- 热传导:不同温度的接触面之间发生的热量交换。
- 热对流:非接触的物体通过空气进行热量交换。

死后尸体热量的散失随时间的延长表现出反"S"曲线(4,7)。尸冷早期呈现短暂的平台期,温度下降较缓慢,这个阶段尸体热量的散失来自于尸体表面。同时,机体的新陈代谢持续产生热量,如果不考虑这一阶段,则会影响通过肛温来推断死亡时间的准确性。随后,肛温表现出线性下降,下降幅度与尸体表面和环境的温差成正比。最后再次变缓,直至达到环境温度。

目前已有各种利用肛温来推断死亡时间的方程、算法和计算预测图(44)。但Henssge等认为"即使增加算法的复杂性,也不保证能提高计算死亡时间的准确性"(7)。有时,简单的经验公式比复杂的数学模型更准确(6,7)。

例如:

(1) 死亡时间 = [死亡时的肛温 − 测量的肛温(°F)] / 1.5

(2) 死亡时间 = [死亡时的肛温 − 测量的肛温(°C)] + 3*

利用尸温变化规律推断死亡时间会受很多因素影响,其中一些因素不可控(1,7)。肛温反应了尸体的核心温度(98.6°F或37°C)。正常的肛温在活体中是不断变化的(在成年人为34.2°C−37.6°C或93.6°F−99.7°F),并取决于很多影响因素[如昼夜变化、运动(7)]。由于新生儿和早产儿的体温调控不够完善,所以新生儿和早产儿的肛温可能会较高。在某些条件下,人体温度也会升高[如败血症、使用某些药物(可卡因、地西泮)、非发热疾病(甲状腺功能亢进)]。环境条件改变,也可使肛温升高或降低。低温会增加死亡时间推断的误差。人体损伤后可出现一段较长的濒死期(6),在这一阶段,人体的体温调节会受到影响,从而在死前就出现体温下降。

尸体温度与周围环境的温差越大,尸温下降速度越快(4)。浸泡在冷水中的尸体温度下降得更快(4)。从死亡到温度记录期间,如果环境温度发生变化,推断死亡时间的不确定性也会增加。法医需要意识到发现尸体的现场不一定是死亡现场。尸体体型大,脂肪多,衣物/覆盖物厚都会减慢尸温下降的速率(4,7)。瘦弱、裸露的尸体在寒冷环境下可能不出现初始温度平台期(4)。尸体的体位(伸展还是蜷缩)也会影响尸体热量的散失(7)。

5 尸体降解

尸体降解是死后尸体逐渐解体的过程,是尸体自溶和腐败的结果(45)。尸体自溶指人死后组织受到自身酶的作用而软化、液化。尸体腐败指人死后肠管内的细菌和其他微生物由血行途径扩散,在这些细菌的作用下,组织和器官逐渐液化和气化。昆虫和动物对尸体的破坏会加快尸体的腐败过程。如果尸体存在开放性皮肤伤口,腐败速度也会加快。新生儿的胎粪是无菌的,故新生儿尸体分解得较慢。

- 意义
  - 尸体降解出现在其他死后变化(尸僵、尸斑、尸温下降)之后,利用尸体降解

---

* 补偿值,用来解释尸体降温过程中可能存在的初始延迟。

来推断死亡时间,更易受各种因素的影响。
- 尸体降解会引起个体识别困难。
- 住宅中降解的尸体反映死者生前存在社会隔离(46)。死者家属对尸体掩埋会减缓尸体降解。

5.1 促进尸体降解的因素

促进尸体降解的因素同样会加快组织自溶和细菌生长,以及尸体的腐败(45)。

- **温度**:温暖的环境会促进尸体降解(47)。体温较高会加快尸体降解,如败血症。但温度过高会降低酶的活性、减少细菌数量,从而减缓尸体降解。冷冻尸体并不一定能减缓尸体降解,在冰冻尸体解冻时,可能因为细菌快速增殖而分解得更快。
- **环境媒介**:尸体所处的环境会影响尸体降解速度。Casper 规则提出:尸体暴露在空气中 1 周,等于淹没在水中 2 周或埋在土壤中 8 周(45)。尸体埋葬得越深,尸体的保存效果就越好(48)。因为埋得越深,环境的温度就越低(延缓尸体降解),而且不易受到昆虫和动物的破坏(45,48)。尸体埋在 1 米(3-4 英尺)深位置时,降解明显延缓(45,47,48)。埋在泥炭中的尸体可完好保存几个世纪(45)。

   当尸体暴露于某些环境媒介中时,尸体导热散失会增加,从而减慢尸体降解。例如,当尸体躺在一个导热平面上(金属)时,尸体降解会减慢。
- **尸体体型**:婴儿和儿童尸温的下降速度快,尸体降解缓慢。肥胖的尸体因脂肪具有良好的绝缘性,尸体热量散失慢,故尸体的降解速度快。但也存在着个体差异性(47)。
- **衣物和其他覆盖物**:厚衣物和覆盖物能保存尸体热量,加速尸体降解。但紧身衣会增加尸体的外部压力,阻止组织内气体膨胀,抑制细菌在血液中的扩散,从而减缓尸体降解(3)。
- **尸体体位——死后淤血**:血管内血量增加(淤血)会促进细菌生长和扩散,反之,失血会减慢尸体腐败。尸体呈俯卧位会引起尸体前侧形成尸斑,肠腔血管淤血,从而加速尸体腐败。当尸体头部处于低位时,头部、颈部和上胸部降解会加速。
- **损伤**:损伤部位提供了细菌进入的通道,从而加速尸体降解(45,49)。

5.2 尸体降解改变

尸体降解的发生、进展易受外界影响,且变动很大。在通常情况下,尸体降解在死后 24-48 小时后开始发生。

5.2.1 变色

厌氧性细菌(如梭状芽胞杆菌)产生的硫化氢气体和溶血产物结合,产生早期的尸体降解改变,如下腹部蓝绿色变(从右至左,因为右下腹临近回盲部;图 2-21,参考文献 50)。尸绿会发展到整个腹部,最终弥漫至身体其余部位。溶血红细胞中血红蛋白色素渗出和血管的气态破裂引起局部皮肤变色(绿色、紫色及黑色),与皮肤挫伤相似(图 2-22)。由于溶血作用,皮肤会呈现沿血管分布的树枝状颜色改变,称为

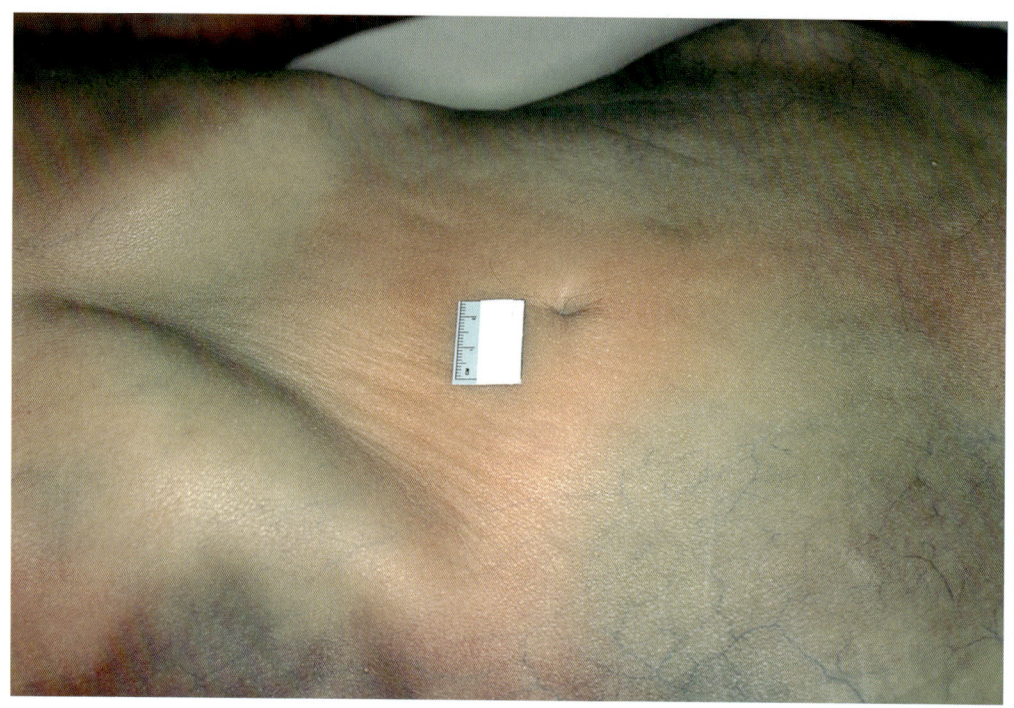

图 2-21 早期尸体降解改变。腹部尸绿形成。

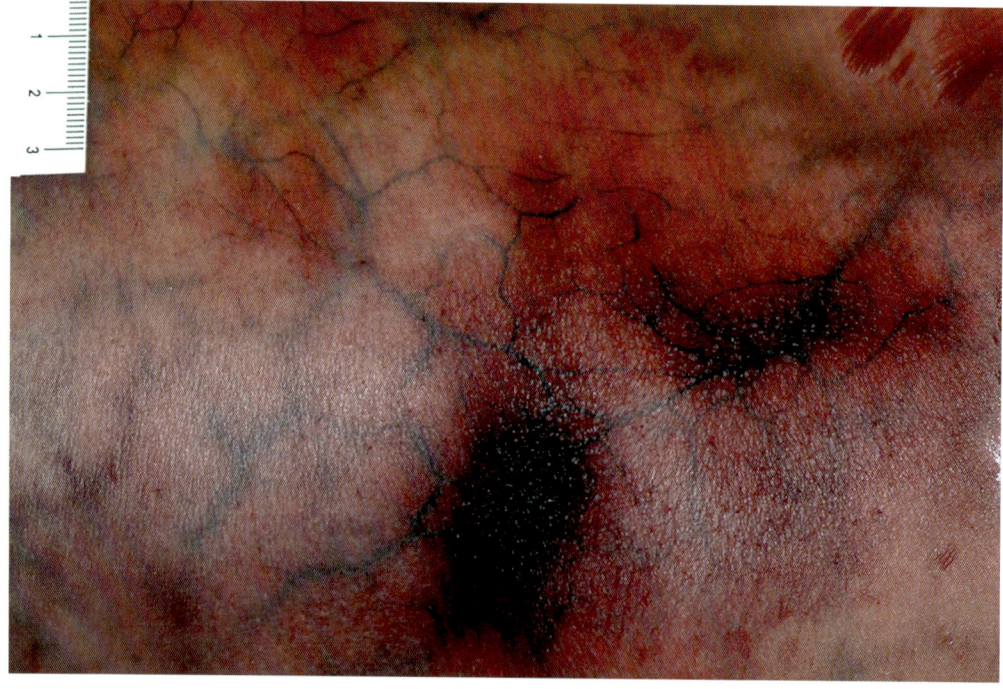

图 2-22 尸体降解引起的局部皮肤变色与生前皮肤挫伤相似。显著的腐败血管网（加拿大安大略省伦敦市伦敦健康科学中心 Dr. M. Moussa 供图）。

第 2 章 | 死后尸体变化——"绝佳的伪装者"

"大理石花纹"（图 2-23）。
- 意义
  ◦ 尸体降解产生的局部皮肤变色会与生前皮肤挫伤混淆（图 2-22，参考文献 51）。有研究试图区分尸体死后的皮肤色变和挫伤，显示血红蛋白色素可轻易渗出血管，但红细胞膜蛋白分子量大，反而不容易渗出（51）。挫伤会破坏血管，导致大量的红细胞膜蛋白渗出（51）。挫伤和死后皮肤变色的免疫组化研究发现，红细胞膜的组成成分血型糖蛋白 A 出现阳性染色，提示为生前损伤（51）。血型糖蛋白 A 在死后皮肤挫伤中不会显现，濒死期可少量出现。
  ◦ 溶血和血液弥散会加重原本的挫伤和出血。
  ◦ 深层软组织和器官内部的血液弥散性渗出提示了疾病和损伤的可能性。例如：仰卧位尸体顶枕部头皮弥漫性"出血"提示可能存在创伤；肺"淤血

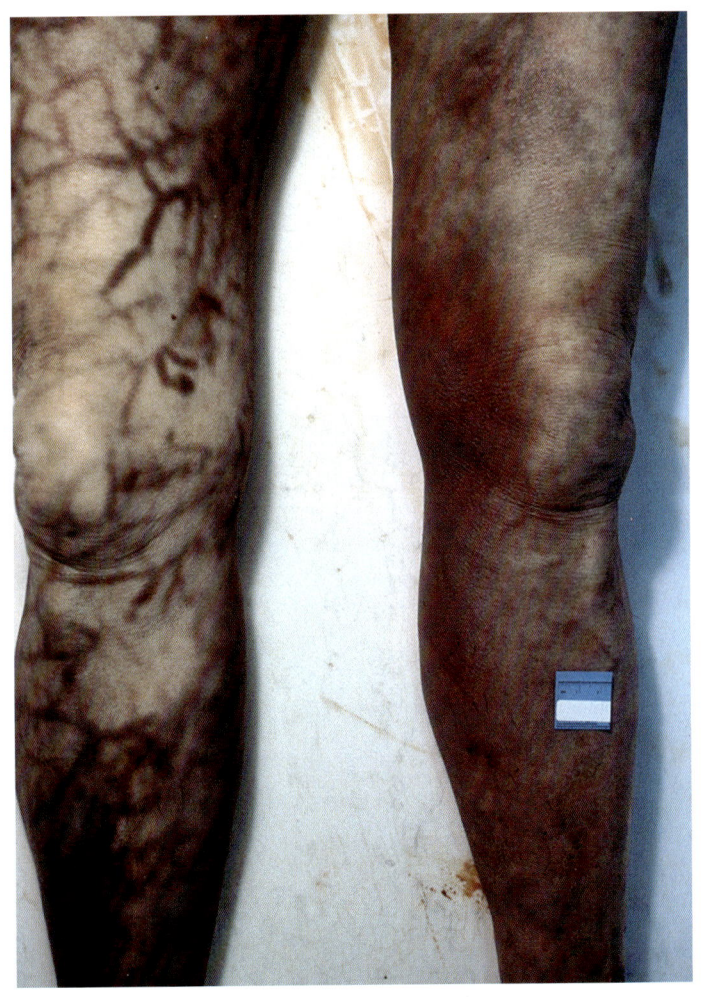

图 2-23　右大腿的腐败静脉网"大理石花纹"，与左大腿的尸斑形成对照。尸体腐败使血管更加明显。

性"出血（镜下检见肺泡内显著出血）；胰腺淤血性"出血"与胰腺炎相似。
- 通常体腔内存在血性液体说明存在生前损伤，但死后尸体降解也会形成某些血性液体淤积现象，如"双侧胸腔积血"（可有数百毫升血性液体）可由尸体降解产生。硬脑膜下和蛛网膜下腔显著的血管淤血和薄层出血在仰卧位尸体的枕叶区域特别明显，这种改变会与蛛网膜下腔出血相混淆（图 2-24）。除去颅骨后需对大脑进行检查，因为组织降解导致大脑软化，大脑移除后其解剖位置和检验均会受到影响。
- 尸体降解过程中会形成玫瑰齿，玫瑰齿是牙本质小管内的渗血自溶所致（图 2-25；参考文献 52-57）。死后产生的碳氧血红蛋白不是产生玫瑰齿的原因（55,57）。头部淤血（头朝下的体位引起）和潮湿环境可促进玫瑰齿的形成（55-57）。由于组织降解死后指甲也可变成粉色（57）。玫瑰齿与死因一般没有必然联系（53,56,57），并可在死后 1-2 周内检见（54,56）。

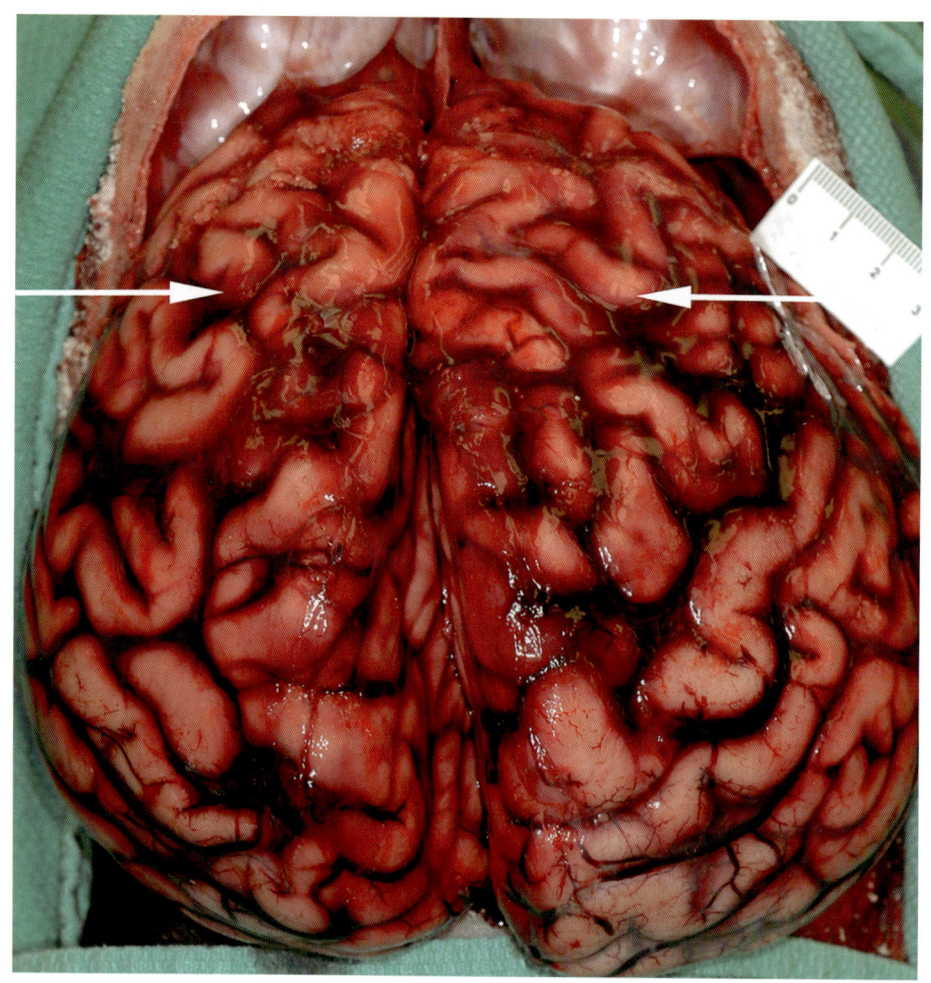

图 2-24 腐败尸体。大脑后部的蛛网膜下腔淤血（在箭头平面下方）。

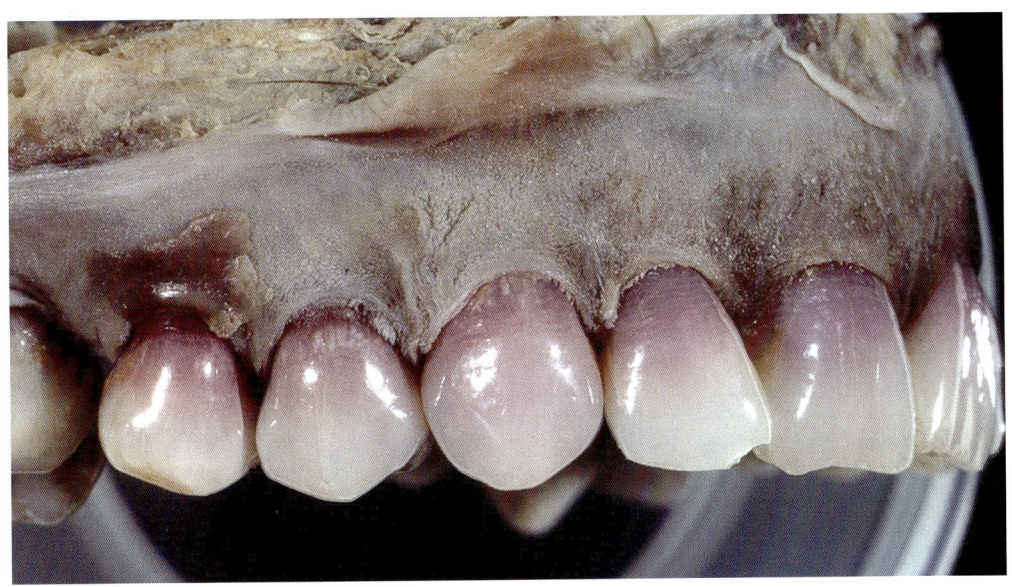

图 2-25 尸体组织降解引起的玫瑰齿。

5.2.2 膨胀

尸体腐败过程中会产生各种气体(如硫化氢、甲烷、氨气、二氧化碳等),气体渗透入皮肤/软组织和器官时,组织会有捻发感和膨胀现象,同时可观察到生殖器、肛门和面部的局部肿胀(眼睛、舌头突出),令死者面目全非,呈巨人观。全身尸体膨胀表现为尸体明显增大。气体蓄积于体腔,打开体腔时可听到明显的放气声,体腔明显缩小。

- 意义
  - 鼻腔血管破裂可引起明显的"鼻衄"。
  - 肺部的气体膨胀会引起血性液体和胃内容物从口腔和鼻腔中溢出,这会影响对面部损伤的观察(图2-26)。腐败气体会使粪便从直肠中排出,即死后排便现象(3)。
  - 外科手术伤口在死后裂开会与锐器伤相混淆。手术病史和伤口中的缝合线(58,59)可说明伤口由外科手术所致。数月前的手术伤口仍可能在死后裂开。

5.2.3 降解

尸体降解可破坏皮肤和其他组织的解剖完整性。局部表皮开始脱落("皮肤滑动")(图2-27),皮肤上会出现气疱或者水疱(图2-28)。皮肤气疱或水疱的破裂区域及皮肤滑动区域干燥后,相应皮肤变成黄色、棕色和红色,呈皮革样改变(图2-29)。尸体降解时毛发和指甲会疏松、脱落,温度较高时头发易聚集成团(47)。手、脚的皮肤疏松并呈现"脱套样"改变(图2-30)。上消化道可检见破裂(食管和胃软化),如破裂处显微镜下可检见炎症改变,这种破裂符合生前形成。脑组织会发生囊状改变(脑软化),易与脑梗死相混淆。

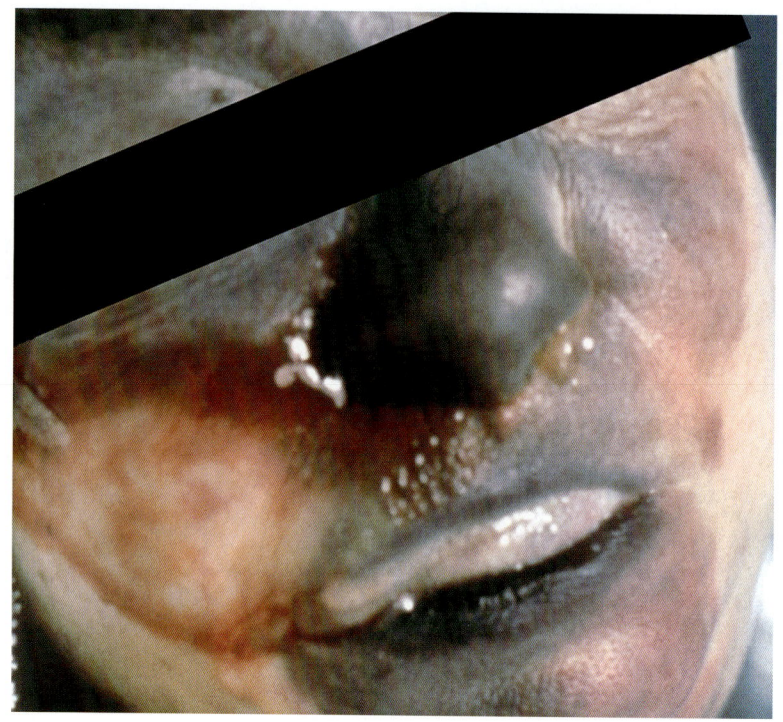

图 2-26 尸体组织降解引起鼻腔和口腔血性液体溢出。

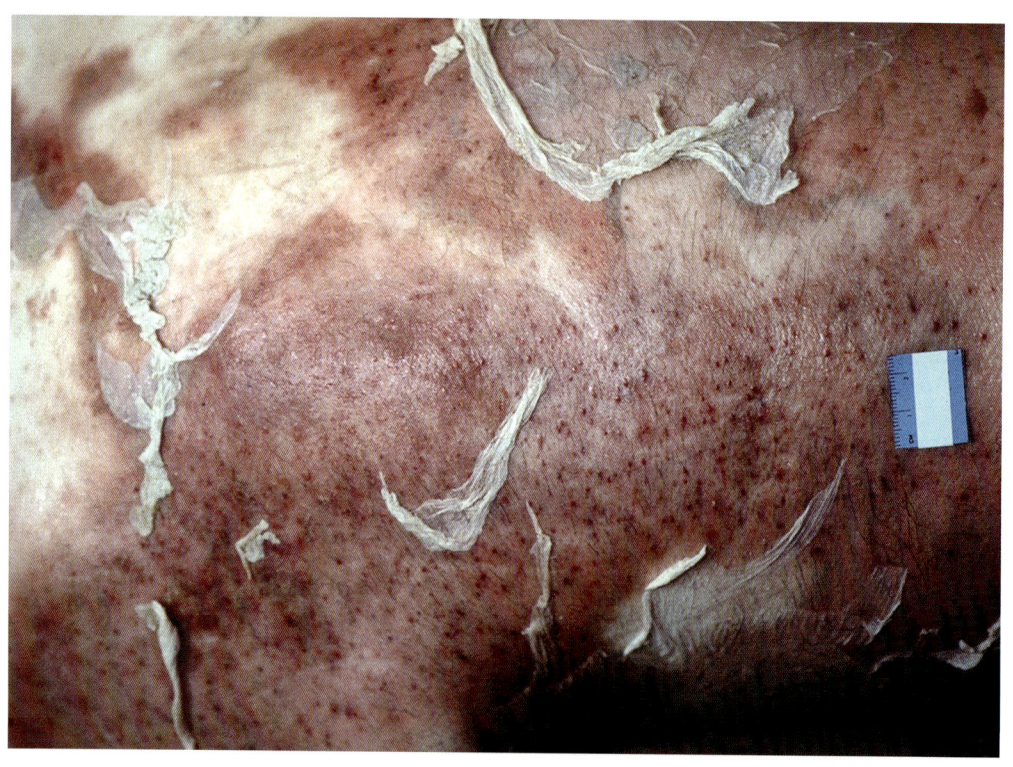

图 2-27 尸体降解,皮肤脱落、移位。

第 2 章 | 死后尸体变化——"绝佳的伪装者"

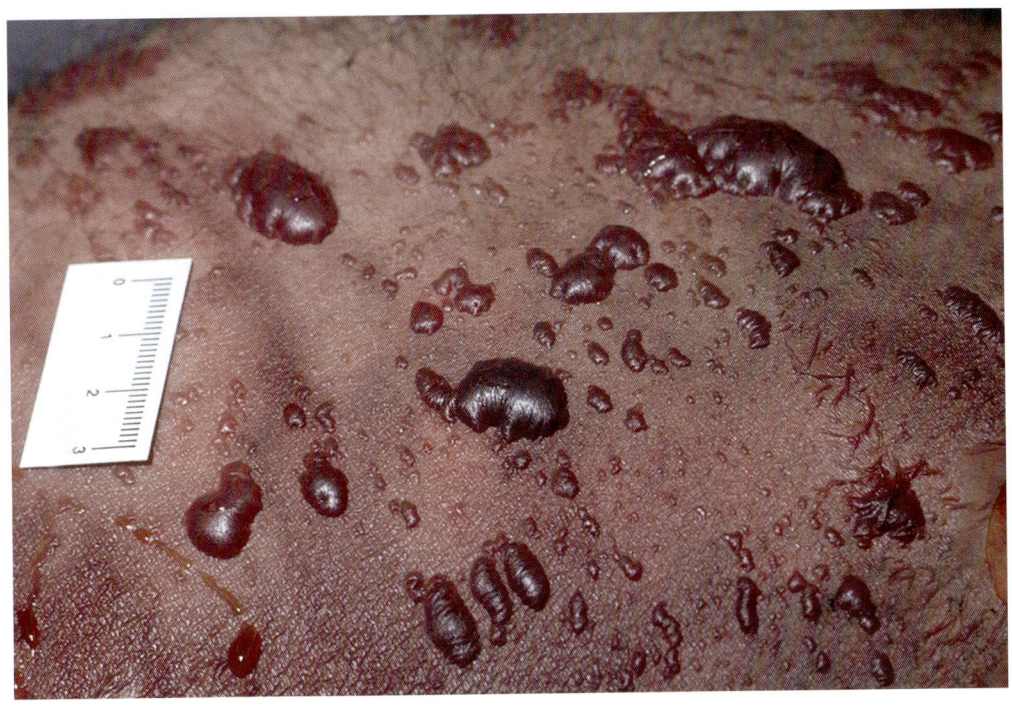

图 2-28 尸体降解,水疱形成。

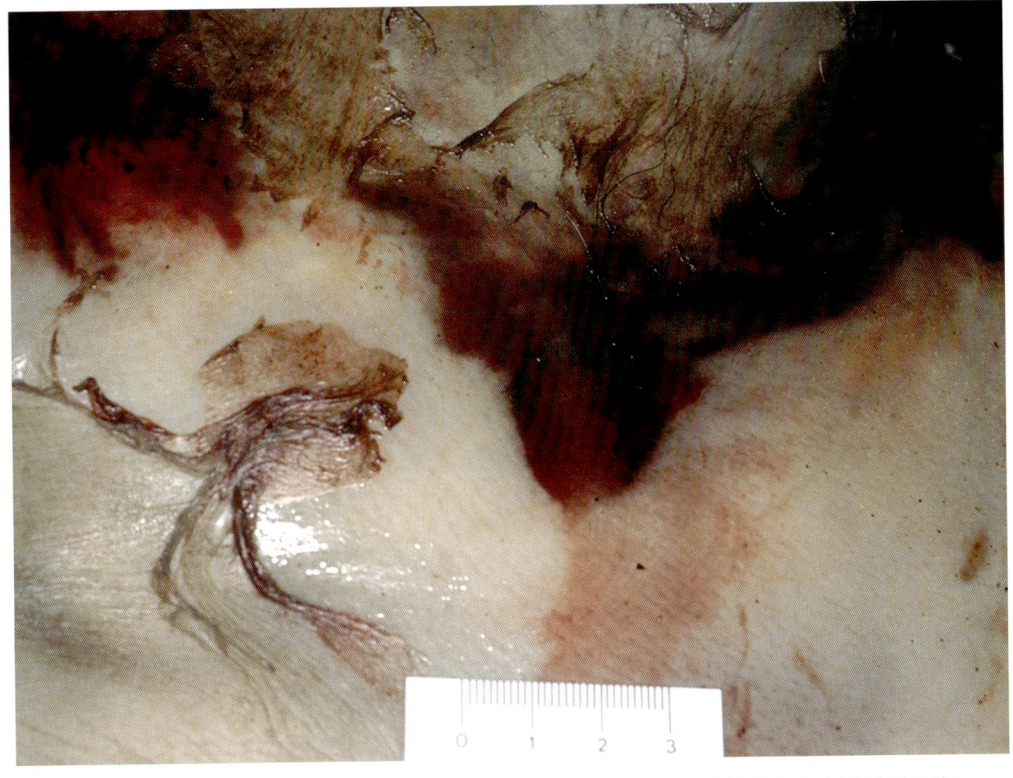

图 2-29 尸体降解,颈部和上胸部皮肤脱落和移位。沿衣领呈带状分布的皮肤棕黄色变。

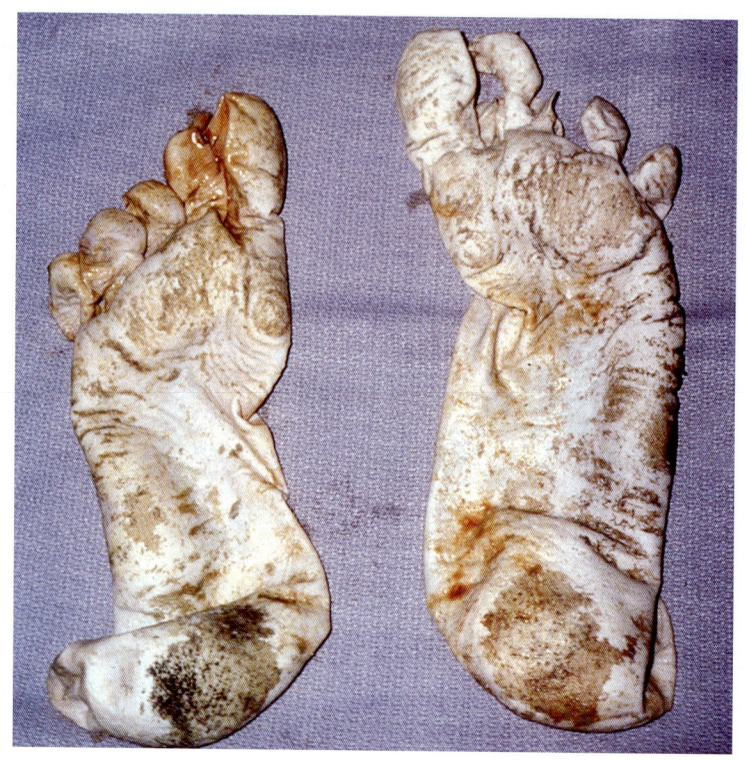

图 2-30 尸体降解,双脚皮肤套状脱落(美国北卡罗来纳州教堂山市法医局供图)。

- 意义
  - 皮肤完整性的破坏会与损伤相混淆(如皮肤擦伤)。
  - 皮肤水疱会与烧伤改变相混淆。
  - 尸体降解使眼睛的出血点消失,可通过干燥保存出血点(42)。

5.2.4 溶解

某些器官和组织(如胰腺)的溶解速度较快,而另一些器官和组织(如骨骼、子宫、前列腺)的溶解速度较慢。随着尸体溶解的进展,组织和器官会逐渐消失,最终仅存骨骼(高温天气需要 2-4 周)(47),骨骼、关节也随之脱离(60)。通常法医需判断残留骨骼是否为人类骨(61)。

5.2.5 "难以解决问题的尸体检验"

色变、膨胀、降解和溶解是尸体腐败的组成部分。尸体腐败让忍受尸体恶臭和蛆虫的法医的工作更具挑战,他们需要通过系统性解剖有条理地处理这些案件,否则会遗漏损伤(图 2-31;参考文献 62)。尸体腐败越严重,死因越可能难以确定("无解剖学上的死因""难以确定死因";参考文献 62)。

5.3 尸体降解的变异

尸体干燥(木乃伊化)是一种尸体降解的变异。局部干燥出现在暴露的舌尖、上下

第2章 | 死后尸体变化——"绝佳的伪装者"

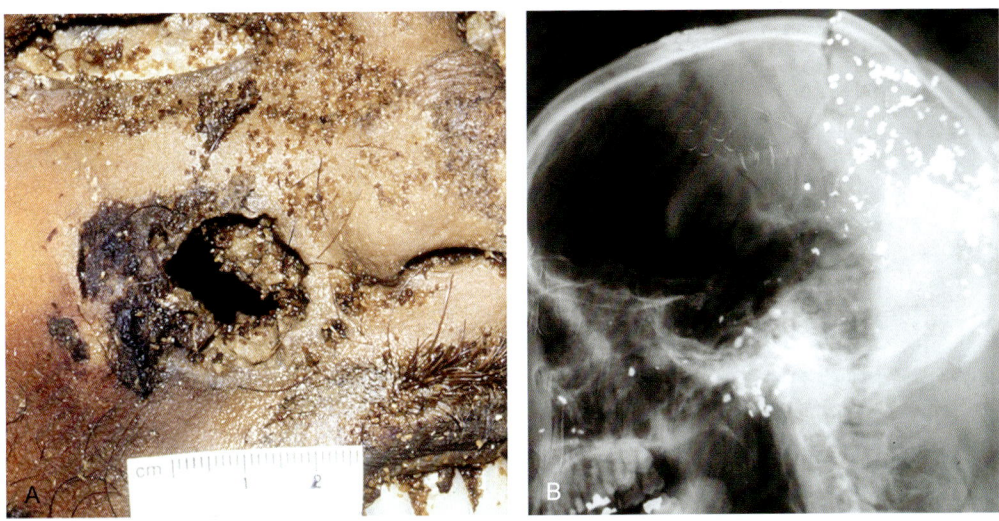

图2-31 他杀案件。由于严重的尸体降解,在启动调查时并没有进行尸体解剖。(A)右面颊枪击伤被大量蛆虫覆盖,案件开始时被认为是自然死亡。(B)头部影像学检查发现霰弹枪的子弹(美国北卡罗来纳州教堂山市法医局供图)。

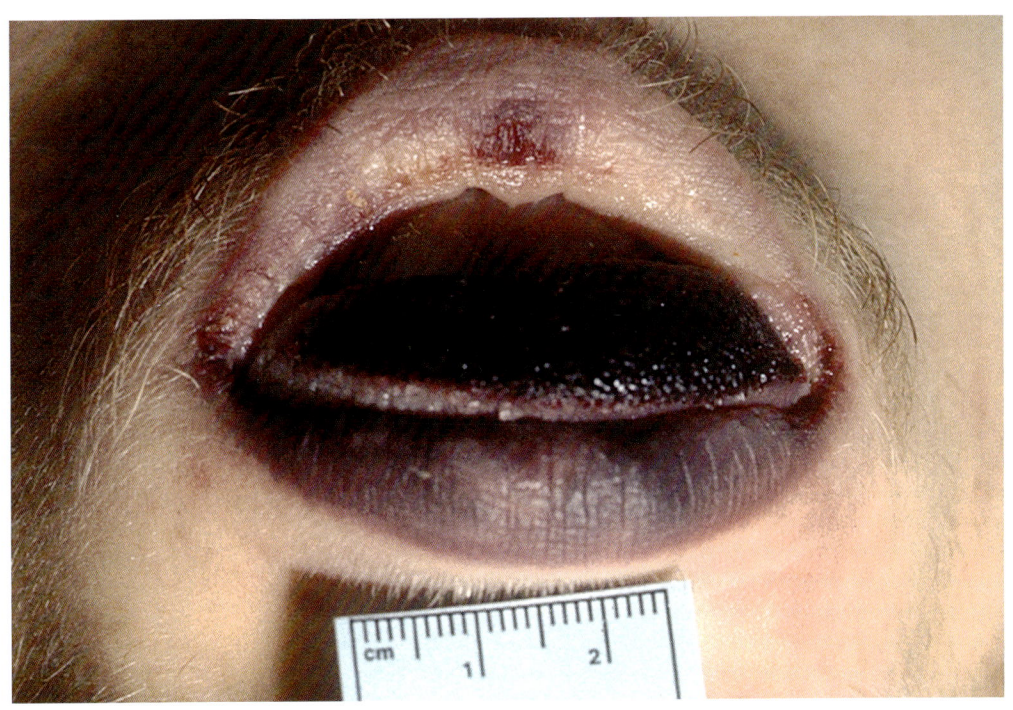

图2-32 暴露的舌尖和下唇在死后干燥。

唇、手指和脚趾末端以及阴囊(图2-32—图2-34)。如果死后眼睑没有闭合,那么巩膜会干燥并表现出棕色的水平线(巩膜黑斑;参阅图2-35)。另一种变化是角膜浑浊。如果死后眼睛是睁开的,角膜浑浊将在死后2—3小时出现;如果双眼是闭合

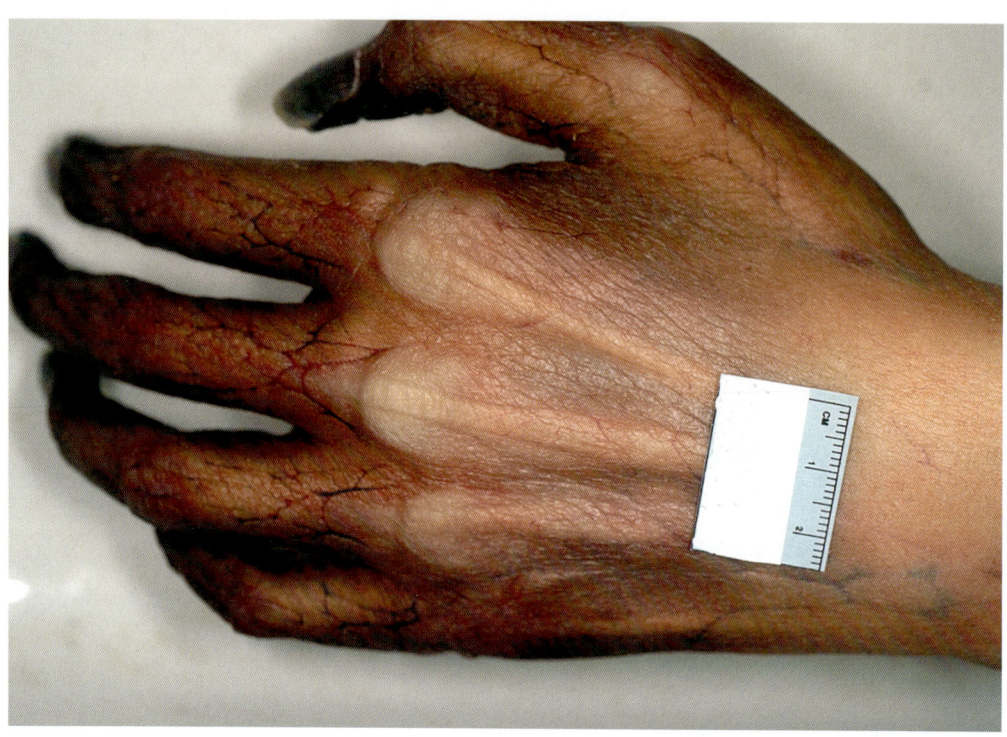

图 2-33　指尖发生死后干燥影响警方采集指纹。

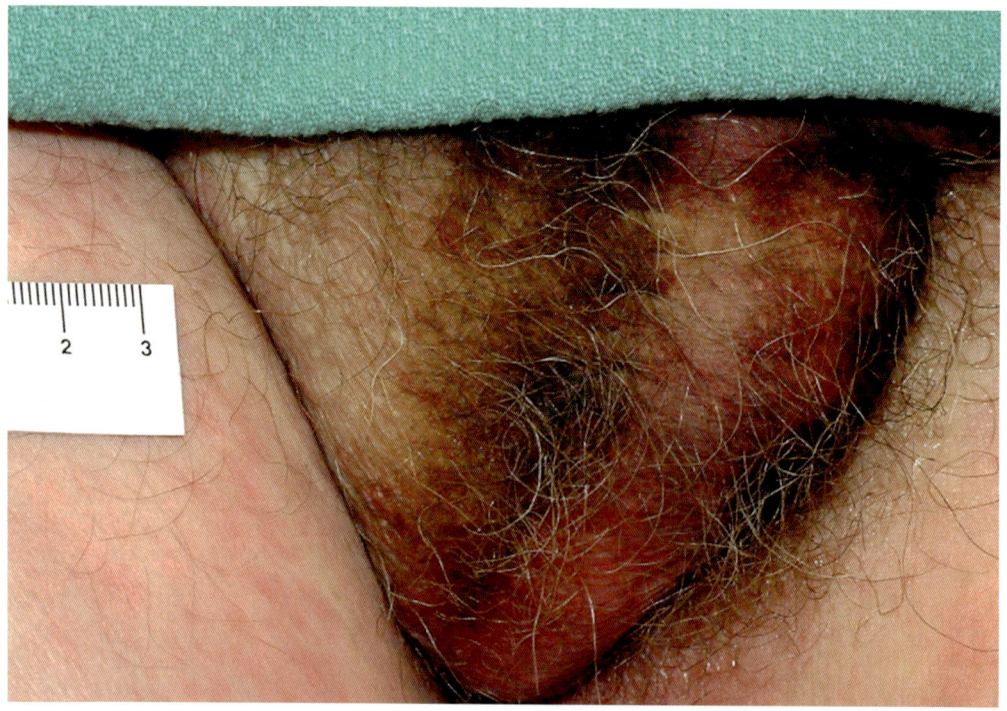

图 2-34　阴囊发生死后干燥,易与皮肤擦伤相混淆。

第 2 章 ｜ 死后尸体变化——"绝佳的伪装者"

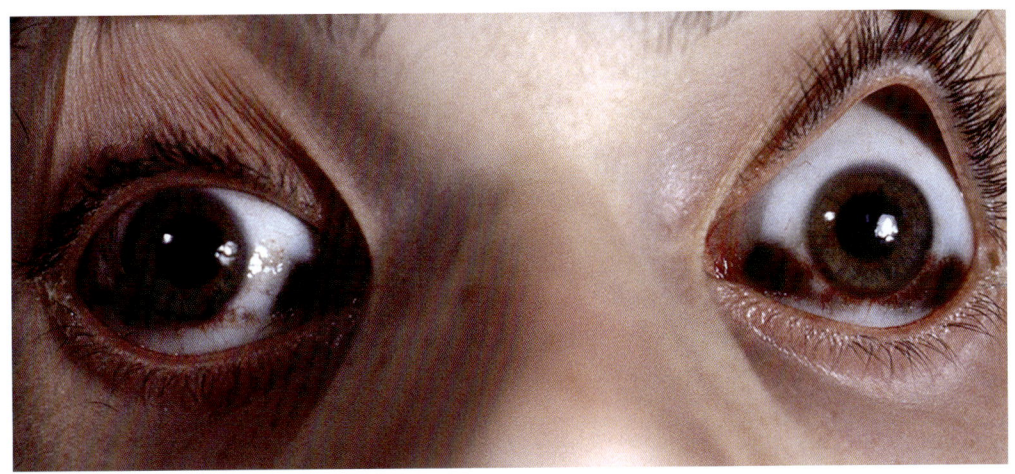

图 2-35 "巩膜黑斑",巩膜干燥。

的,角膜浑浊则在死后 24 小时出现(6,8)。皮肤皮革样变一般也出现在干燥环境中(图 2-36)。有时还能观察到"空"的尸体,即尸体的体腔是空的(63)。即使在温带气候下,形成木乃伊一般仍需要数月,但也有研究者观察到在其他区域(安大略省西南部,夏天)存在死后 1 个月便形成木乃伊的案例。木乃伊化同样可能在雪中形成(64)。

- 意义
  ○ 指尖干燥会对指纹的采集造成影响(图 2-33;参考文献 65,66)。

图 2-36 木乃伊化。部分白骨化残留尸体的骨盆区域可看到皮革样化的皮肤。

- 在阴囊或舌上干燥区域可观察到局部黑色样变,易与损伤相混淆(图2-32 和图2-34)。但切开相应区域不会发现出血,对移除的睾丸进行检查也不会发现异常。
- 巩膜干燥易与生前出血相混淆(图2-35)。但这种现象并不会扩展到巩膜其他位置。

另一种尸体腐败的变异是尸蜡(由脂肪和蜡组成),皮下脂肪在内源性脂肪酶和细菌酶类的作用下,转化为一种灰黄色、油腻的或黏土状的物质(图2-37;参考文献45,67)。甘油三酯发生水解产生液化的中性油脂(储存脂肪),并渗入相邻的软组织(如肌肉)和器官中。不饱和脂肪酸在细菌酶类的作用下转化为饱和形态,主要是软脂酸和硬脂酸。这些脂肪酸比墓地温度(3℃-16℃或37°F-59°F)有更高的熔点(软脂酸63℃或142°F,硬脂酸81℃或176°F),因此会结晶生成一种坚实的固体。尸蜡更常见于肥胖的尸体或女性尸体,因为这类尸体的脂肪含量更高(45)。有多种因素会影响尸蜡的发展(如潮湿的或浸水的土壤)(45)。尸蜡的分布是多变的,可以出现在尸体表面或包绕骨骼;也曾在脂肪肝里发现尸蜡。尸蜡可维持数年(45)。由于尸蜡在水中的溶解度较低,所以尸体可以保留外形。在温带气候,出现尸蜡的预计时间是在死亡几个月之后。

图2-37　尸蜡包裹长骨。

6 胃内容物

在死者最后一次进食时间、进食量、食物种类和性状已知的情况下,通过对胃内容物进行检查可推断死亡时间(68-70)。有时如果药片还没有被消化,通过检验胃内容物可以在毒理学层面上推断出的死亡原因(图2-38;参考文献68)。调查员可

图 2-38 尸体解剖时打开胃。在大部分案件,胃内的药物已经溶解。发现大量药片时支持死者本人摄入的可能。

能会要求法医检查胃部,特别是在现场进行初步尸体检查,而没有记录其他死后变化参数的情况下。

在尸体解剖中,需要记录食物种类、进食量和消化状态。如果胃内容物可被辨认且特殊,可以推断死者在进食后直至死亡都没有再次吃类似特殊的食物。同时摄入的液体、易消化和难消化的固体食物的胃排空速率并不相同(69),液体排空的速率更快(68-70)。胃消化和排空常保持在一个恒定的速率。大容量和高热量的食物排空较慢(如少量食物,2 小时; 中等量食物,3-4 小时; 大量食物,4-6 小时),但不同种类食物的消化是不同的,并且在死后还能被继续消化(5, 68, 69, 71, 72)。某些食物(如富含纤维素的蔬菜)比较难被消化,在胃中滞留时间更长(72)。未嚼碎的、大片状的食物消化较慢且在胃内停留时间较长(71-73)。同一个人的胃排空时间也存在差异,不同人在相似的环境下吃相同食物的胃排空时间也会不同。胃排空时间受各种因素影响,有些因素会延长胃排空时间,包括损伤、休克、疾病、头部损伤引起的颅内压升高、情绪不佳、摄入乙醇和其他药物(如麻醉性镇痛药; 参考文献 68, 70-72)。严重的损伤可延长胃排空时间长达数天(70)。因为受到如此众多因素的影响,所以通过胃内容物很少能有效地推断死亡时间(68, 69, 71, 74)。

7 防腐处理

殡仪馆需要通过防腐处理来保存尸体,以便进行开棺的葬礼,防腐可以尽可能地降低尸体死后的变化(75, 76)。防腐操作会导致软组织的干燥和硬化(75)。经过防腐处理的尸体最终还是会腐败,腐败最先从受压区域开始,如臀部和腿部,因为该区域被防腐液体浸润较少(47,77)。

移除死者衣物,清洗死者头发,修整死者面部,然后清洗尸体(76)。在锁骨下区域作切口,让血液从静脉系统中排空,注入防腐剂,在压力的作用下,防腐剂会进入动脉(图2-39;参考文献75,77)。防腐剂是甲醛、抗凝血剂、香水、表面活化剂(可降低表面张力,增加液体的穿透性)、着色剂、改性剂(如保湿剂或脱水剂)和有机溶剂(乙醇、水、甘油的混合物,用来承载各类防腐化学物质)的混合液体。股动脉和肱动脉同样可以被注射防腐剂(75,76)。目前已经报道了多个穿刺部位用于防腐处理(77)。缝合穿刺切口,在切口底部放置粉末或棉花以吸收渗出液(77)。

为了减少气体膨胀,通常在尸体肚脐周围进行穿刺,用穿刺套管针在肠管上打孔(77)。同样可在其他器官上进行穿刺(图2-39;参考文献76)。阴囊也可以进行穿刺(77)。空腔器官(如心脏、膀胱)在吸出内容物后,可以注入防腐剂(75-77)。缝合或用纽扣堵塞皮肤上的穿刺套管针伤口(图2-39;参考文献77)。有时也可将穿刺套管针直接插入四肢(77)。

在尸体面部涂抹化妆品。用帽子遮住眼睛,固定或缝合下颌关节(77)。将组织填充剂注入眼眶和面部来缓解面容凹陷(76,77)。

更换尸体衣物。服装的背部是开放式的从而使穿衣更为轻松。最内层的衣物需要使用塑料材质,这样可以防止液体渗出(77)。

如果尸体已被解剖,使用金属夹固定颅骨,可起到稳定作用(77)。尸体体腔可能已经被防腐剂浸湿的材料(如衣物、纸毛巾)填充(77)。可能还会有一个存放器官的袋子(77)。体腔内填充的颗粒材料由硬化或脱水混合物和防腐粉末组成。

• 意义

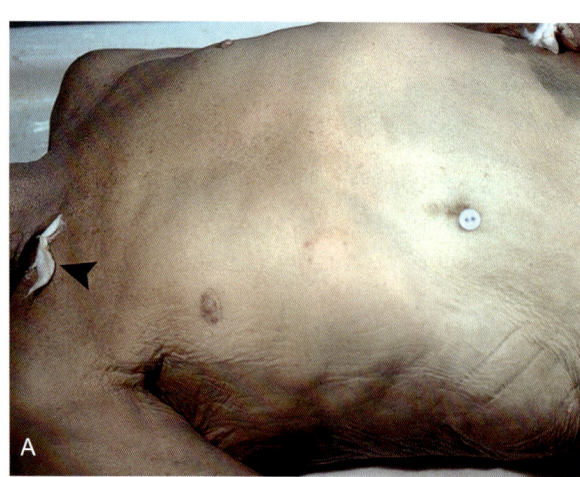
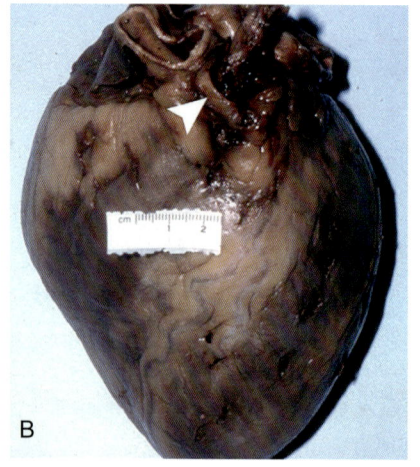

图2-39 经过防腐处理的尸体。(A)用纽扣来隐藏尸体穿刺部位。锁骨下的切口用棉质敷料掩盖(三角箭头)。(B)经过防腐处理的心脏存在人工穿刺创口。值得注意的是在肺动脉中会出现血凝块(三角箭头),可能会与血栓相混淆。

- 防腐后的血液已经不再适合进行毒物分析。玻璃体液可作为替代品(76)。
- 血液凝集会形成"假性血栓",易与肺血栓栓塞相混淆(图2-39;参考文献75,77)。
- 会出现假性损伤(75,76,78,79)。
- 防腐剂的灌注会加重原有的挫伤,形成死后擦伤,或者引起血管破裂,产生死后出血(如颈部区域)(图2-40;参考文献75-77)。血液引流会使尸斑减少,从而使真实的或人为的擦伤更加明显,这个改变会引起死者家属和现场调查员的注意(76)。
- 套管针穿刺不仅会引起腹腔内器官损伤,同时也会影响胸部和骨盆结构(图2-39;参考文献75)。有案例报道生前枪弹伤被死后穿刺套管针的纽扣所掩盖(75,76)。
- 面部化妆会掩盖损伤(图2-41;参考文献75,76)。
- 在检查眼睛出血时,需要移除遮挡眼睛的帽子(76)。
- 损伤可能会改变[如缝合(75,77,79)]。
- 剃须可能会形成颈部擦伤,易与扼颈引起的损伤相混淆(76,77)。
- 着色剂的使用会形成白皙、红润的外观,易与一氧化碳中毒相混淆(76)。

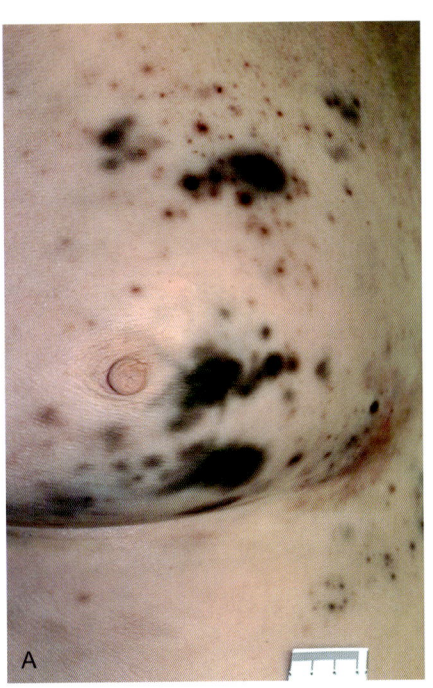
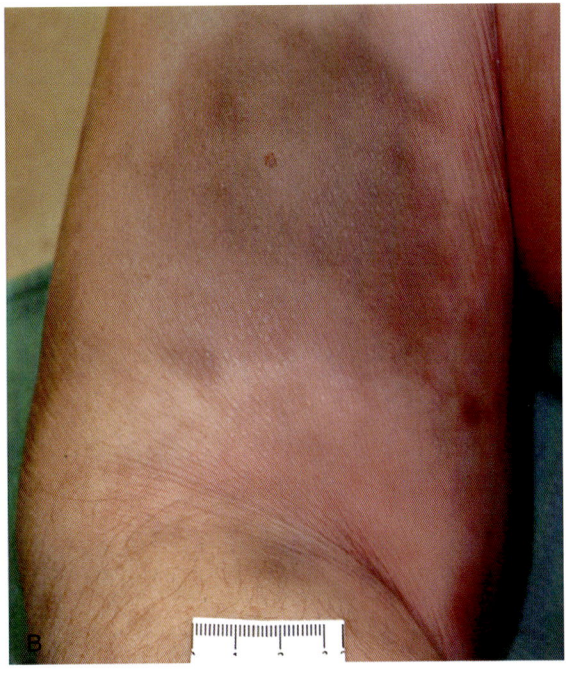

图2-40 经过防腐处理的尸体。死者生前站立不稳。因为前期诊断为肺动脉栓塞,死者生前服用了抗凝剂华法林。在死亡前几天,去医院就医时需要辅助行走。法医在尸体防腐前对尸体进行尸表检查时没有发现挫伤。防腐师指出在进行灌注尸体时发现了挫伤。(A)尸体解剖时,在胸部可以观察到很多擦伤。(B)在右上肢内侧可观察到大片擦伤。

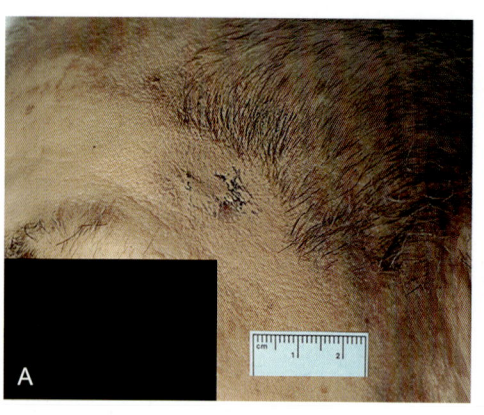
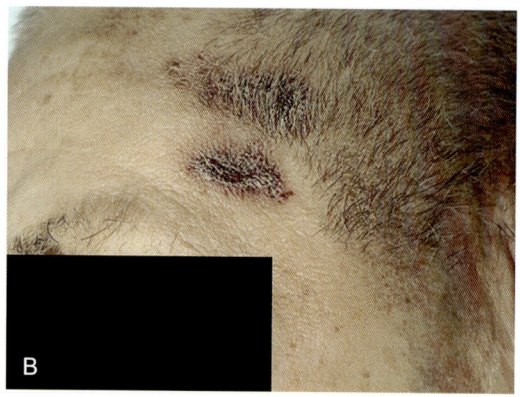

图 2-41 经过防腐处理的尸体。(A)面部使用了化妆品。(B)擦拭面部后暴露了左鬓角处擦伤。

8 法医昆虫学

法医昆虫学是利用昆虫和其他节肢动物来进行法医学的死亡调查(45,80)。法医需要意识到尸体身上昆虫的重要性,从而帮助他们收集信息(49)。法医同时也需要记录昆虫学相关的检查结果(如衣物、明显的伤痕)。

蝇类(双翅目、丽蝇科或绿头蝇)是最先侵入尸体的昆虫(45)。在个体死亡后 1—2 周,这些昆虫的成熟过程(卵—幼虫—蛹—成虫)就像一个生物钟(45,49,80,81)。蝇类的生命演变周期在不同地区有差异(45,80)。富含氨的化合物和硫化氢对虫卵的沉积起到极大的刺激作用(45)。双翅目蝇类偏好于在湿润的组织中产卵,在干燥的组织中不会产卵(45)。蝇类幼虫阶段的生长取决于尸体被发现前死亡现场的温度(45,47,49,80)。在死后几秒,蝇类的虫卵就会出现在尸体的孔洞或伤口上(图 2-31,图 2-42;参考文献 45,47,82)。

需收集蝇类的虫卵、幼虫、蛹和成虫需(80)。幼虫可以保存在福尔马林中。虫卵和蛹可放置于标本瓶中,并放入食物(如肝脏、尸体的肌肉),覆盖纱布,并保持合适的温度和湿度。

- 意义
  - 幼虫会改变伤口形态(36,49,62)。皮肤上幼虫大量聚集提示该部位可能有出血(49,82)。
  - 有活的蛆虫却没有尸体的地点,提示尸体可能曾被放置在这个位置。在幼虫体内发现人类 DNA 说明这些幼虫进食过人体组织(50)。
  - 对蝇类的幼虫进行毒物分析可反映死者生前的药物使用情况(49,50)。
  - 如果蛆虫聚集成团,冷藏环境也难以抑制蛆虫的摄食活动(47,82)。成团蛆虫的温度范围是 27℃—35℃ [81℉—95℉(50)]。
  - 其他昆虫(如蚂蚁、蟑螂、甲虫)也可对尸体造成破坏(图 2-43;参考文献 36,78,81,83,84)。

第 2 章 | 死后尸体变化——"绝佳的伪装者"

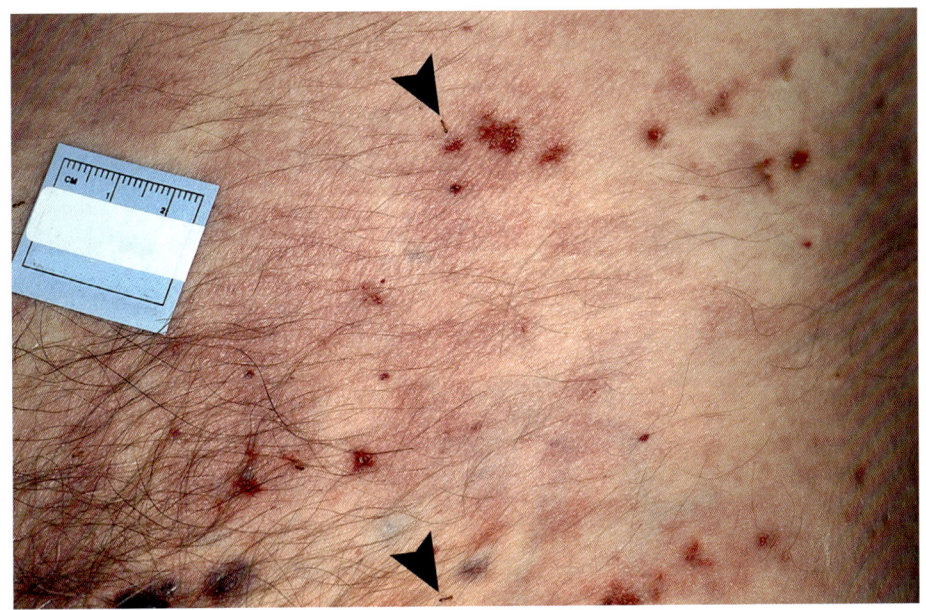

图 2-43　死后蚂蚁咬食（三角箭头）形成的假性"擦伤"。

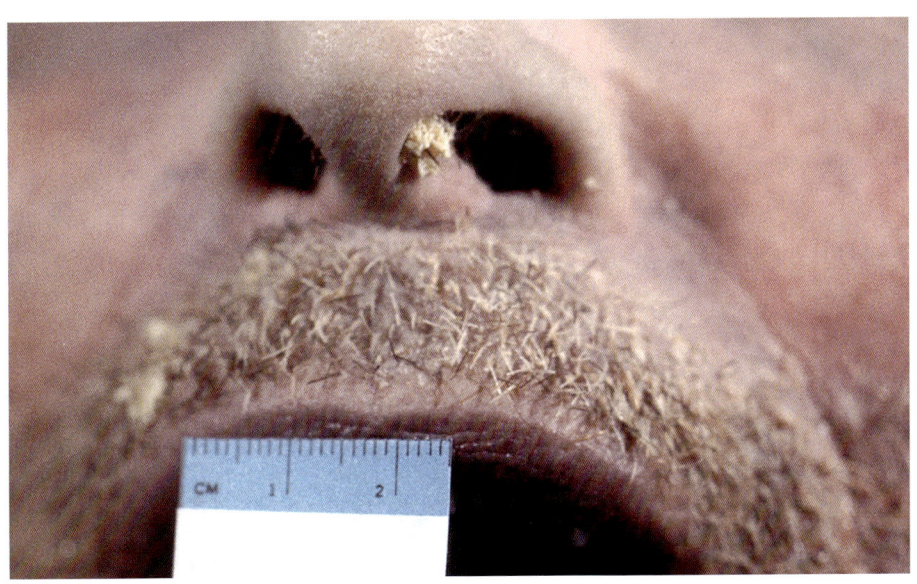

图 2-42　左侧鼻孔的苍蝇虫卵。

9　动物对尸体的毁坏

　　动物毁坏易被误认为生前损伤，从而怀疑案件为他杀（35，36，48，85-89）。动物也可毁坏或改变生前损伤（36）。有案例报道，独居主人自然死亡，家庭宠物也被困于房间内，无法获得食物。有时即使房间内有食物，宠物也有可能因为其他各种原因对尸体进行噬食（85）。宠物可能刚开始只是舔或轻推失去意识的主人，随后可能会撕咬尸体(85,89)。住宅的封闭空间也可以引起宠物对主人攻击(89)。宠物对主人尸体的噬食行为可在主人死后一天内出现(88)。有案例报道,犬在主人死后45分钟内就出现了噬食尸体的行为(89)。

其他动物(如啮齿动物)也会啃咬尸体(85,90,91)。现场啮齿动物的排泄物或毛发可提示损伤形成原因(85,87)。啮齿动物常在社会经济地位低下人群的住所内和室外流浪人群的周围活动。在室外,各种动物均可以毁坏骨骼(36,47)。

9.1 尸体检验

动物常咬食尸体上暴露的柔软部分[如嘴和鼻子(36,87-89)]。大型宠物(如犬;图2-44,参考文献36,85,86,88)咬食尸体后常会导致尸体面部、颈部和躯干部的大面积缺损,并伴有内脏器官不同程度的缺失和骨骼损伤,身体的某些部位(如耳朵)会被全部毁损(图2-44;参考文献91)。啮齿动物可以啃咬尸体衣物覆盖下的区域(87)。动物对尸体的毁损极少情况下会伴有出血或挫伤(85-87,89),在这些损伤中可找到动物的毛发(89)。缺乏明显的抵抗伤(85,87)。在组织缺损的边缘可能观察到由犬齿所引起的咬痕和由脚爪所造成的线性刮痕(图2-44;参考文献85,88,89)。刺创口是食肉动物犬齿留下的典型特征(85)。啮齿动物的噬食具有组织分层损伤的特征(90)。啮齿动物会在某个区域持续啃咬直到所有的皮肤和软组织都被嚼碎,露出肌腱、韧带和骨骼(87)。与犬类啃咬留下的大片不规则的组织缺损边缘相比,啮齿动物造成的损伤更加光滑,呈细锯齿状和扇形(图2-45;参考文献36,85,87,90)。可以观察到牙齿所留下的平行皮肤撕裂创(36,87)。对这些伤口进行显微镜检查不会观察到炎症反应(85,86)。

动物胃内可能存在人体残留组织,这些组织可通过显微镜和DNA分析进行确认(89)。

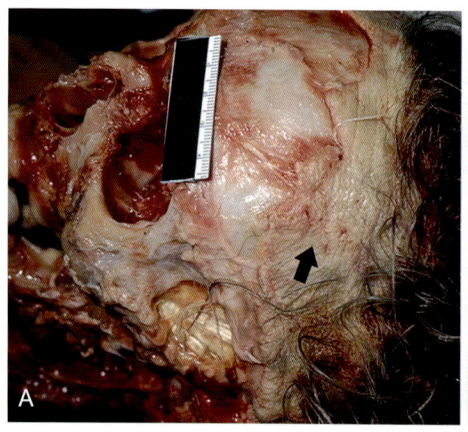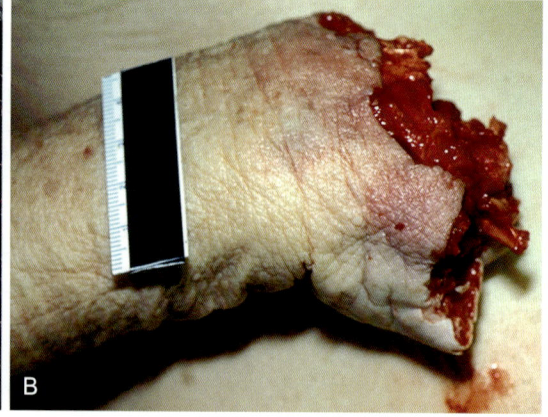

图2-44 死后被犬噬食。(A)面部出现大面积不规则软组织缺损。值得注意的是箭头所指的刺创可能由犬齿所致。(B)动物啃咬导致手的部分缺失(加拿大安大略省汉密尔顿市法医办公室 C. Rao 博士供图)。

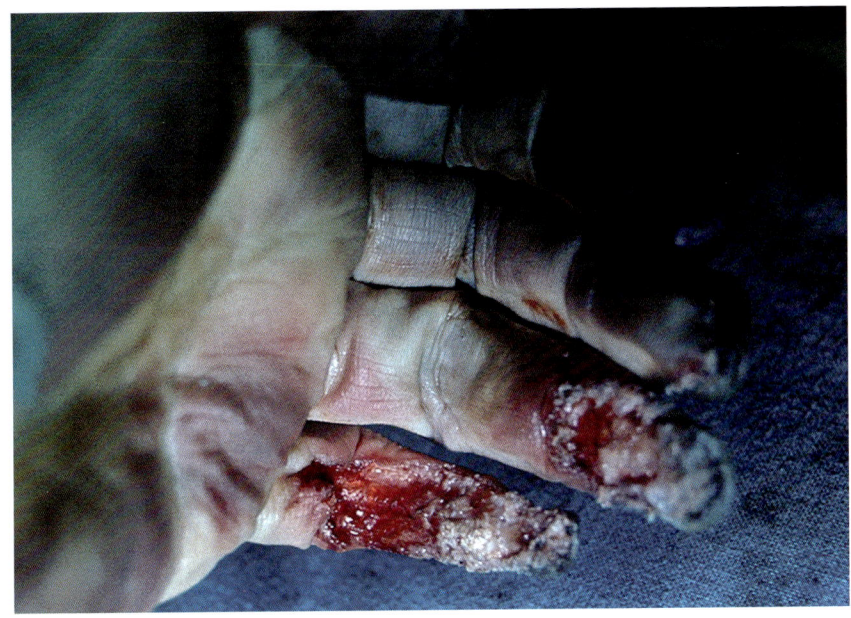

图 2-45 死后手指遭啮齿动物噬食（加拿大安大略省汉密尔顿市法医办公室 D. King 博士供图）。

10 关联性调查

利用死亡现场的信息可推断死亡时间（图 2-46）。家中死亡，在前门廊发现存放了 3 天的报纸，提示死者很可能 3 天前死亡。

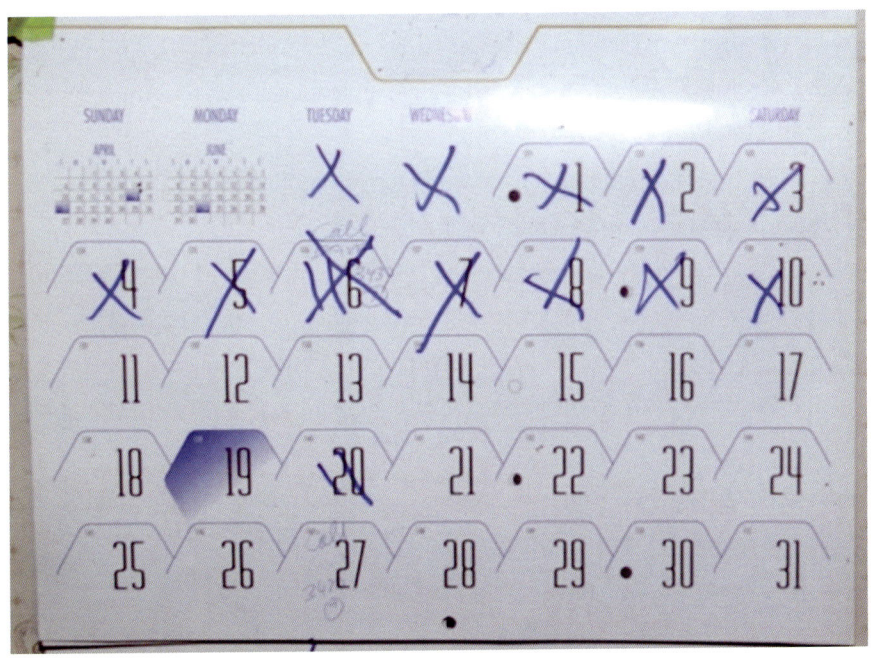

图 2-46 厨房的日历标记到该月 10 号。独居者 1 周后被发现死亡，尸体已腐败。

11 死后其他损伤

死后的人为损伤：

- 针刺吸取眼内玻璃体液时引起巩膜出血；为了获取角膜而进行眼球摘取术所致的眶周软组织出血（参阅标题 3.3；图 2-17；参考文献 92，93）。
- 颅骨未被完全锯断时，暴力移除颅骨会引起颅底骨折。

孙杰　张吉　译

参考文献

1. Burton, J. F. Fallacies in the signs of death. J. Forensic Sci. 19:529–534, 1974.
2. Burton, J. F. The estimated time of death. Leg. Med. Annu. 1976:31–35, 1977.
3. Gonzales, T. A., Vance, M., Helpern, M., Umberger, C. J. Legal Medicine, Pathology and Toxicology. 2nd ed. Appleton Century Crofts, New York, 1954.
4. Camps, F. E. Legal Medicine. 2nd ed. John Wright and Sons, Bristol, UK, 1968.
5. Adelson, L. The Pathology of Homicide. Charles C. Thomas, Springfield, IL, 1974.
6. DiMaio, V. J., DiMaio, D. Forensic Pathology. 2nd ed. CRC Press, New York, 2001.
7. Henssge, C., Knight, B. E., Krompecher, T., Madea, B., Nokes, L. The Estimation of the Time Since Death in the Early Postmortem Period. 2nd ed. Arnold, London, 2002.
8. Perper, J. A. Time of death and changes after death—Part 1. Anatomical considerations. In: Spitz, W. V., ed. Medicolegal Investigation of Death. Guidelines for the Application of Pathology to Crime Investigation. Charles C. Thomas, Springfield, IL, pp. 14–64, 1993
9. Bray, M. Chemical estimation of fresh water immersion intervals. Am. J. Forensic Med Pathol. 6:133–139, 1985.
10. Coe, J. I. Vitreous potassium as a measure of the postmortem interval: an historical review and critical evaluation. Forensic Sci. Int. 42:201–213, 1989.
11. James, R. A., Hoadley, P. A., Sampson, B. G. Determination of postmortem interval by sampling vitreous humour. Am. J. Forensic Med. Pathol. 18:158–162, 1997.
12. Lange, N., Swearer, S., Sturner, W. Q. Human postmortem interval estimation from vitreous potassium: an analysis of original data from six different studies. Forensic Sci. Int. 66:159–174, 1994.
13. Madea, B., Henssge, C., Honig, W., Gerbracht, A. References for determining the time of death by potassium in vitreous humor. Forensic Sci. Int. 40:231–243, 1989.
14. Mulla, A., Massey, K. L., Kalra, J. Vitreous humor biochemical constituents: evaluation of between-eye differences. Am. J. Forensic Med. Pathol. 26:146–149, 2005.
15. Munoz, J. I., Suarez-Penaranda, J. M., Otero, X. L., et al. A new perspective in the

estimation of postmortem interval (PMI) based on vitreous. J. Forensic Sci. 46:209–214, 2001.

16. Pounder, D. J., Carson, D. O., Johnston, K., Orihara, Y. Electrolyte concentration differences between left and right vitreous humor samples. J. Forensic Sci. 43:604–607, 1998.

17. Stephens, R. J., Richards, R. G. Vitreous humor chemistry: the use of potassium concentration for the prediction of the postmortem interval. J. Forensic Sci. 32:503–509, 1987.

18. Vass, A. A., Barshick, S. A., Sega, G., et al. Decomposition chemistry of human remains: a new methodology for determining the postmortem interval. J. Forensic Sci. 47:542–553, 2002.

19. Henssge, C., Althaus, L., Bolt, J., et al. Experiences with a compound method for estimating the time since death. II. Integration of non–temperature–based methods. Int. J. Legal Med. 113:320–331, 2000.

20. Kobayashi, M., Takatori, T., Iwadate, K., Nakajima, M. Reconsideration of the sequence of rigor mortis through postmortem changes in adenosine nucleotides and lactic acid in different rat muscles. Forensic Sci. Int. 82:243–253, 1996.

21. Kobayashi, M., Ikegaya, H., Takase, I., Hatanaka, K., Sakurada, K., Iwase, H. Development of rigor mortis is not affected by muscle volume. Forensic Sci. Int. 117:213–219, 2001.

22. Krompecher, T., Bergerioux, C., Brandt–Casadevall, C., Gujer, H. R. Experimental evaluation of rigor mortis. VI. Effect of various causes of death on the evolution of rigor mortis. Forensic Sci. Int. 22:1–9, 1983.

23. Krompecher, T., Fryc, O. Experimental evaluation of rigor mortis. IV. Change in strength and evolution of rigor mortis in the case of physical exercise preceding death. Forensic Sci. Int. 12:103–107, 1978.

24. Krompecher, T. Experimental evaluation of rigor mortis. V. Effect of various temperatures on the evolution of rigor mortis. Forensic Sci. Int. 17:19–26, 1981.

25. Varetto, L., Curto, O. Long persistence of rigor mortis at constant low temperature. Forensic Sci. Int. 147:31–34, 2005.

26. Krompecher, T., Fryc, O. Experimental evaluation of rigor mortis. III. Comparative study of the evolution of rigor mortis in different sized muscle groups in rats. Forensic Sci. Int. 12:97–102, 1978.

27. Kobayashi, M., Takatori, T., Nakajima, M., et al. Does the sequence of onset of rigor mortis depend on the proportion of muscle fibre types and on intra–muscular glycogen content? Int. J. Legal Med. 112:167–171, 1999.

28. Krompecher, T. Experimental evaluation of rigor mortis. VIII. Estimation of time since

death by repeated measurements of the intensity of rigor mortis on rats. Forensic Sci. Int. 68:149–159, 1994.

29. Suzutani, T., Ishibashi, H., Takatori, T. [Studies on the estimation of the postmortem interval. 2. The postmortem lividity (author's transl.]. Hokkaido Igaku Zasshi 52:259–267, 1978.

30. Noriko, T. Immunohistochemical studies on postmortem lividity. Forensic Sci. Int. 72:179–189, 1995.

31. Inoue, M., Suyama, A., Matuoka, T., Inoue, T., Okada, K., Irizawa, Y. Development of an instrument to measure postmortem lividity and its preliminary application to estimate the time since death. Forensic Sci. Int. 65:185–193, 1994.

32. Sannohe S. Change in the postmortem formation of hypostasis in skin preparations 100 micrometers thick. Am. J. Forensic Med. Pathol. 23:349–354, 2002.

33. Bohnert, M., Weinmann, W., Pollak, S. Spectrophotometric evaluation of postmortem lividity. Forensic Sci. Int. 99:149–158, 1999.

34. Avis SP, Archibald J.T. Asphyxial suicide by propane inhalation and plastic bag suffocation. J. Forensic Sci. 39:253–256, 1994.

35. Prahlow, J. A., Linch, C. A. A baby, a virus, and a rat. Am. J. Forensic Med. Pathol. 21:127–133, 2000.

36. Byard, R. W., James, R. A., Gilbert, J. D. Diagnostic problems associated with cadaveric trauma from animal activity. Am. J. Forensic Med. Pathol. 23:238–244, 2002.

37. Nikolic, S., Atanasijevic, T., Micic, J., Djokic, V., Babic, D. Amount of postmortem bleeding: an experimental autopsy study. Am. J. Forensic Med. Pathol. 25:20–22, 2004.

38. Burke, M. P., Olumbe, A. K., Opeskin, K. Postmortem extravasation of blood potentially simulating antemortem bruising. Am. J. Forensic Med. Pathol. 19:46–49, 1998.

39. Betz, P., Lignitz, E., Eisenmenger, W. The time–dependent appearance of black eyes. Int. J. Legal Med. 108:96–99, 1995.

40. Reh, H., Haarhoff, K. [The significance of the settling of blood into dependent and soft tis– sues as evidence for death by throttling and choking (author's transl.)]. Z Rechtsmed 77:47–60, 1975.

41. Maxeiner, H., Bockholdt, B. Homicidal and suicidal ligature strangulation—a comparison of the post–mortem findings. Forensic Sci. Int. 137:60–66, 2003.

42. Betz, P., Penning, R., Keil, W. The detection of petechial haemorrhages of the conjunctivae in dependency on the postmortem interval. Forensic Sci. Int. 64:61–67, 1994.

43. Carter, N., Ali, F., Green, M. A. Problems in the interpretation of hemorrhage into neck musculature in cases of drowning. Am. J. Forensic Med. Pathol. 19:223–225, 1998.

44. Henssge, C., Madea, B. Estimation of the time since death in the early post–mortem period. Forensic Sci. Int. 144:167–175, 2004.
45. Fiedler, S., Graw, M. Decomposition of buried corpses, with special reference to the formation of adipocere. Naturwissenschaften 90:291–300, 2003.
46. Honigschnabl, S., Schaden, E., Stichenwirth, M., et al. Discovery of decomposed and mummified corpses in the domestic setting—a marker of social isolation? J. Forensic Sci. 47:837–842, 2002.
47. Mann, R. W., Bass, W. M., Meadows, L. Time since death and decomposition of the human body: variables and observations in case and experimental field studies. J. Forensic Sci. 35:103–111, 1990.
48. Rodriguez, W. C. III, Bass, W. M. Decomposition of buried bodies and methods that may aid in their location. J. Forensic Sci. 30:836–852, 1985.
49. Campobasso, C. P., Introna, F. The forensic entomologist in the context of the forensic pathologist's role. Forensic Sci. Int. 120:132–139, 2001.
50. Amendt, J., Krettek, R., Zehner, R. Forensic entomology. Naturwissenschaften 91:51–65, 2004.
51. Kibayashi, K., Hamada, K., Honjyo, K., Tsunenari, S. Differentiation between bruises and putrefactive discolorations of the skin by immunological analysis of glycophorin A. Forensic Sci. Int. 61:111–117, 1993.
52. Kirkham, W. R., Andrews, E. E., Snow, C. C., Grape, P. M., Snyder, L. Postmortem pink teeth. J. Forensic Sci. 22:119–131, 1977.
53. van Wyk, C. W. Postmortem pink teeth. Histochemical identification of the causative pigment. Am. J. Forensic Med. Pathol. 10:134–139, 1989.
54. van Wyk, C. W. Postmortem pink teeth: in vitro production. J. Oral Pathol. 17:568–572, 1988.
55. Brondum, N., Simonsen, J. Postmortem red coloration of teeth. A retrospective investigation of 26 cases. Am. J. Forensic Med. Pathol. 8:127–130, 1987.
56. Borrman, H., Du, C. A., Brinkmann, B. Medico–legal aspects of postmortem pink teeth. Int. J. Legal Med. 106:225–231, 1994.
57. Ortmann, C., DuChesne, A. A partially mummified corpse with pink teeth and pink nails. Int. J. Legal Med. 111:35–37, 1998.
58. Biddinger, P. W. Postmortem wound dehiscence. A report of three cases. Am. J. Forensic Med. Pathol. 8:120–122, 1987.
59. McGee, M. B., Coe, J. I. Postmortem wound dehiscence: a medicolegal masquerade. J. Forensic Sci. 26:216–219, 1981.

60. Haglund, W. D. Disappearance of soft tissue and the disarticulation of human remains from aqueous environments. J. Forensic Sci. 38:806–815, 1993.
61. Byard, R. W., James, R. A., Zuccollo, J. Potential confusion arising from materials presenting as possible human remains. Am. J. Forensic Med. Pathol. 22:391–394, 2001.
62. Meyersohn, J. Putrefaction: a difficulty in forensic medicine. J. Forensic Med. 18:114–117, 1971.
63. Emson, H. E. The case of the empty body. Am. J. Forensic Med. Pathol. 12:332–333, 1991.
64. Ambach, E., Tributsch, W., Ambach, W. Is mummification possible in snow? Forensic Sci. Int. 54:191–192, 1992.
65. Schmidt, C. W., Nawrocki, S. P., Williamson, M. A., Marlin, D.C. Obtaining fingerprints from mummified fingers: a method for tissue rehydration adapted from the archeological literature. J. Forensic Sci. 45:874–875, 2000.
66. Kahana, T., Grande, A., Tancredi, D. M., Penalver, J., Hiss, J. Fingerprinting the deceased: traditional and new techniques. J. Forensic Sci. 46:908–912, 2001.
67. Forbes, S. L., Stuart, B. H., Dadour, I. R., Dent, B. B. A preliminary investigation of the stages of adipocere formation. J. Forensic Sci. 49:566–574, 2004.
68. Horowitz, M., Pounder, D. J. Is the stomach a useful forensic clock? Aust. N. Z. J. Med. 15:273–276, 1985.
69. Horowitz, M., Pounder, D. J. Gastric emptying—forensic implications of current concepts. Med. Sci. Law 25:201–214, 1985.
70. Rose, E. F. Factors influencing gastric emptying. J. Forensic Sci. 24:200–206, 1979.
71. Jaffe, F. A. Stomach contents and the time of death. Reexamination of a persistent question. Am. J. Forensic Med. Pathol. 10:37–41, 1989.
72. Suzuki, S. Experimental studies on the presumption of the time after food intake from stomach contents. Forensic Sci. Int. 35:83–117, 1987.
73. Pera, P., Bucca, C., Borro, R., Bernocco, C., De, L. A., Carossa, S. Influence of mastication on gastric emptying. J. Dent. Res. 81:179–181, 2002.
74. Murphy, G. K. The trials of Steven Truscott. Am. J. Forensic Med. Pathol. 12:344–349, 1991.
75. Oxley, D. W. Examination of the exhumed body and embalming artifacts. Med. Leg. Bull. 33:1–7, 1984.
76. Rivers, R. L. Embalming artifacts. J. Forensic Sci. 23:531–535, 1978.
77. Hanzlick, R. Embalming, body preparation, burial, and disinterment. An overview for forensic pathologists. Am. J. Forensic Med. Pathol. 15:122–131, 1994.

78. Prahlow, J. A., McClain, J. L. Lesions that simulate gunshot wounds. J. Clin Forensic Med. 4:121–125, 1997.
79. Opeskin, K. An unusual injury. Med. Sci. Law 32:58–60, 1992.
80. Kulshrestha, P., Chandra, H. Time since death. An entomological study on corpses. Am. J. Forensic Med. Pathol. 8:233–238, 1987.
81. Benecke, M. A brief history of forensic entomology. Forensic Sci. Int. 120:2–14, 2001.
82. Anderson, G. S. The use of insects to determine time of decapitation: a case–study from British Columbia. J. Forensic Sci. 42:947–950, 1997.
83. Denic, N., Huyer, D. W., Sinal, S. H., Lantz, P. E., Smith, C. R., Silver, M. M. Cockroach: the omnivorous scavenger. Potential misinterpretation of postmortem injuries. Am. J. Forensic Med. Pathol. 18:177–180, 1997.
84. Prahlow, J. A., Barnard, J. J. Fatal anaphylaxis due to fire ant stings. Am. J. Forensic Med. Pathol. 19:137–142, 1998.
85. Tsokos, M., Schulz, F. Indoor postmortem animal interference by carnivores and rodents:report of two cases and review of the literature. Int. J. Legal Med. 112:115–119, 1999.
86. Tsokos, M., Schulz, F., Puschel, K. Unusual injury pattern in a case of postmortem animal depredation by a domestic German shepherd. Am. J. Forensic Med. Pathol. 20:247–250, 1999.
87. Tsokos, M., Matschke, J., Gehl, A., Koops, E., Puschel, K. Skin and soft tissue artifacts due to postmortem damage caused by rodents. Forensic Sci. Int. 104:47–57, 1999.
88. Rossi, M. L., Shahrom, A. W., Chapman, R. C., Vanezis, P. Postmortem injuries by indoor pets. Am. J. Forensic Med. Pathol. 15:105–109, 1994.
89. Rothschild, M. A., Schneider, V. On the temporal onset of postmortem animal scavenging. "Motivation" of the animal. Forensic Sci. Int. 89:57–64, 1997.
90. Haglund, W. D. Contribution of rodents to postmortem artifacts of bone and soft tissue. J. Forensic Sci. 37:1459–1465, 1992.
91. Patel, F. Artefact in forensic medicine: postmortem rodent activity. J. Forensic Sci. 39:257–260, 1994.
92. Harris, L. S. Subscleral hemorrhage. Am. J. Forensic Med. Pathol. 7:177–178, 1986.
93. Di Maio, V. J. Subscleral hemorrhage. Am. J. Forensic Med. Pathol. 6:95, 1985.

第3章
窒 息

概述

　　窒息死的机制为氧和二氧化碳之间的交换发生障碍。机械性窒息［即呼吸和（或）循环被物理性干扰］在法医学的死亡调查中屡见不鲜。虽然尸体表面和内部出现的瘀点性出血被认为是窒息死的标志,但这一表现在不同类型的机械性窒息中并非一成不变。因此,呼吸和循环受阻在瘀点性出血形成中的相对作用至今仍存在争议。缢死是机械性窒息的常见类型之一,可在各种情况下发生,有些比较特殊。本章记录了缢死的一系列尸体内外解剖所见,而其他类型的机械性窒息尸体特征可能更细微,证明在这些特殊情况下用系统方法进行"完整尸检"极其重要。在吸入有毒气体(如一氧化碳)引起的死亡中,死亡原因只能通过毒物化学检测来确认。

　　关键词：窒息；瘀点性出血；一氧化碳

1 前言
1.1 机械性窒息

　　"窒息"(asphyxia)一词是希腊语的派生词,意思是"脉搏停止"(1)。任何死亡在本质上都是"窒息",但在法医病理学中,窒息指体内氧和二氧化碳的交换受到干扰(1)。

　　机械方式可以干扰氧和二氧化碳的交换——即机械性窒息。气流阻塞发生于鼻腔、口腔至肺泡的任何位置——即乏氧性缺氧(anoxic anoxia)(2)。在颈部受压的情况下,可引起喉部气道阻塞和舌头移位致咽后部闭塞,但这并非窒息的唯一原因(3–5)。在缢死者的气管切开位点上方可观察到缢索痕迹(6,7)。有时在自缢者的气道中可见呕吐物(3)。颈部的压迫导致血管受压,颈动脉和椎动脉的变狭减少了流向大脑的含氧血液；颈静脉受压阻碍了二氧化碳和代谢物排出大脑——即循环停滞性缺氧(stagnant hypoxia)(2)。压闭颈部结构所需的力量已经通过实验得到确定：压闭颈静脉需2千克(4.5磅),压闭颈动脉需5千克(11磅),压闭气管需9千克(20

磅),压闭椎动脉需 30 千克(66 磅[8])。上述研究结果意味着在动脉和气道被压闭之前静脉血流已经减少(3)。由于外部压力导致静脉血流受阻,当意识丧失时,肢体肌张力也迅速消失,允许更大的外部压力进一步压闭颈动脉和气道(3)。另外,通过压迫胸壁阻碍呼吸运动也是一种机械性窒息。

吸入异常空气可引起窒息。空气中缺氧也是另一种形式的乏氧性缺氧。吸入有毒气体(化学性窒息)导致氧和血红蛋白之间的相互作用受损,称贫血性缺氧(如吸入一氧化碳);或组织不能利用氧,称组织性缺氧(如氰化物中毒;参阅标题 3.9;第 4 章标题 4.1;参考文献 2)。

1.2 机械性窒息的分类

以下是根据阻塞部位对机械性窒息的分类:

- 捂死(又称闷死)——堵塞性窒息(口、鼻)。
- 哽死(口、口咽、喉)。
- 扼死,缢死(颈部,包括喉、气管和主要血管)。
- 体位性窒息(胸部、颈部)。
- 溺死(上呼吸道及下呼吸道)。
- 外伤性窒息(胸部)。
- 挤压死(胸部)。

1.3 窒息征象

某些死后外部和内部征象与窒息有关,但并非特异性,如:

- 发绀(甲床和面部呈紫色,包括嘴唇和耳垂)。
- 血液呈流动性。
- 肺充血和水肿。
- 右心室扩张(参阅标题 1.5)。
- 浆膜面(心外膜、脏胸膜)和某些器官(如甲状腺;参阅标题 6;图 3-1)出现瘀点性出血。在解释胸膜面明显瘀点性出血时必须小心谨慎,因为胸膜下瘀点性出血会在尸检过程中出现或消失,后者发生在肺自纵隔被移除时。"假性瘀点"可由胸膜静脉充盈、胸膜局部增厚或胸膜下炭色素沉积引起(9)。

1.4 颈部压迫与瘀点性出血的关系

瘀点性出血是由毛细管破裂(10)引起的针尖样、非凸起性、圆形的紫色或红色斑点(<2 毫米或 0.125 英寸)。疏松结缔组织将首先出现瘀点性出血(11)。需要注意的是,各种非窒息死亡也可引起瘀点性出血,如暴发性感染中的脑膜炎球菌血症,该病直接损伤毛细血管致广泛性皮肤和器官瘀点性出血,该征象也可出现于某些消耗性凝血病(10)。

瘀点性出血的形成与窒息相关,其机制是由于血管内压力增加和缺氧引起毛细血管破裂(12-18)。分布在头部和颈部的瘀点性出血可能由颈部受压引起;然而,在

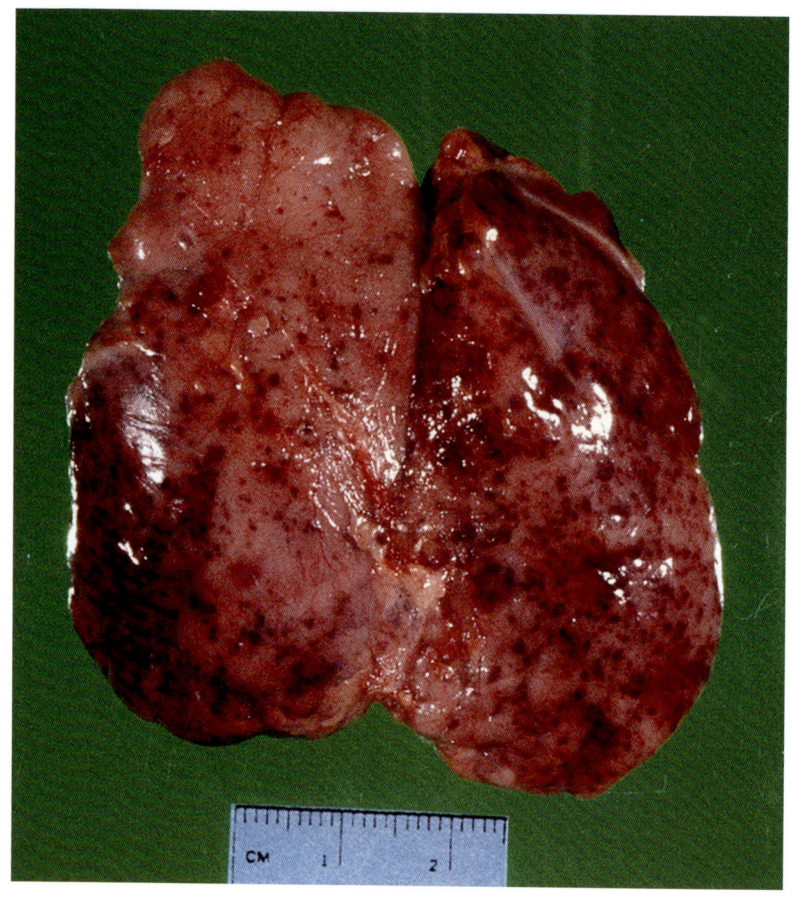

图 3-1 婴儿猝死综合征，死者胸腺呈瘀点性出血，多个瘀点已局部融合。

未失去意识的非缺氧者和勒颈幸存者身上亦可见瘀点性出血 (19)，在参与倒挂的志愿者中也可观察到头部的瘀点性出血和眼内压升高 (20)。

仅压闭头部静脉是导致尸体青灰色部位瘀点性出血的原因，特别是头低位时的瘀点性出血（参阅第 2 章标题 3.3；参考文献 21）。帽状腱膜下瘀点性出血通常是尸检时人为剥除头皮所致。然而，在窒息案件中，这一征象也可指示生前或死后头部静脉压升高（即头部朝下；图 3-2 和参考文献 1, 15, 22 和 23）。在某些类型的机械性窒息中，头部瘀点性出血反映了动脉血流改变所致的静脉压升高 (10, 14, 24, 25)，即存在不完全或间歇性的颈部受压。在颈部受压的情况下，如果头部无瘀点性出血，说明到达头部的动脉和静脉血流被完全阻断（如完全性缢颈；参阅标题 2.1.6）。在某些罕见的情况下，压迫颈部会刺激颈动脉窦，导致迷走神经诱导的心搏骤停，引起猝死 (3, 5)。在这种情况下，头部将不出现瘀点性出血 (5, 26)。某些类型的机械性窒息（如捂死），由于不涉及血管受压，很少出现瘀点性出血，即使观察到也是少量的。

结膜瘀点性出血确实可发生在面部皮肤无瘀点性出血的情况下。尽管也有文献

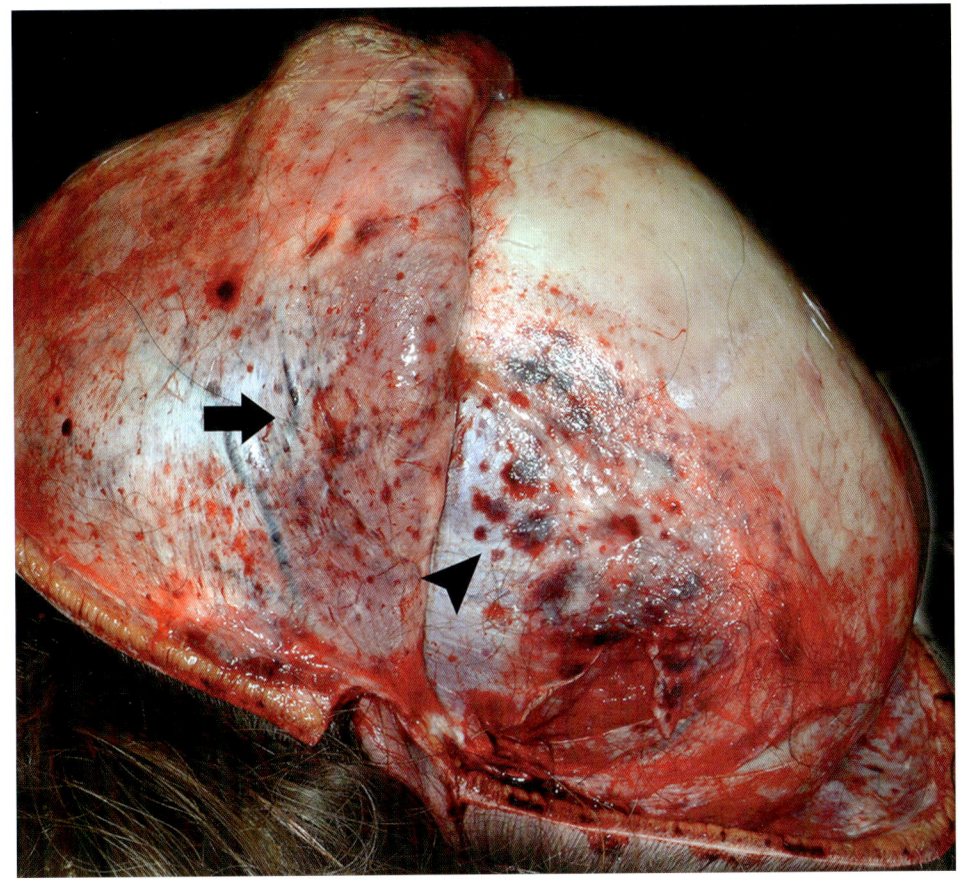

图 3-2 剥除前部头皮后暴露颅骨。头皮下表面（箭头）和颞肌（三角箭头）可见散在的瘀点性出血。死者被发现时面部朝下。

指出，如果面部无瘀点性出血，则眼部亦无瘀点性出血；也有仅出现于面部瘀点性出血的报道［如 1 岁大的婴儿悬于婴儿床死亡、儿童被捂死（24，27，28）］。有研究者（17，29）指出，在儿童窒息死亡中，往往较少发生瘀点性出血。

1.5 胸部压迫与头部瘀点性出血的关系

颈静脉系统分为较浅表的颈外静脉（external jugular vein, EJV）和较深的颈内静脉（internal jugular vein, IJV）。并非所有的头部和颈部的静脉都没有瓣膜，颈内静脉瓣膜位于锁骨下静脉和颈内静脉（30）汇合处上方 0.5－2 厘米（约 0.75 英寸）。当胸内压增加时［如咳嗽（30）］，瓣膜通常能够防止血液逆流至大脑。在中心静脉压（central venous pressure, CVP）正常的个体中，咳嗽时功能正常的瓣膜将产生 6－6.7 千帕（45－50 毫米汞柱）的平均跨瓣压差。解剖研究表明，平均压差达到 10 千帕（75 毫米汞柱）时颈内静脉的瓣膜功能仍然有效。与锁骨下静脉不同，颈内静脉与来自心脏右侧的收缩期静脉回流直接相关。

如果压力超过颈内静脉瓣膜正常范围内的承受能力，则头部压力升高，导致毛细血管破裂，面部和眼部进而出现瘀点性出血。在经历强有力的胸壁和腹部肌肉收缩［如妊娠和分娩、长期严重呕吐或咳嗽（12,21,30）］时，这种散在的瘀点性出血可以发生在正常的、有意识的、非缺氧的个体。通过 Valsalva 动作，即声门紧闭强行呼气以增加胸内压，会影响静脉血回流心脏（12）。

颈内静脉瓣膜损伤将造成跨瓣压差减小。慢性瓣膜损伤是由于三尖瓣反流引起的中心静脉压长期升高所致。急性瓣膜损伤可以发生在中心静脉导管介入术中。

头部瘀点性出血还可发生于急性右心衰竭（即静脉血回流障碍），但左心室功能［即全身动脉循环（12-14）］仍存在的自然死亡中。全心心搏骤停不会导致瘀点性出血（12）。心血管疾病，特别是动脉粥样硬化性心脏病，是和瘀点性出血相关的最常见疾病，但其他疾病（如癫痫）也可引起面部和眼部瘀点性出血。除颈部受压以外的创伤（如头部枪伤所致单纯性颅脑创伤或伴有其他损伤）也与头部瘀点性出血有关（13）。

在疾病和损伤所致死亡中，心肺复苏（cardiopulmonary resuscitation, CPR）也可致头颈部瘀点性出血，并促进结膜瘀点性出血的发展（参阅标题 2.6.1，参考文献 13 及 14）。有报道描述了胸外按压和头部出血的极端情况，一名男性在被实施心肺复苏 45 分钟后发生蛛网膜下腔出血（31）；与此相反，一项研究表明单纯的心肺复苏不会引起瘀点性出血（30）。瘀点性出血已在少数肺部疾病或肺血栓栓塞患者中被发现，这两种情况都与右心室衰竭相关。心肺复苏可以促进心肺复苏前已出现的瘀点性出血的发展。根据复苏中间歇性胸外按压的相关研究发现，颈内静脉瓣膜功能呈现出了不同的结果。在压力为 36-45 千克（80-100 磅）、60 次/分钟的胸部机械按压下，平均跨瓣压差为 2.5 千帕（19 毫米汞柱），即使复苏有所延迟，健康瓣膜也能正常工作以防止血液逆流（30）。相反，另一项研究结果显示，在压力为 32 千克（70 磅）、80 次/分钟的人工或机械心肺复苏下，心脏收缩时发生了血液逆流。很多创伤性窒息案例表现出头部静脉压显著增加的迹象（参阅标题 3.8.3 和标题 3.8.4）。连续胸外按压通常产生相当大的压力［＞454 千克（1 000 磅），或成人体重的 5-10 倍］。

1.6 胸腔内器官瘀点性出血与突发性婴儿猝死综合征的关系

婴儿猝死综合征（sudden infant death syndrome, SIDS）由美国国家儿童健康和人类发展研究所（National Institute of Child Health and Human Development）召集的专家团队定义为"通过彻底的案件调查，包括详尽的尸体解剖、现场勘察及临床病史的检查，仍无法解释的 1 岁以下婴儿猝死"（参阅标题 2.1.5；参考文献 32）。通常，这些婴儿的健康状况良好或有感冒症状，被发现在小床上死亡（33,34）。SIDS 可能代表一种异质性疾病（35）。这些婴儿的解剖结果显示出与窒息相似的非特异性尸体征象（参阅标题 1.3；文献 36-38）：肺充血和肺水肿导致液体从口鼻部流出（34,37），右心室扩张（37），胸腺、脏胸膜和心包有瘀点性出血（图 3-1）（32,34,36,37,39）。这种分布被认为是由于气道存在某些机械性闭塞，呼吸

第 3 章 | 窒　息

运动被迫增强,致胸内压急剧变化引起(参阅标题 3.4；参考文献 9)。一些 SIDS 可能由窒息引起,因此具有类似窒息的非特异性表现(参阅标题 3.1；参考文献 34, 36 和 37)。

1.7　窒息死的镜检指标

已有研究通过对肺组织的显微镜检查来试图诊断和区分不同类型的窒息死。一项研究结果如下：

- 误吸：可见肺淤血,肺间隔有出血灶、异物(参阅标题 3.4)。
- 闷死：管腔过度充盈,间质性水肿(参阅标题 3.1)。
- 溺死：肺泡水肿,肺泡间隙扩张,伴肺间隔毛细血管受压(参阅第 5 章标题 11.4)。
- 勒死(包括缢死)：肺泡出血性水肿伴塌陷、间质性水肿和肺气肿或与支气管扩张/收缩相关的局灶性肺气肿(40, 41)。

肺含铁血黄素沉着已被建议作为窒息死的诊断指标。然而,一项对 206 名婴幼儿死亡[年龄范围包括早产新生儿至 49 个月的幼儿(42)]的研究显示,肺含铁血黄素巨噬细胞的存在与被归类为"窒息死"的案例之间并无相关性。

很多窒息未被及时察觉,发现时个体已死亡。某些案例中,窒息者虽经过抢救,但仍发展为缺血缺氧性脑病,最终死于继发性肺炎(7, 15)。

2　缢死和勒死

2.1　缢死

缢死被定义为全部或部分身体因悬空产生的重量压迫颈部所致的死亡(图 3-3,参考文献 3, 43)。在典型的缢死中,索套通常呈收紧状态,但这并不是必要条件(29, 44)。意外性缢死可能不涉及索套(参阅标题 2.1.5；参考文献 28)。虽然缢死是勒死的一种特殊形式,但后者指紧颈部缢索的力量并非来自身体重量。在极端情况下,仅通过仰卧施加的重量即可收紧颈部索套(45, 46)。有时附加的外力也可收紧索套[如来自机动车辆和电梯的外力(44, 47, 48)]。

缢索承受的体重取决于身体所处的体位。Khokhlov(49)得出以下结论：

体位	缢索承受体重压力百分比
立位,脚趾触及地面	98%
立位,脚平放于地面	>65%
跪位,臀部下沉	74%
跪位,臀部上抬	64%
坐位,背部倾斜	32%
坐位,背部直立	17.5%
卧位,俯卧	18.3%
卧位,仰卧	9.7%

图 3-3　坐位缢死。

澳大利亚和北爱尔兰的缢死相关研究显示,低于半数的死者采取双足离地的完全性缢颈。澳大利亚约 40% 的缢死为立位(16,43),1% 为卧位。北爱尔兰的系列研究中也观察到了类似的结果(50)。如果悬挂点较高,则附近可有登高物(如凳子、箱子或梯子)(50)。

下列为压迫或损伤颈部结构所需的相应重量(8,49):

颈静脉	2 千克(4.4 磅)
颈动脉	2.5—10 千克(5.5—22 磅)
气道(甲状舌骨膜平面)	10 千克(22 磅)
气管	15 千克(33 磅)
椎动脉	8.2—30 千克(18—66 磅)
骨折	
甲状软骨板骨折	14.3 千克(31.5 磅)
环状软骨骨折	18.8 千克(41 磅)

对新鲜尸体喉部的研究表明,造成甲状软骨和环状软骨骨折所需静力的均值分别为 15.8 千克和 20.8 千克(即 34.8 磅和 45.8 磅)(51)。动力(速度达到 11 英里/小时或 18 千米/小时)会产生大于静力均值 30% 以上的力。当作用力均值为 55 千克(121 磅)时,将造成结构性塌陷和致命性气道破坏。

2.1.1 一般人群中的缢死

在多数国家,缢死是窒息性自杀的常见方式(43,42-56)。各项研究显示,至少 70% 的缢死者是男性(24,43,50,57-59)。年龄范围从青少年后期至老年(58,59)。生前可能有尝试自杀史[一项英国研究显示该数量在自杀死亡案例中所占比例超过半数(59)]。同一系列研究显示约三分之一的死亡案例为自杀,这与其他综述报道一致(43,49)。死者住所是最常见的自杀地点,但也会发生在室外其他地点(5,23,43,50,53,58)。

一些自缢常被怀疑为他杀[如在不寻常的地点,像机动车内(60)]。相反,有些自杀被伪装成他杀[如口中有堵塞物(61,62)]。在这些情况下,死者动机为获得人身保险赔偿、以破坏名誉为目的对家庭成员或同事进行报复,以及唤起他人的同情和内疚。有时现场可有多名死者(5,23,63)。缢死者可被伪装成自杀来掩饰他杀罪行[如遭受勒死(64-67)]。除非受害者是婴儿或因疾病、处于睡眠状态、醉酒、遭受过严重创伤(如勒颈和殴打导致失去意识)而丧失行为能力的成年人,否则单人他缢致死是很困难的(8,66,68,69)。单人他缢的情况意味着攻击者和受害者之间存在较大的体格差异(7)。通常情况下,处于清醒状态的成年受害者被他缢致死可能说明案件涉及多个攻击者[如处以私刑(66)]。

进行心理学剖析以评估自杀风险因素有助于确定死亡方式(参阅第 1 章标题 3;参考文献 67,70)。现场调查(如缺乏强行进入迹象,无偷窃或挣扎证据)有助于排除疑点以确认死亡方式为自缢死。

意外性缢死在成年人中较罕见(如被车辆安全带缢死、在电梯运行中发生的缢死;参考文献 44,48 和 71 以及图 3-4)。

2.1.2 拘留期间死亡

监狱中的死亡方式多种多样(72-78),且囚犯的自杀率高于一般人群(72,74,78-85)。

监狱中人口流动性大,而且对于新囚犯(76,78,80)来说由于从未经历过坐牢,自杀的风险随之增加。囚犯可能在狱中服毒自杀(58,78,80,85,86)。虽然一些研究表明,在狱中自杀的多是非暴力罪犯,但另一些研究指出,因刑事犯罪(如持械抢劫、强奸和谋杀等)而入狱的自杀的可能性更高,原因可能是畏惧长期服刑而造成的精神压力(73,76,80,82,87)。就自缢所涉及的关押场所而言(82),关押在拘留所(由警察管理的短期拘留机构)的罪犯通常罪行较轻,有时是强制戒酒或戒毒者(82),而监狱中的囚犯通常因严重的指控被捕入狱(82)。一项审查结果显示,至少

图 3-4 一名独居的女性侧倒在地,被挂在颈部的鞋带缢死,可见鞋带另一端所系的门钥匙已弯曲(箭头)。毒化结果显示乙醇中毒。

75%的自杀者有精神病史(87)。大多数监狱自杀发生在入狱1—2天内(58,73,78,80,85,87)。用锐器自伤较常见,但用缢吊方式自杀后果往往更严重(83-85)。监狱中,床单通常被用作自缢工具(83,87)。

刑期较长的自杀者中,在坐牢前或坐牢期间曾患精神疾病的比例较高(72,76,83,88,89)。漫长的刑期是自杀的主要诱因(81,89)。在德克萨斯州的一项研究中,至少有半数在狱中自杀的死者曾多次尝试过自杀,约三分之二在坐牢期间企图自杀至少一次,或有酒精和药物滥用史(88)。其他研究显示,药物滥用和自杀企图的发生率相似(76,83),这可能由于缺乏酒精和药物会使囚犯不能承受监狱生活的压力(88)。在

第 3 章 | 窒 息

英国的一项研究中,大多数囚犯(60%)在坐牢期间的前3个月实施自杀(89)。研究表明,许多自缢往往发生在监管较松懈的深夜至上午8:00期间(80-82,87)。而选择在白天实施自杀的多是因为希望监狱工作人员能对其立即实施抢救(89)。有报道囚犯策划自缢事件,假装失去意识,以便在随后的住院期间实施越狱(78)。死者多为男性(83,88),且年龄小于35岁,反映了监狱一般群体的特点(76,89)。自杀方式各异(如过量用药、割腕、跳楼和自勒),但是自缢是最常见的方式(76-78,80,81,85,87-90)。一项研究显示,在某个最高安全精神病机构中,95%的自杀者选择缢死(79)。

在监狱和拘留所的死亡案件需要进行仔细的现场调查和完整的尸体解剖,特别是当权力机构未认识到自杀可能而得出他杀结论并遭到质疑时(74-78,80,90)。

2.1.3 精神病院

精神病院中的患者,特别是精神分裂症患者的自杀率高于一般人群(91)。这类自杀通常是由于缺乏正规的治疗和干预(91)。精神病患者选择的自杀方式通常较为极端(如跃入铁轨、跳楼或自缢)。由于患者很少会提前给予警告,因此这种情况下的自杀具有不可预测性,并且在精神治疗后可能有明显的改善(91)。

2.1.4 护理院及其他长期看护机构

居住于护理院及其他长期看护机构者可能受到身体上的束缚。根据下列标准可将死因判定为束缚死:死亡时没有明显的急性疾病;死亡时或前一刻存在限制性体位;处于异常限制性体位致患者难以自救;需排除死后体位被变动的可能性(92)。

此类死亡可能未被及时发现(92-95)。一项回顾性分析显示,体位限制性死亡主要发生在护理院,受害者被发现勒死在椅子或床上(92)。对这些死亡的详细分析表明,死者均患有痴呆症,大部分有冲动性或不自主性运动,且多数死前曾试图挣脱束缚,或被发现时处于束缚状态下的异常体位(92)。坐位患者的约束衣可能起先或之后被不正确地固定,也可能由于未固定底部的束缚带,导致患者从约束衣内滑下,压迫颈部致窒息(图3-5;参考文献92,94-96)。这些患者由于身体和精神上的功能已有所削弱,导致不能自行挣脱(94)。受害者身材较小也为促成因素之一(92)。翻倒的轮椅也可将死者困在约束衣中(参阅标题3.7;参考文献97)。

这种情形所致其他类型的勒死已经有报道,如电动床的床头板升起压迫颈部,导致异常的限制性体位;床的侧杆和床垫之间的滑动,使颈部被侧杆压迫;死者从床上掉下,同时颈部被床头灯的电线缠绕(参阅标题3.2;参考文献48,92,94,98和99)。可采取胸外按压对上述床上缢颈患者实施抢救(参阅标题3.8;参考文献92,100和101)。

由于对患者实施抢救会改变其体位,因此将目击者信息登记在医疗记录中对后期死因确定非常重要(100,101)。在长期看护机构中发生窒息的可能不易被发现且确认患者死亡的医生可能不会深入调查死因(92),或者由于害怕刑事和民事诉讼,存在工作人员企图通过伪装现场或不上报案件而隐瞒非正常死亡的情况(92,96,98)。

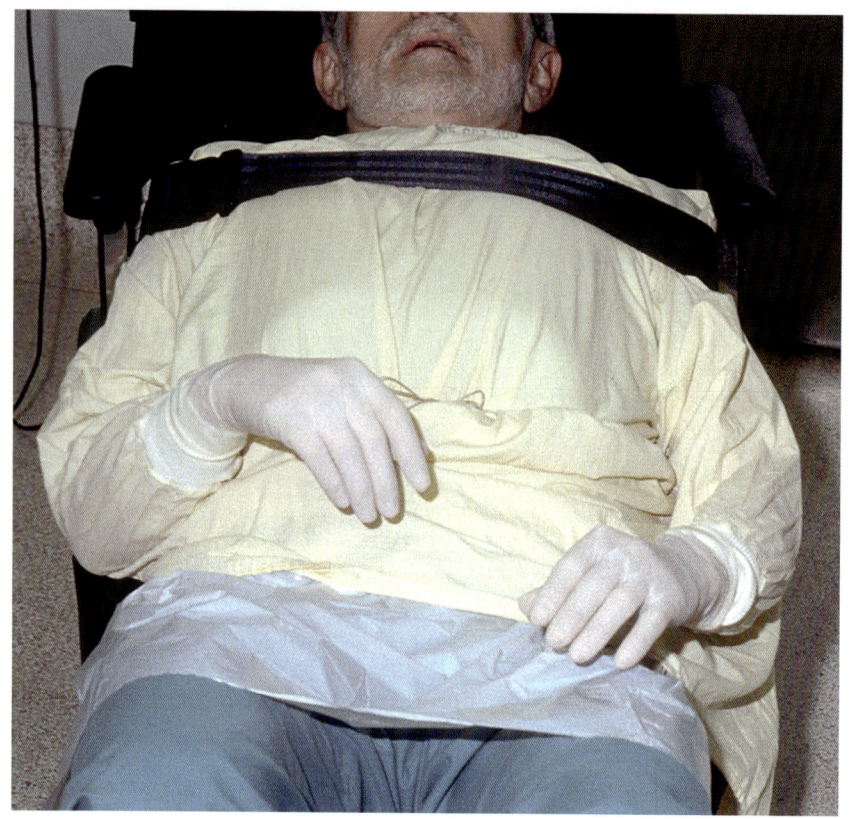

图3-5 仅固定约束衣的胸部位置,患者向下滑动导致勒死的情况模拟(加拿大安大略省斯特拉特福市休伦珀斯医疗联盟 J. Walton 博士供图)。

2.1.5 儿童和青少年

2.1.5.1 自杀

自缢死在儿童中较为罕见。澳大利亚的一项研究显示,在298例自缢死案例中,12岁及以下的儿童占3.7%(28)。美国的一项研究报道了一名8岁男孩的自缢死(15),另一项研究报道了一名9岁男孩的自缢死(102)。北爱尔兰的一项研究报道了一名7岁死者(50)。苏格兰和土耳其的研究显示自缢的死者最小年龄为11岁,男性占多数(103,104)。儿童自杀的原因包括对父母的愤怒、为了获得更多关爱,以及希望追随死去的亲人(102,105)。

在美国各辖区的青少年自杀案例中,死者倾向于使用枪械实施自杀,但在其他国家(106-108),自缢是最常见的自杀方式。

研究发现死者生前多精神不稳定,曾扬言和企图自杀,常有药物和酒精滥用史,有反社会行为,家庭关系混乱(70,106,107)。三分之一的自杀案件死者会留有遗书,且案发现场通常在家中(106),多数未被成年人及时察觉,在某些情况下现场存在其他儿童(103)。

第3章 | 窒 息

2.1.5.2 意外

苏格兰的一项研究显示,每年每 100 000 名儿童中就有 0.7 名发生意外性缢死(103)。6 岁及以下儿童的缢死通常属于意外(15)。在 6—12 岁儿童的缢死中,死亡性质较难明确,因为在这个年龄阶段,儿童对死亡可能没有正确的概念(107)。

- 1 岁或以下的儿童(无法站立)
  - 头部或颈部卡在婴儿床或婴儿车上(参阅标题 3.2;参考文献 15,28,50 和 109–112)。
  - 被婴儿床上的衣服缠绕(4,28)。
  - 被尿布包上的绳索、松紧带、奶嘴绳、链子缠绕(4,43,113–115)。
- 1—3 岁以上的儿童[能够站立(116)]
  - 悬于床脚/床垫之间(29)。
  - 悬于(小孩吃饭时坐的)高脚椅(4)。
  - 被绳索类[如婴儿床或汽车座椅中的束带或安全带、衣服、奶嘴绳、窗帘绳、可卸式晾衣绳、壁灯开关电线、环形秋千索(4,15,28,29,48,103,117–121)]缢死。
  - 颈部卡于车窗上缘(图 3–6;参考文献 4,122 和 123)。
  - 颈部卡在铰链盖和玩具盒之间(114)。

婴儿死亡——摇篮死,包括了婴儿猝死综合征(参阅标题 1.6;参考文献 4)。此类案件必须调查现场,对看护者进行查访,以排除意外性窒息的可能。应检查婴儿床以判断它是否存在安全隐患或设计缺陷(4)。

- 年龄较大的儿童[无人监管(4)]
  - "玩绳套"(如扮演牛仔);"实验"行为(4,15,28,48,50,103,116,124,125)。
  - 在受到惩罚或压力后,由于被孤立或为博得同情而采取缢吊(4,125)。
  - 跳跃时或在床上玩耍时被钥匙挂绳、发带缢吊(125,126)。

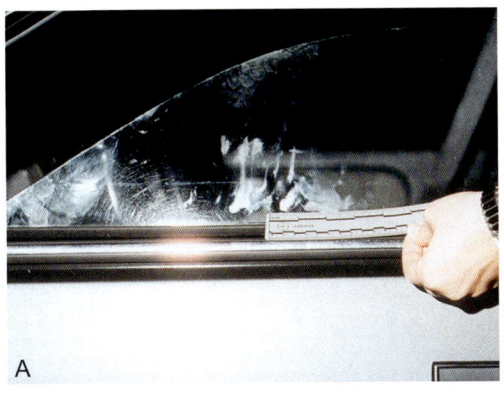 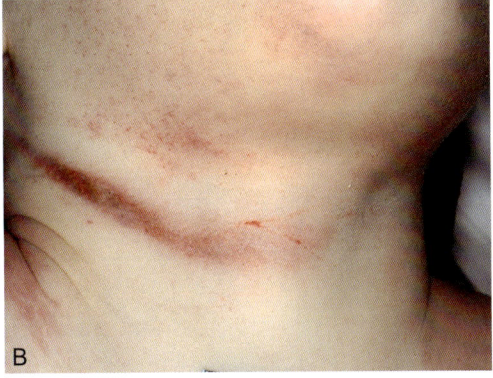

图 3–6 意外性勒死。(A)小女孩被发现时身体悬挂在车外,颈部卡在部分打开的车窗边缘和 A 柱之间;车窗上布满指纹。(B)部分勒沟。

- 颈部卡在窗户玻璃和窗台之间(4)。
- 被操场设备缢吊(4, 48, 103, 114, 127)。
- 身体残疾的儿童被束缚于限制性体位(参阅标题 2.1.4；参考文献 4)。
- 性窒息(参阅标题 2.7；参考文献 4, 43 和 48)。

由于缺乏成人监护,调查时必须考虑所有不自然的死亡方式(图 3-7)。

2.1.5.3 他杀

文献报道的相关案例如下:

- 8 岁女孩被发现缢死于开阔场地(7, 28, 103)。
- 2 岁半男孩缢死[凶手在对儿子实施谋杀后自杀(128)]。
- 4 岁女孩被缢吊于门把手上(128)。

在这种情况下必须考虑性侵的可能性(7, 28, 43, 103)。

2.1.6 缢死的体表检验

前臂和小腿是否发绀取决于缢吊的持续时间(参阅第 2 章图 2-9；参考文献 23)。

2.1.6.1 缢索

绳子、电线和皮带是常见的缢索(23, 24, 43, 50, 57, 58)。缢索可能被人为变

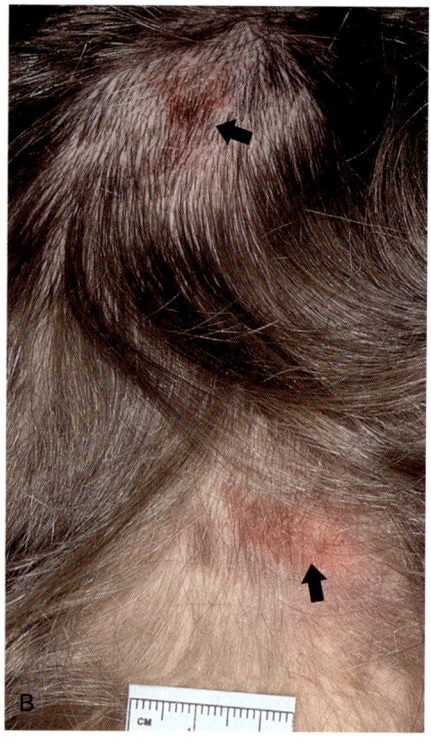

图 3-7 死亡方式不明的缢死。(A)小男孩被发现缢死于可疑场所——学校盥洗室厕所门上的挂钩。(B)在医院存活几天后,因严重缺氧缺血性脑病死亡。颅后部头皮可见擦挫伤(箭头),这是由衣领摩擦皮肤所致,而非由挂钩形成。

动,即被亲属或调查人员解开或切断(16)。缢索可在颈部缠绕多次(图3-8;参考文献5,24和62),也可简单地环绕颈部,或者有一个复杂的绳结[如"绞索活套"(hangman's noose)中的多个环套(16,46)]。澳大利亚的一项研究显示,在使用绳结的案件中,25%为固定型索套,其余为滑动型索套(16)。北爱尔兰的一系列研究显示,69.5%的人使用滑动型索套,8.6%的人使用固定型索套,10.5%的人只是把绳索简单地缠绕颈部(50)。对绳结进行分析有助于确定死亡方式(1)。如果头发被缠绕于绳结中可能存在他杀嫌疑,而自杀者的头发可能会介于套索和颈部皮肤之间(65,67)。

自缢时,死者可通过垫东西来保护颈部减轻疼痛(图3-9;见本章第2.7.1.3节和参考文献23,46)。缢索下可看到所垫衣物(62)。压迫部位的皮肤组织(如表皮、

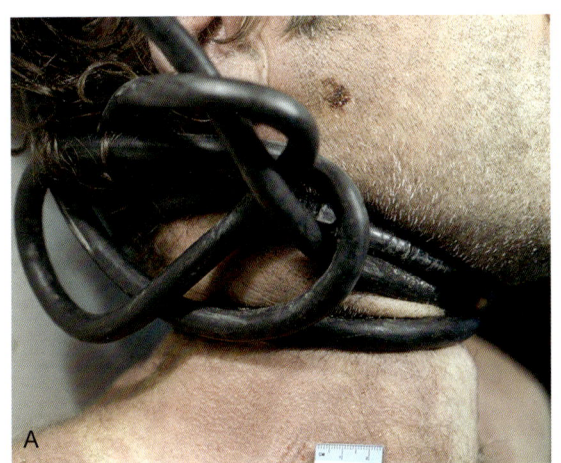 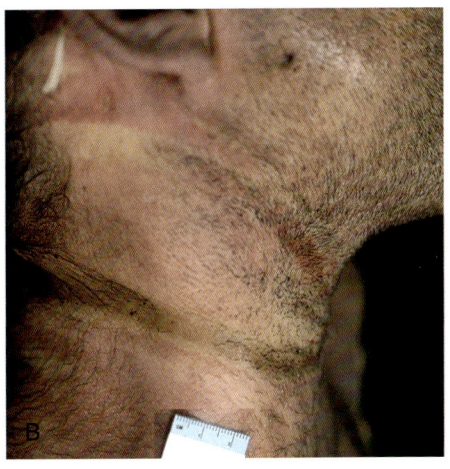

图3-8 自缢。(A)在颈部缠绕3次的延长线;(B)在颈部形成的缢沟。

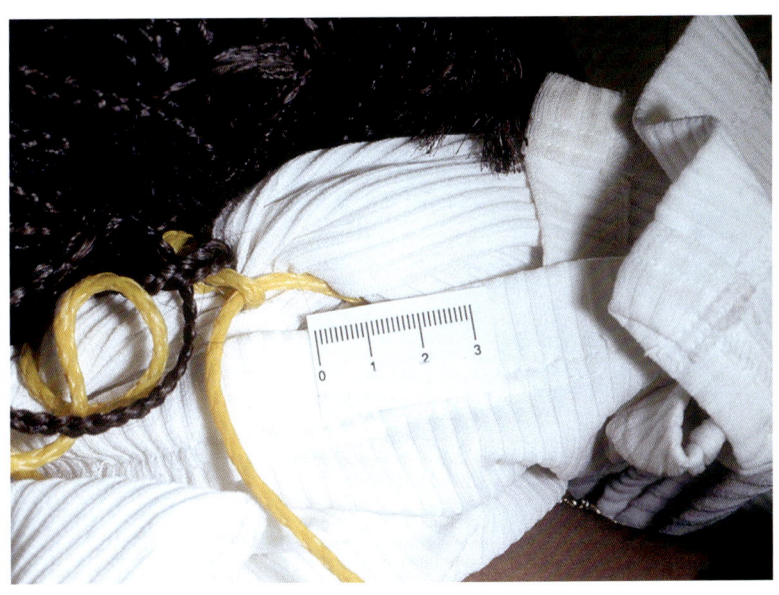

图3-9 自缢。女性死者在缢索和颈部之间垫了一件毛衣。

水疱破裂渗出的脂质）将转移到缢索或衬垫物上（129）。自缢者通常只打单个绳结，但是缢索可能在首次缢吊时发生断裂，导致自缢者打了第二个绳结（128）。

2.1.6.2 身体其他部位

身体其他部位存在捆绑，不能明确是他杀还是自杀（参阅标题 2.7.1.3；参考文献 5, 7 和 130–132）。自缢时四肢可被束缚（图 3–10 和图 3–11），双手可被反绑，甚至可能使用手铐（131, 132）。但类似的捆绑通常较为松散，步骤简单，并且可轻易挣脱（61, 131–133）。

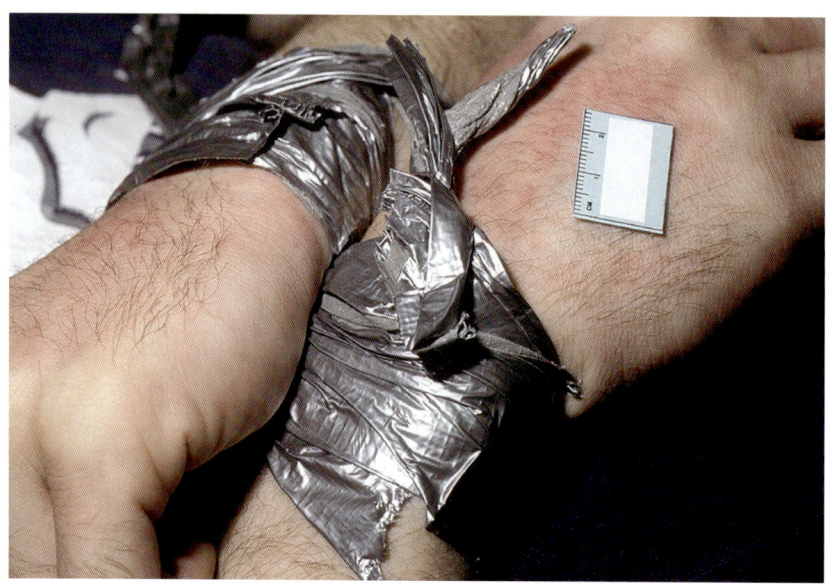

图 3–10 自缢（缢索为绳子）。手腕被胶带捆绑。

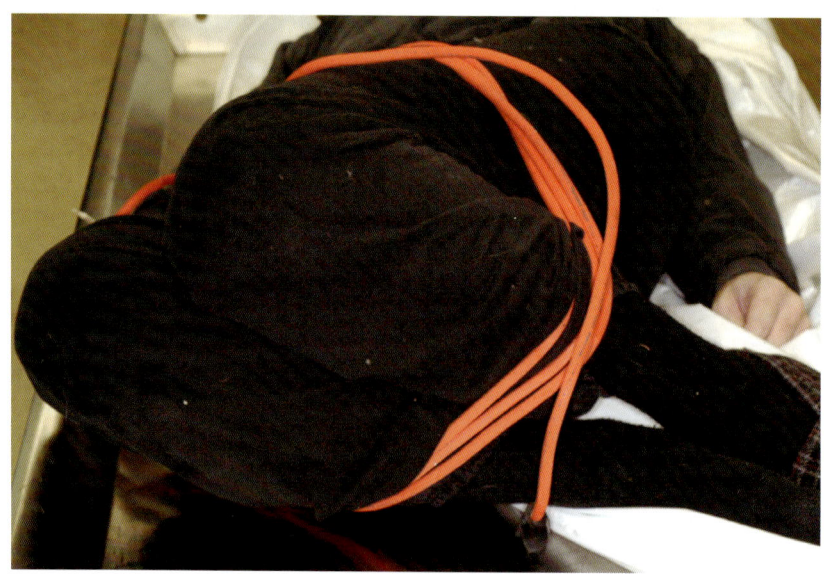

图 3–11 自缢（缢索为电线）。另一根电线用于捆绑膝盖（参阅第 2 章, 图 2–16）。

2.1.6.3 颈部及其他身体部位的压迫性特征

在多数案例中颈部可见缢沟,这是由于缢索的压迫和摩擦所致(23)。缢沟通常呈黄色或棕色,呈皮革样化,并且可以在缢死后很快出现(有案例报道为死后25分钟;图3-12;参考文献28,29,62和134)。红色或粉红色的颈部特征表明死前有皮下出血,但也可能是由于死后血液受到挤压所致(66,134,135)。邻近缢沟部位如有擦挫伤可能是他扼所致(6)。在靠近缢沟的皮肤上可观察到水疱形成(图3-13;参考文献62)。

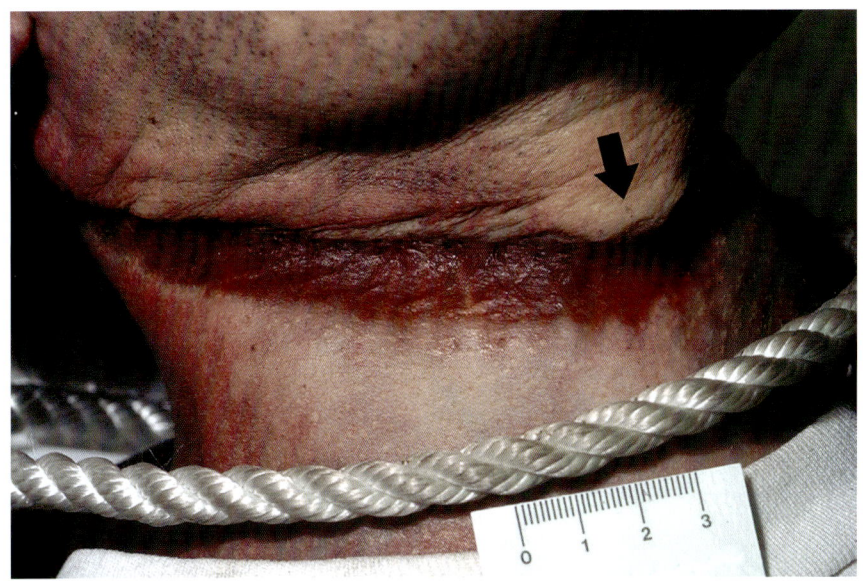

图 3-12 自缢。越过甲状腺软骨凸起部位的典型缢沟(箭头)。

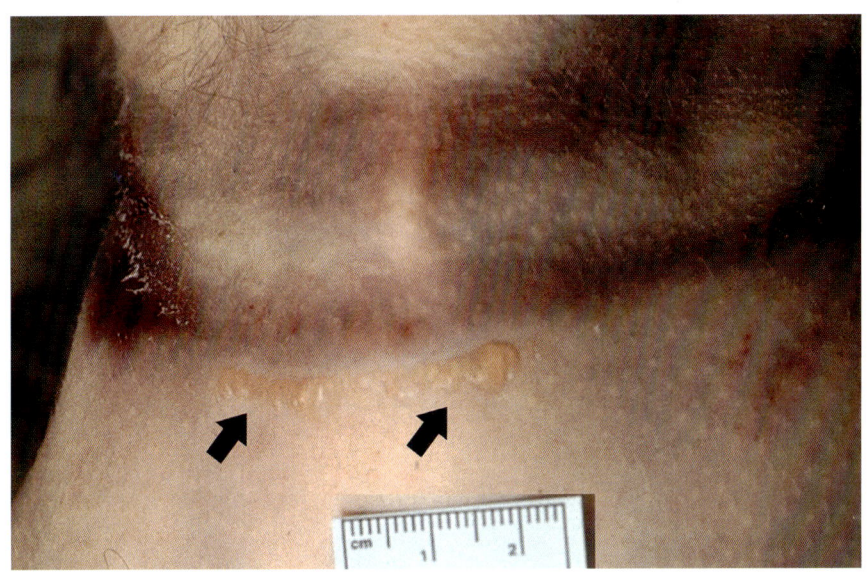

图 3-13 自缢。注意缢沟下缘的皮肤水疱(箭头)。

与勒死相比较,典型缢沟通常位于甲状软骨突起部位(喉结的上切迹)或其上方(图3-12),典型勒沟则通常位于甲状软骨上方或下方(参考文献7,8,15,16和50)。然而,一些自缢案例也存在缢沟位于甲状软骨水平位置的情况(134)。缢沟位置可能取决于缢索类型。一项研究表明,使用硬塑料晾衣绳在完全性缢颈的情况下,缢沟位于甲状腺软骨上方,但使用棉布作为缢索或在不完全性缢颈时,缢沟位于甲状软骨下方(5)。

在一些被衣服缢吊在婴儿床栏上的幼儿缢死案例中,在环状软骨水平位置可观察到缢沟(29)。缢沟下方的皮肤擦伤区域可显示缢索向上的滑动特征,在完全性缢颈时更为明显(7,16,24)。缢沟呈特征性成角或倾斜至缢吊点,即绳结处(图3-14;参考文献28)。缢吊点通常在颈部的侧面,但也有在颈部前方,致颈部出现水平缢沟(图3-15;参考文献5,24)。缢索可先全周环绕颈部,然后再向前或向后环绕打结,最终

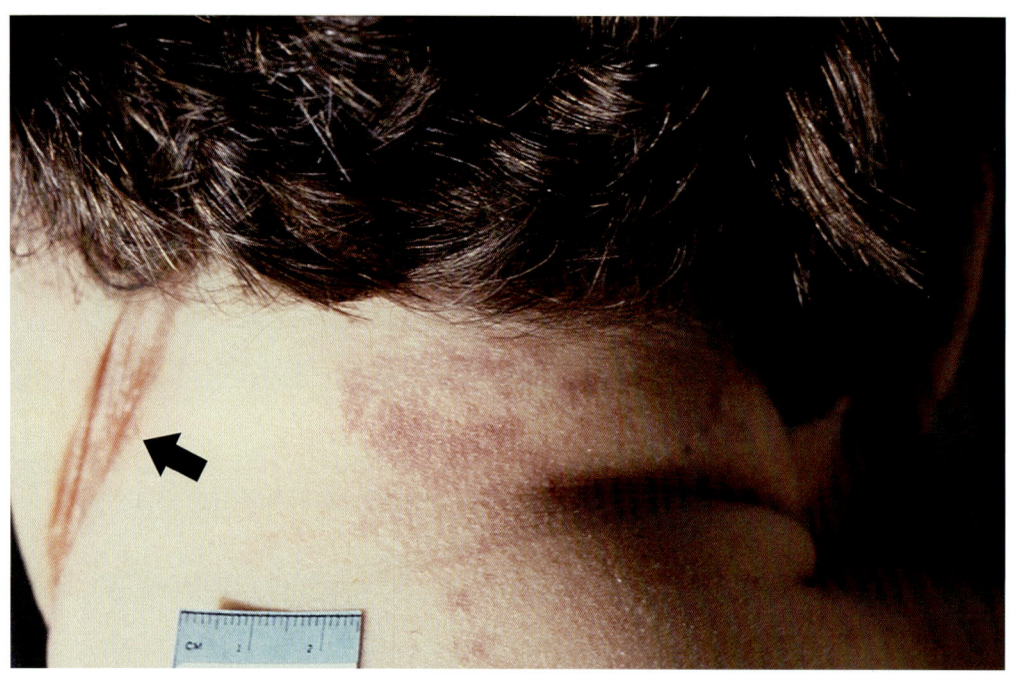

图3-14 自缢。缢吊点在项部。缢沟在左耳后部成角或倾斜(箭头)。

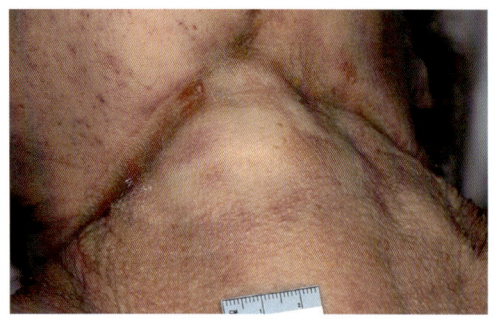 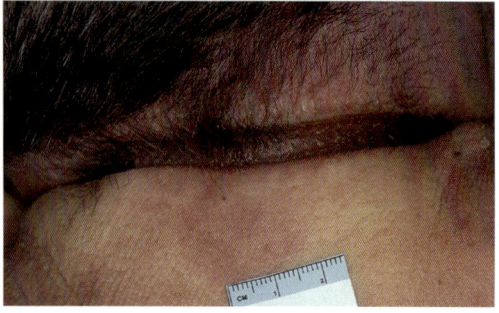

图3-15 自缢。(A)喉部上方的缢吊点(绳结),颈前的成角缢沟。(B)项部的水平缢沟。

形成水平缢沟(图3-16)。水平缢沟易被怀疑为他勒(图3-17；参考文献136)。在使用坚韧的防滑缢索的情况下,从高处跳落可出现水平缢沟(137)。这种情况也出现在特殊缢吊点所致水平缢沟的死者中[如向前跪倒的缢颈体位(50, 138)]。

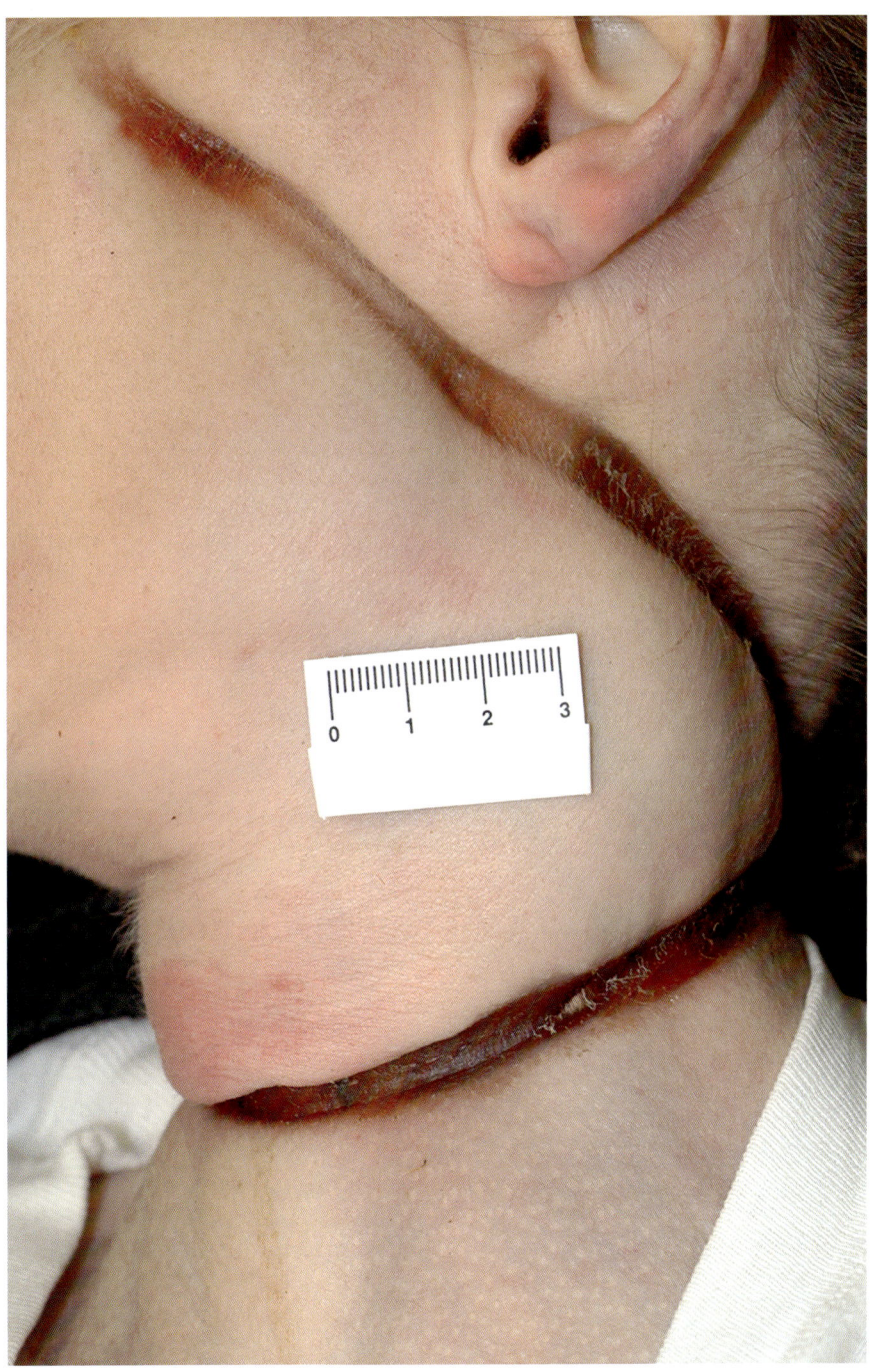

图 3-16 缢索环绕颈部,向后交叉并延伸经过面颊,形成水平缢沟(加拿大安大略省圣托马斯市圣托马斯埃尔金综合医院 E. Rowe 博士供图)。

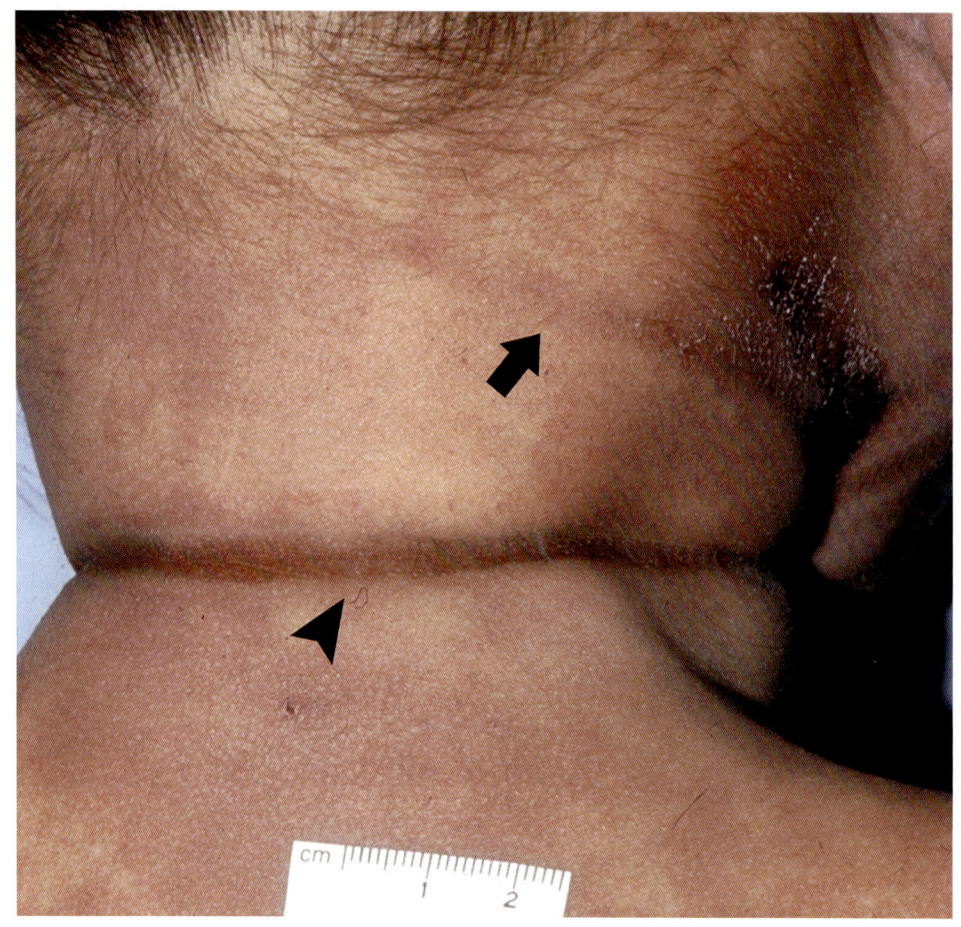

图3-17 年轻女性。他勒伪装成自缢。注意项部的两个逐渐变浅向上倾斜的缢沟（箭头）；水平勒沟（三角箭头）（美国北卡罗来纳州教堂山市法医局供图）。

缢沟处皮肤通常能留下缢索表面纹理的印痕（图3-18）(15,29,128)，其宽度接近缢索(28)宽度。缢索上的纤维可以转移至缢沟处的皮肤上，并黏附其表面(62)。倾斜的缢索在颈部前、后、外侧区域施加恒定的压力(139)。缢沟和其他压迫痕迹有时可能不完整、不清晰，甚至不存在(28)。如果自缢者的缢索被立即"切断"、颈部皮肤和缢索之间有衬垫物、缢吊后存活了一段时间致损伤愈合或使用柔软材料或宽绳作缢索，颈部可不出现缢沟（图3-19；参考文献3,5,6,16,23和78）。如果缢死的死因是迷走神经刺激(5,90,140)，则颈部也将缺乏压痕。最初存在的压痕可能会在移除缢索后数小时内消失(134)。如果颈部出现尸斑，则缢索压迫部位呈苍白色(93)。注意不要将缢沟与颈部皱纹和复苏痕迹相混淆（图3-20）。

可以在身体的其他区域（如穿约束衣者的腋窝处、被捆绑的四肢；参阅标题2.1.4；参考文献96）看到压痕。

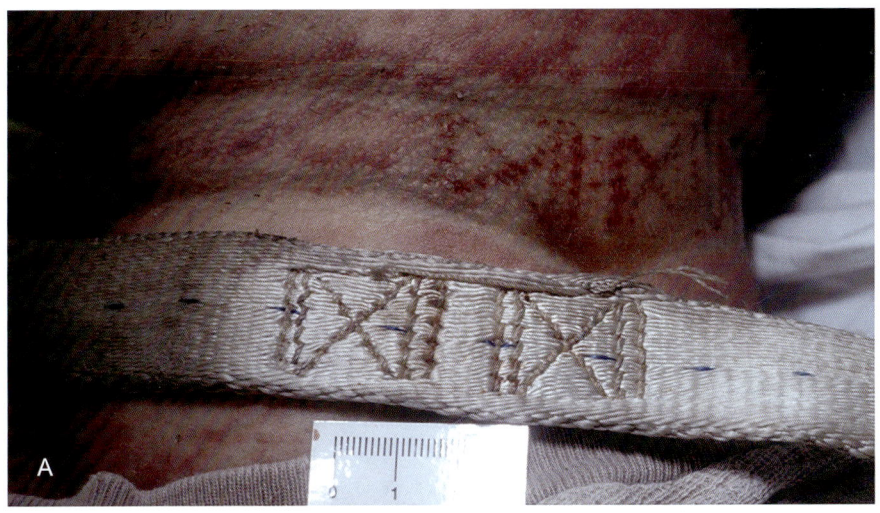
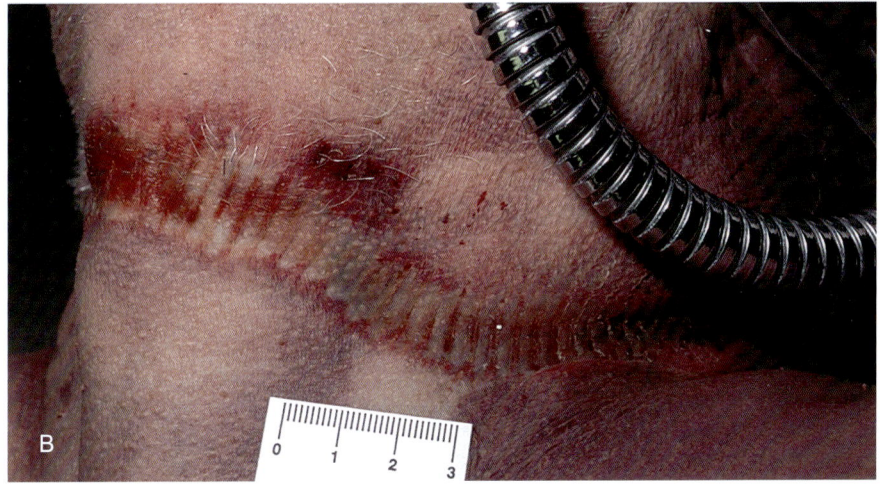

图3-18 自缢。缢沟印痕（A,B）。

2.1.6.4 颜面部

颜面部和颈部发绀是因静脉充血和颈动脉压闭不全引起的（如使用固定型套索、采取不完全性缢颈；参考文献 5, 7, 23, 50 和 78）。颈总动脉被完全压闭的情况（如采取完全性缢颈；图 3-21；参考文献 23, 50, 78）更多见 (50)，面部可呈苍白色，伴有结膜充血和水肿 (7)，鼻腔、嘴角和耳部可能有凝固的血性黏液 (7, 78)，舌可伸出（图 3-21；参考文献 23, 128）。

2.1.6.5 瘀点性出血

瘀点性出血通常分布在眼部及缢索上方的颜面部和颈部的皮肤（图 3-22；参考文献 29）。一项研究 (16) 显示在缢吊案例中，27% 发生眼睑瘀点性出血，33% 有结膜或巩膜瘀点性出血，18% 两者均出现。瘀点性出血表示缢吊发生时死者还存在

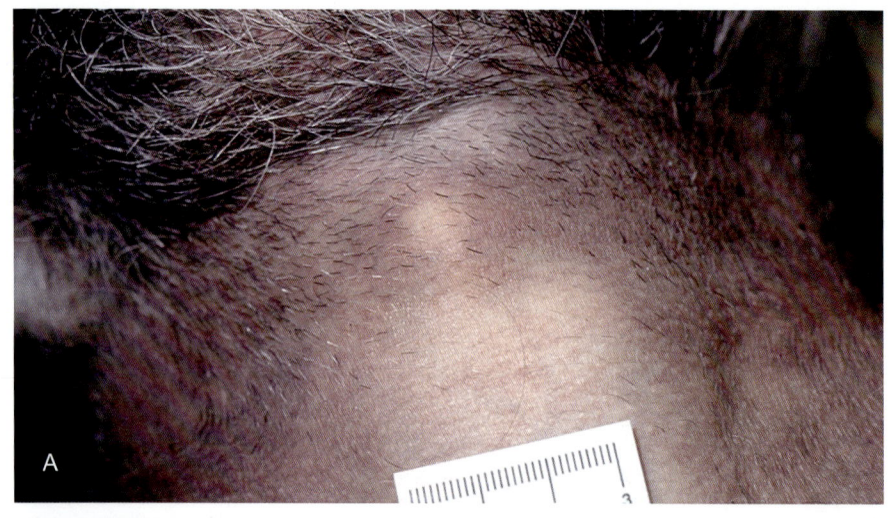

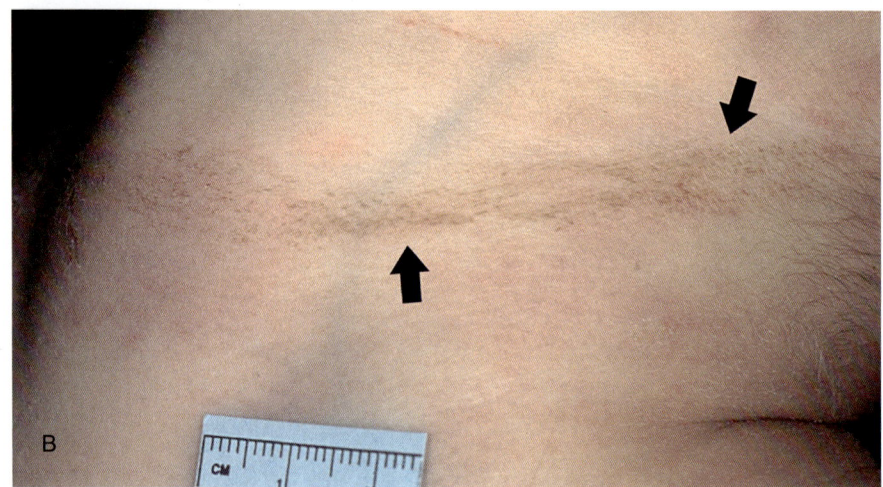

图 3-19 自缢,存活几天后死亡。(A) 缢沟缺失,缢吊时间少于 20 分钟。(B) 缢沟变浅(箭头)。

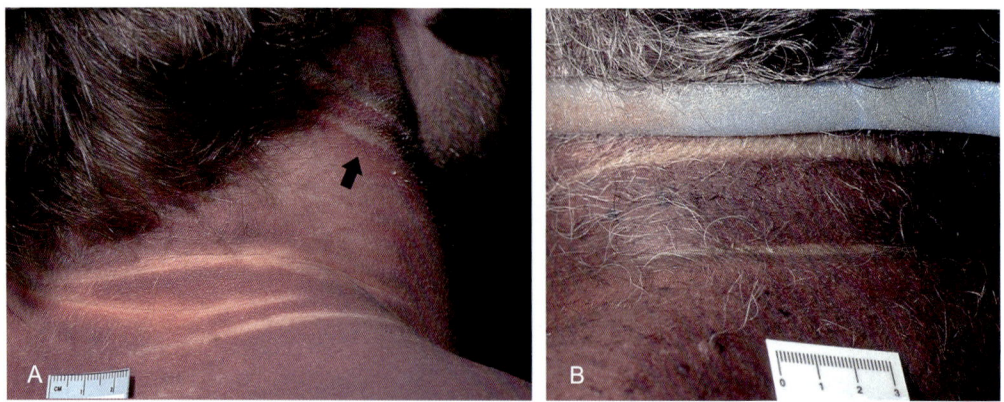

图 3-20 缢死。(A) 尸斑处的苍白缢沟(箭头)由缢索压迫形成,下颈部还可见 3 条皮肤褶皱。(B) 尸斑处的白色"缢痕"由抢救时系于气管插管的软带压迫形成,下方的横向苍白痕迹则是皮肤褶皱。

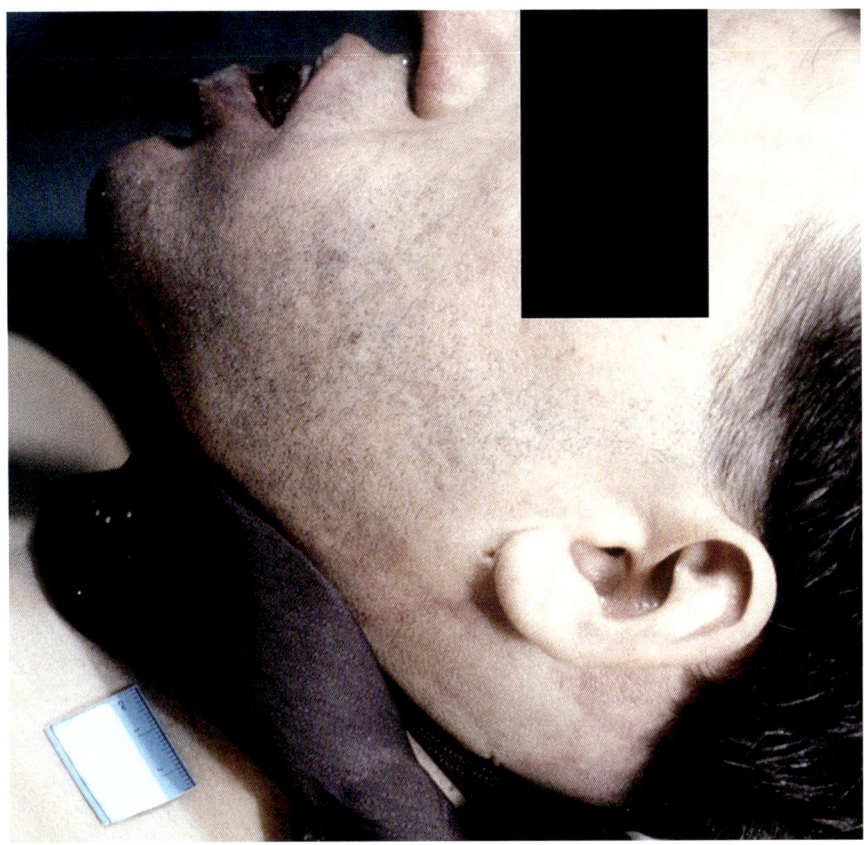

图 3-21 缢死。面部苍白;伸出的舌因干燥变黑。

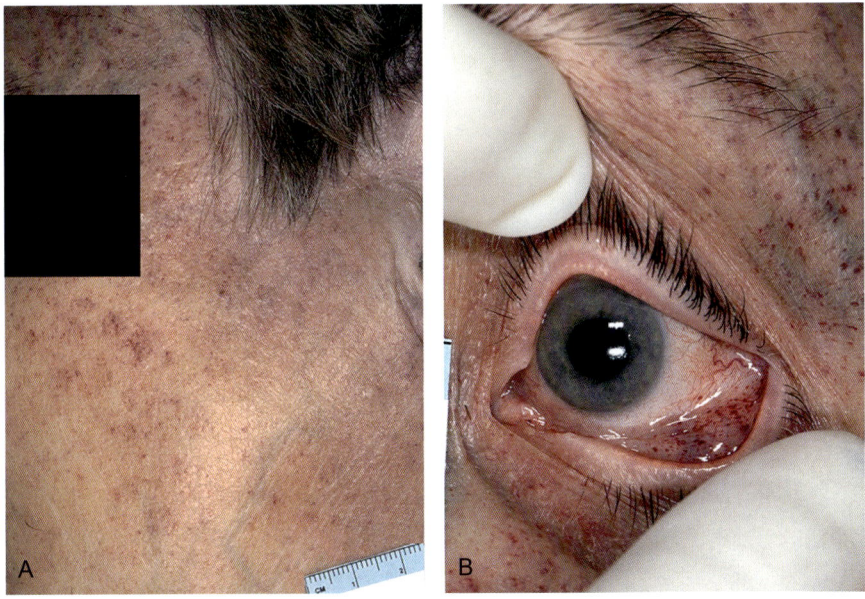

图 3-22 缢死。(A)缢沟上方的皮肤瘀点性出血。(B)结膜和眶周瘀点性出血。

生命体征(129)。在成人和儿童之间,完全性和不完全性缢颈的特征存在差异(5,7,15,24,28,29,61,123,128,141)。瘀点性出血的发生和发展取决于诸多因素,如在施加全身重量时缢索的紧密性和持续时间,以及在不完全性缢颈的情况下未使用滑动型索套(24),或在完全性缢颈时,头部呈一定角度倾斜,使颈部远离绳结部位的动脉血流仅被部分阻断(24)。瘀点性出血也出现在约束衣引起的坐位窒息的情况下(96)。

2.1.6.6 其他损伤征象

死者双手可能位于缢索附近,但是通常看不到试图自救所致的损伤,这表明了意识的快速丧失(图3-23和3-24; 参考文献57)。但颈部也可能存在指甲形成的擦伤(3)。

非致命性创伤可能发生于自杀前,并易引起他杀嫌疑(16)。自己造成的、严重的、正在愈合的或陈旧的非致命性损伤也可能存在(如试切创; 参考文献16,50,61,66和68)。某些损伤可能更令人困惑(如浅表刺伤; 参考文献128)。在精神患者和性倒错者中可观察到自残伤(如男性生殖器被切除)(7)。当自缢者因抢救被抬上担架时,可造成腋窝和小腿部位瘀血(78)。堵塞物可能在自缢前已放入口中(132)。死后伤则可能因实施复苏、动物啃食,以及尸体未被妥善保管(如缢索被切断使尸体掉落至坚硬物体表面)所致(图3-25; 参考文献66,68,78和90)。

缢吊期间可发生其他损伤(如鞭打; 参考文献50,66和68)。在他缢案件中,

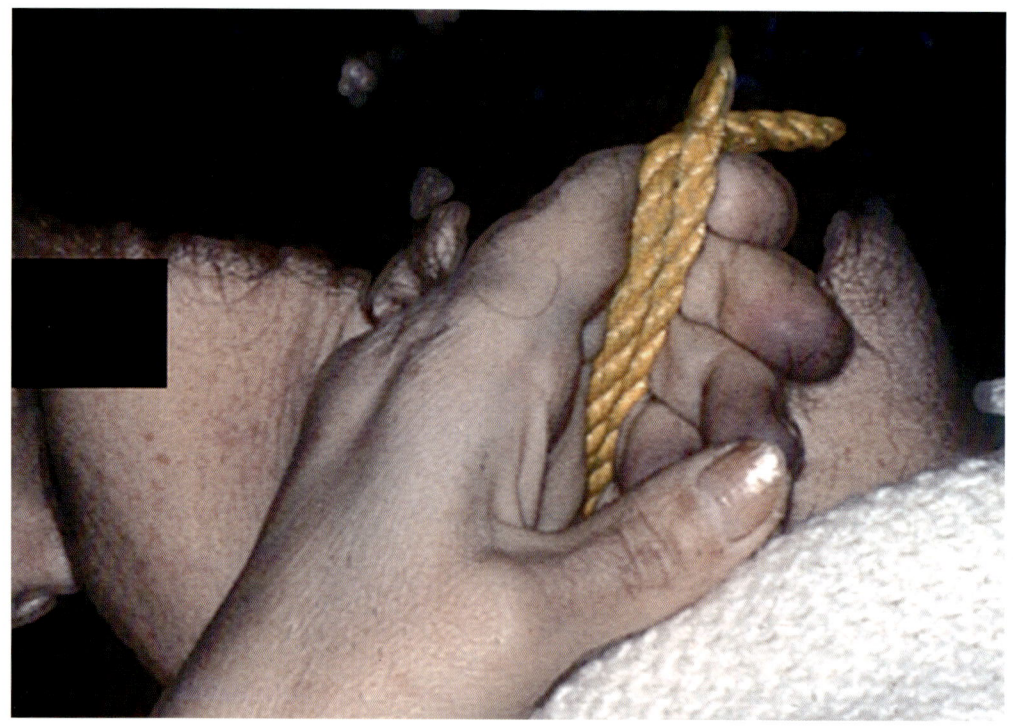

图3-23 自缢时手垫于缢索下。

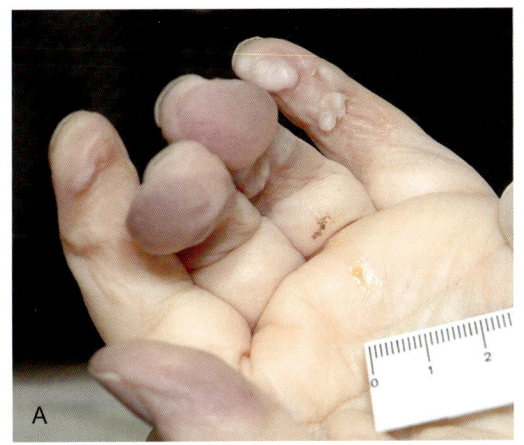
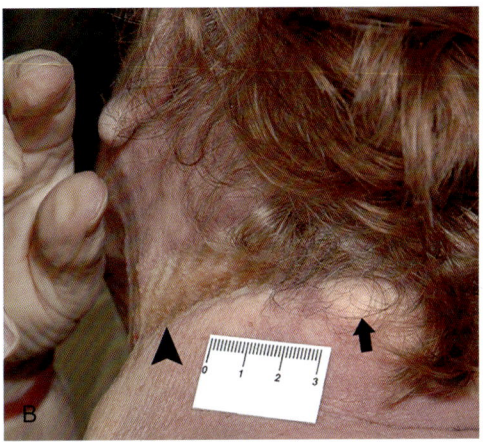

图3-24 缢死。（A）手指垫于收紧的缢索下导致指尖肿胀，出现水疱。（B）靠近缢痕（三角箭头）的尸斑区域有指尖压迹（箭头）。

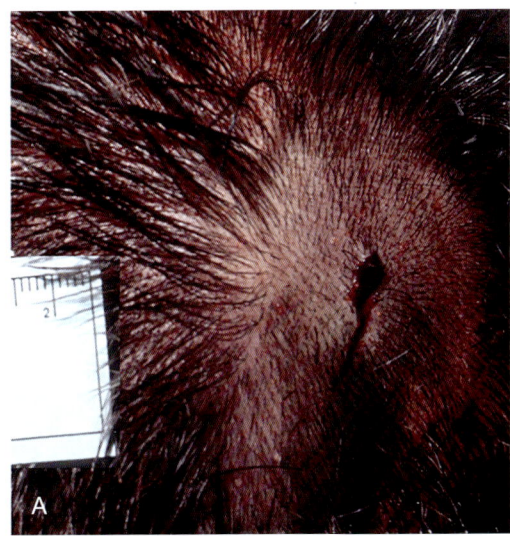
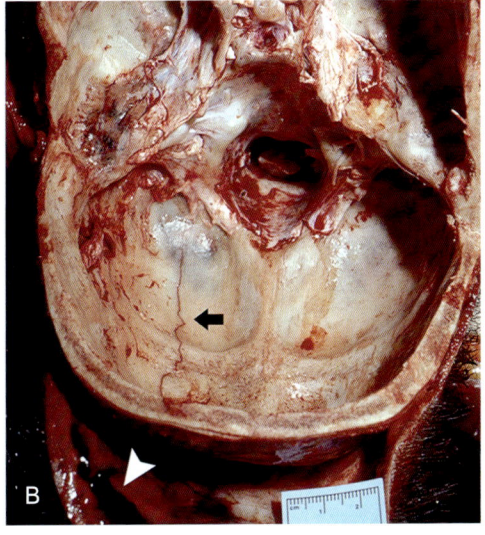

图3-25 缢索在现场被切断时致死者头部撞击混凝土地面。（A）剃去死者毛发后可见左枕部头皮裂创。（B）左枕部头皮内可见挫伤（三角箭头）。剥离硬脑膜后可见枕骨内板线性骨折（箭头）。

如果受害者已意识丧失，则不存在其他创伤（如面部和头皮擦伤）（66，68）；在伪装自杀的他杀案件中可以观察到外部钝挫伤、他勒或锐器伤的迹象（6，7，28，68）。

2.1.7 缢死的内部检查

即使在完全性缢颈的情况下，许多缢死不存在内部损伤，这突显了缢死确实是一种形式"温和"的窒息死，特别是自缢（4，7，15，16，23，24，28，50，93，128）。由于意识迅速丧失，死者没有时间进行有意识的活动（125）。迷走神经刺激致心搏骤停也是原因之一（90）。在一项研究中，约60%的缢死可观察到颈部内的损伤（16）。与不完全性缢颈相比，完全性缢颈的颈部损伤发生率更高（46%-62%）。

2.1.7.1 软组织出血

在少数案例中可见软组织或肌肉出血。多项研究发现,出现软组织出血的情况约为3%至三分之一(16, 23, 24, 50, 57)。颈部骨折、相邻的软组织部位出血表明损伤发生时死者还活着(17, 18, 129)。死后溶血会使软组织出血不那么显著(142)。当尸体已发生腐败时,不能完全排除死后组织出血的可能(参阅第2章标题3.3;参考文献142)。目前未发现软组织出血和舌骨骨折之间存在相关性(24)。失血通常不足以导致死亡(参阅标题2.1.7.2),但在某些情况下(如拔牙),颈部肌肉组织内的广泛性出血可引起窒息(143)。

2.1.7.2 出血部位

出血部位如下:

- 压迫部位的胸锁乳突肌(图3-26;参考文献28)。

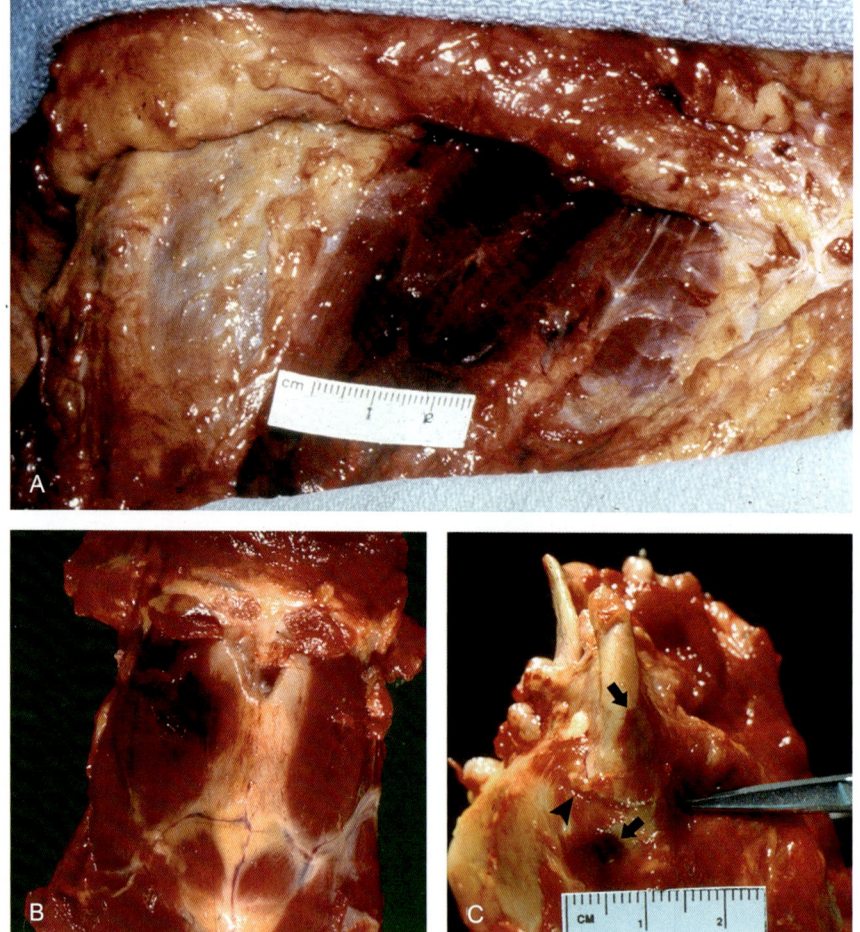

图3-26 自缢,软组织出血。(A)左侧胸锁乳突肌出血(由北卡罗莱纳州教堂山首席法院办公室供图)。(B)喉前面观,甲状软骨右侧毗邻肌肉出血。(C)甲状软骨左上角骨折(三角箭头),周围组织灶状出血(箭头)。

- 颈带状肌(15)。
  - 颈带状肌广泛性出血,伴随声门水肿和出血,会干扰呼吸(144)。
- 甲状舌骨膜。
- 甲状软骨相邻的结缔组织和肌肉组织(图 3-26;参考文献 15)。
- 与完整的舌骨和甲状软骨[上角(28)]相邻的软组织。
- 骨折部位的软组织(如果颈部受压使血液循环完全停止或死后伪造骨折,则骨折部位软组织可不出血;图 3-26;参考文献 145)。
- 由于颈部过度伸展,致胸锁乳突肌下筋膜出血,伴或不伴肌肉受累[在沟痕最高处出血迹象明显(107,129,146)]。
  - 出血不一定肉眼可见,可借用显微切片观察(见本章第 2.4 节和参考文献 142)。
- 环杓后肌出血是非特异性征象,见于多种原因(146–148)。

2.1.7.3 瘀点性出血

瘀点性出血可见于颊黏膜、舌根和会厌处(15,28)。一项系列研究表明,在缢吊案例中,19% 可见心外膜瘀点性出血,6% 可见脏胸膜瘀点性出血(16),4% 两者均出现(16)。在完全性缢颈案例中,10% 可见内部器官瘀点性出血;而在不完全性缢颈案例中内部器官瘀点性出血的发生率为 19%。

2.1.7.4 骨折

缢吊时颈前部骨折的发生率随年龄增加而上升,尽管在一些案例中,这种骨折也会在较小年龄的个体中发生,而在年龄较大的个体中不存在[如在缢吊案件中,14 岁的男孩甲状软骨上角断裂,78 岁的老人虽甲状软骨骨化但并无骨折表现(24,134,145,152–154)]。骨折的发生率亦取决于所使用的解剖方法和解剖时的细致程度(57,134,145,149,154–156)。影像学检查可提高骨折的检出率(145,153,157)。几乎四分之三的自缢可通过立体显微镜检发现舌骨和喉部软骨损伤,检出率高于常规检查方法(触诊、X 线成像和尸体解剖)(156)。

自缢时最常见的骨折为甲状软骨上角骨折(表 3-1;图 3-26;参考文献 16)。缢死者甲状软骨板骨折较少见,如果出现则与完全性缢死或长距离坠落缢吊(一种绞刑方式)有关(16)。通常,舌骨、喉软骨的骨折发生率在扼死或勒死中更高(109)。在 Betz 和 Eisenmenger 对 109 起意外缢死和自缢案件的调查发现中,37% 的死者有双侧甲状软骨上角骨折,15% 有双侧甲状软骨上角骨折合并单侧舌骨大角骨折,10% 有双侧甲状软骨上角骨折合并双侧舌骨大角骨折[包括一名 28 岁死者(155)]。另一篇综述表明,舌骨骨折通常与甲状软骨骨折相关(16)。死者尸体颈外部损伤征象、舌骨喉软骨复合损伤及相关部位出血提示压迫颈部致死的他杀的可能性高。Ubelaker(149)在文献综述后,得出他杀勒死和扼死骨折的发生率为:甲状软骨骨折在勒死中的发生率为 32%,扼死为 34%;舌骨骨折在勒死中的发生率为 11%,扼死为 34%;环状软骨骨折在勒死中的发生率为 9%,扼死为 1%。

表 3-1　自缢案件中骨折情况及发生率

	Ubelaker (149)	Paparo (134)	Simonsen (150)	Luke (24)	DiMaio (151)	Feigin (152)	Samarasekera (16)	James (57)
案例数	综述	167	80	61	83	307	233	84
甲状软骨	15%	11%	28%	13%	11%	5%	30%	25%
舌骨	8%	6%	9%	23%	—	3%	7%	17%
甲状软骨骨折合并舌骨骨折	—	3%	9%	—	—	1%	8%	5%
环状软骨	0.0003%	0.6%	—	—	—	—	1 例	—
颈椎	罕见	—	—	—	1%	1%	1 例	—

舌骨是可移动性结构,前方有下颌骨及软组织保护,后方有颈椎保护(图3-27)。临床上舌骨骨折较少见(144,159)。在勒死和缢死中,很多因素决定了舌骨是否会发生骨折。舌骨大角的形状(即弯曲度)决定了断裂通常会发生在舌骨中后部(160)。大多数舌骨是对称的(136)。尽管舌骨不同的尺寸和形状(如长宽相等

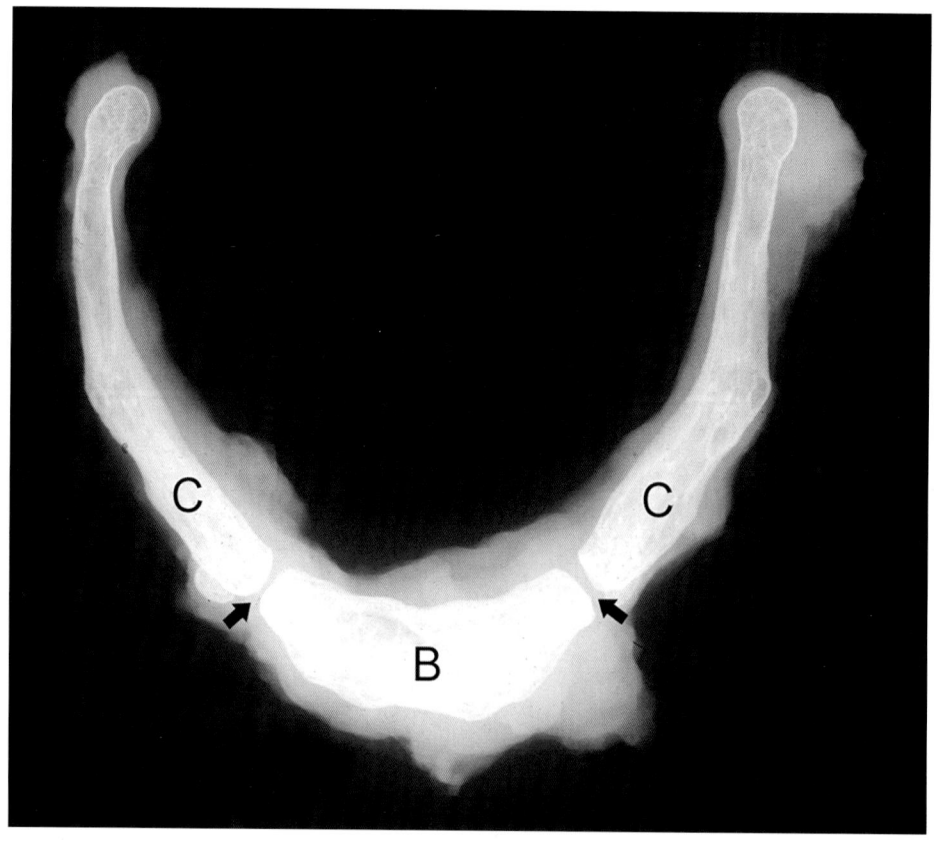

图3-27　舌骨 X 线片显示舌骨体(B)、舌骨大角(C)之间为软骨结合(连结),没有骨性融合(箭头)。

的双曲线形和宽大于长的抛物线形)与骨折类型相关,舌骨的长宽比在人群中也并非呈离散分布。舌骨体与舌骨大角软骨结合(连结)处的骨化或融合使之更易骨折(图3-28;参考文献161),且骨性融合和骨折发生率随年龄增加而上升(145,153,161)。儿童舌骨柔韧度高,罕见舌骨、喉软骨发生骨折(18)。Miller等学者(136)研究发现,舌骨体与舌骨大角骨性融合开始于21-30岁,在此年龄组双侧骨性融合的发生率为16.7%。舌骨体与舌骨大角双侧骨性融合的高峰在60岁,该年龄段60%女性和70%男性的软骨结合处会出现骨化(162)。但另一项研究显示骨性融合的发生率并无性别差异(136)。值得注意的是,相当比例的老年人仍然有高柔韧度的舌骨大角,因此,即使年龄较大的死者无舌骨骨折,亦不可排除颈部受压的可能(162)。舌骨体因与舌骨大角的软骨结合而不融合或不完全融合,会相对地增加此处的活动性,切不可误认为骨折(149)。解剖后舌骨X线检查可用于评估融合程度。Miller的研究显示,在21-30岁的34个研究对象中,12.5%的舌骨发生单侧骨性融合,在

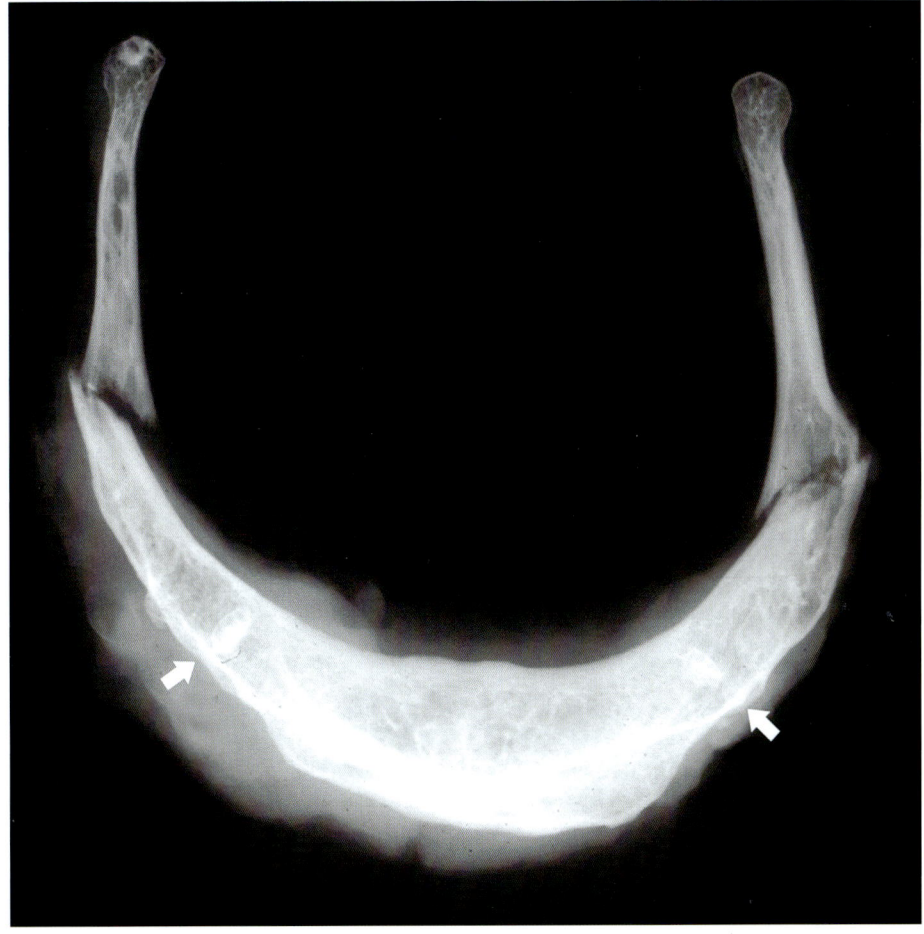

图3-28 自缢,长时间缢吊,死者舌骨X线片显示双侧舌骨大角骨折,双侧舌骨体和舌骨大角骨性融合(箭头)。

大于70岁的个体中,约有30%的舌骨发生单侧骨性融合或不融合(136)。

舌骨骨折还伴有其他因素的影响,即施加于颈部的力的性质、大小和分布情况,以及从施加压力至死亡的时间(161,163)。绳结位于颈部侧面会增加舌骨骨折的可能性(8)。当处于最高点的绳结位于耳后时更易发生舌骨骨折(155)。也有研究发现,以舌骨骨折的部位确定绳结位置是不可靠的(图3-29;参考文献154)。舌骨骨折可在不完全性缢颈时发生(49,96,152),如发生于坐位、穿着约束衣(下滑压迫颈部窒息)的老年死者。一项研究显示,与不完全性缢颈相比,完全性缢颈的骨折发生率更高[22%比10%(16)]。

如果舌骨骨折由钝性暴力(如机动车辆碰撞)引起,通常会合并其他骨折,如下颌骨、甲状软骨、环状软骨等骨折(图3-30;参考文献144,149,159,164和165)。当颈部过伸时,可能仅出现舌骨骨折(159)。慢性乙醇中毒患者易发生舌骨骨折(149)。在自然死亡中也可发现舌骨和喉软骨骨折,推测可能是由心脏停搏濒死期强烈的肌肉收缩或剧烈的咳嗽引起的。舌骨骨折可与咽喉撕裂伤有关(159)。即使没

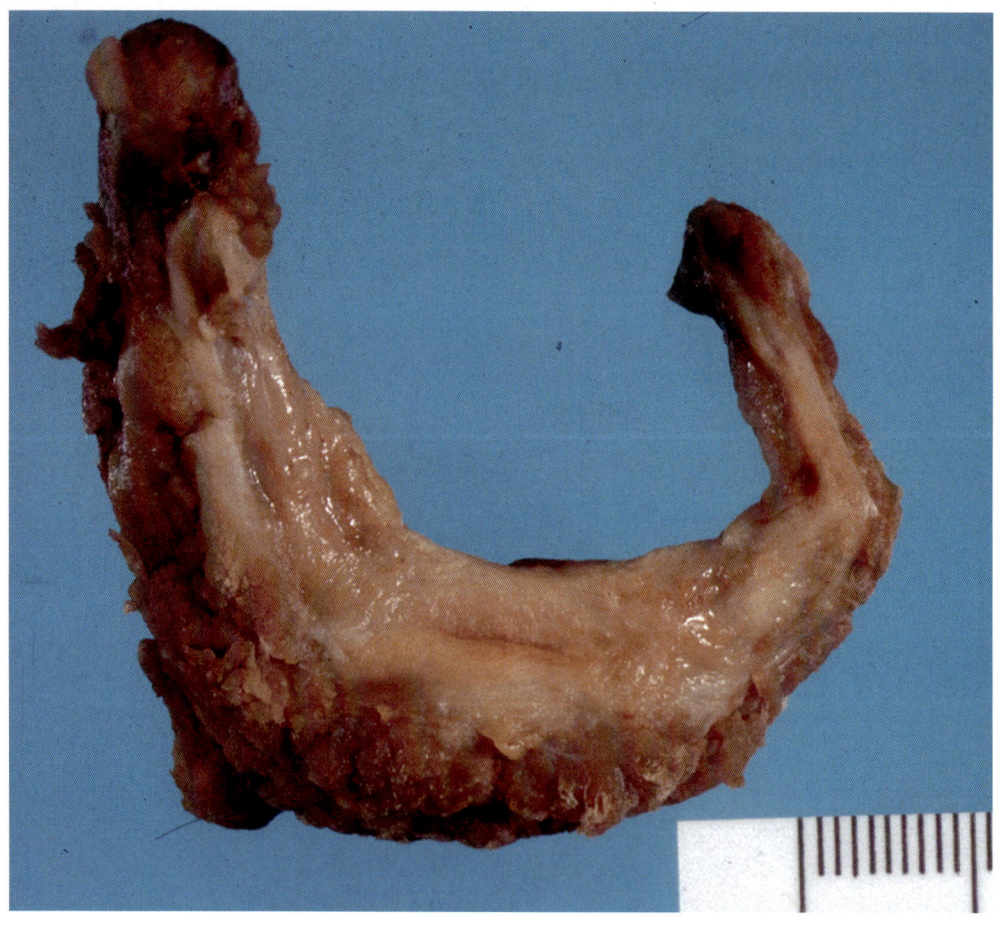

图3-29　自缢。左侧舌骨大角骨折,绳结位于右颈部。

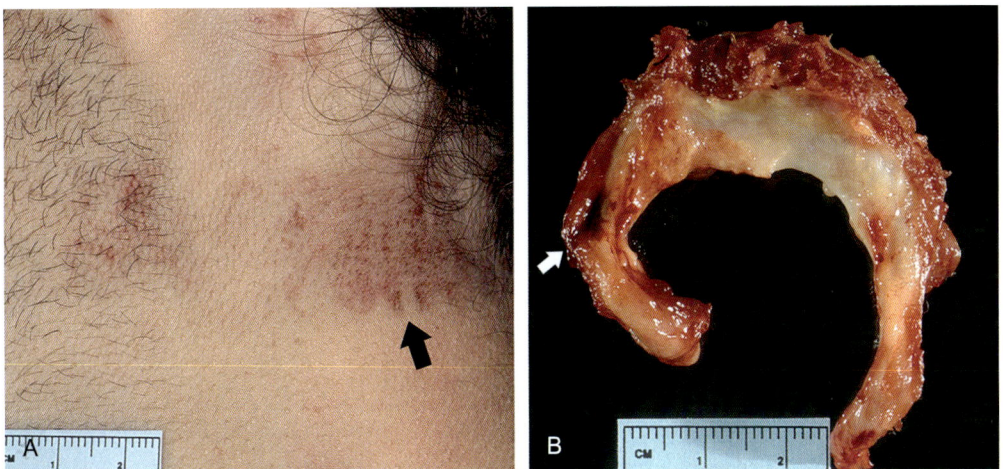

图 3-30 被碾压的行人。(A) 左颈部擦伤 (箭头)。(B) 左侧舌骨大角骨折 (箭头),伴有出血。

有黏膜损伤,喉部水肿也可能导致气道狭窄 (159)。

附着于舌骨小角的茎突舌骨韧带可变异钙化,甚至发生在儿童中,该变异可通过舌骨原位触诊发现。这个部位的骨折较罕见,注意不要与骨化不完全的韧带相混淆 (165)。

任何对甲状软骨上角的检查都必须考虑到解剖变异的可能,不应与骨折相混淆 (图 3-31;参考文献 142, 156, 157, 165 和 166)。此处常见的解剖变异位于上

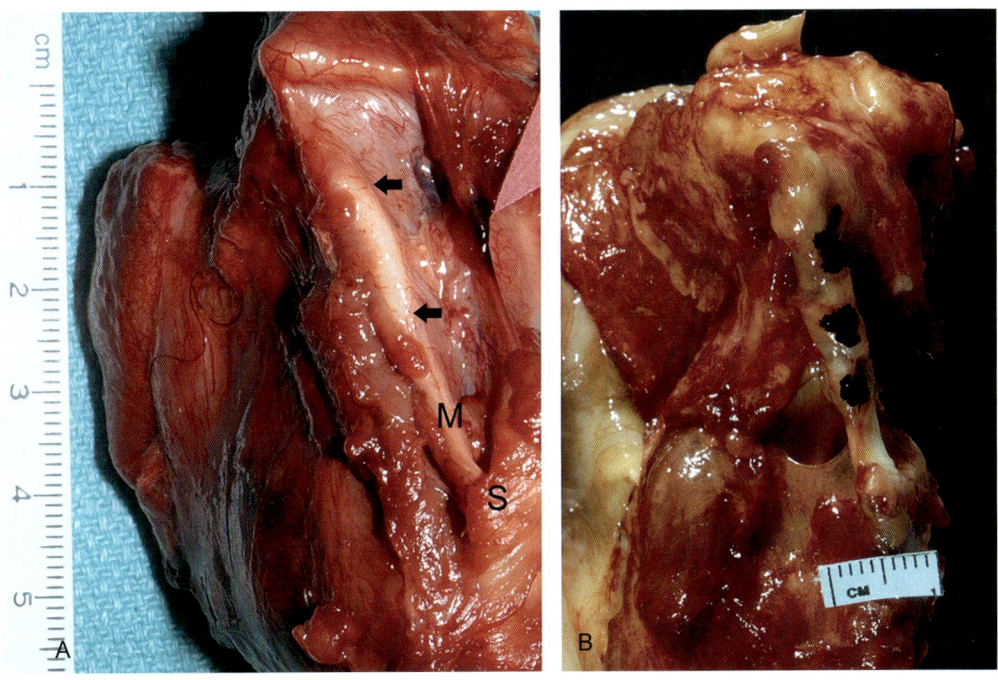

图 3-31 甲状软骨上角的解剖变异。(A) 右上角不附着于甲状软骨板上缘 (S)。纤维膜 (M) 从 S 处延伸至 "浮动" 的甲状软骨上角 (箭头所示的上限和下限)。(B) 由三个活动部分 (墨迹标示) 组成的甲状软骨的右上角。

角上方,是包裹于舌骨甲状侧韧带内移动性的、变异钙化的纤维软骨结节,即麦粒软骨(165)。

随着钙化进展,骨折发生率随着年龄的增加而增加,但存在可变性。因为骨化并不以恒定方式进行(图3-32;参考文献16,50,57,142,145,153和157),且老年人可不存在钙化(64,157)。不完全性缢颈也可见甲状软骨上角骨折[一项研究显示,在完全性缢颈案例中骨折发生率为50%,而在不完全性缢颈案例中为31%(16,49,152)]。骨折的确可发生在与绳结相反的位置(16,154)。研究还表明,较紧缢索所致骨折的发生率(62%)比宽松缢索的(15%)要高。

致命的颈部受压并非是甲状软骨上角骨折的唯一因素,直接钝性损伤(如机动车撞击、从高处跌落等)、抢救复苏和粗暴的尸检操作也可导致上角骨折(51,142,167)。钝性损伤还可导致甲状软骨板骨折(64,168)。愈合的骨折损伤也可在舌骨和喉软骨尸检中被观察到(图3-33)。一项针对骨骼样本尸检的研究表明,有17.3%的样本可见陈旧性骨折,其中,3.2%可见两处陈旧性骨折,陈旧性骨折在甲状软骨的发生率为11.4%,在环状软骨为7.3%,在舌骨为1.6%,在气管软骨为0.2%(168)。

长距离坠落缢吊(绞刑)可导致甲状软骨板骨折(109),但在"一般"缢吊案件

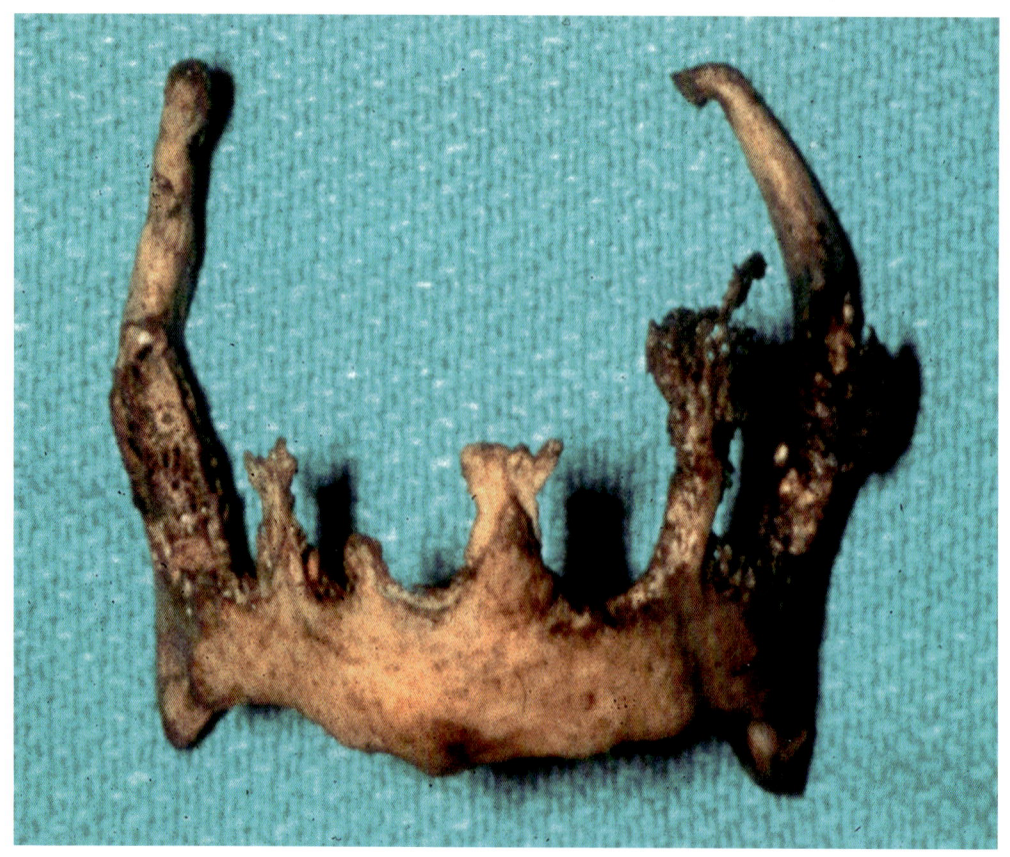

图3-32 遗骸。甲状软骨板不规则骨化。注意突出的上角已完全骨化。

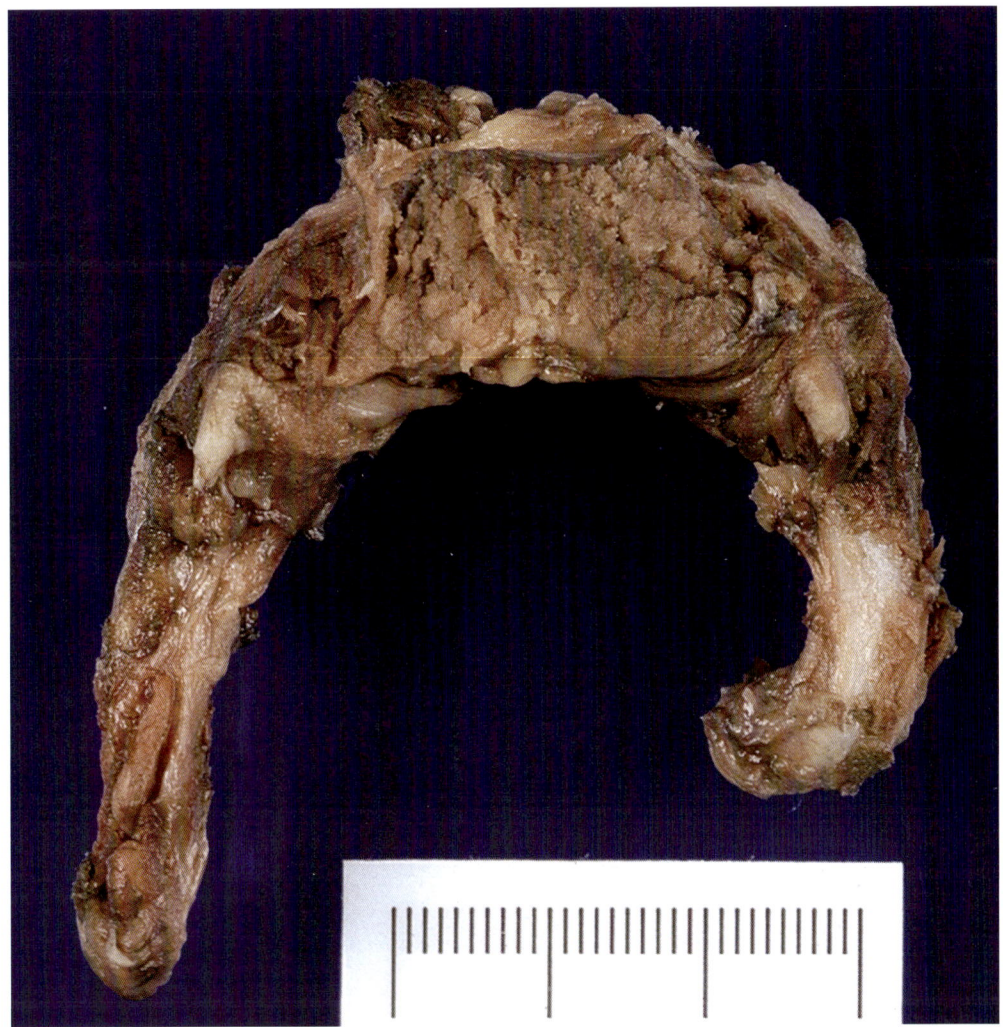

图 3-33 死者右侧甲状软骨上角陈旧性骨折,先前曾尝试自缢。

(非绞刑)中,该类骨折应排除受害者颈部遭受直接暴力致死并被悬尸将他杀伪装成自缢的可能性。自缢案例中环状软骨骨折罕见(表3-1;图3-34;参考文献16)。

颈椎骨折通常与长距离坠落缢吊有关,或者见于骨质疏松的老年缢死者中(图3-35;参考文献7,16,50,152)。然而,也有案例报道一名12岁男孩颈椎(C1-C2)骨折,但案件未涉及长距离缢吊(46)。一名23岁男性C3椎体骨折,被悬吊于4.6米(15英尺)高度,且腰上绑有11千克(25磅)的链条(46)。一名10岁男孩被发现颈椎C1-C2脱臼,死因为在床上跳跃玩耍时被钥匙挂绳悬吊于床头柱上(126)。颈椎骨折时,通常可在颈部观察到广泛的相关损伤(7)。在司法绞刑中,已根据受试者的体重计算出坠落距离在2.44米或8英尺之内,目的是基于人道主义使受刑人颈椎脱臼并瞬间丧失意识(169)。典型的绞刑骨折(hangman's fracture)又称创伤

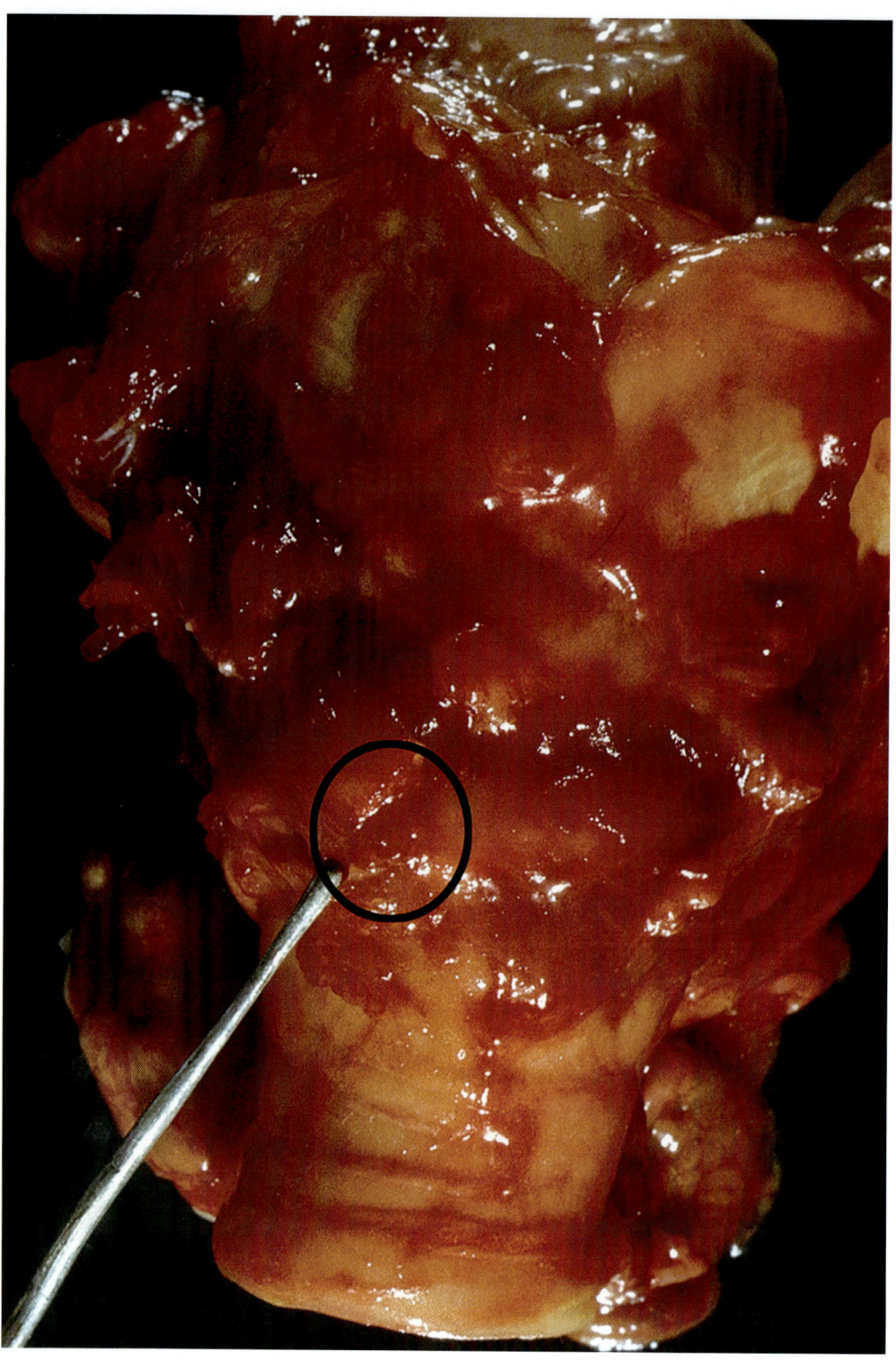

图 3-34 缢死案例中可见环状软骨右侧骨折(靠近探针的圆圈区域指示压迫所致的骨折位置)。

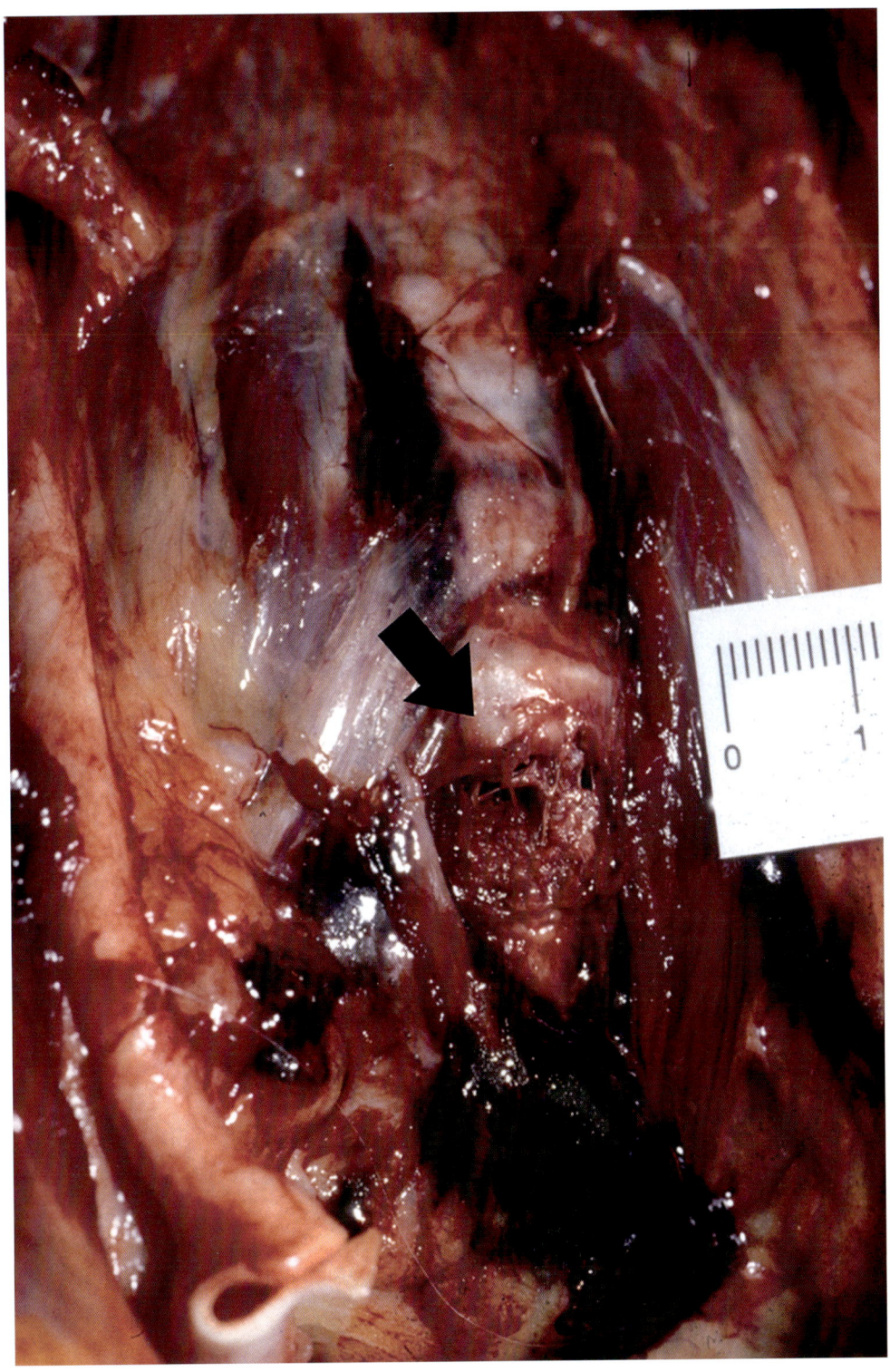

图 3-35 肥胖男性（>100 千克），有精神病史，缢吊于电梯井约 20 分钟。颈椎前区暴露，C6 — C7 颈椎骨折（箭头），骨折区域下软组织出血。

性枢椎前滑脱,指的是C2颈椎(枢椎)椎弓根骨折,但研究表明此种骨折类型多变(如椎弓不完全骨折、C1—C5不稳定性骨折并伴有其他骨性结构损伤等,颅底骨折也有报道;图3-36;参考文献169)。罕见情况下,典型的绞刑骨折也可见于机动车碰撞时系安全带的人员(71,170)。

身体头部断离多见于体型较大的死者遭受外部暴力(如交通事故)的情况,也可见于长距离坠落缢吊时(129,137,169,171,172)。

前额缢吊偶有报道,即缢索经颈后部绕至前方,缢吊点在前额正中(173)。

舌骨和甲状软骨上角骨折表明有外力施加于颈部,也提示窒息可能,但与喉、气管和颈椎的破坏性损伤相比,此处骨折通常并非死亡的直接原因(174)。

2.1.7.5 其他损伤和征象

颈部受压时可见舌部损伤(175)。在缢死者中,舌尖露于咬紧的牙列之间是常见征象(图3-21)。舌部损伤包括不同程度的舌内肌出血,还包括舌尖咬痕——伴有或不伴有黏膜下层微量出血(临界出血)。在一项包含178例他杀扼死和勒死的研究中,28%的扼死案例和16%的勒死案例可见舌尖咬痕;相比之下,在20例自勒案件中未见咬痕,在255例缢死案例中只有1%的案例可见咬痕(175)。在他扼、他勒、自勒和缢死案例中,较深的舌部出血概率分别为53%、42%、50%和4%(175)。观察舌部横断面或纵断面可以检验出血情况。舌中部出血提示淤血严重,

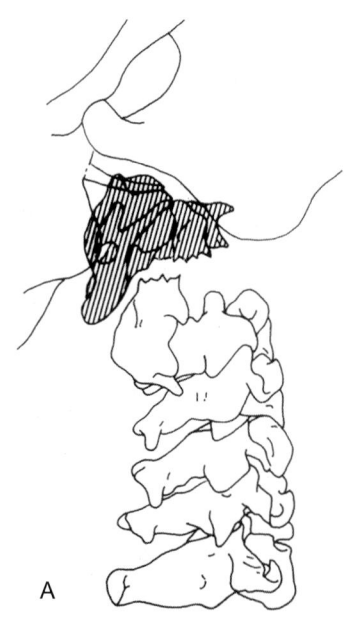 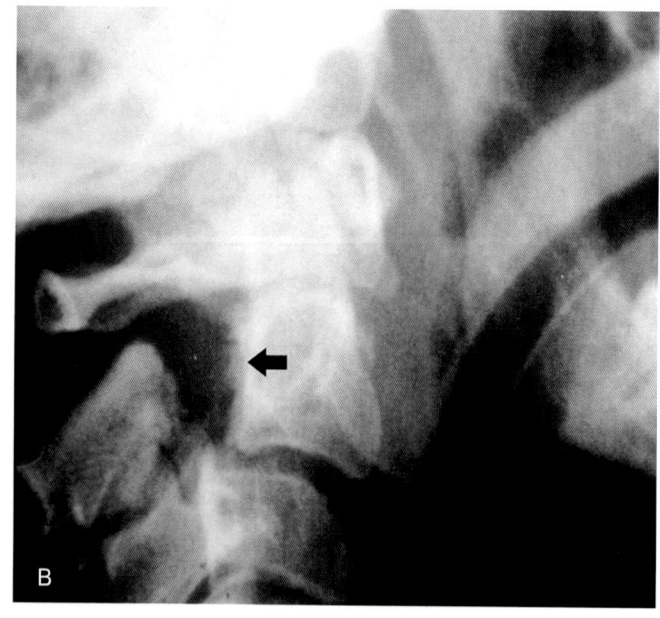

图3-36 典型的绞刑骨折。(A)过伸和轴向负荷导致C2(枢椎)椎弓根骨折。C1(寰椎)和C2椎体(斜线阴影)脱位导致脊髓损伤和死亡[经许可转载自Journal of Forensic Sciences, Vol. 34, No. 2, 参考文献170, 版权归宾夕法尼亚州西康舍霍肯市美国材料与试验协会(ASTM International)所有]。(B)"绞刑骨折"者X线片显示C2椎弓根骨折(箭头)。

多见于扼死和勒死。在一项缢死案例的系列回顾中，2%的案例可见舌尖部局限性出血。在该类案件中部分为不完全性缢颈，或死者处于坐位或跪位（175）。大多数缢死案例都有颅面部淤血的征象，即面部瘀点性出血，压力直接作用于舌骨基底处亦可导致舌部出血（175）。

在缢死中也可观察到上呼吸道撕裂，并导致继发性的皮下和纵隔气肿（图3-37；参考文献174）。

颈动脉内膜撕裂与受害者体重大、采取长距离坠落缢吊和绳结处于后位等因素有关（7，129，154）。一项研究表明，一处或多处颈动脉内膜撕裂在完全性缢颈中

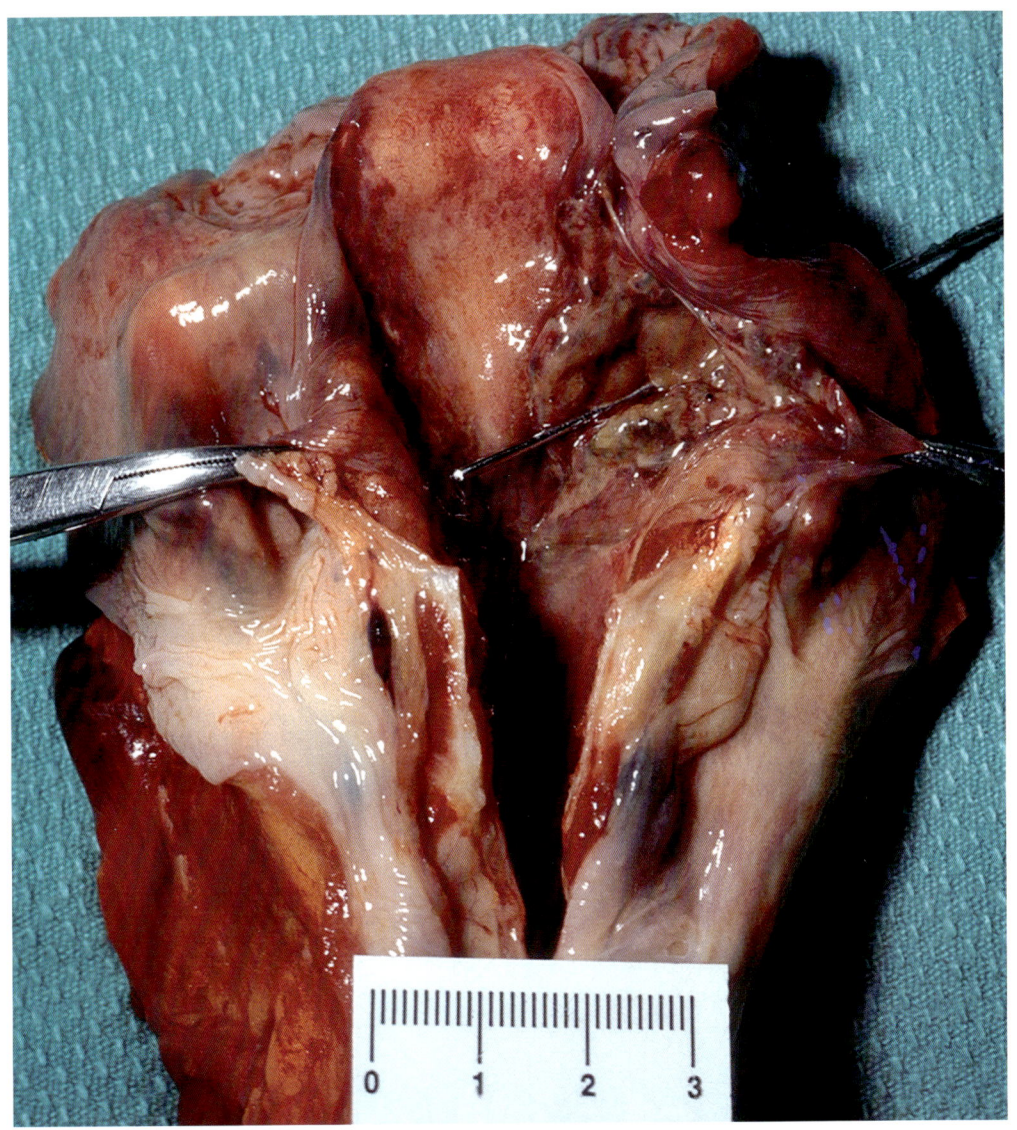

图3-37 缢颈后迟发性死亡。探针指示会厌处透壁裂伤（加拿大安大略省伦敦市伦敦健康科学中心B. Wehrli博士供图）。

的发生率（12%）较不完全性缢颈（2%）更高（16）。他杀勒死和扼死中也可见颈动脉损伤（109）。

一项对 36 例自缢案例的研究显示，四分之一案例中有椎动脉损伤，如破裂、内膜撕裂、内膜下出血等，其中内膜下出血最常见（177）。纵向牵拉负荷被认为是椎动脉损伤的机制，但完全性缢颈并不是引起椎动脉破裂的先决条件。椎动脉损伤也与颈椎损伤有一定关联。

颅脑损伤提示了他杀缢颈的可能，但是尸体未被妥善处理也会造成颅脑损伤（参阅标题 2.1.6.6；图 3-25；参考文献 68，78）。

任何生殖器部位的损伤都可能表明案件性质是性侵杀人（7，28）。

2.2 勒死

勒颈自杀通常易被怀疑为他勒（26），但现场调查通常无挣扎打斗迹象，可能会发现遗书（26）。死者以往的自杀企图、自杀观念及精神病史可提示自勒。

尸体内、外征象有助于区分自勒和他勒（表 3-2；图 3-38）。

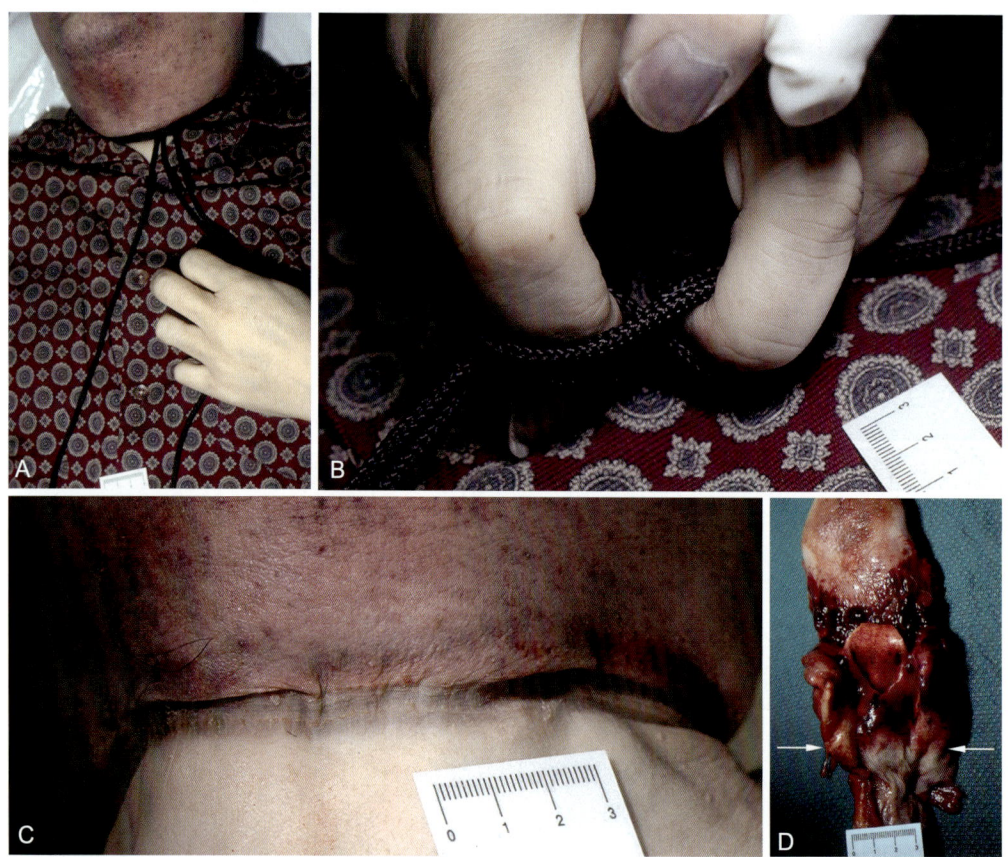

图 3-38 （A）自勒。（B）死者将鞋带（勒索）的两端缠绕手指，围绕颈部后收紧。（C）颈部勒沟水平。注意勒沟上皮肤重度发绀和出现瘀点性出血。眼部瘀点性出血可见（未提供）。（D）舌、喉部后面观。在缢沟（箭头指示）上方，可见严重的充血和出血（点状出血和瘀点融合出血）。

表 3-2 自勒与他勒的鉴别

	他 勒	自 勒
受害者特点	儿童、妇女、老人多见；受害者与攻击者有体格差异(18,65)	均为成人，没有儿童
外部征象		
勒索		
• 缺失或不典型	是，有一案例勒索为受害者头发(140)	否，勒索围绕颈部
• 勒颈超过一匝	是	是(26)
• 多处损伤	是	是，且多见(26,179-181)
• 单个或多个结扣	是	是，勒索不一定有结扣，因自勒者可用手脚固定住两端；也有用棒状物插入勒套扭转制成类似绞盘的装置；身体前倾可增加颈部压力(1,18,109,180-184)
• 结扣位置	后位>侧位>前位	前位>后位(26)
勒沟	有，80%	有，10%(45,179)
		勒沟少见，由于勒索的压迫致颈部出现苍白色条带状区域，也有案例报道勒沟可反映勒索纹理(26)
面部		
瘀点性出血		
• 眼部	是	是
• 面部	是	是
• 颈部	是，可无瘀点性出血(151)	是，眼部和面部瘀点性出血常见，但也可较少见或缺乏。缺乏瘀点性出血表明颈动脉被完全压迫(26,178,179)
面部发绀淤血	是，见于某些勒颈后没有立即移除勒索解除压迫的案例	是(26,179,180)，半数案例出现，缺乏瘀点性出血表明颈动脉被完全压迫(180)
有其他外部损伤	有，80%	有，20%
自我形成	无	如割腕
反抗伤	面部损伤(65)；胸部钝性损伤[攻击者膝部造成(65)]；抵抗伤；生殖器损伤[见于女性(65)]	无
内部征象		
颈前区肌肉出血及喉软骨舌骨骨折	有，超过80% 他勒时出血和骨折的概率高于自勒(178)；骨折见于1/3到1/2的案例，且骨折可为多发性；在一项研究中，勒索材质坚硬与否与颈部损伤的发生率无关	有，少于50% 最易累及的是胸锁乳突肌；喉软骨、舌骨骨折罕见；如有骨折，限于甲状软骨大角骨折；无多处骨折情况

续表

	他 勒	自 勒
舌 由于喉软骨和舌骨向上移位可导致舌底损伤；面部打击可引起舌黏膜损伤		
• 出血	有	有,可能很广泛(175)
• 咬痕	有	无(175)
喉黏膜出血	是	是
声带出血	是	否
喉内肌出血	是	否
颈动脉内膜撕裂	是(109)	有可能

注：改编自参考文献178。

特殊的勒索在勒死案例中也有报道，如橡皮筋、尼龙袜、撕裂的衣服等(26,179,184)。死者的手可靠近勒索或勒索端紧缠于手部(图3-38；参考文献26)。

意外勒死可在多种情况下发生(185)。"围巾"综合征("long-scarf" syndrome)是指围在受害者颈部的围巾、头巾等衣物卷入静止或运动的机械装置（如滑雪索道、雪橇摩托等），并由于机械牵拉使衣物收紧压迫颈部而引起窒息(图3-39；

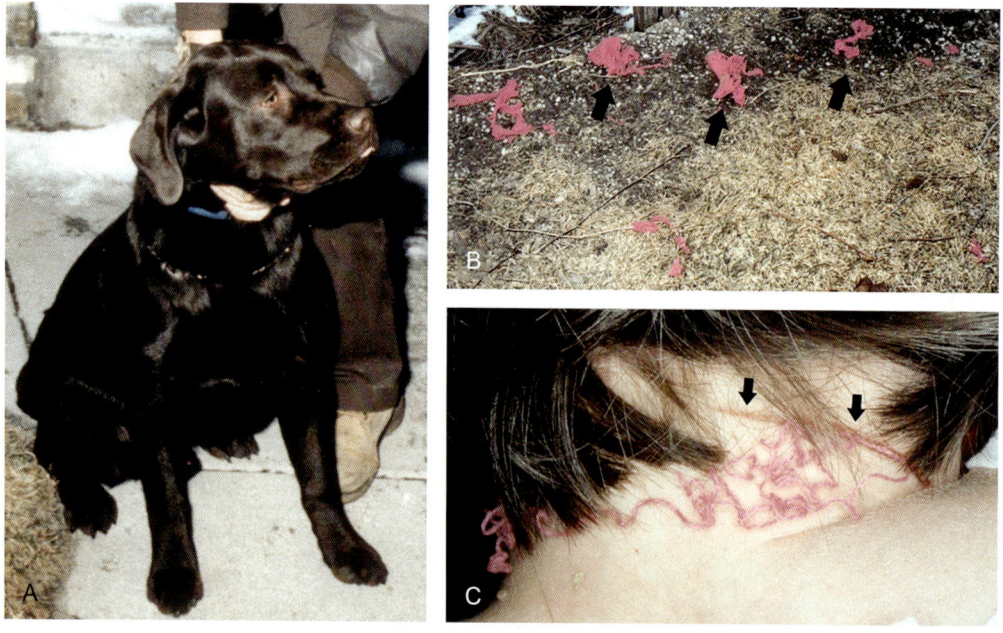

图3-39 意外勒死案例。(A)女童的狗。(B)狗咬住围巾并拖曳女童，地面可见散落围巾碎片（箭头）。(C)后颈部可见勒沟（箭头）和围巾印痕。

参考文献48,109和186–189）。钝性损伤显而易见（190）。意外勒死在性窒息中也有报道（见本章第2.7.1节）。

2.3 扼死

扼死是用单手或双手对颈部施加压力引起的窒息死亡，均为他杀。有时可见用四肢的其他部位［如肘部锁喉（90,191）］对颈部施压（3）。自扼时人在意识丧失后因全身肌肉无力导致颈部压迫解除，所以意外情况下的自扼或自杀扼颈死亡难以实施。扼死可见头面部瘀点性出血，颈部损伤（皮肤擦挫伤，包括指甲划痕）可以非常明显，也可以比较轻微（图3–40；参考文献192）。颈部损伤主要取决于以下几个因素：压力的大小，在小面积上施加压力的持续性；扼颈者指甲的长度、形状和尖锐程度，被扼颈者的皮肤弹性及颈部垫衬的衣物（如衣领）等（19,193,194）。颈部的指甲压痕也可能是死者试图解除压力挣扎所致（参阅标题2.1.6.6和标题2.6.1）。

抢救时颈部也可能受压，并引起相应损伤（138）。

2.4 压迫颈部死亡案例显微病理检查

显微镜检可见缢沟处皮肤表皮层、真皮层擦伤或挫伤（62）。缢沟处皮肤可见充满浆液和脂肪的水疱（图3–13）。

与出血相关的炎症是一种生活反应（142）。无论是否曾实施抢救复苏，镜下发现炎症反应表明死者被压迫颈部后存活过一段时间。在一例作案者承认受害者存活约半小时的他勒案件中，死者舌部出血处可观察到存在炎症反应（175）。在颈部闭

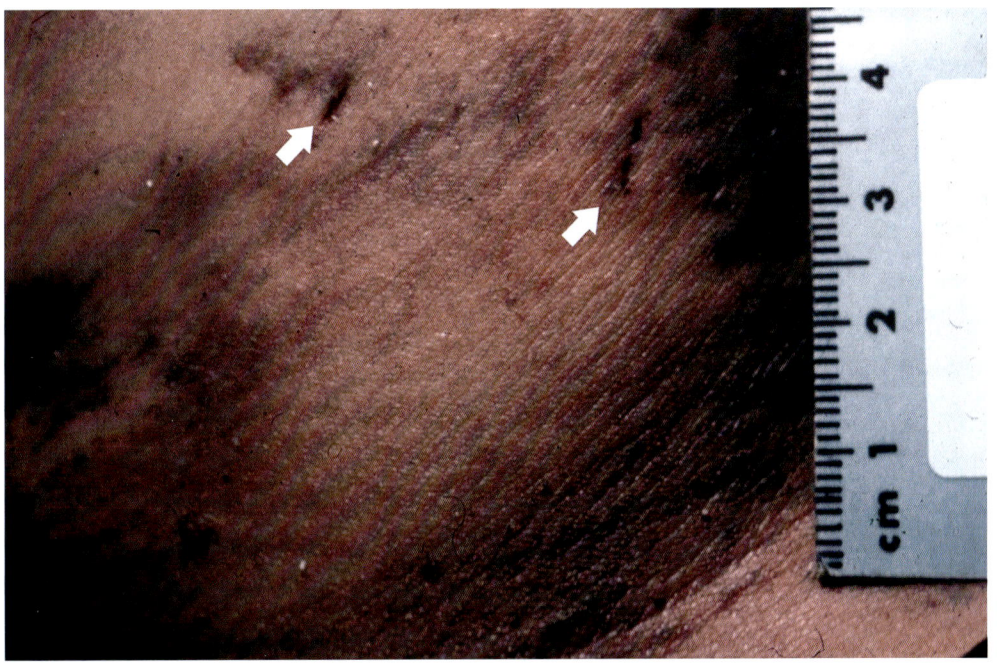

图 3–40 扼死。指甲痕（箭头）。

合或开放的皮肤损伤中,伤后最早 15 分钟即可检测到粒细胞的存在,同时也可证明案发前此处并无损伤(195)。各种组织有不同的变化规律,因此对身体其他部位皮肤创口的研究结果不一定适用于颈部受压的案例。纤维蛋白的存在也是一种生前的变化,在伤口出现后 10-30 分钟内出现(142)。在颈部受压所致损伤和其他类型损伤后数分钟即可出现的生活反应还包括肌组织的改变,如收缩带改变、肌组织透明样变[Zenker 蜡样变性(Zenker's waxy degeneration)(142, 196)]。

在勒死案例和其他钝性暴力作用于颈部的案例中,免疫组织化学技术已被应用于组织损伤的研究中(195, 197-202)。

在颈部受压的案例中,甲状软骨上角纵向切片观察可见软骨膜出血、皱缩和内陷,伴或不伴软骨膜破裂(142)。在扼死和钝性打击颈部的案例中,即使喉部没有明显损伤,镜下仍可见出血。在扼死案例中,用甲醛水溶液固定的侧喉部矢状切片可观察到喉软骨、喉部肌肉和黏膜上皮的出血,此项研究结果也可应用于其他类型的颈部受压案例(158, 192, 205)。

一般缢吊后 5-8 分钟即可死亡,但有复苏存活的可能,甚至有缢吊 30 分钟后抢救成功的案例(206)。缢吊后患者常发生缺血缺氧性脑病和脑水肿引起迟发性死亡(3, 16, 90, 125, 174, 207)。也有罕见案例报道了与脑基底节坏死性病变相关的缢颈后迟发性脑损害(125)。吸入性肺炎也是致患者迟发性死亡的并发症(3)。

2.5 毒理学检查

有文献报道所调查的缢死案例均未进行完整的毒理学分析(107)。约有四分之一到半数的自缢案例检测到乙醇(24, 43, 50, 58, 59)。在自缢死者体内检出高浓度乙醇时需要进一步明确在此浓度死者是否能实施并完成缢颈过程(43)。上消化道剖验若检见过量药物则可表明自杀意图(183)。在已排除使用药物使受害者失去能力实施谋杀的可能性后,死者血液内较高的药物浓度或毒性水平可提示自杀意图(50)。

2.6 抢救过程中颈面部人为损伤

抢救过程会引起一些人为损伤(如口对口人工呼吸引起颈面部擦伤),此种损伤可与颈部受压窒息或捂死时产生的损伤类似。保留抢救设备和明确抢救时所用物品至关重要,可用以分析损伤形成的原因(143)。需要询问医护人员是否在抢救前就有明显的损伤,或明确损伤是否为抢救时人为造成(143)。

2.6.1 尸表检验结果(实施过抢救)

在对 16 岁及以上年龄接受气管插管的患者进行尸表检验时,可以在 24 小时内发现以下检验结果(208, 209):

- 颈部皮肤擦伤。
- 胸外按压所致面部和结膜点状出血。
- 口腔损伤,包括口唇和颊黏膜(包括唇系带)擦伤、挫伤及裂创。

一项关于死前进行心肺复苏的研究表明,大约 4% 的死者(1 677 例法医学尸检

第3章 | 窒　息　　107

中的 21 例) 颈面部可见外部或内部损伤 (210)。外部损伤包括擦伤和挫伤, 分布于鼻尖和鼻孔 (口对口式人工呼吸所致)、颊部 (用指尖抠出死者嘴里的呕吐物所致)、下颌缘处 (实施双手抬颌法所致), 以及颈动脉区 (触诊颈动脉搏动所致)。与此相反, 在他勒案件中, 死者的整个颈前区 (尤其是喉部)、面部下方及项部均可见擦伤。他勒形成的擦伤分布并不一定是相互平行的, 而更具随机性。该研究中, 死者面部和结膜亦未检见点状出血。

在儿科患者 (<1 岁) 中, 各种损伤多由气囊罩、口对口式人工呼吸或气管插管形成 (143)。与面罩相关的擦伤对称分布于鼻梁、鼻底、嘴唇、脸颊及颏前部。在头面部形成的指甲擦伤多与固定患者头颈部以保持呼吸道通畅有关。经现场急救人员实施口对口人工呼吸, 通常会造成鼻翼两侧布满指甲擦伤 (图 3-41), 在面颊、额头和下

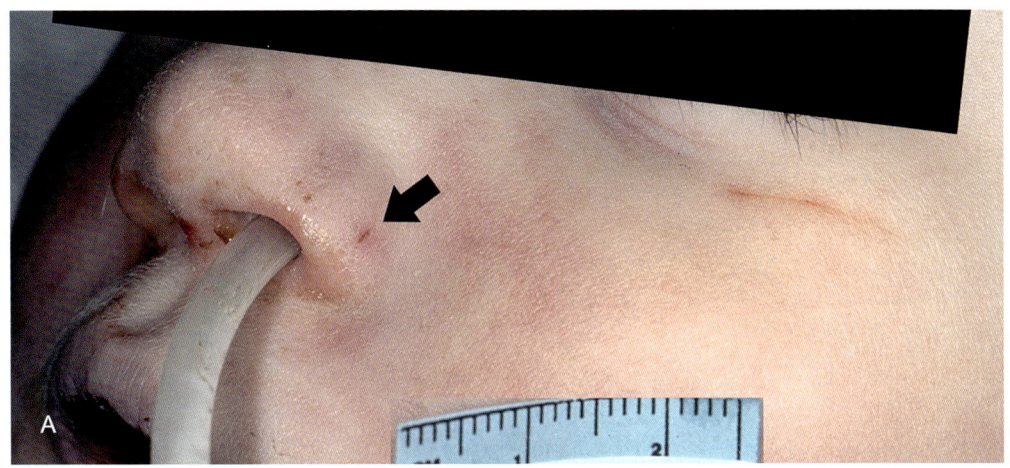

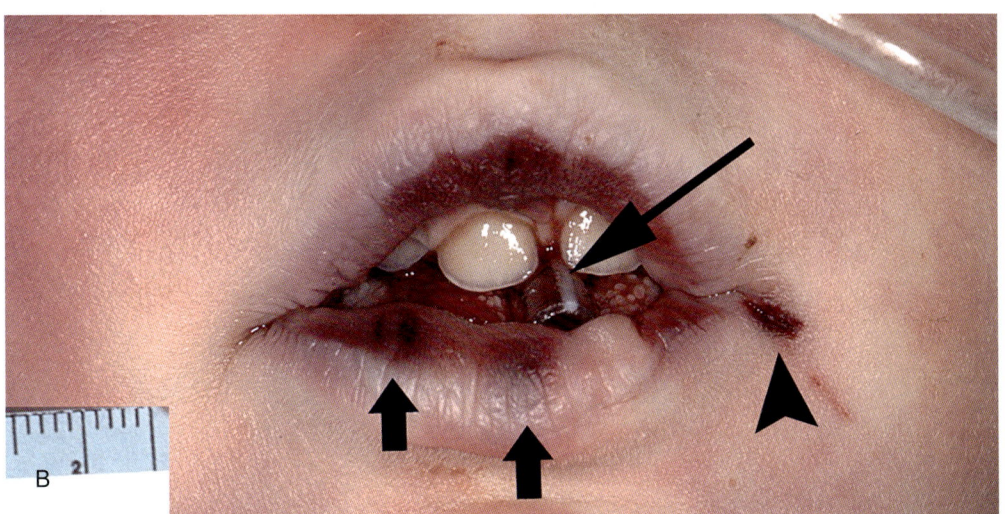

图 3-41　被实施心肺复苏的儿童。(A) 位于左鼻孔的鼻饲管。注意左鼻翼处的小擦伤 (箭头)。(B) 气管内导管 (长箭头)。裸露端已被剪断以便查看唇部损伤。唇部挫伤 (箭头)。位于左侧嘴角附近的擦伤 (三角箭头)。

颌部的分布则较分散。插管可导致唇部损伤（如挫伤,甚至撕裂）,但由于婴幼儿缺少牙齿,该类损伤在婴幼儿中并不常见（图 3-41）。对紧闭的口腔插管会增加受伤的可能性（图 3-42）。

2.6.2 解剖检验结果（实施过插管）

对于插管患者的研究,可以检见以下损伤（208,211,212）：

- 牙齿碎裂或松动。
- 舌根、会厌、梨状隐窝挫伤或撕裂。
- 会厌黏膜点状出血。
- 喉黏膜水肿、挫伤、点状出血［声门和声门下（90,213,214）］。
- 会厌撕裂,其他部位撕裂［声门、喉咽（214-217）］。
- 压迫所致缺血性溃疡引起的声门狭窄是长期并发症；气管造口术也可导致声门下狭窄（213）。
- 气管、支气管撕裂或破裂（218-220）。
- 食管破裂。
- 浅表和深部的颈部肌肉出血（210）。
- 舌骨和甲状软骨骨折较罕见（90,208,221）。

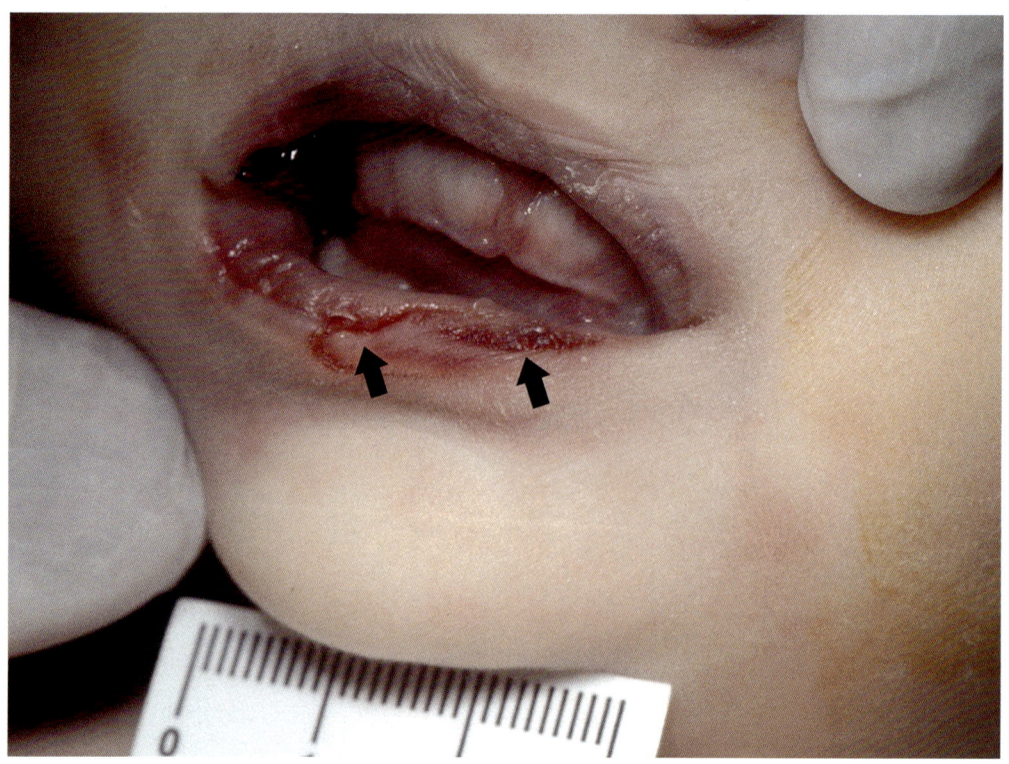

图 3-42 典型的婴儿猝死综合征。由于下颌紧闭,尝试插管导致唇部撕裂（箭头）。

- 环状软骨出血(211)。

对短期气管插管的研究显示,约 6% 的案例存在喉部损伤。这些损伤绝大多数是黏膜下血肿,黏膜撕裂很少见。这些损伤的发生、发展与患者被插管时的放松程度、相关解剖结构的复杂程度及医务人员插管的熟练程度有关(214, 222)。

曾报道有气管插管的误置(误入右主支气管、梨状隐窝、食管,或经颅底骨折处入脑)(211, 212, 223)。

2.7 自淫性死亡

性反常行为是一种非精神病性的精神障碍,不寻常的行为或臆想是性满足所必需的(224, 225)。死者为获取性满足而采取的反常行为,有时会导致自淫性死亡(225, 226)。Hazelwood 等(227)对自淫性死亡的判定提出了 5 个标准:在获得或增加性刺激的活动中存在自救行为;死者企图终止该活动;单独实施性活动;存在危险性行为的预演;没有明显的自杀意图。

2.7.1 自淫性窒息(又称性窒息、窒息式性爱、窒息癖)

自淫性窒息是一种性反常行为,性唤起和性高潮依赖于自我诱导并直至窒息,意识可几近丧失(141, 228, 229)。

自缢是最常用的手段(225, 228–235),颈部受压使脑部血流量减少,导致认知抑制降低,缺氧和高碳酸血症所致眩晕和欣快的主观体验增强了手淫的愉悦感(229, 232–234, 236–238)。当受害者不能自拔时,全身重量使缢索收紧(234, 237, 239–241)。和通常的自缢一样,意识快速丧失最终导致死亡(6, 141, 229)。迷走神经刺激也会导致心脏停搏(227, 231, 233, 236, 237)。

其他自淫性窒息致死方法如下:

- 使用塑料袋/围巾/雨衣/枕头/麻袋造成窒息(224, 228–232, 237, 242–247)。
- 将胶带缠绕头部并使用导管呼吸(240)。
- 口中置入塞口物(袜子)或物体(橡胶球、西葫芦)(141, 243, 248–251)。
- 勒死(案例报道有将女性头发缠绕在滑结中以防松脱;参阅图 3–43;参考文献 109, 224, 228, 230, 241, 247, 249 和 252–254)。
- 用绳索捆绑胸腹部(参阅标题 3.7;参考文献 229, 247 和 255)。
- 用塑料包裹(可使用一根管子呼吸;参阅图 3–44 和参考文献 256)。
- 穿着紧身潜水服(229, 257)。
- 使用液压动力装置缢颈(258)。
- 倒吊缢颈(258)。
- 将身体楔入垃圾箱[压迫胸部(228)]。
- 使用机动车辆[压迫胸部(259)]。
- 身体部分或全部淹没于水中(229, 260)。

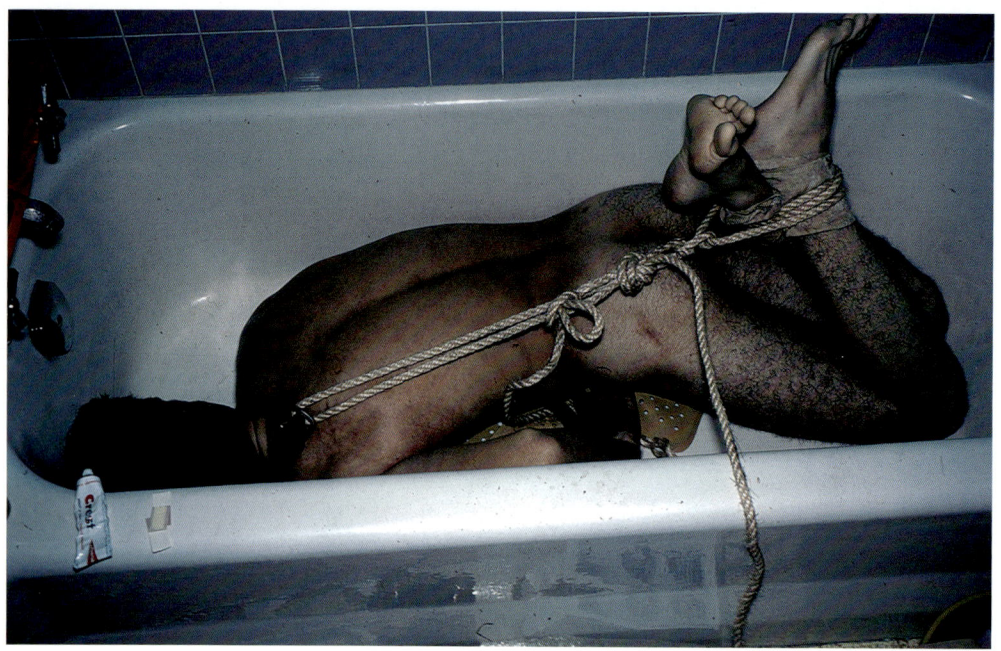

图3-43 自淫性窒息,勒死。脚踝上有衬垫物,浴室地板上放有色情读物。

- 吸入气溶胶喷射剂、化学物质或其他气体,并与面罩、塑料袋、衣物(如袜子)或湿抹布联合使用以达到欣快感(224,229,230,234,236,238,257,261)。

2.7.1.1 流行病学

据报道,美国每年有250-1 000例自淫性死亡案例[即每年1-2人/10^6人;在斯堪的纳维亚半岛为每年0.5人/10^6人(228,229,232,238,262)],死者年龄多在12-25岁(228-230,232,233,238),男性为主,女性极为罕见(男女比例为25:1-50:1(227-229,231-233,235,238,239,241,243,252,262-265)。通常死者独居(229,233,262),以单身为主(228-230,234,238),异性恋者多见,大部分社会适应性良好(227-232,234,238,239,262)。

2.7.1.2 自淫性死亡相关现场发现及现场情况

自淫性缢颈的初步调查结果表现出自杀特点(224,231,232,238,253),具有明显的自杀模式(253)。相反,奇特的现场情况也可能表现为具有虐待倾向或仪式性的他杀。如果死者是女性,易被误认为他杀,且调查线索细微,不易被发现(239,241,252)。深入调查现场情况、死亡形式、死者背景,并对尸体进行外部检查后,不难做出死因为罕见意外性死亡的判断(141,229,234,237,243,250,253,266)。可能还需对死者进行生前精神病学方面的鉴定(参阅第1章标题3;参考文献227,236,253,255,265和266)。自淫性或自虐性自杀实属罕见(225,227,237,249,253,267)。有时他杀可被伪装成自淫性死亡(133,229,262)。一些缢颈并非以性

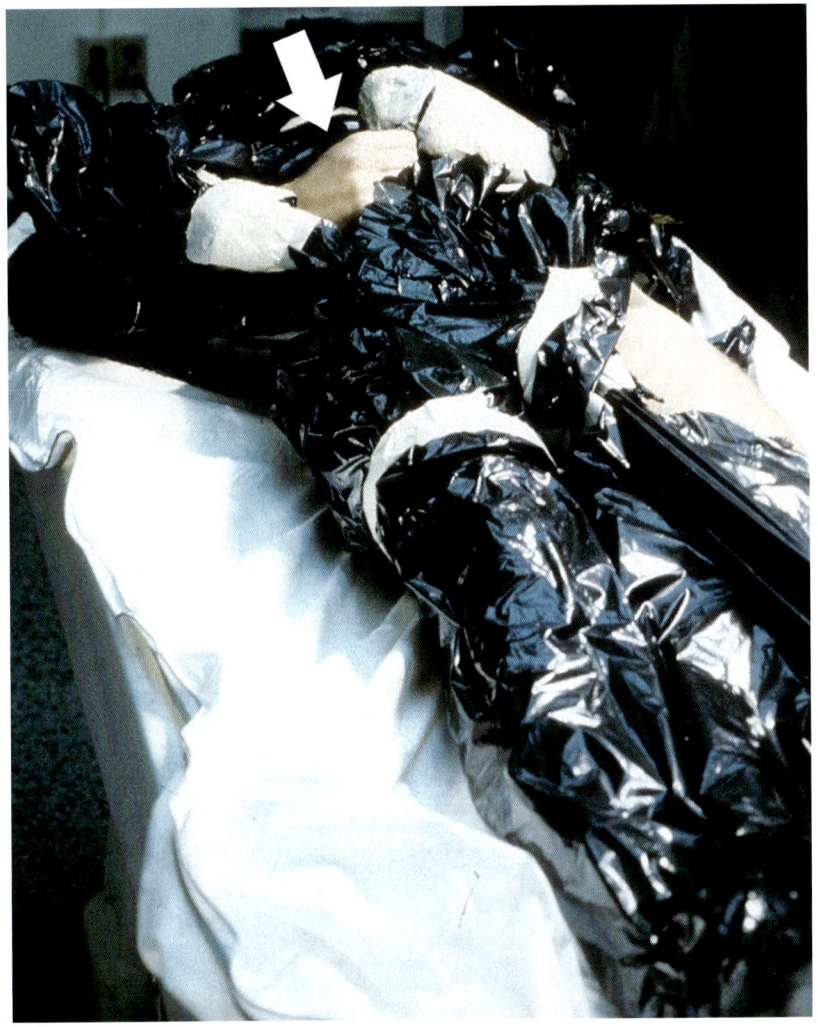

图3-44 自淫性窒息。死者生前将自己包裹在垃圾袋内,只露出右手(箭头)。

为目的[如扮演牛仔套绳套(46)]。由于自淫性死亡涉及个人名誉,亲属可能变动现场,移走自淫活动证据(228,229,231,232,239,268-270)。现场也可能因医疗抢救而被破坏。

场所多为寂静或隐蔽之处[如自家反锁的房间、地下室或阁楼、车间、下班后的工作地点、车内、监狱牢房、汽车旅馆或酒店房间、其他住宅、偏僻的郊外(141,224,227-229,231,232,234,238-240,243,263,271-273)]。所有现场均无类似他杀的搏斗或闯入痕迹,窗户可能被遮掩(227,274)。

死者处于能够解脱自救的体位(229)。通常,死者用腿部接触地面获得部分支撑。坐位、跪位和卧位等体位已有报道(225-227,229,231,238,275)。据丹麦的研究发现,约三分之二的死者为不完全性缢颈,28%为完全性缢颈,4%为倒挂,4%

为勒颈(228)。

现场可能有同性恋或虐待等相关色情物品,并置有镜子以观察自己性活动(141,225,227,228,231–235,238,239,243,261,263,268,273)。有案例报道发现现场有女子与死者性交的照片(48)。自杀现场也可能放有镜子(227,236,239,263)。如果死者是女性(239,241,252,263),性相关物品则较少见。有助于性活动的物品可能在死者身上、体内或身体附近被发现(273),有些物品明显与性活动相关〔如避孕套、振动器、恋物和束缚用物品(227–232,238,241,243,263)〕。其他物品可能与性活动无明显相关性〔如木桌腿、发刷、导尿管、吸尘器(225,268,276,277)〕。死者为老年男性时,现场可观察到更复杂的布置,表现为束缚、易装或两者均出现,且比例较高(230,263)。

死者生前通过与性癖好相似者接触、交流,阅读性知识手册、医疗书籍、色情读物和探案杂志,观看新闻媒体报道、缢颈相关电影,相互模仿,以及采取自发行为等渠道获悉自淫性行为(228,229,232,233,235,239,254,261,266,275,278–280)。现场可能会有描述自淫方法的读物或自淫活动的录像带(243)。已有自淫性行为发生在同族同胞中的报道(281)。

死者的自淫性活动可由配偶或女友、亲属、邻居、医生、性工作者等诱发(46,224,225,227,231,233,235,238,241,243,253,273,276),可伴有其他性反常行为(240)。调查询问(如确认有无抑郁史)和现场勘察(如确认有无遗书)表明死者并非自杀(225,226,229,233,241,262)。现场还可发现以往的自淫性活动所遗留的痕迹(如缢索长期摩擦屋梁留下的痕迹;图3–45;参考文献46,227–229,232–235,239,255,260,262,266和274)。所使用的方法和用具的复杂程度反映了死者具有自缢性活动的经验(227,229)。

2.7.1.3 尸表检查

缢颈是最常见的性窒息方式(图3–46)。缢索和皮肤之间可有柔软材质的衬垫物,但类似的保护性衬垫物并不一定都被使用(图3–46;参考文献141,228,229,231–233,235,238,239,241,252,258,262–264,275和282)。即使使用了衬垫物,缢索仍可在颈部形成缢沟或留下痕迹(141)。

死者也会设置自救机制〔如用刀切断缢索(227,229,231,232,238,243,260)〕,或通过起身缓解颈部压力(图3–46;参考文献232,238)。在颈部和其他身体部位采用的捆绑方式或绳结结构可自行解开(233,281),且这些捆绑通常是宽松的(图3–46;参考文献224,263和281)。

其他性反常行为的证据也已被观察到(229)。可有捆绑束缚,也就是使用或穿着对个人有性意义的、能够束缚身体的物品或衣物〔如塑料、橡胶或皮革材质的服装(225,227,228,230,233–235,238,249,253,258,267,282)〕。男性可能被束缚于女性的服装或用品中(图3–46;参考文献232,240)。四肢和生殖器也可能会

第3章 | 窒　息

图 3-45　通过自缢达到性窒息。屋梁上的压痕与之前的缢吊痕迹一致。

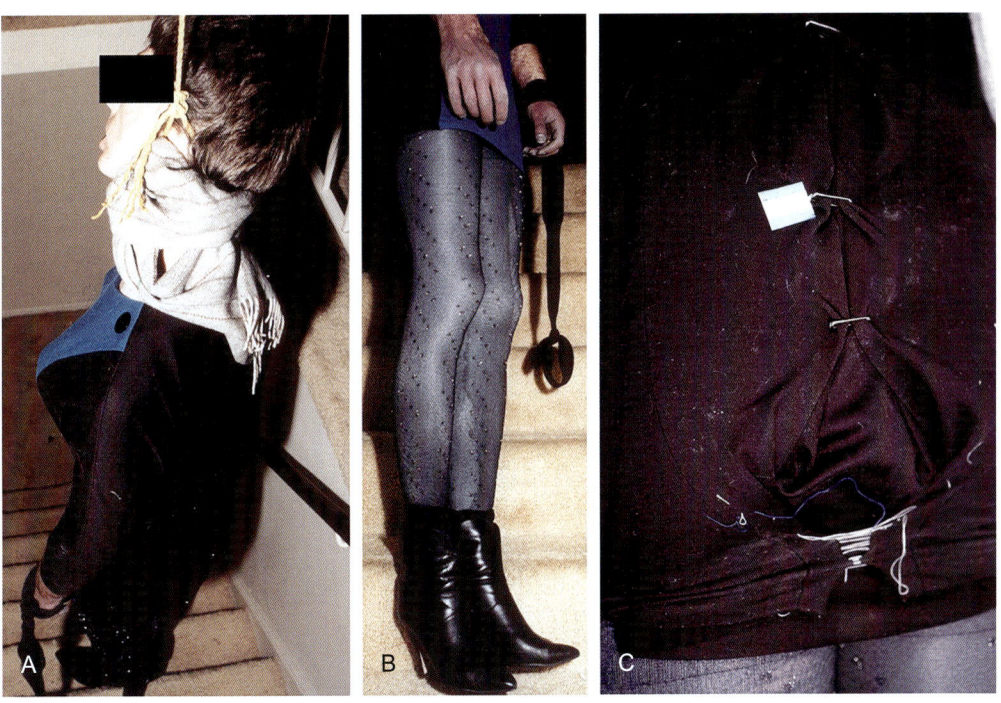

图 3-46　通过缢颈达到自淫性窒息。（A）男性死者被发现于楼梯间，身着女性服装。注意有围巾衬垫于缢索和颈部之间。（B）鞋子几可触及楼梯。腕部缠绕着松解的绳子，两脚踝被捆绑。（C）连衣裙的褶皱处被缝合在一起。

被束缚(图 3-46 和图 3-47；参考文献 141，231，232，235，238 和 266)。过紧的束缚可导致体温过高(283)。捆绑束缚亦被发现于女性死者中(224，241，263，265)。捆绑会在身体的不同部位留下痕迹(图 3-48；参考文献 252，281)。

器具和性器具可被发现于死者身上或体内，这在女性中已有描述(224)。异物可能存在于直肠、阴道或尿道中，可造成相关的创伤(如腹膜炎、出血；参阅第 7 章标题 2.4；参考文献 239，263，265，266 和 282-284)。

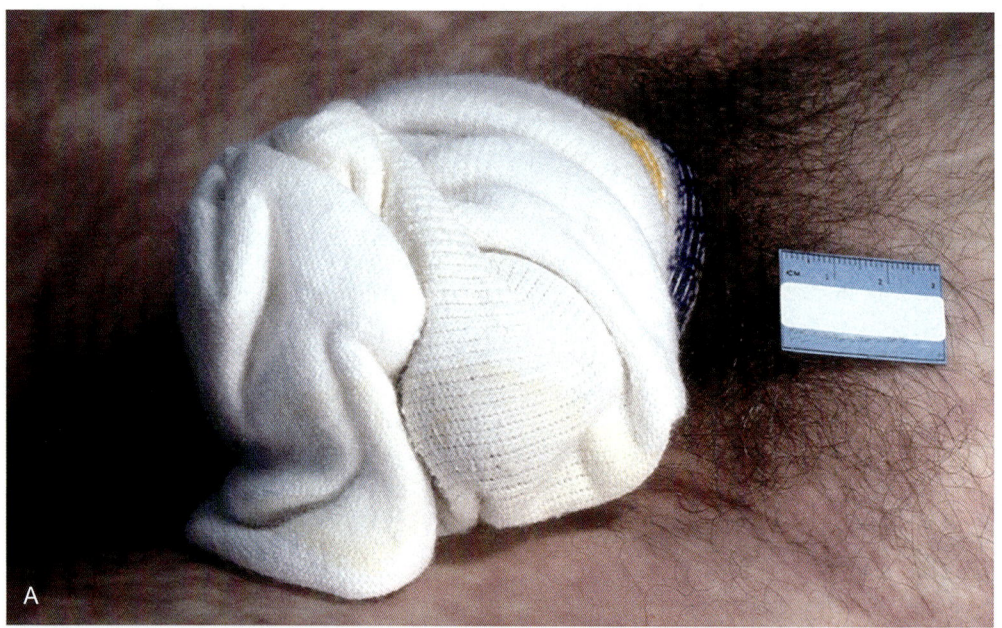

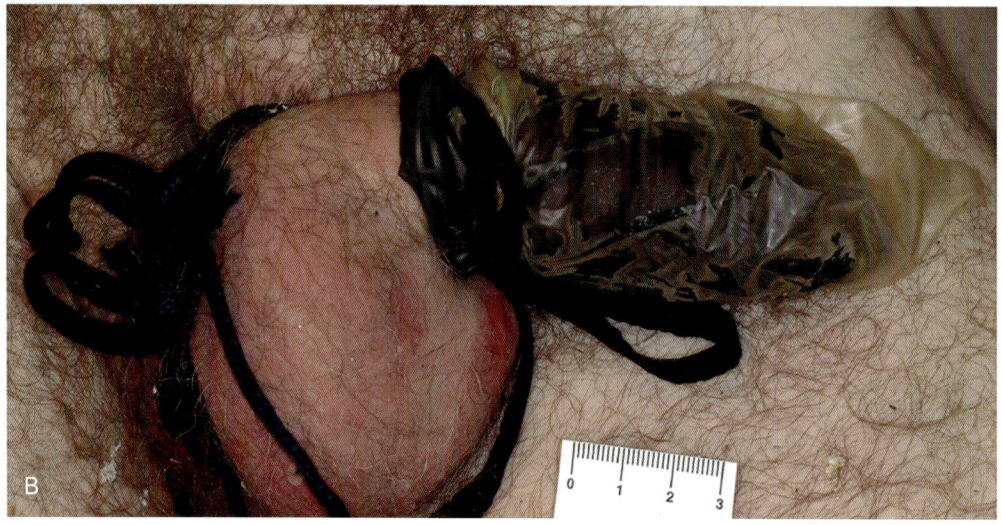

图 3-47 通过缢颈实现自淫性窒息(2 例)。(A)缠绕在阴茎上的袜子。(B)避孕套位于阴茎和阴囊附近(加拿大安大略省伦敦市伦敦健康科学中心 E. Tweedie 博士供图)。

第 3 章 | 窒 息

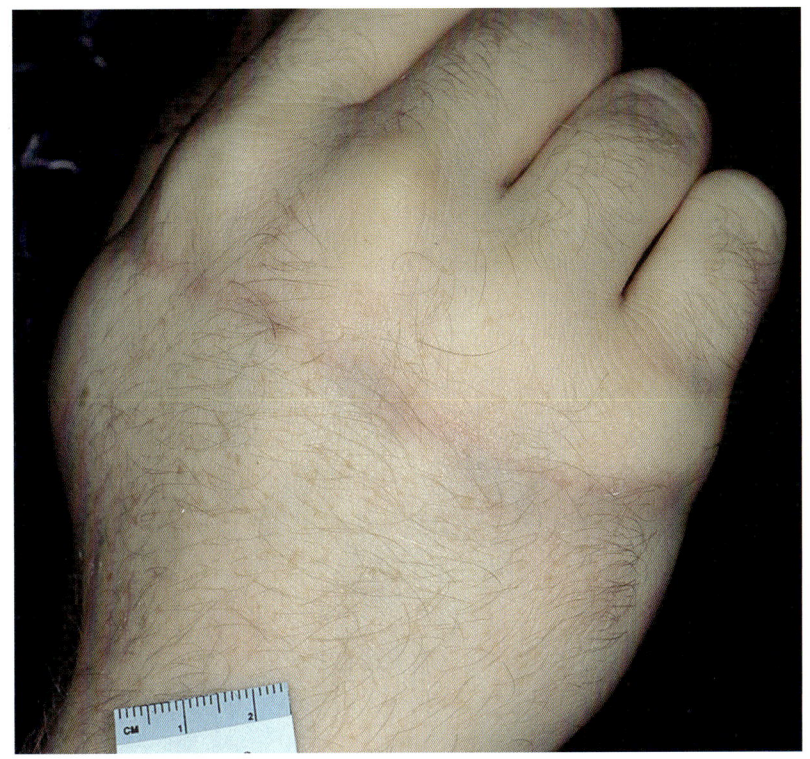

图 3-48 自缢时死者在右手手背上留下的轻微勒痕。

在某些案件中,可发现为引起性刺激而自残造成的近期已愈合的伤口损伤。损伤(如穿孔、烧伤)可存在于生殖器、乳头和其他部位(225,227,228,234,238,239,253,258,263,264,282)。阴毛可以被剃光(230)。性受虐癖在女性中罕见(239,241)。

现场可以发现性活动的证据。受害者的手可能位于生殖器附近(225,234,241,273,275)。自淫行为的目的不一定是实施手淫,即并不总是用手来刺激生殖器(229,258)。生殖器可处于暴露状态(141,226,227,238,239,262,271)。裤子拉链可能处于拉开状态(268)。阴茎附近存在精液不一定表明曾实施过自慰,可能是死后射精(参阅第 2 章标题 2.1;图 2-2;参考文献 28,78,90,225 和 234)。阴茎可能戴有避孕套或其他物品(如包有绵纸的塑料袋)(图 3-47;参考文献 227,238 和 274)。可在衣服或大腿上发现精液(240,243,275)。

男性常穿着女性服装(图 3-46;参考文献 225-227,229,231-234,239,243,258,261,274,276,285),衣服可能属于死者的妻子、女儿或女友(229,238)。死者存在服装不称现象(即衣着与自身职业和社会地位不相符,通常身穿可使其获得性满足的衣服,如牛仔服、骑行"皮革外套")(227,232)。穿着异性服装的男性更可能有使用各种物品进行肛门自慰、用镜子观察自己及自拍等行为(230)。女性则很少穿着特殊服装(239,241,263)。死者身体可能部分或全部裸露(227,229,231,234,241,243,258,268,273,281)。

2.7.2 "非典型"自淫性死亡

"非典型"自淫性死亡是由非缺氧机制的性刺激引起的死亡[约占自淫性死亡的10%(228,247,250,258,273)]。包括：

- 电击(228,229,238,247,250,286–289)。
- 吸入剂。
  - 死亡机制可以是多因素的(273)。缺氧可以由其他气体[如一氧化二氮、丙烷(247,261,268,273)]置换体内氧气引起。一些药物可引起心律失常[如三氯乙烷、氟碳化合物(273,290)]。硝酸盐与重度血管舒张有关(229,273)。某些气体是中枢神经系统的抑制剂[如四氯乙烯、汽油(229,271)]]。上述各类吸入剂也会被用于自杀(291)。
- 使用导尿管所致的膀胱结石引起的肾功能衰竭死亡，其次为支气管肺炎所致的延迟性死亡(292)。
- 枪支引起的直肠内损伤(参阅第6章标题10)。
- 自淫时诱发疾病发作死亡(图3–49；参考文献226,228,243,244,250和276)。

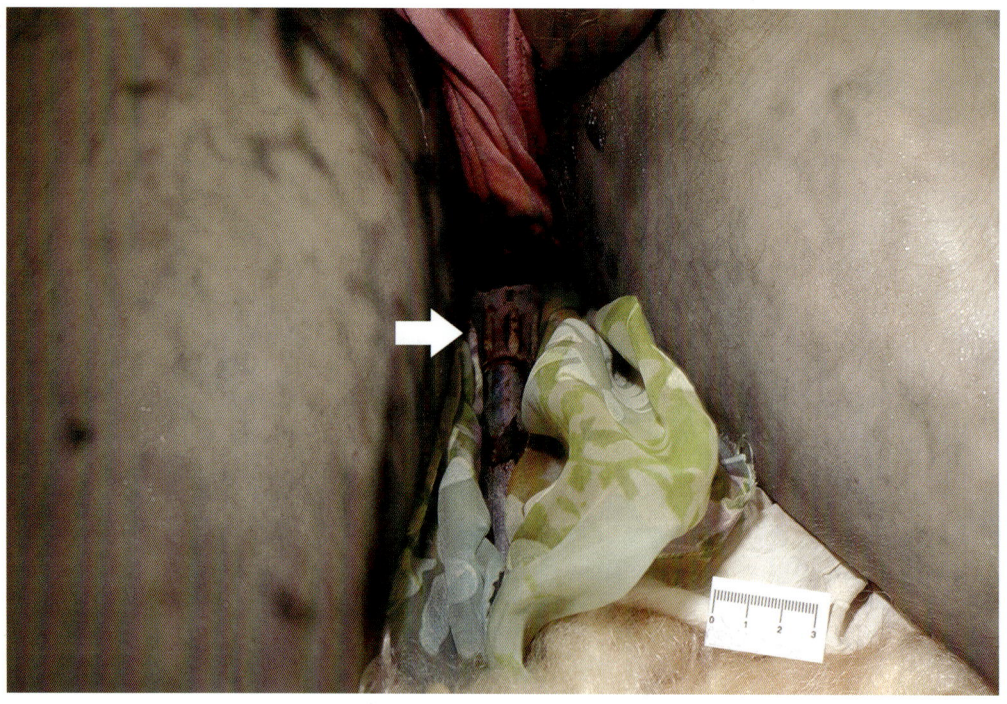

图 3–49　男性死者被发现时身穿女性服装，死因为缺血性心脏病。死者使用金属棒（箭头）进行肛门刺激。

2.7.3 毒物化学检验

死者生前可能使用乙醇、药物及毒品增强自淫快感。毒品或药物的使用可以解释死者为何无法及时摆脱窒息状态（133，225，243，248，255，261，273）。如果通过现场和案情的调查不难得出死亡方式为意外的结论，则毒物化学检验并非必须实施（107）。

2.7.4 自愿性活动

死亡发生在自愿的性活动中，易被怀疑为他杀（244）。死者曾采取某种虐待行为或处于缺氧状态，旨在延长性高潮。包括：

- 束缚和窒息[如通过掐、勒或扼颈，或使用口塞或袋子（191，239，244，249，253，254，262，277，279）]。
- 口交时吸入精液导致窒息（244）。
- 妊娠晚期被口交导致空气栓塞（244）。
- 电击（293，294）。
- 异物插入和拳交致生殖器损伤（295）。
- 自然死亡（247，253）。
- 性交期间非致命性自残和生殖器损伤（244）。

2.8 缢死的法医学检验方法

2.8.1 外部检查

- 对衣着和私人物品进行描述。
- 采集其他损伤的证据；记录损伤的分布。
- 观察现场是否遗留缢索，是处于原位还是已被移动；如果在原位，需注意绳结的位置及索套的匝数。拍照取证后，在远离绳结处剪断缢索，并用胶带连接断端使索套保持原状（图3－50）。注意缢索是重要证据。
- 对缢索进行描述：
  - 缢索的材质类型。
  - 索套周长。
  - 缢索的宽度。
  - 绳结性质（包括打结和固定方式）。
- 观察是否有眼球或面部的淤点性出血。
- 观察牙齿间的舌头伸出部分。
- 对缢沟或皮肤"痕迹"进行描述（62）：
  - 缢沟的特征（角度或倾斜度）。
  - 缢沟的宽度。
  - 缢沟绕颈周长（以确定颈部被勒紧程度；绳套周长＜颈部周长）。
  - 缢沟形成的印痕。
  - 缢索材质的残留。

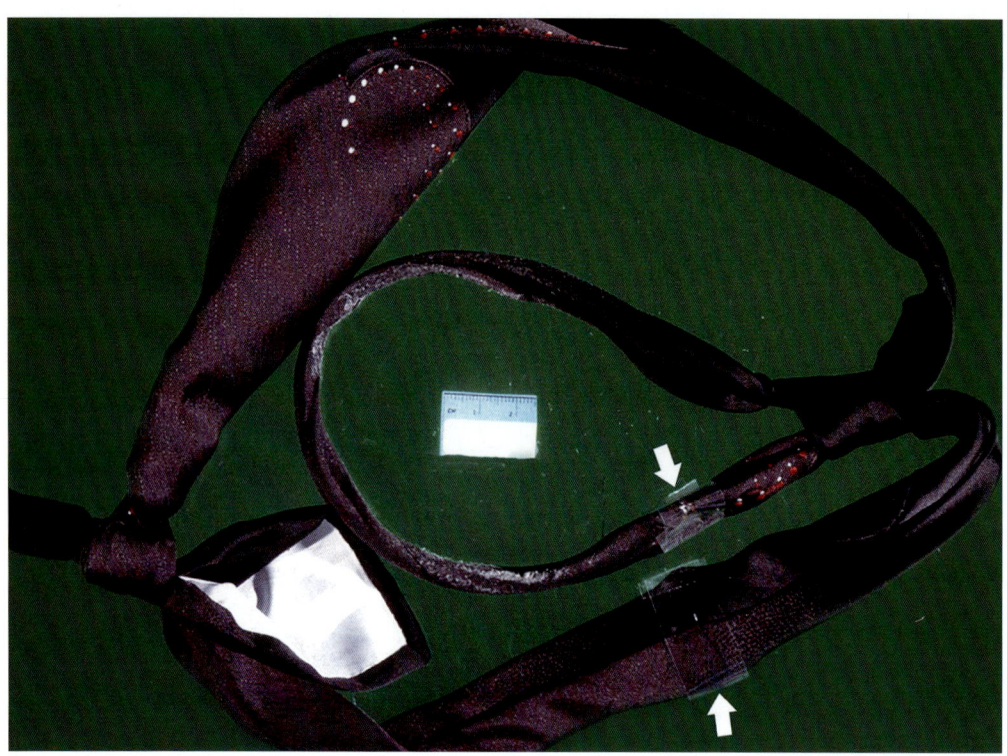

图 3-50 自缢。在远离绳结处剪断缢索,从颈部取下。注意已使用胶带将缢索恢复原状(箭头)。

- 皮肤变化或创伤。
- 与甲状软骨的关系。

2.8.2 解剖检验

- 对窒息死者进行尸体解剖时,在提取毒化样本、去除组织和器官、让血液彻底排出后,再检验颈前结构,以防止解剖时人为造成的出血污染。
- 使用耻骨联合至下颌正中切口或 Y 形胸腹部切口暴露颈前结构。前者为首选方法,但会对殡仪馆修复遗容造成一定困难。如果使用 Y 形切口,开始时应注意切勿切开锁骨上方的皮瓣,否则血液会汇集于皮瓣和下方软组织交界处,造成污染。如果死因可疑,肩膀上的切口可以延伸至耳后,以便更好地清除血液和暴露视野。如果案件存疑,法医须按上述步骤进行解剖检查。
- 移除颈前组织之前,需轻触舌骨,有时可触及钙化的茎突舌骨韧带。需仔细检查颈前肌肉,包括胸锁乳突肌(切开检查是否存在出血)。
- 去除颈前组织结构(舌、喉部、气管与甲状腺及肌肉,可包括下颌下腺)。
- 检查舌部。切开舌(从尖端到底部),检查是否存在出血。
- 检查下颌下腺是否存在出血。
- 分离颈部肌肉,检查有无出血。

- 取出甲状腺,称重并切片。
- 去除环状软骨、甲状软骨板和上角的肌肉组织,检查有无出血或骨折,需注意上角的解剖变异。
- 再次触摸舌骨,检查其活动度。注意舌骨或甲状舌骨韧带临近组织有无出血。取出舌骨(注意避免切断舌骨大角)。
- 如果怀疑有骨折,可以进行舌骨及喉部的X线检查。
- 特殊情况下可将喉部切开,通过检查喉部的纵切面判断是否有软骨内出血。这是一项选择性操作,但有助于鉴定死亡原因是否为缢死。
- 打开食管。
- 打开喉头、气管。如果喉头钙化,需要打开喉头(可能会有碎裂感)。检查是否有黏膜下出血或瘀点、黏膜损伤。
- 必须使用甲醛水溶液固定标本。如果死因可疑,标本有助于后期的法律诉讼和其他专家的审查。

3 "隐匿性"窒息

颈部压迫致死通常具有显著的特征。虽然颈部有时缺乏内部损伤征象,但其表面常见明显的缢沟或印痕。有些类型的窒息死缺乏明显的损伤征象,可以说线索"细微",具有"隐匿性"。经过现场调查,并在尸体解剖时努力搜寻细微的证据,有助于明确窒息方式。涉及使用窒息剂的窒息死,如果在尸体解剖后仍不能明确死因时,应进行毒物分析。

3.1 捂死和闷死

捂死是口、鼻部被阻塞致呼吸障碍而引起的窒息性死亡。闷死是由于被滞留在密闭缺氧环境中发生的窒息性死亡。"捂死"和"闷死"有时涵义相通(116)。由于缺乏特殊征象,确定捂死或闷死的原因和死亡方式取决于详细的案情调查(22)。捂死常为他杀(22, 296),是常见的杀婴手段。

3.1.1 婴幼儿压迫性窒息

婴幼儿压迫性窒息是指较大个体压迫在较小个体上(通常为婴儿)导致后者窒息死亡(27)。压迫除了能阻塞呼吸道外,亦能阻碍颈部和胸部的血流。研究显示,受害者的年龄范围为6天到11个月,且70%的受害者年龄小于3个月(27, 117)。

死因调查时须考虑婴幼儿猝死综合征,以及采用其他方式捂死的可能性(35, 297)。研究显示,婴幼儿猝死综合征在与父母或年长同胞同睡一张床的儿童中有不同的发生率(38, 298)。有文献分析了关于同睡一张床的益处和风险(38, 299–301)。导致婴幼儿猝死综合征风险增加的可能机制包括重复吸入父母呼出的气体、呼吸道阻塞和温度过高引起的缺氧。Blair等(299)指出婴幼儿猝死综合征的发生并

非说明同睡一张床是危险行为,而是在同睡一张床时发生的特殊情况。婴幼儿压迫性窒息案件的调查需要考虑以下几点:

- 死者与成年人同睡一张床,且该成年人可能为肥胖者;或死者与年长同胞同睡一张床。现场可能涉及两人以上(27,113,115,116,302,303)。
- 除非有同床者证实,否则压迫胸腹部所致窒息难以认定(304)。
- 儿童通常睡在成人床(水床、单人床或双人床)或沙发上,偶尔为婴儿床(27,305)。
- 需检查成年人和小孩的衣服及床上用品(见本章第3.1.1.1节)。
- 醉酒或身体状况问题可能造成年长的同床者唤醒反应被抑制,但他们可能不会主动承认这些情况(27,116,304)。

3.1.1.1 外部检查

婴幼儿猝死综合征的部分情况与捂死案件相似(27,297)。死者体表可能会有床上用品或衣服(成年人或儿童的)造成的压痕,但这些压痕也可在死后形成(27)。尸斑形态表明了儿童当时所处的体位,其中,被同床者压迫的部位呈现苍白色。部分案件死者头面部有挫伤,甚至在鼻子和脸颊处有擦伤,这取决于当时接触物表面的硬度(27)。眼睛和面部的瘀点性出血相对少见(27)。唇部或口腔内无破损,特别是在缺少牙齿的儿童中(27,113)。口腔内可能有瘀点性出血(113)。若发现有多处口唇周围皮肤及唇部或口腔内损伤,则增加了他杀的可能性(27)。

3.1.1.2 内部检查

多数案例中可检见胸膜瘀点性出血(27,113)。压迫胸部致椎间静脉丛充血可引起颈椎周围的硬膜外出血,但这在婴儿中属于非特异性的死后征象(306)。

3.1.2 塑料袋套头窒息

塑料袋套头窒息是由于局部吸入低含氧量的空气,以及塑料袋对口鼻部造成物理性阻塞引起的窒息死亡(257)。后者的发生机制为塑料袋因静电吸附于面部,直接阻碍呼吸(242,257),或者塑料袋置于脸部时刺激交感神经系统而引发心律失常。

3.1.2.1 自杀

作为自杀的方式之一,塑料袋套头窒息在老年人中更常见(图3-51;参考文献307-309)。这可能是由于塑料袋具有易获得性和易使用性(307,309)。由于该死亡方式相对无痛苦而被老年人和身体虚弱者采用(307,309)。塑料袋套头窒息已在由Hemlock协会(美国的死亡权利协会)出版的名为《最后的出路:身患绝症之人自杀及协助自杀的履行方案》一书中有所描述(56,307,309,310)。在该书出版后的一年,纽约塑料袋套头窒息的自杀案件数量有所增加,但整体自杀率并没有升高(310)。同样地,在这本书被翻译成丹麦语后,这种自杀方式在该国也有所上升(56)。表3-3总结了3个地区使用塑料袋自杀的案件特点。

第 3 章 | 窒 息

表 3-3 使用塑料袋窒息（自杀）

系列案件	所占百分比	平均年龄	男女比例	案发场所	现场发现遗书比例	阅读"死亡权利"相关书籍的百分比	曾自杀未遂的比例	患有严重或致命疾病的百分比
加拿大安大略省 1993—1997 年 n=110 (307)	1.91%	16—95 岁（平均年龄 60.2 岁），半数年龄大于 60 岁	57%/43%	80% 在家中；10% 在酒店或汽车旅馆；9% 在长期护理机构或医院；1% 在帐篷中	1/2	12%	约 1/3（2 人曾使用塑料袋自杀未遂）	40%
华盛顿州西雅图 1984—1993 年 n=53 (309)	2.6%	18—93 岁（平均年龄 72.5 岁），80% 年龄大于 50 岁	47%/53%	87% 在家中；其他地点：汽车旅馆或酒店、长期护理机构、医院	1/2	11%	约 1/4	38% 其中 15% 处于临终状态
苏格兰 1984—1998 年 n=30 (257)	27/30 自杀死亡占所有死亡案件的 0.2%	31—81 岁（平均年龄 50 岁），男性平均 45 岁，女性平均 71 岁	67%/33%	83% 在家中；其他地点：酒店、医院、工作场所、郊外	1/3	11%	约 1/3	

使用窒息性气体（丙烷、乙醚、氦气）案例的报道显示，在该类案件中，气罐通常位于死者身旁（311–313）。现场可能存在协助者，以帮助死者固定塑料袋。有案件使用了改良型袋子实施自杀，且袋子被协助者移除以伪装成自然死亡（312）。如果同时使用丙烷气体和塑料袋，现场可明显闻到丙烷中所添加的乙硫醇的气味（311，314）。有报道称一名13岁青少年使用充满气溶胶除臭剂的袋子实施自杀（257）。

3.1.2.2 意外

下列情况已被报道：

- 性窒息（见本章第2.7.1节）。
- 药源性危害——挥发性吸入剂[如氯仿、丙烷（257，308，315，316）]。
- 吸入挥发性碳氢化合物（如三氯乙烷）或氟碳燃料。如果袋子没有完全覆盖头部，则死亡机制可能是心律失常（315，317，318）。
- 儿童窒息[如婴儿床上的塑料袋所致的窒息（48，114，115，117）]。
- 塑料床单见于特殊机构中发生的死亡[如患者面部被塑料防尿床单覆盖（48）]。

自杀或他杀现场可能被伪装成意外现场（257）。

3.1.2.3 塑料袋窒息的案例描述

在安大略省的自杀案件中，95%的案件涉及塑料袋的使用（图3–51；参考文献307）。用橡皮筋固定的袋子最常见（22%）。也有使用透明大塑料袋套住头部并将其固定在腰部的报道（311）。安大略省有8例（7%）案件中涉及多个塑料袋的使用（最多使用3个；图3–51）。约有四分之一的案件中使用其他辅助手段实施自杀，如用堵塞物塞住口鼻以确保自杀成功、戴上面罩以防袋子吸附面部而造成不适、绑住手和（或）脚予以制动、吸入袋中的有害气体（如一氧化碳、丙烷）或改良袋子（插入带有电子设备或定时器的呼吸管，以便拉出管子的同时关灯）。呼吸管也可让死者在所摄入的药物开始生效前保持呼吸顺畅，防止恐慌。

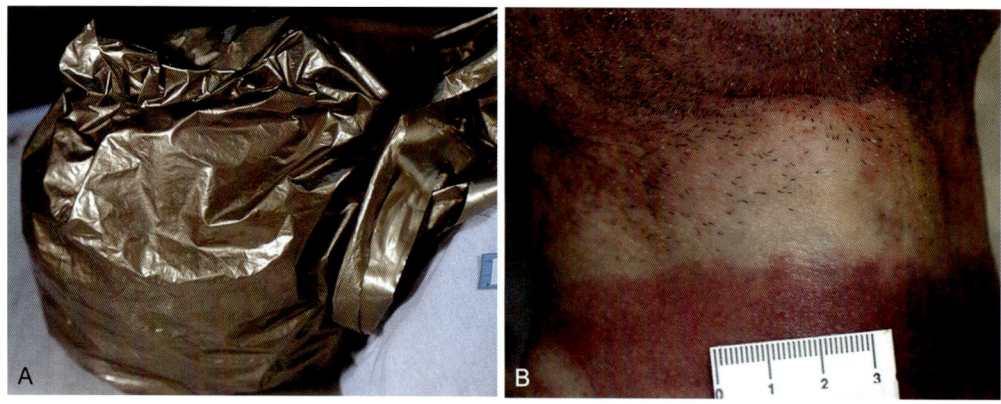

图3–51 塑料袋套头窒息（自杀）。（A）老年妇女。（B）套了3个塑料袋，打结处颈部皮肤局部呈灰白色。

一项西雅图的调查显示，65% 的案件涉及塑料袋的使用，约 80% 的案例仅使用一个袋子（309）。三分之二的案件中塑料袋呈扎紧状态，半数案件中塑料袋吸附于面部，在自杀过程中无其他辅助手段被使用。

另一项苏格兰的案例研究（27 起自杀，3 起意外）显示有 19 例使用了塑料袋（257），其中，5 例使用了两个或两个以上，6 例袋子中含有有毒物质（如气溶胶、氯仿）。

有案例报道一名 40 岁的女子头上套着塑料袋同时自缢（308）。

3.1.2.4 尸表征象

与其他类型的窒息死一样，塑料袋套头窒息死亡通常缺乏明显的尸表征象。如果死者同伴或调查人员移除了现场的塑料袋，则案件调查将会变得异常困难（308）。安大略省的自杀事件中，7.5% 的案例中死者有结膜或面部瘀点性出血（307）。约四分之一的案例中可观察到勒沟（图 3–51）。西雅图的回顾性研究显示，当尸体保存完好时，可在约 10% 的死亡案例中观察到瘀点性出血（309）。通常结膜瘀点性出血较少见（<3 例），但长时间心肺复苏会引起面部和结膜瘀点性出血。约在 20% 的案例中可观察到颈部有系扎（半数案例为橡皮筋）的痕迹。苏格兰的研究发现外部和内部 [结膜、眼睑、面部、颈部和胸膜（257）] 瘀点性出血占 16%。有 3 例发生面部淤血，另有 4 例（13%）颈部存在与塑料袋系扎位置相对应的痕迹。

可能同时存在其他自杀性损伤 [如手腕处的切创（314）]。

3.1.2.5 内部检查

约有半数死者尸检时发现肺水肿和肺淤血（307）。安大略省的调查显示器官瘀点性出血的发生率低于 20%，而西雅图的报道中只占 4%（307，309）。安大略省的案件中没有颈内部组织出血的相关描述，但西雅图的调查发现有一例甲状腺被膜的局灶性出血（307，309）。苏格兰的研究发现，30 名死者中有 9 人患有疾病（冠状动脉粥样硬化、肺部疾病），可能会改变其对缺氧状态的反应（257）。在一些罕见案例中发现了可能导致抑郁症的脑部肿瘤（如额叶区域的脑膜瘤）（319）。

3.1.3 其他捂死或闷死方式（意外和自杀）

- 使用防毒面具（320）、改良的防毒面具和麻醉气体（321）、麻醉面罩和麻醉气体（参阅标题 2.7.1；参考文献 291）、过滤式防毒面具和氦气（322）。
- 摩托车头盔（用胶带封闭面罩，并用浴巾缠绕颈部）结合窒息剂的使用（269）。
- 胶带 [案例描述：将胶带从嘴部左侧开始缠绕，覆盖眼、鼻、口，直至脸颊右下方（296）]。
- 使用枕头 [案例描述：死者为患有慢性精神分裂症的 32 岁男性（22）]。
- 年龄在 1 岁以下的婴幼儿被发现时脸埋在柔软的物体上 [如枕头、豆袋、水床、羊皮地毯、含聚苯乙烯填充物的垫子及悬挂式摇篮等（32，35，113，117，302，323–325）]。婴幼儿由于缺乏自救能力（113，324），口鼻部被阻塞时，分泌的黏液或反流的牛奶将加剧窒息（图 3–52；参考文献 113，323）。实验证明二氧化碳的再吸入可导致婴幼儿窒息(323,326,327),但该窒息方式在成年人中不常见(图3-53)。

俯卧位睡姿是导致婴幼儿猝死综合征的危险因素(38)。已有报道表明二氧化碳浓度增加会引起异常反应(327)。部分婴幼儿睡眠期间发生鼻塞,同时经口呼吸的反射延迟或缺乏被认为是导致窒息的因素(328)。处于上述情况的婴幼儿通常会被惊醒,使其远离潜在的致命环境(327)。然而,当婴儿睡在柔软床垫上时,头部从一侧转到另一侧的动作可能使其面部陷得更深,从而进一步阻碍了呼气(327)。婴儿3个月时才能在俯卧时抬头,6个月时才有能力从俯卧位自行换到仰卧位(327)。儿童

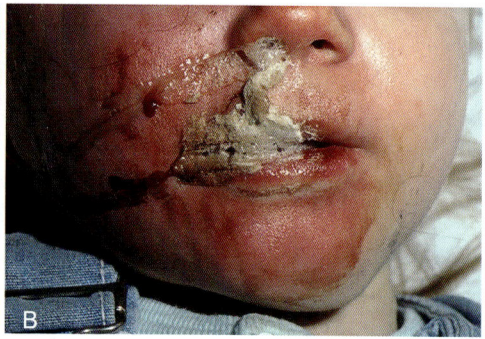

图 3-52 狭窄空间内的窒息。(A)儿童被发现时被厚厚的床单包裹,卡在床和墙壁之间。脸部压迫部位有橙色污点。(B)反流液(牛奶)布满右耳及鼻孔周围。

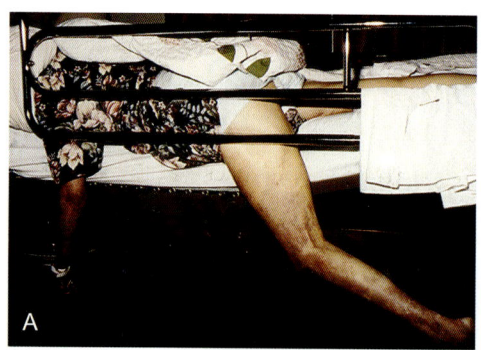
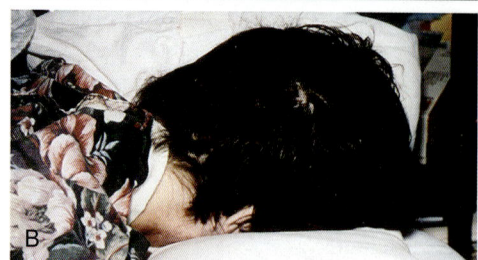
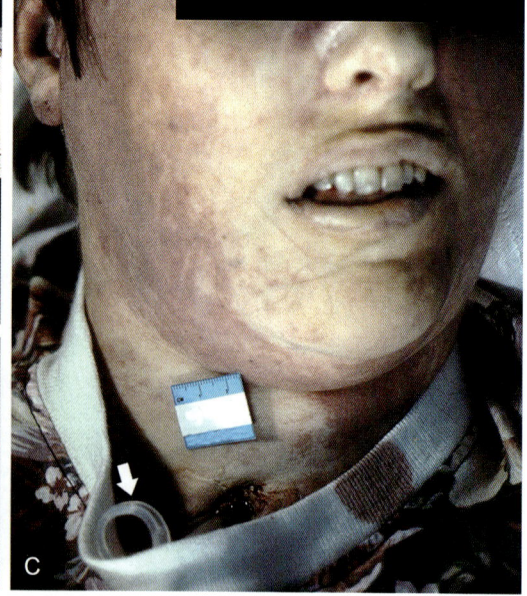

图 3-53 偏瘫的女性死者。(A)被发现时面朝下。手臂和腿卡在床与护栏之间。(B)脸埋在软枕中。(C)口周苍白。气管切开导管(箭头)被压闭。

的翻身动作可被床上物品阻绊(327)。

婴儿咽部和上呼吸道的解剖学特点是呼吸道阻塞的可能因素(32)。俯卧时，婴儿柔软的鼻软骨易被压迫。有些婴儿可能舌的体积较大而口咽相对较小，导致气体流通降低。在睡眠期间，由于肌肉松弛，舌根可能会贴近软腭、会厌和咽部而引起窒息。

婴儿头部是主要的温度调节部位，如被覆盖，可能导致体温过高和通气不足(32, 35, 329, 330)。

潜在的肺部感染可能会增加死亡风险，原因可能是喉痉挛或支气管痉挛(34, 329, 330)。

3.1.3.1 尸表检查

- 防毒面具——有结膜瘀点性出血和面部淤血(面具机械性压迫面部所致)；面部皮肤有压痕(320)。
- 麻醉面罩——面罩覆盖口鼻部(291)。
- 面部被柔软物压迫——压迫部位(鼻尖、口周、前额中央、脸颊、下颚)呈苍白色，周围呈青紫色(称"口周苍白")；鼻尖可能歪斜(图3-53；参考文献22, 325)。可见牙齿造成的嘴唇和颊黏膜擦伤(图3-54)。

如果存在其他创伤(如钝力、穿透性创伤)，则表明可能是他杀(22, 296)，身体其他部位可能被捆绑[如脚踝(296)]。

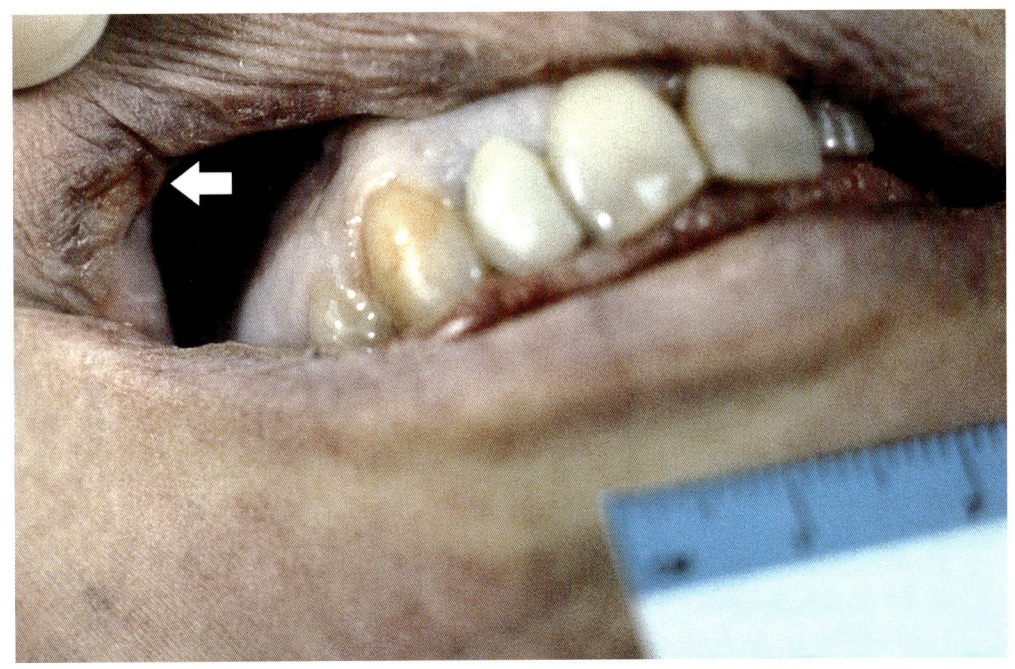

图3-54 捂死(见图3-53)。下牙在右下唇造成的小擦伤(箭头)。

3.1.3.2 器官检查

胸腔内的瘀点性出血在儿童中缺乏或少见(113)。在使用胶带或枕头窒息的自杀案件中没有瘀点性出血的报道(22,296)。解剖中可检见非特异性肺淤血(22)。较大的肺实质出血可由心肺复苏造成(113)。

3.1.4 毒物化学分析：闷死和捂死

如果案情不存在疑点,可不进行毒物化学分析。对可疑的死亡案件需进行毒物化学分析,以判断死者是否因丧失行为能力而遭到攻击(22,269,296,308)。

在使用塑料袋的自杀案件中,约有五分之一至三分之一案例的尸体检测出乙醇(257,307,309),亦可发现某些药物(苯二氮䓬类药物、苯海拉明、抗抑郁药)的使用(307),其浓度通常高于治疗浓度,达到中毒或致死水平(307,309)。

分析塑料袋中挥发物时,需要用氟化物保存死后血液、组织样本(如肺、肝、脑),并将袋子放入密封或玻璃容器中,在检测前冷藏保存(257,269,314,316,321,331)。某些气体(如氦气)不能被检测出,故调查案发现场非常重要(312)。

3.2 嵌入性窒息死

嵌入性窒息死是一种机械性窒息的形式,指面部、颈部或胸部被压迫于两个坚固的结构之间造成的窒息死亡(参阅标题3.7和标题3.8；参考文献27)。成年人可能卡在床栏与床垫之间(参阅标题2.1.4；参考文献99,332)。对美国1980—1997年,年龄小于13个月的2 178名机械性窒息死婴儿的调查结果显示,嵌入性窒息死最常见(40%),其次为口鼻部阻塞或捂死(24%)、婴幼儿压迫性窒息(8%)、悬挂体位性窒息(7%)和缢死[5%(117)]。

3个月至2岁大的婴幼儿通常睡在成人床或婴儿床上(117)。研究表明,嵌入性窒息死主要发生在3—6个月大的婴儿中(117)。在这个阶段,婴儿已有能力移动到成人床或婴儿床的某个角落,但是肌肉尚未发达到能自行脱离所嵌入的位置。父母可能认为将床顶住墙壁可防止孩子在睡觉时掉落,但小孩可能因此嵌入床垫与墙壁、床架、家具、网状物或另一个床垫之间(图3-55；参考文献4,27,35,111,113—117,302和303)。头部卡在床板条或床栏之间则是另一种情况(27,113—115,302)。也可能婴儿床本身存在缺陷或故障(参阅标题2.1.5.2节；参考文献117)。上述情况下吸气障碍为可能的死亡机制(110)。

嵌入性窒息死外部征象较少,也反映了现场调查和询问的重要性。有些案件的死者存在面部挫伤或擦伤(27)。头皮和颈部的线状痕迹和压痕与坚硬的接触面(如床架边缘；图3-55；参考文献27)相吻合。面部瘀点性出血较为少见,这与成年人创伤性窒息的情况相反(27),且无口腔损伤。如果发现多处皮肤和口腔损伤,则应高度怀疑非意外性窒息的可能(27)。

少数案例死者的胸膜检见瘀点性出血,通常仅少量分布(27)。

第3章 | 窒 息

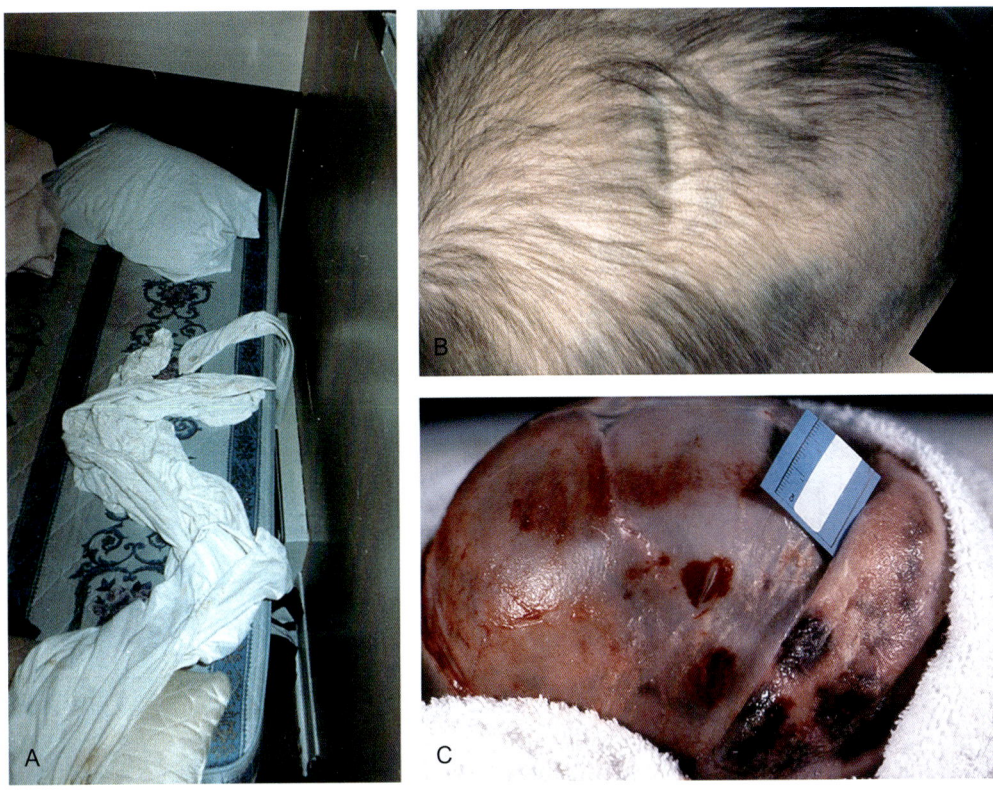

图 3-55 嵌入性窒息。(A) 婴儿嵌入床和墙壁之间,遭受踢脚板电暖器严重灼伤。(B) 床缘在头皮上形成的压痕。(C) 头皮内面显示对应的挫伤。

3.3 哽死:噎死、吸入异物、餐馆冠状动脉综合征(Café Coronary syndrome)或托儿所冠状动脉综合征(Creche Coronary syndrome)。

餐馆冠状动脉综合征是指在进食时由于食物堵塞上呼吸道导致的窒息,发作时症状与心脏病发作相似,所以该类窒息症状经常被误认为由冠状动脉闭塞所致。该综合征也常发生于托儿所的儿童身上,故又称为托儿所冠状动脉综合征。

3.3.1 现场与案情(意外性哽死)

急性致死性呼吸道阻塞发生的不同阶段:

- 异物进入呼吸道。
- 呼吸道阻塞。
- 一旦阻塞发生将难以解除(333)。

该类猝死表现为急性上呼吸道(声门)阻塞征象,如喘鸣、呼吸窘迫、咳嗽、哽咽,受害者也可无法发出声音(334–337)。紧接着的是迅速、频繁的深吸气,导致异物进一步深入呼吸道(333,338),发生喉痉挛(338)。此刻迷走神经受到刺激导致心律失常和呼吸暂停为可能的死亡机制(339)。在某些情况下可发生过敏反应[如吸入胡椒粉(340)],表现为喉黏膜水肿。有时,食管和下呼吸道被异物阻塞时,在呼吸道症状［咳嗽、喘息、呼吸困难（334，336，341，342）］出现前可有一段无征兆期。当吸入高温液体时，可能在长达 8 小时潜伏期之后才出现症状（难以说话、呼吸困难）（343）。当呼吸道黏膜水肿、炎症、出血和支气管痉挛发生时，呼吸道不完全性阻塞变为完全性阻塞（334），之后慢性症状会进一步发生、发展（参阅标题 3.5）。

哽死是 1 岁以下儿童意外死亡的常见原因（116，334，344）。90% 的哽死发生在 5 岁之前。据研究报道发生哽死的年龄范围为 4 个月到 14 岁（344）。老年死者往往由于精神障碍导致哽死，正常的大龄儿童也会发生哽死（334）。1—3 岁的儿童活泼好动，对是否可将小物体放入口中缺乏判断力，进食的食物又较为细小，缺牙致食物不能被充分咀嚼（即门齿先于臼齿萌出，虽能咬断食物但不能适当咀嚼），加上呼吸道较窄咳嗽反射较弱，因此容易发生哽死（托儿所冠状动脉综合征）（116，333，336，337，342，345－348）。

家是儿童发生意外窒息的最常见场所（344）。在许多情况下，儿童从成年人处获得的物品可能具有潜在危险（344，349）。哽死的发生通常是意想不到的（334）。有研究表明，约一半的哽死发生时有成年人在场，但可能缺乏有效的监护（333，344）。在场的其他儿童也可能会分散成年人的注意力［如日托班（347）］。

在进食和玩耍时可能发生哽死［如跑动时（347）］，尝试未吃过的食物也会导致哽死（347）。异食癖指儿童或成年人食用不宜食入的物品（345）。精神障碍或神经障碍患者可大量进食（暴食症；图 3-56；参考文献 340，350）。一岁以下儿童更有可能吸入食物，而年龄较大的儿童往往会吸入非食物类物品（334，348）。婴幼儿猝死有可能是婴幼儿猝死综合征，但仍需考虑哽死的可能性（334）。也有奶嘴引发哽死的报道（图 3-57；参考文献 114，351），研究显示，婴幼儿猝死综合征组的奶嘴使用率低于对照组（352）。

在涉及成年人的哽死案例中，吃饭时突然发生类似于心脏病发作的死亡（餐馆冠状动脉综合征）或无人察觉到的死亡（334，335，350，353）。哽死原因包括衰老所致的保护性呼吸道反射减弱、较差的口腔条件导致习惯性吞咽大块食物、饮酒及摄入抑制咽反射的中枢神经系统抑制剂等（335，341，342，345，350，354，355）。只有三分之一的哽死发生在餐厅（355 人）。大多数成年人哽死发生在家中、养老院或精神病院中（350，355），也有发生在医院里的报道（350）。需长期护理的患者可能有潜在的神经或精神障碍，导致咳嗽反射减弱或吞咽困难（341，345，350，355－358）。

其他哽死案例，包括贪食症患者在催吐时吞入异物［如叉子（359）］、异常体位摄食（350）、口干症（唾液腺功能障碍导致的口腔干燥）引起的吞咽困难（350）、情绪激动（360）、口部被外力击打和癫痫发作或意识丧失（360）。

3.3.2 监押场所死亡案件中辣椒喷雾剂的使用

辣椒油树脂俗称辣椒素，是辣椒（辣椒属）的粗提取物，当接触呼吸道黏膜时，会导致咳嗽或窒息。警察在抓捕罪犯时可以使用辣椒喷雾剂（参阅标题 3.7；参考文献

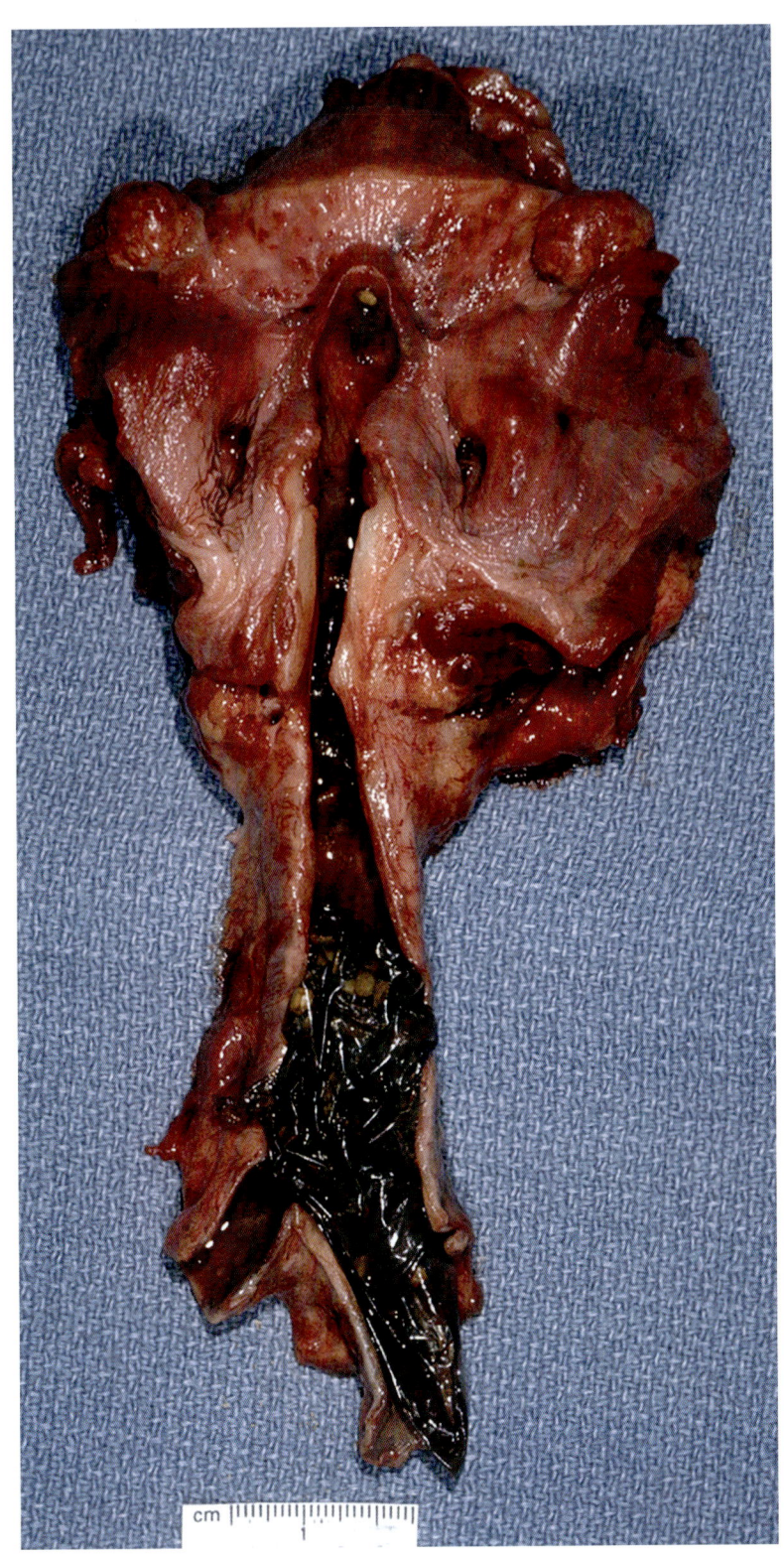

图 3-56 智力障碍者,异食癖。塑料片被气管插管推至气管隆嵴(北卡罗莱纳大学法医室供图)。

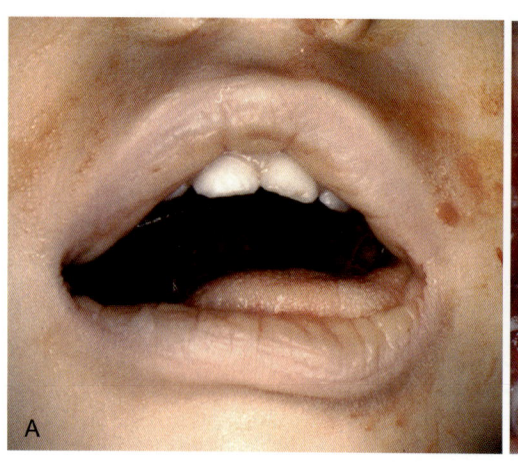 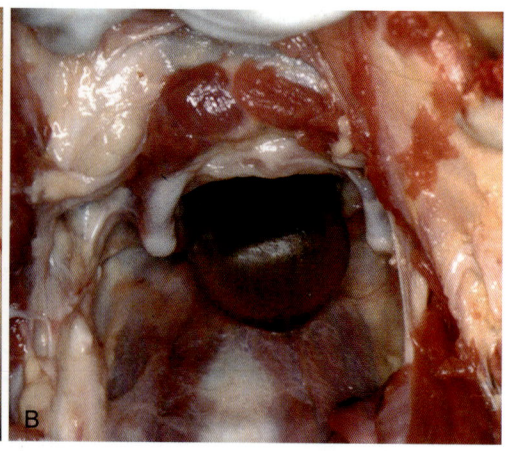

图 3-57 婴儿。奶嘴所致哽死。(A)口腔里的安抚奶嘴。(B)颈前部(喉头已被移除),口咽处的奶嘴。

361),吸入后会发生支气管收缩、呼吸困难和剧烈咳嗽。哮喘患者及其他肺部疾病患者的死亡风险更高(90)。有些受害者在吸入后难以讲话。有报道称一名 11 岁男孩在吸入辣椒素后发生喉头水肿伴呼吸骤停(362)。评价辣椒素在死亡中的作用须考虑各种因素,包括抓捕时的情况、接触辣椒素与症状发作之间的时间关系、症状特点、接触辣椒素后受害者的反应、是否存在导致突发性意识丧失的疾病(如缺血性心脏病),还需进行毒物化学分析以排除乙醇和其他药物中毒的可能性。面部、口腔和上呼吸道拭子检查可以检测到辣椒素。

3.3.3 哽死的死亡方式

虽然大多数哽死属于意外,但也有可能是自杀或他杀(338,363)。自杀性哽死较罕见,通常发生于精神病患者和囚犯中(338)。他杀性哽死的受害者通常为老年人,在因疾病、饮酒或吸食毒品致身体衰弱者及婴儿中也较常见。如果受害者意识清醒,当物体被迫塞入口腔时,可能会有反抗或挣扎的痕迹(338),受害者手上也会有防御伤。如果受害者当时被束缚,四肢可能存在损伤。可能有口周、牙齿、舌头和口腔损伤。在呼吸道和消化道内发现异物是有力的证据,可证明受害者被强行塞入异物导致哽死,尤其当现场大部分物证被凶手或急救人员破坏时。

自身疾病可导致上呼吸道阻塞和猝死。咳嗽或呕吐可使肿瘤移位并进入喉头。阻塞性肿瘤的相关案例报道有:

- 下咽部(喉咽)[脂肪瘤(364)]。
- 食管上段[纤维瘤、息肉(365—367)]。
- 喉[浸润性鳞状细胞癌、初生型乳头瘤样增生(368)]。

导致上呼吸道阻塞的炎症和反应过程包括:

- 急性会厌炎。

- 腭垂、会厌和喉头水肿（过敏反应；参阅第 7 章标题 11）。
- 扁桃体肿大［感染性单核细胞增多症、链球菌扁桃体炎、白喉(369-372)］。
- 声门部位的浆细胞性肉芽肿(373)。

某些疾病（如鼻中隔偏曲、腺样体或舌扁桃体肿大、舌或喉部囊肿）易导致阻塞性睡眠呼吸暂停［睡眠呼吸暂停综合征(374)］。饮酒会加剧上述情况(375,376)。

3.3.4 哽死的外部征象

哽死的外部征象较少。有报道表明有结膜下出血但无皮肤瘀点性出血的征象(334,350)。案件调查时需要对牙齿进行仔细检查。

3.3.5 哽死的内部征象

在进行尸体解剖前无法发现呼吸道中的异物(334,350,377)。如果发现异物，则必须仔细调查案情，可能会获得关于异物存在的"合理"解释［如在死者口中放置硬币是中国葬礼的传统习俗(378)］。有可能阻塞物在急救插管时被发现，但随后被急救人员取出，致使法医无从检查(114,355)。对涉及心肺复苏的案件必须进行详细检查。如果心肺复苏时将呼吸管自口腔插入，可能会人为地将异物推入咽喉部（图 3-56；参考文献 355,360）。气管插管将会使异物深入喉部、气管、支气管或食管。在尸体解剖时，如果未先摘除喉部便检查口咽部，则有可能导致漏检(335,369,379)。

阻塞程度取决于异物的大小、受害者的年龄和呼吸道的宽窄(333,334)。成年人非食物类哽死的异物有：牙科或医疗器具、鼻腔分泌物、滑石粉、零件、粪便、药物和造影剂［如钡剂(341,345,350,356,357,363,380-382)］。异物也可能为非透射性的(360)。致儿童哽死的异物有气球、小玩具、零件、硬币等(114,334,344,346,383-385)。在儿童哽死案件中的异物多为食物(336)。食物通常为圆形且质地坚硬，但也有在呼吸道中逐渐膨胀的柔软物体(114,333,347,349)。豆类等属于在呼吸道内会发生膨胀的异物(379)。能引起儿童哽死的食物种类各异［如热狗、面包、大米、糖果、坚果、口香糖、水果、蔬菜等(114,334,337,344,347,383)］。对成年人而言，肉类、植物、动物骨头和完整的鱼均能引起哽死（图 3-58；参考文献 341,355,356 和 386）。在护理机构中，也有被较软的食物哽死的报道(355)。

哽死表现为会厌充血、喉黏膜出血、充血和瘀点性出血(334,350,360)。在儿童和成年人中，吸入热性液体会导致会厌、喉头和气管水肿、黏膜脱落而需辅助通气(343,387,388)。

鉴定时应对易导致哽死或吸入异物的基础疾病进行评估(340,389)。

尖锐物品（如骨头、牙签）可能在进食时无意中被吞下。故意吞入异物导致呼吸道阻塞的情况多发生在智力障碍者、精神病患者、囚犯和走私违禁物品［如珠宝、毒品(390)］的罪犯中。某些被吞入的异物可滞留于或穿透消化道［如位于食管的别针刺破心脏导致心包积血、牙签刺破小肠进入髂总动脉、骨头刺穿食管插入主动脉或颈总动脉、木螺钉进入腹膜后间隙致败血症、硬币进入食管压迫相邻的气管等(337,379,

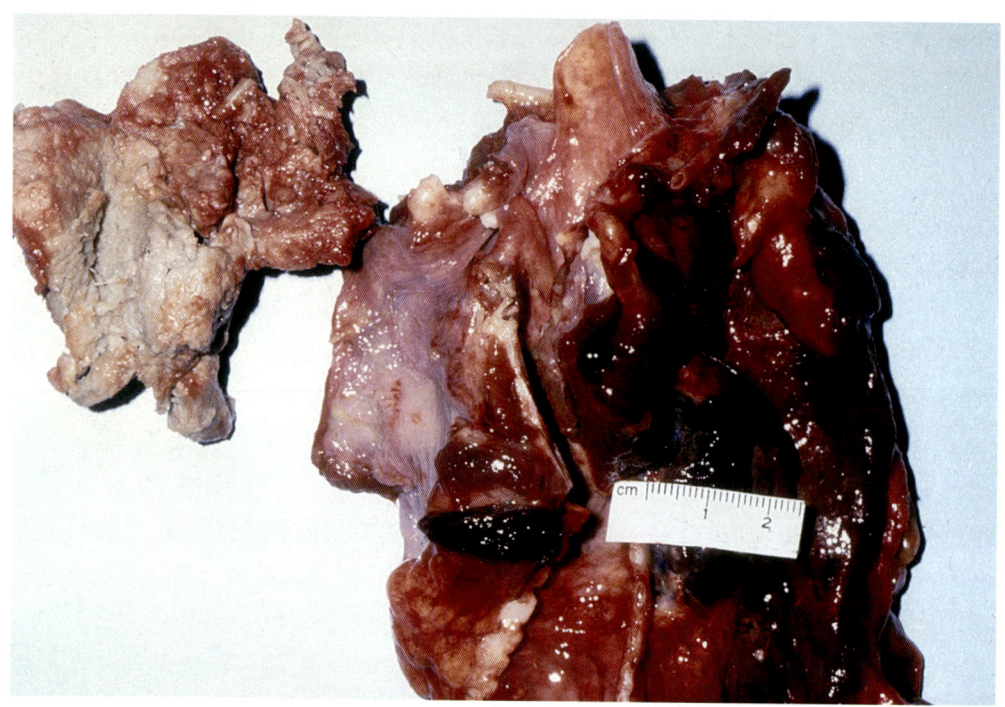

图 3-58 哽死。尸检时从喉部取出一块猪骨（美国北卡罗来纳州教堂山市法医局供图）。

391-394)]。

海姆立克腹部冲击法（Heimlich Maneuver）又称海姆立克急救法、海氏手技，即应用腹压来缓解梗阻，由美国医生 Heimlich 发明。1974 年他首先应用该法成功抢救了一名因食物堵塞呼吸道而发生窒息的患者，从此该法在全世界被广泛应用（353）。

3.4 急性吸入

3.4.1 咽部分泌物和胃内容物

吸入无菌酸性胃内容物或含菌的口咽分泌物时常发生于临终濒死期，并且经常在尸体解剖时被发现（395）。个体死亡时，咳嗽和胃肠反射逐渐丧失，反流物可进入呼吸道（396），这不一定是死因，而是个体反射被抑制的表现（36，209，333，396）。精神和神经障碍均可导致呕吐物被吸入（397）。

胃内容物的误吸常见于意识水平降低的个体［如药物过量、麻醉（395，397，398）］，个体处于仰卧位易导致胃食管反流（398）。危重患者有误吸风险（395）。胃蠕动降低导致胃内容物潴留和胃胀气，增加了胃内容物反流的风险（395）。移除气管插管后镇静药物的残留效应、鼻饲管的使用、上呼吸道感染所致吞咽功能紊乱、声门损伤和喉部肌肉功能障碍等因素增加了误吸的风险（395）。有时尽管使用了鼻饲管，但由于放置位置的原因，仍能导致大量胃酸蓄积（398），且鼻饲管也会影响食管括约肌的功能（398）。胃造口置管和鼻饲管的使用难以有效防止口腔分泌物的吸入

(395)。此外,术后患者更容易在吞咽时发生误吸,而不是在呕吐或反流时,且误吸时通常处于坐位(397)。

误吸可能伴有急性呼吸窘迫的症状,但在许多老年患者中,误吸发生时缺乏明显的症状(395)。咳嗽可能是急性吸入的表征(397),Mendelson综合征即胃酸吸入性肺炎,指吸入酸性胃内容物(pH <2.5)后肺部发生急性"自溶"反应(395,398)。显微镜检可发现终末支气管和肺泡内的水肿液和异物(图3-59;参考文献350,363和397)。细菌侵入发生急性炎症反应(吸入性肺炎),提示死者存活了一段时间。吸入性肺炎如果进一步恶化可导致死亡(395,397)。吸入非阻塞性食物颗粒可在数小时内导致出血性肺炎(398)。在几天内,可观察到肉芽肿反应(参阅标题3.5;参考文献398),随之而来的是弥漫性肺泡损伤(398)。吸入偏碱性液体(pH> 2.5)也可导致肺水肿,但会被迅速分解,几乎无肺损伤和炎症反应(398)。肺水肿在吸入

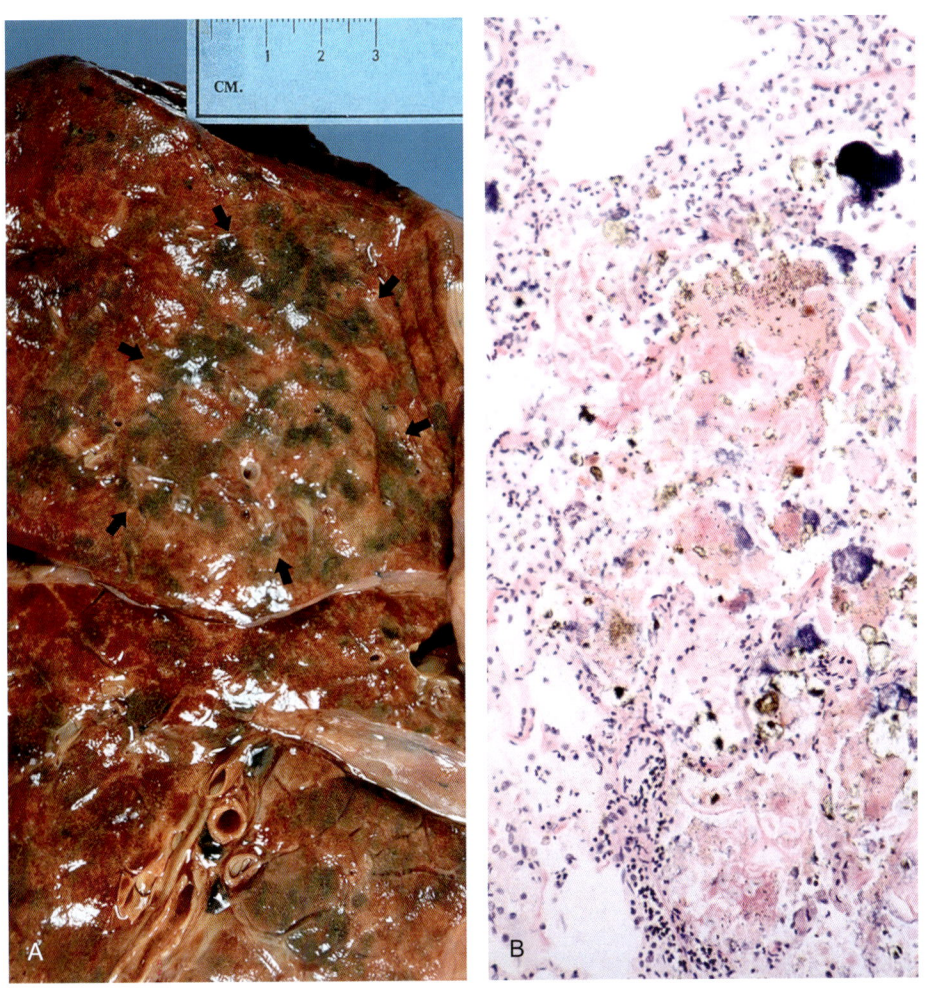

图3-59 急性吸入。(A)因吸入胆汁及胃内容物,肺实质呈绿色变(箭头)。(B)肺镜下观。来自口咽和胃的吸入物(H-E,×100)。

碱性液体几小时后发生,这与吸入酸性液体恰好相反(398)。胃内容物可在死后被动进入呼吸道(396,397)。研究显示在成年人和婴幼儿死亡("婴儿猝死")案件中,约四分之一的尸检发现呼吸道内有胃内容物(396)。尸检时可以观察到肺实质有绿色改变(图3-59),主支气管(通常为右侧)或肺实质内的支气管也可见绿色或棕色物质(图3-60;参考文献337,342,377和389)。

在死因不明时,毒物化学分析是排除乙醇和其他药物导致行为能力丧失的重要检测手段(355)。

尽管研究表明大部分呼吸暂停发作与胃食管反流无关(399),但胃食管反流也是引起呼吸暂停、导致婴幼儿猝死综合征的原因之一(35)。当酸性液体进入食管时可引发心律失常(35,399)。在婴幼儿猝死综合征患儿中,婴儿在清醒状态比睡眠时更易发生反流(399)。有学者认为婴幼儿胃食管反流可能只是发育迟滞的一般表现(35)。虽然俯卧时较少引起反流,但俯卧位却是婴幼儿猝死综合征的一个风险因素(参考文献400;参阅标题3.1.3)。

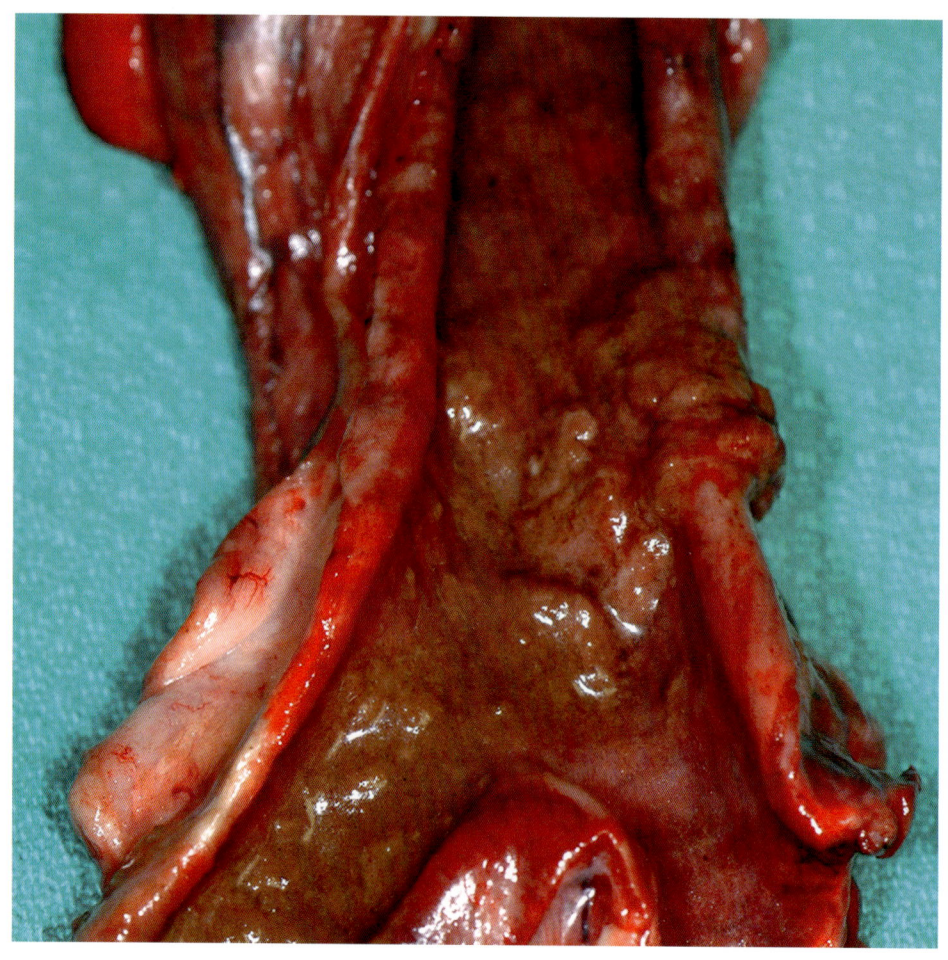

图3-60 急性吸入。喉部和支气管。

3.4.2 颗粒物的吸入

吸入各种颗粒物会引起下呼吸道阻塞。包括:

- 活埋时的沙子和（或）砾石进入呼吸道。抢救时口对口复苏和气管插管均可将颗粒物推入更深的呼吸道（参阅第 5 章标题 10.2；参考文献 401–404）。
- 胡椒。多数为他杀，如通过灌胡椒惩罚孩子（405–407）。死亡机制为胡椒的刺激作用引起的机械性阻塞和黏膜水肿。
- 滑石粉［儿童（408–410）］。滑石颗粒（硅酸镁）具有可极化性，能在肺组织镜检时确认。

3.5 慢性吸入

通常口咽分泌物和食物的慢性吸入会发生在老年人和身体衰弱者中（如癌症、神经障碍患者），以及可能有吞咽困难需长期护理的患者中（354,357,389,395,397,398）。老年人常因口腔卫生不良，导致呼吸道病原菌［肠杆菌科、铜绿假单胞菌、金黄色葡萄球菌（395）］在口腔繁殖。

基于上述情况，死者的异物吸入史可能会被忽视（377,411,412）。这种情况也可见于吸入异物但尚无症状的儿童。反复少量吸入可表现为复发性肺炎、间歇性支气管痉挛、支气管扩张或肺脓肿（336,337,341,342,377,379,389,412–414），最后可能导致呼吸暂停。

慢性吸入，肺镜下表现为细支气管炎、支气管肺炎和（或）异物肉芽肿性炎症（图 3–61；参考文献 337,377 和 389）。

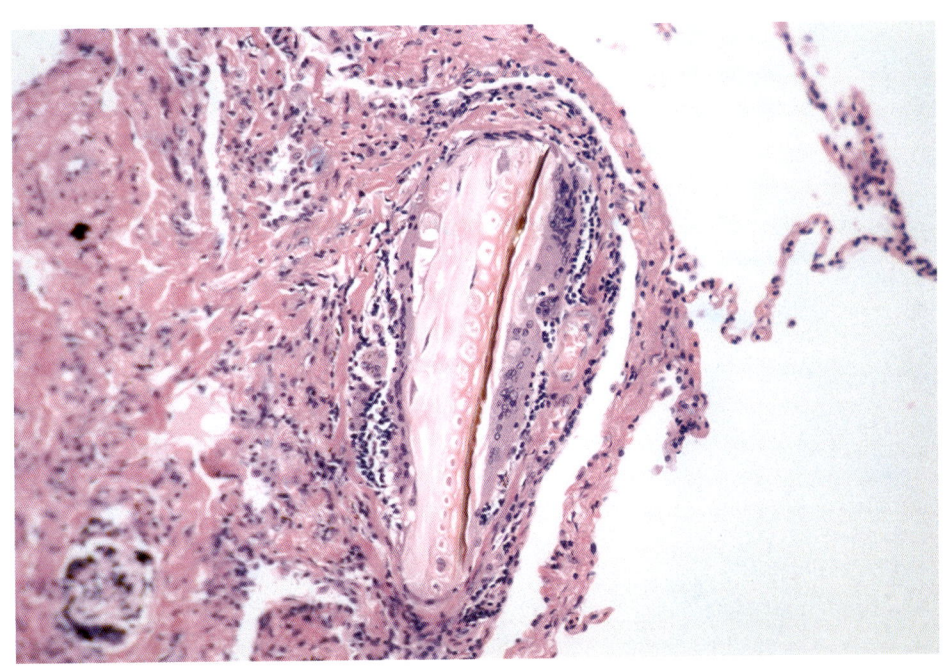

图 3–61 慢性吸入。异物肉芽肿性炎症（植物性异物；H–E,×200）。

3.6 堵死

堵死指受害者口腔内或口鼻周围的堵塞物干扰呼吸及吞咽所致的死亡,具有捂死和哽死的特征(338)。在堵死发生前,异物可能已塞入受害者口中(338)。虽然堵死通常与他杀有关(如抢劫案中的老年受害者、杀婴),但也有通过极端手段自杀时[如自焚(415)]使用堵塞物防止尖叫的情况。

3.7 体位性窒息

体位性窒息是指因身体被动或主动地限制在某种异常体位,机械性地阻塞呼吸道和压迫胸壁,影响呼吸而导致死亡(图3-62;参考文献416,417)。

肺通气功能障碍可能是由中枢呼吸抑制(如服用镇静类药物)、胸壁缺陷(如连枷胸)或呼吸肌疲劳引起(418)。由于各种因素[如摄入酒精或其他药物、身体衰弱、退行性脑病(97,99,246,418-420)],使受害者可能无法自行脱离某种体位。作为中枢神经系统抑制剂的乙醇及其他肌松药,可影响舌部肌肉导致呼吸道阻塞(97,416),达到中毒剂量会抑制呼吸中枢,使其对窒息的反应减弱(417,419,421)。

体位性窒息的相关描述:

- 倒置悬挂位(图3-63;参考文献246,416,419,420和422)。
  - 与以胸部呼吸为主的直立位相反,倒置悬挂时胸壁的活动度受限(246,423-426)。在完全倒置悬挂的情况下,腹腔器官会压迫膈肌,使吸气期延长(427)。起初个体可通过增加呼吸频率补偿供氧不足(427),之后由于呼吸肌逐渐疲劳引起胸壁运动减弱,最终导致缺氧(421,427)。呼吸肌功

图3-62 体位性窒息。

图 3-63 体位性窒息。翻车后受害者被倒置悬挂死亡（加拿大安大略省汉密尔顿地区法医病理室 C.Rao 博士供图）。

能下降,胸内压降低,致静脉血难以有效回流至心脏(246,425)。此外,血液大量涌向头部,使有效回心静脉血量降低(246),减少的血流量进一步加重呼吸肌的疲劳程度,最终心脏停搏(425)。

- 实验动物(兔子)处于倒置悬挂位,半天时间内发生死亡(427)。志愿者被倒挂后可观察到脉搏下降且不规律(427)。死者(如跳伞者、翻倒车辆中的乘客)自事故发生到死亡的时间从几小时到一天不等(246,419)。
- 在临床上,Trendelenburg 卧位(Trendelenburg position,即垂头仰卧位)对心肺功能有影响(419,427)。

- 在倒挂或坐直时颈部或躯干过度屈曲（如颈部过度屈曲压迫气管造口位置、甲状腺肿压迫呼吸道）导致呼吸道阻塞（416，417）。
- 躯干弯曲压在物体上（如浴缸边缘），限制了膈肌和胸廓运动（48，417）。
- 嬉戏时悬挂压迫腹部［如12岁女孩被秋千上的合成编织带悬挂致死亡（421）］。
- 颈部或胸部被压迫（如颈部屈曲卡于床栏间；参阅标题2.1.4、3.2和3.8；参考文献99，332和417）。
- "谵妄""俯卧位限制性窒息"，以及使用"泰瑟枪（电休克枪）"。
  - 由于患精神疾病或兴奋剂（如可卡因、致幻剂、甲基苯丙胺）中毒而极度激动（"谵妄"），受害者因此被采取俯卧位捆绑而导致死亡（428-431）（"俯卧位限制性窒息"）。这类死亡多发生在看护机构和警察监控下，故案件常具有争议性。在谵妄期间，个体会变得偏执，对疼痛不敏感（428，429，431，433），且具有"超出常人"的力气，部分警察因此对其进行捆绑（429，431）。通常情况下，这些受害者在激烈挣扎之后会变得安静，最后发生心肺停止（429，431，433）。各种形式的捆绑均被报道，其中一种将四肢固定捆绑在背部的捆绑方式，即"反绑四肢"（hog-tying 或 hobbling），被认为是主要的致死原因（417）。确认俯卧位限制性窒息必须排除其他死亡原因，即疾病和创伤等（如头部损伤、颈部压迫、器官损伤）（430，431，436）。当遇到明确的俯卧位限制性窒息案件时，以下因素也可能导致死亡（418，428-431，433，436-439）：对颈部施加压力（428，429，431）；胸壁承受体重压力（429）；长时间挣扎导致疲劳、缺氧、酸中毒和高热；可卡因长期滥用者的脑受体功能发生改变，易诱发谵妄和高热（431-434）；长期滥用可卡因还可导致心脏肥大和心肌纤维化，是心律失常的危险因素，且可由急性中毒时的"肾上腺素激增"状态（应激反应）诱发（418，431-433，435）。此外还应注意的是，除上述"反绑四肢"可致体位性窒息外，死亡还可发生在其他限制性体位（439a），亦可发生在无体位性限制时的谵妄状态（432，433）。
  - 有报道提到对俯卧位限制性窒息的志愿者进行捆绑后，观察其处于俯卧位对呼吸过程干扰程度的研究。正常的呼吸过程包括3个关键性的要素（418）：第一是呼吸道；第二是呼吸运动，类似于"风箱"的运作机制，即通过肋骨、肋间肌、膈肌、腹壁及辅助呼吸肌的作用使气体进出呼吸道；第三是肺，保证正常流量的气体能进出呼吸道，并在肺泡壁和血管间进行气体交换。尽管早期研究表明，"反绑四肢"的体位延长了运动后心率和外周血氧饱和度恢复至正常水平的时间（439b），但随后的研究对上述观察结果进行了反驳，它使用了更复杂的方法来测定血氧饱和度以评估肺功能（439）。研究表明，"反绑四肢"确实产生了轻度的、不低于正常预测值

80% 的限制性肺缺血,但这种缺血与缺氧、高碳酸血症或运动后正常心律恢复延迟无关,也与处于仰卧位或俯卧位的非限制性体位个体肺功能的轻微变化差异无关(418,439)。另外,一项由健康志愿者参与"反绑四肢"的研究显示,在背部放置 110 千克(约 50 磅)重物并未进一步降低志愿者呼吸功能(435)。

- 对健康志愿者的观察表明,强制性的限制性体位本身并非导致窒息的唯一原因。据此,Reay 和 Howard(418)认为"死因只能是一种推测,包括由儿茶酚胺激增、抗精神病药物恶性综合征、心因性死亡(包括极度的狂躁和谵妄)及运动等诱发的心脏停搏等";换而言之,即"在(俯卧位限制性窒息死)调查中,涉及了多种因素,所有这些因素都可能在死亡中起一定作用,而不存在任何一个无可辩驳的、可作为死因的独立因素"。在这种情况下,Howard 和 Reay(418)建议通过"概括性描述可确定的致死因素"来进行死因推断。

- 除了限制性体位以外,被制服的个体也可能因吸入胡椒喷雾剂或被泰瑟枪电击而导致极度谵妄,但同时无明显体征(428,429,431)(参阅标题 3.3.2)。

- 泰瑟枪是一种"能使神经肌肉失能"的手持式武器。泰瑟枪可发射两根倒钩至目标上,倒钩通过电线与枪相连。当倒钩穿透或勾住贴近皮肤的衣服时,操作者通过控制电击的持续时间直至目标失去反抗能力,然后将其制服(439c–439f)。泰瑟枪有各种类型,包括警用型、威力较小的民用型,以及更为先进的 M26 型,可快速使目标失去反抗能力(439d)。

- 泰瑟枪造成的主要伤害包括穿刺伤和倒钩勾住部位的烧伤,或电击后目标失去行动能力摔倒所致的二次损伤。另有横纹肌溶解,但其原因尚不明确,因为许多遭到泰瑟枪电击者存在其他潜在的致心肌或肌肉的毒性因素(参阅第 8 章标题 13)。

- 大多数涉及泰瑟枪的死亡发生在电击后几分钟至数小时,但有些死者生前吸食苯环己哌啶(苯基–环己基–哌啶)(439g,439h)和(或)可卡因(439g),该类毒品能单独引起猝死。也有案例报道死者生前患有心脏疾病(439g)。一项为期 5 年半,针对医院急诊室接诊的所有被泰瑟枪电击的案例研究显示:218 例患者中有 3 例死亡,其中 2 例分别在被泰瑟枪电击后的 5–15 分钟发生心脏停搏,1 例在触电 25 分钟后出现呼吸、心搏骤停。上述 3 例死者的血清和肝脏中均检测出高水平的苯环己哌啶(439h)。此外,有案例描述了一名 16 岁男性,在被泰瑟枪电击后发生心室纤颤并被心肺复苏抢救成功,这一案例表明遭泰瑟枪电击与潜在的致命性心律失常之间有着直接联系。但该案例的受害者遭到电击与发生心室纤颤的时间间隔未被记录,报道也未说明受害者是否存在苯环己哌啶、可卡因或其他物质中毒的情况(439i)。然而,也有案例表明,体内植入起搏器者在被泰瑟枪电击后未发生心室纤维性颤动(439j)。

- 对猪的研究证明,诱发心室纤维性颤动所需电荷与体质量直接相关,且要达到泰瑟枪发射电荷的 15－42 倍(439k)。对健康志愿者的研究显示,在电击时或电击后 24 小时内,泰瑟枪放电对心电活动没有影响(439l)。这与之前的观察结果相符,即在急诊室治疗的被泰瑟枪电击的患者中未发现明显的心电图异常(439h)。
- 典型电击死具有即刻死亡的特点(参阅第 4 章标题 7.1.4),上述跟泰瑟枪有关的观察结果表明,遭泰瑟枪电击不太可能是导致死亡的原因。然而,当死者生前处于生理学或毒物化学所致的"谵妄"状态时,被泰瑟枪电击是否是导致死亡的直接原因难以确定,正如本节所讨论的难点——有许多因素决定了俯卧位限制性窒息导致的死亡。因此,有理由认为"对健康成年人使用泰瑟枪通常是安全的,而潜在的心脏病、精神病和药物的使用可能会大大增加死亡的风险"(439m)。

- 婴幼儿猝死综合征(参阅标题 3.1)。

3.7.1 尸检结果: 体位性窒息

体位性窒息死通常缺乏体表征象(417)。由于死者可能被移动,准确地描述尸体所在现场的原始位置对于确定死亡原因至关重要,且需要排除其他死因(97,418)。

如果死者处于倒挂位,其面部、颈部和上胸部皮肤会发绀,可观察到头部充血和肿胀(419),可能存在或缺乏头皮和眼睑瘀点性出血(416,419,440)。皮肤挫伤说明死者生前可能有反抗(416,419)。尸检可发现舌、会厌和气管淤血(416),还可观察到脑和肺淤血。胸壁、膈肌、胰周区域和脾的挫伤与腹部被悬吊的位置一致(421)。

3.8 创伤性窒息

3.8.1 现场

创伤性窒息于 1837 年首次被 Olliver 提出(11, 441–445): 在群体性暴力事件中,受害者被挤压死亡。案发现场的调查有助于确定创伤性窒息的原因,尤其是在缺乏尸体征象时(443,446)。创伤性窒息的共同特点是受害者胸腹部遭到比自身更重的物体挤压。是体位性窒息还是创伤性窒息则与案情有关(参阅标题 3.7;参考文献 416): 如果以胸部压迫为主,是创伤性窒息; 如果死者是由于特殊体位而导致颈部或胸部受压,则是体位性窒息。

- 与机动车相关的创伤性窒息最为常见(445):
  - 在车底修车时,机动车从千斤顶上滑落(443–445)。

第3章 | 窒 息

- 乘客被甩下车后随即被翻覆的车辆压迫(443,446)。
- 前排乘客被压在座椅和方向盘或仪表板之间(422,443,444)。
- 行人被慢行的车辆撞到(443)。
- 在垃圾箱里熟睡或昏迷的流浪汉、醉汉或吸毒人员被垃圾车挤压(447)。
- 衣物缠于车辆传动轴中(448)。
- 重型器械、建筑材料、坠落的残骸、塌方导致的创伤性窒息(参阅标题3.10；图3-64；参考文献441,443-445和449)。
- 倒落的电器、家具导致的创伤性窒息[特别是儿童(443,450)]。这可以作为一种他杀手段。

他杀所致的创伤性窒息可能存在其他窒息方式的证据[如捂死、勒死(451)]。

3.8.2 创伤性窒息的机制

外力挤压胸部、上腹部和(或)背部，严重阻碍胸廓的呼吸运动所致的窒息(441,450)。受害者的胸部与大腿或膝盖相接触的罕见"对折"情况，以及"手风琴"样挤压可发生于儿童(441)。通常，挤压物体与受害者之间存在明显的重量差异[通常>1 000千克(约500磅)(441,444,445)]。发生挤压至死亡的时间长短取决于外力大小。如果外力相当大，个体可以在几秒钟内死亡，但通常存活时间至少2-5分钟(441,446)。

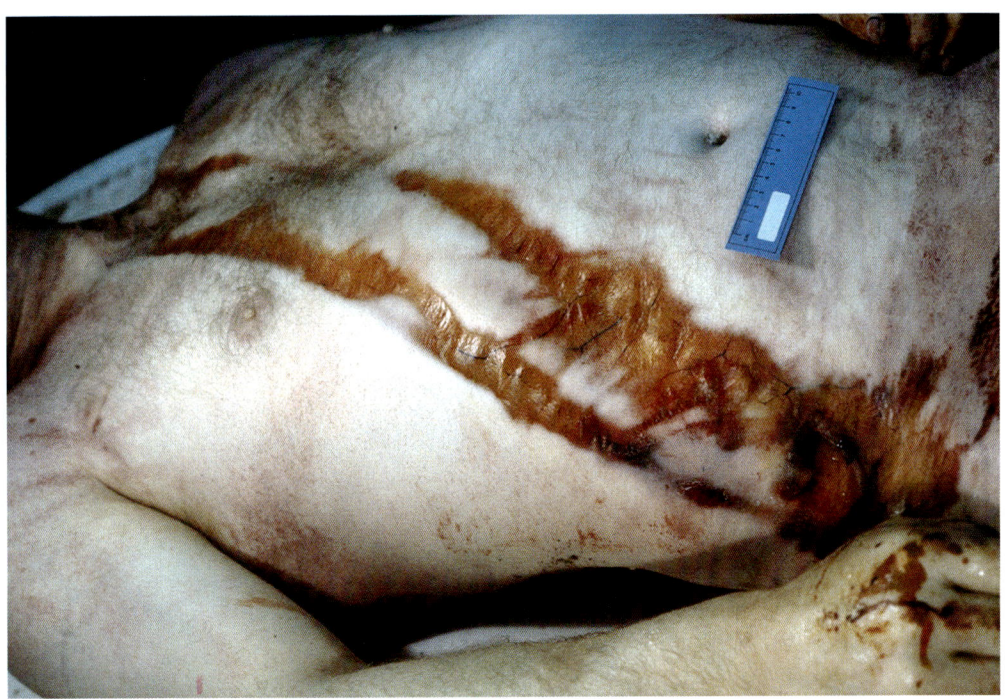

图3-64 创伤性窒息。被农耕机压迫(加拿大安大略省伦敦市伦敦健康科学中心 M. E. Kirk 博士供图)。

系列研究显示，幸存者均在 15 分钟内被救出，而遇难者被挤压或压在车下的时间为 5—15 分钟(443,446)。报道显示遇难者可被缓慢挤压致死(441)。目前缺乏造成创伤性窒息死亡的最小重量的相关信息，文献中描述的负载重量为受害人自身体重 5 倍及以上。动物实验研究显示，有部分受试豚鼠在接受自身 3 倍体重压迫时，于 10 分钟内死亡(452)。有案例报道了一名 13 千克儿童被一名 60 千克成年人用脚（脚上有一个 0.7 千克的护具）踩住约 40 分钟死亡，施暴者施力约 24 千克（假定该名男子腿及护具占其体重的 40%），约为受害儿童体重的 1.8 倍(49,453)。

3.8.3 创伤性窒息外部征象

虽然典型的窒息征象已有案件描述，但并非总是显而易见，有时只能观察到细微的征象（如瘀点性出血）(443,446)。瘀血性面罩指的是挤压后颈、面部出现典型的紫红色至紫黑色肤色改变，且瘀斑、瘀点范围可扩大至上胸部、背部及上肢（图 3-65；参考文献 11,441 和 443–446）。幸存者可能在伤后几天才会有所消退(441)，皮肤受压部位一般不发生变色(441,445)。肤色改变通常在数周内消失，且不会出现类似挫伤愈合时的渐变色(441,444)。给氧治疗也不会改变皮肤

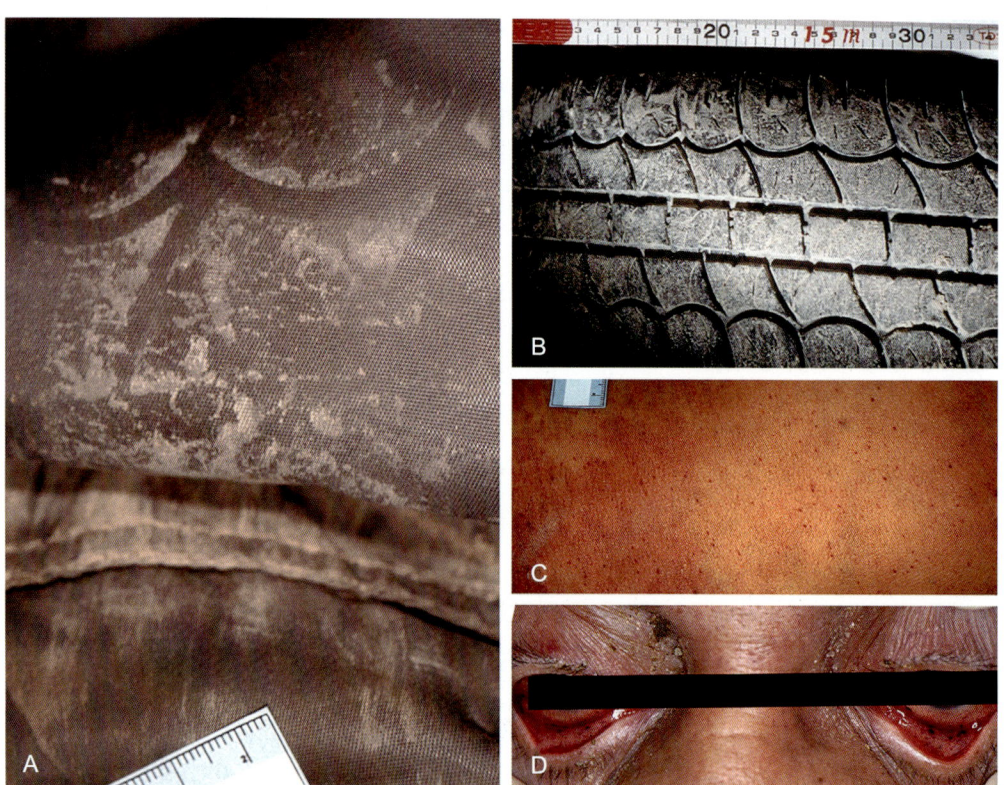

图 3-65 创伤性窒息的细微征象。悬架系统不良且载有 3 名乘客的车辆将一名男性碾压。(A) 受害者的外套，可见轮胎印痕。(B) 汽车轮胎。(C) 背部非挫伤区可见皮肤瘀点性出血。(D) 眼结膜瘀点性出血。

颜色(441)。皮肤瘀点性出血可在几天内消失，但眼结膜点状出血可持续数周，最后褪为黄色并消失(11,441,444)。创伤性窒息也可致面部水肿(11,441,444,445)。在难产、持久性呕吐或咳嗽、癫痫发作和哮喘发作的情况下，也可见类似但较轻微的征象(参阅标题1.5；参考文献441,444)。头部、颈部和躯干部可见钝性损伤(444-446)。

躯干突然遭受巨大压力的挤压后，胸腔内压力升高，血液自上腔静脉回流至右心房受阻(参阅标题1.5；参考文献11,441和443-445)。头颈部静脉血经过颈内和颈外静脉回流，后者主要收集头皮和颈前区浅层的静脉血。颈外静脉虽有一对静脉瓣，但当中心静脉压超过45毫米汞柱时(参考心肺复苏时的最大中心静脉压为40毫米汞柱)，并不足以防止血液反流。相比之下，回流大脑和上呼吸道静脉血的颈内静脉可更有效地对抗中心静脉压的升高。由于硬脑膜静脉窦容量的缓冲作用及坚硬颅骨的保护作用可有效防止颅内出血，且挤压躯干所致升高的静脉压可能不足以使头颈部出现上述典型征象(444)。"恐惧反应"指的是当面对灾难时深吸气并屏气的反射活动，可导致声门关闭和胸腔内压力增高(443,444,450)。压迫胸腹部时机体被动做Valsalva动作(瓦氏呼吸，即深吸气后屏气，再用力做呼气动作)，使胸内压升高并压迫下腔静脉，因此躯干下部可无体征(455)。剧烈呕吐和咳嗽时，胸腹部肌肉强烈收缩对抗闭合的声门，可导致头颈部静脉压升高(441)。高压使毛细血管扩张，血液滞留引起相应部位皮肤颜色变深，继之血管破裂引起皮肤瘀点性出血(441,443,445)。当外力大到能直接损伤全心功能时，可无瘀点性出血出现(442)。

3.8.4 创伤性窒息的内部征象

内部征象较轻微或缺乏，已有描述的各种征象：

- 眼：Purtscher视网膜病变(Purtscher's retinopathy)[视网膜出血(441)]*。
- 口、鼻、耳：咽、舌下腺、鼻腔及耳道瘀点性出血，可有外出血[与颅底骨折时耳鼻出血相似(11,441)]。
- 上呼吸道：会厌、喉及气管瘀点性出血；喉水肿(443,446)。
- 骨骼：肋骨或锁骨骨折；四肢骨和骨盆骨折(441,443,445,446,456)；颅骨骨折少见(441,445)；骨髓栓塞和脂肪栓塞有时可见(446)。
- 肺：挫伤或撕裂；伴血胸或气胸；肺淤血(443-446,456)。
- 心脏：损伤(破裂、挫伤)罕见(445,454,457)。
- 腹部：肝脾破裂(443-445)。
- 中枢神经系统：脑水肿；脑瘀血、脑出血罕见；脊髓缺血性损伤(441,443,444,456)。

---

* 译者注：视网膜受损，通常与严重的头部损伤有关，也可能发生在其他类型的创伤中，如长骨骨折或一些非创伤性的全身性疾病中。

如果损伤严重,死因则为多发性钝性损伤(441,443,450,454)。内部损伤(如肋骨骨折)虽不致命,却是持续受压的证据(443)。死因分析时也应考虑到肺脂肪栓塞(参阅第8章标题12.1;参考文献449)。当缺乏其他致命损伤时,则认为窒息是死亡机制(443,446),右心回心血量减少和脑灌注不足也是可能的机制之一(443)。若要排除酒精和毒品的影响,须进行毒物化学分析(443)。

3.9 一氧化碳中毒

一氧化碳(carbon monoxide, CO)是导致中毒死亡的主要原因之一(458,459)。CO是含碳物质不完全燃烧产生的无色、无味、无刺激性气体(460–468)。在燃烧过程中,如果氧浓度较高且燃烧温度低于710℃(1 310 °F),主要产物为二氧化碳(CO_2);但在氧浓度较低且燃烧温度较高时,开始生成CO(参阅第4章标题2;参考文献469)。CO通常来源于吸烟、汽车尾气、工业废气、火灾及通风不良或故障的供热设备等(460,462,464,466–468,470–472)。工业上用来作为脱漆剂、气溶胶推进喷雾剂和脱脂剂的二氯甲烷,也是CO来源之一(460–462,465,466,468,469)。甲酸与浓硫酸反应可制备CO(473)。

CO与血红蛋白可逆性结合形成碳氧血红蛋白(carboxyhemoglobin, HbCO)(461,474)。CO与血红蛋白的亲和力比氧大300倍左右,因此导致血液携氧能力下降(461,462,464–466,468,471,474–476)。CO与血红蛋白结合占据氧结合位点并修饰剩余的氧结合位点,增加血红蛋白与氧的亲和力,使氧合血红蛋白解离曲线左移,妨碍氧的解离,导致组织细胞缺氧(461,462,465–468,471,472,475,477–480)。组织缺氧引起呼吸加深加快,又增加了对CO的摄取,导致呼吸性碱中毒,进一步使氧解离曲线左移(481)。有10%–15%的CO可与体内其他血红素蛋白、肌红蛋白和线粒体细胞色素氧化酶(细胞色素A3,在ATP生成中起作用)等含铁蛋白可逆性地结合。研究显示CO能损害肌肉功能(475,481),其对其他组织的损伤机制(如脑组织脂质过氧化)也有描述(461,467,472,475,481)。

内源性CO(来源于含铁血红素分解)可产生0.4%–0.7%的HbCO饱和度(461,462,465,479)。正常人体内HbCO的含量与空气中CO的浓度、接触时间及肺通气量有关(461–463,465–471,474,480,486)。

空气中CO的浓度一般低于0.001%(461,463,468),在空气不流通和交通拥堵的城市中,CO的空气浓度可超过0.01%。城市不吸烟人群体内HbCO饱和度为1%–2%,重度吸烟者接近10%,吸雪茄者可至20%(460,462,466,480,487)。处于CO浓度为1%的环境可使体内HbCO饱和度维持在95%左右(462,466)。

静息状态下(肺通气量约6升/分钟),HbCO饱和度 = 3 × % CO(CO环境浓度)× 接触时间(分钟)。在轻度活动状态下(肺通气量9–10升/分钟),HbCO饱和度 = 5 × % CO × 接触时间。在火灾和吸入CO自杀的情况下,高浓度的CO(>1%)会导致机体在无前期症状情况下,短时间内即失去意识并死亡(462,466,

488—491)。空气中 CO 含量为 5% 时,正常人呼吸 10 秒后体内 HbCO 含量约为 10%,30 秒后为 40%(492)。在封闭车库中 CO 含量为 0.5%—1%,接触 10 分钟,HbCO 饱和度就可达致死量(468,470,493)。当 CO 含量为 0.2%—0.3% 时,接触 1—2 小时可导致死亡(465,469,491,494)。外界 CO_2 排放增加(如汽车尾气)可刺激机体呼吸中枢,使呼吸加深加快,并增加 CO 的吸入(491)。CO 中毒时,由于家养宠物体型较小且代谢率较高,会先于主人死亡(471,472,481,495)。

由于心血管系统和中枢神经系统对氧气有固定的需求,在接触相对较低浓度(0.02%—0.12%)的 CO 时,中毒症状在一段时间内(亚急性)具有相似性(表3—4;参考文献 461,467,468,470,477,479,496 和 497)。

表3—4 血液中 HbCO 含量与症状的关系

HbCO 饱和度	健康成年人	有心脏病史者
低于 10%	无明显症状	心绞痛患者更容易引起胸痛
10%—20%	头疼;呼吸困难、费力	心律失常(可致死)
20%—30%	搏动性头疼;恶心;双手灵巧度下降;疲劳;视觉变暗	
30%—40%	严重头疼;恶心呕吐;视觉障碍;意识模糊;身体无力(35% 可致死)	
40%—50%	晕厥;心动过速;呼吸过速	
50%—60%	昏迷;癫痫(威胁生命)	
>60%	心肺功能受损;死亡	

注:引自参考文献 462,465,446,471,482,488,491,498—500。

研究显示,在 HbCO 含量高于 10% 的烧伤患者中,已经可以观察到反映心脏损伤的心电图及生化改变(501)。吸入低浓度的 CO 可加重心绞痛患者的心肌缺血程度(502)。当 HbCO 饱和度急剧升高(但小于 10%)时,冠心病患者冠脉血流量不会增加(470,485)。个人体质和疾病也会影响 CO 的毒性作用(462,465,466,468,474,481,491,503,504)。婴儿、老年人、贫血或肺部疾病患者的中毒症状更明显。在 CO 中毒案例中,有产妇没有死亡,但是腹中胎儿死亡的情况,这是由于相较于母亲体内的血红蛋白(血红蛋白 A),CO 更易与胎儿的血红蛋白结合(463,472)。

处于海平面(常氧分压)、静息状态的成年人 HbCO 的半衰期为 4—5 小时,解离的 HbCO 基本以 CO 原型从肺中被呼出。心肺复苏可减少机体 HbCO 含量。吸入气体的氧分压与 HbCO 半衰期成反比,给予纯氧可使其半衰期减至 80 分钟,而高压氧疗可减至 24 分钟。如果中毒者离开中毒环境一段时间后死亡(或抢救后死亡),体内 HbCO 的含量可较低(已经分解)(463,464,472,475,480)。

3.9.1 现场情况

CO 中毒常见的原因是自杀吸入、火灾及其他意外事故(参阅第 4 章标题 4;参考文献458,463和469)。美国的一项回顾性研究显示,在56 133例CO中毒死亡相关的案例中,约有50%是自杀,28%为火灾,20%为其他意外事故(458人)。CO中毒自杀和意外事故以男性为主(458,494,504)。

吸入汽车尾气是常见的自杀手段(图3-66;参考文献505,506),最常见的是使用某种管道连接排气管到车辆内部,如通过窗口接入软管并保持环境密闭(491,494,507)。车辆可在车库内,也可在开放区域(图3-66;参考文献494,507)。车门可能是锁住的并用胶带密封(507)。现场可能有遗书(494)。当死者被发现时,发动机可能仍在空转;也可能点火装置是开着的,但是发动机因汽油燃尽或封闭环境中氧气耗尽而停转(474,490,494,507,508)。也有一些特殊情况被报道,如点火装置是关闭的,汽车在车库中且没有被发动,死者躺在锁着的后备箱里且身边有钥匙(590)。也有报道描述自杀者躺在车辆排气管附近的区域(周围环境可以开放,也可以封闭),现场不一定遗留连接管(图3-66;参考文献488,510)。

随着家用天然气(甲烷)的普及,通过吸入家用煤气自杀的报道现已减少(464,471,490,494,505,511–513)。"清洁"燃料(丙烷、甲烷)虽燃烧更加完全,仍可能导致CO中毒(468)。利用煤气自杀的现场特征是靠近煤气用具或有连接供气装置的管子(如在厨房里)、为密室、有煤气味,或煤气爆炸。

图3-66 CO中毒。汽车尾气由软管输送到死者车库内的办公区域(自杀现场)。

在与机动车有关的死亡中，CO中毒死亡人数不足1%（514），但系列报道显示CO中毒意外死亡（非火灾性）大多是处于非行驶状态的机动车辆或故障车辆废气泄漏导致的（458，468）。车辆排气系统设计缺陷，排气管道锈蚀穿孔，车厢板、内饰板或后备箱缺损都可导致废气泄漏，引起CO中毒（463，468，515）。事故可涉及在车内睡觉、车内约会、使用车辆取暖及在密闭空间中修车等（514，515）。车窗可部分开启[最多10厘米或4英寸（515）]。也有报道描述汽车在开放的车库里空转（477，515）。案发后，车辆检验通常显示点火装置、加热器或空调器是打开的，燃油表归零，汽车蓄电池耗尽。

其他不常见的与机动车相关的意外CO中毒死亡报道如下：

- 洗车时（天气寒冷时车门关闭，发动机空转）；使用汽油机动力高压清洗机（516，517）。
- 在密闭的工作区域和室内体育赛事中使用汽油机动力设备（463，465，518，519）。
- 工作或生活区与车库相邻（463，477）。
- 汽车尾气通过强制空气流通热风炉（一种供暖装置，空气为传热介质）散布到住宅内（520）。
- 汽车的排气消声器*被泥浆覆盖，CO通过生锈的板材泄漏（515，521）。
- 汽车排气管被雪堵塞（515，522，523）。
- 汽船引擎空转排出的尾气致游泳者中毒（521）。
- 船里的密闭小屋（524）。
- 儿童坐在被檐篷或篷布覆盖的皮卡车尾部（525）。

使用燃料的加热系统发生故障（如烟囱堵塞），可能会导致CO中毒死亡（463，465，475，477，494，504，520，526，527）。现场勘验可确认CO探测器、加热系统有无故障，以及空气中CO的含量（463，480，494，504，520）。CO中毒意外死亡通常发生在冬季（458，477，515，528，529）。奥地利的研究显示，在CO中毒意外事故中，超过半数是60岁以上的老人（504）。在寒冷天气过度使用无烟道燃气热水器是CO中毒在冬季频发的主要原因（461）。有报道显示CO中毒死亡案例与在密闭房间中使用燃料加热或烹饪设备作为替代热源并发生断电故障有关（461，463，465，468，528，530，531）。其他电器故障（如空调机组、电加热器等）在CO中毒死亡案例中也有报道（463，465，468，469，494）。

在接触较低浓度的CO时，症状因人而异，因此在非火灾相关死亡案例中，CO中毒症状可不明显（461）。CO急性中毒的临床症状、体征和预后与HbCO含量相对应（表3-4；参考文献461，463-465，467，471，472，475，483，498和532）。即

---

* 译者注：通过逐渐降低排气压力和衰减排气压力的脉动来消减排气噪声的装置。

使在同一事件中，不同 CO 中毒者也可表现为不同的症状(467)。如果 HbCO 浓度逐渐增加，中毒效应相对较轻(460，520)。此外，当案情不清、现场情况线索不明时，CO 中毒的死因可能会被遗漏(468，527，533)。CO 中毒症状相对而言是非特异性的，如恶心、呕吐、胸痛、意识状态改变及心烦意乱等(461，465，471，475，481，495，503，534)。隐匿性 CO 中毒可引起相应的神经症状(535)，组织相对缺氧反射性地引起血管舒张和脑血流量增加，导致头疼，即文献描述的"冬季头疼(winter headache)"(475，495，536)。有研究显示，最常见的急性体征为头疼(91%)、头晕(77%)、乏力(53%)、恶心(47%)、思维混乱或难以集中精神(43%)，也可引起癫痫发作(465，468，489)。CO 中毒和流感都在冬季多发，症状也相似，因此误诊率会增加(463)。在相对密闭环境中有多人生病或死亡时，应考虑到 CO 中毒(489，537，538)。如未能及时诊断 CO 中毒，意味着 CO 来源仍未被发现，增加了受害者或他人在案发现场再次中毒的风险(461，465，468，495)。

利用 CO 中毒进行他杀较罕见，如利用汽车尾气使被固定的受害者中毒致死(458，490)，也有报道描述 CO 中毒死者被放置在床上伪装成自然死亡(490)。

3.9.2　外部征象

CO 引起血管舒张(482，500)，浅层皮肤血管淤血导致尸斑变红(参考文献 539，参阅第 2 章标题 3.2)，色素沉着、尸体腐败或经过冷藏等因素可能会使尸斑变色不明显(469，490，540)。在深肤色人群中，可以通过检查甲床颜色来判定。

在临床救治过程中，HbCO 浓度相对较低的中毒者可见皮肤、黏膜呈"樱桃红色"，但这与医生观察的仔细程度和经验有关(461，471，481，500)。发绀在临床上更多见(461，532)。CO 与深层血管内血液中的血红蛋白结合形成 HbCO，可使皮肤发绀(539)。身处寒冷环境，CO 中毒者皮肤的浅表血管收缩，导致 HbCO 在深层器官组织中蓄积(540)，加上现场光照条件差或检测不仔细，可能会遗漏上述征象(490)。CO 中毒者的尸斑呈特征性的樱桃红色，通常与体内 HbCO 含量高于 30% 有关，但在某些 HbCO 含量高达 80% 的案例中并无该征象(17，533，540)。有研究表明，98% 的 CO 中毒意外死亡案例中尸斑呈典型的樱桃红色，3 例缺乏此征象的受害者体内，HbCO 的含量分别为 18%、28% 及 31%(533)。在 CO 中毒案件现场，法医仅凭尸斑呈樱桃红色来判断死因的准确率约为 61%，且受害者年龄越大，准确率越低；在受害者年龄大于 80 岁的案件中，有 59% 无法作出准确判断；而在 21-30 岁的案例，仅 19% 的案件无法作出准确判断。

CO 中毒住院患者有皮肤大疱及红斑出现(465，468，541，542)，镜检可见汗腺坏死，以及皮内、皮下均有囊泡形成(465，468，539，542)。

3.9.3　内部征象

CO 中毒尸体的器官及其浆膜、血液呈樱桃红色(图 3-67；参考文献 490，540)是 CO 中毒的重要征象，特别是当通过尸斑无法作出判断时(540)。CO 中毒

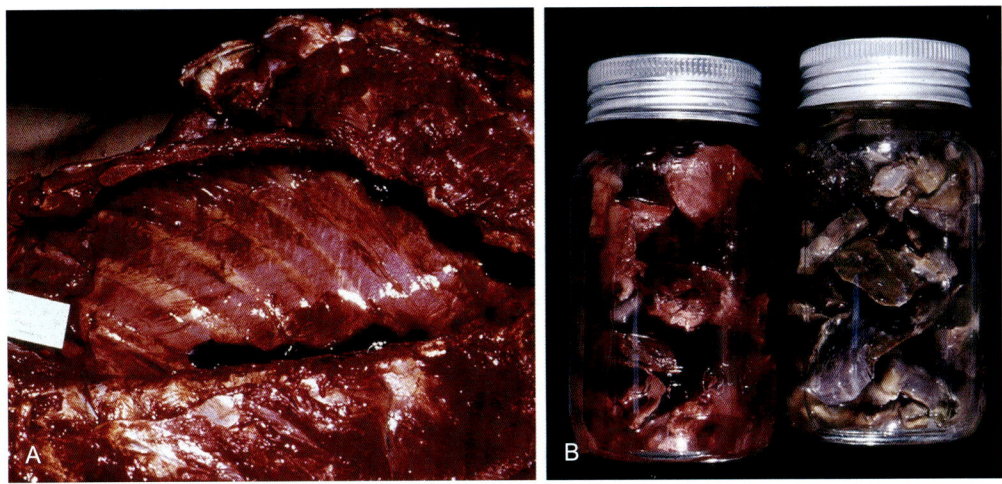

图 3-67 CO 中毒。(A) 深肤色死者的胸膜呈樱桃红色（北卡罗来纳州北卡罗莱纳大学法医室供图）。(B) 甲醛溶液 (35%–40%) 固定的尸体组织：左侧罐中是 CO 中毒组织，呈现出鲜红色。

者的器官经甲醛溶液固定后颜色会更加鲜红（图 3-67；参考文献 490, 540）。

在中毒后接受治疗者中可观察到 CO 中毒的病理变化。心脏病变从灶性出血到心肌坏死不等 (496)。重度 CO 中毒者还可发生横纹肌溶解症，随着病情的进展最终可导致肾衰竭（参阅第 8 章标题 13；参考文献 465, 479 和 543–545）。CO 中毒者脑深层灰质中神经元缺氧损伤最为明显，且通常呈对称性分布，这可能是 CO 中毒相关脑损伤唯一的早期表现 (465, 479, 490, 546, 547)。广泛的神经元和白质变性也有发生 (546–548)。CO 中毒者在初期症状改善后，也可出现迟发性脑病，伴随一系列神经精神症状 (462, 463, 475, 483, 500, 546, 548, 549)。

3.9.4 毒物化学

尸体解剖时采集的全血样本必须加入氟化钠进行预处理并冷藏保存 (460, 461)。血中 HbCO 在妥善保存时相对稳定，但在尸体腐败过程中会受到细菌代谢的影响而分解 (460, 520, 550, 551)。通常情况下，HbCO 含量在心血和外周血中并无差异；但当差异大于 50%（即心血：外周血 =1.5：1）时，表明中毒者循环系统失衡并存活过一段时间 (474, 552)。如果血液样本采集困难，可选用脾脏代替，脾脏内 HbCO 含量与血液中 HbCO 含量度显著相关 (553)。检测肝组织中 HbCO 含量也有报道，即使在救治后也能获得阳性结果 (474, 552, 554)。

急性 CO 中毒者血中 HbCO 含量报道如下：
- 汽车尾气 (460, 494)。
  - HbCO 含量：48% − 93%（平均 72%）；在开放环境中平均为 74%；在车库中平均为 77%。
  - 意外中毒死亡：超过 30% (515)。

- 乙醇是意外死亡的因素之一（515,529）。乙醇可以增强 CO 的毒性作用, 死者血中 HbCO 含量可相对较低（参阅第 4 章标题 4.1；参考文献 520）。丹麦的研究显示, 在家庭火灾中, 死者血中乙醇浓度为 190—200 毫克/分升, HbCO 含量为 60%（494）。相比之下, 利用汽车尾气自杀的中毒者血液乙醇平均浓度为 80 毫克/分升, HbCO 含量为 77%。与乙醇类似, 中枢神经系统抑制剂也可以影响机体精神和体力状态, 更易发生意外性 CO 中毒。（516）。
- 火灾（参阅第 4 章标题 4.1；参考文献 460,480,494 和 520）。
  - HbCO 含量：25%—85%（平均 59%）；炭化尸体中平均为 53%；未炭化的为 63%；另一项研究显示火灾受害者血中 HbCO 含量范围为 3%—94%。
- 密闭空间（参阅标题 3.10；参考文献 494,520）。
  - HbCO 含量：7%—77%（13 例加热系统故障导致的 CO 中毒死亡）；平均 68%（130 例利用 CO 自杀死亡）；平均 72%（19 例燃气用具故障导致的 CO 中毒死亡）。
- 处于开放空间的死亡案件（510）。
  - HbCO 含量：躺在靠近车辆尾气区域自杀的 3 名中毒者, HbCO 含量分别为 79%、81% 和 58%。
  - CO 与空气具有大致相同的密度（1∶0.968）, 故可以形成局部 CO 气体聚集区域（460,475）。
- 老年死者。
  - CO 中毒意外死亡的研究表明, 受害者年龄越大, 体内 HbCO 含量越高（533）。丹麦的研究显示, 64—90 岁的 CO 意外中毒死者血中 HbCO 含量平均为 49%（494）。

吸入汽车尾气自杀的案情较易明确, 但毒物化学检验结果并不一定都能证实是 CO 中毒（474,490,551）。HbCO 含量较低有如下原因：老式车辆排放的尾气中 CO 浓度高达 7%（462,465,507）, 配备有尾气催化器的车辆可以使 CO 排放量降低 90%, 浓度 <0.5%（491,508,555—557）。在有尾气催化器的车辆中自杀, HbCO 的含量较低（<10%）, 窒息主要是由于车内密闭空间中的 CO_2 增加和 O_2 降低所致（458,491,493,508）。但是, 如果发动机冷启动或催化器运转不良（491）, 尾气中 CO 的含量会升高（491）。HbCO 含量较低还可能与存活时间有关。有报道显示, 一名自杀者血中 HbCO 含量低于 5%, 其在车内被发现的汽车尾气排气管通过吸尘器管子连于车内, 且吸尘器管子已从排气管脱落（474）。死者被发现前有 2—3 天昏迷存活期, 大脑有相应的缺氧性改变。在死亡前, 发动机虽已耗尽汽油后停转, 但产生的 CO 量足以导致亚致死性缺氧性脑损伤。

3.10 密闭空间

密闭空间是指进、出口都被封闭的区域。由于通风不良, 密闭空间具有潜在的危险性，不适宜久处，如大容器、下水道、筒仓等（558–560），这类空间需要定期检查、维护、修理或清洁（560）。有些密闭空间顶部虽然敞开，但由于空间较深也会限制通风，如矿井、沟渠等（558）。典型的情况是工人进入密闭空间内发生窒息并死亡，另外一名试图施救的工人也随之中毒死亡（560–562）。

室内空气通常含有79%的氮气、20.9%的氧气、0.1%的二氧化碳、微量水蒸气和其他惰性气体等（2499, 563）。密闭空间中潜在的危害包括但不限于：任何情况下的氧气耗尽（乏氧性缺氧）、存在易燃易爆物质、存在刺激性和腐蚀性化学物质、其他有毒物质的蓄积（558, 559, 563）。密闭空间中的潜在致命危险被定义为：氧气浓度在16%以下；有火源的情况下，可燃气体或蒸汽达到最低可燃浓度；有毒物质蓄积直接危及生命（269, 559, 563–566）。刺激性或腐蚀性物质可以只影响呼吸系统，如氨气，或影响多器官系统，如苯（558）。缺乏氧气是最常见的死因（560），环境中氧气浓度低于5%–10%时，个体可在几分钟内死亡（参阅第4章标题4.1）。所处环境中缺乏氧气，个体可在数秒内失去意识（567）、呼吸停止，心输出量可以持续一段较短时间。即使为缓慢缺乏氧气，受害者也会疲劳乏力，无法逃离（567）。

空气中二氧化碳含量高于10%可致死（2, 493, 499, 562, 564, 566, 568, 569）。二氧化碳的比重是空气的1.5倍，可以形成局部范围内的气体沉积（2, 269）。二氧化碳不仅会导致窒息，还可引起酸中毒（2, 499）。即使空气中氧气含量正常，二氧化碳浓度过高也是致命的（2, 570）。二氧化碳浓度达到30%，个体可在数秒至数分钟内失去意识（568）。高浓度的二氧化碳还可诱导麻醉（568）。

"密闭空间–缺氧综合征"（space-hypoxiasyndrome）被Zugibe等（559, 564）定义为在密闭空间内缺氧导致的死亡（图3–68）。空气中氧气的减少可由以下原因

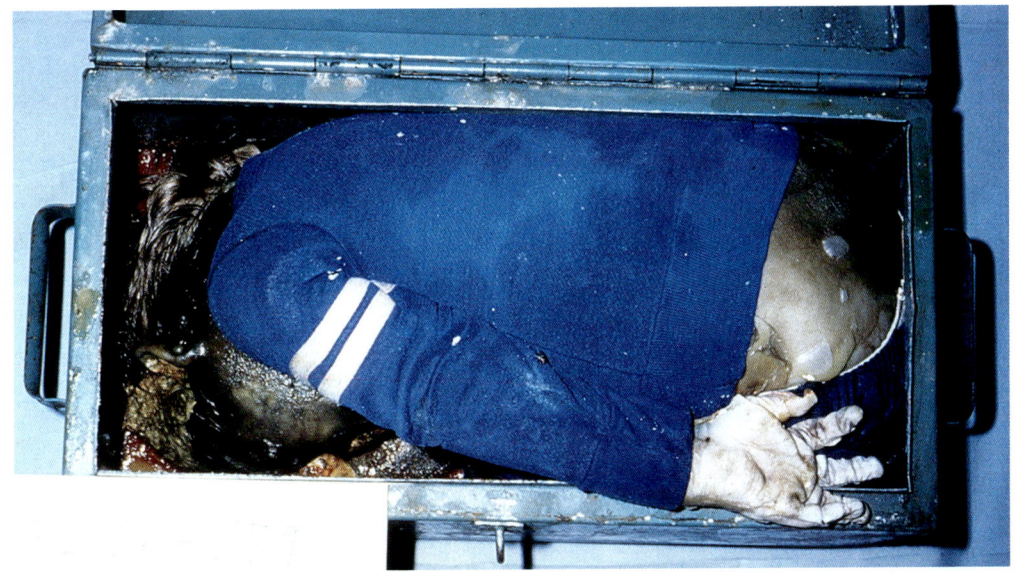

图3–68 被困在工具箱中的儿童（美国北卡罗来纳州教堂山市法医局供图）。

造成(2,269,558,560,563,564,567,571)：微生物消耗；工作活动(如焊接)；化学反应(如氧化锈蚀)；氧气被储存在大容器中的试剂吸收(如活性炭)；被其他气体(如丙烷、氮气等,以及筒仓和下水道蓄积的甲烷等)置换。置换的气体也可能具有毒性,如微生物分解有机物产生的CO,又如处理腐败有机物和工业废物时排放出的硫化氢(558,561,572,573)。有些置换气体,如丙烷,浓度较高时具有中枢神经系统抑制作用并可导致心脏停搏(311)。在密闭空间中工作可能面临机械危害、环境温度不良(过低或高热)和高空坠物等威胁(558,563)。在矿井等密闭空间发生塌方,工人可被掩埋并窒息(参阅标题3.8.1；参考文献574)。亦有儿童被困在冰箱中死亡的案例(48,114,116)。

需要对死亡现场内的有毒气体浓度和氧气浓度进行检测,并对血液及其他组织进行实验室分析(269,561,562,564,572,575)。有时场景模拟是必要的(2)。肺组织应用气密金属容器保存(311)。此外,二氧化碳含量在死后血液中通常会升高,导致不能进行准确定量。

黎世莹　吕叶辉 译

参考文献

1. Spitz, W. V. Asphyxia. In: Spitz, W. V., ed. Medicolegal Investigation of Death: Guidelines for the Application of Pathology to Crime Investigation. Charles C. Thomas, Springfield, IL, pp. 444–497, 1993.
2. Gill, J. R., Ely, S. F., Hua, Z. Environmental gas displacement: three accidental deaths in the workplace. Am. J. Forensic Med. Pathol. 23:26–30, 2002.
3. Iserson, K. V. Strangulation: a review of ligature, manual, and postural neck compression injuries. Ann. Emerg. Med. 13:179–185, 1984.
4. Feldman, K. W., Simms, R. J. Strangulation in childhood: epidemiology and clinical course. Pediatrics 65:1079–1085, 1980.
5. Elfawal, M. A., Awad, O. A. Deaths from hanging in the eastern province of Saudi Arabia. Med. Sci. Law 34:307–312, 1994.
6. Davison, A. M. Medico–legal aspects of accidental and non–accidental hanging. J. R. Nav. Med. Serv. 75:33–36, 1989.
7. Cooke, C. T., Cadden, G. A., Hilton, J. M. Unusual hanging deaths. Am. J. Forensic Med. Pathol. 9:277–282, 1988.
8. Polson, C. J., Gee, D. J. The Essentials of Forensic Medicine. 3rd ed. Pergamon Press, New York, 1973.
9. Zaini, M. R., Knight, B. Sub–pleural petechiae and pseudo petechiae. J. Forensic Sci. Soc. 22:141–145, 1982.

10. Jaffe, F. A. Petechial hemorrhages. A review of pathogenesis. Am. J. Forensic Med. Pathol. 15:203–207, 1994.
11. Lowe, L., Rapini, R. P., Johnson, T. M. Traumatic asphyxia. J. Am. Acad. Dermatol. 23: 972–974, 1990.
12. Ely, S. F., Hirsch, C. S. Asphyxial deaths and petechiae: a review. J. Forensic Sci. 45:1274–1277, 2000. 13. Rao, V. J, Wetli, C. V. The forensic significance of conjunctival petechiae. Am. J. Forensic Med. Pathol. 9:32–34, 1988.
14. Hood, I., Ryan, D., Spitz, W.U. Resuscitation and petechiae. Am. J. Forensic Med. Pathol. 9:35–37, 1988.
15. Clark, M. A., Feczko, J. D., Hawley, D. A., Pless, J. E., Tate, L. R., Fardal, P. M. Asphyxial deaths due to hanging in children. J. Forensic Sci. 38:344–352, 1993.
16. Samarasekera, A., Cooke, C. The pathology of hanging deaths in Western Australia. Pathology 28:334–338, 1996.
17. DiMaio, V. J., DiMaio, D. Forensic Pathology. 2nd ed. CRC Press, New York, 2001.
18. Adelson, L. The Pathology of Homicide. Charles C.Thomas, Springfield, IL, 1974.
19. Harm, T., Rajs, J. Types of injuries and interrelated conditions of victims and assailants in attempted and homicidal strangulation. Forensic Sci. Int. 18:101–123, 1981.
20. Friberg, T. R., Weinreb, R. N. Ocular manifestations of gravity inversion. JAMA 253: 1755–1757, 1985.
21. Betz, P., Penning, R., Keil, W. The detection of petechial haemorrhages of the conjunctivae in dependency on the postmortem interval. Forensic Sci. Int. 64:61–67, 1994.
22. Hicks, L. J., Scanlon, M. J., Bostwick, T. C., Batten, P. J. Death by smothering and its investigation. Am. J. Forensic Med. Pathol. 11:291–293, 1990.
23. Luke, J. L. Asphyxial deaths by hanging in New York City, 1964–1965. J. Forensic Sci. 12:359–369, 1967.
24. Luke, J. L., Reay, D. T., Eisele, J. W., Bonnell, H. J. Correlation of circumstances with pathologic findings in asphyxial deaths by hanging: a prospective study of 61 cases from Seattle, WA. J. Forensic Sci. 30:1140–1147, 1985.
25. Luke, J. L. Strangulation as a method of homicide. Study 1965–1966. in New York City. Arch. Pathol. 83:64–70, 1967.
26. Di Nunno, N., Costantinides, F., Conticchio, G., Mangiatordi, S., Vimercati, L., Di Nunno, C. Self–strangulation: an uncommon but not unprecedented suicide method. Am. J. Forensic Med. Pathol. 23:260–263, 2002.
27. Collins, K. A. Death by overlaying and wedging: a 15–year retrospective study. Am. J. Forensic Med. Pathol. 22:155–159, 2001.

28. Cooke, C. T., Cadden, G. A., Hilton, J. M. Hanging deaths in children. Am. J. Forensic Med. Pathol. 10:98–104, 1989.
29. Moore, L., Byard, R. W. Pathological findings in hanging and wedging deaths in infants and young children. Am. J. Forensic Med. Pathol. 14:296–302, 1993.
30. Maxeiner, H. Congestion bleedings of the face and cardiopulmonary resuscitation—an attempt to evaluate their relationship. Forensic Sci. Int. 117:191–198, 2001.
31. Gueugniaud, P. Y. Subarachnoid hemorrhage: a complication of CPR? Crit. Care. Med. 15:284–285, 1987.
32. Willinger, M., James, L. S., Catz, C. Defining the sudden infant death syndrome SIDS.: deliberations of an expert panel convened by the National Institute of Child Health and Human Development. Pediatr. Pathol. 11:677–684, 1991.
33. Leach, C. E., Blair, P. S., Fleming, P. J., et al. Epidemiology of SIDS and explained sudden infant deaths. CESDI SUDI Research Group. Pediatrics 104:e43, 1999.
34. Handforth, C. P. Sudden unexpected death in infants. Can. Med. Assoc. J. 80:872–873, 1959.
35. Byard, R. W. Possible mechanisms responsible for the sudden infant death syndrome. J. Paediatr. Child Health 27:147–157, 1991.
36. Werne, J., Garrow, I. Sudden apparently unexplained death during infancy. I. Pathologic findings in infants found dead. Am. J. Pathol. 29:633–675, 1953.
37. Valdes–Dapena, M. The sudden infant death syndrome: pathologic findings. Clin. Perinatol. 19:701–716, 1992.
38. Alexander, R. T., Radisch, D. Sudden infant death syndrome risk factors with regards to sleep position, sleep surface, and co–sleeping. J. Forensic Sci. 50:147–151, 2005.
39. Krous, H. F. The microscopic distribution of intrathoracic petechiae in sudden infant death syndrome. Arch. Pathol. Lab. Med. 108:77–79, 1984.
40. Delmonte, C., Capelozzi, V. L. Morphologic determinants of asphyxia in lungs: a semiquantitative study in forensic autopsies. Am. J. Forensic Med. Pathol. 22:139–149, 2001.
41. Brinkmann, B., Fechner, G., Puschel, K. Identification of mechanical asphyxiation in cases of attempted masking of the homicide. Forensic Sci. Int. 26:235–245, 1984.
42. Jackson, C. M., Gilliland, M. G. Frequency of pulmonary hemosiderosis in Eastern North Carolina. Am. J. Forensic Med. Pathol. 21:36–38, 2000.
43. Cooke, C. T., Cadden, G. A., Margolius, K. A. Death by hanging in Western Australia. Pathology 27:268–272, 1995.
44. Verma, S. K., Agarwal, B. B. Accidental hanging with delayed death in a lift. Med. Sci.

Law 39:342–344, 1999.

45. McMaster, A. R., Ward, E. W., Dykeman, A., Warman, M. D. Suicidal ligature strangulation: case report and review of the literature. J. Forensic Sci. 46:386–388, 2001.

46. Clark, M. A., Kerr, F. C. Unusual hanging deaths. J. Forensic Sci. 31:747–755, 1986.

47. Hardwicke, M. B., Taff, M. L., Spitz, W. U. A case of suicidal hanging in an automobile. Am. J. Forensic Med. Pathol. 6:362–364, 1985.

48. Flobecker, P., Ottosson, J., Johansson, L., Hietala, M. A., Gezelius, C., Eriksson A. Accidental deaths from asphyxia. A 10-year retrospective study from Sweden. Am. J. Forensic Med. Pathol. 14:74–79, 1993.

49. Khokhlov, V. D. Calculation of tension exerted on a ligature in incomplete hanging. Forensic Sci. Int. 123:172–177, 2001.

50. Davison, A., Marshall, T. K. Hanging in Northern Ireland—a survey. Med. Sci. Law 26:23–28, 1986.

51. Travis, L. W., Olson, N. R., Melvin, J. W., Snyder, R. G. Static and dynamic impact trauma of the human larynx. Trans. Sect. Otolaryngol. Am. Acad. Opthalmol. Otolaryngol. 80:382–390, 1975.

52. Martinez, A. P., Cameron, J. M. Trends in suicide 1983–1987. Med. Sci. Law 32:289–295, 1992.

53. Copeland, A. R. Suicide among the elderly—the Metro-Dade County experience, 1981–83. Med. Sci. Law 27:32–36, 1987.

54. Bowen, D. A. Hanging—a review. Forensic Sci. Int. 20:247–249, 1982.

55. Pounder, D. J. Why are the British hanging themselves? Am. J. Forensic Med. Pathol. 14:135–140, 1993.

56. Rogde, S., Hougen, H. P., Poulsen, K. Suicides in two Scandinavian capitals—a comparative study. Forensic Sci. Int. 80:211–219, 1996.

57. James, R., Silcocks, P. Suicidal hanging in Cardiff—a 15-year retrospective study. Forensic Sci. Int. 56:167–175, 1992.

58. Guarner, J., Hanzlick, R. Suicide by hanging. A review of 56 cases. Am. J. Forensic Med. Pathol. 8:23–26, 1987.

59. Cooper, P. N., Milroy, C. M. Violent suicide in South Yorkshire, England. J. Forensic Sci. 39:657–667, 1994.

60. Blanco Pampin, J. M., Lopez-Abajo Rodriguez, B. A. Suicidal hanging within an automobile. Am. J. Forensic Med. Pathol. 22:367–369, 2001.

61. Adair, T. W., Dobersen, M. J. A case of suicidal hanging staged as homicide. J. Forensic Sci. 44:1307–1309, 1999.

62. Bohnert, M., Faller–Marquardt, M., Lutz, S., Amberg, R., Weisser, H. J., Pollak, S. Transfer of biological traces in cases of hanging and ligature strangulation. Forensic Sci. Int. 116:107–115, 2001.

63. Avis, S. P., Hutton, C. J. Dyadic suicide. A case study. Am. J. Forensic Med. Pathol. 15:18–20, 1994.

64. Camps, F. E. The case of Emmett Dunne. Med. Leg. J. 27:156–161, 1959.

65. Srivastava, A. K., Das Gupta, S. M., Tripathi, C. B. A study of fatal strangulation cases in Varanasi India.. Am. J. Forensic Med. Pathol. 8:220–224, 1987.

66. Leth, P., Vesterby, A. Homicidal hanging masquerading as suicide. Forensic Sci. Int. 85:65–71, 1997.

67. Simon, R. I. Murder masquerading as suicide: postmortem assessment of suicide risk factors at the time of death. J. Forensic Sci. 43:1119–1123, 1998.

68. Vieira, D. N., Pinto, A. E., Sa, F. O. Homicidal hanging. Am. J. Forensic Med. Pathol. 9:287–289, 1988.

69. Puschel, K., Holtz, W., Hildebrand, E., Naeve, W., Brinkmann, B. [Hanging: suicide or homicide?]. Arch. Kriminol. 174:141–153, 1984.

70. Shafii, M., Carrigan, S., Whittinghill, J. R., Derrick, A. Psychological autopsy of completed suicide in children and adolescents. Am. J. Psychiatry 142:1061–1064, 1985.

71. James, R. A., Byard, R. W. Asphyxiation from shoulder seat belts: an unusual motor vehicle injury. Am. J. Forensic Med. Pathol. 22:193–195, 2001.

72. Wobeser, W. L., Datema, J., Bechard, B., Ford, P. Causes of death among people in custody in Ontario, 1990–1999. CMAJ 167:1109–1113, 2002.

73. Frost, R., Hanzlick, R. Deaths in custody. Atlanta City Jail and Fulton County Jail, 1974–1985. Am. J. Forensic Med. Pathol. 9:207–211, 1988.

74. Smith, R. The state of the prisons. Deaths in prison. Br. Med. J. (Clin. Res. Ed.) 288:208–212, 1984.

75. Copeland, A. R. Deaths in custody revisited. Am. J. Forensic Med. Pathol. 5:121–124, 1984.

76. Novick, L. F., Remmlinger, E. A study of 128 deaths in New York City correctional facilities 1971–1976.: implications for prisoner health care. Med. Care 16:749–756, 1978.

77. Johnson, H. R. Deaths in police custody in England and Wales. Forensic Sci. Int. 19:231–236, 1982.

78. Smialek, J. E., Spitz, W. U. Death behind bars. JAMA 240:2563–2564, 1978.

79. Perez–Carceles, M. D., Inigo, C., Luna, A., Osuna, E. Mortality in maximum security

psychiatric hospital patients. Forensic Sci. Int. 119:279–283, 2001.
80. Hayes, L. M. National study of jail suicides: seven years later. Psychiatr. Q. 60:7–29, 1989.
81. Tuskan, J. J., Jr., Thase, M. E. Suicides in jails and prisons. J. Psychosoc. Nurs. Ment. Health Serv. 21:29–33, 1983.
82. DuRand, C. J., Burtka, G. J., Federman, E. J., Haycox, J. A., Smith, J. W. A quarter century of suicide in a major urban jail: implications for community psychiatry. Am. J. Psychiatry 152:1077–1080, 1995.
83. Green, C., Kendall, K., Andre, G., Looman, T., Polvi, N. A study of 133 suicides among Canadian federal prisoners. Med. Sci. Law 33:121–127, 1993.
84. Joukamaa, M. Prison suicide in Finland, 1969–1992. Forensic Sci. Int. 89:167–174, 1997.
85. McKee, G. R. Lethal vs nonlethal suicide attempts in jail. Psychol. Rep. 82:611–614, 1998.
86. Jordan, F. B., Schmeckpeper, K., Strope, M. Jail suicides by hanging. An epidemiological review and recommendations for prevention. Am. J. Forensic Med. Pathol. 8:27–31, 1987.
87. Copeland, A. R. Fatal suicidal hangings among prisoners in jail. Med. Sci. Law 29: 341–345, 1989.
88. He, X. Y., Felthous, A. R., Holzer, C. E., III, Nathan, P., Veasey, S. Factors in prison suicide: one year study in Texas. J. Forensic Sci. 46:896–901, 2001.
89. Topp, D. O. Suicide in prison. Br. J. Psychiatry 134:24–27, 1979.
90. Reay, D. T. Death in custody. Clin. Lab. Med. 18:1–22, 1998.
91. Shah, A., Ganesvaran, T. Suicide among psychiatric in–patients with schizophrenia in an Australian mental hospital. Med. Sci. Law 39:251–259, 1999.
92. Miles, S. A case of death by physical restraint: new lessons from a photograph. J. Am. Geriatr. Soc. 44:291–292, 1996.
93. Osculati, A., Fassina, G. Two cases of accidental asphyxia by neck compression between bed bars. Am. J. Forensic Med. Pathol. 21:217–219, 2000.
94. Weakley–Jones, B., Wernert, J. Accidental deaths in the aged by protective devices. J. Ky. Med. Assoc. 84:397–398, 1986.
95. Dube, A. H., Mitchell, E. K. Accidental strangulation from vest restraints. JAMA 256: 2725–2726, 1986.
96. Corey, T. S., Weakley–Jones, B., Nichols, G. R., Theuer, H. H. Unnatural deaths in nursing home patients. J. Forensic Sci. 37:222–227, 1992.

97. Bell, M. D., Rao, V. J., Wetli, C. V., Rodriguez, R. N. Positional asphyxiation in adults. A series of 30 cases from the Dade and Broward County Florida Medical Examiner Offices from 1982 to 1990. Am. J. Forensic Med. Pathol. 13:101–107, 1992.
98. DiMaio, V. J., Dana, S. E., Bux, R. C. Deaths caused by restraint vests. JAMA 255:905, 1986.
99. Parker, K., Miles, S. H. Deaths caused by bedrails. J. Am. Geriatr. Soc. 45:797–802, 1997.
100. Miles, S. H., Irvine, P. Deaths caused by physical restraints. Gerontologist 32:762–766, 1992.
101. Emson, H. E. Death in a restraint jacket from mechanical asphyxia. CMAJ 151:985–987, 1994.
102. Copeland, A. R. Childhood suicide: a report of four cases. J. Forensic Sci. 30:965–967, 1985.
103. Wyatt, J. P., Wyatt, P. W., Squires, T. J., Busuttil, A. Hanging deaths in children. Am. J. Forensic Med. Pathol. 19:343–346, 1998.
104. Goren, S., Gurkan, F., Tirasci, Y., Ozen, S. Suicide in children and adolescents at a province in Turkey. Am. J. Forensic Med. Pathol. 24:214–217, 2003.
105. Toolan, J. M. Suicide in children and adolescents. Am. J. Psychother. 29:339–344, 1975.
106. Weinberger, L. E., Sreenivasan, S., Sathyavagiswaran, L., Markowitz, E. Child and adolescent suicide in a large, urban area: psychological, demographic, and situational factors. J. Forensic Sci. 46:902–907, 2001.
107. Schmidt, P., Muller, R., Dettmeyer, R., Madea, B. Suicide in children, adolescents and young adults. Forensic Sci. Int. 127:161–167, 2002.
108. Copeland, A. R. Teenage suicide—the five-year Metro Dade County experience from 1979 until 1983. Forensic Sci. Int. 28:27–33, 1985.
109. Green, M. A. Morbid anatomical findings in strangulation. Forensic Sci. 2:317–323, 1973.
110. Variend, S., Usher, A. Broken cots and infant fatality. Med. Sci. Law 24:111–112, 1984.
111. Bass, M. Asphyxial crib death. N. Engl. J. Med. 296:555–556, 1977.
112. Byard RW, Beal SM, Simpson A, Carter RF, Khong TY. Accidental infant death and stroller-prams. Med. J. Aust. 165:140–141, 1996.
113. Gilbert-Barness, E., Hegstrand, L., Chandra, S., et al. Hazards of mattresses, beds and bedding in deaths of infants. Am. J. Forensic Med. Pathol. 12:27–32, 1991.
114. Baker, S. P., Fisher, R. S. Childhood asphyxiation by choking or suffocation. JAMA 244:1343–1346, 1980.

115. Sturner, W. Q., Spruill, F. G., Smith, R. A., Lene, W. J. Accidental asphyxial deaths involving infants and young children. J. Forensic Sci. 21:483–487, 1976.
116. Nixon, J. W., Kemp, A. M., Levene, S., Sibert, J. R. Suffocation, choking, and strangulation in childhood in England and Wales: epidemiology and prevention. Arch. Dis. Child. 72:6–10, 1995.
117. Drago, D. A., Dannenberg, A. L. Infant mechanical suffocation deaths in the United States, 1980–1997. Pediatrics 103:e59, 1999.
118. Roberton, D., Rookwood, K., Rutter, N. Collapsible washing lines: a strangulation hazard. Br, Med, J, (Clin, Res, Ed.) 282:1664, 1981.
119. Little, A. S. Drapery cord injury and strangulation in babies. Am. Fam. Physician 49:335, 1994.
120. Hord, J. D., Anglin, D. Accidental strangulation of a toddler involving a wall light switch. Am. J. Dis. Child. 147:1038–1039, 1993.
121. Rauchschwalbe, R., Mann, N. C. Pediatric window–cord strangulations in the United States, 1981–1995. JAMA 277:1696–1698, 1997.
122. Byard, R. W., James, R. A. Car window entrapment and accidental childhood asphyxia. J. Paediatr. Child Health 37:201–202, 2001.
123. Calvet, R., Gonzalez–Gil, J., Gonzalez–Azpeitia, C. An unusual fatal case of accidental asphyxia in a child. J. Forensic Sci. 37:1697–1701, 1992.
124. Perrot, L. J., Froede R. C., Jones, A. M. Asphyxiation by hanging in two young Hispanic children—homicide, suicide, or accidental deaths? A review of pediatric hangings. Am. J. Forensic Med. Pathol. 6:284–288, 1985.
125. Digeronimo, R. J., Mayes, T. C. Near–hanging injury in childhood: a literature review and report of three cases. Pediatr. Emerg. Care 10:150–156, 1994.
126. Denton, J. S. Fatal accidental hanging from a lanyard key chain in a 10–year–old boy. J. Forensic Sci. 47:1345–1346, 2002.
127. Petruk, J., Shields, E., Cummings, G. E., Francescutti, L. H. Fatal asphyxiations in children involving drawstrings on clothing. CMAJ 155:1417–1419, 1996.
128. Lew, E. O. Homicidal hanging in a dyadic death. Am. J. Forensic Med. Pathol. 9:283–286, 1988.
129. Rothschild, M. A., Schneider, V. Decapitation as a result of suicidal hanging. Forensic Sci. Int. 106:55–62, 1999.
130. el Khafief, H. Unusual cases from Dubai, United Arab Emirates. Am. J. Forensic Med. Pathol. 12:187–190, 1991.
131. Goonetilleke, U. K. Two unusual cases of suicide by hanging. Forensic Sci. Int. 26:247–

253, 1984.

132. Marsh, T. O., Burkhardt, R. P., Swinehart, J. W. Self-inflicted hanging with bound wrists and a gag. Am. J. Forensic Med. Pathol. 3:367–369, 1982.

133. Wright, R. K., Davis, J. Homicidal hanging masquerading as sexual asphyxia. J. Forensic Sci. 21:387–389, 1976.

134. Paparo, G. P., Siegel, H. Neck markings and fractures in suicidal hangings. Forensic Sci. Int. 24:27–35, 1984.

135. Saukko, P., Knight, B. Knight's Forensic Pathology. 3rd ed. Arnold, London, 2004.

136. Miller, K. W., Walker, P. L., O'Halloran, R. L. Age and sex-related variation in hyoid bone morphology. J. Forensic Sci. 43:1138–1143, 1998.

137. Raja, U., Sivaloganathan, S. Decapitation—a rare complication in hanging. Med. Sci. Law 37:81–83, 1997.

138. Hocking, F. D. Hanging and manual strangulation. Med. Sci. Law 6:49–51, 1966.

139. Khokhlov, V. D. Pressure on the neck calculated for any point along the ligature. Forensic Sci. Int. 123:178–181, 2001.

140. Ruszkiewicz, A. R., Lee, K. A., Landgren, A. J. Homicidal strangulation by victim's own hair presenting as natural death. Am. J. Forensic Med. Pathol. 15:340–343, 1994.

141. Garza-Leal, J. A., Landron, F. J. Autoerotic asphyxial death initially misinterpreted as suicide and a review of the literature. J. Forensic Sci. 36:1753–1759, 1991.

142. Rajs, J., Thiblin, I. Histologic appearance of fractured thyroid cartilage and surrounding tissues. Forensic Sci. Int. 114:155–166, 2000.

143. Kaplan, J. A., Fossum, R. M. Patterns of facial resuscitation injury in infancy. Am. J. Forensic Med. Pathol. 15:187–191, 1994.

144. Guernsey, L. H. Fractures of the hyoid bone. J. Oral Surg. Anesth. Hosp. Dent. Serv. 12:241–246, 1954.

145. Morild, I. Fractures of neck structures in suicidal hanging. Med. Sci. Law 36:80–84, 1996.

146. Keil, W., Forster, A., Meyer, H. J., Peschel, O. Characterization of haemorrhages at the origin of the sternocleidomastoid muscles in hanging. Int. J. Legal Med. 108:140–144, 1995.

147. Keil, W., Kondo, T., Beer, G. M. Haemorrhages in the posterior cricoarytenoid muscles—an unspecific autopsy finding. Forensic Sci. Int. 95:225–230, 1998.

148. Paparo, G. P., Siegel, H. On the significance of posterior crico-arytenoid muscle hemorrhage. Forensic Sci. 7:61–65, 1976.

149. Ubelaker, D. H. Hyoid fracture and strangulation. J. Forensic Sci. 37:1216–1222, 1992.

150. Simonsen, J. Patho-anatomic findings in neck structures in asphyxiation due to hanging: a survey of 80 cases. Forensic Sci. Int. 38:83–91, 1988.

151. DiMaio, V. J. Homicidal asphyxia. Am. J. Forensic Med. Pathol. 21:1–4, 2000.

152. Feigin, G. Frequency of neck organ fractures in hanging. Am. J. Forensic Med. Pathol. 20:128–130, 1999.

153. Hansch, C. F. Throat-skeleton fractures by strangulation. Z. Rechtsmed. 79:143–147, 1977.

154. Nikolic, S., Micic, J., Atanasijevic, T., Djokic, V., Djonic, D. Analysis of neck injuries in hanging. Am. J. Forensic Med. Pathol. 24:179–182, 2003.

155. Betz, P., Eisenmenger, W. Frequency of throat-skeleton fractures in hanging. Am. J. Forensic Med. Pathol. 17:191–193, 1996.

156. Khokhlov, V. D. Injuries to the hyoid bone and laryngeal cartilages: effectiveness of different methods of medico-legal investigation. Forensic Sci. Int. 88:173–183, 1997.

157. Gordon, I., Shapiro, H. A., Taljaard, J. J., Engelbrecht, H. E. Aspects of the hyoid-larynx complex in forensic pathology. Forensic Sci. 7:161–170, 1976.

158. Pollanen, M. S. A triad of laryngeal hemorrhages in strangulation: a report of eight cases. J. Forensic Sci. 45:614–618, 2000.

159. Szeremeta, W., Morovati, S. S. Isolated hyoid bone fracture: a case report and review of the literature. J. Trauma 31:268–271, 1991.

160. Pollanen, M. S., Bulger, B., Chiasson, D. A. The location of hyoid fractures in strangulation revealed by xeroradiography. J. Forensic Sci. 40:303–305, 1995.

161. Pollanen, M. S., Chiasson, D. A. Fracture of the hyoid bone in strangulation: comparison of fractured and unfractured hyoids from victims of strangulation. J. Forensic Sci. 41:110–113, 1996.

162. O'Halloran, R. L., Lundy, J. K. Age and ossification of the hyoid bone: forensic implications. J. Forensic Sci. 32:1655–1659, 1987.

163. Pollanen, M. S., Ubelaker, D. H. Forensic significance of the polymorphism of hyoid bone shape. J. Forensic Sci. 42:890–892, 1997.

164. Whyte, A. M. Fracture of the hyoid bone associated with a mandibular fracture. J. Oral Maxillofac. Surg. 43:805–807, 1985.

165. Porrath, S. Roentgenologic considerations of the hyoid apparatus. Am. J. Roentgenol. Radium Ther. Nucl. Med. 105:63–73, 1969.

166. Watanabe, H., Kurihara, K., Murai, T. A morphometrical study of laryngeal cartilages. Med. Sci. Law 22:255–260, 1982.

167. Mancuso, A. A., Hanafee, W. N. Computed tomography of the injured larynx. Radiology

133:139–144, 1979.

168. Khokhlov, V. D. Knitted fractures of the laryngopharynx framework as a medico–legal matter. Forensic Sci. Int. 104:147–162, 1999.

169. Spence, M. W., Shkrum, M. J., Ariss, A., Regan, J. Craniocervical injuries in judicial hangings: an anthropologic analysis of six cases. Am. J. Forensic Med. Pathol. 20:309–322, 1999.

170. Shkrum, M. J., Green, R. N., Nowak, E. S. Upper cervical trauma in motor vehicle collisions. J. Forensic Sci. 34:381–390, 1989.

171. Prichard, P. D. A suicide by self–decapitation. J. Forensic Sci. 38:981–984, 1993.

172. Tracqui, A., Fonmartin, K., Geraut, A., Pennera, D., Doray, S., Ludes, B. Suicidal hanging resulting in complete decapitation: a case report. Int. J. Legal Med. 112:55–57, 1999.

173. Crompton, M. R. Fronto–cranial suspension—an unusual form of hanging. Med. Sci. Law 26:203–206, 1986.

174. Line, W. S., Jr., Stanley, R. B., Jr., Choi, J. H. Strangulation: a full spectrum of blunt neck trauma. Ann. Otol. Rhinol. Laryngol. 94:542–546, 1985.

175. Bockholdt, B., Maxeiner, H. Hemorrhages of the tongue in the postmortem diagnostics of strangulation. Forensic Sci. Int. 126:214–220, 2002.

176. Suyama, H., Nakasono, I., Yoshitake, T., Narita, K., Yoshida, C. Significance of haemorrhages in central parts of the tongue found in the medicolegal autopsy. Forensic Sci. Int. 20:265–268, 1982.

177. Saternus, K. S. Injury of the vertebral artery in suicidal hanging. Forensic Sci. Int. 25:265–275, 1984.

178. Maxeiner, H., Bockholdt, B. Homicidal and suicidal ligature strangulation—a comparison of the post–mortem findings. Forensic Sci. Int. 137:60–66, 2003.

179. Kogan, Y., Bloom, T. Suicidal ligature strangulation with an elastic band. Am. J. Forensic Med. Pathol. 11:329–330, 1990.

180. Claydon, S. M. Suicidal strangulation by ligature: three case reports. Med. Sci. Law 30:221–224, 1990.

181. Frazer, M., Rosenberg, S. A case of suicidal ligature strangulation. Am. J. Forensic Med. Pathol. 4:351–354, 1983.

182. Gaur, J. R., Verma, R. K., Thakur, G. C. Suicidal strangulation. Med. Sci. Law 32:55–56, 1992.

183. Zecevic, D. Suicidal strangulation with a double–knotted noose. J. Forensic Sci. 27:963–967, 1982.

184. Kennedy, N. M., Whittington, R. M., White, A. C. Suicide by self–strangulation whilst

under observation. Med. Sci. Law 35:174–177, 1995.

185. Shepherd, R. T. Accidental self–strangulation in a young child—a case report and review. Med. Sci. Law 30:119–123, 1990.

186. Deidiker, R. D. Accidental ligature strangulation due to a roller–type massage device. Am. J. Forensic Med. Pathol. 20:354–356, 1999.

187. Habal, M. B., Meguid, M. M., Murray, J. E. The long scarf syndrome—a potentially fatal and preventable hazard. Report of 11 cases. JAMA 221:1269–1270, 1972.

188. Kohli, A., Verma, S. K., Agarwal, B. B. Accidental strangulation in a rickshaw. Forensic Sci. Int. 78:7–11, 1996.

189. Aggarwal, N. K., Agarwal, B. B. Accidental strangulation in a cycle rickshaw. Med. Sci. Law 38:263–265, 1998.

190. Meguid, M. M., Gifford, G. H., Jr. The long free–flowing scarf—a new health hazard to children. Pediatrics 49:290–293, 1972.

191. Michalodimitrakis, M., Frangoulis, M., Koutselinis, A. Accidental sexual strangulation. Am. J. Forensic Med. Pathol. 7:74–75, 1986.

192. Pollanen, M. S. Subtle fatal manual neck compression. Med. Sci. Law 41:135–140, 2001.

193. Shapiro, H. A., Gluckman, J., Gordon, I. The significance of finger nail abrasions of the skin. J. Forensic Med. 9:17–19, 1962.

194. Perper, J. A., Sobel, M. N. Identification of fingernail markings in manual strangulation. Am. J. Forensic Med. Pathol. 2:45–48, 1981.

195. Fieguth, A., Franz, D., Lessig, R., Kleemann, W. J. Fatal trauma to the neck: immunohistochemical study of local injuries. Forensic Sci. Int. 135:218–225, 2003.

196. Tabata, N. Morphological changes in traumatized skeletal muscle: the appearance of "opaque fibers" of cervical muscles as evidence of compression of the neck. Forensic Sci. Int. 96:197–214, 1998.

197. Betz, P., Nerlich, A., Wilske, J., et al. Immunohistochemical localization of fibronectin as a tool for the age determination of human skin wounds. Int. J. Legal Med. 105:21–26, 1992.

198. Fechner, G., Hauser, R., Sepulchre, M. A., Brinkmann, B. Immunohistochemical investigations to demonstrate vital direct traumatic damage of skeletal muscle. Int. J. Legal Med. 104:215–219, 1991.

199. Thomsen, H., Held, H. Susceptibility of C5b–9 m. to postmortem changes. Int. J. Legal Med. 106:291–293, 1994.

200. Fechner, G., Bajanowski, T., Brinkmann, B. Immunohistochemical alterations after

muscle trauma. Int. J. Legal Med. 105:203–207, 1993.
201. Fieguth, A., Kleemann, W. J., von Wasielewski, R., Werner, M., Troger, H. D. Influence of postmortem changes on immunohistochemical reactions in skin. Int. J. Legal Med. 110:18–21, 1997.
202. Grellner, W., Dimmeler, S., Madea, B. Immunohistochemical detection of fibronectin in postmortem incised wounds of porcine skin. Forensic Sci. Int. 97:109–116, 1998.
203. Maxeiner, H. [Injuries to laryngeal articulations in strangulation and throttling]. Arch. Kriminol. 179:38–44, 1987.
204. Maxeiner, H. [Soft tissue hemorrhage within the larynx following strangulation]. Z. Rechtsmed. 94:127–135, 1985.
205. Pollanen, M. S., McAuliffe, D. N. Intra–cartilaginous laryngeal haemorrhages and strangulation. Forensic Sci. Int. 93:13–20, 1998.
206. Pradeep, K. G., Kanthaswamy, V. Survival in hanging. Am. J. Forensic Med. Pathol. 14:80–81, 1993.
207. Aggarwal, N. K., Kishore, U., Agarwal, B. B. Hanging–delayed death a rare phenomenon. Med. Sci. Law 40:270–272, 2000.
208. Raven, K. P., Reay, D. T., Harruff, R. C. Artifactual injuries of the larynx produced by resuscitative intubation. Am. J. Forensic Med. Pathol. 20:31–36, 1999.
209. Leadbeatter, S., Knight, B. Resuscitation artefact. Med. Sci. Law 28:200–204, 1988.
210. Harm, T., Rajs, J. Face and neck injuries due to resuscitation versus throttling. Forensic Sci. Int. 23:109–116, 1983.
211. Krischer, J. P., Fine, E. G., Davis, J. H., Nagel, E. L. Complications of cardiac resuscitation. Chest 92:287–291, 1987.
212. Sommers, M. S. Potential for injury: trauma after cardiopulmonary resuscitation. Heart Lung 20:287–293, 1991.
213. Streitz, J. M., Jr., Shapshay, S. M. Airway injury after tracheotomy and endotracheal intubation. Surg. Clin. North Am. 71:1211–1230, 1991.
214. Peppard, S. B., Dickens, J. H. Laryngeal injury following short–term intubation. Ann. Otol. Rhinol. Laryngol. 92:327–330, 1983.
215. Galvis, A. G., Kelley, C. F. Hypopharynx perforation during infant's resuscitation. JAMA 242:1526–1527, 1979.
216. Hawkins, D. B., Seltzer, D. C., Barnett, T. E., Stoneman, G. B. Endotracheal tube perforation of the hypopharynx. West. J. Med. 120:282–286, 1974.
217. Lee, T. S., Jordan, J. S. Pyriform sinus perforation secondary to traumatic intubation in a difficult airway patient. J. Clin. Anesth. 6:152–155, 1994.

218. Marty-Ane, C. H., Picard, E., Jonquet, O., Mary, H. Membranous tracheal rupture after endotracheal intubation. Ann. Thorac. Surg. 60:1367–1371, 1995.

219. Massard, G., Rouge, C., Dabbagh, A., Kessler, R., Hentz, J. G., Roeslin, N. et al. Tracheobronchial lacerations after intubation and tracheostomy. Ann. Thorac. Surg. 61:1483–148, 1996.

220. Kaloud, H., Smolle-Juettner, F. M., Prause, G., List, W. F. Iatrogenic ruptures of the tracheobronchial tree. Chest 112:774–778, 1997.

221. Gregersen, M., Vesterby, A. Iatrogenic fractures of the hyoid bone and the thyroid cartilage. A case report. Forensic Sci. Int. 17:41–43, 1981.

222. Kambic, V., Radsel, Z. Intubation lesions of the larynx. Br. J. Anaesth. 50:587–590, 1978.

223. Nagel, E. L., Fine, E. G., Krischer, J. P., Davis, J. H. Complications of CPR. Crit. Care. Med. 9:424, 1981.

224. Behrendt, N., Buhl, N., Seidl, S. The lethal paraphiliac syndrome: accidental autoerotic deaths in four women and a review of the literature. Int. J. Legal Med. 116:148–152, 2002.

225. Boglioli, L. R., Taff, M. L., Stephens, P. J., Money, J. A case of autoerotic asphyxia associated with multiplex paraphilia. Am. J. Forensic Med. Pathol. 12:64–73, 1991.

226. Byard, R. W., Bramwell, N. H. Autoerotic death. A definition. Am. J. Forensic Med. Pathol. 12:74–76, 1991.

227. Hazelwood, R. R., Burgess, A. W., Groth, A. N. Death during dangerous autoerotic practice. Soc. Sci Med [E] 15:129–133, 1981.

228. Behrendt, N., Modvig, J. The lethal paraphiliac syndrome. Accidental autoerotic deaths in Denmark 1933–1990. Am. J. Forensic Med. Pathol. 16:232–237, 1995.

229. Uva, J. L. Review: autoerotic asphyxiation in the United States. J. Forensic Sci. 40:574–581, 1995.

230. Blanchard, R., Hucker, S. J. Age, transvestism, bondage, and concurrent paraphilic activities in 117 fatal cases of autoerotic asphyxia. Br. J. Psychiatry 159:371–377, 1991.

231. Diamond, M., Innala, S. M., Ernulf, K. E. Asphyxiophilia and autoerotic death. Hawaii Med. J. 49:11–16, 24, 1990.

232. Innala, S. M., Ernulf, K. E. Asphyxiophilia in Scandinavia. Arch. Sex. Behav. 18:181–189, 1989.

233. Resnik, H. L. Erotized repetitive hangings: a form of self-destructive behavior. Am. J. Psychother. 26:4–21, 1972.

234. Tough, S. C., Butt, J. C., Sanders, G. L. Autoerotic asphyxial deaths: analysis of nineteen

fatalities in Alberta, 1978 to 1989. Can. J.Psychiatry 39:157–160, 1994.
235. Shields, L. B., Hunsaker, D. M., Hunsaker, J. C., III. Autoerotic asphyxia: part I. Am. J. Forensic Med. Pathol. 26:45–5, 2005.
236. Sheehan, W., Garfinkel, B. D. Adolescent autoerotic deaths. J. Am. Acad. Child Adolesc. Psychiatry 27:367–370, 1988.
237. Knight, B. Fatal masochism—accident or suicide? Med. Sci. Law 19:118–120, 1979.
238. Burgess, A. W., Hazelwood, R. R. Autoerotic asphyxial deaths and social network response. Am. J. Orthopsychiatry 53:166–170, 1983.
239. Byard, R. W., Hucker, S. J., Hazelwood, R. R. A comparison of typical death scene features in cases of fatal male and autoerotic asphyxia with a review of the literature. Forensic Sci. Int. 48:113–121, 1990.
240. Sinn, L. E. The silver bullet. Am. J. Forensic Med. Pathol. 14:145–147, 1993.
241. Byard, R. W., Hucker, S. J., Hazelwood, R. R. Fatal and near–fatal autoerotic asphyxia episodes in women. Characteristic features based on a review of nine cases. Am. J. Forensic Med. Pathol. 14:70–73, 1993.
242. Johnstone, J. M., Hunt, A. C., Ward, E. M. Plastic–bag asphyxia in adults. Br. Med. J. 5214:1714–1715, 1960.
243. Breitmeier, D., Mansouri, F., Albrecht, K., Bohm, U., Troger, H. D., Kleemann, W. J. Accidental autoerotic deaths between 1978 and 1997. Institute of Legal Medicine, Medical School Hannover. Forensic Sci. Int. 137:41–44, 2003.
244. Eckert, W. G., Katchis, S., Donovan, W. The pathology and medicolegal aspects of sexual activity. Am. J. Forensic Med. Pathol. 12:3–15, 1991.
245. Ikeda, N., Harada, A., Umetsu, K., Suzuki, T. A case of fatal suffocation during an unusual auto–erotic practice. Med. Sci. Law 28:131–134, 1988.
246. Madea, B. Death in a head–down position. Forensic Sci. Int. 61:119–132, 1993.
247. Shields, L. B., Hunsaker, D. M., Hunsaker, J. C., III, Wetli, C. V., Hutchins, K. D., Holmes, R. M. Atypical autoerotic death: part II. Am. J. Forensic Med. Pathol. 26:53–62, 2005.
248. Breitmeier, D., Passie, T., Mansouri, F., Albrecht, K., Kleemann, W. J. Autoerotic accident associated with self–applied ketamine. Int. J. Legal Med. 116:113–116, 2002.
249. Litman, R. E., Swearingen, C. Bondage and suicide. Arch. Gen. Psychiatry 27:80–85, 1972.
250. Cooke, C. T., Cadden, G. A., Margolius, K. A. Autoerotic deaths: four cases. Pathology 26:276–280, 1994.
251. Burgess, A. W., Hazelwood, R. R. Autoerotic asphyxial deaths and social network

response. Am. J. Orthopsychiatry 53:166–170, 1983.

252. Byard, R. W., Bramwell, N. H. Autoerotic death in females. An underdiagnosed syndrome? Am. J. Forensic Med. Pathol. 9:252–254, 1988.

253. Hazelwood, R. R., Dietz, P. E., Burgess, A. W. Sexual fatalities: behavioral reconstruction in equivocal cases. J. Forensic Sci. 27:763–773, 1982.

254. Burch, P. M., Case, M. E., Turgeon, R. Sexual asphyxiation: an unusual case involving four male adolescents. J. Forensic Sci. 40:490–491, 1995.

255. Thibault, R., Spencer, J. D., Bishop, J. W., Hibler, N. S. An unusual autoerotic death: asphyxia with an abdominal ligature. J. Forensic Sci. 29:679–684, 1984.

256. Minyard, F. Wrapped to death. Unusual autoerotic death. Am. J. Forensic Med. Pathol. 6:151–152, 1985.

257. Jones, L. S., Wyatt, J. P., Busuttil, A. Plastic bag asphyxia in southeast Scotland. Am. J. Forensic Med. Pathol. 21:401–405, 2000.

258. O'Halloran, R. L., Dietz, P. E. Autoerotic fatalities with power hydraulics. J. Forensic Sci. 38:359–364, 1993.

259. Rupp, J. C. The love bug. J. Forensic Sci. 18:259–262, 1973.

260. Sivaloganathan, S. Aqua–eroticum—a case of auto–erotic drowning. Med. Sci. Law 24: 300–302, 1984.

261. Leadbeatter, S. Dental anesthetic death. An unusual autoerotic episode. Am. J. Forensic Med. Pathol. 9:60–63, 1988.

262. Rosenblum, S., Faber, M. M. The adolescent sexual asphyxia syndrome. J. Am. Acad. Child Psychiatry 18:546–558, 1979.

263. Gosink, P. D., Jumbelic, M. I. Autoerotic asphyxiation in a female. Am. J. Forensic Med. Pathol. 21:114–118, 2000.

264. Sass, F. A. Sexual asphyxia in the female. J. Forensic Sci. 20:181–185, 1975.

265. Danto, B. L. A case of female autoerotic death. Am. J. Forensic Med. Pathol. 1:117–121, 1980.

266. Hiss, J., Rosenberg, S. B., Adelson, L. "Swinging in the park". An investigation of an autoerotic death. Am. J. Forensic Med. Pathol. 6:250–255, 1985.

267. Byard, R. W., Botterill, P. Autoerotic asphyxial death—accident or suicide? Am. J. Forensic Med. Pathol. 19:377–380, 1998.

268. McLennan, J. J., Sekula–Perlman, A., Lippstone, M. B., Callery, R. T. Propane–associated autoerotic fatalities. Am. J. Forensic Med. Pathol. 19:381–386, 1998.

269. Downs, J. C., Conradi, S. E., Nichols, C. A. Suicide by environmental hypoxia (forced depletion of oxygen). Am. J. Forensic Med. Pathol. 15:216–223, 1994.

270. Henry, R. I. Suicide by proxy: a case report of juvenile autoerotic sexual asphyxia disguised as suicide. A common occurrence? J. Clin. Forensic Med. 3:55–56, 1996.
271. Isenschmid, D. S., Cassin, B. J., Hepler, B. R., Kanluen, S. Tetrachloroethylene intoxication in an autoerotic fatality. J. Forensic Sci. 43:231–234, 1998.
272. Emson, H. E. Accidental hanging in autoeroticism. An unusual case occurring outdoors. Am. J. Forensic Med. Pathol. 4:337–340, 1983.
273. Gowitt, G. T., Hanzlick, R. L. Atypical autoerotic deaths. Am. J. Forensic Med. Pathol. 13:115–119, 1992.
274. Eriksson, A., Gezelius, C., Bring, G. Rolled up to death. An unusual autoerotic fatality. Am. J. Forensic Med. Pathol. 8:263–265, 1987.
275. O'Halloran, R. L., Lovell, F. W. Autoerotic asphyxial death following television broadcast. J. Forensic Sci. 33:1491–1492, 1988.
276. Imami, R. H., Kemal, M. Vacuum cleaner use in autoerotic death. Am. J. Forensic Med. Pathol. 9:246–248, 1988.
277. Baik, S. O., Uku, J. M. Ligature strangulation of a woman during sadomasochistic sexual activity. Am. J. Forensic Med. Pathol. 9:249–251, 1988.
278. Dietz, P. E., Harry, B., Hazelwood, R. R. Detective magazines: pornography for the sexual sadist? J. Forensic Sci. 31:197–211, 1986.
279. Wesselius, C. L., Bally, R. A male with autoerotic asphyxia syndrome. Am. J. Forensic Med. Pathol. 4:341–344, 1983.
280. Dietz, P. E., Evans, B. Pornographic imagery and prevalence of paraphilia. Am. J. Psychiatry 139:1493–1495, 1982.
281. Bell, M. D., Tate, L. G., Wright, R. K. Sexual asphyxia in siblings. Am. J. Forensic Med. Pathol. 12:77–79, 1991.
282. Tournel, G., Hubert, N., Rouge, C., Hedouin, V., Gosset, D. Complete autoerotic asphyxiation: suicide or accident? Am. J. Forensic Med. Pathol. 22:180–183, 2001.
283. Byard, R. W., Eitzen, D. A., James, R. Unusual fatal mechanisms in nonasphyxial autoerotic death. Am. J. Forensic Med. Pathol. 21:65–68, 2000.
284. Eckert, W. G., Katchis, S. Anorectal trauma. Medicolegal and forensic aspects. Am. J. Forensic Med. Pathol. 10:3–9, 1989.
285. Carr, A. C., Shankel, L. W. Transvestism and hanging episodes in a male adolescent. Psychiatr. Q. 30:478–493, 1956.
286. Tan, C. T., Chao, T. C. A case of fatal electrocution during an unusual autoerotic practice. Med. Sci. Law 23:92–95, 1983.
287. Cairns, F. J., Rainer, S. P. Death from electrocution during auto–erotic procedures. N. Z.

288. Sivaloganathan, S. Curiosum eroticum—a case of fatal electrocution during auto–erotic practice. Med. Sci. Law 21:47–50, 1981.
289. Klintschar, M., Grabuschnigg, P., Beham, A. Death from electrocution during autoerotic practice: case report and review of the literature. Am. J. Forensic Med. Pathol. 19:190–193, 1998.
290. Cordner, S. M. An unusual case of sudden death associated with masturbation. Med. Sci. Law 23:54–56, 1983.
291. Chadly, A., Marc, B., Barres, D., Durigon, M. Suicide by nitrous oxide poisoning. Am. J. Forensic Med. Pathol. 10:330–331, 1989.
292. Sivaloganathan, S. Catheteroticum. Fatal late complication following autoerotic practice. Am. J. Forensic Med. Pathol. 6:340–342, 1985.
293. Ditto, E. W., III. Electrocution during sexual activity. Am. J. Forensic Med. Pathol. 2:271–272, 1981.
294. Schott, J. C., Davis, G. J., Hunsaker, J. C., III. Accidental electrocution during autoeroticism: a shocking case. Am. J. Forensic Med. Pathol. 24:92–95, 2003.
295. Shook, L. L., Whittle, R., Rose, E. F. Rectal fist insertion. An unusual form of sexual behavior. Am. J. Forensic Med. Pathol. 6:319–324, 1985.
296. Avis, S. P. An unusual suicide. The importance of the scene investigation. Am. J. Forensic Med. Pathol. 14:148–150, 1993.
297. Bartholomew, S. E., Macarthur, B. A. The continuing enigma of sudden infant death 1882–91–1977–86. Scott. Med. J. 32:131–132, 1987.
298. Luke, J. L. Sleeping arrangements of sudden infant death syndrome victims in the District of Columbia—a preliminary report. J. Forensic Sci. 23:379–383, 1978.
299. Blair, P. S., Fleming, P. J., Smith, I. J., et al. Babies sleeping with parents: case–control study of factors influencing the risk of the sudden infant death syndrome. CESDI SUDI research group. BMJ 319:1457–1461, 1999.
300. Rosenberg, K. D. Sudden infant death syndrome and co–sleeping. Arch. Pediatr. Adolesc. Med. 154:529–530, 2000.
301. McKenna, J. J., Gartner, L. M. Sleep location and suffocation: how good is the evidence? Pediatrics 105:917–919, 2000.
302. Nakamura, S., Wind, M., Danello, M. A. Review of hazards associated with children placed in adult beds. Arch. Pediatr. Adolesc. Med. 153:1019–1023, 1999.
303. Byard, R. W., Beal, S., Blackbourne, B., Nadeau, J. M., Krous, H. F. Specific dangers associated with infants sleeping on sofas. J. Paediatr. Child Health 37:476–478, 2001.

304. Thach, B. T. Sudden infant death syndrome: old causes rediscovered? N. Engl. J. Med. 315:126–128, 1986.

305. Norvenius, S. G. Sudden infant death syndrome in Sweden in 1973–1977 and 1979. Acta Paediatr. Scand. Suppl. 333:1–138, 1987.

306. Francisco, J. T. Smothering in infancy: its relationship to the "crib death syndrome." South. Med. J. 63:1110–1114, 1970.

307. Bullock, M. J., Diniz, D. Suffocation using plastic bags: a retrospective study of suicides in Ontario, Canada. J. Forensic Sci. 45:608–613, 2000.

308. Perez Martinez, A. L., Chui, P., Cameron, J. M. Plastic bag suffocation. Med. Sci. Law 33:71–75, 1993.

309. Haddix, T. L., Harruff, R. C., Reay, D. T., Haglund, W. D. Asphyxial suicides using plastic bags. Am. J. Forensic Med. Pathol. 17:308–311, 1996.

310. Marzuk, P. M., Tardiff, K., Hirsch, C. S., et al. Increase in suicide by asphyxiation in New York City after the publication of Final Exit. N. Engl. J. Med. 329:1508–1510, 1993.

311. Fonseca, C. A., Auerbach, D. S., Suarez, R. V. The forensic investigation of propane gas asphyxiation. Am. J. Forensic Med. Pathol. 23:167–169, 2002.

312. Ogden, R. D., Wooten, R. H. Asphyxial suicide with helium and a plastic bag. Am. J. Forensic Med. Pathol. 23:234–237, 2002.

313. Winek, C. L., Collom, W. D., Wecht, C. H. Suicide with plastic bag and ethyl ether. Lancet 1:365, 1970.

314. Avis, S. P., Archibald, J. T. Asphyxial suicide by propane inhalation and plastic bag suffocation. J. Forensic Sci. 39:253–256, 1994.

315. Anderson, H. R., Macnair, R. S., Ramsey, J. D. Deaths from abuse of volatile substances: a national epidemiological study. Br. Med. J. Clin. Res. Ed. 290:304–307, 1985.

316. Tsoukali, H., Dimitriou, A., Vassiliades, N. Death during deliberate propane inhalation. Forensic Sci. Int. 93:1–4, 1998.

317. Crawford, W. V. Death due to fluorocarbon inhalation. South. Med. J. 69:506–507, 1976.

318. King, G. S., Smialek, J. E., Troutman, W. G. Sudden death in adolescents resulting from the inhalation of typewriter correction fluid. JAMA 253:1604–1606, 1985.

319. Feigin, G. Suicide and meningioma. Am. J. Forensic Med. Pathol. 9:334–335, 1988.

320. Hiss, J., Kahana, T., Arensburg, B. Suicidal asphyxia by gas mask. Am. J. Forensic Med. Pathol. 15:213–215, 1994.

321. Howard, J. D. Suffocation from use of modified gas mask. Am. J. Forensic Med. Pathol. 16:140–141, 1995.

322. Gallagher, K. E., Smith, D. M., Mellen, P. F. Suicidal asphyxiation by using pure helium

gas: case report, review, and discussion of the influence of the internet. Am. J. Forensic Med. Pathol. 24:361–363, 2003.

323. Emery, J. L., Thornton, J. A. Effects of obstruction to respiration in infants, with particular reference to mattresses, pillows, and their coverings. Br. Med. J. 3:209–213, 1968.

324. Moore, L., Bourne, A. J., Beal, S., Collett, M., Byard, R. W. Unexpected infant death in association with suspended rocking cradles. Am. J. Forensic Med. Pathol. 16:177–180, 1995.

325. Gilbert–Barness, E., Emery, J. L. Deaths of infants on polystyrene–filled beanbags. Am. J. Forensic Med. Pathol. 17:202–206, 1996.

326. Bolton, D. P., Cross, K. W., McKettrick, A. C. Are babies in carry cots at risk from CO_2 accumulation? Br. Med. J. 4:80–81, 1972.

327. Bolton, D. P., Taylor, B. J., Campbell, A. J., Galland, B. C., Cresswell, C. Rebreathing expired gases from bedding: a cause of cot death? Arch. Dis. Child. 69:187–190, 1993.

328. Swift, P. G., Emery, J. L. Clinical observations on response to nasal occlusion in infancy. Arch. Dis. Child. 48:947–951, 1973.

329. Stanton, A. N. Sudden infant death. Overheating and cot death. Lancet 2:1199–1201, 1984.

330. Fleming, P. J., Levine, M. R., Azaz, Y., Wigfield, R., Stewart, A. J. Interactions between thermoregulation and the control of respiration in infants: possible relationship to sudden infant death. Acta Paediatr. Suppl. 82 Suppl 389:57–59, 1993.

331. Imami, R. H., Kemal, M. Propane asphyxiation. Am. J. Forensic Med. Pathol. 7:76–77, 1986.

332. Di Nunno, N., Vacca, M., Costantinides, F., Di Nunno, C. Death following atypical compression of the neck. Am. J. Forensic Med. Pathol. 24:364–368, 2003.

333. Harris, C. S., Baker, S. P., Smith, G. A., Harris, R. M. Childhood asphyxiation by food. A national analysis and overview. JAMA 251:2231–2235, 1984.

334. Bhana, B. D., Gunaselvam, J. G., Dada, M. A. Mechanical airway obstruction caused by accidental aspiration of part of a ballpoint pen. Am. J. Forensic Med. Pathol. 21:362–365, 2000.

335. Haugen, R. K. The cafe coronary: Sudden deaths in restaurants. JAMA 186:142–143, 1963.

336. Blazer, S., Naveh, Y., Friedman, A. Foreign body in the airway. A review of 200 cases. Am. J. Dis. Child. 134:68–71, 1980.

337. Aytac, A., Yurdakul, Y., Ikizler, C., Olga, R., Saylam, A. Inhalation of foreign bodies in children. Report of 500 cases. J. Thorac. Cardiovasc. Surg. 74:145–151, 1977.

338. Taff, M. L., Boglioli, L. R. Homicidal traumatic asphyxia associated with pebble impaction of the upper airway. Am. J. Forensic Med. Pathol. 13:271–274, 1992.

339. Downing, S. E., Lee, J. C. Laryngeal chemosensitivity: a possible mechanism for sudden infant death. Pediatrics 55:640–649, 1975.

340. Sheahan, K., Page, D. V., Kemper, T., Suarez, R. Childhood sudden death secondary to accidental aspiration of black pepper. Am. J. Forensic Med. Pathol. 9:51–53, 1988.

341. Limper, A. H., Prakash, U. B. Tracheobronchial foreign bodies in adults. Ann. Intern. Med. 112:604–609, 1990.

342. McGuirt, W. F., Holmes, K. D., Feehs, R., Browne, J. D. Tracheobronchial foreign bodies. Laryngoscope 98:615–618, 1988.

343. Mellen, P. F., Golle, M. F., Jr., Smialek, J. E. Fatal hot coffee scald of the larynx. Case report. Am. J. Forensic Med. Pathol. 16:117–119, 1995.

344. Lifschultz, B. D., Donoghue, E. R. Deaths due to foreign body aspiration in children: the continuing hazard of toy balloons. J. Forensic Sci. 41:247–251, 1996.

345. Byard, R. W. Coprophagic cafe coronary. Am. J. Forensic Med. Pathol. 22:96–99, 2001.

346. Rimell, F. L., Thome, A., Jr., Stool, S., et al. Characteristics of objects that cause choking in children. JAMA 274:1763–1766, 1995.

347. Byard, R. W. Unexpected death due to acute airway obstruction in daycare centers. Pediatrics 94:113–114, 1994.

348. Altmann, A. E., Ozanne–Smith, J. Non–fatal asphyxiation and foreign body ingestion in children 0–14 years. Inj. Prev. 3:176–182, 1997.

349. Mittleman, R. E. Fatal choking in infants and children. Am. J. Forensic Med. Pathol. 5:201–210, 1984.

350. Hunsaker, D. M., Hunsaker, J. C., III. Therapy–related cafe coronary deaths: two case reports of rare asphyxial deaths in patients under supervised care. Am. J. Forensic Med. Pathol. 23:149–154, 2002.

351. Mihalakis, I. Asphyxia from pacifier. Md., State Med., J., 20:53–54, 1971.

352. Fleming, P. J., Blair, P. S., Pollard, K., et al. Pacifier use and sudden infant death syndrome: results from the CESDI/SUDI case control study. CESDI SUDI Research Team. Arch. Dis. Child. 81:112–116, 1999.

353. Heimlich, H. J. The Heimlich maneuver: prevention of death from choking on foreign bodies. J. Occup. Med. 19:208–210, 1977.

354. Pontoppidan, H., Beecher, H. K. Progressive loss of protective reflexes in the airway with the advance of age. JAMA 174:2209–2213, 1960.

355. Mittleman, R. E., Wetli, C. V. The fatal cafe coronary. Foreign–body airway obstruction.

JAMA 247:1285–1288, 1982.

356. Jacob, B., Huckenbeck, W., Barz, J., Bonte, W. Death, after swallowing and aspiration of a high number of foreign bodies, in a schizophrenic woman. Am. J. Forensic Med. Pathol. 11:331–335, 1990.

357. Leadbeatter, S., Douglas–Jones, A. G. Asphyxiation by glottic impaction of nasal secretions. Am. J. Forensic Med. Pathol. 10:235–238, 1989.

358. Gelperin, A. Sudden death in an elderly population from aspiration of food. J, Am. Geriatr, Soc. 22:135–136, 1974.

359. Jones, T. M., Luke, L. C. Life threatening airway obstruction: a hazard of concealed eating disorders. J. Accid. Emerg. Med. 15:332–333, 1998.

360. Adelman, H. C. Asphyxial deaths as a result of aspiration of dental appliances: a report of three cases. J. Forensic Sci. 33:389–395, 1988.

361. Steffee, C. H., Lantz, P. E., Flannagan, L. M., Thompson, R. L., Jason, D. R. Oleoresin capsicum (pepper) spray and "in–custody deaths." Am. J. Forensic Med. Pathol. 16:185–192, 1995.

362. Winograd, H. L. Acute croup in an older child. An unusual toxic origin. Clin. Pediatr. Phila. 16:884–887, 1977.

363. Steele, A. A. Suicidal death by aspiration of talcum powder. Am. J. Forensic Med. Pathol. 11:316–318, 1990.

364. Fyfe, B., Mittleman, R. E. Hypopharyngeal lipoma as a cause for sudden asphyxial death. Am. J. Forensic Med. Pathol. 12:82–84, 1991.

365. Taff, M. L., Schwartz, I. S., Boglioli, L. R. Sudden asphyxial death due to a prolapsed esophageal fibrolipoma. Am. J. Forensic Med. Pathol. 12:85–88, 1991.

366. Allen, M. S., Jr., Talbot, W. H. Sudden death due to regurgitation of a pedunculated esophageal lipoma. J. Thorac. Cardiovasc. Surg. 54:756–758, 1967.

367. Cochet, B., Hohl, P., Sans, M., Cox, J. N. Asphyxia caused by laryngeal impaction of an esophageal polyp. Arch. Otolaryngol. 106:176–178, 1980.

368. Sperry, K. Lethal asphyxiating juvenile laryngeal papillomatosis. A case report with human papillomavirus in situ hybridization analysis. Am. J. Forensic Med. Pathol. 15:146–150, 1994.

369. Johnson, C. P., Burns, J. Papillary hyperplasia of the lingual tonsil and sudden death in epilepsy. Am. J. Forensic Med. Pathol. 13:335–337, 1992.

370. Guarisco, J. L., Littlewood, S. C., Butcher, R. B., III. Severe upper airway obstruction in children secondary to lingual tonsil hypertrophy. Ann. Otol. Rhinol. Laryngol. 99:621–624, 1990.

371. Cohle, S. D., Jones, D. H., Puri, S. Lingual tonsillar hypertrophy causing failed intubation and cerebral anoxia. Am. J. Forensic Med. Pathol. 14:158–161, 1993.
372. Boglioli, L. R., Taff, M. L. Sudden asphyxial death complicating infectious mononucleosis. Am. J. Forensic Med. Pathol. 19:174–177, 1998.
373. Fonseca, C. A., Suarez, R. V. Plasma cell granuloma of the larynx as a cause of sudden asphyxial death. Am. J. Forensic Med. Pathol. 16:243–245, 1995.
374. Olsen, K. D., Suh, K. W., Staats, B. A. Surgically correctable causes of sleep apnea syndrome. Otolaryngol. Head Neck Surg. 89:726–731, 1981.
375. Robinson, R. W., White, D. P., Zwillich, C. W. Moderate alcohol ingestion increases upper airway resistance in normal subjects. Am. Rev. Respir. Dis. 132:1238–1241, 1985.
376. Krol, R. C., Knuth, S. L., Bartlett, D., Jr. Selective reduction of genioglossal muscle activity by alcohol in normal human subjects. Am. Rev. Respir. Dis. 129:247–250, 1984.
377. Pervez, N. K., Aisen, P. S., Bleiweiss, I. J., Brady, B., Winters, S. Occult aspiration of a nut in an elderly patient: a case report. Am. J. Forensic Med. Pathol. 9:163–165, 1988.
378. Rogers, C., Chang, B., Shibuya, R. A coin in the airway. Am. J. Forensic Med. Pathol. 15:91–92, 1994.
379. Blumberg, J. M., Johnston, E. H. The forensic pathologist and the unsuspected foreign body. J. Forensic Sci. 8:231–249, 1963.
380. Tamura, N., Nakajima, T., Matsumoto, S., Ohyama, T., Ohashi, Y. Foreign bodies of dental origin in the air and food passages. Int. J. Oral Maxillofac. Surg. 15:739–751, 1986.
381. Sherman, B. M., Karliner, J. S., Kikkawa, Y., Oka, M., Goldin, R. Fatal traumatic ingestion of a radiolucent dental prosthesis. N. Engl. J. Med. 279:1275–1276, 1968.
382. Hazelrigg, C. O. Ingestion of mandibular complete denture. J. Am. Dent. Assoc. 108:209, 1984.
383. Jumbelic, M. I. Airway obstruction by a ball. J. Forensic Sci. 44:1079–1081, 1999.
384. Ryan, C. A., Yacoub, W., Paton, T., Avard, D. Childhood deaths from toy balloons. Am. J. Dis. Child. 144:1221–1224, 1990.
385. Anas, N. G., Perkin, R. M. Aspiration of a balloon by a 3–month–old infant. JAMA 250:385–386, 1983.
386. Deidiker, R. Return of the killer fish: accidental choking death on a bluegill Lepomis macrochirus. Am. J. Forensic Med. Pathol. 23:197–198, 2002.
387. Kulick, R. M., Selbst, S. M., Baker, M. D., Woodward, G. A. Thermal epiglottitis after swallowing hot beverages. Pediatrics 81:441–444, 1988.
388. Jung, R. C., Gottlieb, L. S. Respiratory tract burns after aspiration of hot coffee. Chest

72:125–128, 1977.

389. Inayama, Y., Udaka, N., Amano, T., et al. Fatal aspiration of sardine fry in a patient with lung cancer. J. Forensic Sci. 45:478–482, 2000.

390. Simson, L. R., Jr. Sudden death while attempting to conceal illegal drugs: laryngeal obstruction by a package of heroin. J. Forensic Sci. 21:378–380, 1976.

391. Peeler, M. B., Riley, H. D., Jr. Cardiac tamponade due to swallowed foreign body. AMA J. Dis. Child. 93:308–312, 1957.

392. Byard, R. W., Moore, L., Bourne, A. J. Sudden and unexpected death—a late effect of occult intraesophageal foreign body. Pediatr. Pathol. 10:837–841, 1990.

393. Russo, S. S., Taff, M. L., Ratanaproeksa, O., Spitz, W. U. Sudden death resulting from chicken bone perforation of the esophagus. Am. J. Forensic Med. Pathol. 7:263–265, 1986.

394. Norman, M. G., Cass, E. Cardiac tamponade resulting from a swallowed safety pin. Pediatrics 48:832–833, 1971.

395. Marik, P. E. Aspiration pneumonitis and aspiration pneumonia. N. Engl. J. Med. 344:665–671, 2001.

396. Knight, B. H. The significance of the postmortem discovery of gastric contents in the air passages. Forensic Sci. 6:229–234, 1975.

397. Gardner, A. M. Aspiration of food and vomit. Q. J. Med. 27:227–242, 1958.

398. Wynne, J. W., Modell, J. H. Respiratory aspiration of stomach contents. Ann. Intern. Med. 87:466–474, 1977.

399. Gaultier, C. L. Interference between gastroesophageal reflux and sleep in near miss SIDS. Clin. Rev. Allergy 8:395–401, 1990.

400. Anonymous. American Academy of Pediatrics AAP Task Force on Infant Positioning and SIDS: Positioning and SIDS. Pediatrics 89:1120–1126, 1992.

401. Van Dyke, J. J., Lake, K. B. Survival after asphyxia secondary to gravel aspiration. Arch. Intern. Med. 136:471–473, 1976.

402. Avital, A., Springer, C., Mogle, P., Godfrey, S. Successful treatment after 'drowning' in sand. Arch. Dis. Child. 64:615–616, 1989.

403. Bergeson, P. S., Hinchcliffe, W. A., Crawford, R. F., Sorenson, M. J., Trump, D. S. Asphyxia secondary to massive dirt aspiration. J. Pediatr. 92:506–507, 1978.

404. Bender, E. M., Moore, E. E., Kashuk, J. L., Hopeman, A. R. Conservative management of sand aspiration: case report. Mil. Med. 149:98–99, 1984.

405. Adelson, L. Homicide by pepper. J. Forensic Sci. 88:391–395, 1964.

406. Cohle, S. D., Trestrail, J. D., III, Graham, M. A., Oxley, D. W, Walp, B., Jachimczyk, J.

Fatal pepper aspiration. Am. J. Dis. Child. 142:633−636, 1988.

407. Flintoff, W. M., Jr., Poushter, D. L. Aspiration of black pepper. A case report. Arch. Otolaryngol. 100:375−376, 1974.

408. Molnar, J. J., Nathenson, G., Edberg, S. Fatal aspiration of talcum powder by a child, Report of a case. N. Engl. J. Med. 266:36−37, 1962.

409. Brouillette, F., Weber, M. L. Massive aspiration of talcum powder by an infant. Can. Med. Assoc. J. 119:354−355, 1978.

410. Mofenson, H. C., Greensher, J., DiTomasso, A., Okun, S. Baby powder—a hazard! Pediatrics 68:265−266, 1981.

411. Banerjee, A., Rao, K. S., Khanna, S. K., et al. Laryngo−tracheo−bronchial foreign bodies in children. J. Laryngol. Otol. 102:1029−1032, 1988.

412. Gay, B. B., Jr., Atkinson, G. O., Vanderzalm, T., Harmon, J. D., Porubsky, E. S. Subglottic foreign bodies in pediatric patients. Am. J. Dis. Child. 140:165−168, 1986.

413. Weissberg, D., Schwartz, I. Foreign bodies in the tracheobronchial tree. Chest 91:730−733, 1987.

414. Wolkove, N., Kreisman, H., Cohen, C., Frank, H. Occult foreign−body aspiration in adults. JAMA 248:1350−1352, 1982.

415. Shkrum, M. J., Johnston, K. A. Fire and suicide: a three−year study of self−immolation deaths. J. Forensic Sci. 37:208−221, 1992.

416. Belviso, M., De Donno, A., Vitale, L., Introna, F., Jr. Positional asphyxia: reflection on 2 cases. Am. J. Forensic Med. Pathol. 24:292−297, 2003.

417. Reay, D. T., Fligner, C. L., Stilwell, A. D., Arnold, J. Positional asphyxia during law enforcement transport. Am. J. Forensic Med. Pathol. 13:90−97, 1992.

418. Chan, T. C., Vilke, G. M., Neuman, T. Reexamination of custody restraint position and positional asphyxia. Am. J. Forensic Med. Pathol. 19:201−205, 1998.

419. Purdue, B. An unusual accidental death from reverse suspension. Am. J. Forensic Med. Pathol. 13:108−111, 1992.

420. Marshall, T. K. Inverted suspension. Med. Sci. Law 8:49−50, 1968.

421. Busuttil, A., Obafunwa, J. O. Recreational abdominal suspension: a fatal practice. A case report. Am. J. Forensic Med. Pathol. 14:141−144, 1993.

422. Vega, R. S., Adams, V. I. Suffocation in motor vehicle crashes. Am. J. Forensic Med. Pathol. 25:101−107, 2004.

423. Sharp, J. T., Goldberg, N. B., Druz, W. S., Danon, J. Relative contributions of rib cage and abdomen to breathing in normal subjects. J. Appl. Physiol. 39:608−618, 1975.

424. Ward, M., Macklem, P. T. The act of breathing and how it fails. Chest 97:36S−39S, 1990.

425. Roussos, C. Function and fatigue of respiratory muscles. Chest 88:124S–132S, 1985.

426. Roussos, C., Macklem, P. T. The respiratory muscles. N. Engl. J. Med. 307:786–797, 1982.

427. Uchigasaki, S., Takahashi, H., Suzuki, T. An experimental study of death in a reverse suspension. Am. J. Forensic Med. Pathol. 20:116–119, 1999.

428. Pollanen, M. S., Chiasson, D. A., Cairns, J. T., Young, J. G. Unexpected death related to restraint for excited delirium: a retrospective study of deaths in police custody and in the community. CMAJ 158:1603–1607, 1998.

429. O'Halloran, R. L., Lewman, L. V. Restraint asphyxiation in excited delirium. Am. J. Forensic Med. Pathol. 14:289–295, 1993.

430. Glatter, K., Karch, S. B. Positional asphyxia: inadequate oxygen, or inadequate theory? Forensic Sci. Int. 141:201–202, 2004.

431. O'Halloran, R. L., Frank, J. G. Asphyxial death during prone restraint revisited: a report of 21 cases. Am. J. Forensic Med. Pathol. 21:39–52, 2000.

432. Karch, S. B., Wetli, C. V. Agitated delirium versus positional asphyxia. Ann. Emerg. Med. 26:760–761, 1995.

433. Wetli, C. V., Mash, D., Karch, S. B. Cocaine–associated agitated delirium and the neuroleptic malignant syndrome. Am. J. Emerg. Med. 14:425–428, 1996.

434. Karch, S. B., Stephens, B. G. Acute excited states and sudden death. Acute excited states are not caused by high blood concentrations of cocaine. BMJ 316:1171, 1998.

435. Karch, S. B. Cardiac arrest in cocaine users. Am. J. Emerg. Med. 14:79–81, 1996.

436. Reay, D. T., Howard, J. D. Restraint position and positional asphyxia. Am. J. Forensic Med. Pathol. 20:300–301, 1999.

437. Chan, T. C., Vilke, G. M., Neuman, T. Restraint position and positional asphyxia. Am. J. Forensic Med. Pathol. 21:93, 2000.

438. Chan, T. C., Neuman, T., Clausen, J., Eisele, J., Vilke, G. M. Weight force during prone restraint and respiratory function. Am. J. Forensic Med. Pathol. 25:185–189, 2004.

439. Chan, T. C., Vilke, G. M., Neuman, T., Clausen, J. L. Restraint position and positional asphyxia. Ann. Emerg. Med. 30:578–586, 1997.

439a. Park, K. S., Korn, C. S., Henderson, S. O. Agitated delirium and sudden death: two case reports. Prehosp. Emerg. Care 5:214–216, 2001.

439b. Reay, D. T., Howard, J. D., Fligner, C. L., Ward, R. J. Effects of positional restraint on oxygen saturation and heart rate following exercise. Am. J. Forensic Med. Pathol. 9:16–18, 1988.

439c. Koscove, E. M. The Taser weapon: a new emergency medicine problem. Ann. Emerg.

Med. 14:1205–1208, 1985.

439d. Bleetman, A., Steyn, R., Lee, C. Introduction of the Taser into British policing. Implications for UK emergency departments: an overview of electronic weaponry. Emerg. Med. J. 21:136–140, 2004.

439e. Jenkinson, E., Neeson, C., Bleetman, A. The relative risk of police use–of–force options: evaluating the potential for deployment of electronic weaponry. J. Clin. Forensic Med. 2006(epub ahead of print).

439f. Fish, R. M., Geddes, L. A. Effects of stun guns and tasers. Lancet 358:687–688, 2001.

439g. Kornblum, R. N., Reddy, S. K. Effects of the Taser in fatalities involving police confrontation. J. Forensic Sci. 36:434–438, 1991.

439h. Ordog, G. J., Wasserberger, J., Schlater, T., Balasubramanium, S. Electronic gun (Taser) injuries. Ann. Emerg. Med. 16:73–78, 1987.

439i. Kim, P. J., Franklin, W. H. Ventricular fibrillation after stun–gun discharge. N. Engl. J. Med. 353:958–959, 2005.

439j. Haegeli, L. M., Sterns, L. D., Adam, D. C., Leather, R. A. Effect of a Taser shot to the chest of a patient with an implantable defibrillator. Heart Rhythm. 3:339–341, 2006.

439k. McDaniel, W. C., Stratbucker, R. A., Nerheim, M., Brewer, J. E. Cardiac safety of neuromuscular incapacitating defensive devices. Pacing Clin. Electrophysiol. 28:S284–S287, 2005.

439l. Ho, J. D., Miner, J. R., Lakireddy, D. R., Bultman, L. L., Heegaard, W. G. Cardiovascular and physiologic effects of conducted electrical weapon discharge in resting adults. Acad. Emerg. Med. 2006, in press.

439m. Allen, T. B. Discussion of "Effects of the taser in fatalities involving police confrontation."J. Forensic Sci. 37:956–958, 1992.

440. Wilkins, R. W., Bradley, S. E., Friedland, C. K. The acute circulatory effects of the headdown position negative G in normal man, with a note on some measures designed to relieve cranial congestion in this position. J. Clin. Invest. 29:940–949, 1950.

441. Fred, H. L., Chandler, F. W. Traumatic asphyxia. Am. J. Med. 29:508–517, 1960.

442. Gill, J. R., Landi, K. Traumatic asphyxial deaths due to an uncontrolled crowd. Am. J. Forensic Med. Pathol. 25:358–361, 2004.

443. Sklar, D. P., Baack, B., McFeeley, P., Osler, T., Marder, E., Demarest, G. Traumatic asphyxia in New Mexico: a five–year experience. Am. J. Emerg. Med. 6:219–223, 1988.

444. Williams, J. S., Minken, S. L., Adams, J. T. Traumatic asphyxia—reappraised. Ann. Surg. 167:384–392, 1968.

445. Dunne, J. R., Shaked, G., Golocovsky, M. Traumatic asphyxia: an indicator of potentially severe injury in trauma. Injury 27:746–749, 1996.
446. Copeland, A. R. Vehicular-related traumatic asphyxial deaths—caveat scrutator. Z. Rechtsmed. 96:17–22, 1986.
447. Staats, P. N., Jumbelic, M. I., Dignan, C. R. Death by compaction in a garbage truck. J. Forensic Sci. 47:1065–1066, 2002.
448. Wolodzko, A. A., Taff, M. L., Ratanaproeska, O., Spitz, W. U. An unusual case of compression asphyxia and smothering. Am. J. Forensic Med. Pathol. 7:354–355, 1986.
449. Hambeck, W., Pueschel, K. Death by railway accident: incidence of traumatic asphyxia. J. Trauma 21:28–31, 1981.
450. Campbell-Hewson, G., Egleston, C. V., Cope, A. R. Traumatic asphyxia in children. J. Accid. Emerg. Med. 14:47–49, 1997.
451. Lupascu, C., Lupascu, C., Beldiman, D. Mechanical asphyxia by three different mechanisms. Leg. Med. (Tokyo) 5:110–111, 2003.
452. Furuya, Y. Experimental traumatic asphyxia (1)—grades of thoracic compression and mortality. Igaku Kenkyu 51:117–119, 1981.
453. Kohr, R. M. Inflicted compressional asphyxia of a child. J. Forensic Sci. 48:1148–1150, 2003.
454. Rosato, R. M., Shapiro, M. J., Keegan, M. J., Connors, R. H., Minor, C. B. Cardiac injury complicating traumatic asphyxia. J. Trauma 31:1387–1389, 1991.
455. Thompson, A., Jr., Illescas, F. F., Chiu, R. C. Why is the lower torso protected in traumatic asphyxia? A new hypothesis. Ann. Thorac. Surg. 47:247–249, 1989.
456. Lee, M. C., Wong, S. S., Chu, J. J., et al. Traumatic asphyxia. Ann. Thorac. Surg. 51:86–88, 1991.
457. Schiowitz, M. F., Litchman, J., Rizzo, T. F. Traumatic asphyxia and blunt cardiac injury: case report and selected review. Am. J. Emerg. Med. 9:325–327, 1991.
458. Cobb N., Etzel, R. A. Unintentional carbon monoxide-related deaths in the United States, 1979 through 1988. JAMA 266:659–663, 1991.
459. Caplan, Y. H., Ottinger, W. E., Park, J., Smith, T. D. Drug and chemical related deaths: incidence in the state of Maryland—1975 to 1980. J. Forensic Sci. 30:1012–1021, 1985.
460. Baselt, R. C. Disposition of Toxic Drugs and Chemicals in Man. Biomedical Publications, Foster City, CA, 2005.
461. Hawkins, M. Carbon monoxide poisoning. Eur. J. Anaesthesiol. 16:585–589, 1999.
462. Stewart, R. D. The effect of carbon monoxide on humans. Annu. Rev. Pharmacol. 15:409–423, 1975.

463. Abelsohn, A., Sanborn, M. D., Jessiman, B. J., Weir, E. Identifying and managing adverse environmental health effects: 6. Carbon monoxide poisoning. CMAJ 166:1685–1690, 2002.
464. Meredith, T., Vale, A. Carbon monoxide poisoning. Br. Med. J. (Clin. Res. Ed.) 296:77–79, 1988.
465. Dolan, M. C. Carbon monoxide poisoning. CMAJ 133:392–399, 1985.
466. Stewart, R. D. Proceedings: The effect of carbon monoxide on humans. J. Occup. Med. 18:304–309, 1976.
467. Hardy, K. R., Thom, S. R. Pathophysiology and treatment of carbon monoxide poisoning. J. Toxicol. Clin. Toxicol. 32:613–629, 1994.
468. Ernst, A., Zibrak, J. D. Carbon monoxide poisoning. N. Engl. J. Med. 339:1603–1608, 1998.
469. Morgan, D. R., Poon, P., Titley, J., Jagger, S. F., Rutty, G. N. Unique case of fatal carbon monoxide poisoning in the absence of a combustible fossil fuel. Am. J. Forensic Med. Pathol. 22:220–224, 2001.
470. Turino, G. M. Effect of carbon monoxide on the cardiorespiratory system. Carbon monoxide toxicity: physiology and biochemistry. Circulation 63:253A–259A, 1981.
471. Urbanetti, J. S. Carbon monoxide poisoning. Prog. Clin. Biol. Res. 51:355–385, 1981.
472. Varon, J., Marik, P. E., Fromm, R. E., Jr., Gueler, A. Carbon monoxide poisoning: a review for clinicians. J. Emerg. Med. 17:87–93, 1999.
473. Prahlow, J. A., Doyle, B. W. A suicide using a homemade carbon monoxid "death machine". Am. J. Forensic Med. Pathol. 26:177–180, 2005.
474. Opeskin, K., Drummer, O. H. Delayed death following carbon monoxide poisoning. A case report. Am. J. Forensic Med. Pathol. 15:36–39, 1994.
475. Weaver, L. K. Carbon monoxide poisoning. Crit. Care Clin. 15:297–317, viii, 1999.
476. Rodkey, F. L., O'Neal, J. D., Collison, H. A., Uddin, D. E. Relative affinity of hemoglobin S and hemoglobin A for carbon monoxide and oxygen. Clin. Chem. 20:83–84, 1974.
477. Fisher, J. Carbon monoxide poisoning: a disease of a thousand faces. Chest 115:322–323, 1999.
478. Lowry, W. T., Juarez, L., Petty, C. S., Roberts, B. Studies of toxic gas production during actual structural fires in the Dallas area. J. Forensic Sci. 30:59–72, 1985.
479. Jaffe, F. A. Pathogenicity of carbon monoxide. Am. J. Forensic Med. Pathol. 18:406–410, 1997.
480. Dominguez, A. M. Problems of carbon monoxide in fires. J. Forensic Sci. 7:379–392,

1962.

481. Chesney, M. L. Carbon monoxide poisoning in the pediatric population. Air. Med. J. 21:10–13, 2002.

482. Goldbaum, L. R., Ramirez, R. G., Absalon, K. B. What is the mechanism of carbon monoxide toxicity? Aviat. Space Environ. Med. 46:1289–1291, 1975.

483. Thom, S. R., Keim, L. W. Carbon monoxide poisoning: a review epidemiology, pathophysiology, clinical findings, and treatment options including hyperbaric oxygen therapy. J. Toxicol. Clin. Toxicol. 27:141–156, 1989.

484. Somogyi, E., Balogh, I., Rubanyi, G., Sotonyi, P., Szegedi, L. New findings concerning the pathogenesis of acute carbon monoxide (CO) poisoning. Am. J. Forensic Med. Pathol. 2:31–39, 1981.

485. Balraj, E. K. Atherosclerotic coronary artery disease and "low" levels of carboxyhemoglobin; report of fatalities and discussion of pathophysiologic mechanisms of death. J. Forensic Sci. 29:1150–1159, 1984.

486. Peterson, J. E., Stewart, R. D. Predicting the carboxyhemoglobin levels resulting from carbon monoxide exposures. J. Appl. Physiol. 39:633–638, 1975.

487. Stewart, R. D., Baretta, E. D., Platte, L. R., et al. Carboxyhemoglobin levels in American blood donors. JAMA 229:1187–1195, 1974.

488. Landers, D. Unsuccessful suicide by carbon monoxide: a secondary benefit of emissions control. West J Med. 135:360–363, 1981.

489. Burney, R. E., Wu, S. C., Nemiroff, M. J. Mass carbon monoxide poisoning: clinical effects and results of treatment in 184 victims. Ann. Emerg. Med. 11:394–399, 1982.

490. Ruszkiewicz, A., de Boer, B., Robertson, S. Unusual presentation of death due to carbon monoxide poisoning. A report of two cases. Am. J. Forensic Med. Pathol. 18:181–184, 1997.

491. Morgen, C., Schramm, J., Kofoed, P., Steensberg,. J, Theilade, P. Automobile exhaust as a means of suicide: an experimental study with a proposed model. J. Forensic Sci. 43:827–836, 1998.

492. Stewart, R. D., Stewart, R. S., Stamm, W., Seelen, R.P. Rapid estimation of carboxyhemoglobin level in fire fighters. JAMA 235:390–392, 1976.

493. Schmunk, G. A., Kaplan, J. A. Asphyxial deaths caused by automobile exhaust inhalation not attributable to carbon monoxide toxicity: study of 2 cases. Am. J. Forensic Med. Pathol. 23:123–126, 2002.

494. Theilade, P. Carbon monoxide poisoning. Five years' experience in a defined population. Am. J. Forensic Med. Pathol. 11:219–225, 1990.

495. Walker, E., Hay, A. Carbon monoxide poisoning. BMJ 319:1082–1083, 1999.
496. Jaffe, N. Cardiac injury and carbon monoxide poisoning. S. Afr. Med. J. 39:611–615, 1965.
497. Morris, R. D., Naumova, E. N. Carbon monoxide and hospital admissions for congestive heart failure: evidence of an increased effect at low temperatures. Environ. Health Perspect. 106:649–653, 1998.
498. Schulte, J. H. Effests of mild carbon monoxide intoxication. Arch. Environ. Health 38:524–530, 1963.
499. Schulte, J. H. Sealed environments in relation to health and disease. Arch. Environ. Health 85:438–452, 1964.
500. Winter, P. M., Miller, J. N. Carbon monoxide poisoning. JAMA 236:1502, 1976.
501. Williams, J., Lewis, R. W., Kealey, G. P. Carbon monoxide poisoning and myocardial ischemia in patients with burns. J. Burn. Care. Rehabil. 13:210–213, 1992.
502. Allred, E. N., Bleecker, E. R., Chaitman, B. R., et al. Effects of carbon monoxide on myocardial ischemia. Environ. Health Perspect. 91:89–132, 1991.
503. Gemelli, F., Cattani, R. Carbon monoxide poisoning in childhood. Br. Med. J. (Clin. Res. Ed.) 291:1197, 1985.
504. Risser, D., Schneider, B. Carbon monoxide–related deaths from 1984 to 1993 in Vienna, Austria. J. Forensic Sci. 40:368–371, 1995.
505. Farmer, R., Rohde, J. Effect of availability and acceptability of lethal instruments on suicide mortality. An analysis of some international data. Acta Psychiatr. Scand. 62:436–446, 1980.
506. McClure, G. M. Suicide in children and adolescents in England and Wales 1960–1990. Br. J. Psychiatry 165:510–514, 1994.
507. Tsunenari, S., Yonemitsu, K., Kanda, M., Yoshida, S. Suicidal carbon monoxide inhalation of exhaust fumes. Investigation of cases. Am. J. Forensic Med. Pathol. 6:233–239, 1985.
508. Atkinson, P., Langlois, N. E., Adam, B. J., Grieve, J. H. Suicide, carbon dioxide, and suffocation. Lancet 344:192–193, 1994.
509. McAuley, F., Wigmore, J. D. Case report: An unusual case of carbon monoxide poisoning. J. Can. Soc. Forensic Sc. 20:83–86, 1987.
510. DiMaio, V. J., Dana, S. E. Deaths caused by carbon monoxide poisoning in an open environment outdoors. J. Forensic Sci. 32:1794–1795, 1987.
511. Pounder, D. J. Changing patterns of male suicide in Scotland. Forensic Sci. Int. 51:79–87, 1991.
512. Burvill, P. W. The changing pattern of suicide by gassing in Australia, 1910–1987: the

role of natural gas and motor vehicles. Acta Psychiatr. Scand. 81:178–184, 1990.

513. Bowen, D. A., Duffy, P., Callear, A., Fitton, J. Carbon monoxide poisoning. Forensic Sci. Int. 41:163–168, 1989.

514. Copeland, A. R. Non–intentional motor vehicle–related carbon monoxide deaths–revisited. Z. Rechtsmed. 96:145–150, 1986.

515. Baker, S. P., Fisher, R. S., Masemore, W. C., Sopher, I. M. Fatal unintentional carbon monoxide poisoning in motor vehicles. Am. J. Public Health 62:1463–1467, 1972.

516. Carson, H. J., Stephens, P. J. Four deaths due to carbon monoxide poisoning in car washes. Am. J. Forensic Med. Pathol. 20:274–276, 1999.

517. Centers for Disease Control and Prevention. Unintentional carbon monoxide poisoning from indoor use of pressure washers—Iowa, January 1992–January 1993. JAMA 270:2034, 2037, 1993.

518. Centers for Disease Control and Prevention. Leads from MMWR. Carbon monoxide intoxication associated with use of a resurfacing machine at an ice–skating rink. JAMA 251:1016, 1984.

519. Ely, E. W., Moorehead, B., Haponik, E. F. Warehouse workers' headache: emergency evaluation and management of 30 patients with carbon monoxide poisoning. Am. J. Med. 98:145–155, 1995.

520. Caplan, Y. H., Thompson, B. C., Levine, B., Masemore, W. Accidental poisonings involving carbon monoxide, heating systems, and confined spaces. J. Forensic Sci. 31:117–121, 1986.

521. Jumbelic, M. I. Open air carbon monoxide poisoning. J. Forensic Sci. 43:228–230, 1998.

522. Centers for Disease Control and Prevention. Carbon monoxide poisonings associated with snow–obstructed vehicle exhaust systems—Philadelphia and New York City, January 1996. JAMA 275:426–427, 1996.

523. Rao, R., Touger, M., Gennis, P., Tyrrell, J., Roche, J., Gallagher, E. J. Epidemic of accidental carbon monoxide poisonings caused by snow–obstructed exhaust systems. Ann. Emerg. Med. 29:290–292, 1997.

524. Silvers, S. M., Hampson, N. B. Carbon monoxide poisoning among recreational boaters. JAMA 274:1614–1616, 1995.

525. Hampson, N. B., Norkool, D. M. Carbon monoxide poisoning in children riding in the back of pickup trucks. JAMA 267:538–540, 1992.

526. Abu–al Ragheb, S. Y., Battah, A. H. Carbon monoxide fatalities in medicolegal autopsies. Med. Sci. Law 39:243–246, 1999.

527. Bass, M., Kravath, R. E., Glass, L. Death–scene investigation in sudden infant death. N.

Engl. J. Med. 315:100–105, 1986.

528. Hampson, N. B., Kramer, C. C., Dunford, R. G., Norkool, D. M. Carbon monoxide poisoning from indoor burning of charcoal briquets. JAMA 271:52–53, 1994.

529. Yoon, S. S., Macdonald, S. C., Parrish, R. G. Deaths from unintentional carbon monoxide poisoning and potential for prevention with carbon monoxide detectors. JAMA 279:685–687, 1998.

530. Wrenn, K., Conners, G. P. Carbon monoxide poisoning during ice storms: a tale of two cities. J. Emerg. Med. 15:465–467, 1997.

531. Houck, P. M., Hampson, N. B. Epidemic carbon monoxide poisoning following a winter storm. J. Emerg. Med. 15:469–473, 1997.

532. Gorman, D. F., Runciman, W. B. Carbon monoxide poisoning. Anaesth. Intensive Care 19:506–511, 1991.

533. Risser, D., Bonsch, A., Schneider, B. Should coroners be able to recognize unintentional carbon monoxide–related deaths immediately at the death scene? J. Forensic Sci. 40:596–598, 1995.

534. Barret, L., Danel, V., Faure, J. Carbon monoxide poisoning, a diagnosis frequently overlooked. J. Toxicol. Clin. Toxicol. 23:309–313, 1985.

535. Heckerling, P. S., Leikin, J. B., Terzian, C. G., Maturen, A. Occult carbon monoxide poisoning in patients with neurologic illness. J. Toxicol. Clin. Toxicol. 28:29–44, 1990.

536. Grace, T. W., Platt, F. W. Subacute carbon monoxide poisoning. Another great imitator. JAMA 246:1698–1700, 1981.

537. Sadovnikoff, N., Varon, J., Sternbach, G. L. Carbon monoxide poisoning. An occult epidemic. Postgrad. Med. 92:86, 1992.

538. Roy, B., Crawford, R. Pitfalls in diagnosis and management of carbon monoxide poisoning. J. Accid. Emerg. Med. 13:62–63, 1996.

539. Findlay, G. H. Carbon monoxide poisoning: optics and histology of skin and blood. Br. J. Dermatol. 119:45–51, 1988.

540. Carson, H. J., Esslinger, K. Carbon monoxide poisoning without cherry–red livor. Am. J. Forensic Med. Pathol. 22:233–235, 2001.

541. Torne, R., Soyer, H. P., Leb, G., Kerl, H. Skin lesions in carbon monoxide intoxication. Dermatologica 183:212–215, 1991.

542. Leavell, U. W., Farley, C. H., McIntyre, J. S. Cutaneous changes in a patient with carbon monoxide poisoning. Arch. Dermatol. 99:429–433, 1969.

543. Orizaga, M., Ducharme, F. A., Campbell, J. S., Embree, G. H. Muscle infarction and Volkmann's contracture following carbon monoxide poisoning. J. Bone Joint Surg. Am.

49:965−970, 1967.

544. Bessoudo, R., Gray, J. Carbon monoxide poisoning and nonoliguric acute renal failure. Can. Med. Assoc. J. 119:41−44, 1978.

545. Finley, J., VanBeek, A., Glover, J. L. Myonecrosis complicating carbon monoxide poisoning. J. Trauma 17:536−540, 1977.

546. Dutra, F. R. Cerebral residua of acute carbon monoxide poisoning. Am. J. Clin. Pathol. 22:925−935, 1952.

547. Ginsberg, M. D. Delayed neurologic deterioration following hypoxia. Adv. Neurol. 26:21−44, 1979.

548. Smith, J. S., Brandon, S. Morbidity from acute carbon monoxide poisoning at three−year follow−up. Br. Med. J 1:318−321, 1973.

549. Myers, R. A., Snyder, S. K., Emhoff, T. A. Subacute sequelae of carbon monoxide poisoning. Ann. Emerg. Med. 14:1163−1167, 1985.

550. Dominguez, A. M., Halstead, J. R., Domanski, T. J. The effects of postmortem changes on carboxyhemoglobin results. J. Forensic Sci. 88:330−341, 1964.

551. Busuttil, A., Moody, G. H., Obafunwa, J. O., Dewar, C., McIntosh, M. The skeletonized body: suicidal inhalation of motorbike exhaust. Am. J. Forensic Med. Pathol. 18:50−55, 1997.

552. Levine, B., Moore, K. A., Titus, J. M., Fowler, D. A comparison of carboxyhemoglobin saturation values in postmortem heart blood and peripheral blood specimens. J. Forensic Sci. 47:1388−1390, 2002.

553. Wu, S. C., Levine, B., Goodin, J. C., Caplan, Y. H., Smith, M. L. Analysis of spleen specimens for carbon monoxide. J. Anal. Toxicol. 16:42−44, 1992.

554. Kojima, T., Okamoto, I., Yashiki, M., et al. Production of carbon monoxide in cadavers. Forensic Sci. Int. 32:67−77, 1986.

555. O'Brien, J. T., Tarbuck, A. F. Suicide and vehicle exhaust emissions. BMJ 304:1376, 1992.

556. Hays, P., Bornstein, R. A. Failed suicide attempt by emission gas poisoning. Am. J. Psychiatry 141:592−593, 1984.

557. Wagg, A. S., Aylwin, S. J. Catalytic converter and suicide risk. Lancet 342:1295, 1993.

558. Greenberg, S. R. The confined space. A review of a recently discerned medical entity. Am. J. Forensic Med. Pathol. 10:31−36, 1989.

559. Zugibe, F. T., Costello, J. T., Breithaupt, M. K., Zappi, E., Allyn, B. The confined spacehypoxia syndrome. J. Forensic Sci. 32:554−560, 1987.

560. Kleinfeld, M., Feiner, B. Health hazards associated with work in confined spaces. J.

Occup. Med. 8:358–364, 1966.

561. Knight, L. D., Presnell, S. E. Death by sewer gas: case report of a double fatality and review of the literature. Am. J. Forensic Med. Pathol. 26:181–185, 2005.

562. Manning, T. J., Ziminski, K., Hyman, A., Figueroa, G., Lukash, L. Methane deaths? Was it the cause? Am. J. Forensic Med. Pathol. 2:333–336, 1981.

563. Pettit, T. A. Confined spaces: avoiding the hazards. Occup. Health Saf. 52:17–19, 1983.

564. Byard, R. W., Wilson, G. W. Death scene gas analysis in suspected methane asphyxia. Am. J. Forensic Med. Pathol. 13:69–71, 1992.

565. Balding, L. E., Jordan, F. B., Choi, C. S., Rohrig, T. P. Gas flames, closed spaces, and hypoxia. Am. J. Forensic Med. Pathol. 16:229–231, 1995.

566. Guillemin, M. P., Horisberger, B. Fatal intoxication due to an unexpected presence of carbon dioxide. Ann. Occup. Hyg. 38:951–957, 1994.

567. James, P. B., Calder, I. M. Anoxic asphyxia–a cause of industrial fatalities: a review. J. R. Soc. Med. 84:493–495, 1991.

568. Williams, H. I. Carbon dioxide poisoning: report of eight cases, with two deaths. Br. Med. J. 14:1012–1014, 1958.

569. Wagner, G. N., Clark, M. A., Koenigsberg, E. J., Decata, S.J. Medical evaluation of the victims of the 1986 Lake Nyos disaster. J. Forensic Sci. 33:899–909, 1988.

570. Ikeda, N., Takahashi, H., Umetsu, K., Suzuki, T. The course of respiration and circulation in death by carbon dioxide poisoning. Forensic Sci. Int. 41:93–99, 1989.

571. Kernbach–Wighton, G., Kijewski, H., Schwanke, P., Saur, P., Sprung, R. Clinical and morphological aspects of death due to liquid nitrogen. Int. J. Legal Med. 111:191–195, 1998.

572. Kage, S., Kashimura, S., Ikeda, H., Kudo, K., Ikeda, N. Fatal and nonfatal poisoning by hydrogen sulfide at an industrial waste site. J. Forensic Sci. 47:652–655, 2002.

573. Adelson, L., Sunshine, I. Fatal hydrogen sulfide intoxication. Report of three cases occurring in a sewer. Arch. Pathol. 81:375–380, 1966.

574. Centers for Disease Control and Prevention. Occupational fatalities during trenching and excavation work—United States, 1992–2001. MMWR Morb. Mortal. Wkly. Rep. 53:311–314, 2004.

575. Terazawa, K., Takatori, T., Tomii, S., Nakano, K. Methane asphyxia. Coal mine accident investigation of distribution of gas. Am. J. Forensic Med. Pathol. 6:211–214, 1985.

第4章
高温损伤

概述

火、电及爆炸均可直接对人体造成高温损伤。爆炸还可产生"爆炸波效应",间接导致人体损伤。高温损伤致死的案件中,各种死亡方式皆有可能。案发现场的死者可出现诸如尸体炭化、肢体离断等严重损伤,这给法医进行现场物证提取、身份识别、推断死亡原因及区分生前/死后损伤带来极大的困难。在高温致伤环境下存活的受害者,可因一系列损伤并发症最终死于医院。迟发性高温损伤致死案例是区别"直接死因"与"根本死因"概念的典型示例。

关键词: 烧伤; 火; 烟雾吸入性损伤; 一氧化碳(CO); 电流损伤; 雷电损伤; 爆炸; 爆炸伤

1 火灾现场

法医实践中接触最多的烧伤为火焰损伤(1-3)。这类案件中,各种死亡方式皆有可能。死亡原因及死亡方式推断需根据现场勘查、尸体检验结果、火灾调查员及警方提供的案件信息,以及辅助的毒物检验及化学检测结果等综合判断(4)。

北卡罗莱纳州的研究结果显示,四分之三的火场死亡案件由住宅火灾造成(5)。三分之二的死者为男性,火灾发生时约半数死者独自在家。不少死者为5岁以下幼儿或64岁以上老人(5)。火灾起因包括在床上吸烟、使用不合格的加热设备、烹饪及玩火(2,6,7)。成年人中,酗酒、高龄、精神障碍或患有神经系统疾病的个体易成为火灾受害者(参阅第3章标题3.9、标题4;参考文献5,8)。部分研究显示,大量火场死亡案件存在烟雾探测器故障或缺乏烟雾探测器的情况(6,7,9)。虽然烟雾探测器可降低火灾致死的风险,但有研究表明,烟雾探测器并无法有效扼制因儿童玩火所致的火灾死亡(5,6,10),原因可能为此类火灾的始发地常远离烟雾探测器(如卧室)、火势扩大后受害者由于害怕而躲藏及儿童缺乏监护等(6,11,12)。

与工作相关的烧伤受害者大部分为男性(13-15)。美国的研究显示,热烧伤致死事件中占比最高(约四分之一)的死者为交通运输业及公共事业从业人员(15)。交通事故中烧死的死者大部分是卡车司机(15)。这些死者中,65 岁及以上的从业者人数最多。由于老年从业者自身反应及身体功能下降并伴随疾病和药物使用,该类人群更易受伤(15)。

火是自杀的手段之一,多见于自焚或在室内放火。自焚者通常会选择其熟悉的场所,有时亦会选择较偏远的场所(16-19),部分自焚者选择公共场所(17,20)。自焚者也会在机动车内点燃车辆自焚(图 4-1;参考文献 17,18)。对于自焚者的临

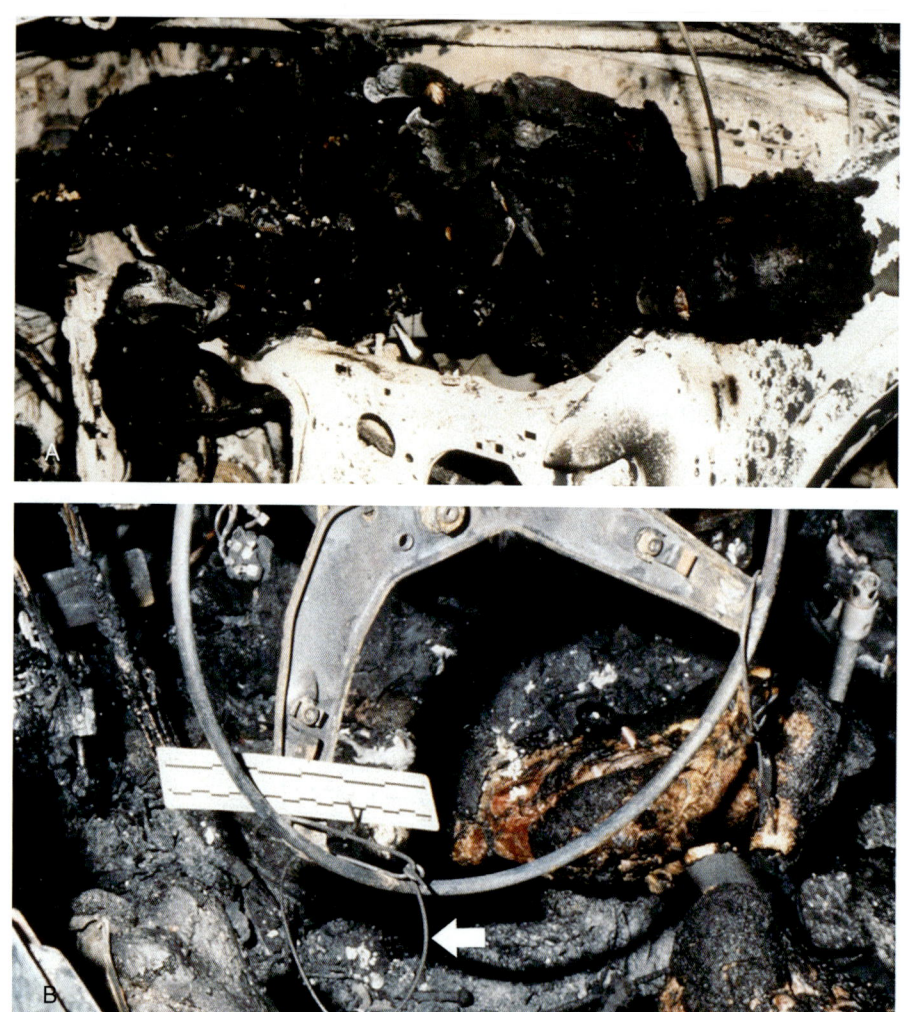

图 4-1 放火自杀(自焚)者为生前烧死(检见烟灰吸入,体内碳氧血红蛋白饱和度升高)。(A)在偏远地区烧毁的车辆引擎盖下方发现尸体。(B)死者曾缚于方向盘上(箭头)[经许可转载自 Journal of Forensic Sciences,参考文献 18,版权归宾夕法尼亚州西康舍霍肯市美国材料与试验协会(ASTM International)所有]。

床及法医学回顾性研究显示,在欧洲及远东国家,自焚者以男性为主,中东国家及印度女性的自焚事件发生率有所上升(21)。在某些国家和地区,自焚占自杀事件的1%(17,18)。许多自焚者有精神病史,但一些欧洲及北美的研究显示,约半数自焚者并无精神病史(17,18,21-23)。自焚者在以往或近期可能已实施过自杀行为,采用的方式包括放火(17,18)。自焚者的动机与采用其他自杀方式的死者类似(17,18,21,24)。在某些国家(如印度),传统婚姻与社会等级制度可能会迫使女性选择自焚(25,26)。宗教因素及政治抗议同样也可作为自焚的动机(17,18,21),自焚抗议会引起媒体关注,并可导致他人效仿(16,18)。对于身处精神病院或收容机构的被监管受控人群,利用身边的点火工具(如火柴)放火可能是其唯一能够实施的自杀手段(16,18)。在某些多种自杀方式并存的"复杂性自杀"案件中,烧死的尸体可伴有其他类型的损伤(如坠落导致的钝性损伤、头部枪弹伤、锐器刺创等),多种类型损伤并存使得死亡原因存疑(图4-2;参考文献16,18,27,和28)。对自焚者的尸表检验可发现异常情况(如口中塞布条以防止喊叫、手臂缚于方向盘上防止逃跑)(图4-1;参考文献18)。自焚者常会使用助燃剂(参阅标题4.2;参考文献18,21)。

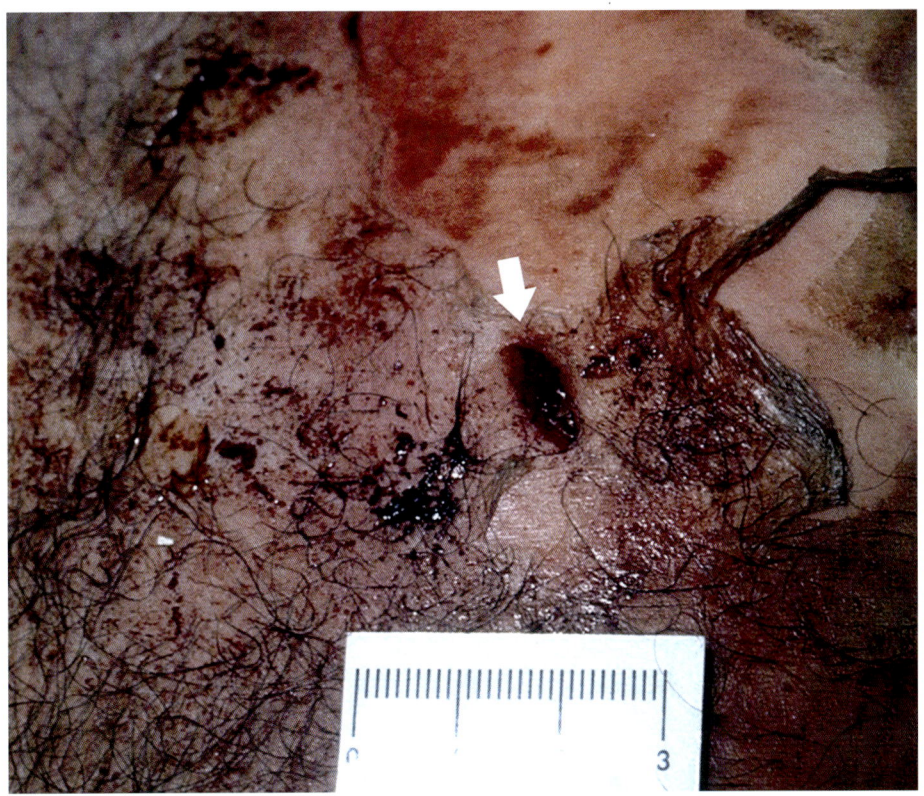

图4-2 住宅火灾死亡。自伤所致非致命性腹部创口(箭头)。烟灰吸入及体内碳氧血红蛋白饱和度升高(39%)。广泛性烧伤。

纵火的其他动机包括纵火癖、蓄意破坏、报复行为、恐吓勒索、财产诈骗等（4）。亦有杀人后企图伪装成意外火灾而纵火（图 4-3；参考文献 4, 29；标题 4.1）。

火灾发生前或火场中同样可发生自然死亡。

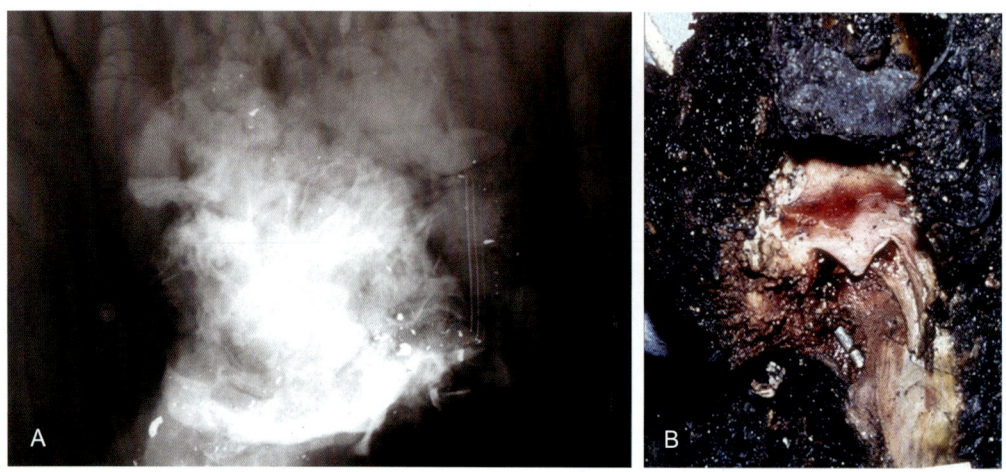

图 4-3 死后焚尸。谋杀案伪造成意外汽车火灾。无证据表明死者存在烟灰及 CO 吸入。(A) 颅骨 X 线图像检见多发性弹片。(B) 部分颅顶骨烧毁缺失。自颅底枪弹创口置入的探针示射入口至颅内最大弹片处的枪弹创道（美国北卡罗来纳州教堂山市法医局供图）。

2 着火

同时具备火源、火源附近足量的可燃物及充足的氧气，即可引发燃烧（4, 30）。燃烧过程中温度升高并产生可见光或火焰（31）。建筑物着火后 5-10 分钟环境温度即可达到 150℃（300°F）以上（32）。某些封闭结构内（如飞机座舱）着火后 5-6 分钟即可产生约 250℃（480°F）的致死性高温（33）。如果此时人为打开门窗，或者封闭结构的完整性遭到高温破坏，突然进入的氧气可引起闪燃，即封闭火场内温度持续升高达到环境内可燃气体及其他可燃物的自燃温度，形成突然爆发性的燃烧（33）。封闭火场内温度达 650℃ [1 200°F (33)] 以上时，也可发生闪燃。飞机飞行过程中发生座舱损坏时，舱内温度数分钟内即可高达 1 000℃（1 832°F）以上（33）。在车内有燃料的情况下，汽车燃烧温度可达 1 100℃（1 980°F）（34-36）。

封闭空间内高温火焰 [980℃（1 800°F）及以上] 产生的热辐射能够点燃家具（4）。

燃烧过程中，含碳物质首先被氧化成 CO_2，此时燃烧产生的 CO 含量较少（参阅第 3 章标题 3.9；参考文献 31）。热解，即物质在热作用下分解，该反应所需空气中的氧含量低于一般燃烧所需的氧含量 [即"不完全燃烧"(31)]。在通风条件差的火场内，当环境中的 O_2 因燃烧而消耗且得不到补充时，物质发生热解并产生烟（空气中的悬浮颗粒）及诸如 CO 等有毒气体（30, 31, 33, 37）。若发生闪燃，热解则会产生化学性质不稳定的复杂化合物及更多 CO（31, 33）。

3 现场尸体

3.1 尸体状态

火场中尸体状态多种多样。部分火场中的尸体可呈现相对无损的状态。尸体被衣物覆盖的区域相对而言受到保护，暴露在外的区域则沾满烟灰。烧伤分级包括Ⅰ度或浅Ⅱ度（皮肤发红或红斑形成），Ⅱ度或深Ⅱ度（烧伤深达真皮层并出现皮肤水疱），Ⅲ度或全层烧伤（表皮及真皮层整体坏死，皮肤呈皮革样化改变；参阅标题6；参考文献38）。部分尸体呈广泛性炭化和碎裂状(39)。某些火场中尸体由于已被烧得无法辨识而未被现场消防人员察觉，消防人员的灭火操作可导致焚毁尸体碎裂。

据将温度控制在670℃－810℃（1240°F－1490°F）焚烧老年死者尸体的研究表明，尸体毁损程度与焚烧时间有关(35,40,41)。焚烧10分钟时，尸体肌肉发生热收缩，由于屈肌较伸肌发达，收缩程度更大，使尸体呈现出一种"拳斗"姿势（图4-4）。约20分钟时，面部及四肢组织炭化。20分钟后，颅骨外板可见骨裂缝，由于颅内蒸汽压增加，使得冠状缝或矢状缝开裂(34)；头部、躯干及四肢皮肤和皮下软组织烧毁，肌肉外露、炭化，四肢骨骼暴露在外；双手烧毁或严重烧伤，手与前臂仅靠炭化的软组织相连。约30分钟后，颅骨外板骨折扩大，并延伸至内板，有时颅骨外板可见粉碎性骨折(34,35)，脑组织表面炭化；胸骨被烧毁，肋骨胸骨端被烧毁，胸、腹腔呈开放状态，胸、腹腔器官炭化、萎缩；前臂远端烧毁，下肢远端软组织基本缺失，长骨外露，在热作用下发生骨折。40分钟后，颅骨烧毁，面颅骨呈碎片状；前臂烧毁，肱骨外露。50分钟后，上肢完全缺失，股骨仅存部分残端；面部组织解体、缺失，颅底外露；椎体煅烧。60分钟后，尸体仅剩面颅及颅底骨，亦可见头部完全缺失；内部器官烧成灰烬；四肢完全缺失。约1.5小时后，躯干部呈碎片状。焚烧约2－3小时后，整具尸体完全焚化（图4-5）。将儿童的尸体在约500℃［930°F(36)］的火炉内焚烧约2小时，整具尸体仅残留焚烧的骨骼。衣物的着火点约为225℃［440°F(4)］。

虽然住宅火灾的环境温度可以达到焚化炉内的温度，但通常难以在室内或户外的火灾现场发现完全炭化的尸体(35,36)。由于消防人员的干预及火场中缺乏足够的燃料来维持燃烧，使得绝大多数火灾不足以维持足够长时间的高温将尸体完全烧尽(35,36)。这使得在大多数火灾案件中，尸体条件允许法医完成个体识别检查、检查内部器官组织判断是否存在疾病与损伤，以及采集体液进行毒物检验（图4-5；参考文献40）。

焚化炉内焚烧的尸体，火焰在尸体表面呈持续、均匀的分布状态，而现实中火灾现场温度存在波动，且火场中人体某些部位并非直接暴露于火焰中（如与硬质物体接触的受压部位），从而受到一定的保护(35,40)。在大多数情况下，尸体背向火焰的一侧的组织炭化程度明显轻于面向火焰的一侧；然而，在某些案件中仍可见到完全炭化的尸体(40,42)。穿衣服的尸体较赤裸的尸体烧毁速度更快(43)。

在某些火灾致死案件中，尸体的炭化部位与其他案件相反，即尸体躯干部烧毁而

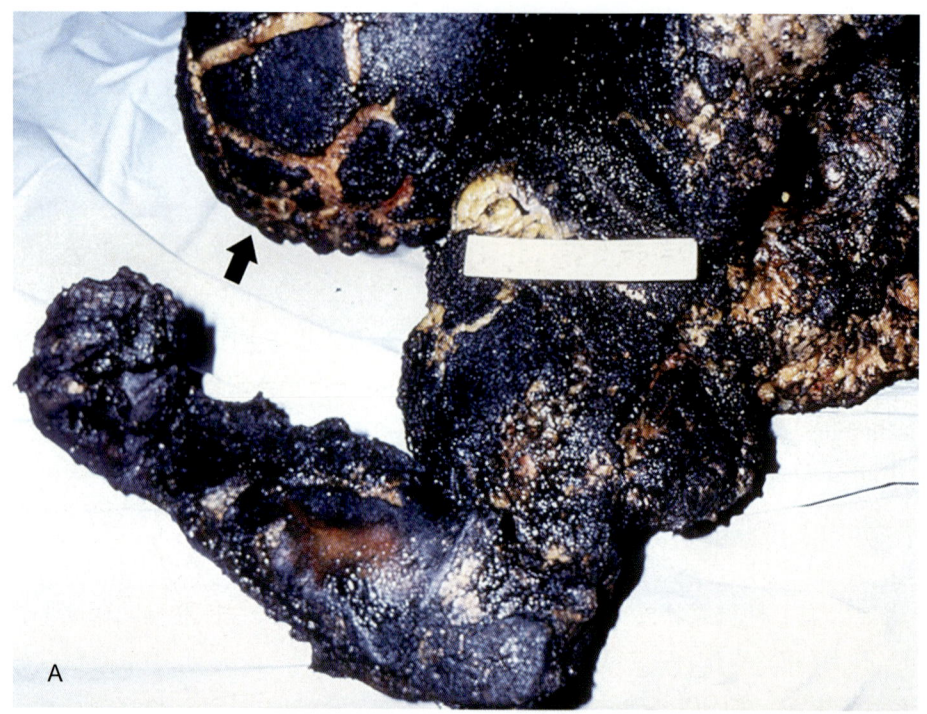

图 4-4 燃烧引起的尸体假象。(A)热作用导致的手臂屈曲、头皮开裂(箭头)。(B)热作用导致的手臂屈曲及胸部皮肤开裂(加拿大安大略省伦敦市伦敦健康科学中心 E. Tweedie 博士供图)。

第 4 章 | 高温损伤

图 4-5 重度炭化尸体。(A) 躯干部炭化。体表广泛性烧伤,但体内器官保存相对完好,能够提取到毒物检验所需检材。(B) 尸体经焚烧后残留的组织(美国北卡罗来纳州教堂山市法医局供图)。

四肢相对保存较好(43,44)。在此类案件中,尸体周边环境过火情况常极其轻微,故推测可能存在"人体自燃"现象(43-45)。此类案件典型的受害者为超重的老年女性(43)。这类死者受疾病影响,日常生活自理能力较差,且尸体位于室内常见的火源附近(如香烟、开放式壁炉、蜡烛、火炉、房间加热器等;参阅标题 4.1;参考文献 43,45)。当所穿衣物或人体周围织物(如地毯)持续燃烧 15 分钟以上,可致皮肤烧裂,皮下脂肪受热融化溢出(44)。脂肪作为最易燃的人体组织(43),其作用就像灯芯,若燃烧的多孔织物吸收了溢出的脂肪组织,可使燃烧持续(44-46)。此种燃烧不足以耗尽房间内 O_2,又不足以产生足够的热辐射来点燃周围环境内的可燃物(44),最终形成上述尸体烧毁、周边环境过火轻微的情况。人体脂肪的燃点约为 250℃

(480°F)，但上述灯芯效应使得脂肪组织能在低于24℃［75°F（45）］的情况下燃烧。此类案件的受害者多肥胖，躯干部的脂肪含量多于四肢，故在躯干部缓慢燃烧的同时，四肢常不燃烧，保存情况较好(44)。

3.2 个体识别

火灾的环境信息（如某居民的住所着火）有助于直接识别受害者。如果火场中尸体体表覆盖烟灰且未遭严重焚毁，清理尸体表面烟灰后可凭肉眼根据尸体面部及其他体表特征进行个体识别（图4-6）。未烧毁的衣着及私人财产同样有助于个体

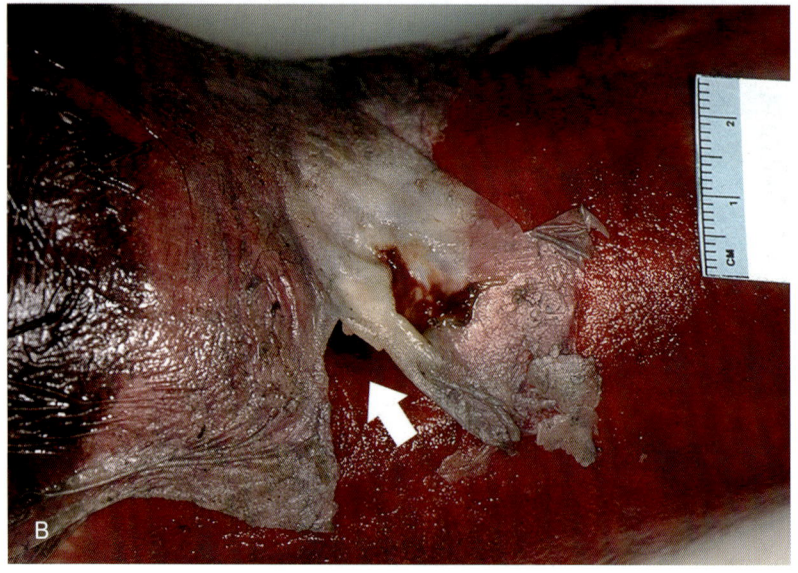

图4-6 火场中尸体的个体识别。(A)将皮肤上覆盖的烟灰擦除后显露具有辨识意义的个体特征（如纹身图案）。(B)尸体部分烧毁。检见骨髓炎皮肤瘘口（箭头），与病史记载一致。

识别(图4-7)。尸体炭化会破坏死者原有的体表特征。热收缩会导致尸体短缩,以至于根据尸长进行个体识别会受到影响。头发颜色的变化同样会影响个体识别(图4-8)。Spitz观察到在约120℃[250°F(47)]时白发会变为金黄色;处于205℃(400°F)温

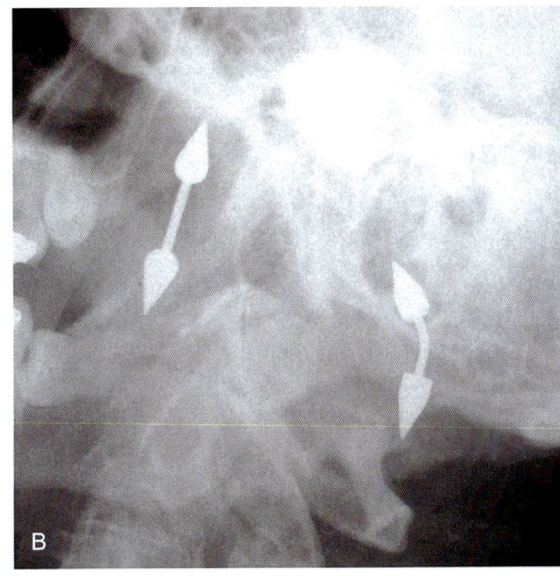

图 4-7 炭化尸体。汽车碰撞事故后起火。根据尸体佩饰进行身份识别。(A)左耳。尸体炭化导致肉眼无法辨识到佩戴的耳环。(B)X线图像示清晰的耳环。

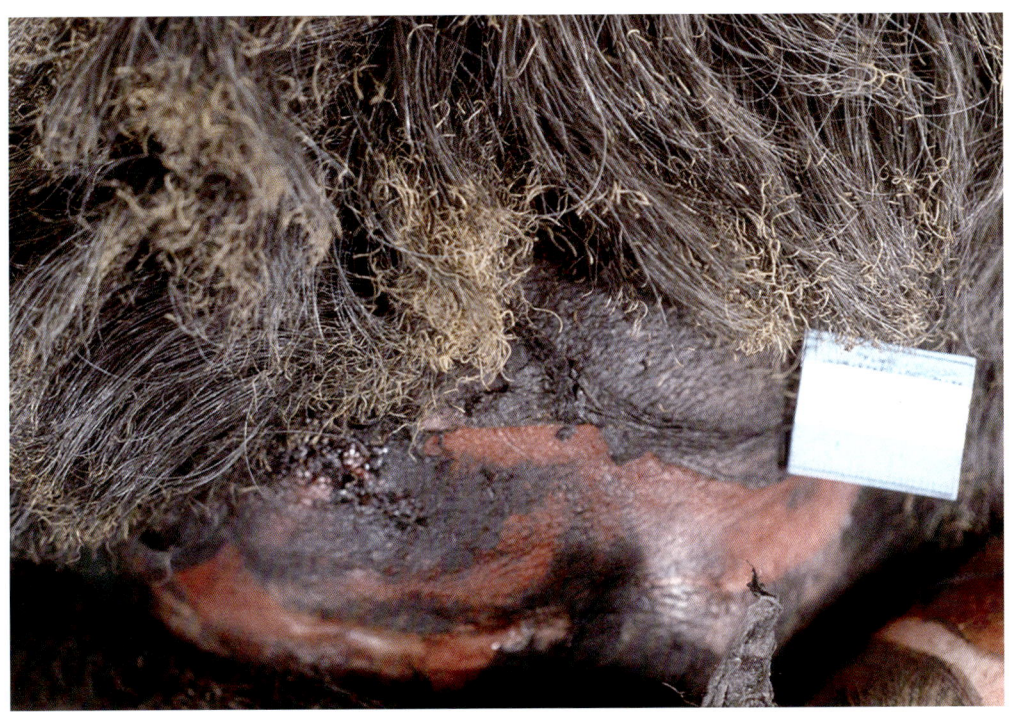

图 4-8 烧灼导致的发色变化。

度下 10–15 分钟后,棕发会呈现出轻微的红色;黑发的颜色不受温度影响(47)。

因热挛缩而握拳的手会留有指纹(图 4–9)可采用比较法进行个体识别。如需对尸体身份进行初步推断,调查人员必须调取尽可能完整的齿科及医疗记录(图 4–10),并根据这些记录的特异性和准确性,有选择性地加以使用(48)。对烧焦尸体进行影像学检查是个体识别的一种手段(如影像学检查可发现体内手术痕迹、陈旧性骨折;参阅标题 4.3)。如果经上述手段获取的死者生前资料与尸体信息难以精确匹配,仍可交由法医及其他专家进行后续的同一性认定(图 4–6,4–11 和 4–12)。如果尸体条件已不允许使用传统的比较法进行个体识别,那么可提取牙齿或骨骼进行 DNA 分析(48)。

3.3 燃烧引起的尸体假象

人体在燃烧过程中能够形成疑似机械性损伤的改变,从而增加了个体识别的难度(参阅标题 3.2):

- 燃烧残留的衣物疑似绕颈的绳索(图 4–13)。
- 由于肌肉收缩而呈现的"拳斗姿势"疑似生前遇到威胁时呈现的"战斗或逃跑"姿态(图 4–4)。
- 皮肤开裂、皮下组织暴露疑似刺创(图 4–4;参考文献 40)。
- 高温可形成皮肤水疱。水疱可保持完整或破裂。皮肤水疱破裂、干燥后可呈黄色至棕黑色。单凭这些水疱不足以认定具有生活反应。助燃剂(煤油、汽油)可加剧水疱形成与表皮滑脱(49)。

图 4–9 炭化尸体。尸体解剖时切下手指用于采集指纹。

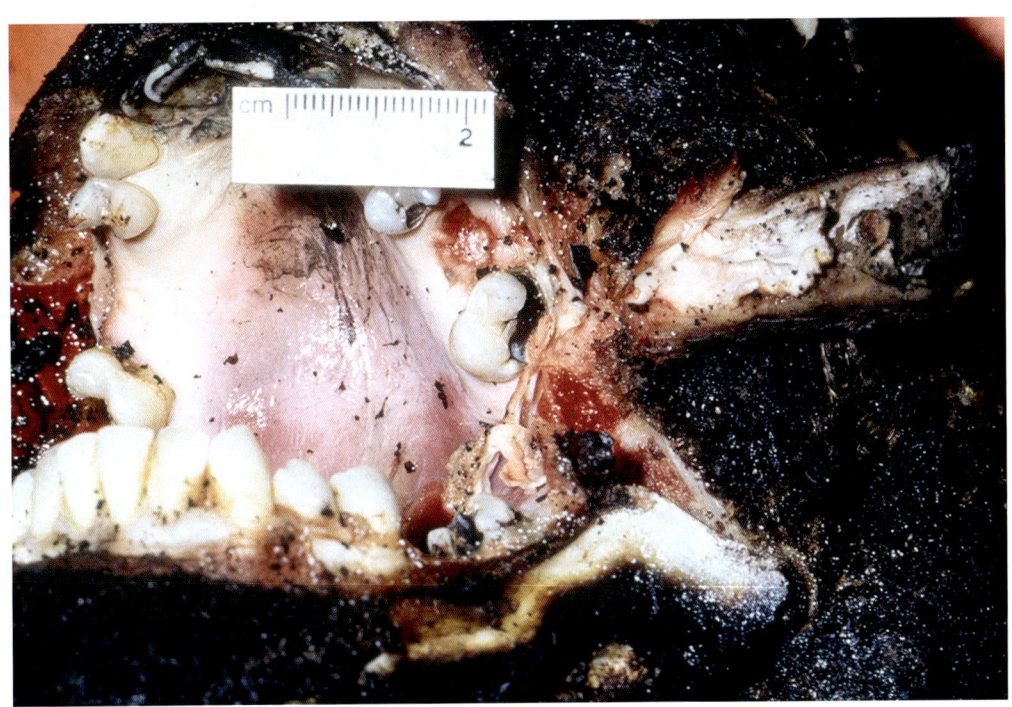

图 4-10　炭化尸体。牙齿较其他组织更耐燃烧,保存情况良好(美国北卡罗来纳州教堂山市法医局供图)。

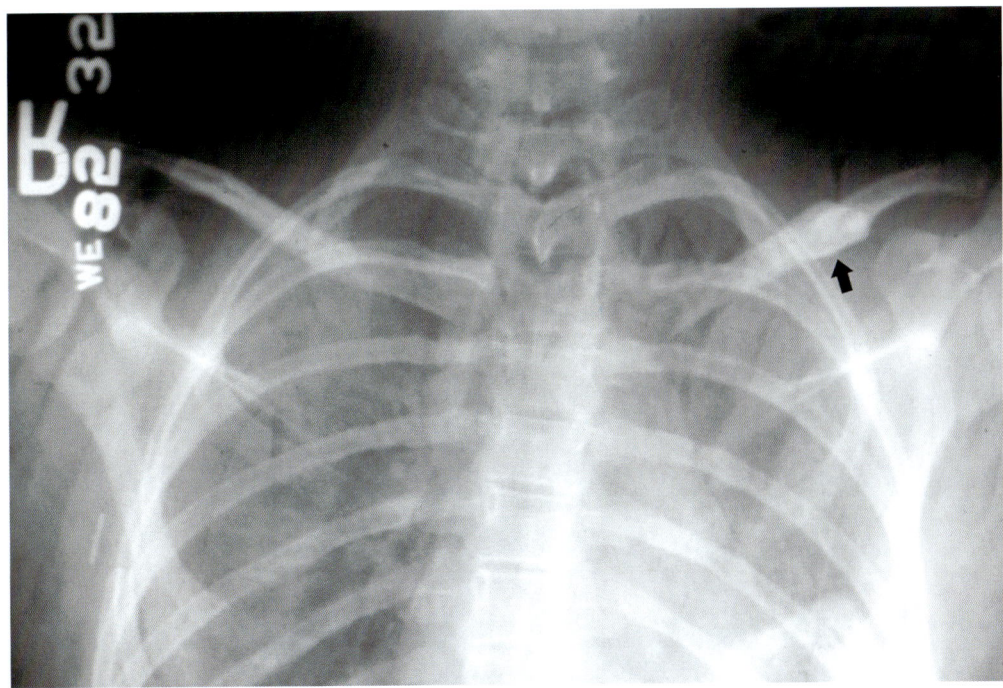

图 4-11　炭化尸体。胸部 X 线图像显示已愈合的锁骨骨折(箭头),若找不到死者生前相应的 X 线图像进行比对,根据相关的病史记载仍可进行一致性比对(美国北卡罗来纳州教堂山市法医局供图)。

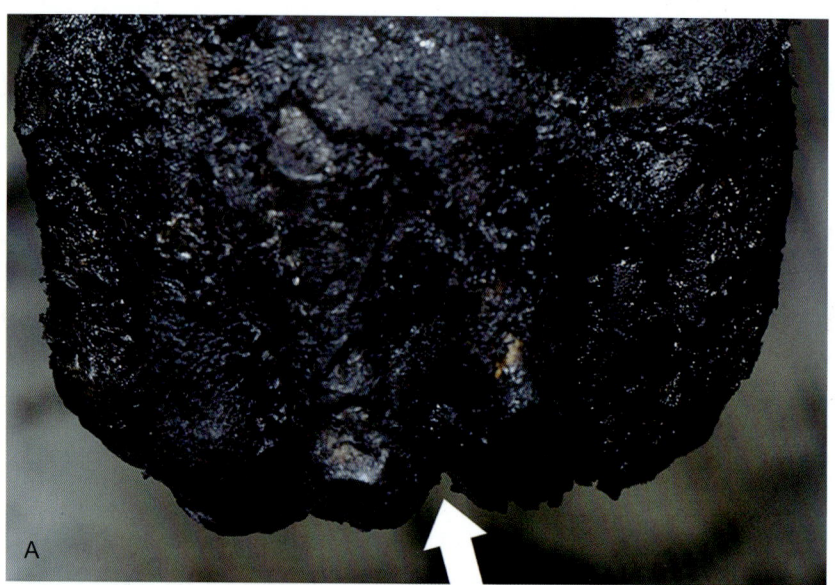

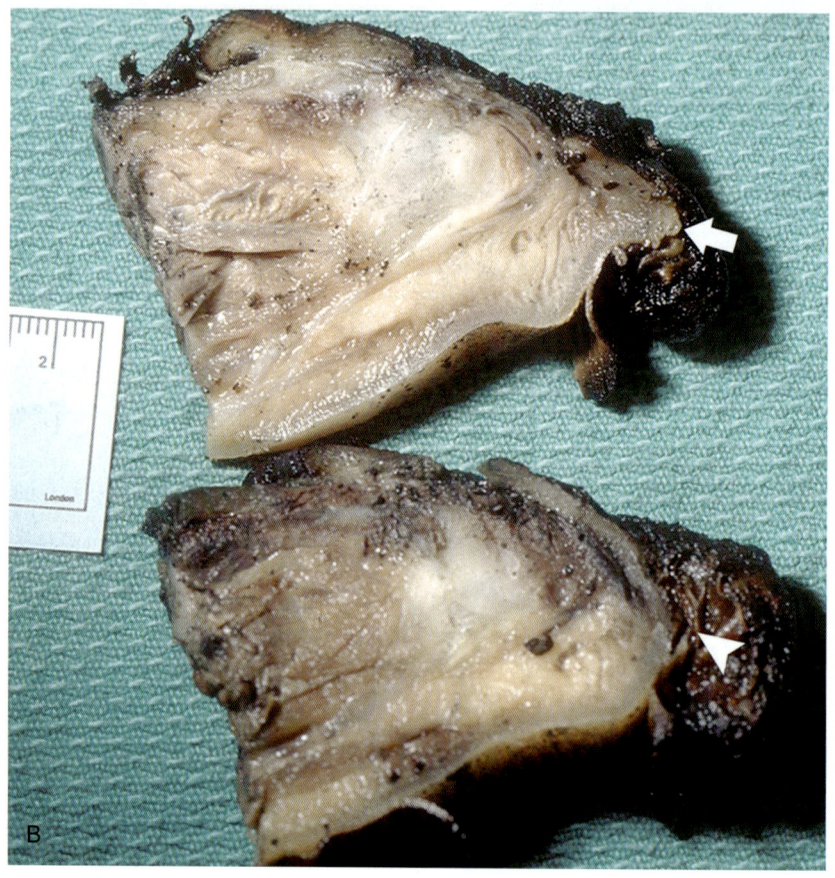

图 4-12 汽车火灾中的炭化尸体。仅存的可用于身份识别的特征是死者的"蹼状"脚趾。(A) 右足前部。第2、3趾间组织部分联合(箭头)。(B) 尸体解剖时纵向剖开趾蹼间隙。上：足趾联合部位的皮肤皱褶(箭头)；下：健侧的趾蹼间隙剖面(三角箭头)。

第 4 章 | 高温损伤

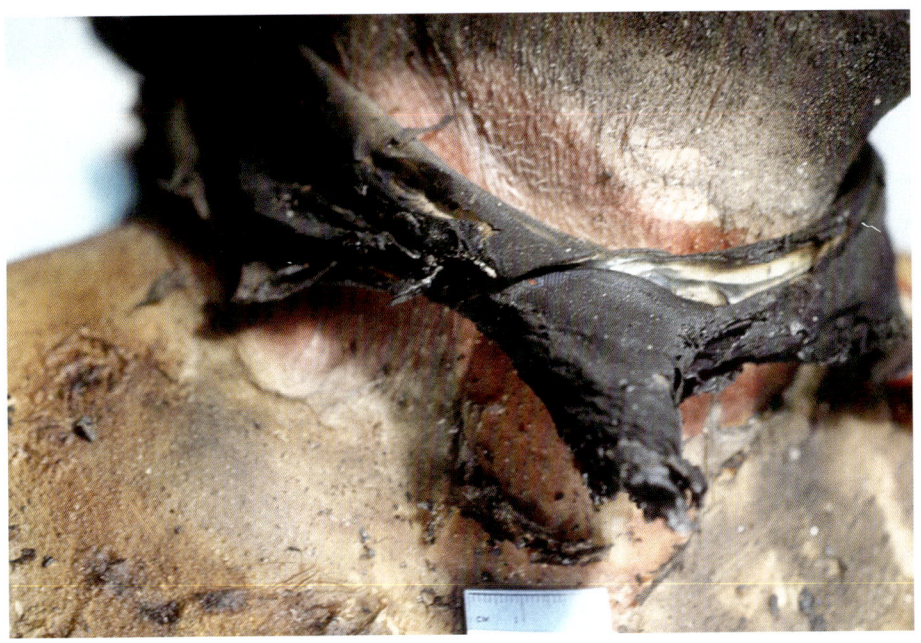

图 4-13 领带燃烧后形似绳索。

- 在严重烧伤或炭化的皮肤周边出现的"红线"为炎症反应的结果,提示受害者在火灾发生时仍存活(图 4-14)。显微镜检查显示红线为表皮下的血液。
- 热骨折并不伴有软组织出血(49)。四肢远端的热截肢被认为是四肢长骨远端炭化的结果(图 4-15)。同理,炭化的颅骨骨折边缘同样可反映出热作用

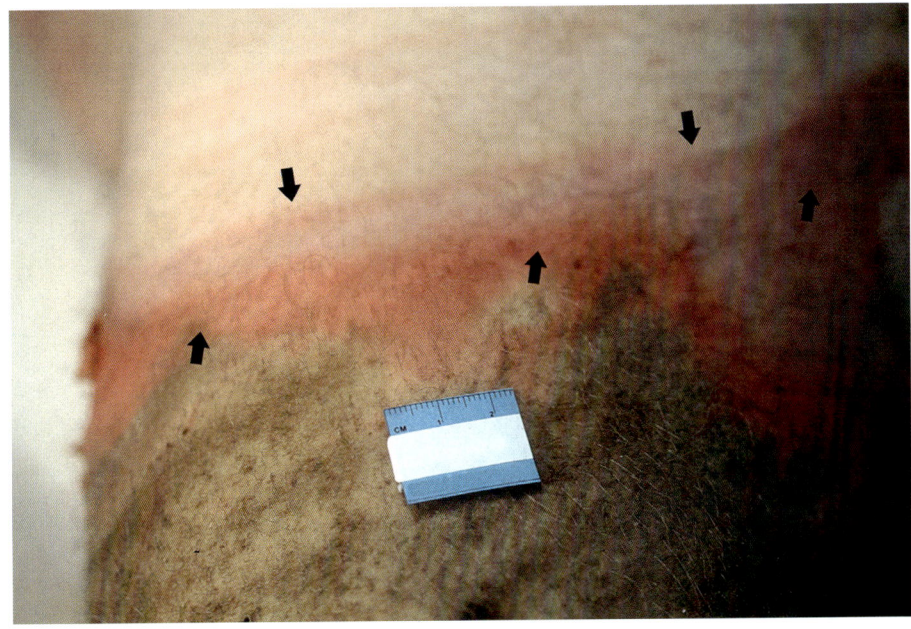

图 4-14 在燃烧与未燃烧皮肤交界处出现的"红线"(箭头)。

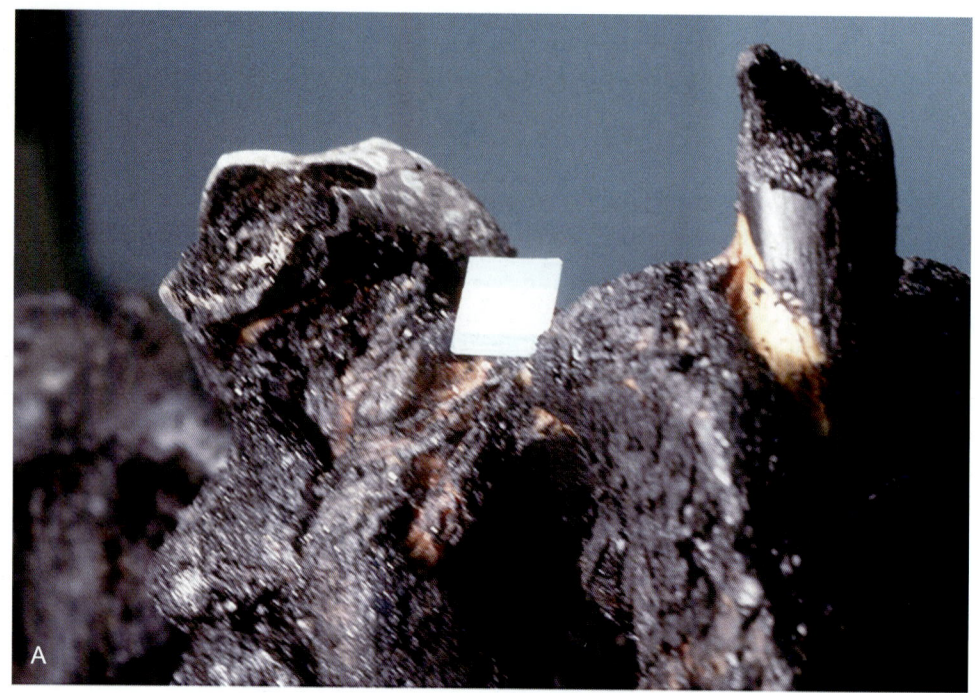

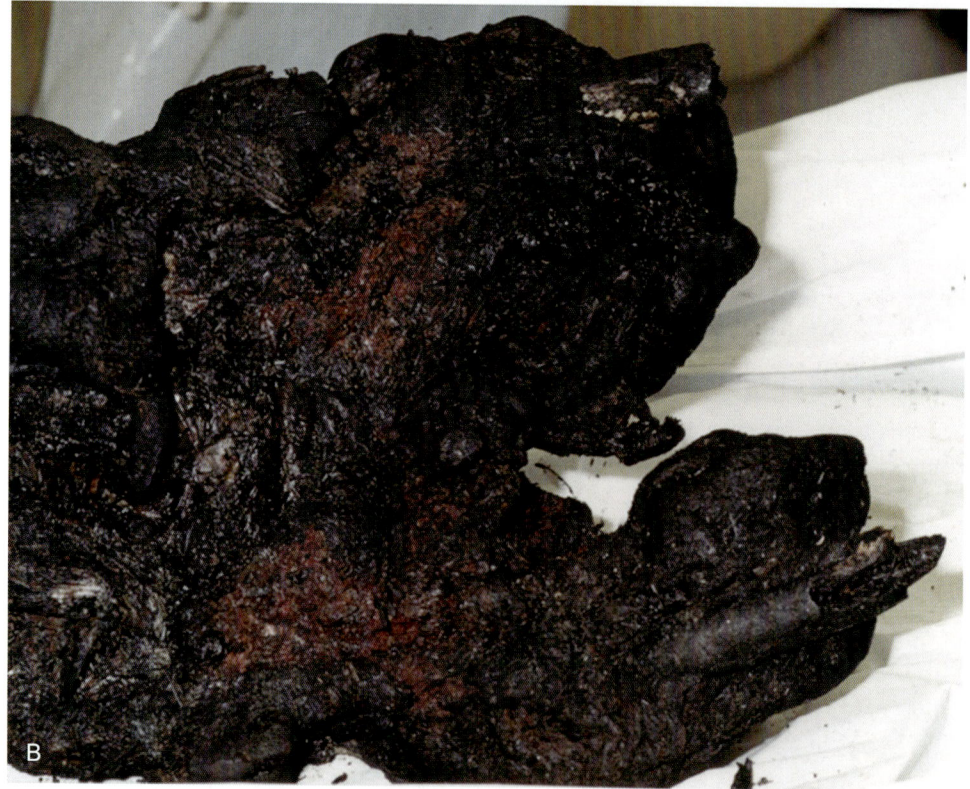

图4-15 燃烧引起的尸体假象。(A)骨折端炭化(热作用导致的骨折)。(B)热作用引起的骨折导致下肢离断(加拿大安大略省伦敦市伦敦健康科学中心 E. Tweedie 博士供图)。

第 4 章 | 高温损伤

效应。四肢长骨的热骨折被认为是由肌肉收缩引起的(47)。骨骼外板燃烧后降低了骨强度。颅内气体受热气压升高可引起"爆裂性"骨折(即骨折片向外膨出),颅盖骨外板受热干燥后同样可发生骨折(34,50)。热作用效应可在颅骨上形成疑似枪弹创的圆形孔洞[图 16(50)]。脑组织常自骨折缺损处疝出(51)。热作用导致的颅骨骨折形态与其他方式形成的颅骨骨折不同,一般机械性损伤导致的颅骨骨折形态为骨折线自颅骨缺损处向外呈放射状分布(36),而热作用导致的颅骨骨折表现为圆形或椭圆形的颅骨缺损,不伴有放射状骨折线(34,35)。也有研究表明在多例热作用颅骨骨折中均观察到多条骨折线从同一个中心放射状向外延伸的现象(47)。热作用导致的颅骨骨折常见于颞骨,有时可发生于双侧颞骨(47),且这类骨折很少仅局限于颅骨外板(47)。生前烧死案件中,即使在年轻死者身上也很难见到颅缝受热开裂;然而在尸体火化过程中可见冠状缝或矢状缝崩裂(34,47)。

- 在灭火过程中,燃烧的尸体迅速冷却或遭高压水柱破坏均会导致肢体分离,从而影响损伤评估(48)。
- 硬脑膜外热血肿,常见于双侧,且伴有头皮及颅骨炭化,并非外伤形成(参考文献 42,49;图 4-17)。
- 脑组织皱缩、质地实、呈黄色或浅棕色变("烤熟状")是热作用引起的尸体现象(47)。

图 4-16　热作用效应所致炭化颅骨上的孔洞。影像学检查未检见子弹残留,未检见颅脑损伤。

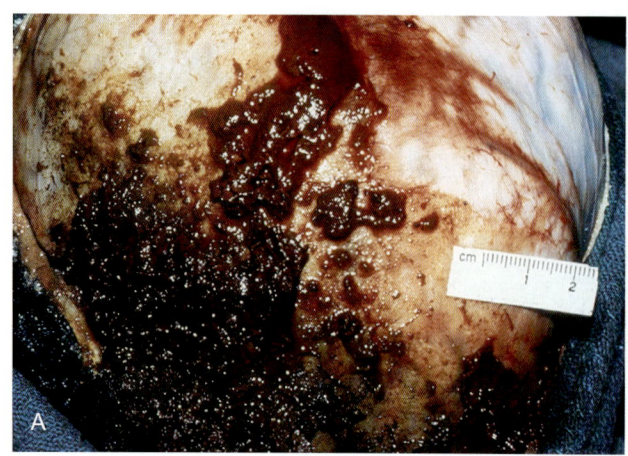

图 4-17 炭化尸体。(A) 去除颅骨后见"硬脑膜外热血肿"(北卡莱罗纳大学法医室供图,北卡莱罗纳州)。(B) 颅骨内侧见双侧"硬脑膜外热血肿"附着。

- 由于热作用将肺组织内血液沿着呼吸道向外挤压,引起口鼻腔内大量积血(参阅标题 4.1;参考文献 47)。
- 尸体解剖时切开炭化的颈部组织或由于燃烧过程中肢体离断,导致体表烟灰掉落至气管内,均可造成生前烟灰吸入的假象(52)。
- 医疗行为造成的尸体假象(参阅标题 5.2,表 4-1)。

4 火灾中机体失能与死亡

4.1 生活反应("受害者是生前烧死还是死后焚烧?")

火灾致死包括多种机制:环境中 O_2 减少、CO 及其他有毒气体含量增加,烟雾及高温气体引起的吸入性损伤,极度高温与休克、烧伤、其他类型的损伤(如逃离火场过程中受到钝性损伤),以及自身原有疾病恶化等均可导致死亡(32,37,52)。有研究指出,在极少数情况下,由于热作用效应而使胸部或颈部挛缩引起呼吸功能障碍同样可致死(52)。高温作用与吸入有毒烟雾是火灾致死的主要原因(49)。

当人体处于高于 150℃(300°F)的环境中,数分钟内即可发生意识丧失或死亡(32)。更高的温度则可立即致死(32)。闪燃或爆炸产生的火焰可吞没受害者(4,32)。若空气中存在燃烧及热裂解产物,受害者吸入少许上述物质可迅速导致死亡。

烟雾及热作用引起的喉痉挛、呼吸骤停和(或)迷走神经反射引起的心脏停搏是火灾中迅速死亡的主要机制(42,52)。

处于火场中仅 1 分钟,烟雾引起的咳嗽、眼部刺激、能见度下降及定向障碍即可导致机体失能(4,33,37)。未受伤的个体通常会试图扑灭火焰,警告他人,并逃离火场,但这些尝试常受到烟雾阻碍而失败(4,33,37)。弥漫的烟雾在房间顶部形成高温烟雾层,然后迅速下降(37),烟雾层内含氧量相对较低,当含氧量低于 7% 时可迅速导致机体失能（参阅第3章标题3.10；参考文献37）。在火场中如果沿着地面爬行，机体受到烟雾影响的时间将推迟（37）。当环境中含氧量低于10%时会引起窒息，但火场中含氧量通常不会低于15%。当环境中含氧量极低时，火焰呈阴燃状态（49，52）。如果存在明显的火焰，则表明环境中有足够的O_2供入呼吸（42）。

当远离火焰后，热作用及空气中O_2消耗对人体的影响显著减小（37，53）。火灾中产生的CO气体会刺激呼吸系统，使人吸入更多其他的有毒气体（32）。吸入这些有毒气体，特别是CO，能够致死（33，37）。火灾中产生的CO含量占火场空气的0.1%—10%（参阅第3章标题3.9.1；参考文献4，33）。火场空气中CO浓度高时可迅速致人死亡（33）。空气中CO浓度较低时，受害者可有自主行动能力（33）。吸入CO可致受害者行为异常 [如返回火场营救其臆想的其他受害者，躲在壁橱里、床下或浴缸中（4）]，受害者在运动或体力劳动时呼吸加剧，则会吸入更多CO气体（参阅第3章标题3.9；参考文献33）。体力劳动时机体需氧量大，相比静息状态下的机体，体力劳动过程中即使体内碳氧血红蛋白饱和度较低也可发生死亡（31）。体内碳氧血红蛋白饱和度达30%时可引起精神异常及肌肉功能受损，并引起昏迷（参阅第3章表3-4；参考文献37）。受害者在失能的状态下仍可继续吸入CO（33）。

对于那些远离起火源的受害者，体内较低的CO含量增加了其因吸入其他有毒气体致死的可能性（37，54）。在各种涉及吸入CO导致死亡的案件类型中，非火灾死亡的受害者体内碳氧血红蛋白饱和度普遍较高，提示除CO外其他有毒气体等因素在火灾死亡中起到重要作用（参阅第3章标题3.9.4；参考文献37）。氰化物致机体失能较CO更迅速（33，37）。氰化物可被人体快速吸收，其呼吸抑制作用可能会限制机体吸入CO（37）。含有含氮化合物的可燃材料 [如聚乙烯聚氨酯、羊毛、尼龙、尿素甲醛树脂（4，37）] 燃烧会产生氰化物。氰化物通过抑制线粒体呼吸链中还原态细胞色素a3的氧化而产生毒性（55）。氰化物能刺激呼吸系统，增加机体吸入其他有毒气体的可能性（30）。大量研究表明，CO与氰化物之间并无协同作用（30，37，55–58）。有研究指出，尚无依据表明受害者体内CO含量、乙醇含量、年龄、心脏疾病等因素与其血液中氰化物含量有相关性（57）。在诸多火灾死亡案件中，死者体内CO含量已达致死量，而体内氰化物含量尚未达中毒浓度，说明较氰化物而言，CO中毒才是多数火灾受害者的重要致死原因（58，59）。血液中氰化物浓度达到50微摩尔/升时可致机体失能（57）。在某些情况下（如火场中有含氮塑料燃烧），死者血氰化物浓度可达100微摩尔/升，严重威胁生命，而体内碳氧血红蛋白含量则相对较低（57，58）。氰化物的致死血浓度为1—3毫摩尔/升（1 000—3 000微摩尔/升）（37）。如果燃烧的物质中含有氟、氯或溴（如聚氯乙烯、阻燃剂），则在燃烧过程中会产生相应的卤化氢气体。这些腐蚀性气体会损伤呼吸道黏膜并对人体造成迟发性损害（37）。燃烧过程中同样会产生其他刺激性物质（甲醛、丙烯醛）（31）。此外，燃烧中产生的高反应性自由基会导致弥漫性肺泡损伤（33）。

药物与酒精会影响火灾受害者的意识水平与逃脱能力(4,37)。虽然有研究指出药物或乙醇中毒会与 CO 一同对人体产生协同作用,但更多的是由于乙醇中毒后自我逃脱及帮助他人逃脱的能力减退而导致死亡(参阅第 3 章标题 3.9.4;参考文献 4, 59-62)。某案例报道中一名火灾受害者被发现死于床上,现场勘查表明其并无逃离火场意图,该死者血液乙醇含量为 268 毫克/分升;另一名于火场出口附近发现的死者血液乙醇含量为 88 毫克/分升(59)。对于火灾致死的研究表明,约 1/3 至 1/2 的死者曾摄入酒精(7,62-65)。

血液中 CO(碳氧血红蛋白饱和度>10%)及其他有毒气体含量增加,口腔、上呼吸道烟灰吸入及胃肠道内的烟灰等现象提示死者在火场中有生活反应(图 4-18;参考文献 4,52)。血中碳氧血红蛋白饱和度≥ 50% 被认为达到致死量,但不加分析、严格按照碳氧血红蛋白饱和度来判断死因会对案件调查造成误导(参阅第 3 章标题 3.9.4;参考文献 37,66)。大多数火灾现场的死者中,能够同时检见呼吸道烟灰、血中碳氧血红蛋白饱和度升高(>10%)及胃肠道烟灰中的几项。其中胃肠道烟灰检出率较低[据某研究报道约三分之一的死者捡出胃肠道烟灰(42)]。据另一项研究报道四分之三的火灾死者呼吸道中检见烟灰,约半数死者胃肠道中检见烟灰,约三分之

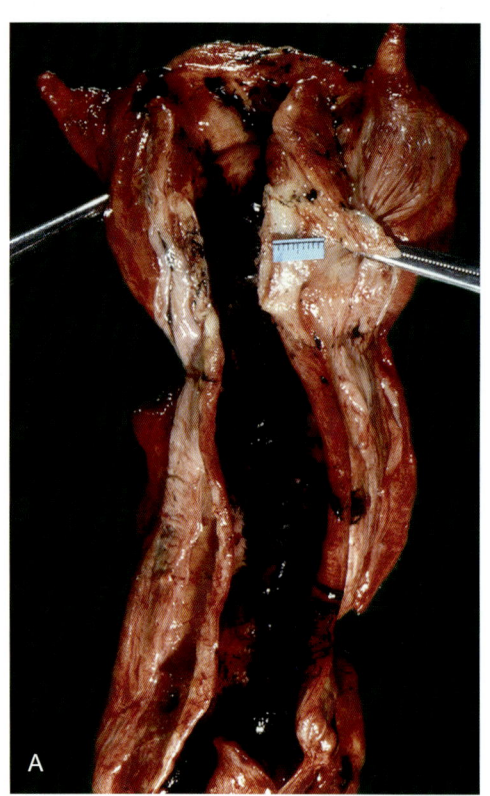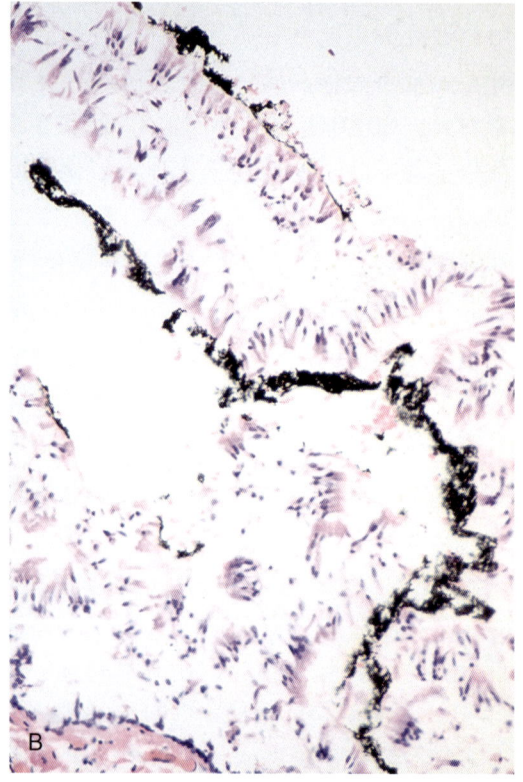

图 4-18 生前烧死的尸体。(A)喉腔及气管腔内烟灰(烟灰吸入)。(B)镜下见主支气管黏膜上皮脱落伴烟灰附着(H-E 染色,×100)。

二的死者血中碳氧血红蛋白饱和度＞10%(52)。胃肠道烟灰与呼吸道烟灰常同时存在(52)。许多死者同时检见血中碳氧血红蛋白饱和度升高及烟灰吸入，但在某些案例中上述阳性发现并不同时存在(42,52,67)。

有研究显示，多名火灾死者血中碳氧血红蛋白饱和度已达致死量，但呼吸道内均未检见烟灰(65)。上述死者中半数死于阴燃火灾，一例使用了助燃剂(65)。在一些阴燃火灾中死者呼吸道内未检见烟灰(42,68)。虽然某些放火自杀的死者血中碳氧血红蛋白饱和度较低且体内未检见烟灰，但大多数火灾死者血中碳氧血红蛋白饱和度均有升高。血中低碳氧血红蛋白饱和度案例常见于非闪燃火灾的死者中(69)。较低的碳氧血红蛋白饱和度可见于在户外自焚的死者(17,18)。车内烧死的死者常检见血中高碳氧血红蛋白饱和度(17,18)。血中碳氧血红蛋白饱和度轻度升高的死者体内可检见烟灰(70)，这种情况多见于年老、无助且由于衣服着火而烧死的案例(52)。

前牙列炭化并不代表受害者在火灾发生时嘴唇处于张开状态(71)。即使血液中碳氧血红蛋白饱和度未升高，死者呼吸道中大量的黏液依然提示其存在生活反应(49)。烟雾刺激导致肺水肿并形成大量泡沫从口鼻腔溢出，提示死者在火灾发生时仍有呼吸(图4-19，参考文献47)。在某些烧死尸体中可检见吸入的灭火器内容物及其他外源性物质(72)。

其他火灾中常见的生活反应包括眼角处皮肤未遭灼伤和（或）未被烟雾熏黑（"鹅爪状"改变），睫毛未完全烧毁，仅尖端被烧焦，提示火场中机体受烟雾刺激而紧闭双眼。气管、支气管、咽部、会厌或食管黏膜脱落及会厌肿胀等同样为常见的生活反应(见标题4.5；参考文献52)。空气是热的不良导体，热作用损伤常局限于上呼吸道。烟雾吸入导致肺损伤(49)。有研究显示，约半数火灾死者被检见上呼吸道及食管的热作用损伤，其中部分死者呼吸道内检见烟灰(图4-20、图4-21；参考文献52)。眼结膜及颈部肌肉出血被认为是烧伤的生活反应(73)。在某些烧死尸体中，尤其是血中碳氧血红蛋白饱和度较低(<30%)的死者，可观察到舌根出血，有观点认为上述舌根出血是由热作用导致颈部或胸部压力升高引起的颅内血管淤血所致(74)。尸体舌外凸程度与气道内烟灰含量无关(74)。

4.2 证据支持

采集尸体心血管及股动、静脉血后需置于添加了氟化钠防腐剂的试管中。未做防腐处理的血液中的碳氧血红蛋白及氰化物含量会随时间发生改变(75-77)。有研究发现，烧死尸体的左心室血液中碳氧血红蛋白与氰化物的含量较右心室血液中的高(56)。可能的机制为受害者生前于火场中吸入的有毒气体经肺进入血循环并循环至左心(56,78)。有研究通过对上述火灾中人体吸入有毒物质后的"首过效应"(first-pass phenomenon，一种药物代谢现象，指药物进入人体后，在进入体循环之前其浓度会大大降低，通常与药物的肝脏代谢和肠道吸收有关)进行评估后指出，烧死尸体中左、右心室血液内碳氧血红蛋白饱和度无明显差异。即使在火灾中人体呼吸运动迅速

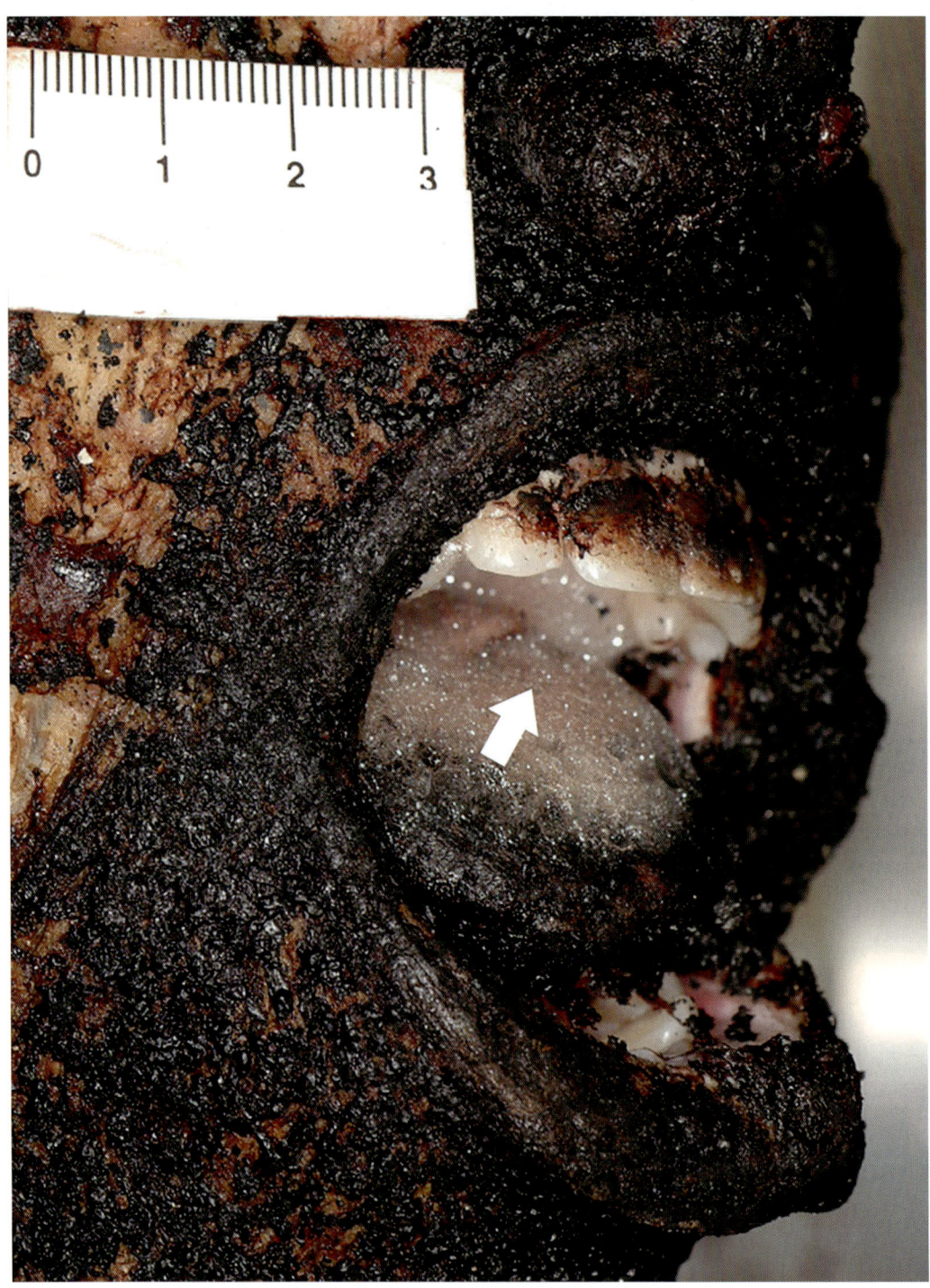

图 4-19 机动车碰撞后起火案例。炭化尸体口腔内泡沫(箭头)——肺水肿征象,提示存在生活反应。死亡原因为颅脑损伤,死者血中碳氧血红蛋白饱和度低于 10%。

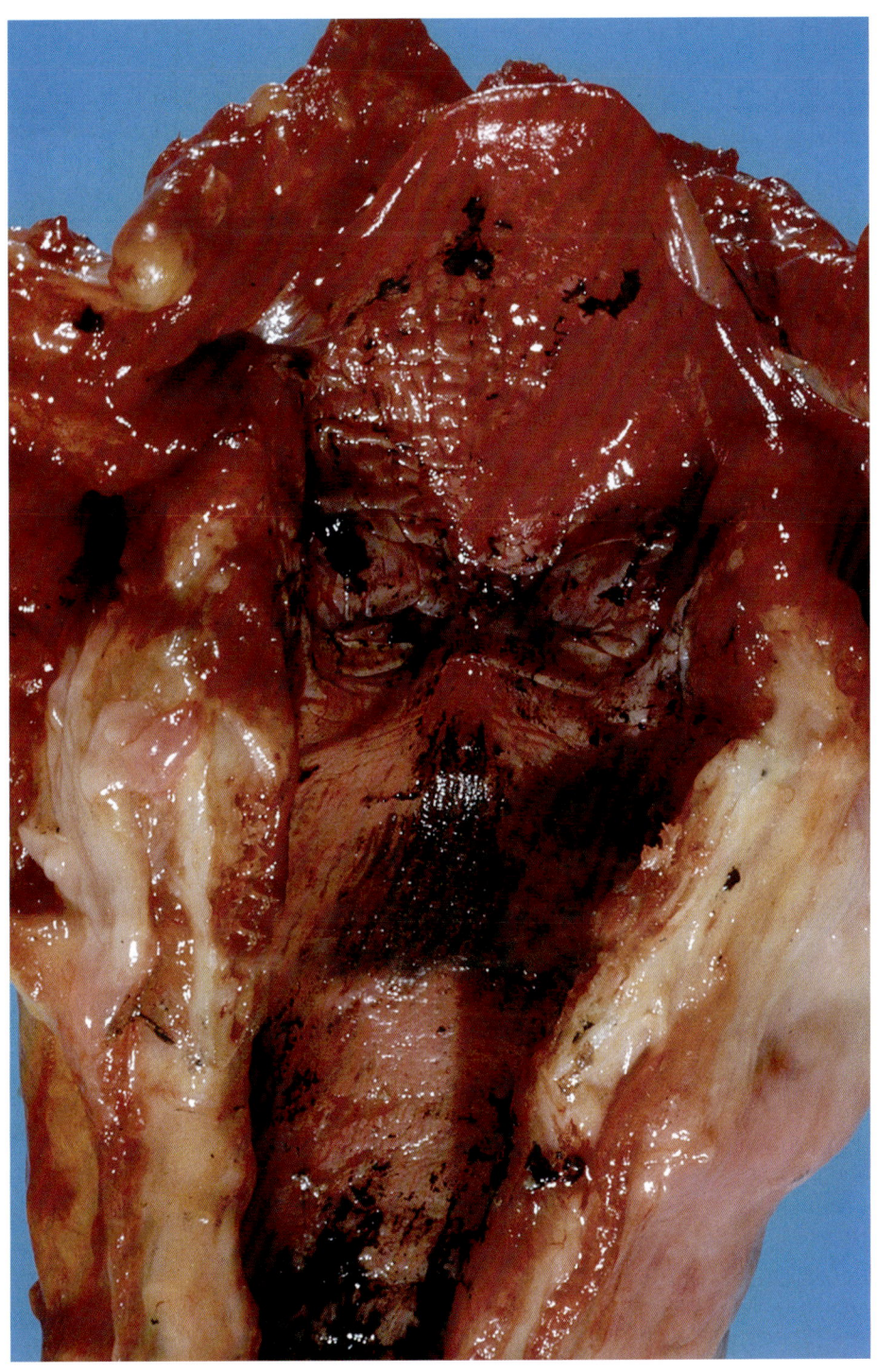

图 4-20 吸入性损伤。会厌粘膜红肿、血管淤血。气道中检见烟灰。

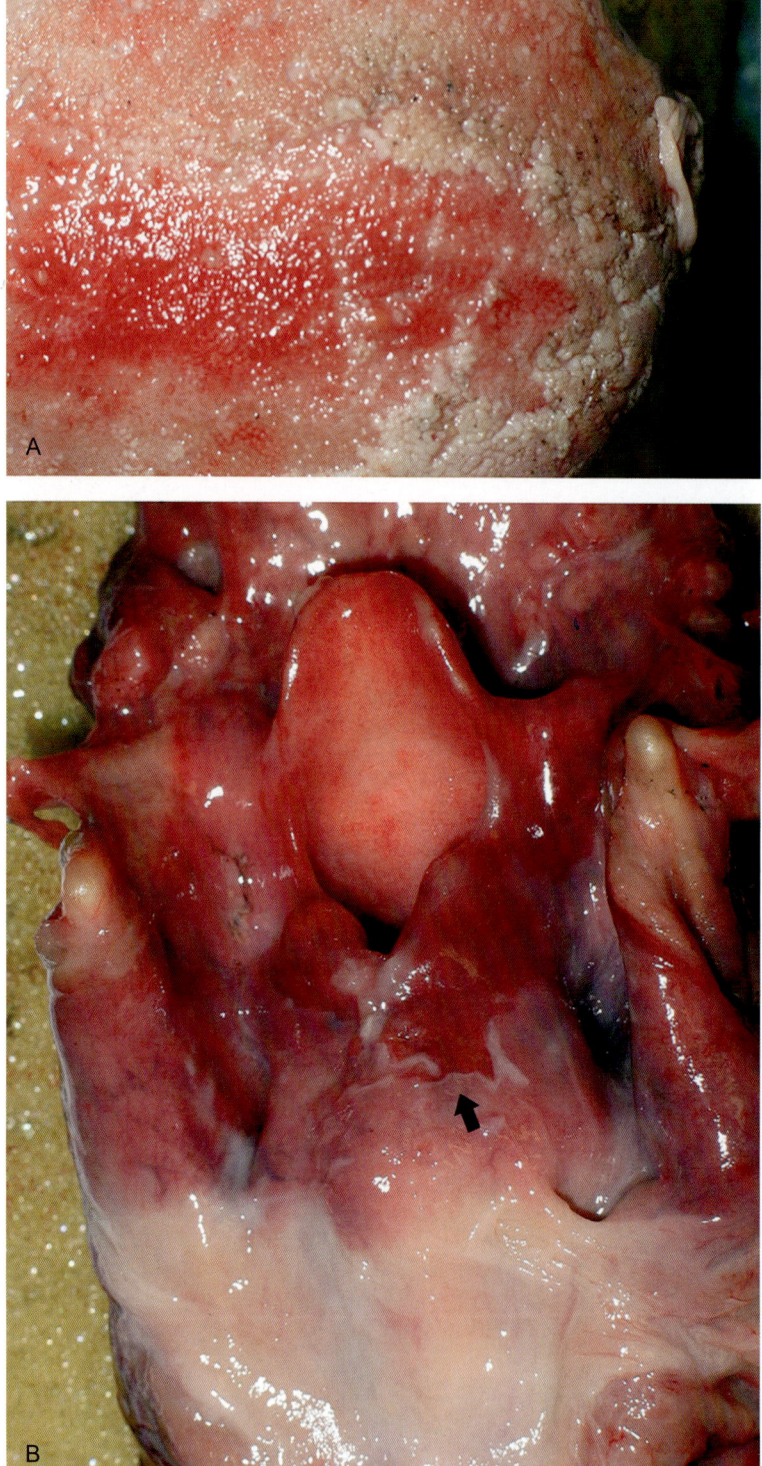

图 4-21 吸入性损伤。（A）舌黏膜糜烂。（B）原位喉－气管。热损伤导致杓会厌襞糜烂（箭头）（加拿大安大略省伦敦市伦敦健康科学中心的 C.Armstrong 博士供图）。

停止,血液循环仍将持续一段时间,导致左、右心室血液中毒物浓度一致(79)。

在火灾现场收集可疑物质用于判断是否使用了助燃剂。当尸体被闻及芳香烃或其他气味时需高度怀疑使用了助燃剂。解剖时冲洗尸体可见其体表薄膜状物质脱落(80)。因助燃剂多为挥发性物质,解剖时应尽快提取检材[皮肤和(或)软组织、烧毁的衣物](80,81)。部分自杀的死者会喝下助燃剂,可在其血液中检出(16,82)。在使用助燃剂的情况下,尸体呼吸道内可能无明显烟灰,血中碳氧血红蛋白饱和度亦不升高。对这类案件,死者血液中助燃剂的检测有助于判断其是否为生前烧死。自焚案件中常会使用助燃剂(19,21,83)。有研究表明使用助燃剂自杀或他杀的烧死尸体中,左心室血液内助燃剂(如汽油、煤油)含量较右心室血液内的高(78,79,84)。这种左、右心室血液中助燃剂含量的差异可能源于心室纤颤导致的全身血液循环停止(79)。在一些使用助燃剂的火灾案件中,死者体内检见烟灰且(或)血中碳氧血红蛋白饱和度升高(>10%),但血中却未检出助燃剂。

4.3 其他损伤

发生于火灾前的致死性损伤(图4-22、图4-23)。尸体解剖前应先进行影像学检查,便于排除某些类型的损伤(如枪弹创,参阅图4-3及参考文献4)。尸体炭化会掩盖体表损伤(图4-24;参考文献67),需运用人类学知识区分生前与死后形成的热作用骨折(85)。基于解剖学特点,颅底受到热直接作用相对较少。未炭化的颅底骨折提示生前损伤,如果同时伴有骨折部位及周围软组织出血、相应硬脑膜下及蛛网膜下腔出血则更支持生前伤(图4-25;参考文献34,86)。硬脑膜下血肿为生前损伤的特征(参阅标题3.3及参考文献4,47)。硬脑膜下出血通常为单侧(49),可检见脑内损伤(图4-25)。

在具有致死性机械性损伤的尸体中未检见烟灰及血液中碳氧血红蛋白含量增加(42)。机械性损伤亦可于火灾中形成(4)。对于机动车相关火灾的研究显示,尸体检验常见3类阳性发现:烟灰吸入及血中碳氧血红蛋白含量增加、呼吸道热作用损伤及机械性损伤(67)。此类死者如果血中碳氧血红蛋白饱和度超过30%,则强烈提示其因吸入大量燃烧产物致死(67);如果血中碳氧血红蛋白饱和度低于20%,则需考虑是否有其他的致死原因,如在机动车碰撞过程中所受机械性损伤及热作用损伤(67)。在机动车碰撞并着火的案件中受伤死亡的车内乘客体内可检见烟灰及较低的血中碳氧血红蛋白饱和度(52)。

4.4 疾病

火场中的死者可在火灾前或火灾发生时死于疾病,可能无法检见血中碳氧血红蛋白含量增加及呼吸道内烟灰(图4-26;参考文献4,33,42,52)。较健康人而言,患有贫血、心脏及呼吸系统疾病或脑卒中的个体在体内碳氧血红蛋白饱和度轻度升高时即可死亡(4)。无证据表明火灾死者的年龄与血中碳氧血红蛋白饱和度有相关性(56)。

图 4-22 死后焚尸。未检见烟雾吸入，血中碳氧血红蛋白饱和度极低。棚车卸货时车厢壁倒塌将死者压在底下。火灾源于工人使用的乙炔火源。尸体解剖检见锁骨下动脉撕裂。

第 4 章 | 高温损伤

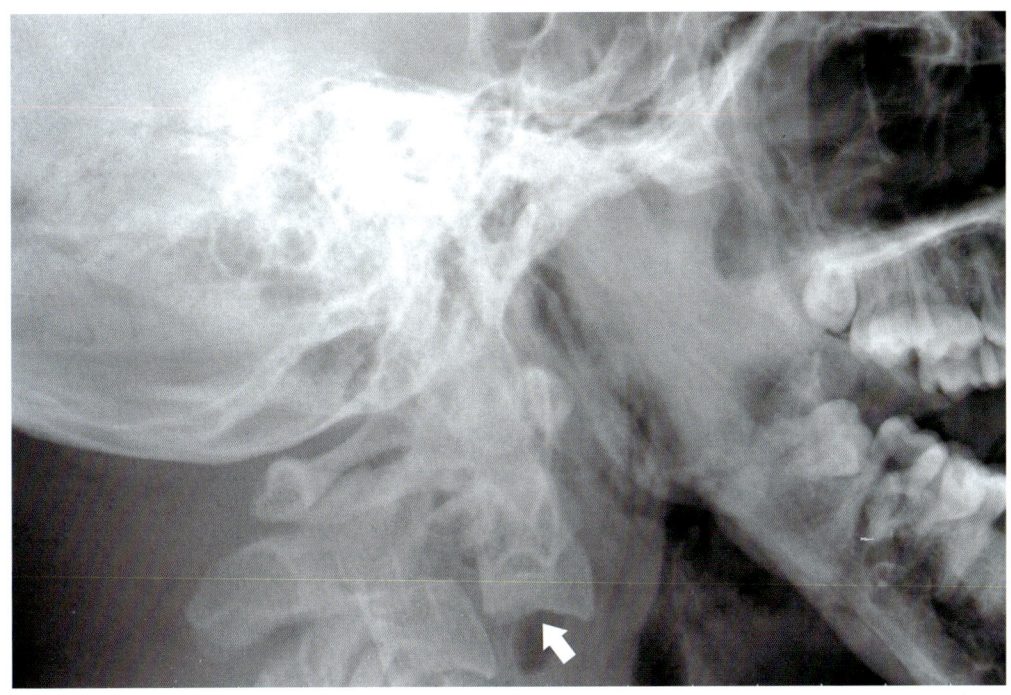

图 4-23 机动车碰撞事故起火，火场中发现炭化尸体。影像学检查示 C2－C3 椎体脱位（箭头）。

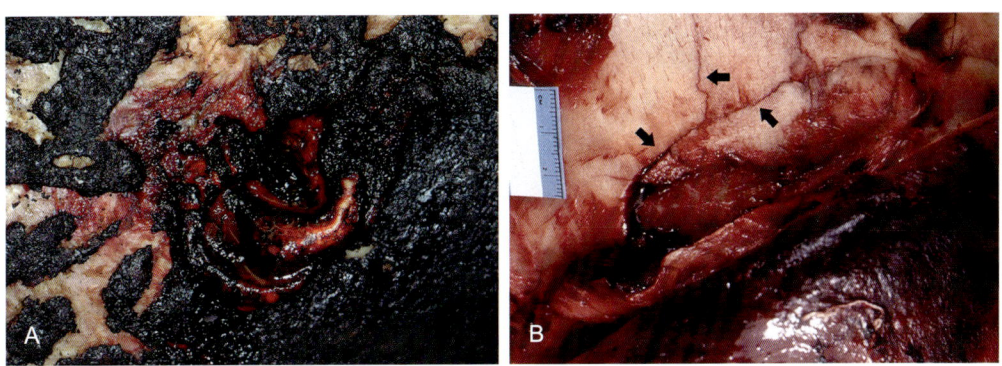

图 4-24 机动车碰撞后起火。(A) 炭化尸体耳道内的凝血块（箭头）。检见颅底骨折。注意炭化引起的耳部附近皮肤开裂。(B) 炭化尸体。翻开头皮检见颅骨线性骨折（箭头），未见炭化等热作用迹象。

4.5 显微镜检查

解剖时，大体检见呼吸道黏膜上烟灰覆盖及镜检见黏膜中炭末沉积可以明确死者存在烟灰吸入（图 4-18，参考文献 52）。对烧伤组织的镜检可以评估烧伤时个体是否存活。烧伤后存活 4 小时的组织镜检可见数个中性粒细胞自血管内向外迁移（52，87）。存活 6 小时的烧伤组织周围可见大量粒细胞浸润。在大多数火灾现场死亡的案件中，受害者在吸入 CO 及烟雾后迅速死亡，烧伤为死后形成。

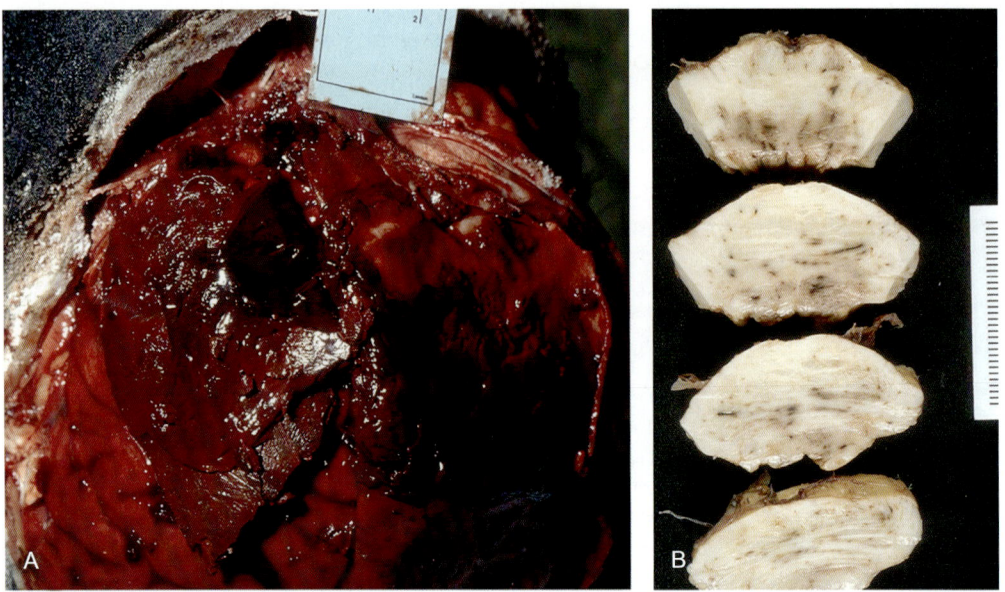

图 4-25 机动车碰撞后起火,炭化尸体。(A)常规开颅。硬脑膜下血肿。(B)脑干(脑桥)多发点状出血提示弥漫性血管损伤。

图 4-26 火灾发生前死亡的尸体。尸体解剖明确其患有缺血性心脏病。未检见烟雾吸入,血中碳氧血红蛋白饱和度极低。

第4章 | 高温损伤

镜检所见的上呼吸道黏膜脱落等可由组织自溶引起（见标题4.1及参考文献52）。呼吸道上皮细胞核拉长并呈栅栏状排列是一种热作用效应的表现(52)。呼吸道黏膜水肿、血管淤血是一种非特异性的生活反应表现(52)。检见假性杯状细胞、黏液分泌增多及呼吸道黏膜上皮细胞的水泡状脱落被认为是生前组织受到热作用的表现，即使尸体内未检见烟灰及血中碳氧血红蛋白含量增加(52)。对迅速死亡尸体的肺进行检查，可见非特异性改变［急性肺淤血、水肿(52)］。骨折后脂肪组织可进入血循环，但在某些未检见钝性损伤的火灾死亡尸体的肺内也可检见轻至中度的脂肪栓塞（参阅第8章标题12.1；参考文献42,47,52）。

5 入院治疗（烧伤患者）

5.1 流行病学

被送医后最终死亡的烧伤患者，可能存在多种类型的损伤(1,61)。年龄的增长会伴随记忆力下降与行动不便，这是意外火灾受害者的一项高危因素，但某些类型的火灾具有特定的受害者群体(61)。例如，一项研究指出，机动车及有机溶剂相关的火灾的受害者多为青少年或20出头的人群(61)。烫伤是门诊就诊及儿童和成人住院的常见原因。大多数重度烧伤及死亡的患者由火灾引起(1,88-90)。患有身体残疾及精神障碍的个体（如养老院居民）无法从滚烫的浴缸或淋浴中离开，是成年患者烫伤的一项典型的原因(2,61,91)。乙醇中毒也是烧伤发生的危险因素之一(2)。儿童在洗澡或厨房玩耍时缺乏监护（如儿童触碰灶具上煮沸的锅具）会引起烫伤(89,91)，这些烫伤可能缘于水温设定过高，将家用热水器水温调低至54.4℃［130°F(92)］以下可减少烫伤的发生。

大量的研究期望明确烧伤患者死亡的危险因素。一项回顾性研究对1990—1994年间马萨诸塞州总医院及Shriners烧伤研究所接诊的1 665名急性烧伤病例进行分析后，明确了3个烧伤患者死亡的危险因素：年龄大于60岁、烧伤体表面积超过40%及吸入性损伤(93)。根据死亡率预测公式计算，不存在或存在上述3个危险因素中的一项、两项或三项的烧伤患者死亡率分别为0.3%、3%、33%及90%左右。关于其他预后影响因素［如Ⅲ度烧伤的程度及潜在的慢性呼吸系统疾病等(1,94-98)］也有相关报道。个体所患疾病（如心脏病）及其他健康状况（如酒精滥用、抽烟）对烧伤的预后可能具有一定影响或没有影响(1)。年幼及年老的患者心肺功能储备有限，对循环血容量变化十分敏感，这类患者在复苏期间可能出现循环血量不足或过多(98)。患者出现肺淤血、水肿是非特异性的表现，未必与容量复苏有关（参阅标题5.2，表4-1及参考文献99）。鉴于烧伤死亡的复杂性，尽管已有研究建立相关数学模型，但烧伤死亡率的危险因素仍未完全明确(97)。此外，一个研究机构提出的数学模型可能无法在其他研究机构中得到复制(1,97)。随着医疗技术的发展，烧伤死亡率随之下降，而预后影响因素也会发生改变(94)。对于长期住院后死亡的烧伤患者，无论其是否存在相关的预后影响因素，法医病理学工作者都需根据相关信息及检验所见对具体案例进行死因鉴定，这是一项巨大的挑战。

5.2 烧伤并发症

烧伤患者可有多种并发症，一种或多种并发症均可成为致死原因（见表4-1及参考文献98,100,101）。

随着对重度烧伤患者进行有效液体复苏手段的发展，败血症逐渐成为致死的重要原因（1,94,100,101,103）。败血症来源具有多样性（表4-1），可源于烧伤创面感染、肺炎、插导尿管后尿路感染、开放静脉通路后感染及皮肤移植供皮区创面感染（101,111）。

即使在临床治疗中已经消除了任何感染，感染及烧伤仍能触发一种难以控制的系统性炎症反应，从而导致多器官功能衰竭，这是另一种常见的致死原因（参阅第1章标题4.3；参考文献1,88,103,131）。低血容量性休克也可导致多器官功能衰竭（88,103）。有研究表明，发生多器官功能衰竭的患者往往存在较大创面的烧伤，并且年龄较大，但其他研究并未得出此种关联性（1,103）。

呼吸衰竭[吸入性损伤、肺炎、成人呼吸窘迫综合征（ARDS）]同样是致死的重要原因（1,88,98,100,102,103,110,113,116,131,132）。

5.3 烟雾吸入性损伤

吸入烟雾会影响呼吸道上皮的气道清除功能，引起支气管痉挛，并会影响肺泡细胞产生表面活性物质（104,108,112）。

吸入的烟雾或其他燃烧产物能影响上呼吸道或包括肺组织在内的整个呼吸道的正常功能（98,99,101,102,104,113）。

除吸入沸水、蒸汽或其他炙热气体（如爆炸产生的挥发性气体）之外，热空气通常不会引起气管损伤（99,101,102,113,133）。上呼吸道吸入的热气体将在到达肺泡前冷却（102,104,133）。面部烧伤、呼吸道内烟灰、密闭空间内的火灾及无意识地吸入烟雾等情况均会增加吸入性损伤的可能性（102,104,110,116,132,133）。吸入性损伤可不伴有皮肤烧伤（102,104）。临床上，吸入性损伤患者可在吸入后数日方出现症状（98,104,110,113）。

上呼吸道水肿、炎症及24小时内并发呼吸衰竭者，需进行气管插管（98,101,102,108,133）。呼吸道内烟灰通常会在住院后次日消失（110,113）。吸入性气管损伤可进展为气管壁溃疡，最终导致严重、广泛的黏膜坏死，患者需用机械通气辅助呼吸并可能需进行气管切开（98,100,102,113,116）。既往有气管/支气管炎者易继发肺炎（98,109,110,113）。气管插管及气管切开术后可并发上呼吸道溃疡及炎症（99,100,116,134）。晚期并发症包括声门及声门下狭窄（134）。严重烧伤患者易患下呼吸道感染（116）。急性呼吸窘迫综合征同样是吸入性损伤的并发症（参阅第1章标题4.3；参考文献104）。

表 4–1　死因鉴定中需要注意的烧伤后严重并发症

发生于 3 天内
- CO 中毒后的神经系统并发症；缺血缺氧性脑病 (100)
- 吸入性损伤 (烟雾, 有毒物质, 炙热气体如蒸汽) (94, 98, 100, 102, 103)
  - 急性咽喉水肿
  - 黏膜 "烧伤"
  - 坏死性或 "假膜性" 喉/气管/支气管炎、肺炎及呼吸衰竭 (104)
- 休克 (大面积烧伤；参考文献 94, 98, 100, 101 及 103)
- 组织水肿—紧缩致四肢 ("筋膜室综合征")、躯干内部器官组织受压 ("腹腔间隙综合征") 及颈部呼吸道受压所致呼吸窘迫需要进行焦痂及筋膜切开减压术[a] (参阅第 8 章标题 8.4；图 4–27；参考文献 98, 105–109)
- 肌红蛋白尿及肾衰竭 (电流作用或挤压伤引起) (参阅第 8 章标题 13)
- 麻痹性肠梗阻 (98)

发生于 7 天内
- 左心室心内膜下出血 (濒死期改变)[b]
- 肺炎
  - 继发于吸入性损伤 (空气媒介；参考文献 98–100, 108, 110 和 111)[b]
  - 吸入 ± 肺炎 (88)[b]
- 肺出血、水肿或不张 (可为即时性；参考文献 98, 99, 101, 102, 108, 112 和 113)[b,c]
- 肾衰竭 (血容量不足) — 急性肾小管坏死[b]；肾皮质坏死 (100, 101)[b,d]
- 烧伤伤口感染 (如铜绿假单胞菌等革兰阴性菌、金黄色葡萄球菌；参考文献 89, 100, 101 和 111)[b,e]

发生于 7 天后
- 急性心肌梗死 (98, 103, 114, 115)[f]
- 感染性心内膜炎及化脓性血栓性静脉炎 (可由血管插管引起)
- 肺炎 (见 3 天及 7 天内并发症)
  - 血行感染 (革兰阴性菌, 如烧伤伤口铜绿假单胞菌感染, 血管插管部位感染引起化脓性血栓性静脉炎, 内脏隐匿性穿孔引起腹膜炎, 尿路感染, 内脏或外周血管注射部位脓肿 [98–100, 116])[g]
- 弥漫性肺泡损伤 (成人呼吸窘迫综合征；参阅第 1 章标题 4.3；参考文献 99, 116 和 117)
- 血栓栓塞[d,h]
- 胃、十二指肠糜烂/溃疡 (柯林溃疡)[d]；出血性胃炎前期表现 (98, 100, 118)[d]
- 胃扩张, 败血症并发症 (101)
- 肠梗阻, 败血症并发症 (88, 98, 101)
- 肠系膜上动脉综合征致十二指肠梗阻 (98, 119)[d,i]
- 结肠扩张 (假性肠梗阻) 并发盲肠穿孔 (120)[d]
- 缺血性 (伪膜性) 肠炎 (100, 101, 121)[d]
- 肝衰竭[j]
- 急性胆囊炎 (结石性, 非结石性；参考文献 98, 122 和 123)[k]
- 急性出血性胰腺炎 (98)[d]
- 肾衰竭 (见 3 天及 7 天内并发症)[d,l]
- 急性肾盂肾炎 (101) — 上行性,[d] 血行性[d]

- 肾动脉血栓形成［肾皮质梗死(115)］ᵈ
- 坏死性前列腺炎ᵈ
- 烧伤，其他损伤，脓毒血症并发弥散性血管内凝血(DIC)(参阅第1章标题4.3；参考文献98,100)ᵐ
- 急性脾炎，败血症表现(100)
- 儿童应激性胸腺退化(100)
- 肾上腺出血［Waterhouse-Friderichsen综合征(98,100,101,124)］ᵈ·ⁿ
- 血容量不足致垂体梗死ᵈ
- 烧伤伤口感染［见7天内并发症，由少见的真菌引起，如念珠菌(111)］
- 内脏脓肿(败血症表现)
- 病毒感染［巨细胞病毒，单纯疱疹病毒，腺病毒(125,126)］ᵈ

注：a 焦痂及筋膜切开后皮肤边缘回缩的程度(达到4—9 cm或1.5—3.5 in时)提示组织水肿。

b 并发症可发生于烧伤1周后。

c 肺出血存在多种原因：肺动脉高压(如头部损伤、充血性心力衰竭)，胃液吸入，脂肪栓塞，DIC，吸入性损伤，血栓栓塞性梗死，感染性(如铜绿假单胞菌)血管坏死。血容量超负荷可导致肺水肿，且是心衰的表现之一。

d 非常见死因。

e 烧伤伤口可通过与医院工作人员的手或带菌物体(如被污染的褥垫)接触而感染，也可由受害者自身的粪便污染。开放性烧伤伤口感染的表现包括：组织变为深褐色或黑色、烧伤区域皮下脂肪组织出血变色，以及远离烧伤部位的软组织灶性出血(98,101)。镜下可见烧伤部位有大量的微生物聚集(98)，微生物侵入周围未坏死组织，未烧伤组织内可见血管炎、坏死及出血(98)。

f 可能不伴有冠状动脉粥样硬化。血液高凝状态(如DIC)并发冠状动脉血栓形成可能是导致梗死的原因之一。血栓也可见于其他血管中(101,115)。

g 血源性肺炎的特征为类似于肺梗死的肺膜下出血(101,116)。镜下可见明显的肺实质坏死(116)。若铜绿假单胞菌感染，在肺血管及支气管周围肺间质内可见大量革兰阴性菌(116)。可检见炎性栓子(116)。早期病变可无渗出性改变。

h 研究表明肺动脉血栓栓塞与中心静脉导管有关(127)。尽管在这些患者的无名静脉中未检见血栓，但不能排除锁骨下静脉内血栓形成的可能。血栓栓塞的风险与烧伤面积无相关性(101)。

i 对于全身烧伤面积超过30%的患者，发生肠系膜上动脉综合征的特征性表现为十二指肠部分或完全梗阻(119)。十二指肠远端被卡压在前部结构(肠系膜上动脉)与后部结构(脊柱、主动脉)之间。该综合征与患者长期卧床及体重迅速下降，引起肠系膜及腹膜后脂肪组织减少及腹部肌肉力量减弱有关。为烧伤患者补充营养可以减少体重下降。

j 肝小叶中央性出血性坏死、肝内淤胆及非特异性肝炎是败血症、休克、多次输血、充血性心力衰竭和肝肾综合征的表现。胆汁淤积型肝炎可能为药源性(98,100,128,129)。

k 败血症、脱水、多次外科手术、胆汁及胃肠道淤积、胰腺炎等均可导致非结石性胆囊炎(98,123)。

l 败血症和充血性心力衰竭是肾衰竭的原因。肾衰竭与高压电损伤、挤压伤或延迟复苏有关(98)。

m 表现为血管穿刺部位出血及黏膜出血，广泛性皮肤瘀斑，包括肾上腺在内的内脏出血(130)。

n 与DIC、败血症、抗凝治疗和直接损伤等有关。烧伤后早期也可观察到。罕见广泛性腹膜后出血(124)。

(改编自参考文献3。)

6 法医对烧伤住院后死亡患者的评估

尸体解剖不仅有助于明确死亡原因,并且能够发现临床上未检出的病变。华盛顿大学烧伤中心的研究指出,在 1989—1994 年,88 例患者的尸体解剖结果表明有 18% 的患者存在临床误诊。这些病例中有 4 例若误诊被早期发现并改变治疗方案,很可能会有较好的预后(135)。

高温损伤鉴定时,法医需注意以下几点:

(1)审查临床病史资料。根据案件情况,向多方收集信息(如警方、火灾调查员)。

(2)尸表检验中,记录医疗行为引起的尸体改变,包括焦痂切开术/筋膜切开术(图 4-27)。

(3)记录高温损伤的程度与外观(图 4-28)。伤者是否存在特征性损伤?例如,热水浴缸中烫伤者,其烫伤往往位于身体低下部位(91)。这类伤者中部分伤者存在局部身体烫伤,这是因为烫伤部位恰好紧贴浴缸的侧面或底部(136)。必须对损伤进行拍照。

(4)排除其他类型损伤的可能性(137)。

(5)开展包括组织病理学检查在内的系统性尸体解剖,阐明多种死亡参与因素(表 4-1)。可对烧伤组织进行显微镜检(图 4-29)。

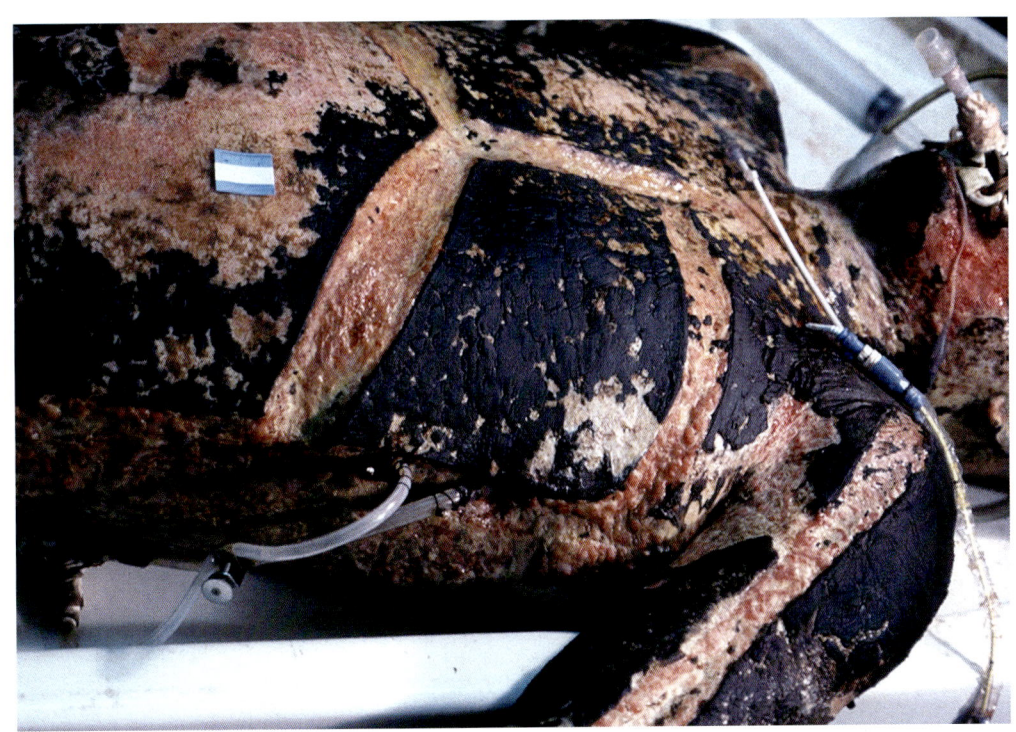

图 4-27　烧伤者。焦痂切开术后。

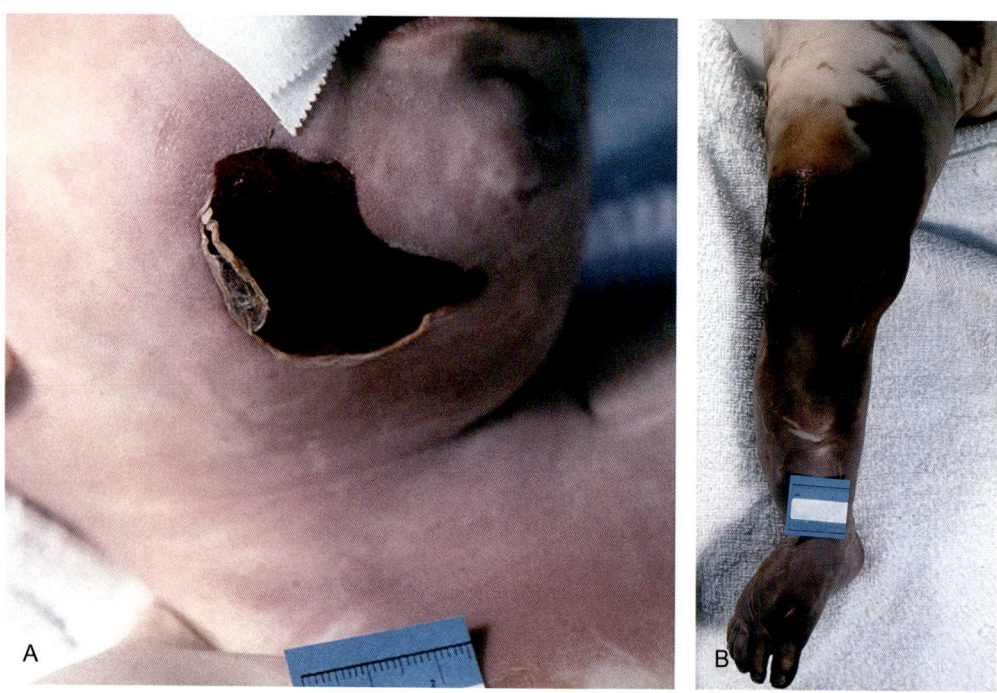

图 4-28 热辐射引起的烧伤。(A) 皮肤水疱,破裂(Ⅱ度烧伤)。(B) 下肢皮肤广泛性皮革样化改变(Ⅲ度烧伤)。

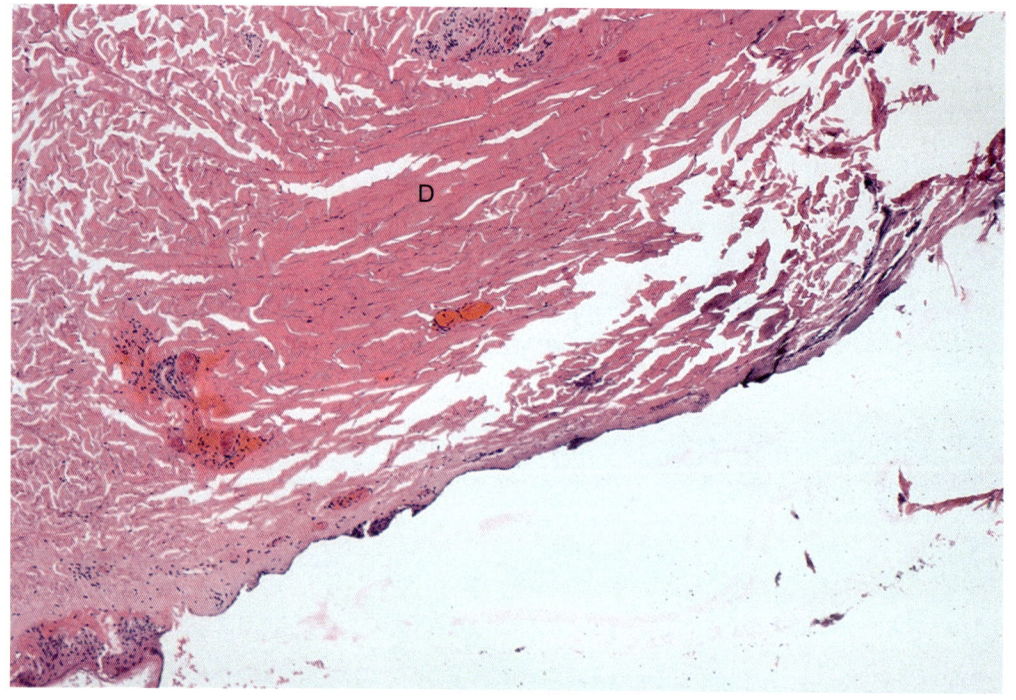

图 4-29 Ⅱ度烧伤。表皮脱落,真皮凝固性坏死(D)(H-E 染色,放大倍数 ×25)。

(6) 长时间住院的烧伤患者可能已经进行了大量的微生物学检查并进行了多种抗生素治疗,如果有需要,可提取生物学样本(如血液、肺组织、脓肿组织)进行微生物培养。

7 电击死

7.1 电流损伤的物理学与病理生理学特征

在同一电路中,通过某段导体的电流与导体两端的电压成正比,与导体的电阻成反比(138–140)。即欧姆(Ohm)定律:$I = V / R$,其中"I"是电流[安培(A)],"V"是电压[伏特(V)],"R"是电阻[欧米伽(Ω);参考文献 138,139 和 141–145]。

电流作用于人体产生两大影响:神经肌肉细胞去极化及组织热效应,热效应的产生需要更长的电流持续作用时间(38,140,142,144,146–149)。电流通过人体时,大多数骨骼肌细胞及神经元轴突的长轴平行于电流方向,细胞跨膜电位会受影响(147)。电流作用于神经肌肉细胞将会破坏细胞膜的磷脂双分子层结构,改变细胞膜的通透性,从而导致细胞结构缺陷或产生"微孔"(电穿孔),电流作用可导致细胞膜蛋白质变性(142,145–147)。当电流产生高于 60℃(140°F)的温度时会破坏组织(150)。电流产生的热损伤通过凝固性坏死作用使组织变性(38,151)。

多种因素决定了电流作用于人体后的损伤机制及损伤特征。上述因素包括电路类型、接触时间、人体电阻、电压、电流大小、电流传导途径及接触面积(电流强度与接触面积呈反比;参考文献 38,138,141,143,151–154,标题 7.3 和 7.4.)。

7.1.1 电路类型

交流电(alternating current, AC),是一种极性不停变换的电场,在美国和加拿大频率为 60 赫[在欧洲频率为 50 赫(138–140,142,147,152,155,156)]。交流电可见于家庭住宅(低压;美国和加拿大为 15 安)和公共事业线(高压),这也是最常见的两类电击死亡的发生地点(139,145,147,156)。交流电会引起细胞去极化(140),肌肉完成一次生理性收缩-松弛时间为 20–40 毫秒(147)。当肌纤维受到频率在 40–110 次/秒(40–110 赫)的电流持续性作用时,会产生持续性收缩[强直(152,157)]。60 赫的交流电每秒钟变换 120 次电流方向[即每 8 毫秒变换 1 次(147)]。交流电在较低电流下即可导致肌强直,故比直流电(direct current, DC)更危险(参考文献 139,141,142,144,145,149,152 和 158–160)。如果手握交流电源,手及前臂屈肌会产生强直性收缩,这会增强手的握力并延长电流接触时间,增强电流损伤程度(139,141,142,147,152,157,158)。尸僵可在高压电电击死后即刻产生,且仅局限于四肢中的单个肢体(参阅第 2 章图 2–8;参考文献 140,147,和 161–163)。

与交流电不同,电子沿单一方向流动称为直流电(138,139)。直流电作用于人体会引起单次肌肉收缩,电流接触时间较短,但增加了钝性损伤的风险(139,141,142,145,147,152,157)。直流电损伤可发生于雷电活动及与某些特定设备接触的过程中(如除颤器[139,140,145,152,164-166])。

7.1.2 电阻

电阻(R)与导电性相反,是组织对电流的阻碍作用,取决于组织的含水量、温度和其他物理性质(142,152)。电流恒定时,电阻越大,电能转换为热能的程度越大(38,142,144,145,151,152,167,168)。这可以用焦耳(Joule)定律表示:$Q = I^2 \times R \times T$($Q$=热量;$I$=电流;$R$=电阻;$T$=接触持续时间)。人体的最小电阻约为500欧(139,159,163)。良好的导电组织包括神经、血液、黏膜和肌肉(139-141,152,158)。黏膜(口、直肠、阴道)为低电阻组织,电阻变动范围为100欧[139,141,169,170])。肌腱和脂肪电阻较大,骨骼电阻最大(139,141,142,144,152,158,168)。皮肤是电流最先接触的部位,其电阻大小中等,电流接触皮肤后将有大量电能耗散(138,139,141,142,152,155)。潮湿皮肤的电阻会下降[出汗皮肤电阻约为2 500欧/平方厘米;浸没在水中的皮肤电阻为1 200-1 500欧/平方厘米(139,141,142,152,171)]。潮湿皮肤不会被烧伤,更多的电流将会进入体内(152),手掌上茧化皮肤的电阻可高达2×10^6欧/平方厘米(141,147,152,158)。当皮肤烧伤炭化后,电阻下降,更多电流将进入体内(139,142,145,152)。

电流产生的热量大小取决于电流强度,其与电流经过人体的横断面直径成反比,手指、脚趾的电烧伤程度较手臂、腿部更严重(38,141,145,146,148,168)。随着电流在体内积聚,电流将逐渐克服低导电性组织的电阻(152),整个人体将成为导体,电流将经过除骨骼以外的所有组织,导致不同程度的电流损伤与热损伤(38,139,147,152,155,168)。骨骼肌在四肢软组织中所占的体积最大,也承载了大部分电流作用(147)。肌肉既受到电流的直接热作用,又受到热容较高的骨骼的热作用(38,139,147,148,172)。

7.1.3 电流

电流是单位时间内通过导体横断面的电量。在电击中,由于仅能估算电流接触部位的人体皮肤表面电阻,而电流进入体内后所流经组织的电阻大小难以估算,故无法准确计算实际经过人体的电流大小(141,147,149)。电流经过人体会造成损伤(141,149,152,159,171),非致死性的电击会使人震颤,并可能引发高坠(159)。

7.1.4 电流通路

低压交流电会通过引起窒息(呼吸肌麻痹)或心跳、呼吸骤停而致死(表4-2)。通过心脏的电流(如手-手通路)可直接导致心肌损伤和心律失常(139,142,144,152,158-160)。心室纤颤是最常见的心律失常(144,150,159,173)。触电后发生心室纤颤者,在瘫倒之前可保持约10秒的意识清醒,并可在此期间做出保护性行为(如关闭电器电源)(140,159-161)。

第 4 章 | 高温损伤

表 4-2　交流电（60 Hz）对人体产生的影响

效应	电流 [毫安（mA），安（A）]
刺痛 / 疼痛	1—2 毫安
摆脱电流（平均水平）	
• 成年男性	7—9 毫安
• 成年女性	6—8 毫安
• 儿童	3—5 毫安
人体能自行抓握并摆脱的最大电流强度（50% 成年男性水平）	16 毫安
抽搐，肌僵直（触电后人体僵麻）	16—20 毫安
胸部肌肉强直致呼吸骤停	20—50 毫安
心室纤颤	50—100 毫安
心室停搏	＞2 000 毫安（＞2 安）
常用家用断路器	15 安
（美国）家用电流最大强度	240 安
高压电	＜1 000 安
雷电	＞200 000 安

注：改编自参考文献 38，140，142，150，157，159 和 160。

在雷击中，大量直流电沿着身体表面传播并进入体内，可导致心脏停搏、呼吸骤停、血管痉挛及自主神经功能障碍（141，167，174）。由于电流较大，雷击和高压电触电致心室停搏比心律失常更为多见（139，140，143，145，163，165，167）。心脏的自律性使其呈周期性、节律性搏动，在心脏停搏期间发生呼吸骤停导致的缺氧可引起心室纤颤及缺血缺氧性脑病（139，141—143，145，152，153，163，166，174，175）。约有三分之二的雷击受害者存活（142，147，153，164，174，176，177）。

电流通过脑可致呼吸骤停、麻痹、癫痫和直接性脑（脑干）损伤（如头 - 肢体通路（38，141—143，145，152，158—160，164，173，174，178）。约 100 毫安电流从头部流向肢体即可导致呼吸骤停（159）。高压电可产生大量热能并致不可逆的脑死亡（163）。即使呼吸中枢不在电流通路上，接触 60 赫、5 安以上的电流 1 秒钟即可致呼吸停止[如手 - 脚通路（159）]。电流经手臂 - 手臂或手臂 - 腿通路，也可致呼吸肌强直性收缩而引起窒息死亡（38，173）。

7.1.5 电压

在电损伤案件中，电压（V）通常是唯一已知的信息（142，143，145，149）。电损伤分为低压电损伤（≤1 000 伏）和高压电损伤（38，141，142，145，147，152，158，163）。电压越高，损伤越严重，但 110 伏家庭用电仍然具有足够的电流强度引起心室纤颤（144，158）。高压电触电案例中热效应是导致损伤或死亡的一种重要机制（140）。不同地区的民用电压大小不同：120 伏（美国和加拿大），220 伏（欧洲）或 240 伏[澳大利亚，英国（139，140，144，147，179）]。工业用电常为 220—440 伏（147）。高压电线电压可达数千伏。闪电在云端和地面之间的电压差达百万伏(143,164,167,176,180)。

7.2 流行病学与触电环境

对佛罗里达州戴德县217例意外触电事件的研究发现,其中93例为高压电(>1 000伏)触电,108例为低压电触电(163),16例为雷击死。另一项研究发现,39%的电击死为低压电触电[民用电最常见(171)]。对澳大利亚104例电击死的研究发现,88%的死者为低压电触电,12%的死者为高压电触电(181)。美国每年有大约1 000人死于电击伤(142,147,152,157,159,161)。美国医院烧伤科患者中有3%-6.5%为电烧伤(142,147,148,152)。约有一半的电击伤发生于工作场所中,其余发生于家中(181)。

多种情况均会形成低压电损伤[如使用有故障的工具或设备、修理电器、触碰外表破损的电线或带电物体(142,163,182,183)]。约三分之二的死者年龄在15—40岁,男性居多(174)。使用未接地(即电路或设备与地面或其替代物之间的导电连接)的工具或设备和靠近水的设备是触电的高危因素(142,181)。受害者可能不具备带电作业的资质(183)。高压电损伤通常发生在工作场所,主要涉及男性(142,147,158,161)。因高压电致死的工伤死者中,高压电工往往比其他职业的死者年轻(148,182,184)。夏季工伤触电死亡人数最多,原因包括:户外作业增加;因天气炎热而未穿戴厚重的绝缘服(包括手套和靴子);出汗导致皮肤电阻下降(181,184)。多种情况均会导致人体与工作场所的高压电器直接接触(如起重机触碰高压电线,金属杆、天线、梯子升起时触碰高压电线;参考文献142,151,158,161,163,185和186)。建筑业、采矿业人员的触电死亡率最高(182,187)。

盆浴时遭电击与家用电器有关,通常是由于吹风机浸泡在水中。安装接地故障断路器(漏电保护器)可降低遭电击的风险(161,188,189)。接地故障断路器探测到接地线和电流线之间5毫安大小的电流差时便会起保护作用。

超过20%的电击受害者是儿童(142)。由于幼儿在爬行和触摸时常会咀嚼物体(如电线),所以幼儿易受低压电损伤(139,141,142,145,147,152,189,190)。数日后在去除口唇部位电流损伤痂皮时,可能会损伤唇动脉引起大出血(139,157,189)。家长可能未做好充分的预防措施以防止幼儿接触电线(183)。幼儿还可通过直接(即嘴或手指)或间接(如使用金属叉)与电源插座接触而触电(190)。

对于在使用电器时突然死亡的案件,须考虑存在低压电触电的可能,并且需对电器设备和接线进行检测(140,161,163,184)。触电现场的设备并不一定处于开启状态,因为电线可能存在故障或受害者触电后有时间关闭设备(161)。死者可被目击在喊叫后瘫倒在地(140,161,163,181,184)。电击也会发生在自体性行为及两性性行为过程中(参阅第3章标题2.7.2;参考文献169,170,191和192)。

在工作场所以外,触碰完整的或垂落的高压电线也可触电(163)。儿童和青少年可因意外而触碰高压电线(142,145,151,152,189,190,193)。在家中或娱乐活动时通过接触导电体(如天线、风筝)也可触电(163,182,183,194)。接电话时由于电话线与 15 厘米(6 英寸)外的高压线之间产生电弧,可引起电烧伤(155,195)。如果触电者与高压或低压电源保持接触,上前施救的人员也可遭电击(139,151,196)。切换或断开带电线路可引起非接触性"闪光"性烧伤(158)。

电击死可涉及所有的死亡方式。对 220 例电击死案例的研究表明,其中 217 例为意外,2 例为自杀,1 例为他杀(163)。选择电击的自杀者相对较少(图 4-30;参考文献 161,163,181,188 和 197-199)。自杀者有时会使用定时器(200,201)。电源与皮肤之间可由电线相连(161,200)。有时他杀会被伪装成电击自杀(202)。采用电击杀人非常罕见(161,163,197,203,204)。

在美国,雷击每年造成 30-100 人死亡(139,152,159,174,177)。由于潮湿的暖空气与冷空气发生对流,形成积雨云(164,174,176,180)。粒子运动产生静电(144,167,180)。云层底部形成负电荷中心,而地面变为正电荷中心(144,164,174,176,180),形成巨大的电位差。当云层与地面间电位差达 30 000 伏或以上时,雷电可以从云层向地面延伸,并击中地面上物体(如站立的人)(164,174,176,205)。闪电常见于雷雨天气,但也见于暴风雪、沙尘暴和火山喷发等情况(144)。晴朗天气中也可能遭雷击,此时雷雨云离事发地非常遥远(167,177,206)。大部分雷击事件出现在夏天(174)。一次雷击可造成多人受伤(141-143)。

男性因为更多地参与户外工作和活动而面临更大的雷击风险(177,205)。一般来说,采取避雷措施的建筑物内不会发生雷击死亡事件;然而,闪电可通过铅管固定装置、电话线或其他通过金属导体连接到房屋外墙的设备进行侧向放电并对屋内人员进行间接雷击(174)。处于空旷区域或部分遮蔽区域者[如帐篷(174,205)]会面临更大的雷击风险。新加坡的学者经研究发现,三分之二的雷击死发生于部分遮蔽区域内(205)。闪电并不总是击中最高的物体(174)。雷击受害者无法维持带电状态(139,174)。

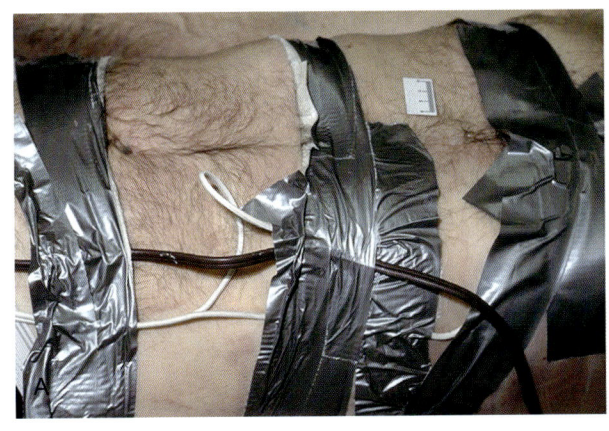 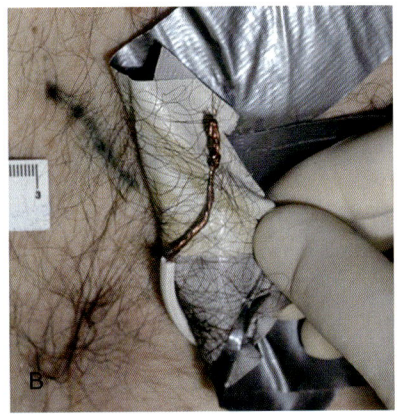

图 4-30　电击自杀。(A)胶带将电线固定在躯干部。(B)外露的铜线。电烧伤皮肤呈绿色。

7.3 电烧伤及其他体表损伤

直接接触带电体是最常见的电烧伤致伤机制(158)。皮肤电阻越大，烧伤程度越严重(141)。接触面积越小，电流强度越大，电流损伤越严重(158,163)。若接触面积大、接触时间短，即使高压电击也可能不形成皮肤电烧伤(140,142,149,163)。最常见的接触部位(电流入口)是手(图4-31；参考文献141,145和149)。低压交流电触电者可不伴有皮肤电流损伤(140,147,161,163,181)。澳大利亚的研究发现，约有90%的电击受害者伴有皮肤烧伤，可能是因为该国的家庭电压为240伏(181)。最常见的接地部位(电流出口)是脚(图4-32；参考文献141,149,152和158)。对于低压电击死案例的研究发现，位于皮肤较薄的部位(胸部、颈部、面部或手臂)而非手的电流接触性烧伤可能是由于皮肤潮湿所致(184)。触电后产生多枚电弧而形成多条电流通路时，人体表面可观察到多个电流入口及出口(图4-32；参考文献147,152和207)。

暴露在水中会使皮肤电阻降低、接触面积增加，从而减小电流强度，触电后没有明显的皮肤损伤；然而，低压电仍可致命[如潮湿的皮肤电阻为1 000欧，接触110伏的电源后产生0.1伏或100毫安的电流，该电流大小恰为引起心室纤颤的阈值(138,139,141,145,147,152,208)]。泡澡时如果身体的一部分伸出水面并接触到接地的金属物体，在浴缸中也可发生电流损伤(188)。个别案例报道了与水相关的特殊触电方式[如饮用地下电缆周围喷出的水；向电气化铁路上小便(209)]。

高压电触电更易导致重度烧伤(141)。直接接触高压电会引起深层软组织烧伤，甚至造成骨骼的热损伤(38)。触电时由于带电物体接触部位的金属发生汽化，高压电触电者皮肤接触部位常见黑色金属物质覆盖(147)。有时皮肤烧伤显露出特殊的损伤形态，与带电体接触部位形态一致，或与身上的金属饰品形态一致(161,210)。

电流入口与出口的电烧伤可小似针尖而被漏检，亦可形成巨大烧伤(图4-31和图4-32；参考文献38,147和158)。电流出口损伤面积并不一定大于电流入口(147)。电流斑中央组织炭化，周围环绕灰白色坏死组织(140,158)，坏死区域周围组织呈红色(140,158,161)。该皮肤红斑并不一定是生活反应(参阅标题3.3和参考文献163)。90℃(194℉)以上的温度会造成组织炭化，人体需要与低压电源持续接触约30秒才能达到该温度(163)。54℃(130℉)的温度40秒可造成表皮坏死(211)。触电后引发的致死性心律失常早于皮肤烧伤，这意味着典型的皮肤电流斑可能是死后形成的(139,163)。持续1-10毫秒的交流电刺激可引起心室纤颤，而Ⅰ度烧伤或皮肤红斑的形成至少需要与20毫安/平方毫米大小的电流持续接触20秒(139,163)。相比之下，用交流电(115伏)电击死猪的皮肤，电烧伤皮肤周围未见充血带。充血带只能在生前电流损伤中被观察到(212)。

未与电源直接接触也可引起电烧伤(38,147,157,207)。高压电(>300伏，包括闪电)触电会产生电弧(139,140,147)。人体的手臂与7 500千伏电力线之

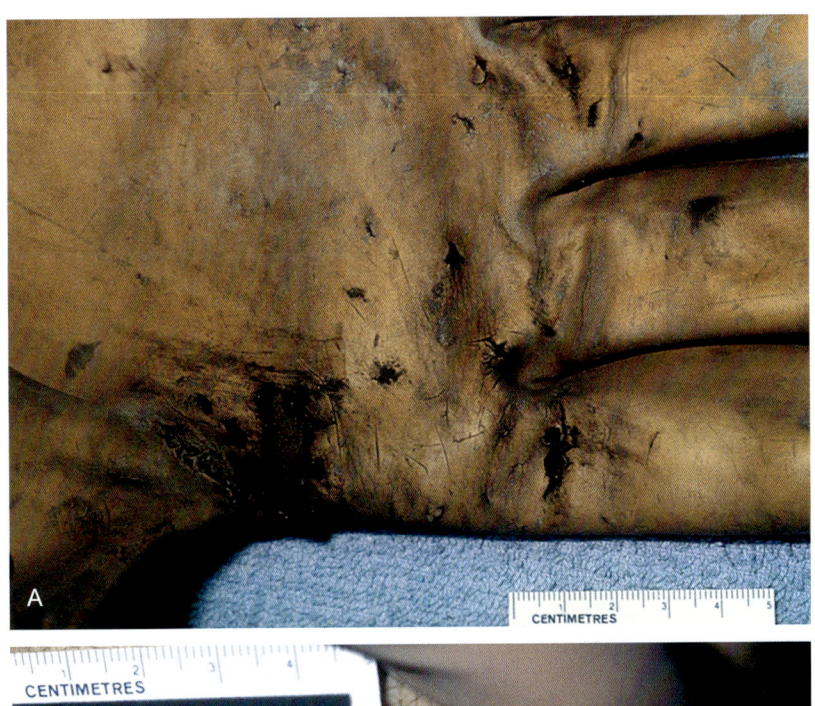

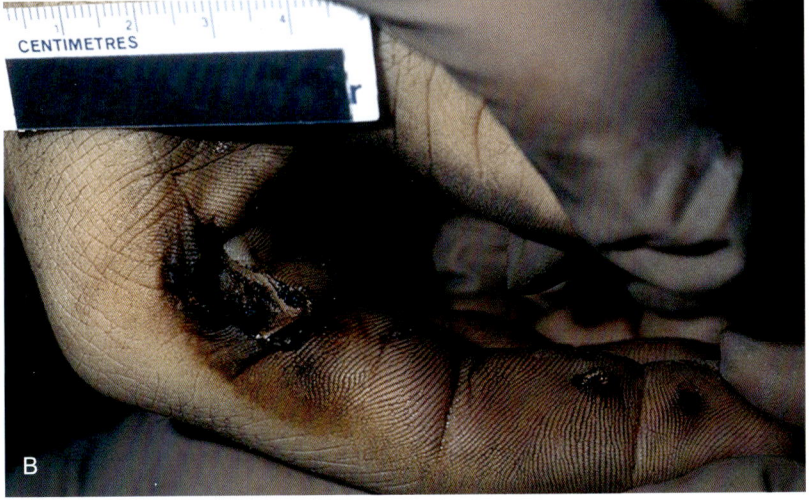

图4-31 电流损伤（接触部位或电流入口）。（A）工人手套。（B）手部烧伤（加拿大安大略省汉密尔顿市法医病理办公室 D.King 博士供图）。

间距离为3—4毫米时可引出电弧（147）。当手指伸出或手握尖锐物体（如螺丝刀）时，引出电弧的距离可以更远（147, 207, 209）。电弧温度接近2 500℃－5 000℃（4 500°F－9 000°F）时，可造成严重烧伤（139, 141, 145, 149, 150, 152, 157, 161, 209）。衣物，特别是鞋袜上可以留有电弧烧灼痕迹（139－141, 149, 150, 157, 161, 163, 209）。电弧烧伤可深达软组织甚至骨骼；然而有时皮肤表面电弧损伤轻微，尸表检验时可能会漏检（139, 141, 158, 207, 209, 210）。当电流经过屈肌并在皱褶部位（肘关节、腋窝、腕关节；参考文献 144, 145, 147, 152, 158 和 210）形成电弧时，

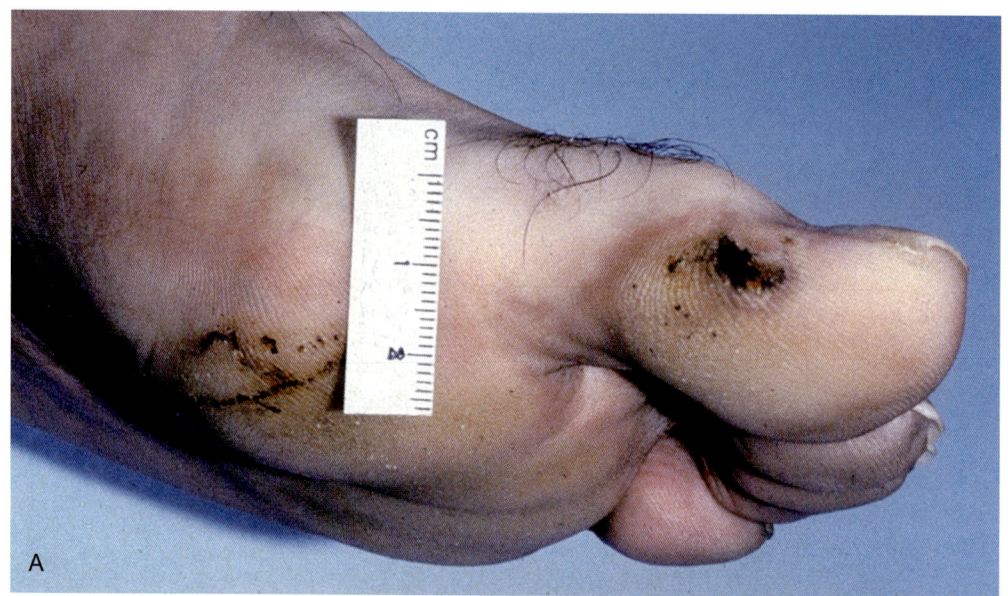

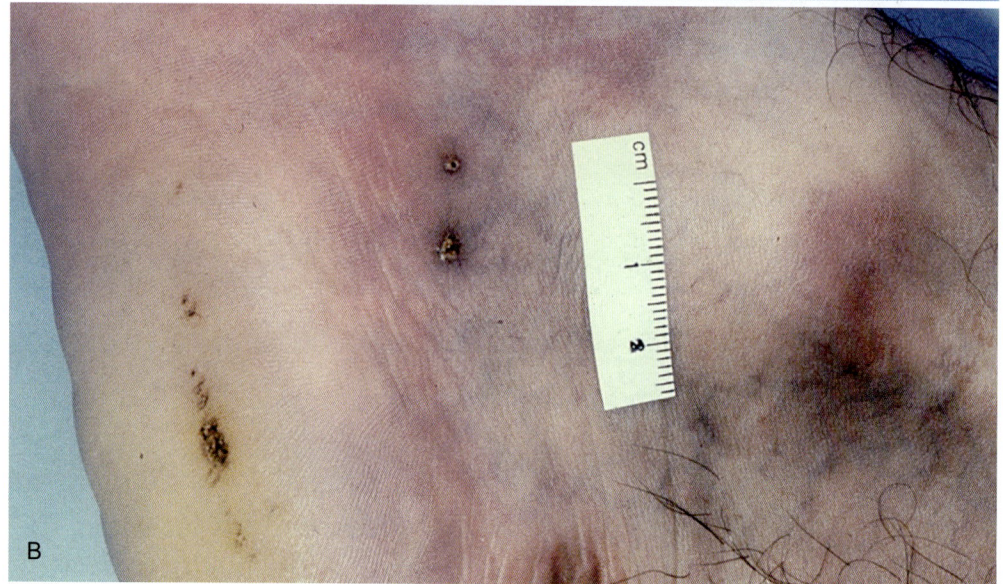

图4-32 电击伤（电流出口）。(A) 死亡原因为电流作用于心脏致心搏骤停。拇趾的电流出口损伤（美国北卡罗来纳州教堂山市法医局供图）。(B) 踝关节下方及足跟见多处电流出口损伤（加拿大安大略省汉密尔顿市法医病理办公室 D.King 博士供图）。

可造成"亲吻样"烧伤。电流入口与出口可能难以区分，因为入口与出口间可形成电弧（图4-31和图4-32；参考文献38,151）。当电弧接地时，地面上的受害者可以间接地暴露在强大的电弧中（139,158）。

雷电相关损伤可由直接雷击、接触被雷击的物体、闪电侧向传导（"放电"）、地面电流（跨步电压）、钝性损伤等因素造成（表4-3；参考文献141,142,147,176和213）。

第 4 章 | 高温损伤

表 4-3　雷电损伤

皮肤烧伤（139, 143, 152, 153, 165, 167, 174, 205）
　未见（分散的电流入口，出口不明显）
　表浅烧伤
　　• 线性烧伤（由汗液或水积聚形成）
　　• 闪络效应导致红斑性烧伤
　　• 点状烧伤
　热作用[衣物起火，金属皮带扣或拉链熔化（214）]
　头发烧焦（205, 215）
Lichtenberg 图案[即雷击纹，蕨类植物状、羽毛状、树枝状"烧伤"（143, 153, 174, 216）]
鼓膜破裂[继发于直接电烧伤、冲击波、颅底骨折（143, 152, 153, 165, 167, 174, 217–219）]
肺挫伤[钝性损伤，冲击波效应（152, 153, 174, 220）]
心肌梗死（罕见）；心肌收缩带（143, 153, 165–167, 174, 175, 178, 221–223）
肌肉坏死，肌红蛋白尿，肾衰竭[与高压交流电触电相比，罕见于雷击（143, 153, 165, 180, 224）]
脊髓坏死[雷电直接作用，继发于骨折（167）]
直接脑损伤[与颅脑烧伤有关（143, 164, 166, 174）]
　• 脑实质凝固性坏死
　• 硬脑膜外及硬脑膜下出血[? 钝力性损伤（155, 166, 174, 224）]
　• 脑室内及脑室周围出血（155, 174）
　• 蛛网膜下腔出血[? 钝性损伤（166, 224）]
　• 基底节出血（雷电直接作用或热作用）；脑干出血（166, 224, 225）
　• 脑颅骨骨折[钝性损伤（155）]
面颅骨骨折[冲击波效应（226）]
心搏骤停后缺血缺氧性脑病（224）
　• 相关性脑梗死

　　闪电电流的持续时间很短[100 ms（147）]。闪电直接击中头部后可进入头部孔隙[眼、耳和口部（152, 205）]。这类受害者即刻死亡（166, 224）。当人体触碰闪电流经的物体（如帐篷杆）时，形成接触性损伤（152）。空中放电是指雷电从初始击中的物体（如树木）跃迁或发出电弧延伸至电阻更低的物体[如树旁的人体（152, 176）]。当雷电击中地面后，电流会沿径向扩散。由于双脚存在电位差，电流可流经双腿及躯干形成损伤（147, 152）。闪电在空中放电及地面电流扩散可导致多人受伤（153）。

　　空中放电和地面电流往往不引起头部损伤（166）。闪电导致空气过热并快速冷却，形成爆炸冲击波作用于人体导致平滑肌收缩并形成钝性损伤，钝性损伤也可见于雷击后的高坠（147, 152, 167, 174）。

　　电流通常沿金属导体的外部传导（164, 165, 174），电流沿体表的潮湿衣服传导可引起衣物撕裂（图 4-33；参考文献 139, 141, 143, 144, 147, 150, 153, 174, 178, 205, 215 和 227），而衣物撕裂易被怀疑存在性侵害，尤其当尸体在空旷地区被发现时（161, 174, 205）。雷击时温度可达 30 000℃[54,000°F（153, 176）]。薄的金属物体可被烧毁,死者体表可见黑色物质覆盖(图4-33;参考文献38,214和228)。高压电触电的电火花烧伤为浅表烧伤,呈红色或棕色,常见于体表暴露部位("鳄鱼皮样改变;"图4-34; 参考文献38,141,152,157,158,165和229)。相比较,雷击少见受害者深层组织烧伤;雷击引起的人体热作用烧伤是由衣物或周围物体燃烧所致(38,38,139,144,145,147,158,230,231)。研究表明,90%的雷击受害者存在烧伤(三分之二的受害者躯干部烧伤,半数受害者头部烧伤),但仅有5%的受害者存在深层组织烧伤(143,153,164,167,174)。雷击时传递至体内的电流强度有限,除了直接接触部位外,热效应一般不会造成人体内部器官损伤(139,141,142,147,150,174,180,229)。

利希滕贝格(Lichtenberg)图案(蕨类植物样图案,雷击纹)是一种物理现象,指人体遭雷击后皮肤上出现的树枝状红色区域,其出现于遭雷击后1小时内,并且通常于24-48小时后消失(图4-35;参考文献38,180,205,213和216)。利希滕贝格(Lichtenberg)图案并非烧伤所致,不沿血管或神经分布。利希滕贝格图案的形成与正电荷有关,这是由附近的物体发生的次级正闪络效应引起的,与负电荷闪电击中的人有关。利希滕贝格(Lichtenberg)图案与分形行为一致,由皮肤内正极放电吸引周围皮肤的电子形成。分形是一个数学对象,它随着放大倍数的增加而显示出越来越多的细节,且放大倍数较小的结构与放大倍数较大的结构相同(38,213,216)。

7.4 电击导致的体内损伤(表4-3)

遭电击住院的受害者可出现心肌缺血或心律失常的表现(139,141,145,147,149,152,158)。由于心律失常可为迟发性,上述患者入院后需进行24小时心电监护,尤其是对有心脏病史、遭电击后意识丧失或电流经过心脏的伤者而言(139,141,142,145,232,233)。部分死者尸体解剖时心脏未见明显异常(181)。部分死者可

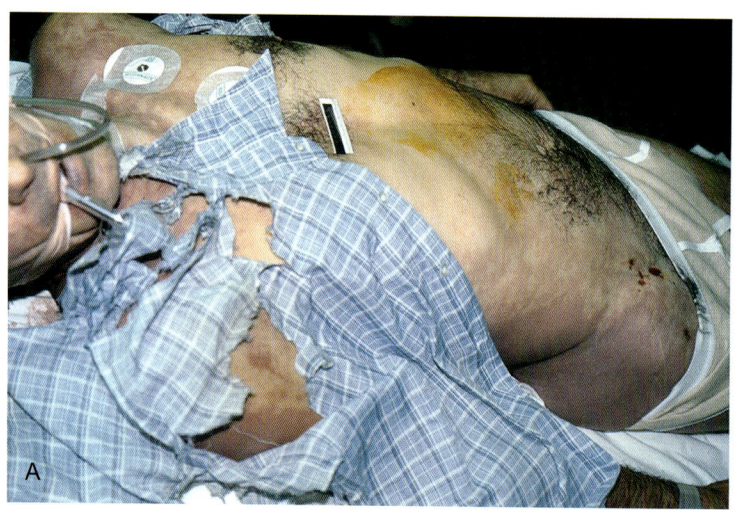
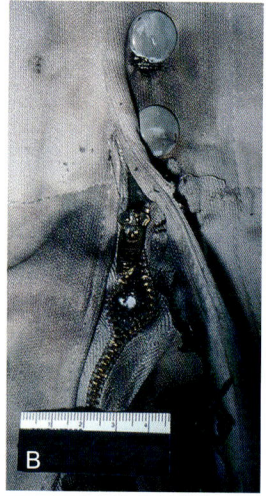

图4-33 雷击死。(A)衣服撕裂。(B)拉链烧毁(加拿大安大略省汉密尔顿市法医病理办公室D. King博士供图)。

第 4 章 | 高温损伤

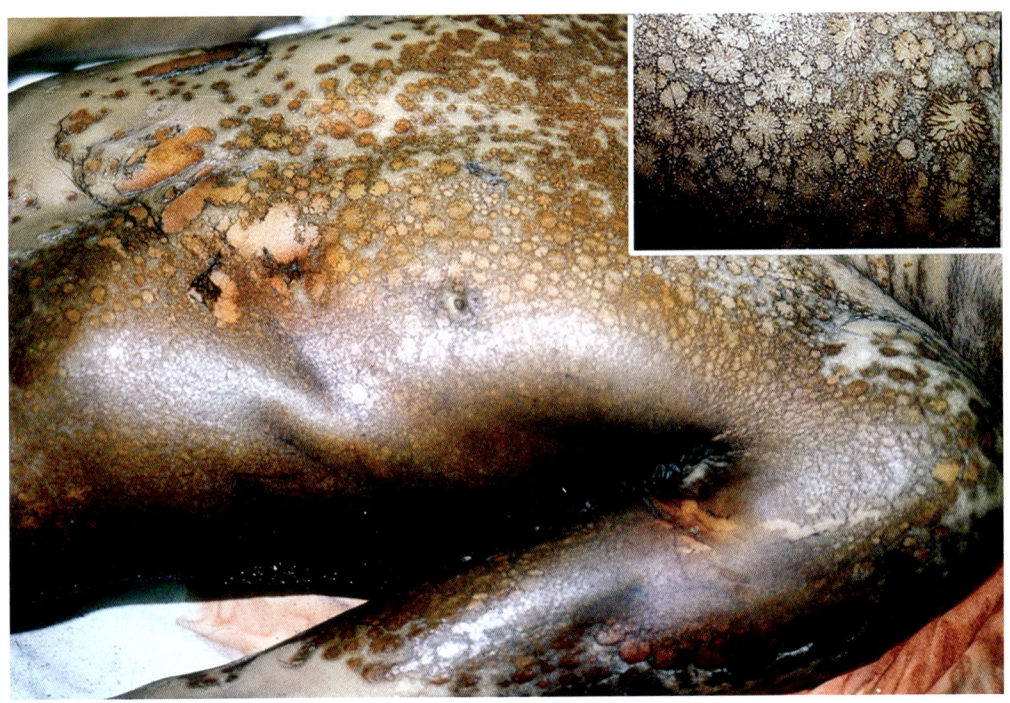

图 4-34 电击死（触碰高压电线）。闪络效应导致皮肤烧伤（右上角图示"鳄鱼皮样改变"）。

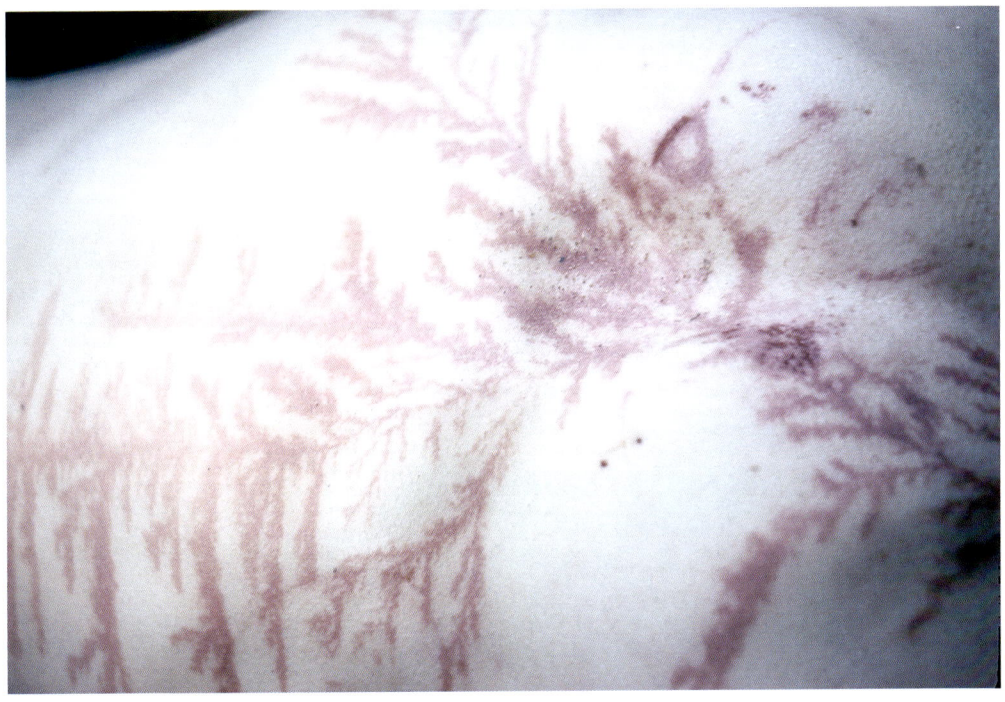

图 4-35 雷击死。利希滕贝格（Lichtenberg）图案。（加拿大安大略省汉密尔顿市法医病理办公室 D. King 博士供图）

检见心肌点状出血，并可见心包与心内膜斑片状出血（181）。眼睑、球结膜、胸膜及心外膜的点状出血为电击死的征象之一（197，234）。上述尸体征象与遭电击时的电压及电流路径无相关性（197）。点状出血的形成机制可能与遭电击时心脏停搏引起静脉淤血及肌肉收缩导致的血压升高有关（197）。电击死者可见心肌及传导系统内大面积或局灶性坏死伴出血及急性心肌收缩带，这些改变与迟发性心律失常有关（图4-36；参考文献 139，142，232，235 和 236）。心肌梗死与冠状动脉痉挛可见于无冠状动脉粥样硬化病变的死者（236-238）。雷击可引起全身血管痉挛（167）。电击引起冠状动脉血栓并致心肌梗死较为罕见（142）。

高压及低压电流流经血管会造成血管内膜与中膜损伤（收缩带坏死），导致即时性或迟发性血栓形成并引起器官组织缺血（38，139-142，144，145，147，151，152，157，158，161，235）。由于四肢大动脉的血流量大、散热性好，遭电击时常不发生损伤，但肌内小动脉可因热作用或自身血管闭塞而坏死，即使其对应的体表皮肤未见明显坏死（139，149，154，168，172）。血管中膜损伤可形成动脉瘤（149）。骨骼肌收缩导致的血压升高和电流作用引起的血管收缩可致原有的脑动脉瘤破裂（149，234）。

电击所致肌肉损伤是由热量、电流、缺血和创伤引起的（145）。高压电会造成严重的肌肉、血管及神经损伤（38，150，152）。低压电击致肌肉坏死的程度难以用皮肤

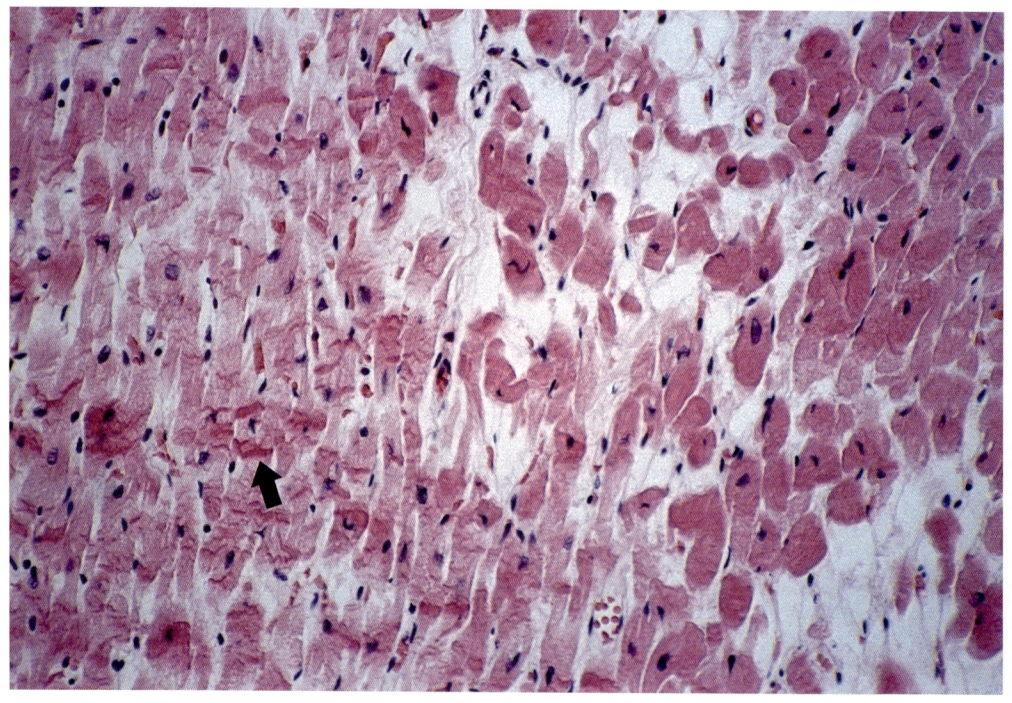

图 4-36 电击死。图片左侧心肌可见收缩带（箭头；H-E 染色，放大倍数 ×100）（加拿大安大略省汉密尔顿市法医病理办公室 D.King 博士供图）。

第 4 章｜高温损伤

烧伤的程度来评估(139,141,144,145,147,150,152,157,158,172)。肌间隔综合征可继发于组织水肿与血管缺血(139,141,147,152)。肌红蛋白尿可致肾衰竭(参阅第 8 章标题 13；参考文献 38,141,142,144,145,147,152,157 和 158)。尸体血液内肌红蛋白含量与电击无显著相关性(239,240)。死后组织自溶可导致血液内肌红蛋白含量增多(239)。电击死者亦可检见高钾血症(147)。骨骼肌细胞膜的电损伤并非肉眼可见的急性大面积坏死(147,168)，缺血改变可以延迟出现(141,146,150)。电损伤组织常呈不规则分布，损伤部位可远离肉眼可见的电流入口及出口(141,146,148)。尽管肌组织在遭电击后初期看似正常，但细胞已发生不可逆转的电穿孔及热变性(146)。上述细胞的持续性损伤可致广泛性肌坏死(147)。高压电所致的广泛性肌组织烧伤可能使伤者需要截肢(148,149,189,193,210,230)。电击也可造成组织气性坏疽(241)。

电击直接导致肺损伤较罕见(157)，更多的是遭电击时形成的肺钝性损伤(如肺挫伤)(157,167)。肺损伤后遗症中包括成人呼吸窘迫综合征(145)。

也有部分高压电及罕见的低压电造成腹腔空腔器官(如胃、肠、食管、膀胱)破裂的案例报道，器官破裂被认为是爆炸效应的结果(145,176,242,243)。有电击致膀胱瘘的案例报道(244)。肠壁小血管凝固性坏死可致肠道缺血(154,242)。有电击引起麻痹性肠梗阻的报道(154)。实质性器官(如肝、胰腺)坏死常由钝性损伤或烧伤导致(157,167,210,242,245)。电流引起实质性器官损伤的案例亦有报道(246)。

遭直流电(如闪电)和高压交流电电击的个体可被直接击飞或由于强烈的肌肉收缩而跌落(38,141,142,145,147,150,152,157,182)。与交流电触电不同，遭雷击时不会出现由于肌肉强直性收缩而增加触电时长的情况(153,164,165,174)。电弧闪络形成的高温迅速加热空气，形成爆炸效应并击飞受害者(147,209)。

电击可致头部损伤(147,166,209,210)。无论电流是否经过头部，均可见中枢神经系统后遗症(38,147,166,247)。电击过程中心搏呼吸骤停可致脑缺氧性损伤(139,147,152,174)。电击受害者可见脑静脉血栓形成(247)。电击损伤会引起长期神经性及精神性后遗症，可不伴有中枢神经系统损伤(38,147,247)。低压及高压电击可致脊髓长时间损伤(38,178,248)。遭雷击后受害者可因心跳呼吸骤停而暂时意识丧失，心肺复苏对其有效(147)。遭电击后受害者可出现行为举止异常及记忆遗忘(143)。

交流电引起的肌肉痉挛可致颈椎及长骨骨折、脱位[如肩关节(38,144,145,147,152,157,161,210,249,250)]。电击中发生高坠可致骨折(152,158)。

7.5 显微镜检查及微量物证

皮肤电流斑镜检示表皮、真皮及皮下空泡形成，表皮细胞极化，细胞核细长、深染，呈核流现象，真皮胶原纤维凝固性坏死(161,170,207,209,251,252)。若存在烧伤,可见皮肤炭化。电损伤皮肤内可见钙沉积[直流电或交流电作用于动物和人体(253-256)]。

软组织内异位成骨现象被视为一种重度电损伤的后果(147)。与金属类导电物体接触可在完整或缺损皮肤处留下金属颗粒(如铜、铁),进行电镜超微组织结构检查和微量组织化学染色可显示上述颗粒(161,200,234,251,257,258)。元素分析可确认金属沉积(228)。接触物或导体上可能存在生物学检材供 DNA 分析(259)。

8 爆炸

8.1 损伤机制

"爆炸"伤是指爆炸及产生的冲击波作用于人体后,人体发生的生物物理学现象及造成的病理生理学改变(260)。爆炸发生后,爆炸力自炸点迅速下降(261,262)。化学性爆炸涉及浓缩的反应物,如烟火等低量级反应物(<16 psi 或 Ib/in^2)或高量级反应物[如炸药(263,264)]。分散反应物爆炸涉及气体和(或)空气中的微粒物质[如发射井和煤矿的爆炸(263,265)]。爆炸可由火源(如火柴)、摩擦、静电或过热引发(265,266)。爆炸死存在多种死亡方式(267,268)。

爆炸可致单纯性器官损伤,不伴有体表损伤(260)。冲击波对人体造成直接效应[一级爆炸伤(260,261,265,269-271)]。冲击波作用于人体后部分被人体吸收并转为压力波在体内传播(260,272)。大于 300 psi 的压力波会破坏人体组织(263)。从波传播的角度分析,人体组织为高黏性组织,当压力波经过不同组织器官时会发生改变(260)。

人体最脆弱的部位是含有空气或气体的器官(260,261)。压力波具有碎裂效应,人体空腔结构更易受损,因压力波会集中于密度差异较大的介质之间的界面上(260,261)。

压力波从液相介质进入气相环境(如肺泡,胃肠道;参考文献260,273 和 274)时,该效应会增强。当胸壁被20米/秒(46英里/小时)以上的速度向内挤压时,0.5毫秒内即会造成肺损伤(260,261)。冲击波还产生纵向的剪切效应,通过相邻的连接结构破坏组织和器官的正常弹性(261)。实质性器官对这种加速-减速运动较为敏感(275)。与空气中爆炸相比,水下爆炸可对更远距离的人体造成损害(260)。

其他致伤机制包括爆炸投射物形成的贯通伤(二次损伤)、受害者遭爆炸气浪击飞后与其他物体碰撞或摔跌伤(三次损伤)、爆炸闪光或建筑物着火所致烧伤、暴露于有毒气体环境中致伤,以及挤压伤(260,261,263,265-272,276)。如果爆炸后形成火焰,火焰边缘扩散速度最高可达200米/秒(450英里/小时)(266)。

爆炸可形成特征性的损伤(表4-4)。

表 4-4　爆炸损伤

- 体表损伤
    - 人体完全爆碎提示存在高量级浓缩爆炸物近距离爆炸（260，262，263，274）
    - 邻近爆炸点的人体组织碎裂伴有四肢部分离断（262，274）；自杀者可见头面部损伤（267）下肢离断为典型的站立位或坐位爆炸伤（图 4-37；参考文献 277）。如果手握爆炸物，可见手部损伤（图 4-38；参考文献 267，271，278 和 279）
    - 爆炸投射物损伤（263，265，274；图 4-39）
    - 点状裂创（274）
    - 粉尘附着（274）。体表沾有源自爆炸物的黑色污渍（263）
    - 瓦砾倒塌所致损伤（274）
    - 烧伤（爆炸后位于附近的受害者可即刻出现闪光灼伤及头发烧焦；图 4-40 和参考文献 274）
    - 受害者被炸飞至其他建筑形成二次爆炸伤（271）
- 颅骨骨折（265）
- 中枢神经系统的出血 [脑膜，脑，神经根（260）]
- 视网膜出血（271）
- 鼓膜破裂 [主要爆炸效应之一（260，271，272，275，276，280，281）]
- 面部骨折（265）
- 颈部裂创及喉部骨折（265）
- 肋骨骨折（265）
- 肺损伤（主要爆炸效应之一；图 4-41 和参考文献 281）
    - 破裂、出血（除呼吸道内大量积血引起窒息）并不足以致死，爆炸的幸存者会出现成人呼吸窘迫综合征（参阅第 1 章标题 4.3；参考文献 260，261，265，271，276 和 280）
    - 胸膜及肺膜下出血 [出现于冲击波应力集中区——两肺后侧及邻近心、膈肌处（261）]
    - 急性肺气肿，肺大疱，张力性气胸（261）
    - 气体栓塞（参阅第 5 章标题 14.3；第 7 章标题 12.1；第 8 章标题 12.4；参考文献 261）
- 心脏节律障碍（282）
    - 心动过缓 [肺损伤引起迷走神经反射所致（260，283）]
    - 心脏震荡（可见于无明显致命伤的爆炸受害者；参阅第 8 章标题 6.4；参考文献 260，261）
- 心肌出血（260）
- 心脏破裂（275）
- 主动脉破裂（265）
- 肝破裂（265，275，276）
- 食管、胃或肠管破裂 [也可发生消化道壁内出血，消化道非游离部位横断（260，265，271，276，280）]
- 胆囊破裂（275）
- 肾破裂（265，275）
- 膀胱破裂（271，275）
- 脾破裂（265，275）
- 肾上腺破裂（275）
- 四肢骨折，脊椎骨折（260，265，271）

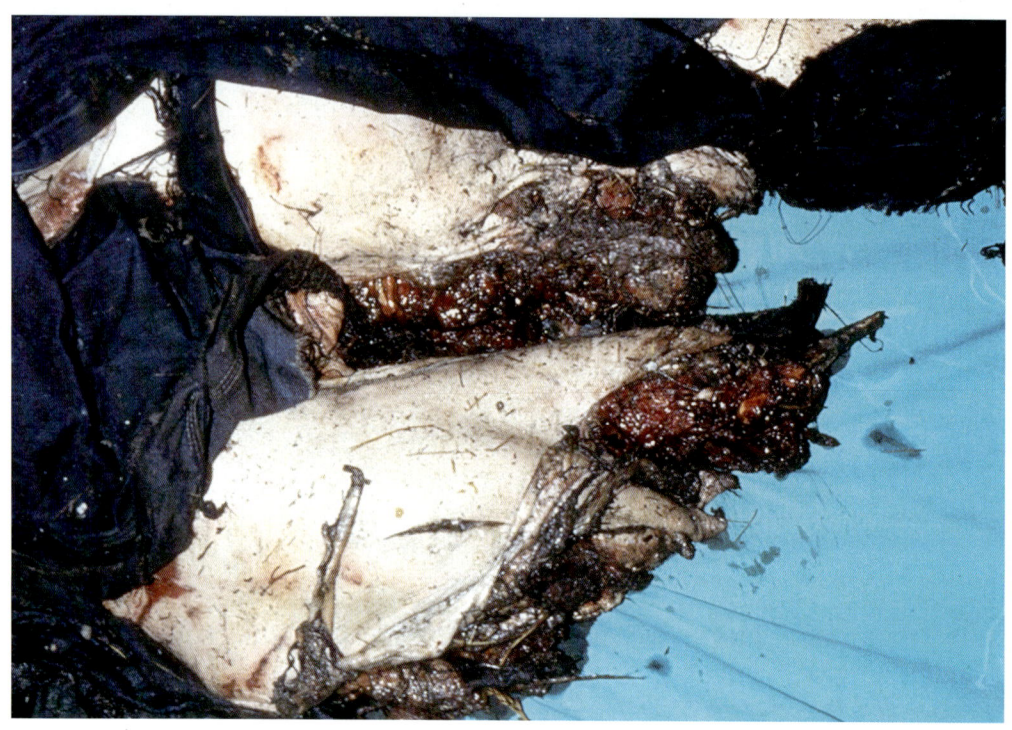

图 4-37 机动车内置于死者腿下的爆炸物。双腿创伤性离断。（美国北卡罗来纳州教堂山市法医局供图）

8.2 爆炸受害者检验步骤

- 复原死者全部组织及衣物(263)。衣物需置于隔绝空气的容器内[如未使用的油漆罐或成分为尼龙、聚酯或聚丙烯的袋子(263,284,285)]。
- 注意投射物损伤的方向(263)。
- 检查受害者双手以明确爆炸时是否手握爆炸物(267,271,278,279)。
- 收集爆炸残留物，包括已燃烧（呈黑色或灰色）及未燃烧物质（呈黄色、棕色及灰色）。提取皮肤拭子，提取部位包括有明显黑色污渍附着部位、无明显附着物部位及手部(267)。收集头发、指甲（缝）刮取物(263,284)。提取阴性对照(284)。
- 在皮肤表面及创道内提取 X 线可透过的残留物（如纸屑、木头、塑料），它们可能是爆炸物的成分(263,267,284)。其他外源性异物可能来自周边环境(284)。
- 拍摄尸体全身照。
- 进行尸体全身 X 线检查(267,284)。提取尸体内所有 X 线无法透过的碎片。这些物体可能是爆炸装置的组成部分、身体内假体的部件或周围环境内金属结构（如车辆部件）。反复进行 X 线扫描以确保体内碎片已被取尽(263,284)。

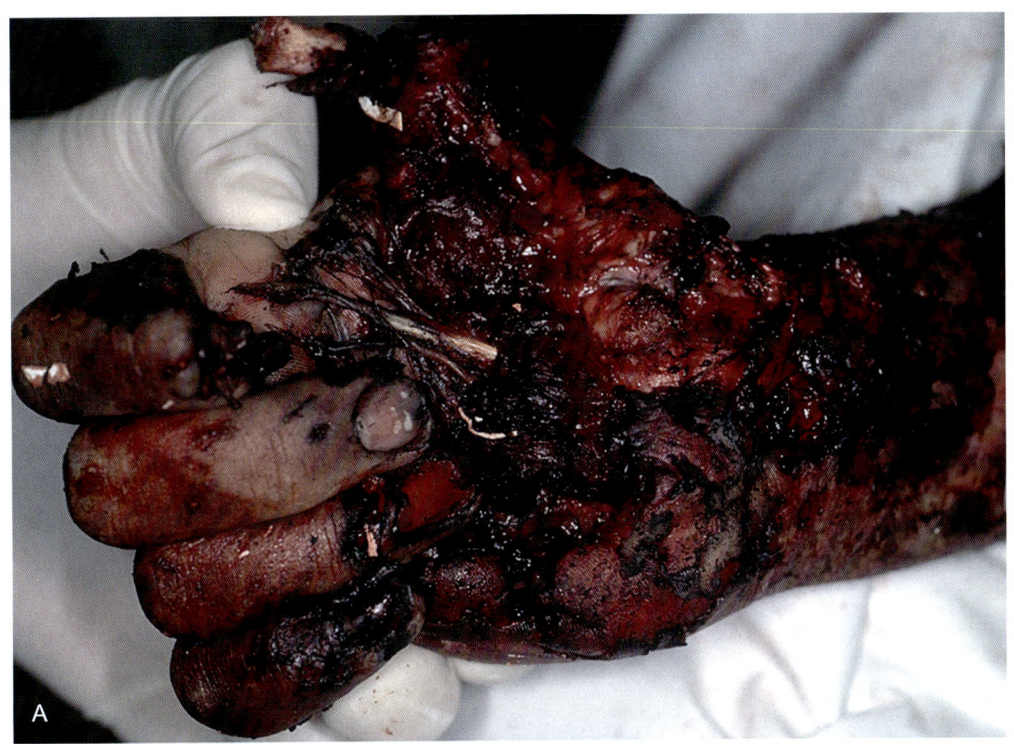

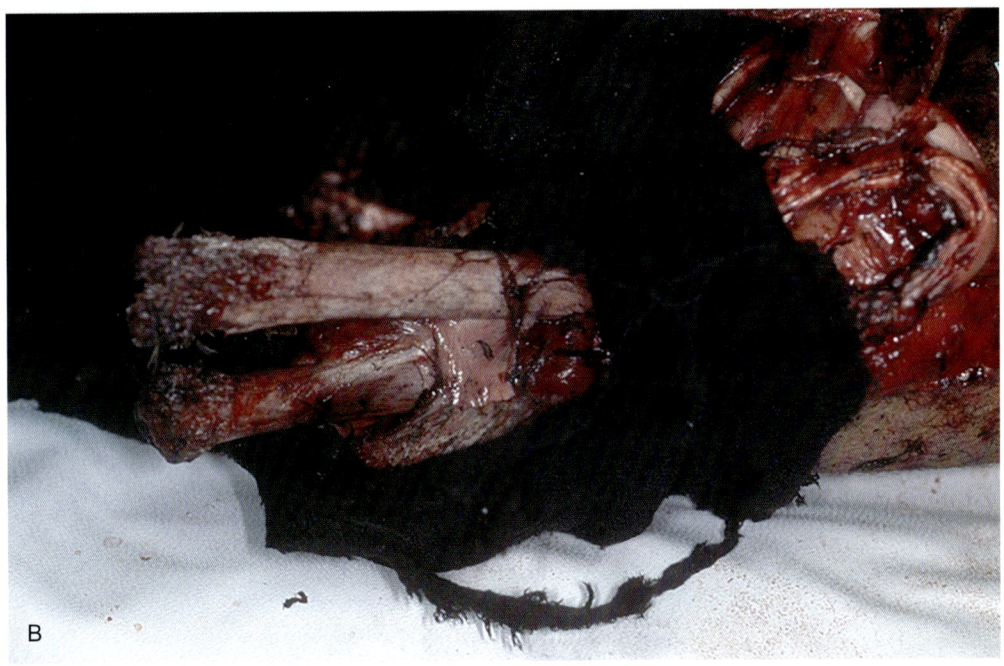

图4-38 手握爆炸物（手榴弹）形成的损伤。（A）手部严重烧伤，部分手指离断。（B）手部创伤性离断。尺、桡骨外露。

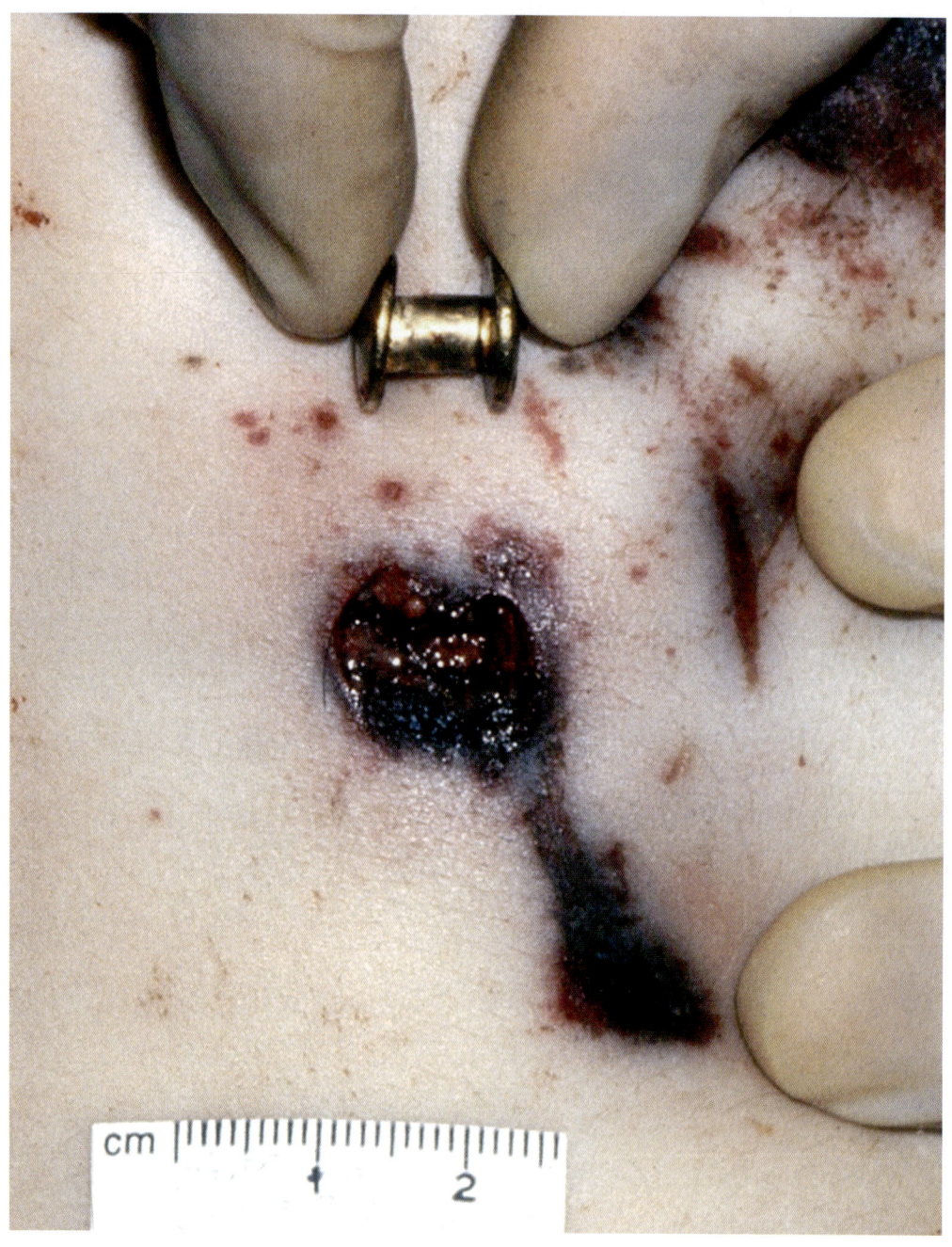

图 4-39 爆炸。爆炸子弹损伤(美国北卡罗来纳州教堂山市法医局供图)。

第 4 章 | 高温损伤

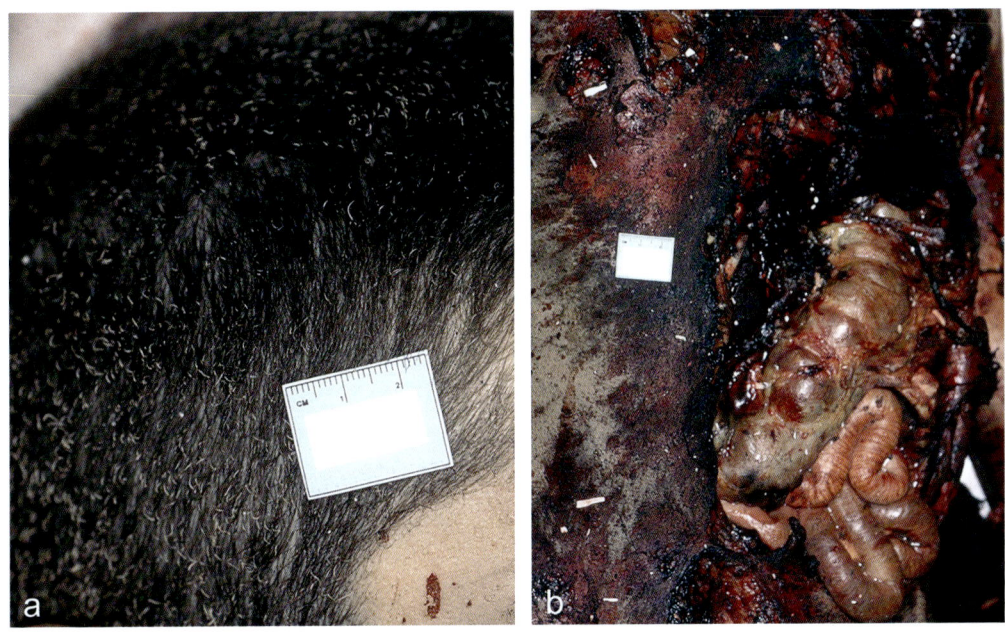

图 4-40　爆炸效应。(A) 头发烧焦。(B) 皮肤烧伤；肠管外露。

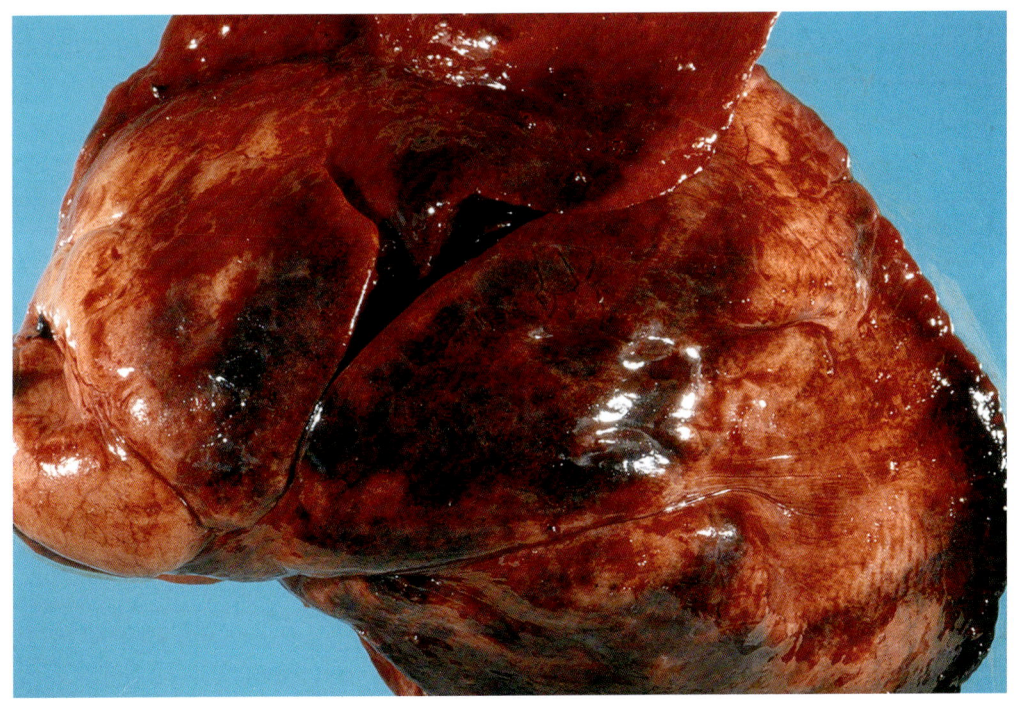

图 4-41　爆炸效应。右肺表面；肺出血。

- 毒物分析。富含 CO 的环境内发生爆炸（如煤矿爆炸）可导致受害者体内碳氧血红蛋白浓度升高（265,266）。

秦志强　邵煜　译

参考文献

1. Barret, J. P., Gomez, P., Solano, I., Gonzalez–Dorrego, M., Crisol, F. J. Epidemiology and mortality of adult burns in Catalonia. Burns 25:325–329, 1999.
2. Crikelair, G. F., Symonds, F. C., Ollstein, R. N., Kirsner, A. I. Burn causation: its many sides. J. Trauma 8:572–582, 1968.
3. Panke, T. W., McLeod, C. G. Pathology of Thermal Injury. A Practical Approach. Grune and Stratton, Orlando, FL, 1985.
4. Eckert, W. G. The medicolegal and forensic aspects of fires. Am. J. Forensic Med. Pathol. 2:347–357, 1981.
5. Marshall, S. W., Runyan, C. W., Bangdiwala, S. I., Linzer, M. A., Sacks, J. J., Butts, J. D. Fatal residential fires: who dies and who survives? JAMA 279:1633–1637, 1998.
6. Istre, G. R., McCoy, M. A., Osborn, L., Barnard, J. J., Bolton, A. Deaths and injuries from house fires. N. Engl. J. Med. 344:1911–1916, 2001.
7. McGwin, G., Jr., Chapman, V., Rousculp, M., Robison, J., Fine, P. The epidemiology of fire–related deaths in Alabama, 1992–1997. J. Burn Care Rehabil. 21:75–83, 2000.
8. MacArthur, J. D., Moore, F. D. Epidemiology of burns. The burn–prone patient. JAMA 231:259–263, 1975.
9. Runyan, C. W., Bangdiwala, S. I., Linzer, M. A., Sacks, J. J., Butts, J. Risk factors for fatal residential fires. N. Engl. J. Med. 327:859–863, 1992.
10. Mallonee, S., Istre, G. R., Rosenberg, M., et al. Surveillance and prevention of residential–fire injuries. N. Engl. J. Med. 335:27–31, 1996.
11. Istre, G. R., McCoy, M., Carlin, D. K., McClain, J. Residential fire related deaths and injuries among children: fireplay, smoke alarms, and prevention. Inj. Prev. 8:128–132, 2002.
12. Squires, T., Busuttil, A. Can child fatalities in house fires be prevented? Inj. Prev. 2:109–113, 1996.
13. Biddle, E. A., Hartley, D. Fire and flame related events with multiple occupational injury fatalities in the United States, 1980–1995. In. j Control Saf. Promot. 9:9–18, 2002.
14. Mandelcorn, E., Gomez, M., Cartotto, R. C. Work–related burn injuries in Ontario, Canada: has anything changed in the last 10 years? Burns 29:469–472, 2003.
15. Quinney, B., McGwin, G., Jr., Cross, J. M., Valent, F., Taylor, A. J., Rue, L. W. III.

Thermal burn fatalities in the workplace, United States, 1992 to 1999. J. Burn Care Rehabil. 23:305–310, 2002.

16. Leth, P., Hart–Madsen, M. Suicide by self–incineration. Am. J. Forensic Med. Pathol. 18:113–118, 1997.
17. Rothschild, M. A., Raatschen, H. J., Schneider, V. Suicide by self–immolation in Berlin from 1990 to 2000. Forensic Sci. Int. 124:163–166, 2001.
18. Shkrum, M. J., Johnston, K. A. Fire and suicide: a three–year study of self–immolation deaths. J. Forensic Sci. 37:208–221, 1992.
19. Sukhai, A., Harris, C., Moorad, R. G., Dada, M. A. Suicide by self–immolation in Durban, South Africa: a five–year retrospective review. Am. J. Forensic Med. Pathol. 23:295–298, 2002.
20. Suk, J. H., Han, C. H., Yeon, B. K. Suicide by burning in Korea. Int. J. Soc. Psychiatry 37:141–145, 1991.
21. Laloe, V. Patterns of deliberate self–burning in various parts of the world. A review. Burns 30:207–215, 2004.
22. Prosser, D. Suicides by burning in England and Wales. Br. J. Psychiatry 168:175–182, 1996.
23. Meir, P. B., Sagi, A., Ben Yakar, Y., Rosenberg, L. Suicide attempts by self–immolation— our experience. Burns 16:257–258, 1990.
24. Gupta, R. K., Srivastava, A. K. Study of fatal burns cases in Kanpur (India). Forensic Sci. Int. 37:81–89, 1988.
25. Mzezewa, S., Jonsson, K., Aberg, M., Salemark, L. A prospective study of suicidal burns admitted to the Harare burns unit. Burns 26:460–464, 2000.
26. Kumar, V. Burnt wives—a study of suicides. Burns 29:31–35, 2003.
27. Bohnert, M., Rothschild, M. A. Complex suicides by self–incineration. Forensic Sci. Int. 131:197–201, 2003.
28. Cingolani, M., Tsakri, D. Planned complex suicide: report of three cases. Am. J. Forensic Med. Pathol. 21:255–260, 2000.
29. Suarez–Penaranda, J. M., Munoz, J. I., Lopez, D. A., et al. Concealed homicidal strangula– tion by burning. Am. J. Forensic Med. Pathol. 20:141–144, 1999.
30. Wetherell, H. R. The occurrence of cyanide in the blood of fire victims. J. Forensic Sci. 11:167–173, 1966.
31. Hartzell, G. E. Overview of combustion toxicology. Toxicology 115:7–23, 1996.
32. Einhorn, I. N. Physiological and toxicological aspects of smoke produced during the com– bustion of polymeric materials. Environ. Health Perspect. 11:163–189, 1975.

33. Hill, I. R. An analysis of factors impeding passenger escape from aircraft fires. Aviat. Space Environ. Med. 61:261–265, 1990.
34. Bohnert, M., Rost, T., Faller–Marquardt, M., Ropohl, D., Pollak, S. Fractures of the base of the skull in charred bodies—post–mortem heat injuries or signs of mechanical trauma– tisation? Forensic Sci. Int. 87:55–62, 1997.
35. Bohnert, M., Rost, T., Pollak, S. The degree of destruction of human bodies in relation to the duration of the fire. Forensic Sci. Int. 95:11–21, 1998.
36. Bohnert, M., Schmidt, U., Perdekamp, M. G., Pollak, S. Diagnosis of a captive–bolt injury in a skull extremely destroyed by fire. Forensic Sci. Int. 127:192–197, 2002.
37. Alarie, Y. Toxicity of fire smoke. Crit. Rev. Toxicol. 32:259–289, 2002.
38. ten Duis, H. J. Acute electrical burns. Semin. Neurol. 15:381–386, 1995.
39. Glassman, D. M., Crow, R. M. Standardization model for describing the extent of burn injury to human remains. J. Forensic Sci. 41:152–154, 1996.
40. Eckert, W. G., James, S., Katchis, S. Investigation of cremations and severely burned bod– ies. Am. J. Forensic Med. Pathol. 9:188–200, 1988.
41. Richards, N. F. Fire investigation—destruction of corpses. Med. Sci. Law. 17:79–82, 1977.
42. Gerling, I., Meissner, C., Reiter, A., Oehmichen, M. Death from thermal effects and burns. Forensic Sci. Int. 115:33–41, 2001.
43. Christensen, A. M. Experiments in the combustibility of the human body. J. Forensic Sci. 47:466–470, 2002.
44. DeHaan, J. D., Nurbakhsh, S. Sustained combustion of an animal carcass and its implica– tions for the consumption of human bodies in fires. J. Forensic Sci. 46:1076–1081, 2001.
45. Gee, D. J. A case of "spontaneous combustion." Med. Sci. Law 18:37–38, 1965.
46. DeHaan, J. D., Campbell, S. J., Nurbakhsh, S. Combustion of animal fat and its implica– tions for the consumption of human bodies in fires. Sci. Justice 39:27–38, 1999.
47. Spitz, W. U. Thermal injuries. In: Spitz, W. U., ed. Spitz and Fisher's Medicolegal Investigation of Sudden Death. Guidelines for the Application of Pathology to Crime Investigation. 3rd ed. Charles C. Thomas, Springfield, IL, pp. 413–443, 1993.
48. Bassed, R. Identification of severely incinerated human remains: the need for a coopera– tive approach between forensic specialities. A case report. Med. Sci. Law 43:356–361, 2003.
49. Hill, IR. Immediate causes of death in fires. Med. Sci. Law 29:287–292, 1989.
50. Hausmann, R., Betz, P. Thermally induced entrance wound–like defect of the skull. Forensic Sci. Int. 128:159–161, 2002.

51. Kondo, T., Ohshima, T. Epidural herniation of the cerebral tissue in a burned body: a case report. Forensic Sci. Int. 66:197–202, 1994.
52. Bohnert, M., Werner, C. R., Pollak, S. Problems associated with the diagnosis of vitality in burned bodies. Forensic Sci. Int. 135:197–205, 2003.
53. Levin, B. C., Rechani, P. R., Gurman, J. L., et al. Analysis of carboxyhemoglobin and cyanide in blood from victims of the Dupont Plaza Hotel fire in Puerto Rico. J. Forensic Sci. 35:151–168, 1990.
54. Birky, M., Malek, D., Paabo, M. Study of biological samples obtained from victims of MGM Grand Hotel fire. J. Anal. Toxicol. 7:265–271, 1983.
55. Barillo, D. J., Goode, R., Rush, B. F., Jr., Lin, R. L., Freda, A., Anderson, E. J., Jr. Lack of correlation between carboxyhemoglobin and cyanide in smoke inhalation injury. Curr. Surg. 43:421–423, 1986.
56. Yoshida, M., Adachi, J., Watabiki, T., Tatsuno, Y., Ishida, N. A study on house fire victims: age, carboxyhemoglobin, hydrogen cyanide and hemolysis. Forensic Sci. Int. 52:13–20, 1991.
57. Anderson, R. A., Harland, W. A. Fire deaths in the Glasgow area: III. The role of hydrogen cyanide. Med. Sci. Law 22:35–40, 1982.
58. Lundquist, P., Rammer, L., Sorbo, B. The role of hydrogen cyanide and carbon monoxide in fire casualties: a prospective study. Forensic Sci. Int. 43:9–14, 1989.
59. Barillo, D. J., Rush, B. F., Jr., Goode, R., Lin, R. L., Freda, A., Anderson, E. J., Jr. Is ethanol the unknown toxin in smoke inhalation injury? Am. Surg. 52:641–645, 1986.
60. Levine, B., Moore, K. A., Fowler, D. Interaction between carbon monoxide and ethanol in fire fatalities. Forensic Sci. Int. 124:115–116, 2001.
61. Parks, J. G., Noguchi, T. T., Klatt, E. C. The epidemiology of fatal burn injuries. J. Forensic Sci. 34:399–406, 1989.
62. Squires, T., Busuttil, A. Alcohol and house fire fatalities in Scotland, 1980–1990. Med. Sci. Law 37:321–325, 1997.
63. Gerson, L., Wingard, D. Fire deaths and drinking: data from the Ontario fire reporting sys- tem. Am. J. Drug Alcohol Abuse 6:125–133, 1979.
64. Gormsen, H., Jeppesen, N., Lund, A. The causes of death in fire victims. Forensic Sci. Int. 24:107–111, 1984.
65. Rogde, S., Olving, J. H. Characteristics of fire victims in different sorts of fires. Forensic Sci. Int. 77:93–99, 1996.
66. Menchel, S. M., Dunn, W. A. Hydrofluoric acid poisoning. Am. J. Forensic Med. Pathol. 5:245–248, 1984.

67. Wirthwein, D. P., Pless, J. E. Carboxyhemoglobin levels in a series of automobile fires. Death due to crash or fire? Am. J. Forensic Med. Pathol. 17:117–123, 1996.

68. Walter, J. E., Hirsch, C. S., Zumwalt, R. E. Never say never. Negligible carboxyhemoglobin in the victim of a smoldering mattress fire. Am. J. Forensic Med. Pathol. 5:239–244, 1984.

69. Hirsch, C. S., Adelson, L. Absence of carboxyhemoglobin in flash fire victims. JAMA 210:2279–2280, 1969.

70. Betz, P., Roider, G., von Meyer, L., Drasch, G., Eisenmenger, W. Carboxyhemoglobin blood concentrations in suicides by fire. Med. Sci. Law 36:313–316, 1996.

71. O'Halloran, R. L., Lundy, J. K. Three fatalities in flash fire with variable dental charring. Am. J. Forensic Med. Pathol. 6:248–249, 1985.

72. Suzuki, T., Takahashi, H., Umetsu, K. Unusual aspirations in fire death. Forensic Sci. Int. 72:71–76. 1995.

73. Scharschmidt, A., Bratzke, H. (Congestive hemorrhage caused by burns?). Arch. Kriminol. 182:94–100, 1988.

74. Quan, L., Zhu, B. L, Ishida, K., et al. Hemorrhages in the root of the tongue in fire fatalities: the incidence and diagnostic value. Leg Med (Tokyo) 5 Suppl. 1:S332–S334, 2003.

75. Fechner, G. G., Gee, D. J. Study on the effects of heat on blood and on the post–mortem estimation of carboxyhaemoglobin and methaemoglobin. Forensic Sci. Int. 40:63–67, 1989.

76. Curry, A. S., Price, D. E., Rutter, E. R. The production of cyanide in post mortem material. Acta Pharmacol. Toxicol. (Copenh.) 25:339–344, 1967.

77. Ballantyne, B., Bright, J. E., Williams, P. The post–mortem rate of transformation of cyanide. Forensic Sci. 3:71–76, 1974.

78. Matsubara, K., Akane, A., Maseda, C., Shiono, H. "First pass phenomenon" of inhaled gas in the fire victims. Forensic Sci. Int. 46:203–208, 1990.

79. Miyazaki, T., Kojima, T., Yashiki, M., Chikasue, F., Iwasaki, Y. Interpretation of COHb con– centrations in the left and right heart blood of cadavers. Int. J. Legal Med. 105:65–68, 1992.

80. Roh, L., Paparo G. Detection of accelerants on a burn victim. J. Forensic Sci. 28:292, 1983.

81. Ettling, B. V., Adams, M. F. The study of accelerant residues in fire remains. J. Forensic Sci. 13:76–89, 1968.

82. Shiono, H., Matsubara, K., Akane, A., Fukushima, S., Takahashi, S. Immolation after drinking kerosene. Am. J. Forensic Med. Pathol. 10:229–231, 1989.

83. Ho, W. S., Ying, S. Y. Suicidal burns in Hong Kong Chinese. Burns 27:125–127, 2001.
84. Kojima, T., Yashiki, M., Chikasue, F., Miyazaki, T. Analysis of inflammable substances to determine whether death has occurred before or after burning. Z. Rechtsmed. 103:613–619, 1990.
85. Herrmann, N. P., Bennett, J. L. The differentiation of traumatic and heat–related fractures in burned bone. J. Forensic Sci. 44:461–469, 1999.
86. Iwase, H., Yamada, Y., Ootani, S., et al. Evidence for an antemortem injury of a burned head dissected from a burned body. Forensic Sci. Int. 94:9–14, 1998.
87. Raekallio, J. Histological estimation of the age of injuries. In: Perper, J. A., Wecht, C. H., eds. Microscopic diagnosis in forensic pathology. Charles C. Thomas, Springfield, IL, pp. 3–16, 1980.
88. Davies, M. R., Cywes, S., Van der Riet, R. L., Davies, D., Rode, H. A review of deaths in a paediatric burns unit. S. Afr. Med. J. 50:1479–1483, 1976.
89. Stitz, R. W. Burns in children. A three–year survey. Med. J. Aust. 1:357–361, 1972.
90. Jay, K. M., Bartlett, R. H., Danet, R., Allyn, P. A. Burn epidemiology: a basis for burn pre–vention. J. Trauma 17:943–947, 1977.
91. Cerovac, S., Roberts, A. H. Burns sustained by hot bath and shower water. Burns 26:251–259, 2000.
92. Katcher, M. L. Scald burns from hot tap water. JAMA 246:1219–1222, 1981.
93. Ryan, C. M., Schoenfeld, D. A., Thorpe, W. P., Sheridan, R. L., Cassem, E. H., Tompkins, R. G. Objective estimates of the probability of death from burn injuries. N. Engl. J. Med. 338:362–366, 1998.
94. Curreri, P. W., Luterman, A., Braun, D. W., Jr., Shires, G. T. Burn injury. Analysis of sur–vival and hospitalization time for 937 patients. Ann. Surg. 192:472–478, 1980.
95. Feller, I., Flora, J. D., Jr., Bawol, R. Baseline results of therapy for burned patients. JAMA 236:1943–1947, 1976.
96. Roi, L. D., Flora, J. D., Jr., Davis, T. M., Wolfe, R. A. Two new burn severity indices. J. Trauma 23:1023–1029, 1983.
97. Zawacki, B. E., Azen, S. P., Imbus, S. H., Chang, Y. T. Multifactorial probit analysis of mortality in burned patients. Ann. Surg. 189:1–5, 1979.
98. Pruitt, B. A., Jr. Complications of thermal injury. Clin. Plast. Surg. 1:667–691, 1974.
99. Pruitt, B. A., Jr., Flemma, R. J., DiVincenti, F. C., Foley, F. D., Mason, A. D., Jr., Young, W. G., Jr. Pulmonary complications in burn patients. A comparative study of 697 patients. J. Thorac. Cardiovasc. Surg. 59:7–20, 1970.
100. Linares, H. A. A report of 115 consecutive autopsies in burned children: 1966–80. Burns

Incl. Therm. Inj. 8:263–270, 1982.

101. Sevitt, S. A review of the complications of burns, their origin and importance for illness and death. J. Trauma 19:358–369, 1979.
102. Heimbach, D. M., Waeckerle, J. F. Inhalation injuries. Ann. Emerg. Med. 17:1316–1320, 1988.
103. Marshall, W. G., Jr., Dimick, A. R. The natural history of major burns with multiple sub-system failure. J. Trauma 23:102–105, 1983.
104. Hill, I. Inhalational injury in fires. Med. Sci. Law 29:91–99, 1989.
105. Hobson, K. G., Young, K. M., Ciraulo, A., Palmieri, T. L., Greenhalgh, D. G. Release of abdominal compartment syndrome improves survival in patients with burn injury. J. Trauma 53:1129–1133, 2002.
106. Ivy, M. E., Possenti, P. P., Kepros, J., et al. Abdominal compartment syndrome in patients with burns. J. Burn Care Rehabil. 20:351–353, 1999.
107. Quinby, W. C., Jr. Restrictive effects of thoracic burns in children. J. Trauma 12: 646–655, 1972.
108. Ruddy, R. M. Smoke inhalation injury. Pediatr. Clin. North Am. 41:317–336, 1994.
109. Stone, H. H. Pulmonary burns in children. J. Pediatr. Surg. 14:48–52, 1979.
110. DiVincenti, F. C., Pruitt, B. A., Jr., Reckler, J. M. Inhalation injuries. J. Trauma 11:109–117, 1971.
111. Santucci, S. G., Gobara, S., Santos, C. R., Fontana, C., Levin, A S. Infections in a burn intensive care unit: experience of seven years. J. Hosp. Infect. 53:6–13, 2003.
112. Nieman, G. F., Clark, W. R., Jr., Wax, S. D., Webb, S. R. The effect of smoke inhalation on pulmonary surfactant. Ann. Surg. 191:171–181, 1980.
113. Whitelock–Jones, L., Bass, D. H., Millar, A. J., Rode, H. Inhalation burns in children. Pediatr. Surg. Int. 15:50–55, 1999.
114. Meyers, D. G., Hoestje, S. M., Korentager, R. A. Incidence of cardiac events in burned patients. Burns 29:367–368, 2003.
115. Sevitt, S. Coronary thrombosis following injury and burns. Med. Sci. Law 13:185–191, 1973.
116. Foley, F. D., Moncrief, J. A., Mason, A. D., Jr. Pathology of the lung in fatally burned pat– ints. Ann. Surg. 167:251–264, 1968.
117. Paret, G., Ziv, T., Augarten, A., et al. Acute respiratory distress syndrome in children: a 10 year experience. Isr. Med. Assoc. J. 1:149–153, 1999.
118. Pruitt, B. A., Jr., Foley, F. D., Moncrief, J. A. Curling's ulcer: a clinical–pathology study of 323 cases. Ann. Surg. 172:523–539, 1970.

119. Reckler, J. M., Bruck, H. M., Munster, A. M., Curreri, P. W., Pruitt, B. A., Jr. Superior mesenteric artery syndrome as a consequence of burn injury. J. Trauma 12:979–985, 1972.
120. Lescher, T. J., Teegarden, D. K., Pruitt, B. A., Jr. Acute pseudo–obstruction of the colon in thermally injured patients. Dis. Colon Rectum 21:618–622, 1978.
121. Desai, M. H., Herndon, D. N., Rutan, R. L., Abston, S., Linares, H. A. Ischemic intestinal complications in patients with burns. Surg. Gynecol. Obstet. 172:257–261, 1991.
122. DuPriest, R. W., Jr., Khaneja, S. C., Cowley, R. A. Acute cholecystitis complicating trauma. Ann. Surg. 189:84–89, 1979.
123. Munster, A. M., Goodwin, M. N., Pruitt, B. A., Jr. Acalculous cholecystitis in burned patients. Am. J. Surg. 122:591–593, 1971.
124. Foley, F. D., Pruitt, B. A., Jr., Moncrief, J. A. Adrenal hemorrhage and necrosis in seriously burned patients. J. Trauma 7:863–870, 1967.
125. Linnemann, C. C., Jr., MacMillan, B. G. Viral infections in pediatric burn patients. Am. J. Dis. Child. 135:750–753, 1981.
126. Seeman, J., Konigova, R. Cytomegalovirus infection in severely burned patients. Acta Chir. Plast. 18:142–151, 1976.
127. Coleman, J. B., Chang, F. C. Pulmonary embolism. An unrecognized event in severely burned patients. Am. J. Surg. 130:697–699, 1975.
128. Champion, H. R., Jones, R. T., Trump, B. F., et al. Post–traumatic hepatic dysfunction as a major etiology in post–traumatic jaundice. J. Trauma 16:650–657, 1976.
129. Czaja, A. J., Rizzo, T. A., Smith, W. R., Jr., Pruitt, B. A., Jr. Acute liver disease after cutaneous thermal injury. J. Trauma 15:887–894, 1975.
130. McManus, W. F., Eurenius, K., Pruitt, B. A., Jr. Disseminated intravascular coagulation in burned patients. J. Trauma 13:416–422, 1973.
131. Sheridan, R. L., Ryan, C. M., Yin, L. M., Hurley, J., Tompkins, R. G. Death in the burn unit: sterile multiple organ failure. Burns 24:307–311, 1998.
132. Tweed, A., Ross, J. F. A review of the mortality in the burns units at the Victoria General Hospital and the Izaak Walton Killam Hospital, January, 1967, to April, 1977. Ann. Plast. Surg. 2:491–498, 1979.
133. Crapo, R. O. Smoke–inhalation injuries. JAMA 246:1694–1696, 1981.
134. Moylan, J. A., Jr., West, J. T., Nash, G., Bowen, J. A., Pruitt, B. A., Jr. Tracheostomy in thermally injured patients: a review of five years' experience. Am. Surg. 38:119–123, 1972.
135. Fish, J., Hartshorne, N., Reay, D., Heimbach, D. The role of autopsy on patients with

burns. J. Burn Care Rehabil. 21:339–344, 2000.

136. Balakrishnan, C., Greer, K. A., Tse, K. G., Hardaway, M. Y. Specific pattern burn in a psy– chiatric patient. Burns 19:439–440, 1993.

137. Varghese, T. K., Kim, A. W., Kowal–Vern, A., Latenser, B. A. Frequency of burn–trauma patients in an urban setting. Arch. Surg. 138:1292–1296, 2003.

138. Bruner, J. M. Hazards of electrical apparatus. Anesthesiology 28:396–425, 1967.

139. Koumbourlis, A. C. Electrical injuries. Crit. Care Med. 30:S424–S430, 2002.

140. Wright, R. K. Death or injury caused by electrocution. Clin. Lab. Med. 3:343–353, 1983.

141. Cooper, M. A. Electrical and lightning injuries. Emerg. Med. Clin. North Am. 2:489–501, 1984.

142. Fontanarosa, P. B. Electrical shock and lightning strike. Ann. Emerg. Med. 22:378–387, 1993.

143. Ghezzi, K. T. Lightning injuries. A unique treatment challenge. Postgrad. Med. 85:197–198, 201–203, 207–208, 1989.

144. Kobernick, M. Electrical injuries: pathophysiology and emergency management. Ann. Emerg. Med. 11:633–638, 1982.

145. Leibovici, D., Shemer, J., Shapira, S. C. Electrical injuries: current concepts. Injury 26:623–627, 1995.

146. DeBono, R. A histological analysis of a high voltage electric current injury to an upper limb. Burns 25:541–547, 1999.

147. Lee, R. C. Injury by electrical forces: pathophysiology, manifestations, and therapy. Curr. Probl. Surg. 34:677–764, 1997.

148. Luce, E. A., Gottlieb, S. E. "True" high–tension electrical injuries. Ann. Plast. Surg. 12:321–326, 1984.

149. Solem, L., Fischer, R. P., Strate, R. G. The natural history of electrical injury. J. Trauma 17:487–492, 1977.

150. Sances, A., Jr., Larson, S. J., Myklebust, J., Cusick, J. F. Electrical injuries. Surg. Gynecol. Obstet. 149:97–108, 1979.

151. DiVincenti, F. C., Moncrief, J. A., Pruitt, B. A., Jr. Electrical injuries: a review of 65 cases. J. Trauma 9:497–507, 1969.

152. Cooper, M. A. Emergent care of lightning and electrical injuries. Semin. Neurol. 15: 268–278, 1995.

153. Blount, B. W. Lightning injuries. Am. Fam. Physician 42:405–415, 1990.

154. Williams, D. B., Karl, R. C. Intestinal injury associated with low–voltage electrocution. J. Trauma 21:246–250, 1981.

155. Morgan, Z. V., Jr., Headley, R. N., Alexander, E. A., Sawyer, C. G. Atrial fibrillation and epidural hematoma associated with lightning stroke; report of a case. N. Engl. J. Med. 259:956–959, 1958.
156. Bligh–Glover, W. Z., Miller, F. P., Balraj, E. K. Two cases of suicidal electrocution. Am. J. Forensic Med. Pathol. 25:255–258, 2004.
157. Martinez, J. A., Nguyen, T. Electrical injuries. South. Med. J. 93:1165–1168, 2000.
158. Butler, E. D., Gant, T. D. Electrical injuries, with special reference to the upper extremities. A review of 182 cases. Am. J. Surg. 134:95–101, 1977.
159. Bernstein, T. Effects of electricity and lightning on man and animals. J. Forensic Sci. 18:3–11, 1973.
160. Lee, W. R. The mechanisms of death from electric shock. Med. Sci. Law 18:23–28, 1965.
161. Jumbelic, M. I. Forensic perspectives of electrical and lightning injuries. Semin. Neurol. 15:342–350, 1995.
162. Krompecher, T., Bergerioux, C. Experimental evaluation of rigor mortis. VII. Effect of ante– and post–mortem electrocution on the evolution of rigor mortis. Forensic Sci. Int. 38:27–35, 1988.
163. Wright, R. K., Davis, J. H. The investigation of electrical deaths: a report of 220 fatalities. J. Forensic Sci. 25:514–521, 1980.
164. Cooper, M. A. Lightning injuries: prognostic signs for death. Ann. Emerg. Med. 9:134–138, 1980.
165. Craig, S. R. When lightning strikes. Pathophysiology and treatment of lightning injuries. Postgrad. Med. 79:109–112;121–124, 1986.
166. Kleinschmidt–DeMasters, B. K. Neuropathology of lightning–strike injuries. Semin. Neurol. 15:323–328, 1995.
167. Whitcomb, D., Martinez, J. A., Daberkow, D. Lightning injuries. South. Med. J. 95:1331–1334, 2002.
168. Hunt, J. L., Mason, A. D., Jr., Masterson, T. S., Pruitt, B. A., Jr. The pathophysiology of acute electric injuries. J. Trauma 16:335–340, 1976.
169. Ditto, E. W., III. Electrocution during sexual activity. Am. J. Forensic Med. Pathol. 2:271–272, 1981.
170. Cooke, C. T., Cadden, G. A., Margolius, K. A. Autoerotic deaths: four cases. Pathology 26:276–280, 1994.
171. Bailey, B., Forget, S., Gaudreault, P. Prevalence of potential risk factors in victims of elec– trocution. Forensic Sci. Int. 123:58–62, 2001.
172. Hunt, J. L., McManus, W. F., Haney, W. P., Pruitt, B. A., Jr. Vascular lesions in acute elec–

tric injuries. J. Trauma 14:461–473, 1974.

173. Levy, L. S. Physiological changes during electrical asphyxiation. Br. J. Ind. Med. 28:164–171, 1971.

174. O'Keefe, G. M., Zane, R. D. Lightning injuries. Emerg. Med. Clin. N. Am. 22:369–403, 2004.

175. Kleiner, J. P., Wilkin, J. H. Cardiac effects of lightning stroke. JAMA 240:2757–2759, 1978.

176. Moran, K. T., Thupari, J. N., Munster, A. M. Lightning injury: physics, pathophysiology and clinical features. Ir. Med. J. 79:120–122, 1986.

177. Centers for Disease Control and Prevention. Lightning–associated deaths—United States, 1980–1995. MMWR Morb. Mortal. Wkly. Rep. 47:391–394, 1998.

178. Myers, G. J., Colgan, M. T., VanDyke, D. H. Lightning–strike disaster among children. JAMA 238:1045–1046, 1977.

179. Mackenzie, E. C. Electrocution in a bath. Sci. Justice 35:253–258, 1995.

180. Bartholome, C. W., Jacoby, W. D., Ramchand, S. C. Cutaneous manifestations of lightning injury. Arch. Dermatol. 111:1466–1468, 1975.

181. Fatovich, D. M. Electrocution in Western Australia, 1976–1990. Med. J. Aust. 157: 762–764, 1992.

182. Rossignol, M., Pineault, M. Classification of fatal occupational electrocutions. Can. J. Public Health 85:322–325, 1994.

183. Brokenshire, B., Cairns, F. J., Koelmeyer, T. D., Smeeton, W. M., Tie, A. B. Deaths from electricity. N. Z. Med. J. 97:139–142, 1984.

184. Zhang, P., Cai, S. Study on electrocution death by low–voltage. Forensic Sci. Int. 76: 115–119, 1995.

185. Still, J., Orlet, H., Law, E., Wheeler, M., Pickens, H. Electrocution due to contact of indus– trial equipment with power lines. Burns 23:573–575, 1997.

186. Moghtader, J. C., Himel, H. N., Demun, E. M., Bellian, K. T., Edlich, R. F. Electrical burn injuries of workers using portable aluminium ladders near overhead power lines. Burns 19:441–443, 1993.

187. Taylor, A. J., McGwin, G., Jr., Valent, F., Rue, L. W., III. Fatal occupational electrocutions in the United States. Inj. Prev. 8:306–312, 2002.

188. Lawrence, R. D., Spitz, W. U., Taff, M. L. Suicidal electrocution in a bathtub. Am. J. Forensic Med. Pathol. 6:276–278, 1985.

189. Rai, J., Jeschke, M. G., Barrow, R. E., Herndon, D. N. Electrical injuries: a 30–year review. J. Trauma 46:933–936, 1999.

190. Nguyen, B. H., MacKay, M., Bailey, B., Klassen, T. P. Epidemiology of electrical and lightning related deaths and injuries among Canadian children and youth. Inj. Prev. 10:122–124, 2004.
191. Tan, C. T., Chao, T. C. A case of fatal electrocution during an unusual autoerotic practice. Med. Sci. Law 23:92–95, 1983.
192. Cairns, F. J., Rainer, S. P. Death from electrocution during auto–erotic procedures. N. Z. Med. J. 94:259–260, 1981.
193. McLoughlin, E., Joseph, M. P., Crawford, J. D. Epidemiology of high–tension electrical injuries in children. J. Pediatr. 89:62–65, 1976.
194. McConnell, T. S., Zumwalt, R. E., Wahe, J., Haikal, N. A., McFeeley, P. J. Rare electrocution due to powerline contact in a hot–air balloon: comparison with fatalities from blunt trauma. J. Forensic Sci. 37:1393–1400, 1992.
195. Thomas, P. C., Kumar, P. High tension electrical injury from a telephone receiver. Burns 27:502–503, 2001.
196. Mitchell, E. K., Davis, J. H. Electrocution by street lighting. J. Forensic Sci. 29:836–842, 1984.
197. Karger, B., Suggeler, O., Brinkmann, B. Electrocution—autopsy study with emphasis on "electrical petechiae." Forensic Sci. Int. 126:210–213, 2002.
198. Fernando, R., Liyanage, S. Suicide by electrocution. Med. Sci. Law 30:219–220, 1990.
199. Bligh–Glover, W. Z., Miller, F. P., Balraj, E. K. Two cases of suicidal electrocution. Am. J. Forensic Med. Pathol. 25:255–258, 2004.
200. Yamazaki, M., Terada, M., Ogura, Y., Wakusugi, C., Mitsukuni, Y. (A suicidal case of elec– trocution with hypnotic drug poisoning: an autopsy report). Nippon Hoigaku Zasshi 51:95–101, 1997.
201. Risse, M., Weiler, G., Kaiser, H. (Rare suicidal death by electrocution using a timer and vital reaction). Arch. Kriminol. 197:149–154, 1996.
202. Troger, H. D., Urban, R., Weller, J. P. (Homicide simulating electrocution suicide by spinal anesthesia). Beitr. Gerichtl. Med. 50:1–5, 1992.
203. al Alousi, L. M. Homicide by electrocution. Med. Sci. Law 30:239–246, 1990.
204. Pfeiffer, H., Karger, B. Attempted homicide by electrocution. Int. J. Legal Med. 111:331–333, 1998.
205. Chao, T. C., Pakiam, J. E., Chia, J. A study of lightning deaths in Singapore. Singapore Med. J. 22:150–157, 1981.
206. Cherington, M., Krider, E. P., Yarnell, P. R., Breed, D W. A bolt from the blue: lightning strike to the head. Neurology 48:683–686, 1997.

207. Chandrasiri, N. Electrocution by dielectric breakdown (arcing) from overhead high tension cables. Med. Sci. Law 28:237–240, 1988.
208. Goodson, M. E. Electrically induced deaths involving water immersion. Am. J. Forensic Med. Pathol. 14:330–333, 1993.
209. Moar, J. J., Hunt, J. B. Death from electrical arc flash burns. A report of 2 cases. S. Afr. Med. J. 71:181–182, 1987.
210. Taylor, P. H., Pugsley, L. Q., Vogel, E. H., Jr. The intriguing electrical burn. A review of thirty–one electrical burn cases. J. Trauma 2:309–326, 1962.
211. Danielsen, L., Gniadecka, M., Thomsen, H. K., et al. Skin changes following defibrillation. The effect of high voltage direct current. Forensic Sci. Int. 134:134–141, 2003.
212. Dutra, F. R. Electrical burns of the skin. Medicolegal investigation. Am. J. Forensic Med. Pathol. 2:309–312, 1981.
213. ten Duis, H. J., Klasen, H. J., Nijsten, M. W., Pietronero, L. Superficial lightning injuries—their "fractal" shape and origin. Burns Incl. Therm. Inj. 13:141–146, 1987.
214. Herrero, F., Garcia–Morato, V., Salinas, V., Alonso, S. An unusual case of lightning injury: a melted silver necklace causing a full thickness linear burn. Burns 21:308–309, 1995.
215. Blumenthal, R. Lightning fatalities on the South African Highveld: a retrospective descrip– tive study for the period 1997 to 2000. Am. J. Forensic Med. Pathol. 26:66–69, 2005.
216. Cherington, M., Olson, S., Yarnell, P. R. Lightning and Lichtenberg figures. Injury 34:367–371, 2003.
217. Weiss, K. S. Otologic lightning bolts. Am. J. Otolaryngol. 1:334–337, 1980.
218. Gordon, M. A., Silverstein, H., Willcox, T. O., Rosenberg, S. I. Lightning injury of the tym– panic membrane. Am. J. Otol. 16:373–376, 1995.
219. Qureshi, N. H. Indirect lightning strike via telephone wire. Injury 26:629–630, 1995.
220. Moulson, A. M. Blast injury of the lungs due to lightning. Br. Med. J. (Clin. Res. Ed.) 289:1270–1271, 1984.
221. Ekoe, J. M., Cunningham, M., Jaques, O., et al. Disseminated intravascular coagulation and acute myocardial necrosis caused by lightning. Intensive Care Med. 11:160–162, 1985.
222. Sinha, A. K. Lightning–induced myocardial injury. A case report with management. Angiology 36:327–331, 1985.
223. Zack, F., Hammer, U., Klett, I., Wegener, R. Myocardial injury due to lightning. Int. J. Legal Med. 110:326–328, 1997.

224. Cherington, M. Neurologic manifestations of lightning strikes. Neurology 60:182–185, 2003.
225. Kint, P. A., Stroy, J. P., Parizel, P. M. Basal ganglia hemorrhage secondary to lightning stroke. JBR –BTR 82:113, 1999.
226. Tibesar, R. J., Roy, S., Hom, D. B. Bilateral Le Fort I fracture from a lightning strike injury to the face. Otolaryngol. Head Neck Surg. 123:647–649, 2000.
227. Hocking, B., Andrews, C. Fractals and lightning injury. Med. J. Aust. 150:409–410, 1989.
228. Jonas, L., Fulda, G., Nizze, H., et al. Detection of gold particles in the neck skin after light- ning stroke with evaporation of an ornamental chain. Ultrastruct. Pathol. 26:153–159, 2002.
229. Ohashi, M., Kitagawa, N., Ishikawa, T. Lightning injury caused by discharges accompany- ing flashovers—a clinical and experimental study of death and survival. Burns Incl. Therm. Inj. 12:496–501, 1986.
230. Burke, J. F., Quinby, W. C., Jr., Bondoc, C., McLaughlin, E., Trelstad, R. L. Patterns of high tension electrical injury in children and adolescents and their management. Am. J. Surg. 133:492–497, 1977.
231. Moran, K. T., Munster, A. M. Low voltage electrical injuries: the hidden morbidity. J. R. Coll. Surg. Edinb. 31:227–228, 1986.
232. Jensen, P. J., Thomsen, P. E., Bagger, J. P., Norgaard, A., Baandrup, U. Electrical injury causing ventricular arrhythmias. Br. Heart J. 57:279–283, 1987.
233. Bailey, B., Gaudreault, P., Thivierge, R. L., Turgeon, J. P. Cardiac monitoring of children with household electrical injuries. Ann. Emerg. Med. 25:612–617, 1995.
234. Sprecher, W., Wenz, W., Haffner, H. T. Rupture of an intracranial aneurysm—unusual com- plication of an electric shock. Forensic Sci. Int. 122:85–88, 2001.
235. James, T. N., Riddick, L., Embry, J. H. Cardiac abnormalities demonstrated postmortem in four cases of accidental electrocution and their potential significance relative to nonfatal electrical injuries of the heart. Am. Heart J. 120:143–157, 1990.
236. Xenopoulos, N., Movahed, A., Hudson, P., Reeves, W. C. Myocardial injury in electrocu- tion. Am. Heart J. 122:1481–1484, 1991.
237. Walton, A. S., Harper, R. W., Coggins, G. L. Myocardial infarction after electrocution. Med. J. Aust. 148:365–367, 1988.
238. Colonna, M., Caruso, G., Nardulli, F., Altamura, B. Myocardial haemorrhagic necrosis in delayed death from electrocution. Acta Med. Leg. Soc. (Liege) 39:145–147, 1989.
239. Fieguth, A., Schumann, G., Troger, H. D., Kleemann, W. J. The effect of lethal electrical shock on postmortem serum myoglobin concentrations. Forensic Sci. Int. 105:75–82,

1999.

240. Puschel, K., Lockemann, U., Bartel, J. Postmortem investigation of serum myoglobin lev- els with special reference to electrical fatalities. Forensic Sci. Int. 72:171-177, 1995.

241. Poate, W. J., Macafee, A. L. Gas gangrene following electrical burns. A report of two cases. Br. J. Plast. Surg. 15:17-19, 1962.

242. Kumar, S., Thomas, S., Lehri, S. Abdominal wall and stomach perforation following acciden- tal electrocution with high tension wire: a unique case. J. Emerg. Med. 11:141-145, 1993.

243. Carvajal, H. F., Feinstein, R., Traber, D. L, et al. An objective method for early diagnosis of gram-negative septicemia in burned children. J. Trauma 21:221-227, 1981.

244. Chari, P. S., Bapna, B. C., Balakrishnan, C. Electrical burns causing a urinary bladder fis- tula. Case report. Plast. Reconstr. Surg. 61:446-448, 1978.

245. Sinha, J. K., Roy, S. K. Perforation of the caecum caused by an electrical burn. Br. J. Plast. Surg. 29:179-181, 1976.

246. Newsome, T. W., Curreri, P. W., Eurenius, K. Visceral injuries: an unusual complication of an electrical burn. Arch. Surg. 105:494-497, 1972.

247. Patel, A., Lo, R. Electric injury with cerebral venous thrombosis. Case report and review of the literature. Stroke 24:903-905, 1993.

248. Levine, N. S., Atkins, A., McKeel, D. W., Jr., Peck, S. D., Pruitt, B. A., Jr. Spinal cord injury following electrical accidents: case reports. J. Trauma 15:459-463, 1975.

249. Kotak, B. P., Haddo, O., Iqbal, M., Chissell, H. Bilateral scapular fractures after electrocu- tion. J. R. Soc. Med. 93:143-144, 2000.

250. Brown, R. J. Bilateral dislocation of the shoulders. Injury 15:267-273, 1984.

251. Jacobsen, H. Electrically induced deposition of metal on the human skin. Forensic Sci. Int. 90:85-92, 1997.

252. Odesanmi, W. O. Things are not always what they seem! Joule burns in electrocution—a report of four cases. Med. Sci. Law 27:63-67, 1987.

253. Karlsmark, T., Thomsen, H. K., Danielsen, L., et al. The morphogenesis of electrically and heat-induced dermal changes in pig skin. Forensic Sci. Int. 39:175-188, 1988.

254. Karlsmark, T., Thomsen, H. K., Danielsen, L., et al. Tracing the use of electrical torture. Am. J. Forensic Med. Pathol. 5:333-337, 1984.

255. Karlsmark, T., Aalund, O., Danielsen, L., et al. The occurrence of calcium salt deposition on dermal collagen fibres following electrical injury to porcine skin. Forensic Sci. Int. 39:245-255, 1988.

256. Karlsmark, T., Danielsen, L., Aalund, O., et al. Electrically-induced collagen calcification

257. Adjutantis, G., Dritsas, C., Iordanidis, P. An unusual occurrence of electric burns in a case of fatal electrocution. Forensic Sci. 2:255–257, 1973.
258. Marcinkowski, T., Pankowski, M. Significance of skin metallization in the diagnosis of electrocution. Forensic Sci. Int. 16:1–6, 1980.
259. Ortmann, C., Rolf, B., Fechner, G. DNA–typing of cellular material on current conductors. Int. J. Legal Med. 111:177–179, 1998.
260. Clemedson, C. J. Blast injury. Physiol. Rev. 36:336–354, 1956.
261. Guy, R. J., Glover, M. A., Cripps, N. P. The pathophysiology of primary blast injury and its implications for treatment. Part I: The thorax. J. R. Nav. Med. Serv. 84:79–86, 1998.
262. Marshall, T. A pathologist's view of terrorist violence. Forensic Sci. Int. 36:57–67, 1988.
263. Wright, R. K. Death or injury caused by explosion. Clin. Lab. Med. 3:309–319, 1983.
264. Makitie, I., Paloneva, H., Tikka, S. Explosion injuries in Finland 1991–1995. Ann. Chir. Gynaecol. 86:209–213, 1997.
265. Botti, K., Grosleron–Gros, N., Khaldi, N., Oliviera, A., Gromb, S. Postmortem findings in 22 victims due to two grain silo explosions in France. J. Forensic Sci. 48:827–831, 2003.
266. Nicholas, E. J. Underground explosions in coal mines. Med. Sci. Law 16:240–243, 1976.
267. Shields, L. B., Hunsaker, D. M., Hunsaker, J. C., III, Humbert, K. A. Nonterrorist suicidal deaths involving explosives. Am. J. Forensic Med. Pathol. 24:107–113, 2003.
268. Tsokos, M., Turk, E. E., Madea, B., et al. Pathologic features of suicidal deaths caused by explosives. Am. J. Forensic Med. Pathol. 24:55–63, 2003.
269. Karmy–Jones, R., Kissinger, D., Golocovsky, M., Jordan, M., Champion, H. R. Bomb-related injuries. Mil. Med. 159:536–539, 1994.
270. Mellor, S. G., Cooper, G. J. Analysis of 828 servicemen killed or injured by explosion in Northern Ireland 1970–84: the Hostile Action Casualty System. Br. J. Surg. 76:1006–1010, 1989.
271. Clark, M. A. The pathology of terrorism. Acts of violence directed against citizens of the United States while abroad. Clin. Lab. Med. 18:99–114, 1998.
272. Cooper, G. J., Maynard, R. L., Cross, N. L., Hill, J. F. Casualties from terrorist bombings. J. Trauma 23:955–967, 1983.
273. Andersen, P., Loken, S. Lung damage and lethality by underwater detonations. Acta Physiol. Scand. 72:6–14, 1968.
274. Marshall, T. K. Deaths from explosive devices. Med. Sci. Law 16:235–239, 1976.
275. Cripps, N. P., Glover, M. A., Guy, R. J. The pathophysiology of primary blast injury and

its implications for treatment. Part II: The auditory structures and abdomen. J. R. Nav. Med. Serv. 85:13–24, 1999.
276. Saravanapavananthan, N. Injuries caused by home–made explosives. Forensic Sci. Int. 12:131–136, 1978.
277. Hull, J. B., Bowyer, G. W., Cooper, G. J., Crane, J. Pattern of injury in those dying from traumatic amputation caused by bomb blast. Br. J. Surg. 81:1132–1135, 1994.
278. Varga, M., Csabai, G. A suicidal death by explosives. Int. J. Legal Med. 105:35–37, 1992.
279. Karger, B., Zweihoff, R. F., DuChesne, A. Injuries from hand grenades in civilian settings. Int. J. Legal Med. 112:372–375, 1999.
280. Katz, E., Ofek, B., Adler, J., Abramowitz, H. B., Krausz, M. M. Primary blast injury after a bomb explosion in a civilian bus. Ann. Surg. 209:484–488, 1989.
281. Brismar, B., Bergenwald, L. The terrorist bomb explosion in Bologna, Italy, 1980: an analysis of the effects and injuries sustained. J. Trauma 22:216–220, 1982.
282. Guy, R. J., Watkins, P. E., Edmondstone, W. M. Electrocardiographic changes following primary blast injury to the thorax. J. R. Nav. Med. Serv. 86:125–133, 2000.
283. Guy, R. J., Kirkman, E., Watkins, P. E., Cooper, G. J. Physiologic responses to primary blast. J. Trauma 45:983–987, 1998.
284. Laposata, E. A. Collection of trace evidence from bombing victims at autopsy. J. Forensic Sci. 30:789–797, 1985.
285. Yallop, H. J. Loss of clothes in an explosion. J. Forensic Sci. Soc. 22:399–400, 1982.

第5章
水中尸体

概述

在水中被发现的尸体并不意味着溺死,其他死因如损伤后被人抛尸入水也有可能。溺死是窒息死亡的一种类型,其死亡机制涉及复杂的病理生理学,而某些疾病发作(如缺血性心脏病、癫痫、酒精中毒)等也会增加发生溺死的风险。尽管溺死的过程很复杂,但与之相关的外部和内部的线索却非常少。缺少特异性改变和水中物体所造成的损伤都会对溺水者死因的推断产生影响。因此,便有各种针对溺死的检验方法被用来帮助判断。由于可能存在各种死亡方式,人们总觉得查明浴缸中尸体的死因更具挑战性。然而令人感到讽刺的是,对于潜水员的遇难却毫无疑问地认为是由于氧气瓶中的人造空气供给不足所致。

关键词:窒息;溺死;淹没;硅藻;低温;潜水

1 前言

对于法医和侦查员而言,明确水中尸体的死亡原因和死亡方式非常具有挑战性(1–5)。在所有可能的死亡原因中,首先会怀疑溺死(6),但溺死的方式却难以明确(7)。因为关于溺死前的情况,有时由于缺少目击者而对溺死者如何入水知之甚少(1, 3, 8–10)。在案件中往往只有1/2至3/4的溺死者有目击证人(11, 12)。对1 590具水中尸体调查后发现,在这些意外、自杀、他杀、灾害及死因不明的案件中,分别有37.3%、30.8%、12.4%、11.9%及5.3%的案件有目击者[占总数的25.3%(3)]。但在超过半数的案件中目击者的证词均未得到证实,这涉及到目击者和受害者之间的关系,甚至多位证人的证词还相互矛盾。对于某些未明确性质的案件,其有一小部分(6.9%)即使有目击者,侦查员仍然无法明确死者是自己失足落水还是被他人推入水中(7)。

大多数淹没在水中的尸体,包括那些未明确性质的,都可先归类为溺死(5, 7, 13)。但即使高度怀疑为溺死,也应注意排除其他死亡原因(如疾病、损伤等)(参阅标题 5-7；参考文献 1,9,10 及 14-16）。自然死亡和其他非自然死亡的落水者在濒死期都会吸入溺液，所以对溺死的诊断须排除这些可能的因素（2,4,7,17-20）。因此，尸体解剖便成为明确死亡原因和死亡方式的金标准（21,22）。通过尸体各种非特异性的外部和内部征象，并结合死亡现场，可明确判断死者是否符合溺死的（1,3,5,5-10,19,20,23,24）。但尸体长时间浸泡在水中会发生腐败并破坏原本就不多的病理学证据，从而增加了判断溺死的难度（10,25-27）。此外法医还需分析死者在水中无法存活的原因（1）。尽管有时对水中尸体的检验缺乏阳性发现，但溺死确实涉及了复杂的病理生理机制，并与被害人和现场的各类因素有关。

2 流行病学与环境

2.1 死亡方式

一项对芬兰 1 590 具水中尸体的研究表明，其中 56.2% 的死者系意外溺死，23.8% 系自杀溺死，16.5% 系死因不明，0.8% 系他杀溺死，还有 2.6% 系自然灾害溺死（3）。而从另一项对纽约下水道内发现的 123 具尸体的 4 年研究获悉，其中 42% 的死者系自杀溺死，41% 系死因不明，13% 系意外溺死，还有 4% 系他杀溺死（5）。在对 1 201 件溺水案件的研究中也有 11% 的死者无法明确死亡方式（13）。因此，对溺水死亡方式的判断取决于法律证明的标准，不同司法管辖区有不同的判断标准（7）。

研究表明，在各年龄阶段的溺死（相对于其他死亡原因死后抛尸入水而言）案件中有大约 90% 死者由意外造成（4,13,18,28-30），其余案件中大部分死者为自杀身亡。然而，一些北美洲地区以外的研究表明自杀溺死的比例更高（参阅标题 3；参考文献 4,9,13,18,24,28 及 31-34），他杀溺死则很少见（13,18,28,30,33,35,36）。诸多研究显示，30 岁以下年轻女性自杀溺死者为零，这就意味着对于此类案件仍需排除意外和他杀（37）。

2.2 高危人群

溺死者往往都是男性［大于 65%（11-13,28,30,33,38-48）］，男性溺死者比例较高可能反映出男性在水中更活跃、更愿意冒险（42）。

溺死通常发生在夏季，多见于河流、湖泊、池塘及小溪中（11-13,32,38,44,45,48）。而在北方地区，人们驾驶摩托雪橇和机动车时由于冰面破裂而落水，也会发生溺死（44）。游泳、潜水、涉水都是与溺死紧密相关的活动（12,28,30,44,49,50）。溺死的高危人群主要是 20 岁左右的青年（11,12,30,44,45,47,48,51）。很多青少年在游泳时溺水（13），他们中大多数会游泳，却由于其他原因（如乙醇中毒）而溺水（13）。药物和酒精是主要原因之一，特别在缺乏成年人监护时（29,39,41,45,48,52）。其他与溺死相关的"正常"活动还包括钓鱼、赛艇和沐浴（12,28,33）。年龄较大的男性常会在这些活动中溺水［如钓鱼、赛艇（12,13,47）］，这些人大部分都没有救生衣（13,19,44,45,47）。在船舶事故［超载、超速、危险驾驶（19,45）］中也会发生溺水。有时意外落水（如车祸、失足落水）同样也会发生溺死（13,30,32,38,

44),过量饮酒也可能是主要原因之一(19,47)。这些死者往往都身穿私服,而不是泳衣(41)。所以侦查员仍需要甄别他们是自杀还是意外溺水(4,37)。

儿童也是溺死的高危人群(28,43,44,47,48,53),尤其是 2 岁以下的低龄儿童,更易发生危险(54—56)。由于缺乏娴熟的活动技能及平衡能力,他们无法依靠自身的力量脱离险境(55),他们也不会游泳,无法大声呼救和保存体力(55)。游泳池溺水的风险取决于人们去游泳池游泳的风靡程度,这是由气候因素所决定的(43,44,57)。天气较凉爽时,溺死往往发生在自然水域中(48)。

在家中,泳池和浴缸都是婴幼儿发生溺死的高危场所(参阅标题 13.1;参考文献 11,13,29,38—40,53—56 及 58—60)。1 岁以下的婴儿是浴缸内溺死的高危人群,而泳池则对 1 岁以上的婴幼儿更危险。儿童在地下注水的泳池内游泳要比在地上注水的泳池内更易发生溺水(61)。泳池安装完成后的前 6 个月幼儿发生溺水的风险最高(62)。因为幼儿溺水可能只是在游泳池边缘玩耍时失足落水发生,而不是直接嬉水造成(12,39,55,57,63),同样在海滩边玩耍的幼儿有被海浪卷走的危险(46,64)。踏上覆在泳池上的太阳能毯也是儿童溺水的潜在危险(48)。

值得注意的是,私人住宅的泳池周围缺少监管(11—13,19,42,48,57,60,63,65,66),有时监护的成年人也会出现醉酒状况(48)。在一系列溺水案件中,尽管 84% 的案件有成年人在泳池旁监护儿童,却只有 18% 的成年人发现儿童溺水,这说明成年人也会出现一过性的注意力缺失(67)。对于溺水案件,在泳池中失去意识的儿童的存活率为 65%,而在河流或小溪中溺水的儿童的存活率只有 21%(40),因为在泳池旁边一般都有成年人,能尽快发现儿童溺水并迅速实施心肺复苏抢救(39,57)。

泳池缺少安全防护栏也是造成儿童溺水事故的一个安全隐患(13,29,38,39,45,48,56,58—61,63,65,68,69)。即使安装了防护栏也可能存在问题〔如防护栏的锁损坏、防护栏变形都能使儿童轻易进出泳池(42)〕。这些存在隐患的防护栏会给家长带来"安全错觉",从而放松对儿童的监管,同时也会延误抢救的时机(61)。

青少年往往在公共泳池中发生溺死事故,即使救生员在场,也难以避免(13)。成人有时也会因为救生员没有有效地观察和救护而溺死(49),更不用说救生员在游泳人群中察觉到大龄儿童的溺水(61)。

有研究已显示,儿童在 5 加仑(1 加仑 = 3.785 升)容量的水桶内发生溺水的频率也非常高(38,53,55,56)。当幼儿蹒跚学步时,由于重心高,站不稳,很容易从高处落入水桶中(53,70)。而 8—15 个月的婴幼儿是发生此类事故的高危人群(71)。在大多数情况下,这类水桶都是用来保洁或清洗尿布的(53,70)。桶里往往已倒入至少 10% 容量的液体(53,70),通常是水,有时也会加入洗涤剂、清洁剂或漂白剂(70)。水桶的高度为 34—38 厘米(14—15 英寸),而本章"水中尸体"所研究的 245 名溺死儿童的身高在 67—79 厘米(27—32 英寸)之间(53,55,70)。水桶本身有很强的稳固性,即使是空桶也不容易发生倾倒(53,70)。放在水桶内的物品(如玩具、衣物)会吸引儿童的注意力

(70),而他们的运动控制能力尚未完全成熟,失足落入水桶后无法独自摆脱困境(53)。有时,熟睡的婴儿在床上翻滚也会落入床旁装满液体的水桶中(70)。

3 自杀溺死

系列案件研究显示很多信息有助于确定自杀:证人;遗书和轻生意念;癌症或疾病晚期(已知道或感觉到);近期奇怪的行为或抑郁症;自伤等(表 5-1;参考文献 3)。通过现场勘查发现死者的衣物和个人物品被整齐地堆放在水边,也可作为其自杀的佐证(4,31)。而在水岸边发现单独的鞋印,或者积雪中有雪橇的踪迹,也暗示死者是经过深思熟虑后才跃入寒冷水中的(3)。有时现场勘查还会有不寻常的发现,让人怀疑死者系自杀(如将重物与身体捆绑在一起,或者夫妻俩的腰捆绑在一起)(图 5-1;参考文献 4,37)。

对溺水尸体的识别有助于推断死者是否系自杀(1,5)。若能够对溺水者进行有效的个体识别,以及确认死者生前是否有精神疾病史,将有助于诊断(7)。即使有提示死者自杀的证据(如手腕上试切伤的皮肤瘢痕或某些药物的毒理学检测结果),若没有对个体进行正确的识别,要想获取更多的信息就显得十分困难(参阅标题 8.1)。在鉴定过程中进行死亡方式分析时,要对疑似自杀地点和死者的既往史(如自杀未遂、精神失常)进行全面、仔细的调查(7)。自杀是唯一需要论证死者动机的死亡方式。

图 5-1 自杀溺死。重物与身体捆绑在一起。

表 5–1 自杀溺死

案件	数量	自杀比	溺死比	男:女	年龄范围	落水点	精神病史	毒物分析	其他备注/发现
佛罗里达州；Copeland (9)	70	4.5% (70/1569)	13.4% (70/521)	41:29	38.6%>70岁 1.43% (n=1) 0—20岁	海洋/海湾: 31.4% 河道: 21.4% 住宅: 21.4% (泳池: 10件; 浴缸: 5件)	抑郁症患者: 70% 有精神病史或行为异常者 15.7%	• 在70起案件中有68起 (97.1%) 进行乙醇检测，有50起 (71.4%) 进行药物检测 • 乙醇检测中39起案件阴性 (55.7%) 阳性,17起 (24.3%) 阳性, 12起 (17.1%) 乙醇含量达100毫克/分升或更高 • 药物检测中30起案件阴性 (42.8%) 阳性, 20起 (28.6%) 阳性 (镇静剂最为常见; 其中3起案件的死者药系药物临床试验志愿者)	遗书: 28.6% 遗言: 25.7% 死者大都穿戴整齐
佛罗里达州；Davis (31)	25	2.9% (25/873)	9% (25/267)	14:11	25—91岁 64%超过65岁	住宅内泳池: 28.0% 河道: 24.0% 湖泊: 20.0% 海洋: 12.0%	抑郁症患者阳性 76% 严重精神疾病 20%	• 6/24 (25%) 乙醇检测阳性 (50—350毫克/分升) • 8/25 (32%) 检测处方药阳性,其中3起案件超出治疗浓度 (2起发生在住宅浴缸,1起发生在住宅泳池)	• 约有20%的居民超过65岁 • 5人驾车至事发地点 (其中2人驾车落水); • 60%身着便服; 28%仅穿着较少; 12%赤裸 (参阅第5章标题13)

续表

案件	数量	自杀比	溺死比	男:女	年龄范围	落水点	精神病史	毒物分析	其他备注/发现
德克萨斯州；Wirthwein等(4)	52	0.85%(52/6082)	4%(52/1303)	28:24	21—84岁 54%男性>40岁 67%女性>40岁	湖泊/池塘：56% 泳池：17%	有精神病史者和/或酗酒者/药物滥用者：50%	• 52名死者中有21人乙醇检测阳性，其中13位对乙醇更易代谢分解 • 24（46%）名死者检测出其他药物，其中4人接近或超出致死浓度范围	2人在被淹没的车中
纽芬兰，加拿大；Avis(72)	22	8.9%(22/247)	—	14:8	77%超过50岁 在所有自杀者中有约四分之一的人在此年龄范围内	海洋：86.4% 无人在浴缸内溺死	—	• 2/22（9.1%）乙醇检测阳性（41毫摩尔/升或189毫克%，29.6毫摩尔/升或136.5毫克%） • 3/18（16.7%）药物检测阳性（曲米帕明、溴西泮、氟西泮），都在治疗浓度范围内	23.5%的女性和6.6%的男性选择溺死作为自杀的方式
阿德莱德，澳大利亚；Byard等(37)	123	—	—	76:47	男性：16—88岁（平均50.5岁） 女性：34—88岁（平均60.6岁）	淡水：53.7% 海水：46.3%	精神疾病患者—43.1%	至少有25人乙醇检测阳性（20.3%），20起案件中死者体内检出处方药	遗书：14.6% 健康问题：8.1% 有5起汽车驶入水中的案件
芬兰；Auer(34)	51	—	17.8%(51/285)	—	21岁至70岁 21—30岁占27.5%，70岁以上占19.6%	户外自来水（泳池）：5.9% 浴缸：—	精神错乱者—15.7%；接受心理干预治疗者—49%；抑郁症患者—35.3% 自杀未遂者—37.3%	—	遗书：7.8%

4 溺水的死亡机制

4.1 溺死("湿性"溺死,"典型"溺死)

溺死被定义为液体通过口鼻被吸入呼吸道而引起的窒息死亡(6,16,47,48,58,79-76)。该定义中所吸入的液体并不包括呕吐物、血液、唾液、胆汁及胎粪(73)。溺死案件中大多数属于"湿性"溺死(参阅标题10;参考文献75)。一般认为,全身浸入液体中才会溺死,其实只要将头面部甚至口鼻腔浸入液体,即能溺死。例如:酒醉、昏倒、癫痫发作的成人或幼儿跌倒在5—6厘米(2英寸)的水洼内也会溺死(77)。溺死的主要死亡机制是体内缺氧(47,48,78-84)。溺液的多少和性质等因素决定了死亡机制是缺氧还是心搏骤停(47,74,78,81,85,86)。

通过目击者的证词、人体研究和动物实验,我们能够还原溺死的过程(8)。一名清醒的受害者全身浸入水中时会本能地屏气(58,60,76),这可以通过呼吸肌运动和防止吞咽液体而紧闭声门来增强(68,87)。有些人溺水后吞咽大量液体(58,60,76,87),这会增加呕吐反应和吸入胃内容物的概率(58,60,73,88)。同时落水者也会在水中挣扎,儿童会挣扎10—20秒,或者平静地沉入水中,而成人能够挣扎60秒(58,73,76),持续屏气直到不可控制的呼吸("断点")发生,继而出现不自主的急促呼吸(60,76,86)。受害者在屏气时也无法呼喊求助(73,88)。受过专业训练的人员在水中屏气的平均持续时间大约为1.5分钟,普通人大约只有1分钟(89)。在寒冷的水中屏气的时间还会缩短(参阅标题4.5;参考文献60)。

随着不自主的急促呼吸的出现,溺液刺激咽喉部引起呛咳(47,58,76,86)。这个阶段溺液被大量吸入(47)。溺液会刺激副交感神经(迷走神经)反射引起外周性气道阻塞,从而使肺的顺应性下降(参阅标题4.3;参考文献58,60,76,90及91)。在淡水与咸水肺内分流的机制的形成不同。吸入的溺液渗入肺泡,会影响肺表面活性物质的功能(76,78)。通过对犬的实验发现高渗性液体(如海水)的渗透压大于人体的血液,渗透性盐溶液可稀释或洗去肺表面活性物质(58,60,76,81)。而含氯或不含氯的淡水则会损害肺泡膜并使肺表面活性物质变性。水中的杂质(污物、污水、清洁剂)同样也是有害的(参阅标题4.4)。肺表面活性物质的变性、含量降低可导致肺泡萎陷(肺不张),继而出现肺内分流和换气-灌注不协调而加重缺氧(58,76,78,82,83,85,92)。肺牵张反射在临床上是极其重要的生理反应(73,83)。在海水中溺死,大量含盐溶液通过血液循环迅速渗入肺泡,产生肺水肿,从而形成肺内分流(47,78,83,86,92)。肺水肿不仅在海水溺死者中会发生,在淡水溺死者中也会发生。淡水被迅速吸收进入血液循环,由于缺氧使心脏负担加重,使得肺泡毛细血管通透性改变,导致肺泡腔内渗出液增多,继而发生肺水肿(84,93,94)。由于喉痉挛会减少通气,泡沫(溺液和空气混合的水肿液)、黏液及外来物质造成气道阻塞、肺不张和肺水肿,这些多重因素又加重了人体缺氧(60,74,78,90)。淡水溺水者的生还率与海水溺水者相比并无差异。然而,与内陆水体相比,海岸的救援服务可能更好,能迅速实施心肺复苏,提高溺水者的生还概率(46,73,88)。

尽管肺水肿很常见,动物实验(将血液浓缩的动物放入海水中,出现溶血、血液稀释、低钠血症的情况,在淡水中则会出现高钾血症)显示血容量变化及电解质紊乱在临床上通常并不重要(47,50,58,60,78,80−82,85,88,92,94−97)。由于人体自身的代偿机制,淡水溺水或海水溺水时在临床上会发生一过性的血容量变化(47),因此吸入溺液后心血管和肺部的变化与液体的渗透压并不相关(98,99),但吸入大量溺液会引起电解质失衡。通过动物实验发现,吸入大量淡水(44毫升/千克或20毫升/磅)会造成电解质紊乱和溶血,但人体无法吸收如此大容量的液体(2,73,100)。研究表明,人体摄入22毫升/千克(10毫升/磅)的液体与维持正常的电解质水平相关(74,78)。通过对犬的相关实验发现,电解质的变化都很短暂,而高钾血症也不会引起心室纤颤(82,95)。关于淡水和海水溺死的研究发现,15%的死者吸入了超过22毫升/千克(或10毫升/磅)的水,造成左心室中氯含量显著变化(80)。但在临床上由于电解质紊乱引起的心室纤颤并不常见(85,88,95)。通过动物实验发现,在几分钟内吸入2.2毫升/千克(1毫升/磅)的水便会引起缺氧(58,73,76,82,85,92−94)。而吸入少量的水有时也会导致濒死。有临床案例显示由血容量和电解质变化引起的异常情况,如严重的溶血会导致弥散性血管内凝血[DIC(101)]。吸入海水所引起的电解质变化与液体的体积和浓度呈函数变化(79)。吸入过咸的水(如淹没在死海中)会导致血清电解质变化,但溺水后肺部并发症的病理生理变化在临床处理中依旧最为重要(102)。

人落水后,会引起反射性吸气运动,将液体吸入气道引起呛咳,然后本能地出现呼吸暂停(60)。在水中几分钟后就会出现不自主的急促呼吸,继而吸入大量溺液,最终引起呼吸暂停(88)。如果心肺复苏不及时,持续性缺氧会导致心律失常、心搏骤停甚至脑死亡。人体淹没于水中通常在3分钟内便会因脑缺氧而失去意识(103)。持续性缺氧引起的大脑不可逆损伤的程度与溺水者的年龄相关。目击者对致命性溺死的浸泡时间大多数是估计的,且浸泡时间会随着年龄和水温的差异而变化[如果水温在15℃−20℃(59℉−68℉)或以上,浸泡时间为3−10分钟;水温在0℃−15℃(32℉−59℉)之间浸泡时间为5−40分钟;有些生还的儿童甚至能够恢复正常的神经功能;(参阅标题4.5;参考文献60,76和103)。对浴缸内溺水案件的研究发现,生还儿童最长溺水时间为3−5分钟(中位数为4分钟),而死亡往往发生在溺水后3−20分钟之间[中位数为5分钟(77)]。

4.2 潜泳和屏气

所谓"断点",即随着机体动脉血氧分压(PaO_2)的降低和动脉血二氧化碳分压

($PaCO_2$)的升高,出现了不自主的急促呼吸(89,104)。发生断点时动脉血二氧化碳分压平均为60毫米汞柱,动脉血氧分压约为80毫米汞柱(58,104)。过度通气会使体内动脉血二氧化碳分压降至50毫米汞柱以下,假如游泳者在进行剧烈活动时过度通气并屏住呼吸,即潜泳,会在二氧化碳潴留发生断点刺激呼吸之前就因缺氧而失去意识(PaO_2 < 60毫米汞柱)(8,58,60,78,105–107),继而溺死。对于受过训练的潜水者,他们对高碳酸血症具有更高的耐受性并能有意识地避开断点(106,107)。高碳酸血症还会引起心律失常(89)。

4.3 溺水后猝死("干性"溺死,浸入综合征)

在10%−20%的案件中,会出现溺死者不吸入溺液而没有"湿性"溺死的尸体征象(肺淤血、呼吸道内产生泡沫)(6,8,58,74–76,86)。由于外界刺激导致的喉痉挛被认为是阻止溺液吸入的原因(6,8,47,58,60,74,76,86)。

目击者对此类案件受害人溺水的描述大都是他们在游泳、涉水或落水后,挣扎不久便消失在水中(2,11,15,17–19,78,108)。即使迅速从水中被救起,但死亡已难以避免。对34起溺死案例的研究显示,有一人两次浮出水面,有三人一次浮出水面,另有30人没有浮出水面(11)。呼吸暂停会刺激颈动脉化学感受器,使迷走神经兴奋,反射性引起心搏骤停(参阅标题4.1;参考文献109)。原本就只有少量溺液被吸入,发生心搏骤停后就更难被吸入呼吸道内(6,8,58,76,108)。此外,当受害者突然入水后,冷水的刺激使迷走神经兴奋,也会反射性引起心搏骤停(86)。上述这些综合征尤其会对醉酒的中老年人产生影响(2,15,18,110)。如果患有潜在的心脏疾病也会增加猝死的风险(参阅标题7;参考文献78),因为这些人容易发生心脏传导系统异常而溺死(111)。

4.4 围溺死期

溺死往往发生在水中(75),而围溺死期指的是复苏和治疗后的一段生存期(6,32,47,48,56,73,75,87,97)。众所周知,并发症也能致人死亡(如成人呼吸窘迫综合征、肺炎、败血症、缺血缺氧性脑病、脑水肿、弥散性血管内凝血等,参阅第1章标题4.3;参考文献58,60,76,87和112)。"继发性溺死"指溺水者被抢救复苏后情况好转,却因呼吸代偿失调而死亡(46)。然而现在均不建议使用"继发性溺死"这种表述(75)。因为,受害者因疾病或意外(如高坠[47,48,73,78])跌入水中后死亡也可被称为继发性溺死。

在没有意识丧失或呼吸停止的情况下也会出现肺部并发症(87)。吸入淡水或海水的溺水者被成功复苏后,肺泡表面活性物质的变化仍持续进行(76,87)。围溺水期后,急性肺水肿和肺泡损伤可以持续长达12小时(76,87,88)。溺水者还会有吸入胃内容物的风险(参阅标题4.1;参考文献87,113)。吸入溺液、异物或感染均可引起成人呼吸窘迫综合征(48,59)。即使使用呼吸机抢救,低氧血症也会对全身多器官造成损伤(59)。肺表面活性物质的含量降低或改变、肺不张、肺内分流增多、通气灌注不均和肺水肿都会导致缺氧。大约有三分之一的围溺死期生还者被发现因缺氧导致中度至重度脑损伤(87)。同时,寒冷和损伤所诱发的横纹肌溶解会导致急性肾功能衰竭(参阅第8章标题13;参考文献87,97),而缺氧也会促进急性肾小管坏死(97)。

围溺死期的良好预后因素包括年轻、淹没时间较短(＜10分钟)、淹没在冷水中(＜10℃)、没有吸入大量溺液、及时现场急救、短时间内复苏成功(＜10分钟)、快速自发地恢复心输出量、入院时意识恢复及瞳孔对光反应存在、核心体温低于33℃－35℃(91℉－95℉;59,87,114)。但这些因素并非都可以预料。因此,对所有围溺死期的受害者都应该尽力复苏抢救(87,115)。

围溺死期的死亡率往往比溺水时更高(58,116)。在各类溺水事故中,受害者在水中的时间越长,成功复苏的机会就越渺茫。研究发现只有22%溺死案件中受害者的溺水时间在30分钟以内(30)。

4.5 浸入冷水中

4.5.1 冷休克反应

突然淹没在冷水中会引起持续2－3分钟的心肺反射(87,117)。

对健康的落水者而言,呼吸道的应激反应是对生存最大的威胁(117)。当体表温度迅速下降时会通过冷敏感受体直接刺激呼吸中枢,而在10℃[50℉(117,118)]的冷水中这种刺激会达到最高峰(119)。但当水温进一步降至冰点(32℉)时反应反而不那么强烈(120)。对成人而言,从最开始的喘气演变成不自主的急促呼吸(17,74,87,117,118,121),这会使体内的动脉血二氧化碳分压下降,导致室性心律失常(117)。正常着装的落水者最长屏气时间一旦小于10秒就会增加其在水中吸入溺液的可能性(17,87,117)。因此游泳时如果动作和换气不协调,就会在冷水中溺水(87,117)。而剧烈运动(如打水)和随之发生的血管舒张也加快了机体热量的流失(60)。

早期的心血管反应为交感神经系统被激活的表现,如外周血管收缩、心动过速及心输出量增加(17,87,117,118,121)。心脏负荷及儿茶酚胺水平增加会导致心律失常,患有心血管疾病的老年受害者尤为显著(参阅标题4.5.3;参考文献17,96,97和117)。当全身浸入寒冷的水中时,屏气会增加室性心律失常的发生率(121)。

4.5.2 体温过低

在冷水中持续浸泡超过30分钟便会导致人体体温过低,体温过低的定义为人体体温低于35℃(95℉;87,117)。健康且穿衣服的成年人即便在只有5℃(41℉)的水中浸泡15－30分钟,只要头面部露出水面也不会出现体温过低(122)。在实验室条件下,把头露出水面的成年人在5℃的水中浸泡1小时,或者在15℃(59℉;87)的水中浸泡3－6个小时,其核心体温平均下降至35℃(95℉)。

有研究显示,在 0℃(32℉;120)水中存活的极限时间为 90—120 分钟。现实生活中,风和蒸发作用会加速未受保护的头部热量的流失(87)。若头部被水淹没,体温则下降得更快。虽然乙醇有扩张血管的作用,人饮酒后会感到全身发热,但不会增加热量的流失(13,14,17,60,123)。乙醇还会使人在沉入水中后的颤抖减少(123)。

随着核心体温下降至 30℃—34℃(86℉—93℉),人的意识也会逐渐模糊(87,112,120)。在这种情况下,除非落水者身穿救生衣并且头部露出水面,否则便会吸入溺液。之后会出现颤抖直至体温降至 29℃(84℉),此时游泳也会变得无济于事(87)。当核心体温继续降至 28℃(82℉)以下时会出现心室纤颤,并在 24℃—26℃时继发心律失常。最终当体温降至 22℃(72℉)时,脑活动停止。

"水中环境救援衰竭"指的是淹没于冷水中的受害者在救援期间或不久之后出现衰竭的情况(87,116,124)。观察 18℃(64℉)以下水中人体发现,人体浸没在水中时会收缩下肢外周静脉,而使血液重新分布到上半部分身体("浸没反应";125),中心血容量的增加会促进利尿而导致全身血容量不足,同时在冷水中,外周血管收缩,又加重了血容量的再分配。当人从水的浮力环境中脱离后,身体便只受到重力作用,静脉血汇集又重新回到下肢,致回心血量减少,心脏便出现反射性心动过速以代偿所需增加的血量。如果心脏功能受到低温和心肌缺血的影响,尤其是冠状动脉粥样硬化病变者,可能就无法耐受这种情况。当人体处于垂直体位时,心脏需要更多能量将血液送至大脑,否则就会出现室颤。溺水者为了配合救援所付出的体力也会增加心脏代谢的需求。"复温衰竭"是指由于冷利尿而导致血容量不足的受害者不能耐受复温期间血管收缩消退引起的动脉压降低(124)。

在某些情况下,长时间浸没在 10℃(50℉)以下的水中,生存概率反而因为低温而增加。尽管有成年幸存者被报道,但主要还是常见于儿童和青少年(47,48,78,113,116)。如果急性窒息发生 10 分钟以上,常温下的大脑就会受到不可逆的缺氧损害(122),因此存活的关键在于体温下降的速度。与医疗环境中受控的低体温不同,意外的低体温是可变的(116,126)。为提高存活率,低体温必须在心脏功能障碍发展为严重缺氧之前快速产生(59,87)。儿童往往由于其体表面积与身体质量之比更大、皮肤更薄而更易降温,但在受控条件下(如心脏开放手术),其核心体温降至 24℃—25℃(75℉—77℉)仍需要约 30 分钟,而冷却大脑所需的时间太长则无法保护其免受溺水所诱发的缺氧损害(59,60,87,126)。如前所述,体表降温的幅度和速度都不足以起到保护作用(122)。虽然可以用人体循环摄取吸入和吞入的冷水来解释核心体温的快速下降,但人体吸收大量的冷水只发生于少数情况之下(60,87,96,122)。人体需要摄取相当于自身体重 20% 的冷水才会使体温降至 30℃(122)。潜水反射会在淹没水中最初的 10 分钟内出现,随后是低体温,这些生理过程协同作用,可能会使溺水者存活(122)。

4.5.3 哺乳动物潜水反射

大多数人淹没于冷水中都会出现冷休克反应,但约有 15% 的个体表现出潜水反射(参阅标题 4.5.1;参考文献 122)。这种反射在儿童中尤为常见,随着年龄的增长而减少发生(28, 58, 76)。虽然关于"哺乳动物潜水反射"在冷水中保护大脑免于缺氧,究竟是单独作用还是与低温联合作用仍存在争论(48, 76, 116, 122),但随着水温的降低,潜水反射反而会增强(122)。当头面部浸入冷水中时三叉神经的眼神经分支受到刺激,使延髓的呼吸中枢受到反射性抑制并在几秒内出现呼吸骤停(28, 56, 76, 117, 122, 127)。而面部的感觉传导通路与呼吸中枢抑制又会引起心血管反射,即由交感神经和迷走神经刺激介导的全身性外周血管收缩和心动过缓(122, 127)。屏气又会进一步加重心动过缓(122, 127, 128)。恐惧也会增强这种反射,但过度焦虑引起的心动过速却会减缓反射(28, 122)。自身神经系统变性(如糖尿病性神经病变)和中枢神经系统抑制(如乙醇)则会使这种反射钝化(122, 127)。在意识丧失前,机体在 30 秒内便会出现心动过缓,外周血流到心脑的血液也会发生分流(76, 122)。从外周向重要器官供血的再分配和心动过缓的程度会保护大脑免受缺氧的影响(28, 58, 117, 122),同时发生呼吸暂停,而不是屏气,是为了防止溺液被吸入。因此,在接近 0°C(或 32°F)的冷水中发生心律失常的概率更大(28, 127)。

5 溺死的其他死亡机制

- 潜水:在所有与水有关的活动中,潜水导致的脊髓损伤最多,特别是年龄在 20 岁以下的男性(8, 45, 47, 78)。相关因素包括缺乏潜水经验、不熟悉潜水地域和摄入酒精(47)。
- 失足落水:马里兰州的一项研究中约有四分之一的溺水发生于与溺水不太相关的活动(在水边捕鱼、玩耍、靠近水边行走 [11])之中。救生索的缺乏是工人溺水身亡的罪魁祸首。
- 被船撞或与水下危险物体碰撞:会产生头部损伤引起意识丧失(11)。
- 水下被困(如水草纠缠 [47])。
- 电击(参阅标题 13.6;第 4 章标题 7):不存在电灼伤。电击可能是非致死的,但会引起肌肉麻痹,抑制游泳的能力。死亡是由溺水造成的。
- 汽车落水:钝性外伤可能导致死亡(30, 52)。轻微的头部受伤可能导致意识的短暂丧失(30, 52)。
- 可疑伤害:可能会观察到凶杀(例如窒息)或自杀的损伤征象(例如试切创)(6, 8, 9, 37)。

6 癫痫与溺水

癫痫患者存在溺水的风险(14, 32, 38, 41, 45, 47, 48, 66, 112, 129-132)。已知的触发机制包括水面闪烁的光影、热水浴、玩耍中被惊吓以及过度换气(参阅标题 13.1；参考文献 129, 131)。各种研究表明,3%-6% 的溺水者有癫痫病史(11, 12, 30, 33, 131, 132)。这些溺水事件在自然水体和家庭环境中都有发生(132)。癫痫发作时,癫痫患者可以从船上落入水中,如果其没有穿着救生衣便会溺死(132)。

有研究发现,癫痫病史(9 个月至 39 年)和癫痫发作的持续时间以及患者最后一次癫痫发作至死亡的时间间隔(1 周至 15 年)并不是预测溺水风险的因素(132)。也有研究显示,一名 11 岁的女孩在其第一次癫痫发作时就发生了溺水(14)。

对溺水者进行抗惊厥药物的毒物分析通常无法检出用药或治疗初始剂量(132),药物的治疗水平不能防止癫痫发作(13, 42)。

7 其他潜在性疾病

在明确死亡原因的时候,必须根据情况仔细权衡疾病的作用(1)。基础疾病(例如缺血性心脏病)的发作有时是巧合,有时则会引起溺水(8, 11, 32, 38, 49, 66)。有些溺水者就叙述自己曾出现心脏传导系统异常(133)。临床记录和 DNA 分析的研究证实了一些溺水者会发生 QT 间期延长的情况(7)。神经系统疾病则可能会影响肢体活动(9, 32)。疾病往往会成为自杀溺水的诱发因素,特别是发生在老年人身上(见标题 3 [133])。

8 乙醇

乙醇中毒会影响人们的判断力、方向感、反射和肢体活动度,导致处理意外情况的能力下降(8, 12, 108, 134)。即使血液中乙醇浓度较低[20 毫克/分升或 4.3 毫摩尔/升(108)]也会影响视力观察。当血液中乙醇浓度达到 50 毫克/分升[11 毫摩尔/升(108)]时,任何人发生意外的风险均会增加。与水接触后,乙醇可能会增强某些呼吸道反射(如喉痉挛),导致"干性溺死"(参阅标题 4.3；参考文献 76, 110 和 134)。空腹饮酒加上剧烈活动,会引起低血糖和体温调节功能受损(108, 135, 136)。血管舒张引起皮肤温度上升而导致皮肤和水之间的温度梯度升高,使冷感受器得到更显著的刺激(17)。这可能会增强心肺反射,增加心律失常的可能性以及突然无法控制的呼吸(参阅标题 4.5；参考文献 17)。

在对不同情况下溺死的青少年与成人的研究中发现,40%-60% 的人都有乙醇摄入的毒物分析证据。

8.1 乙醇及药物在自杀溺水中的作用

确定是否存在中毒浓度或致死浓度的药物可帮助明确死者是否系自杀（表5-1；图5-2；参考文献4,5），但在死者体内发现精神治疗药物并不一定能证明其为自杀（5）。这种观察仅能证明死者生前有抑郁症病史，但并不一定存在自杀意念（5）。这些药物也可用于治疗其他疾病（如偏头痛，癫痫[5]）。纽约的一项研究表明，25%的自杀溺死者有醉酒情况（5），在41%的自杀案件中发现了乙醇和（或）非法药物，而10%的自杀案件中则发现了治疗睡眠问题的抗组胺类药物，但在意外死亡案件中却鲜有发现。

9 溺水尸体的尸表检查

在典型的"湿性"溺死中，口、鼻孔部及其周围会涌出泡沫（"蛋白霜样"）（参阅标题10和12；图5-3；参考文献6,16）。但这些泡沫也会在尸体被发现前被水冲走，或者在尸体被发现后已消失，或者在尸体转运途中被擦去（3）。以上情况下法医无法观察到泡沫（3）。有研究发现，只有在19%的案件中观察到涌出的泡沫（3）。

一位醉汉滑入水中溺死而他身穿的裤子却没有被拉上拉链，这点需要深思。（1,9）。溺死者手中紧握的异物（如杂草、沙子）证明其曾在水中挣扎（6）。指甲缝

图5-2 在浴缸中溺死的女士。现场调查发现空的安眠药药瓶。毒物分析发现较高浓度的苯海拉明，未达致死量。

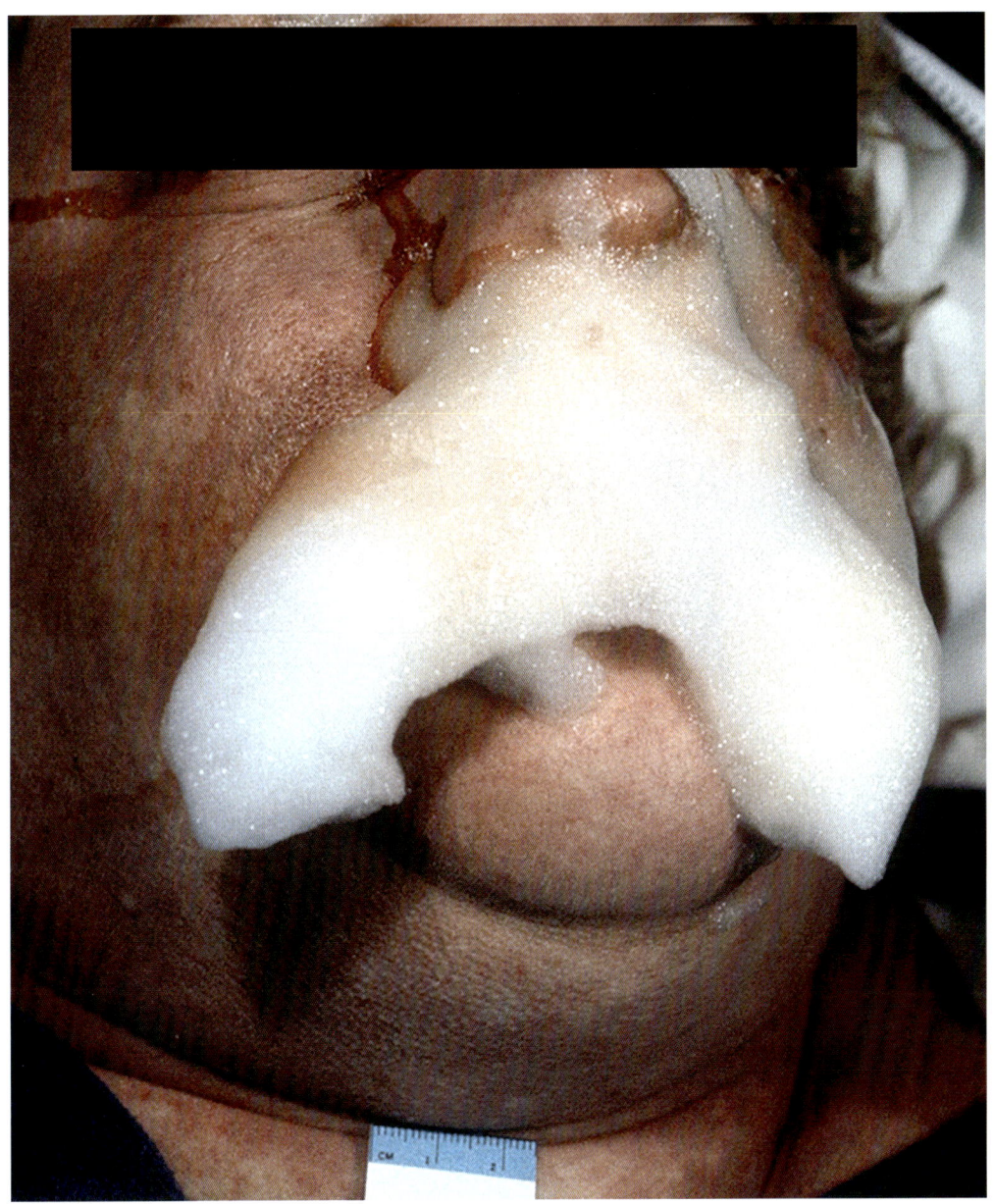

图 5-3 "湿性"溺死。口、鼻腔蕈样泡沫。

的污垢可能表明溺死者悬起的双手接触过水底的淤泥(图5-4)。溺死者手腕的瘢痕或近期新鲜的自创切口均显示其有自杀意念(参阅标题3；参考文献9,137)。面部或头皮钝性损伤则意味着要排除溺死者潜在的颅脑和颈椎损伤；然而，当溺死者是头部倒栽入水并与水底发生刮蹭时，这些皮肤受损也可能发生(参阅第2章标题3.3；图5-5；参考文献11,29)。此外，在没有目击证人的溺水案件中，即使死者体表未发现损伤也并不意味着其死亡原因就一定是溺死(13)。

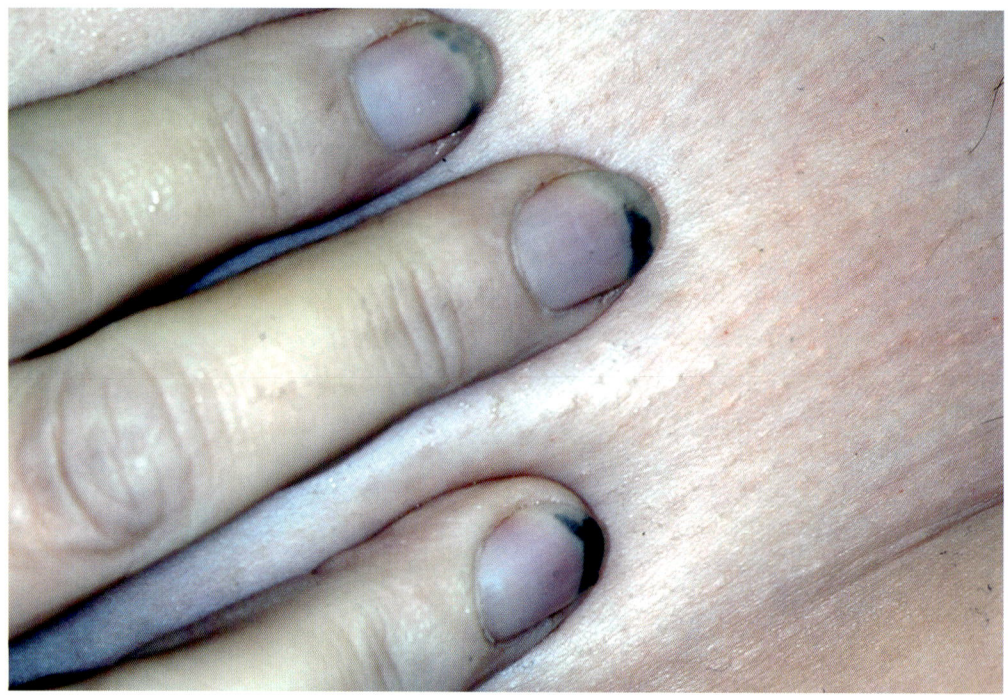

图 5-4 指甲缝内的污垢可能表明受害者的双手曾与河道泥泞的河床发生接触,但需要排除死后人为改变。

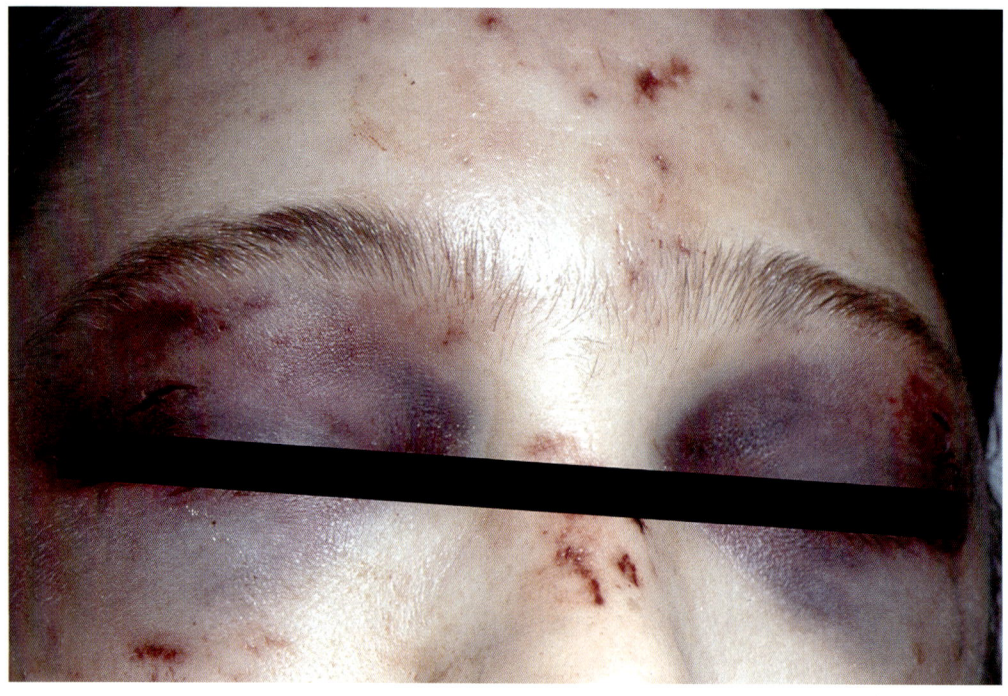

图 5-5 面部皮肤擦伤和眼眶周围皮肤挫伤。尸体面朝下漂浮在岩质海岸。

第 5 章 | 水中尸体

10 溺水尸体的内部器官检查

某些非特异性的发现往往也能证明溺水者吸入溺液（如湿性溺死；参阅标题 4.1, 标题 12）。

10.1 胸腔积液

非溺死案件中［如中毒、勒死、捂死、刺伤（138）］都会发现 80 毫升或更多的胸腔积液（也就是每个胸腔各有大于 40 毫升的液体）。如果尸体解剖证实了死者存在心脏异常［如心肌肥大或心肌瘢痕形成（138）］，则证明胸腔积液可能由于自身疾病所致。对浸泡时间小于 30 天的案件研究发现，其中四分之三案件中的死者肺和胸腔积液的总重量在 1 000－2 000 克之间，这可以有助于诊断是否是溺死（22）。有研究表明，淡水和海水溺死者的胸腔积液量没有显著差异［淡水,（521±340 毫升；海水, 768±536 毫升）］。在没有腐败或仅有早期腐败征象的溺死尸体中，大约三分之二的海水溺死尸体和三分之一的淡水溺死尸体的胸腔积液会增加（138）。也有研究表明，与淡水溺死案例相比［33%（24）］，海水溺死案例（38%）出现胸腔积液的比例会轻度增加。淡水溺死者和海水溺死者的肺脏总重量与胸腔积液重量之间并无相关性（24, 138）。在有或没有胸腔积液增加的情况下，肺的平均重量分别为（1 326±436）克和（1 310±358）克（138）。在溺死案件和水中非溺死案件中，由于水的被动渗透作用，随着尸体腐败程度增加，胸腔积液也会增加，但当尸体进一步腐败后，积液量却出现下降（22, 24, 138）。腐败尸体胸腔积液总量超过 250 毫升提示可能为溺死（139）。从发现尸体到解剖的时间间隔与胸腔积液量无关（138）。较短时间的水中浸泡便可出现大量胸腔积液，但是在大多数案例中通常超过 8 小时的浸泡才会出现胸腔积液［67% vs 39% ＜ 8 小时（138）］。短时间浸泡（20 分钟以内）与积液量有关（24）。胸腔积液量与性别、体重和身高及心脏重量均不相关（24），血液中乙醇的含量也与胸腔积液量不相关（138）。

10.2 肺

肺水肿并不是溺死的特异性改变，在自然死亡（如心脏病）和其他非自然死亡［如急性阿片类药物中毒、癫痫（4, 5, 8, 14）］中也可以发现。因此，肺部解剖所发现的改变需要与环境因素相结合（22）。在湿性溺死中，两肺膨隆，重量增加，呈淤血状改变（6, 16, 138）。两肺在胸腔内膨胀，表面会有肋骨压迹，这些都是溺水的死后征象（8）。肺膜表面可见出血点（16），表面肺大疱（胸膜下肺气肿）形成（3, 16, 138）。肺切面可见大量泡沫样液体（水肿）（图 5-6；参考文献 16）。成年人肺的总重量达 1 000 克（＞18 岁），这对于区分溺水和非溺水案件具有重要意义；然而，由于吸入溺液的量是可变的，这种重量的辨别可能也是变动的（138, 140）。其他的研究显示如下：

- 溺水组两肺的重量为 1 411（平均）±396.4 克；对照组 20 个样本两肺的重量为（994±133.0）克［年龄＞ 18 岁；水中浸泡时间＜ 24 小时；对照组为头部枪弹伤（22）］。

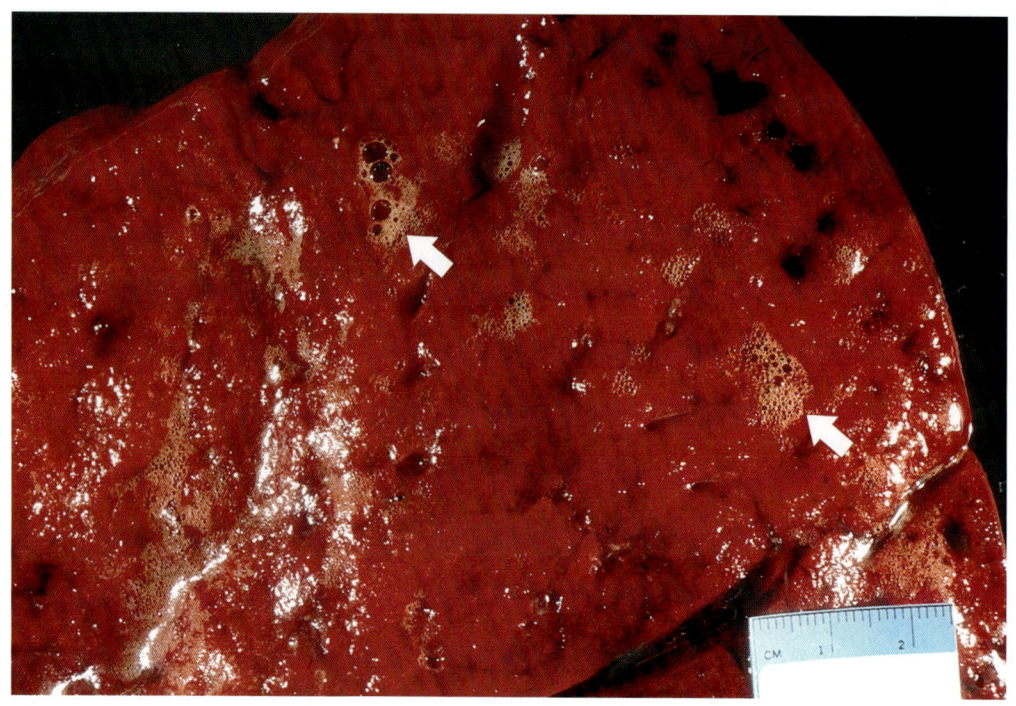

图 5-6　溺死后淤血的肺脏，注意肺切面可见泡沫水肿液（箭头所示）。

- 溺水组两肺的平均重量约为 1 400 克；对照组 50 个样本两肺的重量为 780 克［年龄＞18 岁；对照组为头部枪弹伤（20）］。

观察发现淡水和海水溺死者之间两肺的重量并没有明显的差异（20，22，24，138）。少数案例（2 项研究中最多 20%）中死者肺的重量不足 1 000 克（20，22，24，138，140）。这些可能都是干性溺死案件，但事实情况并非如此（3）。淹没水中的时间与肺的重量并无显著关系；然而，芬兰学者经过系列研究发现，有目击证人且非腐败尸体的溺死案件中有 13% 的尸体，肺脏和渗出物的重量少于 1 000 克，而腐败尸体溺死案件中的比例则为 35.6%（3，24）。另一项对水中尸体的研究显示，保存良好的新鲜尸体肺脏的总重量平均为 1 439（720－2 740 克），而在腐败尸体中肺脏的总重量平均仅为 1 049 克（380－1 900 克）（5）。非腐败尸体案件中发现"干性"肺脏（＜1 000 克）的百分比为 17%，而腐败尸体案件中这个比例则为 51%。在其他案件中，也有类似的观察结果，即尸体在水中浸泡的时间越长肺脏的重量反而越轻（22）。

如果尸体在短时内就被发现（＜6 小时），与引起窒息死亡的其他情况相比较，溺死者肺脏的平均重量的增加明显高于预期。然而，除非肺脏出现严重淤血［如总重量＞2 500 克（141）］，仅根据肺脏的重量不可能区分溺死和被投水之前发生的窒息死。

溺死者的喉腔、气管和支气管中都可观察到血性泡沫状液体（参阅标题 9；图 5-7；参考文献 16）。这是一种濒死期的反射现象（22），这些泡沫是水肿液、表面活性物质及支气管分泌物的混合物（3，90）。淹没在淡水中时上呼吸道内的水肿液往往都是血性的,因为低渗性液体会破坏红细胞(8)。而浸泡在海水中的溺死者体内的红细胞往往能够保持完整性(8)。在没有发现上呼吸道泡沫状液体的情况下,难以对溺死作出明确的诊断(8)。溺死者的上呼吸道和肺实质中可检出来自水中的异物,但是在口腔或上呼吸道内发现水或异物则不足以诊断溺死(图5-8;参考文献2,16,21和142)。溺水仅仅几分钟便可以形成呼吸道泡沫液体(22),但随着死亡时间的增加,这些泡沫会消失(143)。对1 590起溺水案件的研究显示,对于水中浸泡

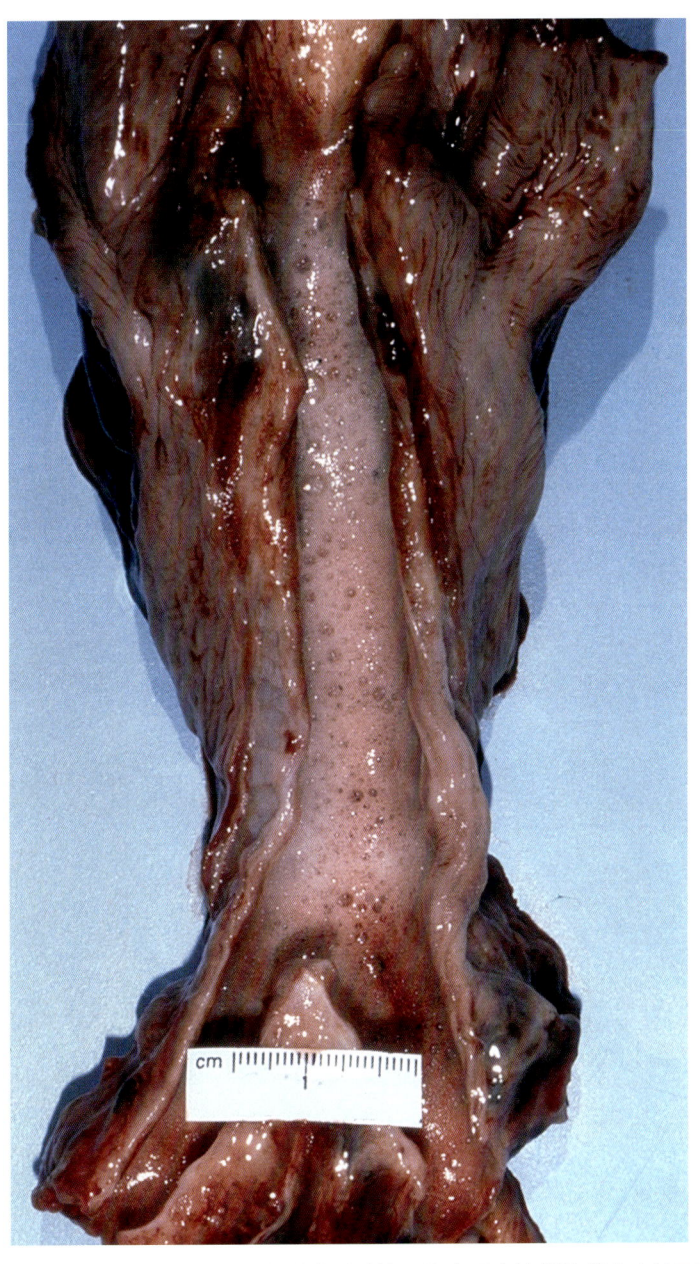

图5-7 "湿性"溺死。上呼吸道内的泡沫(美国北卡罗来纳州教堂山市法医局供图)。

时间小于 1 天的尸体,发现外部泡沫、呼吸道内泡沫状液体以及肺内侧缘重叠的百分比分别为 17.3%、46.5% 及 42.1%。这些发现在水中浸泡长达 1 周的尸体中仍然存在,然后才逐渐消失(3)。到了第 3 个月,这些变化已不明显［如仅有 4% 的肺组织边缘重叠(3)］。抢救复苏的行为也会掩盖肺部溺水征象［如肺气肿、水肿(142)］。

10.3 其他器官重量

与其他类型的损伤致死案件相比,死亡后 6 小时内窒息死和溺死的某些器官的重

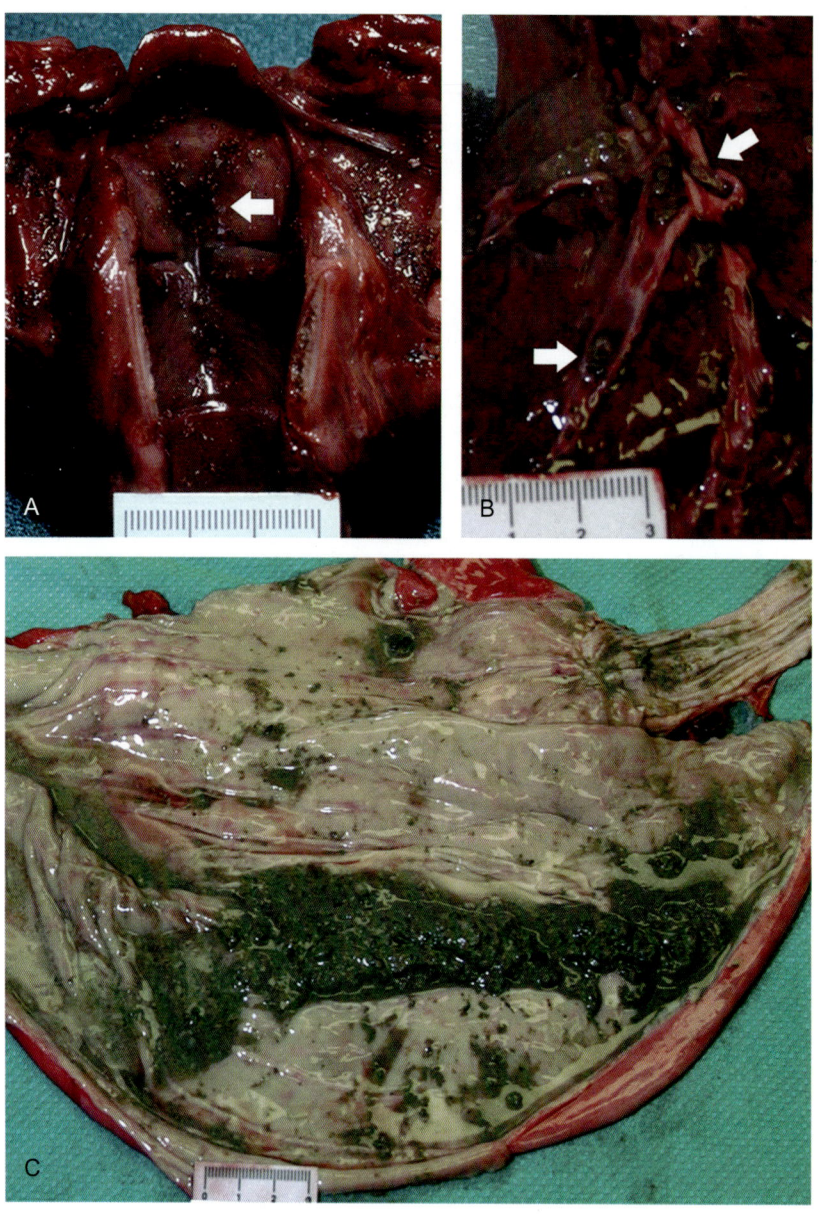

图 5-8 被激流冲入排水管道内溺死案例。(A)喉腔内的异物(箭头所示)。(B)支气管吸入的异物(两处箭头所示)。(C)吞咽入胃中的异物。

量可能会增加（141）。窒息死案件的尸体中肺、肾、肝和脾的平均重量会增加（141），而在损伤、窒息和溺死案件的尸体中心脏和脑的平均重量相对保持不变。长时间浸泡在水中会减少尸体器官的重量（141），溺死者也会出现"贫血状"的小脾脏（144）。器官缩小的机制可能与交感神经兴奋有关（144），但显微镜检查发现脾窦内红细胞含量没有明显减少（144）。溺死者"贫血状"缩小的脾脏可能是长时间在水中浸泡所致的死后变化（141）。

10.4 胃肠道

溺液和溺液中的异物可被吞咽入胃和肠；然而，水压和水流的冲击力也可以将少量的溺液灌入死后被抛的尸体胃内（参阅标题 4.1；图 5-8；参考文献 6, 16 和 138）。

10.5 颈部出血

关于颈部出血内容参阅第 2 章标题 3.3。

10.6 溺死尸体的颅骨检查

当中耳和乳突发生淤血或出血时，检查颅骨剥离硬脑膜后会发现颞骨岩部表面有蓝色斑点（图 5-9；参考文献 6, 25 和 138）。并不是在所有情况下都能检出这种蓝色斑点，只有在至少约 75 厘米（2.5 英尺）深的水中溺死才会发生（25）。由于溺液被咽喉管阻塞造成中耳与外界环境之间压力差而引起中耳出血（25）。中耳炎的早期瘢痕以及乳突气房气腔的形成可能会降低颞骨岩部的出血（25）。因此中耳淤血或出血是生前溺死的诊断依据之一，而且能解释即便是经验丰富的泳者，中耳淤血或出血也会

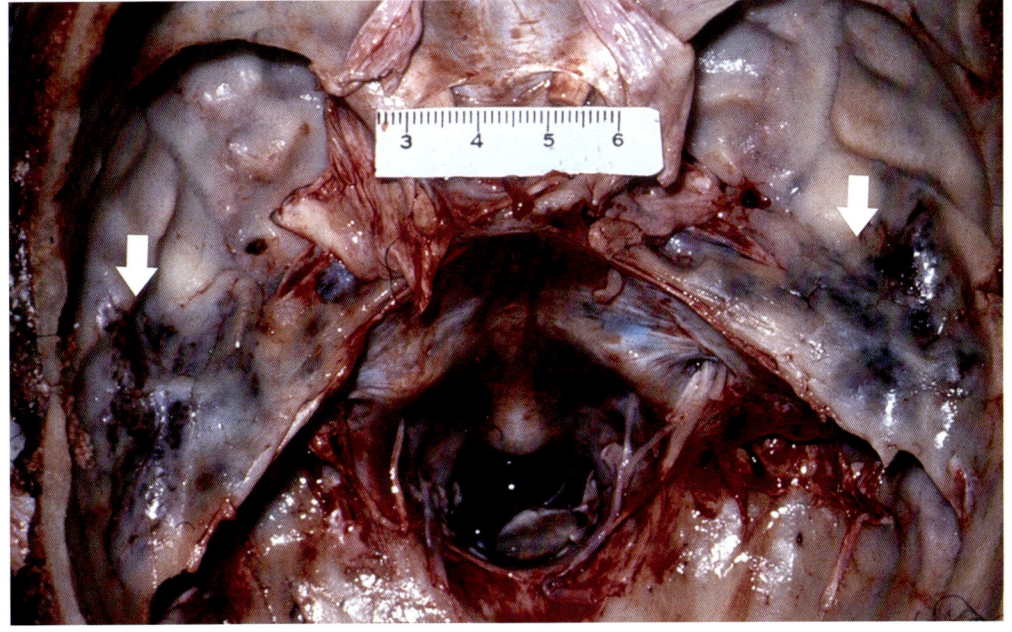

图 5-9　颞骨岩部青紫色变（两处箭头）。溺死者中耳"出血"（美国北卡罗来纳州教堂山市法医局供图）。

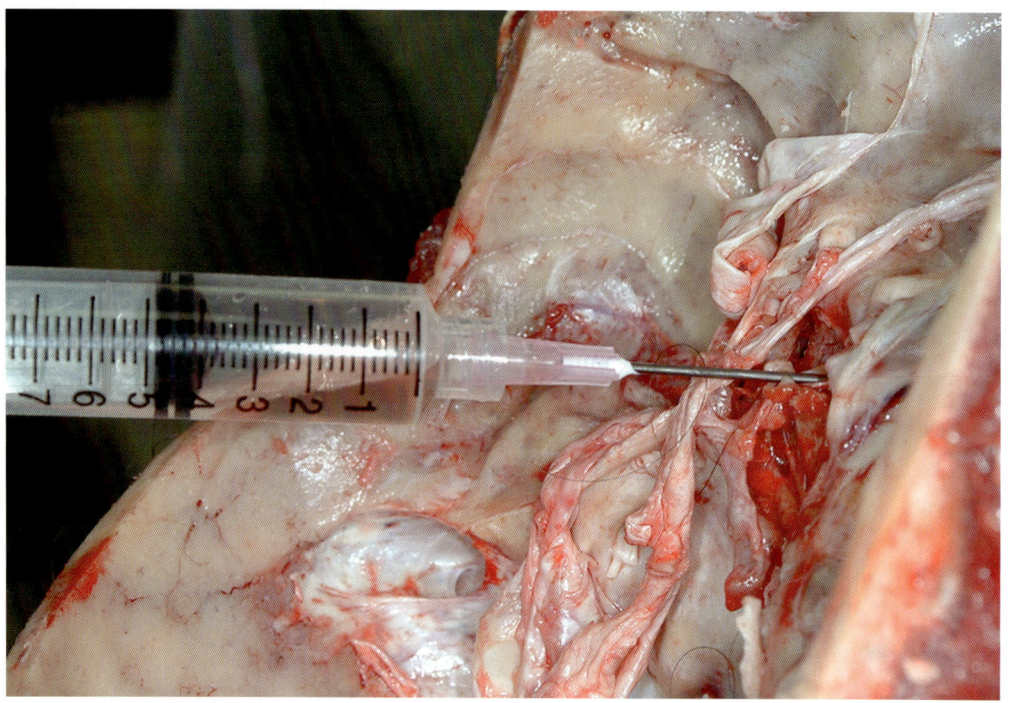

图 5-10　从溺死者蝶窦中抽出的液体。

使人体失去平衡而溺水(参阅标题 14.3；参考文献 6)。另一方面,这种变化也可能是由于头部位置朝下而产生的死后变化(参阅标题 12,第 2 章标题 3.3)。从鼻窦(如蝶窦)中抽出液体也可能是诊断溺死的依据之一(图 5-10；参考文献 8,138)。

11　溺死的实验室检验

在生前入水还是死后抛尸入水的鉴定中,实验室检验显得尤为重要(18,8)。尸体因在水中时间延长而腐败分解,其中一些检验方法由于缺乏特异性仍需改进,故仅具有参考意义(2,25-27,80,110,145-147)。

11.1　血浆比重和渗透压测定

淡水溺死者吸入肺部的溺液会稀释左心房的血液,使得左心房血液密度低于右心房(6,15,148,149)。但死后溶血或自溶会影响这一检验结果(146)。

11.2　氯离子浓度的测定(Gettler 试验)

淡水溺死者左心腔内血液的氯、钠离子浓度水平较右心腔或股静脉低,海水溺死者则恰好相反(6,8,148)。实际上氯、钠离子浓度的检验结果没有明显的意义,特别是淡水溺死者的血液可能没有显著的电解质变化,且往往难以检测(80)。其他学者对电解质的研究也提出了不同的观点(150)。

11.3　硅藻检验

硅藻是由二氧化硅构成细胞壁的多种微观单细胞藻类,它们广泛分布于淡水和海水中(图5-11)(146, 151-154),且种类极其丰富,现已知的种类超过十万种(155)。对于长时间淹没水中的溺死者,当尸体发生腐败、窒息征象不明显时,依赖硅藻检验辅助判断是否为生前溺死显得尤为重要(26, 27, 151, 152)。

溺水者将溺液吸入肺中,硅藻经肺泡毛细血管随血液循环进入人体循环系统(153, 156)。肺和其他器官内均检见硅藻说明死者符合生前溺水(27, 146, 151, 157)。体内检出硅藻取决于水中硅藻的浓度及死者吸入溺液的量(27, 143, 146, 152, 154),对于干性溺死者由于吸入液体量较少,内部器官就难以检出硅藻(26, 143)。即使同一水体中的溺死者,水中硅藻的类型和含量也会随着区域和季节的变化而不同,会影响组织样本中硅藻的检出(143, 146, 152-154, 158, 159)。经验表明,大多数情况下只需单次提取水样,但通常需要在不同时间和不同水深对疑似落水点进行多次取样(143, 152, 155)。

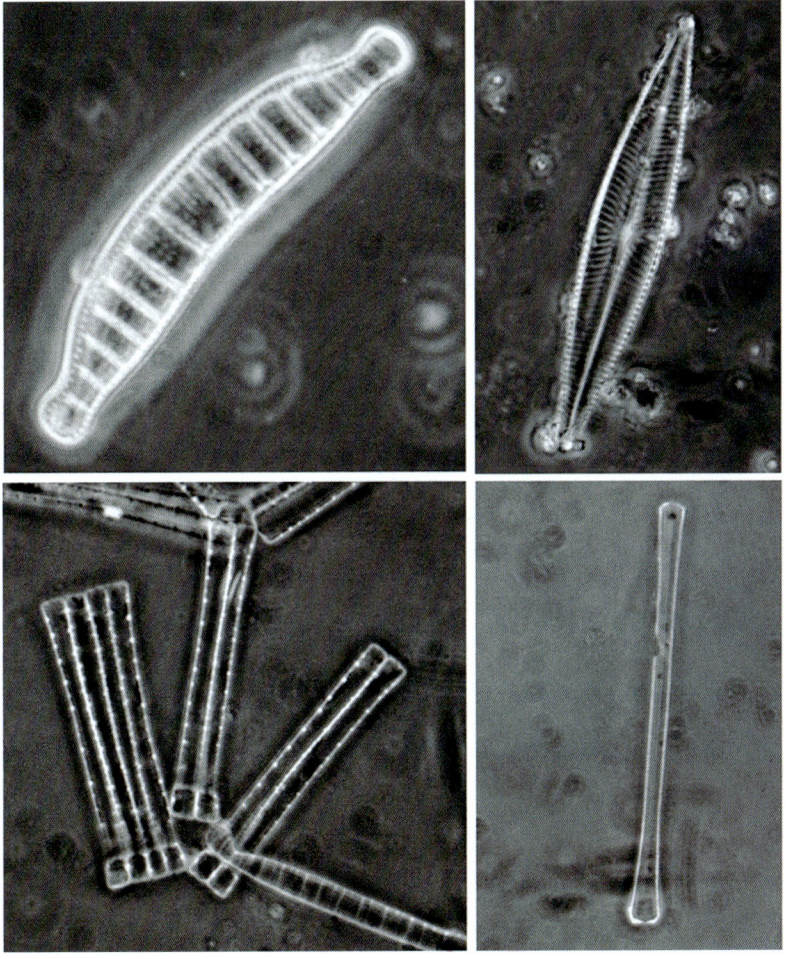

图 5-11 使用相差显微镜观察的各类硅藻。按原始比例放大 250 倍(加拿大多伦多市法医病理办公室 M. Pollanen 博士供图)。

可以从人体不同器官中提取检材进行硅藻检验,如肺、心、脑、肝、肾和骨髓(2,154,155,157)。如果仅在肺及其他内脏器官内检出硅藻时要慎重判断,为了防止外源性硅藻污染,需对实验试剂和设备定期检测(6,26,27,151-153,155,157)。空气中硅藻含量高时,可通过空气被吸入,所以部分非溺死者的内脏器官中也可检出硅藻(1,6,146,151,153,157,160-163)。摄入富含硅藻的食物和水的人体也可能被检出硅藻(146,151,152,161,162,164)。当长时间在水中活动时,硅藻也会被动地进入上呼吸道和肺中(2,26,27,143,146,153,154,164)。溺死者的肺内会检出大量硅藻(143,163),但尸体发生腐败时,水中的硅藻会污染内脏器官(2,143,154,157)而出现假阳性,故可以取不易受污染的骨组织(如完整的股骨或胸骨和脊椎)替代作为检材(2,152,153,160)。经常游泳的人死后其内部器官可被检出硅藻,这可能是由于其长期暴露于水体中所致,判断溺死需格外谨慎(165),如果在其骨髓中也发现硅藻,就能判定其为生前溺死(153)。

将股骨沿长轴锯开,刮取约 50 克骨髓进行检验(153,155)。骨髓中检出的硅藻或硅藻碎片往往很小(< 30 微米),少于在肺和水样中所检出的数量(26,151,153,159,164),这表明只有体积微小的硅藻才会留存于骨髓内(159)。溺死者的器官中能检出最低限度的硅藻(定量分析),能与死后抛尸入水相区分(26,27,143)。骨髓用酸(如硝酸)(153,155,157)处理,待组织完全液化,离心样品分离出含有耐酸材料的沉淀颗粒,即富含二氧化硅成分的硅藻(146,153,155,166)。将沉淀物均匀涂抹于玻璃片上并使用相差显微镜检查(153,155)。

鼻窦(蝶骨、上颌骨)中的溺液、胃内容物和疑似溺死者的介质也能用同样的方法检测(153,155)。但在胃内容物中发现硅藻可能说明检验过程中有污染(参阅标题 10.4;参考文献 155)。

对死者全身多器官内硅藻的定性、定量检查可以判断其是否为生前溺死:
- 凡不同器官中所检出的硅藻种类与水样一致,即可诊断为溺死[定性分析(6,26,27,143,153-155,166)]。
- 当溺水征象不显著或缺乏时(如尸体腐败)(34,155,158),硅藻检验可以作为死者生前溺死的有效证据。但硅藻检验的缺陷在于其灵敏度。有研究发现,738 例野外淡水溺死者中只有 28% 的人体内检出硅藻,33 例室内用水[即水经过过滤或加工(浴缸、泳池、厕所等)]溺死者中只有 12% 的人体内检出硅藻(153)。也有研究发现,只有三分之一的案件通过硅藻定性检验可诊断为生前溺死(26),但在浴缸中的溺死者基本无法检出硅藻(146,166)。由于硅藻都在自来水厂被过滤,硅藻检验对自来水中溺死者的诊断意义不大(26)。安大略省的研究发现,4 名室内用水溺死者中有 2 名死者曾在水中添加了硅藻(磨砂清洁剂、砾石)。如果泳池过滤器内含硅藻泥,则泳池中的水会富含硅藻(8),溺死者的肺也可以检出硅藻。

内部器官没有检出硅藻并不能完全排除死者溺死的可能性,而应当根据系统尸体解剖结果综合分析其死亡原因(27, 146, 153, 157, 158),也可能死亡过程迅速,硅藻来不及通过体内大循环进入全身各个内脏器官。未检出硅藻也可能说明死者符合干性溺死或溺液中并无硅藻(157, 163)。股骨骨髓中没有检出硅藻可能是由于骨中的循环血量太少(153)。

- 即使尸体解剖及环境均不支持溺死,硅藻对于生前溺死的诊断仍具有重要的意义(153, 155)。
- 这有助于对可疑死亡案件或谋杀案件提供关键的证据(155)。尸体解剖能够检见损伤(如窒息、颅脑损伤等),但硅藻检验阳性才能说明死者落水时有自主呼吸,判断是否为生前溺水(155)。
- 检验打捞尸体水域疑似溺水点水样中的硅藻种类,然后对比水样和尸体各内部器官内的硅藻,以确定落水点。
水样中硅藻比对有助于确定死者溺水的地点[如浴缸或天然水域(153, 155, 157)]。
- 水中尸体发生腐败时,硅藻检验是诊断溺死的唯一有效手段(153, 163)。
由于溺死者尸体会在远离落水点处被打捞,且水具有流动性,从死者体内检出的硅藻可能会与落水区域水样中的硅藻有所不同(159)。

11.4 硅藻的显微镜检查

各类与溺死相关征象的光镜下检查(参阅第 3 章标题 1.7;参考文献 145):

- "肺气肿"是指肺泡扩张,肺泡间隔变薄,肺泡毛细血管压缩(2, 167)。
- 肺淤血、水肿,肺泡出血,肺泡壁破裂(2, 145)。
- 对于尚未腐败的尸体,由于溺液的冲刷作用,肺泡内的巨噬细胞会减少(167)。而在腐败尸体中,肺泡巨噬细胞会从分解的肺泡壁中被释放,也会随自溶的发生而消失,因此镜下的数量会发生变动(145, 167)。
- 在尸体尚未腐败的情况下,溺死、窒息的死者均会被检见肺泡出血(145)。

显微镜检查是确定肉眼难以发现的潜在病理改变的必要手段,对溺死的判断尤为重要(145)。

12 水中尸体征象

- 鹅皮样改变(鸡皮疙瘩、鸡皮样皮肤)。由于皮肤受冷水刺激,立毛肌收缩,毛囊隆起,毛根竖立,故皮肤呈鸡皮样改变或称鹅皮样改变(参阅第 2 章标题 2;参考文献 16)。
- 手掌皮肤皱褶("洗衣妇手")和足底皮肤皱褶(图 5–12,图 7–31;参考文献 16)。
- 在淡水中浸没 4 小时后眼结膜的出血点会消失,这可能与低渗介质引起的溶血有关(168)。
- 尸体腐败分解会掩盖或影响溺死征象(参阅第 2 章标题 5.2;参考文献 6, 15

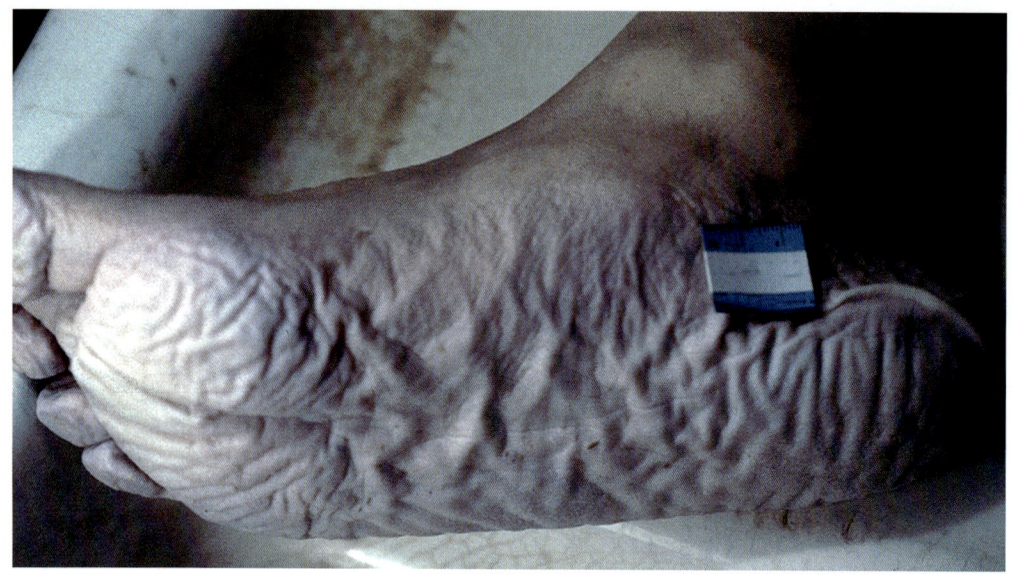

图 5-12 尸体长期浸泡在水中，足底皮肤呈皱褶样改变（参阅第 7 章及图 7-31）。

和 17）。
- 明显的肺淤血（16）。
- 呼吸道及胸腔内可见血性积液（16）。
- 腐败气体混合腐败液呈泡沫状从口、鼻腔溢出（16）。
- 尸体腐败所引起的腹胀能导致伤口（最多 6 个月）再次裂开（169）。
- 大部分早期溺水尸体征象消失（3）。

- 头朝下体位
 由于头部的比重大于脚，当尸体浮出水面时都是头部向下。
  - 头、颈部区域以及身体的前侧均会出现尸斑（参阅第 2 章标题 3.3；参考文献 6）。乳突 / 中耳"出血"可能是尸斑的另外一种表现形式（图 5-9；参阅标题 10.6 及 14.3）。
  - 人为颈部出血（排除抢救过程中由于人工复苏形成；图 5-13）。
- 损伤（16）
  - 致命损伤难以解释（3）。
  - 长时间浸泡会使开放的皮肤伤口出血。
  - 野生动物、水中和岸边的致伤危险因素也可能对尸体造成损伤（图 5-14；参考文献 2，6）。
  - 在浅水区域，俯卧位可能导致身体的某些区域（如脸部、前臂外侧、膝部前侧）与河床发生撞击（参阅标题 9；图 5-5；参考文献 170）。
  - 前额的擦伤和挫伤可能是从水中打捞出来时形成的 [如泳池边缘（11）]。

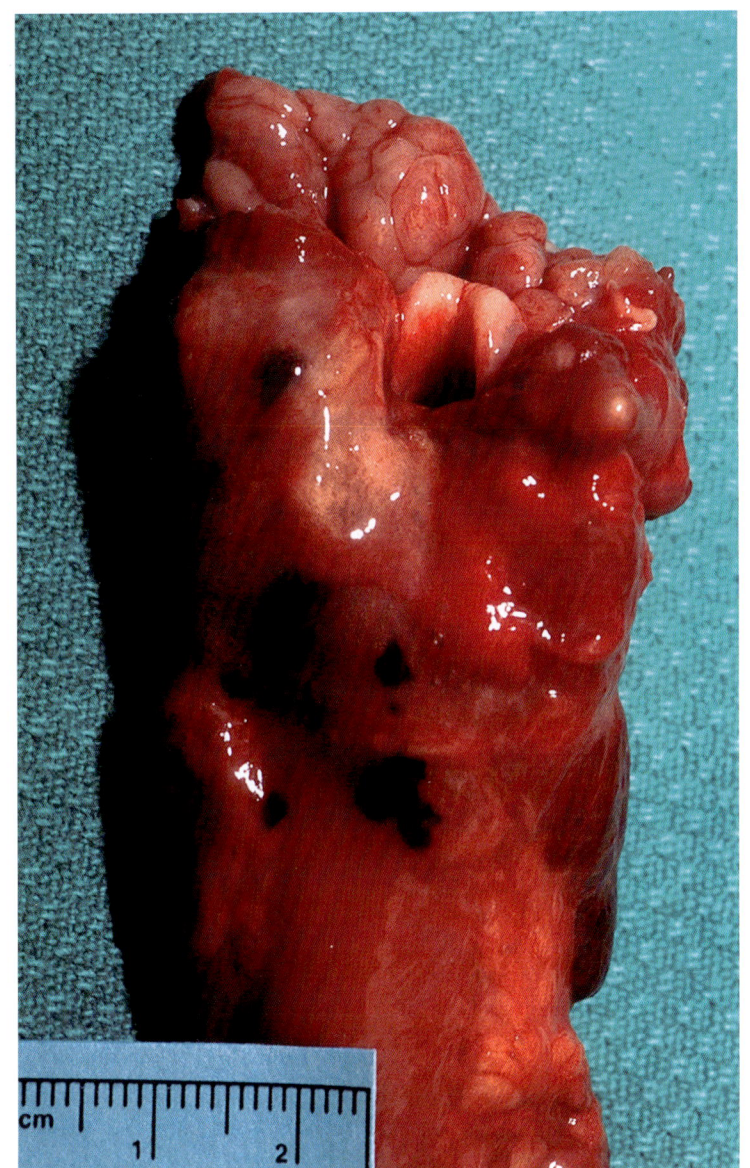

图 5-13 年轻的男性溺水者从泳池中被救起,经过复苏后,喉头及食管后部局部软组织出血。

○ 复苏效应(参阅第 3 章标题 2.6;参考文献 2)。

• 水中尸体上浮

水中尸体腐败分解产生大量气体,使得尸体相对密度下降,当尸体相对平均密度小于水的密度时,尸体开始上浮。但是对漂浮在纽约水道中的 104 具尸体进行研究后发现,其中 28 具尸体并没有腐败分解(5)。当身体的相对平均密度超过水密度时(淡水 = 1.000;海水 = 1.026)就会沉入水中(104)。人体密度会因各种因素增加(如随着溺水过程中吸入大量的溺液,体重也逐渐增加)。浮力会受肺容量(肺容纳的

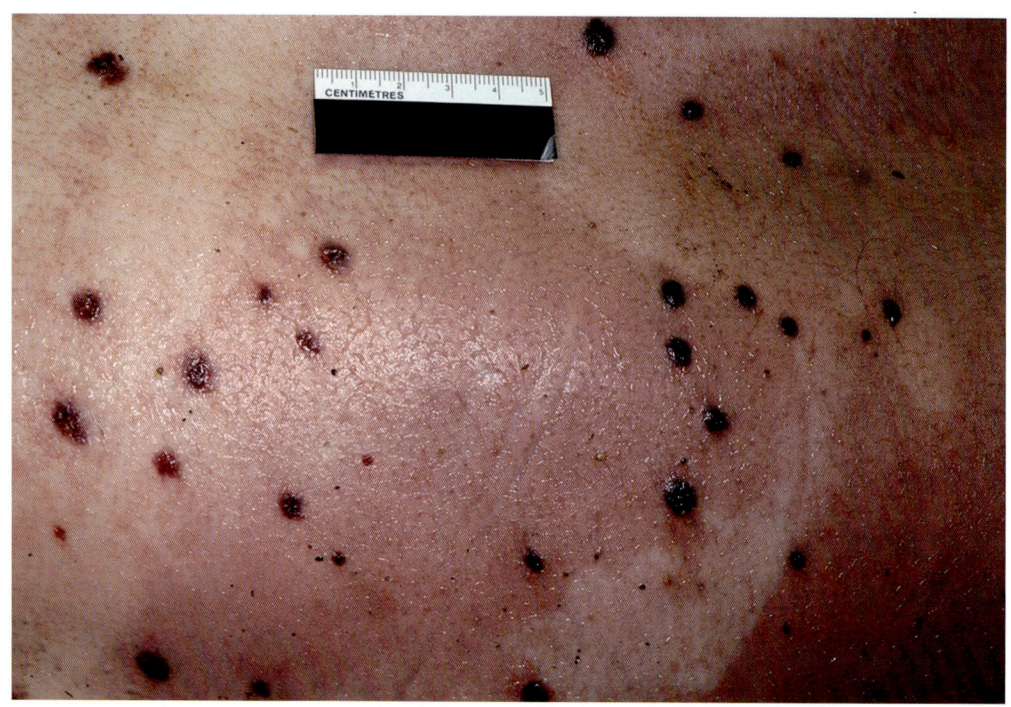

图 5-14 身体淹没在水中被水蛭咬伤（加拿大安大略省汉密尔顿市法医病理办公室 C. Rao 博士供图）。

气体量）的影响（104）。有研究表明，在人体尽力吸气终末，当肺内气体达到最大容量时，近乎所有的个体均会漂浮在淡水和海水中（171）。在功能残气量状态下（平静呼气末存留于肺内的气量，一般接近于无意识或死亡个体的肺容量），7% 的个体能在淡水中浮起，69% 的个体能在海水中浮起。无论肺容量大小如何，在淡水中任何人加重 5 千克（11 磅）便会下沉，海水中则要加重 6.8 千克（15 磅）才能下沉。一旦身体下沉，静水压便会压缩胸、腹部器官中的气体而使身体持续下沉。随着水中压力持续压缩胸部，残余肺容量逐渐减少，从而形成负浮力（104）。

13 浴缸中溺死

浴室可能是室内最危险的场所（172）。浴缸中溺死的发生率各不相同。在溺死案件中，浴缸中溺死的发生率为 1%-8%（11, 12, 30, 31, 33, 44, 173）。对澳大利亚布里斯班市溺死案件的研究发现，55 例儿童溺死案件中有 8 例（15%）发生在浴缸中（54）。

对于浴缸中的尸体，所有死亡方式都是可能的（表 5-2）。

一系列溺水自杀案件显示，有 10%-15% 的案件发生在浴缸内（表 5-1；参考文献 4, 9, 22 及 37）。浴缸中他杀虽不常见，但也需要考虑他杀的可能性（177）。案件发生后，需尽快展开调查（172），调查人员也需充分考虑由报案人和救援人员所致的案发现场的变化。

第 5 章 | 水中尸体

表 5-2 浴缸中死亡

案件来源	数目	溺水所占百分比	年龄范围(男：女)	死亡方式（数目）					注解
				N	A	S	H	U	
芬兰，1976—2000；Lunetta 等报道 (173)	116	7%	—	2.6% (3)	30.2% (35)	53.4% (62)	0.9% (1)	12.9% (15)	—
丹麦和瑞典，1961—1969；Geertinger, Voigt 报道 (174)	51[a]	—	22—85 岁 (11:31)	9.5% (4)	11.9% (5)	71.4% (30)	2.4% (1)	—	2 例 (4.8%) "疑似"自杀，包括自残，药物过量和溺水；意外 (2 例跌倒，1 例溺水，1 例一氧化碳中毒，1 例癫痫)；自然死亡 - 心源性。
比利时，1934—1983；Devos 等报道 (175)	36	—	6 个月至 78 岁 (12:24) 9 名儿童	8.3% (3)	63.9% (23)	19.4% (7)	5.6% (2)	2.8% (1)	19 例采暖系统致一氧化碳中毒的意外身亡死。大多数自杀者体内均检测到乙醇或镇静剂的中毒浓度。自然死亡：2 例癫痫，1 例心脏病。
北卡罗来纳州，1982—1983；Shkrum 和 Hudson 报道 (176)	70 (67 例死于普通浴缸，2 例死于漩涡式浴缸，1 例死于按摩式浴缸)	—	59 名成人，11 名儿童	44% (31)	36% (25)	11% (8)	6% (4)	3% (2)	死亡方式 反映出在法医学的管辖下调查人口的总体发生率。自然死亡：主要是缺血性心脏病。意外：参阅标题 13.1。自杀：4 例枪击，4 例溺水。他杀：2 例勒死，1 例儿童服药后溺死，1 例浴缸中分娩的孩子在塑料袋中窒息而死。

注：a：9 人没有毒物分析，42 人均有准确死亡方式。N(Nature)：自然死亡；A(Accident)：意外；S(Suicide)：自杀；H(Homicide)：他杀；U(Undetermined)：难以明确。

13.1 意外死亡：诱发因素

导致成人意外溺水的因素有很多，包括乙醇或其他药物中毒、因疾病丧失行动能力（如卒中、癫痫、心脏病）、病残、摔跌、遭受收容机构不良影响的个体和儿童（参阅标题 2.2，标题 6-8；参考文献 12，43 和 176）。

Dietz 和 Baker 通过对 10 名浴缸中溺死者的调查发现，其中有 2 人曾饮酒[1 名发生了摔跌，另 1 名有癫痫病史（11）]。Wintemute 等通过对 15 岁及以上年龄的 12 起浴缸中溺死的案件研究发现，只有 2 人的体内检测到乙醇（≥1 毫克/分升）[其中 1 人≥200 毫克/分升或 34 毫摩尔/升（178）]。

癫痫患者是浴缸中溺死的高危人群，尤其在无人监护的情况下（103，112，131，179）。马里兰州在浴缸中溺死的 8 人中，有 6 人既往有癫痫发作史（11）。在萨克拉门托县 17 例癫痫患者溺死案件中有 7 人死于浴缸（30）。新西兰的溺死案件报道中有 5 名癫痫患者，其中 1 人死在浴缸中（33）。Gardner 和 Devos 等在他们案例的研究中发现浴缸中溺死的 2 人均是癫痫患者（172，175）。加拿大的研究显示，25 名在浴缸中溺死的癫痫患者，有 60%（15 名）无人监护。癫痫患者即使淋浴也会存在溺水风险，癫痫发作时受害人会瘫倒在浴缸中（131），身体堵住了浴缸排水口从而发生溺水（132）。其他潜在的受伤还包括撞及淋浴房或其他固定装置，以及癫痫发作时不小心撞到热水龙头（132）。癫痫发作并不一定表现为无意识性的肌肉收缩，所以当人体在浴缸中抽搐时也可能不留下挣扎的迹象或溅水的证据等（112）。当癫痫发作时牙关紧闭会咬伤口唇黏膜，严重时舌头会被咬断（图 5-15 和图 5-16）。

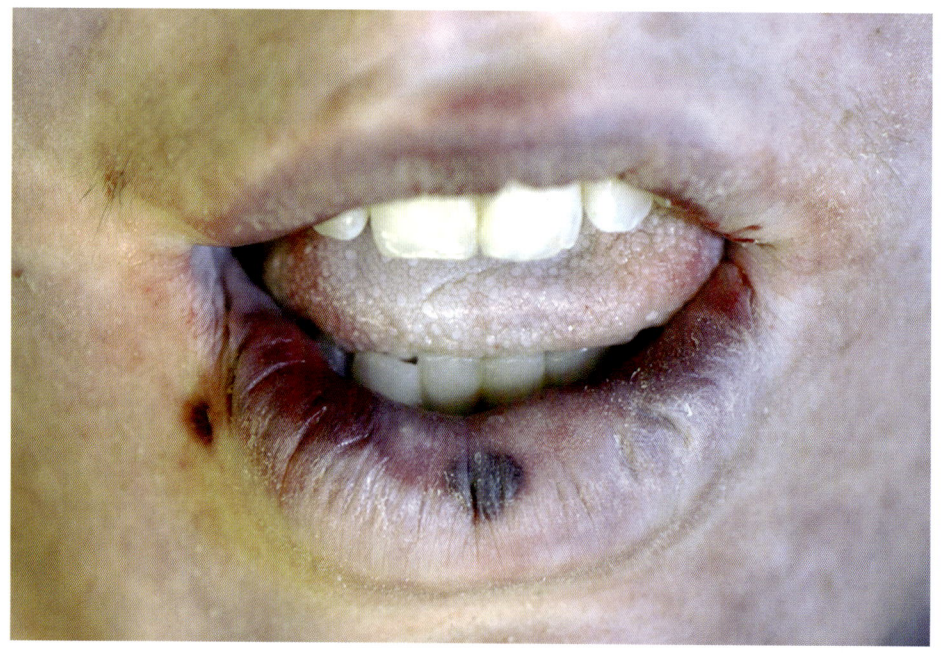

图 5-15　癫痫发作时溺死在浴缸中；口唇黏膜挫伤。

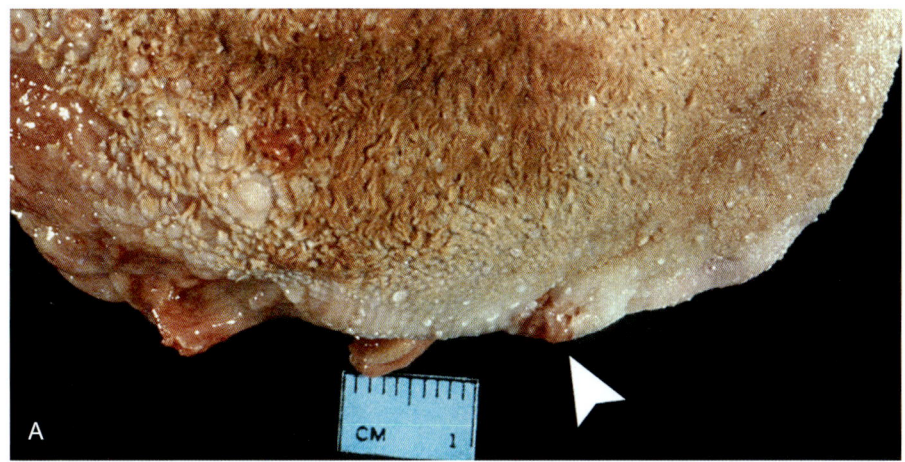

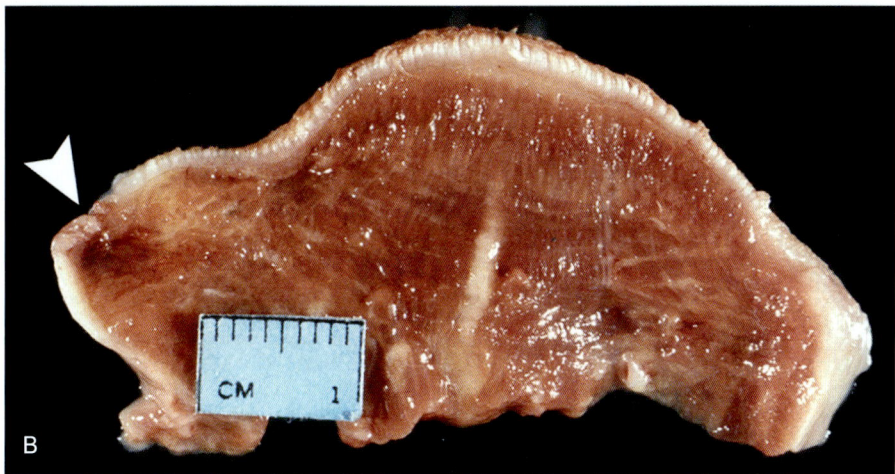

图 5-16 癫痫溺死者。(A)舌右侧边缘撕裂伤(三角箭头)。(B)舌冠状面显示对应撕裂伤部位的肌肉出血(三角箭头)。

对于死者缺乏癫痫发作史的溺死案件,尸体解剖时可能难以发现癫痫的神经病理学证据,但是通过对固定后大脑的检查能更好地发现其中细微的病理学异常(图 5-17;参考文献 11,12)。对那些开始服用抗癫痫药物的浴缸中溺死者进行毒理学检测,通常未发现药物或者药物仅处于亚治疗浓度,此时要通过对医学史及毒理学的结果推断癫痫在浴缸溺死者中的作用(30,132,176)。但即使是服用了治疗浓度药物的癫痫患者也有发生溺死的可能性(132)。

如果死亡现场是干燥的浴缸,死因就要考虑是摔跌引起的颅脑损伤或酒后跌倒在浴缸中引起的体位性窒息(176)。

经调查发现美国北卡罗来纳州大部分浴缸中溺死的儿童年龄在 6 个月至 2 岁之间(176),因为这个年龄段的儿童往往会出现无人看管的情况(图 5-18; 参考文献 12,42,55,103,175,176 及 180)。儿童溺死案件中浴缸的水深 5—35 厘米[2—14 英寸

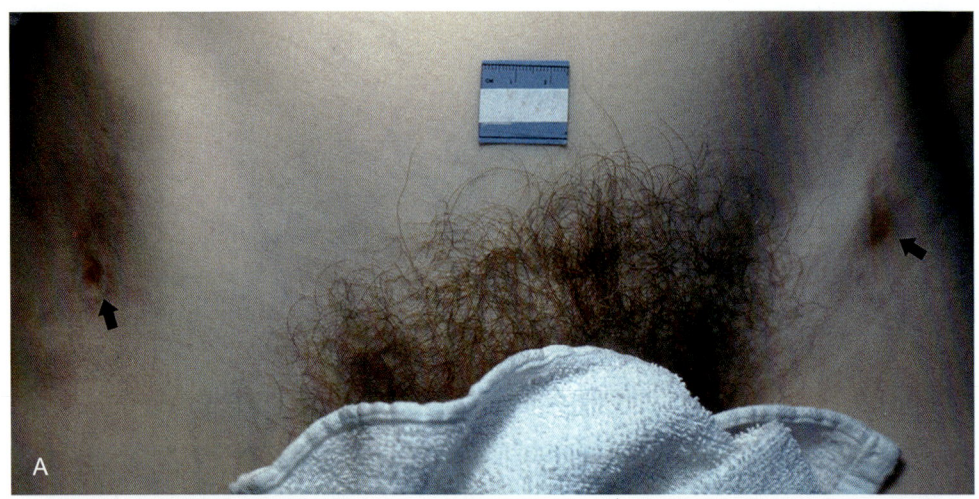

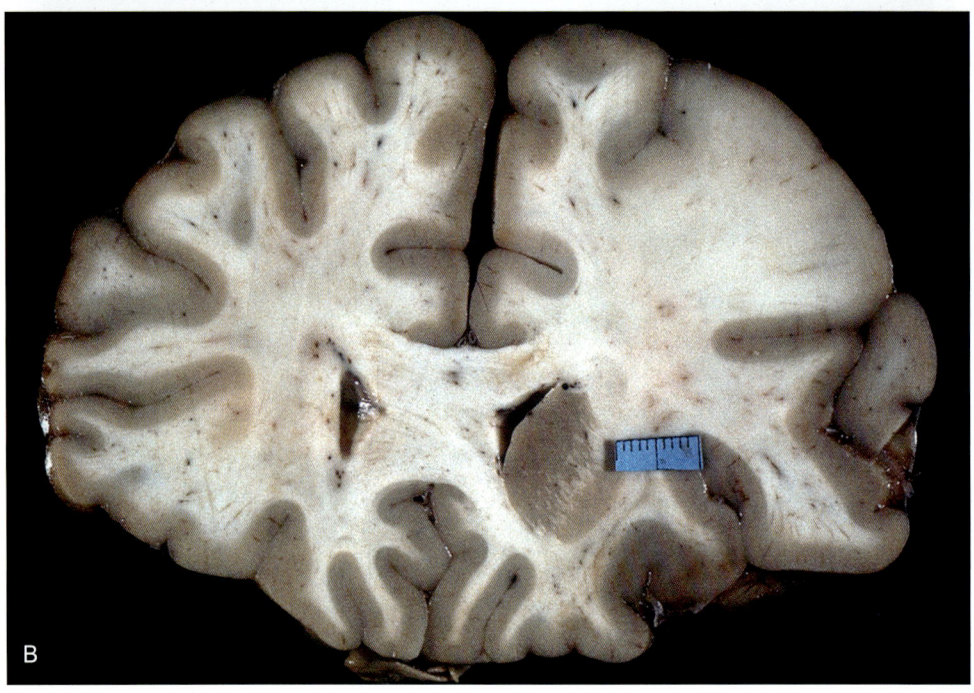

图 5-17 女性死者被发现跌倒在放满水的浴缸边缘。尸体解剖发现溺死征象,而死者生前 1 年内身体看似健康。(A) 双侧髂嵴皮肤擦伤,提示死者与浴缸边缘发生碰擦(箭头所示)。(B) 死者大脑经甲醛溶液固定后,右额叶取材制片,显微镜检查示星形细胞瘤(加拿大法庭科学学会杂志供图)。

(77)],平均为 20 厘米(8 英寸),死者的年龄大都不足 1 岁(77)。由于这个年龄的儿童已经能够端坐或站立(55),家长就将这些幼儿交给家里年长的儿童照顾,以代替家长监护的责任,但年长儿童自己也存在受伤的风险(103),因此溺死往往由于年长儿童或玩伴监护不力所致(55)。有时候家庭因素也会成为儿童非意外伤害死亡的原因,把儿童浸没在水中就是一种虐待方式,应视为他杀(图 5-19;参考文献 103,180 及 181)。

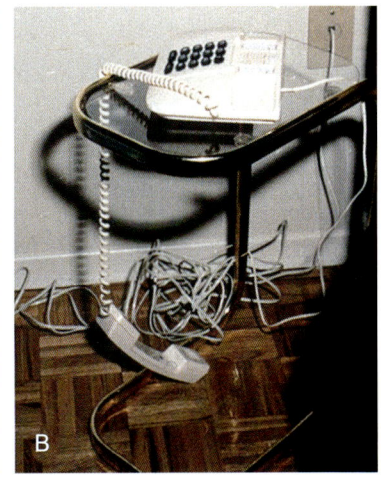

图 5-18 意外婴儿溺死。案件及现场调查结果显示：母亲在浴缸中睡着了，而婴儿趴在她身上，当母亲醒后发现婴儿浸没在水中。(A) 注意清洁剂倒在地上，烟灰散落一地，母亲记不清碰翻了烟灰缸。(B) 疯狂呼救。

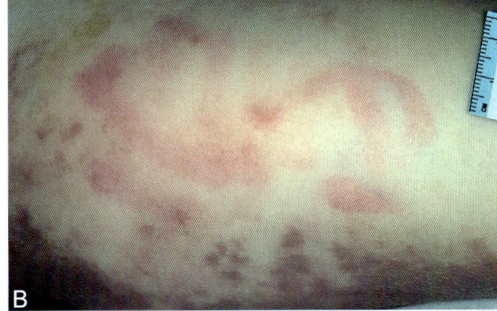

图 5-19 有精神病史的母亲将婴儿溺死的案件。(A) 浴室墙上用口红涂的字。(B) 婴儿身上也能看见用口红涂的字。

13.2 自杀

自杀者以年长者居多，而且可能有精神病史（参阅标题 3；参考文献 182）。当其他自杀方法因疾病或不易行动难以实施时，老年人可能会选择自溺（182）。有些人身上会看到自残的证据（如手腕割伤；参阅第 7 章标题 2.1 及参考文献 182），有些人则会通过各种手段使自己沉入水中［如保龄球（182）］。将自己反锁在浴室内自溺的情况则比较少见（174）。浴室中的自溺者会饮酒或使用药物镇静，然而对于有意溺死自杀者而言，并非必须使自己意识水平下降（182）。

13.3 他杀

凶手可以在浴缸内杀人，也可以将被害人藏尸于浴缸内（177）。在后一种情况下，凶手会将浴缸放满水伪造现场，让死者看上去像自溺身亡，且可以抹除痕迹证据（177）。溺水和其他损伤既能单独发生也能同时发生（如扼颈、触电）（174，177），如在扼死的情况下，体表征象就不易被察觉。大多数他杀案件的被害人是年龄在 20—40 岁的年轻女性（177）。如果生前溺死征象十分明显，则说明被害人被放入装满水的浴缸时仍然活着（177），酒精中毒可能是导致被害人丧失反抗能力的一个因素（177）。

13.4 浴缸中的水

当发现尸体在放满水的浴缸内时，首先都会考虑是溺死，但有时浴缸中的水会通过排水管流尽（176）。潮湿的头发和衣服表明尸体曾浸在水中，但仅头面部浸入水中并不一定意味着溺死（176）。北卡罗来纳州的研究发现有近一半在浴缸中自然死亡的案件中，浴缸中都有水（176），所以仍需要排除其他可能的死亡原因。

13.5 衣着情况：成年人

死于疾病、意外或他杀者要么穿着衣服，要么赤身裸体（176,177），而自杀者大多穿着衣服。但在浴缸中发现赤裸尸体时也不能排除其自杀的可能（4,31,173,176,182）。

13.6 触电死亡

在浴缸中触电身亡的案件中，意外、自杀或他杀都有可能（参阅本章标题 5；第 4 章标题 7；参考文献 176,177,183 及 184）。

14 潜水活动相关的死亡

潜水者的主要死因是溺死，且在潜水的任何一个阶段都会发生（185–187）。1974—1985 年，在加利福尼亚州萨克拉门托县共有 244 位潜水者溺死，其中 3% 是携带轻便潜水器潜水时发生的（30）。60% 的潜水死亡是由于医疗、环境或潜水装备的问题所致，其余则无法解释（185）。即使潜水员的装备运转正常，空气补给充足，也没有外伤或明显的医疗问题，无法解释的死亡仍会发生（185）。在水中惶恐不安会影响自己的呼吸，可能是其中的一个因素（185），不同经历的潜水员都可能会因为恐慌而不合时宜地脱掉潜水装备（185）。

14.1 潜水的分类

14.1.1 休闲潜水活动

休闲潜水时发生的死亡是法医最常见的案件（187）。

- 屏息潜水（浮潜）：没有换气装置，利用呼吸管进行换气，成人平均能下潜 6—10 米（20 至 30 英尺），长矛捕鱼者可以下潜至 30 米（100 英尺）或更深（参阅标题 4.2）。
- 自行携带水下呼吸装备（自给式水下呼吸器）潜水：携带常规压缩空气装备可以下潜至水下 40 米（130 英尺）；更深的潜水活动则需要更复杂精密的装备（"技术潜水"）。

14.1.2 专业/商业潜水活动

- 专业潜水：包括进行科学研究的潜水员、负责公共安全的潜水员（如警方蛙人）和潜水教练/潜水向导。
- 商业潜水：在水底进行作业的潜水（如水下打捞、石油钻机维修等）。

专业和商业潜水员在深海活动时都使用水面供气潜水装备——由水面的供气机通过专用长软管为潜水员输送空气。水面供气潜水活动在海水中只能下潜至水下60米（190英尺），而且持续时间也较短（小于30分钟）。水面供混合气体装备则使用了氦气、氧气和氮气（三种混合气体）或使用氦气和氧气来防止潜水员出现氮气麻醉，使用这种设备的潜水员能下潜至水下90米（300英尺）。而进行饱和潜水还需要使用潜水钟和减压室进行深度潜水活动。在潜水活动最初24小时内，潜水员的身体会完全充满惰性气体，每30米（100英尺）深度大约需要减压1天。

14.2 氮麻醉和氧中毒现象

在专业和商业潜水活动中可能会发生氮麻醉和氧中毒现象。Henry定律指出，在恒定温度下，溶解在液体（如血液、组织液）中的气体量与其分压成正比（104，188-190）。在海平面（大气压 = 1.0 atm），氮气和氧气的分压分别为大约0.8 atm（空气中含量达79%）和0.2 atm（空气中含量达21%）。下潜超过30米[100英尺（188，189，191）]后随时可能发生氮麻醉现象。潜水员在水下40米或132英尺（5.0 atm）时使用的压缩空气供给装备中的氮气分压为4.0 atm（104）。在这个深度，潜水员就面临着氮麻醉的风险（"深海晕眩"），这与乙醇的影响类似（188，189，191）。当潜水员下潜至90米[300英尺（189）]以下时就会出现意识不清。

在水下60米或233英尺（8 atm），即超出了运动潜水者所能达到的深度，此时氧分压是1.6 atm（氮气分压 = 6.4 atm）。在这个深度，潜水员存在氧中毒的风险[如癫痫症状（104，189）]。

14.3 肺泡外气体综合征

Boyle定律指出，如果气体的温度保持不变，它的体积与绝对压强成反比（如压力 × 体积 = 常数；参考文献104，188-190和192）。气压性损伤反映出压力和体积的反比关系（188，189）。气压性损伤是由于环境气压突然变化时，人体空腔器官不能迅速平衡内外压力变化而引起的损伤（188，191）。它在潜水活动事故中引起死亡的原因仅次于溺水（186，189）。

潜水员下潜得越深所受到的压力越大。在海平面上，人体所承受的是1 atm（14.7磅/平房英寸或760毫米汞柱）（104，188，191），当潜到海下10米（33英尺）（相当于淡水下34英尺），人体就要多承受相当于2个自动柜员机重量的压力（104，187，193）。随着潜水员下潜时的压力增大，容积减小，导致人体内出现相对真空的状态，尤其是在刚性骨腔内[如当呼吸道感染导致咽鼓管和鼻窦阻塞时，中耳和鼻窦会出血，继而出现鼻腔出血（104，188，189，191，194）]。内耳气压性损伤的产生是为了平衡中耳压力和眩晕的结果（188，189），在潜水员上升时也可以观察到中耳和内耳出现了气压性损伤（194）。当潜水员在潜水面罩内感觉呼吸困难时意味着罩内压力相对较低，这会引起眼睛出血["面罩挤压"（104）]。

在水下10米（33英尺），潜水员屏息时肺容量会减半，但是如果使用了常规压缩空气装备（水中呼吸装置）(195)，则肺容量不会变化。即使携带了这种装备，当潜水员从水下 1.8－2.4 米（6－8 英尺）迅速下潜时，也可能因为焦虑没有呼气，而导致肺容量增加(104, 185, 188, 189, 191, 192, 195－197)。当吸入水时，呼气也可能会被声门反射性关闭或支气管收缩所阻碍(197)。由于装备所供应冷气的刺激，哮喘患者可能会出现支气管痉挛(198)。过度扩张导致肺泡破裂，继而空气进入肺间质、胸膜和相邻腔室(104, 189)，引起皮下和纵隔气肿，继而引起气胸(104, 188, 189)。如果空气通过膈肌(199－201)，甚至可能引起气腹。如果有慢性阻塞性肺疾病（肺气肿、哮喘）会加剧肺内空气潴留，也会引起肺部病变恶化（如肺大疱），从而使肺更易破裂(104, 189, 196)。当空气经肺泡毛细血管进入肺静脉，最终会导致冠状动脉和大脑动脉的空气栓塞，即引起动脉空气栓塞（图 5-20；参

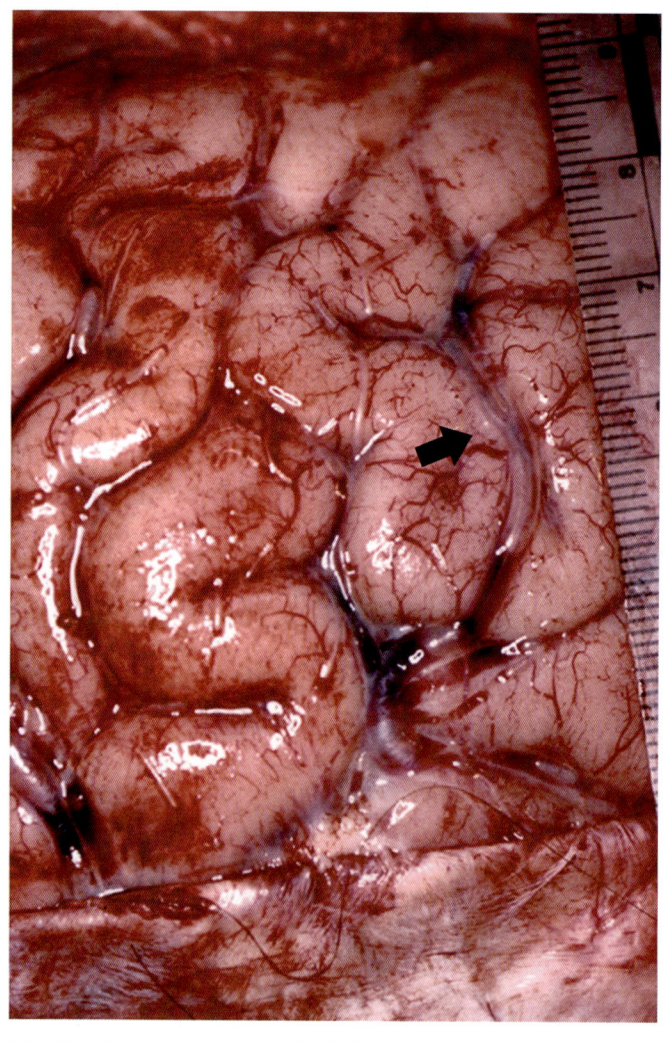

图 5-20 潜水意外事故。死者大脑中动脉内空气栓塞（箭头所示）（加拿大安大略省欧文桑德市格雷布鲁斯医疗中心 B. Sawka 博士供图）。

考文献 104, 188, 191, 195, 197, 202 和 203）。抬头时血管内的气泡也随之上升（189），导致潜水员在水中立即或 1 分钟内丧失意识（189, 195, 196, 202, 204）。气泡也会机械性阻塞心脏流出道（192, 195, 204），只需几毫升的空气就可能导致致命的动脉空气栓塞（192）。

胃的最大容积约为 5 升（193, 200）。当潜水员在短暂潜水［平均（8±5）分钟］后迅速上浮至少 6 米或 20 英尺［通常是（43±12）米或（140±40）英尺］便会引起胃扩张，导致黏膜撕裂伤（图 5-21；参考文献 193, 199-201 和 205-207）。潜水员的胃可能已经因饱餐或苏打水（199）而膨胀，当上升过程中又吞入空气和水时（193, 199-201, 206），胃便会进一步扩张。黏膜皱褶较少处只有肌肉层，又缺乏弹性，因此胃小弯处容易发生撕裂（199, 200, 205）。胃壁撕裂并不常见，

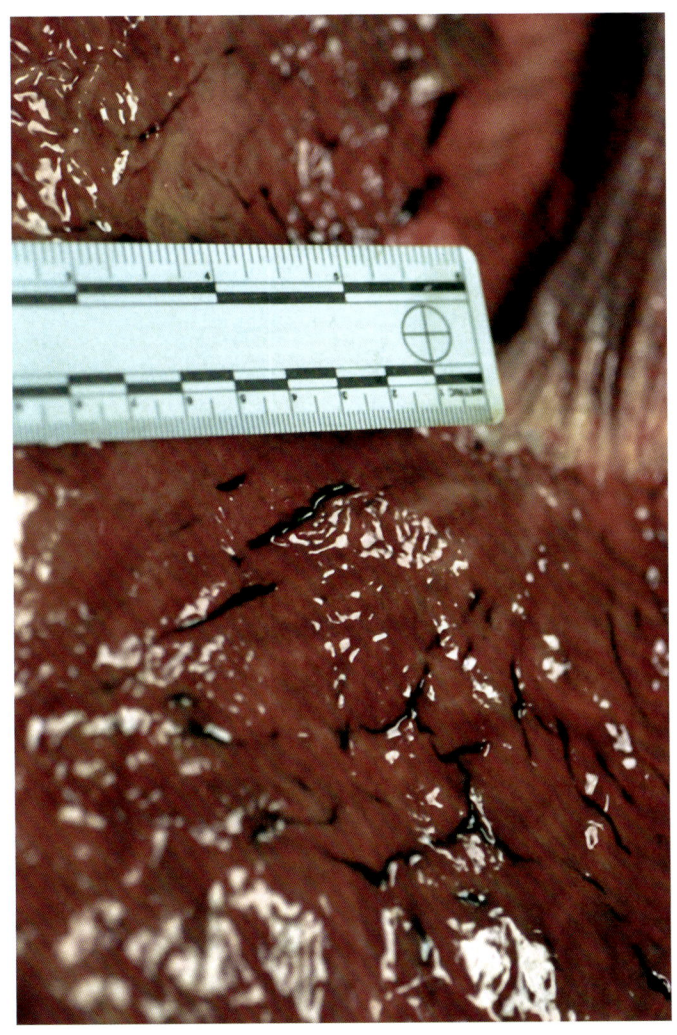

图 5-21 潜水意外事故。死者快速上升后引起胃黏膜撕裂伤（加拿大安大略省欧文桑德市格雷布鲁斯医疗中心的 B. Sawka 博士供图）。

因为胃内气体通常会进入食管和十二指肠（193），但随着胃进一步扩张，角度会增大，胃食管交界处可能会闭合，也可能会引起反射性幽门痉挛（199，200，205），继而胃黏膜和胃壁发生多处撕裂，大小2－15厘米[0.75－6英寸；(200)]。潜水员出现呕血可能是胃黏膜多处撕裂的征象（200）。在没有炎症的情况下，胃扩张会加重门静脉高压，导致食管胃底静脉曲张出血（125）。撕裂伤也可能会延伸至胃食管交界处（207）。抢救时的心肺复苏也可能导致胃破裂（参阅第8章标题6.2；参考文献193）甚至肠破裂（200）。需要与肺泡外气体综合征的症状进行鉴别（193）。

14.4 减压症

潜水员呼吸的空气内含有79%的氮气以及21%的氧气。氮分压升高意味着潜水员在水下较长时间内吸收了更多的氮气（104）。氮气是一种惰性气体，在脂肪中溶解的速度比在血液中更快（188），两者所溶解的氮气有不同的饱和度，而决定血液中含氮饱和度的是下潜时间的长短，而不是深度（104，189，195）。但潜水的深度却决定了所吸收氮气的总量，反复潜水便会增加风险（188）。当潜水员快速上浮时，无法继续维持溶解状态，继而出现气泡聚集于血液和脂肪中的情况（104，189）。血液和脂肪中的氮气气泡，就像打开苏打水时冒出的气泡（104，188，189）。在脂肪组织的毛细血管中混入氮气气泡会引起静脉气体栓塞（104，195，196）。当下潜深度小于10米（33英尺）时，渐进式减压在上浮时是不需要的（104）。当深度超过40米（130英尺）时，上浮时便需要停下减压。即使经过适当的停顿减压，减压病仍可能在上浮过程中发生（188，189）。潜水后的飞行行为会令减压病症状加剧（189）。

氮气气泡膨胀可能引起身体疼痛，通常影响人体致密结缔组织，如关节周围韧带或肌腱（"弯曲"）（104，188，189，195）。关节症状通常在24小时内发生，但更严重的症状在半小时内便会发生（188，195）。当脊髓周围的硬脑膜外静脉丛中形成气泡（104，188，189，195，202，203）时，由于脊髓受到压迫便会引起瘫痪。大量静脉气体（80－100毫升）进入右心室会导致严重的后果（参阅第7章标题12.1.1；参考文献192）。肺循环中的气泡会引起"窒息"（104，188，189，195，208），气体还能通过未闭的卵圆孔进入人体重要器官（脑、心脏），从而引起空气栓塞（188，195，208）。还可能诱发癫痫症状。减压病甚至会使人体出现弥散性血管内凝血（191，195，208）。减压病可与空气栓塞同时发生（188，195，208）。

14.5 肺水肿

大约有1%的潜水员潜水时会出现肺水肿（209）。肺水肿的原因可以是心源性（毛细血管静压力增加）或非心源性的（血管通透性增加），也可能没有明显的诱发因素，潜水员在任何深度或温度的水中潜水时，均可能出现肺水肿。目前所知的各种诱

第 5 章 ｜ 水中尸体

发因素有：浸没效应（参阅标题 4.5）；大力呼吸引起胸内负压增加以及身着紧身潜水衣等；高血压病也可能是潜在的诱发因素。

14.6 与潜水活动死亡有关的情况

下述信息对潜水死亡案件的调查十分重要（187，190，191）。

- 既往病史
  - 心脏疾病，肺疾病（慢性阻塞性肺病）。
  - 近期是否有呼吸道感染。
  - 糖尿病。
  - 癫痫。
  - 药物治疗史。
  - 酒精或毒品。
  - 精神疾病史。
- 既往潜水史。
- 目击者 / 潜水同伴。
  - 潜水情况。
  - 死亡前情况。
- 复苏的结果。
- 饮食史。
- 是否遵守潜水规则，是否因水下危险因素导致钝性外伤或落入陷阱。
- 水面上的危险因素（船壳或螺旋桨）。
- 环境因素。

14.7 潜水设备

所有设备必须被扣押并妥善保存以供后期专家检查（187）。因为设备可能失灵、被更改或使用不当（190，191）。用于填充潜水员空气罐的高压空气压缩机也可能会发生故障（如从压缩机发动机吸入一氧化碳 [104，190，191]）。可能是潜水员用尽空气，也可能由于罐体的内衬被锈蚀腐化，氧气耗尽（104，190，191，211），因此需要对压缩机和气缸内的空气取样。控制漂浮的浮力补偿器也可能有缺陷（208），潜水员在紧急情况下有时无法使用充气补偿器（190）。潜水计算器是一种用于测量潜水深度和时间的佩戴装备，可用来评估潜水员的减压状态。该装备可以提供有关潜水深度、潜水各个阶段的持续时间（包括上升）和水温（191）等数据。

14.8 潜水死亡案件的尸检注意事项

对于尸检所见需要运用多学科的知识进行解释和分析，并充分了解潜水活动及其危险因素，综合分析后才能得出可靠的结论（190，191，212，213）。

- 如果尸体上的潜水装备没有被移走，则需要对该装备拍照取证。
- 确保正确识别个人信息，注意任何辨认特征。

- 注意尸斑的颜色（在一氧化碳中毒和体温过低时会出现粉红色）；活体身上出现大理石花纹斑块提示可能有动脉空气栓塞（紫斑状）(195)。由于空气罐重量的原因，尸斑往往出现在潜水员的背部，而普通溺死者的尸斑通常出现在前侧。尸体腐败会阻碍在软组织、体腔和循环系统中检验气体。
- 检验任何创伤的迹象。
- 检验脸上是否有"面罩挤压"的征象。检验其他气压损伤的迹象，如鼻道出血。若有条件使用耳镜，应检查耳膜。观察溺死征象（从口、鼻腔流出的泡沫）。
- 如果有条件使用眼底镜，应检查死者视网膜动脉中是否进入空气。
- 触摸颈部和胸部的皮肤，检查是否有皮下气肿。
- 在胸部侧面肋间插入 14 或 16 号针头的 50 毫升注射器，注射器内装入几毫升水，用以检查气胸。回抽注射器活塞观察注射器内是否有气泡产生，并评估气胸程度。如果解剖室不进行气胸检查，移除胸骨后就难以观察气胸。注意复苏过程，也就是气管插管和人工通气过程，伴有或不伴有心肺复苏引起的肋骨骨折，这也可引起医源性气胸。从胸部抽吸空气时未夹住气管导管可能导致错误地观察到明显的气胸。
- 使用影像学技术检查头、颈及躯干部血管内外是否有空气。取尸体左侧卧位的胸片。血管内发现大量空气说明与动脉空气栓塞有关 (196, 214)。
- 在取出心脏前先检查大脑。在颅骨被打开前，在其两侧颞顶部开 5 平方厘米的骨窗。移除颅盖骨时，可以用手压住骨窗，保持大脑和硬脑膜于原位，检查大脑表面是否有空气栓塞。为防止空气进入动脉，取出大脑前先双重夹闭颈内动脉和基底动脉。注意详细检查双侧颞骨及颞肌 (194)。
- 在心脏前侧的胸骨处开一个小的骨窗，骨窗内放满水并将注射器插入心包内，检查心包内是否积气。打开心包，观察冠状动脉各分支内是否有空气。在心包中灌满水，10 毫升注射器内吸入少量的水，在水面下针头插入心室腔，观察是否有气泡（参阅第 7 章图 5-38）。原位检查肺胸膜血管时，即使在心腔内和血管中发现气泡并不是动脉空气栓塞或减压病的特异性表现。死后即使人体处于正常大气压，氮气也会从体液中挥发出来 (204, 212)。尸体腐败也会产生气体，需通过微生物培养来确定是否存在微生物产气。
- 特别是在干性溺死案件中，需考虑其他创伤和自然死亡的原因。使用探针检查心脏内卵圆孔是否闭合。发现死者舌头撕裂，表明可能是癫痫发作所致。斑纹灰的舌头（Leibermeister 征象）提示可能存在空气栓塞。
- 复苏过程会产生人为干预，将增加解释的难度（如瘀斑，脂肪/骨髓栓塞）。
- 取下心、肺时，可以先将心脏及肺门处主要的血管结扎。将肺放置在盛满水的容器中，用注射器将空气注入到支气管中检查胸膜破裂位置。检查是否存在肺大疱和肺气肿。检查支气管和胃是否分别存在泡沫和泥沙。

- 在某些案件中可视情况对骨组织（如股骨）进行硅藻检验（参阅标题11.3）。
- 保留脑和脊髓。
- 进行毒物分析检测（乙醇、毒药物筛选）。

张建华 陈敏 译

参考文献

1. Davis, J. H. Bodies found in the water. An investigative approach. Am. J. Forensic Med. Pathol. 7:291–297, 1986.
2. Timperman, J. The diagnosis of drowning. A review. Forensic Sci. 1:397–409, 1972.
3. Lunetta, P., Penttila, A., Sajantila, A. Circumstances and macropathologic findings in 1590 consecutive cases of bodies found in water. Am. J. Forensic Med. Pathol. 23:371–376, 2002.
4. Wirthwein, D. P., Barnard, J. J., Prahlow, J. A. Suicide by drowning: a 20-year review. J. Forensic Sci. 47:131–136, 2002.
5. Lucas, J., Goldfeder, L. B., Gill, J. R. Bodies found in the waterways of New York City. J. Forensic Sci. 47:137–141, 2002.
6. Moar, J. J. Drowning—postmortem appearances and forensic significance. A case report. S. Afr. Med. J. 64:792–795, 1983.
7. Lunetta, P., Smith, G. S., Penttila, A., Sajantila, A. Undetermined drowning. Med. Sci. Law 43:207–214, 2003.
8. Modell, J. H., Bellefleur, M., Davis, J. H. Drowning without aspiration: is this an appropriate diagnosis? J. Forensic Sci. 44:1119–1123, 1999.
9. Copeland, A. R. Suicide by drowning. Am. J. Forensic Med. Pathol. 8:18–22, 1987. 10. Pachar, J. V., Cameron, J. M. Submersion cases: a retrospective study—1988–1990. Med. Sci. Law 32:15–17, 1992.
11. Dietz, P. E., Baker, S. P. Drowning: epidemiology and prevention. Am. J. Public Health 64:303–312, 1974.
12. Patetta, M. J., Biddinger, P. W. Characteristics of drowning deaths in North Carolina. Public Health Rep. 103:406–411, 1988.
13. Press, E., Walker, J., Crawford, I. An interstate drowning study. Am. J. Public Health Nations Health 58:2275–2289, 1968.
14. Smith, N. M., Byard, R. W., Bourne, A. J. Death during immersion in water in childhood. Am. J. Forensic Med. Pathol. 12:219–221, 1991.
15. Plueckhahn, V. D. The aetiology of 134 deaths due to "drowning" in Geelong during the years 1957 to 1971. Med. J. Aust. 2:1183–1187, 1972.
16. Gordon, I. The anatomical signs in drowning. A critical evaluation. Forensic Sci. 1:389–

395, 1972.

17. Giertsen, J. C. Drowning while under the influnce of alcohol. Med. Sci. Law 10:216−219, 1970.

18. Plueckhahn, V. D. Alcohol and accidental drowning. A 25−year study. Med. J. Aust. 141:22−25, 1984.

19. Plueckhahn, V. D. Death by drowning? Geelong 1959 to 1974. Med. J. Aust. 2:904−−906, 1975.

20. Copeland, A. R. An assessment of lung weights in drowning cases. The Metro Dade County experience from 1978 to 1982. Am. J. Forensic Med. Pathol. 6:301−304, 1985.

21. Lau, G. Did he drown or was he murdered? Med. Sci. Law 42:172−180, 2002. 22. Kringsholm, B., Filskov, A., Kock, K. Autopsied cases of drowning in Denmark 1987−1989. Forensic Sci. Int. 52:85−92, 1991.

23. Davis, J. H. Bodies in water. Solving the puzzle. J. Fla. Med. Assoc. 79:630−632, 1992. 24. Morild, I. Pleural effusion in drowning. Am. J. Forensic Med. Pathol. 16:253−256, 1995.

25. Mueller, W. F. Pathology of temporal bone hemorrhage in drowning. J. Forensic Sci. 14:327−336, 1969.

26. Pachar, J. V., Cameron, J. M. The diagnosis of drowning by quantitative and qualitative diatom analysis. Med. Sci. Law 33:291−299, 1993.

27. Ludes, B., Quantin, S., Coste, M., Mangin, P. Application of a simple enzymatic digestion method for diatom detection in the diagnosis of drowning in putrified corpses by diatom analysis. Int. J. Legal Med. 107:37−41, 1994.

28. Gooden, B. A. Drowning and the diving reflex in man. Med. J. Aust. 2:583−587, 1972. 29. Wintemute, G. J., Kraus, J. F., Teret, S. P., Wright, M. Drowning in childhood and adolescence: a population−based study. Am. J. Public Health 77:830−832, 1987.

30. Wintemute, G. J., Kraus, J. F., Teret, S. P., Wright, M. A. The epidemiology of drowning in adulthood: implications for prevention. Am. J. Prev. Med. 4:343−348, 1988.

31. Davis, L. G. Suicidal drowning in south Florida. J. Forensic Sci. 44:902−905, 1999. 32. Bierens, J. J., van der Velde, E. A., van Berkel, M., van Zanten, J. J. Submersion cases in the Netherlands. Ann. Emerg. Med. 18:366−373, 1989.

33. Cairns, F. J., Koelmeyer, T. D., Smeeton, W. M. Deaths from drowning. N. Z. Med. J. 97:65−67, 1984.

34. Auer, A. Suicide by drowning in Uusimaa province in southern Finland. Med. Sci. Law 30:175−179, 1990.

35. Copeland, A. R. Homicidal drowning. Forensic Sci. Int. 31:247−252, 1986. 36. Griest, K. J., Zumwalt, R. E. Child abuse by drowning. Pediatrics 83:41−46, 1989.

37. Byard, R. W., Houldsworth, G., James, R. A., Gilbert, J. D. Characteristic features of suicidal drownings: a 20-year study. Am. J. Forensic Med. Pathol. 22:134–138, 2001.

38. Davis, S., Smith, L. S. The epidemiology of drowning in Cape Town—1980–1983. S. Afr. Med. J. 68:739–742, 1985.

39. Wintemute, G. J. Childhood drowning and near-drowning in the United States. Am. J. Dis. Child. 144:663–669, 1990.

40. Nixon, J., Pearn, J., Wilkey, I., Corcoran A. Fifteen years of child drowning—a 1967–1981 analysis of all fatal cases from the Brisbane Drowning Study and an 11 year study of consecutive near-drowning cases. Accid. Anal. Prev. 18:199–203, 1986.

41. Davis, S., Ledman, J., Kilgore, J. Drownings of children and youth in a desert state. West. J. Med. 143:196–201, 1985.

42. Cass, D. T., Ross, F., Lam, L. T. Childhood drowning in New South Wales 1990–1995: a population-based study. Med. J. Aust. 165:610–612, 1996.

43. O'Carroll, P. W., Alkon, E., Weiss, B. Drowning mortality in Los Angeles County, 1976 to 1984. JAMA 260:380–383, 1988.

44. Hedberg, K., Gunderson, P. D., Vargas, C., Osterholm, M. T., MacDonald, K. L. Drownings in Minnesota, 1980–85: a population-based study. Am. J. Public Health 80:1071–1074, 1990.

45. MacLachlan, J. Drownings, other aquatic injuries and young Canadians. Can. J. Public Health 75:218–222, 1984.

46. Pearn, J. H., Wong, R. Y., Brown, J., III, Ching, Y. C., Bart, R., Jr., Hammar, S. Drowning and near-drowning involving children: a five-year total population study from the City and County of Honolulu. Am. J. Public Health 69:450–454, 1979.

47. Orlowski, J. P. Drowning, near-drowning, and ice-water submersions. Pediatr. Clin. N. Am. 34:75–92, 1987.

48. DeNicola, L. K., Falk, J. L., Swanson, M. E., Gayle, M. O., Kissoon, N. Submersion injuries in children and adults. Crit. Care Clin. 13:477–502, 1997.

49. Copeland, A. R. Deaths during recreational activity. Forensic Sci. Int. 25:117–122, 1984.

50. Wong, L. L., McNamara, J. J. Salt water drowning. Hawaii Med. J. 43:208, 210, 1984.

51. O'Shea, J. S. House-fire and drowning deaths among children and young adults. Am. J. Forensic Med. Pathol. 12:33–35, 1991.

52. Wintemute, G. J., Kraus, J. F., Teret, S. P., Wright, M. A. Death resulting from motor vehicle immersions: the nature of the injuries, personal and environmental contributing factors, and potential interventions. Am. J. Public Health 80:1068–1070, 1990.

53. Jumbelic, M. I., Chambliss, M. Accidental toddler drowning in 5-gallon buckets. JAMA

263:1952–1953, 1990.

54. Pearn, J., Nixon, J., Wilkey, I. Freshwater drowning and near–drowning accidents involving children: a five–year total population study. Med. J. Aust. 2:942––946, 1976.
55. Byard, R. W., Lipsett, J. Drowning deaths in toddlers and preambulatory children in South Australia. Am. J. Forensic Med. Pathol. 20:328–332, 1999.
56. Kibel, S. M., Nagel, F. O., Myers, J., Cywes, S. Childhood near–drowning—a 12–year retrospective review. S. Afr. Med. J. 78:418–421, 1990.
57. Wintemute, G. J. Drowning in early childhood. Pediatr. Ann. 21:417–421, 1992.
58. Levin, D. L., Morriss, F. C., Toro, L. O., Brink, L. W., Turner, G. R. Drowning and near–drowning. Pediatr. Clin. N. Am. 40:321–336, 1993.
59. Kallas, H. J., O'Rourke, P. P. Drowning and immersion injuries in children. Curr. Opin. Pediatr. 5:295–302, 1993.
60. Shaw, K. N., Briede, C. A. Submersion injuries: drowning and near–drowning. Emerg. Med. Clin. N. Am. 7:355–370, 1989.
61. Pearn, J. H., Nixon, J. Swimming pool immersion accidents: an analysis from the Brisbane Drowning Study. 1977. Inj. Prev. 3:307–309, 1997.
62. Wintemute, G. J., Drake, C., Wright, M. Immersion events in residential swimming pools. Evidence for an experience effect. Am. J. Dis. Child. 145:1200–1203, 1991.
63. Pearn, J., Nixon, J. Prevention of childhood drowning accidents. Med. J. Aust. 1:616–618, 1977.
64. Patrick, M., Bint, M., Pearn, J. Saltwater drowning and near–drowning accidents involving children. A five–year total population study in south–east Queensland. Med. J. Aust. 1:61–64, 1979.
65. Pitt, W. R., Balanda, K. P. Childhood drowning and near–drowning in Brisbane: the contribution of domestic pools. Med. J. Aust. 154:661–665, 1991.
66. Corbin, D. O., Fraser, H. S. A review of 98 cases of near–drowning at the Queen Elizabeth Hospital, Barbados. West Indian Med. J. 30:22–29, 1981.
67. Quan, L., Gore, E. J., Wentz, K., Allen, J., Novack, A. H. Ten–year study of pediatric drownings and near–drownings in King County, Washington: lessons in injury prevention. Pediatrics 83:1035–1040, 1989.
68. Fergusson, D. M., Horwood, L. J. Risks of drowning in fenced and unfenced domestic swimming pools. N. Z. Med. J. 97:777–779, 1984.
69. Pearn, J. H., Nixon, J. Swimming pool immersion accidents: an analysis from the Brisbane drowning study. Med. J. Aust. 1:432–437, 1977.
70. Mann, N. C., Weller, S. C., Rauchschwalbe, R. Bucket–related drownings in the United

States, 1984 through 1990. Pediatrics 89:1068–1071, 1992.
71. Scott, P. H., Eigen H. Immersion accidents involving pails of water in the home. J. Pediatr. 96:282–284, 1980.
72. Avis, S. P. Suicidal drowning. J. Forensic Sci. 38:1422–1426, 1993.
73. Orlowski, J. P., Szpilman, D. Drowning. Rescue, resuscitation, and reanimation. Pediatr. Clin. North Am. 48:627–646, 2001.
74. Ritchie, B. C. The physiology of drowning. Med. J. Aust. 2:1187–1189, 1972. 75. Modell, J. H. Drown versus near–drown: a discussion of definitions. Crit. Care Med. 9:351–352, 1981.
76. Pearn, J. Pathophysiology of drowning. Med. J. Aust. 142:586–588, 1985.
77. Pearn, J., Nixon, J. Bathtub immersion accidents involving children. Med. J. Aust. 1:211–213, 1977.
78. Modell, J. H. Drowning. N. Engl. J. Med. 328:253–256, 1993.
79. Modell, J. H., Moya, F., Newby, E. J., Ruiz, B. C., Showers, A. V. The effects of fluid volume in seawater drowning. Ann. Intern. Med. 67:68–80, 1967.
80. Modell, J. H., Davis, J. H. Electrolyte changes in human drowning victims. Anesthesiology 30:414–420, 1969.
81. Giammona, S. T., Modell, J. H. Drowning by total immersion. Effects on pulmonary surfactant of distilled water, isotonic saline, and sea water. Am. J. Dis. Child. 114:612–616, 1967.
82. Modell, J. H. Near–drowning. Int. Anesthesiol. Clin. 15:107–115, 1977.
83. Modell, J. H. Biology of drowning. Annu. Rev. Med. 29:1–8, 1978.
84. Modell, J. H., Kuck, E. J., Ruiz, B. C., Heinitsh, H. Effect of intravenous vs. aspirated distilled water on serum electrolytes and blood gas tensions. J. Appl. Physiol. 32:579–584, 1972.
85. Modell, J. H. The pathophysiology and treatment of drowning. Acta Anaesthesiol. Scand. Suppl. 29:263–279, 1968.
86. Noble, C. S., Sharpe, N. Drowning: Its mechanism and treatment. Can. Med. Assoc. J. 89:402–405, 1963.
87. Golden, F. S., Tipton, M. J., Scott, R. C. Immersion, near–drowning and drowning. Br. J. Anaesth. 79:214–225, 1997.
88. Harries, M. G. Drowning in man. Crit. Care Med. 9:407–408, 1981.
89. Davis JH. Fatal underwater breath holding in trained swimmers. J. Forensic Sci. 1961; 6:301–306.
90. Colebatch, H. J., Halmagyi, D. F. Lung mechanics and resuscitation after fluid aspiration. J. Appl. Physiol. 16:684–696. 1961.

91. Colebatch, H. J., Halmagyi, D. F. Effect of vagotomy and vagal stimulation on lung mechanics and circulation. J. Appl. Physiol. 18:881–887, 1963.

92. Modell, J. H. Near drowning. Circulation 74:IV27–IV28, 1986.

93. Halmagyi, D. F., Colebatch, H. J. Ventilation and circulation after fluid aspiration. J. Appl. Physiol. 16:35–40, 1961.

94. Halmagyi, D. F., Colebatch, H. J., Starzecki, B. Inhalation of blood, saliva, and alcohol: consequences, mechanism, and treatment. Thorax 17:244–250, 1962.

95. Modell, J. H., Gaub, M,, Moya, F., Vestal, B., Swarz, H. Physiologic effects of near drowning with chlorinated fresh water, distilled water and isotonic saline. Anesthesiology 27:33–41, 1966.

96. Conn, A. W., Miyasaka, K., Katayama, M., et al. A canine study of cold water drowning in fresh versus salt water. Crit. Care Med. 23:2029–2037, 1995.

97. Segarra, F., Redding, R. A. Modern concepts about drowning. Can. Med. Assoc. J. 110:1057, 1974.

98. Orlowski, J. P., Abulleil, M. M., Phillips, J. M. The hemodynamic and cardiovascular effects of near–drowning in hypotonic, isotonic, or hypertonic solutions. Ann. Emerg. Med. 18:1044–1049, 1989.

99. Orlowski, J. P., Abulleil, M. M., Phillips, J. M. Effects of tonicities of saline solutions on pulmonary injury in drowning. Crit. Care Med. 15:126–130, 1987.

100. Modell, J. H., Moya, F. Effects of volume of aspirated fluid during chlorinated fresh water drowning. Anesthesiology 27:662–672, 1966.

101. Culpepper, R. M. Letter: Bleeding diathesis in fresh water drowning. Ann. Intern. Med. 83:675, 1975.

102. Modell, J. H. Serum electrolyte changes in near–drowning victims. JAMA 253:557, 1985. 103. Schmidt, P., Madea, B. Death in the bathtub involving children. Forensic Sci. Int. 72:147–155, 1995.

104. Sanford, J. P. Medical aspects of recreational skin and scuba diving. Annu. Rev. Med. 25:401–410, 1974.

105. Craig, A. B., Jr. Underwater swimming and drowning. J. Sports Med. Phys. Fitness 2:23–26, 1962.

106. Craig, A. B., Jr. Causes of loss of consciousness during underwater swimming. J. Appl. Physiol. 16:583–586, 1961.

107. Craig, A. B., Jr. Underwater swimming and loss of consciousness. JAMA 176:255–258, 1961.

108. Plueckhahn, V. D. Alcohol consumption and death by drowning in adults; a 24–year epi–

demiological analysis. J. Stud. Alcohol. 43:445-452, 1982.
109. Daly, M. D., Angell-James, J. E., Elsner, R. Role of carotid-body chemoreceptors and their reflex interactions in bradycardia and cardiac arrest. Lancet 1:764-767, 1979.
110. Plueckhahn, V. D. Alcohol and accidental submersion from watercraft and surrounds. Med. Sci. Law 17:246-250, 1977.
111. Lunetta, P., Levo, A., Laitinen, P. J., Fodstad, H., Kontula, K., Sajantila, A. Molecularscreening of selected long QT syndrome (LQTS) mutations in 165 consecutive bodies found in water. Int. J. Legal Med. 117:115-117, 2003.
112. Saxena, A., Ang, L. C. Epilepsy and bathtub drowning. Important neuropathological obser-vations. Am. J. Forensic Med. Pathol. 14:125-129, 1993.
113. Edwards, N. D., Timmins, A. C., Randalls, B., Morgan, G. A., Simcock, A. D. Survival inadults after cardiac arrest due to drowning. Intensive Care Med. 16:336-337, 1990.
114. Modell, J. H., Graves, S. A., Ketover, A. Clinical course of 91 consecutive near-drowningvictims. Chest 70:231-238, 1976.
115. Waugh, J. H., O'Callaghan, M. J., Pitt, W. R. Prognostic factors and long-term outcomesfor children who have nearly drowned. Med. J. Aust. 161:594-599, 1994.
116. Orlowski, J. P. Drowning, near-drowning, and ice-water drowning. JAMA 260:390-391, 1988.
117. Tipton, M. J. The initial responses to cold-water immersion in man. Clin. Sci. (Lond.) 77:581-588, 1989.
118. Tipton, M. J., Golden, F. S., Higenbottam, C., Mekjavic, I. B., Eglin, C. M. Temperaturedependence of habituation of the initial responses to cold-water immersion. Eur. J. Appl. Physiol. Occup. Physiol. 78:253-257, 1998.
119. Tipton, M. J., Stubbs, D. A., Elliott, D. H. The effect of clothing on the initial responses to cold water immersion in man. J. R. Nav. Med. Serv. 76:89-95, 1990.
120. Hayward, J. S., Eckerson, J. D. Physiological responses and survival time prediction forhumans in ice-water. Aviat. Space Environ. Med. 55:206-211, 1984.
121. Tipton, M. J., Mekjavic, I. B., Eglin, C. M. Permanence of the habituation of the initialresponses to cold-water immersion in humans. Eur. J. Appl. Physiol. 83:17-21, 2000.
122. Gooden, B. A. Why some people do not drown. Hypothermia versus the diving response. Med. J. Aust. 157:629-632, 1992.
123. Graham, T., Baulk, K. Effect of alcohol ingestion on man's thermoregulatory responsesduring cold water immersion. Aviat. Space Environ. Med. 51:155-159, 1980.
124. Golden, F. S., Hervey, G. R., Tipton, M. J. Circum-rescue collapse: collapse, sometimes

fatal, associated with rescue of immersion victims. J. R. Nav. Med. Serv. 77:139–149, 1991.

125. Nguyen, M. H., Ernsting, K. S., Proctor, D. D. Massive variceal bleeding caused by scuba diving. Am. J. Gastroenterol. 95:3677–3678, 2000.

126. Mohri, H., Dillard, D. H., Crawford, E. W., Martin, W. E., Merendino, K. A. Method of surface–induced deep hypothermia for open–heart surgery in infants. J. Thorac. Cardiovasc. Surg. 58:262–270, 1969.

127. Gooden, B. A. The diving response in clinical medicine. Aviat. Space Environ. Med. 53:273–276, 1982.

128. Campbell, L. B., Gooden, B. A., Horowitz, J. D. Cardiovascular responses to partial and total immersion in man. J. Physiol. 202:239–250, 1969.

129. Orlowski, J. P., Rothner, A. D., Lueders, H. Submersion accidents in children with epilepsy. Am. J. Dis. Child. 136:777–780, 1982.

130. Pearn, J., Bart, R., Yamaoka, R. Drowning risks to epileptic children: a study from Hawaii. Br. Med. J. 2:1284–1285, 1978.

131. Pearn, J. M. Epilepsy and drowning in childhood. Br. Med. J. 1:1510–1511, 1977.

132. Ryan, C. A., Dowling, G. Drowning deaths in people with epilepsy. CMAJ 148:781–784. 1993.

133. Stumpp, J. W., Schneider, J., Bar, W. Drowning of a girl with anomaly of the bundle of His and the right bundle branch. Am. J. Forensic Med. Pathol. 18:208–210, 1997.

134. Pearn, J. Drowning and alcohol. Med. J. Aust. 141:6–7, 1984.

135. Mackie, I. Alcohol and aquatic disasters. Med. J. Aust. 1:652–653, 1978.

136. Haight, J. S., Keatinge, W. R. Failure of thermoregulation in the cold during hypoglycaemia induced by exercise and ethanol. J. Physiol. 229:87–97, 1973.

137. Kurihara, K., Kuroda, N., Murai, T., Matsuo, Y., Yanagida, J., Watanabe, H. A case of suicide by drowning with hesitation marks on the back. Nippon Hoigaku Zasshi 43:517–521, 1989.

138. Yorulmaz, C., Arican, N., Afacan, I., Dokgoz, H., Asirdizer, M. Pleural effusion in bodies recovered from water. Forensic Sci. Int. 136:16–21, 2003.

139. Terazawa, K., Haga, K. The role of pleural effusion in drowning. Am. J. Forensic Med. Pathol. 17:173–174, 1996.

140. Lunetta, P., Modell, J. H., Sajantila, A. What is the incidence and significance of "dry–lungs" in bodies found in water? Am. J. Forensic Med. Pathol. 25:291–301, 2004.

141. Hadley, J. A., Fowler, D. R. Organ weight effects of drowning and asphyxiation on the lungs, liver, brain, heart, kidneys, and spleen. Forensic Sci. Int. 133:190–196, 2003.

142. Mukaida, M., Kimura, H., Takada, Y. Detection of bathsalts in the lungs of a baby

drowned in a bathtub: a case report. Forensic Sci. Int. 93:5–11, 1998.
143. Auer, A., Mottonen, M. Diatoms and drowning. Z. Rechtsmed. 101:87–98, 1988.
144. Haffner, H. T., Graw, M., Erdelkamp, J. Spleen findings in drowning. Forensic Sci. Int. 66:95–104, 1994.
145. Fornes, P., Pepin, G., Heudes, D., Lecomte, D. Diagnosis of drowning by combined computer–assisted histomorphometry of lungs with blood strontium determination. J. Forensic Sci. 43:772–776, 1998.
146. Neidhart, D. A., Greendyke, R. M. The significance of diatom demonstration in the diagnosis of death by drowning. Am. J. Clin. Pathol. 48:377–382, 1967.
147. Durlacher, S. H., Freimuth, H. C., Swan, H. E., Jr. Blood changes in man following death due to drowning, with comments on tests for drowning. AMA Arch, Pathol. 56:454–461, 1953.
148. Foroughi, E. Serum changes in drowning. J. Forensic Sci. 16:269–282, 1971.
149. Freimuth, H. C., Swann, H. E., Jr. Plasma specific gravity changes in sudden deaths; observations with specific reference to drowning. AMA Arch. Pathol. 59:214–218, 1955.
150. Farmer, J. G., Benomran, F., Watson, A. A., Harland, W. A. Magnesium, potassium, sodium and calcium in post–mortem vitreous humour from humans. Forensic Sci. Int. 27:1–13, 1985.
151. Peabody, A. J. Diatoms and drowning—a review. Med. Sci. Law 20:254–261, 1980.
152. Hendey, N. I. The diagnostic value of diatoms in cases of drowning. Med. Sci. Law 13:23–34, 1973.
153. Pollanen, M. S., Cheung, C., Chiasson, D. A. The diagnostic value of the diatom test for drowning, I. Utility: a retrospective analysis of 771 cases of drowning in Ontario, Canada. J. Forensic Sci. 42:281–285, 1997.
154. Ludes, B., Coste, M., Tracqui, A., Mangin, P. Continuous river monitoring of the diatoms in the diagnosis of drowning. J. Forensic Sci. 41:425–428, 1996.
155. Pollanen, M. S. Diatoms and homicide. Forensic Sci. Int. 91:29–34, 1998.
156. Lunetta, P., Penttila, A., Hallfors, G. Scanning and transmission electron microscopical evidence of the capacity of diatoms to penetrate the alveolo–capillary barrier in drowning. Int. J. Legal Med. 111:229–237, 1998.
157. Krstic, S., Duma, A., Janevska, B., Levkov, Z., Nikolova, K., Noveska, M. Diatoms in forensic expertise of drowning—a Macedonian experience. Forensic Sci. Int. 127:198–203, 2002.
158. Gruspier, K. L., Pollanen, M. S. Limbs found in water: investigation using anthropological analysis and the diatom test. Forensic Sci. Int. 112:1–9, 2000.
159. Pollanen, M. S. The diagnostic value of the diatom test for drowning, II. Validity: analysis of diatoms in bone marrow and drowning medium. J. Forensic Sci. 42:286–290, 1997.

160. Porawski, R. Investigations on the occurrence of diatoms in organs in death from various causes. J. Forensic Med. 13:134–137, 1966.
161. Foged, N. Diatoms and drowning—once more. Forensic Sci. Int. 21:153–159, 1983.
162. Gylseth, B., Mowe, G. Diatoms in lung tissue. Lancet 2:1375, 1979.
163. Auer, A. Qualitative diatom analysis as a tool to diagnose drowning. Am. J. Forensic Med. Pathol. 12:213–218, 1991.
164. Spitz, W. U., Schneider. V. The significance of diatoms in the diagnosis of death by drowning. J. Forensic Sci. 67:11–18, 1964.
165. Taylor, J. J. Diatoms and drowning—a cautionary case note. Med. Sci. Law 34:78–79, 1994.
166. Goonetilleke, U. K. Diatoms in drowning. Med. Sci. Law 21:194–195, 1981.
167. Betz, P., Nerlich, A., Penning, R., Eisenmenger, W. Alveolar macrophages and the diagnosis of drowning. Forensic Sci. Int. 62:217–224, 1993.
168. Betz, P., Penning, R., Keil, W. The detection of petechial haemorrhages of the conjunctivae in dependency on the postmortem interval. Forensic Sci. Int. 64:61–67, 1994.
169. Biddinger, P. W. Postmortem wound dehiscence. A report of three cases. Am. J. Forensic Med. Pathol. 8:120–122, 1987.
170. Spitz, W. V. Drowning. In: Spitz, W. V., ed. Medicolegal Investigation of Death:Guidelines for the Application of Pathology to Crime Investigation. Charles C. Thomas, Springfield, IL, pp. 498–515, 1993.
171. Donoghue, E. R., Minnigerode, S. C. Human body buoyancy: a study of 98 men. J. Forensic Sci. 22:573–579, 1977.
172. Gardner, E. Death in the bathroom. Med. Leg. Criminologic Rev. 12:180–195, 1944.
173. Lunetta, P., Levo, A., Mannikko, A., Penttila, A., Sajantila, A. Death in bathtub revisited with molecular genetics: a victim with suicidal traits and a LQTS gene mutation. Forensic Sci. Int. 130:122–124, 2002.
174. Geertinger, P., Voigt, J. Death in the bath. A survey of bathtub deaths in Copenhagen, Denmark, and Gothenburg, Sweden, from 1961 to 1969. J. Forensic Med. 17:136–147, 1970.
175. Devos, C., Timperman, J., Piette, M. Deaths in the bath. Med. Sci. Law 25:189–200, 1985. 176. Shkrum, M. J., Hudson, P. The body in the bathtub. Proceedings of 37th Annual Meeting of American Academy of Forensic Sciences. Las Vegas, NV, 1985.
177. Schmidt, P., Madea, B. Homicide in the bathtub. Forensic Sci. Int. 72:135–146, 1995.
178. Wintemute, G. J., Teret, S. P., Kraus, J. F., Wright, M. Alcohol and drowning: an analysis of contributing factors and a discussion of criteria for case selection. Accid. Anal. Prev. 22:291–296, 1990.

179. Livingston, S., Pauli, L. L., Pruce, I., Kramer, I. I. Drowning in epilepsy. Ann. Neurol. 7:495, 1980.

180. Pearn, J. H., Brown, J., III, Wong, R., Bart, R. Bathtub drownings: report of seven cases. Pediatrics 64:68–70, 1979.

181. Pearn, J., Nixon, J. Attempted drowning as a form of non–accidental injury. Aust. Paediatr. J. 13:110–113, 1977.

182. Nowers, M. P. Suicide by drowning in the bath. Med. Sci. Law 39:349–353, 1999.

183. Budnick, L. D. Bathtub–related electrocutions in the United States, 1979 to 1982. JAMA 252:918–920, 1984.

184. Lawrence, R. D., Spitz, W. U., Taff, M. L. Suicidal electrocution in a bathtub. Am. J. Forensic Med. Pathol. 6:276–278, 1985.

185. Morgan, W. P. Anxiety and panic in recreational scuba divers. Sports Med. 20:398–421, 1995.

186. Nichols, G. R., Davis, G. J., Parola, A. C. Dirty diving. Sudden death of a SCUBA diver in a water treatment facility. Am. J. Forensic Med. Pathol. 13:72–75, 1992.

187. Barsky, S., Neuman, T. Investigating Recreational and Commercial Diving Accidents. Hammerhead Press, Ventura, CA, 2003.

188. Melamed, Y., Shupak, A., Bitterman, H. Medical problems associated with underwater diving. N. Engl. J. Med. 326:30–35, 1992.

189. Neuman, T. S. Diving medicine. Clin. Sports Med. 6:647–661, 1987.

190. Obafunwa, J. O., Busuttil, A., Purdue, B. Deaths of amateur scuba divers. Med. Sci. Law 34:123–129, 1994.

191. Busuttil, A., Obafunwa, J. A review of the forensic investigation of scuba diving deaths. Sci. Justice 35:87–95, 1995.

192. Cooperman, E. M., Hogg, J., Thurlbeck, W. M. Mechanisms of death in shallow–water scuba diving. Can. Med. Assoc. J. 99:1128–1131, 1968.

193. Halpern, P., Sorkine, P., Leykin, Y., Geller, E. Rupture of the stomach in a diving accident with attempted resuscitation. A case report. Br. J. Anaesth. 58:1059–1061, 1986.

194. Antonelli, P. J., Parell, G. J., Becker, G. D., Paparella, M. M. Temporal bone pathology in scuba diving deaths. Otolaryngol. Head Neck Surg. 109:514–521, 1993.

195. Neuman, T. S. Arterial gas embolism and decompression sickness. News Physiol. Sci. 17:77–81, 2002.

196. Harker, C. P., Neuman, T. S., Olson, L. K., Jacoby, I., Santos, A. The roentgenographic findings associated with air embolism in sport scuba divers. J. Emerg. Med. 11:443–449, 1993. 197. Kanter, A. S., Stewart, B. F., Costello, J. A., Hampson, N. B. Myocardial infarction during

scuba diving: a case report and review. Am. Heart J. 130:1292–1294, 1995.

198. Weiss, L. D., Van Meter, K. W. Cerebral air embolism in asthmatic scuba divers in a swimming pool. Chest 107:1653–1654, 1995. 199. Petri, N. M., Vranjkovic–Petri, L., Aras, N., Druzijanic, N. Gastric rupture in a diver due to rapid ascent. Croat. Med. J. 43:42–44, 2002. 200. Molenat, F. A., Boussuges, A. H. Rupture of the stomach complicating diving accidents. Undersea Hyperb. Med. 22:87–96, 1995.

201. Titu, L. V., Laden, G., Purdy, G. M., Wedgwood, K. R. Gastric barotrauma in a scuba diver: report of a case. Surg. Today 33:299–301, 2003.

202. Warren, L. P., Jr., Djang, W. T., Moon, R. E., et al. Neuroimaging of scuba diving injuries to the CNS. AJR Am. J. Roentgenol 151:1003–1008, 1988.

203. Reuter, M., Tetzlaff, K., Hutzelmann, A., et al. MR imaging of the central nervous system in diving–related decompression illness. Acta Radiol. 38:940–944, 1997.

204. Neuman, T. S., Jacoby, I., Bove, A. A. Fatal pulmonary barotrauma due to obstruction of the central circulation with air. J. Emerg. Med. 16:413–417, 1998.

205. Yeung, P., Crowe, P., Bennett, M. Barogenic rupture of the stomach: a case for non–operative management. Aust. N. Z. J. Surg. 68:76–77, 1998.

206. Cramer, F. S., Heimbach, R. D. Stomach rupture as a result of gastrointestinal barotrauma in a SCUBA diver. J. Trauma 22:238–240, 1982.

207. Novomesky, F. Gastro–esophageal barotrauma in diving: similarities with Mallory–Weiss syndrome. Soud. Lek. 44:21–24, 1999.

208. Strauss, M. B., Borer, R. C., Jr. Diving medicine: contemporary topics and their controversies. Am. J. Emerg. Med. 19:232–238, 2001.

209. Slade, J. B., Jr., Hattori, T., Ray, C. S., Bove, A. A., Cianci, P. Pulmonary edema associated with scuba diving: case reports and review. Chest 120:1686–1694, 2001.

210. Byrd, J. H., Hamilton, W. F. Underwater cave diving fatalities in Florida: a review and analysis. J. Forensic Sci. 42:807–811, 1997.

211. Temple, J. D., Bosshardt, R. T., Davis, J. H. SCUBA tank corrosion as a cause of death. J. Forensic Sci. 20:571–575, 1975.

212. Brown, C. D., Kime, W., Sherrer, E. L., Jr. Postmortem intravascular bubbling: a decompression artifact? J. Forensic Sci. 23:511–518, 1978.

213. Findley, T. P. An autopsy protocol for skin– and scuba–diving deaths. Am. J. Clin Pathol. 67:440–443, 1977.

214. Roobottom, C. A., Hunter, J. D., Bryson, P. J. The diagnosis of fatal gas embolism: detection by plain film radiography. Clin. Radiol. 49:805–807, 1994.

第6章
穿透性损伤——近距离火器创

概述

火器伤死亡是最常见的自伤致死方式。判定自杀不仅要有近距离枪弹创的损伤形态特征,还需结合现场勘察和案件信息综合判断。通过全面的尸表检验可能在死者身上找到火器自杀的证据,即溅落血迹和烟晕沉着。自伤性枪弹创最常见于头部,枪弹所致的颅脑损伤有其特征性表现(如回弹性)。某些特殊因素可使近距离火器损伤鉴定的难度增加,如医疗处理措施和衣物遮挡可导致枪弹创的形态发生改变。创伤部位异常或多处创伤应考虑他杀可能,通过创道分析可以明确死因。对于有多处创道的案件,在判定死亡方式时需对相对致命伤和致残伤进行评定。

关键词:枪弹创;枪击;自杀;颅脑损伤;穿透性

1 人口统计学

2001年英格兰和威尔士枪击致死案件的发生率为0.14/10万(自杀65%;他杀7%;无法确定或意外28%),2002年加拿大的发生率为2.6/10万(自杀80%;他杀15%;无法确定或意外5%),2001年美国发生率为10.2/10万[自杀67%;他杀27%;无法确定或意外6%(1—3)]。

使用枪械自杀主要是由于枪械容易获取(4—15)。在美国,枪械自杀是最常见的自杀方式(9,16)。例如:美国南部各州的调查研究显示,有65%—87%自杀案件涉及枪械的使用(17—20)。欧洲各项研究表明,4%—8%的自杀使用了枪械(21—23)。在美国,有75%—96%的谋杀后自杀(murder-suicide,嫌疑人枪击他人后使用枪支自杀)案件涉及枪械使用(24—29)。

自伤性火器损伤发生于各年龄段的成年人中(21)。各项涉及火器损伤的研究表明,成年人中自杀者的平均年龄要高于他杀受害者(18,30—37)。例如:新墨西哥州/南卡罗来纳州关于自伤性头部枪弹创的研究显示,自杀者的平均年龄为39.2岁,而他杀受害者的平均年龄为33.7岁(30)。在谋杀后自杀的案件中罪犯也具有相似的年龄分布,但如果受害者是儿童,则罪犯(同时为自杀者)的平均年龄相对降低,澳大利亚的研究显示其平均年龄在31岁(12,28,29,38)。

儿童的枪弹损伤方式多样(39,40)。儿童玩弄枪支时发生意外(39,41–44)。青少年也许会因一时冲动使用枪械"干蠢事",醉酒可能是此类案件的一个重要因素(42)。枪械易用性和易获取性,与玩具枪械的相似性,以及枪械故障都是发生枪击意外死亡的因素(4,41,43),所以也存在意外自伤性枪弹创(41)。头部是枪弹创最常见部位(41,44)。在儿童和青少年中自杀性枪弹创并不常见,例如在对伊利诺州库克县9年内45例10岁以下儿童枪击致死案件的回顾性研究中,就没有发现自杀案件(45)。在其他研究中,自伤性火器损伤受害者的最小年龄相对一致:南卡罗莱纳州为12岁;南卡罗来纳州 – 新墨西哥州为14岁,德克萨斯为11岁,纽约市为13岁(6,18,30,32)。该类案件的涉案枪支多属借取或盗窃所得(12,17)。

虽然在某些地区女性自杀案件的发生更加频繁,但总体上自伤性枪弹创的发生率在男性中更显著(9,14,23,33–36,46–49)。在美国以外的其他国家,只有不到10%的枪击自杀事件发生于女性,而在美国各地区其发生率为5%–17%(6,18,21,32,37,50,51)。在一些国家,女性难以接触枪械,因而枪械自杀案件在性别上存在差异。此外,由于女性会意识到火器损伤从头部射入时可能毁容(21),故女性的头部枪械自杀率偏低。

在谋杀后自杀案件中,女性受害者占有较大比例(12,52)。美国和其他国家的研究显示,在相同年龄范围内,85%–100%的案件中罪犯(同时为自杀者)是男性(12,24–26,28,29,52)。如果受害者是儿童,则案件为女性犯罪的概率会增加(53)。

2 案发现场

无论调查涉及的是单个死者的自杀案件,还是多个受害者被谋杀后的自杀案件,案发现场通常相似。在大多数案件中,死亡发生在家中或在住所附近(17,21,24,26,28,34,35,37,46,48–50,54,55)。在案发现场,通常门从里边被反锁或从里边被椅子顶住。如果现场环境异常,则有助于案件的调查,特别是多发枪弹创案件(37,56–60)。也有案件发生在不常见的地方,如汽车内(55,61,62)。

3 枪械种类

美国和大多数国家的研究显示,手枪最常见(20–22,30,32,63–66)。在美国拥有枪支是受保护的。在德克萨斯州自杀案件的枪械分布如下:

	手枪[a]	步枪	霰弹枪[b]
男性	76.1%	13.7%	10.2%
女性	87.4%	6.7%	6%

[a] 最常见的是0.38英寸特种手枪;
[b] 半数以上案例使用的是12号霰弹枪;

在其他国家或地区（加拿大、英国、斯堪的纳维亚、澳大利亚），由于枪支持有受到管制，长管枪械（步枪和霰弹枪）的使用最常见(23,34-37,46-49)。小口径枪械（手枪和步枪）通常出现于多次射击的自杀现场，但较大口径的手枪和猎枪也有使用(67)。

下面列举出自伤性枪弹创中一些不常见的枪械、子弹：
- 霰弹（铅弹）手枪[68]；
- 黑火药枪(69)；
- 气动枪/气动步枪(16,70-75)；
- "强力弹头枪"[带有枪弹和铅弹的短滑膛枪管，用于捕鱼或防御鲨鱼攻击(16,76)]；
- 笔式枪(77,78)；
- 自制装置(34,73,79,80)；
- 晕眩枪[即屠宰动物用枪(16,23,26,34,65,81,82)]；
- 气压锤(83)；
- 钉/钉枪(16,84-91)；
- 发令枪(73)；
- 空包弹或催泪瓦斯弹药筒(21,22,92,93)。

4 枪械位置

如果能找到枪械，特别是在靠近死者的位置找到，则更有理由推断为自杀案件(59)。德克萨斯州的研究显示，24%的案件可以发现自杀者手中持有枪支，即其一根手指位于枪械的扳机扣环上或至少一只手轻握或紧握枪管(94)。25.7%使用手枪的自杀案件可以在死者手中发现枪支。在那些使用霰弹枪、步枪等长枪自杀案件中，19.5%的案件发现死者手中持有枪支，且通常位于左手。另有研究表明，20%的死者手中持有手枪，其中11%的死者手中持有长枪(95)。德国的研究显示，三分之一的自杀者手中持有枪械(21)。然而，也有将枪支放于受害者手中以掩盖谋杀的(94)。

德克萨斯州的研究显示，69%的案件中枪支位于身体上或接触体表或位于身体附近30厘米（12英寸）的范围内，而枪支距身体30厘米（12英寸）外占7%[其中34起案件中有4起涉及长枪(94)]。死者性别、枪弹创射入口的位置、枪械口径大小，以及是否在死者手中发现枪支等因素之间并无联系。在多次射击的自杀案件中，多见在死者手中或尸体旁发现枪械(55,56,96)。同时使用两支枪械的自杀案件较罕见，此类案件中近一半的死者手中持有枪械(97)。

枪弹创通常位于死者身体的主利手一侧，即右利手的人射击自己右侧太阳穴，但从相反的左侧太阳穴射击也有报道(16,63,98)：据报道有8%的右利手人从左侧太阳穴射击(98)。使用非主利手的情况也可见到(99)，此时枪械多会停置在身体主利手的对侧(100)。

以其他方式扣动扳机也有发生，比如使用脚趾、长物体或长绳扣动长管枪的扳机等(图6-1；参考文献37)。死者可通过操作射击装置自杀(46,60)，此时枪械多被支撑或固定在一个稳固的表面上(图6-2；参考文献46,60)。

枪械"失踪"会使警方对自杀案件的调查愈加困难(16)。此类情况中，枪械多是被死者的亲友拿走，但急救人员和警察也会有此举动(94,101)。拿走枪械出于对死者的考虑和其他顾虑，包括害怕自杀影响声誉、社会和宗教方面的担忧，以及被认定为自杀对保险索赔存在不利因素等。自杀者有时也有以嫁祸仇家(如伪装为凶杀)为目的的举动(37,102)：死者利用辅助装置将武器从自杀现场移除[如死者开枪自杀后手枪因重力因素沉入河中，或使用橡皮筋弹走武器(102-104)]。火器损伤也可能不会立即致命或致残，令死者有机会将枪械带离现场或隐藏在其他地方(22,46,105)。枪

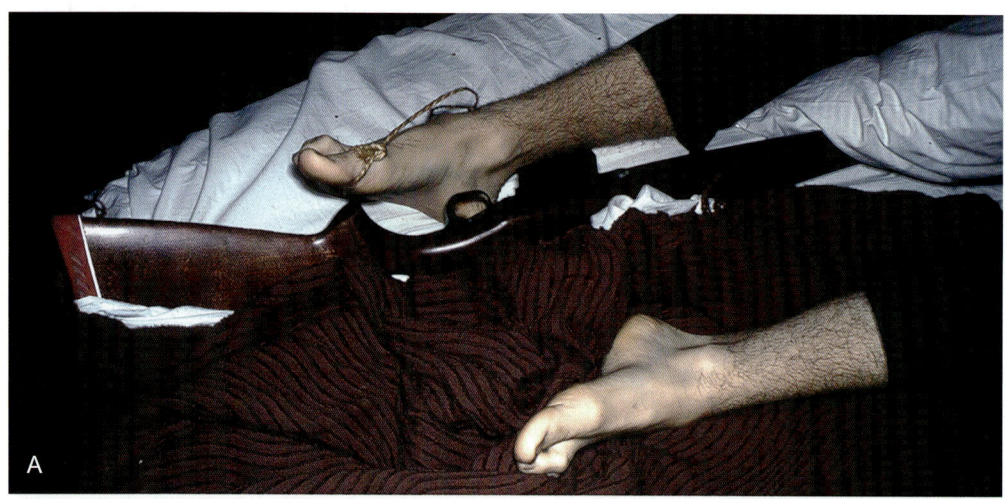

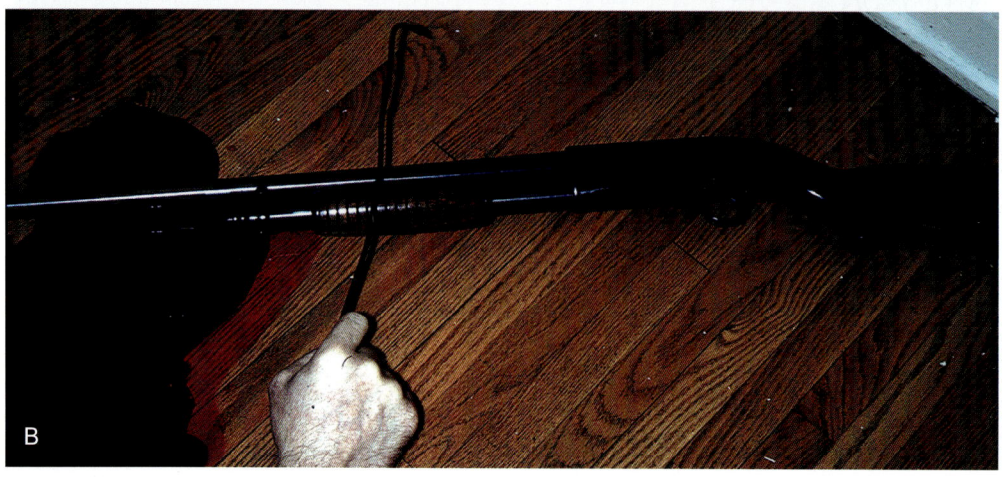

图6-1 自伤性枪弹创。扣动长管枪扳机的方式：(A)用细绳系在脚趾上；(B)辅助装置。

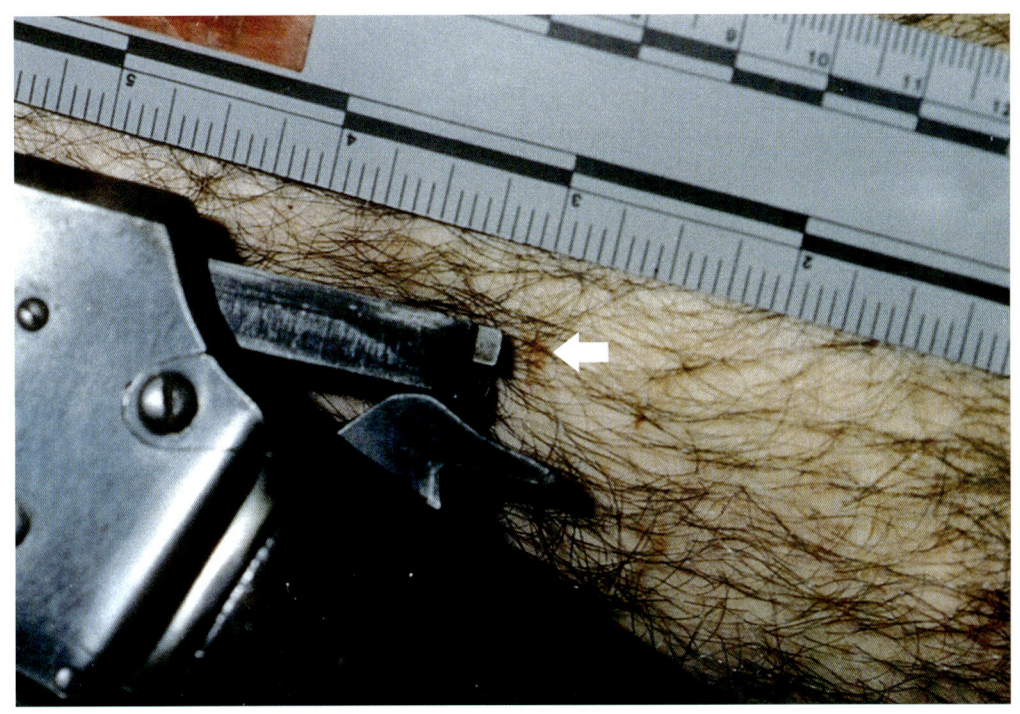

图 6-2　头部自杀枪弹创。用腿部稳定枪支时,后膛在接触部位形成的擦伤(箭头所示)。

械也可被他人从案发现场带走(94,102),可能在案件调查明确后被销毁(106)。

枪械状态的变化可提示自杀或他杀(107,108)。

5 自杀案件中特殊现场或背景信息

如果自伤性枪弹创不立即致命,血液会遗留在不同位置,显示出死者生前具有目的性的活动(图 6-3; 参考文献 16,22,105,109)。在现场血迹勘探中,死者的足迹更为重要(60)。

案发现场可发现遗书。在美国和其他国家大多数自伤性枪弹创的研究中,10%—40%的案件可在现场找到遗书(6,16-19,21,32,35,46,49,50,110)。英国的研究显示 55%的案件现场发现遗书。当然,也可在现场发现其他类似物品,包括遗嘱、丧葬信息、保险保单或其他个人证件(56,110)。遗书大多可成为现场照相证据,或电脑提取证据的一部分(57,111)。但如果发现手写遗书,需要通过笔迹鉴定以明确遗书是否为死者本人所写(111)。

案件中可能会缺乏既往自杀史或企图自杀史的信息。在美国各类枪击自杀案件中,以往企图自杀或声称自杀的案件占 16%—38%(18,110)。低于 19 岁的人群中,有该类记录的案件则高达 42%(6,17)。德克萨斯州的研究发现,以往有自杀史的案件中,死者既往采用的自杀方式包括服用过量药物(38%)或使用枪支[9%(32)]自杀。

图6-3 多次射击自杀，非致命性口腔内枪弹创，枪弹创形成后大量血液流入桶内。另一个房间内发现死者，死于胸部枪弹创（加拿大安大略省伦敦市伦敦健康科学中心 E. Tweedie 博士供图）。

在各类案件中大约有 1/5 到 2/3 死（伤）者存在精神病史或精神障碍（12，17-19，26，32，46，110），其中抑郁症最常见。死（伤）者中有少数为精神病已确诊患者［如谋杀后自杀案件中，多为杀害子女的母亲或死者的直系亲属（12）］。

自杀案件中自杀者和谋杀后自杀者有着相似的刺激因素（28），其中包括人际关系紧张、金融/经济压力、健康状况不佳或患有不治之症、酗酒和药物滥用、法律无助（包括待定的监禁）、精神疾病、自卑、有身体虐待和性虐待史（18，21，24，37，110）。谋杀后自杀案件罪犯的驱动因素依据不同处境而变化，包括嫉妒、报复、利他主义（将家人从这个世界的罪恶中拯救出来）或怜悯［如配偶身患疾病（12，24，25，27，28，38，53）］。南卡罗来纳州的研究显示，低于 18 岁的自伤性火器致死人群中 42% 有危险行为史［如玩弄枪械、吸毒和酗酒（17）］，而在 65 岁及以上的自杀者中则有约 3/4 的死者生前患有高发性癌症和其他慢性、退行性疾病（18）。

自伤性枪弹创可有目击者（16）。澳大利亚的研究发现，10% 的自杀案件有目击者（36，46）。自伤性枪弹创也可能在被警察追击或逮捕过程中形成（112-114）。德克萨斯州的研究发现，15% 的谋杀后自杀案件的罪犯自杀时有目击者，而在新罕布什尔州有超过一半的枪弹创案件存在目击者（26，32）。

自杀者可能会将自杀掩饰为"清洁枪支"或"狩猎"事故（参阅标题21；参考文献 16，23，115）。在这些情况下，应该细致调查，确定是否为意外枪击死亡（图6-4；

第6章 | 穿透性损伤——近距离火器创 313

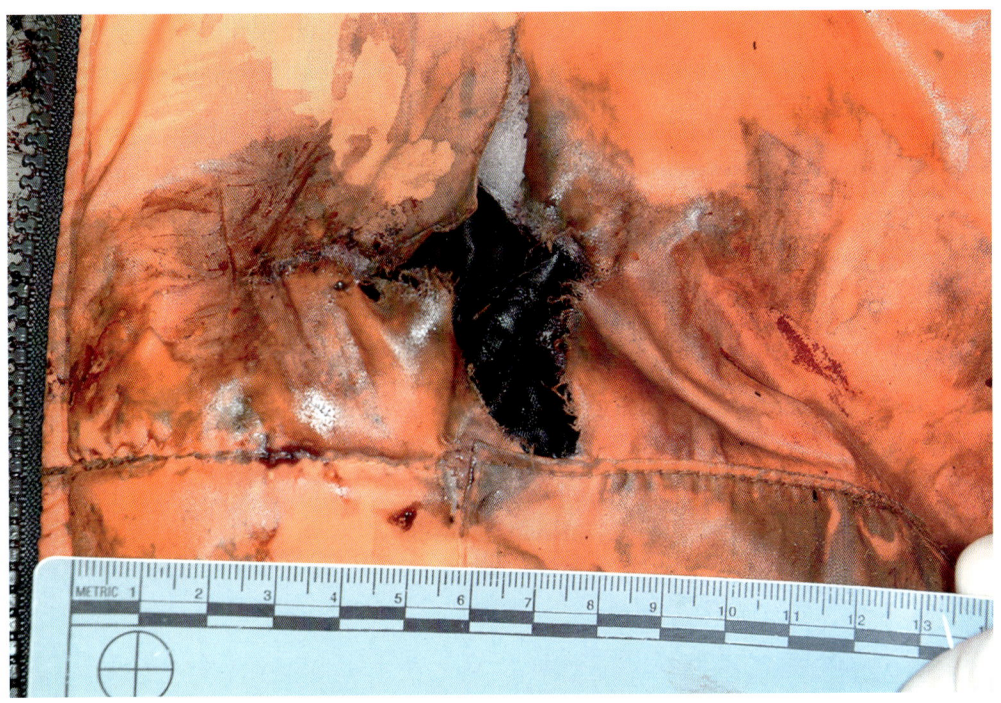

图6-4 狩猎意外案件：狩猎者夹克上的烟晕。死者手握枪管挥舞猎枪驱赶两只打斗的犬时，枪械意外发射（加拿大安大略省伦敦市伦敦健康科学中心 E. Tweedie 博士供图）。

参考文献44）。如果涉及狩猎时手枪造成的死亡案件应引起怀疑（42），无论是自伤还是由他人造成，霰弹枪都是最可能造成意外死亡的武器（42,115）。

在复合性自杀案件中，也就是使用不止一支枪械或采用多种方式自杀，需要留心观察自伤性枪弹损伤（图6-5；参考文献16,77,116-118）。这类自杀可能并非是预谋的，通常在尝试自杀（如一氧化碳中毒或缢颈）失败后，死者到其他场所使用枪械自杀（47,119）。自杀也可以是计划好的，有案例报道，存在合并使用不同枪械（如在霰弹枪后使用气步枪，两把枪械同时使用）或者使用枪械并采用其他方式（缢颈、中毒），以降低仅使用一种方式自杀失败的可能性（21,22,36,72,97,116,120）。

谋杀后自杀案件可按凶手与受害者的关系进行分类（12,24,27,29）。大部分受害者在被发现时已经死亡（28,29,53），其中最常见的情况是婚姻关系或性伴侣关系［40%-85%（24-26,29,53,121）］。在这类案件中嫉妒和疾病是常见动机（52,121,122），也可存在家庭暴力的背景（26,29）。在其他类型的谋杀后自杀案件情形中有多个受害者出现［如杀亲或血亲复仇（28,53,122）］。

在谋杀后自杀案件中时序关系可能会有变化。在杀死一人或多人后往往伴随着杀人者自杀［“多重死亡现场"（123）］，80%的罪犯在杀害他人1小时后自杀，然而，年纪大的杀人者甚至会把自杀推迟达1个月（12,28）。

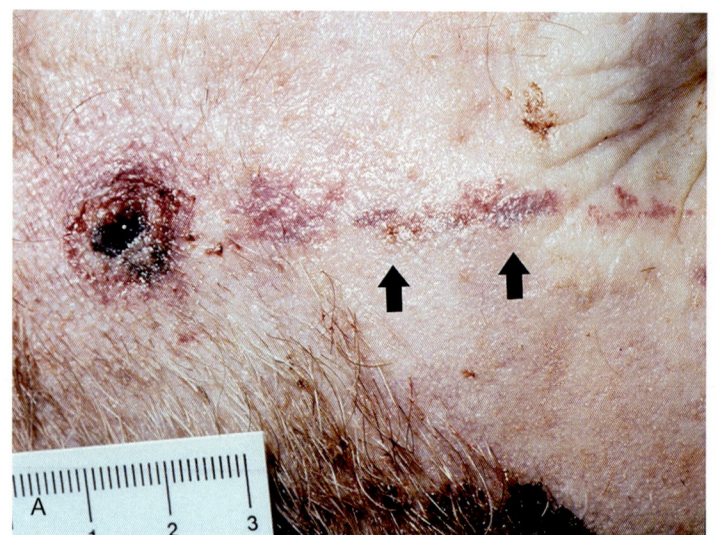
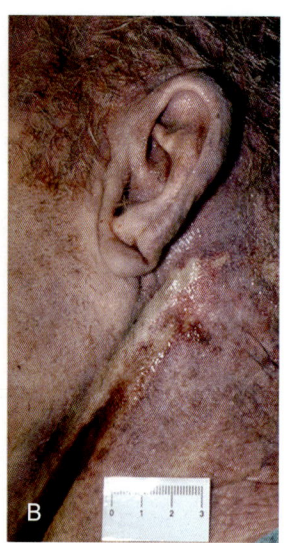

图 6-5 复合性自杀案件。(A) 右侧额顶部接触性枪弹创：明显的条形擦伤（箭头所示）从创口延伸并与骨折线相一致。(B) 缢死,缢沟。

6 枪械

步枪和手枪膛线的设计使子弹高速旋转并保持既定的轨道运行(16)。大部分霰弹枪的枪管是光滑的,常见的子弹是铅弹(16)。铅弹可以是鸟(枪)弹也可以是鹿(枪)弹,后者的直径通常大于 0.6 厘米［0.25 英寸(16,124)］。如果使用鸟(枪)弹,填充的铅弹可达数百个(124)。手枪或步枪的口径指的是枪管的近似直径或基于子弹大小的直径(16)。霰弹枪的口径指的是霰弹枪枪管的直径(124)。12 号霰弹枪具有 0.729 英寸的口径,其可装备 12 颗大小相等、总重量为 1 磅的铅弹(124)。410 号口径霰弹枪是例外,指的是膛径为 0.410 英寸的霰弹枪(16)。霰弹枪枪弹中唯一子弹直径与枪管口径相同的是附膛线重弹头(16)。

触发手枪/步枪或霰弹枪的扳机导致撞针击发弹壳或枪弹药筒底部的底火。底火由大量不等的锑酸铅、硝酸钡和硫化锑组成。弹壳或枪弹药筒内的火药颗粒被底火引爆。标准的火药颗粒的直径为 1 毫米(16)。火药燃烧产生高温、高压气体,迫使弹头脱离弹壳,一氧化碳是气体的成分之一(16)。当弹头或其他类型的枪弹（如铅弹、霰弹枪的附膛线重弹头）离开枪口时,伴随着火焰、气体、各种不同程度燃烧的火药颗粒、烟（烟晕）、底火残渣以及射弹和弹壳中喷射而出的金属(16,124,125)。如果使用的是左轮手枪,从这个圆孔中喷射出的是除弹头以外的各种物质,包括子弹中的填充物和弹壳(16)。

枪弹创的形态取决于枪口到体表皮肤的距离。该距离决定了枪口喷发物在枪弹创射入口的沉积样式。

7 枪弹创射入口的分类

枪弹创射入口可按照如下方式分类(16):

- 接触射入口(参阅标题9和12)
  - 部分枪口抵住体表皮肤。
  - 以枪弹创烧焦组织周围有烟晕嵌入为特征。
  - 如果是紧密接触射入口,皮肤表面的烟晕沉着一般较轻微。
- 贴近接触射入口
  - 枪口轻轻接触体表,可让烟晕沉着在创周(图6-6)。烟晕较宽区域可能会被不经意地抹去。
- 近距离射入口
  - 这类枪弹创与贴近接触的枪弹创相似,当枪口和皮肤表面存在较短距离时产生。
- 中距离射入口
  - 枪口在该距离内可让火药颗粒分散,导致火药颗粒分散之后分别碰撞皮肤。
  - 火药颗粒与皮肤擦挫形成棕红或棕橘色点状擦伤,被称为火药斑纹或火药颗粒(图6-7)。
  - 创周烟晕沉着与射击距离有关,但由于烟晕密度相对较低,随着枪口到皮肤

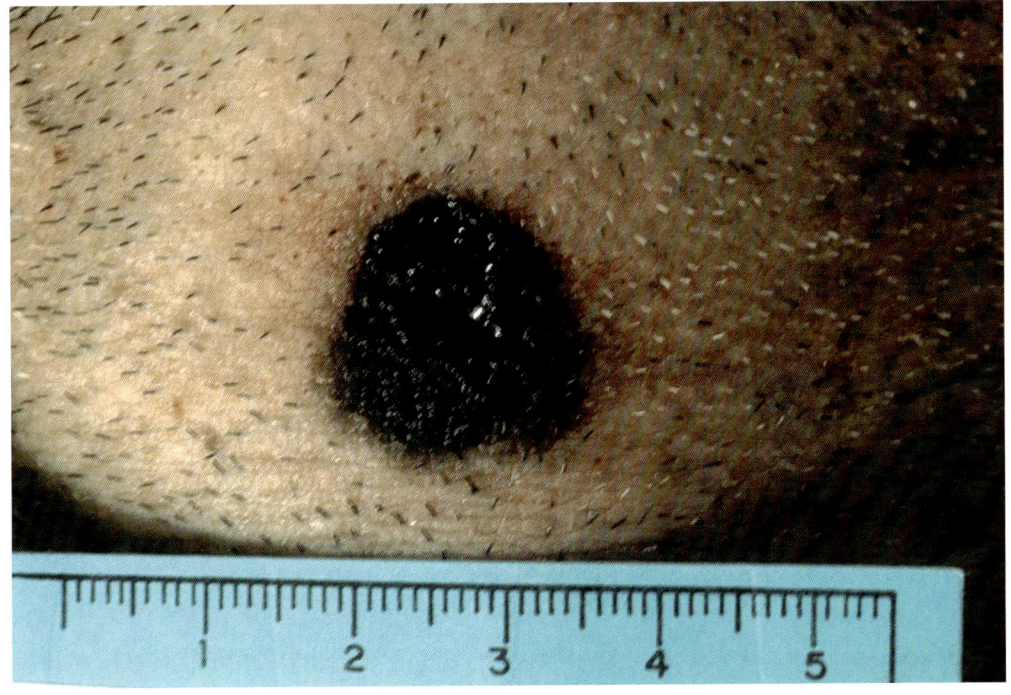

图6-6 下颌半接触或轻微接触枪弹创,创周烟晕沉积。

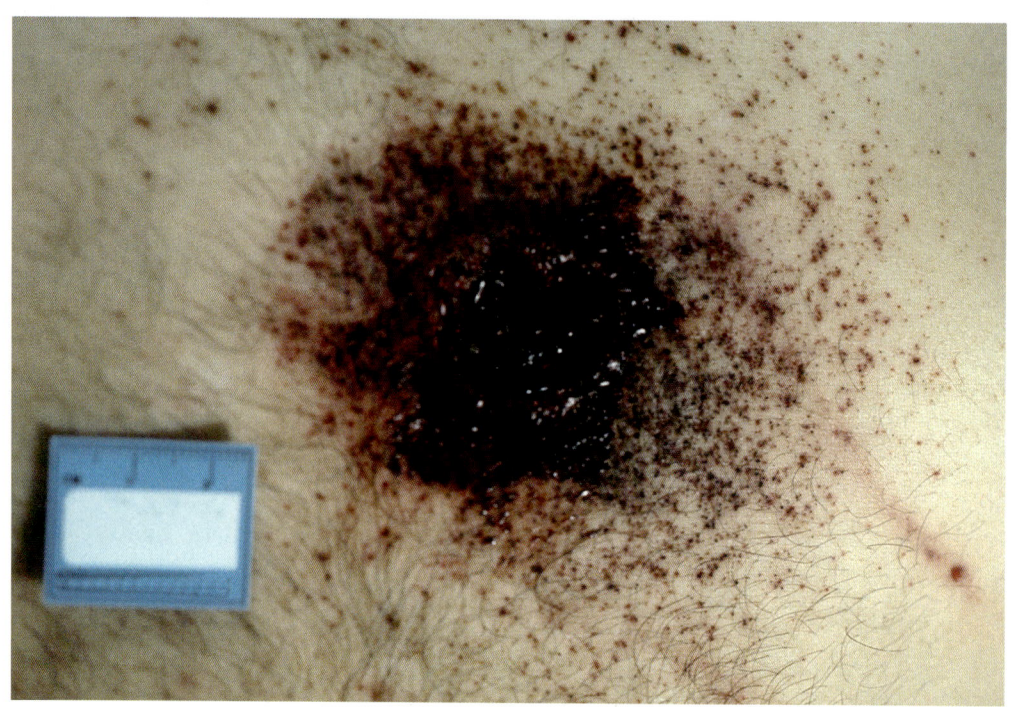

图6-7 中距离霰弹枪创。火药颗粒。

的距离增加,烟晕的浓度逐渐降低。
- 远距离射入口
  ○ 枪口距离皮肤表面距离较远时,不会有烟晕沉着或火药斑纹形成。
  ○ 擦拭轮明显(图6-8)。

霰弹枪的损伤形态特征是由中远距离射击时弹丸分散形成的(16,124)。当中距离射击时,少量弹丸从主弹柱中分离并在中心射入口周围呈扇形分布,形成在密集弹丸产生的主创口周围的,一些由散布的弹丸造成的小孔状射入口。远距离射击会使弹丸完全分散。霰弹枪内的弹丸被包裹在毡制弹塞中或装在塑料弹壳中(图6-9;参考文献16,124),毡制弹塞的直径与霰弹枪的膛径(规格)相同。近距离和中距离射击时弹塞可随弹丸一同射入人体。

大部分的枪创射入口都被擦拭轮围绕(高速步枪子弹和半被甲手枪子弹除外),擦拭轮由弹头进入机体时的机械性创伤造成(16,125)。由于皮肤收缩和变形,射入口的大小与弹头的口径之间并没有关联(125)。

8 枪弹创射出口

射出口比射入口大且形状不规则,反映出弹头在射出时翻滚、变形或破碎致更大的损伤(图6-10;参考文献16,125)。除有硬物衬垫以外,其他射出口都没有擦拭

第6章 | 穿透性损伤——近距离火器创

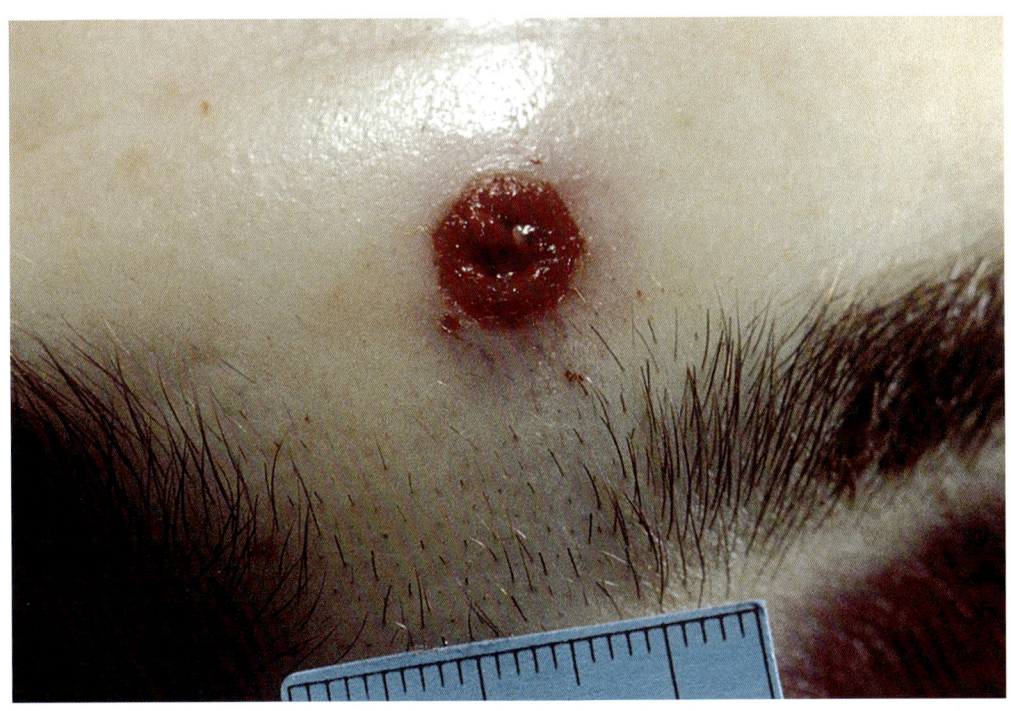

图 6-8 远距离枪弹创。同轴型擦拭轮提示子弹以垂直角度射入体内。

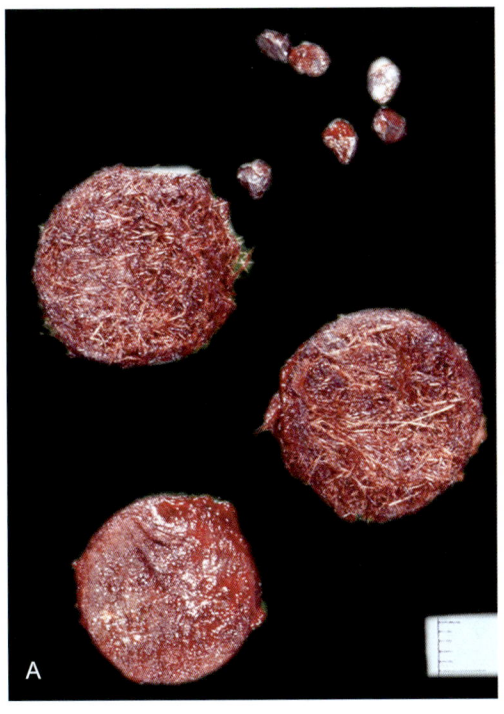
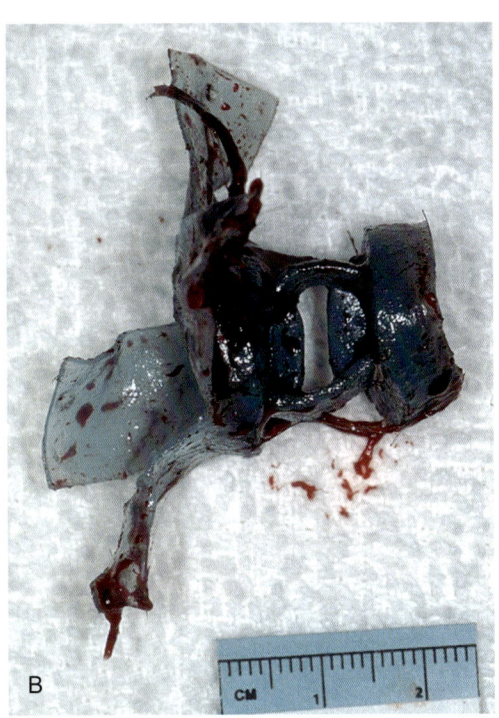

图 6-9 尸体解剖发现的各种霰弹枪弹塞。（A）毡制弹塞和铅弹；（B）变形的塑料弹壳。

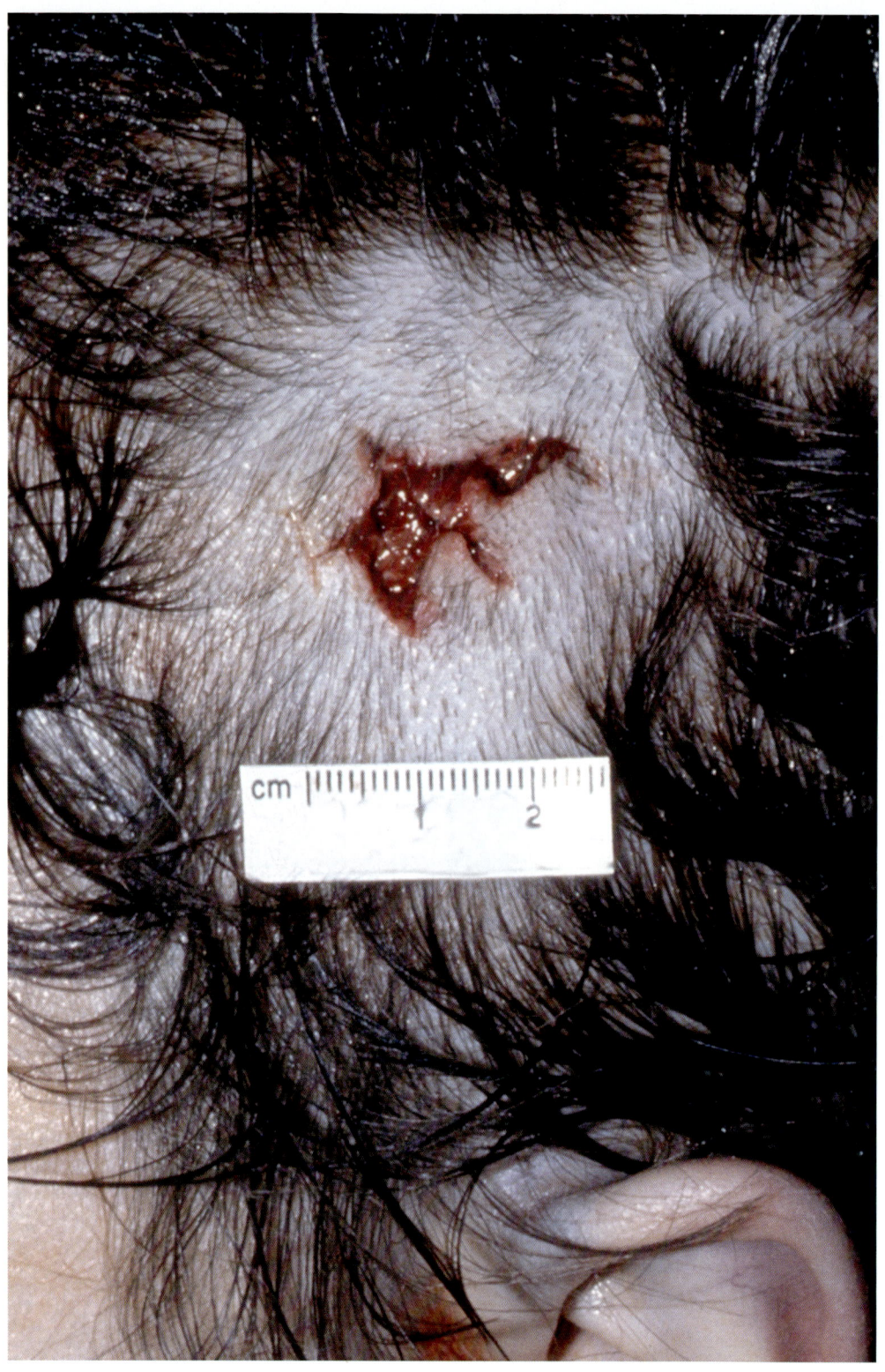

图 6-10 典型的不规则枪弹创射出口,左颞部(创周头发已剃除)。

轮。如果皮肤外有硬物（如墙、椅子；图6-11和参考文献16, 126, 127）衬垫，在射出口位置可有不规则擦伤。射出口创缘皮肤常向外翻。皮肤的弹性可阻抗弹头射出（参阅标题16；图6-12）。对于头部接触性霰弹枪弹创，大部分弹头在射入口对侧的躯体射出（124）。通过对自杀和他杀案件中不同口径枪械造成的头部枪弹创进行回顾，近一半的自杀者中有射出口，而他杀案件中大约有20%存在射出口（16）。

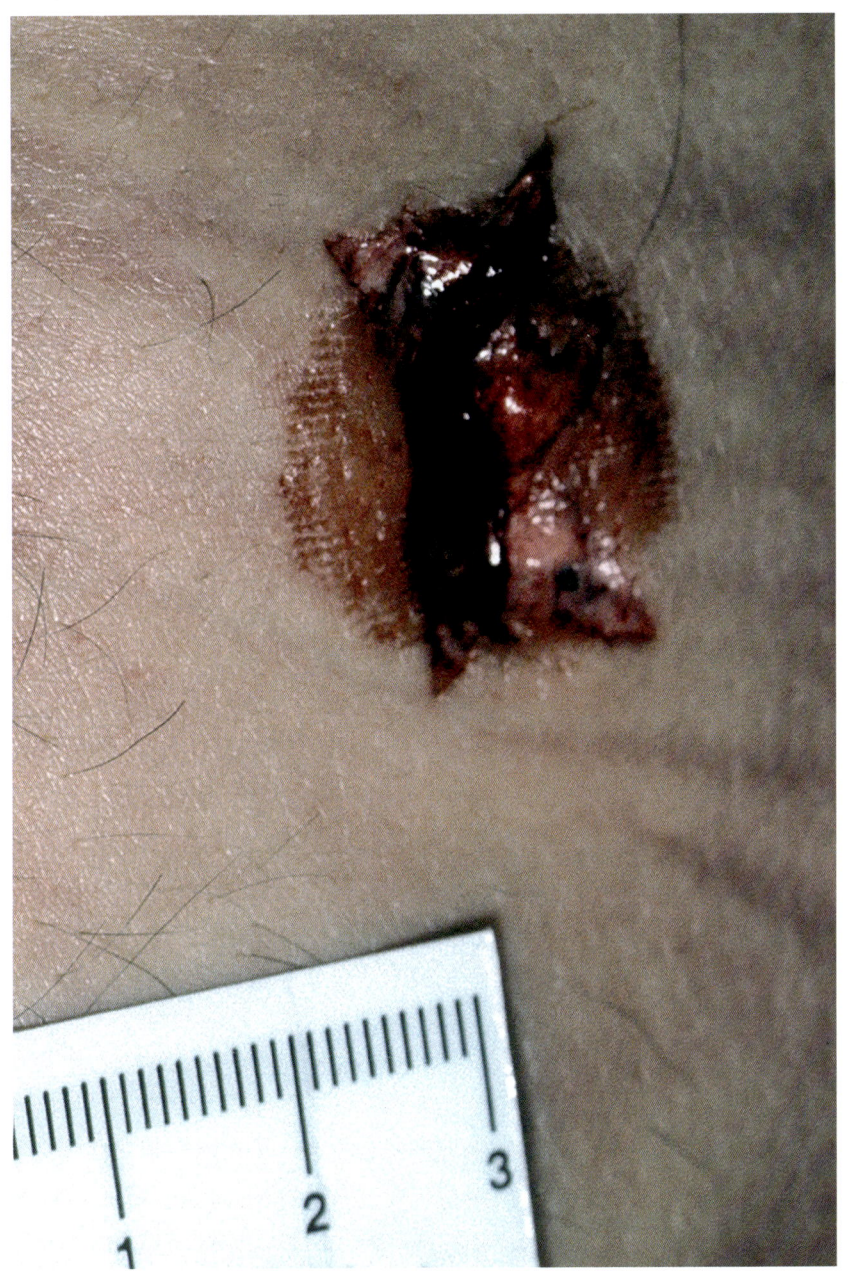

图6-11 背部有衬垫的射出口。胸部自伤性霰弹枪弹创（带有来复线的单丸猎枪弹）。死者背部有汽车座椅支撑。

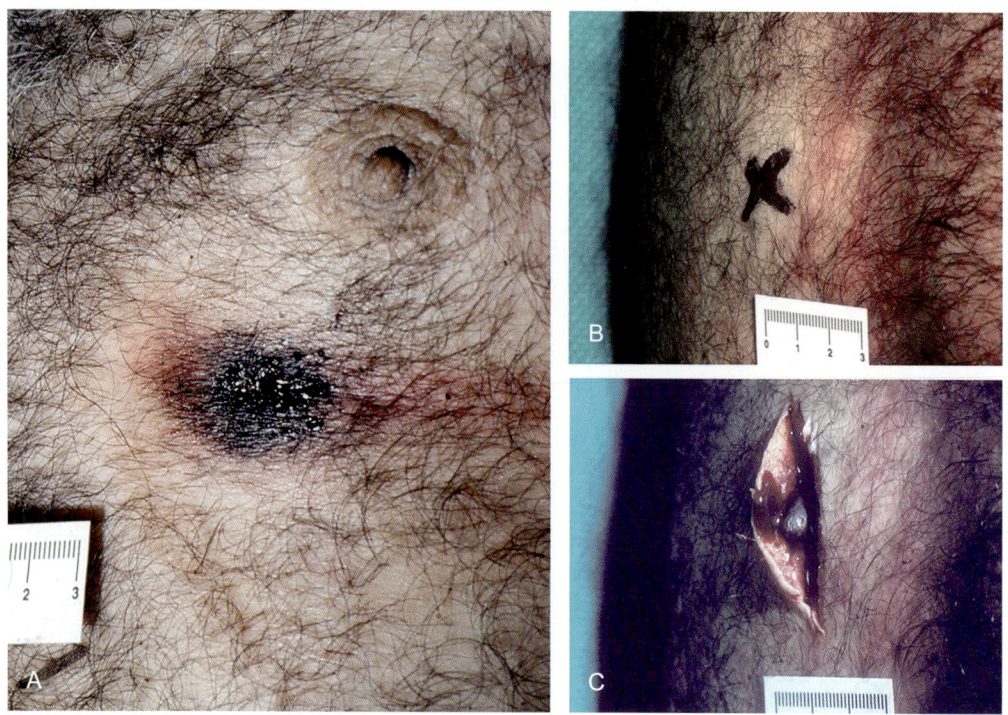

图6-12 皮肤阻抗致子弹停留在人体内部。(A)胸部接触枪弹创。(B)背部皮肤下可触及子弹(用墨汁标记"X")。(C)切开皮肤暴露子弹。

9 自杀案件射击距离

有接触射入口通常更支持自杀的推断(37,49,55,63)。大部分多处自伤性火器损伤表现为接触性的(22,51,55,57,67,96,101,109,111,117,120,128,129)。枪口到靶面的其他射击距离也可能存在(16,128,130)。据达拉斯的研究记载,在199起自杀案件中,头部的单个枪弹创全部是接触射入口,而在119起他杀案件中只有11起(10%)为接触射入口(63)。在1 200起枪械自杀案件的数据库中只发现2起是非接触射入口。据新墨西哥州－南卡罗来纳州的一份研究表明,77例自杀枪弹创中,97%为接触射入口,3%为中距离射入口。他杀枪弹创中有10%为接触射入口。有研究显示,有四分之一的意外枪弹创为接触性的,其余四分之三属于中距离射击形成(图6-4;参考文献30)。德克萨斯州的枪弹创研究发现,97%为接触射入口,2%为中距离射入口,1%为接触或中距离射入口(32)。

接触枪弹创以在弹创外部或内部有烟晕沉着为特征(16,73,92,93)。在某些情况下烟晕可以很明显:火药未彻底燃烧;使用比枪械更小口径的子弹,导致大量未燃火药粉末残留;枪械不止一次地向同一入口射击(图6-13;参考文献69,131)。

血痂或皮肤的干燥、腐烂和炭化都可掩盖烟晕(图6-14),皮下出血也可导致创缘颜色加深。如果是长枪管的接触枪弹创也可没有烟晕:0.22英寸口径步枪可存在

第 6 章 | 穿透性损伤——近距离火器创

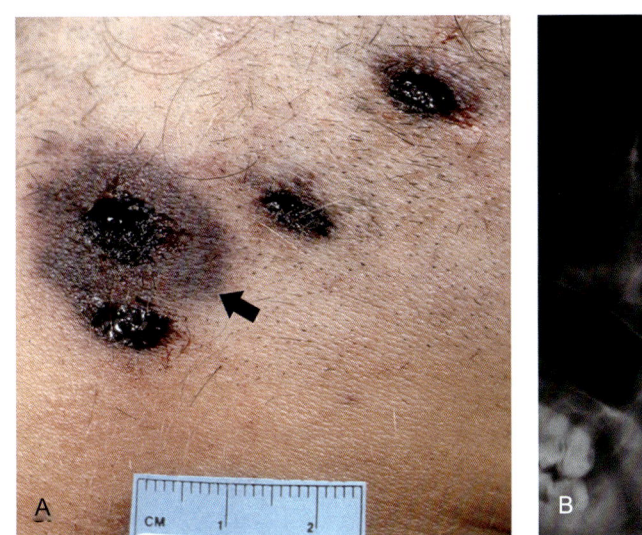
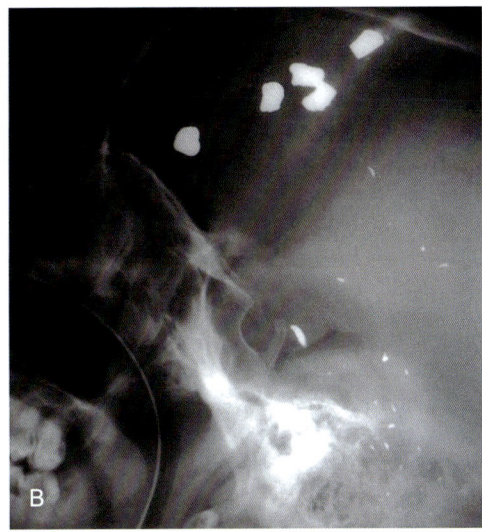

图 6-13 手枪从相同部位多次射击；他杀。（A）后颈 4 处硬接触枪弹创。射入口（箭头所示）显著的烟晕沉着和挫伤。（B）头部 X 线片：5 颗子弹。

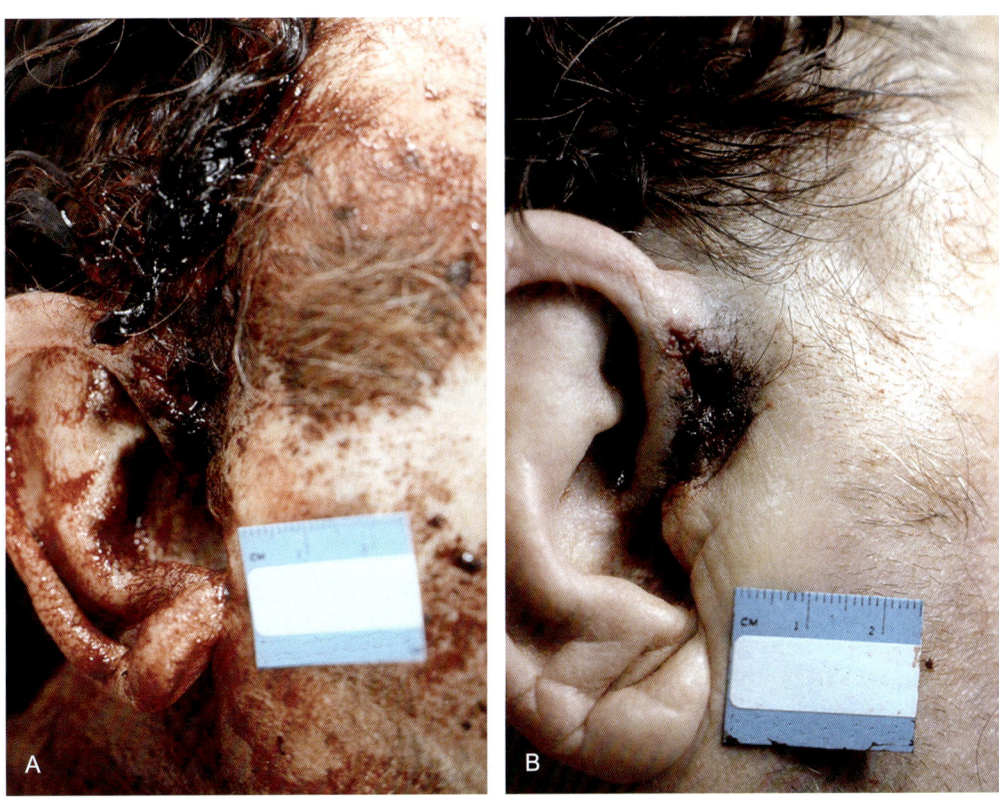

图 6-14 耳前硬接触枪弹创入口。（A）创口被血痂遮盖。（B）清洁后的创口。

没有烟晕的情况，因为少量火药在枪管中燃烧会更加彻底（参阅标题24；图6-15；参考文献16，132）。在某些情况下，枪弹创内会有异物出现［如特殊的雷瑟安全弹往往会留下蓝色的特氟龙颗粒印痕（119）］。

成角接触和半接触枪弹创会导致烟晕呈偏心性形态沉着。当枪口与体表成一定角度并接触时，火药颗粒沉积在射入口离枪口较远部位，该形态可提示子弹运行方向（图6-16）。当枪口与体表成一定角度但没有接触时，火药颗粒仅沉积在射入口离枪口较近部位，因为火药颗粒没有足够的浓度到达射入口离枪口较远部位，该形态也可指示弹头的来源方向（图6-17）。X线检查和创道分析有助于区分成角的接触枪弹创和半接触枪弹创（参阅标题16）。

0.22英寸口径缘发式步枪在前额、太阳穴和颈部位置形成接触性枪弹创时，约50%有"铅笔头"样黑变区和从射入口向下延伸的皮肤烧焦（图6-18）。这是由于枪口喷发的高温气体和烟晕灼烧皮肤，以及枪口下缘未接触皮肤（"不完全"接触）或

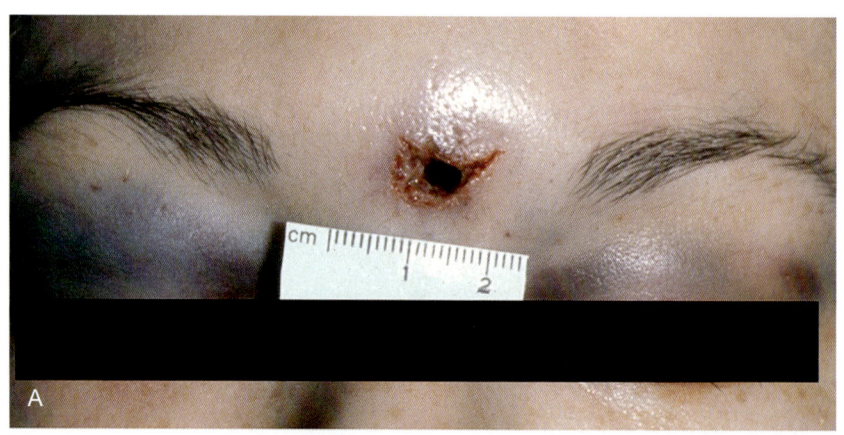

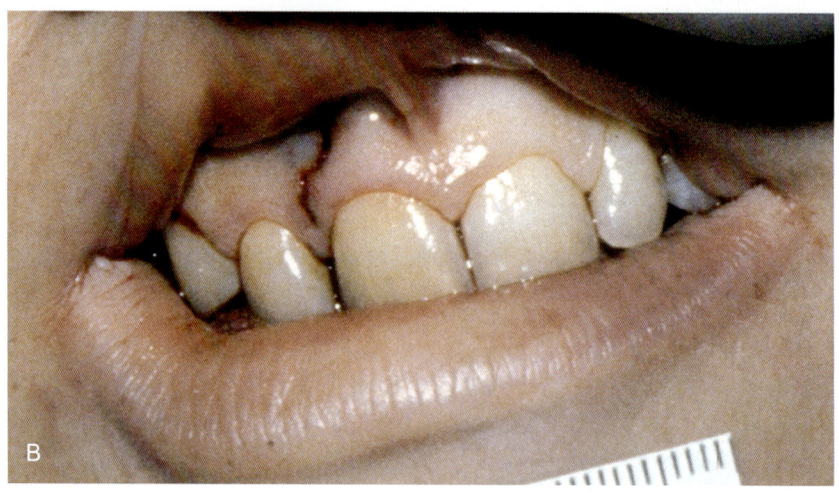

图6-15 他杀（22口径步枪）。（A）眉间（轻微撕裂）接触性枪弹创。创口见少量火药颗粒。（B）其他损伤。嘴被打后牙龈挫裂创（美国北卡罗来纳州教堂山市法医局供图）。

第6章｜穿透性损伤——近距离火器创　　323

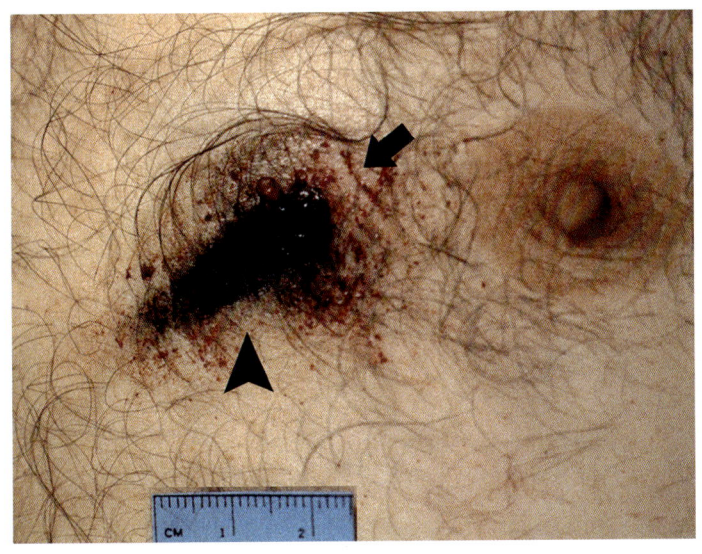

图6-16　左胸部成角接触枪弹创射入口（箭头）。烟晕（三角箭头）见于射入口内下方，提示子弹向右下方射入死者。

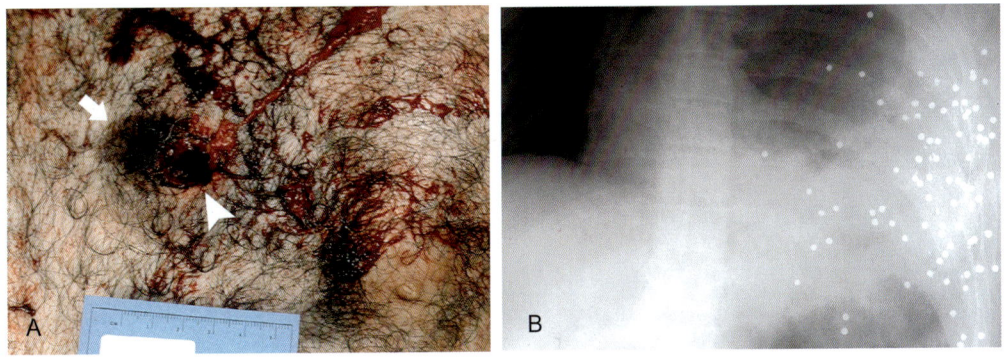

图6-17　左胸部成角接触枪弹创（射入口；三角箭头所示）。(A)烟晕（箭头所示）见于创口内侧，靠近成角的枪口。(B) X线片显示铅弹呈一侧分布，在死者身体左侧，即"撞球"效应。

重力导致枪口下滑所致（16，133，134）。

　　射入口附近皮肤可检见烟晕沉着和火药颗粒（弹膛间隙效应）（图6-19；参考文献16，119，135）。非常见武器（如螺栓枪、射钉枪）可形成气体出口烧伤（73）。如果枪械带有枪口制退器或排气口则可见均匀的烟晕沉着（86）。

　　"假性火药颗粒损伤"是由于弹膛和枪管不重合导致弹头碎裂，其细小的碎裂片可随弹头一起射入皮肤组织，在创口周围形成散在性点片状皮肤擦伤（16，58）。如果有物体置于枪口和皮肤之间也可使子弹碎裂形成假性火药损伤（136）。织物介入也会造成颗粒状皮肤损伤（参阅标题15；图6-20；参考文献16，59）。

　　远距离自杀性枪弹创较罕见（如枪械离身体的距离已接近手臂的长度或使用辅助装置）。

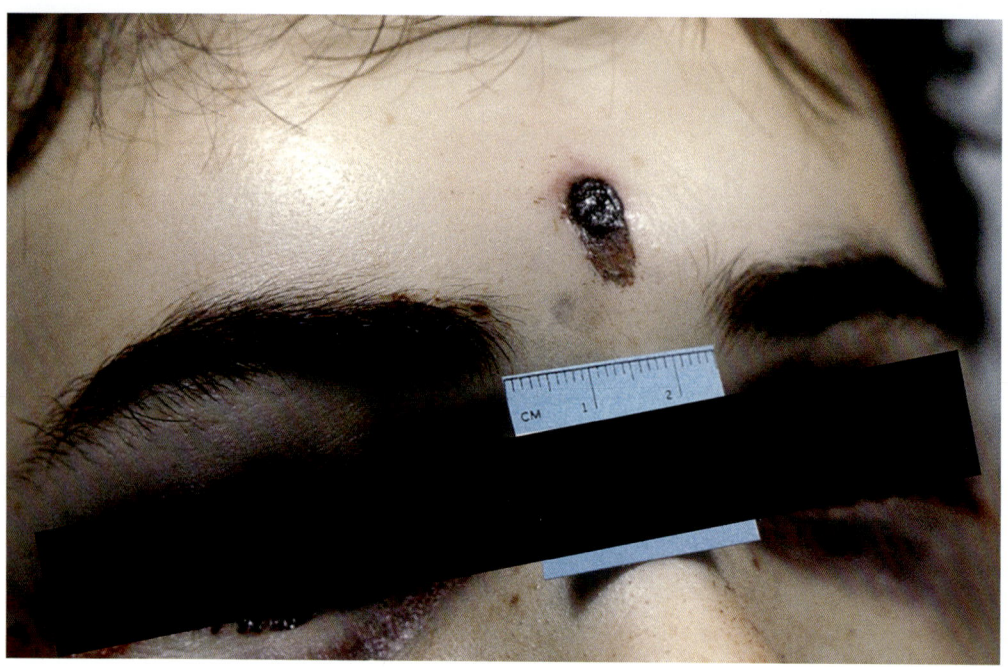

图 6-18 硬接触枪弹创射入口（0.22 英寸口径步枪）。从射入口向下延伸的"铅笔头"样灼烧区。

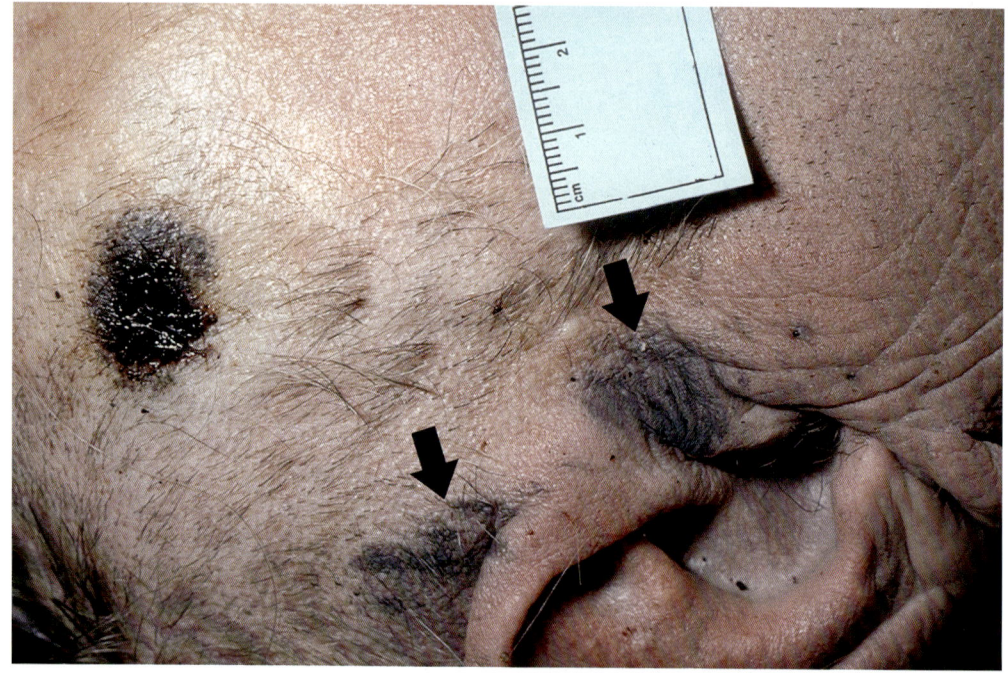

图 6-19 右侧太阳穴接触性枪弹创。注意耳前火药烟晕区域（箭头所示），由左轮手枪的旋转枪膛间隙所沉积。

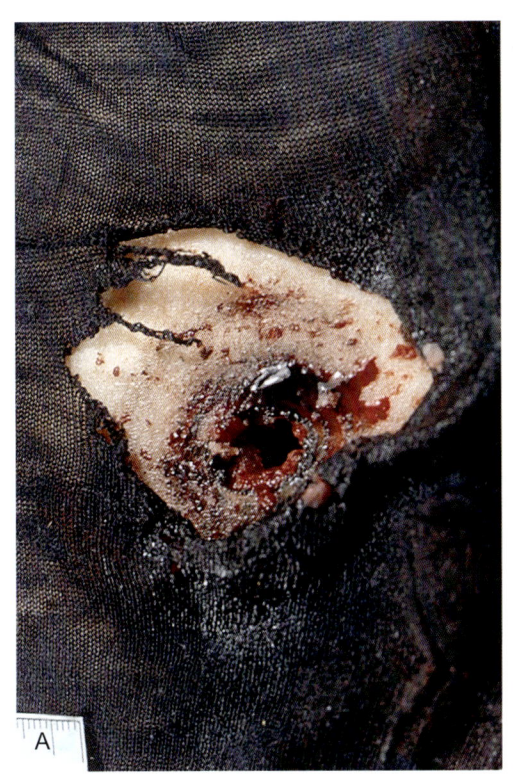 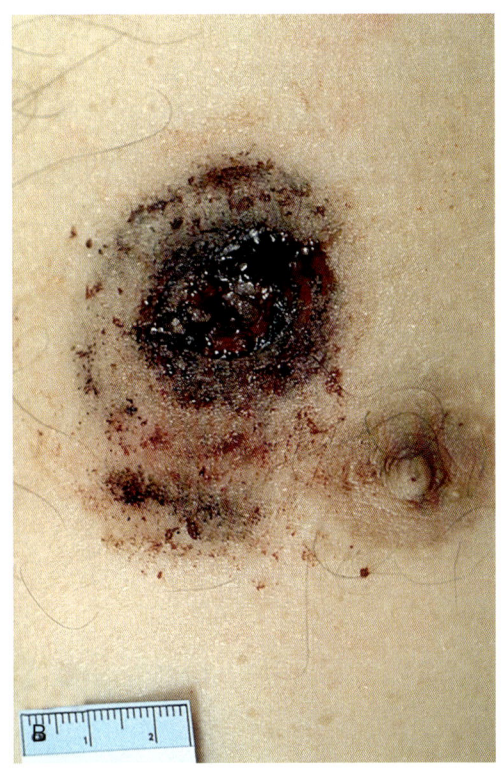

图 6-20 胸部接触枪弹创。衬衫充当了"中间"物。(A)深色衬衫和血痂遮盖烟晕。(B)去除衬衫及清洗创口后,可检见颗粒状的皮肤损伤。

10 自伤性火器伤的部位

自杀案件的枪弹创射入口位置具有特征性(37,59)。部位多为死者易接触处,如头部、胸部和腹部(20,35,59,102)。头部枪弹射入口的比例最高(18,19,21,23,33,34,49,59,63,66,95,98,102,117)。太阳穴部位(从右至左)是最常见的位置(21,46,50,51,66,101)。据德克萨斯州的自杀性枪伤研究发现枪弹创的分布存在差异:头部枪弹创占83.7%(右侧太阳穴51.5%;口腔20.6%;前额8.7%;左侧太阳穴6.3%;下颌部4.8%;枕部4%;颈部1.8%;眼部0.5%;其他1.8%);胸部占14%;腹部占1.9%;复合部位占0.4%(32)。Eisele等人研究枪弹创的位置分布如下:头部占74%(右颞部39%;左颞部5%;口腔9%;额中部8%;颏下3%;右顶部3%;头部左侧非特异部位2%;颏部、眼眶、前额其他部位、头部右侧非特异部位各1%;鼻部、枕部、左顶部各<1%);颈部占4%;胸部占18%;腹部占4%(98)。太阳穴部位的枪弹创倾向于自杀,但也不能排除他杀和意外。研究显示,47%自杀案件中的枪弹创位于太阳穴部位,他杀案件为18%,自杀案件为25%(30,37)。如果使用长管枪(步枪、霰弹枪),从口腔射入更常见。但土耳其的研究显示,涉及手枪案件的这类情况更为显著(32,34,35,37,49,137,138)。

使用步枪的案件中，枪弹创出现在颞顶部和太阳穴区域较普遍（98）。瑞士的研究显示，颈部射入口和长管枪存在一定关系（37）。新墨西哥州的系列研究表明，长管枪多见于面部损伤［面颊及颏下（139）］，颏部射入创更倾向于自伤（30）。

口腔内自伤性枪弹创的死者会有嘴唇、牙齿或舌头的烟晕沉着（图 6-21）。枪弹创可能不易被检见，特别是在尸僵形成后口腔难以打开的情况下（图 6-22；参考文献 137）。口腔内枪弹创往往由自杀所致，但他杀也有可能（30, 37, 137, 140, 141）。与他杀案件不同，自杀者口腔内的枪弹创易在舌头上检见烟晕沉着（图 6-23；参考文献 140）。

枕部枪弹创常出现在他杀案件，在自杀案件中较罕见（16, 142）。德克萨斯州的研究表明，10 例枕部枪弹创案件中 7 例为手枪、2 例为步枪、1 例为霰弹枪造成（32）。仅有 2.5% 自伤性枪弹创出现在项部，而他杀案件中有 14% 的枪弹创在项部（30）。

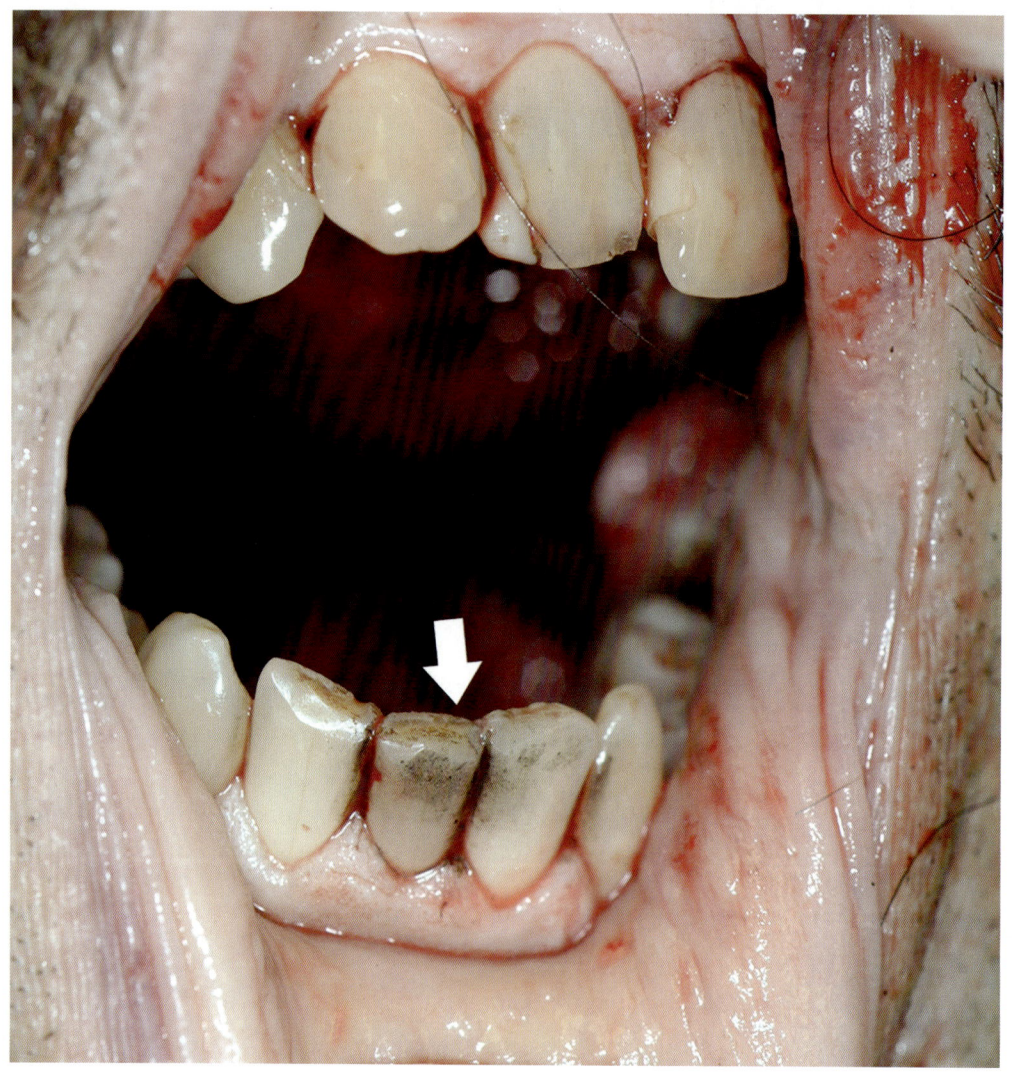

图 6-21　口腔内自伤性射击。下切牙上烟晕（箭头所示）。

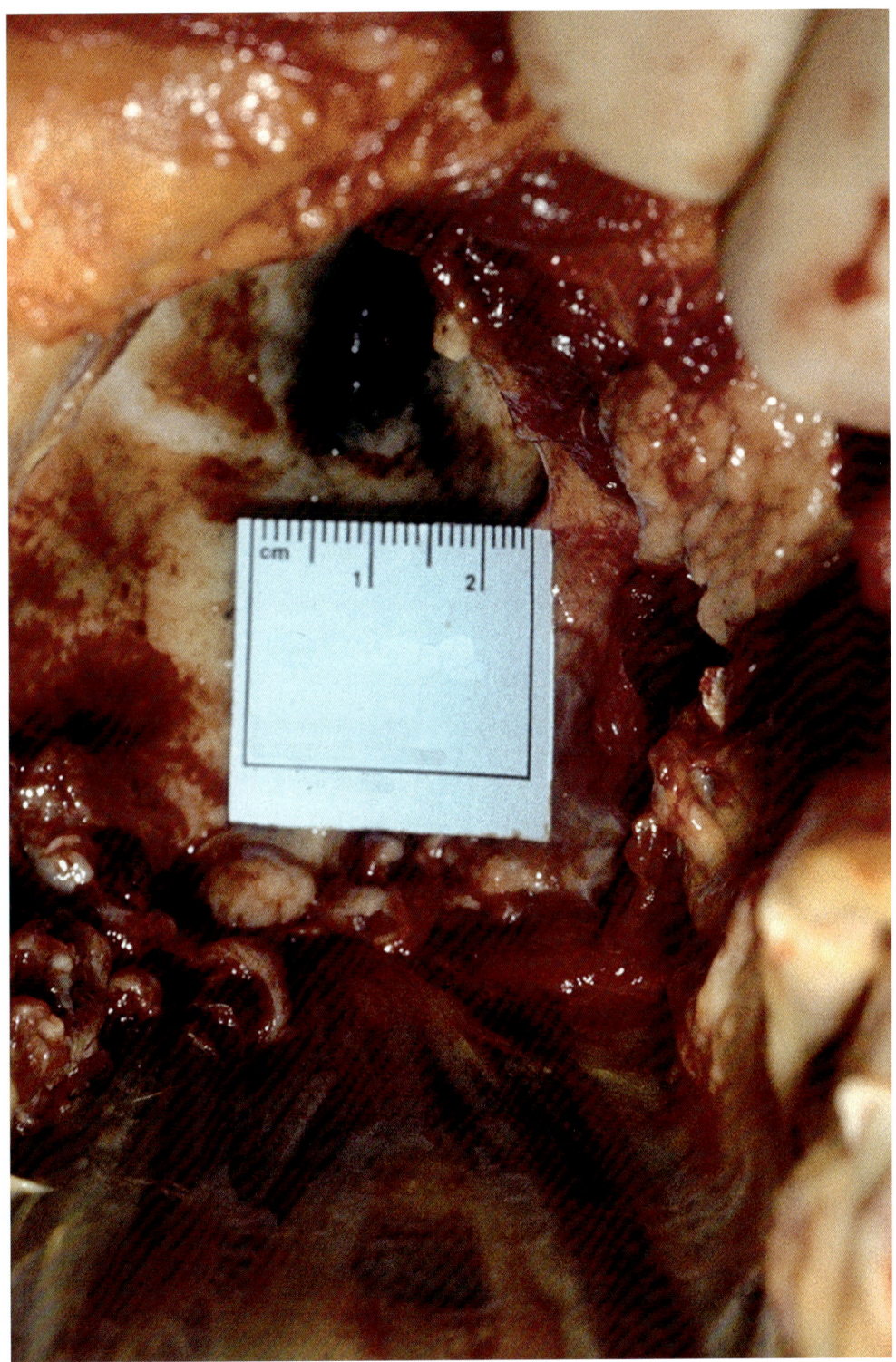

图 6-22 口腔（硬腭）接触枪弹创。由于尸僵致口腔紧闭，图为由下向上的内部观，舌及颈前软组织已去除。

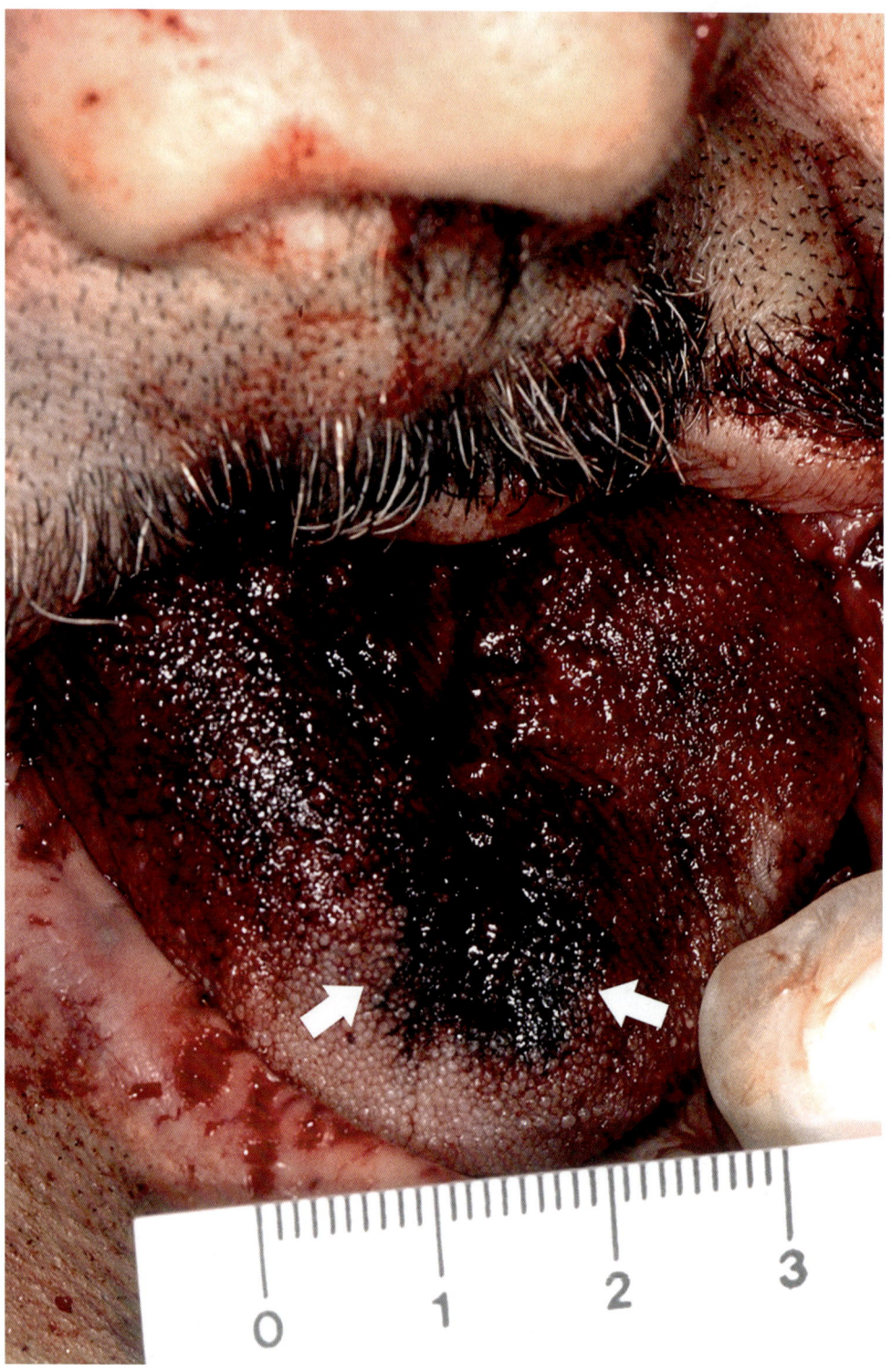

图 6-23 口腔内枪弹创,舌头上烟晕(箭头所示)。向后延伸的撕裂创。

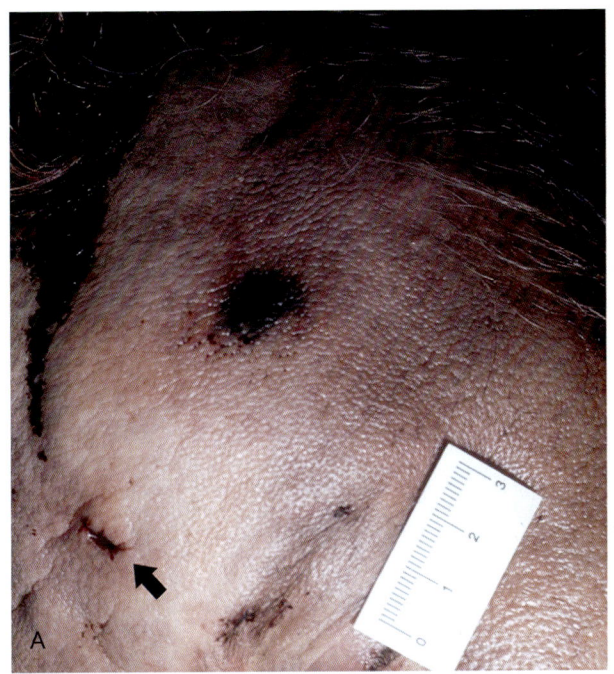 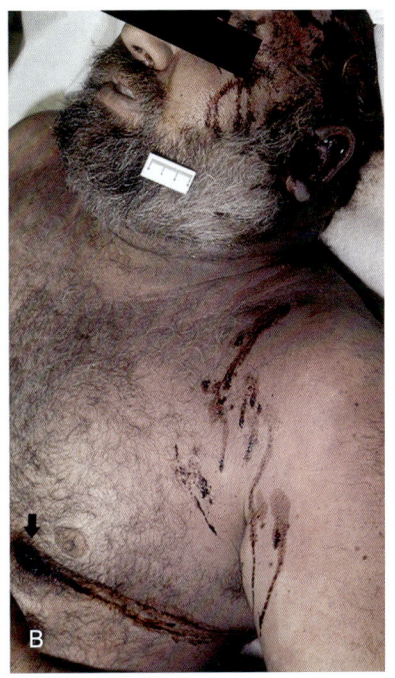

图6-24 多次枪击自杀（图6-51）。(A) 左前额接触枪弹创：弹道位于皮下且颅骨完整。射出口（箭头所示）。(B) 面部和肩部血迹说明死者直立姿势时头部受到非致命性枪击。从胸部创伤部位流向肩部的血迹说明死者在胸部致命性枪弹创（箭头所示）形成后改为仰卧姿势。

其他非常见的射入口部位(16)包括头顶、鼻、耳、眼、腹部和背部等(37,46,51,57,66,117,143)。直肠内的枪弹创应考虑性反常行为（参阅第3章标题2.7.2；参考文献56）。

胸部自伤性枪弹创多见于心前区，他杀案件中胸部损伤的分布范围更广(37,59,102)。

腹部自伤性枪弹创常见于上腹部(144)。

11 多次枪击自杀

多次枪击自杀需考虑他杀的可能性，尸体解剖是排除他杀的重要环节(22,55,57,59,60,67,72,109,111,128,129,145)。据北卡罗莱纳州的多次枪击自杀案件研究发现，58例多次枪击自杀案件中包括1.6%的火器自伤和0.7%制式枪支自杀死亡(67)。瑞士的研究发现多次枪击自杀案件仅占3%，而他杀案件的多次枪击占57%(37)。德国的研究显示5.6%的自杀案件中有不止一处枪击伤，而此类情况在他杀案件中占到了54%(51)。

多次枪击自杀案件的原因有多种：自杀者往往因解剖学知识匮乏而不了解人体致命部位（参阅标题14）；扣动扳机时自杀者畏惧；使用有缺陷、不恰当的或低速弹药，子弹仅贯穿体表（如皮肤）；某些类型的武器（16，22，33，46，55，57，59，67，109，111，117，146）。刮擦伤和浅表贯穿伤也常被检见。

多次枪击自杀的部位通常在心前区，或合并头部、腹部损伤（55，67，145）。带有弹夹的 0.22 英寸口径步枪在胸部可形成多达 14 个射入口（60）。在多次枪击自杀案件中，枪弹创均出现在头部的情况并不常见（图 6-25；参考文献 22，67，111，117，120，146）。0.32 英寸口径左轮手枪可造成多达 5 个枪击射入口（57）。同样

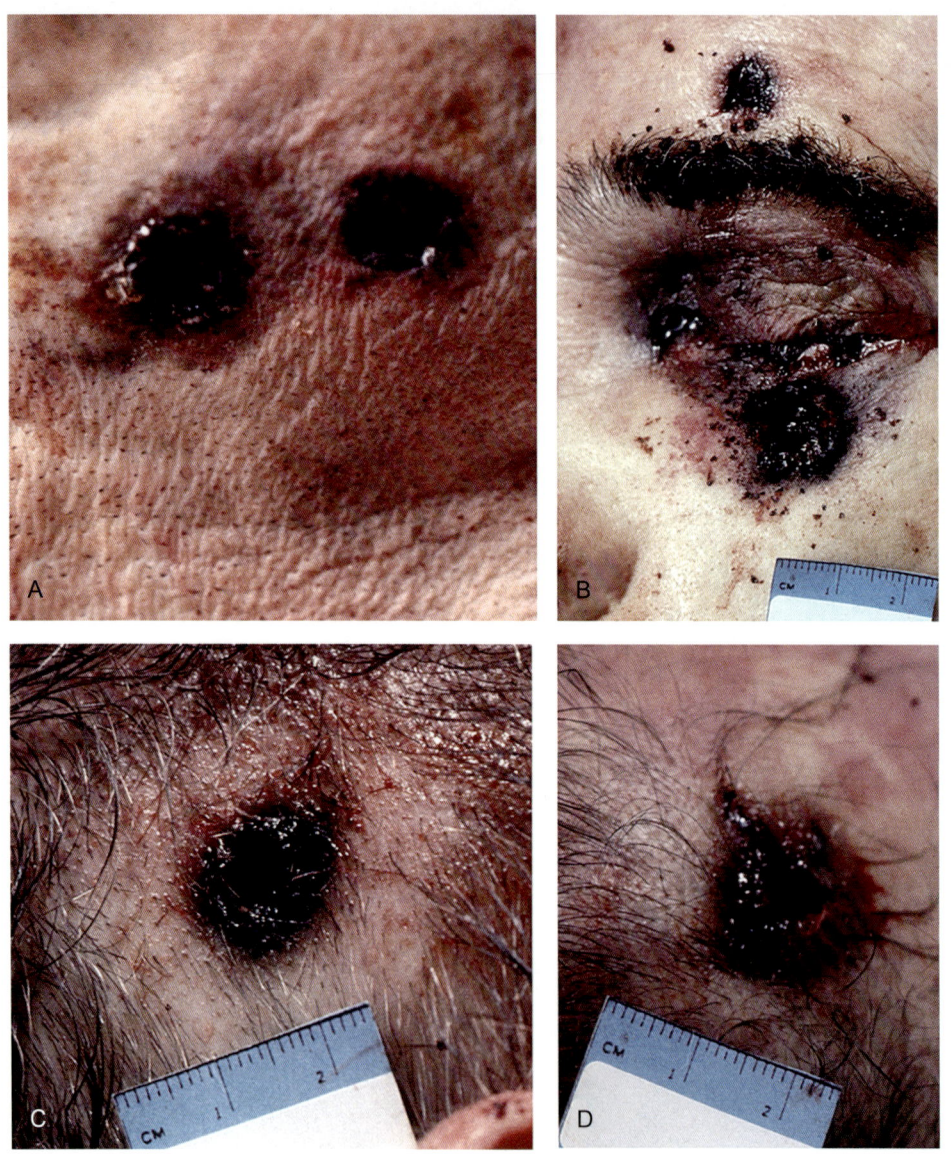

图 6-25 多次射击自杀，头部枪弹创。（A）颏下两处硬接触枪弹创。（B）创道从口腔和面颅中部贯穿，从眼眶上方和下方穿出。颅腔未穿透。（C）位于右耳上方的第三处硬接触枪弹创。（D）创道从右侧大脑贯穿并从左侧头皮射出（加拿大法医学会杂志社供图）。

也有报道称使用空包弹枪械在头部和颈部可形成 8 处创伤(73)。

多次枪击也可以使用不止一支枪械并同时射击(16,55,147,148)。在多次枪击自杀案件中也有口腔内枪弹创的记载(22)。

子弹先后从同一入口射入可能是由于子弹未引爆,未引爆可能因火药的污染或变质导致火药不足或残损所致(149,150)。也有研究报道从单一入口多次射击的案例(96,145)。

12 接触射击入射口的外部特征

在皮肤和软组织较薄且有骨衬垫的部位(如头部;图 6-14,图 6-15,图 6-26,图 6-27;参考文献 16),接触射击枪弹创可出现星芒状皮肤裂创。这和射出口的损伤形态相似。气体的反冲作用和能量的耗散导致骨组织表面的皮肤短时间抬升并裂开(16)。在高速损伤中,组织可从入口喷出,这会造成组织是从射出口被挤压出的假象(16,151)。如果皮下气体体积较大可形成严重撕裂创,如催泪瓦斯弹药筒、高速步枪、霰弹枪(16,93)。口腔高速射击枪弹创可与广泛性皮肤破裂和鼻部、眼部、口部周围撕裂有关(16)。口周"伸展"撕裂创受限于口腔射入口(图 6-28;参考文献 138)。大面积的撕裂创需要通过分析皮肤边缘来确定入口的位置(图 6-29;参考文献 16)。如果远距离击中骨质突出部位(如眉弓、颧骨、下颌骨),创口可能呈现星芒状。若弹头

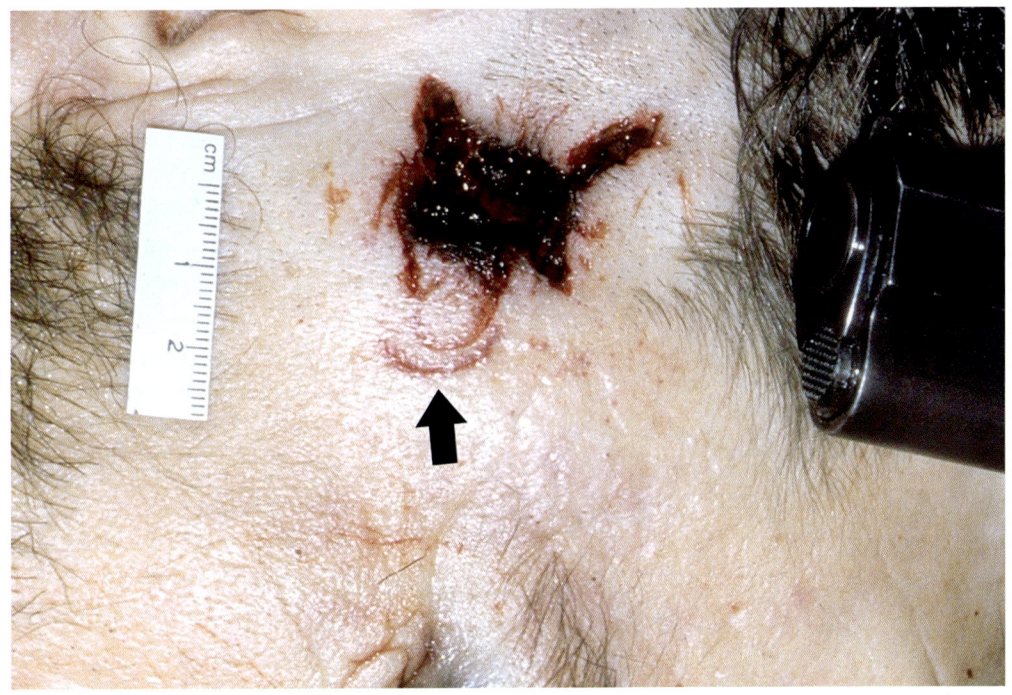

图 6-26 右侧太阳穴硬接触枪击创入口。皮肤表面未见烟晕,伤口边缘呈星状。枪口印痕(箭头)很明显(美国北卡罗来纳州教堂山市法医局供图)。

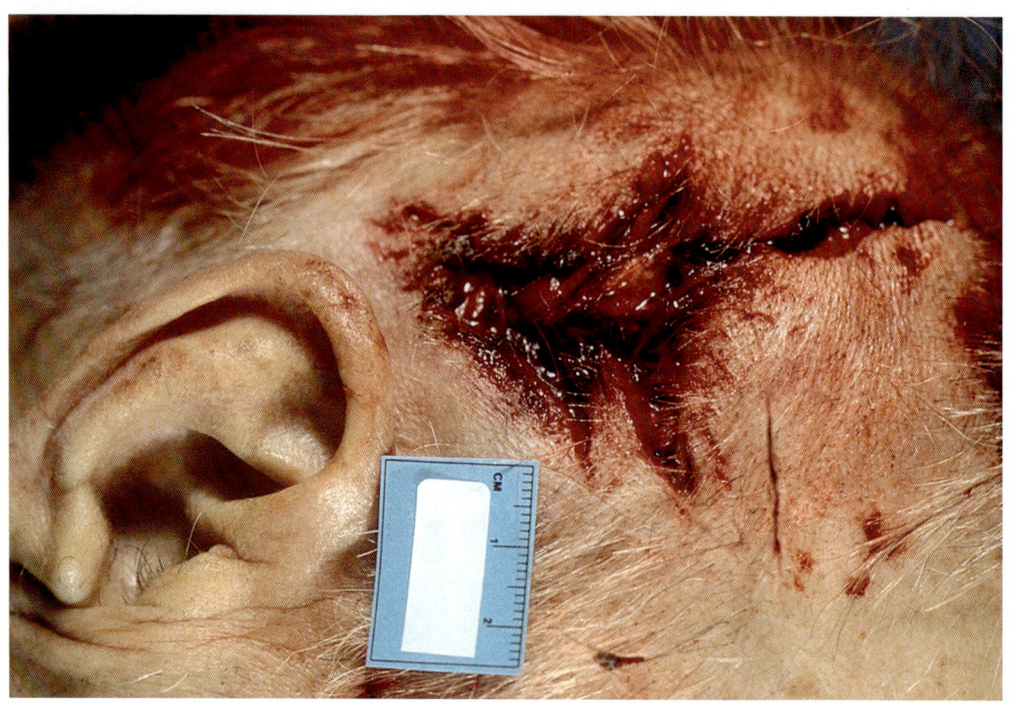

图 6-27 右侧太阳穴硬接触枪弹创射入口大范围的星芒状形态和不规则射出口较为相似。

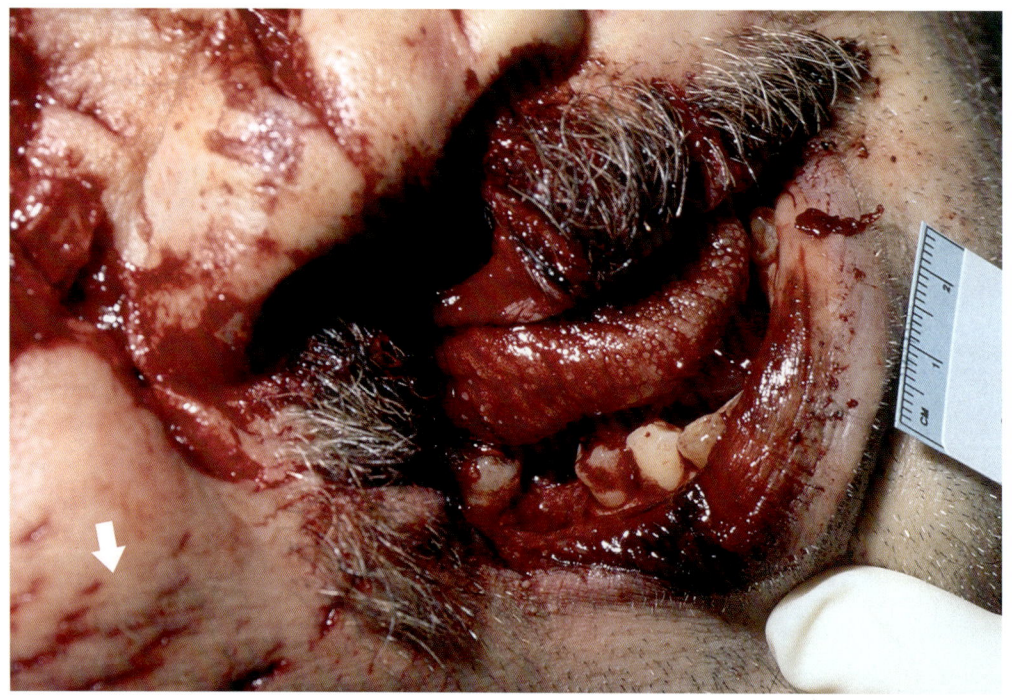

图 6-28 口腔霰弹枪创。口周撕裂创(箭头所示)。

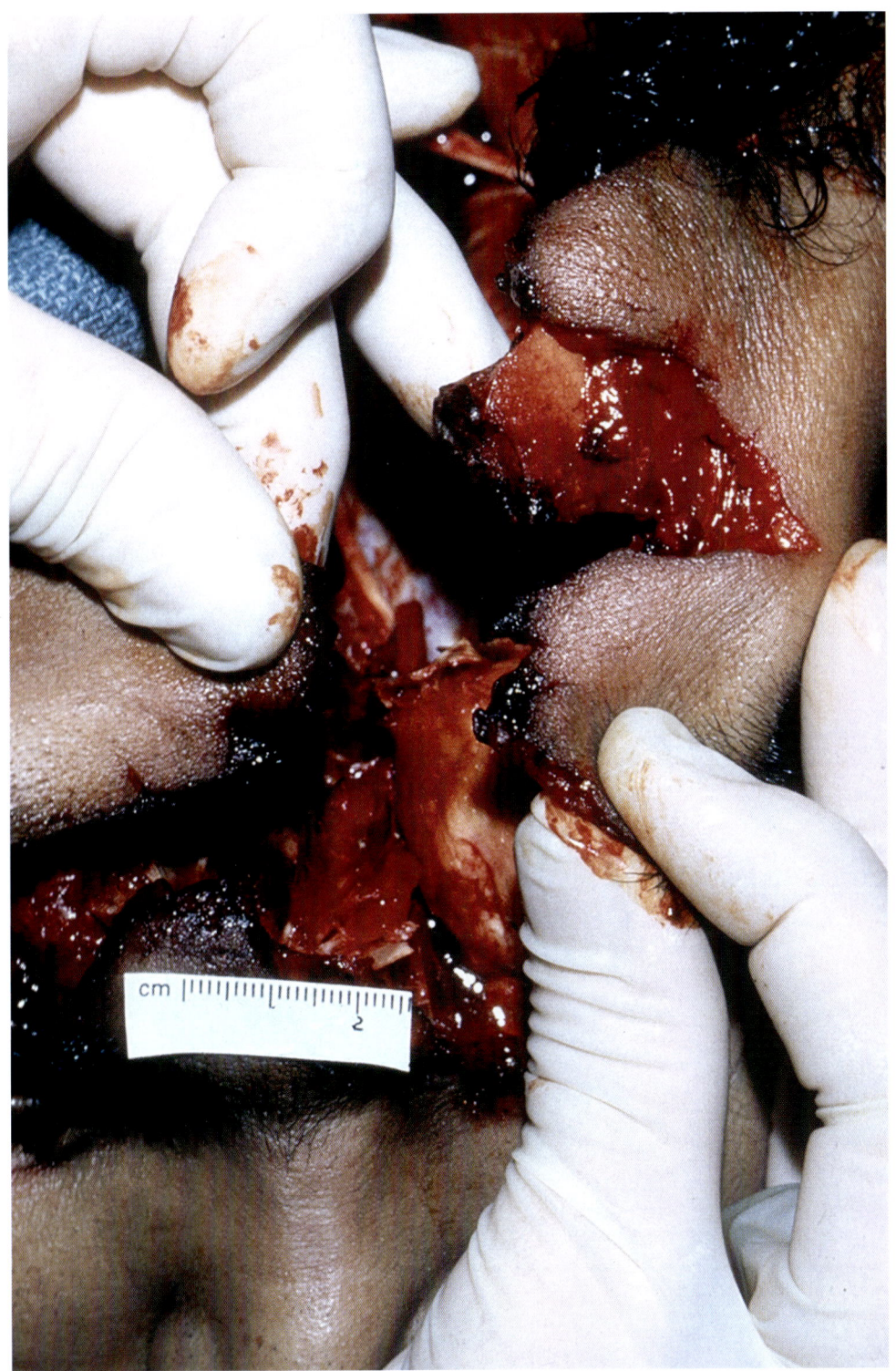

图 6-29 前额大口径子弹枪弹创,颅骨被广泛性破坏。对射入创进行还原(美国北卡罗来纳州教堂山市法医局供图)。

变形或翻滚,撕裂创则更严重。弹头从同一位置射入并射出会在一定程度上撕扯创口边缘[如38口径左轮手枪,从右侧太阳穴射入(153)]。某些类型的武器也可形成"不规则"射入口(119)。枪击后摔跌也会造成皮肤损伤[如面部擦伤(145)]。

枪口喷射的气体将皮肤向外冲起并紧贴于手枪、步枪或霰弹枪口形成枪口印痕(图6-26、图6-30;参考文献16)。此类损伤可考虑枪械造成,特别是在没有找到弹头的时候;然而,枪口印痕可大于枪口的实际大小(16,113)。枪口印痕也会由多

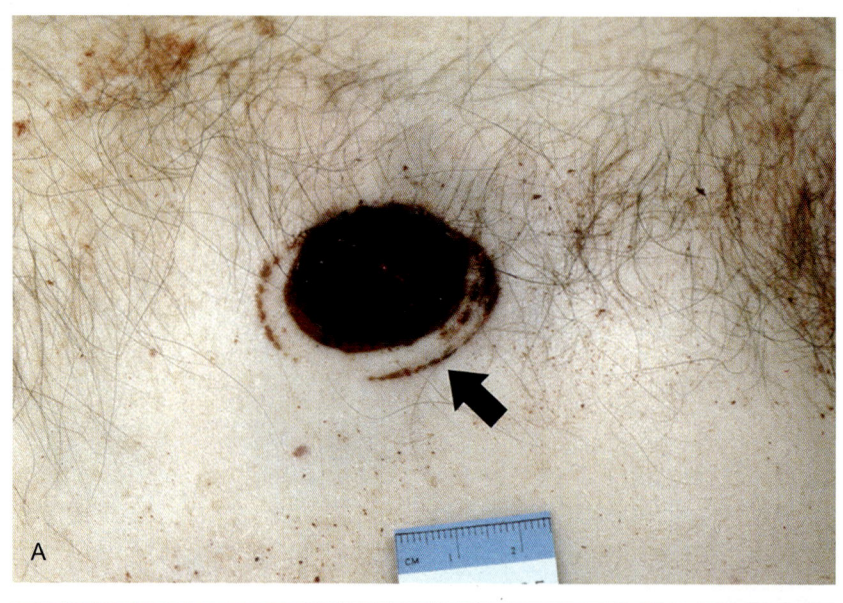

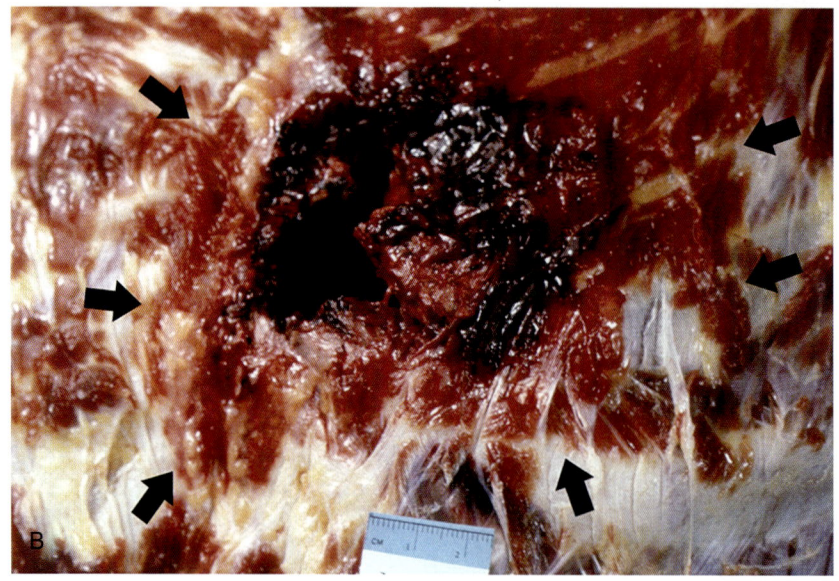

图6-30 胸部接触性霰弹枪射入口。(A)皮肤上火药烟晕并不明显,可见枪口印痕(箭头所示)。(B)胸壁射入口。鲜红色变(边缘被箭头标识)提示一氧化碳从枪口喷出。

第6章 | 穿透性损伤——近距离火器创　　335

次射击自杀所致(22,57,59,62)。空包弹、射钉枪或弹射杆也会检见不同的枪口印痕(73,85,92,107)。

13 火器自杀的手部检查

手部的某些特征为自杀推断提供证据,特别是对于多次射击的案件(55,154)。对于死亡存在疑点的案件,手部需用纸袋包裹以保护证据(图6-31；参考文献16)。如果使用塑料袋包裹,尸体冰冻时会产生凝结水汽(16)。作为尸检前的准备工作,指纹采集和手部清洗会破坏证据并影响证据收集(图6-32；参考文献16,154)。

手上的底漆残留物肉眼难以发现(参阅标题24；参考文献16,155)。因反冲作用("回溅作用"),在扣动扳机一侧的手背或用于固定枪口的另一侧手背可能发现血液和(或)组织(如头部枪弹创的脑组织)(参阅标题23；图6-33；参考文献16,111、154)。接触性枪弹创创周放射状皮肤撕裂与手部的回溅血迹没有必然联系。

如果用非射击手固定手枪、步枪或霰弹枪的枪口末端,并且枪口未与皮肤紧密接触,手掌大鱼际周围(即食指和拇指)可检见烟晕("枪口间隙效应"；图6-34—图6-36；参考文献16,55)。如果武器是左轮手枪,则烟晕可见于小鱼际周围,即小指和环指("旋转枪膛间隙效应"；图6-34)。如果使用的是高速射击武器,会形

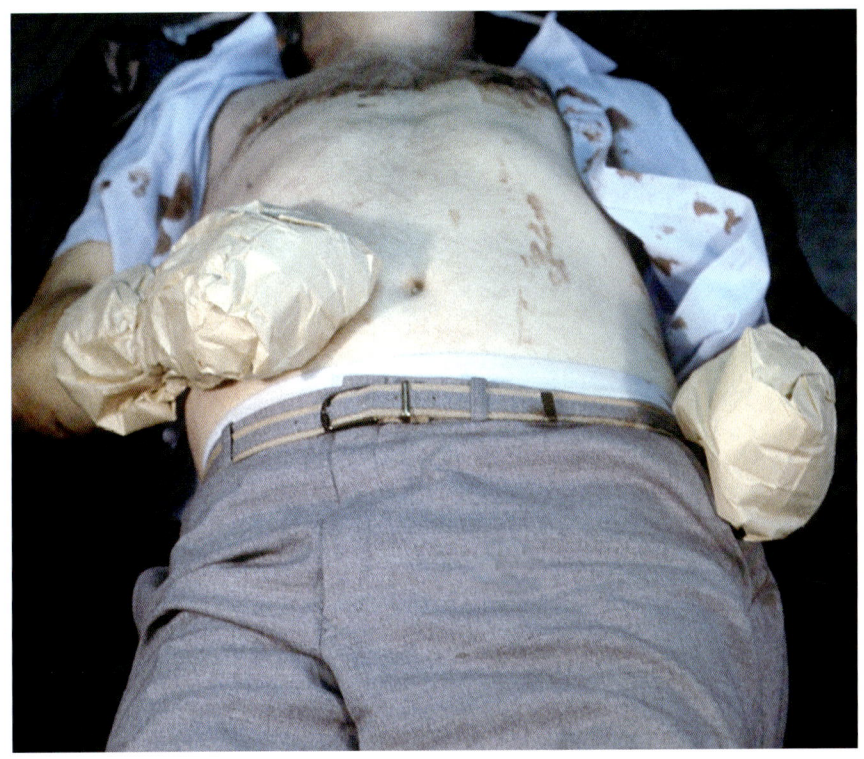

图6-31　自己造成的枪伤。手上包着纸袋以保存证据。

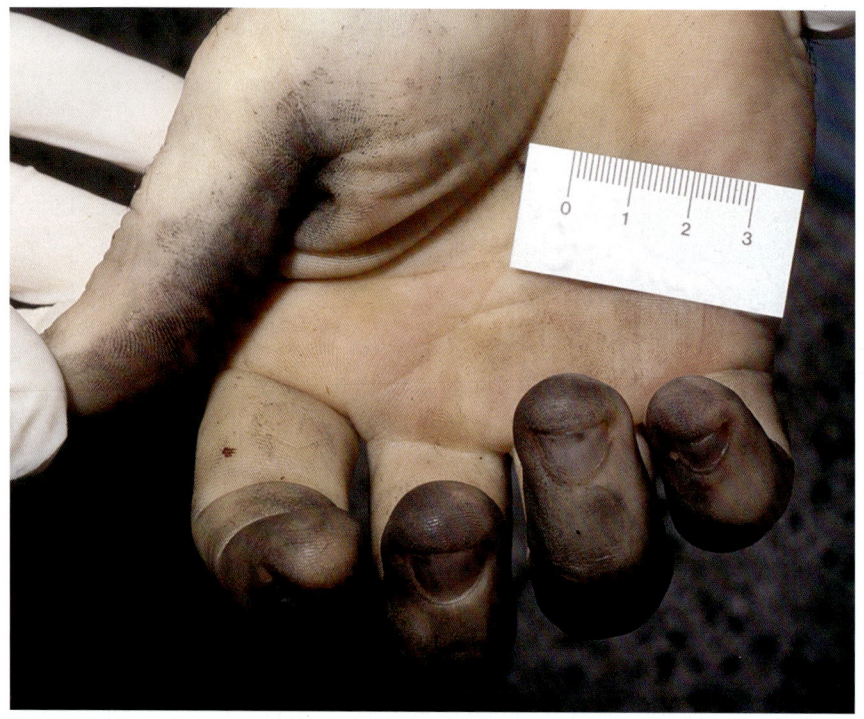

图 6-32 指纹采集与烟灰附着较为相似。

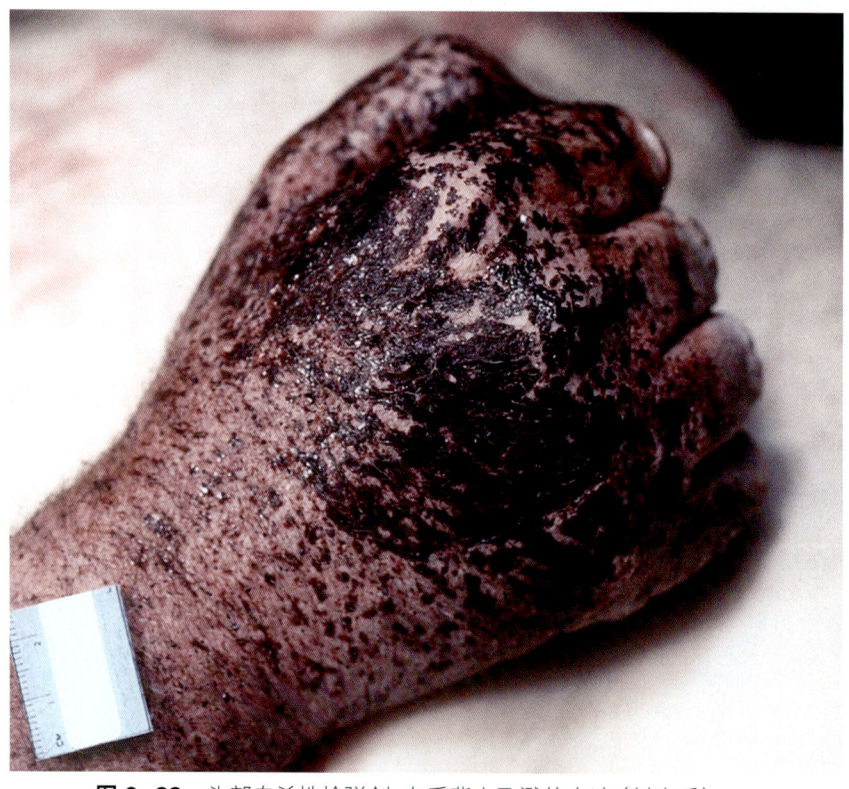

图 6-33 头部自杀性枪弹创,右手背上飞溅的血迹(射击手)。

成撕裂创（图6-34，图6-35）。握住武器的手掌面会出现黄褐色变，这种皮肤色变是潮湿和汗水作用产生"锈渍"的沾染（图6-37；参考文献16）。

手腕有条形切口皮肤瘢痕说明既往有自杀的企图（73）。

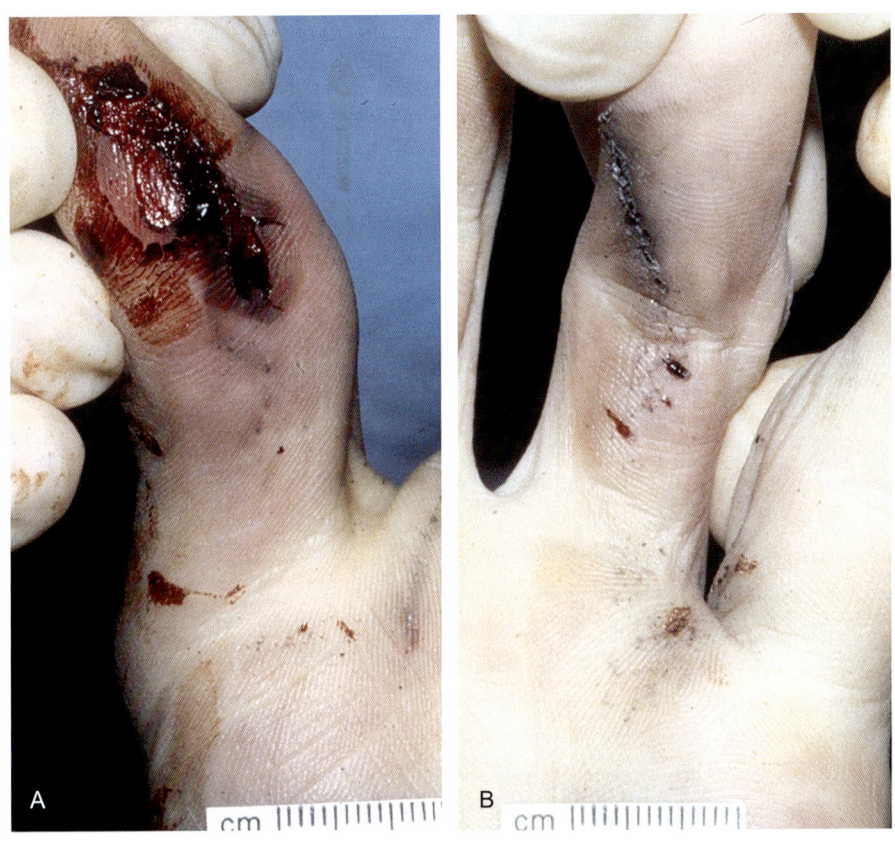

图6-34 大口径手枪头部接触性枪弹创。对固定枪口的手（非射击手）进行检查。（A）拇指创口周围火药烟晕（枪口空隙作用）。（B）环指创口周围火药烟晕（枪膛空隙作用）。

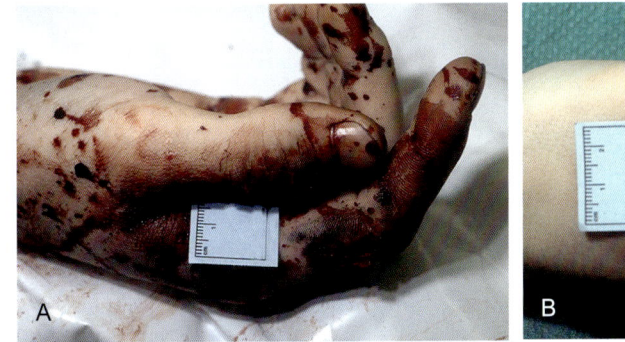 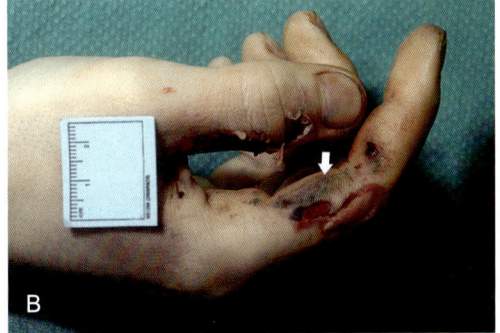

图6-35 头部接触性枪弹创。（A）固定枪口端手掌侧的飞溅血液。（B）手部清洁后可见火药烟晕（箭头）和裂创（枪口空隙作用）。

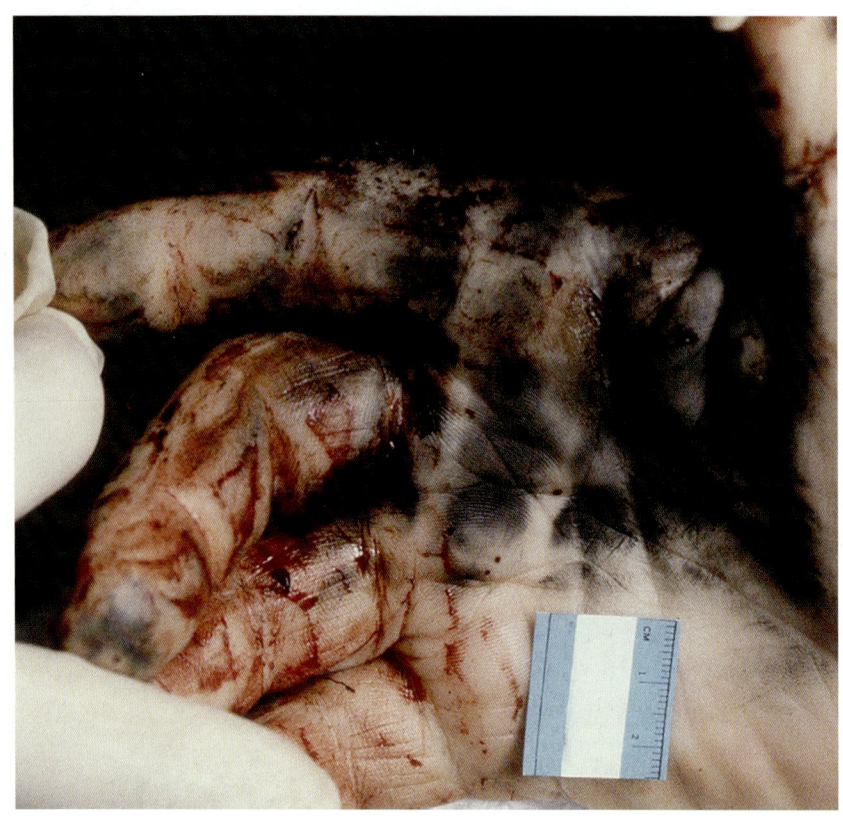

图 6-36 手握枪口末端时,火药烟晕沉积于手掌(枪口空隙作用)。

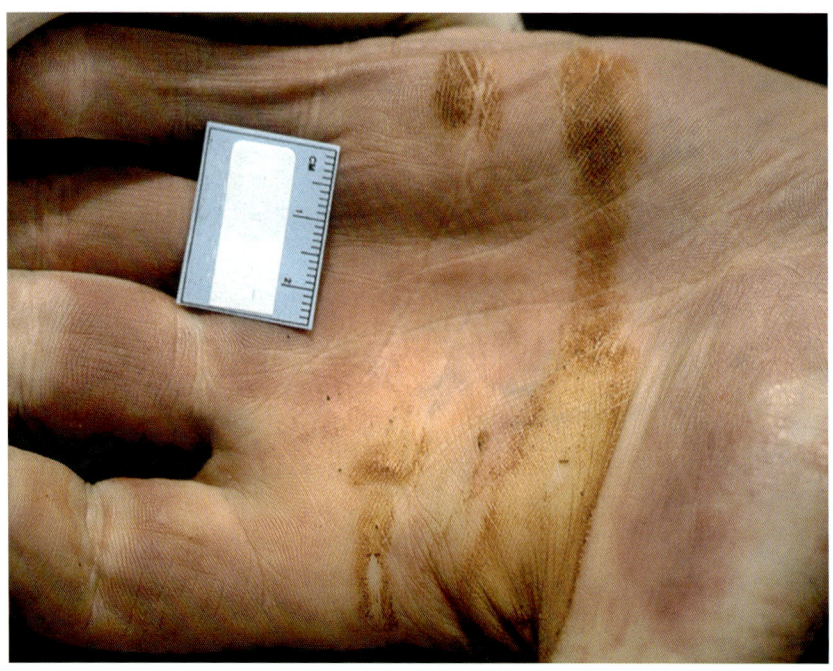

图 6-37 枪击自杀。手握步枪枪管时,潮湿手掌沾染的锈迹。

14 血迹的意义

手部回溅血迹有助于推断枪弹伤是否由自杀造成（参阅标题 13）。

血液垂直溅落在身体、衣物和相近环境，提示死者在枪弹伤形成时是直立姿势（坐姿或站姿）（图 6-24；参考文献 57，58，94，130）。如果血液轨迹是从创伤部位流向身体背侧，提示死者处于仰卧姿势（图 6-24；参考文献 106）。在多次射击的自杀案件中，血迹分布和范围有助于推断枪弹伤导致的人体活动能力丧失程度。例如：根据案件中对口腔内枪弹创的描述，死者身体前侧有大量血迹而肩部有少量血迹，说明口内创伤的作用比从太阳穴射入更持久（22）。多次枪击自杀案件中，死亡现场不同位置的血迹提示了枪弹伤致受害者活动能力丧失前的行为目的（参阅标题 18；图 6-3）。

15 衣着情况

自伤性火器伤的死者可以全身赤裸，或衣物敞开暴露射击部位，或射击后自己再穿上衣物或由他人穿上（55，59，73，105，112，117，158）。透过衣物的烟晕不能作为他杀的依据（158）。保存好死者的衣物对警方调查至关重要（16）。

衣物作为中间靶物会改变枪弹创的形态（参阅标题 9）。衣物或其他物体介于枪口和皮肤之间，烟晕会附着在衣物上，使得接触区域的损伤特征通常会改变（图 6-20；参考文献 16，55，59）。衣物充当中间靶物时所形成的损伤也会和接触枪弹创相似（图 6-38）。此时，衣物和任何介入物体的收集是必不可少的（159）。烟晕

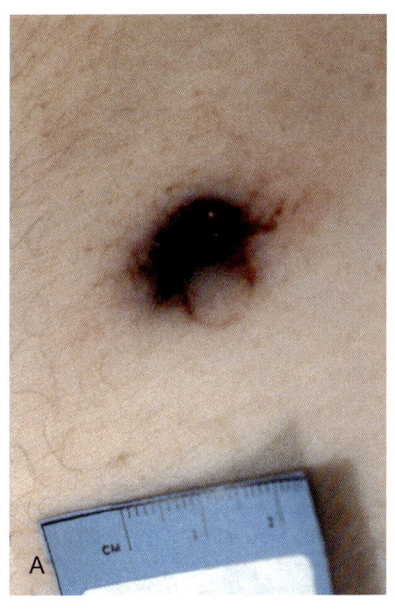 

图 6-38 他杀。躯干 3 处步枪创口。（A）射入口位于左下腹部。半圆形擦伤提示枪口印痕，说明罪犯在两次远距离射击后，最后一次近距离射击致受害人死亡。（B）对死者裤子检查发现，子弹击中裤腰附近的金属扣，纽扣发生了变形。

有时不会在损伤处检见(55),也可能被深色的衣物和血液掩盖(图6-20;参考文献103,160)。通常小口径武器会引起射入口少量血液流出。射入口周围的布料边缘会被烧焦(60)。

16 尸体影像学检查

影像学检查是火器损伤检查中必不可少的。正位和侧位X线片有助于推断体内弹头的位置、形态和运行轨迹(16)。如果弹头从躯体前侧射入并未从背侧射出,侧位X线片尤为重要。正位X线片可产生弹头在身体停留深度的误判,以至于法医需耗费大量时间寻找弹头。当侧位X线片提示弹头位于身体较后位置时,通过简单的触摸并在背部切开皮肤就能轻易地发现弹头(图6-12)。MRI和CT在火器损伤的评估上起到了更为重要的作用(161)。

创口会被血迹、浓密的头发、皮肤色素所掩盖,同时,腐败、临床治疗和昆虫或动物也会破坏损伤,通过对接触射击枪弹创或创周的铅进行检测,有助于区分射入口和射出口(160,162,163)。扫描电镜/X线能谱可以有效地检测出铅。枪击所致的颅骨损伤在外板会有铅残留(16)。铅不仅可以有效反映出创道通路,还可以探查出颅内跳弹的路径(参阅标题19.4;参考文献16)。

高速弹药碎片(如霰弹枪射击)会形成"暴风雪"样损伤(图6-39)。尽管部分夹克式中心点火的子弹金属碎片呈圆锥形分布,圆锥的顶部朝向射入口,但研究显示仅根据X线片中弹片呈"暴风雪"样分布难以预测弹头的行进方向(162)。

霰弹枪子弹内的弹塞通常为透射材料,除非有铅残留在这些纤维弹塞中(16,124)。铅弹散布("台球效应")在体内并不是远距离霰弹枪创伤的特有现象,在接触

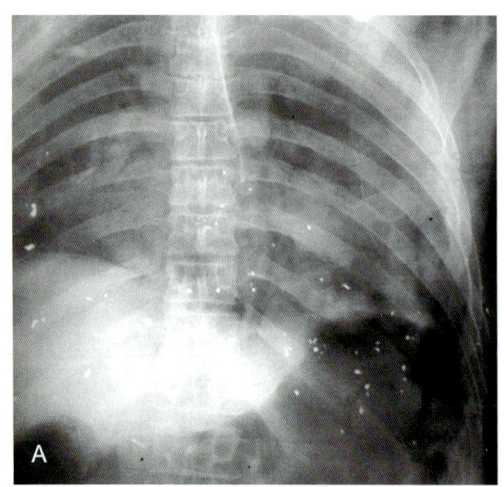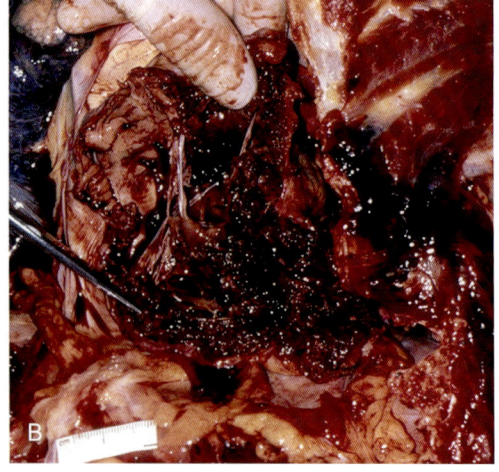

图6-39 高速猎枪他杀。(A)X线片显示子弹碎片形成的"暴风雪"样特征。(B)创道上的心脏严重破裂,这是由于子弹行进过程中产生的巨大瞬时空腔将就所致(美国北卡罗来纳州教堂山市法医局供图)。

第6章 | 穿透性损伤——近距离火器创

性枪弹创中也可检见(图6-17；参考文献16,124)。同样,铅弹在体内也可发生形变(164)。

X线片对外来异物和损伤形态有较好的反映(56),可显示某些类型子弹的损伤特点(119)。目前也有串联式投射物(22口径子弹和枪管清洁刷从步枪中射出)致伤的相关报道。射钉枪自杀案件中,可在创道内发现钢钉；相反,在被射钉反弹意外损伤的旁观者或使用者的体内可发现弯曲的钢钉(85,166-168)。如果钢钉射穿墙壁或在半空中发射,则旁观者受伤处的钢钉是直的。

体表未发现明显射出口时,须行影像学检查,射出口可以由破碎的弹片或碎骨片形成(16)。假如部分夹克式子弹的外壳和弹芯在体内发生分离,X线将有助于发现子弹的金属外壳,外壳能呈现出膛线条纹(参阅标题21；图6-40；参考文献16)。即使霰弹枪铅弹造成了大范围的颅脑损坏,X线检查仍可发现少量铅弹碎片残留(16)。贯穿枪伤中,X线检查可定位子弹的微小残留碎片。对这些碎片进行分析,并与可能使用的弹药进行比对(16)。如果子弹在X线片中不明显,而且皮肤上缺少射出口,则可能是射出口位置隐秘而被忽略或未被发现,也可能由于子弹为可透射线的材质(如塑料子弹),或是子弹进入血液循环形成栓塞(常为霰弹枪或小口径子弹),或是空包弹(16,73,92,93,169,170)。

提取脑组织后仍未发现子弹及其碎片,须对脑组织进行X线检查,以证实子弹的存在,子弹在颅脑内是可移动的(171,172)。

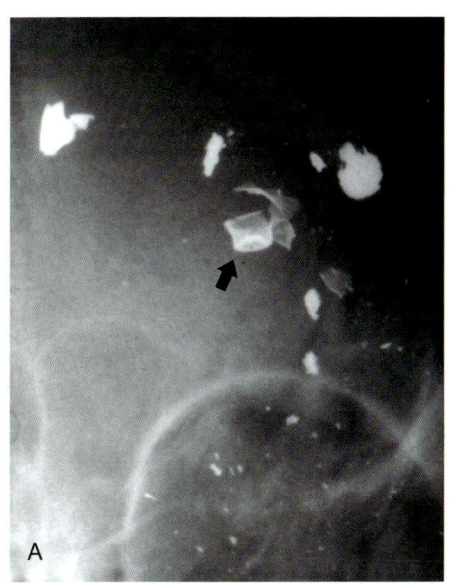 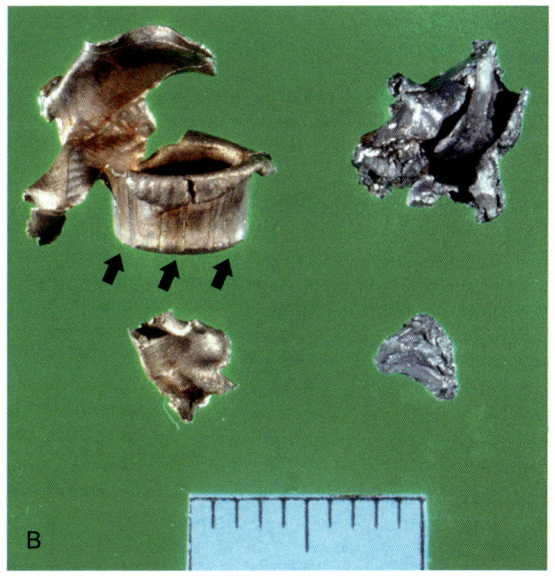

图6-40 头部接触射击所致的枪弹创。部分夹克式子弹。(A)弹头外壳(箭头所示)。X线片显示其与内芯分离。(B)提取的子弹。弹头外壳有显著的线性条纹(箭头所示),与膛线枪管内条纹一致。

17 医疗处理后射入创变化

如果射入创在医疗处理后发生变化,法医须从相关医生和护士处了解其具体的治疗方案,以获取更多信息(图6-41; 参考文献16,66,99,134)。在火器伤急救过程中,医生主要关注的是伤者的致命性损伤,治疗焦点在于内部器官的损伤。但对法医来讲,火器伤的体表检查极为重要,特别在伤者存活的情况下(173)。医生因为没有经过法医专业的培训和学习,难以对火器伤的特征进行专业性描述。由于抢救伤者时间紧急,医生完全有可能遗漏损伤或将射入创和射出创相混淆(16,99,132,174)。临床病

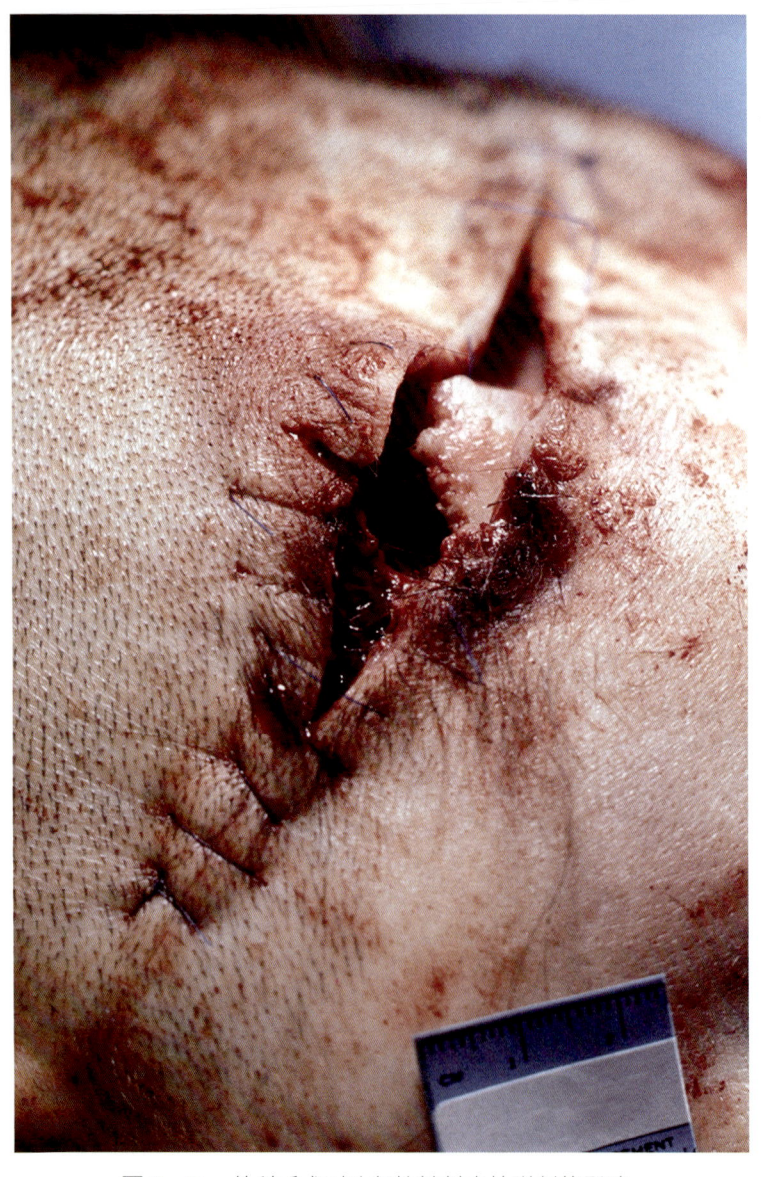

图6-41 外科手术对头部接触射击枪弹创的影响。

历记载的枪弹创可能有不同的描述,大小、形状、范围、位置、射击方向可能与实际情况均有差异(173,174)。伤者住院治疗期间,创伤也会受感染和治疗因素的影响而发生改变(16)。因此,在临床治疗过程中,枪弹创证据采集会受到极大的影响(174)。

法医需要对枪伤的创口和创道进行取样检查(175)。法医学实验室需要配备相应的检测系统以确保证据完整性,枪伤检材应由经验丰富的法医开展检验工作并拍照取证。警方应就案件涉及的样本及子弹进行质询,而向警方提供的证据需要伤者同意或法律授权,而且必须记录在案。

18 损伤的能量和致命性

子弹可以直接击碎组织(176)。当子弹穿过机体时,组织瞬间获得径向(大约10毫秒)加速(16,176)。"瞬时空腔"的最大径向取决于弹头所释放的能量和组织弹性程度(16,142,176—178)。弹头能量与其速度的平方成正比[$E = mv^2/2$,E 为弹头动能;m 为弹头质量,v 为弹头速度(16,176—178)]。民用猎枪弹头的速度在600—1 200米/秒(2 000—4 000英尺/秒),民用手枪弹头的速度低于300米/秒(1 000英尺/秒),22口径步枪速度在300—380米/秒[1 000—1 250英尺/秒(177)]。猎枪弹头会形成较大的瞬时空腔(图6-39;参考文献179),瞬时空腔坍塌后形成"永久性创道",创道通常比弹头的直径宽(图6-42;参考文献16,177)。永久性创道的直径和形态未必与弹头口径有关(177)。低速枪支(如手枪)形成的永

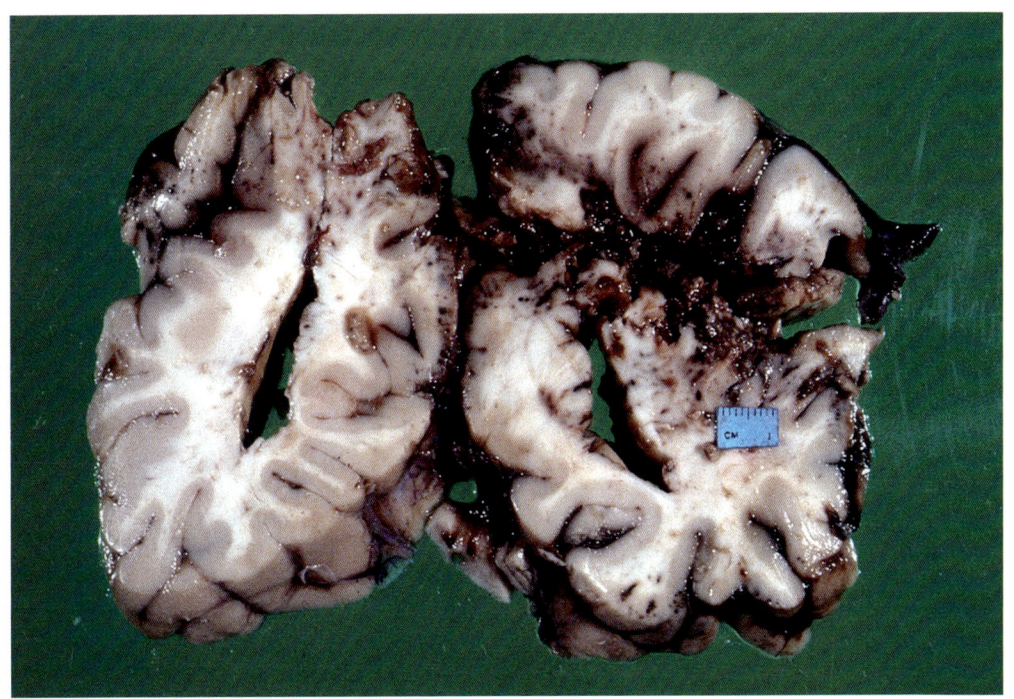

图6-42 自杀枪弹创。甲醛溶液固定大脑的冠状切片。低口径手枪造成的割伤痕迹。

久性创道直径常比弹头口径小,是由于人体组织的弹性导致了创道缩小。瞬时空腔和永久性创道的大小可能与组织特性有关。弹性较小的组织(如相对肌肉和皮肤而言的脑组织)产生大面积瞬时空腔后,会形成一个更宽的永久性创道(16,176)。弹头在体内可发生形变,偏离原来轨道,致其能量扩散至更远的部位(16,176),这可导致创道出现不规则形态(177)。弹片与骨组织接触后使其破碎程度更加严重(176)。由于射入口骨折碎片可导致组织撕裂,因此创道靠近射入口的一端较宽。如果弹头出现翻滚,则创道靠近射出口处较宽(142)。

子弹往往破坏局部组织结构,即使低能量子弹也会对整个机体和微观结构产生更广泛的影响(16,177,180,181),如头部受到低速致命性枪弹伤,通常情况是在几秒到几分钟内呼吸、心搏停止(142,180,182)。脑部永久性创道周围2—4毫米内可以检见脑出血和坏死。脑出血和坏死区域可见神经元深染固缩,免疫组织化学染色显示星形胶质细胞蛋白及G型淀粉样前体蛋白缺失(161,183)。颅骨限制了瞬时空腔体积的增大,空腔内压力相对升高(129,176)。当子弹穿过大脑时,可以使远离创道的部位产生损伤,称为远达效应或远隔损伤。压痕(凹槽)可见于脑钩回和小脑扁桃体(177),压痕在枪弹创形成后的数分钟内便可被观察到,但压痕不一定是脑水肿所致(177)。脑挫伤可见于射入口附近(冲击伤)和对侧部位脑组织(对冲伤),包括射出口处(图6—43;参考文献177)。在额叶、颞叶和枕叶的底部可检见脑挫伤,类似于钝性损伤;小脑扁桃体与颅骨、小脑幕的接触部位可检见脑挫伤(图6—44;参考文献176)。颅后窝位置的脑组织损伤与胼胝体的撕裂有关,这是由于该部位与大脑镰腹侧缘发生了碰撞。脑挫伤间接提示颅骨骨折(参阅标题19.3),脑血管周围出血是颅内压升高的标志,死亡机制为脑干功能障碍(176,177,182)。肉眼和显微镜下可检见远离创道的大脑基底部、脑干、小脑局部出血(图6—44)。也有文献报道,远离创道的脑组织可检见弥漫性轴索损伤(176,180)。如果子弹释放的能量超过了器官组织弹性阈值就会发生爆裂(16,179),引起严重的破坏性损伤。相反,低速子弹仅引起穿透组织器官的损伤(16,72)。

火器损伤评估包括个体的死亡速度。行为能力丧失是指脑损伤或大失血导致个体不能进行复杂性和持续性运动(参阅标题14;参考文献129,176)。存活时间和意识水平决定了伤者在枪伤后是否具有目的的行为能力(如自杀案件中多次射击;参阅图6—3;参考文献55,109)。多次射击案件中如果发现两处即刻致命损伤应高度怀疑他杀,除非发现了两支枪械(55,129)。

大部分枪弹创所致的死亡和脑损伤有关:1989—1998年,在美国,枪支是造成致命性脑损伤的主要原因(184)。脑组织某些部位的损伤(内囊、间脑、大脑基底部、小脑、脑干、高位颈髓)可以引起瞬间死亡(16,55,57,111,129,182,185)。就贯穿冠状面和矢状面的脑损伤而言,涉及单个脑叶的损伤具有较高存活率(186)。蝶鞍和颅前窝底部充当着骨性屏障,以降低来自额部损伤所致的径向组织位移和向后的过

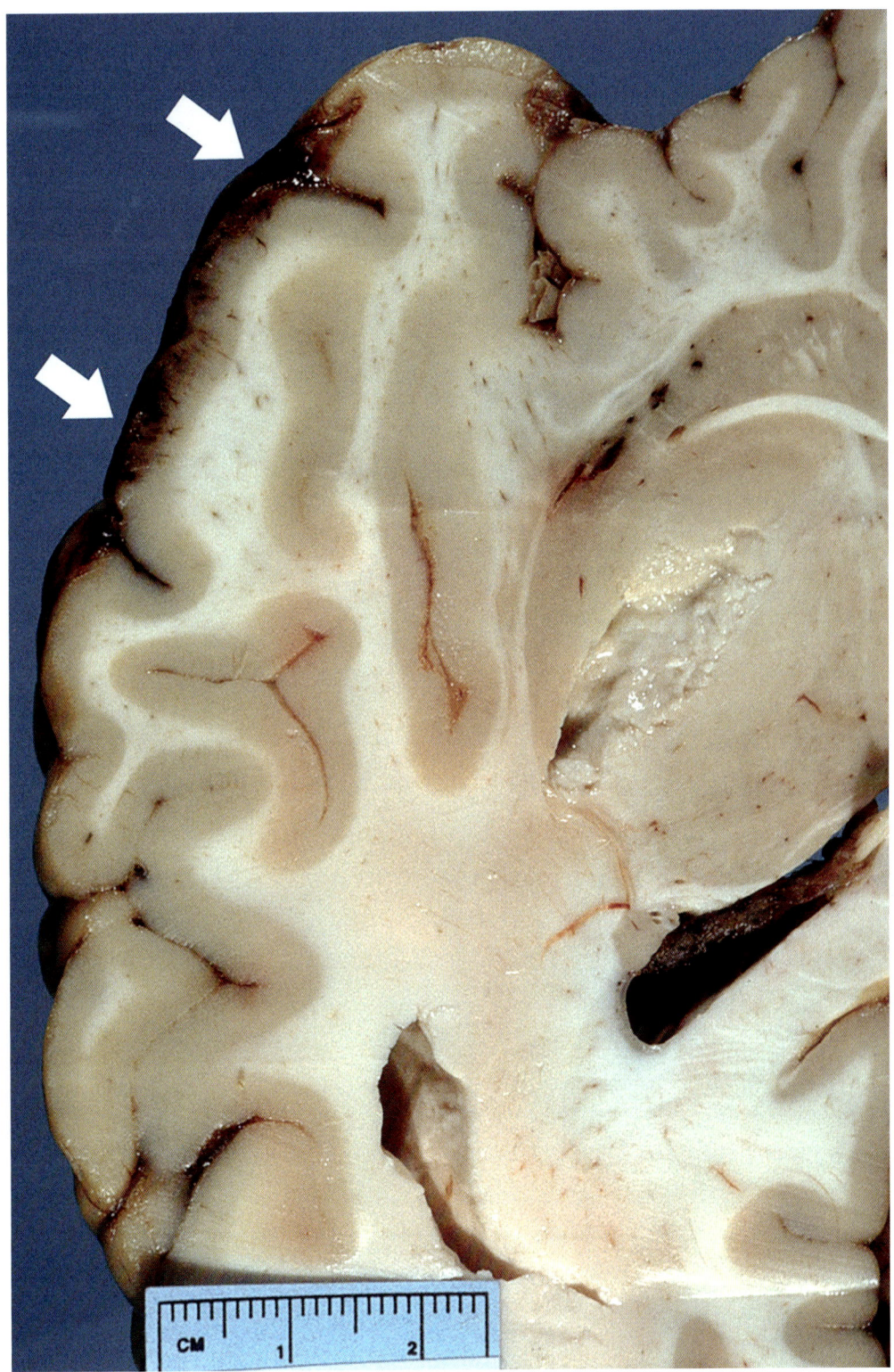

图 6-43 射入口（右太阳穴）对面（对冲）的大脑挫伤（箭头）。甲醛溶液固定脑。

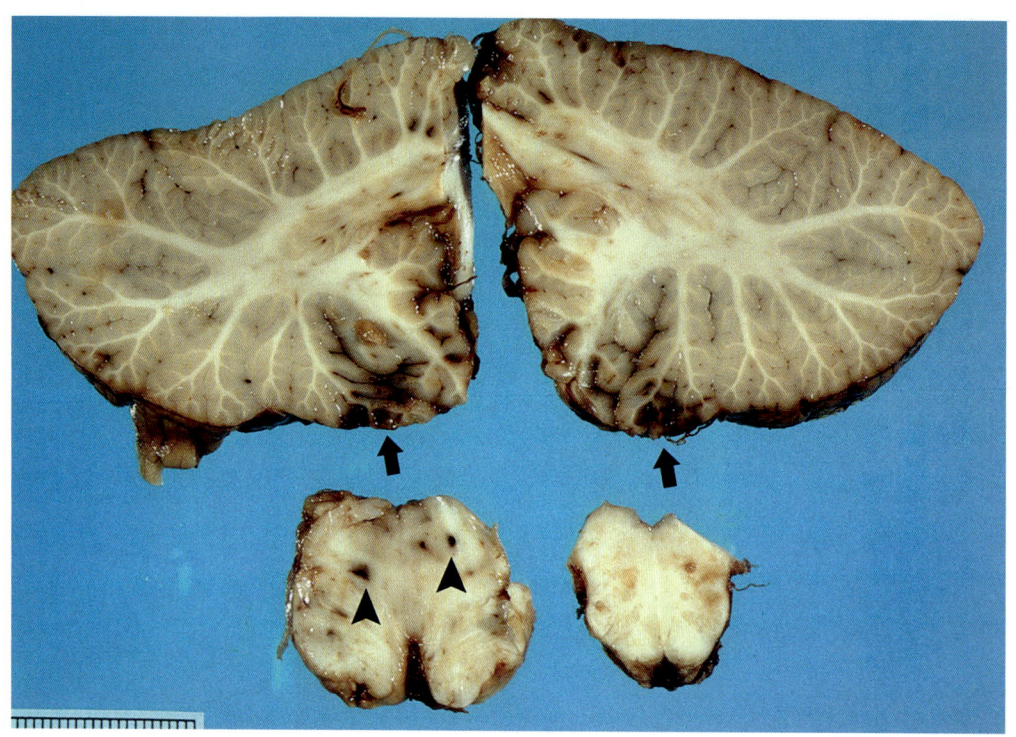

图6-44 自杀,口腔内枪弹创。远离创道部位的损伤:小脑扁桃体挫伤(箭头)、脑干出血(三角箭头)。福尔马林固定后的脑组织。

度挤压(182)。额叶损伤有时并不致命(47,67)。额叶并非大脑支配活动或意识的重要中枢,但是基于子弹口径大小的差异,该部位的创伤可以导致瞬间或非瞬间死亡(111,129,182)。有研究表明,无论弹头是横穿大脑冠状面和矢状面,还是射入颅后窝,往往都是致命的(186),而且与子弹口径无关(186)。

脊椎枪弹创往往致穿过的椎骨骨折或破碎,但是椎间盘韧带的不完全参与维持着脊柱的稳定性(187,188)。脊髓因主创道组织破碎和撕裂而产生较严重的的损伤,由于脊髓被紧紧限制在椎管内,瞬时空腔效应对脊髓的影响较小。椎动脉可发生损伤,包括双侧椎动脉血栓向基底动脉延伸(189)。

枪弹创形成后几小时内出现明显的继发性缺血性脑损伤、脑水肿和脑血肿,与严重的钝性脑损伤相同(142)。

颅内静脉窦出血允许伤者存在短期的有意识活动(182)。

心脏和大动脉损伤会迅速致死,通常允许产生10—15秒的随意活动,但在某些案例中可观察到更持久的活动(16,55,105,129,145,176)。在次要器官(如肝、肾、肺)受损后,出血更广泛,伤者存在意识并存活一段时间(数分钟)(129)。

非致命性自伤性枪弹创出现的部位包括面部较低位置、口腔(上颚)和额骨(16,22,111,182)。枪弹伤也可引起感染致迟发性死亡(图6-45;参考文献66,70,

第6章 | 穿透性损伤——近距离火器创

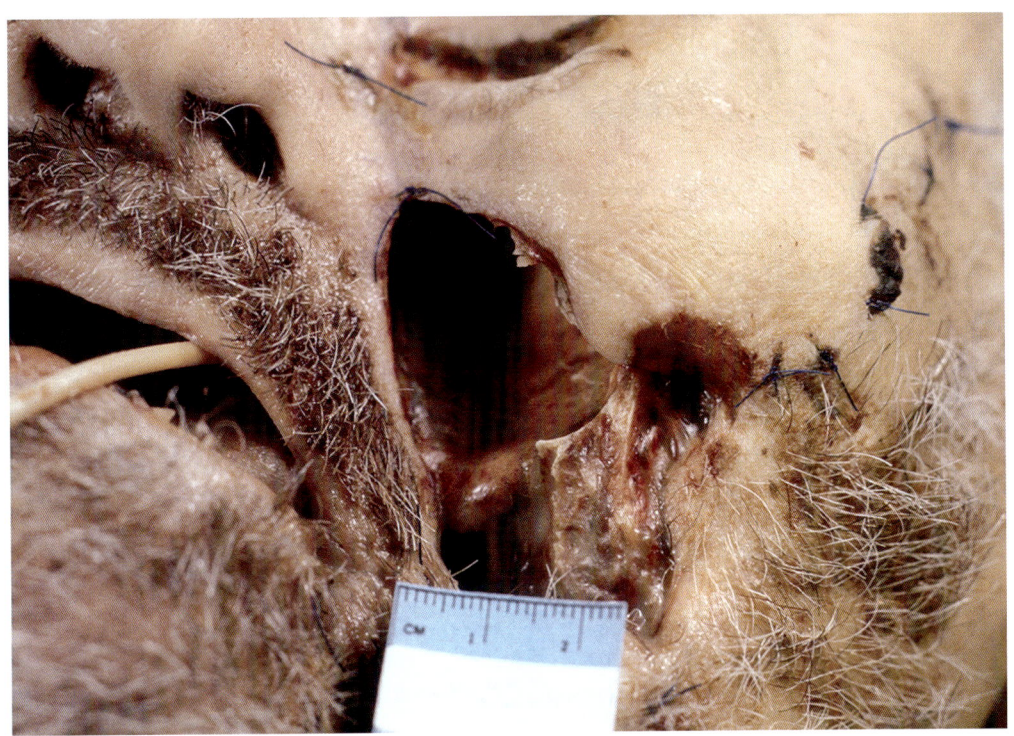

图 6-45 面部自伤性霰弹枪创。迟发性败血症死亡。

139,186)。

19 颅骨枪弹损伤

随着子弹口径增大和速度增加,射击时枪械与头部越贴近,颅骨穿透性损伤的可能性就越大(142,190)。

颅骨射入口和射出口的形状多变,但通常大部分射入口呈圆形或椭圆形(191,192)。因为弹头在颅内翻滚和变形,故射出口往往不规则且相对较大(191,192)。颅骨碎片也会形成脑内多处创道(16,177)。

19.1 斜面

出现在骨组织内板("内斜面")或外板("外斜面")的孔状颅骨缺损分别见于枪弹创射入口和射出口。典型的斜面见于颅骨枪弹创,但也可见于其他骨骼(图6-46)。射入口的大小与斜面程度并无直接的联系(194)。非对称性内板斜面对创道轨迹的推断没有价值(194)。

斜面可以作为确定射击方向的依据(如射入口或射出口的判断),当射入口皮肤损伤形态为非特异性或组织结构受到破坏、腐败、手术治疗的影响时,通过斜面确定射击方向尤为重要(193,194)。如果涉及的是薄骨(如眶壁、上颌骨)或坚硬的骨质[颞骨岩部(16,191,193)],可不形成斜面。有时射入口也可伴有外板斜面(16),包

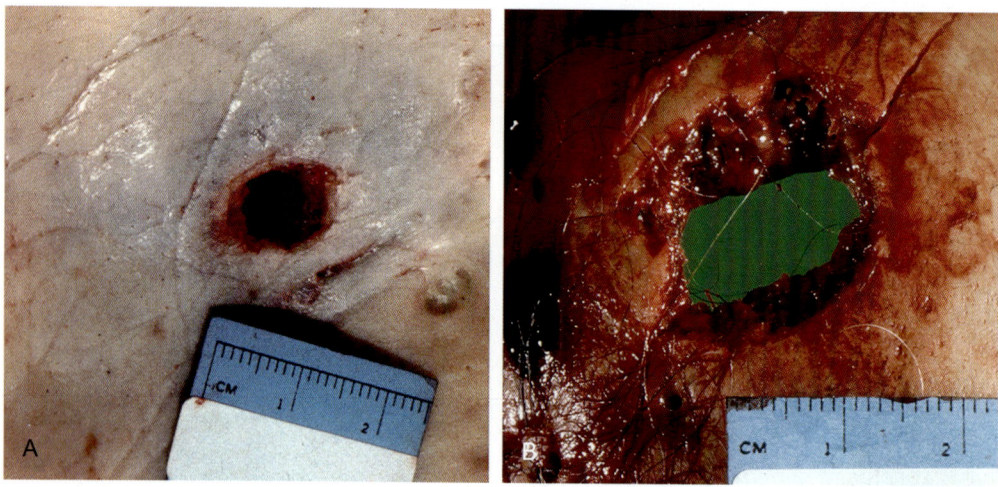

图6-46 颅内枪弹创。(A) 射入口。颅骨内板:"入口斜面"。(B) 射出口。颅骨外板:"出口斜面"。

括切线方向射击形成的锁孔状骨折、垂直射击枪弹创、远距离射击创(图6-47;参考文献193-196)。罕见情况下,子弹可以从射入口穿出,表现为外斜面。射入口外斜面的形成机制有多种解释,包括高速弹头的瞬时空腔形成和气体反冲作用。后者可通过对颅骨外板碎片的观察得到验证但子弹变形的解释可被排除。

头部枪弹创射出口也可显示出内斜面(191,197)。射出口会显示出与切线射击方向无关的锁孔状骨折(197,198)。

19.2 颅骨与弹头接触点的骨折形态

如果子弹的动能在射入口全部被吸收,则不会出现骨折(191)。射入口和射出口周围环形紧箍应力的释放形成了放射状骨折(图6-5;参考文献191,199)。放射状骨折的骨折线在射出口处长度并不长,因为子弹在射出口位置所具能量较小。弹

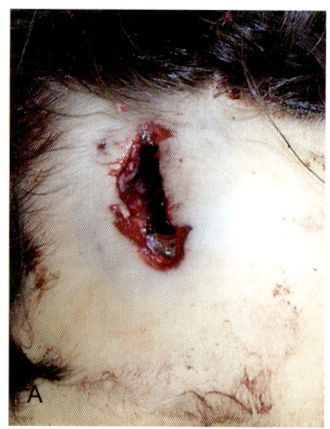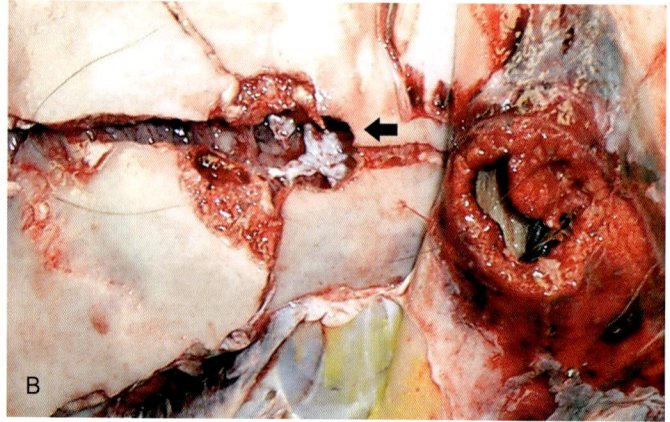

图6-47 颅骨锁孔状骨折。(A) 右前额远距离枪弹创。(B) 颅骨锁孔状骨折(箭头示子弹方向)(加拿大安大略省伦敦市伦敦健康科学中心 E. Tweedie 博士供图)。

头经过颅内所产生的瞬间颅内高压导致射入口和射出口周围环形骨折(176,200)。环形骨折和已经形成的放射状骨折相连,环形骨折是在放射状骨折之后形成的,且不能单独形成(176,200),邻近射出口的环形骨折没射入口那么明显(200)。

由于颅骨骨板抗压性强、抗拉性弱,因此环形骨折会出现外斜面(200)。放射状骨折很少有广泛性斜面(200)。射出口的骨折线会被更早出现的射入口骨折线终止,说明骨折传播速度比子弹行进速度快(191,197,200,201)。如果出现多处射入口(如多次射击自杀),中断的骨折线有助于推断射击顺序(22,201)。如果皮肤表面射入口和射出口发生了改变(如腐败),那么斜面以及骨折线的交叉有助于鉴别射入口和射出口。

19.3 颅底和全颅骨折

颅底各区域的厚度不同,加之颅底存在神经、血管穿过的孔道导致颅底易于骨折(65)。如子弹直接射中颅底,通常会出现颅中窝骨折(65)。瞬时空腔效应导致颅骨骨折远离射入口。低、高动能子弹均可导致颅前窝(如菲薄的眶壁和筛板;图6-48;参考文献65,176,177,182)的"间接"骨折。高速子弹更易致颅中窝

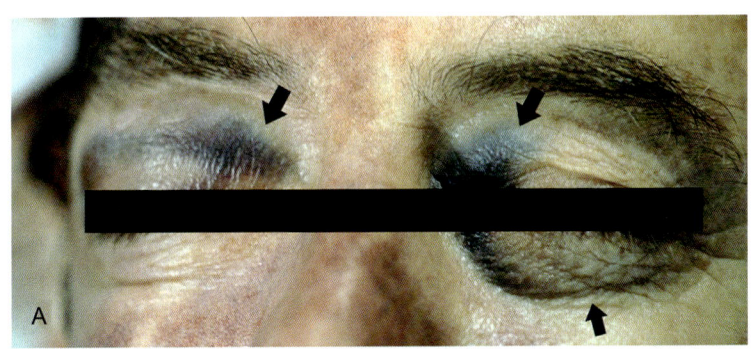

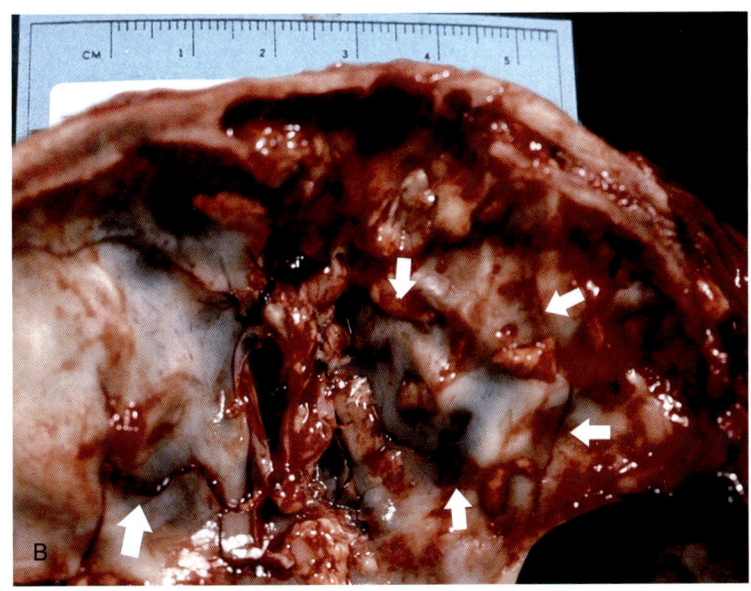

图6-48 头部接触射击枪弹创。(A)眶周出血(箭头所示)提示眶板骨折。(B)眶板骨折(箭头所示)。

和颅后窝骨折(65)。"铰链式"骨折横贯颅中窝,与霰弹枪和猎枪枪弹创引起的颅内高压有关(65)。太阳穴位置接触射击枪弹创可导致颅脑前部区域气体性"爆裂"(202)。即使子弹不贯穿大脑,头部枪弹创也可导致颅底骨折和致命性脑挫伤(参阅标题19.5;参考文献16)。

接触射击枪弹创常导致严重的颅骨破坏,颅骨破坏程度主要取决于子弹的动能和高压气体量(图6-29;参考文献16,124,138,176,177)。可产生严重破坏的枪械包括:大口径左轮手枪、狩猎/军用步枪和霰弹枪(59,69,119,120,137,138,203)。霰弹枪在太阳穴、前额和头皮上接触射击时面部可不完全损毁,而在口腔和颏下区域射击时可破坏整个面部。

脑组织严重破坏时可伴有脑组织喷溅(16,124,176,203,204)。即使严重脑损伤也需进行神经病理学检查,以确定是否存在潜在疾病(205,206)。

19.4 颅内跳弹

在穿透性枪弹创中,颅内穿行的子弹通常在抵达对侧颅骨前就会停止前进(142)。在特殊情况下,子弹穿过脑组织并触及颅骨后会发生折返,形成颅内跳弹创。颅内跳弹的形成多见于小口径武器(16)。自颅骨射入口开始,子弹在脑组织的运行路径呈一直线(图6-49;参考文献177),当弹头穿透脑组织并击中内板后,可发生折返,从而在脑组织表面形成浅表"凹槽"(图6-50),该折返路径可以很长。投射物沿初始路径穿行至折返点,碰撞内板后可形成印痕或发生浅表位移性骨折(图6-50;参考文献16)。在大部分从对侧颅骨表面折返的跳弹案件中,子弹的初始轨迹常较明显。然而,部分案件中投射物发生碎裂,此时推断子弹的初始方向可能存在困难。

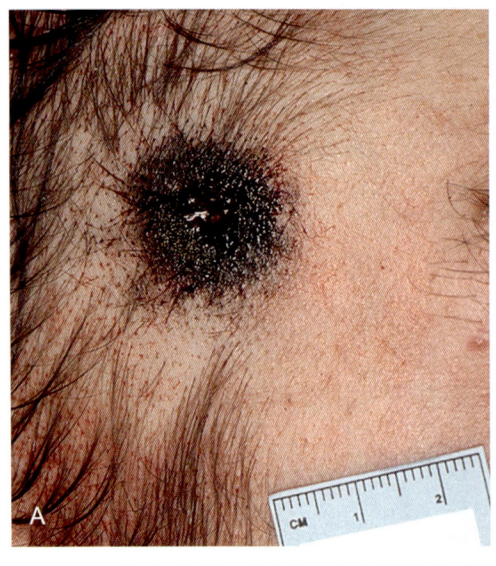 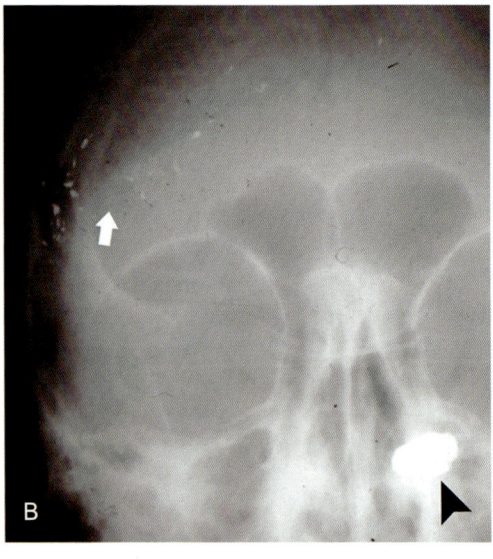

图6-49 颅内跳弹。(A)右颞部半接触枪弹创。(B)颅骨X线片显示弹片从射入口一直沿着创道的通路(箭头)。颅底左侧见大块弹片(三角箭头)。

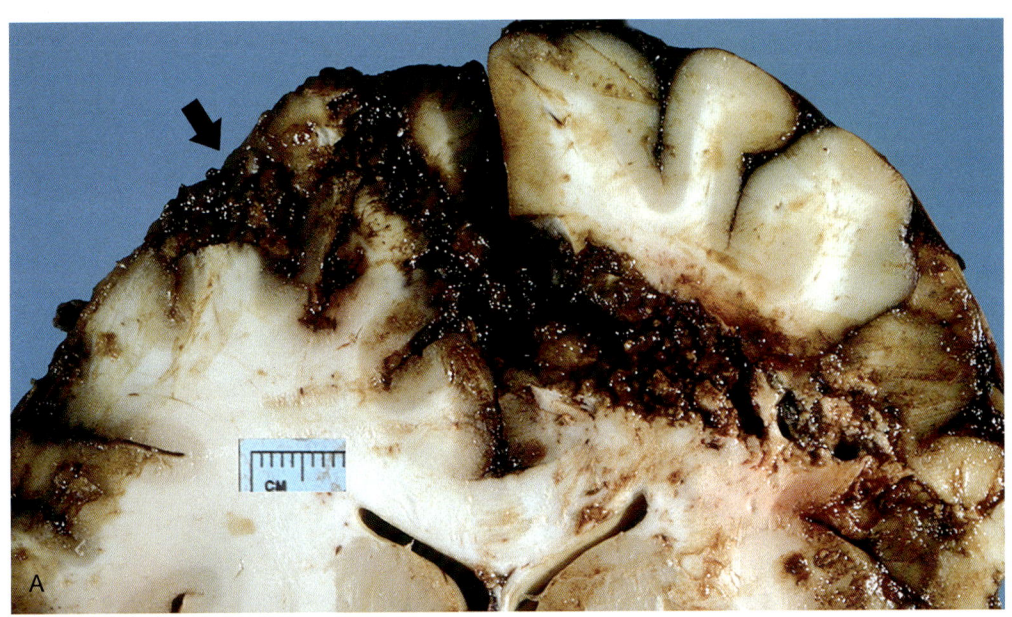
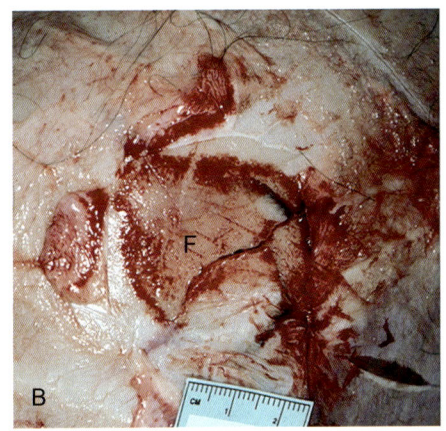
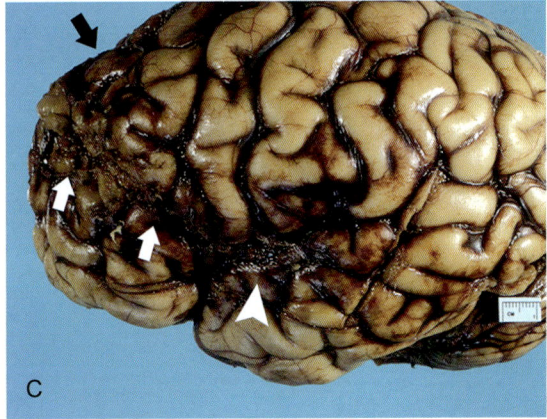

图 6-50 颅内子弹折返,与图 6-49 为同一案件。用甲醛溶液固定后的大脑。(A)脑组织冠状切面,创道相对于死者向左向前(出口;箭头所示)。(B)颅骨突出性骨折(F)标志着子弹从左侧大脑半球穿出。(C)浅表路径("凹槽";白色箭头所示)从出口(黑色箭头所示)开始,沿着脑组织表面找到子弹最终位置(三角箭头所示)。

19.5 切线枪弹创

头部切线枪弹创是指子弹或弹片未穿透颅骨内板而形成的枪弹创。虽然这种损伤有时会致命,但更多见于因其他损伤而导致受害者死亡。临床研究显示,25%的切线枪弹创的伤者 CT 检查可见颅骨骨折、单纯性头皮挫伤,以及单纯性蛛网膜下腔出血、硬脑膜下出血或脑出血(图 6-51;参考文献 207)。另外,43%伤者的 CT 检查显示多处颅内出血,也会存在硬脑膜外出血,但较为少见。故在临床上,如果受害者在伤后出现意识丧失,或 Glasgow 昏迷评分低于 15 分,则高度提示伤者存在颅内

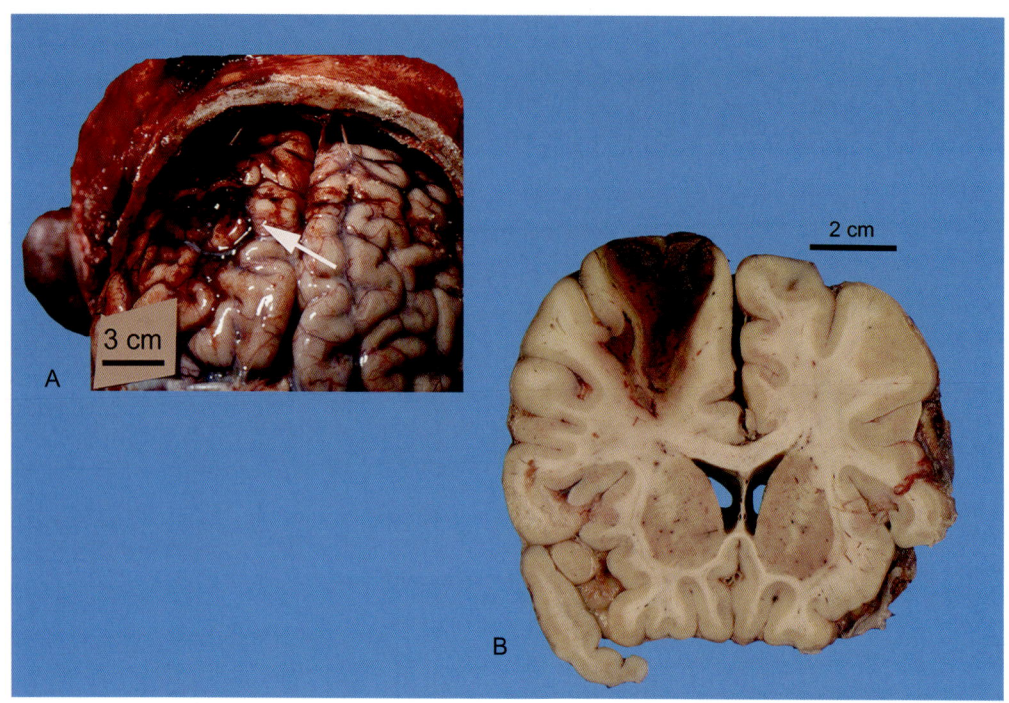

图 6-51 多次射击自杀（参阅图 24）。（A）颅骨并未穿透，脑额叶蛛网膜下腔出血（箭头所示），为前额自伤性切线创伤所致。（B）福尔马林固定后脑组织冠状切面的显示类似于打击性脑挫伤。

出血。颞部或顶部为子弹作用部位、颅骨骨折以及头皮或颅骨内有弹片残留，均为颅内出血的高危因素。

20 体内远离射击部位的损伤

头部接触射击枪弹创可伴有眼部损伤，可见眶周出血（"熊猫眼"），系颅脑遭枪击后形成的眶壁骨折和颅内压增加所致（参阅标题 19.3；图 6-48）。眼内出血多与头、颈部接触射击枪弹创有关，可能因膨胀的气流所致，而越接近眼眶的枪弹创，出血可能性越大（155）。眼内出血也见于颈部霰弹枪损伤（155）。357 玛格南左轮手枪（9.07 毫米或 0.357 英寸子弹直径的左轮手枪）的胸部接触性损伤可形成静脉压力波，导致巩膜和结膜出血。

近距离射击的气体作用或"冲击伤"可导致血管撕裂，如催泪瓦斯弹爆炸，可见血管破裂，但体内未发现与之对应的创道（93）。已有报道称，射于颈部的空包弹可导致颈动脉和颈静脉撕裂（92），射于胸部的空包弹可导致心脏破裂（73）。

心脏室间隔区域肉眼可见的心内膜下出血，往往与头部和其他部位（如腹部）的枪弹创密切相关（图 6-52；参考文献 208），不过头部钝性外伤也可引起类似改变。一般认为其形成机制是交感神经过度兴奋和儿茶酚胺过量分泌（208）。另外，有案例报道头部遭发令枪致伤后镜下可见心肌收缩带（73）。

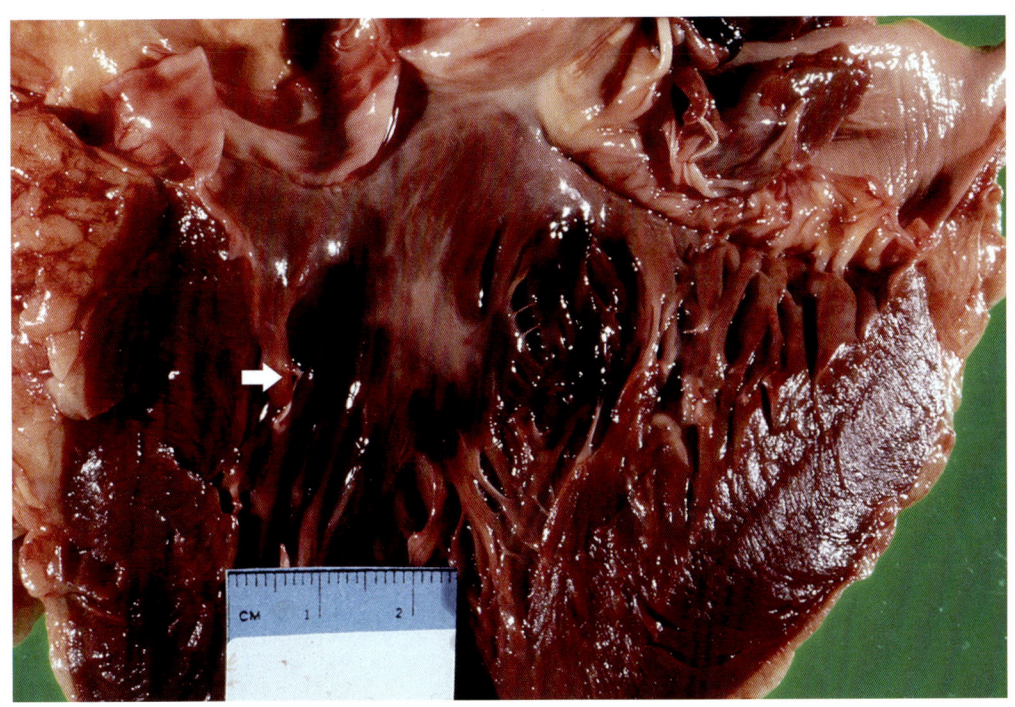

图6-52 头部枪弹创。左心室流出道心内膜下出血（箭头所示）。

21 体内创道的其他检查方法

如果创道涉及深层软组织和骨骼，则需要对其探查和取样，以确定是否存在火药烟晕（16, 57, 59, 141），这对自杀案例尤其是多次射击的自杀案例，可以有效地推断射击范围。软组织（如肌肉等）可被从枪口喷射出的一氧化碳染为鲜红色（图6-30；参考文献16），甚至在特殊情况下（如催泪瓦斯弹）创道可有捻发感（93）。

如果创道方向提示自伤，须仔细记录（101），创道是自伤的重要证据（37, 51）。在自杀案例中，通向身体前侧的创道（从后侧到前侧）或自右颞向下的创道较为罕见（51, 137, 140）；胸部自伤性损伤方向可以为向上、向下或水平方向，而自左向右的创道较为罕见（51, 55, 59, 105）。当发现罕见的创道时，要根据死者的体位进行射击方向的重建（209）。有些看似狩猎意外的案件，实际为自杀，关键在于发现了接触射击枪弹创（参阅标题5；参考文献16）。如果受害者俯身于步枪或霰弹枪上，则其创道方向可以向下（16）。根据受害者握枪方式的不同，或右手逆时针扣动扳机，或左手顺时针扣扳机，可分别形成通向身体左侧或右侧的创道。如果发现完整子弹，可根据子弹上膛线痕迹与可疑枪支进行比对（16）。注意不要用金属工具夹取质地较软的铅质子弹，否则会破坏子弹的膛线痕迹。如果子弹为部分披甲，则弹壳上的膛线痕迹会比在较软的铅质弹芯上更明显（图6-40；参考文献16）。

尽管霰弹枪是滑膛枪管，但如能发现弹垫则可获取推断枪支口径和火药成分等信息的线索（图6-9；参考文献16）。子弹破裂成碎片时，其证据价值会变小（如22口径弹头较小，可能与其他特殊类型武器相似），通过成分分析可以将收集的子弹碎片与可疑枪支发射的已知子弹进行比对、验证（16，63）。子弹变形和破碎的程度取决于创伤位置［如头部（63）］。子弹碎片也会形成多个创道（176，210）。

22 枪弹创的固定和显微镜检查

如果创伤组织结构较完整，可直接分离并固定在甲醛中（124）。如果大量组织破碎，则需尽可能远离创伤边缘提取。疑似自杀案件，是否需要提取损伤组织进一步分析火药烟晕和底火残留，取决于案件要求。如果死亡性质存疑，那么必须提取损伤组织做进一步分析。法医可提取射入口皮肤和软组织来检测是否存在火药烟晕，例如：在创道表面或创道内部可看到黑褐色的非晶体或颗粒状的物质以及更大的火药颗粒（图6-53；参考文献16，125，211）。除皮肤破口外，真皮胶原蛋白同样会发生改变（图6-53；参考文献16，125）。如果对射出口创伤组织进行镜下观察，法医必须意识到在创道深部也可能见到少量火药烟晕和较大火药颗粒，特别在近距离射击时（16，125）。与射入口渐进式的表皮损伤不同，射出口的损伤边界线更明显（125）。

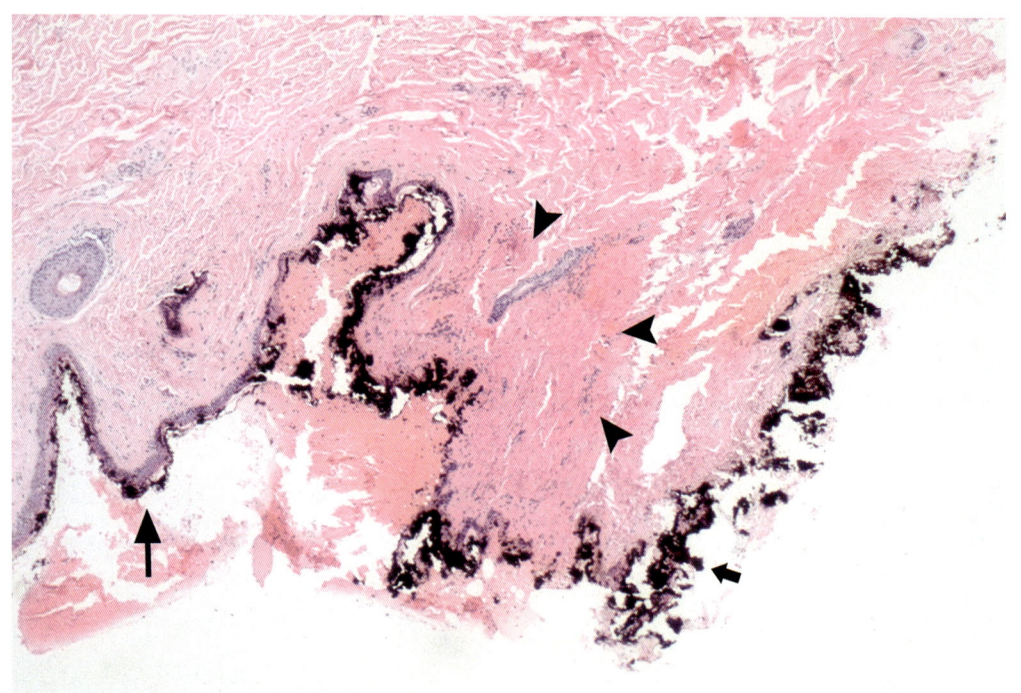

图6-53 接触性枪弹创入口边缘组织显微照片。完整表皮上的炭颗粒沉积（长箭头）和裸露真皮上的炭颗粒沉积（短箭头），以及真皮胶原改变（三角箭头；H-E染色，原始放大倍数×25）

23 枪械的检查

必要情况下,需要其他学科的专家协助寻找枪械是否存在走火的证据(212)。当尸体解剖、现场勘查和周围环境存在不一致现象时,需要对案件进行综合分析(58,130)。死者指纹可能出现在弹盒或枪械上(60,101,105)。有研究显示,12%案件中枪械上会发现指纹(106)。

死者血迹出现在枪管上或枪管内有助于推断射击距离。近距离射击时,火药和气体射入机体,紧接着瞬时空腔闭合,形成反溅效应,如血液、组织气溶胶、骨质和子弹微粒从创伤处逆向膨出(95,155,213,214)。手上有反向飞溅物提示死者自己开枪(参阅标题13;参考文献213)。必要时,进行DNA分析可以验证两者间的联系。反溅效应常见于近距离射击,但未发现此类现象并不意味着一定是中距离或远距离射击(213)。即便是枪械二次发射,仍然可在枪械上检测到溅落物(63)。

德克萨斯州达拉斯县法医局的研究发现:

血液检出(利用隐色孔雀石绿检测)	左轮手枪/手枪/步枪	霰弹枪
枪管内	约1/2[a]	约3/4
枪管外	约3/4[b]	约85%[b]

[a] 阳性结果可在枪管表面7.5 cm(3英寸)范围内。
[b] 血液可沉积在长枪枪管几英尺的远处(大约1 m)。

24 枪弹残留物推断

射击残留物包括燃尽和未燃尽火药颗粒、底火成分(铅、钡、锑或其他成分),以及来自弹头、枪械和弹壳的微粒(16,159,215,216)。

射击残留物检测可推断是否是从同一个枪械发射。残留物可从枪口或后膛漏出并附着在枪械或持有枪械的手上(159,215-218),双手均需检测(22)。与手枪相比,长枪残留物的沉淀较少(216)。不同射击残留物可附着在射击者的手掌或手背上或固定枪口末端的非射击手上(103,215,216)。如果拾起并移动刚射击的手枪,或手掌接触了创伤区域,底火残留物可转移至手掌(63,215,216)。射击残留物可用于推断皮肤和衣物上的孔洞是否为射入口(132,215),射击残留物还可用于提示射击距离。基于不同类型及口径的信号枪和左轮手枪,在射击目标3—4英寸(大约1米)外可检测到残留物(钡、锑)(219)。

射击残留物检测可通过原子吸收光谱进行无机化学分析或扫描电镜/X线能谱进行微粒分析(16,159,215,216,220)。使用拭子、擦拭或胶带吸附的方法从手部收集物证(16,159,215,216),最有效的方法是用纸袋保护未被污染的手(图6-31)。对手上飞溅的血液也可进行分析(221)。研究显示在44%左轮手枪和24%信号枪所涉及的案件中检测出射击残留物(95)。还有研究显示,所有自杀者射击手和非射击手的阳性检出概率为38%（221）。如果排除0.22英寸口径左轮手枪和信号枪，则阳性率分别为50%和29%。其他研究也显示0.22英寸口径信号枪/左轮手枪检出的阳性率较低（参阅标题9；参考文献63,221）。对于多次射击，检出率会升至50%。涉及步枪和霰弹枪时，残留物难以在射击手上检出，但可在固定枪口的非射击手上检出（16）。利用原子吸收光谱可在近距离射击手上发现微量金属沉积。如果组织干燥或腐败、死者存活一段时间或衣物阻挡导致创缘改变，则射击残留物的检测尤为重要（159）。

25 毒化检验

并非所有自杀案件都需要进行毒化检验（37,110）。自杀案件常可检出乙醇，研究表明1/4到1/2的自伤性案件有乙醇检出（19,30,32,34,35,37,49）。德克萨斯州的系列研究显示，谋杀后自杀的犯罪嫌疑人中有65%（13/20）可检出乙醇（以20毫克/分升为基准浓度）（24）。自杀者中1/4可检出其他毒（药）物（37）。在特殊情况下，也可检出其他中间代谢物[如血液中检出氰化物、催泪瓦斯代谢产物（73,93）]。尽管在谋杀后自杀案件中，一些年老犯罪嫌疑人存在抑郁症病史，但几乎无法检出抗抑郁药物（52）。

26 近距离火器损伤的法医学检查方法

1. 脱去衣物和清洗前需进行尸体检查。有明显的火器射入口或射出口的衣服需要保存。有时侦查员会在尸检前去除死者衣物，法医应该尝试将衣物上所见孔洞与尸体上出现的创伤进行比对。检查时一定不能随意变动衣物位置，特别是需要当作证据使用时。如果衣物被弄湿（如血液浸湿），则检查可以在其干燥后完成。尸检报告衣物记录的内容包括孔洞的数量、尺寸、相关特征和位置，衣物上孔洞的数量未必等同于射入口的数量。由于衣服上有褶皱，射穿的衣服并不总是接触皮肤表面。因此，衣物上的孔洞比皮肤射入口多。此外，受害者是自由体位，接触射击时衣物内层射出口可被机体组织、投射物碎片甚至火药掩盖（132）。

2. 脱去衣物后，尸体检验前不要清洗尸体。对尸体和创伤以及其他损伤要拍整体照和细目照。

3. 在提取指纹或清洗手部之前，对其进行检查（图6-32）。如果手部有纸袋包裹，则去除纸袋，让警方提取物证（图6-31）。注意观察血液溅落的形态或火药烟晕所致的颜色改变。警方需要对射击残留物的胶带进行分析。特别在有阳性发现的时候（图6-33－图6-37），需要对手部进行全面拍照。

4. 检查射入口和射出口。射入口周围的清洗要小心（图6-14）。对皮肤破损的大小进行测量。如果皮肤表面有任何烟晕沉积或火药颗粒，测量大小时要格外注意。以解剖标志定位创伤的位置，并测量创伤到头顶和人体中线的距离。

5. 对相关部位进行 X 线检查。

6. 切取创伤处组织（用手术刀在创面正上方部位切下一小块）并用福尔马林固定送检。如果需要对创伤做进一步分析，法医需提取有代表性的软组织来确定镜下的物质是否是火药烟晕（图 6-53）。检查过程必须小心细致，不能改变或破坏创伤。如果不能提取创伤处组织送检，则可在创伤皮肤边缘的外围切取。创伤剩余组织需要保留备份，以防案件再次调查及出现法律问题。

7. 尸体内部检查需要记录创道，即路径、方向、与死者相关性，测量相应部位体腔内的积血量。在头部创伤的案件中，应该尽量将脑组织切片，按顺序依次切开自大脑射入口和射出口之间的组织，以准确暴露子弹在大脑中路径。

8. 对于霰弹枪案件，必须找到子弹或有特征性的弹丸和弹垫（图 6-9）。如果子弹破裂，需要收集最大的弹片。如果有弹壳，则须尽量找到弹壳（图 6-40）。不能用金属钳夹取任何铅类子弹，用手指和塑料钳操作可避免破坏膛线痕迹。如果颅骨 X 线片中提示有子弹，应在头部下放置器皿接住子弹，以防止提取脑组织时子弹遗落。

刘宁国　简俊祺 译

参考文献

1. Anonymous. Review of the Registrar General on Deaths by Cause, Sex and Age, in England and Wales 2001. Her Majesty's Stationery Office. National Statistics Publication, London, 2002.

2. Wilkins, K. Deaths involving firearms. Statistics Canada Health Reports, 14:37–43, 2005.

3. Anderson, R. N., Minino, A. M., Fingerhut, L. A., Warner, M., Heinen, M. A. Deaths: injuries, 2001. Natl. Vital Stat. Rep. 52:1–86, 2004.

4. Miller, M., Azrael, D., Hemenway, D. Firearm availability and unintentional firearm deaths, suicide, and homicide among 5–14 year olds. J. Trauma 52:267–274, 2002.

5. Miller, M., Azrael, D., Hemenway, D. Firearm availability and suicide, homicide, and unin- tentional firearm deaths among women. J. Urban Health 79:26–38, 2002.

6. Gill, J. R., Lenz, K. A., Amolat, M. J. Gunshot fatalities in children and adolescents in New York City. J. Forensic Sci. 48:832–835, 2003.

7. Meehan, P. J., Saltzman, L. E., Sattin, R. W. Suicides among older United States residents:epidemiologic characteristics and trends. Am. J. Public Health 81:1198–1200, 1991.

8. Sloan, J. H., Rivara, F. P., Reay, D. T., Ferris, J. A., Kellermann, A. L. Firearm regulations and rates of suicide. A comparison of two metropolitan areas. N. Engl. J. Med. 322:369–373, 1990.

9. Wintemute, G. J. Firearms as a cause of death in the United States, 1920–1982. J. Trauma

27:532−536, 1987.

10. Boyd, J. H., Moscicki, E. K. Firearms and youth suicide. Am. J. Public Health 76: 1240−1242, 1986.

11. Boyd, J. H. The increasing rate of suicide by firearms. N. Engl. J. Med. 308:872−874, 1983.

12. Felthous, A. R., Hempel, A. Combined homicide−suicides: a review. J. Forensic Sci. 40:846−857, 1995.

13. Brent, D. A., Perper, J. A., Allman, C. J., Moritz, G. M., Wartella, M. E., Zelenak, J. P. The presence and accessibility of firearms in the homes of adolescent suicides. A case−control study. JAMA 266:2989−2995, 1991.

14. Goren, S., Subasi, M., Tirasci, Y., Ozen, S. Female suicides in Diyarbakir, Turkey. J. Forensic Sci. 49:796−798, 2004.

15. Goren, S., Gurkan, F., Tirasci, Y., Ozen, S. Suicide in children and adolescents at a province in Turkey. Am. J. Forensic Med. Pathol. 24:214−217, 2003.

16. DiMaio, V. J. Practical Aspects of Firearms, Ballistics and Forensic Techniques. 2nd ed. CRC Press, New York, 1999.

17. Lee, C. J., Collins, K. A., Burgess, S. E. Suicide under the age of eighteen: a 10−year retrospective study. Am. J. Forensic Med. Pathol. 20:27−30, 1999.

18. Bennett, A. T., Collins, K. A. Suicide: a ten−year retrospective study. J. Forensic Sci. 45:1256−1258, 2000.

19. Bennett, A. T., Collins, K. A. Elderly suicide: a 10−year retrospective study. Am. J. Forensic Med. Pathol. 22:169−172, 2001.

20. Riddick, L., Wanger, G. P., Fackler, M. L., et al. Gunshot injuries in Mobile County, Alabama: 1985−1987. Am. J. Forensic Med. Pathol. 14:215−225, 1993.

21. Schmeling, A., Strauch, H., Rothschild, M. A. Female suicides in Berlin with the use of firearms. Forensic Sci. Int. 124:178−181, 2001.

22. Jacob, B., Barz, J., Haarhoff, K., Sprick, C., Worz, D., Bonte, W. Multiple suicidal gunshots to the head. Am. J. Forensic Med. Pathol. 10:289−294, 1989.

23. Hansen, J. P. Fatalities from firearms in Denmark. Forensic Sci. 4:239−245, 1974.

24. Felthous, A. R., Hempel, A. G., Heredia, A., et al. Combined homicide−suicide in Galveston County. J. Forensic Sci. 46:586−592, 2001.

25. Malphurs, J. E., Cohen, D. A newspaper surveillance study of homicide−suicide in the United States. Am. J. Forensic Med. Pathol. 23:142−148, 2002.

26. Campanelli, C., Gilson, T. Murder−suicide in New Hampshire, 1995−2000. Am. J. Forensic Med. Pathol. 23:248−251, 2002.

27. Hanzlick, R., Koponen, M. Murder–suicide in Fulton County, Georgia, 1988–1991. Comparison with a recent report and proposed typology. Am. J. Forensic Med. Pathol. 15:168–173, 1994.
28. Palermo, G. B., Smith, M. B., Jenzten, J. M., et al. Murder–suicide of the jealous paranoia type: a multicenter statistical pilot study. Am. J. Forensic Med. Pathol. 18:374–383, 1997.
29. Hannah, S. G., Turf, E. E., Fierro, M. F. Murder–suicide in central Virginia: a descriptive epidemiologic study and empiric validation of the Hanzlick–Koponen typology. Am. J. Forensic Med. Pathol. 19:275–283, 1998.
30. Cina, S. J., Ward, M. E., Hopkins, M. A., Nichols, C. A. Multifactorial analysis of firearm wounds to the head with attention to anatomic location. Am. J. Forensic Med. Pathol. 20:109–115, 1999.
31. Moug, S. J., Lyle, J. A., Black, M. A review of gunshot deaths in Strathclyde—1989 to 1998. Med. Sci. Law 41:260–265, 2001.
32. Kohlmeier, R. E., McMahan, C. A., DiMaio, V. J. Suicide by firearms: a 15–year experience. Am. J. Forensic Med. Pathol. 22:337–340, 2001.
33. Rouse, D., Dunn, L. Firearm fatalities. Forensic Sci. Int. 56:59–64, 1992.
34. Chapman, J., Milroy, C. M. Firearm deaths in Yorkshire and Humberside. Forensic Sci. Int. 57:181–191, 1992.
35. Thomsen, J. L., Albrektsen, S. B. An investigation of the pattern of firearms fatalities before and after the introduction of new legislation in Denmark. Med. Sci. Law 31:162–166, 1991.
36. Selway, R. Firearm fatalities in Victoria, Australia 1988. Med. Sci. Law 31:167–174, 1991.
37. Druid, H. Site of entrance wound and direction of bullet path in firearm fatalities as indicators of homicide versus suicide. Forensic Sci. Int. 88:147–162, 1997.
38. Byard, R. W., Knight, D., James, R. A., Gilbert, J. Murder–suicides involving children: a 29–year study. Am. J. Forensic Med. Pathol. 20:323–327, 1999.
39. Ordog, G. J., Wasserberger, J., Schatz, I., et al. Gunshot wounds in children under 10 years of age. A new epidemic. Am. J. Dis. Child. 142:618–622, 1988.
40. Wintemute, G. J., Teret, S. P., Kraus, J. F. The epidemiology of firearm deaths among residents of California. West. J. Med. 146:374–377, 1987.
41. Wintemute, G. J., Teret, S. P., Kraus, J. F., Wright, M. A., Bradfield, G. When children shoot children. 88 unintended deaths in California. JAMA 257:3107–3109, 1987.
42. Morrow, P. L., Hudson, P. Accidental firearm fatalities in North Carolina, 1976–80. Am. J.

Public Health 76:1120–1123, 1986.

43. Heins, M., Kahn, R., Bjordnal, J. Gunshot wounds in children. Am. J. Public Health 64:326–330, 1974.

44. Copeland, A. R. Accidental death by gunshot wound—fact or fiction. Forensic Sci. Int. 26:25–32, 1984.

45. Choi, E., Donoghue, E. R., Lifschultz, B. D. Deaths due to firearms injuries in children. J. Forensic Sci. 39:685–692, 1994.

46. Selway, R. Gunshot suicides in Victoria, Australia, 1988. Med. Sci. Law 31:76–80, 1991.

47. Thoresen, S. Fatal head injuries from firearms. An autopsy study of 270 cases. Z. Rechtsmed. 93:65–69, 1984.

48. Nowers, M. Gunshot suicide in the County of Avon, England. Med. Sci. Law 34:95–98, 1994.

49. Avis, S. P. Suicidal gunshot wounds. Forensic Sci. Int. 67:41–47, 1994.

50. Elfawal, M. A., Awad, O. A. Firearm fatalities in Eastern Saudi Arabia: impact of culture and legislation. Am. J. Forensic Med. Pathol. 18:391–396, 1997.

51. Karger, B., Billeb, E., Koops, E., Brinkmann, B. Autopsy features relevant for discrimination between suicidal and homicidal gunshot injuries. Int. J. Legal Med. 116:273–278, 2002.

52. Cohen, D., Llorente, M., Eisdorfer, C. Homicide–suicide in older persons. Am. J. Psychiatry 155:390–396, 1998.

53. Milroy, C. M., Dratsas, M., Ranson, D. L. Homicide–suicide in Victoria, Australia. Am. J. Forensic Med. Pathol. 18:369–373, 1997.

54. Copeland, A. R. Teenage suicide—the five-year Metro Dade County experience from 1979 until 1983. Forensic Sci. Int. 28:27–33, 1985.

55. Introna, F., Jr., Smialek, J. E. Suicide from multiple gunshot wounds. Am. J. Forensic Med. Pathol. 10:275–284, 1989.

56. Prahlow, J. A. Suicide by intrarectal gunshot wound. Am. J. Forensic Med. Pathol. 19:356–361, 1998.

57. Sekula–Perlman, A., Tobin, J. G., Pretzler, E., Ingle, J., Callery, R. T. Three unusual cases of multiple suicidal gunshot wounds to the head. Am. J. Forensic Med. Pathol. 19:23–29, 1998.

58. Jones, E. G., Hawley, D. A., Thompson, E. J. Atypical gunshot wound caused by cylinder index error. Am. J. Forensic Med. Pathol. 14:226–229, 1993.

59. al Alousi, L. M. Automatic rifle injuries: suicide by eight bullets. Report of an unusual case and a literature review. Am. J. Forensic Med. Pathol. 11:275–281, 1990.

60. Boxho, P. Fourteen shots for a suicide. Forensic Sci. Int. 101:71–77, 1999.
61. Murphy, G. K. Suicide by gunshot while driving a motor vehicle. Two additional cases. Am. J. Forensic Med. Pathol. 18:295–298, 1997.
62. Murphy, G. K. Suicide by gunshot while driving an automobile. Am. J. Forensic Med. Pathol. 10:285–288, 1989.
63. Stone, I. C. Characteristics of firearms and gunshot wounds as markers of suicide. Am. J. Forensic Med. Pathol. 13:275–280, 1992.
64. Wintemute, G. J., Teret, S. P., Kraus, J. F., Wright, M. W. The choice of weapons in firearm suicides. Am. J. Public Health 78:824–826, 1988.
65. Betz, P., Stiefel, D., Hausmann, R., Eisenmenger, W. Fractures at the base of the skull in gunshots to the head. Forensic Sci. Int. 86:155–161, 1997.
66. Azmak, D., Altun, G., Bilgi, S., Yilmaz, A. Firearm fatalities in Edirne, 1984–1997. Forensic Sci. Int. 95:231–239, 1998.
67. Hudson, P. Multishot firearm suicide. Examination of 58 cases. Am. J. Forensic Med. Pathol. 2:239–242, 1981.
68. Rouge, D., Telmon, N., Alengrin, D., Marril, G., Bras, P. M., Arbus, L. Fatal injuries caused by guns using shotshell: case reports and ballistic studies. J. Forensic Sci. 39:650–656, 1994.
69. Karger, B., Teige, K. Fatalities from black powder percussion handguns. Forensic Sci. Int. 98:143–149, 1998.
70. Shaw, M. D., Galbraith, S. Penetrating airgun injuries of the head. Br. J. Surg. 64:221–224, 1977.
71. Vaquero, J., Martinez, R., Areitio, E., Leunda, G. Pneumocephalus after air rifle wound of the brain. Neuroradiology 23:161–162, 1982.
72. Cohle, S. D., Pickelman, J., Connolly, J. T., Bauserman, S. C. Suicide by air rifle and shot–gun. J. Forensic Sci. 32:1113–1117, 1987.
73. Jacob, B., Huckenbeck, W., Daldrup, T., Haarhoff, K., Bonte, W. Suicides by starter's pis–tols and air guns. Am. J. Forensic Med. Pathol. 11:285–290, 1990.
74. Ng'walali, P. M., Ohtsu, Y., Muraoka, N., Tsunenari, S. Unusual homicide by air gun with pellet embolisation. Forensic Sci. Int. 124:17–21, 2001.
75. Barnes, F. C., Helson, R. A. A death from an air gun. J. Forensic Sci. 21:653–658, 1976.
76. Frost, R. E. A suicidal wound inflicted by a "power head." J. Forensic Sci. 39:1321–1324, 1994.
77. Cingolani, M., Tsakri, D. Planned complex suicide: report of three cases. Am. J. Forensic Med. Pathol. 21:255–260, 2000.

78. Karger, B., DuChesne, A. Suicide with a signal pen gun. Int. J. Legal Med. 107:323–325, 1995.
79. Goonetilleke, U. K. Suicide by home-made gun. Med. Sci. Law 22:111–114, 1982.
80. Maglietta, R. A., Di Fazio, A., Greco, M. G., Introna, F., Jr., De Donno, A. A singular case of murder-suicide committed with a homemade firearm. Am. J. Forensic Med. Pathol. 26:89–91, 2005.
81. Hochmeister, M. N., Seifert, D., Smetana, R., Czernin, J. Suicide attempted by aiming slaughtering gun at pacemaker. Am. J. Forensic Med. Pathol. 10:268, 1989.
82. Viola, L., Costantinides, F., Di Nunno, C., Battista, G. M., Di Nunno, N. Suicide with a butcher's bolt. J. Forensic Sci. 49:595–597, 2004.
83. De Letter, E. A., Piette, M. H. An unusual case of suicide by means of a pneumatic hammer. J. Forensic Sci. 46:962–965, 2001.
84. Shakir, A., Koehler, S. A., Wecht, C. H. A review of nail gun suicides and an atypical case report. J. Forensic Sci. 48:409–413, 2003.
85. Opeskin, K., Cordner, S. Nail-gun suicide. Am. J. Forensic Med. Pathol. 11:282–284, 1990.
86. DiMaio, V. J., Spitz, W. U. Variations in wounding due to unusual firearms and recently available ammunition. J. Forensic Sci. 17:377–386, 1972.
87. Spitz, W. U., Wilhelm, R. M. Stud gun injuries. J. Forensic Med. 17:5–11, 1970.
88. Weedn, V. W, Mittleman, R. E. Stud guns revisited: report of a suicide and literature review. J. Forensic Sci. 29:670–678, 1984.
89. Stanbridge, R. D. Self-inflicted nail-gun injury of the heart and lung: a short report. Injury 14:285–286, 1982.
90. Viswanathan, R., MacArthur, D. C., Whittle, I.R. Nail gun injury to the brain: an unusual case of suicide. Scott. Med. J. 39:83, 1994.
91. Goonetilleke, U. K. A stud (cartridge) gun suicide (a case report). Med. Sci. Law 16: 181–184, 1976.
92. Rothschild, M. A., Vendura, K. Fatal neck injuries caused by blank cartridges. Forensic Sci. Int. 101:151–159, 1999.
93. Clarot, F., Vaz, E., Papin, F., Clin, B., Vicomte, C., Proust, B. Lethal head injury due to tear- gas cartridge gunshots. Forensic Sci. Int. 137:45–51, 2003.
94. Garavaglia, J. C., Talkington, B. Weapon location following suicidal gunshot wounds. Am. J. Forensic Med. Pathol. 20:1–5, 1999.
95. Stone, I. C. Observations and statistics relating to suicide weapons. J. Forensic Sci. 32:711–716, 1987.

96. Habbe, D., Thomas, G. E., Gould, J. Nine-gunshot suicide. Am. J. Forensic Med. Pathol. 10:335–337, 1989.
97. Parroni, E., Caringi, C., Ciallella, C. Suicide with two guns represents a special type of combined suicide. Am. J. Forensic Med. Pathol. 23:329–333, 2002.
98. Eisele, J. W., Reay, D. T., Cook, A. Sites of suicidal gunshot wounds. J. Forensic Sci. 26:480–485, 1981.
99. Collins, K. A., Lantz, P. E. Interpretation of fatal, multiple, and exiting gunshot wounds by trauma specialists. J. Forensic Sci. 39:94–99, 1994.
100. Ventura, F., Blasi, C., Celesti, R. Suicide with the latest type of slaughterer's gun. Am. J. Forensic Med. Pathol. 23:326–328, 2002.
101. Suwanjutha, T. Direction, site and the muzzle target distance of bullet in the head and neck at close range as an indication of suicide or homicide. Forensic Sci. Int. 37:223–229, 1988.
102. Gross, A., Kunz, J. Suicidal shooting masked using a method described in Conan Doyle's novel. Am. J. Forensic Med. Pathol. 16:164–167, 1995.
103. Prahlow, J. A., Long, S., Barnard, J. J. A suicide disguised as a homicide: return to Thor Bridge. Am. J. Forensic Med. Pathol. 19:186–189, 1998.
104. Gerdin, B. A case of disguised suicide. Forensic Sci. Int. 16:29–34, 1980.
105. Juvin, P., Brion, F., Teissiere, F., Durigon, M. Prolonged activity after an ultimately fatal gunshot wound to the heart: case report. Am. J. Forensic Med. Pathol. 20:10–12, 1999.
106. Danto, B. L., Streed, T. Death investigation after the destruction of evidence. J. Forensic Sci. 39:863–870, 1994.
107. Wetli, C. V., Krivosta, G., Sturiano, J. V. Open revolver cylinder at the suicide death scene. Am. J. Forensic Med. Pathol. 23:229–233, 2002.
108. Lew, E. O., Kennington, R. H. Not under the hammer: a revolver suicide. J. Forensic Sci. 41:317–319, 1996.
109. Fatteh, A. Murder or suicide? A case report. J. Forensic Med. 18:122–123, 1971.
110. Weinberger, L. E., Sreenivasan, S., Gross, E. A., Markowitz, E., Gross, B. H. Psychological factors in the determination of suicide in self-inflicted gunshot head wounds. J. Forensic Sci. 45:815–819, 2000.
111. Kury, G., Weiner, J., Duval, J. V. Multiple self-inflicted gunshot wounds to the head: report of a case and review of the literature. Am. J. Forensic Med. Pathol. 21:32–35, 2000.
112. Sperry, K. Scleral and conjunctival hemorrhages arising from a gunshot wound of the chest: a case report. J. Forensic Sci. 38:203–209, 1993.

113. Harruff, R. C., Llewellyn, A. L., Clark, M. A., Hawley, D. A., Pless, J. E. Firearm suicides during confrontations with police. J. Forensic Sci. 39:402–411, 1994.
114. Jenet, R. N., Segal, R. J. Provoked shooting by police as a mechanism for suicide. Am. J. Forensic Med. Pathol. 6:274–275, 1985.
115. Carter, G. L. Accidental firearm fatalities and injuries among recreational hunters. Ann. Emerg. Med. 18:406–409, 1989.
116. Blanco–Pampin, J. M., Suarez–Penaranda, J. M., Rico–Boquete, R., Concheiro–Carro, L. Planned complex suicide. An unusual suicide by hanging and gunshot. Am. J. Forensic Med. Pathol. 18:104–106, 1997.
117. Hirsch, C. S., Adelson, L. A suicidal gunshot wound of the back. J. Forensic Sci. 21:659–666, 1976.
118. Padosch, S. A., Schmidt, P. H., Madea, B. Planned complex suicide by self–poisoning and a manipulated blank revolver: remarkable findings due to multiple gunshot wounds and self–made wooden projectiles. J. Forensic Sci. 48:1371–1378, 2003.
119. Jones, A. M., Reyna, M., Jr., Sperry, K., Hock, D. Suicidal contact gunshot wounds to the head with. 38 Special Glaser Safety Slug ammunition. J. Forensic Sci. 32:1604–1621, 1987.
120. Rogers, D. R. Simultaneous temporal and frontal suicidal gunshots. Am. J. Forensic Med. Pathol. 10:338–339, 1989.
121. Milroy, C. M. The epidemiology of homicide–suicide (dyadic death). Forensic Sci. Int. 71:117–122, 1995.
122. Marzuk, P. M., Tardiff, K., Hirsch, C. S. The epidemiology of murder–suicide. JAMA 267:3179–3183, 1992.
123. Betz, P., Eisenmenger, W. Comparison of wound patterns in homicide and dyadic death. Med. Sci. Law 37:19–22, 1997.
124. Breitenecker, R. Shotgun wound patterns. Am. J.Clin. Pathol. 52:258–269, 1969.
125. Adelson, L. A microscopic study of dermal gunshot wounds. Am. J. Clin. Pathol. 35:393–402, 1961.
126. Aguilar, J. C. Shored gunshot wound of exit. A phenomenon with identity crisis. Am. J. Forensic Med. Pathol. 4:199–204, 1983.
127. Dixon, D. S. Characteristics of shored exit wounds. J. Forensic Sci. 26:691–698, 1981.
128. Hanzlick, R. L., Eskew, R. Suicide by three shots with different muzzle to target distances. Am. J. Forensic Med. Pathol. 5:95, 1984.
129. Karger, B., Brinkmann, B. Multiple gunshot suicides: potential for physical activity and medico–legal aspects. Int. J. Legal Med. 110:188–192, 1997.

130. Dowling, G. P., Dickinson, J. A., Cooke, C. T. Shotcup petal abrasions in close range. 410-caliber shotgun injuries. J. Forensic Sci. 33:260–266, 1988.
131. Thogmartin, J. R., Start, D. A. 9 mm ammunition used in a 40 caliber Glock pistol: an atyp-ical gunshot wound. J. Forensic Sci. 43:712–714, 1998.
132. Stone, I. C., Petty, C. S. Interpretation of unusual wounds caused by firearms. J. Forensic Sci. 36:736–74, 1991.
133. King, D. E. An unusual entrance wound associated with rimfire rifles. Am. J. Forensic Med. Pathol. 13:177, 1992.
134. Di Maio, V. J., Kaplan, J. A. An unusual entrance wound associated with rimfire rifles. Am. J. Forensic Med. Pathol. 12:207–208, 1991.
135. Rogers, D. R. Wounds caused by tight contact with the barrel–cylinder gap of revolvers. Am. J. Forensic Med. Pathol. 5:131–136, 1984.
136. Skinker, D. M., Coyne, C. M., Lanham, C., Hunsaker, J. C., III. Chasing the casing: a 38 special suicide. J. Forensic Sci. 41:709–712, 1996.
137. Azmak, D., Altun, G., Koc, S., Yorulmaz, C., Ozaslan, A. Intra- and perioral shooting fatal-ities. Forensic Sci. Int. 101:217–227, 1999.
138. Harruff, R. C. Comparison of contact shotgun wounds of the head produced by different gauge shotguns. J. Forensic Sci. 40:801–804, 1995.
139. Shuck, L. W., Orgel, M. G., Vogel, A. V. Self–inflicted gunshot wounds to the face: a review of 18 cases. J. Trauma 20:370–377, 1980.
140. Fatteh, A. Homicidal gunshot wound of mouth. J. Forensic Sci. Soc. 12:347–349, 1972.
141. Zietlow, C., Hawley, D. A. Unexpectedly homicide. Three intraoral gunshot wounds. Am. J. Forensic Med. Pathol. 14:230–233, 1993.
142. Freytag, E. Autopsy findings in head injuries from firearms. Statistical evaluation of 254 cases. Arch. Pathol. 76:215–225, 1963.
143. Lee, K. A., Opeskin, K. Gunshot suicide with nasal entry. Forensic Sci. Int. 71:25–31, 1995.
144. Canfield, T. M. Suicidal gunshot wounds of the abdomen. J. Forensic Sci. 14:445–452, 1969.
145. Marsh, T. O., Brown, E. R., Burkhardt, R. P., Davis, J. H. Two six–shot suicides in close geographic and temporal proximity. J. Forensic Sci. 34:491–494, 1989.
146. Shkrum, M. J. Suicide involving mulitple cranial gunshot wounds. Can. Soc. Forensic Sci. J. 29:137–142, 1996.
147. Fatteh, A., Gore, S. B., Mann, G. T., Garvin, K. Suicide with two guns: a unique case. J. Forensic Sci. 25:883–885, 1980.

148. Hudson, P. Suicide with two guns fired simultaneously. J. Forensic Sci. 27:6–7, 1982.
149. Timperman, J., Cnops, L. Tandem bullet in the head in a case of suicide. Med. Sci. Law 15:280–283, 1975.
150. Simmons, G. T. Findings in gunshot wounds from tandem projectiles. J. Forensic Sci. 42:678–681, 1997.
151. Clark, M. A., Micik, W. Confusing wounds of entrance and exit with an unusual weapon. Am. J. Forensic Med. Pathol. 5:75–78, 1984.
152. Lantz, P. E. An atypical, indeterminate–range, cranial gunshot wound of entrance resembling an exit wound. Am. J. Forensic Med. Pathol. 15:5–9, 1994.
153. Grey, T. C. The incredible bouncing bullet: projectile exit through the entrance wound. J. Forensic Sci. 38:1222–1226, 1993.
154. Yen, K., Thali, M. J., Kneubuehl, B. P., Peschel, O., Zollinger, U., Dirnhofer, R. Blood–spatter patterns: hands hold clues for the forensic reconstruction of the sequence of events. Am. J. Forensic Med. Pathol. 24:132–140, 2003.
155. Betz, P., Peschel, O., Stiefel, D., Eisenmenger, W. Frequency of blood spatters on the shooting hand and of conjunctival petechiae following suicidal gunshots wounds to the head. Forensic Sci. Int. 76:47–53, 1995.
156. Karger, B., Nusse, R., Schroeder, G., Wustenbecker, S., Brinkmann, B. Backspatter from experimental close–range shots to the head. I. Macrobackspatter. Int. J. Legal Med. 109:66–74, 1996.
157. Karger, B., Nusse, R., Troger, H. D., Brinkmann, B. Backspatter from experimental close– range shots to the head. II. Microbackspatter and the morphology of bloodstains. Int. J. Legal Med. 110:27–30, 1997.
158. Karger, B., Kersting, C., Brinkmann, B. Prior exposure of the entrance wound region from clothing is uncommon in firearm suicides. Int. J. Legal Med. 110:79–81, 1997.
159. Stone, I. C., DiMaio, V. J., Petty, C. S. Gunshot wounds: visual and analytical procedures. J. Forensic Sci. 23:361–367, 1978.
160. Lantz, P. E., Jerome, W. G., Jaworski, J. A. Radiopaque deposits surrounding a contact small–caliber gunshot wound. Am. J. Forensic Med. Pathol. 15:10–13, 1994.
161. Oehmichen, M., Meissner, C., Konig, H. G., Gehl, H. B. Gunshot injuries to the head and brain caused by low–velocity handguns and rifles A review. Forensic Sci. Int. 146:111–120, 2004.
162. Straathof, D., Bannach, B. G., Wilson, A. J., Dowling, G. P. Radiography of perforating centerfire rifle wounds of the trunk. J. Forensic Sci. 45:597–601, 2000.
163. Rivers, R. L., Miller, L. B., Loquvam, G. S. Soft tissue radiography in determining contact

and near-contact gunshot wounds. J. Forensic Sci. 21:373–377, 1976.
164. Froede, R. C., Pitt, M. J., Bridgemon, R. R. Shotgun diagnosis: "it ought to be something else." J. Forensic Sci. 27:428–432, 1982.
165. Ellis, P. S. Fatal gunshot injury caused by an unusual projectile—a barrel-cleaning brush as a tandem bullet. Am. J. Forensic Med. Pathol. 18:168–171, 1997.
166. Nadesan, K. A fatal nail gun injury—an unusual ricochet? Med. Sci. Law 40:83–87, 2000.
167. McCorkell, S. J., Harley, J. D., Cummings, D. Nail-gun injuries. Accident, homicide, or suicide? Am. J. Forensic Med. Pathol. 7:192–195, 1986.
168. Goldin, M. D., Economou, S. G. Stud gun injuries. J. Trauma 5:670–677, 1965.
169. Michelassi, F., Pietrabissa, A., Ferrari, M., Mosca, F., Vargish, T., Moosa, H. H. Bullet emboli to the systemic and venous circulation. Surgery 107:239–245, 1990.
170. DiMaio, V. J., DiMaio, D. J. Bullet embolism: six cases and a review of the literature. J. Forensic Sci. 17:394–398, 1972.
171. Zafonte, R. D., Watanabe, T., Mann, N. R. Moving bullet syndrome: a complication of pen- etrating head injury. Arch. Phys. Med. Rehabil. 79:1469–1472, 1998.
172. Kocak, A., Ozer, M. H. Intracranial migrating bullet. Am. J. Forensic Med. Pathol. 25:246–250, 2004.
173. Shuman, M., Wright, R. K. Evaluation of clinician accuracy in describing gunshot wound injuries. J. Forensic Sci. 44:339–342, 1999.
174. Bhana, B. D., Kirk, G. M., Dada, M. A. Fatal firearm wounds: a clinicopathologic study. Am. J. Forensic Med. Pathol. 24:273–276, 2003.
175. Murphy, G. K. The study of gunshot wounds in surgical pathology. Am. J. Forensic Med. Pathol. 1:123–130, 1980.
176. Karger, B. Penetrating gunshots to the head and lack of immediate incapacitation. I. Wound ballistics and mechanisms of incapacitation. Int. J. Legal Med. 108:53–61, 1995.
177. Kirkpatrick, J. B., Di Maio, V. Civilian gunshot wounds of the brain. J. Neurosurg. 49:185–198, 1978.
178. Fackler, M. L., Malinowski, J. A. The wound profile: a visual method for quantifying gun- shot wound components. J. Trauma 25:522–529, 1985.
179. DiMaio, V. J., Zumwalt, R. E. Rifle wounds from high velocity, center-fire hunting ammu- nition. J. Forensic Sci. 22:132–140, 1977.
180. Oehmichen, M., Meissner, C., Konig, H. G. Brain injury after survived gunshot to the head: reactive alterations at sites remote from the missile track. Forensic Sci. Int. 115:189–197, 2001.

181. Povlishock, J. T. Traumatically induced axonal injury: pathogenesis and pathobiological implications. Brain Pathol. 2:1–12, 1992.
182. Karger, B. Penetrating gunshots to the head and lack of immediate incapacitation. II. Review of case reports. Int. J. Legal Med. 108:117–126, 1995.
183. Oehmichen, M., Meissner, C., Konig, H. G. Brain injury after gunshot wounding: morpho-metric analysis of cell destruction caused by temporary cavitation. J. Neurotrauma 17:155–162, 2000.
184. Adekoya, N., Thurman, D. J., White, D. D., Webb, K. W. Surveillance for traumatic brain injury deaths—United States, 1989–1998. MMWR Surveill. Summ. 51:1–14, 2002.
185. Schmidt, P., Madea, B. Reflex mechanisms of death in missile injuries of the neck. Forensic Sci. Int. 66:53–60, 1994.
186. Selden, B. S., Goodman, J. M., Cordell, W., Rodman, G. H., Jr., Schnitzer, P. G. Outcome of self-inflicted gunshot wounds of the brain. Ann. Emerg. Med. 17:247–253, 1988.
187. Yoshida, G. M., Garland, D., Waters, R. L. Gunshot wounds to the spine. Orthop. Clin. North Am. 26:109–116, 1995.
188. Bono, C. M., Heary, R. F. Gunshot wounds to the spine. Spine J. 4:230–240, 2004.
189. Fitzgerald, L. F., Simpson, R. K., Trask, T. Locked-in syndrome resulting from cervical spine gunshot wound. J. Trauma 42:147–149, 1997.
190. Kirkpatrick, J. B. Gunshots and other penetrating wounds of the central nervous system. In: Leestma, J. E., ed. Forensic Neuropathology. Raven Press, New York, pp. 276–299, 1988.
191. Quatrehomme, G., Iscan, M. Y. Characteristics of gunshot wounds in the skull. J. Forensic Sci. 44:568–576, 1999.
192. Quatrehomme, G., Iscan, M. Y. Gunshot wounds to the skull: comparison of entries and exits. Forensic Sci. Int. 94:141–146, 1998.
193. Dixon, D. S. Keyhole lesions in gunshot wounds of the skull and direction of fire. J. Forensic Sci. 27:555–566, 1982.
194. Quatrehomme, G., Iscan, M. Y. Analysis of beveling in gunshot entrance wounds. Forensic Sci. Int. 93:45–60, 1998.
195. Coe, J. I. External beveling of entrance wounds by handguns. Am. J. Forensic Med. Pathol. 3:215–219, 1982.
196. Baik, S. O., Uku, J. M., Sikirica, M. A case of external beveling with an entrance gunshot wound to the skull made by a small caliber rifle bullet. Am. J. Forensic Med. Pathol. 12:334–336, 1991.
197. Bhoopat, T. A case of internal beveling with an exit gunshot wound to the skull. Forensic

198. Dixon, D. S. Exit keyhole lesion and direction of fire in a gunshot wound of the skull. J. Forensic Sci. 29:336–339, 1984.

199. Oehmichen, M., Gehl, H. B., Meissner, C., et al. Forensic pathological aspects of post-mortem imaging of gunshot injury to the head: documentation and biometric data. Acta Neuropathol. (Berl) 105:570–580, 2003.

200. Smith, O. C., Berryman, H. E., Lahren, C. H. Cranial fracture patterns and estimate of direction from low velocity gunshot wounds. J. Forensic Sci. 32:1416–1421, 1987.

201. Dixon, D. S. Pattern of intersecting fractures and direction of fire. J. Forensic Sci. 29:651–654, 1984.

202. Johnson, G. C. Unusual shotgun injury. Gas blowout of anterior head region. Am. J. Forensic Med. Pathol. 6:244–247, 1985.

203. Shepard, G. H. High-energy, low-velocity close-range shotgun wounds. J. Trauma 20:1065–1067, 1980.

204. Sights, W. P., Jr. Ballistic analysis of shotgun injuries to the central nervous system. J. Neurosurg. 31:25–33, 1969.

205. Lecso, P. A. Murder-suicide in Alzheimer's disease. J. Am. Geriatr. Soc. 37:167–168, 1989.

206. Cina, S. J., Smith, M. T., Collins, K. A., Conradi, S. E. Dyadic deaths involving Huntington's disease: a case report. Am. J. Forensic Med. Pathol. 17:49–52. 1996.

207. Anglin, D., Hutson, H. R., Luftman, J., Qualls, S., Moradzadeh, D. Intracranial hemorrhage associated with tangential gunshot wounds to the head. Acad. Emerg. Med. 5:672–678, 1998.

208. Harruff, R. C. Subendocardial hemorrhages in forensic pathology autopsies. Am. J. Forensic Med. Pathol. 14:284–288, 1993.

209. Karger, B., DuChesne, A. Who fired the gun? A casuistic contribution to the differentiation between self-inflicted and non-self-inflicted gunshot wounds. Int. J. Legal Med. 110:33–35, 1997.

210. Fackler, M. L., Surinchak, J. S., Malinowski, J. A., Bowen, R. E. Bullet fragmentation: a major cause of tissue disruption. J. Trauma 24:35–39, 1984.

211. Torre, C., Varetto, L., Ricchiardi, P. New observations on cutaneous firearm wounds. Am. J. Forensic Med. Pathol. 7:186–191, 1986.

212. McKinney, C. D., Brinkhous, W. K., Butts, J. D. Accidental deaths involving derringer handguns: a report of three cases. J. Forensic Sci. 35:730–734, 1990.

213. Karger, B., Nusse, R., Bajanowski, T. Backspatter on the firearm and hand in experimen-

tal close-range gunshots to the head. Am. J. Forensic Med. Pathol. 23:211–213, 2002.
214. Burnett, B. R. Detection of bone and bone-plus-bullet particles in backspatter from close-range shots to heads. J. Forensic Sci. 36:1745–1752, 1991.
215. Saverio, R. F., Margot, P. Identification of gunshot residue: a critical review. Forensic Sci. Int. 119:195–211, 2001.
216. Krishnan, S. S. Detection of gunshot residues on the hands by trace element analysis. J. Forensic Sci. 22:304–324, 1977.
217. Basu, S., Ferriss, S., Horn, R. Suicide reconstruction by glue-lift of gunshot residue. J. Forensic Sci. 29:843–864, 1984.
218. Kilty, J. W. Activity after shooting and its effect on the retention of primer residue. J. Forensic Sci. 20:219–230, 1975.
219. Cooper, R., Guileyardo, J. M., Stone, I. C., Hall, V., Fletcher, L. Primer residues deposited by handguns. Am. J. Forensic Med. Pathol. 15:325–327, 1994.
220. Andrasko, J., Maehly, A. C. Detection of gunshot residues on hands by scanning electron microscopy. J. Forensic Sci. 22:279–287, 1977.
221. Reed, G. E., McGuire, P. J., Boehm, A. Analysis of gunshot residue test results in 112 suicides. J. Forensic Sci. 35:62–68, 1990.

第7章
穿透性损伤——锐器损伤

概述 法医病理鉴定实践中经常遇到不同类型的锐器损伤（如切创、刺创、动物咬伤，以及医疗或非法用途的静脉穿刺）。遭受切创和刺创的死者大多数为他杀，但任何死亡方式皆有可能。在自杀者中也会观察到毁损性的多发性损伤。在尸体检验中，衣物和损伤部位的详细记录尤为重要，包括损伤及其对应部位衣物破损的形态、类型和走行方向，以及其他类型的损伤（"试切创"及"抵抗伤"），这有助于判断和认定自残行为。刺创大小受多种因素影响。

关键词： 刺创；咬伤；刺

1 定义

切创和刺创均为锐性外力所致。一般可通过比较创道深度和皮肤创口长度区分刺创和切创。刺创创道深度常大于创口长度，而切创创道深度则显著小于创口长度。刺创由捅刺行为所致，从人体动作的角度而言，可以是过肩式，也可以是低手式。挥砍也可形成切创。如果工具既有刃缘又有锋利尖端（如刀），则既能切割又能刺戳；仅有锋利尖端但无刃缘（如针），则仅能刺戳，不能切割；而仅有锐利刃缘但无锋利尖端，则仅能砍切，无法刺戳（图7-1）。锐器损伤可伴有钝性外力损伤，通常取决于锐器边缘的锋利程度（如斧头砍切）。刺穿属于另一类型的穿透性损伤，指尖锐或狭窄物体刺入身体并牢牢滞留在体内。

2 锐器损伤的方式

2.1 他杀与自杀

在欧洲刺伤案件比枪械案件更常见，而在美国则相反（1–6）。判断死亡方式需全面详细地调查案情（7）。达拉斯县立法医办公室进行的研究表明，在630例锐器

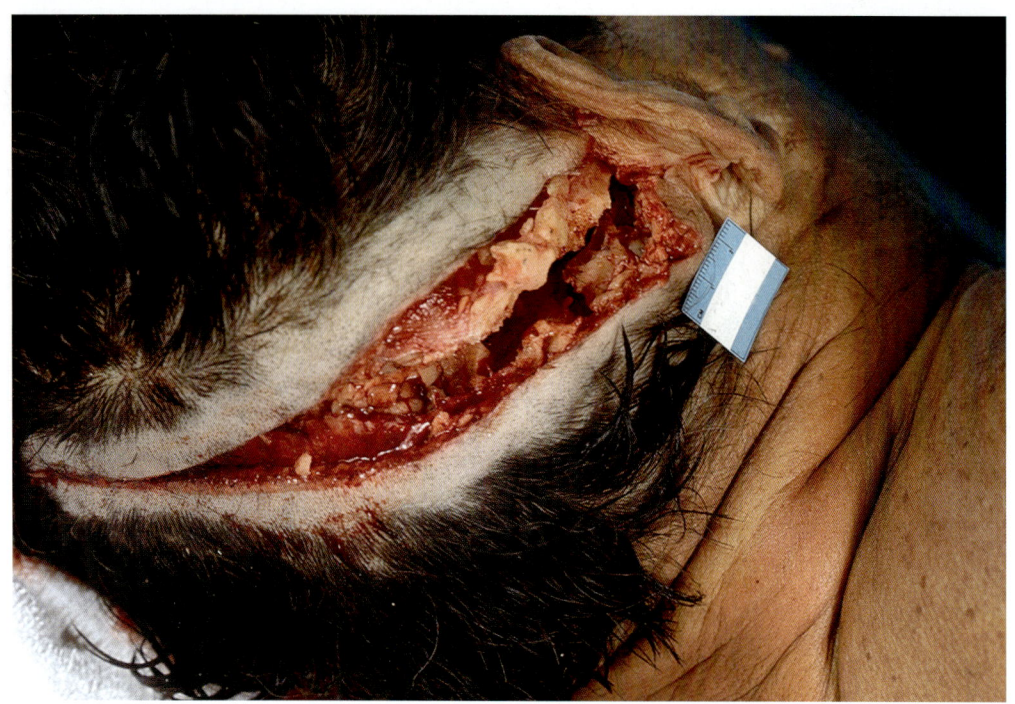

图 7-1 后枕部头皮砍切创伴开放性颅骨骨折（飞机螺旋桨所致）。

损伤（如刺创、切创、砍创）死亡案件中，90% 为他杀，7.5% 为自杀，3.5% 为意外死，有 2 例死因不明（7）。该研究还表明，锐器损伤在 1990－1999 年 10 年间所有意外死亡案例中仅占 0.29%。纽约市一项关于 120 例锐器损伤死亡案件的回顾性分析显示，84% 为他杀，14% 为自杀，2% 为意外死（8）。德国一份关于 376 例锐器损伤致死的案例分析显示，80% 为他杀，17% 为自杀，3% 为意外死（9）。尽管对单一及多发锐器损伤死者而言各种死亡方式均有可能，但基于上述研究中他杀发生的概率极高，在其他死亡方式未被证实前，均不应当排除他杀可能（表 7-1；参考文献 5, 6, 8 和 10）。

自杀可能并不显而易见。例如，在仅有单一刺创、刺创部位不典型（如背部）、衣物遭切割、致伤物远离身体、距离致命伤较远处有其他锐器损伤以及存在其他类型损伤（如复杂的自杀）等情况下应提高警惕（2, 8, 10, 14, 25）。否则会将他杀误判为自杀（8）。

多项研究显示，锐器损伤死者大多数为男性（1-8, 12, 13, 18）。自杀者平均年龄（50 岁）比他杀者大 15 岁左右（6）。大多数自杀案发生在自杀者家中，其中浴室和卧室为最常见的场所（2, 6, 8, 13, 18, 26），其他场所包括医院、酒店客房、拘留所及工作场所。浴缸内自杀者可能认为热水可以扩张血管、防止血液凝固（参阅第 5 章标题 13.2；参考文献 8）。监狱中的自杀者通常是初犯，常因轻微指控被捕，常有醉酒、被脱光衣服搜查/被隔离(26),极少有自杀史,自残多在24小时监禁期内发生,常使用简易的工具(如玻璃碎片)。

表7-1 锐器损伤与死亡方式

	他杀	自杀	意外
死亡方式(%) (7-9, 11)	80%-90%	<20% 2%-4%自杀者(12, 13)	<5%
现场致伤物/尖锐器	+(62%)"家庭访问"(4)	+(参阅标题2.1)	+
1种以上致伤物	+	+(18%)(2, 14)	+
衣物受损	+(79%)(6)例外情况 (参阅标题4.1)	不常见(5%)(6) 常见于一些情况28%(2) 52%的躯干部损伤案件(9)	+
锐器损伤			
• 类型	刺创>切创	切创>刺创:2:1(6) 切创40%,刺创37% 两者皆有23%(9)	切创或刺创
• 部位	单一和多发的胸部刺创最为常见(1, 4-6) 仅有面部和咽喉部创伤(多发性创伤)(4) 手腕、肘窝少见(6)	切创—上肢(包括肘窝、手腕)(6, 9, 12, 13) 双臂(12) 下肢(股区,足背部)少见(13) (参阅标题5)(13) 刺创—胸部>腹部>颈部>面部(2, 6-8, 15-17) 一项研究中颈部"损伤"最常发生(18) 颈部刺创不常见(10, 13, 19-21) 生殖区少见(6, 18)	任何部位,手腕/肘窝>颈部、躯干部(6, 12)
• 易造成致命损伤,但又难以触及或接近受害人的部位	+/- 头部,背部常见(6)	− 头部及背部刺创/切创,罕见(6, 18)	+/-
• 单一刺创	34%-45%(1, 3-6) 女性20%,男性55%(3);女性18%,男性45%(1);多数女性受害者身体有3或4处创伤(1)	多发伤可能(10) 19%(6) 37%(9) 64%(2)	+
抵抗伤	+(7, 8, 23) 总体—38.5%(24),41%(6),45%(5) 上肢刺创	罕见(参阅标题4.4)	−

续表

	他杀	自杀	意外
	单一—2.6%(7), 15%(3), 22%(6); 多发—54%(3); 3—9处刺创—54.7%(7) 男性27%；女性55%(3)；一项研究中无性别差异(5)；乙醇阳性受害者, 44%(7)		
试切创	罕见(参阅标题 4.4)	55%(16), 62%(6), 64%(2), 77%[9] 单一创伤, 20%(6)	—
其他类型锐性外力损伤	生殖器损伤不常见(6)	自残可能(16) (参考文献 16；标题 5)	—
其他类型外伤	+ 17%(3), 28%(6) 女性 39%；男性 34%(1)	"复杂"自杀 (2, 4, 6, 16)	+

据瑞典的研究显示,超过50%的锐器损伤致死的他杀案发生在被害人或凶手家中(4)。北欧地区的研究显示,78%的女性受害人在自己家中被杀,而男性为49%(1)。男性被害人有21%在户外被杀,而女性仅为6%(1)。他杀经常发生在双方熟悉的地点,说明约80%的案件中受害者和行凶者可能相互认识(4)。还有研究表明,在86%的案件中被害人与凶手彼此认识(1)。单一创伤常为饮酒后同伴争吵或打架形成,但对于多发性损伤案件,60%的被害人和凶手间存在情感关系(4)。厨房刀具和剃须刀片常被见于自杀案件(2, 6, 9, 13, 18, 27)。在一项日本关于923例刺伤自杀案件的研究中,57.2%用刀自杀,17.7%用剃须刀自杀(18)。用剪刀和剑的自杀案件较罕见(13, 18)。使用玻璃碎片等很少被使用的致伤工具通常表明是草率决定自杀的(13, 18)。有案例描述一名外科医生在局部麻醉下切了一条长切口,露出股动脉以自杀(13)。

有精神病、饮酒和药物滥用史以及先前试图自杀未果的人很可能自杀(6, 22)。研究表明,大概有一半的自杀者有酗酒史和(或)精神或心理疾病(9, 13)。在少数案例中会发现自杀笔记(6)。斯德哥尔摩的一项研究表明, 19%的男性和31%的女性(总体为28%)会留下自杀笔记(13),而纽约的一项研究揭示约有50%的死者会留自杀笔记(8)。言语表达自杀意图更为常见。上述关于斯德哥尔摩105例锐器自杀案件的研究显示, 53%的死者会利用语言表达出自杀倾向, 27%的死者曾尝试自杀(6)。

有人在场的情况下用锐器自杀不常见,这通常表明锐器自杀者有精神障碍或是情绪激动时的一时冲动(28)。在英国 28 例刺伤自己的案件中,有一半有亲属或朋友在场,但实际上仅有 2 例自伤过程被目击(2)。

2.2 意外

意外导致的锐器损伤相对罕见,包括切创、刺创和砍创(7)。意外刺创和切创常是单一的(图 7-2;参考文献 7)。切创通常会造成颈部和四肢大动脉或静脉的破损,但刺伤和多发性皮肤创伤也会导致致命性出血(11,29,30)。乙醇(酒精)是成年人发生意外的重要因素(11,29)。

玻璃碎片造成的损伤通常为意外(图 7-2;参考文献 7,29,31)。利用玻璃碎片进行自杀和他杀较罕见(32)。不同类型的玻璃描述如下:退火玻璃(碟、盘)可碎裂成刺伤/穿刺机体的微小尖锐碎片;钢化(淬火)玻璃,通常可破碎成不规则的矩形碎片;夹层玻璃,在玻璃层和裂缝间插入一层塑料可保持其完整性;夹丝玻璃,与金属丝网夹在一起(30)。玻璃门和玻璃窗会导致人体严重锐性损伤(33),这经常发生于儿童和年轻人中(7,30)。一项前瞻性研究显示,在 1 086 例玻璃造成的损伤事件中,伤者年龄在 5-31 岁之间(15 岁最常见),其中约三分之二为男性(33)。最常发生的地点是家中(39%)、公共场所(31.3%)以及工作场合(21.1%)。家庭意外包括摔跌、穿过门板或窗户、打翻玻璃家具、破窗而入(图 7-2;参考文献 8,11,31,34,35)。

创缘整齐还是不规则伴刮擦痕,取决于玻璃的性状和死者受伤时的运动状态

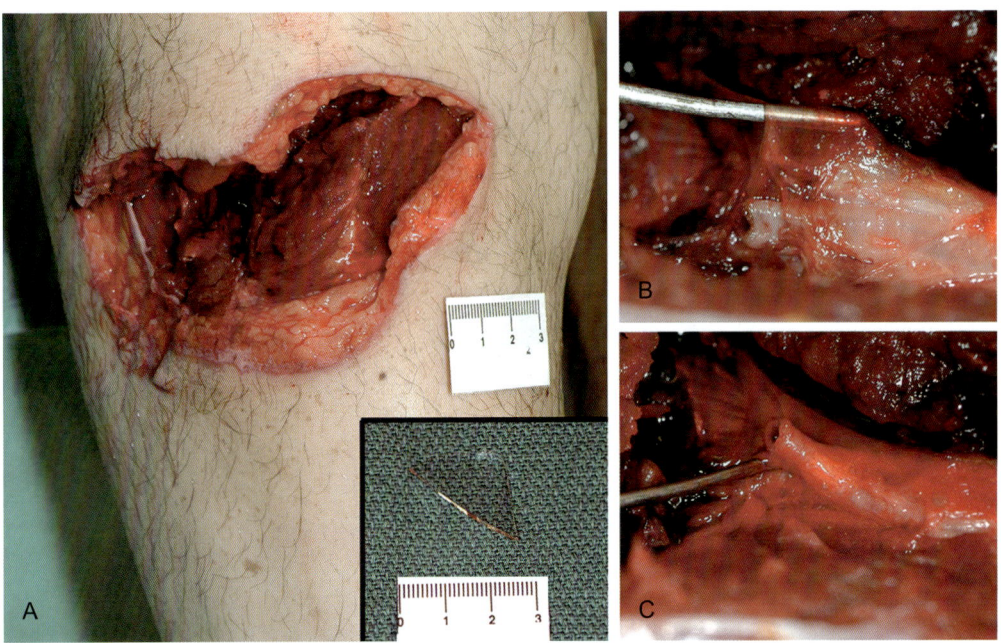

图 7-2 意外锐性外力损伤。酒精中毒。(A)小腿部切创。小插图:破损餐桌上的玻璃碎片。(B)创道探查。探针置于横断的静脉内。(C)邻近的腓动脉被截断(探针挑起腓动脉)。

(11,31,35)。伤者不慎跌倒时,常形成多发性皮肤擦伤和浅表创(11)。伤口深处的碎玻璃尖端可堵住伤口,止住出血(31)。刀、匕首等所致的意外刺创前文已有描述(11,36),其他锐器(如缝纫针)也可意外刺入躯干(35,37,38)。此外,抛掷的锐器也能致人死亡(39)。

2.3 戳伤

戳伤在各类死亡方式中均存在,但在他杀中不常见(40,41)。跌落可导致成人和儿童戳伤(42−45)。戳伤常在儿童玩耍过程中发生。成人跌落可能由饮酒和药物治疗引起(46)。潜在性疾病(如癫痫)也是人摔跌造成戳伤的因素(46)。戳伤也会发生在工作场合(如跌落在钢筋上)。发生交通事故时,乘客可能会被坚固的部件(如栅栏、立柱、树枝)戳伤(图7−3;参考文献47−51)。自伤性戳伤常见于精神病患者/痴呆症及智障人士(参阅标题6.2;参考文献52−56)。

2.4 肛门直肠损伤

穿透性肛门直肠损伤可在不同情况下发生。由于外伤不明显或症状进展缓慢,可能会延误临床诊断(34,41,42)。自慰时可能会把异物插入阴道和直肠导致损伤(参阅第3章标题2.7;参考文献50)。儿童遭受"骑跨式"损伤时(42,57,58),被戳部位可能是阴道、会阴或肛门(42,57),而衣物难以阻止戳穿的发生(42)。这类损伤有性侵嫌疑(42,57,58)。腹腔内插入物会损伤膀胱、肠道及腹腔实质器官和大血管(41,42,57,58),进而可能戳进胸腔(42)。曾有研究特别报道发生在儿童身上的医源性损伤(如插入温度计)(图7−4;参考文献42)。

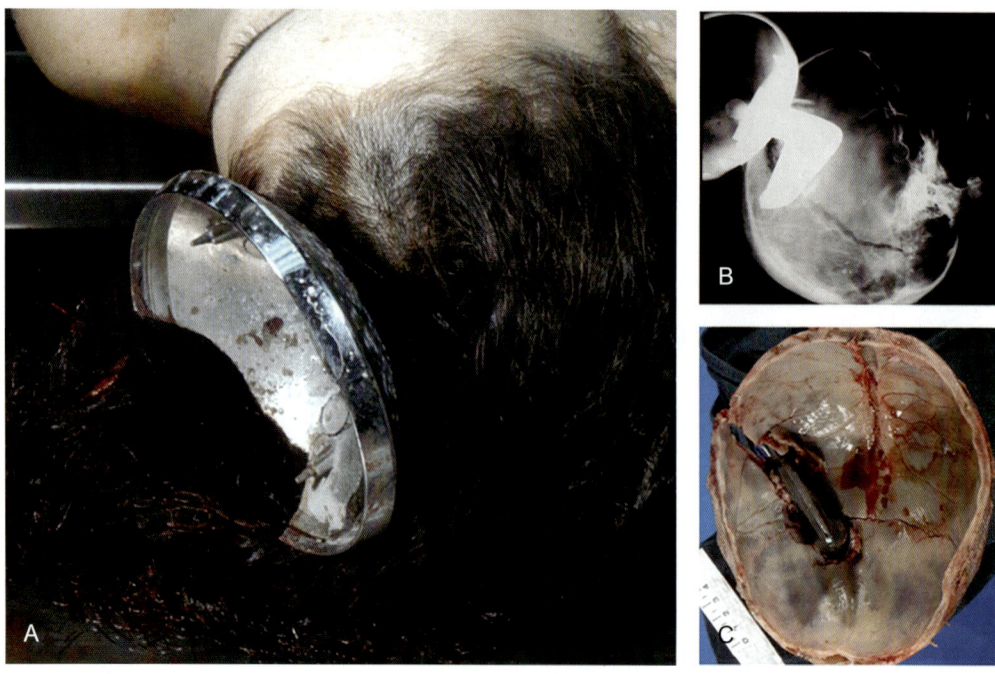

图7−3 汽车碰撞。(A)汽车反光镜戳伤。(B)头颅X线片。(C)穿透颅盖骨。

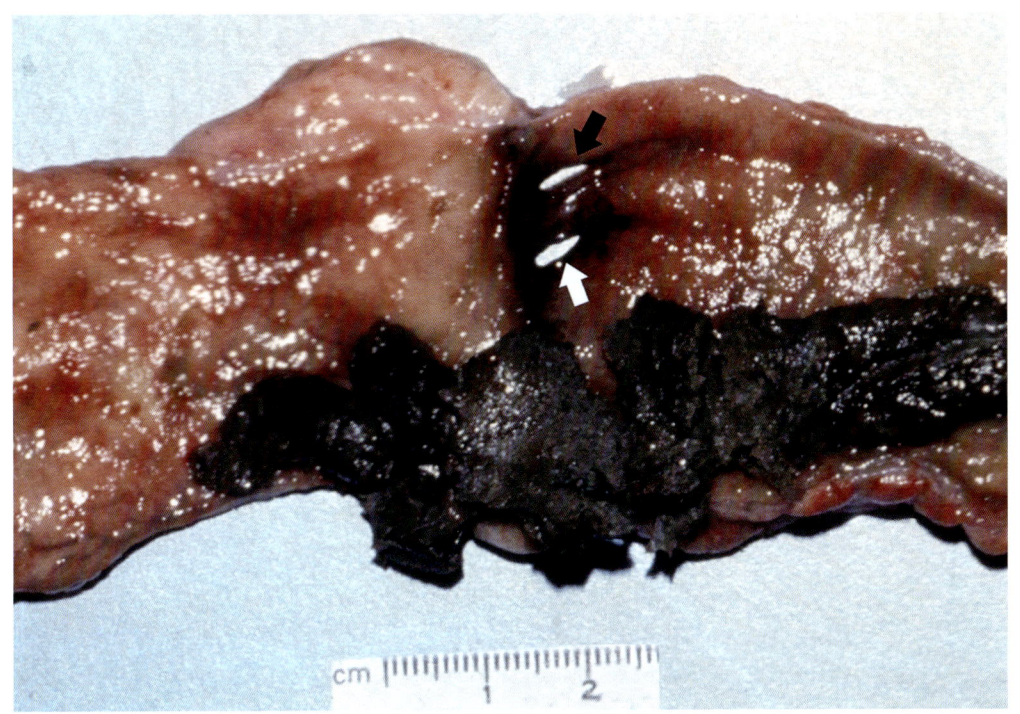

图 7-4　儿童远端大肠穿孔继发腹膜炎。有温度计插入史（美国北卡罗来纳州教堂山市法医局供图）。

2.5 电动工具

链条锯是为右利手而设计的，损伤常在身体左侧（59）。当锯片或锯条与坚硬物体接触时，链条锯会被反冲至上半身或向下到膝部或足部（59-61）。它造成的皮肤创伤的边缘光滑或呈锯齿状（60-62）。链条锯其他部件对颈部和四肢的再次刮擦有助于重建死者姿势（62）。链条锯常形成伴有挫伤和尖锐皮瓣的特有的平行性皮肤损伤（60，61）。面部创伤以撕裂伤和骨裂为特征（59）。颈部血管和上呼吸道也会受损（59，61）。胸部损伤会引起肺气肿（肺大疱），继而破裂形成致命性气胸（63）。手部损伤也较常见。单独的意外性手指截断常见于远端（64），一般不伴有手指和手的损伤，手指近端截断通常不会意外发生（64）。大多数自伤性链条锯损伤的伤者有职业经历和精神病史（63）。可疑和他杀案中的死亡也会涉及链条锯（60）。

其他工具（如带锯、圆锯、电钻）导致的损伤，自伤及意外都有可能造成（图 7-5；参考文献 9，65-69）。某些装置（如螺旋桨）能造成多发性砍切伤（图 7-1；参考文献 7，70，71）。

3　刺创、切创与锐器的关系

某些情况下，致伤刀具会留在人体创口内（图 7-6）。在极少数情况下，刀尖与

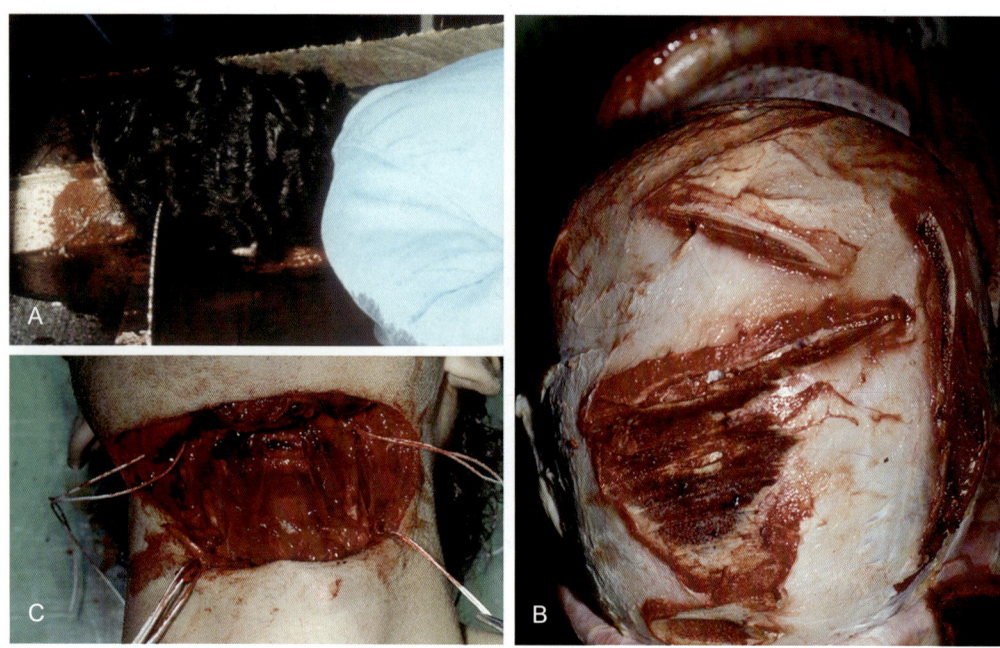

图 7-5 用台锯自杀。(A) 受害者面部朝下,俯卧于台锯上,锯机仍在运转。(B) 颅顶骨。几把锯子从不同方向锯切,部分已锯透颅骨,贯穿大脑。(C) 颈部切创。颈动脉被切断(结扎处)(加拿大安大略省汉密尔顿市法医病理办公室 D. King 博士供图)。

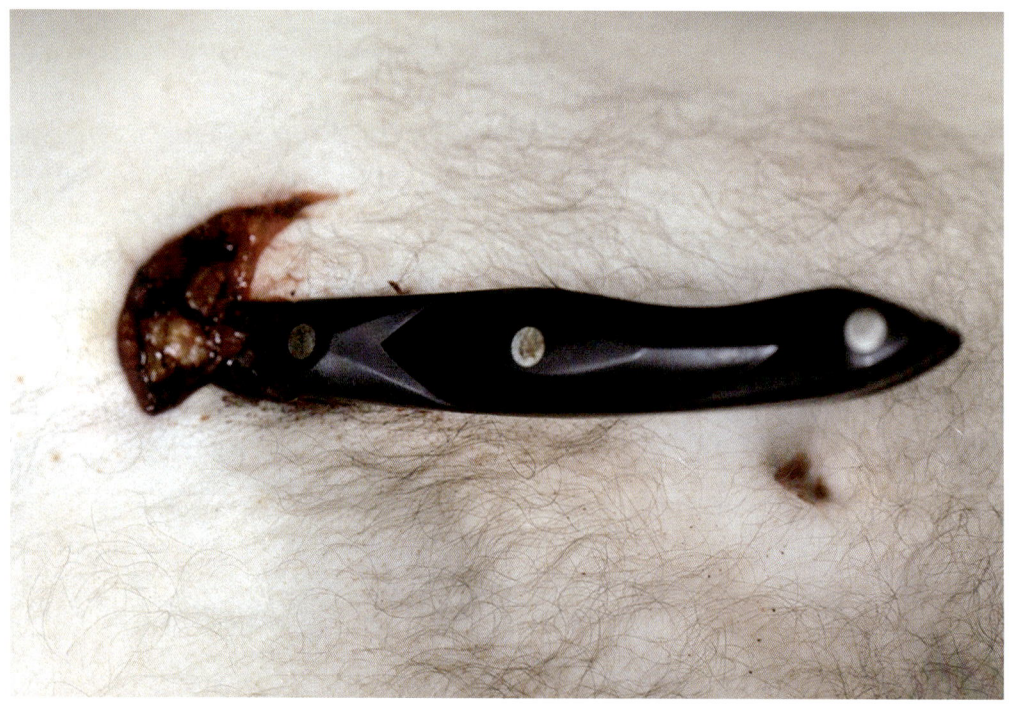

图 7-6 自伤性腹部刺创。刀仍在创伤原位。

第 7 章 | 穿透性损伤——锐器损伤

骨骼接触会折断,可通过 X 线检查判断。可疑刀具上的血迹需与损伤处组织进行 DNA 比对分析(图 7-7)。若现场无致伤刀具,则需对创伤与可疑锐器进行比较,分析对比刺创与凶器在深度、长度和宽度方面的关联性。家用刀具类型多样,这些参数有助于检查者锁定方向,寻找凶器。由于很多刀具能造成相同损伤,而法医仅能分析创伤的外观、形态与特定工具/致伤物接触面是否一致或符合,因此有时即使能准确测量和对比刺创的长度和宽度,也难以认定致伤工具类型。测量切创深度与长度,只能了解损伤的严重程度。

刺戳物嵌入体内时(46),异物末端可能在现场就被急救人员截断,而剩余部分仍留在体内,以确保填塞内部损伤(47)。影像学检查可显示、记录刺戳物在体内的位置,有时需要较大的外力或锯子来移除刺戳物(46)。

刀片与刺创尺寸的相关性受以下诸多因素影响:

- **皮肤弹性:** 由于大多数刀片厚度在 1—2 毫米(约 0.0625 英寸),故测量刺创的宽度不是非常重要。创口方向与由皮肤弹性所产生的张力线(皮纹分裂线、朗格线)平行时创口相对较窄,垂直时则创口长度会变短(图 7-8),为获得这种创伤更为准确的长度,需要以其创缘的近似值来确定(72)。研究发现,即使测量的是哆开创口创缘的长度,位于胸、腹、腰侧的皮肤创口长度也往往达不到刀片的宽度(72)。
- **刀刺入角度:** 许多刀片是单刃的,即一面为锋利的可切割的刃缘,另一面为钝性的不能切割的背部。通常情况下,刀垂直刺入皮肤时,皮肤创伤的创角为一锐一钝,这与刀片两侧边缘的构型相符(图 7-9)。如果刀以一定角度刺入皮

图 7-7 刀口上受害者的血渍(箭头)。

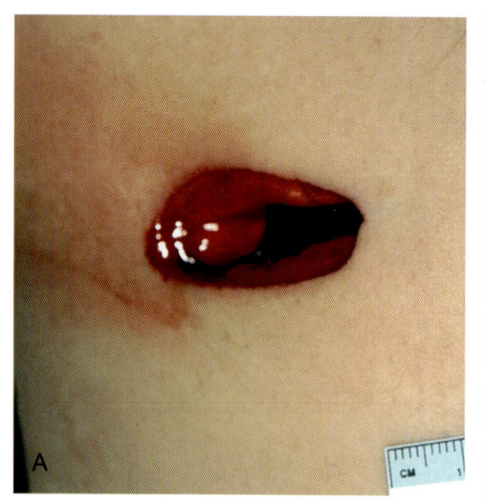
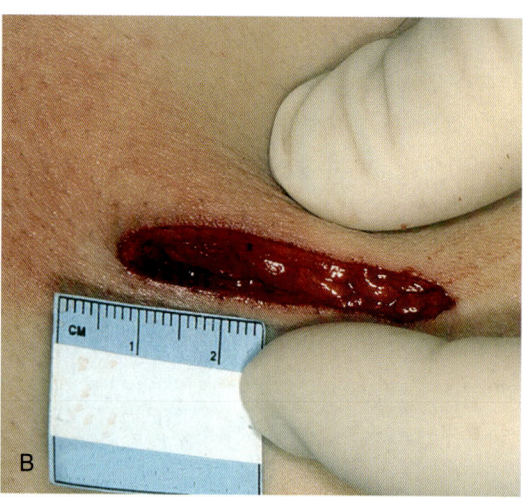

图7-8 刺创长度的测量。(A)裂开的刺创。刺创长度变短。(B)用手合拢刺创创缘。

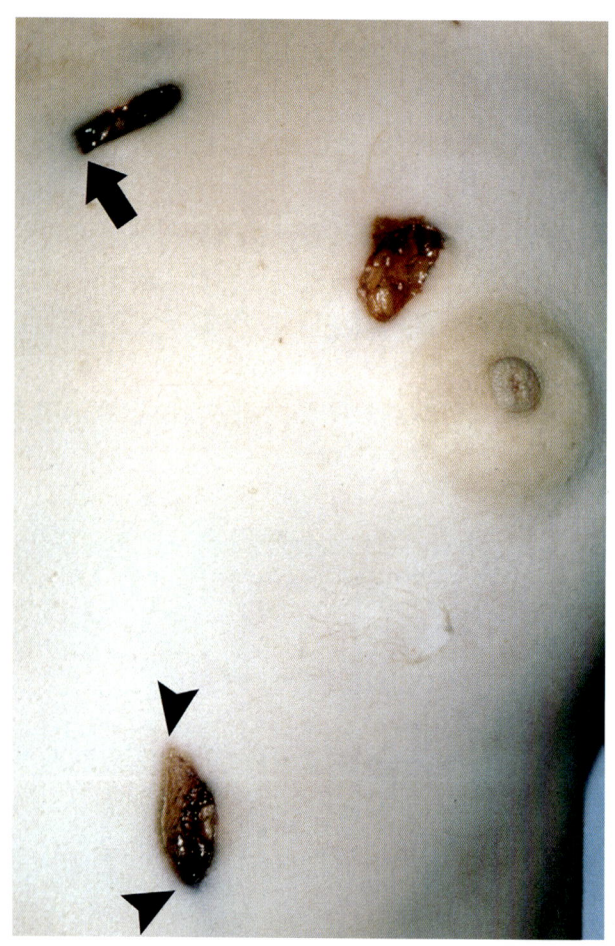

图7-9 胸部多处刺创。刀垂直刺入——锐端和钝端(箭头所示)。刀以一定角度刺入——两个锐端(三角箭头所示)(美国北卡罗来纳州教堂山市法医局供图)。

肤，创口长度变长，同时创口两端（创角）变尖，一端由刀尖初始刺入形成，另一端则由刀刃所致（图 7-9）。"摇摆型/变异型"刺创最小的创口长度应与刀宽相对应（图 7-10）。刀和伤者的运动会导致刀片相对于刺入口或刺出口转动，从而造成创口延长及皮肤创口一端可能出现凹陷（图 7-11）。刀身大幅度的转动会造成较大的和不规则的创伤（图 7-12）。如果重复刺入或刀身在体内转动，那么单一皮肤创伤也可能形成多发性创道（图 7-13；参考文献 2，73）。单一的和多发性创道伴随出血，说明为生前伤（图 7-14；参考文献 10）。多发性创道表明行凶意图（19）。

- **解剖学变化（生前和死后）**：对于刀片长度，创口深度可提供重要的信息。一般情况下，刺创最深尺寸提示刀身的最短长度。创道深度在死后可能会发生

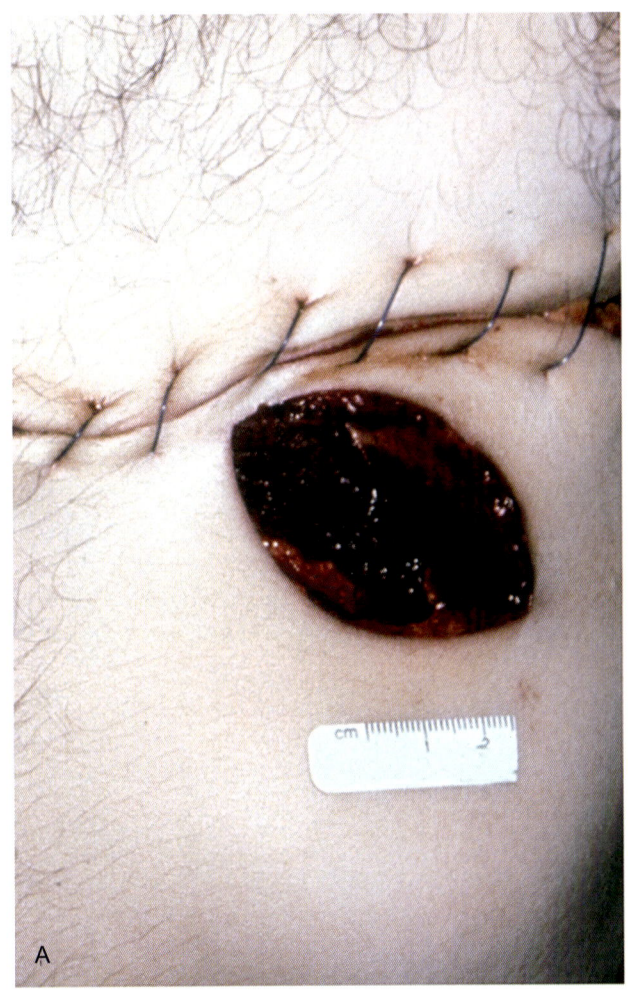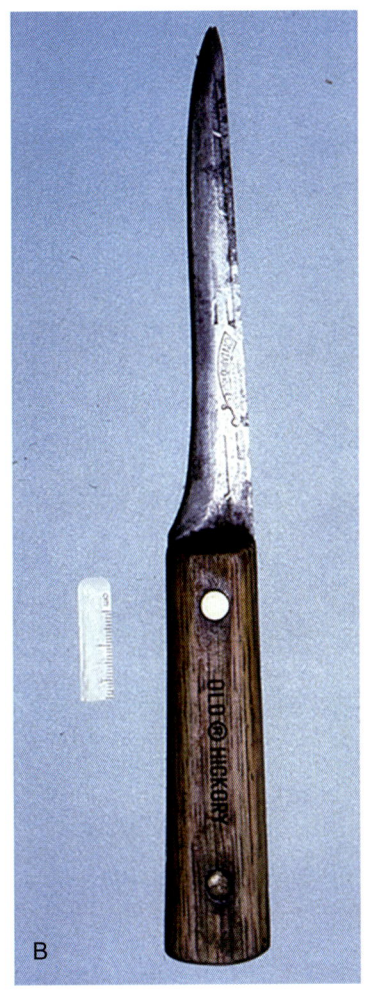

图 7-10 "摇摆型/变异型"刺创。（A）胸部哆开的单一刺创（胸廓切开术创口下方）。伤者和刀的相对运动改变了刺创长度。（B）致伤刀具。其刀片宽度较窄（美国北卡罗来纳州教堂山市法医局供图）。

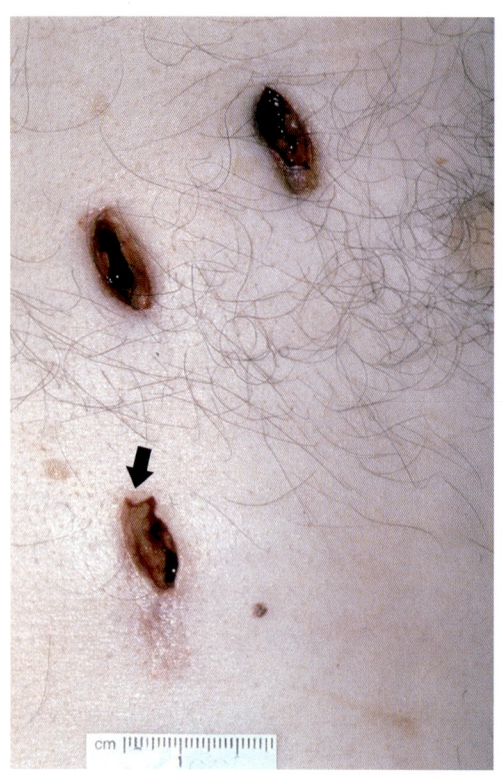

图 7-11 多处刺创。下方刺创因刀体扭转而使创缘凹凸不平（箭头所示）（美国北卡罗来纳州教堂山市法医局供图）。

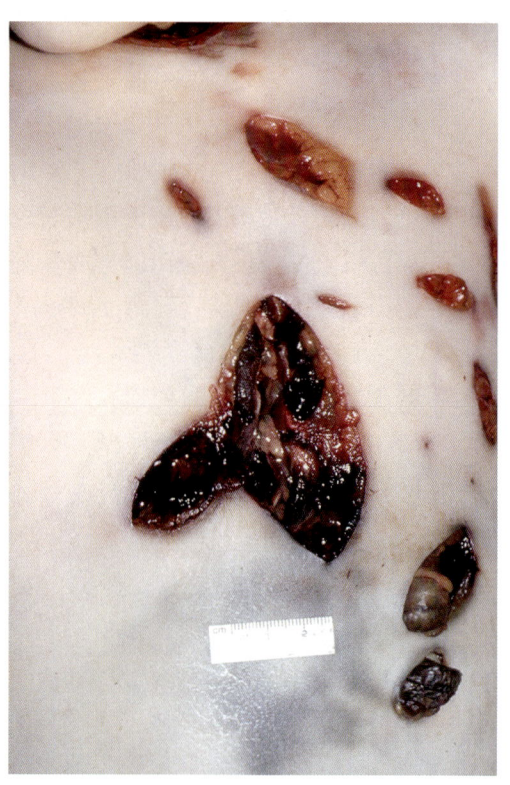

图 7-12 多处大小不一的刺创。大的创口由刀体的大幅度扭转所致（美国北卡罗来纳州教堂山市法医局供图）。

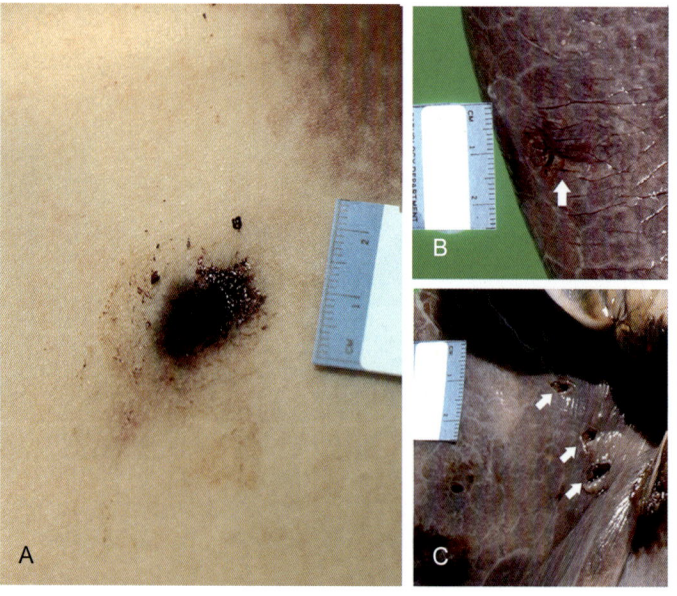

图 7-13 他杀。（A）背部单一刺创。（B）创道一直延伸至右肺下叶上方（箭头所示）。（C）右肺下叶底部多处创道（箭头所示），提示锐器从同一刺入口反复多次刺入胸腔。

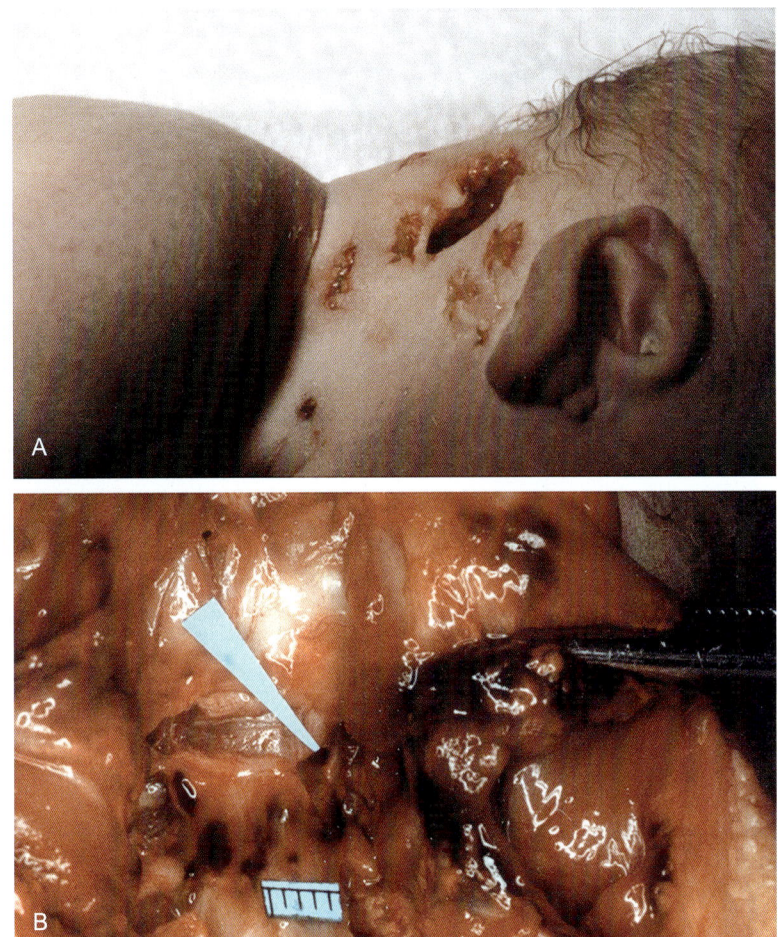

图 7-14 杀婴。多处刺创。(A) 右颈部刺创。(B) 后颈部检见创道延伸至颈髓(解剖,三角箭头所示)。创腔周围的出血说明为生前伤。

改变。尸体检验刺创时,尤其是心脏前侧,测量刺创深度仅仅是刺器长度的估值(74)。尸体解剖时摘除胸骨使得心包前侧与胸骨分离,导致心脏陷入胸腔,这增加了前胸壁与心脏的距离[研究显示为 7 毫米或约 0.25 英寸(74)]。如果创道触及心脏,心包积血会增加胸壁与心脏创伤之间的距离[1-4 厘米或 0.5-1.5 英寸(74)]。如果有心脏压塞,心搏在收缩期停止,就会造成尸检时创道深度比损伤时更深,当然,心脏也可能在损伤时处于舒张期(74)。

- **作用力的大小:** 刀的宽度向刀尖方向逐渐变窄。如果仅是刀的尖端刺入体表,则体表创口的长度要小于刀的最大宽度。若用力将刀捅入胸、腹部,创道深度会超过刀体的长度。刀体全部刺入身体,创口周围皮肤可见由刀柄所致的二次钝性损伤(如刀柄、护手或刀体固定装置;图 7-15;参考文献 75)。对 74 例致死性刺创的研究发现,仅有 5 例检见刺创周围伴有刀柄所致的皮肤印痕(76)。捅刺过程中除刀柄外,持刀手亦会造成皮肤损伤(3)。自杀者可通过多种方式支撑使用的刀具而自伤(如身体前倾时紧握刀具刺入身体,进而锤击刀柄;图 7-16;参考文献 9)。

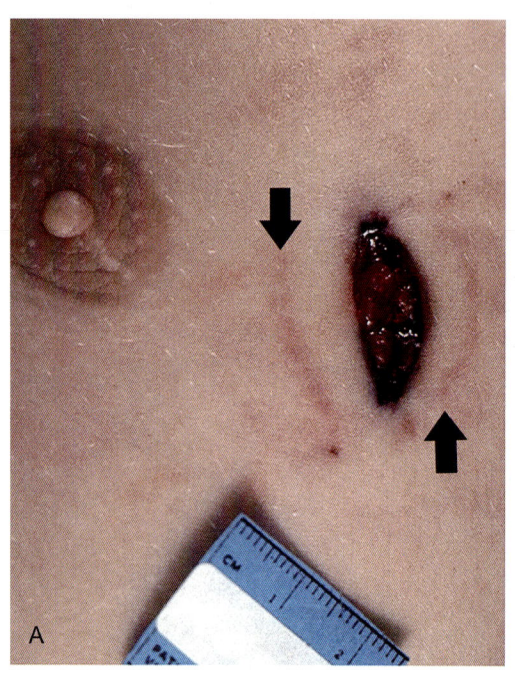

图 7-15 猛力将刀捅入身体时皮肤表面的刀柄印痕。刺创深度超过刀身长度。(A)胸部单一刺创,伴创口两侧线性挫伤(箭头所示)。(B)挫伤是在用力将刀刺入身体时,由木制刀柄边缘与皮肤碰撞所致。

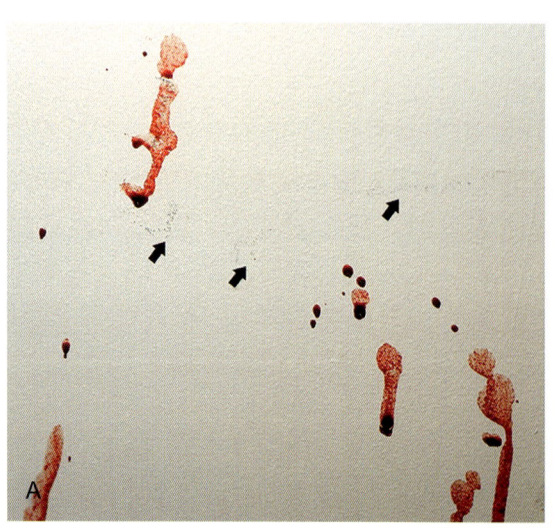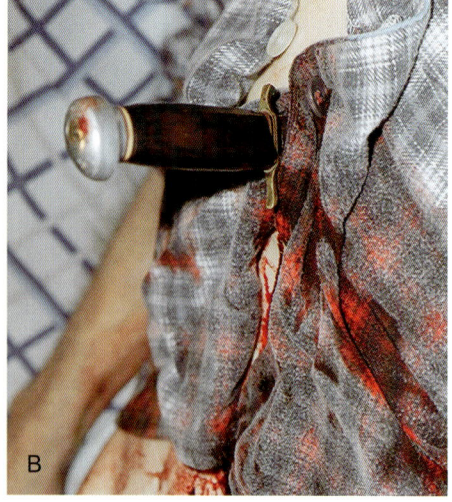

图 7-16 自杀性刺创。(A)死者将刀柄抵在墙上。墙面上可见与溅落血迹相邻的浅灰色印痕(箭头所示),印痕是由刀柄上的金属转移于墙面所致。(B)刺入身体的刀,刀柄末端为灰色金属。

- 刺穿身体所需外力大小的评估往往难以确定,这涉及多种因素:锐器锋利程度、锐器捅刺速度、死者衣服的数量和性质,以及受损部位的组织类型(77-79)。锐器尖端的锋利程度是影响刺穿身体的最重要因素。若锐器尖端足够锋利,单个手指施加的压力就足以刺入机体(77-79)。若刺器尖端圆钝,则需施加足够大的外力,同时也会增加受损部位钝性损伤的可能性。除骨骼和钙化软骨外,皮肤是对锐器抵抗最强的组织。一旦刺穿皮肤,进一步刺入机体所需的外力会变小(77,78,80)。身体不同部位的抗穿透性存在差异(77),如肋间隙比上腹部更容易被刺穿,这是由于肋间隙组织的张力更强。有人利用尸体和截肢标本进行研究,发现肌肉被刺穿时可产生显著的抵抗力(79,81)。

- 无论是接触皮肤表面(静止的),还是在距离皮肤 15 厘米(6 英寸)处,刀仅需 0.5-3 千克(1.1-6.6 磅)的压力(0.5-3 牛的外力)即可刺穿胸腹部皮肤(15,77,78)。Knight 发现,尸体在向距离 10 厘米(4 英寸)被固定的刀前倾时,刀很容易刺入(77)。Green 发现,当刀距离尸体 15 厘米(6 英寸)时,突然从尸体后方推动尸体,皮肤极易被刺穿[类似"意外跌倒"(78)]。有案例描述,42 岁男性自杀时利用从 10 厘米(4 英寸)高处自由下落的匕首(2.72 千克或 6 磅)刺穿胸腔,刺入肺部深达 12 厘米[4.75 英寸(15)]。若刀处于运动状态,刺向身体的瞬间作用力会更大。与小幅度的低手刺入方式相比,大幅度的过肩抢摆刺入时产生的终末平均速度和能量要大得多(82,83)。此外,垂直皮肤表面刺入机体要比成角刺入时产生的作用力大(80)。

- 使用锋利的锐器,单手即可刺破衣物,但如果锐器较钝则需两手一起发力[如螺丝刀(84)]。钝器可在不刺破衣物的情况下造成皮肤损伤,同时可伴有部分衣物嵌入创腔内。创缘不整的创口提示致伤物为钝器或带有锯齿缘,而血液会黏附于衣物纤维上,使得创缘看上去相对"整洁"。Green 发现,向锐器施加 2-3 千克(4.4-6.6 磅)的压力即可刺穿衣物(78)。

- 将刀从体内拔出可能需要更大的外力[对于着装尸体而言,外力可高达 15 千克或 33 磅(78)]。如果尸体检验发现不止一处损伤,可提示作案动机(78)。但也有研究显示从猪皮肤内拔除刀具并不需要太大的力量(79)。

- 医疗护理:随着住院治疗时间的延长,创口会逐渐愈合(图 7-17)。医疗手段(如开胸手术)的介入会影响创伤愈合或造成创伤(如置入胸腔引流管,图 7-17 和图 7-18)。法医需从病史材料中获取准确的信息,从而对损伤进行有效评估。

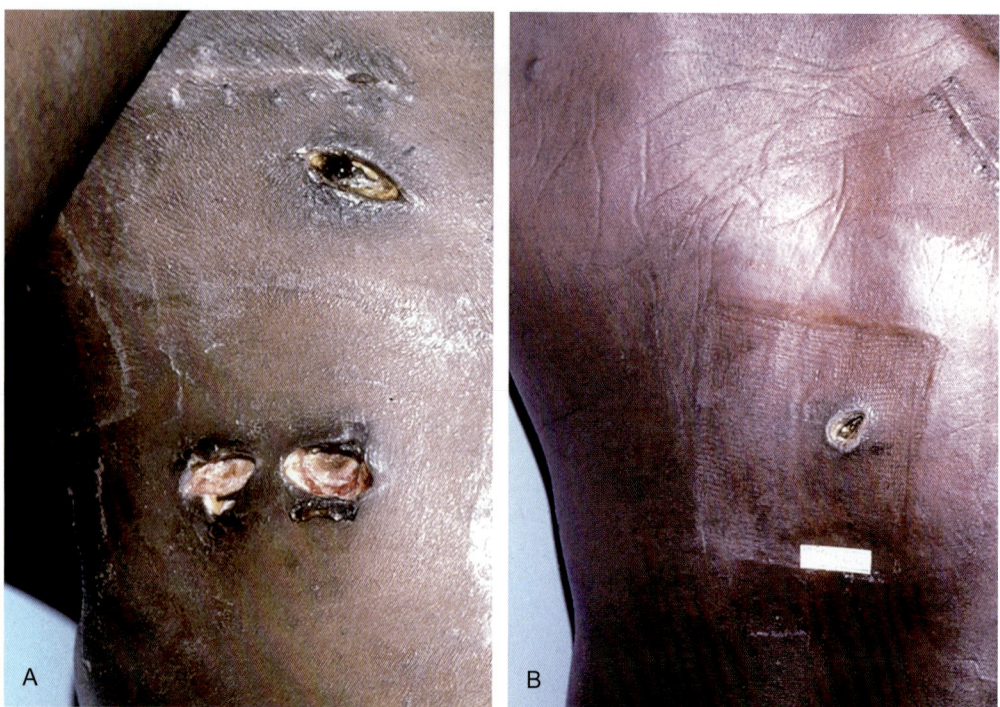

图 7-17 多发性刺创引起败血症导致的迟发性死亡。(A) 多处愈合中的胸腔引流口。(B) 愈合中的背部刺创,为与他人发生争执时受的伤(美国北卡罗来纳州教堂山市法医局供图)。

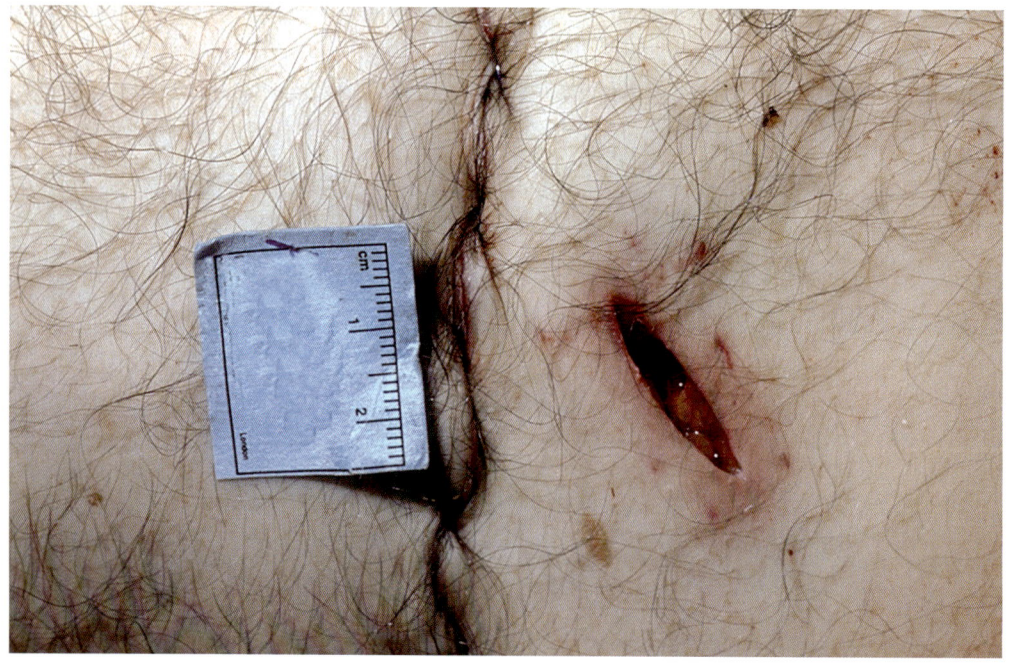

图 7-18 "刺创",为开胸术胸壁手术切口上方的胸腔引流口。

4 锐器伤外部检查的其他特点（表7-1）

4.1 衣着

在他杀案例中,受害者的衣服通常被损坏,但是有些受害者的衣服也可能被推至一定部位[如儿童(6,23)]。在自杀案例中,死者一般会将衣物推至一定部位暴露皮肤,但是也可能在其自杀过程中衣物被损坏(图7-19;参考文献2,6,7,10,13,23,85和86)。自杀案例中,尤其当皮肤损伤较少时,衣物的损坏情况可为死者的试探性自伤提供重要线索。因此,法医对死者的衣着检查要高度重视,不但要将衣物上的纤维缺口位置与皮肤伤口对应,还应分析无皮肤损伤处的衣服破损情况。此外,在锐器刺入身体过程中衣物碎片也会被带入创腔(46)。

4.2 数量、方向及分类

在自杀和他杀案件中,单一的致命性刺创多位于死者胸部(6),多发性锐器伤一

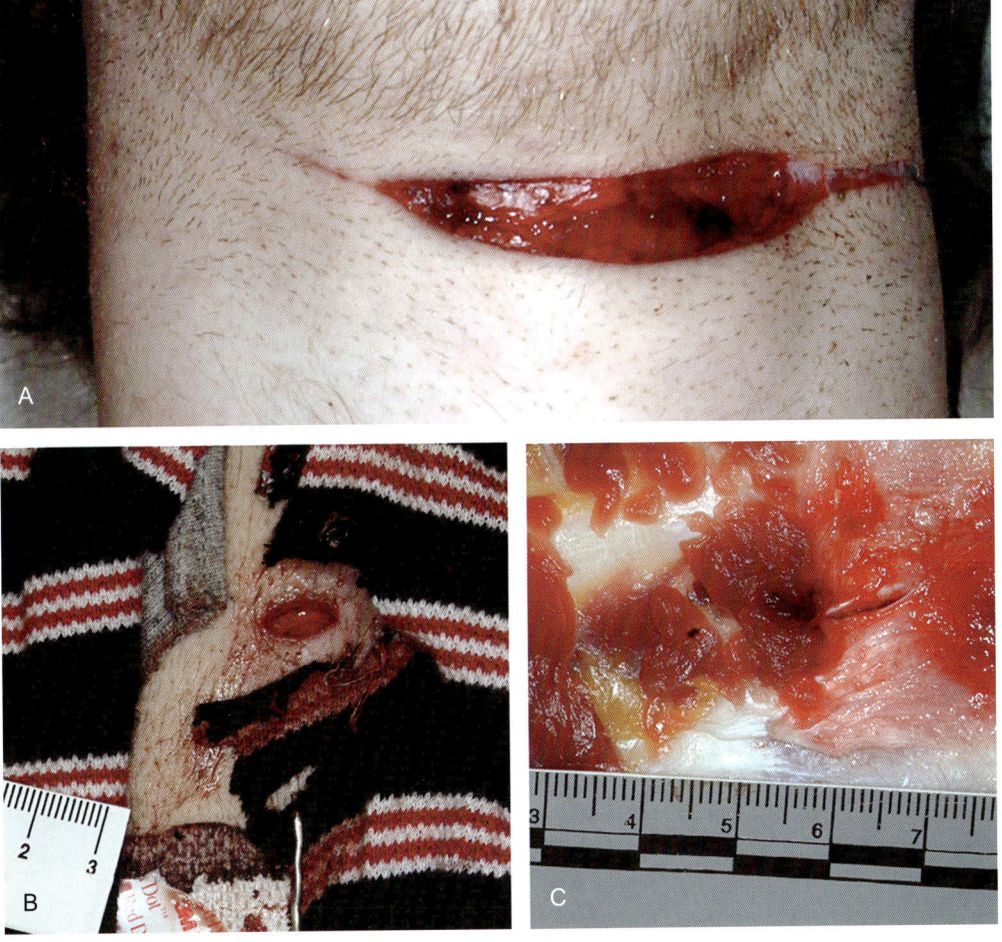

图7-19 自杀性锐器伤。(A)颈部浅表切创。(B)穿透针织衫致胸部致命性刺创(探针所示)。(C)刀具刺穿胸骨(加拿大安大略省伦敦市伦敦健康科学中心 E.Tweedie 博士供图)。

般常见于自杀者的四肢(6),而多发离断性损伤则提示他杀(17)。有案例报道在他杀者身上发现98处伤口(3)。研究显示,自杀者平均存在14.4处锐器伤,而他杀者身上平均只有8.8处(人均体表刺创数目:自杀案件6.8处;他杀案件5.6处;人均体表切创数目:自杀案件15.0处,他杀案件3.5处)(8)。自杀案件中自杀者常存在多处锐器伤,但是单一锐器伤也不能排除自杀的可能(8,12,13,22)。四肢的单一自伤性刺创也有报道(如股动脉刺创)(8)。自杀案件中亦可检见单一切创(如手腕的桡动脉或尺动脉切创)(图7-20和图7-21;参考文献13)。自杀案件中单一的腹部刺创在下文有详细的描述(参阅标题4.3.1;图7-6;参考文献8)。

垂直于胸部所致的刺创常见于他杀(6,87)。一项斯德哥尔摩的研究发现,他杀刺创多见于死者身体右侧上部且垂直走向,而自杀性刺创更多位于受害者身体左侧上部且为水平走向(图7-22;参考文献13)。位于胸部水平走向的创伤数目在自杀和他杀案件中并无统计学差异,但也有研究发现大多数自杀者左胸部的刺创常为水平走向(6,9)。然而,自杀者的颈部刺创方向常向下(10),上腹部的刺创创道常向上,这反映出自杀者刺向心脏的意图(9)。

判断切创走行方向仍是个难题(88)。切创一般在起始处较深,在末端较浅,但并非绝对(参阅标题4.4;图7-23;参考文献88)。通过电镜扫描发现,在切创的起始部存在侧向的副尾,当创口方向垂直于朗格线时尤其明显(88)。

自伤性锐器伤常集中于身体的某一区域(图7-22;参考文献10)。

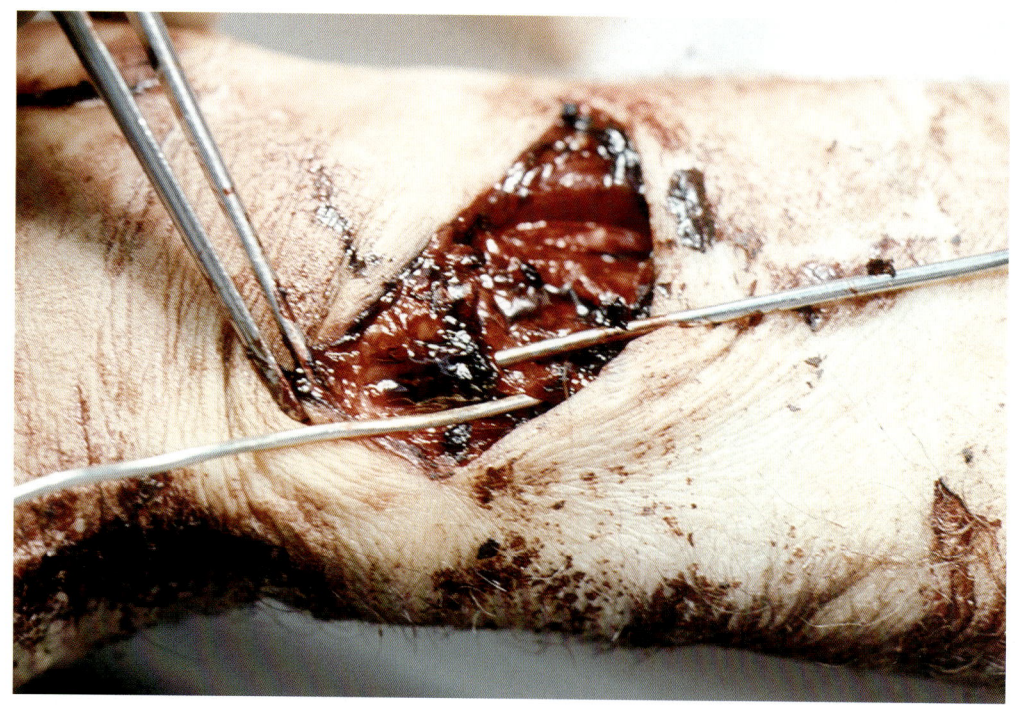

图7-20　自杀者手腕切创造成的桡动脉损伤(插入桡动脉的探针所示)出血。

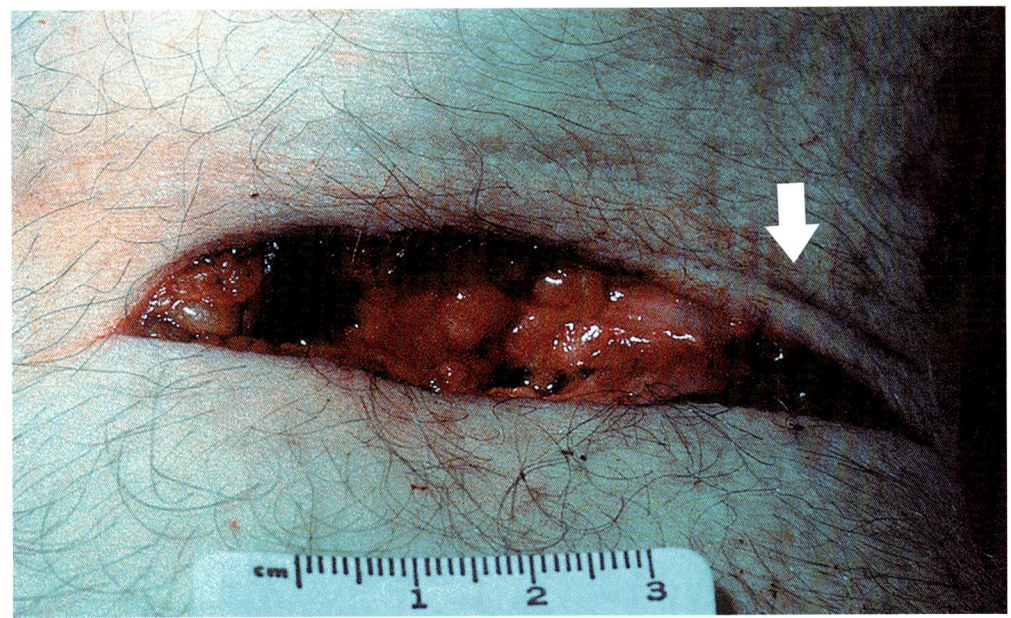

图 7-21 肘窝自伤性切创。与深部创口平行走行的表浅切创（试切创；箭头所示）。

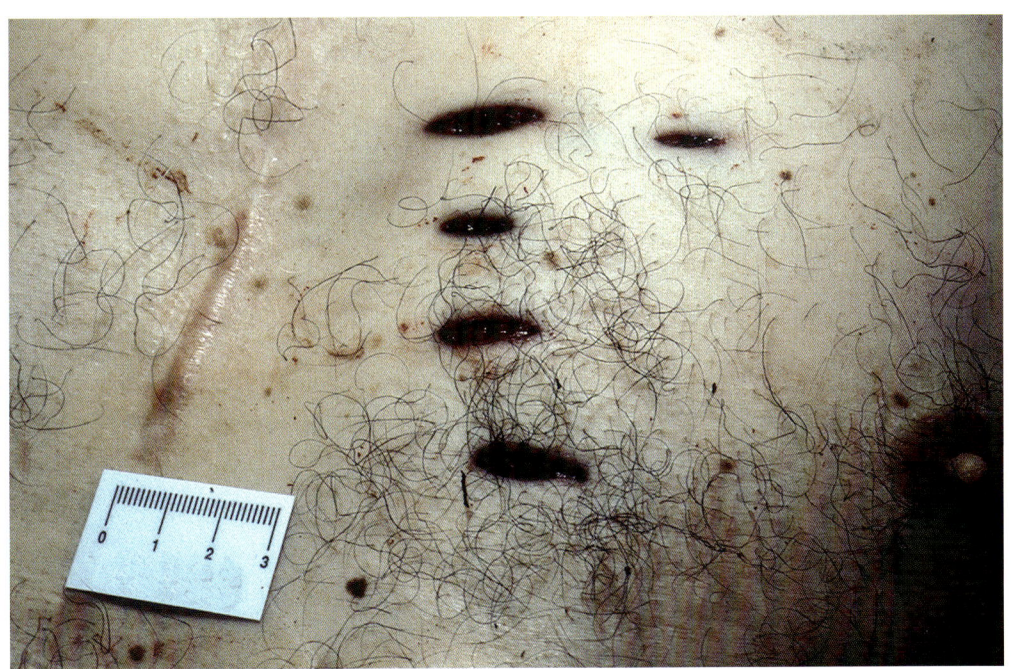

图 7-22 心前区多处水平方向的自伤性刺创。

4.3 创伤部位

按照死亡方式,创伤部位的描述见表 7-1。

4.3.1 剖腹自杀

剖腹自杀（harakiri，hara：腹部，kiri：切，日文）是日本传统的自杀形式，是一种不常见的自伤性腹部创伤（27，85）。自杀者用剑刃或刀刃刺入左下腹并向右水平切割，第二刀向上切割（27，85，89），从而在腹壁形成疼痛难忍的 L 形创口，但并未伤及腹腔器官（85，89）。这样不会导致立刻死亡，随后的自残行为造成颈部、胸部和上肢的切割伤则会加速死亡（18，27，85，89）。传统情况下，在剖腹自杀者切腹后，在场的介错人会将其斩首（18，27）。从事这种仪式的人可能患有精神疾病或处于醉酒状态（85）。

4.4 试切创和抵抗伤

尝试性或"试切"伤由自身所致，其特征是在较深的致命伤附近伴有浅表切创或刺创（图 7-19，图 7-21，图 7-23－图 7-26，参考文献 6，8，13，16，17，23，85，86）。浅表切创一般相互平行并延伸至皮下（16，90）。刺创周围可能伴有多处簇聚的细小刺痕并存在擦挫伤（16）。刺创周围会伴有线性尾部擦伤或较深的切创（图 7-24）

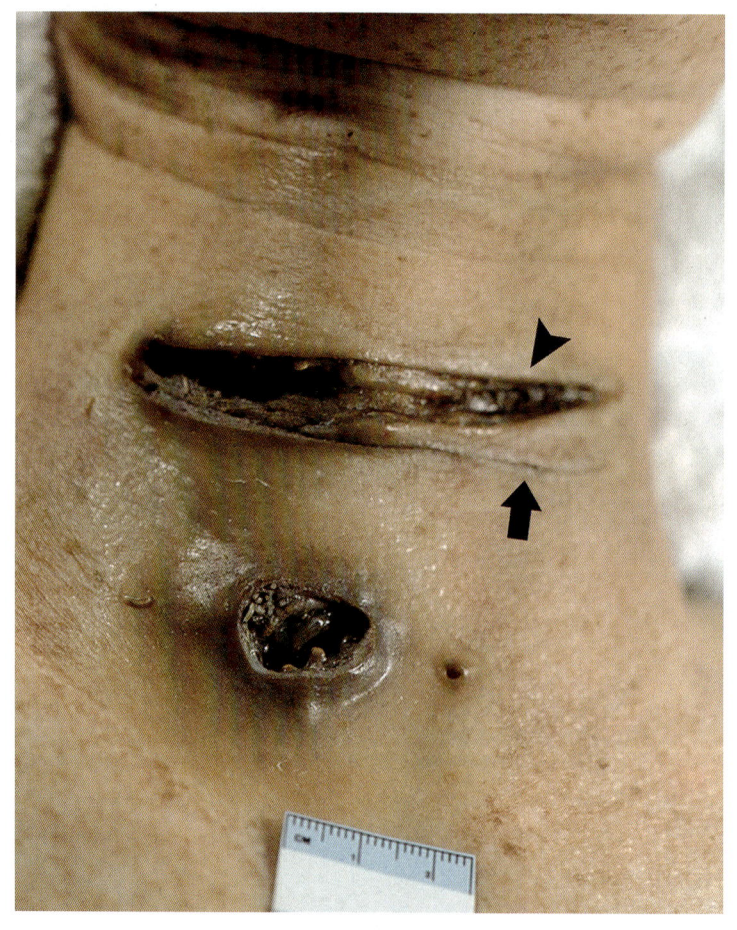

图 7-23 自伤性颈部刺创和切创。深切创一侧的"浅尾"（三角箭头所示）及与其相邻的浅切创（"试切"伤；箭头所示）。

第 7 章 | 穿透性损伤——锐器损伤

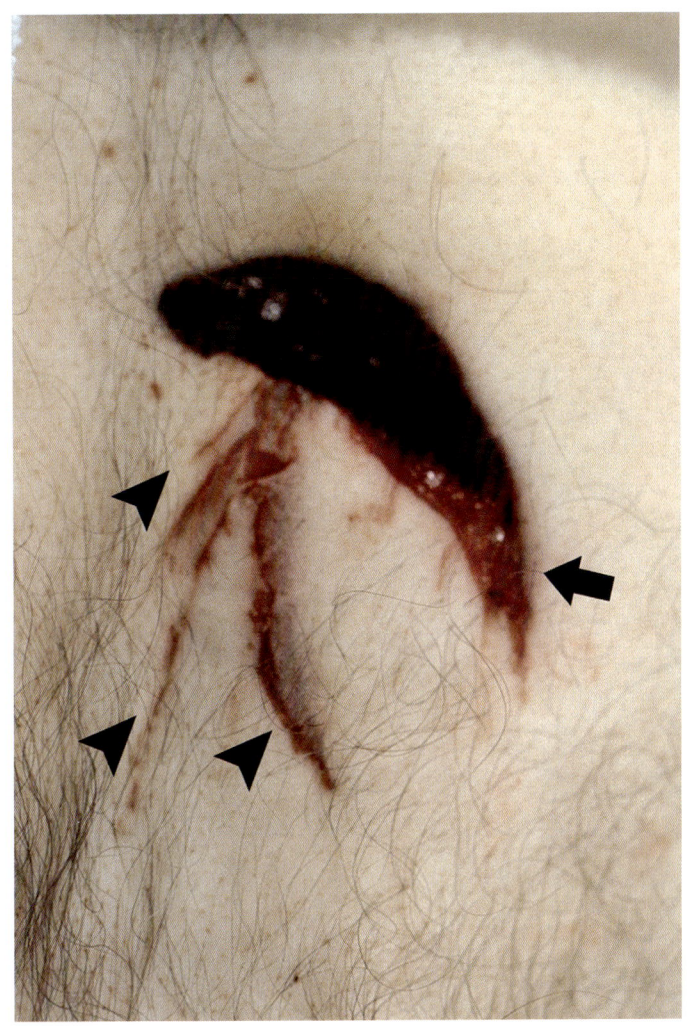

图 7-24 自伤性腹部创伤。深创伤伴有一处浅表的尾部擦伤（箭头所示）。浅表切创提示为"试切"伤（三角箭头所示）。

(16)。当损伤涉及身体多个部位时，可以检见多处试切创(16)。自杀者的手指上会发现浅表切口，与抵抗伤形态相似(5,6,9,16,27)，这些浅表切割伤为错误使用刀具或其他锐器［如剃须刀(10,16)］所致。在被谋杀的儿童体表可以检见尝试性损伤，这些损伤在成年人中较罕见，但在因疾病、中毒或其他残障而丧失行为能力的成年人中也可检见(6,17,23,90)。试切伤出血提示为生前所致，电动工具自伤案件中也会检见浅表或较深的试切创（如带锯或圆锯；参阅图 7-5；参考文献 65,69）。

抵抗伤常见于四肢，手臂损伤最常见，由伤者在自卫或抵抗过程中移动身体保护躯干致命部位所引起（图 7-27；参考文献 3,8）。伤者在抵抗中也可能会因夺取刀具而受伤（图 7-28）。抵抗伤在女性中更常见，因为女性更易受到长期的家庭暴力，会在自卫过程中受伤(3)。

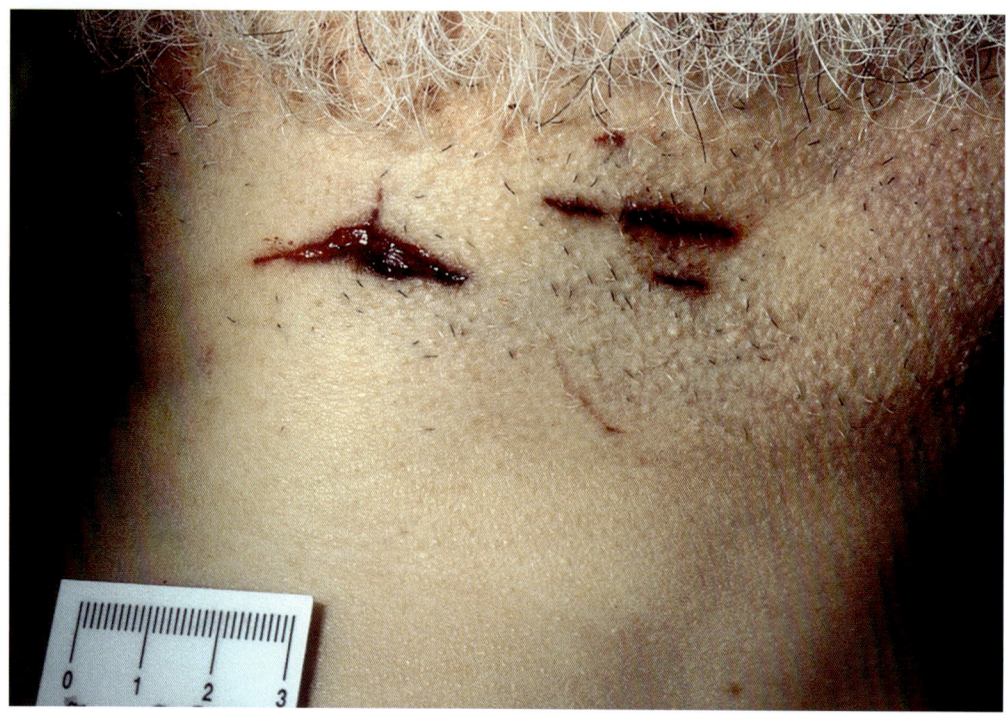

图 7-25 自伤性颈部浅表刺创（"试切"创）。

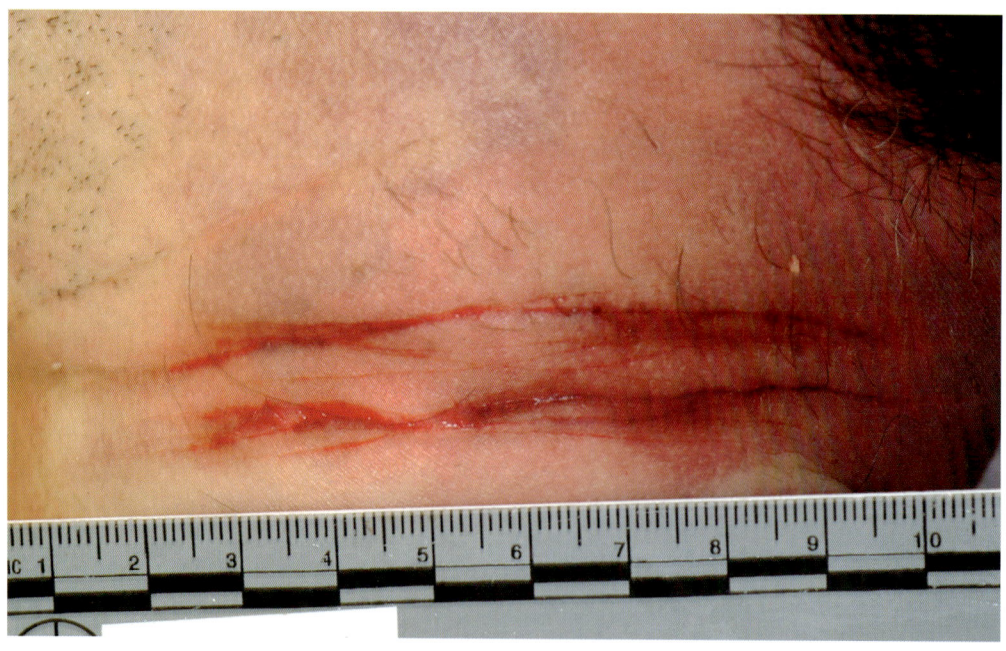

图 7-26 颈部浅表"试切"创（加拿大安大略省伦敦市伦敦健康科学中心 E.Tweedie 博士供图）。

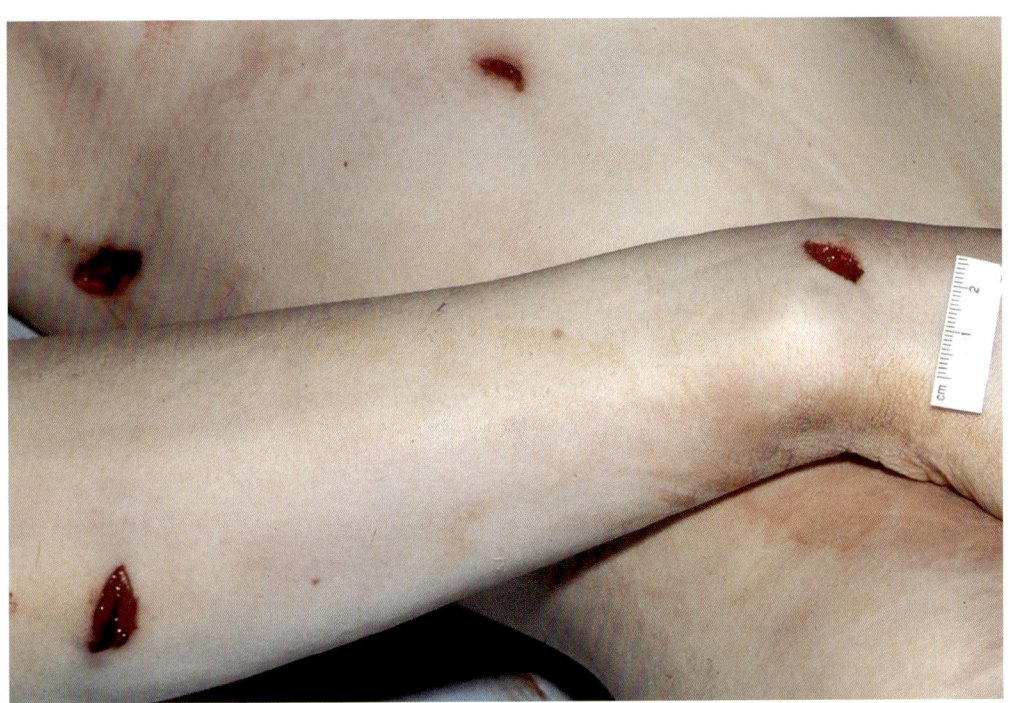

图7-27 他杀,多处刺创。手臂上的刺创说明受害人曾有过自卫行为("抵抗"伤)(美国北卡罗来纳州教堂山市法医局供图)。

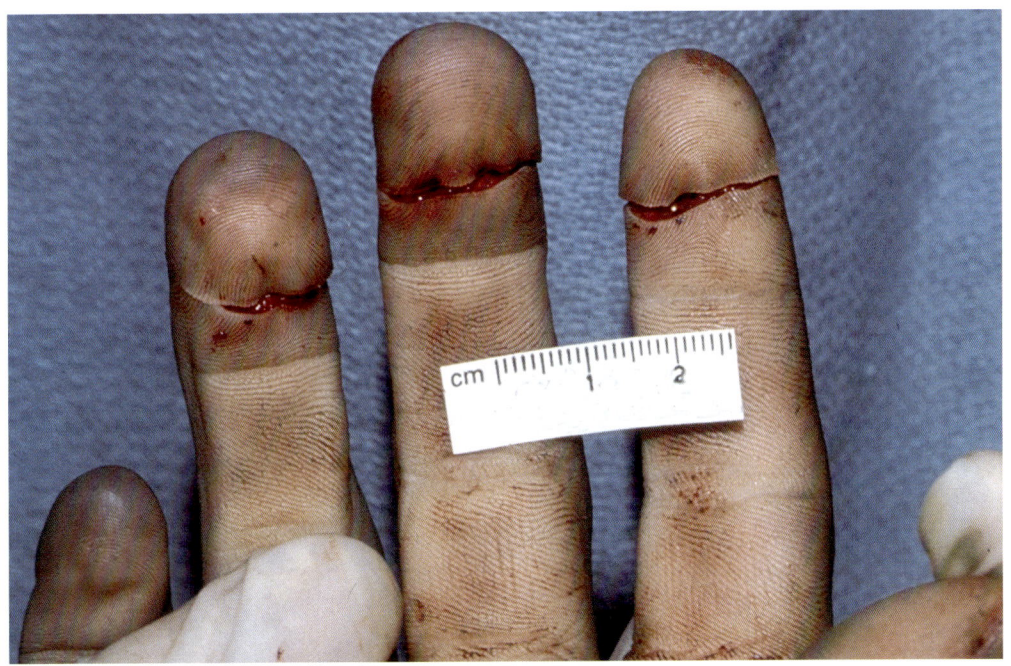

图7-28 抵抗伤。受害人伸手抓刀时手指遭切割(美国北卡罗来纳州教堂山市法医局供图)。

4.5 他杀还是自杀

Karlsson 采用多元分析模型研究他杀刺创的阳性预测因素,按重要性降序排列分别为: 衣物破损、血液乙醇含量、抵抗伤、其他暴力性损伤、垂直于胸部的刺创、上肢的锐器伤(手腕和肘窝除外)、头部和背部锐器伤(91)。与自杀性刺死呈正相关的因素依次为: 肘窝锐器伤(手臂弯曲)、自杀者家中的现场、自杀笔记、自杀者年龄、手腕部锐器伤、自杀意念以及试切伤(91)。

5 自伤和自残

在尸检时会发现一些经专业处理或自己处理的身体穿孔装饰(如在身体某些部位穿孔并插入饰品,如舌头、乳头和生殖器)(56,92)。这些身体穿孔装饰常受社会、文化或宗教习俗的影响(93-95)。

自伤性切割可由于精神异常所致,也可以是非精神异常行为造成的,酒精或药物均会增强这种损伤行为(图7-29;参考文献56,93,95-101)。自伤性切割可以是宗教仪式行为,也可以是获取经济利益的手段[如诈病、保险欺诈(56,64,93,95,96)]。四肢自伤(如割腕)很常见(56,99,101)。自伤性损伤通常相对较小,且为分布于身体非疼痛敏感区的浅表皮肤损伤。多发重复的浅表伤提示为反应性或习惯性行为(95,96,98)。有些人会采用注射药物(如利多卡因)的方式获取镇痛作用(102)。尽管在致命性自杀案中这些损伤会以不同形式或类型出现,但自伤性损伤常不足以引起死亡(图7-30;参考文献10,56,95,97)。愈合的手腕切创表明受害者曾试图自杀,提示调查人员,其死亡方式可能为自杀(图7-31;参考文献7,12)。

更多的致残性损伤通常与精神疾病有关,损伤常造成重要器官解剖结构破坏,常需要外科手术治疗,严重者可能导致死亡(图7-32;参考文献56,99)。但也

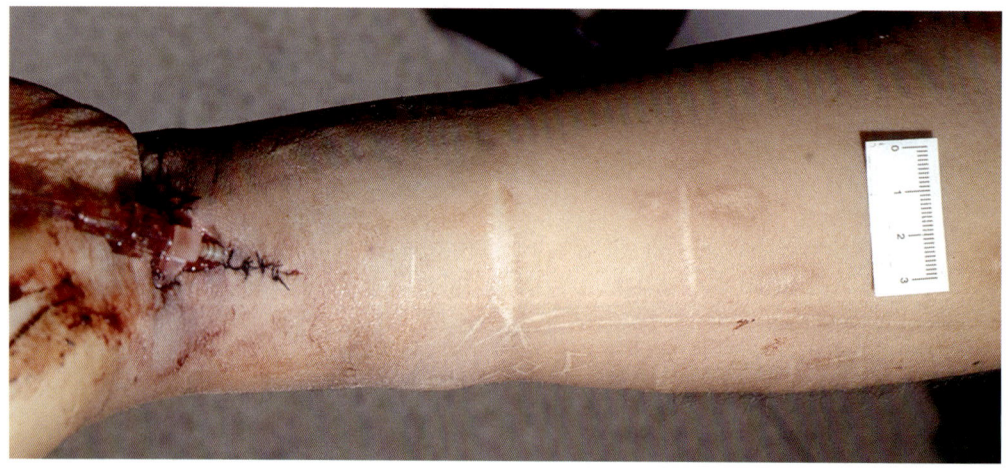

图7-29 住院期间死于乙酰氨基酚中毒。径向插入。先前自伤所致的前臂多处线性和不规则瘢痕。

第 7 章 | 穿透性损伤——锐器损伤

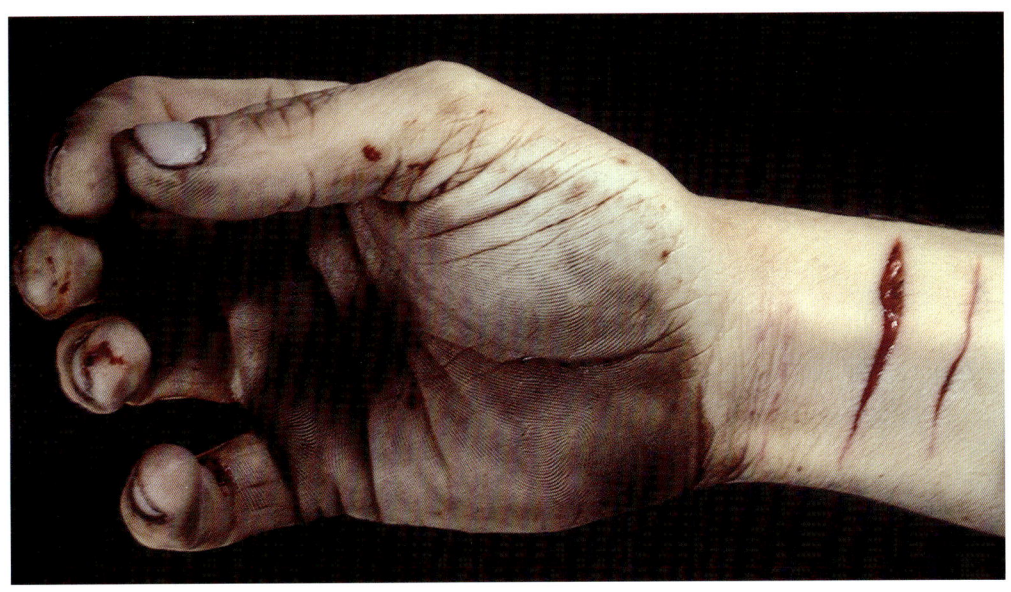

图 7-30　新鲜的自伤性手腕切创。发生于胸部枪弹射击自杀案。

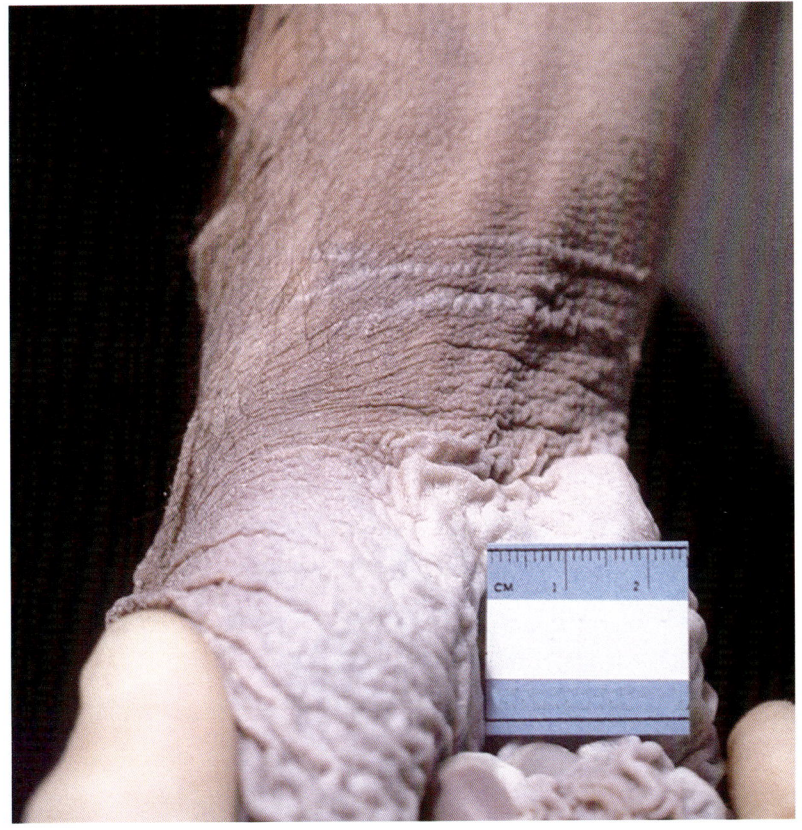

图 7-31　愈合的手腕切创。死于浴缸（水浸泡作用导致手的皮肤明显皱缩），服用了过量盐酸苯海拉明自杀。

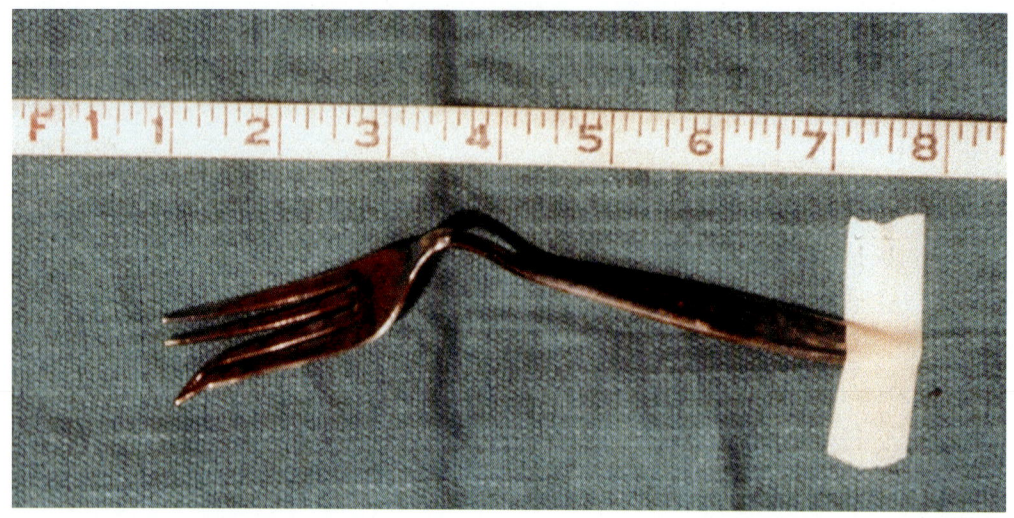

图 7-32 精神分裂症患者。餐叉插入头部所致的自伤性创伤。眼球被挖和颅顶骨穿透引起硬脑膜下出血。穿透颅顶骨的餐叉弯曲变形。

有一些为非精神障碍人群所致(94),醉酒、中毒或精神错乱者也可能有自残行为(95,99)。自残可能属于 Munchausen 综合征的一部分(56,95,96)。精神病患者能够承受非同一般的伤痛: 自己摘除眼球、锐器创伤或指甲创除、自身离断、器械导致的内脏穿孔、颅骨穿透以及阉割(参阅标题 6.2;参考文献 53,54,56,94,99,103,104)。前文已描述使用菜刀或电锯对手臂进行的自体离断(69,103)。

生殖器自残者分为 3 类: 精神病患者(精神分裂症患者)、异装癖者以及具有复杂宗教或文化信仰的患者(93)。这些案例通常发生在男性中(93)。妇女可能会毁损她们的生殖器官以实现堕胎(93)。前文已描述将针头插入腹壁以引起流产的自伤性损伤(105)。

6 内部检查

6.1 骨和软骨损伤

在自杀和他杀的锐器伤中均可见骨和软骨损伤(6,106)。在涉及儿童的他杀案件中胸骨、肋骨损伤较少见(23)。胸壁损伤更多为多发性皮肤创伤(106)。骨/软骨损伤部位常与致命性损伤位置相对应(106)。在一项研究中,喉软骨损伤可发生在自杀和他杀案件中,而肋骨、脊椎和颅骨损伤常限于他杀案件中(参阅标题 6.2,参考文献 23,106)。穿透性/横断性胸、肋骨损伤常提示自杀的可能(图 7-19)。在严重的精神病患者中会发生胸骨横断性损伤(6)。胸、肋骨损伤可能会伴有肋间动脉或乳内动脉(即胸廓内动脉,搭桥最常用的血管)损伤(参阅第 8 章标题 6.1,参考文献 38,73,107)。

评价锐器伤时,包括肋软骨损伤,可能需要对刀具进行分类(108)。刀具作用身体所致的条状损伤可能仅具有一般性特征,但是刀具本身的某些小缺陷可形成独特的损伤标记(108,109)。应用特殊技术可将这些条状损伤与刀刃部相对照匹配以判定致伤刀具(109)。提取受损的骨和软骨并保存于甲醛液中,以备用作致伤刀具的推断(109)。

6.2 颅脑损伤

6.2.1 颅骨损伤

他杀引起的头部刺创与自伤性头部刺创显著不同(110),自伤性颅骨穿透伤很罕见(参阅标题2.3;图7-32;参考文献14),但多次锤式撞击于一把被固定的刀也可能造成颅骨穿透伤。具有锋利尖端的物体(如钉子)能够钉入颅内(111)。某些物体(如铅笔、撬棍等)也可刺穿颅骨(45,112)。坠落的锋利物体能轻易地刺穿相对薄弱的颞骨鳞部(45)。电动工具(如带状电锯或圆盘锯)亦可造成自伤性颅脑损伤(图7-5;参考文献65,69),且电动工具引起的意外损伤有时与枪弹伤入口较相似(67)。

6.2.2 眶壁穿透

经眶壁穿透颅脑的情形较罕见(54,113),大多数情况为意外,包括儿童或成人跌倒或滑倒在尖端物体上[如铅笔(7,11,31,53,54,110,113-118)]。有时自杀和他杀也可形成眶壁穿透伤(52,117,119,120)。

由于成人眼窝的平均深度为4-4.5厘米或约1.75英寸,穿透物长度常需大于5厘米(2英寸)才能穿过眼窝(52,117)。眼窝的解剖结构会使致伤物沿着内侧壁向内刺入(52)。眼球距内侧壁比外侧壁远[距内侧壁6.5毫米或约0.25英寸,距外侧壁4.5毫米或约0.2英寸(52)]。致伤物可沿经眶上裂或眶板的薄弱处继续刺入(52,77,114,117)。由于巩膜具有较好的韧性,且致伤物刺入时眼睛会移动,故眼球通常不易受伤,但较大致伤物仍会造成眼球损伤(117-119)。致伤物穿透眶上裂便可直接刺入大脑额叶下方的海绵窦,向内则伤及颞骨岩部上方和脑干外侧的颞叶(52,119),同时颈内动脉和视神经亦会受损(119)。而意外创伤通常趋于向上向内走行,损伤大脑额叶(119)。自伤性刺创的创道则趋向颅后窝(117,121)。

外部检查往往难以发现眶内损伤,尤其是眶周组织明显肿胀并伴有神经症状时(118,119)。利用影像学检查(X线,CT)能显示不透射线的物体(122)。MRI检查可显现出木制异物(123)。

眼眶损伤能通过不同反射活动抑制迷走神经,从而引起致命性心律失常:眼心反射、眼睑和三叉神经-心脏反射(124-126)。

6.2.3 其他颅骨孔隙(图7-33)

腭部贯通伤极少致命(127),造成该类损伤的常见情况为:儿童向前摔倒时嘴里含有致伤物(127)。扁桃体周围区域的损伤会导致颈内动脉血栓形成(127)。

圆珠笔经鼻孔插入可刺入脑内(120)。

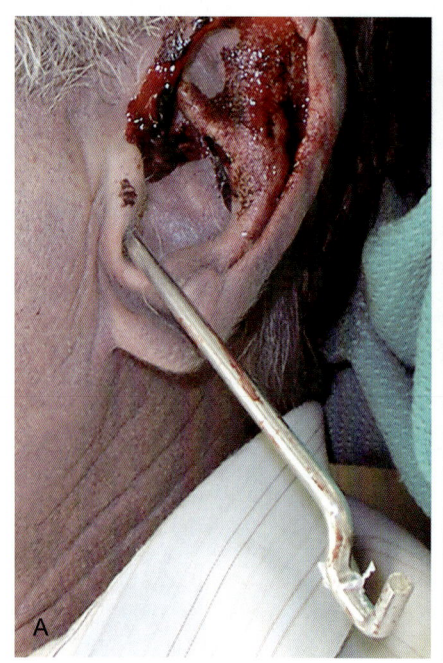 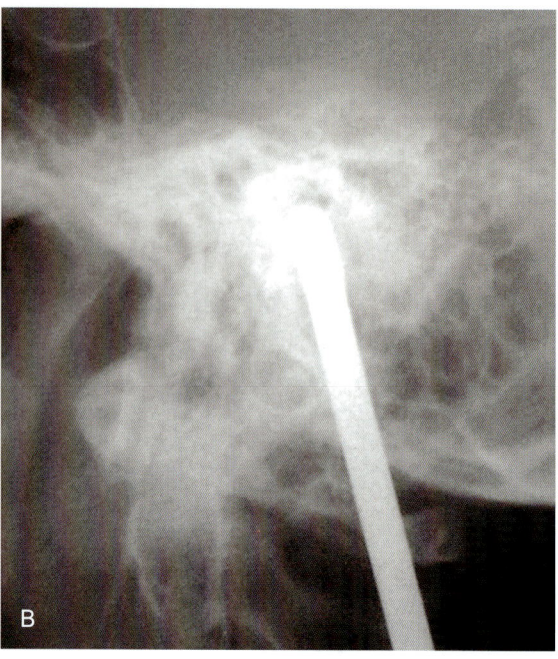

图 7-33 自伤性刺伤,头部损伤(致命性胸部损伤以外的损伤)。(A)金属棒刺入耳内,未穿透颅骨。(B)X线片显示金属棒位置(加拿大安大略省伦敦市伦敦健康科学中心 E.Tweedie 博士供图)。

7 伤后目的性活动和存活时间

受害者死亡之前可能会有不同程度的目的性活动(91)。

有研究表明,仅21%的锐器伤死者伤后还有身体活动(128)。尽管他们的活动能力会受到很大影响(如在机体功能衰竭之前爬楼梯),有些伤者的存活时间从5分钟到42小时不等(128)。另有研究表明,在致命性刺伤案件中某些机体活动仍可能发生(28)。相对于他杀案件中的受害者而言,自杀者因能预期到损伤的严重性,故其身体活动更明显(28)。酒精中毒不一定会影响目的性活动和存活时间(128)。

心脏遭受穿透伤时受害者常立即死亡,然而心脏损伤后血流动力学的不稳定取决于许多因素(参阅标题8;参考文献73,128)。其他血管损伤(如主动脉)可引起休克(73,129),冠状动脉损伤则导致心肌缺血(73)。与心包毗邻的纵隔结构可封闭心包损伤部位,如果心包伤口很小,血液则难以溢入胸腔。当心包积血量达150-200毫升时,心脏压塞会非常严重(128)。与枪弹创相比,裂隙样心脏刺创会随心肌收缩而使创口变窄、缩小(图7-34;参考文献28)。心室壁长度小于1厘米(约0.5英寸)的裂隙样刺创可自发性闭合。与较大的破口(达2厘米或0.75英寸)相比,心肌的小穿孔或小裂口(0.7-1厘米;0.25-0.5英寸)可使受害者的存活时间延长(28)。与枪弹伤相比,锐器伤受害者的生存时间更长,死亡率较低(28,130)。在心脏穿透伤的研究中,由于锐器刺伤的受害者存活时间较长,因此更有可能被送到医院

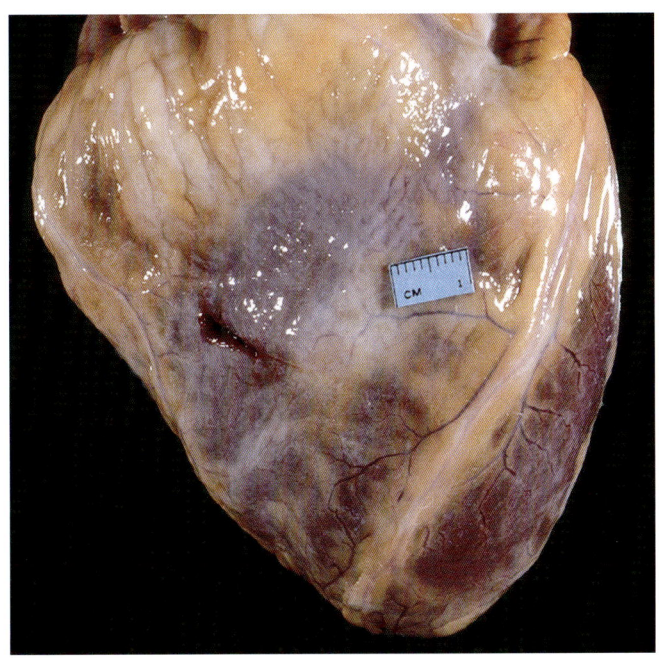

图7-34 裂隙样心脏刺创。

接受抢救(73)。即使心脏遭受穿透伤,甚至多发伤,受害者在短时间内仍然有目的性活动(128)。据案例报道,一名44岁男性自杀者刺伤胸部造成左心前壁6处刺创(长达0.5-1厘米或约0.5英寸),尸检发现心包积血300毫升,左、右胸腔积血分别为320毫升和90毫升。这名44岁男性在伤后还能清洗刀具、换掉血腥衣服、在亲属面前吃午饭,于伤后2小时死亡(131)。

单侧颈动脉和椎动脉横断会使受害者在几秒钟内多器官功能衰竭,但如果单侧动脉血流未完全中断,受害者则可能维持数分钟的生命活动(28)。外周静脉(如大隐静脉)大出血的情况比较罕见,出血后伤者可能存活数小时(28)。有案例报道,一名49岁女性在汽车里刺伤自己后步行100米(330英尺),再自缢死亡,后在汽车副驾驶位发现一把带血的登山刀。尸检发现这名女子的胸部有3处伤口,导致肺被刺破、右侧颈内静脉被切断(132)。外周动脉切断后有时受害者也可能存活数小时之久(28)。

除心脏和大血管损伤外,在其他多器官(如肝、肾、肺)损伤的情况下,人体可存活数小时(128)。

在现场受伤后很快便死亡的人的内部出血往往并不严重,而存活时间较长的伤者会有大量的失血(128),但失血量达1.5升的伤者仍会有意识行为(128)。体外失血量可通过称量受害者血液浸渍的衣服和其他亚麻制品,再称量洗涤烘干后的上述衣物,将两者的重量相减进行失血量估计(26)。

8 死亡机制

刺创和切创均为"低速"损伤,其损伤后果通常受不连续创道的影响。需要探测创道以明确死亡原因,死因确定需要通过创伤部位和失血量加以判断,如胸、腹腔内失血量。死亡机制如下:

- 失血性休克。
- 空气栓塞(涉及颈部结构时;参阅本章标题 12.1;第 5 章标题 14.8;参考文献 11,73,129)。
- 吸入血液所致的吸入性窒息[如肺、气管或椎动脉损伤(图 7-35;参考文献 15,19)]。
- 心脏压塞。
- 血和(或)气胸。
- 脑和脊髓损伤(图 7-14;参考文献 9,11,31,32,90,133,134)。
- 并发症:术后明显的低血压;各种术后并发症包括肺栓塞、肺炎、伤口脓毒症(图 7-17)、再出血和心肌缺血(73);颅骨骨折导致脑膜炎(119)。

对上述案件,法医须明确受害者的直接死因(参阅第 1 章标题 11)。

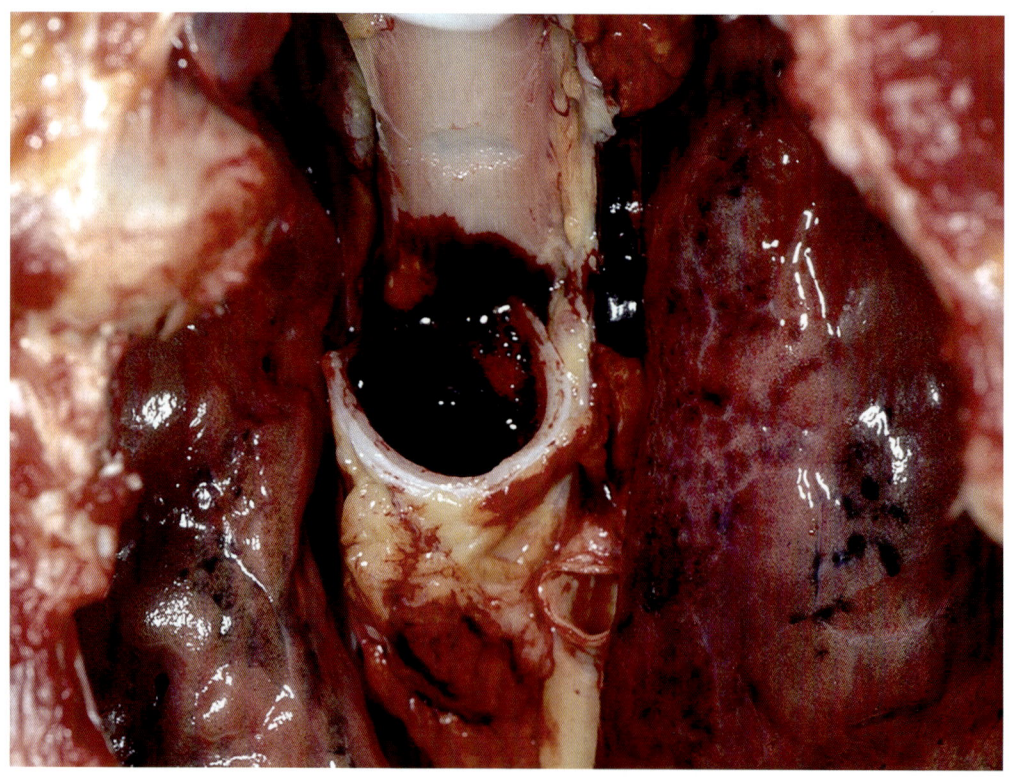

图 7-35 颈部刺创。尸体解剖见气管腔内大量血液。

9 刺创和切创的法医学鉴定方法

1. 脱掉衣物之前应先拍摄全身照。注意血液溅落的形态特征。
2. 需对死者衣物做证据保留。记录衣物的破口与撕裂情况,分析衣服破损与皮肤损伤的关系。
3. 在清洗尸体前,应先对尸体拍照,包括不同部位的损伤。
4. 锐器损伤记录:
   a. 创伤的长度、宽度和深度。如果伤口呈裂开或哆开状,应将创缘合并、对齐后重新测量长度。创口深度可使用探针探查,了解创道轨迹和方向,注意操作过程中可能会改变创道本来的轨迹。
   b. 相对于死者位置,创道方向可呈现水平、垂直和倾斜。
   c. 创角是尖锐的还是圆钝的?需要区分锐器伤还是钝器伤。
   d. 创伤的位置。需测量伤口与头顶、身体中线或某解剖学位置之间的距离,以进行解剖定位。如果不止一处损伤,可对损伤进行编号标记。
5. 检查身体其余部位,尤其需要关注手部。
6. 对身体受伤部位进行影像学检查以排除残留于伤口内断裂的刀尖。
7. 清洗尸体并重新检验伤口,对损伤部位进行拍照。
8. 如果刀仍留在损伤原位,在尸体检验时应用塑料袋将其封存。在尸体解剖过程中应尝试确定刀尖所在的位置。
9. 记录创道、出血情况,以及颅腔、胸、腹腔等处的出血量。
10. 记录其他类型的损伤和病变。
11. 提取毒化检材。必要时提取血样进行 DNA 分析。

10 犬咬伤

遭犬攻击并被咬死的案例极少[在美国,每年估计约 10 人(135,136)]。尽管重度损伤常与大型犬(如比特犬、罗特韦尔犬、德国牧羊犬)有关,但不同类型的犬均可造成严重咬伤(136−140)。年轻的雄性犬(1−5 岁)更有攻击性(140)。受害者身体弱小是被犬攻击咬伤的因素之一。大多数受害者为幼儿或老年人(135−143),熟睡中的婴儿同样容易受攻击(136,137)。

宠物犬攻击最常见(138,140)。在犬主人的领地,犬更具有攻击性,这些犬名为散养或缺乏约束(136,144)。各种不同的原因均会挑衅或激怒犬:犬在家中的地位受到了威胁(如新生儿影响了它的家庭地位);犬担心它的地盘、食物或玩具受到威胁,而且人类难以识别犬的痛苦,特别是幼儿;犬的攻击性也会受人的活动或声音刺激而产生;疾病亦会改变犬的行为[如狂犬病(136,138,140,143,145)]。饥饿不一定是引起犬发起攻击的刺激因素(135,145)。犬的攻击行为常可被预先察觉

(135,137,144)。

犬群攻击不常见(135,143,145)。犬天生具有结群的本能(143,145)。过去,犬与人类之间的关系不稳定,当犬群参与捕食并察觉受到威胁或受人类活动刺激时[如奔跑(135,143,145)],更易发生群体性攻击行为。有时受害者的防御行为(如挥舞手臂)也可能导致犬的攻击更加猛烈(135)。

最常见的咬伤部位是下肢,其次为上肢、头部、面部、颈部和躯干(140)。流浪犬往往咬伤上肢,尤其是当儿童试图触摸流浪犬头部时,上肢会被咬伤(140)。宠物犬一般与儿童较为亲近,且儿童常趴在动物身上,故宠物犬往往咬伤儿童的头面部或颈部(140,143,144,146)。头、颈部咬伤往往具有致命性(135,143,147)。犬群攻击更能造成严重的损伤(135)。犬先咬伤受害者的下肢使其难以站立和行动,伤者跌倒后犬再攻击其头部、颈部和胸部(138,140,143,145)。

犬的咬痕比猫的更长、更窄(148)。受激惹的犬咬住人体后会大幅度晃动头部,造成受损部位软组织广泛性损毁、器官和四肢损毁(135,143,147),严重时会导致伤者截肢,衣物会被咬碎(135,149)。对于儿童,可能会造成颅骨凹陷性骨折和颅骨穿孔(136,150,151)。伤者会引起感染(如蜂窝织炎)(143,147)。犬咬伤所致的广泛性损伤有时与他杀性锐器伤相似(图7-36)(149)。

在犬身上或嘴中可以发现受害者的血液、衣物和毛发(135,138)。通过对犬的

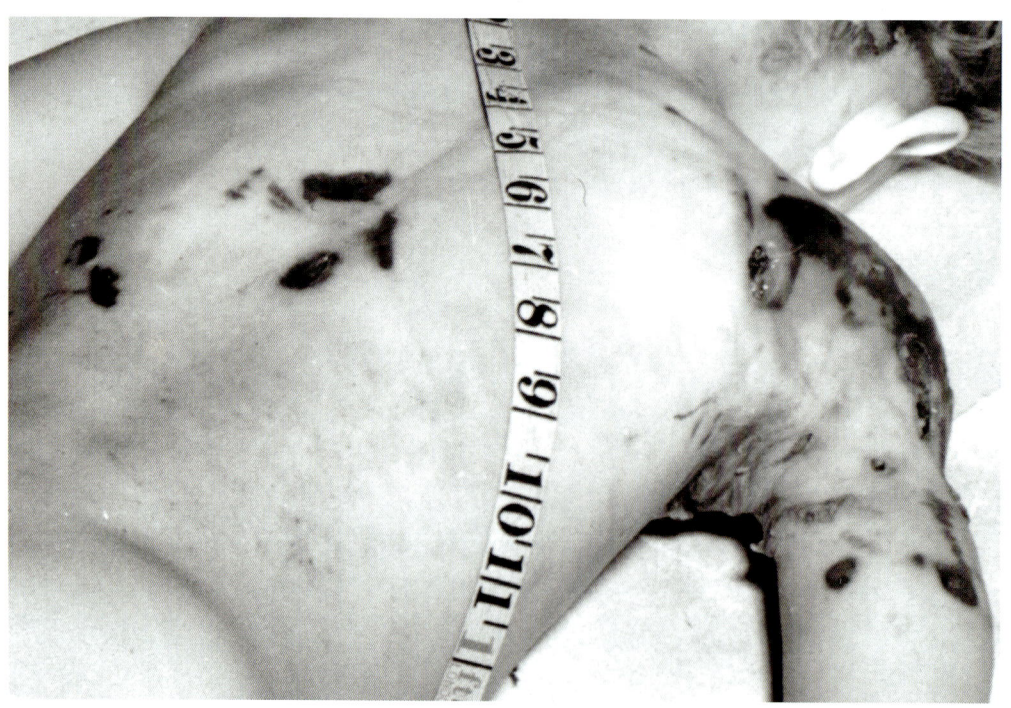

图7-36 犬攻击幼儿所致的多发性损伤(加拿大安大略省伦敦市西安大略大学 J.C.E. Kaufmann 博士供图)。

影像学检查和尸体解剖,在其胃肠道内可发现吞食的人体器官组织(136,138,143)。对犬的尸体解剖可以发现犬产生攻击行为的病理原因(138)。可将动物牙齿与受害者身上的咬痕进行比对(136,138,142,148,149)。如果是犬群攻击,会发现多种不同的咬痕(145)。通过显微镜检查,犬嘴内的物质在受害者创口部位也可能会被发现(149)。

11 过敏性反应:昆虫叮咬和药物注射

过敏反应(过敏性休克)是一种导致外周循环衰竭的速发型超敏反应(152)。在美国,每年死于过敏反应的人估计约有 500 例(153)。过敏反应由组织的肥大细胞释放组胺和其他炎症介质所触发(152)。肥大细胞的活化是过敏原与特异性 IgE 抗体在肥大细胞上相互作用的结果,但某些药物和诊断剂也可直接引起肥大细胞释放组胺(152,154)。引起过敏反应的情况很多,包括昆虫叮咬[如膜翅目昆虫蚊子(黄蜂)]、药物注射(如抗生素)、食物摄取(如贝壳类)和花粉吸入(152,154)。肥大细胞介质的释放会引起平滑肌收缩(如支气管痉挛)、血管扩张和毛细血管通透性增加(152)。最常见的症状和体征表现为急性呼吸或循环功能衰竭[呼吸困难、哮喘及胸痛(152,155)],也会出现肢体抽搐、恶心呕吐和皮疹(152)。过敏症状通常在接触过敏原 20 分钟内产生,但也可能延迟至 2.5 小时(152)。

由于组胺的半衰期很短,故不适于进行死后分析(156)。类胰蛋白酶是一种在肥大细胞分泌颗粒中发现的中性蛋白酶,具有较长的半衰期,可作为一种过敏反应中检测活化肥大细胞的指标(153,154,156,157)。过敏反应发生 1 小时后,血清中类胰蛋白酶含量开始升高,并维持数小时。如果伤者发生过敏反应后未死,则其体内的类胰蛋白酶水平会逐渐下降到正常水平(154)。类胰蛋白酶正常一般意味着并未发生过敏反应,但也可能是由于血样提取得过早或过晚。如果患者存活或 24 小时内死亡,能最准确地检测到其血清中的类胰蛋白酶水平(153,154)。尸检时提取的血清应在冷藏环境下运输,而后 −20℃冷冻保存。非过敏性休克死亡尸体的类胰蛋白酶水平也会升高,这必须结合案情加以严谨的解释说明(156,158)。其中 β− 胰蛋白酶测定的特异性较高。但胸腔液和心包液不能用于分析测定(154)。IgE 特异性抗体水平升高表明症状发生前已致敏(154,159)。

过敏死亡案件的尸检有时缺乏明显的特异性改变(152),或无任何特异性改变(152,155)。肺和其他器官淤血在该类案件中均可检见,也可能是唯一的发现(152,154,155)。有些案件会发现受害者气道阻塞引起的肺气肿(152,154,155)。肺气肿可能与肺不张相互交替(152,155)。喉头水肿是较特异性的发现,但并不总是很明显(152,153,155)。有时也可能观察到舌头和声门区水肿(155)。关于此类案例,声门区的镜下特点一般为固有层水肿(152,155)。气管和支气管黏膜也会出现水肿改变(155)。高度严重的肺气肿也会被检见(152,155)。有时还会发现哮喘的病理学改变(如呼吸道上皮基底膜增厚)(155)。肝脏和脾脏内的嗜酸性粒细胞数目会增加,但这也可能是死者生前患过敏性疾病所致(155),而此时嗜酸性粒细胞在肺和上呼吸道组织内可能更加显著(152,155)。

12 医疗意外

医疗意外死亡是由医疗意外相关的损伤所致或在医疗过程中或即刻出现的不良后果引起。先天性伤残或治疗之前的身体状况、副作用,或者涉及医疗过程的并发症不属于医疗意外(160)。医疗意外包括诊疗过程中刻板的诊断和治疗;错误的、不规范的诊疗行为;不合适的药物剂量或给药方式;医疗设备的错误使用;使用不适当的或有故障的医疗设备(160)。医源性疾病是指由诊疗行为引起的疾病(161)。医源性疾病和医疗意外并非疏忽所致(161,162)。

如果患者死于医疗意外,而处理案件的病理医生或法医是该医院职工,那么就会有潜在的利益冲突。因此,尸体解剖需由其他机构完成,如果难以实现,为了确保案件公正性,案件调查过程需要法医全程参与。必须全面系统地进行尸体解剖,包括显微镜检查和其他必要的辅助检查(162,163)。对于麻醉/外科手术死亡的案件,明确死亡原因时不仅需要考虑手术方式和潜在的并发症,还应考虑可能促进患者死亡的潜在性疾病(163)。手术过程中引起医源性并发症而导致患者的死亡,需要考虑手术的选择及实施是否针对危及生命的病情。

对纽约州住院患者的调查研究表明,3.7%的住院患者会发生诊疗的不良后果(164),其中约四分之一为疏忽造成的(164)。对一所医学院附属医院815例住院患者的研究发现,36%的患者存在医源性疾病(161),9%的患者会有威胁生命或造成残疾的严重后果,2%的患者会死亡。其中最主要的原因是药物的使用。然而,严重并发症常在诊疗过程中产生。心导管介入术发生并发症最常见。此外,从养老院转入重症监护室的患者并发症的发生率较高。

在宾夕法尼亚州涉及医疗意外死亡的案件中,大约有四分之三由治疗引起,而其他常见于诊断过程(160)。大约一半的医疗意外为医疗损伤所致(导管插入引起的致命性出血最常见),17.5%为药物毒性,约13%为过敏反应(抗生素或放射造影剂),气道阻塞与过敏反应的发生比例相似[气管切开术(160)]。其中90%以上发生在医院,大学附属医院并发症的发生率是其他医疗机构的两倍(160)。涉及法医学的调查可能首先由医院的病理医生处理(160)。

俄亥俄州代顿市法医办公室对9 497例案件的研究发现,44例(发生率0.46%)为医疗意外:手术占36%(最常见的为术中造成血管或内脏损伤并引起致命性大出血,其他原因包括心搏呼吸骤停、气管切开并发症、空气栓塞、严重的基础疾病下的外科手术、失血后凝血障碍、血液吸入);30%为麻醉并发症(最常见的为麻醉中急性心搏呼吸骤停,其他原因包括吸入性肺炎、术中或术后呼吸停止、迟发性肝衰竭、药物过量);18%为治疗性操作(最常见的为内脏穿孔、电休克治疗后心脏停搏;其他原因包括透析方法不当、治疗性血管超负荷、血液吸入、血管撕裂);14%为诊断失误(最常见的为血管或心脏撕裂;其他原因包括静脉造影剂急性反应、腐蚀性物质食管内浸润、脑血管意外、空气栓塞);药物反应(青霉素过敏)占2%(162)。

12.1 医源性穿透伤(中央静脉导管)

留置的静脉导管对医源性损伤的判断尤为重要(165)。多个穿刺点是反复尝试插入导管的证据(图7-37;参考文献166)。中央静脉和肺动脉导管通过锁骨下静脉穿刺置入体内。中央静脉导管的用途包括测量中心静脉压,快速、大量的静脉输液,不适宜的外周静脉用药,长期肠外营养和药物注射,以及起搏器和肺动脉导管的置入(167)。锁骨下静脉导管置入也可用于血液透析,尤其是急救患者(168,169)。肺动脉导管可测量肺血管内压力,进而监测心功能。胸部X线片可确定导管的位置(167)。

12.1.1 并发症死亡

- 空气栓塞(参阅第5章标题14.8)
  - 胸部和神经外科手术中,颈部的中心静脉置管有发生空气栓塞的风险,也

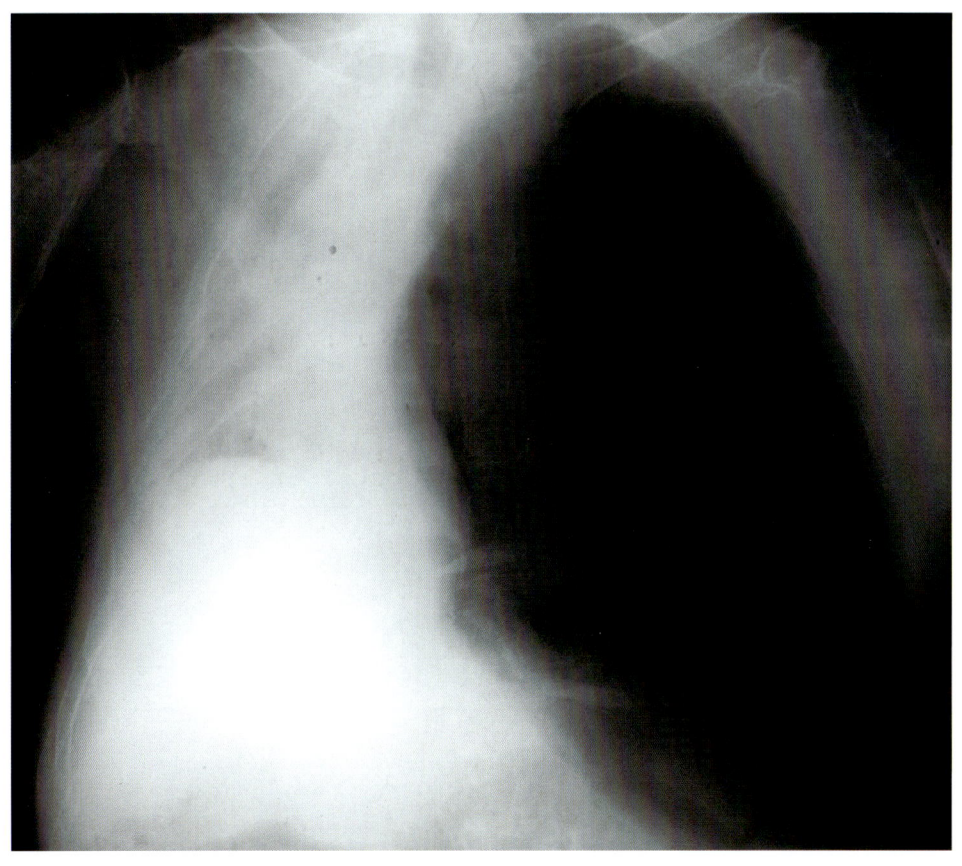

图7-37 尸体X线片显示气胸。多次锁骨下静脉穿刺,中央静脉导管置入。

可能引起气胸(170–173)。导管需在患者身体保持水平或头向下倾斜的位置置入(170–172, 174)。造成死亡的静脉内空气栓塞气体量为10－480毫升(171, 175)。当空气缓慢进入血液循环时，人体可以耐受较大的气体量(176)。右心室内的空气会阻碍血流进入肺脏，引发心力衰竭(173)。在插管过程中导管断裂会使空气进入血液循环(170)。静脉内的气体可以通过心脏房室间的分流或经肺毛细血管床进入体循环(173, 174, 177)。

- 空气栓塞死亡尸体的征象如下(173, 178)：
  - 头、颈部皮肤发绀。
  - 静脉回流受阻导致口、鼻腔溢出血性液体。
  - 眼睑水肿。
  - 舌头伸出。
  - 皮下气肿。
  - 广泛瘀点性出血。
- 空气栓塞死亡尸体的内部特征如下：
  - 从右心可以抽吸出气体(图7–38)。
  - 左心室内也会有空气。
  - 静脉中气泡较明显(如冠状静脉)。

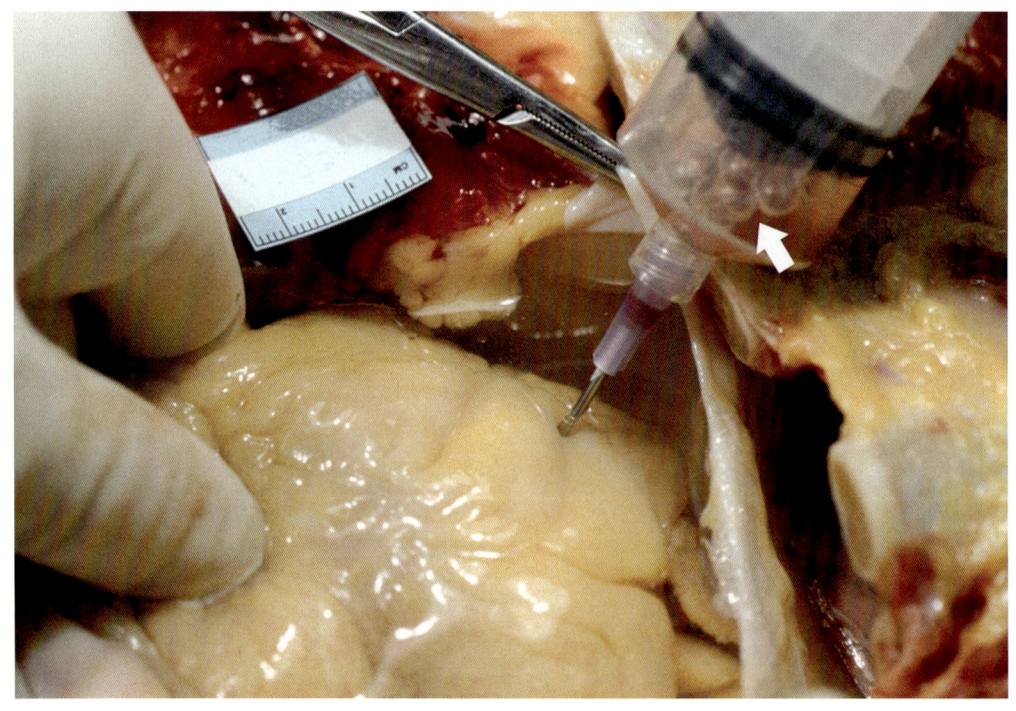

图7–38 空气栓塞。从右心室抽吸出空气。注射器内的气泡(箭头所示)。

- 肺显微镜检查发现血管内有粒细胞和血小板环绕的气泡(179)。
- 穿孔是导致死亡的常见原因(172)。
- 胸腔积液(血液透析)、心包积液、纵隔积液、乳糜胸、血胸(心脏或大静脉被刺破)、气胸(锁骨下穿刺；图 7-37；参考文献 165,167,168,170,171,180-184)。
  - 左颈内静脉中心静脉导管置入时可能会损伤胸导管(172)。
- 血管内导管置入时会刺穿大静脉、心脏或肺动脉分支,导致血液进入纵隔、胸腔或心包腔(图 7-39；参考文献 167,168,170,171,183)；穿刺时很可能会意外刺穿颈部的主要动脉(图 7-40)。
- 由于肺上叶尖部邻近锁骨下静脉,气胸是最常见的并发症(图 7-37；参考文献 167)。
  - 血栓形成(167,172,180)。
  - 导管残片滞留体内(167,170,180)。
- 最常见的原因是具有锋利尖端和斜面的穿刺针切断导管(医源性或患者因素所致)(170,180)。
- 能造成心脏穿孔、肺栓塞,以及血栓栓塞。
  - 感染/败血症(172,180)。
  - 心律失常。
  - 心内导管插入时刺激心脏(167)。

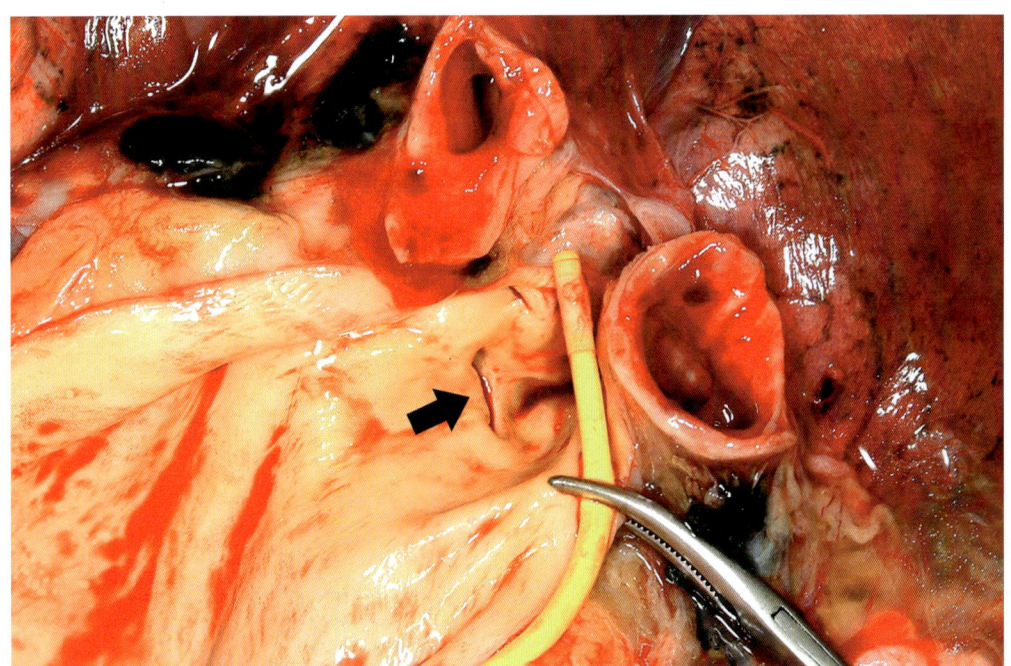

图 7-39 Swan-Ganz 导管(即肺动脉导管,尸检中止血钳夹持处)尖端刺穿肺动脉(箭头所示)(加拿大安大略省伦敦市伦敦健康科学中心 E. Tweedie 博士供图)。

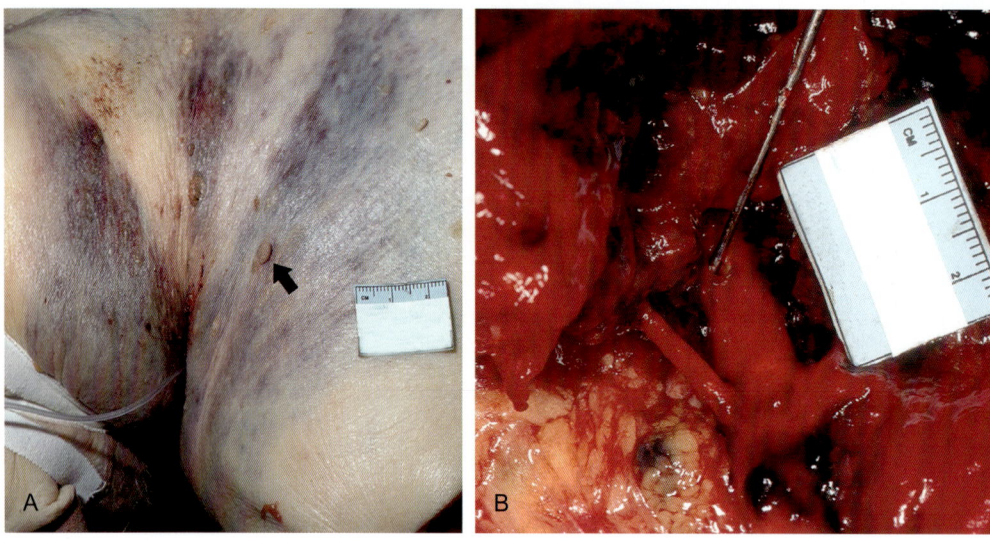

图 7-40　中心静脉导管置入进行血液透析。(A) 锁骨下静脉穿刺处(箭头所示),周围大面积皮肤青紫。(B) 探针所示锁骨下动脉被意外刺穿。

13　自己造成的静脉穿刺

在静脉注射吸毒者身上经常能发现一个或多个自己造成的静脉穿刺针眼。穿刺针眼不仅在常见部位(如肘窝)被检见,在不明显部位也能观察到(图 7-41)。需要排除复苏抢救时形成的静脉穿刺针眼,如果静脉留置针已被拔除,则其判定会更困难(图 7-42)。观察到的点状皮肤瘢痕提示先前注射所形成(图 7-43)。

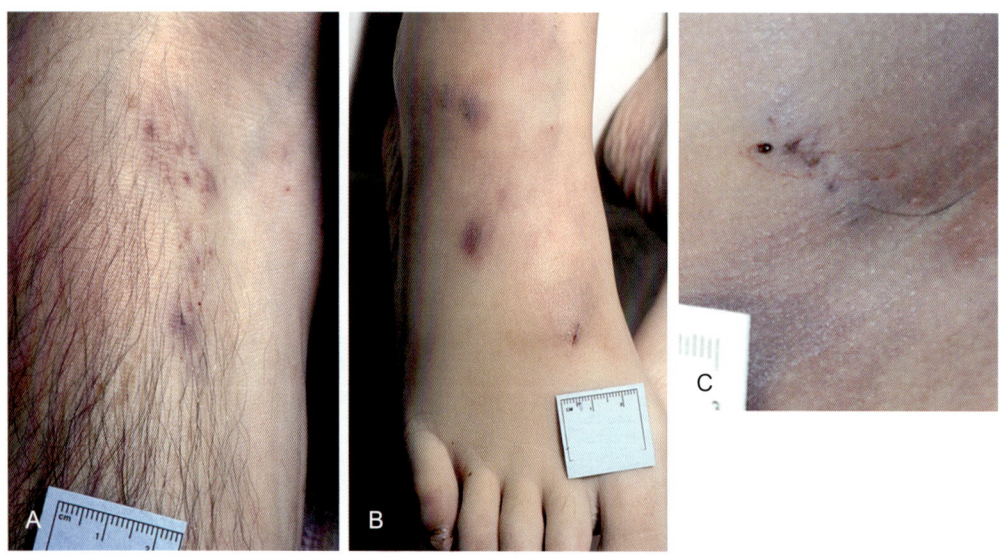

图 7-41　吸毒者体表近期的穿刺针眼。(A) 肘窝。(B) 足背部。(C) 颈部(加拿大安大略省伦敦市伦敦健康科学中心 E. Tweedie 博士供图)。

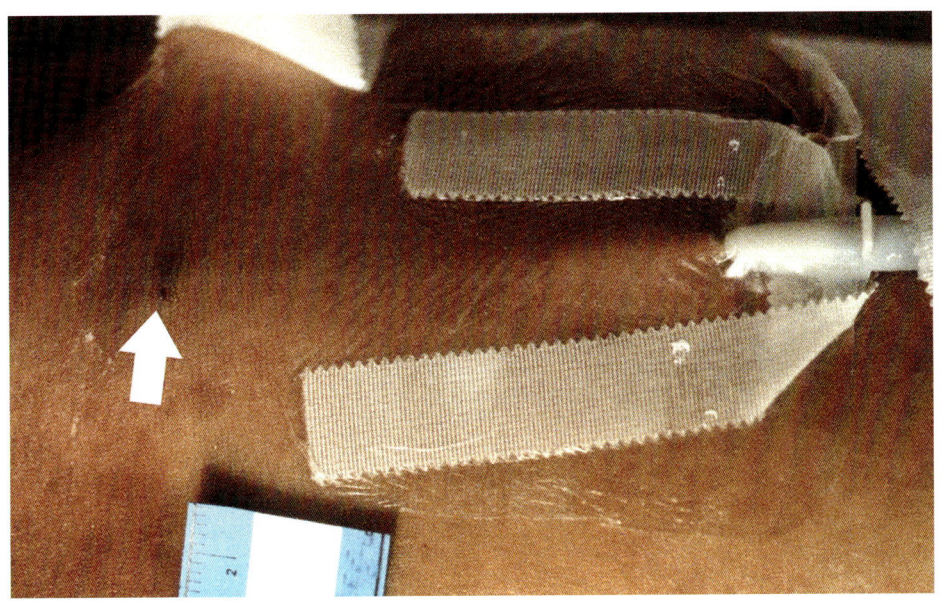

图 7-42 吸毒者身上的穿刺针眼也可能是复苏抢救时所致。静脉留置针。目击证人指出死者注射可卡因的位置(箭头所示)。

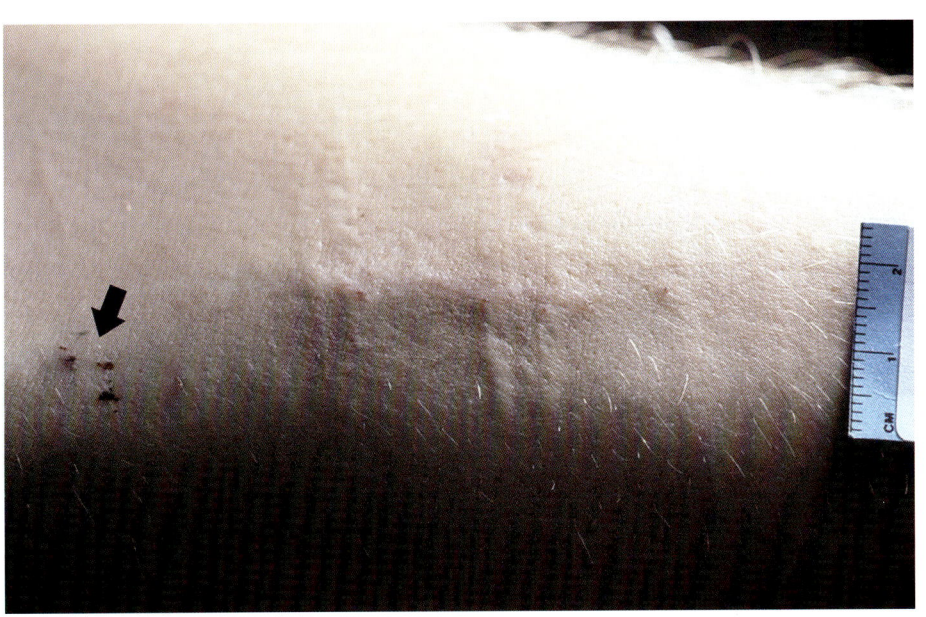

图 7-43 "残留标记"(前臂点状皮肤瘢痕)表明有静脉毒品滥用情况。近期的穿刺针眼(箭头所示)。

田志岭　邓恺飞 译

参考文献

1. Rogde, S., Hougen, H. P., Poulsen, K. Homicide by sharp-force in two Scandinavian

capitals. Forensic Sci. Int. 109:135–145, 2000.

2. Start, R. D., Milroy, C. M., Green, M. A. Suicide by self-stabbing. Forensic Sci. Int. 56:89–94, 1992.

3. Hunt, A. C., Cowling, R. J. Murder by stabbing. Forensic Sci. Int. 52:107–112, 1991.

4. Ormstad, K., Karlsson, T., Enkler, L., Law, B., Rajs, J. Patterns in sharp-force fatalities a comprehensive forensic medical study. J. Forensic Sci. 31:529–542, 1986.

5. Rouse, D. A. Patterns of stab wounds: a six year study. Med. Sci. Law 34:67–71, 1994.

6. Karlsson, T. Homicidal and suicidal sharp-force fatalities in Stockholm, Sweden. Orientation of entrance wounds in stabs gives information in the classification. Forensic Sci. Int. 93:21–32, 1998.

7. Prahlow, J. A., Ross, K. F., Lene, W. J., Kirby, D. B. Accidental sharp-force injury fatalities. Am. J. Forensic Med. Pathol. 22:358–366, 2001.

8. Gill, J. R., Catanese, C. Sharp injury fatalities in New York City. J. Forensic Sci. 47:554–557, 2002.

9. Karger, B., Niemeyer, J., Brinkmann, B. Suicides by sharp-force: typical and atypical features. Int. J. Legal Med. 113:259–262, 2000.

10. West, I. Single suicidal stab wounds—a study of three cases. Med. Sci. Law 21:198–201, 1981.

11. Karger, B., Rothschild, M. A., Pfeiffer, H. Accidental sharp-force fatalities—beware of architectural glass, not knives. Forensic Sci. Int. 123:135–139, 2001.

12. Byard, R. W., Klitte, A., Gilbert, J. D., James, R. A. Clinicopathologic features of fatal self-inflicted incised and stab wounds: a 20-year study. Am. J. Forensic Med. Pathol. 23:15–18, 2002.

13. Karlsson, T., Ormstad, K., Rajs, J. Patterns in sharp-force fatalities—a comprehensive forensic medical study: Part 2. Suicidal sharp-force injury in the Stockholm area 1972–1984. J. Forensic Sci. 33:448–461, 1988.

14. Fekete, J. F., Fox, A. D. Successful suicide by self-inflicted multiple stab wounds of the skull, abdomen, and chest. J. Forensic Sci. 25:634–637, 1980.

15. Ueno, Y., Asano, M., Nushida, H., Adachi, J., Tatsuno, Y. An unusual case of suicide by stabbing with a falling weighted dagger. Forensic Sci. Int. 101:229–236, 1999.

16. Vanezis, P., West, I. E. Tentative injuries in self stabbing. Forensic Sci. Int. 21:65–70, 1983.

17. Betz, P., Tutsch-Bauer, E., Eisenmenger, W. "Tentative" injuries in a homicide. Am. J. Forensic Med. Pathol. 16:246–248, 1995.

18. Kuroda, N., Saito, K., Takada, A., et al. Suicide by self-stabbing in the city of Tokyo—

19. Hasekura, H., Fukushima, H., Yonemura, I., Ota, M. A rare suicidal case of a ten-year-old child stabbing himself in the throat. J. Forensic Sci. 30:1269–1271, 1985.
20. Gee, D. J. Two suicidal transfixions of the neck. Med. Sci. Law 12:171–172, 1972.
21. Chadly, A., Marc, B., Paraire, F., Durigon, M. Suicidal stab wounds of the throat. Med. Sci. Law 31:355–356, 1991.
22. Marc, B., Baudry, F., Zerrouki, L., Ghaith, A., Garnier, M. Suicidal incised wound of a fistula for hemodialysis access in an elderly woman: case report. Am. J. Forensic Med. Pathol. 21:270–272, 2000.
23. Dettling, A., Althaus, L., Haffner, H. T. Criteria for homicide and suicide on victims of extended suicide due to sharp-force injury. Forensic Sci. Int. 134:142–146, 2003.
24. Katkici, U., Ozkok, M. S., Orsal, M. An autopsy evaluation of defence wounds in 195 homicidal deaths due to stabbing. J. Forensic Sci. Soc. 34:237–240, 1994.
25. Urban, R., Eidam, J., Kleemann, W., Troger, H. D. [Isolated stab wound without preliminary stab wounds—suicide or homicide?]. Beitr. Gerichtl. Med. 47:272–277, 1989.
26. Porter, K. K., Jones, M. J. Wrist slashing in a detention center. Case report and review of the literature. Am. J. Forensic Med. Pathol. 11:319–323, 1990.
27. Watanabe, T., Kobayashi, Y., Hata, S. Harakiri and suicide by sharp instruments in Japan. Forensic Sci. 2:191–199, 1973.
28. Karger, B., Niemeyer, J., Brinkmann, B. Physical activity following fatal injury from sharp pointed weapons. Int. J. Legal Med. 112:188–191, 1999.
29. Johnston, S. E., Langley, J. D., Chalmers, D. J. Serious unintentional injuries associated with architectural glass. N. Z. Med. J. 103:117–119, 1990.
30. Evans, R. Injuries produced by shattering annealed glass. Resuscitation 7:119–126, 1979.
31. Rothschild, M. A., Karger, B., Schneider, V. Puncture wounds caused by glass mistaken for with stab wounds with a knife. Forensic Sci. Int. 121:161–165, 2001.
32. Klose, W., Pribilla, O. [Unusual suicide caused by a stab wound in the neck]. Arch. Kriminol. 183:157–162, 1989.
33. Ousby, J., Wilson, D. H. 1086 consecutive injuries caused by glass. Injury 13:427–430, 1982.
34. Kelly, S. B. Penetrating injury of rectum caused by fall in shower. Arch. Emerg. Med. 3:115–118, 1986.
35. Shiono, H., Fujiwara, M., Tabata, N., Azumi, J., Morita, M. A single fatal penetrating chest

wound caused by a dagger−shaped fragment of broken door glass. Am. J. Forensic Med. Pathol. 8:346–349, 1987.

36. Frazer, M., Rosenberg, S. Russian roulette with a knife. J. Forensic Sci. 28:268–272, 1983. 37. Shiono, H., Akane, A., Tanabe, K., Matsubara, K. Cardiac tamponade caused by a stab wound with a sewing needle left in a kimono. Am. J. Forensic Med. Pathol. 14:155–157, 1993.

38. Murphy, G. K. A single fatal penetrating chest wound from shattered wind−blown glass. Am. J. Forensic Med. Pathol. 6:332–335, 1985.

39. Katanick, D., Taff, M. L., Spitz, W. U. A work−related death due to a penetrating chest injury. Am. J. Forensic Med. Pathol. 7:163–164, 1986.

40. Torre, C., Varetto, L. A case of murder by impalement. Z. Rechtsmed. 91:83–84, 1983.

41. Marti, M. C., Morel, P., Rohner, A. Traumatic lesions of the rectum. Int. J. Colorectal Dis. 1:152–154, 1986.

42. Jona, J. Z. Accidental anorectal impalement in children. Pediatr. Emerg. Care 13:40–43, 1997.

43. Evans, R. J., Richmond, J. M. An unusual death due to screwdriver impalement: A case report. Am. J. Forensic Med. Pathol. 17:70–72, 1996.

44. Okumori, M., Futamura, A., Tsukuura, T., et al. Impalement wounds of the head and chest by reinforced steel bars with recovery: an unusual case report. J. Trauma 21:240–241, 1981.

45. Kaiser, M. C., Rodesch, G., Capesius, P. CT in a case of intracranial penetration of a pencil. A case report. Neuroradiology 24:229–231, 1983.

46. Missliwetz, J. Fatal impalement injuries after falls at construction sites. Am. J. Forensic Med. Pathol. 16:81–83, 1995.

47. Vaslef, S. N., Dragelin, J. B., Takla, M. W., Saliba, E. J., Jr. Multiple impalement with survival. Am. J. Emerg. Med. 15:70–72, 1997.

48. Ahmad, N., Busuttil, A. Impaling−type head injury in a road traffic incident. Med. Sci. Law 33:261–263, 1993.

49. Giusti, G. V., Bacci, M. Chain link fence impalements in a traffic accident. Am. J. Forensic Med. Pathol. 7:167–168, 1986.

50. Karger, B., Teige, K., Bajanowski, T. Bizarre impalement fatalities—where is the implement? J. Forensic Sci. 47:389–391, 2002.

51. Di Nunno, N., Solarino, B., Costantinides, F., Di Nunno, C. Fatal impalement with transfixion of the neck in a road traffic accident. Am. J. Forensic Med. Pathol. 25:164–168, 2004.

52. Lasky, J. B., Epley, K. D., Karesh, J. W. Household objects as a cause of self-inflicted orbital apex syndrome. J. Trauma 42:555–558, 1997.

53. Field, H. L., Waldfogel, S. Severe ocular self-injury. Gen. Hosp. Psychiatry 17:224–227, 1995.

54. Bowen, D. I. Self-inflicted orbitocranial injury with a plastic ballpoint pen. Br. J. Ophthalmol. 55:427–430, 1971.

55. Johansson, B., Eriksson, A. Suicide by driving an awl into the brain. Am. J. Forensic Med. Pathol. 9:331–333, 1988.

56. Eckert, W. G. The pathology of self-mutilation and destructive acts: a forensic study and review. J. Forensic Sci. 22:242–250, 1977.

57. Beiler, H. A., Zachariou, Z., Daum, R. Impalement and anorectal injuries in childhood: a retrospective study of 12 cases. J. Pediatr. Surg. 33:1287–1291, 1998.

58. Weber, S., Mauch, W., Kalayoglu, M., Moon, T. D. Intraperitoneal and extraperitoneal bladder rupture secondary to rectal impalement. J. Trauma 38:818–819, 1995.

59. Haynes, C. D., Webb, W. A., Fenno, C. R. Chain saw injuries: review of 330 cases. J. Trauma 20:772–776, 1980.

60. Reuhl, J., Bratzke, H. Death caused by a chain saw—homicide, suicide or accident? A case report with a literature review with 11 illustrations.. Forensic Sci. Int. 105:45–59, 1999.

61. Koehler, S. A., Luckasevic, T. M., Rozin, L., et al. Death by chainsaw: fatal kickback injuries to the neck. J. Forensic Sci. 49:345–350, 2004.

62. Campman, S. C., Springer, F. A., Henrikson, D. M. The chain saw: an uncommon means of committing suicide. J. Forensic Sci. 45:471–473, 2000.

63. Segerberg-Konttinen, M. Suicide by the use of a chain saw. J. Forensic Sci. 29:1249–1252, 1984.

64. Bonte, W. Self-mutilation and private accident insurance. J. Forensic Sci. 28:70–82, 1983.

65. Rainov, N. G., Burkert, W. L. An unusual suicide attempt using a circular saw. Int. J. Legal Med. 106:223–224, 1994.

66. Lim, R. Y. Chain saw injury to the larynx. W. V. Med. J. 83:118–119, 1987.

67. Costantinides, F. A fatal case of accidental cerebral injury due to power drill. Am. J. Forensic Med. Pathol. 3:241–243, 1982.

68. Clark, S. P., Delahunt, B., Thomson, K. J., Fernando, T. L. Suicide by band saw. Am. J. Forensic Med. Pathol. 10:332–334, 1989.

69. Betz, P., Eisenmenger, W. Unusual suicides with electric saws. Forensic Sci. Int. 75:173–

179, 1995.

70. Jackson, F. E. High speed propeller injuries of the brain. Report of two cases. Am. J. Surg. 110:473–476, 1965.

71. Hargarten, S. W., Karlson, T., Vernick. J. S., Aprahamian, C. Motorboat propeller injuries in Wisconsin: enumeration and prevention. J. Trauma 37:187–190, 1994.

72. Pollak, S., Fischer, A. [Morphometric findings of stab wounds]. Beitr. Gerichtl. Med. 49:219–225, 1991.

73. Demetriades, D., van der Veen, B. W. Penetrating injuries of the heart: experience over two years in South Africa. J. Trauma 23:1034–1041, 1983.

74. Ormstad, K., Rajs, J., Calissendorff, B., Ahlberg, N. E. Difference between in vivo and postmortem distances between anterior chest and heart surface. A combined autopsy and in vivo computerized tomography study. Am. J. Forensic Med. Pathol. 5:31–35, 1984.

75. Pollak, S., La Harpe, R. [Defined contusion marks caused by the knife handle]. Arch. Kriminol. 190:1–8, 1992.

76. Murray, L. A., Green, M. A. Hilts and knives: a survey of ten years of fatal stabbings. Med. Sci. Law 27:182–184, 1987.

77. Knight, B. The dynamics of stab wounds. Forensic Sci. 6:249–255, 1975.

78. Green, M. A. Stab wound dynamics—a recording technique for use in medico-legal investigations. J. Forensic Sci. Soc. 18:161–163, 1978.

79. Jones, S., Nokes, L., Leadbeatter, S. The mechanics of stab wounding. Forensic Sci. Int. 67:59–63, 1994.

80. Careless, C. M., Acland, P. R. The resistance of human skin to compressive cutting. Med. Sci. Law 22:99–106, 1982.

81. O'Callaghan, P. T., Jones, M. D., James, D. S., Leadbeatter, S., Holt, C. A., Nokes, L. D. Dynamics of stab wounds: force required for penetration of various cadaveric human tissues. Forensic Sci. Int. 104:173–178, 1999.

82. Chadwick, E. K., Nicol, A. C., Lane, J. V., Gray, T. G. Biomechanics of knife stab attacks. Forensic Sci. Int. 105:35–44, 1999.

83. Horsfall, I., Prosser, P. D., Watson, C. H., Champion, S. M. An assessment of human performance in stabbing. Forensic Sci. Int. 102:79–89, 1999.

84. Monahan, D. L., Harding, H. W. J. Damage to clothing—cuts and tears. J. Forensic Sci. 35:901–912, 1990.

85. Di Nunno, N., Costantinides, F., Bernasconi, P., Di Nunno, C. Suicide by hara-kiri: a series of four cases. Am. J. Forensic Med. Pathol. 22:68–72, 2001.

86. Marcikic, M., Mandic, N. Homicide-suicide by stabbing. Am. J. Forensic Med. Pathol.

11:312–315, 1990.
87. Scolan, V., Telmon, N., Blanc, A., Allery, J. P., Charlet, D., Rouge, D. Homicide–suicide by stabbing study over 10 years in the Toulouse region. Am. J. Forensic Med. Pathol. 25:33–36, 2004.
88. Luna, A., Solano, C., Gomez, M., Banon, R. Incised wound margins caused by steel blades. Scanning electron microscopy to determine wound direction. Forensic Sci. Int. 43:21–26, 1989.
89. Moriani, S., Cecchi, R., Cipolloni, L. Suicide by sharp instruments: a case of harakiri. Int. J. Legal Med. 108:219–220, 1996.
90. Herbst, J., Haffner, H. T. Tentative injuries to exposed skin in a homicide case. Forensic Sci. Int. 102:193–196, 1999.
91. Karlsson, T. Multivariate analysis ('forensiometrics')—a new tool in forensic medicine. Differentiation between sharp–force homicide and suicide. Forensic Sci. Int. 94:183–200, 1998.
92. Rothschild, M. A., Ehrlich, E., Klevno, W. A., Schneider, V. Self–implanted subcutaneous penile balls—a new phenomenon in Western Europe. Int. J. Legal Med. 110:88–91, 1997.
93. Catalano, G., Morejon, M., Alberts, V. A., Catalano, M. C. Report of a case of male genital self–mutilation and review of the literature, with special emphasis on the effects of the media. J. Sex Marital. Ther. 22:35–46, 1996.
94. Kennedy, B. L., Feldmann, T. B. Self–inflicted eye injuries: case presentations and a literature review. Hosp. Community Psychiatry 45:470–474, 1994.
95. Tantam, D., Whittaker, J. Personality disorder and self–wounding. Br. J. Psychiatry 161:451–464, 1992.
96. Kernbach–Wighton, G., Thomas, R. S., Saternus, K. S. The discrimination between overt and non–overt self–inflicted lesions. Forensic Sci. Int. 89:203–209, 1997.
97. Patel, V., de Moore, G. Harakiri: a clinical study of deliberate self–stabbing. J. Clin. Psychiatry 55:98–103, 1994.
98. Sachsse, U. Overt self–injury. Psychother. Psychosom. 62:82–90, 1994.
99. Leslie, J., Taff, M. L., Patel, I., Sternberg, A., Fernando, M. M. Self–inflicted ocular injuries. A rare form of self–mutilation. Am. J. Forensic Med. Pathol. 5:83–88, 1984.
100. Benecke, M. First report of nonpsychotic self–cannibalism (autophagy), tongue splitting, and scar patterns(scarification) as an extreme form of cultural body modification in a western civilization. Am. J. Forensic Med. Pathol. 20:281–285, 1999.
101. Favazza, A. R., Conterio, K. Female habitual self–mutilators. Acta Psychiatr. Scand. 79:283–289, 1989.

102. Gaillard, Y., Pepin, G. Case report of an unusual use of lidocaine during episodes of self mutilation. J. Forensic Sci. 43:235–238, 1998.
103. Rogers, D. R. Autoamputation of the left arm—a bizarre suicide. Am. J. Forensic Med. Pathol. 9:64–65, 1988.
104. Karabatsou, K., Kandasami, J., Rainov, N. G. Self–inflicted penetrating head injury in a patient with manic–depressive disorder. Am. J. Forensic Med. Pathol. 26:174–176, 2005.
105. Osuna, E., Toucedo, M. A., Sanchez–Espigares, G., et al. A case of self–inflicted wounding by the introduction of needles through the abdominal wall to induce abortion. Forensic Sci. Int. 128:141–145, 2002.
106. Banasr, A., de la Grandmaison, G. L., Durigon, M. Frequency of bone/cartilage lesions in stab and incised wounds fatalities. Forensic Sci. Int. 131:131–133, 2003.
107. Gupta, R. L., Keen, R. I. An unusual case of cardiac injury. Lancet 1:1157, 1958.
108. Bonte, W. Tool marks in bones and cartilage. J. Forensic Sci. 20:315–325, 1975.
109. Rao, V. J., Hart, R. Tool mark determination in cartilage of stabbing victim. J. Forensic Sci. 28:794–799, 1983.
110. Smrkolj, V., Balazic, J., Princic, J. Intracranial injuries by a screwdriver. Forensic Sci. Int. 76:211–216, 1995.
111. Hemphill, R. E. Attempted suicide by hammering a nail into the brain. S. Afr. Med. J. 57:477–478, 1980.
112. Jacobs, L. M., Berrizbeitia, L. D., Ordia, J. Crowbar impalement of the brain. J. Trauma 25:359–361, 1985.
113. Sebag, J., Shillito, J., Robb, R. Transorbital penetrating injuries to the frontal lobe. Ophthalmic Surg. 17:631–634, 1986.
114. Siegel, E. B., Bastek, J. V., Mehringer, C. M., Yee, R. D. Fatal intracranial extension of an orbital umbrella stab injury. Ann. Ophthalmol. 15:99–102, 1983.
115. Albert, D. M., Burns, W. P., Scheie, H. G. Severe orbitocranial foreign–body injury. Am. J. Ophthalmol. 60:1109–1111, 1965.
116. Kirkby, G. R. Penetrating orbitocranial injury with a snooker cue. Br. Med. J. (Clin. Res. Ed.) 293:1646, 1986.
117. Lunetta, P., Ohberg, A., Sajantila, A. Suicide by intracerebellar ballpoint pen. Am. J. Forensic Med. Pathol. 23:334–337, 2002.
118. Rompen, J. C., Meek, M. F., van Andel, M. V. A cause celebre: the so–called "ballpoint murder." J. Forensic Sci. 45:1144–1147, 2000.
119. De Villiers, J. C., Sevel, D. Intracranial complications of transorbital stab wounds. Br. J. Ophthalmol. 59:52–56, 1975.

120. Sharif, S., Roberts, G., Phillips, J. Transnasal penetrating brain injury with a ball–pen. Br. J. Neurosurg. 14:159–160, 2000.

121. Lynch, M. J., Parker, H. Forensic aspects of ocular injury. Am. J. Forensic Med. Pathol. 21:124–126, 2000.

122. Davis, N. L., Kahana, T., Hiss, J. Souvenir knife: a retained transcranial knife blade. Am. J. Forensic Med. Pathol. 25:259–261, 2004.

123. Specht, C. S., Varga, J. H., Jalali, M. M., Edelstein, J. P. Orbitocranial wooden foreign body diagnosed by magnetic resonance imaging. Dry wood can be isodense with air and orbital fat by computed tomography. Surv. Ophthalmol. 36:341–344, 1992.

124. Schaller, B., Probst, R., Strebel, S., Gratzl, O. Trigeminocardiac reflex during surgery in the cerebellopontine angle. J. Neurosurg. 90:215–220, 1999.

125. Anderson, R. L. The blepharocardiac reflex. Arch. Ophthalmol. 96:1418–1420, 1978.

126. Lang, S., Lanigan, D. T., van der Wal M. Trigeminocardiac reflexes: maxillary and mandibular variants of the oculocardiac reflex. Can. J. Anaesth. 38:757–760, 1991.

127. von Domarus, H., Poeschel, W. Impalement injuries of the palate. Plast. Reconstr. Surg. 72:656–658, 1983.

128. Thoresen, S. O., Rognum, T. O. Survival time and acting capability after fatal injury by sharp weapons. Forensic Sci. Int. 31:181–187, 1986.

129. Sugg, W. L., Rea, W. J., Ecker, R. R., Webb, W. R., Rose, E. F., Shaw, R. R. Penetrating wounds of the heart. An analysis of 459 cases. J. Thorac. Cardiovasc. Surg. 56:531–545, 1968.

130. Thourani, V. H., Feliciano, D. V., Cooper, W. A., et al. Penetrating cardiac trauma at an urban trauma center: a 22–year perspective. Am. Surg. 65:811–816, 1999.

131. Shiono, H., Takaesu, Y. Suicide by self–inflicted stab wound of the chest. Am. J. Forensic Med. Pathol. 7:72–73, 1986.

132. Maeda, H., Imura, M., Higuchi, T., Noguchi, K. An autopsy case of suicide by hanging with multiple stab wounds of the neck and chest. Med. Sci. Law 33:67–69, 1993.

133. Baghai, P., Sheptak, P. E. Penetrating spinal injury by a glass fragment: case report and review. Neurosurgery 11:419–422, 1982.

134. Hirt, M., Karger, B. Fatal brain injury caused by the free–flying blade of a knife—case report and evaluation of the unusual weapon. Int. J. Legal Med. 112:313–314, 1999.

135. Borchelt, P. L., Lockwood, R., Beck, A. M., Voith, V. L. Attacks by packs of dogs involving predation on human beings. Public Health Rep. 98:57–66, 1983.

136. Boglioli, L. R., Taff, M. L., Turkel, S. J., Taylor, J. V., Peterson, C. D. Unusual infant death: dog attack or postmortem mutilation after child abuse? Am. J. Forensic Med.

Pathol. 21:389–394, 2000.

137. Sacks, J. J., Lockwood, R., Hornreich, J., Sattin, R. W. Fatal dog attacks, 1989–1994. Pediatrics 97:891–895, 1996.

138. Lauridson, J. R., Myers, L. Evaluation of fatal dog bites: the view of the medical examiner and animal behaviorist. J. Forensic Sci. 38:726–731, 1993.

139. Sacks, J. J., Sattin, R. W., Bonzo, S. E. Dog bite–related fatalities from 1979 through 1988. JAMA 262:1489–1492, 1989.

140. Wright, J. C. Canine aggression toward people. Bite scenarios and prevention. Vet. Clin. North Am. Small Anim. Pract. 21:299–314, 1991.

141. Langley, R. L. Fatal animal attacks in North Carolina over an 18–year period. Am. J. Forensic Med. Pathol. 15:160–167, 1994.

142. Bux, R. C., McDowell, J. D. Death due to attack from chow dog. Am. J. Forensic Med. Pathol. 13:305–308, 1992.

143. Kneafsey, B., Condon, K. C. Severe dog–bite injuries, introducing the concept of pack attack: a literature review and seven case reports. Injury 26:37–41, 1995.

144. Wright, J. C. Severe attacks by dogs: characteristics of the dogs, the victims, and the attack settings. Public Health Rep. 100:55–61, 1985.

145. Avis, S. P. Dog pack attack: hunting humans. Am. J. Forensic Med. Pathol. 20:243–246, 1999.

146. Wiseman, N. E., Chochinov, H., Fraser, V. Major dog attack injuries in children. J. Pediatr. Surg. 18:533–536, 1983.

147. Falconieri, G., Zanella, M., Malannino, S. Pulmonary thromboembolism following calf cellulitis: report of an unusual complication of dog bite. Am. J. Forensic Med. Pathol. 20:240–242, 1999.

148. Clark, M. A., Sandusky, G. E., Hawley, D. A., Pless, J. E., Fardal, P. M., Tate, L. R. Fatal and near–fatal animal bite injuries. J. Forensic Sci. 36:1256–1261, 1991.

149. Glass, R. T., Jordan, F. B., Andrews, E. E. Multiple animal bite wounds: A case report. J. Forensic Sci. 20:305–314, 1975.

150. Wilberger, J. E., Jr., Pang, D. Craniocerebral injuries from dog bites. JAMA 249:2685–2688, 1983.

151. Wilberger, J. E., Jr., Pang, D. Craniocerebral injuries from dog bite in an infant. Neurosurgery 9:426–428, 1981.

152. Delage, C., Irey, N. S. Anaphylactic deaths: a clinicopathologic study of 43 cases. J. Forensic Sci. 17:525–540, 1972.

153. Ansari, M. Q., Zamora, J. L., Lipscomb, M. F. Postmortem diagnosis of acute anaphylaxis

by serum tryptase analysis. A case report. Am. J. Clin. Pathol. 99:101–103, 1993.

154. Yunginger, J. W., Nelson, D. R., Squillace, D. L., et al. Laboratory investigation of deaths due to anaphylaxis. J. Forensic Sci. 36:857–865, 1991.

155. James, L. P., Jr., Austen, K. F. Fatal systemic anaphylaxis in man. N. Engl. J. Med. 270:597–603, 1964.

156. Randall, B., Butts, J., Halsey, J. F. Elevated postmortem tryptase in the absence of anaphylaxis. J. Forensic Sci. 40:208–211, 1995.

157. Schwartz, L. B., Metcalfe, D. D., Miller, J. S., Earl, H., Sullivan, T. Tryptase levels as an indicator of mast–cell activation in systemic anaphylaxis and mastocytosis. N. Engl. J. Med. 316:1622–1626, 1987.

158. Edston, E., Hage–Hamsten, M. Mast cell tryptase and hemolysis after trauma. Forensic Sci. Int. 131:8–13, 2003.

159. Hoffman, D. R., Wood, C. L., Hudson, P. Demonstration of IgE and IgG antibodies against venoms in the blood of victims of fatal sting anaphylaxis. J. Allergy Clin. Immunol. 71:193–196, 1983.

160. Perper, J. A., Kuller, L. H., Shim, Y. K. Detection of fatal therapeutic misadventures by an urban medico–legal system. J. Forensic Sci. 38:327–338, 1993.

161. Steel, K., Gertman, P. M., Crescenzi, C., Anderson, J. Iatrogenic illness on a general medical service at a university hospital. N. Engl. J. Med. 304:638–642, 1981.

162. Murphy, G. K. Therapeutic misadventure. An 11–year study from a metropolitan coroner's office. Am. J. Forensic Med. Pathol. 7:115–119, 1986.

163. Reay, D. T., Eisele, J. W., Ward, R., Horton, W., Bonnell, H. J. A procedure for the investigation of anesthetic/surgical deaths. J. Forensic Sci. 30:822–827, 1985.

164. Brennan, T. A., Leape, L. L., Laird, N. M., et al. Incidence of adverse events and negligence in hospitalized patients. Results of the Harvard Medical Practice Study I. N. Engl. J. Med. 324:370–376, 1991.

165. Zeien, L. B., Noguchi, T. T. Fatal hydrothorax associated with subclavian vein catheterization for hemodialysis. Am. J. Forensic Med. Pathol. 13:326–328, 1992.

166. Kontozoglou, T., Mambo, N. Fatal retropleural hematoma complicating internal jugular vein catheterization. A case report. Am. J. Forensic Med. Pathol. 4:125–127, 1983.

167. Conces, D. J., Jr., Holden, R. W. Aberrant locations and complications in initial placement of subclavian vein catheters. Arch. Surg. 119:293–295, 1984.

168. Tapson, J. S., Uldall, P. R. Fatal hemothorax caused by a subclavian hemodialysis catheter. Thoughts on prevention. Arch. Intern. Med. 144:1685–1687, 1984.

169. Cohle, S. D., Graham, M. A. Sudden death in hemodialysis patients. J. Forensic Sci.

30:158-166, 1985.

170. Feliciano, D. V., Mattox, K. L., Graham, J. M., Beall, A. C., Jr., Jordan, G. L., Jr. Major complications of percutaneous subclavian vein catheters. Am. J. Surg. 138:869-874, 1979.

171. Borja, A. R., Masri, Z., Shruck, L., Pejo, S. Unusual and lethal complications of infraclavicular subclavian vein catheterization. Int. Surg. 57:42-45, 1972.

172. Scott, W. L. Complications associated with central venous catheters. A survey. Chest 94:1221-1224, 1988.

173. Cohen, A. C., Glinsky, G. C., Martin, G. E., Fetterhoff, K. I. Air embolism. Ann. Intern. Med. 35:779-784, 1951.

174. McGill, M. P., Kumar, A., Rahko, P. S. Venous air embolism. Echocardiographic diagnosis of air bubbles in the left side of the heart in a patient with a previously diagnosed intrapulmonary shunt. Chest 111:826-828, 1997.

175. Saukko, P., Knight, B. Knight's Forensic Pathology. 3rd ed. Arnold, London, 2004.

176. Oppenheimer, M. J., Durant, T M., Lynch, P. Body position in relation to venous air embolism and the associated cardiovascular-respiratory changes. Am. J. Med. Sci. 225:362-373, 1953.

177. Butler, B. D., Hills, B. A. Transpulmonary passage of venous air emboli. J. Appl. Physiol. 59:543-547, 1985.

178. Bunai, Y., Nagai, A., Nakamura, I., Kanno, S., Yamada, S., Ohya, I. An unusual case of fatal gas embolism. Am. J. Forensic Med. Pathol. 20:256-260, 1999.

179. Ritz-Timme, S., Eckelt, N., Schmidtke, E., Thomsen, H. Genesis and diagnostic value of leukocyte and platelet accumulations around "air bubbles" in blood after venous air embolism. Int. J. Legal Med. 111:22-26, 1998.

180. Doering, R. B., Stemmer, E. A., Connolly, J. E. Complications of indwelling venous catheters, with particular reference to catheter embolus. Am. J. Surg. 114:259-266, 1967.

181. Foley, F. D., Moncrief, J. A., Mason, A. D., Jr. Pathology of the lung in fatally burned patints. Ann. Surg. 167:251-264, 1968.

182. Pruitt, B. A., Jr., Flemma, R. J., DiVincenti, F. C., Foley, F. D., Mason, A. D., Jr., Young, W. G., Jr. Pulmonary complications in burn patients. A comparative study of 697 patients. J. Thorac. Cardiovasc. Surg. 59:7-20, 1970.

183. Adar, R., Mozes, M.. Fatal complications of central venous catheters. Br. Med. J. 3:746, 1971.

184. Moylan, J. A., Jr., West, J. T., Nash, G., Bowen, J. A., Pruitt, B. A., Jr. Tracheostomy in thermally injured patients: a review of five years' experience. Am. Surg. 38:119-123, 1972.

第 8 章
钝器损伤
——包括航空器、火车和机动车辆损伤

概述

  钝器损伤是法医病理学实践中最常见的损伤。由钝器所致的皮肤损伤并不致命且看似不重要,然而钝器损伤却具有极大的证据价值。锐器伤和火器伤的形态可以较明显地反映致伤工具的特征,但钝器损伤形态多样,在交通事故中可常观察到特征性的钝器损伤形态,如安全带损伤,但这种典型的钝器损伤在平时的鉴定中并不多见。因此,分析和判断钝器损伤的困难和挑战极大,一直是法医病理学实践中的重点和难点。此外,钝器损伤的肉眼大体观察是法医病理学实践中最常用的方法,对于大多数钝器损伤(如大出血、身体损毁)案件,通过损伤形态观察可以较明确地对死亡原因与机制作出合理、正确的解释。然而,某些特殊损伤(如震荡性损伤、脂肪栓塞等)则需要更多的检验方法,显微镜检查将有助于法医观察到肉眼难以检见的损伤,对死因判断具有极大的诊断价值。

  关键词: 非穿透伤; 钝器损伤; 车辆; 交通事故; 安全气囊; 安全带; 飞机; 铁路; 高坠; 心肺复苏; 褥疮; 脂肪栓塞; 横纹肌溶解症

1 前言

  钝器损伤是法医尸检中最常见的损伤类型,大量的钝器损伤案件都会出现体表和体内损伤,法医需要解释这些损伤在致死性方面的作用。然而,观察到这些钝器损伤的意义不仅在于确定死因,还有其他问题需要解决。在某些案件中,钝器损伤微不足道。然而,根据法医学检验结果,较大和较小的钝器损伤均能引起死亡。

  当人体撞击钝性物体或受钝物打击时,较大的局部机械性外力会破坏人体解剖结构的完整性,从而造成损伤。通过拉伸(张力)、挤压(压力)或使用差异应力(摩擦力或剪切力),人体组织结构发生改变。体表损伤和内部损伤位置相邻证明是外

力直接作用,但内部严重损伤却可在无体表症状的情况下发生。如果缺乏体表损伤,而只有内部损伤,则说明外力从较远处作用于损伤部位。尸检中或显微镜下观察到损伤,尤其是内部损伤,是致死性病理生理紊乱的征兆。通常致命性损伤很少会不明显。

损伤的程度和范围取决于施加外力的大小,力等于物体质量和运动加速度的乘积(牛顿第二定律),加速度是单位时间(δt)内速度(δt)的变化程度。人体或致伤物移动表面的速度增加,作用力就会成正比地增加。如果物体的运动速度在较短时间内改变(也就是 δt 减小),作用力也会成正比地增大(1-3)。外力作用于较小面积时更易发生损伤(也就是应力与力除以面积的商成正比)(2,3)。人体形变速度(v)和压力(C)的相互关系是引起损伤的重要因素(4),已有人用两者的乘积($v\times c$)来描述损伤的严重性(4-6)。如果形变速度高,即使作用于胸部的压力极小,也会发生内部器官损伤,如肺挫伤,而仅伴有轻微肋骨骨折甚至没有骨折。器官或组织对压力和撞击速度的抵抗力可反映其"黏性耐受度"。

物体与运动相关的能量称为动能(kinetic energy, $Ek = 0.5\ mv^2$;公式中 m 为质

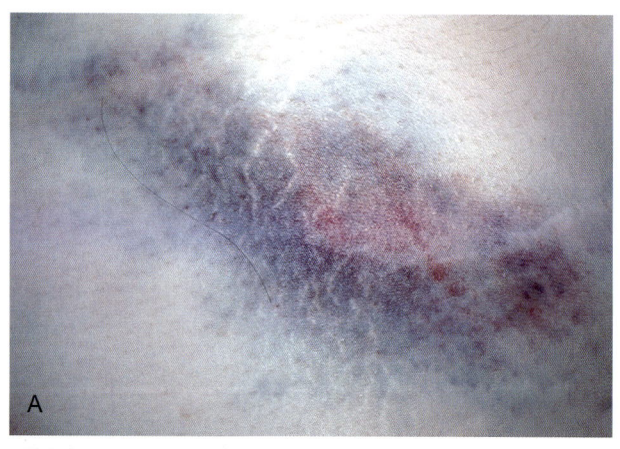

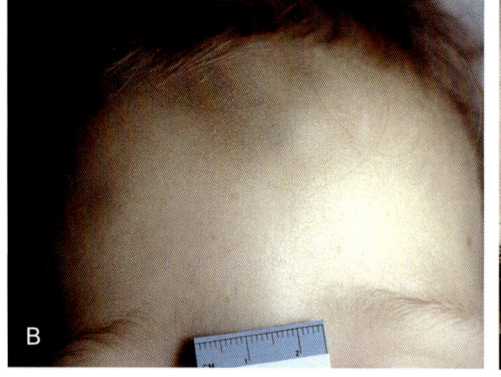 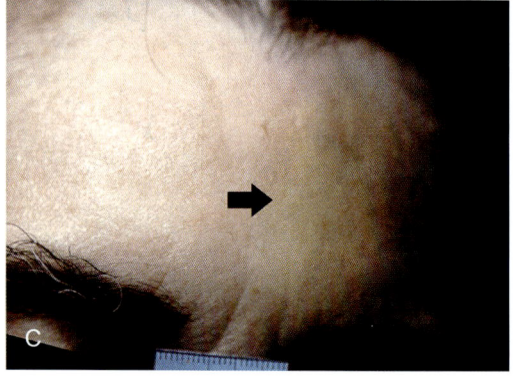

图 8-1 不同时期的挫伤。(A)早期挫伤:呈紫红色。(B)愈合中的挫伤:呈棕色。(C)愈合后期的挫伤(箭头):呈黄色。

量, v 为运动速度)。动能越大,损伤程度越严重。此外,动能的吸收取决于冲击表面的性质 [3]。接触的表面坚硬说明有大量的机械能在人体内消散 (2)。年轻人的皮肤和肋骨弹性较大,意味着损伤较小;但弹性较弱的器官(如肝脏)会受到严重损害。人体的某些器官和部位由于结构和构造导致其更易受到损伤。例如,位移差异会在活动的主动脉弓和固定的降主动脉过渡处引起剪应力(参阅标题 6.5;参考文献 7)。充气结构中的能量吸收会因冲击波效应而放大,充满液体的器官(如心脏)会由于流体静压增加而破裂(参阅标题 6.4)。

2 皮肤损伤

有三种皮肤损伤较常见:挫伤(碰撞)、擦伤(刮擦)及挫/撕裂创(撕裂)。各种挫伤有一致的特点(8-12),表现为由于损伤或疾病引起血管破裂,导致皮肤因潜在的血液外渗而变色(参阅标题 3.2 和图 8-1),但表面完好无损。不同于与擦伤和挫/撕裂创,挫伤为"闭合性"损伤,不易引起感染。如果表皮由于摩擦、挤压或拉伸而剥脱,则形成擦伤(图 8-2)。挫/撕裂创则是组织表面被撕裂。挫裂创与锐器创区别显著,其创缘不规则、创腔内可见组织间桥(图 8-3),形成破坏,而锐器创由皮肤被提

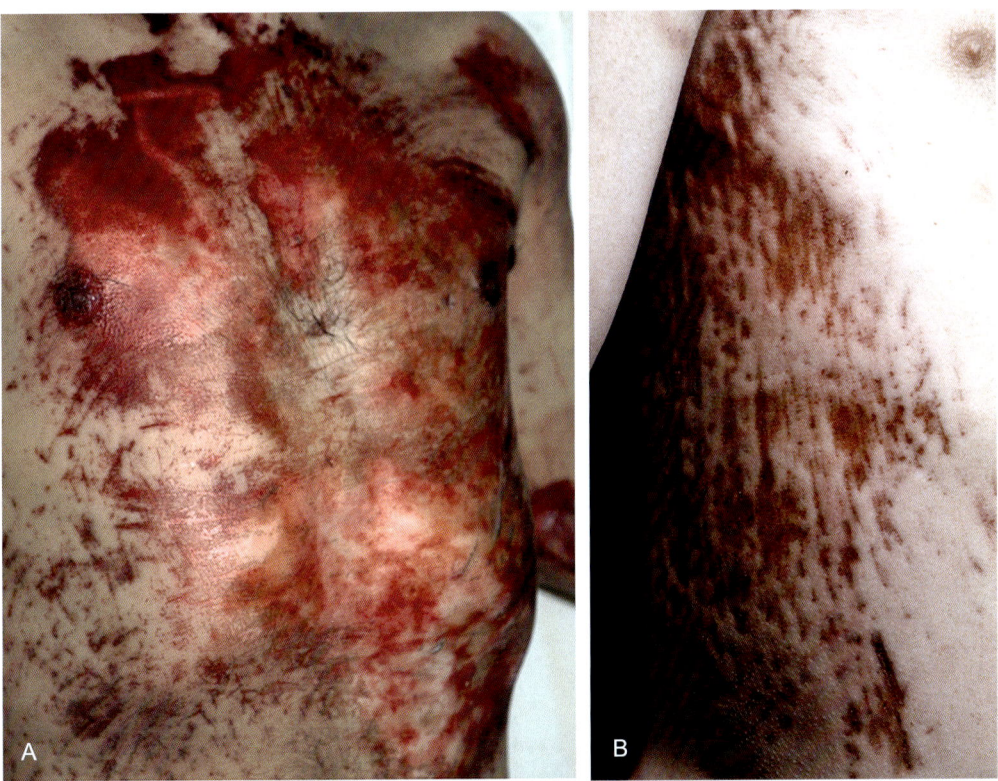

图 8-2 各类擦伤。(A)相对光滑平面的物体摩擦所致的刷状擦伤(如柏油路)。(B)凹凸平面的物体摩擦所致的点状和条形擦伤(如砂石路)。

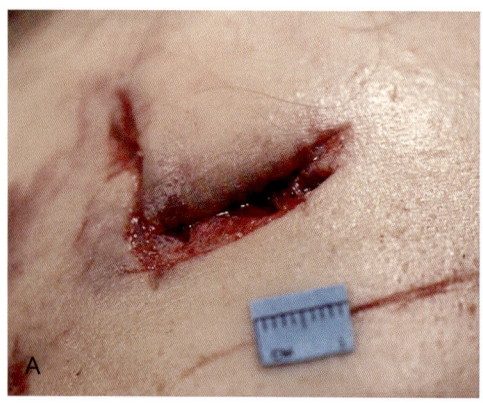
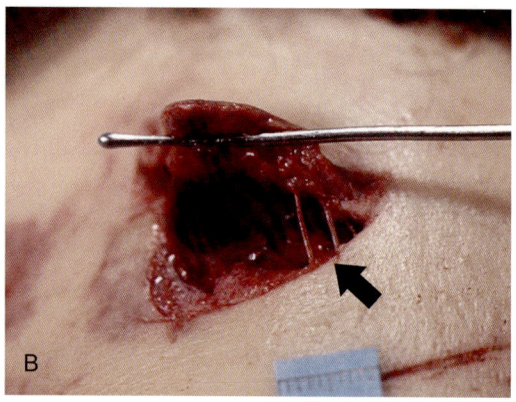

图 8-3 挫/撕裂创。(A) 不整齐的创缘。(B) 皮下延伸性损伤和组织间桥（剪头所示）。

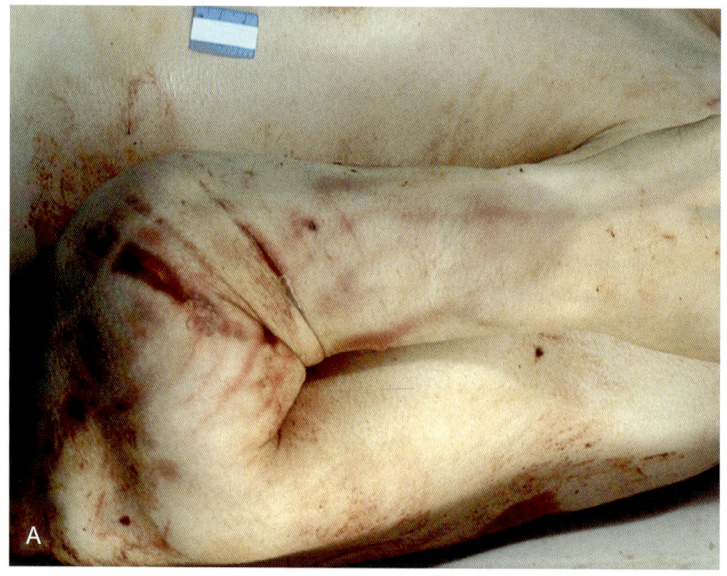

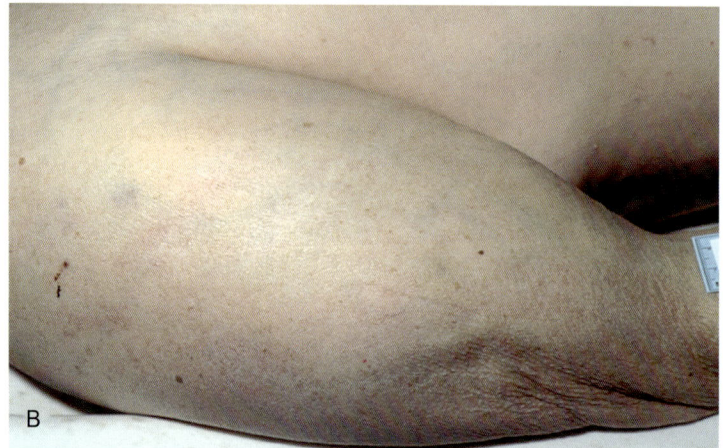

图 8-4 上肢骨折。(A) 尺、桡骨骨折引起上肢变形。(B) 肿胀：肱骨骨折。

拉引起,会造成软组织破裂形成皮瓣。

变形和肿胀是急性骨折的外部征象(图 8-4 和图 8-5),死后影像学检查可明确诊断骨折(图 8-5)。

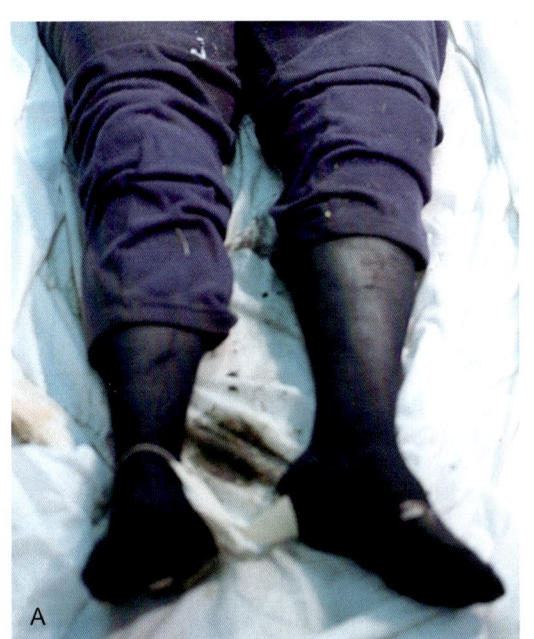
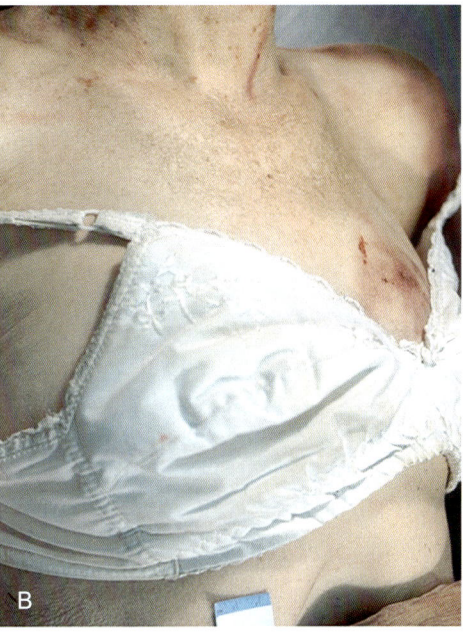
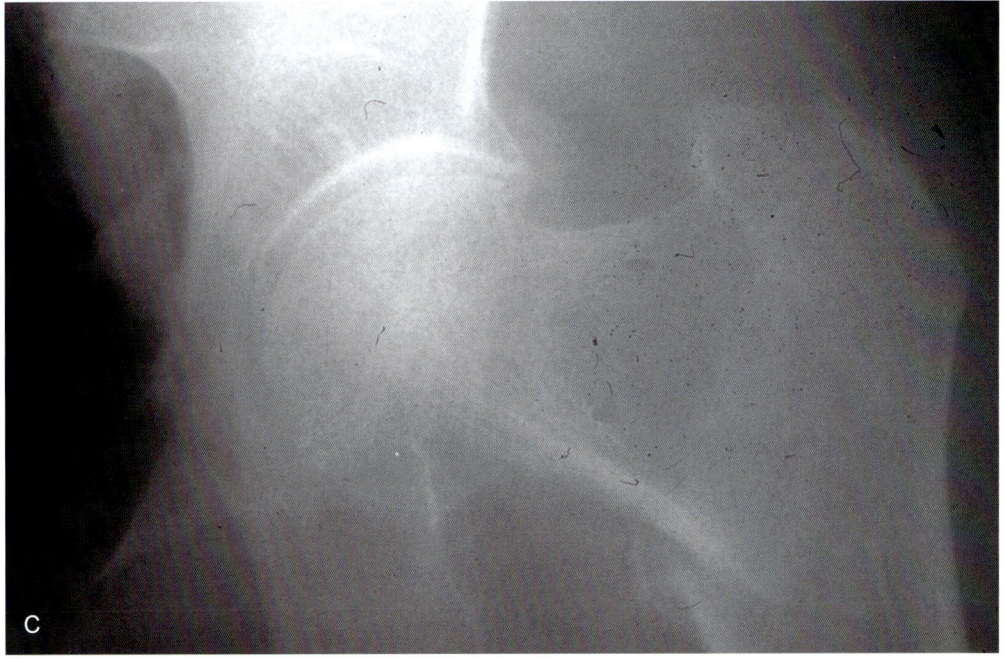

图 8-5 老年女性冬季被发现死于庭院天井中。体温过低(图 8-9)。(A)左腿缩短、外旋畸形。(B)反常脱衣现象。(C)死后 X 线片提示左股骨骨折,骨折后受害人丧失活动能力。

3 钝器所致皮肤损伤的意义

皮肤损伤检查的首要步骤是通过文字描述、绘图及照相对损伤进行准确记录,然后对损伤进行恰当的解释。要认识到即使轻微的损伤也具有重要的法医学意义(13)。

3.1 生前或死后伤判断

发现的损伤可能发生在死后。皮肤挫伤,无论单独出现还是与其他皮肤损伤合并出现,都提示伤者有心脏排血。然而,出血量在濒死期由于心功能减弱而相应减少。在致命损伤后也可发生进一步损伤(图 8-6),死后尸体变化也会改变或造成类似损伤(参阅第 2 章标题 3.2、3.3 和 5.2)。

3.2 力的程度、方向及死亡原因

多处、广泛、开放性皮肤损伤通常提示所受的外力较大。分布在人体不同部位的损伤取决于致伤环境,可能表示多处同时发生的损伤或重复性创伤。皮肤损伤是严重内部器官损伤的外部征兆,表明该部位吸收能量显著。皮肤挫裂很少会引发致命性大出血(图 8-7)。软组织广泛受损可引起死亡(参阅标题 12.1;参考文献 3,14)。

虽然挫伤程度反映出施加外力的大小,但很多因素会改变这一解释(13)。

身体遭受轻微外力,也可导致较广范围的皮肤挫伤如果有人在服药(如阿司匹林、抗凝剂)或有出血倾向(如肝硬化、血友病),则更容易出血(参阅标题 3.4.1.1;图 8-7;参考文献 8,13)。儿童由于皮肤松弛、细腻而更易发生挫伤(8,13),老年人

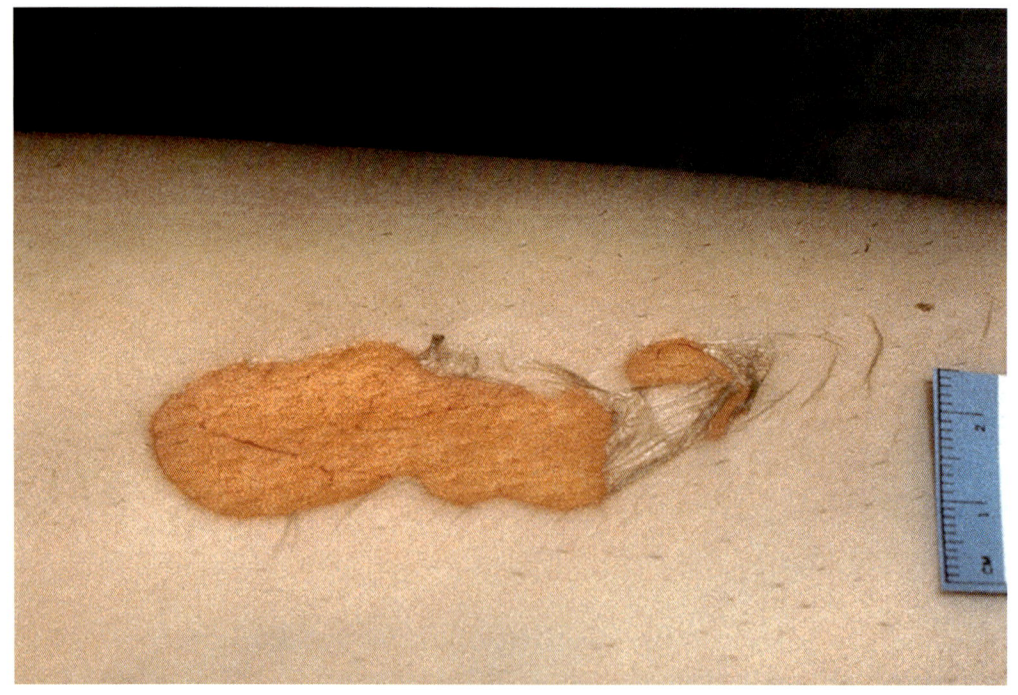

图 8-6 死后皮肤擦伤呈现典型的黄色。

第 8 章｜钝器损伤——包括航空器、火车和机动车辆损伤　　　　　　　　　　　　　　　　　　　　*427*

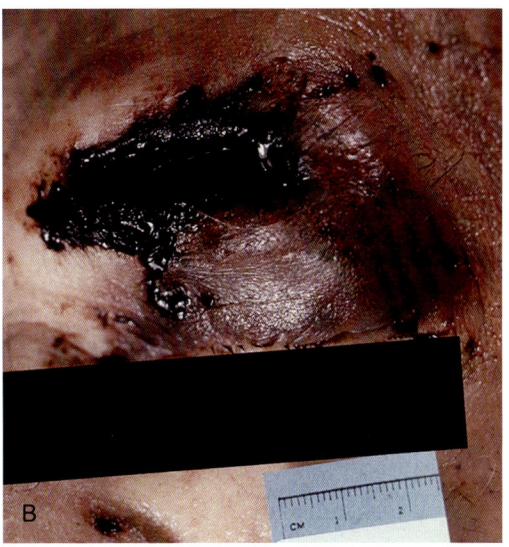

图 8-7　嗜酒者死于家中。急性酒精中毒（血液中酒精浓度 240 毫克/分升），尸检发现肝硬化。(A) 现场大量血液。(B) 左侧眉弓挫裂创致大出血，上眼睑皮下出血。

则由于皮肤组织萎缩和毛细血管支持减少而易形成老年性瘀伤（8，13，15）。这些挫伤常发生于 60 岁以上老人，疑似虐待案件（15）。老年性瘀斑的特征是出血点不明显、边缘不规则，通常分布于上肢，其次为颈部和下肢侧面（图 8-8）。主要出现于疗养院的老人，急救医院和住家老人中也可见。轻微的创伤（如提举或其他身体支撑方式）可引起瘀伤，肥胖会加剧挫伤（8，13）。

损伤部位的特征会影响所见的皮肤损伤。外力作用在骨突部位（如眼眶）更易引起挫裂创（图 8-7）。

与擦伤和挫裂创不同，由于血液具有流动性，皮肤挫伤并非总能指示外力的直接作用部位（图 8-9）。擦伤和挫裂创可反映力的方向［如擦伤的皮肤层被推向一侧，不均匀的挫裂与剪切力方向一致（3）］。如果渗血淤积在深部软组织（血肿），瘀伤在初期并不明显，只有通过切开可疑的受伤部位才能被发现（图 8-10；参考文献 3，8）。头皮的挫伤会被头发覆盖（图 8-11），只有翻开头皮才可能充分暴露挫伤。出血常发生于受钝性撞击的头皮与颅骨的交接处。如果伤者幸存，血液可到达皮肤表面，随后出现瘀伤。如果损伤部位组织疏松、富含血管，或两者兼有（如眼眶部、生殖器区域。图 8-7；参考文献 3，8，13），则出血程度会加剧。对损伤部位持续按压可减少出血（8）。

3.3 损伤时间

在尸检和法律程序中常被问及的一个问题是："损伤形成时间多久"。在尸检过程中，法医通过使用显微镜和其他特殊检验手段推断损伤形成时间。通常皮肤损伤与致伤时间之间很难存在精确的关系（3）。法医还需考虑损伤时间为同期型（死亡

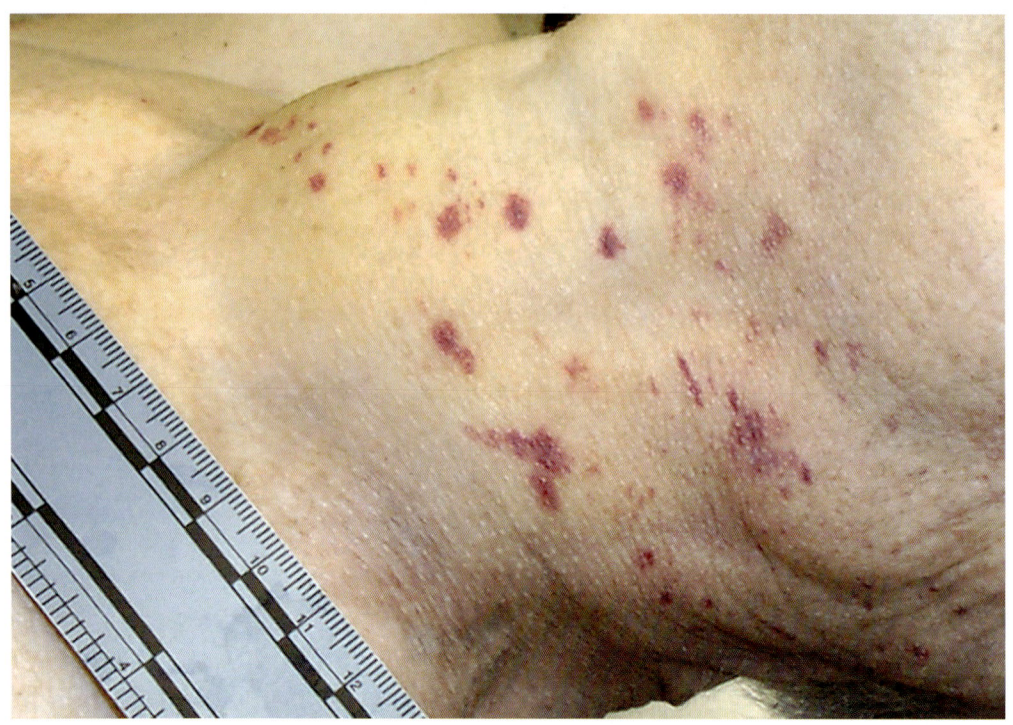

图 8-8　颈部的老年性瘀斑（加拿大安大略省伦敦市伦敦健康科学中心 E. Tweedie 博士供图）。

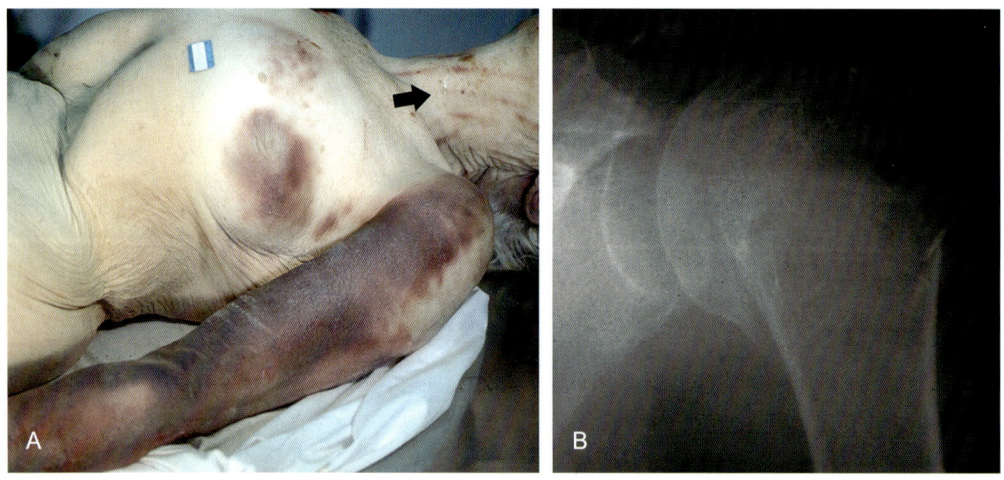

图 8-9　老年女性因体温过低而死于户外（参阅图 8-5）。（A）发生于死前 2 周的肱骨骨折导致左上臂和前臂大量出血。颈部擦伤（箭头）提示可能受到勒压，但无外部出血点，也没有内部损伤。（B）死后 X 线片提示肱骨骨折。

时发生）、巧合型（致命事件前发生但与其无关），还是演进型（损伤存在一段时间并在存活期间有所发展，如硬脑膜下出血）。

在各种皮肤损伤中，推断皮肤挫伤时间最具挑战性。血红蛋白随巨噬细胞吞噬

第 8 章 | 钝器损伤——包括航空器、火车和机动车辆损伤

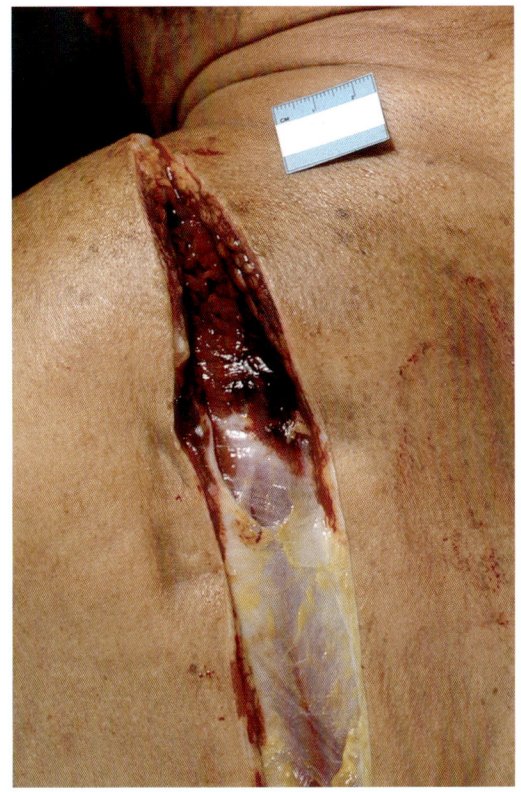

图 8-10 背部软组织血肿,注意皮肤表面未检见瘀伤。

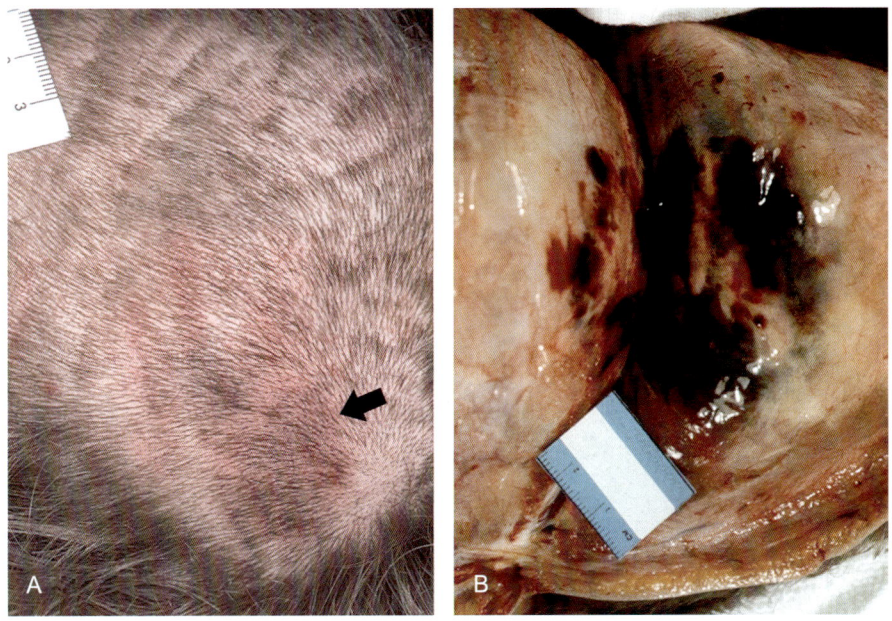

图 8-11 "隐藏"的头皮挫伤。(A)头皮挫伤(箭头)被头发遮盖,尸检时被部分切开。(B)另一案例显示枕部头皮翻开,头皮和颅骨交界处可见挫伤,体表损伤不明显。

而减少,挫伤会经历一系列颜色改变,这一作用曾被用于推断挫伤时间(图8-1)。挫伤外观会受多种因素影响,深色皮肤色素沉着说明挫伤颜色缺失或改变,光照类型和色觉亦会影响挫伤的观察结果(16,17)。由于影响因素较多,挫伤的颜色最多只能作为一种推断损伤时间的参考依据(8-11,18-20)。游离血红蛋白呈红色(9,11),胆绿素和胆红素分别呈绿色和黄色,含铁血黄素也呈黄色。较暗的颜色,如蓝色和紫色,反映了皮肤不同深度的血液对光的反射(9),绿色可以是黄、蓝色改变的综合效果(9)。通常而言,皮肤红、紫、黑色变发生于损伤早期,即损伤后24小时内(8,12)。损伤后24-72小时生存期,皮肤挫伤会发生蓝、紫或棕色变。这期间也可观察到淡黄色,可持续数天。一项对皮肤挫伤照片的研究发现,超过18小时的挫伤皮肤可呈现淡黄色(9)。皮肤绿色变发生于损伤后第一周并可持续至伤后10天。挫伤处在7-10天后变黄,2周或更长时间后开始退色(12)。

对皮肤挫伤不同颜色出现的时间存在不同的观点[如棕色变出现在伤后1-3天而非伤后1周,黄色变出现在伤后数日而非2周(11,20)]。不同身体部位在同一时间遭受的挫伤可呈现不同特征,主要取决于出血位置、致伤物性状、个体对损伤的反应(10)。挫伤愈合的速度也各不相同(9),愈合开始于挫伤的外周,大面积挫伤的中心区域最晚被吸收(10,11)。如果挫伤发生在原先损伤部位,血液吸收会加剧。挫伤部位的血管越富集,其愈合速度也越快;受伤个体越年轻,修复速度也更快(11,21)。

"新鲜"损伤的形态(红、蓝、紫色变)可持续数日(9,10),法医虽然无法说出挫伤的确切形成时间,但可根据某些色变(黄、绿、棕)判断挫伤"较旧"(9,10,18,20)。临床上根据照片评估损伤时间,但儿童损伤,往往不准确(10,16)。

如需要推断皮肤损伤形成时间,要对具有代表性损伤的皮肤采样进行显微镜检查。组织学检验对评估开放性体表损伤(擦伤和挫裂创)更加精确。挫伤愈合分为3期: 炎症期(损伤后1-3天)、增生期(损伤后10-14天)及再生或重塑期[损伤后2周到1个月;图8-12,(8)]。开放性皮肤损伤的愈合过程归纳如下(8,12,21,22):

1. 结痂
   a. 伤后4小时,血清、红细胞及纤维蛋白沉积在损伤部位(提示生前伤)。
   b. 伤后2-6小时,血管周围出现中性粒细胞。
   c. 伤后8小时,损伤表面及皮下组织可见中性粒细胞层。
   d. 伤后12小时,呈现3个区域。
      i. 表层(表面有纤维蛋白和红细胞)。
      ii. 中间层(中性粒细胞)。
      iii. 深层(受损且异常染色的胶原蛋白处出现中性粒细胞浸润,至伤后18小时)。

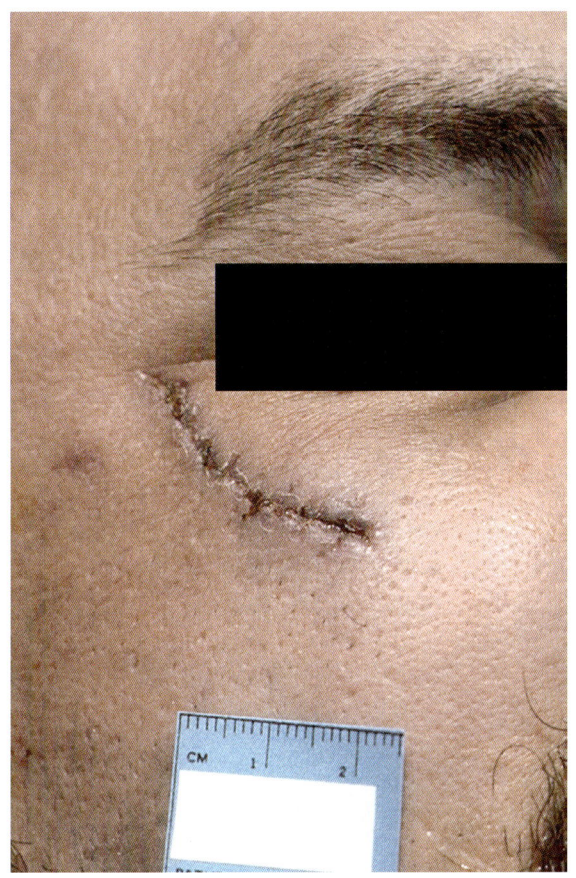

图 8-12 愈合中的挫裂创。注意皮肤缺损处的表皮向内不规则生长。

  e. 伤后 16—24 小时，巨噬细胞数量超过中性粒细胞。
2. 表皮再生（起源于毛囊和创缘）
  a. 浅表损伤后 30 小时出现。
  b. 多数擦伤后 72 小时可见。
3. 皮下肉芽组织（擦伤处表皮全层覆盖）
  a. 最早伤后 1 天，一般伤后 5 天出现纤维母细胞。
  b. 伤后 5—8 天，形成肉芽组织。
  c. 伤后 9—12 天，表皮增生。
4. 愈合
  a. 伤后 8—12 天，细胞活性（如炎症反应、毛细血管增生、纤维母细胞数）下降。
  b. 伤后约 12 天，表皮变薄，胶原纤维增加。
  c. 伤后 14 天以上，结缔组织收缩与成熟。

  擦伤时间难以准确推断。各类损伤中，中性粒细胞出现在损伤早期的 20—30 分钟（皮下脂肪组织不超过 4 小时），通常持续 1—24 小时(8,21)。用显微镜检查评估出血时间时也要注意谨慎,因为炎症细胞会随着淤血被动地进入软组织。远离红细胞聚集的渗出液也十分重要(21)。巨噬细胞在伤后数小时出现,伤后 1－2 天明显增多。含铁血黄素巨噬细胞在挫伤后 24－72 小时出现并可通过普鲁士蓝染色显现(8,21,23,24)。含铁血黄素巨噬细胞的出现与损伤部位相关[如在大脑最短 3－5 天出现,在肺脏最短 17 小时出现(8)]。损伤部位未检出含铁血黄素并不能反映损伤时间,因为含铁血黄素出现与否取决于最初出血量,如果是陈旧性损伤,含铁血黄素可能被全部吸收(8,24)。

多种酶组织化学、生物化学、免疫组织化学及其他技术都被用于推断损伤时间(8,9,19,25-29)。

3.4 损伤形态/印痕样损伤

3.4.1 损伤形态

很多钝器伤形态不典型,难以推断致伤物接触面情况。通过损伤形态通常可以推断出致伤原因,但某些非特异性的损伤需要结合案情和致伤过程综合判断。(图 8-13)。在某些类型的死亡中也会出现一些钝器伤形态。

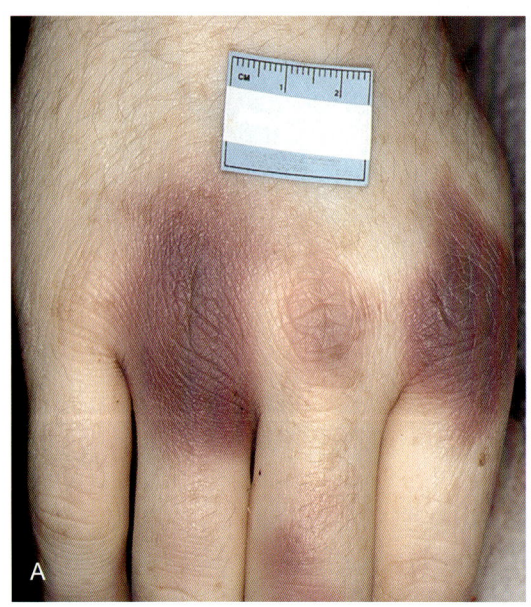 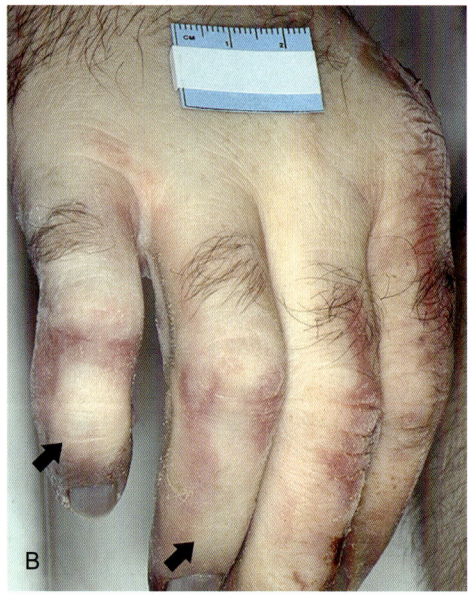

图 8-13 损伤形状。(A)与拳击有关的掌指关节皮肤挫伤。(B)中指皮肤挫伤,死者生前用力敲门导致挫伤中心区域呈灰白色变(箭头)。

3.4.1.1 慢性酒精中毒

长期嗜酒者醉酒时反复摔跌,并由于肝硬化导致凝血功能障碍而容易出血(图 8-7)。会出现四肢、躯干及面部的多发性损伤,提示受到袭击(图 8-14)(30),也会出现更受关注的内部损伤。根据不同时间的体表损伤和内部损伤检验结果,结合毒理学分析和死亡现场勘查,可对致伤过程提供有效证据。

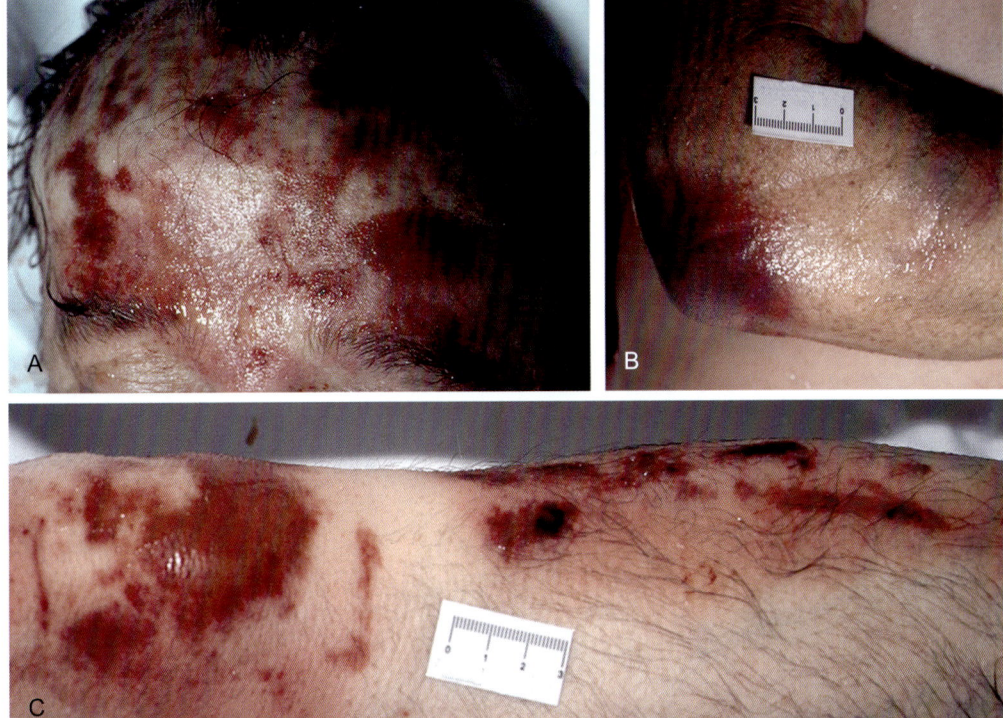

图 8-14 多发性挫伤。长期嗜酒者易反复摔跌。(A)额部。(B)肘部。(C)膝部和小腿胫骨前(加拿大安大略省伦敦市伦敦健康科学中心 A. Tuck 博士供图)。

3.4.1.2 体温过低

人体体温低于 35℃ [95℉ (31-33)] 时称为体温过低。室内供暖差、冷水浸泡(参阅第 5 章标题 4.5)及户外暴露是常见原因(31, 34)。某些诱因也会致体温过低,幼儿和老年人都很脆弱(图 8-5; 参考文献 31, 34-36),潜在疾病和外伤会使他们更加脆弱。缺血性心肌病容易引发低温诱导的心律失常(36)。内分泌功能紊乱(如甲状腺功能减退、糖尿病)会改变低温感知度,降低代偿能力(31)。神经、精神疾病(如精神分裂症、痴呆)会使避寒欲望变得迟钝(31, 37, 38)。穿湿衣服或衣服穿太少的醉酒者都是寒冷环境中冻死的典型案例(31, 34-36, 38, 39)。

这些病例可表现出钝性外伤的特征。擦伤常出现在四肢,但也可能涉及身体其他部位(图 8-5、图 8-9 和图 8-15; 参考文献 35, 36, 38)。这些擦伤可由摔跌或摩擦形成。手背擦伤提示生前可能存在打斗(图 8-15)。如果死者衣服被脱除,提示案件存在疑点。反常脱衣现象从仅脱去鞋子到全身裸露皆有可能,提示性侵可能(图 8-5)(35, 36, 38-40)。反常脱衣现象是由于低温诱导血管收缩后丧失张力进而发生血管扩张所致(35, 36, 38, 40),其结果是产生热感幻觉,死者甚至会有生前在雪地里打滚的迹象(35, 39)。精神疾病患者和自杀者也会有反常脱衣现象(37, 39)。冻死者也可

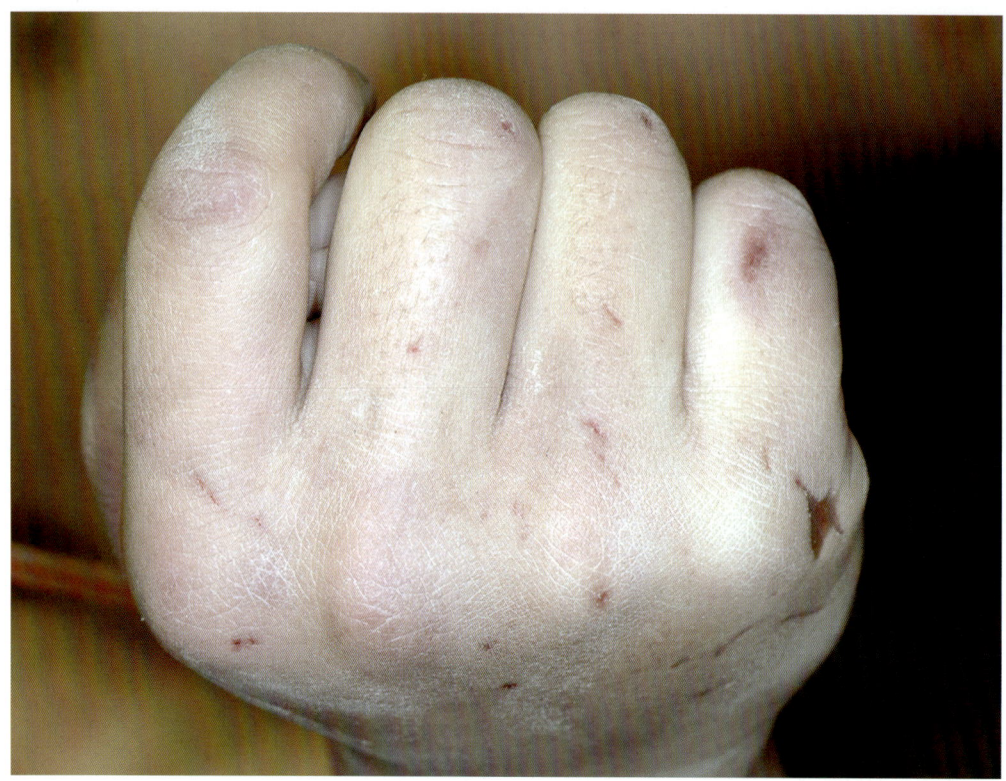

图8-15 低温死亡。死者脸朝下趴在冰面上,手背上散在分布多处细微擦伤(参阅图8-9)。

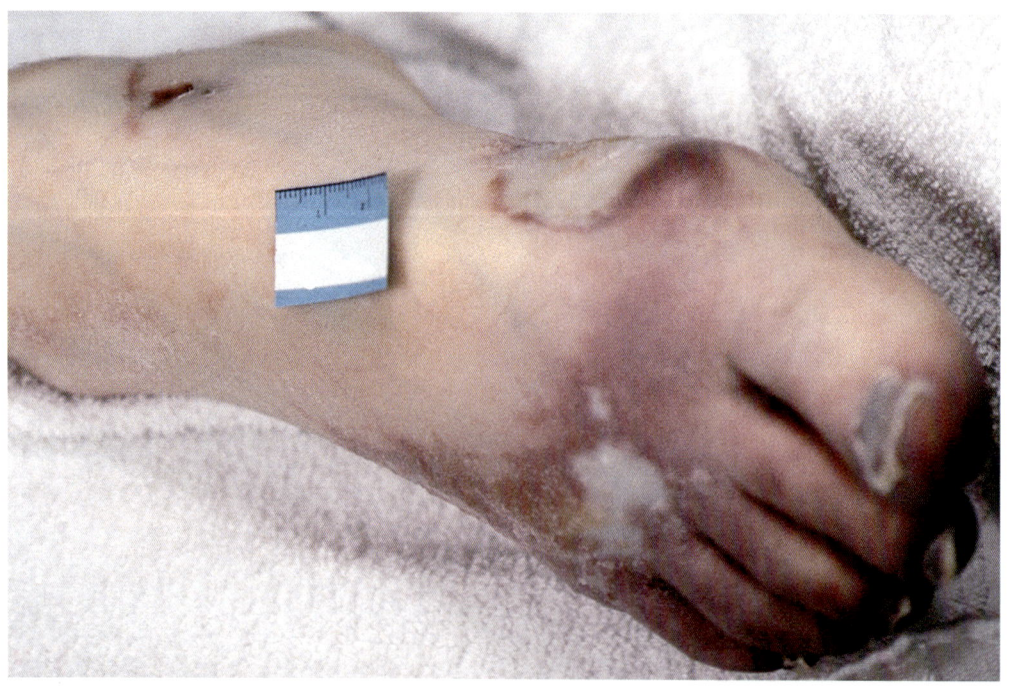

图8-16 冻伤引起右脚缺血性改变。

因为"临终挖掘行为"而被发现死于不寻常之处（如躺在床下）(38)。

相关尸表检查结果包括冻伤、面部及四肢水肿、鲜红色尸斑（图8-16；参考文献35,36,41）。出现紫色或紫红色变，尤其是在膝部和肘部，可能是死后的尸体变化(35,36,41)。尸体解冻后，四肢静脉显现更加显著，出现大理石状花纹(41)。

尸体内部器官检验的结果可能很少。急性器官病变包括：浅表胃黏膜糜烂、胰腺出血、肺水肿及髂腰肌"条带状"出血（图8-17；参考文献35,36,38,40,41）。胃部损伤可能是由于血管收缩引起缺血所致(40)。延长生存期可并发凝血病、横纹肌溶解症及肾功能衰竭（参阅第8章标题13；参考文献31）。

必须进行毒理学分析才能确定受害人是否中毒。尿液中检出丙酮提示可能存在低温致酮中毒(38)。

3.4.2 印痕样损伤

印痕样损伤（即致伤物的痕迹在皮肤表面反复出现）并不常见，但具有重要的证据价值，尤其是在凶杀案的调查中（图8-18—图8-23；参考文献8,42-47）。损伤有时表现为致伤物的镜像(44)，需要通过多种方法确定印痕样损伤与致伤物间的关系［如1:1叠加分析、损伤和致伤物或其铸件模型的影像对比分析、紫外光照射分析(44-48)］。

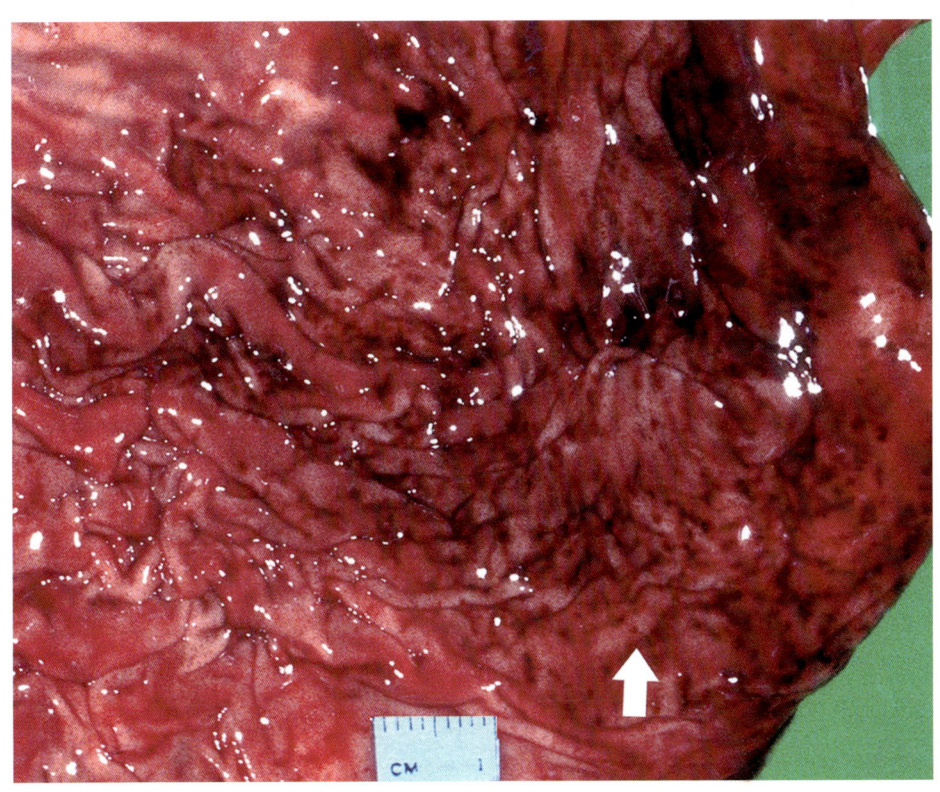

图8-17 低温死亡。胃溃疡呈矩形分布（箭头）。

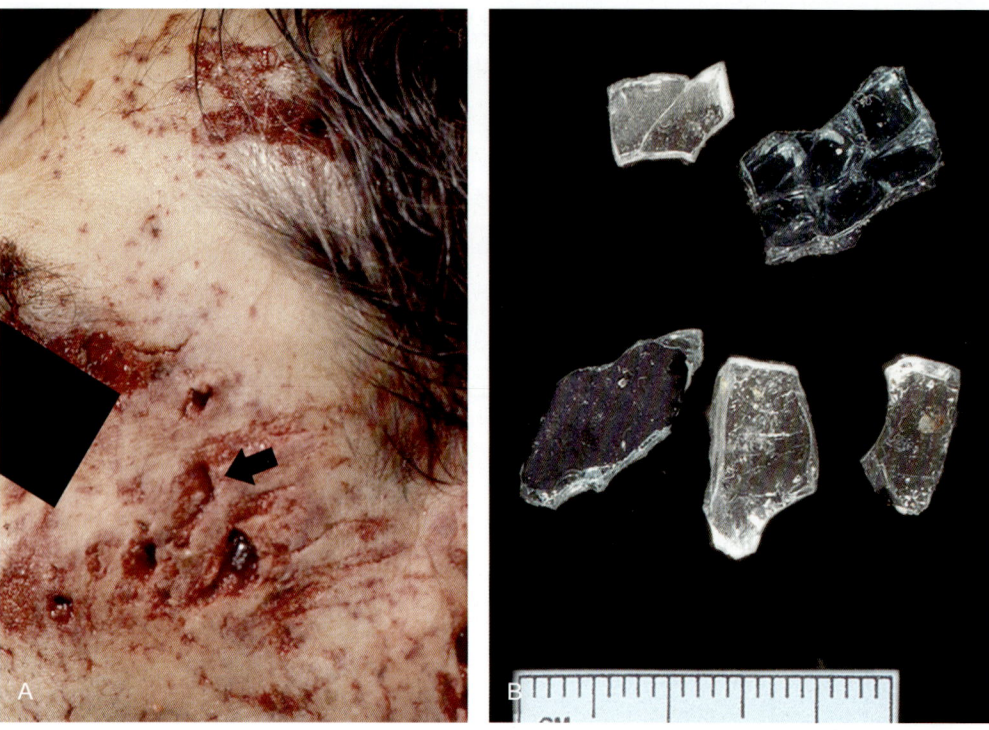

图 8-18 交通事故中遭受外侧面碰撞的车辆驾驶员。(A) 左侧面颊多处挫裂创,反 L 形挫裂创(箭头),创伤处可见钢化玻璃碎片。(B) 汽车侧门典型的矩形钢化玻璃碎片。

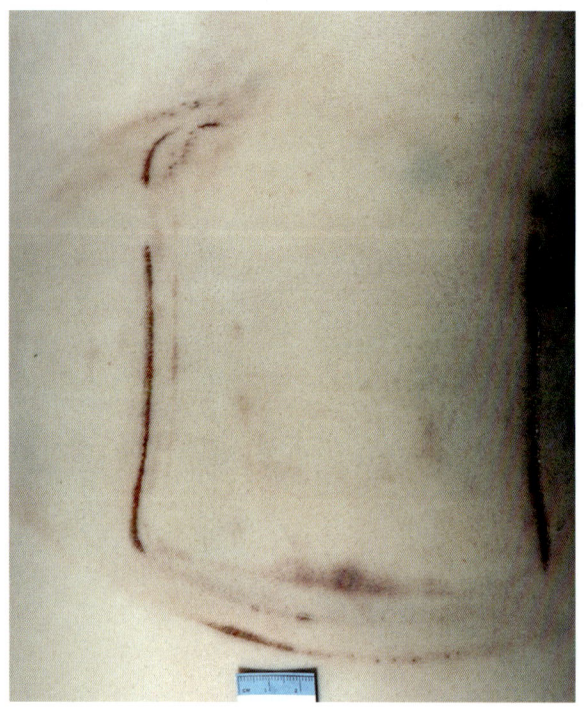

图 8-19 汽车方向盘所致的胸部印痕样损伤。

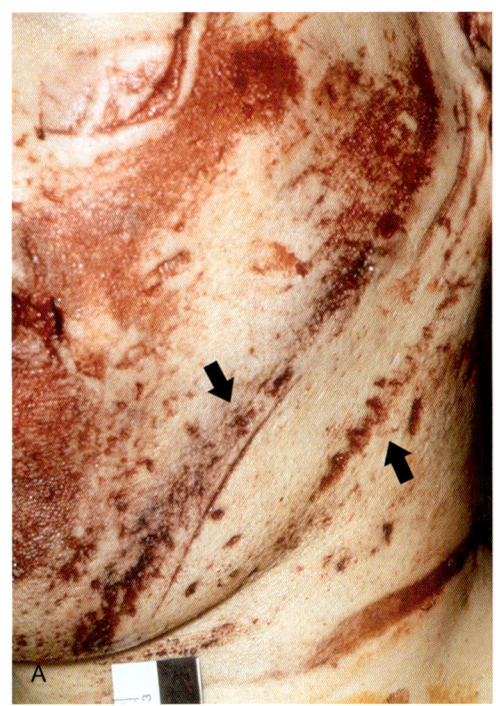 

图 8-20 车辆驾驶员死亡。（A）驾驶员左侧面颊两处平行的线形擦伤（箭头）（加拿大安大略省伦敦市伦敦健康科学中心 C. McLean 博士供图）。（B）印痕样损伤由汽车 A 柱造成。

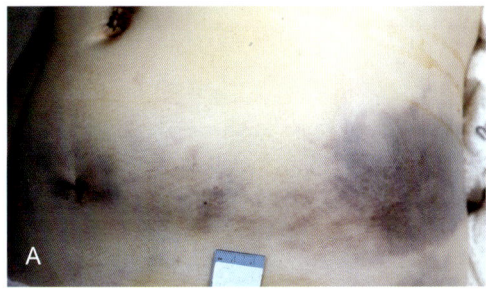 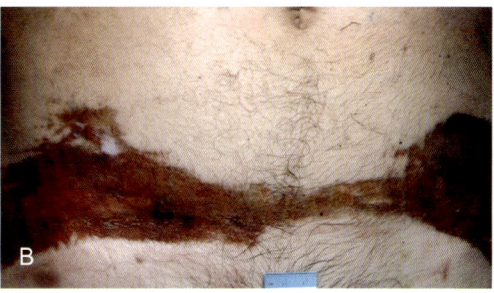

图 8-21 腰式安全带导致下腹部皮肤受伤（"安全带损伤"）（A）挫伤。（B）擦伤。

 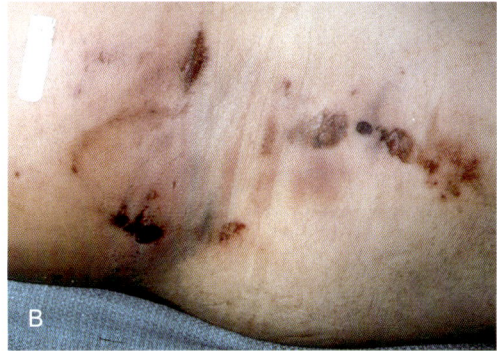

图 8-22 行人被机动车撞击的"二次"损伤。（A）与发动机罩边缘和前大灯碰撞。（B）显示右臀部上方的半圆形擦伤，可能由前灯接触所致（美国北卡罗来纳州教堂山市法医局供图）。

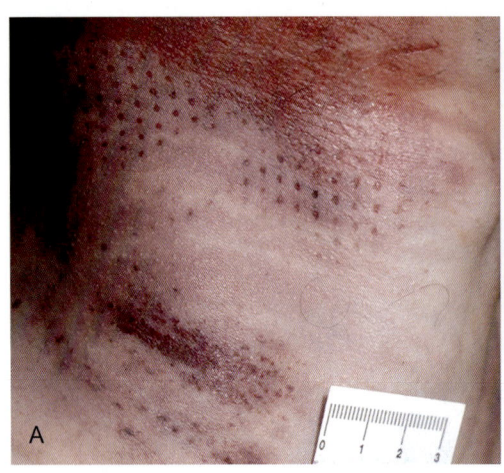 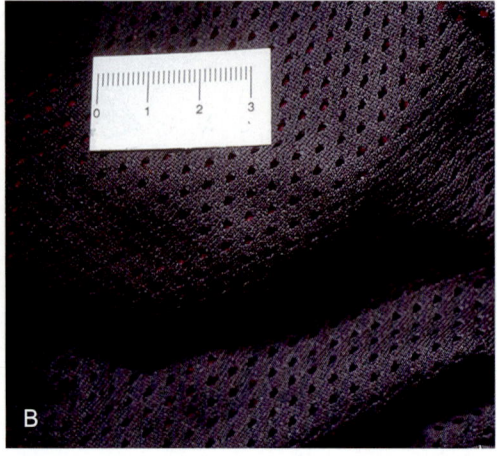

图 8-23 碾压伤。（A）颈部印痕样擦伤。（B）运动衫的编织纹样。

3.4.2.1 人咬痕

性侵、儿童虐待、某些性行为、自卫过程中会出现人咬伤。有些咬痕易被加以无罪解释［如自伤、儿童之间互咬（12,49-56）］。人类咬合过程中的撕扯或挤压会导致圆形或椭圆形排列的挫伤、擦伤和撕裂创（49,57）。咬痕通常呈 2 个与上、下颌牙列相对应的 U 形印痕，中间存在空隙（长 25-40 毫米或 0.125 英寸），可被牙齿咬切形成挫伤（49）。

皮肤由于被吮吸可出现瘀斑（55），咬痕通常由位于前面的 6 颗牙齿咬切所致（从一侧犬齿到另一侧犬齿（49,55））。对咬痕的研究显示大多数受害者是女性（53,58），乳房是最易受伤的部位。男性手臂更易被发现咬痕（53,58）。男童外阴可出现咬痕，女童则会在身体多个部位发现咬痕，会同时出现多重咬痕（58）。

如果发现疑似咬痕，需向法医齿科学专家咨询（54,58,59），最好在现场进行咬痕检验（57）。如果案件涉及暴力侵犯，需擦取咬痕获取唾液进行 DNA 分析（43,49,60）。咬痕处也可发现牙齿碎片和牙结石（54）。嫌疑人牙列模型需要与带有比例尺参考（美国法医学会）的咬痕照片（彩色或黑白）进行对比（49,61,62）。咬痕印记是牙齿压痕的负向复制，用于创建牙列模型（图 8-24；参考文献 59,62）。犯罪嫌疑人的牙列模型可以直接与咬痕照片比对，也可以间接与电脑、拍照或描摹生成的牙痕进行重合比对（49,59,61,63-65）。虽然咬痕是一种印痕样损伤，但对于个体来说并非总是具有特异性（49,68）。

4 褥疮（压疮）

骨性突起处皮肤受压可导致褥疮（如包括骶骨的脊柱、肩胛部、肘部、股骨大转子处、足跟及足踝处）（69-75）。褥疮常发生于养老院、医院和家中的患者（73,76），有研究显示其发生率约为 11%（73），另一项前瞻性尸体研究结果显示了相似的发生

第 8 章 | 钝器损伤——包括航空器、火车和机动车辆损伤

图 8-24　背部咬痕,磨具上是牙印痕。

率(72)。褥疮发生率从一般人群的 0.1% 到脊髓康复患者的 30% 不等(73)。

任何长期卧床的个体都可能产生褥疮,营养不良、血管功能不全(如糖尿病)、大小便失禁引起的粪尿积聚、护理过程中的摩擦(如帮患者翻身)是造成褥疮的原因(69,71-75,77)。皮肤摩擦可能会除去已经失活的表皮(78)。受压区域首先显示出红斑(第 1 阶段),然后发展为水疱或浅表溃烂(第 2 阶段),进一步引起皮肤全层坏死并延伸至皮下组织和筋膜(第 3 阶段),最终累及下面的肌肉和支撑结构(骨骼、肌腱、关节囊;第 4 阶段)(69,71,73-75)。

深度褥疮有继发蜂窝织炎和骨髓炎败血症的风险(71-74,76,79-81)。显微镜检查可确定是否存在软组织和骨性炎症;然而,败血症的临床症状和微生物培养结果(即血液培养呈阳性)支持了褥疮在死亡原因中的作用(70,72,74,75,78,80,81)。损伤处常见细菌污染(69,75),需氧菌(如金黄色葡萄球菌)和厌氧菌(如类杆菌(81))都可存活于伤口处。微生物菌血症不一定表示感染,必须排除其他感染源(80)。

住院患者有褥疮溃疡与死亡风险增加相关(73,75,76,79,82)。无论什么阶段的褥疮,都是身体衰弱的表现,表明多种与绝症有关的因素导致了患者死亡(79,82)。晚期溃疡的发展需引起对个人护理的关注(图 8-25;参考文献 71,72,74,76,80,83,84)。动物研究表明,压力持续 1-2 小时便会引起肌肉坏死(74,75)。医院里

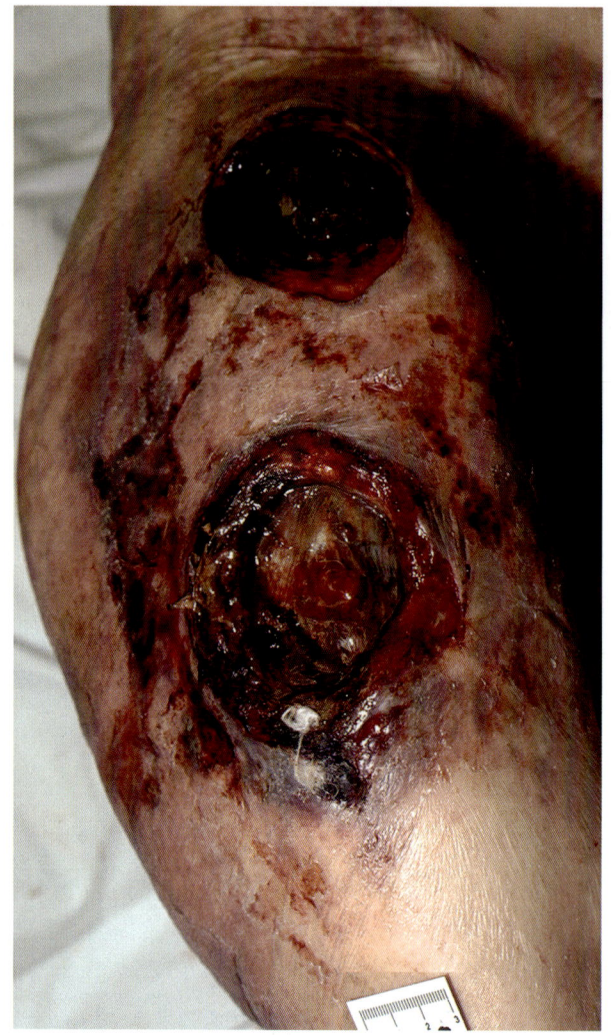

图 8-25 老年患者在家中长期卧床,右臀部褥疮。

护理人员工作繁忙,给患者频繁翻身是一种挑战,可能没有特别有效的干预措施能完全减少褥疮发生(77)。

5 高坠

各种死亡方式都可发生(7, 85-89),其中某些较为常见。

- "跳楼者": 女性约占自杀总人数的 25% - 50%(7, 87, 90)。某些情况下,出现受害者为较年长者的趋势,很可能反映了某社区的人口统计特征(91, 92)。大多数案例发生在自杀者住所(89),但有些自杀者也会选择远离住所的地点(85, 90, 93)。许多自杀者有精神疾病史、药物滥用史或衰竭性疾病(90, 92-95)。抑郁症比精神病更为普遍,约三分之一的自杀者写有遗书

(85,92)。其他现场调查结果也会支持自杀意图［如高坠前脱鞋、爬过窄窗、从高于人体重心的障碍物上掉落(85,89)］。也有精神病患者跃过窗户(96)。虽然有不少研究表明自杀与坠落高度的关联性高于意外高坠,但研究结果并不一致(85,91,92,97,98)。根据尸体发现位置与建筑物间的距离判断坠落意图(即跳楼还是坠落)不一定可靠,但一项理论研究表明,距离与起跳角度相关,如果距离有 40 米(130 英尺)说明有助跑起跳,而距离为 10 米(330 英尺)则为原地起跳(85,88)。会出现尸体可能在被发现之前已被移动的情况(89)。

- 工作场所事故和其他意外坠落：从建筑物、脚手架及梯子上坠落是建筑行业中最主要的致死原因(85,99,100)。20-30 岁的男性是最常见的受害者(7,85,87,99,100),坠落原因涉及工作场地安全性、本人意图、醉酒和疾病(85,87,100,101)。醉酒和鲁莽行为是非工作因素坠落的主要原因,意外和自杀高坠者中有超过三分之一被发现有饮酒和吸食毒品史(85,90)。

防护措施有缺陷和缺乏成年人监管是导致儿童坠楼的主要原因(102,103)。高坠案件中他杀占 2%(85,87)。

多种因素决定损伤的程度和范围(2,104),坠落高度是主要因素,但也并非唯一因素(2,103-107)。一般而言,高度越高,发生多处致命性损伤的可能性就越大(85,87,97,106,108-111)。坠落速度的计算公式为：$V = \sqrt{2gh}$,其中 g 为重力加速度(9.8 米/秒²),h 为坠落高度(103,112,113)。从 2 层(1 层为 3-4.5 米或 10-14.5 英尺)坠落的速度可达 15 米/秒(30 英里/小时),从 40 层坠落则速度可达到约 60 米/秒(120 英里/小时)(1,2,86,90,108,114)。成人从 5 层以上坠落往往会致命,尽管从 8 层坠落也有生还的可能(2,85,86,97,114,115)。一项关于儿童高坠的研究显示,儿童从 3 层或低于 3 层坠落均可存活(116),从 5-6 层坠落儿童的死亡率推断为 50%。另一项研究显示,15 岁或更低年龄的青少年从 5 层坠落,有 75% 当场死亡(117)。有些从较低楼层坠落的受害者由于诊治延迟而死亡(如硬脑外血肿)。从 5 层以上坠落则会导致受害者多重致命性头部损伤。

虽然脚部着地的坠落力与面积比较大,但这种姿势通常损伤较轻(87,105,112,118,119),而头部着地则大多数为致命性损伤(90)。

坠落在可变形的表面(如水、雪)上会增加冲击时间,从而减轻损伤程度,但无论坠落于何种表面,都会发生一定范围的损伤(1,2,85,87,90,91,98,105,106,114)。已有从高度为 75 米(250 英尺)的桥上跳入水中幸存的案例(90,119-121),也有从高空(7 000 米或 23 000 英尺)坠落至雪中生还的报道(122)。

儿童对坠落伤的耐受程度高于成人(2,103),因为儿童体重轻、骨骼韧性大、皮下脂肪多。儿童坠落时姿态更加放松,而且心肺功能储备更好,容易康复(90,105,106,114,123)。

衣服能增加身体受到的阻力,高空中的空气阻力也能延缓坠落时间(90,112)。

坠落伤是包括直接碰撞引起的垂直性减速暴力、坠落中或初次碰撞后中介物体引起的二次碰撞、能量传递到身体远离碰撞的部位等(1,7,86,97,106,109,113,114,119)。垂直减速运动会导致严重的胸部(如主动脉撕裂、心脏破裂)和腹部器官损伤(1,2,7,119,120)。碰撞后身体反弹也可在高坠中发生(2,106,124)。直接碰撞会发生在头部、臀部、体侧及下肢，但直接碰撞部位通常难以明确判定(7,110,113)。有研究显示，从较低楼层起跳坠落常足部着地(一般不超过12层)，体侧着地一般在13层以下，头部着地则发生在更高楼层(90)。

根据碰撞部位的不同，损伤特征可有以下几种情况(7)：

- 头部：对于意外坠落，由于人体的重心位于上半身，故成人和儿童均会发生头部碰撞(2,102,103)，可观察到颅骨骨折和脑损伤(2,7,113,118)。对于其他的落地姿势，身体撞击地面后的二次碰撞也会导致头部损伤。无论坠落高度如何，头部损伤都是最主要的致死因素(7,87,90–92,115,116,125)。一项研究显示致命性头部损伤易出现在从低于7米(23英尺)和高于30米[97英尺(111)]的坠落事件中，还有一项研究表明严重头部损伤主要出现在低于10米(33英尺)和高于25米(81英尺)的坠落(89)。
- 臀部：骨盆和胸腰部骨折最常见(2,7,104)，腹膜后会大量出血(115)。脊柱骨折常由压迫引起(7,109,115,125)，外力通过脊柱传递而造成颅底骨折(围绕枕骨大孔的"环状"骨折)(7,104,113)。
- 体侧：肋骨骨折会直接撕裂胸膜，胸椎外伤可发生在碰撞部位的对侧(7,119)。有研究表明，肋骨骨折数目随坠落高度的增加而增多，从超过40米(130英尺)的高空坠落会引起多发性肋骨骨折(111)。
- 下肢(足部着地)：骨折可出现在足部、踝部及胫部，但坠落至水中可能不发生骨折(2,7,85,105)。外力可以传导至股骨、胸腰椎及颅底(1,2,7)。不同于坠落在较硬表面上对躯干、臀部和下肢的撞击，坠落于水中皮肤损伤较轻，但内部器官损伤严重(85)。坠落水于中会产生"冲击波"效应(肋骨骨折、肺挫伤、气胸；参阅第4章标题8.1；参考文献1,2,105,112,113,118,119,126,127)。如果伤者由于下肢骨折无法游泳，则会导致溺死(87,105,118–120,126)。

碰撞侧通常会形成损伤[即一个损伤面(89)]。如果身体多面都出现皮肤损伤，但没有对应的四肢和胸部骨折，则疑似谋杀罪行(85,98)，儿童多发性致命性损伤提示可能有虐待案情(117)。

如果受害人在坠落过程中撞击到障碍物或着陆时试图用手撑地，就可能引起上肢骨折(图8-26；参考文献85,113)。如果受害人因握力不足页松手，则可在其手掌发现皮肤损伤(图8-27；参考文献85)。

坠落案件中也常观察到舌骨和喉部骨折(89,118)。

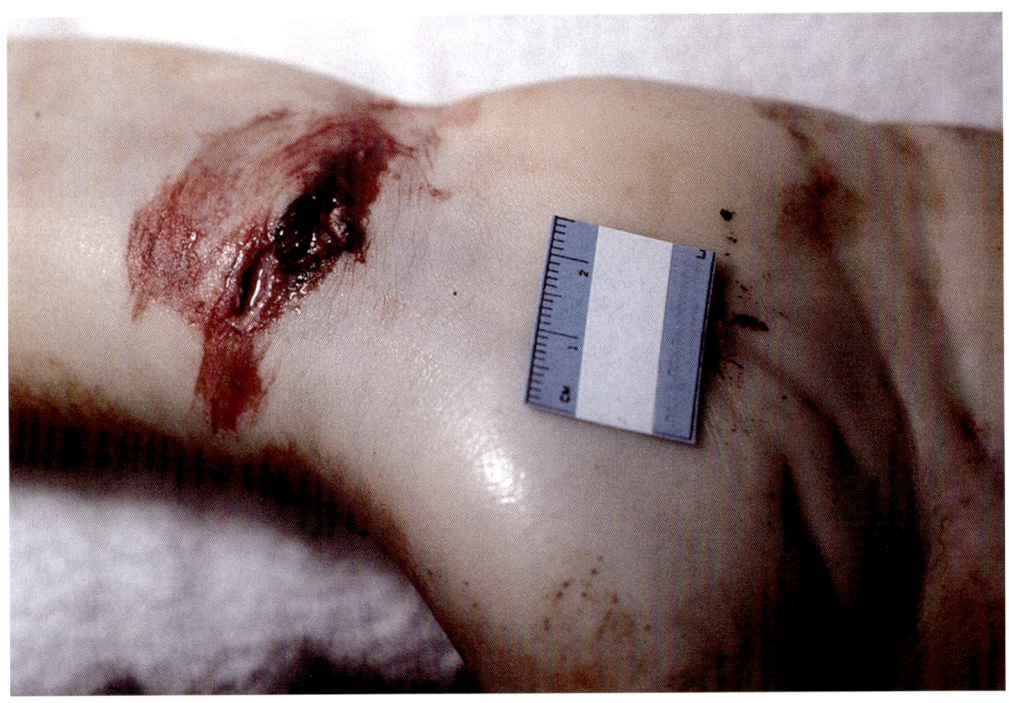

图 8-26 高坠。死者腕部擦伤及相应骨折,可能着地时试图用手撑地。

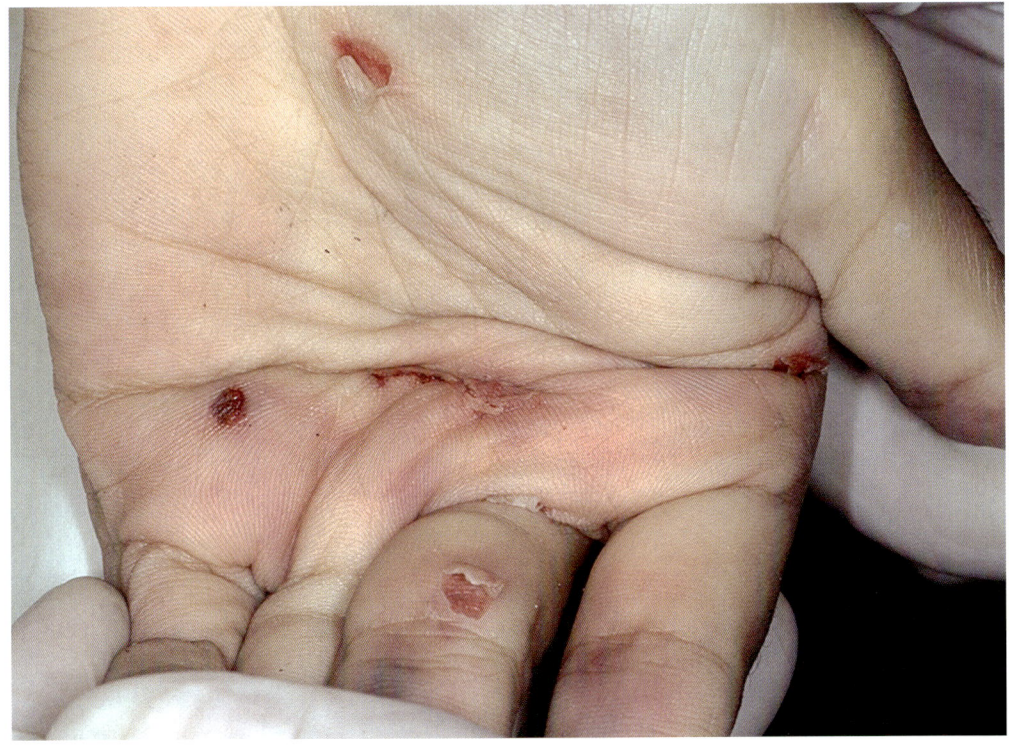

图 8-27 死者坠落前手抓阳台栏杆,手掌皮肤擦伤。

6 胸部损伤

6.1 胸壁

直接按压会导致肋骨和胸骨骨折(128)。如果发生骨折,说明所受外力的能量耗散(129)。胸壁侧边最为脆弱(128)。受压的部位不同,骨折会有多种典型的表现形式:前胸受压,引起胸骨和前外侧肋骨骨折;后背受压,导致后侧肋骨骨折;侧面受压,造成后侧肋骨骨折和肋软骨连接处分离(128)。老年人由于骨质疏松和肌肉组织减少,损伤后更容易发生胸壁骨折(128,130-133)。儿童发生胸壁骨折,则提示相对弹性较好的肋骨受到的外力非常大(如机动车辆碰撞)(128,134)。

由于胸壁损伤可直接或间接引起死亡,因此,尸体解剖时不应局限于解剖器官,还必须检查胸壁的完整性(图8-28)。

连续性骨折包括至少3根肋骨发生骨折,且每根肋骨有两个骨折部位,使局部胸壁变得松散而出现反常于呼吸运动的移位[即"连枷胸"(128,135)]。胸廓任何部位骨折都可造成连枷胸(128,136)。胸骨横断骨折可加重反常位移(135)。背部肌肉和肩胛骨可为后肋骨骨折提供更好的支撑(135)。连枷胸可伴有呼吸功能不全,伤者住院后可能出现肺不张,随后发生肺炎(128,135,137-139)。

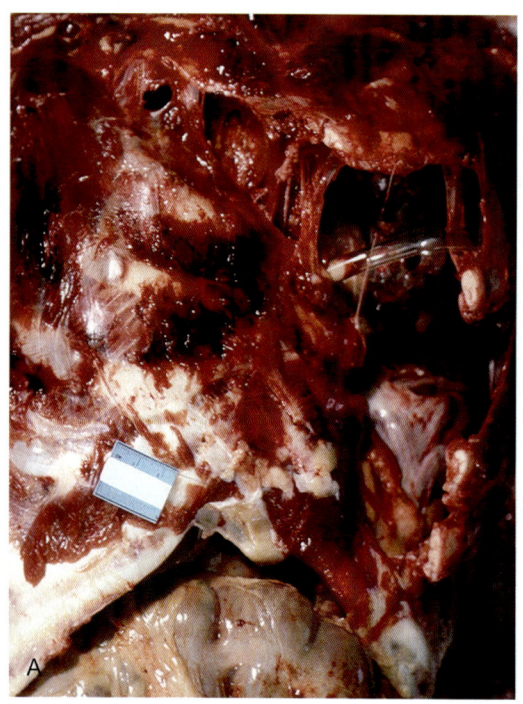 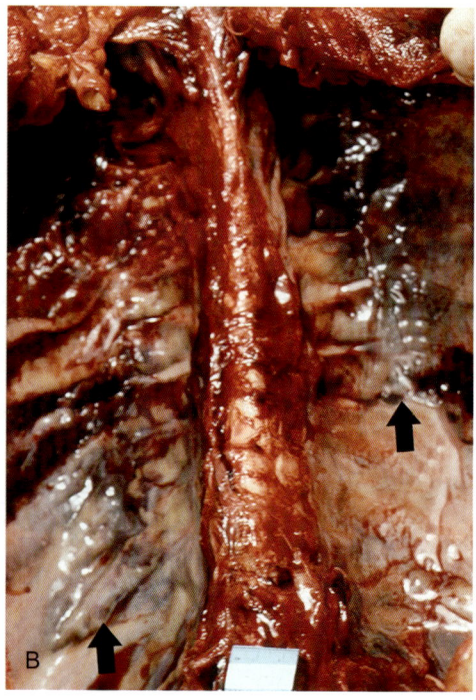

图8-28 肋骨骨折。(A)前肋骨和胸骨大范围骨折(从左胸壁缺损处插入胸管)。(B)胸膜下出血(箭头),表明多发性后肋骨骨折。这些损伤只有在摘除器官后检查胸腔时才可发现。

肋骨骨折的分布和程度可提示外力的方向、大小及潜在的内脏损伤情况（128，136，139，140）。器官损伤并非总伴有胸壁骨折，特别是在年轻人中（140）。胸骨骨折提示有纵隔损伤，下肋骨骨折则提示存在膈肌和腹部器官损伤，而 3 根或更多肋骨骨折则说明内脏损伤与死亡的风险提高（130，141）。一项临床综述研究表明：在 1 490 例胸部钝性损伤患者中，2 根以上肋骨骨折患者的死亡率为 4.7%，而连枷胸患者的死亡率为 17%（131）。当外部压力增大到足以破坏胸壁完整性（胸廓稳定性极限）时，会导致胸壁塌陷和内部器官严重损伤（6）。根据尸体研究，"极限"为至少 6 处肋骨骨折（参阅参考文献 6 和标题 6.5）。

胸壁骨折时常出现血胸和气胸（137，140，141），如果肋骨骨折数量增加，这些并发症的风险也会升高（131，139）。气胸通常由肺破裂引起，而血胸通常由肺、心脏和大血管损伤引起（参阅标题 6.4.2，6.5—6.7；参考文献 140）。

检查胸腔时，法医不仅要记录所有的骨折，而且还要意识到肋间血管损伤是导致血胸的另一个原因（142）。肋骨骨折后，血胸可能延迟发生（143—146）。出血来源通常是肋间动脉（143—145）。在临床症状改善期间，当胸廓运动因深呼吸和咳嗽加强时，可能发生迟发性出血（144）。血胸且不伴肋骨骨折的情况，很少发生（145）。如果在尸体解剖时从胸部分离胸骨后未做检查，意味着胸廓内动脉或静脉撕裂可能被遗漏（图 8-29）。这类损伤极为少见（147，148），也可能与锁骨或肋骨骨折有关（149）。突然减速可以使胸廓内动脉从锁骨下动脉发出处撕脱，随后发生血胸或纵隔血肿，并于数小时内导致休克（147，149，150）。

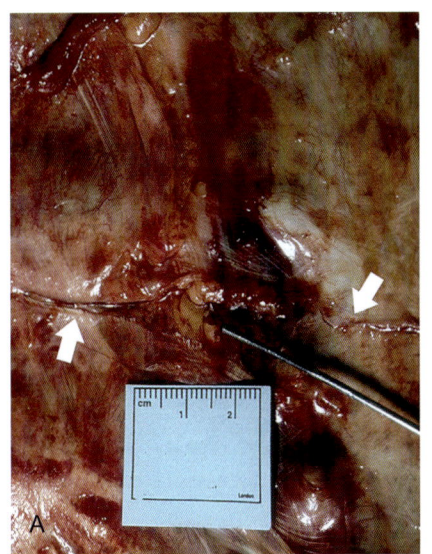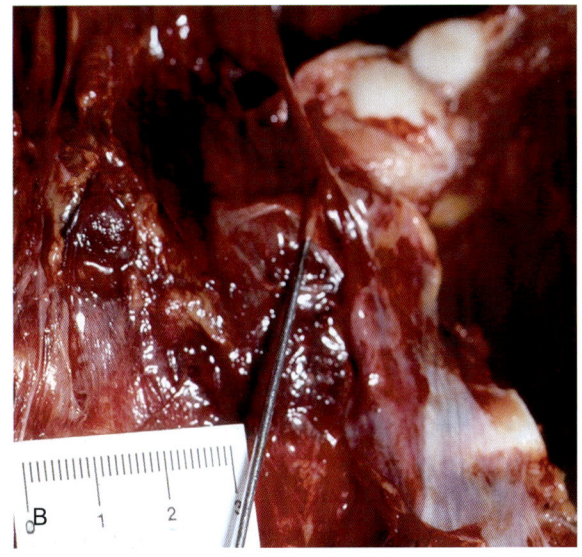

图 8-29 胸骨骨折 2 例。（A）胸骨背面可见明显的胸廓内动脉"撕裂"（探针尖端），但这其实是由解剖刀在分离胸骨时人为造成的（剪头）。（B）碾压。胸骨向上翻开（部分被标签遮挡）。胸骨背面显示胸廓内静脉撕裂（探针插入撕裂口底端）。

6.2 胸外心肺复苏损伤

上文已经描述了心肺复苏（cardiopulmonary resuscitation, CPR）过程中由于手动操作和装置辅助的胸外按压导致的并发症（表 8-1）[151 和 152]。

表 8-1　胸外心脏按压的并发症

胸壁
　肋骨、胸骨骨折或脱位（151-160）
　　• 连枷胸（155, 161-163）
　　• 肋软骨连接处分离（163-165）
　胸壁出血（166, 167）
　血胸（151, 152, 155, 164, 168, 169）
　其他骨折［锁骨、肩胛骨、颈椎、胸腰椎（155, 162, 164, 170）］

膈肌破裂（167）

心血管系统
　心包撕裂（152, 156, 171）
　心包积血（151, 153, 155, 158, 164, 172）
　　• 心脏破裂
　　• 心包穿刺术、心脏起搏器、中央静脉导管（157, 173-175）
　心肌挫伤（152, 155, 158）
　室间隔出血［左心室后室间隔部位最常见（154, 155, 157, 164, 169）］
　心肌破裂
　　• 心房（152, 155, 156, 176）
　　• 心室
　　　◦ 正常心肌（156, 157, 160, 168, 171, 177）
　　　◦ 心肌梗死（156, 172, 173, 178）
　　　◦ 由肋骨骨折或椎骨骨折所致（171, 179）
　　• 乳头肌（180）
　冠状动脉破裂（152）
　主动脉内膜撕裂/破裂［升/降胸主动脉粥样硬化（152, 156, 164, 168, 181）］
　主动脉夹层及相关的动脉粥样硬化（182）
　静脉撕裂［如下腔静脉、脾静脉、肾静脉、胸廓内静脉（155, 159, 164, 169, 183）］

呼吸系统
　胸膜破裂（152）
　肺挫伤/挫裂创（157, 160, 164, 183）
　肺气压伤［气胸、心包积气、腹腔积气、纵隔气肿、肺间质和皮下气肿（151, 155, 164, 168, 169, 173, 174, 184）］
　气管裂创/出血（157, 184）

腹腔器官
　食管、胃、结肠破裂（151, 158, 167, 179, 185-189）

续表

食管、胃撕裂(167, 184, 189, 190)
胃扩张(155, 158)
肝破裂(151, 154, 155, 158, 159, 164, 168, 169, 191)
• 肝动脉撕裂(192)
肝包膜下血肿(155, 164)
脾脏破裂(154, 155, 159, 164, 168, 169)
胰腺出血、胰腺炎(159, 193–195)
网膜出血(155)
腹膜后间隙
腹膜后间隙出血(155, 159, 164, 184, 194)
肾上腺出血(169)
骨髓和脂肪栓塞(参阅标题12.1和12.2)
横纹肌溶解症——肾衰竭(参阅标题13；参考文献196)
视网膜出血(儿童)(参阅标题6.2；参考文献197)

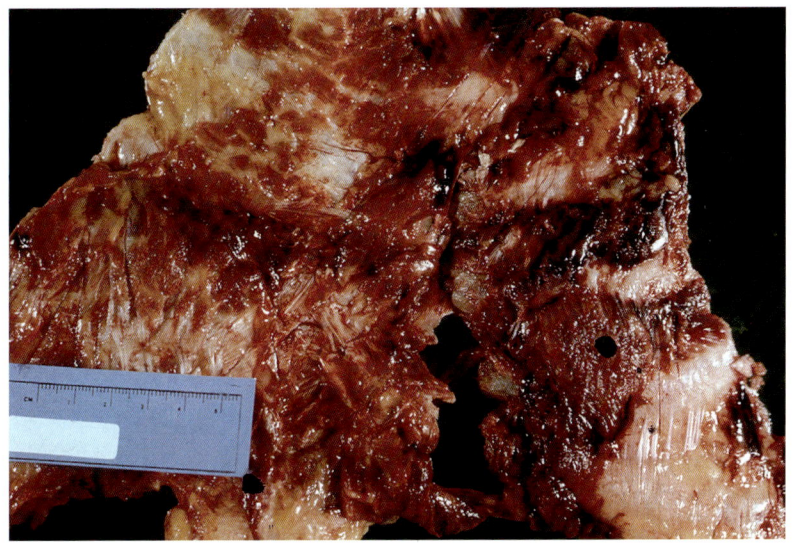

图8-30 尸检中检查移出的胸骨，发现心肺复苏导致中线垂直骨折。

胸壁骨折是最常见的损伤(图8-30)(152, 155, 164, 168, 169, 173, 174)。在一项针对705名复苏患者的研究中，有63%发生5处或5处以上肋骨骨折，其中75%的骨折累及双侧胸廓(155)。有尸检研究显示：成人案件中有8.4%因心肺复苏造成1–4处肋骨骨折，有2.6%超过5处肋骨骨折(164)。更早的一项研究发现，31%的案例中有2–8处骨折，3.8%有超过8处骨折(153)。骨质疏松、按压力度过大及胸部按压姿势错误都会增加胸壁骨折和器官损伤的可能性(132, 134, 155–

157,160,169,198)。通常,典型的骨折发生于前外侧第3—7肋骨和胸骨中段(132)。按压时手的位置过高会导致上肋骨(第1、第2肋骨)和胸骨骨折(155),手的位置过低则可能导致下肋骨(低于第6肋骨)和胸骨骨折及腹内损伤(155,159)。骨折部位出血表明在胸部按压过程中心脏搏动恢复。

儿童肋骨骨折很罕见,通常被认为有虐待儿童的可能;但也有案例报道CRP导致的儿童肋骨骨折(134,159,169)。CPR后儿童视网膜出血与先前的严重创伤有关(197)。

血管和器官破裂可能是被骨折碎片穿透所致(160),也可能是流体静压力增加所致。任何心肺复苏引发的严重损伤通常在濒死期形成(152,155)。即使患者复苏,其复苏相关的创伤也可能导致患者发病和死亡。复苏可能会导致一种以上的损伤。有研究显示,CPR相关胸外伤患者中有33%有腹部并发症,有23%出现上呼吸道创伤,约15%出现肺或心血管后遗症(155),还有不到1%的患者出现危及生命的并发症。

6.3 心包膜

心包破裂通常与胸壁骨折穿透有关(199),心脏破裂和大血管损伤也较常见,但并非总相伴发生(199,200)。心包破裂可以发生在心包膜的膈肌面、上纵隔面或其两侧(199),其中左侧心包膜最常见(199)。胸膜心包膜侧面撕裂通常为垂直方向,有时会累及膈神经(199)。

心包破裂可阻止心脏压塞的发生(199,201),否则会出现胸腔积血、腹腔积血或纵隔出血。通过膈肌薄弱部位(尤其是左侧膈肌顶)引起的心脏疝可导致严重的血液动力学改变(199,200,202),可能会延迟死亡(199)。腹部器官可通过膈肌缺损处膨出,导致心脏压塞(199,203)。

6.4 心脏

心脏钝性损伤可由外界暴力作用于心前区胸壁直接导致(伴或不伴肋骨和胸骨骨折),也可由外界压迫和运动减速引起心内压升高而间接形成(129,204-209)。

6.4.1 心脏挫伤

临床和尸检中经常会遇到心脏挫伤(129,204,205,210,211)。临床上,心脏挫伤往往会被更严重的损伤掩盖(205,210,212),如果其他严重损伤导致患者立即死亡,则心脏损伤会被忽略(210,211)。

暂时性心律失常会在住院24小时内出现,但也可延迟出现(204,205,207,208,210-214)。心脏挫伤本身很少致患者死亡,但致死性心律失常和心力衰竭会在损伤后几天内出现(210-212,215)。在心肌挫伤和血液高酒精浓度的动物实验模型中可观察到致死性机电分离现象(204)。

尸体解剖观察到的挫伤位置多局限于右心室,类似于心肌梗死,但与心肌梗死相比出血更明显(图8-31)(204,207,210和211)。程度较轻的心脏挫伤多表现为

第 8 章 | 钝器损伤——包括航空器、火车和机动车辆损伤

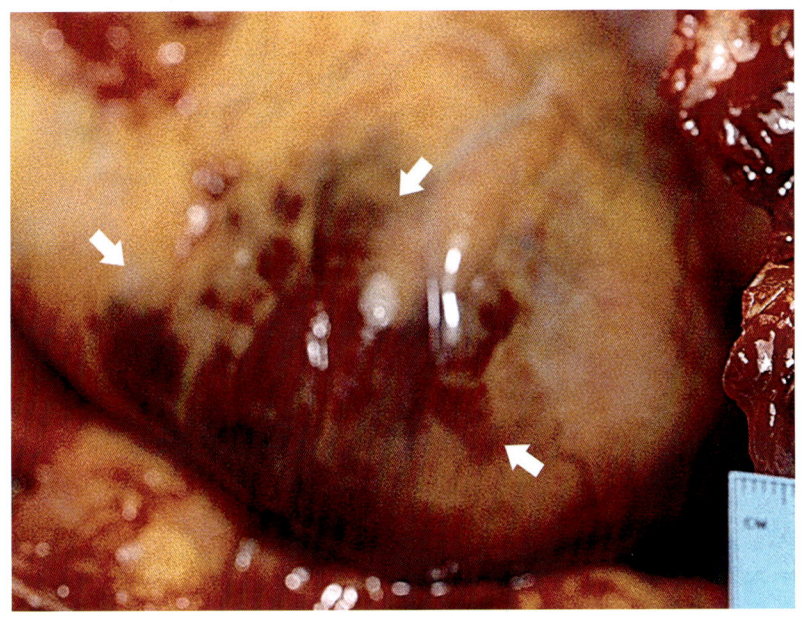

图 8-31 心肌挫伤（箭头界定区域）。

心外膜或心内膜下出血(205)，挫伤部位的坏死区可恶化并引起心脏破裂(216)，但很少形成动脉瘤或假性动脉瘤并发生破裂(216)。

6.4.2 心脏破裂

胸壁下心前区的构成如下：55% 右心室，20% 左心室，10% 右心房，10% 升主动脉和肺动脉，5% 腔静脉(205)。心脏不同部位破裂的概率反映出各自的表面解剖结构(129,206,217-220)。心脏室间隔和房间隔破裂相对少见。心房破裂最可能发生在心脏收缩期(204)，患者心房破裂尚有可能存活(206,209,219,221-223)。心前区在舒张期遭受外界暴力打击可发生心室破裂(204,224)。心脏破裂的其他机制还包括腹部和四肢创伤及减速运动间接引发的心内压升高(224-226)。心脏破裂可以愈合并形成室壁瘤(227)，心动脉瘤可并发于心脏破裂、充血性心力衰竭、心律不齐和全身性栓塞，愈合过程中可能发生迟发性破裂(225,228)。

6.4.3 心脏震荡

心脏震荡的特点是在没有严重结构性心血管疾病或创伤的情况下，心前区遭受看似轻微的打击后心脏停搏而猝死(208,214,229-236)。某些情况下，在心前区可观察到皮肤挫伤(229,235)，通常观察不到胸壁骨折(231,232,235)。肺挫伤可能是胸部受撞击的唯一形态学依据(237)。受害者遭受撞击后立即昏倒或暂时保持清醒意识之后心脏停搏(229,232,233,235)。通常，心肺复苏无法使受害者的心率恢复正常(229,233,235)，即使心率恢复也已经发生了不可逆的缺氧性脑损伤(235)。在某些情况下，如果及时给予复苏和除颤(229,231,232,238)，也可能完全恢复。

在极少数情况下,心脏震荡能自行恢复(231)。

室性心律失常的机制是心前区在心脏周期复极化(T波)的易颤期遭受打击(229,230,232,234-236,239),从而触发早搏,导致心室颤动(231,232,235)。心脏震荡的发生取决于外力的类型、强度和部位[胸骨中下段(230)]。中高强度的快速外力最可能导致心脏震荡(230)。

心脏震荡通常与儿童和青少年的运动或娱乐活动有关,但不仅限于此(图8-32)(231,232和235)。年轻人因为胸壁顺应性增加,作用于心前区的力量被更多地传递至心脏,故更容易发生心脏震荡(207,234,235)。实心物体比充气球体更容易引发致命性心律失常(231),在棒球和垒球比赛中最为常见(229,231)。曾有研究报道,从12-14米(40-45英尺)以外以48-80千米/小时(30-50英里/小时)的速度飞来的棒球击打到人体胸部[231,235]。对猪的损伤研究发现,以40千米/小时(64英里/小时)的速度撞击胸部最有可能引起心脏震荡(232-234,240)。还有研究描述过其他物体或表面(如曲棍球棒、石头、上肢或下肢)与胸部接触性碰撞(175,207,231,232,234,235,241),如曲棍球和长曲棍球以144千米/小时(90英里/小时)的高速击打到人体胸部。在少数情况下(如足球比赛中的抢断、冰球等比赛中的身体阻截)可发生胸部表面更大面积的损伤(229,231,232,235)。使用护

图8-32 心脏震荡。一名儿童在打棒球时被坚硬的塑料球击中胸部,当场心脏停搏,经过40分钟心肺复苏后被宣告死亡。

胸并不一定会降低心脏震荡发生的风险(229,231)。心脏震荡是机动车碰撞中的一种损伤机制(参阅标题14.2.2；参考文献241)。

6.4.4 冠状动脉

冠状动脉钝性损伤很少见到诸如主动脉夹层、血栓形成、破裂-撕裂、瘘管及动脉瘤等后遗症(211,242-249)，但可能存在相关的心肌挫伤(211,250)。冠状动脉3条主要分支都可能受伤(245,250-252)。冠状动脉损伤可表现为心肌缺血，但很少出现动脉粥样硬化(243-245,248,249,251-254)。

6.4.5 心脏瓣膜

钝性损伤可导致二尖瓣、三尖瓣及其乳头肌和腱索破裂(255-269)，也可导致主动脉瓣膜破裂(270,271)。主动脉内膜破裂导致瓣膜功能不全也曾有报道(272)。

6.5 主动脉(包括腹主动脉)

机动车交通事故创伤是主动脉损伤的主要原因(273-275)。车内死者中有高达四分之一者被发现主动脉破裂(273,274,276-282)。绝大部分主动脉破裂的伤者当场死亡(273,276,283,284)。主动脉破裂很少单独出现，常伴有其他严重损伤(273,275,283,285-287)。

峡部(即降主动脉于左锁骨下动脉开口下方区域)最易发生损伤(图8-33)(273-275和283)。峡部是依附于脊柱的降主动脉与活动的近端主动脉连接部位的"固定"点(275,283)。由于峡部是胎儿出生后动脉导管闭锁的遗迹，因此成为主动脉固有的薄弱区域(275)。年龄增长和疾病(如动脉粥样硬化)会使峡部退变(288)，因此主动脉破裂很少发生在年轻群体中(275,289,290)。

已有许多理论用于解释主动脉这一相对受保护区域更易发生外伤性破裂的原因

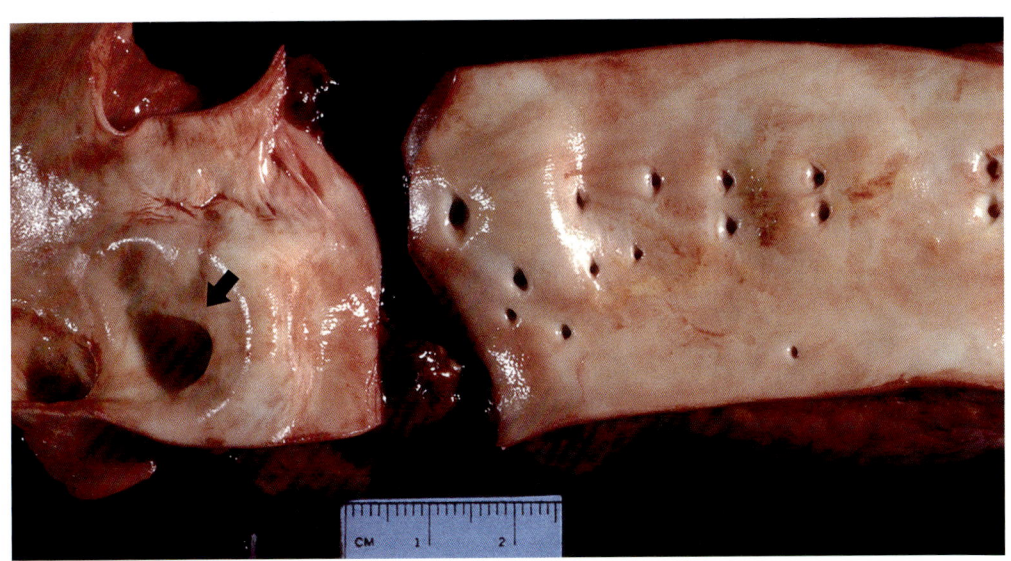

图 8-33 降主动脉横断面(峡部)。左锁骨下动脉开口(箭头)。

(274，275，283，291），包括胸壁挤压、机体运动减速、血管内压增加及其他血流动力学作用（图 8-34），其共同途径可能是作用于主动脉峡部的纵向压力导致典型的主动脉壁横向撕裂，轻则引起动脉内膜撕裂，重则导致动脉全层破裂（275）。尸体解剖中可见的左侧胸腔积血通常由峡部撕裂引起。在确定积血量之后、取出脏器之前，应该沿着胸部脊柱下行方向检查降主动脉全段，暴露胸膜破裂部位及下方的峡部破裂。主动脉破裂可为多发性的（273，275），破裂口也可自行愈合（292）。主动脉破裂并不总伴有肋骨骨折（140，275，283）。一项针对成年人的研究显示，主动脉破裂至少伴有 5-7 处肋骨骨折（参阅标题 6.1，参考文献 275）。

升主动脉作为另一个固定点，是第二处易发生损伤的部位（图 8-35）（274，275）。其他固定部位包括胸主动脉横隔膜开口处、主动脉弓及腹主动脉分叉处附近（273，275）。

腹主动脉破裂并不常见[发生率仅为胸主动脉损伤的 5%（293-295）]，因为它贴合在脊柱上且受后腹膜保护。椎骨骨折可直接导致腹主动脉破裂。腹壁受到挤压可导致主动脉压升高。作用于腹主动脉的主要附着点（如肠系膜下动脉）和髂动脉分叉处的减速力量可引发血管撕裂（293）。先前存在的动脉粥样硬化可能是诱发动脉

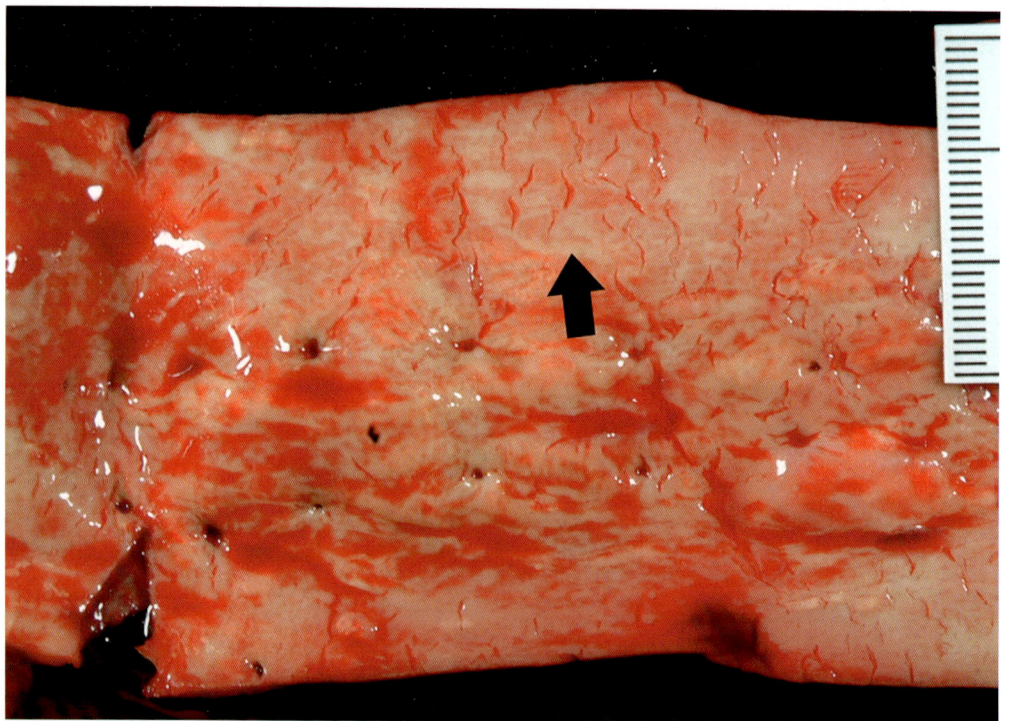

图 8-34　降主动脉峡部一处破裂的下方多处创伤性内膜破裂（箭头）。多发性动脉外膜损伤被认为是撞击时主动脉压力升高的征兆（加拿大安大略省伦敦市伦敦健康科学中心 E. Tweedie 博士供图）。

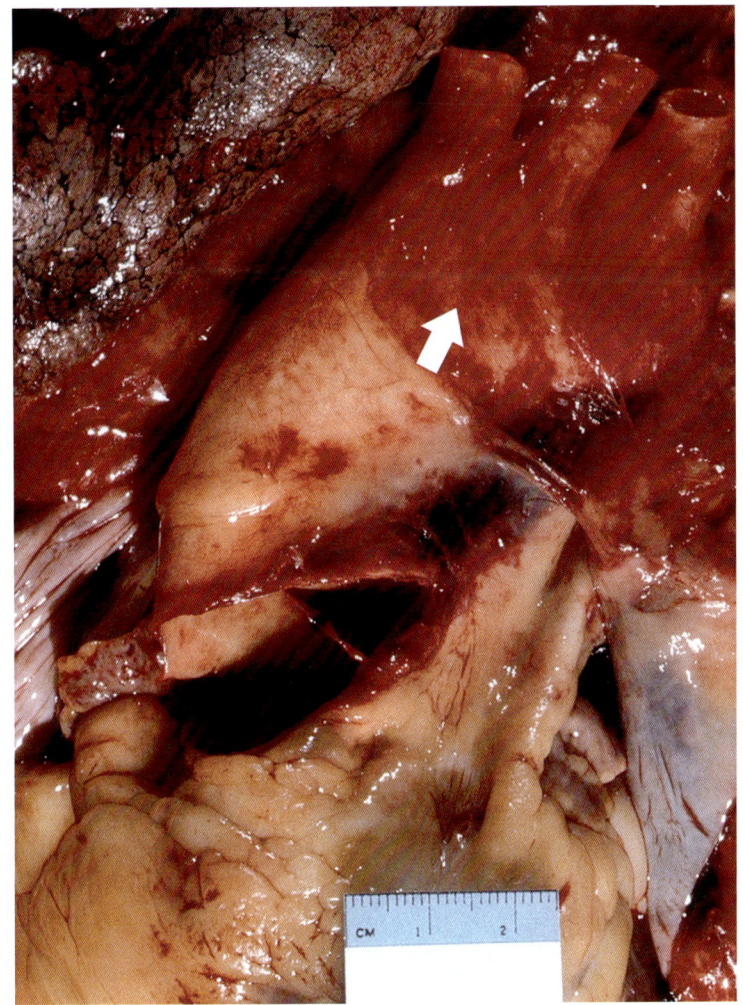

图 8-35 升主动脉撕裂。主动脉弓部主要的大血管（箭头）。

破裂的因素。腹主动脉发生破裂时不会马上发生腹膜后出血，而是首先出现假性动脉瘤，但现存的动脉瘤可能立即破裂(295)。

正面和近侧机动车碰撞会增加主动脉破裂的风险(274,296)。有研究表明，要导致主动脉峡部和降主动脉破裂，正面和侧面碰撞的最小等效碰撞速度分别为54公里/小时（34英里/小时）和31公里/小时（19英里/小时）(275)。另一项主动脉损伤的研究用 v（速度变化）表示平均事故严重程度，要导致主动脉损伤，δv 在正面碰撞时为57公里/小时或35英里/小时（范围：21-160公里/小时或13-100英里/小时），在侧面碰撞时为43公里/小时或27英里/小时（范围：21-68公里/小时或13-42英里/小时）(284)。还有研究表明，v 在正面碰撞中为48公里/小时（30英里/小时）、侧面碰撞时为36公里/小时（24英里/小时）就会导致主动脉破裂(283)。在许多事故案例中可观察到车内人员受到严重碰撞(275,296)。遭受近侧碰撞的车内人员比遭受正面及远侧碰撞者更易发生主动脉损伤(284)。安全带和安全气囊可降低、但不能完全消除主动脉损伤的风险(276,283,284)。

6.5.1 主动脉夹层

主动脉及其主要分支可动脉夹层(如肾动脉)(293,294,297–300)。夹层可发生在主动脉任何部位,最初的诱因可能是粥样硬化导致的动脉内膜破裂(301)。确定主动脉夹层在损伤之前发生还是由外伤引起,取决于案情与病理检查结果。如果事故前有胸背部疼痛及主动脉退行性病变的证据(如主动脉中层坏死),则倾向于判定其为自发性主动脉夹层。

6.5.2 主动脉弓血管

钝性损伤造成的主动脉弓血管破裂和夹层较为少见(148,302–306)。颈部过伸引起的拉伸和旋转压力可能在这类损伤中起作用(302,307)。锁骨下动脉被锁骨和第1肋骨保护得很好。如果锁骨和第1肋骨发生骨折且出现血胸,锁骨下动脉破裂的可能性就会增高(307–309)。

6.6 其他主要胸腔内血管

6.6.1 主要的肺血管

胸部钝性损伤很少导致肺动脉及其主要分支或肺静脉的单一性破裂(310–316)。

6.6.2 上、下腔静脉

上、下腔静脉很少因为钝性损伤而破裂(参阅标题14.2;参考文献317–321),也很少形成血栓(322)。

6.6.3 奇静脉

奇静脉沿胸椎右侧行走于胸膜下,在第4胸椎高度处形成奇静脉弓,转向注入上腔静脉(图8-36)(323)。

钝性损伤造成的奇静脉破裂很少见,但如果要对出现的血胸和纵隔积血进行鉴别诊断,则必须考虑奇静脉破裂的可能(323–327)。这些情况大多发生在机动车辆碰撞事故中(326),其特点是在存活的几个小时内,无论实施心肺复苏还是手术修补其他出血区,患者仍持续存在低血压(323,326)。奇静脉破裂可能由胸中段脊柱骨折直接导致,但大多数发生在上腔静脉和奇静脉交界附近或奇静脉弓处(图8-36)(323和326)。奇静脉损伤的机制可能为运动减速导致的剪切作用(323,326,328)。

如果观察到死者右侧胸腔积血,则有必要在清除胸腔积血后于原处仔细检查奇静脉。如果没有在取出心脏和肺之前检查奇静脉,则奇静脉的破裂位置将被后续的解剖所破坏。

6.7 呼吸道

机动车辆碰撞是造成气管、支气管和肺损伤最常见的原因(329–331)。

6.7.1 气管及主要支气管

呼吸道损伤较少见,在成年人钝性胸部损伤中仅占不到1%(332),单一性呼

第 8 章 | 钝器损伤——包括航空器、火车和机动车辆损伤　　455

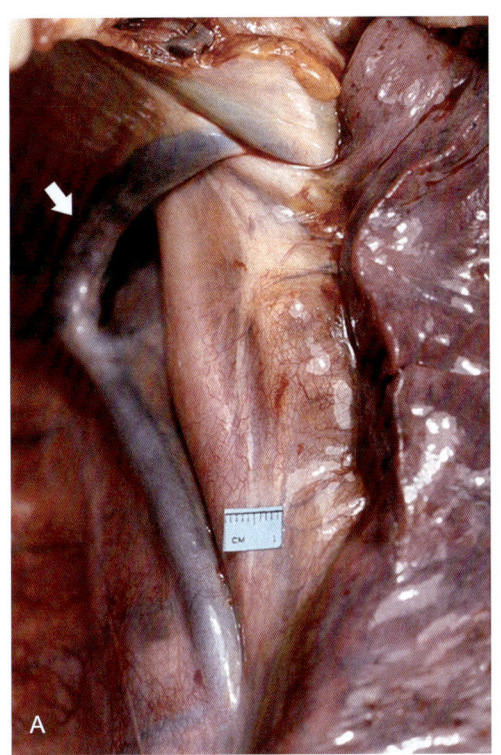
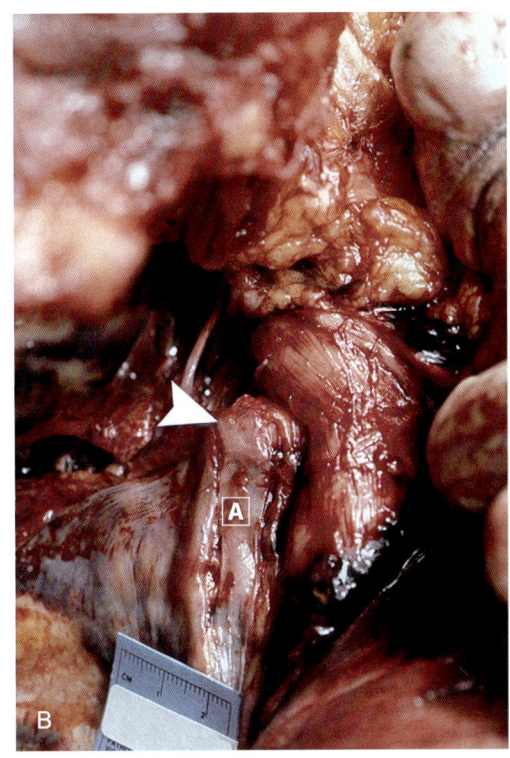

图 8-36　奇静脉。(A) 将右肺拉开,可以在此处发现明显的呈弓形的奇静脉(箭头)。(B) 同样在此处检查奇静脉弓与降部连接处的横断面(箭头)。奇静脉已被打开(A)。

道损伤则更少见(332)。呼吸道损伤的机制可能是外力作用于胸部纵隔入口处固定的气管或撞到脊柱的主支气管(332,333)。声门关闭可导致支气管内压力增加(332),气管隆凸以内 2 厘米与右主支气管是最常见的损伤部位(330,332)。

6.7.2　肺

肺挫伤是最常见的胸腔器官损伤,常伴肋骨骨折(参阅标题 6.1;参考文献 128,136,329,334),已有研究描述了多种损伤机制(329,334)。胸部撞击导致的正压震荡波会过度扩张肺并引起肺泡破裂,震荡波传递至气液界面时可导致肺泡壁破裂。突然减速引起的惯性压力可导致低密度区的肺泡从依附的支气管结构中撕裂。

大多数肺挫伤可在 2 周内自愈,且不留后遗症。如果挫伤累及肺实质的 20% 及以上,发生成人呼吸窘迫综合征 [82% vs 22%(如果累及肺实质 <20%)] 和肺部感染 [50% vs 28%] 的风险就会升高(参阅第 1 章标题 4.3;参考文献 128,329,335)。还有研究显示,当肺实质为 18%－28% 时,某些患者就需要辅助呼吸;超过 28% 时,所有患者都需要辅助呼吸(336)。

6.7.3　血胸和气胸

血胸和气胸通常由肋骨骨折断端刺破肺导致(尸体气胸检查技术参阅第 5 章标

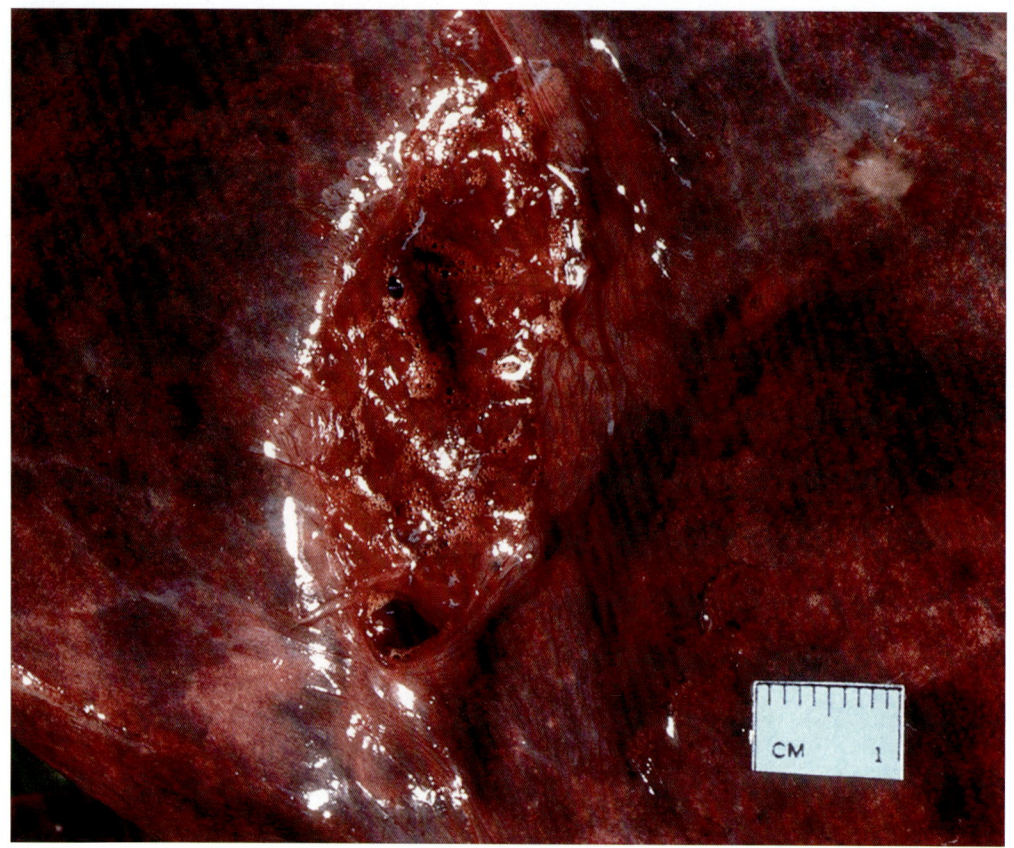

图 8-37 肺裂创。

题 14.8；图 8-37；参考文献 140,32 9,331 和 334），剪切力会造成远离骨折部位的肺部撕裂（331）。导致气胸的其他机制包括由胸壁撞击所致的肺泡内压增加及气管、支气管树和食管的破裂（140,331,334,337），随之可出现皮下气肿和纵隔积气（332,337）。肋骨骨折会导致胸膜表面的撕裂，而由其他原因导致的撕裂创伤通常发生在肺门处（334）。肺裂创出血可以自行停止或持续，也可复发（329）。

7 膈肌

钝性损伤致膈肌破裂的发生率约为 2%（203,338,339）。最常见的原因是机动车交通事故损伤，车内人员近侧面碰撞比正面碰撞更易造成膈肌破裂（339-344）。对 1995—1999 年美国国家汽车采样系统数据库的回顾表明：在发生正面或近侧面机动车碰撞时，如果车被撞入超过 30 厘米（12 英寸）或速度变化值（δv）超过 40 公里/小时（25 英里/小时），较易发生膈肌损伤（345）。损伤的机制包括：剪切力作用于紧张状态的膈肌、膈肌附着缘撕裂以及腹腔器官间力的突然传递（203,344）。

各种膈肌损伤都以左侧为主（203,339,343,346-348），因为右侧膈肌有肝

第 8 章 | 钝器损伤——包括航空器、火车和机动车辆损伤

脏保护(203,338)。膈肌双侧破裂较少见(203,339,346,347,349,350)。钝性损伤可能引起膈疝和腹腔器官(如胃、小肠、网膜、脾和肝)绞窄(图 8-38)(346 和 351)。腹腔压力和最大呼吸力的作用会导致腹腔和胸腔间压力差增大,使得腹腔器官进入胸腔形成膈疝(203,338),有研究显示膈疝可通过 10 厘米(4 英寸)或更大的膈肌破裂口形成(339)。膈肌破裂可导致通气减少,伴腹腔器官进入胸腔而压迫肺(203)。纵隔错位可影响心脏静脉血回流(203),但立即死亡并不常见(338)。

膈肌破裂很少单独出现,通常与其他严重损伤相关(203,338,339,341-343,347,348,350,352),有相当数量无并发症的膈肌破裂未被明确诊断(203,339)。一篇综述文献显示,有 44% 的病例术前诊断出膈肌破裂,41% 的病例在尸检或开胸

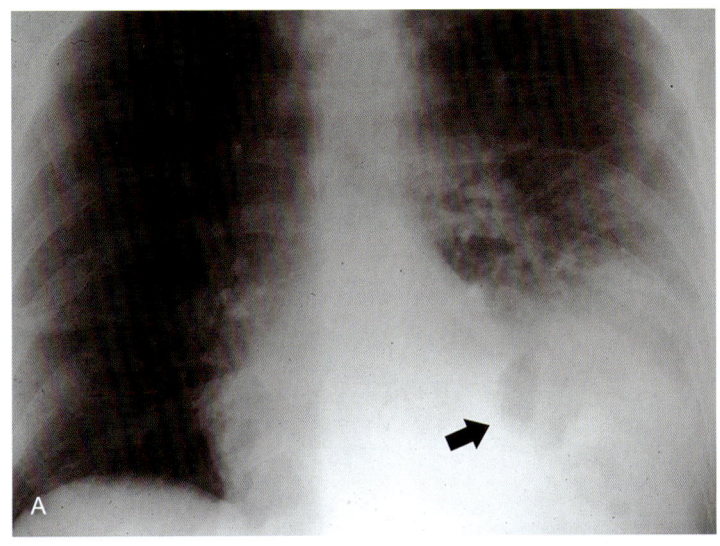

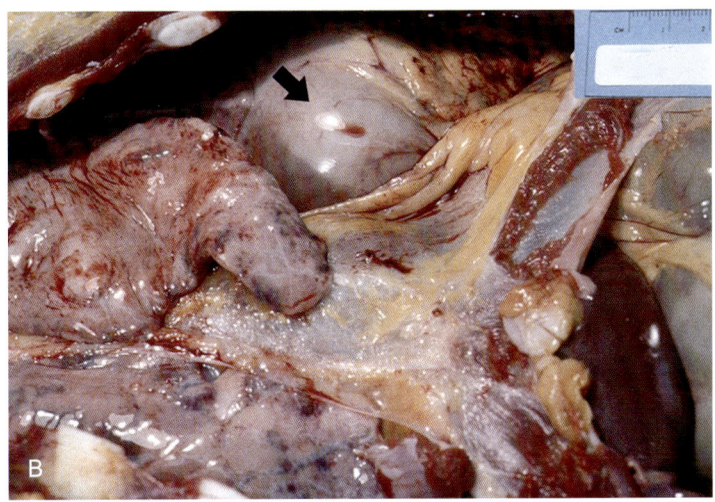

图 8-38 两起机动车辆碰撞案件致膈肌创伤性破裂。(A)胸部 X 线片显示肠段脱入胸腔形成膈疝,可见肠腔积气(箭头)。(B)胃壁通过左侧膈肌破裂口进入胸腔形成膈疝(箭头)。

手术时才被诊断出膈肌破裂,还有15%病例的膈肌破裂被延迟诊断。膈肌破裂如果不进行外科手术修补很难自愈(338,339,341),形成膈疝的腹腔器官发生绞窄,会发生迟发性并发症(338,347)。

8 腹部损伤

8.1 胃肠道

8.1.1 胃

腹部左侧遭钝性外力撞击很少引起胃部损伤(353)。一项研究表明,在1 300例腹部钝性损伤患者中仅有7例患者出现胃损伤[发生率为0.5%(353)]。机动车辆碰撞是引起胃损伤最常见的原因(参阅标题6.2,14.2;参考文献353)。胃损伤通常伴有相邻的实质脏器(如脾)和胸壁损伤(353,354)。如果胃内充盈过多食物和液体则更易破裂(353,354)。钝性外力致胃破裂可发生在胃壁任意部位,通常为单个部位,胃前壁最常见,之后依次是胃大弯、胃小弯、胃后壁(353)。胃破裂可继发气腹和化学性腹膜炎,取决于存活时间的长短(353)。如果在胃、食管交界处附近有破裂,则会出现皮下气肿和纵隔气肿(353)。

8.1.2 小肠和肠系膜

小肠和肠系膜损伤常由机动车碰撞事故引起,车内人员安全保护系统出现问题可能是造成这种损伤的原因之一(参阅标题14.2)。尸检中法医应在移除小肠前仔细检查肠系膜,以了解是否出现破裂及破裂程度(图8-39)。

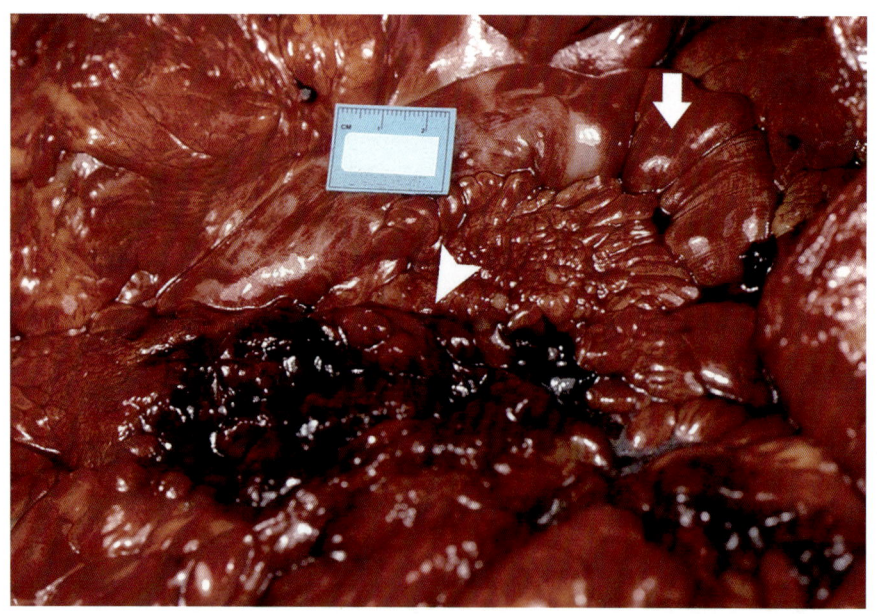

图8-39 机动车碰撞导致的肠系膜破裂。小肠(箭头)在腹腔内向上翻起,露出被撕裂的肠系膜(三角)。

8.2 肝

机动车碰撞是肝损伤的常见原因之一(355,356)。肝损伤通常合并其他损伤(355,357),但合并右侧肋骨骨折并不常见(355)。肝右叶后上区域是损伤常发部位(356)。方向盘等物品压迫肝区可造成典型的肝挫裂(图8-40)(356),其他肝损伤类型包括不同深度的肝条状撕裂、肝被膜下血肿,以及肝实质撕裂(图8-40)(356和358)。肝主要的血管损伤很少见。肝具备双重血供,因此不易发生梗死(356,359)。肝损伤几小时到数天后可发生迟发性出血(如不断发展的血肿)(358,360,361)。

8.3 脾

脾是腹部遭受钝性外力(尤其是机动车碰撞事故)最常见的受损器官(图8-41)(355,362-364)。脾损伤常伴有其他严重外伤(355,363-366),随后会引起急性或迟发性腹腔积血(363)。

McIndoe将迟发性脾破裂定义为腹部遭受钝性外力48小时后脾破裂,引起腹腔大出血(367,368)。还可能出现两种情况:急性脾破裂被延误诊断,脾损伤不断发展并最终破裂,即延迟性症状(363,368-373)。

过去,创伤性脾破裂误诊的发生率为2%-40%(363,368,370,374-377),因为当时缺乏精密的检查设备,仅根据患者的症状(如左上腹部疼痛)和体征(如腹壁僵硬)来判断,往往会与其他损伤、昏迷和中毒相混淆(362,367,368,378)。近年来,由于深腹腔灌洗技术及CT扫描成像技术的发展,脾破裂误诊的发生率已降至1%(368,370,374,376,377,379-381)。即使如此,由于休克或填塞效应可引起暂时性出血停止,急性脾破裂所致的腹腔积血也可能不明显。发生填塞效应的填塞物可以为血凝块、邻近的网膜脂肪和内脏以及通过破裂膈肌的腹内脏器疝(365,367,368,375,382-384)。

基于手术及影像检查结果可对脾损伤进行分级(378):程度较轻的损伤包括脾被膜下血肿、脾实质血肿和脾被膜破裂;严重的损伤包括累及脾实质或脾主要血

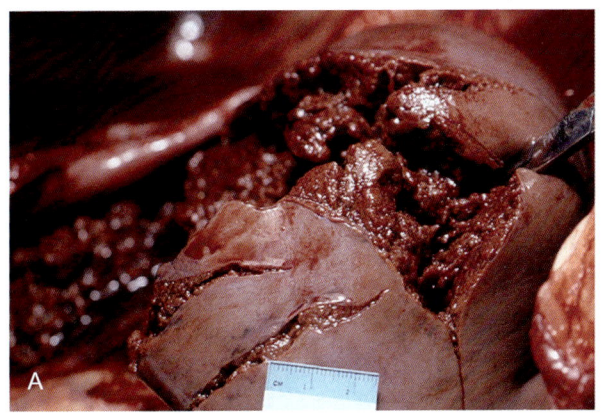
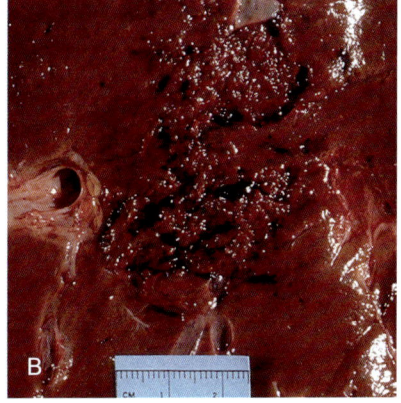

图8-40 机动车碰撞导致的肝破裂。(A)大面积的肝挫裂,胸腔完整。(B)肝实质撕裂。

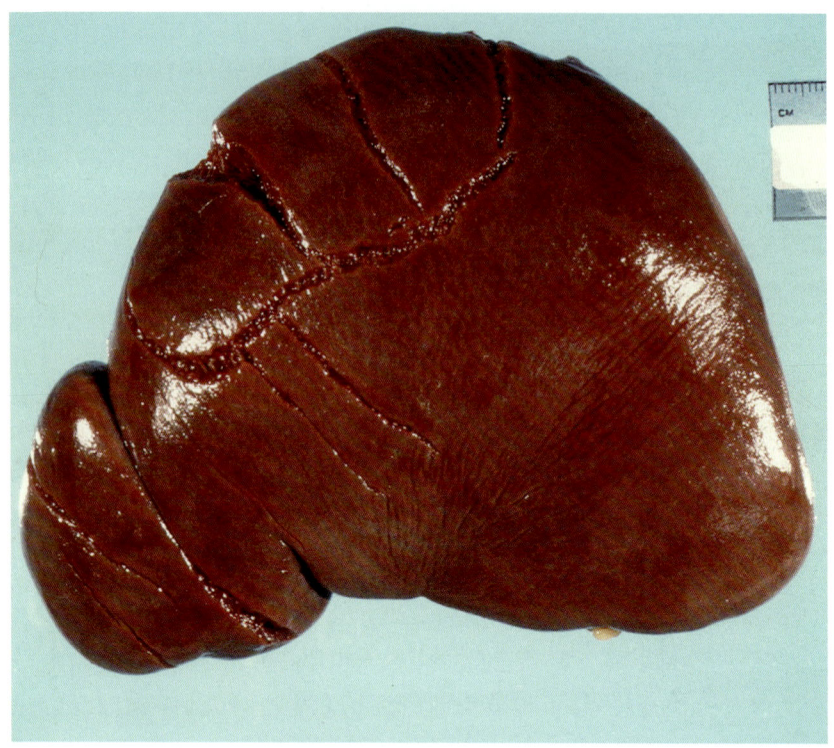

图 8-41 创伤性脾破裂。

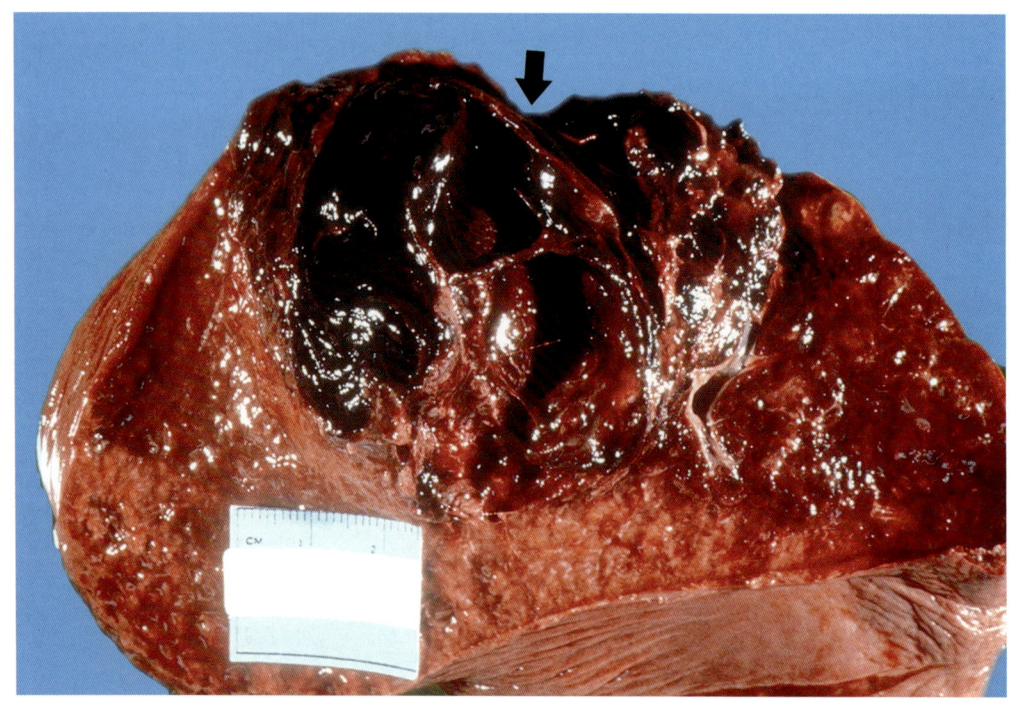

图 8-42 创伤性迟发性脾破裂的一种表现。可见大面积血肿、脾被膜破裂（箭头）。

管的广泛性破裂。对程度较轻、血流动力学稳定的脾损伤可进行保守性治疗(363,378)。

轻微损伤或腹腔内压轻度升高(如用力排便、咳嗽、呕吐、弯腰)都会使完整的脾被膜下自发性脾内血肿不断膨胀然后破裂,导致症状延迟出现(图8-42)(367,370,371,380,381)。脾被膜下-脾内血肿的患者可以无症状,且无法通过深腹腔灌洗技术被发现(362,368,372,379,382,383,385,386)。

脾内假性动脉瘤(即血管壁因血块或血栓而破裂,以及腹膜纤维粘连牵引引起的脾被膜剥离)是导致脾脏迟发性破裂的其他原因之一(图8-43)(374和387)。尽管创伤后脾破裂或自发性脾破裂者往往有脾的基础性疾病,但通常观察不到创伤之外的其他微观病变(368,369,388-390)。

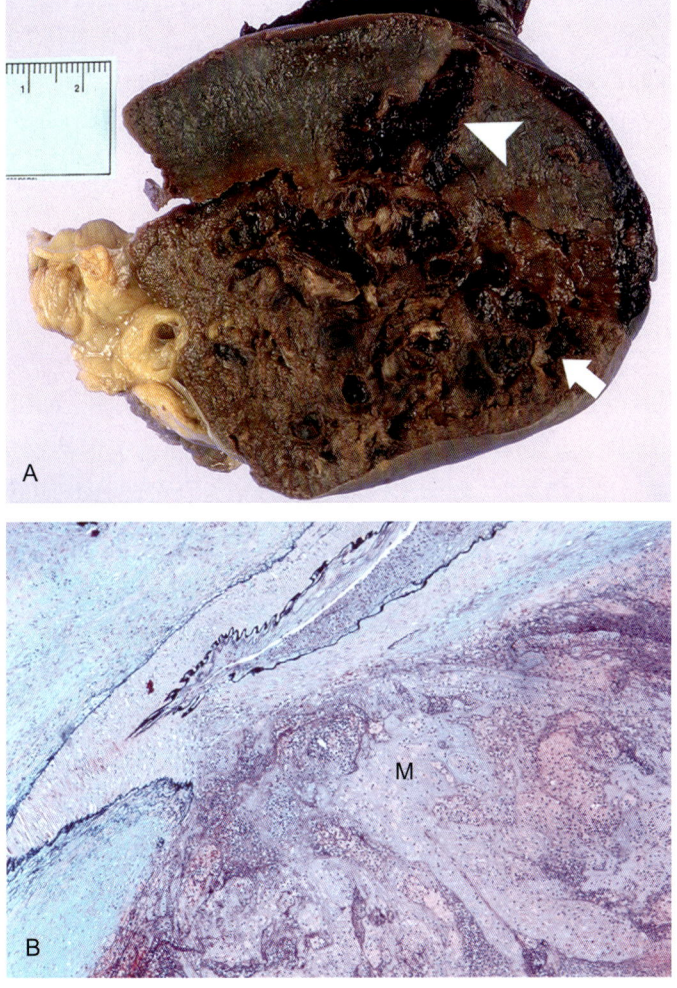

图 8-43 创伤后迟发性脾破裂的另一种表现。(A) 多发性"微动脉瘤"(箭头),导致被膜破裂的实质内出血踪迹(三角)。(B) 破裂的脾动脉分支伴有血液溢出。M:微小动脉瘤(Movat 染色,放大倍数 ×100)。

约 95% 的迟发性脾破裂在伤后一个月内发生,但也有案例报道脾损伤痊愈 5 年半后仍发生迟发性破裂(367,370,385,387,391,392)。脾损伤可在这段潜伏期愈合(367,370,371,378,393)。多次腹部 CT 检查显示脾损伤未愈合或损伤程度加重,提示可能会发生脾破裂(362,376,394)。

巨大外力会导致正常的脾发生破裂,通常情况突然、严重,且集中于腹部左上象限(367)。在机动车碰撞中,受到左侧车门碰撞最容易导致脾损伤(395)。在某些案件中,安全带负荷也会引起脾损伤(395)。机动车侧面碰撞程度与脾损伤程度并非总是成正比(396)。一项研究表明,无论车内人员是否系安全带,脾损伤大都发生在挤压程度超过 30 厘米(12 英寸)的车辆中。这项研究表明,系安全带的小型车辆驾驶员最易与碰撞的车辆接触。重型车辆的侧门提供的安全保障更大。如果车内人员不系安全带,也可能因为方向盘和仪表板触压而使脾受伤(395)。

尽管脾损伤通常伴左侧肋骨骨折,但有时也会伴右侧肋骨骨折(355,363,368,397)。肋骨骨折更易发生于老年群体(368)。如果脾损伤伴有最小程度的胸壁外伤或无胸壁外伤,预示粘性器官反应,即器官变形的敏感性(参阅标题 1)。这种反应在诸如脾被覆包膜并受到肋骨保护的软器官中发生改变,导致损伤不断发展,造成症状延迟出现。

8.4 腹腔间隔室综合征

腹腔的正常压力最多为大气压力,在呼吸过程中与胸腔内压力成反比(398)。腹部损伤合并、大量补液、腹腔积血、肠水肿、腹壁顺应性降低的闭合性手术、腹腔填充物的使用均会引起腹内压升高。体表的烧伤焦痂可导致外源性压迫(参阅第 4 章标题 5.2)。腹内压升高与腹围增加及肥胖并存。当腹内压升高与器官功能障碍(即心肺功能和肾功能下降)相关时,就会出现腹腔间隔室综合征。出现腹腔间隔室综合征的患者大多最终死于败血症或多器官功能衰竭。

9 腹膜后出血

骨盆骨折最容易造成创伤性腹膜后出血(399),且常伴有尿道、膀胱撕裂及盆腔主要血管破裂(399)。肾周出血需要在原位检查肾动脉及肾静脉,以排除血管破裂的可能(图 8-44)。肾皮质撕裂也可导致出血(图 8-44),也曾有报道单纯的腰大肌出血(400),损伤位置未知的腹膜后出血也曾发生(399)。

10 骨盆

骨盆骨折的生物力学分析中需要考虑以下几点(401-406):
- 骨盆是刚性环状结构。骨盆不稳定提示存在多发性骨折或脱位。
- 骨盆可受垂直剪切和挤压作用的影响。挤压作用可以是前后或横向的,力可直接或间接地作用于骨盆壁(如通过膝盖接触加载于股骨,导致髋关节脱位)。

第8章 | 钝器损伤——包括航空器、火车和机动车辆损伤

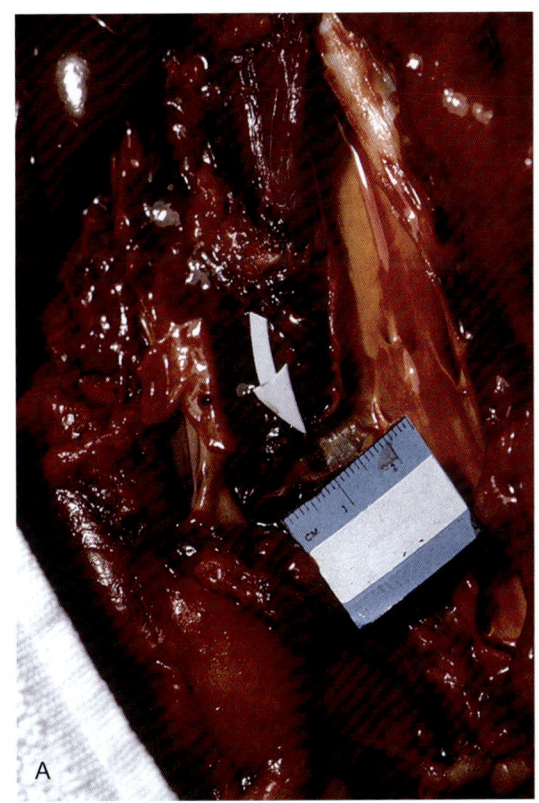 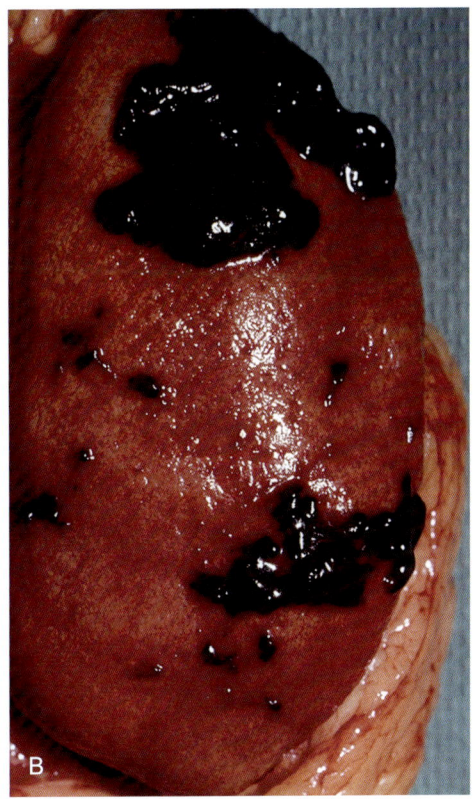

图 8-44 腹膜后出血。(A) 肾脏原位显示肾动脉破裂 (箭头)。(B) 血凝块覆盖下的肾皮质破裂。

- 骨盆的稳定性取决于骶髂关节复合体和主要韧带的完整性。基于骨盆后侧的稳定性进行骨盆骨折的分型。

三种类型的骨盆骨折如下:

A 型: 骨折不涉及或最小程度涉及环状结构移位。

B 型: 旋转不稳定但垂直稳定的骨折(如耻骨联合分离、耻骨支骨折)。 如果后骨盆稳定性部分保留,则骶骨压缩性骨折也可归类于此型。

C 型: 盆骨后壁不稳定(如髂骨的垂直骨折、骶髂关节脱位、垂直骶骨骨折)会引起旋转和垂直均不稳定。盆骨后壁损伤几乎总是与骨盆前壁损伤相关。

骨盆骨折最常发生于机动车的碰撞中(403,407),发生率在近侧碰撞中更高,因为会和碰撞的车门相接触(402,408)。约25%的交通事故死亡者有骨盆骨折(401,409),大多数是C型骨折(401,409)。骨盆骨折会引起腹膜后出血,从而导致死亡(403,407,410,411)。骨盆骨折伴发其他损伤也很常见(401,403,406,407,411-413)。

骨盆骨折发生时,体表可见腹部和大腿肿胀(404),也可看到或触及骨盆畸形。法医在检查盆腔时可触诊骨盆环,但要注意避免手套被刺破。如有必要,可行尸体影

像学检查可以提供更准确的诊断(401,402,404,409,414)。X 线向足部和头部倾斜 45°照射，而不是常规的前后照射，可以更好地观察盆腔入口和骶骨(404)。

11 四肢

根据下肢损伤情况可以判断行人受伤时的状态是站位还是卧位(参阅标题 14.6)。

11.1 止血带综合征

肢体持续受压(如机器压迫)也可导致死亡(图 8-45)(415)。失血和低氧代谢产物引起的休克及高钾血症都可能是造成死亡的因素。

12 栓塞

12.1 脂肪栓塞

脂肪栓塞(fat embolism, FE)指脂肪进入血液循环(416-418)。脂肪栓塞综合征(fat embolism syndrome, FES)表明脂肪栓塞与病理生理作用相关(416-419)。各种创伤和非创伤性疾病都与 FE 和 FES 相关(416,417,419-424)。

12.1.1 创伤

- 骨折[骨髓/骨中的脂肪，尤其是下肢长骨和骨盆(423)]。
- 仅有软组织损伤(425,426)。
- 脂肪肝损伤。

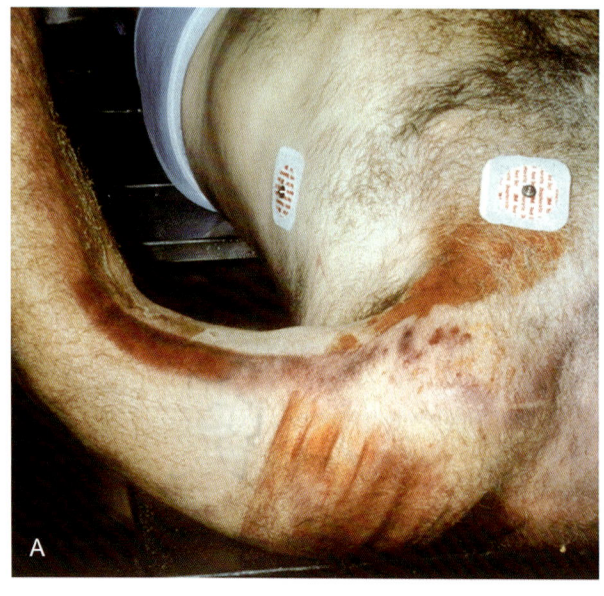
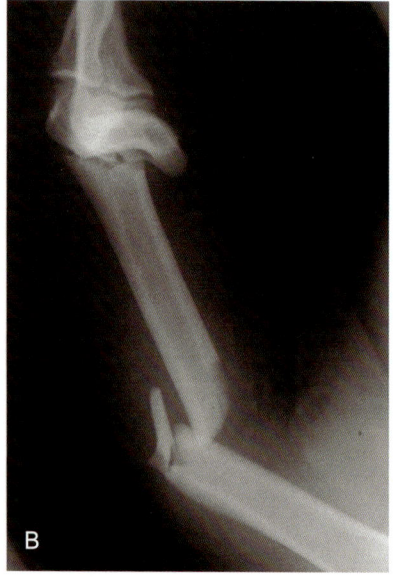

图 8-45 工伤事故：手臂卡在机器里。伤者当场死亡，其余部位未见损伤。(A)受压的手臂。(B)死后 X 线片显示肱骨骨折(加拿大安大略省伦敦市伦敦健康科学中心 M. Moussa 博士供图)。

- 严重烧伤（参阅第 4 章标题 4.5）。
- 爆炸伤（参阅第 4 章标题 8）。
- 高原反应。
- 减压病（参阅第 5 章标题 14.4）。

12.1.2 手术操作

- 骨科手术。虽然 FES 与某些手术方式有关（如髓内钉），但骨折的固定方式对伤者发展为呼吸功能障碍的影响甚小（418, 427, 428）。
- 抽脂术。
- 骨髓移植。
- 肾移植。

12.1.3 诊疗过程

- 心肺复苏术（表 8–1）。尽管对心肺复苏者进行了胸腔检查，也可能未发现明显的肋骨/胸骨骨折，但高达 80% 的心肺复苏失败患者有脂肪栓塞（424）。
- 骨内注射。一项动物研究显示，在复苏期间使用骨内注射发生脂肪栓塞的概率没有增加（429）。该研究还在未成功复苏的婴儿中观察到肺脂肪栓塞。
- 长期静脉高营养疗法。
- 影像学检查（如淋巴管造影）。
- 心肺旁路循环。
- 长期类固醇治疗。

12.1.4 疾病和中毒

- 不同的疾病［如急性胰腺炎、酒精性脂肪肝、肝衰竭、急性骨髓炎、镰状细胞病引起的骨坏死、癫痫、糖尿病、严重感染、高脂血症等（430）］。
- 四氯化碳中毒。

"机械"理论认为脂肪组织分解无论发生在骨外还是骨内（即骨折），都可以使脂肪进入破裂的静脉（416, 417, 421–424, 427, 431, 432）。如果存在骨折，骨髓会伴脂肪栓子一并进入血液循环（参阅标题 12.2）。髓内压增加可进一步促使骨髓/脂肪进入血液循环（416, 421, 432）。"贮存脂肪源性"的栓塞也会发生在炎症和退行性疾病中（如急性胰腺炎、脂肪肝）。脂肪微粒直径变化范围为 2–200 微米（420），大多数脂肪栓子可阻塞直径小于 75 微米的肺血管（420, 421）。广泛肺血管栓塞可引起急性右心衰竭，但血管内脂肪含量与临床病程严重程度之间无相关性（423）。较小的脂肪栓子（直径 7–10 微米）可发生形变，因此可通过肺毛细血管进入体循环［如脑、肾（420, 422, 427）］。体循环栓塞提示已发生大量肺脂肪栓塞，但没有肺部表现，也可发生体循环栓塞症状（416, 421, 422, 431）。脂肪栓子也可以通过心内分流（如未闭的卵圆孔）或从肺毛细血管前分流入肺静脉，再进入体循环（416, 420, 422）。肺内活化脂肪酶分解栓子中存在中性脂肪（417, 420–423,

431,433),产生的游离脂肪酸(FFA)对Ⅱ型肺泡上皮细胞有毒性作用,引起炎症发生(416,421-423,427,431-433),随即可引发成人呼吸窘迫综合征(ARDS)(参阅第1章标题4.3;参考文献423,427)。从损伤发生到症状出现的潜伏期长度与毒性游离脂肪酸的生成相关(424)。脂肪栓子可能会激发血管内凝血(434-436)。

"生化"理论则认为,由于应激引发代谢反应,脂滴可能来自血液循环("血源性")(424,431)。应急刺激后儿茶酚胺释放,动员了FFA(416,417,420,431),循环中血脂的乳化稳定性也随之改变(426,437)。在任何组织损伤的24-48小时内,C反应蛋白(一种急性期反应物)水平升高,引起乳糜微粒和极低密度脂蛋白凝集,形成直径2-35微米的团块(416,421,422,424,430,438)。

以上两种理论中,机械理论被接受的程度更高,因为脂肪栓子的游离脂肪酸特性比循环中的血浆脂质更像骨髓脂肪(417,420,422,432)。

脂肪栓塞在损伤案件中较为常见(发生率为50%-100%)(416-421,44),但FES不常见,有报道显示FES与骨折数目直接相关(单一型长骨骨折中的发生率仅为0.25%-3%,多发型长骨骨折合并骨盆骨折中的发生率则可达10%-30%),也与手术固定延误直接相关(416-418,420-423,427,428,438,439)。FES更容易由下肢和骨盆骨折诱发,而在上肢损伤病例中则不易发生(418,420,422)。一项综述研究显示,FES在闭合性骨折患者中更常见,提示开放性骨折中髓腔内压力较低,因此脂肪栓塞较少发生(418,439)。其他研究则观察到相反的情况(418)。儿童脂肪栓塞发生率很低,因为儿童骨髓腔中具有造血功能的结构相对于脂肪的比例高于成人,而且儿童骨髓脂肪中的三油酸甘油酯的含量较少,而这种脂肪酸对肺具有毒性作用(420-423,427)。不能仅根据栓塞的脂肪含量来预测FES的发生率。其他因素(如休克、败血症和弥散性血管内凝血)对FES的发生都有促进作用(参阅第1章标题4.3;参考文献421,438)。多达10%的外伤致死者都有FES发生(418,431),而非外伤性疾病患者极少发生FES。

盆腔骨折或长骨骨折后6-72小时内通常会出现FES(416-424,427,428,432,438)。约90%的FES病例发生在骨折后3天以内,但直到2周后才出现症状的情况也有过报道(420,421)。FES的临床表现如下:

- 急性呼吸窘迫最常见(417,418,421,431,432),会发生于75%的FES患者。有10%的患者最终由于急性呼吸窘迫综合征而需要通气支持(417,422,423)。
- 多达86%的患者会出现脑部症状(意识模糊、嗜睡、昏睡、谵妄及昏迷),有时脑部症状可能是FES的唯一表现(417,418,422,423)。
- 多达60%的患者在胸部和颈前处可见结膜、黏膜和皮肤的瘀斑(416-418,420-423,432)。分布在颈部和腋下的出血点由主动脉弓内脂肪滴聚集所致;

当患者直立时，这些脂肪滴便流向锁骨下动脉和颈动脉各分支（416，417，423，427）。另外，肺内脂肪可造成血小板聚集和裂解，继而导致血小板减少，诱发皮肤、黏膜点状出血（参阅第 3 章标题 1.4；参考文献 416，417，431）。

各种 FES 的临床表现不尽相同，患者可在受伤后突然而迅速地暴发症状，数小时内死亡（416，418，419，423）。死亡机制包括呼吸衰竭和急性右心衰竭（419），暴发性病程与多发性骨折有关（419，421），神经系统症状可能是主要的临床表现（418，419）。

FES 在临床上没有特异性的实验室或放射学检查结果（427，428），尸检时也不是总能观察到脂肪栓子（图 8-46）。显微镜下观察肺组织的 H-E 染色切片仅显示血管内清晰透亮区域，无法识别脂肪栓子（图 8-47）。但是死后肉眼可观察到肺和其他组织（如肾、脑）中的脂肪（图 8-47）。冷冻组织用 oil-red-O 染色可显示脂肪（417），用 35%－40% 甲醛溶液固定后的组织用四氧化锇再固定也可显示脂肪（426，440）。

判断脂肪栓塞是否参与构成死亡原因，需要通过案情分析，需要死者生前临床症状的支持和脂肪栓塞免疫组化检测结果的确认来做出最终判定。在猝死案件中，如果存在骨折和软组织损伤，并且排除了其他致命损伤，脂肪栓塞可作为是死亡原因。

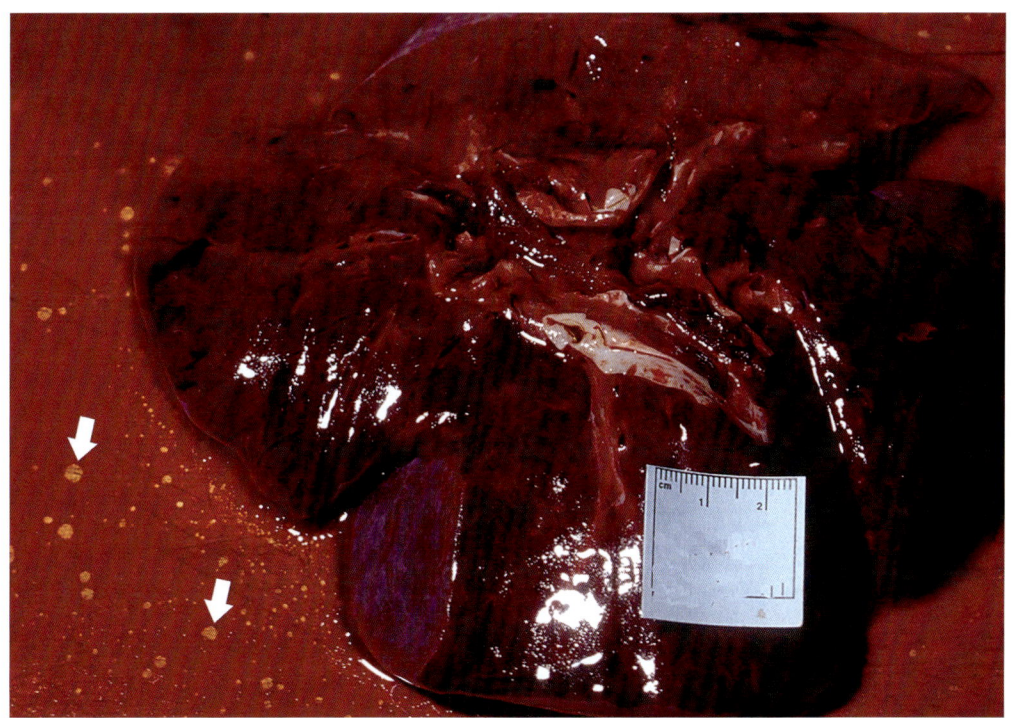

图 8-46 一例肺脂肪栓塞的创伤案例。尸检时将肺切除，解剖板上有大量脂肪滴（箭头）（加拿大安大略省伦敦市伦敦健康科学中心 C. Armstrong 博士供图）。

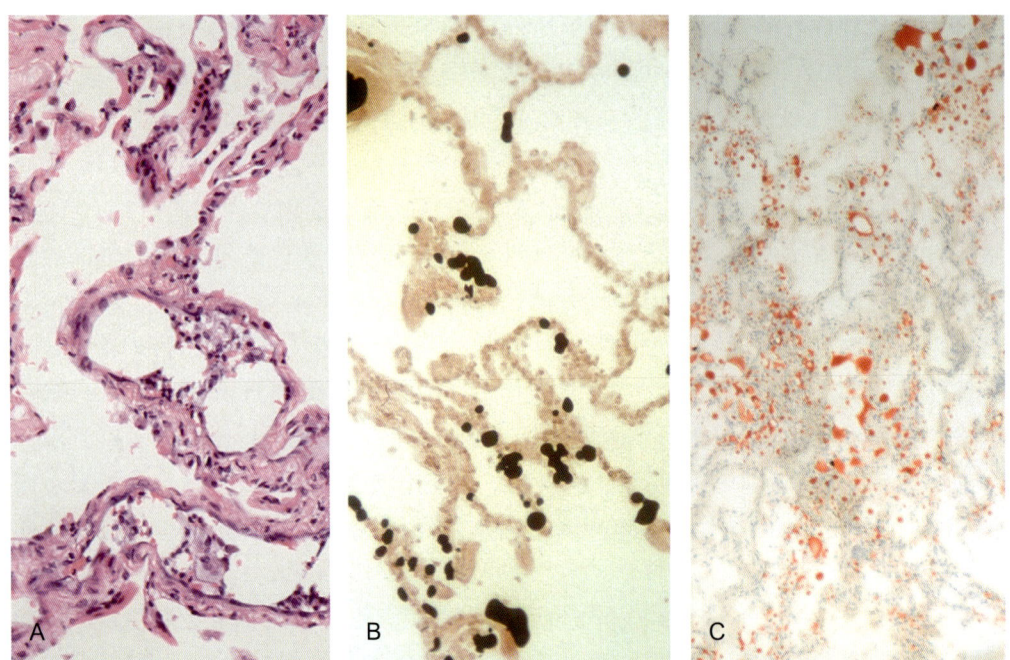

图 8-47 肺脂肪栓塞的显微镜检查。(A)血管内空泡(35%—40%甲醛溶液固定组织经 H-E 染色。放大倍数 ×200)。(B)多个脂肪栓子(35%—40%甲醛溶液固定组织再经四氧化锇固定,放大倍数 ×100)。(C)多个脂肪栓子(冷冻组织经 oil-red-O 染色,放大倍数 ×100)。

12.2 骨髓栓塞

肺部发生骨髓栓塞提示有骨损伤(441,442)。心肺复苏期间发生人为的肋骨骨折、造成骨髓栓塞的案例占 10%—50%(表 8-1;参考文献 157,167,172,173,176,441)。骨髓栓塞通常仅在肺部发生(图 8-48)(151,443),且并不总伴脂肪栓塞(167)。显微镜下观察到骨髓栓子并不总是与明显外伤相关(153,167,172)。无明显外伤的老年个体发生骨髓栓塞,是由骨质疏松性骨的微创伤引起的(443)。肺部骨髓栓塞通常不会造成不良临床结果,除非有大量血管发生闭塞(153,167)。

12.3 肺血栓栓塞

受伤患者容易出现深静脉血栓(deep venous thrombosis,DVT)及随后的肺栓塞(pulmonary thromboembolism,PTE)(444—446)。DVT 的发生、发展涉及血流缓慢、内皮损伤和高凝状态 3 种因素的相互作用。DVT 和 PTE 的风险因素包括损伤类型(下肢或骨盆骨折、头部或脊髓损伤、静脉创伤)、年龄超过 40 岁、有血栓形成倾向、使用呼吸机时间较长(大于 3 天)、昏迷、中央静脉导管留置,以及进行过大手术(444—451)。

大多数 DVT 病例都起始于小腿静脉,且血栓可自行溶解(452),也有 DVT 发

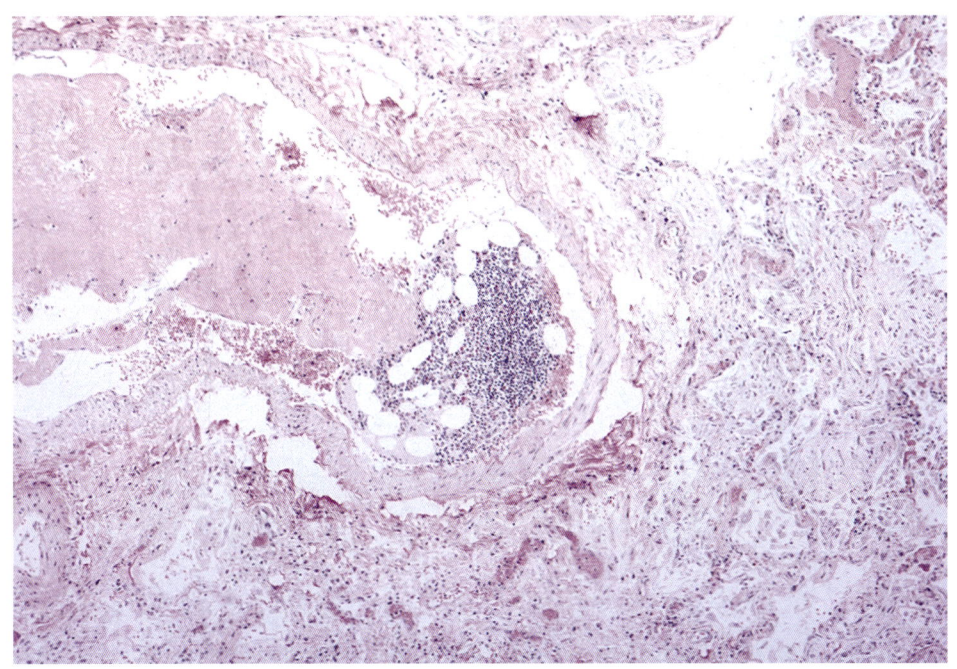

图 8-48　骨髓栓子(H-E 染色,放大倍数 × 100)。

生在受伤肢体对侧的正常肢体中(448)。借助静脉造影技术发现受伤病例下肢出现无症状 DVT 的发生率很高。一项对 716 例外伤案件的研究发现,约有半数头部、面部、胸部或腹部受伤的患者、2/3 盆腔和脊髓受伤的患者,以及超过 3/4 股骨和胫骨骨折的患者会出现 DVT(451)。DVT 向静脉近心端延伸容易发生栓塞(452),但 PTE 不一定必须先有 DVT 的临床证据(451)。半数近心端 DVT 患者没有 PTE 症状,但肺通气与血液灌注扫描的结果提示这些患者发生栓塞的可能性极高(452)。有研究显示,美国创伤中心入院患者静脉血栓栓塞(DVT、PTE)的临床发生率不到 1%(447)。其他研究显示 PTE 的发生率低于 1%(445,451)。美国国家儿科创伤登记处的系列记录显示,年龄小于 19 岁的受伤患者 PTE 的总体发生率为 0.000 069%〔脊髓损伤患者 PTE 的发生率为 1.85%(449)〕。

尸检研究从另一个侧面说明了 DVT 和 PTE 的发生率(448)。在致死性暴力伤害案件中,有 65% 的受害者在尸检过程中发现 DVT,20% 的受害者直接死于 PTE(453,454)。没有心肺疾病的年轻健康个体可以耐受 PTE(452)。约 10% 的 PTE 患者猝死(452)。肺动脉分叉处大血栓堵塞(鞍状栓子)或其主要分支大血栓堵塞通常可以迅速致死(图 8-49)(455),较小的血栓堵塞一半以上的肺动脉二级分支也可迅速致死(455)。

法医在尸解时必须在取出心脏前打开并指检肺动脉分叉。如果触诊怀疑 PTE,可以夹紧肺动脉防止栓子脱落,然后将心脏和肺一并取出,再进一步打开肺动脉分支。

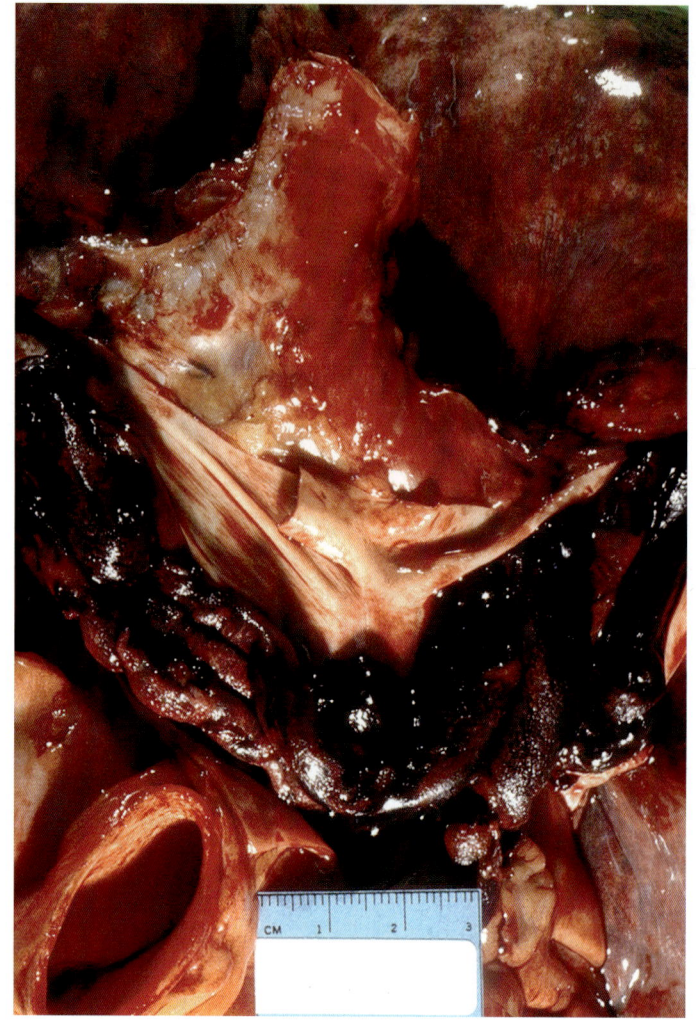

图 8-49 打开肺动脉分叉,显示"鞍状"血栓栓塞。

血栓栓塞需再在显微镜下观察并确认。比较大腿和小腿周长以评估 DVT 是否发生继发水肿。如果存在差异,则要打开双侧股静脉和腘静脉,即近端静脉。这种有限的解剖可能无效,因为血栓可能已经完全脱落、裂解或栓塞到其他位置。

12.4 与损伤相关的其他类型栓塞

12.4.1 脑

严重的颅脑损伤很少在肺部形成肉眼或显微镜下可见的脑组织栓子,但也曾有案例报道有出生时脑创伤和成人脑损伤患者肺部有脑组织栓塞(图 8-50)(456-462)。严重的颅脑损伤后,肺的脑组织栓塞发生率为2%-10%(458,459)。硬脑膜窦撕裂并非肺部脑组织栓塞的必要条件(460)。脑组织也可以进入大脑静脉和脑膜静脉。

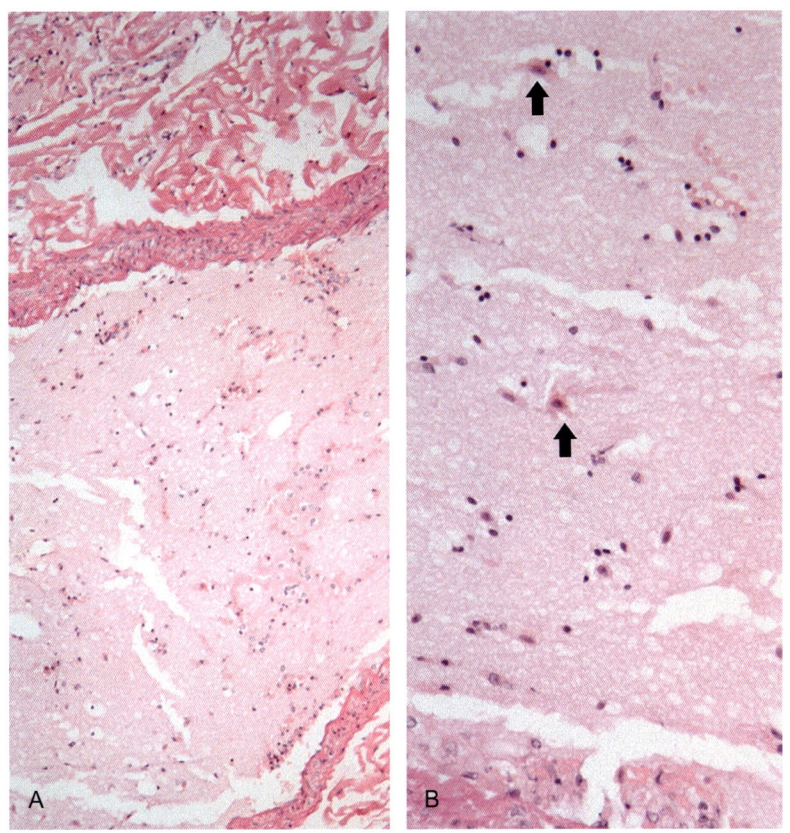

图 8-50 颅脑损伤。(A) 肺中的脑组织栓子 (H-E 染色,放大倍数 ×200)。(B) 脑组织栓子。退化的神经元 (箭头, H-E 染色,放大倍数 ×400)。

12.4.2 肝

下腔静脉损伤与肝严重损伤相关 (463-465)。下腔静脉破裂后, 肝组织进入血液循环, 在肺部形成明显的严重栓塞 (463-465)。有时在肺血管中检见肝的细微组织, 提示肝组织栓子可能由于外力作用被挤入心脏和肺血管 (463)。肺血管内微小的肝组织栓子反映出强烈的生活反应, 即受伤时血液循环非常活跃 (图 8-51)(参考文献 466)。

12.4.3 羊水

在钝性损伤致死的孕妇中可观察到羊水栓塞 (图 8-52)。羊水栓塞可发展为循环衰竭、呼吸衰竭和凝血功能障碍 (417, 467-469)。可在肺血管中检见胎儿角化上皮细胞, 有时也可以在体循环血管中发现 (468), 且在妊娠晚期更容易发现。进行肺多部位检查有助于检出胎儿角化上皮细胞。

12.4.4 软骨

有案例报道描述了由外伤引起的肺部软骨栓塞, 包括胸外心肺复苏术和矫形外科手术 (470, 471)。

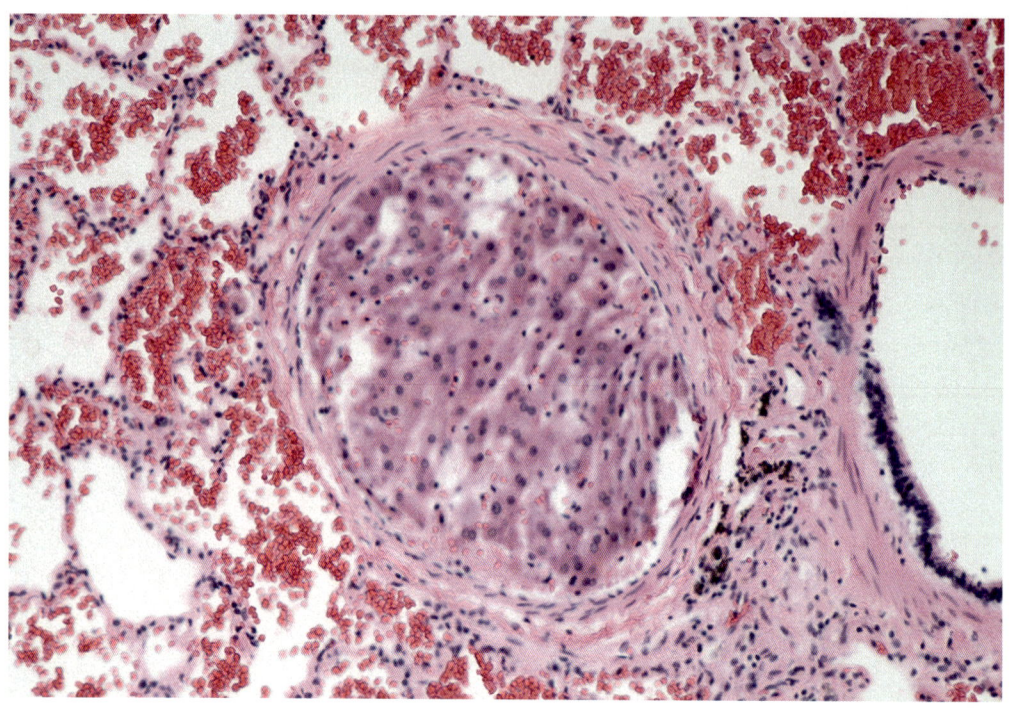

图 8-51 肝损伤。肺的肝组织栓塞（H-E 染色，放大倍数 ×200）。

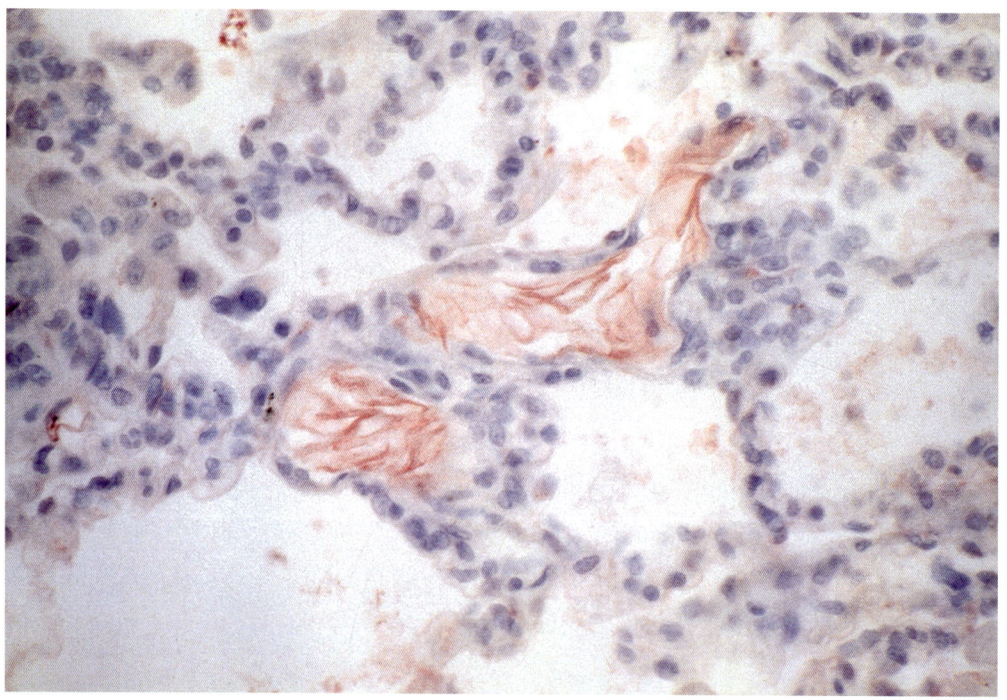

图 8-52 孕妇驾车发生交通事故，因多发伤死于现场。肺羊水栓塞：肺泡毛细血管中的胎儿角化上皮细胞（免疫过氧化物酶技术显示角蛋白阳性）（放大倍数 ×200）。

12.4.5 空气

外伤可导致空气栓塞(参阅第 7 章标题 12.1)(417,420,472)。当静脉向大气开放时,由于存在负压梯度,空气就会进入静脉。大量空气可阻塞右心室和肺流出道,少量空气可导致肺动脉阻塞。如果空气通过心脏(如卵圆孔未闭)和肺内分流,则可引发体循环空气栓塞。

12.4.6 巨核细胞栓塞

肺毛细血管中会发现显著的巨核细胞的细胞核,这是血小板正常产物的一部分,尽管有研究认为其可作为死者生前发生骨骼肌损伤的指标(图 8-53)(442 和 473)。

13 横纹肌溶解

横纹肌溶解是肌肉坏死的结果,可发生于各种情况,如吸毒(可卡因)和外伤[钝性外伤、烧伤、触电、低体温及淹溺(474-480)]。身体特定部位长期受压可出现横纹肌溶解,尤其在昏迷个体[如药物过量及酒精中毒(478,481,482)]中应考虑这种可能性。肾功能衰竭的临床表现与急性肾小管坏死和肌红蛋白变性有关(图 8-54)。横纹肌溶解并非一定导致肌红蛋白尿(478)。

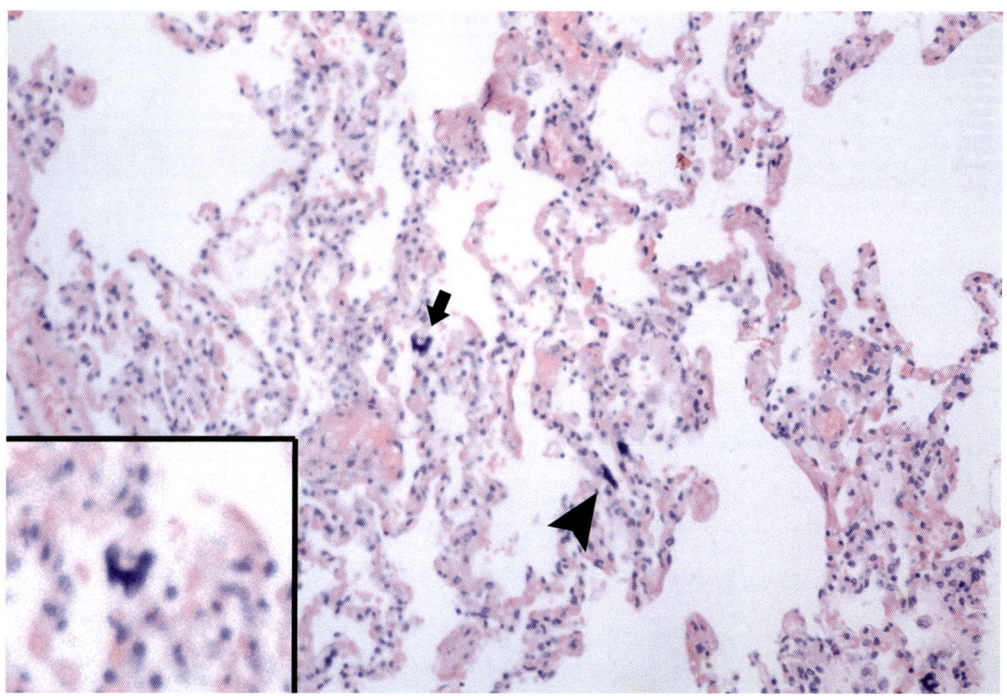

图 8-53 肺泡毛细血管中的巨核细胞(箭头和三角箭头)(H-E 染色,放大倍数 ×50)。左下角插入的图片显示放大的巨核细胞。

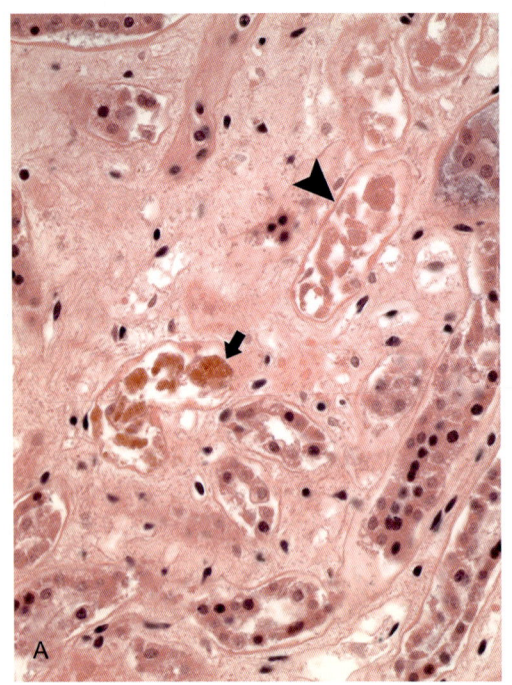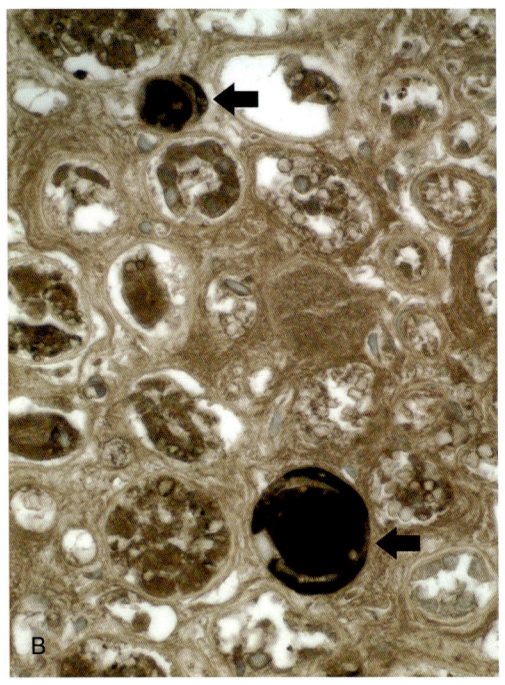

图 8-54 横纹肌溶解症者的肾。(A)肌红蛋白(箭头),肾小管坏死(三角;H-E 染色;放大倍数 ×200)。(B)免疫过氧化物酶技术显示肌红蛋白反应阳性(箭头,放大倍数 ×400)(加拿大安大略省伦敦市伦敦健康科学中心 M. Moussa 博士供图)。

14 机动车辆碰撞

常见的机动车辆碰撞有正面撞击、侧面碰撞与擦撞、追尾和翻滚。机动车损伤是钝性损伤的主要原因,致伤方式和形态主要与碰撞类型有关(483,484)。要理解车辆损伤的机制,需要将损伤与车辆、车内人员的动态变化联系起来综合分析(483),有助于鉴别驾驶员和乘客的损伤。

14.1 正面碰撞

正面撞击事故中,外力主要沿机动车中轴线撞击车辆。碰撞发生时,如果车内人员未系安全带,就会极速向前与车内部件发生碰撞。尸检时可以清理血液和其他组织,然后标记受害者在车内撞击的部位。车内部件受到撞击可以发生变形。车内人员的头面部可撞击前挡风玻璃、A 柱或前部联箱(Ⅰ类损伤或高位损伤,参阅图 8-20 和图 8-55)(487-489)。能量由颅骨传导至脊柱,可造成颈椎骨折。乘车人员或司机的躯干可能撞击仪表盘和方向盘(Ⅱ类损伤或中位损伤;参阅图 8-19)(489 和 490),导致方向盘严重变形(图 8-56)(491)。车内人员的头面部和颈部也可能撞击仪表盘和方向盘(492)。如果转向柱两侧的仪表盘下方受损,说明司机膝盖撞击到仪表板。如果车内人员未系安全带,则膝盖受撞击可导致股骨和骨盆骨折[Ⅲ类损伤或低位损伤(489)]。无论是否系安全带,车内人员脚趾尖在车底板受到撞击都

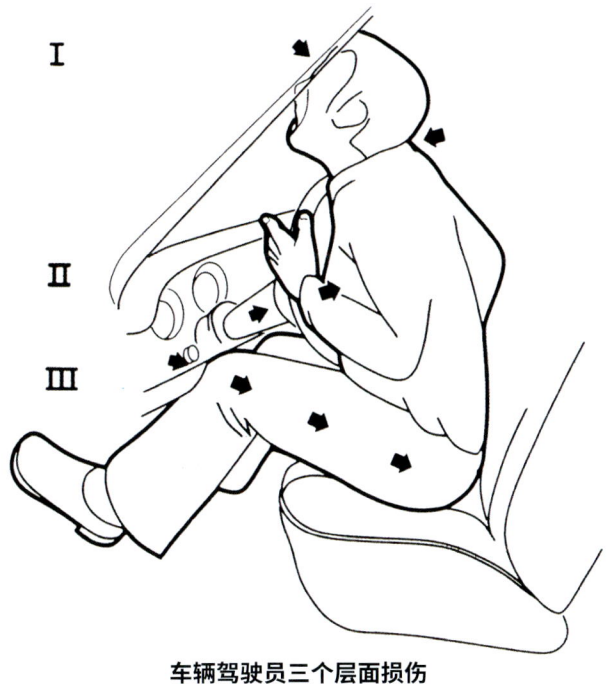

车辆驾驶员三个层面损伤

图 8-55 正面碰撞中,未系安全带的驾驶员遭受来自不同平面的碰撞损伤。法医需意识到即使乘车人员系了安全带,也会由于外物侵入车舱而受伤(经 Lippincott Williams 和 Wilkins 许可,引自参考文献 489)。

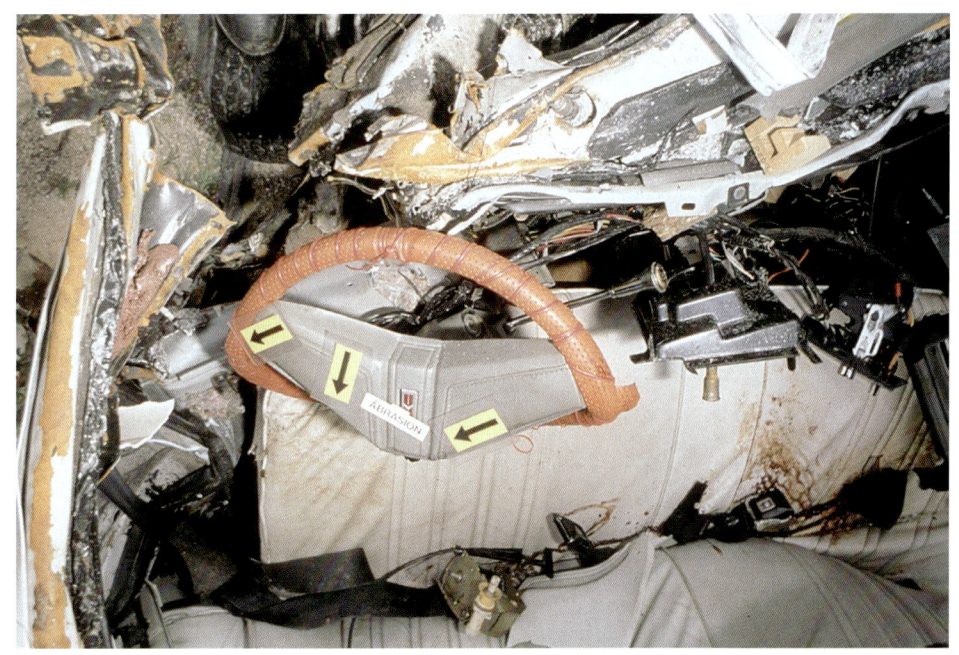

图 8-56 正面碰撞;方向盘侵入并变形(加拿大运输署道路安全及车辆管理局供图)。

会导致足和踝关节损伤(图 8-57)(408,487 和 493-496)。车舱侵入和变形会增加车内人员遭受触碰的可能性(491,495,497),且触碰也可以来自外部(如侵入的车辆和固定的物体)。

14.2 车内人员限制系统

14.2.1 安全带

在几乎所有类型的碰撞中,正确佩戴安全带能给车内人员带来各种保护:有效防止车内人员被抛甩,减少车内碰撞,使车内人员在车辆变形、碰撞时能量消散而"克服"碰撞的危害(484,487,498-502)。车内人员应尽早系好安全带,以便发生碰撞时充分利用车辆挤碰持续的时间。车辆正面碰撞时,安全带紧急自动束紧装置启动,驾驶员突然向前移动时安全带锁死。安全带的腰部和肩部组建能分别有效地限制骨盆和躯干前移。在安全带系统中,大部分拉伸都在肩带部分,因此车内人员上身在腰带上发生枢转。在剧烈的正面碰撞中,即使车内人员正确系好了安全带,也可能造成面部和头部受伤。如果安全带相对松弛,会增加车内人员对它的负荷。松弛的安全带使得碰撞中车内人员前倾的幅度加大,增加了车内碰撞的风险(503),新型车辆中的信号预警器可消除安全带松弛现象。负载限制器和安全气囊联合使用会提供强大的阻力,也允许身体前倾触及安全气囊。在极少数负荷过重的情况下,安全带会发生断裂,使得车内人员被抛出(500)。

如果有外界物体撞入车舱,所有约束系统的保护作用都会因为高强度碰撞而明显下降(497-500,504-507)。

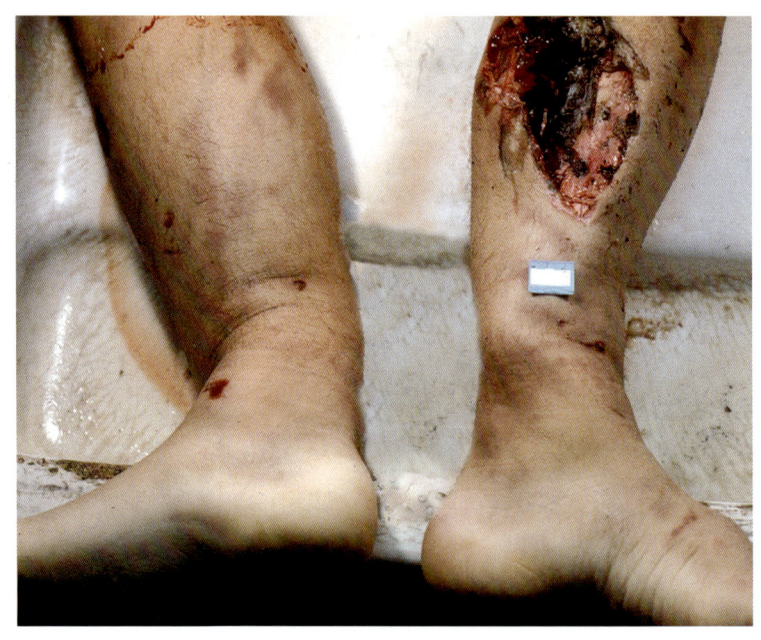

图 8-57　脚趾平面受侵。踝关节骨折脱位畸形,左腿胫侧撕裂创。

第 8 章 | 钝器损伤——包括航空器、火车和机动车辆损伤

安全带相关损伤见表 8-2。

表 8-2 安全带相关损伤

腰部安全带相关伤

腹壁软组织破裂 (499, 501, 508-510)
- 躯干离断 (511)

膈肌破裂 [腹腔脏器继发疝 (512)]

胃破裂 (353)

大小肠创伤 [挫伤、浆膜撕裂、穿孔、横断、继发性梗死 (499, 502, 505, 510, 513-521)]
- 附属脏器破裂 (522)

大网膜破裂 (499)

肠系膜损伤 [挫伤、撕裂、内疝 (499, 501, 502, 508, 510, 515)]

胰损伤 [离断、炎症 (523)]

腹主动脉损伤 [挫伤、内膜破裂、夹层、血栓、继发性栓塞、急性或迟发性动脉瘤破裂 (293, 294, 301, 524-530)]
- 髂动脉损伤 [内膜破裂 (499, 941)]

下腔静脉破裂 (319, 532)
- 肾静脉破裂

肾破裂 (532)

腰椎骨折 (499, 505, 510, 513, 519, 520, 533)

骨盆骨折 (499, 500)

妊娠相关损伤
- 子宫破裂 (499, 534-540)
- 胎儿继发性死亡
  - 胎盘早剥
  - 创伤 (颅脑损伤、其他脏器损伤)

肩部安全带相关伤

寰椎脱位 (545)

颈椎骨折 [包括 hangman 骨折,又称创伤性枢椎滑脱、第 2 颈椎 (枢椎) 椎弓根骨折]

颈部离断 (499, 548, 549)

窒息 (499, 550)

喉损伤 [骨折、横断 (499, 546, 548)]

气管横断 (548, 551-553)

颈段食管穿孔 (554)

胸壁骨折 [肋骨、胸骨、锁骨、胸肋关节脱位 (499, 502, 555)]

胸椎骨折 (546, 547, 556, 557)

胸主动脉损伤 [裂伤、横断 (275, 502, 556)]

大动脉损伤
- 颈动脉 [横断、破裂 (530, 546, 551, 558, 559)]

续表

- 椎动脉损伤(560)
- 锁骨下动脉[内膜撕裂(555,560)]
- 无名动脉破裂(561)

心脏[挫伤、撕裂(502,562,563)]
肺[挫伤、撕裂(502)]
胸膜、心包膜破裂(502)
肝破裂(502,555)
- 肝静脉撕裂

脾破裂(395,499,502)
肾包括肾动脉和肾静脉破裂(499)

安全带所致的内脏严重损伤很少见,一般是由于安全带使用不当所致(502,503)。严重损伤反映出碰撞强度高(时速>40公里/小时或30英里/小时)、碰撞性质严重[如车辆翻转会增加身体局部受到抛甩和"悬挂"于安全带上的可能性(499,

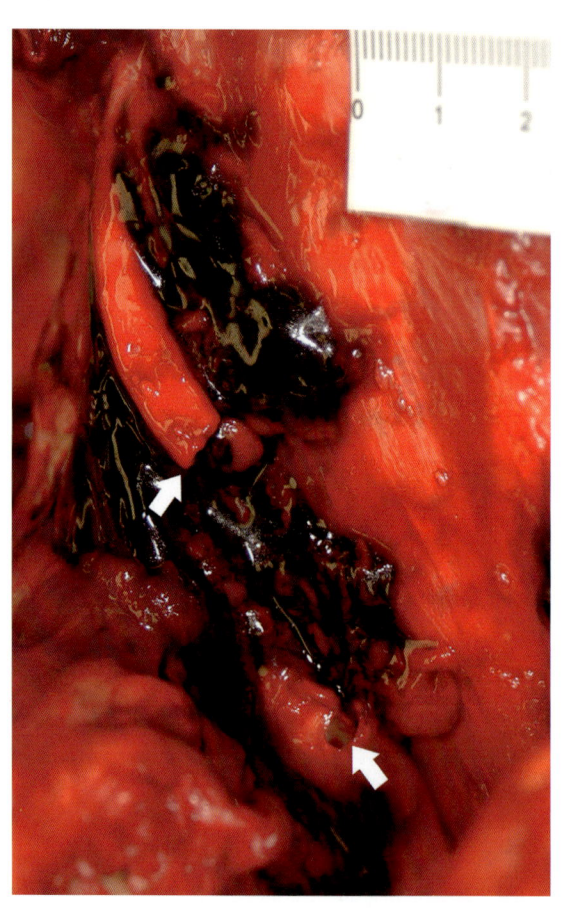

图8-58 身材矮小的驾驶员系一斜跨式安全带,可见左侧颈部擦伤,左侧颈总动脉断端(箭头)。

500, 550)。腰跨式安全带必需通过盆部, 斜挎式安全带则必需斜行穿过胸部(500, 501, 515)。如果腰跨式安全带系得过高会引起损伤, 因为这样产生的负荷不会作用于较为强壮的骨盆, 而会传导至腹部器官和腰椎。某些身体因素(肥胖、怀孕)会导致腰跨式安全带束于腹部(502, 564, 565)。肩带可能会致身材矮小人员颈部损伤(图8-58)(515)。安全带相关损伤可见于所有年龄段, 两点式(腰部)和三点式(腰-肩部)安全带均可发生(510)。成人安全带无法为儿童提供足够的保护(530, 566)。

皮肤损伤可反映安全带的使用和负荷情况(图8-21和图8-59), 安全带上的痕迹也可反映负荷情况(567)。安全带放置不当可造成皮肤损伤, 形成"安全带特征性损伤", 提高引起内部器官受损的可能性(500, 501, 515, 518, 519, 521, 547, 558, 568)。各种皮肤损伤不尽相同, 并非总与内脏损伤绝对关联(500, 501)。相反, 即使未检见外部损伤(如伤者身着厚重衣服), 也不能排除内脏损伤(图8-60)(499, 501, 514, 515和568)。两点式安全带比三点式安全带更易造成腹部器官严重损伤(569)。

已提出的安全带引起腹部损伤的机制如下:

1. 固定结构撕裂(如十二指肠-空肠结合处、空肠Treitz韧带、回肠末端、横结肠乙状结肠连接处、纤维粘连区)。

2. 内部器官压迫脊柱。

3. 局部压力引起闭合性肠穿孔。

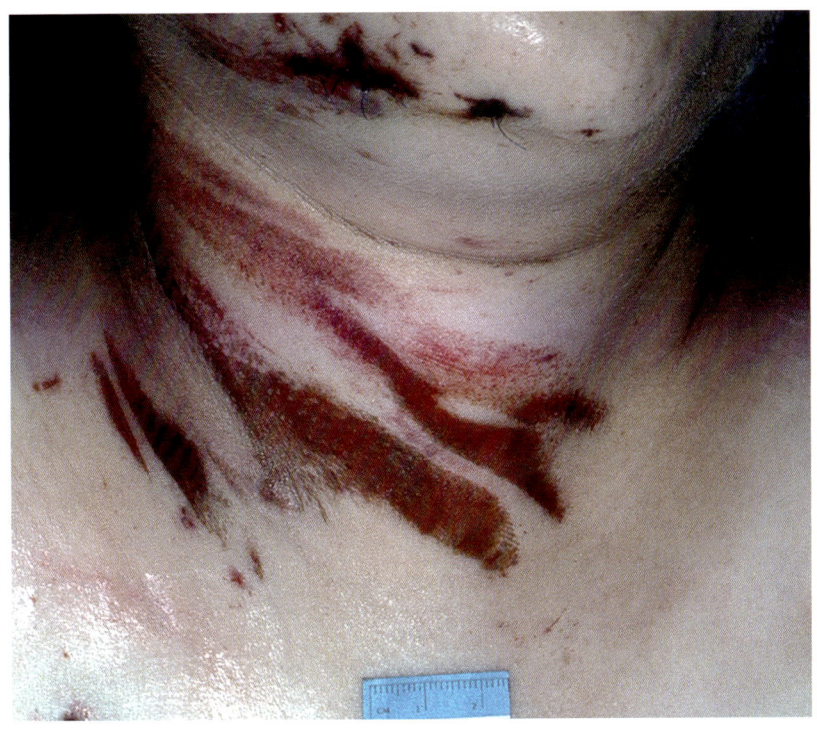

图8-59　前排乘员。安全带肩带引起颈部右侧皮肤擦伤。

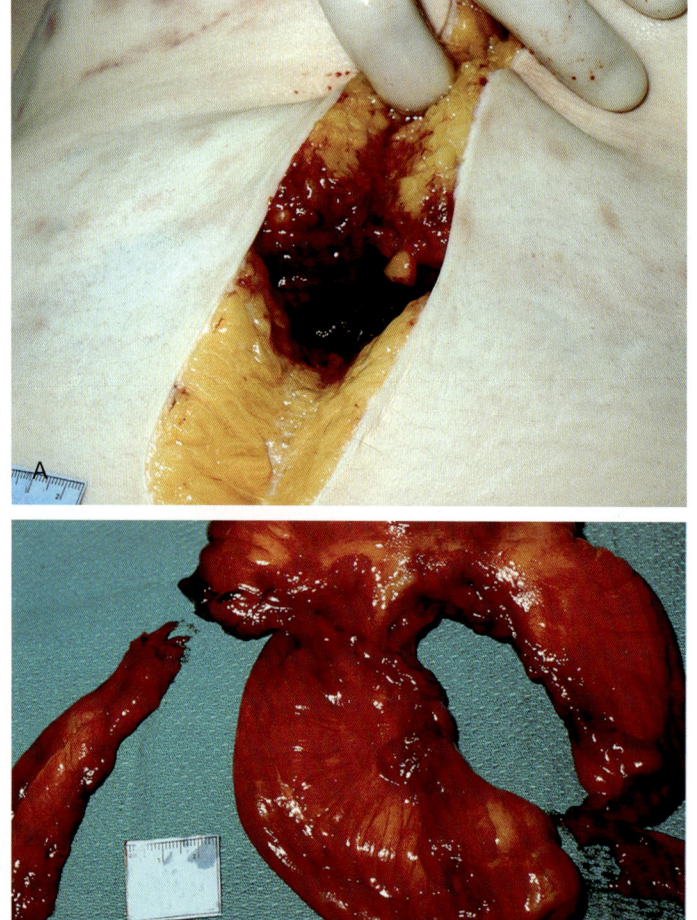

图 8-60　腰式安全带损伤。（A）腹部切口处可见下腹壁血肿，周围散在皮肤挫伤。（B）小肠肠管横断。

4. 腹腔内压力增加，对空腔和固体器官造成冲击波效应（505，515，516，518，521，570）。

腰带更易造成空腔脏器损伤（509，513）。安全带引起的腰椎骨折（Chance 骨折：脊椎的屈曲性损伤，1948 年由 G.Q.Chance 首先提出，包括椎体前部分的压缩性骨折和椎体后部的横向骨折）是由于腰带在脐部不正确固定所致，这种不正确固定方式引起了脊柱过度屈曲（505）。骨折涉及椎体和其后部，常发生在第 2、3、4 腰椎（500，510，533）。不使用安全腰带的车内人员也会发生压缩性骨折（533）。车辆旋转所产生的向心力、多次碰撞和车辆坠落均会导致腰椎骨折（500，533）。

汽车碰撞中孕妇死亡会导致胎儿死亡（571）。在较轻的碰撞中，对孕妇最好的保护是使用安全带，这能有效降低车内碰撞（538，542，571，572）。在某些轻微的碰撞事故中,孕妇受轻微伤也可造成胎儿死亡(539,572–576)。安全带对腹部的作用会增加受孕子宫的压力(539),由于子宫膨胀会引起弹性较低的胎盘剥离,导致胎盘早剥(571)。值得注意的是,不使用安全带的孕妇也会发生类似安全带造成的损伤,如子宫破裂、胎盘早剥、胎儿损伤(571,572)。孕妇也会有骨盆和股骨粗隆骨折(577)。

与安全气囊引起的前肋骨折相比,安全肩带所致的前肋骨折呈不对称分布(133,504,578)。

14.2.2 安全气囊相关损伤

前置安全气囊与安全带协同发挥作用,在车辆中度及重度正面碰撞中为前排人员提供保护。安全气囊展开,缓冲了前排人员头胸部与方向盘、仪表板的碰撞。车辆在纵向轴方向突然减速,会激活安全气囊,大多数气囊展开都发生在正面碰撞中(579)。正面碰撞会触发"第一代"安全气囊展开,其临界速度为11—25公里/小时[7—16英里/小时(579)],车身侧面和底盘遭受撞击也可触发安全气囊打开(图8-61)(579)。

安全气囊造成的损伤大都很轻微[如面部皮肤损伤(580,581)],有研究曾报道眼部损伤和面部骨折(580)。如果驾驶员在转动方向盘时手臂位于气囊装置上方,可发生上肢骨折(580),如果车内人员"潜于"安全气囊之下,则下肢会缺乏保护(582–585)。

由于安全气囊是电子点火装置,所以可以通过独特的机制造成孤立性伤(580,581,586)。如果车内人员"位置不当",即驾驶员胸部与方向盘距离小于25厘米

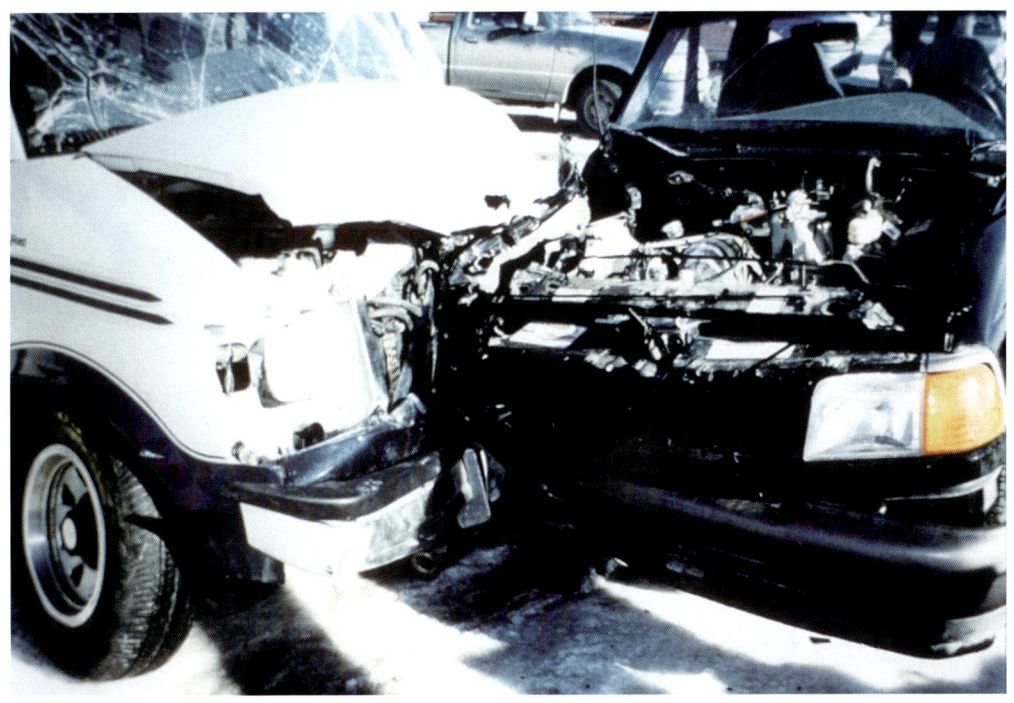

图8-61 驾驶员在车辆远侧面(副驾驶一侧)碰撞事故中死亡,碰撞触发安全气囊打开。被撞车辆中的前排乘客存活(图8-63和图8-64)(加拿大运输署道路安全及车辆管理局供图)。

（10英寸），就容易受伤（579，586，587）。有多种因素可导致车内前排人员位置不正确，见表8-3（图8-62和图8-63）。

表8-3 前排乘员"不规范乘坐"的原因

身体肥胖

身材矮小者为踩到踏板而向前调整座椅

　骨骼疾病（如脊柱侧弯、软骨发育不全）

　驾驶员身高≤160厘米（5英尺4英寸）

其他位置变化

　各年龄段乘客坐姿不当，伸手、身体前倾

　驾驶员由于困倦、疾病、中毒等原因趴在方向盘上

　各年龄段乘客向前移动，原因如下：

- 碰撞前制动
- 车辆轻微碰撞（猛烈程度低于安全气囊打开的阈值），以及如果安全带则碰撞加重
  ○ 没有使用
  ○ 松弛（身着厚重衣物）；安全带延缓锁死
  ○ 轻微碰撞后由于惯性作用引起安全带松弛，然后安全气囊在猛烈碰撞中展开
  ○ 不正确佩戴安全带；仅使用腰式安全带

　儿童安全座椅安装于前排右方

注：表格内容源于参考文献586，经 *Journal of Forensic Sciences* 期刊授权。

图8-62 轻微碰撞。安全气囊打开，司机当场死亡，疑似酒精中毒而过度转动方向盘。尸体解剖发现死者左侧肺动脉撕裂（经许可转载自 *Journal of Forensic Sciences*，参考文献579）。

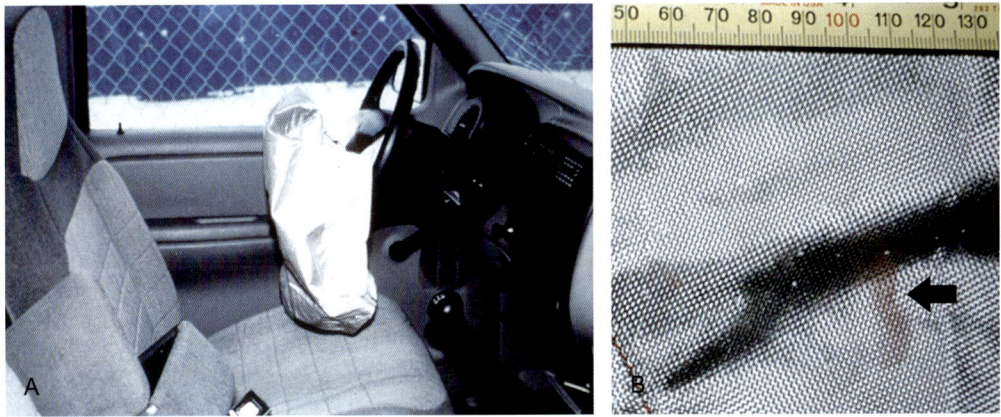

图 8-63 身材矮小的女性司机将座椅向前调节。(A)受害者身体向前倾,以便更好地观察结冰的路面。受害者驾驶的车辆由于打滑与迎面而来的车辆发生碰撞,安全气囊打开(图 8-61)(经许可转载自 Journal of Forensic Sciences,参考文献 579)。(B)气囊上可见唇印(箭头)。

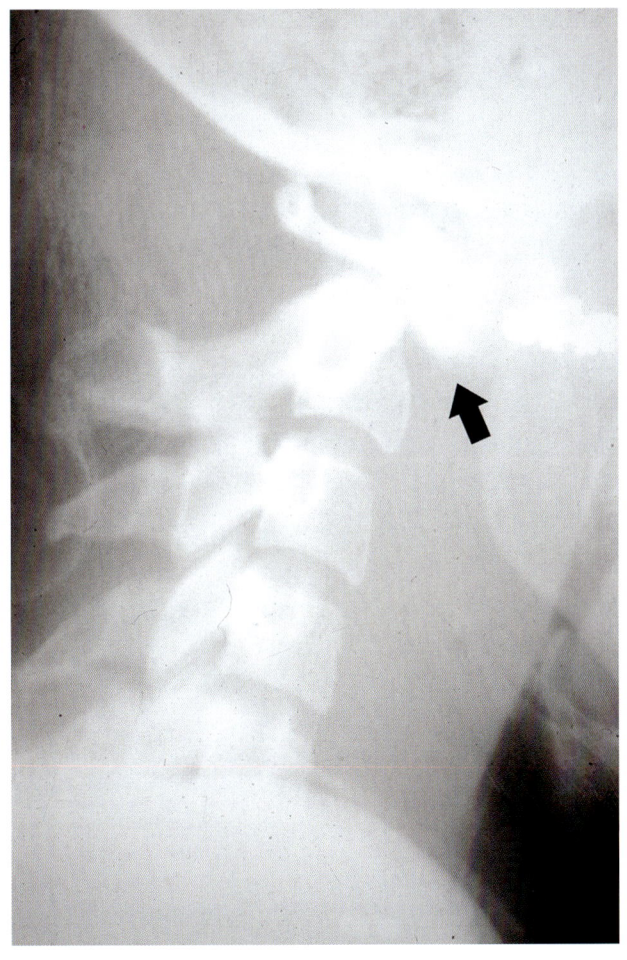

图 8-64 尸体 X 线片显示安全气囊展开导致 C1-C2 椎骨脱位(寰枢椎脱位;箭头)(图 8-61 和图 8-63)(经许可转载自 Journal of Forensic Sciences,参考文献 579)。

在安全气囊"冲出"阶段，如果人体躯干趴在安全气囊上或与安全气囊装置之间的距离太近，安全气囊充气会受阻（588）。如果安全气囊部分充气且进一步伸展受限，就会引起损伤（图8-64）（588）。因为外力在被高速传递时（145—328公里/小时或90—211英里/小时），会发生包括爆炸型损伤在内的一系列损伤（表8-4）（579）。

表8-4　与安全气囊展开相关的驾驶员和前排乘客致命和非致命性损伤（文献综述）

颅脑损伤
　颅骨骨折，nos[a]（589-591）
　　颅底（nos，环形，裂隙）±颅顶[a]（579, 589, 592-595）
　　　相关血管撕裂［海绵窦、颈动脉（589, 596）］
　　凹陷性损伤，nos[b]（589）
　　枕骨[a]（589, 597）
　　仅颅盖骨[b]（598）
　硬膜外、硬膜下/蛛网膜下腔/脑室内出血[a]（589, 590, 595, 597, 599-604）
　脑损伤、头部受伤，nos[a]（589, 591）
　　脑组织软化[b]（589）
　　脑水肿[a]（589, 590, 598, 601）
　　闭合性颅脑损伤[a]（579, 589, 598, 605）
　　弥散性轴索损伤[a]（590, 603, 606）
　　脑挫伤[a]（589, 590）
　　脑出血，nos[a]（589, 594, 598）

脑干－颈椎损伤
　断头或颈部横断[b]（589）
　颈椎损伤或颈部骨折，nos[a]（589, 595）
　　寰枕或寰枢椎脱位[a]（579, 589, 590, 594, 595, 602, 604, 606-614）
　　其他颈椎骨折或脱位（C2—C7）[a]（579, 589, 590, 593, 594, 600, 610, 615, 616）
　脑干损伤，nos（595）
　　脑桥、延髓撕裂或断裂[a]（602, 604, 606）
　　延髓出血/撕裂/横断（589）
　　撕裂伤或横断，nos[a]（589, 593, 595）
　　脑干或桥脑挫伤/出血[a]（589, 590, 600）
　颈椎脊髓损伤，nos[a]（589, 590）
　　挤压、撕裂或横断[a]（589, 590, 594, 595, 607-609, 612）
　　挫伤[b]（594）

其他颈部损伤
　气管－喉横断或压碎[a]（589, 617, 618）
　颈部钝性损伤致窒息、颈部肿胀致气道闭合、咽后壁血肿、颈椎骨折所致气道移位（589, 593, 607, 619, 620）
　颈部损伤，nos（589）

续表

椎动脉破裂 a(621)
颈内动脉夹层(622)

胸部受伤
胸腔大出血(589)
心脏损伤, nos(589)
　心脏或心肌撕裂, nos(589, 590, 595, 623)
　心房/心室撕裂(579, 589, 595, 600, 611, 623–626)
　瓣膜撕裂, nos(589, 595)
　　三尖瓣(589, 627)
　　主动脉瓣(270, 628, 629)
　　挫伤(589, 600, 611, 623)
　引起心脏停搏的胸部钝性损伤(589)
大血管撕裂
　主动脉, nos(579, 589, 595, 605)
　　胸主动脉, nos(589, 611)
　　升主动脉(589, 630, 631)
　　主动脉弓(589, 623)
　　降主动脉(602, 625)
　　腹主动脉(589, 632)
　　主动脉夹层(589)
　腔静脉
　　上腔静脉(589, 623)
　　下腔静脉 a(317, 594)
　头臂动脉(内膜)(625)
　肺静脉(589)
　肺动脉(579, 607, 619, 633)
奇静脉撕裂(634)
隔肌破裂(635)
肺损伤
　挫伤 a(589, 590, 594, 595, 600, 611)
　出血＝冲击伤(579)
　撕裂(589, 611)
　血气胸(589, 590, 594, 600, 602, 636)
食管破裂(637)
多发性肋骨骨折－胸部挤压伤, 连枷胸(579, 589, 593, 600, 623) c, d
胸椎骨折－脊髓撕裂伤 a(589, 594, 595, 615)
脾、肝、胰腺、肠、肠系膜撕裂(589, 593, 595, 599, 600, 602, 611, 623, 632, 638, 639)
肾撕脱 b(640)

续表

妊娠相关损伤
    胎盘早剥、胎儿死亡（641）
    胎膜早破（642）
    包括冲击伤在内的胎儿外伤（576,643）

注：a 损伤也在儿童中检见。
    b 损伤仅在儿童中检见。
    c 79岁男性，患有肺癌，交通事故中系腰式安全带，肋骨骨折致呼吸衰竭，碰撞速度为35公里/小时（22英里/小时）。
    d 74岁女性，体重100千克（220磅），身高163厘米（65英寸）。
    nos（not otherwise specified）：未另行说明。
    表格内容经许可转载自 *Journal of Forensic Sciences*，参考文献586。

评估气囊是否为致伤原因，法医必需认识到在严重的交通事故中，车内人员的挤压负载可能会超过安全气囊的保护能力（586,644）。在多次碰撞后，安全气囊可能会提前打开，随后就无法有效地保护车内人员（图8-65）。

碰撞中如果车内有多人受伤且难以确定谁是驾驶员，可以通过检查安全气囊（包括提取擦拭生物样本进行DNA分析）来协助确定。

图8-65 撞车过程中多次轻微碰撞引起安全气囊较早打开，方向盘与司机碰撞发生形变，驾驶员主动脉横断（加拿大运输署道路安全及车辆管理局供图）。

14.3 侧面碰撞和擦刮

在正面或后面的车辆碰撞中,车辆吸收碰撞能量而发生明显变形,从而减少传递到车舱的碰撞能量。其他装置(如能量吸收式转向柱、垫板仪表板)也可吸收能量。相反,由于车身侧面结构不耐碰撞(图 8-66),即使碰撞不严重,也会有较强的外力直接传导至车舱内,加之时常发生车舱内陷,从而增加了车内人员受伤的风险(490, 646-649)。当被撞车辆的重量小于撞击车辆时,被撞车内人员受伤的风险会更高(648)。如果存在外物侵入车舱而内陷,则安全带的保护作用就会相应减小(648)。

侧面碰撞时,车内人员会向碰撞的一侧横向移动;如果被撞车辆原本还向前运动,则车内人员同时也会向前移动。在近侧(车内人员乘坐于碰撞侧)碰撞时,车辆碰撞部位常见于侧面车窗、B 柱和车门内侧(图 8-18)(4, 650)。车内人员,特别是不系安全带者,可被完全或部分弹出,与地面、撞击车辆或固定物体发生碰撞(图 8-67)(651)。如果车辆碰撞后发生内陷变形(651),可能导致车内人员头部严重损伤。在远侧(车内人员乘坐于碰撞对侧)碰撞时,未系安全带的人员可在车辆中移动并与系安全带的乘客发生碰撞而引起损伤(652, 653)。系安全带人员在远侧碰撞中也可与对侧的车内部件、其他乘客发生碰撞,或发生安全带损伤(651, 654)。远侧碰撞中乘客也可从安全带的肩部脱出(651)。对于远侧碰撞的人员,由于近侧人员的阻挡作

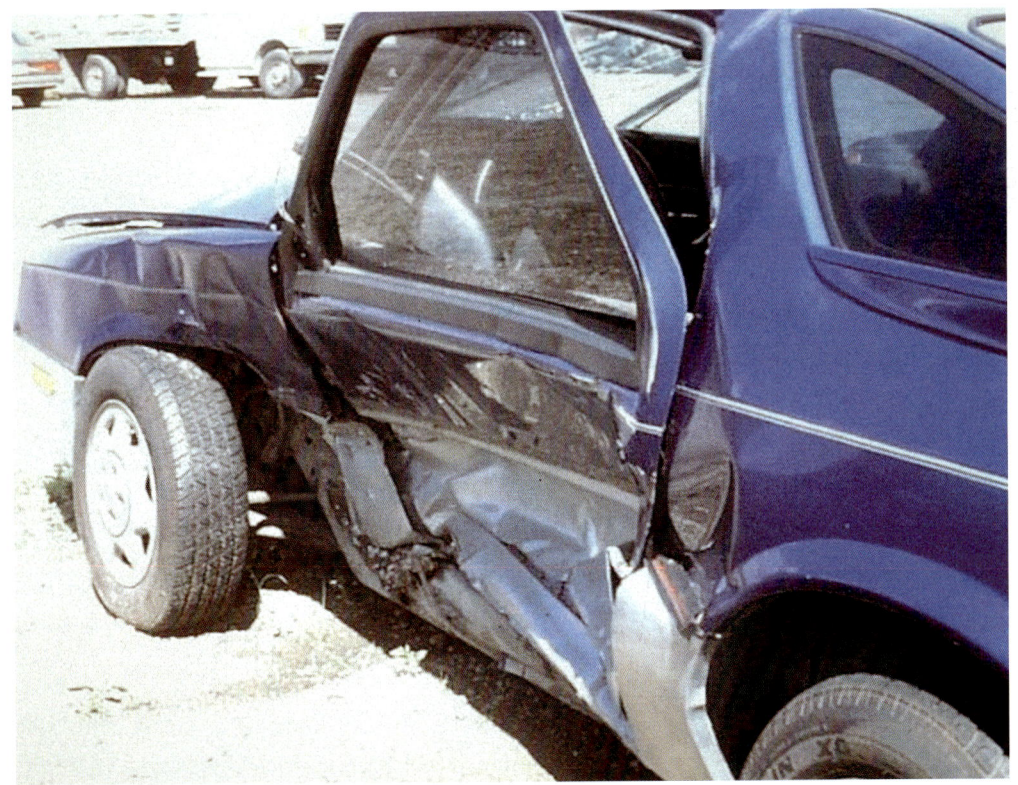

图 8-66 侧面碰撞,驾驶室车门内陷(加拿大运输署道路安全及车辆管理局供图)。

图 8-67 侧面碰撞；卡车侵入车舱。箭头指示机动车乘员头部接触（加拿大运输署道路安全及车辆管理局供图）。

用,其与碰撞侧车内部件的碰撞损伤得以减轻(651,654)。

　　侧面碰撞的损伤特征不同于正面碰撞。近侧碰撞中常见头部、颈部、胸部和腹部损伤(4,647)。车顶和 B 柱内陷变形常直接导致头部损伤,这是造成死亡的主要原因(650,655)。侧向撞击造成躯干损伤也很常见,车辆侧面碰撞时会导致多发性肋骨和骨盆骨折(495),也会发生严重的胸部、腹部和盆腔器官损伤(490,646)。远侧碰撞时主要为头部和躯干部损伤(654)。

　　车辆在移动中掠过其他车辆或固定物体时会发生侧擦碰撞。如果有外物侵入车舱或巨大能量通过坚硬的车辆结构传递时,会对乘员造成伤害。此类损伤与近侧碰撞事故的损伤类似。

14.4 追尾

　　车辆高速追尾事故并不常见,被追尾车辆车厢凹陷可导致后排乘员受伤。事故中,前排座椅损坏会向后塌陷,造成后排乘员的挤压伤,也有可能将前排乘员向后摔出。

14.5 翻车

　　翻滚是车辆在高速(>65 公里/小时或 40 英里/小时)行驶过程中发生的一系列复杂的交通事故,通常由于车辆失控引起(656)。以下是不同的翻滚类型(657):

- 绊翻,是最常见的机动车翻滚类型。由于车轮接触到某物表面(如砾石),车辆的横向移动突然减慢,引起车辆翻滚。
- 坠翻,车辆重心离开车轮支撑,使车辆从斜坡滚下。
- 抛翻,车辆一侧被凸出的物体(如护栏)抬升引起车辆翻滚。
- 爬翻,车辆完全越过障碍物(如护栏)引起翻滚。
- 弹翻,车辆与固定物接触并受其反弹作用而发生翻滚。
- 转翻,车辆急速转弯或快速转向产生的离心力(尤其是车辆重心较高时)引起车辆翻滚。
- 撞翻,与其他辆车相撞引起翻滚。
- 空翻,车辆绕其横轴的翻滚,最为少见。

车辆翻滚期间,动能随着翻滚时间和距离的增加而逐渐减弱。车辆翻滚的冲击力分布于车辆多个表面上。如果乘员系了安全带且未被抛掷出车外,存活的概率会升高(484,658,659)。乘员可由侧面车窗(关闭或打开)、前挡风玻璃以及在坠落过程中被暴力损毁的车门和天窗(658)被抛掷出车外。死亡事故中乘员通过侧面车窗被抛掷出车外的情况最常见。关闭的车窗可在外力作用下发生破裂。如果乘员在车辆翻滚过程中身体部分被抛出并且困在车体和外部之间,也会引起乘员受伤(658)。

翻滚事故中常见乘员的头部和胸部损伤(657),前者是由于乘员与车顶及车厢立柱发生碰撞所致,后者是由于乘员与车内部件发生碰撞所致(图 8-68 和图 8-69)(656 和 657)。颅脑损伤可由车顶凹陷或弯曲引起,但主要还是由乘员被抛掷所引

图 8-68 车辆翻滚事故;驾驶员部分身体被弹出车外,头部与车顶边缘发生碰撞。车厢顶部可见血迹(箭头)(加拿大运输署道路安全及车辆管理局供图)。

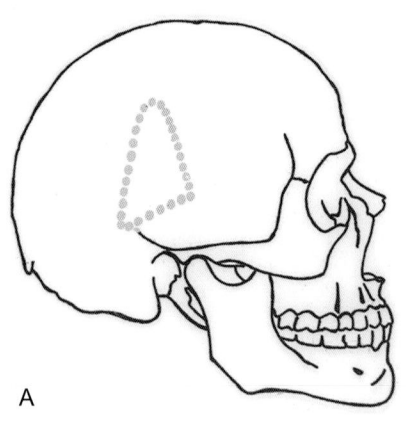

图 8-69 车辆翻滚；驾驶员系安全带，在车内死亡。(A)尸体解剖发现右侧颞顶骨三角形骨折。(B)相应部位头皮破裂，车顶内部可见大量血迹。驾驶员部分身体曾被抛甩到驾驶室车厢一侧车顶受外力碰撞的部位，被发现时死于驾驶室座椅上（图 8-70D）（经许可转载自 Journal of Forensic Sciences, 参考文献 656）。

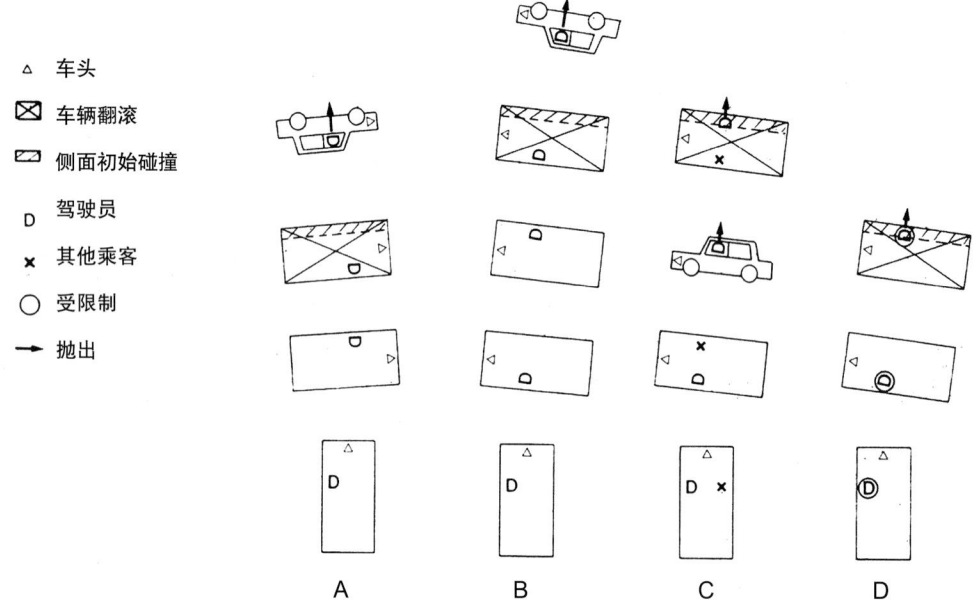

图 8-70 车辆翻车事故；车辆翻转导致驾驶员被抛掷，估计车辆行驶速度≥ 100 公里/小时（60 英里/小时）。(A)车内仅驾驶员（未系安全带）一人，副驾驶一侧受到碰撞，车辆顺时针翻转，驾驶员从前排左侧（驾驶侧）车窗被抛出。(B)车内仅驾驶员（未系安全带）一人，车辆逆时针翻转，驾驶员被甩到副驾驶侧并从前排右侧（副驾驶侧）车窗被抛出。(C)驾驶员（未系安全带），副驾驶位乘员（系/未系安全带），车辆逆时针翻转，驾驶员在翻滚初期身体完全从前排左侧车窗被抛出或在碰撞初期以车辆驾驶侧部分身体就被抛出。(D)驾驶员系安全带，车辆逆时针翻转，驾驶员从撞击侧（驾驶侧）被抛出（图 8-69）（经许可转载自 Journal of Forensic Sciences, 参考文献 656）。

起(656)。乘员头部损伤可以是与车内部件(如车顶横梁、车顶)、车外物体或地面发生碰撞的结果,具体取决于车辆翻滚方向,车顶首次着地侧(即与翻车方向相反的一侧),车内人员的数量、位置、活动情况及安全带使用等因素(图8-70)(656和657)。在一些事故中,乘员有可能在车内发生位移(656)。被困在车内的乘员可因体位性窒息而死亡(参阅第3章标题3.7;图8-63)(660)。

14.6 行人

14.6.1 站位的行人

面对行人死亡事故,法医需在确定死亡原因之外弄清以下其他问题:

- 行人被撞时是否处于站立状态?
- 是否有行人醉酒的证据?已有研究证明行人醉酒后受伤更严重(661)。

正面碰撞在行人被碰撞的交通事故中最常见(662)。

图8-71描述了机动车正面-行人碰撞时的各种运动轨迹(656,662,663)。

车辆初次撞击的行人为站立位时可导致"保险杠"骨折,通常为胫骨和腓骨骨折(664-666)。骨折断端通常向外伸展、拉伸甚至刺穿皮肤(图8-72)。撞击点对侧体表可能未见损伤,但切开皮肤后可见软组织损伤并出血(图8-73)(665)。从

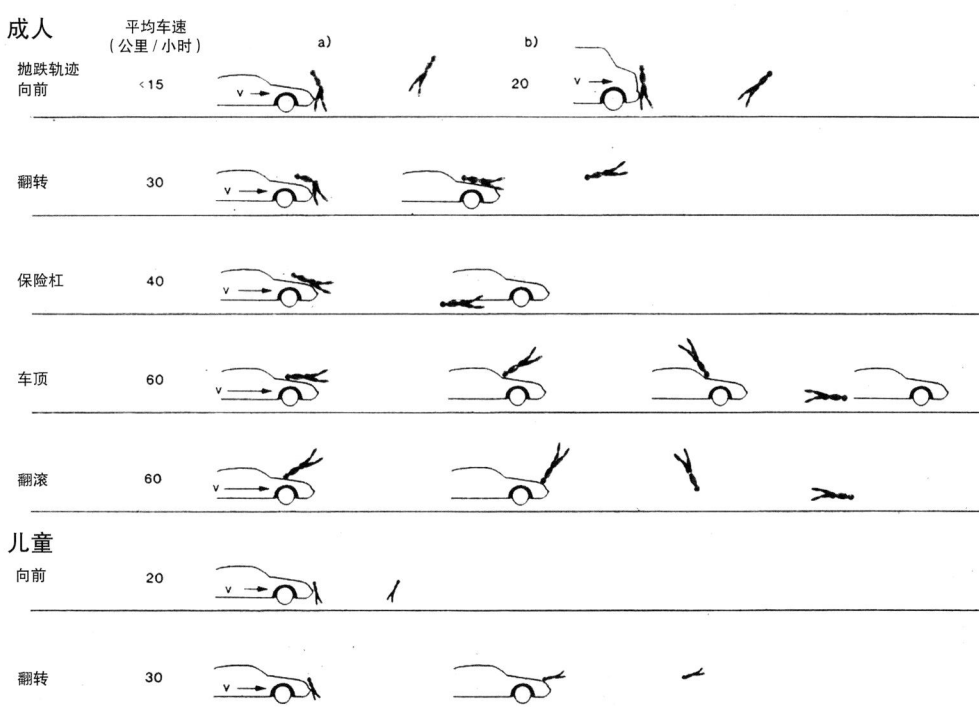

图8-71 车辆与行人在机动车(正面)-行人碰撞事故中的运动轨迹(经许可转载自 *Journal of Forensic Sciences*,参考文献656)。

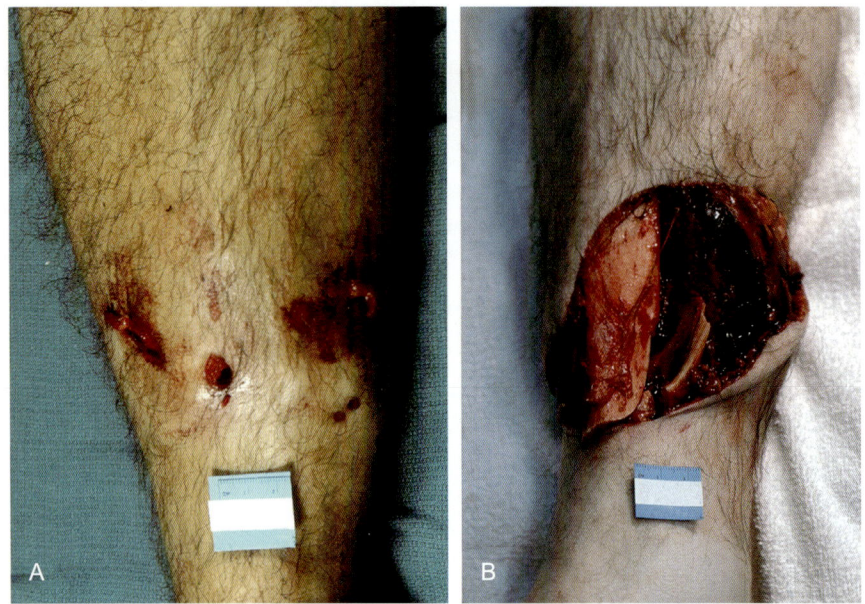

图 8-72 保险杠撞击点对侧骨折断端移位（移位方向与撞击方向相反）引起胫部皮肤损伤。（A）伸展创和小裂创。（B）大面积裂创，可见胫骨骨折。

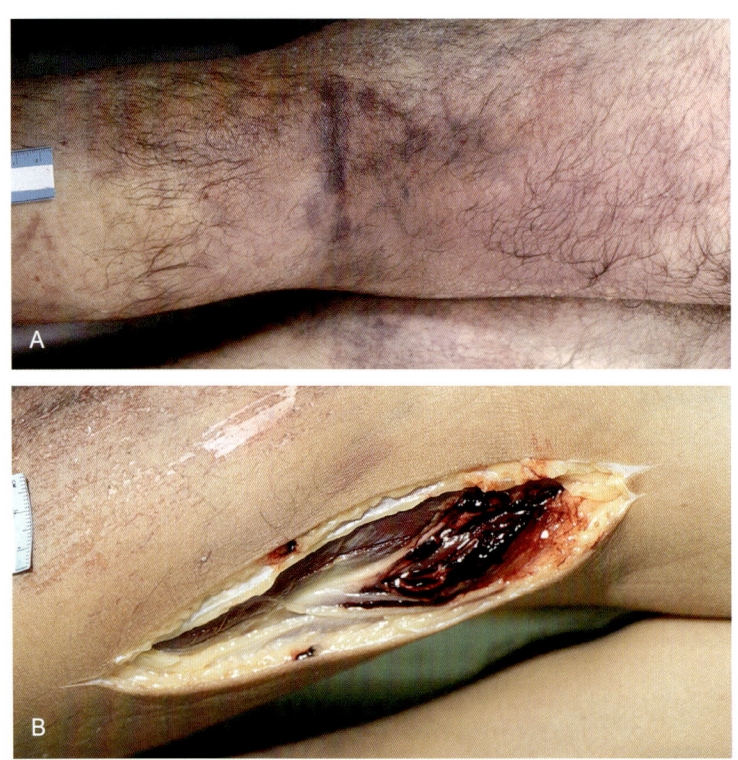

图 8-73 下肢保险杠损伤部位。（A）腘窝挫伤。（B）另一案例显示软组织血肿，为保险杠撞击的证据。这类损伤在体表没有明显的皮肤擦伤，切开皮肤可检见损伤。

第 8 章 | 钝器损伤——包括航空器、火车和机动车辆损伤　　493

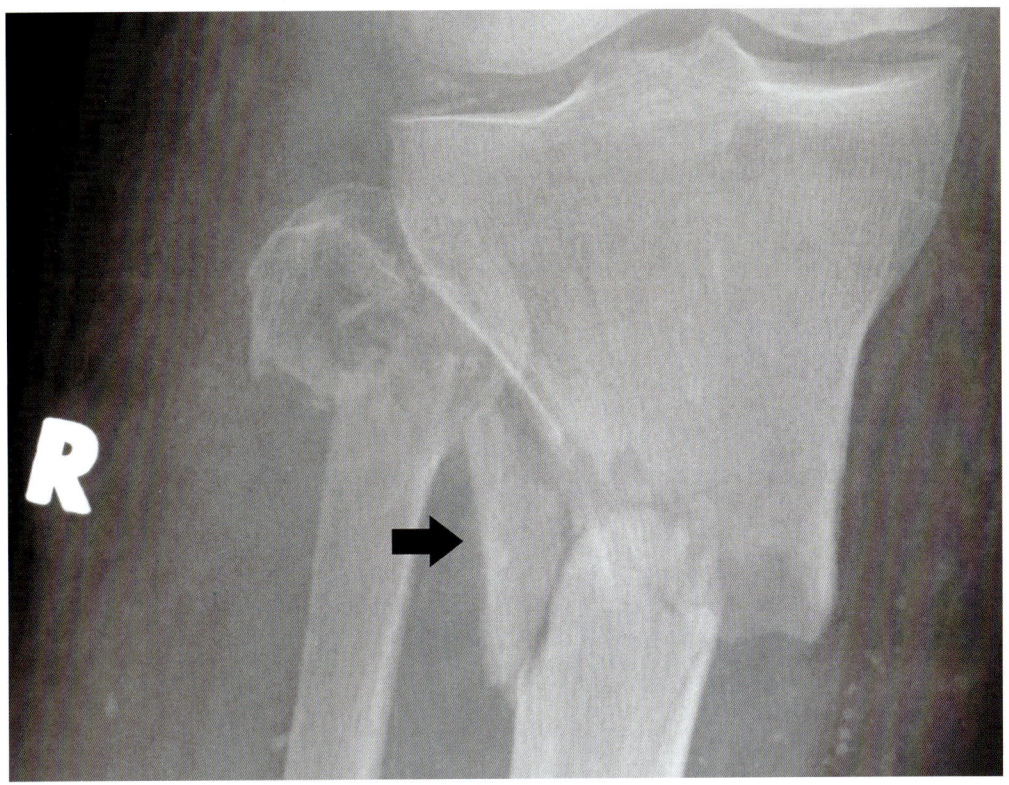

图 8-74　行人被车辆撞击。胫骨楔形骨折（箭头）（加拿大安大略省伦敦市伦敦健康科学中心 E. Tweedie 博士供图）。

足底到骨折部位的距离可以大致反映撞击时车辆保险杠的高度。X 线平片可证实肉眼可见或可触摸的骨折及隐匿性骨折。骨折可能呈现为楔形骨折（"蝴蝶状"骨折或 Messerer 骨折；图 8-74）。有研究报道楔形骨折的尖端指向车辆行驶方向，但其他研究也曾观察到指向相反方向（667-669）。行人股骨骨折由车辆发动机罩或地面接触碰撞导致（670）。撞击伤也会造成肢体离断（664，665，671）。可以不出现保险杠骨折，但可影响一侧下肢的多处部位，也可影响双侧下肢（672）。站立位的行人腿部受撞击可导致"骨挫伤"，多见于胫骨和腓骨骨骺端（665，666）。膝关节损伤的主要机制包括下肢过度屈曲 / 伸展和脱位，分别导致胫骨骨髁压缩性骨折和膝关节韧带撕裂。

前一种机制造成的骨挫伤面积大、位置居中，后一种机制造成的骨挫伤面积小，多分布于外周。踝关节损伤（如踝骨骨折）可由外旋、内旋或屈曲引发，也能说明行人处于站立状态（669）。与膝关节损伤类似，踝关节损伤的机制和位置也取决于碰撞方向（665，666，669）。其他能提示行人处于站立姿势的征象包括腿上有汽车油漆痕迹、鞋底拖擦痕等（664）。脚趾有擦伤说明腿部受到撞击后鞋内发生强烈摩擦（图 8-75）。

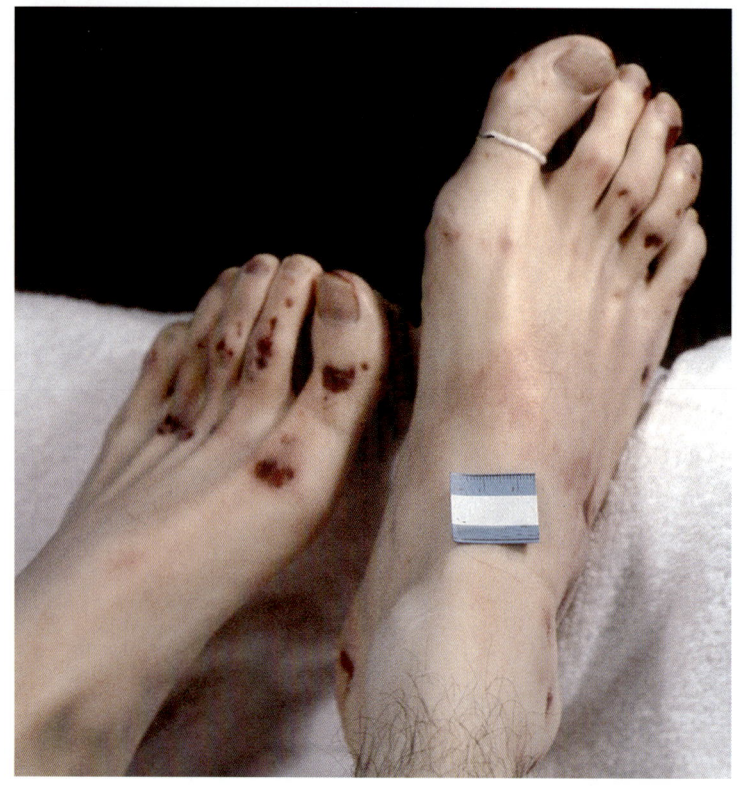

图 8-75 人体站立时被车辆撞击，足趾与鞋剧烈摩擦导致足趾擦伤。

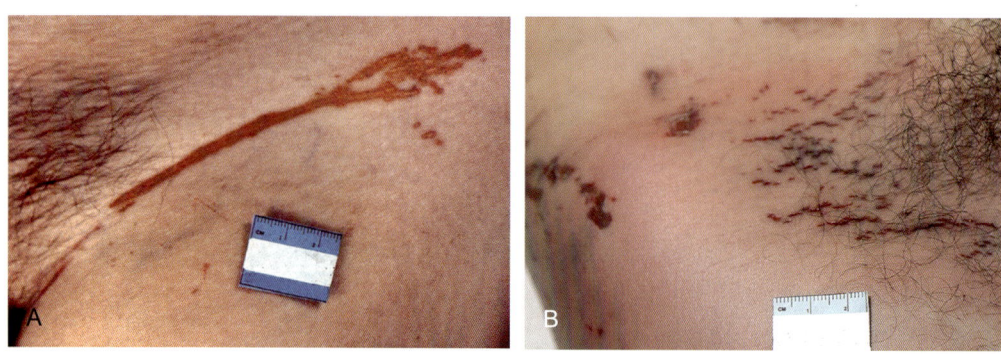

图 8-76 行人被车辆撞击。与发动机罩"二次"碰撞导致骨盆骨折。（A）和（B）腹股沟-股骨区"伸展创"。

车辆发动机罩边缘或车头灯的二次撞击可导致骨盆和髋关节损伤（图 8-22）（670）。腹股沟区皮肤伸展创提示这些部位发生骨折（图 8-76）。交通事故中最常出现抛举性碰撞（图 8-71）（656 和 673）：当减速行驶的车辆撞击成年人时，会使其上身屈曲，与发动机罩相撞（图 8-77 和图 8-78）；车辆停止后，行人倒在地上（674）。儿童由于重心较低，常因与发动机罩边缘碰撞而导致头部受伤

第 8 章 | 钝器损伤——包括航空器、火车和机动车辆损伤　　495

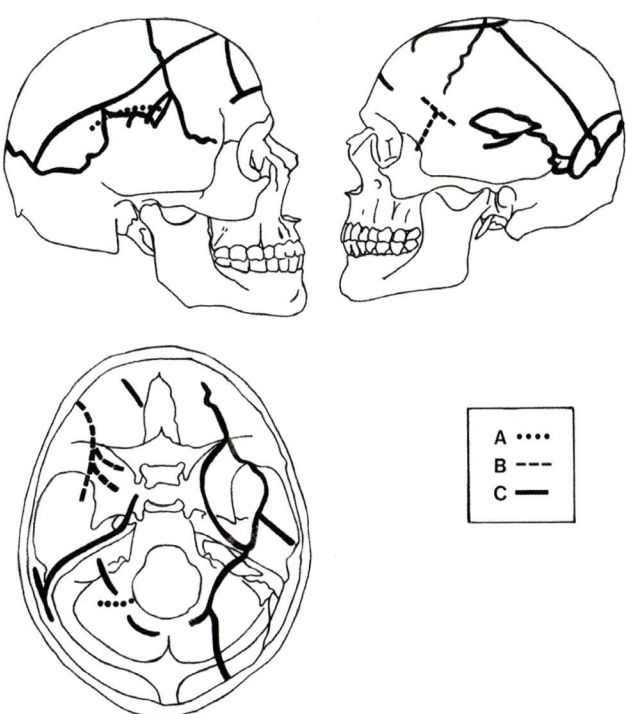

图 8-77　在某些车辆撞击行人的事故中,颅骨骨折情况可反映撞击的运动轨迹(A-C;参阅图 8-78—图 8-80)(经许可转载自 *Journal of Forensic Sciences*,参考文献 656)。

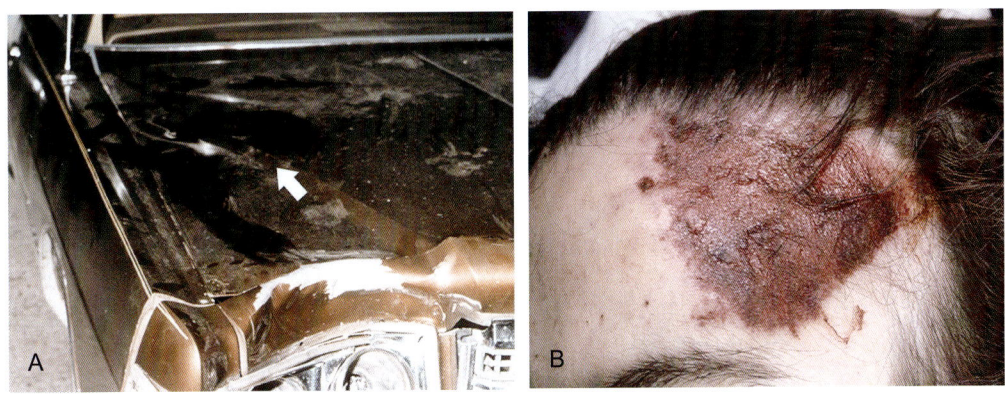

图 8-78　场景 B(图 8-77)。(A) 20 岁男子被行驶速度为 35 公里／小时(22 英里／小时)的车辆撞击,车辆撞击部位如箭头所示(图片源于经 *Journal of Forensic Sciences* 参考文献 656)。(B) 额部左侧大片擦伤("碰撞点")。

(图 8-79)(656,675 和 676)。儿童容易在停放的车辆间跑动时或在住宅区车道上被撞倒(675,677)。行人严重交通伤多与抛举性碰撞相关,高速行驶的车辆将行人抛举到发动机罩、挡风玻璃、车顶甚至行李厢上(图 8-80)(656)。行人向前扑倒主要发生于儿童或者被卡车／面包车撞击的成年人。低速(30 公里／小时或 19 英里

图 8-79 场景 A（图 8-77）。两岁女童，头部被行驶速度为 50 公里/小时（30 英里/小时）的汽车撞击。碰撞点为车辆发动机罩边缘撞击（箭头所示）。（经许可转载自 Journal of Forensic Sciences 期刊授权参考文献 656）。

图 8-80 场景 C（图 8-77）。29 岁男子被行驶速度为 80 公里/小时（50 英里/小时）的汽车撞击。碰撞点见于发动机罩、挡风玻璃和车顶（箭头）。（经许可转载自 Journal of Forensic Sciences 期刊授权参考文献 656）。

/小时)行驶的运动型多用途汽车(SUV)、轻型卡车和货车比小型客车更容易导致行人重伤和死亡。

行人头部损伤较常见(673, 674, 676)。颈部过伸可引起上位颈椎脱位(寰枕水平, C1－C2, C2－C3)与单纯性脑干损伤(图8-81)(679和680),也可引发基底血管(如基底动脉)撕裂(680)。有研究显示斜角肌和胸锁乳突肌下段出血与受力方向相关(681)。法医需意识到脑干撕裂(如原发性撕裂)可能不明显,脑组织从颅骨中取出后如果受到剧烈拉扯,可能会造成人为的脑干撕裂。

一项关于机动车－行人正面碰撞的研究确定了撞击速度与损伤模式之间的关系(682)。某些损伤与最低撞击速度的关系为:脊柱骨折(27.5公里/小时或17英里/小时);胸主动脉破裂合并胸椎骨折(63公里/小时或39英里/小时);腹股沟皮肤撕裂(66公里/小时或41英里/小时);颈部、躯干或肢体离断(98公里/小时或61英里/小时)。发生保险杠撞击导致的腿部骨折的撞击速度在18.5－142公里/小时(12－88英里/小时)范围内,但在某些情况下不出现(最高冲击速度为67公里/小时或42英里/小时)。

在验尸过程中,警方调查人员也可记录各种尸体测量结果,有助于确定受害者的重心和被撞击后的运动轨迹。

14.6.2 卧位的行人

躺在道路上的行人被车辆碾压后没有保险杠撞击所致的骨折,一种例外情况是:

图8-81 行人下肢被机动车撞击(二次碰撞)导致高位颈椎受到高强度剪切力的作用(经许可转载自 *Journal of Forensic Sciences* 期刊授权参考文献679)。

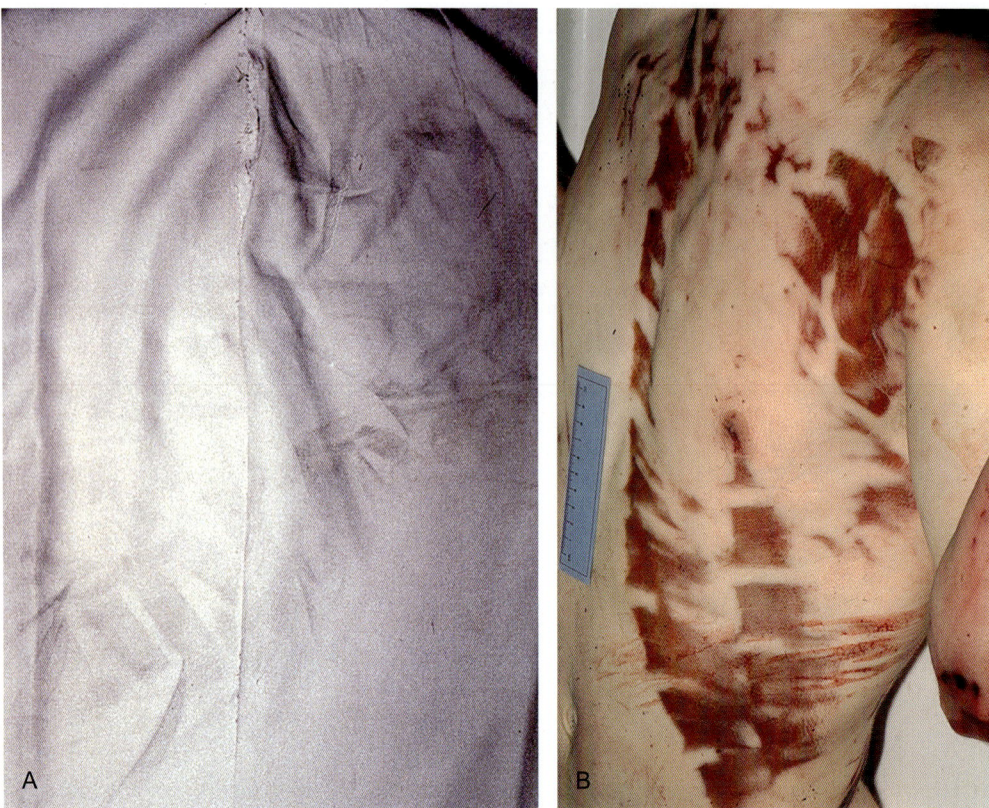

图 8-82 行人被车辆辗压。（A）裤子上的轮胎花纹印痕（北卡莱罗纳法医局供图）。（B）轮胎凸面花纹造成的躯干擦伤。

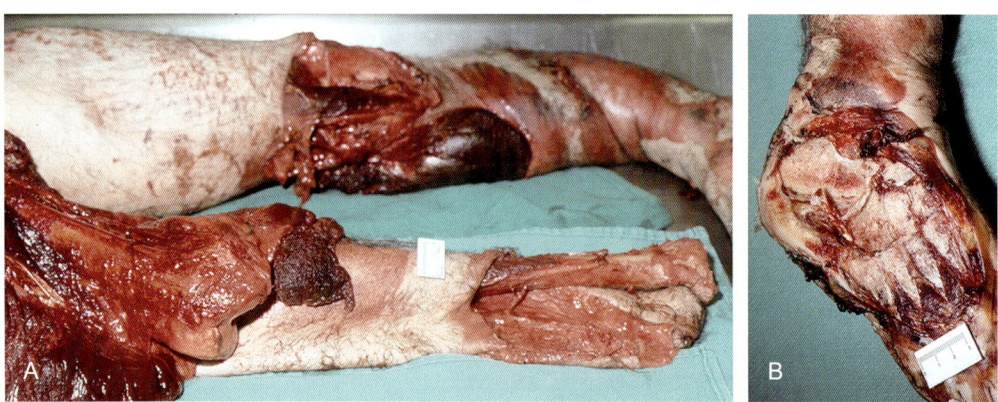

图 8-83 行人被碾压和拖擦。（A）下肢撕脱伤，右足离断。（B）左足骨摩损擦伤。

最初站立的行人被车辆撞倒后又被其他车辆反复碾压。可见髋关节脱位和骨盆损伤（665）。皮肤表面可见车辆下表面图案和衣服的印痕（图 8-23 和图 8-82）（683）。人体可因路面和车轮的打磨而发生严重损伤，衣服被大面积撕破（683，684），并可见轮胎印痕。皮肤可与皮下脂肪分离，可能发生肢体离断（图 8-83）（665）。如果车辆沿切线方向撞击直立的行人（665），也可导致受害者皮肤撕脱。拖曳和刮擦可产生广泛的"刷状擦伤"（图8-2）（683和685）。黑色擦伤可能由摩擦热效应所致（686），常见于骨骼凸起部位［颅骨、关节、肋骨（683，685）］。拖擦甚至可使内脏暴露（683，684），也可发生骨骼磨损（图8-83）（683）。颈部受压会导致喉软骨和舌骨骨折（图8-84；参阅图3-30）（687）。胸部受压则会导致眼睑淤血，严重压迫可导致内脏撕裂或撕脱。拖擦部位出血表明为生前伤（683）。吸入泥土是伤者被拖擦时还存活的另一个征象（683）。躺卧在地上的行人常会被检出酒精中毒（664）。

14.7 机动车事故中的死亡方式

虽然大多数涉及机动车辆的死亡案件都是交通事故，但法医必须意识到其他死亡方式也可能存在（484，688，689）。驾驶员自然死亡（如心肌梗死或心脏病发作）的确会发生。驾驶员可能会有前驱症状，使他们能采取适当的措施来防止对自己和他人造成的严重伤害（690-693）。有些驾驶员在停车前就失去意识（693），这种情况下的创伤不足以解释死亡原因（693）。心律读取植入装置有助于确定死亡前的身体状况（694）。法医需要评估疾病在事故中的作用或加剧疾病的创伤（695）。尽管许多死亡案件都发生于交通事故后不久，但是有些死亡可因各种并发症而延迟发生（参阅第1章标题11）。交通事故中的一些损伤可能类似于凶杀案件（图8-85），其他形式的意外也可能与机动车有关（如因车辆排气系统故障导致一氧化碳中毒；参

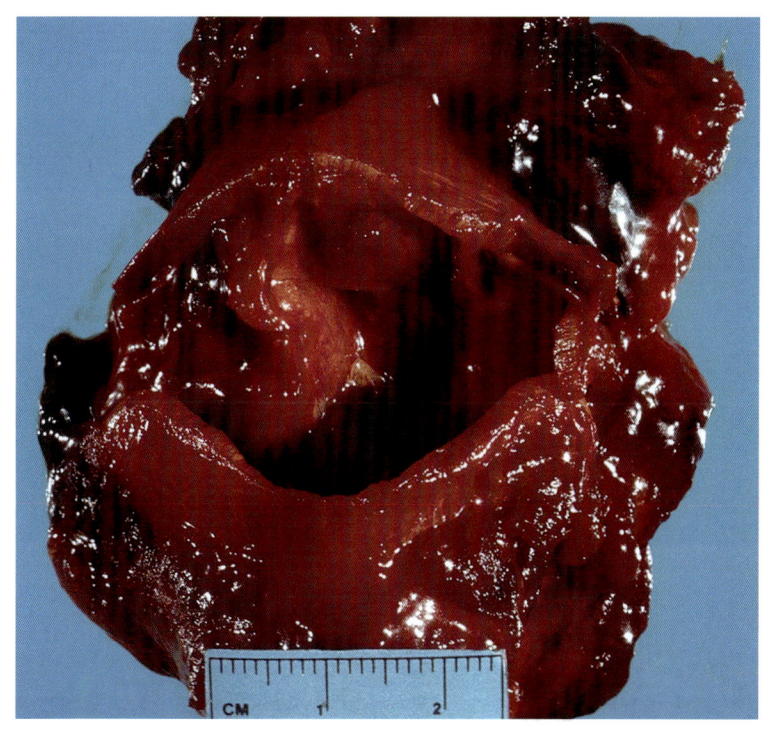

图8-84 车辆碾压致喉部横断损伤。

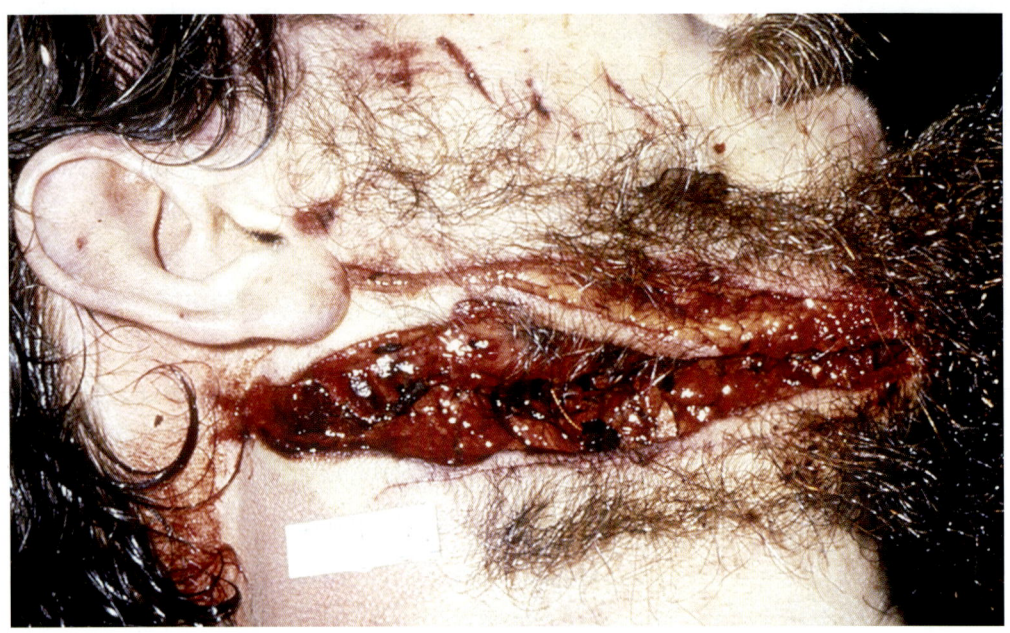

图 8-85 司机单独在州际公路上驾驶卡车,颈部见可疑伤口。发现车辆偏离行驶道路。损伤可能由碎玻璃片割划所致(美国北卡罗来纳州教堂山市法医局供图)。

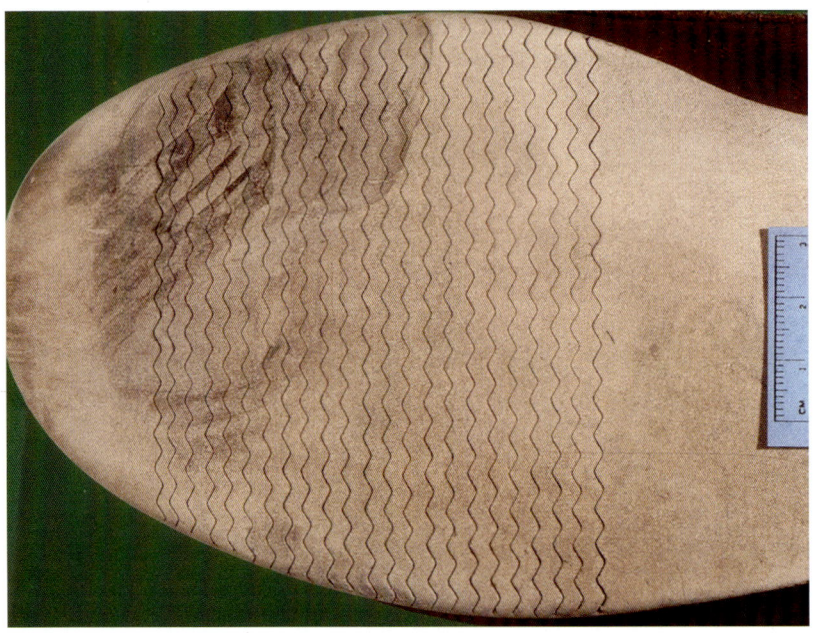

图 8-86 死亡驾驶员右脚鞋底可见刹车踏板印痕,说明在碰撞前采取过制动。

阅第 3 章标题 3.9.1)。乙醇和其他药物导致的急性中毒、酗酒、精神损害都可增加交通事故发生的风险(696, 697)。机动车也可以被用作自杀工具(697),驾驶员可能故意驶离道路(如撞向固定设施、其他车辆,驶入河道)或从高处坠落(553, 689,

697–700)。这些情况中,没有车辆制动痕迹,表明驾驶员未采取制动,驾驶员鞋底可能有加速器踏板印痕(图8-86)(483,688,689,697,701,702)。车辆加速行驶可能会有目击者。车辆可能被故意停在铁轨上(参阅标题15),行人可能会主动冲向行驶车辆,也有人会蓄意制造一氧化碳窒息(如在封闭的车库内运行发动机;参阅第3章标题3.9.1;图8-66;参考文献698,699)。非常规手段自杀(如枪弹伤、自焚、自缢)会引人怀疑(图4-1)(698,699,701,703-705),机动车可能会被用作实施他杀的工具(563),受害人可能会被车辆故意碾压。更常见的情况是"肇事逃逸",在这些案例中必须寻找痕迹证据(706,707)。谋杀案可能会被伪装成意外事故(图4-3)。

15 铁路交通事故死亡

铁路交通事故死亡指在铁路设施上发生或发现的死亡案件,铁路设施包括列车、轨道和公用通道(708)。各种场景和各类死亡方式均有被报道(708-713):

- 机动车辆与列车相撞(图8-87)。
- 机动车辆在轨道上抛锚或故意停靠;机动车驾驶员在通过没有保护设施的交叉路口时可能不知道有火车驶入;机动车驾驶员忽略或绕过交叉路口安全栅栏。
- 行人被列车撞击。

图8-87 机动车和列车相撞。

- 在铁轨或附近发现尸体。没有目击证人的死亡会给案件的性质带来较大的争议;有目击者的,会发现行人坐、卧在列车轨道上,在列车轨道上或靠近轨道行走,绕过交叉路口降低的保护门或跳到行驶的火车前方。酒精和其他药物是造成意外死亡的重要因素,特别是卧轨者(708,710,712,714-716)。自杀者可能有精神病病史(709)。
- 列车乘客死亡。
- 列车合法乘客及非法乘坐者可从列车上坠落摔伤或被列车碾轧。会发生列车脱轨。受害者在列车上被谋杀后抛尸于列车轨道。

在任何情况下,尸检时都要排除潜在疾病作为死亡或交通事故发生的原因(图8-88)(708)。

大多数案件的死亡原因是多发钝性损伤(708,709,711,713,716),死者多为男性(713,714,717)。铁路交通事故中,行人比机动车车内乘客更易发生创伤性肢体离断(图8-89)(708,714,717)。尽管站立位行人被认为不太可能发生肢体离断,但行人可能先被撞倒再被推到铁轨上(713)。还有其他类型的铁路死亡事故没有发现明显的损伤特征(711,717)。高速行驶的列车撞击行人会导致广泛的颅脑损伤、腹腔破裂、器官暴露和肢体离断(包括躯干离断)(图8-90)(713),头颈离断多见于自杀,但也可能发生于高速碰撞的事故中(图8-89)(709,713,716)。如果行人身体上附着污垢和油渍,表明被列车撞击过(图8-89)(713)。

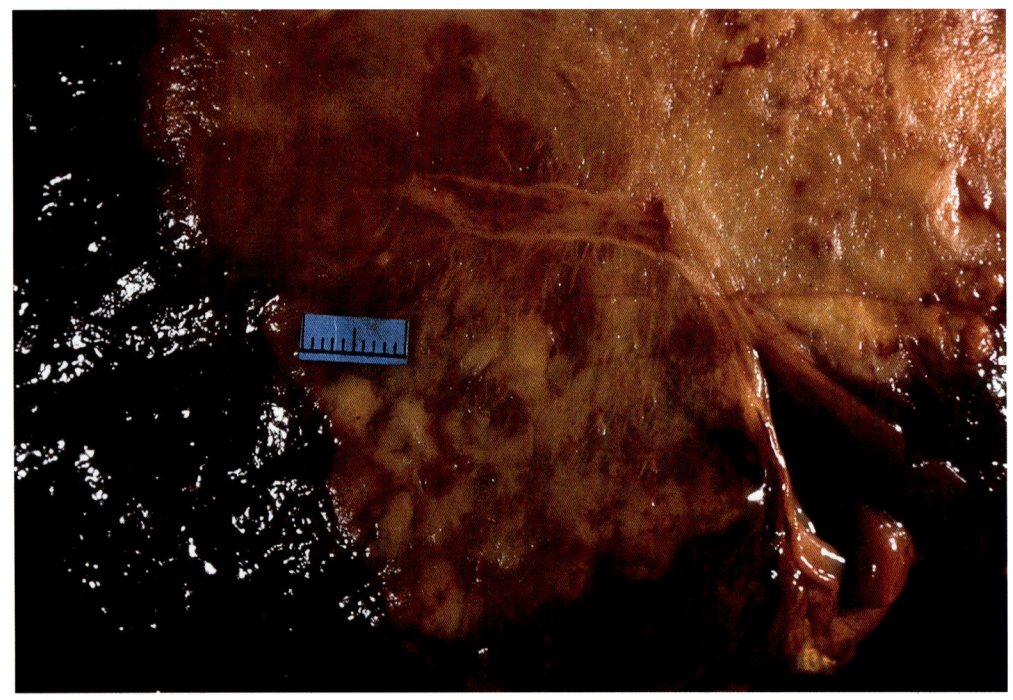

图8-88 机动车和列车相撞,机动车驾驶员多发性损伤,尸检中意外地发现死者患有胆管癌。

由于列车撞击可造成身体广泛性破坏,凶手可能试图抛尸于铁路来掩盖凶杀案件(708,709,711,716)。除了钝性损伤外,还可能有其他类型的损伤(710)。通常列车撞击会造成瞬间死亡,所以发现伴出血的钝性损伤可说明为生前伤(708)。与头皮损伤和颅脑外伤相关的广泛性出血,也需被高度怀疑(709,716)。

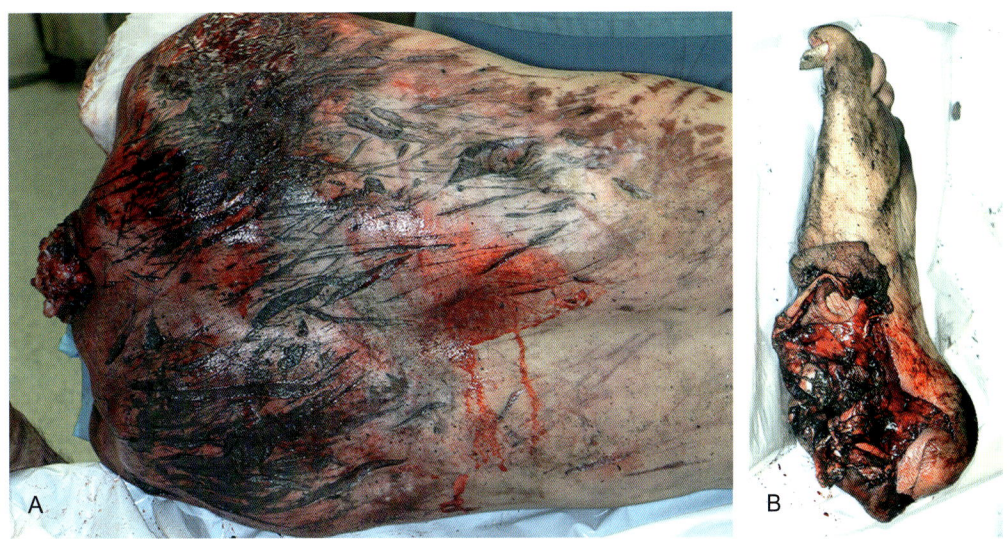

图 8-89 行人被火车撞击;自杀。(A)头颈离断;背部有广泛性皮肤擦伤和污垢附着。(B)足部离断。

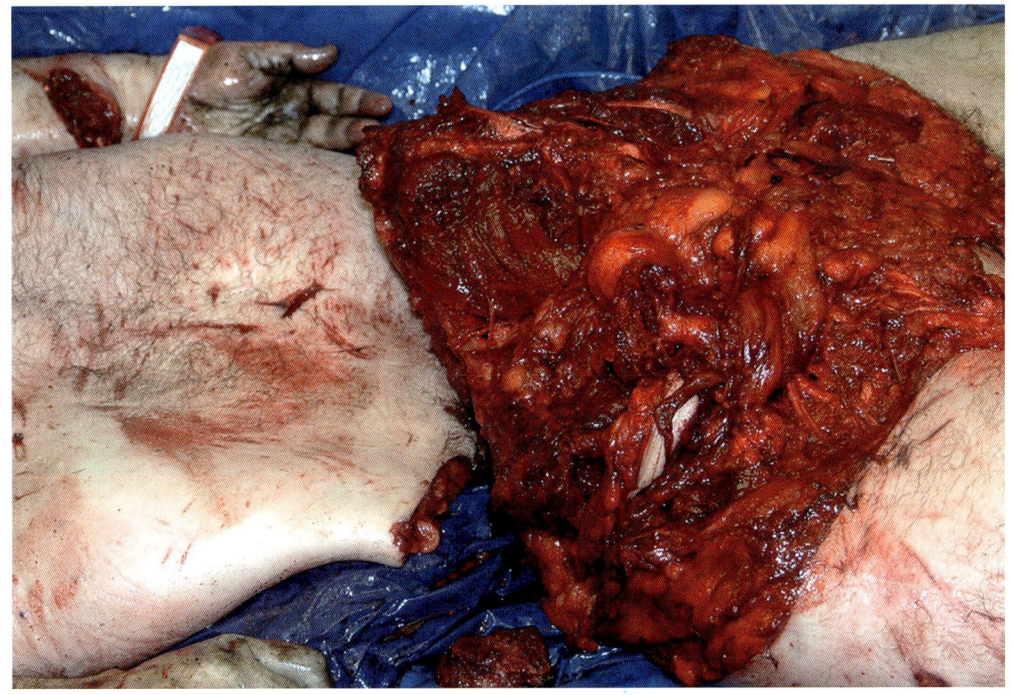

图 8-90 行人与列车相撞;自杀。腹部被横断。

16 轻型飞机

轻型飞机包括通用航空飞机（单引擎或多引擎活塞动力飞机，最大起飞重量为5 700千克或12 500磅）、旋翼机、超轻型飞机和滑翔机（718）。法医和警察及交通运输调查员间的沟通对于查明损伤、死亡和坠机的原因至关重要。必须进行完整的尸体解剖（719）。多发性外伤是最常见的死亡原因（表8-5）（720和721），损伤可能非常广泛（722）。

表8-5　轻型飞机事故死亡研究中损伤发生率的比较

	安大略省研究[a] %(n)	Reals等的研究[b] %(n)	Stevens等的研究[c] %(n)
骨折			
颅骨	53（20）	70（104）	67（63）
面骨	55（21）	—	48（45）
脊柱			
颈椎	29（11）	13（19）	12（11）
胸椎	8（3）	12（18）	23（21）
腰椎	5（2）	10（15）	18（17）
肋骨	63（24）	56（83）	63（59）
四肢			
上肢	42（16）	63（94）	56（52）
下肢	71（27）	74（110）	73（68）
骨盆	21（8）	—	—
内脏损伤（破裂/挫伤）			
脑	39（15）	53（78）	56（52）
脑干[d]	13（5）		
颈髓[d]	16（6）		
肺	66（25）	34（50）	36（33）
心	53（20）	34（51）	35（33）
主动脉	34（13）	23（34）	39（36）
肝	47（18）	49（72）	35（33）
肠系膜	13（5）	—	—
胃肠道	18（7）	—	—
脾	29（11）	41（61）	34（32）
肾[e]	18（7）	19（28）	23（21）

注：根据以下尸检结果：
　　a 38名受伤人员[25名飞行员，13名乘客；27人死于多发伤（717），11人仅有头颈部损伤]。
　　b 148名遇难者[未确定为飞行员还是乘员（723）]。
　　c 93名死者[70名飞行员，23名乘员（724）]。
　　d 包括肢体离断。
　　e 包括肾周血肿、血管破裂。
　　（图片经许可转载自 Journal of Forensic Sciences, 参考文献718）

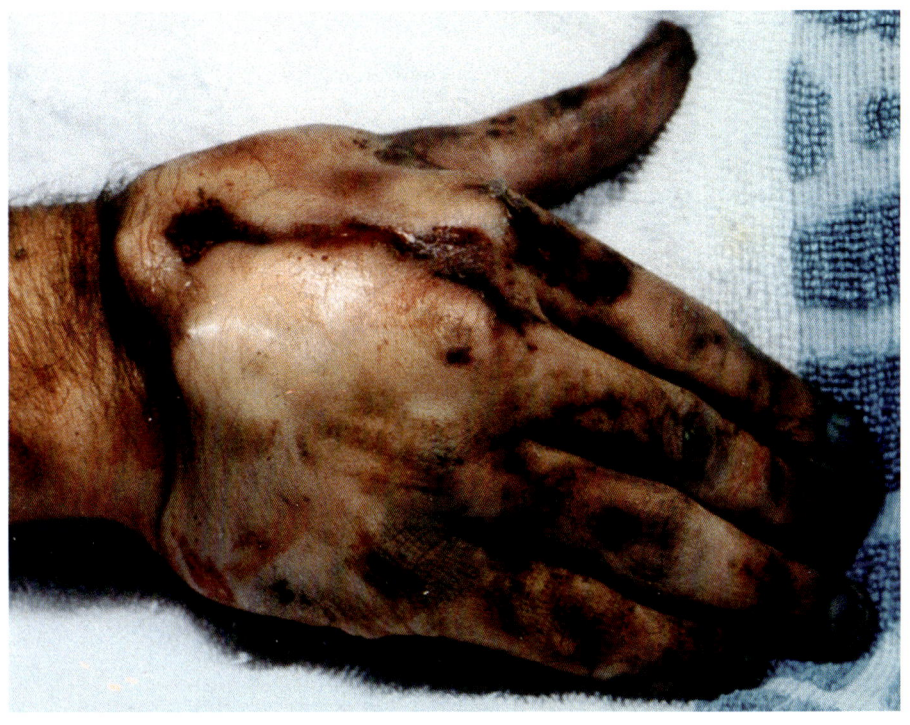

图 8-91　飞行员机毁人亡,右手手腕骨折引起畸形;操纵杆损伤(加拿大安大略省伦敦市伦敦健康科学中心 M. Joseph 博士供图)。

胸壁骨折是最常见的肌肉骨骼损伤类型。上肢和下肢骨折分别表示操纵杆和地板冲击伤(图 8-91)(725)。需要评估疾病或中毒导致能力丧失的可能性(718)。

黄平　林汉成　于笑天 译

参考文献

1. Lowenstein, S. R., Yaron, M., Carrero, R., Devereux, D., Jacobs, L. M. Vertical trauma: injuries to patients who fall and land on their feet. Ann. Emerg. Med. 18:161–165, 1989.

2. Warner, K. G., Demling, R. H. The pathophysiology of free-fall injury. Ann. Emerg. Med. 15:1088–1093, 1986.

3. Davis, G. J. Patterns of injury. Blunt and sharp. Clin. Lab. Med. 18:339–350, 1998.

4. Viano, D. C., Lau, I. V, Asbury, C., King, A. I., Begeman, P. Biomechanics of the human chest, abdomen, and pelvis in lateral impact. Accid. Anal. Prev. 21:553–574, 1989.

5. Rouhana, S. W., Lau, I. V., Ridella, S. A. Influence of velocity and forced compression on the severity of abdominal injury in blunt, nonpenetrating lateral impact. J. Trauma 25:490–500, 1985.

6. Viano DC, Lau VK. Role of impact velocity and chest compression in thoracic injury.

Aviat. Space Environ. Med. 54:16−21, 1983.

7. Goonetilleke, U. K. Injuries caused by falls from heights. Med. Sci. Law 20:262−275, 1980.

8. Vanezis, P. Interpreting bruises at necropsy. J. Clin. Pathol. 54:348−355, 2001.

9. Langlois, N. E., Gresham, G. A. The ageing of bruises: a review and study of the colour changes with time. J. Forensic Sci. 50:227−238, 1991.

10. Stephenson, T., Bialas, Y. Estimation of the age of bruising. Arch. Dis. Child. 74:53−55, 1996.

11. Wilson, E. F. Estimation of the age of cutaneous contusions in child abuse. Pediatrics 60:750−752, 1977.

12. Dailey, J. C., Bowers, C. M. Aging of bitemarks: a literature review. J. Forensic Sci. 42:792−795, 1997.

13. Camps, F. E. Interpretation of wounds. Br. Med. J. 2:770−772, 1952.

14. Hiss, J., Kahana, T., Kugel, C. Beaten to death: why do they die? J. Trauma 40:27−30, 1996.

15. Giles, T. E., Williams, A. R. The postmortem incidence of senile ecchymoses. Am. J. Forensic Med. Pathol. 15:208−210, 1994.

16. Munang, L. A., Leonard, P. A., Mok, J. Y. Lack of agreement on colour description between clinicians examining childhood bruising. J. Clin. Forensic Med. 9:171−174, 2002.

17. Hughes, V. K., Ellis, P S., Langlois, N. E. The perception of yellow in bruises. J. Clin. Forensic Med. 11:257−259, 2004.

18. Bariciak, E. D., Plint, A. C., Gaboury, I., Bennett, S. Dating of bruises in children: an assessment of physician accuracy. Pediatrics 112:804−807, 2003.

19. Raekallio, J. Estimation of time in forensic biology and pathology. An introductory review. Am. J. Forensic Med. Pathol. 1:213−218, 1980.

20. Schwartz, A. J., Ricci, L. R. How accurately can bruises be aged in abused children? Literature review and synthesis. Pediatrics 97:254−257, 1996.

21. Betz, P. Histological and enzyme histochemical parameters for the age estimation of human skin wounds. Int. J. Legal Med. 107:60−68, 1994.

22. Robertson, I., Hodge, P. R. Histopathology of healing abrasions. J. Forensic Sci. 1:17−25, 1972.

23. Spitz, W. V. Blunt force injury. In: Spitz W. V., ed. Medicolegal Investigation of Death: Guidelines for the Application of Pathology to Crime Investigation. Charles C. Thomas, Springfield, IL, pp. 199−251, 1993.

24. Betz, P., Eisenmenger, W. Morphometrical analysis of hemosiderin deposits in relation to wound age. Int. J. Legal Med. 108:262–264, 1996.
25. Ohshima, T. Forensic wound examination. Forensic Sci. Int. 113:153–164, 2000.
26. Ortiz-Rey, J. A., Suarez-Penaranda, J. M., Da Silva, E. A., et al. Immunohistochemical detection of fibronectin and tenascin in incised human skin injuries. Forensic Sci. Int. 126:118–122, 2002.
27. Fieguth, A., Feldbrugge, H., Gerich, T., Kleemann, W. J., Troger, H. D. The time-dependent expression of fibronectin, MRP8, MRP14 and defensin in surgically treated human skin wounds. Forensic Sci. Int. 131:156–161, 2003.
28. Raekallio, J. Timing of wounds—an introductory review. Ann. Acad. Med. Singapore 13:77–84, 1984.
29. Betz, P. Immunohistochemical parameters for the age estimation of human skin wounds. A review. Am. J. Forensic Med. Pathol. 16:203–209, 1995.
30. Thomsen, J. L., Albrektsen, S. B. External appearance of forensic autopsy material of alcoholics. Forensic Sci.. Int. 71:65–71, 1995.
31. Centers for Disease Control and Prevention. Hypothermia-related deaths—United States, 2003. MMWR Morb. Mortal. Wkly. Rep. 53:172–173, 2004.
32. Tipton, M. J. The initial responses to cold-water immersion in man. Clin. Sci. (Lond.) 77:581–588, 1989.
33. Golden, F. S., Tipton, M. J., Scott, R. C. Immersion, near-drowning and drowning. Br. J. Anaesth. 79:214–225, 1997.
34. Taylor, A. J., McGwin, G., Jr., Davis, G. G., Brissie, R. M., Holley, T. D., Rue, L. W., III. Hypothermia deaths in Jefferson County, Alabama. Inj. Prev. 7:141–145, 2001.
35. Wedin, B., Vanggaard, L., Hirvonen, J. "Paradoxical undressing" in fatal hypothermia. J. Forensic Sci. 24:543–553, 1979.
36. Albiin, N., Eriksson, A. Fatal accidental hypothermia and alcohol. Alcohol Alcohol. 19:13–22, 1984.
37. Kibayashi, K., Shojo, H. Accidental fatal hypothermia in elderly people with Alzheimer's disease. Med. Sci. Law 43:127–131, 2003.
38. Rothschild, M. A., Schneider, V. "Terminal burrowing behaviour" — a phenomenon of lethal hypothermia. Int. J. Legal Med. 107:250–256, 1995.
39. Gormsen, H. Why have some victims of death from cold undressed? Med. Sci. Law 12:200–202, 1972.
40. Mizukami, H., Shimizu, K., Shiono, H., Uezono, T., Sasaki, M. Forensic diagnosis of death from cold. Leg. Med. (Tokyo) 1:204–209, 1999.

41. Hirvonen, J. Necropsy findings in fatal hypothermia cases. J. Forensic Sci. 8:155–164, 1976.
42. McGee, M. B. Unusual blunt force wound patterns due to a hexagonal steel bar. Am. J. Forensic Med. Pathol. 12:149–152, 1991.
43. Perper, J. A., Menges, D. J. The skin as a repository and masker of evidence. Am. J. Forensic Med. Pathol. 11:56–62, 1990.
44. Takizawa, H., Nakamura, I., Hashimoto, M., Maekawa, N., Yamamura, M. Toolmarks and peculiar blunt force injuries related to an adjustable wrench. J. Forensic Sci. 34:258–262, 1989.
45. Rao, V. J. Patterned injury and its evidentiary value. J. Forensic Sci. 31:768–772, 1986.
46. Zugibe, F. T., Costello, J. T. Identification of the murder weapon by intricate patterned injury measurements. J. Forensic Sci. 31:773–777, 1986.
47. Zugibe, F. T., Costello, J., Breithaupt, M. Identification of a killer by a definitive sneaker pattern and his beating instruments by their distinctive patterns. J. Forensic Sci. 41:310–313, 1996.
48. Zugibe, F. T., Costello, J. T. Identification of a murder weapon by a peculiar blunt force injury pattern and histochemical analysis. J. Forensic Sci. 30:239–242, 1985.
49. Pretty, I. A., Hall, R. C. Forensic dentistry and human bite marks: issues for doctors. Hosp. Med. 63:476–482, 2002.
50. Anderson, W. R., Hudson, R. P. Self–inflicted bite marks in battered child syndrome. J. Forensic Sci. 7:71–74, 1976.
51. Warnick, A. J., Biedrzycki, L., Russanow, G. Not all bite marks are associated with abuse, sexual activities, or homicides: a case study of a self–inflicted bite mark. J. Forensic Sci. 32:788–792, 1987.
52. Sobel, M. N., Perper, J. A. Self–inflicted bite mark on the breast of a suicide victim. Am. J. Forensic Med. Pathol. 6:336–339, 1985.
53. Vale, G. L., Noguchi, T. T. Anatomical distribution of human bite marks in a series of 67 cases. J. Forensic Sci. 28:61–69, 1983.
54. Dorion, R. B. Bite mark evidence. J. Can. Dent. Assoc. 48:795–798, 1982.
55. Furness, J. A general review of bite–mark evidence. Am. J. Forensic Med. Pathol. 2:49–52, 1981.
56. Beckstead, J. W., Rawson, R. D., Giles, W. S. Review of bite mark evidence. J. Am. Dent. Assoc. 99:69–74, 1979.
57. Sperry K, Campbell HR, Jr. An elliptical incised wound of the breast misinterpreted as a bite injury. J. Forensic Sci. 35:1226–1235, 1990.

58. Pretty, I. A., Sweet, D. Anatomical location of bitemarks and associated findings in 101 cases from the United States. J. Forensic Sci. 45:812–814, 2000.

59. American Board of Forensic Odontology. Guidelines for bite mark analysis. J. Am. Dent. Assoc. 112:383–386, 1986.

60. Sweet, D., Lorente, M., Lorente, J. A., Valenzuela, A., Villanueva, E. An improved method to recover saliva from human skin: the double swab technique. J. Forensic Sci. 42:320–322, 1997.

61. Kouble, R. F., Craig, G. T. A comparison between direct and indirect methods available for human bite mark analysis. J. Forensic Sci. 49:111–118, 2004.

62. Benson, B. W., Cottone, J. A., Bomberg, T. J., Sperber, N. D. Bite mark impressions: a review of techniques and materials. J. Forensic Sci. 33:1238–1243, 1988.

63. Sweet, D., Bowers, C. M. Accuracy of bite mark overlays: a comparison of five common methods to produce exemplars from a suspect's dentition. J. Forensic Sci. 43:362–367, 1998.

64. Pretty, I. A., Sweet, D. Digital bite mark overlays—an analysis of effectiveness. J. Forensic Sci. 46:1385–1391, 2001.

65. Dailey, J. C. A practical technique for the fabrication of transparent bite mark overlays. J. Forensic Sci. 36:565–570, 1991.

66. Grey, T. C. Defibrillator injury suggesting bite mark. Am. J. Forensic Med. Pathol. 10:144–145, 1989.

67. James, H., Cirillo, G. N. Bite mark or bottle top? J. Forensic Sci. 49:119–121, 2004.

68. Pretty, I. A., Turnbull, M. D. Lack of dental uniqueness between two bite mark suspects. J. Forensic Sci. 46:1487–1491, 2001.

69. Walker, P. Management of pressure ulcers. Oncology (Williston Park) 15:1499–1508, 1511, 2001.

70. Sugarman, B., Hawes, S., Musher, D. M., Klima, M., Young, E. J., Pircher, F. Osteomyelitis beneath pressure sores. Arch. Intern. Med. 143:683–688, 1983.

71. Di Maio, V. J., Di Maio, T. G. Homicide by decubitus ulcers. Am. J. Forensic Med. Pathol. 23:14, 2002.

72. Tsokos, M., Heinemann, A., Puschel, K. Pressure sores: epidemiology, medico–legal implications and forensic argumentation concerning causality. Int. J. Legal Med. 113:283–287, 2000.

73. Allman, R. M. Pressure ulcer prevalence, incidence, risk factors, and impact. Clin. Geriatr. Med. 13:421436, 1997.

74. Evans, J. M., Andrews, K. L., Chutka, D. S., Fleming, K. C., Garness, S. L. Pressure

ulcers: prevention and management. Mayo Clin. Proc. 70:789–799, 1995.
75. Allman, R. M. Pressure ulcers among the elderly. N. Engl. J. Med. 320:850–853, 1989.
76. Turk, E. E., Tsokos, M., Delling, G. Autopsy–based assessment of extent and type of osteomyelitis in advanced–grade sacral decubitus ulcers: a histopathologic study. Arch. Pathol. Lab. Med. 127:1599–1602, 2003.
77. Thomas, D. R. Are all pressure ulcers avoidable? J. Am. Med. Dir. Assoc. 4:S43–S48, 2003.
78. Witkowski, J. A., Parish, L. C. Histopathology of the decubitus ulcer. J. Am. Acad. Dermatol. 6:1014–1021, 1982.
79. Berlowitz, D. R., Brandeis, G. H., Anderson, J., Du, W., Brand, H. Effect of pressure ulcers on the survival of long–term care residents. J. Gerontol. A. Biol. Sci. Med. Sci. 52:M106–M110, 1997.
80. Heinemann, A., Tsokos, M., Puschel, K. Medico–legal aspects of pressure sores. Leg. Med. (Tokyo) 5 Suppl 1:S263–S266, 2003.
81. Galpin, J. E., Chow, A. W., Bayer, A. S., Guze, L. B. Sepsis associated with decubitus ulcers. Am. J. Med. 61:346–350, 1976.
82. Thomas, D. R., Goode, P. S., Tarquine, P. H., Allman, R. M. Hospital–acquired pressure ulcers and risk of death. J. Am. Geriatr. Soc. 44:1435–1440, 1996.
83. Holmes, J. H., Guileyardo, J. M., Barnard, J. J., DiMaio, V. J. Pressure sores in a Christian Science sanatorium. Am. J. Forensic Med. Pathol. 14:10–11, 1993.
84. Shields, L. B., Hunsaker, D. M., Hunsaker, J. C., III. Abuse and neglect: a ten–year review of mortality and morbidity in our elders in a large metropolitan area. J. Forensic Sci. 49:122–127, 2004.
85. Gill, J. R. Fatal descent from height in New York City. J. Forensic Sci. 46:1132–1137, 2001.
86. Lewis, W. S., Lee, A. B., Jr., Grantham, S. A. "Jumpers syndrome." The trauma of high free fall as seen at Harlem Hospital. J. Trauma 5:812–818, 1965.
87. Li, L., Smialek, J. E. The investigation of fatal falls and jumps from heights in Maryland 1987–1992.. Am. J. Forensic Med. Pathol. 15:295–299, 1994.
88. Shaw, K. P., Hsu, S. Y. Horizontal distance and height determining falling pattern. J. Forensic Sci. 43:765–771, 1998.
89. Turk, E. E., Tsokos, M. Pathologic features of fatal falls from height. Am. J. Forensic Med. Pathol. 25:194–199, 2004.
90. Isbister, E. S., Roberts, J. A. Autokabalesis: a study of intentional vertical deceleration injuries. Injury 23:119–122, 1992.

91. Perret, G., Flomenbaum, M., La Harpe, R. Suicides by fall from height in Geneva, Switzerland, from 1991 to 2000. J. Forensic Sci. 48:821–826, 2003.

92. Copeland, A. R. Suicide by jumping from buildings. Am. J. Forensic Med. Pathol. 10:295–298, 1989.

93. Gunnell, D., Nowers, M. Suicide by jumping. Acta Psychiatr. Scand. 96:1–6, 1997.

94. Hanzlick, R., Masterson, K., Walker, B. Suicide by jumping from high–rise hotels. Fulton County, Georgia, 1967–1986. Am. J. Forensic Med. Pathol. 11:294–297, 1990.

95. Pounder, D. J. Suicide by leaping from multistorey car parks. Med. Sci. Law 25:179–188, 1985.

96. Sims, A., O'Brien, K. Autokabalesis: an account of mentally ill people who jump from buildings. Med. Sci. Law 19:195–198, 1979.

97. Risser, D., Bonsch, A., Schneider, B., Bauer, G. Risk of dying after a free fall from height. Forensic Sci. Int. 78:187–191, 1996.

98. Goren, S., Subasi, M., Tyrasci, Y., Gurkan, F. Fatal falls from heights in and around Diyarbakir, Turkey. Forensic Sci. Int. 137:3740, 2003.

99. Kisner, S. M., Fosbroke, D. E. Injury hazards in the construction industry. J. Occup. Med. 36:137–143, 1994.

100. Cattledge, G. H., Hendricks, S., Stanevich, R. Fatal occupational falls in the U.S. construction industry, 1980–1989. Accid. Anal. Prev. 28:647–654, 1996.

101. Copeland, A. R. Accidental death due to falls at work. Am. J. Forensic Med. Pathol. 10:17–20, 1989.

102. Smith, M. D., Burrington, J. D., Woolf, A. D. Injuries in children sustained in free falls: an analysis of 66 cases. J. Trauma 15:987–991, 1975.

103. Roshkow, J. E., Haller, J. O., Hotson, G. C., Sclafani, S. J., Mezzacappa, P. M., Rachlin, S. Imaging evaluation of children after falls from a height: review of 45 cases. Radiology 175:359–363, 1990.

104. Steedman, D. J. Severity of free–fall injury. Injury 20:259–261, 1989.

105. Snyder, R. G. Human tolerance limits in water impact. Aerosp. Med. 36:940–947, 1965.

106. Kazarian, K. K., Bole, P., Ketchum, S. A., III, Mersheimer, W. L. High–flyer syndrome: survival after 17–story fall. N. Y. State J. Med. 76:982–985, 1976.

107. Mathis, R. D., Levine, S. H., Phifer, S. An analysis of accidental free falls from a height: the 'spring break' syndrome. J. Trauma 34:123–126, 1993.

108. Mellen, P. F., Sohn, S. S. Military parachute mishap fatalities: a retrospective study. Aviat. Space Environ. Med. 61:1149–1152, 1990.

109. Tomczak, P. D., Buikstra, J. E. Analysis of blunt trauma injuries: vertical deceleration

versus horizontal deceleration injuries. J. Forensic Sci. 44:253–262, 1999.
110. Lau, G., Ooi, P. L., Phoon, B. Fatal falls from a height: the use of mathematical models to estimate the height of fall from the injuries sustained. Forensic Sci. Int. 93:3344, 1998.
111. Atanasijevic, T. C., Savic, S. N., Nikolic, S. D., Djoki, V. M. Frequency and severity of injuries in correlation with the height of fall. J. Forensic Sci. 50:608–612, 2005.
112. Harvey, P. M., Solomons, B. J. Survival after free falls of 59 metres into water from the Sydney Harbour Bridge, 1930–1982. Med. J. Aust. 1:504–511, 1983.
113. Gupta, S. M., Chandra, J., Dogra, T. D. Blunt force lesions related to the heights of a fall. Am. J. Forensic Med. Pathol. 3:35–43, 1982.
114. Layton, T. R., Villella, E. R., Kelly, E. G. High free fall with survival. J. Trauma 21:983–985, 1981.
115. Scalea, T., Goldstein, A., Phillips, T., et al. An analysis of 161 falls from a height: the 'jumper syndrome'. J. Trauma 26:706–712, 1986.
116. Barlow, B., Niemirska, M., Gandhi, R. P., Leblanc, W. Ten years of experience with falls from a height in children. J. Pediatr. Surg. 18:509–511, 1983.
117. Hall, J. R., Reyes, H. M., Horvat, M., Meller, J. L., Stein, R. The mortality of childhood falls. J. Trauma 29:1273–1275, 1989.
118. Cetin, G., Gunay, Y., Fincanci, S. K., Ozdemir, K. R. Suicides by jumping from Bosphorus Bridge in Istanbul. Forensic Sci. Int. 116:157–162, 2001.
119. Lukas, G. M., Hutton, J. E., Jr., Lim, R. C., Mathewson, C., Jr. Injuries sustained from high velocity impact with water: an experience from the Golden Gate Bridge. J. Trauma 21:612–618, 1981.
120. Kurtz, R. J., Pizzi, W. F., Richman, H., Tiefenbrun, J. Jumping from the Brooklyn Bridge. Surg. Gynecol. Obstet. 165:60–62, 1987.
121. Snyder, R. G., Snow, C. C. Fatal injuries resulting from extreme water impact. Aerosp. Med. 38:779–783, 1967.
122. Snyder R. G. Terminal velocity impacts into snow. Mil. Med. 131:1290–1298, 1966.
123. Rozycki, G. S., Maull, K. I. Injuries sustained by falls. Arch. Emerg. Med. 8:245–252, 1991.
124. Thogmartin, J. R. Fatal fall of an aircraft stowaway: a demonstration of the importance of death scene investigation. J. Forensic Sci. 45:211–215, 2000.
125. Velmahos, G. C., Demetriades, D., Theodorou, D., et al. Patterns of injury in victims of urban free-falls. World J. Surg. 21:816–820, 1997.
126. Simonsen, J. Injuries sustained from high-velocity impact with water after jumps from high bridges. A preliminary report of 10 cases. Am. J. Forensic Med. Pathol. 4:139–142,

1983.

127. Robertson, H. T., Lakshminarayan, S., Hudson, L. D. Lung injury following a 50-metre fall into water. Thorax 33:175–180, 1978.

128. Wanek, S., Mayberry, J. C. Blunt thoracic trauma: flail chest, pulmonary contusion, and blast injury. Crit. Care. Clin. 20:71–81, 2004.

129. Bintz, M., Gall, W. E., Harbin, D. Blunt myocardial disruption: report of an unusual case and literature review. J. Trauma 33:933–934, 1992.

130. Lee, R. B., Bass, S. M., Morris, J. A., Jr., MacKenzie, E. J. Three or more rib fractures as an indicator for transfer to a Level I trauma center: a population-based study. J. Trauma 30:689–694, 1990.

131. Liman, S. T., Kuzucu, A., Tastepe, A. I., Ulasan, G. N., Topcu, S. Chest injury due to blunt trauma. Eur. J. Cardiothorac. Surg. 23:374–378, 2003.

132. Sperry, K. Anterior thoracic wall trauma in elderly homicide victims. The "CPR defense". Am. J. Forensic Med. Pathol. 11:50–55, 1990.

133. Schmidt, G. Rib-cage injuries indicating the direction and strength of impact. Forensic Sci. Int. 13:103–110, 1979.

134. Feldman, K. W., Brewer, D. K. Child abuse, cardiopulmonary resuscitation, and rib fractures. Pediatrics 73:339–342, 1984.

135. Myllynen, P., Kivioja, A., Wilppula, E., Rokkanen, P., Mattila, S., Laakso, E. Flail chest—pathophysiology, treatment and prognosis. Ann. Chir. Gynaecol. 72:43–46, 1983.

136. Campbell, D. B. Trauma to the chest wall, lung, and major airways. Semin. Thorac. Cardiovasc. Surg. 4:234–240, 1992.

137. Duff, J. H., Goldstein, M., McLean, A. P., Agrawal, S. N., Munro, D. D., Gutelius, J. R. Flail chest: a clinical review and physiological study. J. Trauma 8:63–74, 1968.

138. Relihan, M., Litwin, M. S. Morbidity and mortality associated with flail chest injury: a review of 85 cases. J. Trauma 13:663–671, 1973.

139. Ciraulo, D. L., Elliott, D., Mitchell, K. A., Rodriguez, A. Flail chest as a marker for significant injuries. J. Am. Coll. Surg. 178:466–470, 1994.

140. Shorr, R. M., Crittenden, M., Indeck, M., Hartunian, S. L., Rodriguez, A. Blunt thoracic trauma. Analysis of 515 patients. Ann. Surg. 206:200–205, 1987.

141. Sirmali, M., Turut, H., Topcu, S., et al. A comprehensive analysis of traumatic rib fractures: morbidity, mortality and management. Eur. J. Cardiothorac. Surg. 24:133–138, 2003.

142. Kessel, B., Alfici, R., Ashkenazi, I., et al. Massive hemothorax caused by intercostal artery bleeding: selective embolization may be an alternative to thoracotomy in selected patients.

Thorac. Cardiovasc. Surg. 52:234−236, 2004.

143. Ross, R. M., Cordoba, A. Delayed life−threatening hemothorax associated with rib fractures. J. Trauma 26:576−578, 1986.

144. Simon, B. J., Chu, Q., Emhoff, T. A., Fiallo, V. M., Lee, K. F. Delayed hemothorax after blunt thoracic trauma: an uncommon entity with significant morbidity. J. Trauma 45:673−676, 1998.

145. Bundy, D. W., Tilton, D. M. Delayed hemothorax after blunt trauma without rib fractures. Mil. Med. 168:501−502, 2003.

146. Sinha, P., Sarkar, P. Late clotted haemothorax after blunt chest trauma. J. Accid. Emerg. Med. 15:189−191, 1998.

147. Irgau, I., Fulda, G. J., Hailstone, D., Tinkoff, G. H. Internal mammary artery injury, anterior mediastinal hematoma, and cardiac compromise after blunt chest trauma. J. Trauma 39:1018−1021, 1995.

148. Madoff, D. C., Brathwaite, C. E., Manzione, J. V., et al. Coexistent rupture of the proximal right subclavian and internal mammary arteries after blunt chest trauma. J. Trauma 48:521−524, 2000.

149. Wilkinson, J., Jacob, T. D., Armitage, J., Zajko, A., Udekwu, A. O., Peitzman, A. B. Avulsion of the internal mammary artery caused by blunt trauma. Ann. Emerg. Med. 22:1762−1765, 1993.

150. Nomori, H., Ootsuka, T., Horio, H., Naruke, T., Suemasu, K. Bilateral internal thoracic artery injury induced by blunt trauma. Jpn. J. Thorac. Cardiovasc. Surg. 51:214−216, 2003.

151. Atcheson, S. G., Fred, H. L. Letter: Complications of cardiac resuscitation. Am. Heart J. 89:263−265, 1975.

152. Rabl, W., Baubin, M., Broinger, G., Scheithauer, R. Serious complications from active compression−decompression cardiopulmonary resuscitation. Int. J. Legal Med. 109:84−89, 1996.

153. Himmelhoch, S. R., Dekker, A., Gazzaniga, A. B., Like, A. A. Closed−chest cardiac resuscitation. A prospective clinical and pathological study. N. Engl. J. Med. 270:118−122, 1964.

154. Bynum, W. R., Connell, R. M., Hawk, W. A. Causes of death after external cardiac massage. Analysis of observations of fifty consecutive autopsies. Cleve. Clin. Q. 30:147−151, 1963.

155. Krischer, J. P., Fine, E. G., Davis, J. H., Nagel, E. L. Complications of cardiac resuscitation. Chest 92:287−291, 1987.

156. Klintschar, M., Darok, M., Radner, H. Massive injury to the heart after attempted active compression–decompression cardiopulmonary resuscitation. Int. J. Legal Med. 111:93–96, 1998.

157. Bedell, S. E., Fulton, E. J. Unexpected findings and complications at autopsy after cardiopulmonary resuscitation (CPR). Arch. Intern. Med. 146:1725–1728, 1986.

158. Nagel, E. L., Fine, E. G., Krischer, J. P., Davis, J. H. Complications of CPR. Crit. Care Med. 9:424, 1981.

159. Clark, D. T. Complications following closed–chest cardiac massage. JAMA 181:337–338, 1962.

160. Sokolove, P. E., Willis–Shore, J., Panacek, E. A. Exsanguination due to right ventricular rupture during closed–chest cardiopulmonary resuscitation. J. Emerg. Med. 23:161–164, 2002.

161. Enarson, D. A., Didier, E. P., Gracey, D. R. Flail chest as a complication of cardiopulmonary resuscitation. Heart Lung 6:1020–1022, 1977.

162. Kaplan, B. M., Knott, A. P., Jr. Closed–chest cardiac massage for circulatory arrest. Effectiveness in 100 consecutive cases. Arch. Intern. Med. 114:5–12, 1964.

163. Roser, L. A. Cardiopulmonary resuscitation experience in a general hospital. Review of 116 consecutive resuscitative attempts during a 2 1/2–year period. Arch. Surg. 95:658–663, 1967.

164. Patterson, R. H., Burns, W. A, Jannotta, F.S. Complications of external cardiac resuscitation: a retrospective review and survey of the literature. Med. Ann. Dist. Columbia 43:389–394, 1974.

165. Lawrence, R. M., Haley, E. M., Gillies, A. J. Closed–chest cardiopulmonary resuscitation: results and criteria for application. N. Y. State J. Med. 64:2523–2532, 1964.

166. Haugeberg, G., Bonarjee, V., Dickstein, K. Fatal intrathoracic haemorrhage after cardiopulmonary resuscitation and treatment with streptokinase and heparin. Br. Heart J. 62:157–158, 1989.

167. Silberberg, B., Rachmaninoff, N. Complications following external cardiac massage. Surg. Gynecol. Obstet. 119:6–10, 1964.

168. Bodily, K., Fischer, R. P. Aortic rupture and right ventricular rupture induced by closed chest cardiac massage. Minn. Med. 62:225–227, 1979.

169. Paaske, F., Hansen, J. P., Koudahl, G., Olsen, J. Complications of closed–chest cardiac massage in a forensic autopsy material. Dan. Med. Bull. 15:225–230, 1968.

170. Azuma, S. S., Mashiyama, E. T., Goldsmith, C. I., Abbasi, A. S. Chest compression–induced vertebral fractures. Chest 89:154–155, 1986.

171. Agdal, N., Jorgensen, T. G. Penetrating laceration of the pericardium and myocardium and myocardial rupture following closed-chest cardiac massage. Acta Med. Scand. 194:477-479, 1973.
172. Yamada, E. Y., Fukunaga, F. H. Cardiopulmonary complications of external cardiac massage. Hawaii Med. J. 29:114-117, 1969.
173. Powner, D. J., Holcombe, P. A., Mello, L. A. Cardiopulmonary resuscitation-related injuries. Crit. Care Med. 12:54-55, 1984.
174. Sommers, M. S. Potential for injury: trauma after cardiopulmonary resuscitation. Heart Lung 20:287-293, 1991.
175. Thakore, S., Johnston, M., Rogena, E., Peng, Z., Sadler, D. Non-penetrating chest blows and sudden death in the young. J. Accid. Emerg. Med. 17:421-422, 2000.
176. Wolfe, W. G., Dudley, A. W., Jr., Wallace, A. G. A pathological study of unsuccessful cardiac resuscitation. Arch. Surg. 96:123-126, 1968.
177. Baldwin, J. J., Edwards, J. E. Clinical conference: Rupture of right ventricle complicating closed chest cardiac massage. Circulation 53:562-564, 1976.
178. Noffsinger, A. E., Blisard, K. S., Balko, M. G. Cardiac laceration and pericardial tamponade due to cardiopulmonary resuscitation after myocardial infarction. J. Forensic Sci. 36:1760-1764, 1991.
179. Atcheson, S. G., Petersen, G. V., Fred, H. L. Ill-effects of cardiac resuscitation: report of two unusual cases. Chest 67:615-616, 1975.
180. Meyers, D. S., Rogers, W. Papillary muscle rupture due to external cardiac massage. Case report. Mo. Med. 70:721-722, 1973.
181. Nelson, D. A., Ashley, P. F. Rupture of the aorta during closed-chest cardiac massage. JAMA 193:681-683, 1965.
182. Mayers, C. P. Aortic aneurysm following external cardiac massage. Br. J. Surg. 59:238-239, 1972.
183. Cohn, L. H., Sayer, W. J. Multiple complications from external cardiac massage. Report of a case. Calif. Med. 98:220-221, 1963.
184. Moe, N. Complications following resuscitation. Acta Med. Scand. 182:773-779, 1967.
185. McClure, J. N., Jr., Skardasis, G. M., Brown, J. M. Cardiac arrest in the operating area. Am. Surg. 38:241-246, 1972.
186. Custer, J. R., Polley, T. Z., Jr., Moler, F. Gastric perforation following cardiopulmonary resuscitation in a child: report of a case and review of the literature. Pediatr. Emerg. Care 3:24-27, 1987.
187. Demos, N. J., Poticha, S. M. Gastric rupture occurring during external cardiac

resuscitation. Surgery 55:364–366, 1964.

188. Tobias, S. Perforation of the transverse colon following external cardiac massage. Arch. Surg. 94:335–336, 1967.

189. Aguilar, J. C. Fatal gastric hemorrhage: a complication of cardiorespiratory resuscitation. J. Trauma 21:573–575, 1981.

190. Anthony, P. P., Tattersfield, A. E. Gastric mucosal lacerations after cardiac resuscitation. Br. Heart J. 31:72–75, 1969.

191. Lau, G. A case of sudden maternal death associated with resuscitative liver injury. Forensic Sci. Int. 67:127–132, 1994.

192. Barrowcliffe, M. P. Visceral injuries following external cardiac massage. Anaesthesia 39:347–350, 1984.

193. Jeresaty, R. M., Godar, T. J., Liss, J. P. External cardiac resuscitation in a community hospital. A three-year experience. Arch. Intern. Med. 124:588–592, 1969.

194. Cowan, D. Pancreatitis and pulmonary hemorrhage complicating closed-chest cardiac massage. Can. Med. Assoc. J. 95:976–977, 1966.

195. Waldman, P. J., Walters, B. L., Grunau, C. F. Pancreatic injury associated with interposed abdominal compressions in pediatric cardiopulmonary resuscitation. Am. J. Emerg. Med. 2:510–512, 1984.

196. Hojs, R., Sinkovic, A., Hojs-Fabjan, T. Rhabdomyolysis and acute renal failure following cardioversion and cardiopulmonary resuscitation. Ren. Fail. 17:765–768, 1995.

197. Kanter, R. K. Retinal hemorrhage after cardiopulmonary resuscitation or child abuse. J. Pediatr. 108:430–432, 1986.

198. Baubin, M., Rabl, W., Pfeiffer, K. P., Benzer, A., Gilly, H. Chest injuries after active compression-decompression cardiopulmonary resuscitation (ACD-CPR) in cadavers. Resuscitation 43:9–15, 1999.

199. Clark, D. E., Wiles, C. S., III, Lim, M. K., Dunham, C. M., Rodriguez, A. Traumatic rupture of the pericardium. Surgery 93:495–503, 1983.

200. Levine, A. J., Collins, F. J. Blunt traumatic pericardial rupture. J. Accid. Emerg. Med. 12:55–56, 1995.

201. May, A. K., Patterson, M. A., Rue, L. W., III, Schiller, H. J., Rotondo, M. F., Schwab, C. W. Combined blunt cardiac and pericardial rupture: review of the literature and report of a new diagnostic algorithm. Am. Surg. 65:568–574, 1999.

202. Janson, J. T., Harris, D. G., Pretorius, J., Rossouw, G. J. Pericardial rupture and cardiac herniation after blunt chest trauma. Ann. Thorac. Surg. 75:581–582, 2003.

203. Shah, R., Sabanathan, S., Mearns, A. J., Choudhury, A. K. Traumatic rupture of

diaphragm. Ann. Thorac. Surg. 60:1444−1449, 1995.

204. Nirgiotis, J. G., Colon, R., Sweeney, M. S. Blunt trauma to the heart: the pathophysiology of injury. J. Emerg. Med. 8:617−623, 1990.

205. Salehian, O., Teoh, K., Mulji, A. Blunt and penetrating cardiac trauma: a review. Can. J. Cardiol. 19:1054−1059, 2003.

206. Banning, A. P., Pillai, R. Non−penetrating cardiac and aortic trauma. Heart 78:226−229, 1997.

207. Boglioli, L. R., Taff, M. L., Harleman, G. Child homicide caused by commotio cordis. Pediatr. Cardiol. 19:436438, 1998.

208. Froede, R. C., Lindsey, D., Steinbronn, K. Sudden unexpected death from cardiac concussion (commotio cordis) with unusual legal complications. J. Forensic Sci. 24:752−756, 1979.

209. Martin, T. D., Flynn, T. C., Rowlands, B. J., Ward, R. E., Fischer, R. P. Blunt cardiac rupture. J. Trauma 24:287−290, 1984.

210. Vougiouklakis, T., Peschos, D., Doulis, A., Batistatou, A., Mitselou, A., Agnantis, N. J. Sudden death from contusion of the right atrium after blunt chest trauma: case report and review of the literature. Injury 36:213−217, 2005.

211. Darok, M., Beham−Schmid, C., Gatternig, R., Roll, P. Sudden death from myocardial contusion following an isolated blunt force trauma to the chest. Int. J. Legal Med. 115:85−89, 2001.

212. Macdonald, R. C., O'Neill, D., Hanning, C. D., Ledingham, I. M. Myocardial contusion in blunt chest trauma: a ten−year review. Intensive Care Med. 7:265−268, 1981.

213. Lindstaedt, M., Germing, A., Lawo, T., et al. Acute and long−term clinical significance of myocardial contusion following blunt thoracic trauma: results of a prospective study. J. Trauma 52:479485, 2002.

214. Koehler, S. A., Shakir, A., Ladham, S., et al. Cardiac concussion: definition, differential diagnosis, and cases presentation and the legal ramification of a misdiagnosis. Am. J. Forensic Med. Pathol. 25:205−208, 2004.

215. Shanklin, D. R. Delayed fatal impact cardiopathy. Forensic Sci. Int. 25:283−291, 1984.

216. RuDusky, B. M. Myocardial contusion culminating in a ruptured pseudoaneurysm of the left ventricle—a case report. Angiology 54:359−362, 2003.

217. Ansari, M. Z., Chaudhry, M. A., Singal, A., Joshi, R. Unusual cardiac injury following blunt chest trauma. Eur. J. Emerg. Med. 8:229−231, 2001.

218. Chou, T. F., Hwang, J. J., Chu, S. H. Interventricular septum rupture due to falling from a height. Thorac. Cardiovasc. Surg. 39:379−381, 1991.

219. Degiannis, E., Brink, J., Haagensen, M., Williams, P., Boffard, K. Rupture of the auricle of the right atrium of the heart and pericardium after blunt trauma. Eur. J. Surg. 167:472–474, 2001.

220. Rao, G., Garvey, J., Gupta, M., Wisoff, G. Atrial septal defect due to blunt thoracic trauma. J. Trauma 17:405–406, 1977.

221. Hermans, K., Vermeulen, J., Meyns, B. Isolated rupture of the left atrial appendage after blunt chest trauma. Acta Cardiol. 59:663–664, 2004.

222. Tobin, H. M., Hiratzka, L. F., Vargish, T. Ruptured right atrium from nonpenetrating trauma of the chest. South. Med. J. 79:499–501, 1986.

223. Brathwaite, C. E., Rodriguez, A., Turney, S. Z., Dunham, C. M., Cowley, R. Blunt traumatic cardiac rupture. A 5-year experience. Ann. Surg. 212:701–704, 1990.

224. Durak, D. Cardiac rupture following blunt trauma. J. Forensic Sci. 46:171–172, 2001.

225. Pollak, S., Stellwag-Carion, C. Delayed cardiac rupture due to blunt chest trauma. Am. J. Forensic Med. Pathol. 12:153–156, 1991.

226. Cumberland, G. D., Riddick, L., McConnell, C. F. Intimal tears of the right atrium of the heart due to blunt force injuries to the abdomen. Its mechanism and implications. Am. J. Forensic Med. Pathol. 12:102–104, 1991.

227. Arcudi, G., Marchetti, D. Left ventricular aneurysm caused by blunt chest trauma. Am. J. Forensic Med. Pathol. 17:194–196, 1996.

228. Veinot, J. P., Acharya, V. Post-traumatic left ventricular false aneurysm. J. Forensic Sci. 46:396–398, 2001.

229. Futterman, L. G., Lemberg, L. Commotio cordis: sudden cardiac death in athletes. Am. J. Crit. Care 8:270–272, 1999.

230. Kohl, P., Nesbitt, A. D., Cooper, P. J., Lei, M. Sudden cardiac death by commotio cordis: role of mechano-electric feedback. Cardiovasc. Res. 50:280–289, 2001.

231. Maron, B. J., Gohman, T. E., Kyle, S. B., Estes, N. A., III, Link, M. S. Clinical profile and spectrum of commotio cordis. JAMA 287:1142–1146, 2002.

232. Link, M. S., Wang, P. J., Maron, B. J., Estes, N. A. What is commotio cordis? Cardiol. Rev. 7:265–269, 1999.

233. Link, M. S. Mechanically induced sudden death in chest wall impact (commotio cordis). Prog. Biophys. Mol. Biol. 82:175–186, 2003.

234. Link, M. S., Maron, B. J., Wang, P. J., Pandian, N. G., VanderBrink, B. A., Estes, N. A., III. Reduced risk of sudden death from chest wall blows (commotio cordis) with safety baseballs. Pediatrics 109:873–877, 2002.

235. Maron, B. J., Poliac, L. C., Kaplan, J. A., Mueller, F. O. Blunt impact to the chest leading

to sudden death from cardiac arrest during sports activities. N. Engl. J. Med. 333:337–342, 1995.

236. McCrory, P. Commotio cordis. Br. J. Sports Med. 36:236–237, 2002.

237. Wang, N. D., Stevens, M. H., Doty, D. B., Hammond, E. H. Blunt chest trauma: an experimental model for heart and lung contusion. J. Trauma 54:744–748, 2003.

238. Wang, J. N., Tsai, Y. C., Chen, S. L., Chen, Y., Lin, C. S., Wu, J. M. Dangerous impact—commotio cordis. Cardiology 93:124–126, 2000.

239. Maron, B. J. Sudden death in young athletes. N. Engl. J. Med. 349:1064–1075, 2003.

240. Link, M. S., Maron, B. J., Wang, P. J., VanderBrink, B. A., Zhu, W., Estes, N. A., III. Upper and lower limits of vulnerability to sudden arrhythmic death with chest–wall impact (commotio cordis). J. Am. Coll. Cardiol. 41:99–104, 2003.

241. Frazer, M., Mirchandani, H. Commotio cordis, revisited. Am. J. Forensic Med. Pathol. 5:249–251, 1984.

242. Hirose, H. Posttraumatic right coronary artery aneurysm complicated with acute myocardial infarction shortly after blunt chest trauma. J. Trauma 44:937, 1998.

243. Straub, A., Beierlein, W., Kuttner, A., Hahn, U., Raygrotzki, S., Ziemer, G. Isolated coronary artery rupture after blunt chest trauma. Thorac. Cardiovasc. Surg. 51:97–98, 2003.

244. Mairesse, G. H., Timmermans, P. Post–traumatic myocardial infarction. Acta Clin. Belg. 48:128–131, 1993.

245. Fang, B. R., Li, C. T. Acute myocardial infarction following blunt chest trauma. Eur. Heart J. 15:705–707, 1994.

246. Dueholm, S., Fabrin, J. Isolated coronary artery rupture following blunt chest trauma. A case report. Scand. J. Thorac. Cardiovasc. Surg. 20:183–184, 1986.

247. Suzuki, I., Sato, M., Hoshi, N., Nanjo, H. Coronary arterial laceration after blunt chest trauma. N. Engl. J. Med. 343:742–743, 2000.

248. Fu, M., Wu, C. J., Hsieh, M. J. Coronary dissection and myocardial infarction following blunt chest trauma. J. Formos. Med. Assoc. 98:136–140, 1999.

249. Yoon, S. J., Kwon, H. M., Kim, D. S., et al. Acute myocardial infarction caused by coronary artery dissection following blunt chest trauma. Yonsei Med. J. 44:736–739, 2003.

250. Goktekin, O., Unalir, A., Gorenek, B., et al. Traumatic total occlusion of left main coronary artery caused by blunt chest trauma. J. Invasive Cardiol. 14:463–465, 2002.

251. Naseer, N., Aronow, W. S., McClung, J. A., et al. Circumflex coronary artery occlusion after blunt chest trauma. Heart Dis. 5:184–186, 2003.

252. Banzo, I., Montero, A., Uriarte, I., et al. Coronary artery occlusion and myocardial infarction: a seldom encountered complication of blunt chest trauma. Clin. Nucl. Med. 24:94—96, 1999.
253. Patel, R., Samaha, F. F. Right coronary artery occlusion caused by blunt trauma. J. Invasive Cardiol. 12:376–378, 2000.
254. Shapiro, M. J., Wittgen, C., Flynn, M. S., Zuckerman, D. A., Durham, R. M., Mazuski, J. E. Right coronary artery occlusion secondary to blunt trauma. Clin. Cardiol. 17:157–159, 1994.
255. Kugai, T., Chibana, M. Rupture in a mitral papillary muscle following blunt chest trauma. Jpn. J. Thorac. Cardiovasc. Surg. 48:394–397, 2000.
256. Wilke, A., Kruse, T., Hesse, H., Bittinger, A., Moosdorf, R., Maisch, B. Papillary muscle injury after blunt chest trauma. J. Trauma 43:360–361, 1997.
257. Grinberg, A. R., Finkielman, J. D., Pineiro, D., Festa, H., Cazenave, C. Rupture of mitral chorda tendinea following blunt chest trauma. Clin. Cardiol. 21:300–301, 1998.
258. Bruschi, G., Agati, S., Iorio, F., Vitali, E. Papillary muscle rupture and pericardial injuries after blunt chest trauma. Eur. J. Cardiothorac. Surg. 20:200–202, 2001.
259. Simmers, T. A., Meijburg, H. W., de la Riviere, A. B. Traumatic papillary muscle rupture. Ann. Thorac. Surg. 72:257–259, 2001.
260. McDonald, M. L., Orszulak, T. A., Bannon, M. P., Zietlow, S. P. Mitral valve injury after blunt chest trauma. Ann. Thorac. Surg. 61:1024–1029, 1996.
261. Munim, A., Chodoff, P. Traumatic acute mitral regurgitation secondary to blunt chest trauma. Crit. Care Med. 11:311–312, 1983.
262. Pathi, V., Jones, B., Davidson, K. G. Mitral valve disruption following blunt trauma: case report and review of the literature. Eur. J. Cardiothorac. Surg. 10:806–808, 1996.
263. Trotter, T. H., Knott–Craig, C. J., Ward, K. E. Blunt injury rupture of tricuspid valve and right coronary artery. Ann. Thorac. Surg. 66:1814–1816, 1998.
264. RuDusky, B. M., Cimochowski, G. Traumatic tricuspid insufficiency—a case report. Angiology 53:229–233, 2002.
265. Reardon, M. J., Conklin, L. D., Letsou, G. V., Safi, H. J., Espada, R., Baldwin, J. C. Mitral valve injury from blunt trauma. J. Heart Valve Dis. 7:467–470, 1998.
266. Salehian, O., Mulji, A. Tricuspid valve disruption and ventricular septal defect secondary to blunt chest trauma. Can. J. Cardiol. 20:231–232, 2004.
267. Bayezid, O., Mete, A., Turkay, C., Yanat, F., Deger, N., Isin, E. Traumatic tricuspid insufficiency following blunt chest trauma. J. Cardiovasc. Surg. (Torino) 34:69–71, 1993.
268. dos Santos J., Jr., de Marchi, C. H., Bestetti, R. B., Corbucci, H. A., Pavarino, P. R.

Ruptured chordae tendineae of the posterior leaflet of the tricuspid valve as a cause of tricuspid regurgitation following blunt chest trauma. Cardiovasc. Pathol. 10:97–98, 2001.

269. Banning, A. P., Durrani, A,. Pillai, R. Rupture of the atrial septum and tricuspid valve after blunt chest trauma. Ann. Thorac. Surg. 64:240–242, 1997.

270. Unal, M., Demirsoy, E., Gogus, A., Arbatli, H,. Hamzaoglu, A., Sonmez, B. Acute aortic valve regurgitation secondary to blunt chest trauma. Tex. Heart Inst. J. 28:312–314, 2001.

271. ten Berg, J. M., Jaarsma, W., Hamerlynck, R. P., Suttorp, M. J. Rupture of the left coronary cusp of the aortic valve caused by blunt chest trauma: early diagnosis by transesophageal echocardiography. J. Am. Soc. Echocardiogr. 8:766–769, 1995.

272. Chang, J. P., Chu, J. J., Chang, C. H. Aortic regurgitation due to aortic root intimal tear as a result of blunt chest trauma. J. Formos. Med. Assoc. 89:41–43, 1990.

273. Burkhart, H. M., Gomez, G. A., Jacobson, L. E., Pless, J. E., Broadie, T. A. Fatal blunt aortic injuries: a review of 242 autopsy cases. J. Trauma 50:113–115, 2001.

274. Katyal, D., McLellan, B. A., Brenneman, F. D., Boulanger, B. R., Sharkey, P. W., Waddell, J. P. Lateral impact motor vehicle collisions: significant cause of blunt traumatic rupture of the thoracic aorta. J. Trauma 42:769–772, 1997.

275. Shkrum, M. J., McClafferty, K. J., Green, R. N., Nowak, E. S., Young, J. G. Mechanisms of aortic injury in fatalities occurring in motor vehicle collisions. J. Forensic Sci. 44:44–56, 1999.

276. Richens, D., Kotidis, K., Neale, M., Oakley, C., Fails, A. Rupture of the aorta following road traffic accidents in the United Kingdom 1992–1999. The results of the co–operative crash injury study. Eur. J. Cardiothorac. Surg. 23:143–148, 2003.

277. Newman, R. J., Rastogi, S. Rupture of the thoracic aorta and its relationship to road traffic accident characteristics. Injury 15:296–299, 1984.

278. Feczko, J. D., Lynch, L., Pless, J. E., Clark, M. A., McClain, J., Hawley, D. A. An autopsy case review of 142 nonpenetrating (blunt) injuries of the aorta. J. Trauma; 33:846–849, 1992.

279. Hossack, D. W. The pattern of injuries received by 500 drivers and passengers killed in road accidents. Med. J. Aust. 2:193–195, 1972.

280. Sevitt, S. Fatal road accidents in Birmingham: times to death and their causes. Injury 4:281–293, 1973.

281. Greendyke, R. M. Traumatic rupture of aorta; special reference to automobile accidents. JAMA 195:527–530, 1966.

282. Dischinger, P., Cowley, R., Shankar, B., Smialek, J. The incidence of ruptured aorta among vehicular fatalities. Proceedings of the 32nd AAAM Conference. Association for

the Advancement of Automotive Medicine, Des Plaines, IL, 1988.

283. Siegel, J. H., Smith, J. A., Siddiqi, S. Q. Change in velocity and energy dissipation on impact in motor vehicle crashes as a function of the direction of crash: key factors in the production of thoracic aortic injuries, their pattern of associated injuries and patient survival. A Crash Injury Research Engineering Network (CIREN) study. J. Trauma 57:760–777, 2004.

284. Fitzharris, M., Franklyn, M., Frampton, R., Yang, K., Morris, A., Fildes, B. Thoracic aortic injury in motor vehicle crashes: the effect of impact direction, side of body struck, and seat belt use. J. Trauma 57:582–590, 2004.

285. Brundage, S. I., Harruff, R., Jurkovich, G. J., Maier, R. V. The epidemiology of thoracic aortic injuries in pedestrians. J. Trauma 45:1010–1014, 1998.

286. Siegel, J. H., Smith, J. A., Tenenbaum, N., et al. Deceleration energy and change in velocity on impact: key factors in fatal versus potentially survivable motor vehicle crash (mvc) aortic injuries (AI): the role of associated injuries as determinants of outcome. Annu. Proc. Assoc. Adv. Automot. Med. 46:315–338, 2002.

287. Hossack, D. W. Rupture of the aorta in road crash victims. Aust. N. Z. J. Surg. 50:136–137, 1980.

288. McGwin, G., Jr., Reiff, D. A., Moran, S. G., Rue, L. W., III. Incidence and characteristics of motor vehicle collision–related blunt thoracic aortic injury according to age. J. Trauma 52:859–865, 2002.

289. Eddy, A. C., Rusch, V. W., Fligner, C. L., Reay, D. T., Rice, C. L. The epidemiology of traumatic rupture of the thoracic aorta in children: a 13–year review. J. Trauma 30:989–991, 1990.

290. Strassmann, G. Traumatic rupture of the aorta. Am. Heart J. 33:508–515, 1947.

291. Richens, D., Field, M., Hashim, S., Neale, M., Oakley, C. A finite element model of blunt traumatic aortic rupture. Eur. J. Cardiothorac. Surg. 25:1039–1047, 2004.

292. Jensen, B. T. Fourteen years' survival with an untreated traumatic rupture of the thoracal aorta. Am. J. Forensic Med. Pathol. 9:58–59, 1988.

293. Roth, S. M., Wheeler, J. R., Gregory, R. T., et al. Blunt injury of the abdominal aorta: a review. J. Trauma 42:748–755, 1997.

294. Reisman, J. D., Morgan, A. S. Analysis of 46 intra–abdominal aortic injuries from blunt trauma: case reports and literature review. J. Trauma 30:1294—1297, 1990.

295. Bunai, Y., Nagai, A., Nakamura, I., Ohya, I. Traumatic rupture of an abdominal aortic aneurysm associated with the use of a seatbelt. J. Forensic Sci. 44:1304–1306, 1999.

296. McGwin, G., Jr., Metzger, J., Moran, S. G., Rue, L. W., III. Occupant– and collision–

related risk factors for blunt thoracic aorta injury. J. Trauma 54:655–660, 2003.

297. Gammie, J. S., Katz, W. E., Swanson, E. R., Peitzman, A. B. Acute aortic dissection after blunt chest trauma. J. Trauma 40:126–127, 1996.

298. Munshi, I. A. Aortic dissection after blunt trauma. J. Trauma 55:1181, 2003.

299. Mimasaka, S., Yajima, Y., Hashiyada, M., Nata, M., Oba, M., Funayama, M. A case of aortic dissection caused by blunt chest trauma. Forensic Sci. Int. 132:5–8, 2003.

300. Sharples, E. J., Sobeh, M., Matson, M., Yaqoob, M. M. Renal artery dissection after blunt abdominal trauma: a rare cause of acute cortical necrosis. Am. J. Kidney Dis. 40:E11, 2002.

301. Mangiante, E. C., Voeller, G. R., Kidsk, K. A., Fabian, T. C. Blunt injury of the abdominal aorta. J. Tenn. Med. Assoc. 82:255–256, 1989.

302. Hirose, H., Gill, I. S. Blunt injury of proximal innominate artery. Ann. Thorac. Cardiovasc. Surg. 10:130–132, 2004.

303. Karmy–Jones, R., DuBose, R., King, S. Traumatic rupture of the innominate artery. Eur. J. Cardiothorac. Surg. 23:782–787, 2003.

304. Sturm, J. T., Strate, R. G., Mowlem, A., Quattlebaum, F. W., Perry, J. F., Jr. Blunt trauma to the subclavian artery. Surg. Gynecol. Obstet. 138:915–918, 1974.

305. Yoak, M. B., Beaver, B. L., Denning, D. A. Blunt traumatic subclavian artery injury. W. V. Med. J. 96:403–404, 2000.

306. Kaplan, J. A. Delayed fatal hemothorax due to traumatic carotid dissection: a case report of a previously unreported cause of death. J. Forensic Sci. 39:552–556, 1994.

307. Posner, M. P., Deitrick, J., McGrath, P., et al. Nonpenetrating vascular injury to the subclavian artery. J. Vasc. Surg. 8:611–617, 1988.

308. Rozendaal, F. W., Bonjer, H. J., Bruining, H. A. Late haemorrhage from the subclavian vein due to a fracture of the first rib. Injury 26:57–58, 1995.

309. Galbraith, N. F., Urschel, H. C., Jr., Wood, R. E., Razzuk, M. A., Paulson, D. L. Fracture of first rib associated with laceration of subclavian artery. Report of a case and review of the literature. J. Thorac. Cardiovasc. Surg. 65:649–652, 1973.

310. Clements, R. H., Wagmeister, L. S., Carraway, R. P. Blunt intrapericardial rupture of the pulmonary artery in a surviving patient. Ann. Thorac. Surg. 64:258–260, 1997.

311. Katz, D. S., Groskin, S. A. Pulmonary artery laceration and tension pneumothorax in blunt chest trauma. J. Thorac. Imaging 8:156–158, 1993.

312. Collins, M. P., Robinson, G. C. Traumatic rupture of the pulmonary artery. Ann. Thorac. Surg. 47:612–613, 1989.

313. Ambrose, G., Barrett, L. O., Angus, G. L., Absi, T., Shaftan, G. W. Main pulmonary

artery laceration after blunt trauma: accurate preoperative diagnosis. Ann. Thorac. Surg. 70:955–957, 2000.

314. Hanline, M. H., Jr. Blunt traumatic rupture of the main pulmonary vessels. South. Med. J. 76:541–542, 1983.

315. Le Guyader, A., Bertin, F., Laskar, M., Cornu, E. Blunt chest trauma: a right pulmonary vein rupture. Eur. J. Cardiothorac. Surg. 20:1054–1056, 2001.

316. Varghese, D., Patel, H., Cameron, E. W., Robson, M. Repair of pulmonary vein rupture after deceleration injury. Ann. Thorac. Surg. 70:656–658, 2000.

317. Kluth, M., Luiz, T., Lehnert, S., Boettcher, M. [Airbag associated deceleration trauma with complete infradiaphragmatic dissection of the inferior vena cava (IVC) and tear of liver veins]. Anasthesiol. Intensivmed. Notfallmed. Schmerzther 39:24–27, 2004.

318. Peitzman, A. B., Udekwu, A. O., Pevec, W., Albrink, M. Transection of the inferior vena cava from blunt thoracic trauma: case reports. J. Trauma 29:534–536, 1989.

319. van de Wal, H. J., Draaisma, J. M., Vincent, J. G., Goris, R. J. Rupture of the supradiaphragmatic inferior vena cava by blunt decelerating trauma: case report. J. Trauma 30:111–113, 1990.

320. Couves, C. M., Heughan, C. Laceration of superior vena cava due to blunt trauma: successful surgical management. Can. J. Surg. 24:402–403, 1981.

321. Fey, G. L., Deren, M. M., Wesolek, J. H. Intrapericardial caval injury due to blunt trauma. Conn. Med. 63:259–260, 1999.

322. Takeuchi, M., Maruyama, K., Nakamura, M., et al. Posttraumatic inferior vena caval thrombosis: case report and review of the literature. J. Trauma 39:605–608, 1995.

323. Shkrum, M. J., Green, R. N., Shum, D. T. Azygos vein laceration due to blunt trauma. J. Forensic Sci. 36:410–421, 1991.

324. Cagini, L., Boaron, M., Corneli, G., et al. Rupture of the azygos vein in blunt chest trauma. J. Cardiovasc. Surg. (Torino) 39:249–250, 1998.

325. Sharma, O. P., Rawitscher, R. E. Blunt vena azygos trauma: report of a case and review of world literature. J. Trauma 46:192–195, 1999.

326. Bowles, B. J., Teruya, T., Belzberg, H., Rivkind, A. I. Blunt traumatic azygous vein injury diagnosed by computed tomography: case report and review of the literature. J. Trauma 49:776–779, 2000.

327. Sugimoto, K., Asari, Y., Hirata, M., Imai, H., Ohwada, T. The diagnostic problem associated with blunt traumatic azygous vein injury: delayed appearance of right haemothorax after blunt chest trauma. Injury 29:380–382, 1998.

328. Inoue, H., Iwasaki, M., Shirota, S., Ogawa, J., Shohtsu, A. Total avulsion of the azygos

vein and longitudinal laceration of the mediastinal pleura due to blunt chest trauma: a case report. J. Cardiovasc. Surg. (Torino) 34:67–68, 1993.

329. Boyd, A. D., Glassman, L. R. Trauma to the lung. Chest Surg. Clin. N. Am. 7:263–284, 1997.

330. Kiser, A. C., O'Brien, S. M., Detterbeck, F. C. Blunt tracheobronchial injuries: treatment and outcomes. Ann. Thorac. Surg. 71:2059–2065, 2001.

331. Hankins, J. R., McAslan, T. C., Shin, B., Ayella, R., Cowley, R. A., McLaughlin, J. S. Extensive pulmonary laceration caused by blunt trauma. J. Thorac. Cardiovasc. Surg. 74:519–527, 1977.

332. Mordehai, J., Kurzbart, E., Kapuller, V., Mares, A. J. Tracheal rupture after blunt chest trauma in a child. J. Pediatr. Surg. 32:104–105, 1997.

333. Pratt, L. W., Smith, R. J., Guite, L. A., Jr., Tryzelaar, J. F. Blunt chest trauma with tracheobronchial rupture. Ann. Otol. Rhinol. Laryngol. 93:357–363, 1984.

334. Tomlanovich, M. C. Pulmonary parenchymal injuries. Emerg. Med. Clin. North Am. 1:379–392, 1983.

335. Miller, P. R., Croce, M. A., Bee, T. K., et al. ARDS after pulmonary contusion: accurate measurement of contusion volume identifies high–risk patients. J. Trauma 51:223–228, 2001.

336. Wagner, R. B., Crawford, W. O., Jr., Schimpf, P. P., Jamieson, P. M., Rao, K. C. Quantitation and pattern of parenchymal lung injury in blunt chest trauma. Diagnostic and therapeutic implications. J. Comput. Tomogr. 12:270–281, 1988.

337. Kunisch–Hoppe, M., Hoppe, M., Rauber, K., Popella, C., Rau, W. S. Tracheal rupture caused by blunt chest trauma: radiological and clinical features. Eur. Radiol. 10:480–483, 2000.

338. Mansour, K. A. Trauma to the diaphragm. Chest Surg. Clin. N. Am. 7:373–383, 1997.

339. Rubikas, R. Diaphragmatic injuries. Eur. J. Cardiothorac Surg. 20:53–57, 2001.

340. Rodriguez–Morales, G., Rodriguez, A., Shatney, C. H. Acute rupture of the diaphragm in blunt trauma: analysis of 60 patients. J. Trauma 26:438–444, 1986.

341. Rosati, C. Acute traumatic injury of the diaphragm. Chest Surg. Clin. N. Am. 8:371–379, 1998.

342. Sarna, S., Kivioja, A. Blunt rupture of the diaphragm. A retrospective analysis of 41 patients. Ann. Chir. Gynaecol. 84:261–265, 1995.

343. Lee, W. C., Chen, R. J., Fang, J. F., et al. Rupture of the diaphragm after blunt trauma. Eur. J. Surg. 160:479483, 1994.

344. Kearney, P. A., Rouhana, S. W., Burney, R. E. Blunt rupture of the diaphragm: mechanism,

diagnosis, and treatment. Ann. Emerg. Med. 18:1326–1330, 1989.

345. Reiff, D. A., McGwin, G., Jr., Metzger, J., Windham, S. T., Doss, M., Rue, L. W., III. Identifying injuries and motor vehicle collision characteristics that together are suggestive of diaphragmatic rupture. J. Trauma 53:1139–1145, 2002.

346. Leppaniemi, A., Pohjankyro, A., Haapiainen, R. Acute diaphragmatic rupture after blunt trauma. Ann. Chir. Gynaecol. 83:17–21, 1994.

347. Athanassiadi, K., Kalavrouziotis, G., Athanassiou, M., et al. Blunt diaphragmatic rupture. Eur. J. Cardiothorac. Surg. 15:469–474, 1999.

348. Holm, A., Bessey, P. Q., Aldrete, J. S. Diaphragmatic rupture due to blunt trauma: morbidity and mortality in 42 cases. South. Med. J. 81:956–962, 1988.

349. Humphreys, T. R., Abbuhl, S. Massive bilateral diaphragmatic rupture after an apparently minor automobile accident. Am. J. Emerg. Med. 9:246–249, 1991.

350. Chen, J. C., Wilson, S. E. Diaphragmatic injuries: recognition and management in sixty-two patients. Am. Surg. 57:810–815, 1991.

351. Estrera, A. S., Landay, M. J., McClelland, R. N. Blunt traumatic rupture of the right hemidiaphragm: experience in 12 patients. Ann. Thorac. Surg. 39:525–530, 1985.

352. Meyers, B. F., McCabe, C. J. Traumatic diaphragmatic hernia. Occult marker of serious injury. Ann. Surg. 218:783–790, 1993.

353. Tejerina Alvarez, E. E., Holanda, M. S., Lopez–Espadas, F., Dominguez, M. J., Ots, E., Diaz–Reganon, J. Gastric rupture from blunt abdominal trauma. Injury 35:228–231, 2004.

354. Shinkawa, H., Yasuhara, H., Naka, S., et al. Characteristic features of abdominal organ injuries associated with gastric rupture in blunt abdominal trauma. Am. J. Surg. 187:394–397, 2004.

355. Evers, K., DeGaeta, L. R. Abdominal trauma. Emerg. Med. Clin. North Am. 3:525–539, 1985.

356. Hardy, K. J. Patterns of liver injury after fatal blunt trauma. Surg. Gynecol. Obstet. 134:3943, 1972.

357. Cox, E. F., Flancbaum, L., Dauterive, A. H., Paulson, R. L. Blunt trauma to the liver. Analysis of management and mortality in 323 consecutive patients. Ann. Surg. 207:126–134, 1988.

358. Taff, M. L., Wolodzko, A. A., Boglioli, L. R. Sudden death due to delayed rupture of hepatic subcapsular hematoma following blunt abdominal trauma. Am. J. Forensic Med. Pathol. 11:270–274, 1990.

359. Francque, S., Condat, B., Asselah, T., et al. Multifactorial aetiology of hepatic infarction: a

case report with literature review. Eur. J. Gastroenterol. Hepatol. 16:411–415, 2004.

360. Aoki, Y., Nata, M., Hashiyada, M., Sagisaka, K. Laceration of the liver with delayed massive intra–abdominal hemorrhage: a case report of child abuse. Nippon Hoigaku Zasshi 51:4447, 1997.

361. Goettler, C. E., Stallion, A., Grisoni, E. R., Dudgeon, D. L. Delayed hemorrhage after blunt hepatic trauma: case report. J. Trauma 52:556–559, 2002.

362. Cathey, K. L., Brady, W. J., Jr., Butler, K., Blow, O., Cephas, G. A., Young, J. S. Blunt splenic trauma: characteristics of patients requiring urgent laparotomy. Am. Surg. 64:450–454, 1998.

363. Bellemore, M. C., Power, A. R. Splenic trauma from blunt abdominal injury. Aust. N. Z. J. Surg. 51:3945, 1981.

364. Arden, G. P., Christian, M. S., Williams, E. J. Traumatic rupture of the spleen. Int. Surg. 66:149–153, 1981.

365. Traub, A. C., Perry, J. F., Jr. Injuries associated with splenic trauma. J. Trauma 21:840–847, 1981.

366. Kairaluoma, M. I., Tarkka, M., Mokka, R. E., et al. Traumatic splenic rupture. Ann. Chir. Gynaecol. 66:154–159, 1977.

367. Mclndoe, A. H. Delayed haemorrhage following traumatic rupture of the spleen. Br. J. Surg. 20:249–267, 1931.

368. Dang, C., Schlater, T., Bui, H., Oshita, T. Delayed rupture of the spleen. Ann. Emerg. Med. 19:399–403, 1990.

369. Parithivel, V. S., Sajja, S. B., Basu, A., Schein, M., Gerst, P. H. Delayed presentation of splenic injury: still a common syndrome. Int. Surg. 87:120–124, 2002.

370. Black, J. J., Sinow, R. M., Wilson, S. E., Williams, R. A. Subcapsular hematoma as a predictor of delayed splenic rupture. Am. Surg. 58:732–735, 1992.

371. Washburn, M. E., Balk, M. W., Mazat, B. A., Zurlo, J. A. Experimental subcapsular hematoma of the spleen: natural history and radioisotope scan correlation. Ann. Surg. 187:407–410, 1978.

372. Berlatzky, Y., Shiloni, E., Anner, H., Weiss, Y. "Delayed rupture of the spleen" or delayed diagnosis of the splenic injury? Isr. J. Med. Sci. 16:659–664, 1980.

373. Bergqvist, D., Hedelin, H., Lindblad, B. Traumatic splenic rupture during 30 years. An analysis of 88 cases with special attention to delayed rupture. Acta Chir. Scand. 146:4145, 1980.

374. Hiraide, A., Yamamoto, H., Yahata, K., Yoshioka, T., Sugimoto, T. Delayed rupture of the spleen caused by an intrasplenic pseudoaneurysm following blunt trauma: case report. J.

Trauma 36:743–744, 1994.

375. Clark, O. H., Lim, R. C., Jr., Margaretten, W. Spontaneous delayed splenic rupture–case report of a five–year interval between trauma and diagnosis. J. Trauma 15:245–249, 1975.

376. Fagelman, D., Hertz, M. A., Ross, A. S. Delayed development of splenic subcapsular hematoma: CT evaluation. J. Comput. Assist. Tomogr. 9:815–816, 1985.

377. Benjamin, C. I., Engrav, L. H., Perry, J. F., Jr. Delayed rupture or delayed diagnosis of rupture of the spleen. Surg. Gynecol. Obstet. 142:171–172, 1976.

378. Krause, K. R., Howells, G. A., Bair, H. A., et al. Nonoperative management of blunt splenic injury in adults 55 years and older: a twenty–year experience. Am. Surg. 66:636–640, 2000.

379. Gruenberg, J. C., Horan, D. P. Delayed splenic rupture: the phoenix. J. Trauma 23:159–160, 1983.

380. Brown, R. L., Irish, M. S., McCabe, A. J., Glick, P. L., Caty, M. G. Observation of splenic trauma: when is a little too much? J. Pediatr. Surg. 34:1124–1126, 1999.

381. Farhat, G. A., Abdu, R. A., Vanek, V. W. Delayed splenic rupture: real or imaginary? Am. Surg. 58:340–345, 1992.

382. Blatt, C. J., Meng, C. H. Traumatic subcapsular hematoma in delayed splenic rupture. Am. J. Gastroenterol. 60:592–601, 1973.

383. Jean–Baptiste, C., Suarez, J. R. Subcapsular hematoma of spleen. N. Y. State J. Med. 72:739–741, 1972.

384. Olsen, W. R. Editorial: Delayed rupture of the spleen as an index of diagnostic accuracy. Surg. Gynecol. Obstet. 138:82, 1974.

385. Leppaniemi, A., Haapiainen, R., Standertskjold–Nordenstam, C. G., Taavitsainen, M., Hastbacka, J. Delayed presentation of blunt splenic injury. Am. J. Surg. 155:745–749, 1988.

386. Lieberman, R. C., Welch, C. S. A study of 248 instances of traumatic rupture of the spleen. Surg. Gynecol. Obstet. 127:961–965, 1968.

387. Deva, A. K., Thompson, J. F. Delayed rupture of the spleen 5 1/2 years after conservative management of traumatic splenic injury. Aust. N. Z. J. Surg. 66:494–495, 1996.

388. Andersen, R., Pratt, D., Hitchcock, C. Splenectomy following abdominal trauma. Proceedings of the 13th AAAM Conference 1969. Association for the Advancement of Automotive Medicine, Des Plaines, IL, 1969.

389. Farhi, D. C., Ashfaq, R. Splenic pathology after traumatic injury. Am. J. Clin. Pathol. 105:474–478, 1996.

390. McMahon, M. J., Lintott, J. D., Mair, W. S., Lee, P. W., Duthie, J. S. Occult rupture of the spleen. Br. J. Surg. 64:641–643, 1977.
391. Sizer, J. S., Wayne, E. R., Frederick, P. L. Delayed rupture of the spleen. Review of the literature and report of six cases. Arch. Surg. 92:362–366, 1966.
392. Fernandes, C. M. Splenic rupture manifesting two years after diagnosis of injury. Acad. Emerg. Med. 3:946–947, 1996.
393. Lynch, J. M., Meza, M. P., Newman, B., Gardner, M. J., Albanese, C. T. Computed tomography grade of splenic injury is predictive of the time required for radiographic healing. J. Pediatr. Surg. 32:1093–1095, 1997.
394. Sziklas, J. J., Spencer, R. P., Rosenberg, R. J. Delayed splenic rupture: a suggestion for "predictive monitoring." J. Nucl. Med. 26:609–611, 1985.
395. Reiff, D. A., McGwin, G., Jr., Rue, L. W., III. Splenic injury in side impact motor vehicle collisions: effect of occupant restraints. J. Trauma 51:340–345, 2001.
396. Huelke, D. F., Sherman, H. W., Steigmeyer, J. L. Side impacts to the passenger compartment–clinical studies from field accident investigations. SAE Report 890379. Society of Automotive Engineers, Inc., Warrendale, PA, 1989.
397. Magee, R. B., D'Luzansky, J. J. Acute blunt traumatic rupture of the spleen. Arch. Surg. 99:121–122, 1969.
398. Bailey, J., Shapiro, M. J. Abdominal compartment syndrome. Crit. Care 4:23–29, 2000.
399. Baylis, S. M., Lansing, E. H., Glas, W. W. Traumatic retroperitoneal hematoma. Am. J. Surg. 103:477–480, 1962.
400. Arrizabalaga, M., Benitez, J., Gallardo, C., Garrido, R., Casanueva, T. [Retroperitoneal hematoma secondary to traumatic rupture of the psoas muscle]. Actas Urol. Esp. 14:36–38, 1990.
401. Adams, J. E., Davis, G. G., Heidepriem, R. W., III, Alonso, J. E., Alexander, C. B. Analysis of the incidence of pelvic trauma in fatal automobile accidents. Am. J. Forensic Med. Pathol. 23:132–136, 2002.
402. Richter, M., Otte, D., Gansslen, A., Bartram, H., Pohlemann, T. Injuries of the pelvic ring in road traffic accidents: a medical and technical analysis. Injury 32:123–128, 2001.
403. Dalal SA, Burgess AR, Siegel JH, et al. Pelvic fracture in multiple trauma: classification by mechanism is key to pattern of organ injury, resuscitative requirements, and outcome. J. Trauma 29:981–1000, 1989.
404. MacLeod, M., Powell, J. N. Evaluation of pelvic fractures. Clinical and radiologic. Orthop. Clin. North Am. 28:299–319, 1997.
405. Tile, M. Pelvic ring fractures: should they be fixed? J. Bone Joint Surg. Br. 70:1–12,

1988.

406. McCoy, G. F., Johnstone, R. A., Kenwright, J. Biomechanical aspects of pelvic and hip injuries in road traffic accidents. J. Orthop. Trauma 3:118–123, 1989.
407. Demetriades, D., Karaiskakis, M., Toutouzas, K., Alo, K., Velmahos, G., Chan, L. Pelvic fractures: epidemiology and predictors of associated abdominal injuries and outcomes. J. Am. Coll. Surg. 195:1–10, 2002.
408. Banglmaier, R. F., Rouhana, S. W., Beillas, P., Yang, K. H. Lower extremity injuries in lateral impact: a retrospective study. Annu. Proc. Assoc. Adv. Automot. Med. 47:425–444, 2003.
409. Adams, J. E., Davis, G. G., Alexander, C. B., Alonso, J. E. Pelvic trauma in rapidly fatal motor vehicle accidents. J. Orthop. Trauma 17:406–410, 2003.
410. Rittmeister, M., Lindsey, R. W., Kohl, H. W., III. Pelvic fracture among polytrauma decedents. Trauma–based mortality with pelvic fracture—a case series of 74 patients. Arch. Orthop. Trauma Surg. 121:4349, 2001.
411. Demetriades, D., Karaiskakis, M., Velmahos, G. C., Alo, K., Murray, J., Chan, L. Pelvic fractures in pediatric and adult trauma patients: are they different injuries? J. Trauma 54:1146–1151, 2003.
412. Gansslen, A., Pohlemann, T., Paul, C., Lobenhoffer, P., Tscherne, H. Epidemiology of pelvic ring injuries. Injury 27 Suppl. 1:S–A13–20, 1996.
413. Eastridge, B. J., Burgess, A. R. Pedestrian pelvic fractures: 5–year experience of a major urban trauma center. J. Trauma 42:695–700, 1997.
414. Isler, B., Ganz, R. Classification of pelvic ring injuries. Injury 27 Suppl. 1:S–12, 1996.
415. Suzuki, T., Yoshikawa, K., Umetsu, K., Harada, A. Sudden death from tourniquet shock. Forensic Sci. Int. 61:185–190, 1993.
416. Mellor, A., Soni, N. Fat embolism. Anaesthesia 56:145–154, 2001.
417. Dudney, T. M., Elliott, C. G. Pulmonary embolism from amniotic fluid, fat, and air. Prog. Cardiovasc. Dis. 36:447–474, 1994.
418. Bulger, E. M., Smith, D. G., Maier, R. V, Jurkovich, G. J. Fat embolism syndrome. A 10–year review. Arch. Surg. 132:435–439, 1997.
419. Fulde, G. W., Harrison, P. Fat embolism—a review. Arch. Emerg. Med. 8:233–239, 1991.
420. King, M. B., Harmon, K. R. Unusual forms of pulmonary embolism. Clin. Chest Med. 15:561–580, 1994.
421. Levy, D. The fat embolism syndrome. A review. Clin. Orthop. Relat. Res. 281–286, 1990.
422. ten Duis, H. J. The fat embolism syndrome. Injury 28:77–85, 1997.
423. Johnson, M. J., Lucas, G. L. Fat embolism syndrome. Orthopedics 19:41–48, 1996.

424. Hulman, G. The pathogenesis of fat embolism. J. Pathol. 176:3–9, 1995.
425. Lee, K. A., Opeskin, K. Death due to superficial soft tissue injuries. Am. J. Forensic Med. Pathol. 13:179–185, 1992.
426. Nichols, G. R., Corey, T. S., Davis, G. J. Nonfracture–associated fatal fat embolism in a case of child abuse. J. Forensic Sci. 35:493–499, 1990.
427. Richards, R. R. Fat embolism syndrome. Can. J. Surg. 40:334–339, 1997.
428. Parisi, D. M., Koval, K., Ego,l K. Fat embolism syndrome. Am. J. Orthop. 31:507–512, 2002.
429. Fiallos, M., Kissoon, N., Abdelmoneim, T., et al. Fat embolism with the use of intraosseous infusion during cardiopulmonary resuscitation. Am. J. Med. Sci. 314:73–79, 1997.
430. Hulman, G. Pathogenesis of non–traumatic fat embolism. Lancet 1:1366–1367, 1988.
431. Peltier, L. F. Fat embolism. A current concept. Clin. Orthop. Relat. Res. 66:241–253, 1969.
432. Gossling, H. R., Donohue, T. A. The fat embolism syndrome. JAMA 241:2740–2742, 1979.
433. King, E. G., Wagner, W. W., Jr., Ashbaugh, D. G., Latham, L. P., Halsey, D. R. Alterations in pulmonary microanatomy after fat embolism. In vivo observations via thoracic window of the oleic acid–embolized canine lung. Chest 59:524—530, 1971.
434. Saldeen, T. The importance of intravascular coagulation and inhibition of the fibrinolytic system in experimental fat embolism. J. Trauma 10:287–298, 1970.
435. King, E. G., Weily, H. S., Genton, E., Ashbaugh, D. G. Consumption coagulopathy in the canine oleic acid model of fat embolism. Surgery 69:533–541, 1971.
436. Bradford, D. S., Foster, R. R., Nossel, H. L. Coagulation alterations, hypoxemia, and fat embolism in fracture patients. J. Trauma 10:307–321, 1970.
437. Tedeschi, C. G., Castelli, W., Kropp, G., Tedeschi, L. G. Fat macroglobulinemia and fat embolism. Surg. Gynecol. Obstet. 126:83–90, 1968.
438. Muller, C., Rahn, B. A., Pfister, U., Meinig, R. P. The incidence, pathogenesis, diagnosis, and treatment of fat embolism. Orthop. Rev. 23:107–117, 1994.
439. Robert, J. H., Hoffmeyer, P., Broquet, P. E., Cerutti, P., Vasey, H. Fat embolism syndrome. Orthop. Rev. 22:567–571, 1993.
440. Davison, P. R., Cohle, S. D. Histologic detection of fat emboli. J. Forensic Sci. 32:1426–1430, 1987.
441. Buchanan, D., Mason, J. K. Occurrence of pulmonary fat and bone marrow embolism. Am. J. Forensic Med. Pathol. 3:73–78, 1982.
442. Suzuki, T., Ikeda, N., Umetsu, K. Pulmonary bone marrow embolic phenomena.

Antemortem reactions in traumatic immediate death. Am. J. Forensic Med. Pathol. 8:283–286, 1987.

443. Dzieciol, J., Kemona, A., Gorska, M., et al. Widespread myocardial and pulmonary bone marrow embolism following cardiac massage. Forensic Sci. Int. 56:195–199, 1992.

444. Shackford, S. R., Davis, J. W., Hollingsworth–Fridlund, P., Brewer, N. S., Hoyt, D. B., Mackersie, R. C. Venous thromboembolism in patients with major trauma. Am. J. Surg. 159:365–369, 1990.

445. Knudson, M. M., Ikossi, D. G. Venous thromboembolism after trauma. Curr. Opin. Crit. Care 10:539–548, 2004.

446. Anderson, F. A., Jr., Spencer, F. A. Risk factors for venous thromboembolism. Circulation 107:I9–I16, 2003.

447. Knudson, M. M., Ikossi, D. G., Khaw, L., Morabito, D., Speetzen, L. S. Thromboembolism after trauma: an analysis of 1602 episodes from the American College of Surgeons National Trauma Data Bank. Ann. Surg. 240:490–496, 2004.

448. Meissner, M. H. Deep venous thrombosis in the trauma patient. Semin. Vasc. Surg. 11:274–282, 1998.

449. McBride, W. J., Gadowski, G. R., Keller, M. S., Vane, D. W. Pulmonary embolism in pediatric trauma patients. J. Trauma 37:913–915, 1994.

450. Vavilala, M. S., Nathens, A. B., Jurkovich, G. J., Mackenzie, E., Rivara, F. P. Risk factors for venous thromboembolism in pediatric trauma. J. Trauma 52:922–927, 2002.

451. Geerts, W. H., Code, K. I., Jay, R. M., Chen, E., Szalai, J. P. A prospective study of venous thromboembolism after major trauma. N. Engl. J. Med. 331:1601–1606, 1994.

452. Kearon, C. Natural history of venous thromboembolism. Circulation 107:I22–I30, 2003.

453. Sevitt, S., Gallagher, N. Venous thrombosis and pulmonary embolism. A clinico–patholog–ical study in injured and burned patients. Br. J. Surg. 48:475–489, 1961.

454. Sevitt, S. Fatal road accidents. Injuries, complications, and causes of death in 250 subjects. Br. J. Surg. 55:481–505, 1968.

455. McManus, B. M., Allard, M. F., Yanagawa, B. Hemodynamic disorders. In: Rubin, E., Gorstein, F., Rubin, R., Schwarting, R., Strayer, D., eds. Rubin's Pathology: Clinicopathologic Foundations of Medicine. 4th edition. Lippincott Williams and Wilkins, Baltimore, pp. 280–311, 2005.

456. Davis, G. J., McCloud, L. C., Nichols, G. R., Martin, A. W. Cerebral tissue pulmonary embolization due to head trauma: a case report with immunohistochemical confirmation. J. Forensic Sci. 36:921–925, 1991.

457. King, D. E. Discussion of "Cerebral tissue embolization due to head trauma: a case report

with immunohistochemical confirmation." J. Forensic Sci. 37:682–684, 1992.
458. Collins, K. A., Davis, G. J. A retrospective and prospective study of cerebral tissue pulmonary embolism in severe head trauma. J. Forensic Sci. 39:624–628, 1994.
459. McMillan, J. B. Emboli of cerebral tissue in the lungs following severe head injury. Am. J. Pathol. 32:405–415, 1956.
460. Tackett, L. R. Brain tissue pulmonary emboli. Arch. Pathol. 78:292–294, 1964.
461. Karkola, K., Mottonen, M. Embolism of brain tissue to the pulmonary arteries after head injury. Med. Sci. Law 11:149–150, 1971.
462. Torry, J. M. Massive brain tissue and fat pulmonary embolism following severe head injury. Med. Sci. Law 27:128–131, 1987.
463. Takatsu, A., Shigeta, A., Abe, M., Kitune, K., Kawai, T. Embolism of massive hepatic tissue in inferior vena cava and right atrium after closed liver injury. Am. J. Forensic Med. Pathol. 9:233–235, 1988.
464. Voitk, A. J., Munkittrick, R. C. A fatal pulmonary embolus composed of gross liver tissue. Can. J. Surg. 29:218–219, 1986.
465. Michalodimitrakis, M., Tsatsakis, A. Massive pulmonary embolism by liver tissue. Med. Sci. Law 38:85–87, 1998.
466. Moar, J. J. Pulmonary embolism due to hepatic tissue—a forensic vital sign? A case report. S. Afr. Med. J. 66:699–700, 1984.
467. Olcott, C., Robinson, A. J., Maxwell, T. M., Griffin, H. A. Amniotic fluid embolism and disseminated intravascular coagulation after blunt abdominal trauma. J. Trauma 13:737–740, 1973.
468. Lau, G., Chui, P. P. Amniotic fluid embolism: a review of 10 fatal cases. Singapore Med. J. 35:180–183, 1994.
469. Judich, A., Kuriansky, J., Engelberg, I., Haik, J., Shabtai, M., Czerniak, A. Amniotic fluid embolism following blunt abdominal trauma in pregnancy. Injury 29:475–477, 1998.
470. Lau, G. Pulmonary cartilage embolism: fact or artefact? Am. J. Forensic Med. Pathol. 16:51–53, 1995.
471. Veinot, J. P., Edwards, W. D. Trauma–related embolization of cartilage to the lungs. Case report of a 41–year–old man. Am. J. Forensic Med. Pathol. 15:138–141, 1994.
472. Messmer, J. M. Massive head trauma as a cause of intravascular air. J. Forensic Sci. 29:418424, 1984.
473. Slater, D. N. Bone marrow emboli. Am. J. Forensic Med. Pathol. 9:357–358, 1988.
474. Merigian, K. S., Roberts, J. R. Cocaine intoxication: hyperpyrexia, rhabdomyolysis and acute renal failure. J. Toxicol. Clin. Toxicol. 25:135–148, 1987.

475. Nolte, K. B. Rhabdomyolysis associated with cocaine abuse. Hum. Pathol. 22:1141–1145, 1991.

476. Korantzopoulos, P., Papaioannides, D., Sinapidis, D., Kolios, P. Acute rhabdomyolysis due to prolonged exposure to the cold. Int. J. Clin. Pract. 57:243–244, 2003.

477. Lazarus, D., Hudson, D. A. Fatal rhabdomyolysis in a flame burn patient. Burns 23:446–450, 1997.

478. Poels, P. J., Gabreels, F. J. Rhabdomyolysis: a review of the literature. Clin. Neurol. Neurosurg. 95:175–192, 1993.

479. Brumback, R. A., Feeback, D. L., Leech, R. W. Rhabdomyolysis following electrical injury. Semin. Neurol. 15:329–334, 1995.

480. Bonnor, R., Siddiqui, M., Ahuja, T. S. Rhabdomyolysis associated with near-drowning. Am. J. Med. Sci. 318:201–202, 1999.

481. Chaikin, H. L. Rhabdomyolysis secondary to drug overdose and prolonged coma. South. Med. J. 73:990–994, 1980.

482. Mercieca, J., Brown, E.A. Acute renal failure due to rhabdomyolysis associated with use of a straitjacket in lysergide intoxication. Br. Med. J. (Clin. Res. Ed.) 288:1949–1950, 1984.

483. Horowitz, R., Siegel, J., Flaster, M., Maldonado, W. E. Injury patterns in motor vehicle fatalities. J. Forensic Sci. 32:167–172, 1987.

484. Tonge, J. I., O'Reilly, M. J., Davison, A., Johnston, N. G., Wilkey, I. S. Traffic-crash fatalities 1968–73.: injury patterns and other factors. Med. Sci. Law 17:9–24, 1977.

485. Akane, A., Shiono, H., Matsubara, K., Takahashi, S. Identification of the driver in an automobile collision. Am. J. Forensic Med. Pathol. 11:246–251, 1990.

486. Smock, W. S., Nichols, G. R., Fuller, P. M., Weakley-Jones, B. The forensic pathologist and the determination of driver versus passenger in motor vehicle collisions. The need to examine injury mechanisms, occupant kinematics, vehicle dynamics, and trace evidence. Am. J. Forensic Med. Pathol. 10:105–114, 1989.

487. Daffner, R. H., Deeb, Z. L., Lupetin, A. R., Rothfus, W. E. Patterns of high-speed impact injuries in motor vehicle occupants. J. Trauma 28:498–501, 1988.

488. Sweitzer, R. E., Rink, R. D., Corey, T., Goldsmith, J. Children in motor vehicle collisions: analysis of injury by restraint use and seat location. J. Forensic Sci. 47:1049–1054, 2002.

489. Weisz, G. M., Schramek, A., Barzilai, A. Injury to the driver. J. Trauma 14:212–215, 1974.

490. Yoganandan, N., Pintar, F. A., Gennarelli, T. A., Maltese, M. R. Patterns of abdominal injuries in frontal and side impacts. Annu. Proc. Assoc. Adv. Automot. Med. 44:17–36,

2000.

491. Stefanopoulos, N., Vagianos, C., Stavropoulos, M., Panagiotopoulos, E., Androulakis, J. Deformations and intrusions of the passenger compartment as indicators of injury severity and triage in head−on collisions of non−airbag−carrying vehicles. Injury 34:487−492, 2003.

492. Mittleman, R. E. Cervical airway injuries as a result of impact with steering wheel rim. J. Forensic Sci. 33:1198−1205, 1988.

493. Fildes, B., Lenard, J., Lane, J., Vulcan, P., Seyer, K. Lower limb injuries to passenger car occupants. Accid. Anal. Prev. 29:785−791, 1997.

494. Acierno, S., Kaufman, R., Rivara, F. P., Grossman, D. C., Mock, C. Vehicle mismatch: injury patterns and severity. Accid. Anal. Prev. 36:761−772, 2004.

495. Siegel, J. H., Mason−Gonzalez, S., Dischinger, P., et al. Safety belt restraints and compartment intrusions in frontal and lateral motor vehicle crashes: mechanisms of injuries, complications, and acute care costs. J. Trauma 34:736−758, 1993.

496. Richter, M., Thermann, H., Wippermann, B., Otte, D., Schratt, H. E., Tscherne, H. Foot fractures in restrained front seat car occupants: a long−term study over twenty−three years. J. Orthop. Trauma 15:287−293, 2001.

497. Thomas, P., Bradford, M. The nature and source of the head injuries sustained by restrained front−seat car occupants in frontal collisions. Accid. Anal. Prev. 27:561−570, 1995.

498. Swierzewski, M. J., Feliciano, D. V., Lillis, R. P., Illig, K. A., States, J. D. Deaths from motor vehicle crashes: patterns of injury in restrained and unrestrained victims. J. Trauma 37:404−407, 1994.

499. Williams, J. S., Kirkpatrick, J. R. The nature of seat belt injuries. J. Trauma 11:207−218, 1971.

500. Garrett, J. W., Braunstein, P. W. The seat belt syndrome. J. Trauma 2:220−238, 1962.

501. Asbun, H. J., Irani, H., Roe, E. J., Bloch, J. H. Intra−abdominal seatbelt injury. J. Trauma 30:189−193, 1990.

502. Hill, J. R., Mackay, G. M., Morris, A. P. Chest and abdominal injuries caused by seat belt loading. Accid. Anal. Prev. 26:11−26, 1994.

503. Sato, T. B. Effects of seat belts and injuries resulting from improper use. J. Trauma 27:754−758, 1987.

504. Arajarvi, E., Santavirta, S. Chest injuries sustained in severe traffic accidents by seatbelt wearers. J. Trauma 29:37−41, 1989.

505. Reid, A. B., Letts, R. M., Black, G. B. Pediatric Chance fractures: association with

intraabdominal injuries and seatbelt use. J. Trauma 30:384–391, 1990.

506. Miltner, E., Salwender, H. J. Influencing factors on the injury severity of restrained front seat occupants in car–to–car head–on collisions. Accid. Anal. Prev. 27:143–150, 1995.

507. Santavirta, S., Arajarvi, E. Ruptures of the heart in seatbelt wearers. J. Trauma 32:275–279, 1992.

508. Munshi, I. A., Patton, W. A unique pattern of injury secondary to seatbelt–related blunt abdominal trauma. J. Emerg. Med. 27:183–185, 2004.

509. Rutledge, R., Thomason, M., Oller, D., et al. The spectrum of abdominal injuries associated with the use of seat belts. J. Trauma 31:820–825, 1991.

510. Prince, J. S., LoSasso, B. E., Senac, M. O., Jr. Unusual seat–belt injuries in children. J. Trauma 56:420–427, 2004.

511. Nadjem, H., Ropohl, D. Complete transection of the trunk of passengers in car accidents. Am. J. Forensic Med. Pathol. 17:167–171, 1996.

512. Bergqvist, D., Dahlgren, S., Hedelin, H. Rupture of the diaphragm in patients wearing seatbelts. J. Trauma 18:781–783, 1978.

513. Anderson, P. A., Rivara, F. P., Maier, R. V., Drake, C. The epidemiology of seatbelt–associated injuries. J. Trauma 31:60–67, 1991.

514. Tso, E. L., Beaver, B. L., Haller, J. A., Jr. Abdominal injuries in restrained pediatric passengers. J. Pediatr. Surg. 28:915–919, 1993.

515. Pedersen, S., Jansen, U. Intestinal lesions caused by incorrectly placed seat belts. Acta Chir. Scand. 145:15–18, 1979.

516. Arajarvi, E., Santavirta, S., Tolonen, J. Abdominal injuries sustained in severe traffic accidents by seatbelt wearers. J. Trauma 27:393–397, 1987.

517. Gaines, B. A., Shultz, B. S., Morrison, K., Ford, H. R. Duodenal injuries in children: beware of child abuse. J. Pediatr. Surg. 39:600–602, 2004.

518. Hughes, T. M., Elton, C. The pathophysiology and management of bowel and mesenteric injuries due to blunt trauma. Injury 33:295–302, 2002.

519. Vandersluis, R., O'Connor, H. M. The seat–belt syndrome. CMAJ 137:1023–1024, 1987.

520. Hudson, I., Kavanagh, T. G. Duodenal transection and vertebral injury occurring in combination in a patient wearing a seat belt. Injury 15:6–9, 1983.

521. Slavin, R. E., Borzotta, A. P. The seromuscular tear and other intestinal lesions in the seatbelt syndrome: a clinical and pathologic study of 29 cases. Am. J. Forensic Med. Pathol. 23:214–222, 2002.

522. Statter, M. B., Coran, A. G. Appendiceal transection in a child associated with a lap belt restraint: case report. J. Trauma 33:765–766, 1992.

523. Freeman, C. P. Isolated pancreatic damage following seat belt injury. Injury 16:478–480, 1985.

524. Warrian, R. K., Shoenut, J. P., Iannicello, C. M., Sharma, G. P., Trenholm, B. G. Seatbelt injury to the abdominal aorta. J. Trauma 28:1505–1507, 1988.

525. Randhawa, M. P., Jr., Menzoian, J. O. Seat belt aorta. Ann. Vasc. Surg. 4:370–377, 1990.

526. Siriwardena, A. K. Seat–belt aortic injury. Eur. J. Vasc. Surg. 4:649–650, 1990.

527. Ali, M. R., Jr., Norcross, E. D., Brothers TE. Iliac and femoral artery occlusion by thromboemboli from an abdominal aortic aneurysm in the setting of blunt abdominal trauma. J. Vasc. Surg. 27:545–548, 1998.

528. Dajee, H., Richardson, I. W., Iype, M. O. Seat belt aorta: acute dissection and thrombosis of the abdominal aorta. Surgery 85:263–267, 1979.

529. Naude, G. P., Back, M., Perry, M. O., Bongard, F. S. Blunt disruption of the abdominal aorta: report of a case and review of the literature. J. Vasc. Surg. 25:931–935, 1997.

530. Riches, K. J., James, R. A., Gilbert, J. D., Byard, R. W. Fatal childhood vascular injuries associated with seat belt use. Am. J. Forensic Med. Pathol. 23:45–47, 2002.

531. Dell'Erba, A., Di Vella, G., Giardino, N. Seatbelt injury to the common iliac artery: case report. J. Forensic Sci. 43:215–217, 1998.

532. DeCou, J. M., Abrams, R. S., Gauderer, M. W. Seat–belt transection of the pararenal vena cava in a 5–year–old child: survival with caval ligation. J. Pediatr. Surg. 34:1074–1076, 1999.

533. Huelke, D. F., Kaufer, H. Vertebral column injuries and seat belts. J. Trauma 15:304—318, 1975.

534. Astarita, D. C., Feldman, B. Seat belt placement resulting in uterine rupture. J. Trauma 42:738–740, 1997.

535. Matthews, C. D. Incorrectly used seat belt associated with uterine rupture following vehicular collision. Am. J. Obstet. Gynecol. 121:1115–1116, 1975.

536. Pepperell, R. J., Rubinstein, E., MacIsaac, I. A. Motor–car accidents during pregnancy. Med. J. Aust. 1:203–205, 1977.

537. van Enk, A., van Zwam, W. Uterine rupture. A seat belt hazard. Acta Obstet. Gynecol. Scand. 73:432–433, 1994.

538. Klinich, K. D., Schneider, L. W., Moore, J. L., Pearlman, M. D. Investigations of crashes involving pregnant occupants. Annu. Proc. Assoc. Adv. Automot. Med. 44:37–55, 2000.

539. Lavin, J. P., Jr., Polsky, S. S. Abdominal trauma during pregnancy. Clin. Perinatol. 10:423–438, 1983.

540. Lifschultz, B. D., Donoghue, E. R. Fetal death following maternal trauma: two case

reports and a survey of the literature. J. Forensic Sci. 36:1740–1744, 1991.

541. Bunai, Y., Nagai, A., Nakamura, I., Ohya, I. Fetal death from abruptio placentae associated with incorrect use of a seatbelt. Am. J. Forensic Med. Pathol. 21:207–209, 2000.

542. Evrard, J. R., Sturner, W. Q., Murray, E. J. Fetal skull fracture from an automobile accident. Am. J. Forensic Med. Pathol. 10:232–234, 1989.

543. Fries, M. H., Hankins, G. D. Motor vehicle accident associated with minimal maternal trauma but subsequent fetal demise. Ann. Emerg. Med. 18:301–304, 1989.

544. Ford, R. M., Picker, R. H. Fetal head injury following motor vehicle accident; an unusual case of intrauterine death. Aust. N. Z. J. Obstet. Gynaecol. 29:72–73, 1989.

545. Gogler, H., Athanasiadis, S. Fatal cervical dislocation related to wearing a seat belt: a case report. Injury 10:196–200, 1979.

546. Skold, G., Voigt, G. E. Spinal injuries in belt-wearing car occupants killed by head-on collisions. Injury 9:151–161, 1977.

547. Sumchai, A., Eliastam, M., Werner, P. Seatbelt cervical injury in an intersection type vehicular collision. J. Trauma 28:1384–1388, 1988.

548. Spitz, D. J., Prator, P. C., Stratton, J. E., et al. Neck injuries caused by automatic two-point seat belts: an analysis of four cases. J. Forensic Sci. 50:159–163, 2005.

549. Saldeen, T. Fatal neck injuries caused by use of diagonal safety belts. J. Trauma 7:856–862, 1967.

550. Veenema, K. R. Strangulation associated with a passive restraint shoulder harness seatbelt: case report. J. Emerg. Med. 12:317–320, 1994.

551. McConnell, E. J., Macbeth, G. A. Common carotid artery and tracheal injury from shoulder strap seat belt. J. Trauma 43:150–152, 1997.

552. Roh, L. S., Fazzalaro, W. Transection of trachea due to improper application of automatic seat belt (submarine effect). J. Forensic Sci. 38:972–977, 1993.

553. Uemura, K., Yoshida, K. Seat belt induced transection of the trachea in a child on the lap of an adult. J. Forensic Sci. 46:714–716, 2001.

554. Gill, S. S., Dierking, J. M., Nguyen, K. T., Woollen, C. D., Morrow, C. E. Seatbelt injury causing perforation of the cervical esophagus: a case report and review of the literature. Am. Surg. 70:32–34, 2004.

555. Woelfel, G. F., Moore, E. E., Cogbill, T. H., Van, W. C., III. Severe thoracic and abdominal injuries associated with lap-harness seatbelts. J. Trauma 24:166–167, 1984.

556. Arajarvi, E., Santavirta, S., Tolonen, J. Aortic ruptures in seat belt wearers. J. Thorac. Cardiovasc. Surg. 98:355–361, 1989.

557. Hampson, S., Coombs, R., Hemingway, A. Fractures of the upper thoracic spine—an

addition to the "seat–belt" syndrome. Br. J. Radiol. 1984; 57:1033–1034.

558. Reddy, K., Furer, M., West, M., Hamonic, M. Carotid artery dissection secondary to seatbelt trauma: case report. J. Trauma 30:630–633, 1990.

559. Baik, S., Uku, J. M., Joo, K. G. Seat–belt injuries to the left common carotid artery and left internal carotid artery. Am. J. Forensic Med. Pathol. 9:38–39, 1988.

560. Ruskey, J., Lieberman, M. E., Shaikh, K. A., Talucci, R. C. Unusual subclavian artery lacerations resulting from lap–shoulder seatbelt trauma: case reports. J. Trauma 29:1598–1600, 1989.

561. Wexler, L., Silverman, J. Traumatic rupture of the innominate artery—a seat–belt injury. N. Engl. J. Med. 282:1186–1187, 1970.

562. Hamilton, J. R., Dearden, C., Rutherford, W. H. Myocardial contusion associated with fracture of the sternum: important features of the seat belt syndrome. Injury 16:155–156, 1984.

563. Nadesan, K. Murder and robbery by vehicular impact: true vehicular homicide. Am. J. Forensic Med. Pathol. 21:107–113, 2000.

564. Pearlman, M. D., Phillips, M. E. Safety belt use during pregnancy. Obstet. Gynecol. 88:1026–1029, 1996.

565. Tyroch, A. H., Kaups, K. L., Rohan, J., Song, S., Beingesser, K. Pregnant women and car restraints: beliefs and practices. J. Trauma 46:241–245, 1999.

566. Agran, P. F., Dunkle, D. E., Winn, D. G. Injuries to a sample of seatbelted children evaluated and treated in a hospital emergency room. J. Trauma 27:58–64, 1987.

567. Gorski, Z. M., German, A., Nowak, E. S. Examination and analysis of seat belt loading marks. J. Forensic Sci. 35:69–79, 1990.

568. Chandler, C. F., Lane, J. S., Waxman, K. S. Seatbelt sign following blunt trauma is associated with increased incidence of abdominal injury. Am. Surg. 63:885–888, 1997.

569. Ball, S. T., Vaccaro, A. R., Albert, T. J., Cotler, J. M. Injuries of the thoracolumbar spine associated with restraint use in head–on motor vehicle accidents. J. Spinal Disord. 13:297–304, 2000.

570. Williams, R. D., Sargent, F. T. The mechanism of intestinal injury in trauma. J. Trauma 3:288–294, 1963.

571. Crosby, W. M., Costiloe, J. P. Safety of lap–belt restraint for pregnant victims of automobile collisions. N. Engl. J. Med. 284:632–636, 1971.

572. Agran, P. F., Dunkle, D. E., Winn, D. G., Kent, D. Fetal death in motor vehicle accidents. Ann. Emerg. Med. 16:1355–1358, 1987.

573. Sidky, I. H., Daikoku, N. H., Gopal, J. Insignificant blunt maternal trauma with lethal fetal

outcome: a case report. Md. Med. J. 40:1083–1085, 1991.

574. Hagmann, C. F., Schmitt-Mechelke, T., Caduff, J. H., Berger, T. M. Fetal intracranial injuries in a preterm infant after maternal motor vehicle accident: a case report. Pediatr. Crit. Care Med. 5:396–398, 2004.

575. Lane, P. L. Traumatic fetal deaths. J. Emerg. Med. 7:433435, 1989.

576. Karimi, P., Ramus, R., Urban, J., Perlman, J. M. Extensive brain injury in a premature infant following a relatively minor maternal motor vehicle accident with airbag deployment. J. Perinatol. 24:454–457, 2004.

577. Bowdler, N., Faix, R. G., Elkins, T. Fetal skull fracture and brain injury after a maternal automobile accident. A case report. J. Reprod. Med. 32:375–378, 1987.

578. Yoganandan, N., Morgan, R. M., Eppinger, R. H., Pintar, F. A., Sances, A., Jr., Williams, A. Mechanisms of thoracic injury in frontal impact. J. Biomech. Eng. 118:595–597, 1996.

579. Shkrum, M. J., McClafferty, K. J., Nowak, E. S., German, A. Driver and front seat passenger fatalities associated with air bag deployment. Part 1: A Canadian study. J. Forensic Sci. 47:1028–1034, 2002.

580. Sato, Y., Ohshima, T., Kondo, T. Air bag injuries — a literature review in consideration of demands in forensic autopsies. Forensic Sci. Int. 128:162–167, 2002.

581. Wallis, L. A., Greaves, I. Injuries associated with airbag deployment. Emerg. Med. J. 19:490–493, 2002.

582. McGwin, G., Jr., Metzger, J., Alonso, J. E., Rue, L. W., III. The association between occupant restraint systems and risk of injury in frontal motor vehicle collisions. J. Trauma 54:1182–1187, 2003.

583. Martin, P. G., Crandall, J. R., Pilkey, W. D. Injury trends of passenger car drivers in frontal crashes in the USA. Accid. Anal. Prev. 32:541–557, 2000.

584. Estrada, L. S., Alonso, J. E., McGwin, G., Jr., Metzger, J., Rue, L. W., III. Restraint use and lower extremity fractures in frontal motor vehicle collisions. J. Trauma 57:323–328, 2004.

585. McGovern, M. K., Murphy, R. X., Jr., Okunski, W. J., Wasser, T. E. The influence of air bags and restraining devices on extremity injuries in motor vehicle collisions. Ann. Plast. Surg. 44:481–485, 2000.

586. Shkrum, M. J., McClafferty, K. J., Nowak, E. S., German, A. Driver and front seat passenger fatalities associated with air bag deployment. Part 2: A review of injury patterns and investigative issues. J. Forensic Sci. 47:1035–1040, 2002.

587. McKay, M. P., Jolly, B. T. A retrospective review of air bag deaths. Acad. Emerg. Med. 6:708–714, 1999.

588. Lau, I. V., Horsch, J. D., Viano, D. C., Andrzejak, D. V. Mechanism of injury from air bag deployment loads. Accid. Anal. Prev. 25:29–45, 1993.

589. National Highway Traffic Safety Administration. Various reports provided at: http://www-nrd.nhtsa.dot.gov/departments/nrd-30/ncsa/TextVer/SCI.html, 2005.

590. Chidester, A. B., Rutland, K. W. Air bag crash investigations. Paper 98–S6–O–02. Proceedings of the 16th International Technical Conference on the Enhanced Safety of Vehicles. National Highway Traffic Safety Administration, Washington, DC, 1998.

591. Centers for Disease Control and Prevention. Air–bag–associated fatal injuries to infants and children riding in front passenger seats—United States. JAMA 274:1752–1753, 1995.

592. Werner, J. V., Sorenson, W. W. Survey of airbag involved accidents. An analysis of collision characteristics, system effectiveness and injuries. SAE Report 940802. Society of Automotive Engineers, Inc., Warrendale, PA, 1994.

593. Dalmotas, D. J., German, A., Hendrick, B. E., Hurley, R. M. Airbag deployments: the Canadian experience. J. Trauma 38:476–481, 1995.

594. Huelke, D. F., Reed, R. T. Front seat passenger and air bag deployments. Paper 96–S1–O–2. Proceedings of the 15th International Technical Conference on the Enhanced Safety of Vehicles. National Highway Traffic Safety Administration, Washington, DC, 1996.

595. Huelke, D. F., Reed, R. T. Cranial–vertebral fractures and dislocations associated with steering wheel airbag deployment. Paper 96–S1–O–01. Proceedings of the 15th International Technical Conference on the Enhanced Safety of Vehicles. National Highway Traffic Safety Administration, Washington, DC, 1996.

596. Perez, J., Palmatier, T. Air bag–related fatality in a short, forward–positioned driver. Ann. Emerg. Med. 28:722–724, 1996.

597. Hansen, T. P., Nielsen, A. L., Thomsen, T. K., Knudsen, P. J. Avulsion of the occipital bone—an airbag–specific injury. Lancet 353:1409–1410, 1999.

598. Huff, G. F., Bagwell, S. P., Bachman, D. Airbag injuries in infants and children: a case report and review of the literature. Pediatrics 102:e2, 1998.

599. Augenstein, J. S., Digges, K. H., Lombardo, L. V., et al. Occult abdominal injuries to airbag– protected crash victims: a challenge to trauma systems. J. Trauma 38:502–508, 1995.

600. Augenstein, J. S., Perdeck, E. B., Murtha, M., et al. Injuries sustained by drivers in air bag crashes. Paper 96–S10–O–01. Proceedings of the 15th International Technical Conference on the Enhanced Safety of Vehicles. National Highway Traffic Safety Administration, Washington, DC, 1996.

601. Smock, W. S., Nichols, G. R. Airbag module cover injuries. J. Trauma 38:489–493, 1995.

602. Brown, D. K., Roe, E. J., Henry, T. E. A fatality associated with the deployment of an automobile airbag. J. Trauma 39:1204–1206, 1995.

603. Hollands, C. M., Winston, F. K., Stafford, P. W., Shochat, S. J. Severe head injury caused by airbag deployment. J. Trauma 41:920–922, 1996.

604. Cooper, J. T., Balding, L. E., Jordan, F. B. Airbag mediated death of a two-year-old child wearing a shoulder/lap belt. J. Forensic Sci. 43:1077–1081, 1998.

605. German, A., Dalmotas, D. J., Hurley, R. M. Air bag collision performance in a restrained occupant population. Paper 98-S5-O-04. Proceedings of the 16th International Technical Conference on the Enhanced Safety of Vehicles. National Highway Traffic Safety Administration, Washington, DC, 1998.

606. Maxeiner, H., Hahn, M. Airbag-induced lethal cervical trauma. J. Trauma 42:1148–1151, 1997.

607. Dalmotas, D. J., Hurley, R. M., German, A. Supplemental restraint systems: friend or foe to belted occupants? Proceedings of the 40th AAAM Conference. Association for the Advancement of Automotive Medicine, Des Plaines, IL, 1996.

608. McCaffrey, M., German, A., Lalonde, F., Letts, M. Air bags and children: a potentially lethal combination. J. Pediatr. Orthop. 19:60–64, 1999.

609. German, A., Dalmotas, D. J., Comeau, J. L., Monk, B., Contant, P., Gou, M. In-depth investigation and reconstruction of an air bag induced child fatality. Paper 98-S5-W-19. Proceedings of the 16th International Technical Conference on the Enhanced Safety of Vehicles. National Highway Traffic Safety Administration, Washington, DC, 1998.

610. Morrison, A. L., Chute, D., Radentz, S., Golle, M., Troncoso, J. C., Smialek, J. E. Air bag-associated injury to a child in the front passenger seat. Am. J. Forensic Med. Pathol. 19:218–222, 1998.

611. Huelke, D. F. An overview of air bag deployment and related injuries. Case studies and a review of the literature. SAE Report 950866. Society of Automotive Engineers, Inc., Warrendale, PA, 1995.

612. Giguere, J. F., St. Vil, D., Turmel, A., et al. Airbags and children: a spectrum of C-spine injuries. J. Pediatr. Surg. 33:811–816, 1998.

613. Gossman, W., June, R. A., Wallace, D. Fatal atlanto-occipital dislocation secondary to airbag deployment. Am. J. Emerg. Med. 17:741–742, 1999.

614. Bailey, H., Perez, N., Blank-Reid, C., Kaplan, L. J. Atlanto-occipital dislocation: an unusual lethal airbag injury. J. Emerg. Med. 18:215–219, 2000.

615. Blacksin, M. F. Patterns of fracture after air bag deployment. J. Trauma 35:840–843, 1993.

616. Traynelis, V. C., Gold, M. Cervical spine injury in an air–bag–equipped vehicle. J. Spinal Disord. 6:60–61, 1993.
617. Perdikis, G., Schmitt, T., Chait, D., Richards, A. T. Blunt laryngeal fracture: another airbag injury. J. Trauma 48:544–546, 2000.
618. Roberts, D., Pexa, C., Clarkowski, B., Morey, M., Murphy, M. Fatal laryngeal injury in an achondroplastic dwarf secondary to airbag deployment. Pediatr. Emerg. Care 15:260–261, 1999.
619. Dalmotas, D. J., Hurley, J., German, A., Digges, K. Air bag deployment crashes in Canada. Paper 96–S1–O–05. Proceedings of the 15th International Technical Conference on the Enhanced Safety of Vehicles. National Highway Traffic Safety Administration, Washington, DC, 1996.
620. Tenofsky, P. L., Porter, S. W., Shaw, J. W. Fatal airway compromise due to retropharyngeal hematoma after airbag deployment. Am. Surg. 66:692–694, 2000.
621. Willis, B. K., Smith, J. L., Falkner, L. D., Vernon, D. D., Walker, M. L. Fatal air bag mediated craniocervical trauma in a child. Pediatr. Neurosurg. 24:323–327, 1996.
622. Duncan, M. A., Dowd, N., Rawluk, D., Cunningham, A. J. Traumatic bilateral internal carotid artery dissection following airbag deployment in a patient with fibromuscular dysplasia. Br. J. Anaesth. 85:476–478, 2000.
623. Augenstein, J. S., Perdeck, E., Williamson, J., et al. Heart injuries among restrained occupants in frontal crashes. SAE Report 970392. Society of Automotive Engineers, Inc., Warrendale, PA, 1997.
624. Lancaster, G. I., DeFrance, J. H., Borruso, J. J. Air–bag–associated rupture of the right atrium. N. Engl. J. Med. 328:358, 1993.
625. Pillgram–Larsen, J., Geiran, O. [Air bags influence the pattern of injury in severe thoracic trauma]. Tidsskr. Nor. Laegeforen117:2437–2439, 1997.
626. Jumbelic, M. I. Fatal injuries in a minor traffic collision. J. Forensic Sci. 40:492–494, 1995.
627. Sharma, O. P., Mousset, X. R. Review of tricuspid valve injury after airbag deployment: presentation of a case and discussion of mechanism of injury. J. Trauma 48:152–156, 2000.
628. Hanna, K. M., Weiman, D. S., Pate, J. W., Wolf, B. A., Fabian, T. C. Aortic valve injury secondary to blunt trauma from an air bag. Tenn. Med. 90:195–196, 1997.
629. Reiland–Smith, J., Weintraub, R. M., Sellke, F. W. Traumatic aortic valve injury sustained despite the deployment of an automobile air bag. Chest 103:1603, 1993.
630. DeGuzman, B. J., Morgan, A. S., Pharr, W. F. Aortic transection following air–bag

deployment. N. Engl. J. Med. 337:573–574, 1997.

631. Dunn, J. A., Williams, M. G. Occult ascending aortic rupture in the presence of an air bag. Ann. Thorac. Surg. 62:577–578, 1996.

632. Coben, L. E. The risk and benefits of air bag systems: are they needlessly killing and injuring motorists? SAE Report 970492. Society of Automotive Engineers, Inc., Warrendale, PA, 1997.

633. McClafferty, K. J., Shkrum, M. J., Chan, J., German, A. A multi–disciplinary study of a Canadian airbag fatality. Proceedings of the Canadian Multi–disciplinary Road Safety Conference X. Vehicle Safety Research Centre, Ryerson Polytechnic University, Toronto, 1997.

634. Rebel, A., Ellinger, K., van Ackern, K. [New airbag–associated injuries in traffic accidents]. Anaesthesist 45:359–362, 1996.

635. Sharma, O. P. Pericardio–diaphragmatic rupture: five new cases and literature review. J. Emerg. Med. 17:963–968, 1999.

636. Morgenstern, K., Talucci, R., Kaufman, M. S., Samuels, L. E. Bilateral pneumothorax following air bag deployment. Chest 114:624–626, 1998.

637. Cullinan, M., Merriman, T. Oesophageal rupture resulting from airbag deployment during a motor vehicle accident. Aust. N. Z. J. Surg. 71:554–555, 2001.

638. Augenstein, J. S., Perdeck, E., Williamson, J., Stratton, J., Horton, T., Digges, K. Injury patterns in air bag equipped vehicles. Paper 98–S1–O–06. Proceedings of the 16th International Technical Conference on the Enhanced Safety of Vehicles., National Highway Traffic Safety Administration, Washington, DC, 1998.

639. Mbamalu, D., Banerjee, A., Shankar, A., Grant, D. Air bag associated fatal intra–abdominal injury. Injury 31:121–122, 2000.

640. Smith, D. P., Klein, F. A. Renal injury in a child with airbag deployment. J. Trauma 42:341–342, 1997.

641. Schultze, P. M., Stamm, C. A., Roger, J. Placental abruption and fetal death with airbag deployment in a motor vehicle accident. Obstet. Gynecol. 92:719, 1998.

642. Gimovsky, M. L., Nunez, G., Beck, P. Fetal heart rate monitoring casebook. Airbag–associated rupture of membranes: evaluation of trauma in pregnancy. J. Perinatol. 20:270–273, 2000.

643. Sherer, D. M., Abramowicz, J. S., Babkowski, R., Metlay, L. A., Ron, M., Woods, J. R., Jr. Extensive fetal intrathoracic injuries sustained in a motor vehicle accident. Am. J. Perinatol. 10:414–416, 1993.

644. Tanno, K., Kohno, M., Ono, K., et al. Fatal cardiovascular injuries to the unbelted

occupant associated with airbag deployment: two case-reports. Leg. Med. (Tokyo) 2:227-231, 2000.
645. Grubwieser, P., Pavlic, M., Gunther, M., Rabl, W. Airbag contact in traffic accidents: DNA detection to determine the driver identity. Int. J. Legal Med. 118:9-13, 2004.
646. Miltner, E., Wiedmann, H. P., Leutwein, B., et al. Liver and spleen ruptures in authentic car-to-car side collisions with main impact at front door or B-pillar. Am. J. Forensic Med. Pathol. 13:2-6, 1992.
647. McLellan, B. A., Rizoli, S. B., Brenneman, F. D., Boulanger, B. R., Sharkey, P. W., Szalai, J. P. Injury pattern and severity in lateral motor vehicle collisions: a Canadian experience. J. Trauma 41:708-713, 1996.
648. Chipman, M. L. Side impact crashes—factors affecting incidence and severity: review of the literature. Traffic Inj. Prev. 5:67-75, 2004.
649. Howard, A., Rothman, L., McKeag, A. M., et al. Children in side-impact motor vehicle crashes: seating positions and injury mechanisms. J. Trauma 56:1276-1285, 2004.
650. Nirula, R., Mock, C., Kaufman, R., Rivara, F. P., Grossman, D. C. Correlation of head injury to vehicle contact points using crash injury research and engineering network data. Accid. Anal. Prev. 35:201-210, 2003.
651. Mackay, G. M., Hill, J., Parkin, S., Munns, J. A. Restrained occupants on the nonstruck side in lateral collisions. Accid. Anal. Prev. 25:147-152, 1993.
652. MacLennan, P. A., McGwin, G., Jr., Metzger, J., Moran, S. G., Rue, L. W., III. Risk of injury for occupants of motor vehicle collisions from unbelted occupants. Inj. Prev. 10:363-367, 2004.
653. Cummings, P., Rivara, F. P. Car occupant death according to the restraint use of other occupants: a matched cohort study. JAMA 291:343-349, 2004.
654. Augenstein, J. S., Perdeck, E. B., Martin, P., et al. Injuries to restrained occupants in far-side crashes. Annu. Proc. Assoc. Adv. Automot. Med. 44:57-66, 2000.
655. Miltner, E., Salwender, H. J. Injury severity of restrained front seat occupants in car-to-car side impacts. Accid. Anal. Prev. 27:105-110, 1995.
656. Shkrum, M. J., Green, R. N., McClafferty, K. J., Nowak, E. S. Skull fractures in fatalities due to motor vehicle collisions. J. Forensic Sci. 39:107-122, 1994.
657. Parenteau, C. S., Viano, D. C., Shah, M., et al. Field relevance of a suite of rollover tests to real-world crashes and injuries. Accid. Anal. Prev. 35:103-110, 2003.
658. Malliaris, A. C., DeBlois, J. H., Digges, K. H. Light vehicle occupant ejections—a comprehensive investigation. Accid. Anal. Prev. 28:1-14, 1996.
659. Howard, A., McKeag, A. M., Rothman, L., Comeau, J. L., Monk, B., German, A.

Ejections of young children in motor vehicle crashes. J. Trauma 55:126–129, 2003.

660. Byard, R. W., Gilbert, J. D., Klitte, A., Felgate, P. Gasoline exposure in motor vehicle accident fatalities. Am. J. Forensic Med. Pathol. 23:42–44, 2002.

661. Williams, J. S., Graff, J. A., Uku, J. M. Pedestrian intoxication and fatal traffic accident injury patterns. Prehospital Disaster Med. 10:30–35, 1995.

662. Schlumpf, M. R., Niederer, P. F. Motion patterns of pedestrian surrogates in simulated vehicle–pedestrian collisions. J. Biomech. 20:371–384, 1987.

663. Ravani, B., Brougham, D., Mason, R. T. Pedestrian post–impact kinematics and injury patterns. SAE Report 811024. Society of Automotive Engineers, Inc., Warrendale, PA, 1981.

664. Karger, B., Teige, K., Fuchs, M., Brinkmann, B. Was the pedestrian hit in an erect position before being run over? Forensic Sci. Int. 119:217–220, 2001.

665. Teresinski, G., Madro, R. Evidential value of injuries useful for reconstruction of the pedestrian–vehicle location at the moment of collision. Forensic Sci. Int. 128:127–135, 2002.

666. Teresinski, G., Madro, R. Knee joint injuries as a reconstructive factors in car–to–pedestrian accidents. Forensic Sci. Int. 124:74–82, 2001.

667. Ubelaker, D. H., Adams, B. J. Differentiation of perimortem and postmortem trauma using taphonomic indicators. J. Forensic Sci. 40:509–512, 1995.

668. Spitz, W. V. The road traffic victim. In: Spitz, W. V., ed. Medicolegal Investigation of Death: Guidelines for the Application of Pathology to Crime Investigation. Charles C.Thomas, Springfield, IL, pp. 528–565, 1993.

669. Teresinski, G., Madro, R. Ankle joint injuries as a reconstruction parameter in car–to–pedestrian accidents. Forensic Sci. Int. 118:65–73, 2001.

670. Waddell, J. P., Drucker, W. R. Occult injuries in pedestrian accidents. J. Trauma 11:844–852, 1971.

671. Zivot, U., Di Maio, V. J. Motor vehicle–pedestrian accidents in adults. Relationship between impact speed, injuries, and distance thrown. Am. J. Forensic Med. Pathol. 14:185–186, 1993.

672. Copeland, A. R. Pedestrian fatalities. The Metropolitan Dade County experience, 1984–1988. Am. J. Forensic Med. Pathol. 12:40–44, 1991.

673. Lane, P. L., McClafferty, K. J., Nowak, E. S. Pedestrians in real world collisions. J. Trauma 36:231–236, 1994.

674. Roudsari, B. S., Mock, C. N., Kaufman, R., Grossman, D., Henary, B. Y., Crandall, J. Pedestrian crashes: higher injury severity and mortality rate for light truck vehicles

compared with passenger vehicles. Inj. Prev. 10:154–158, 2004.

675. Byard, R. W., Green, H., James, R. A., Gilbert, J. D. Pathologic features of childhood pedestrian fatalities. Am. J. Forensic Med. Pathol. 21:101–106, 2000.

676. Harruff, R. C., Avery, A., Alter–Pandya, A. S. Analysis of circumstances and injuries in 217 pedestrian traffic fatalities. Accid. Anal. Prev. 30:11–20, 1998.

677. Brison, R. J., Wicklund, K., Mueller, B. A. Fatal pedestrian injuries to young children: a different pattern of injury. Am. J. Public Health 78:793–795, 1988.

678. Wyatt, J. P., Martin, A., Beard, D., Busuttil, A. Pedestrian deaths following collisions with heavy goods vehicles. Med. Sci. Law 41:21–25, 2001.

679. Shkrum, M.J., Green, R.N., Nowak, E.S. Upper cervical trauma in motor vehicle collisions. J. Forensic Sci. 34:381–390, 1989.

680. Ohshima, T., Kondo, T. Forensic pathological observations on fatal injuries to the brain stem and/or upper cervical spinal cord in traffic accidents. J. Clin. Forensic Med. 5:129–134, 1998.

681. Madro, R., Teresinski, G. Neck injuries as a reconstructive parameter in car–to–pedestrian accidents. Forensic Sci. Int. 118:57–63, 2001.

682. Karger, B., Teige, K., Buhren, W., DuChesne, A. Relationship between impact velocity and injuries in fatal pedestrian–car collisions. Int. J. Legal Med. 113:84–88, 2000.

683. Klintschar, M., Darok, M., Roll, P. Fatal truck–bicycle accident involving dragging for 45 km. Int. J. Legal Med. 117:226–228, 2003.

684. Dix, J. D., Bolesta, S. Dragging deaths: a case in point. J. Forensic Sci. 33:826–828, 1988.

685. Fukushima, H., Yonemura, I., Ota, M., Hasekura, H. A case of death due to dragging by a car: establishment of a homicide because of conscious negligence. Nippon Hoigaku Zasshi 44:186–190, 1990.

686. Fujiwara, S., Nishimura, A., Ueno, Y., Nakagawa, K., Tatsuno, Y., Mizoi, Y. Histo–patho– logical findings of abraded skins in the cases of automobile dragging. Nippon Hoigaku Zasshi 47:398–405, 1993.

687. Maxeiner, H., Ehrlich, E., Schyma, C. Neck injuries caused by being run over by a motor vehicle. J. Forensic Sci. 45:31–35, 2000.

688. Murphy, G. K. Suicide by gunshot while driving a motor vehicle. Two additional cases. Am. J. Forensic Med. Pathol. 18:295–298, 1997.

689. Macdonald, J. M. Suicide and homicide by automobile. Am. J. Psychiatry 121:366–370, 1964.

690. Kerwin, A. J. Sudden death while driving. Can. Med. Assoc. J. 131:312–314, 1984.

691. Kerwin, A. J. The electrophysiologic features of sudden death. Can. Med. Assoc. J.

131:315–317, 1984.

692. Baker, S. P., Spitz, W. U. An evaluation of the hazard created by natural death at the wheel. N. Engl. J. Med. 283:405–409, 1970.

693. Ostrom, M., Eriksson, A. Natural death while driving. J. Forensic Sci. 32:988–998, 1987.

694. Dolinak, D., Guileyardo, J. Automatic implantable cardioverter defibrillator rhythm strip data as used in interpretation of a motor vehicle accident. Am. J. Forensic Med. Pathol. 22:256–260, 2001.

695. Suarez-Penaranda, J. M., de la Calle, M. C., Rodriguez-Calvo, M. S., Munoz, J. I., Concheiro, L. Rupture of liver cell adenoma with fatal massive hemoperitoneum resulting from minor road accident. Am. J. Forensic Med. Pathol. 22:275–277, 2001.

696. Noyes, R., Jr. Motor vehicle accidents related to psychiatric impairment. Psychosomatics 26:569–6, 579, 1985.

697. Imajo, T. Suicide by motor vehicle. J. Forensic Sci. 28:83–89, 1983.

698. Byard, R. W., Gilbert, J. D. Cervical fracture, decapitation, and vehicle–assisted suicide. J. Forensic Sci. 47:392–394, 2002.

699. Hardwicke, M. B., Taff, M. L., Spitz, W. U. A case of suicidal hanging in an automobile. Am. J. Forensic Med. Pathol. 6:362–364, 1985.

700. Schmidt, C. W., Jr., Shaffer, J. W., Zlotowitz, H. I., Fisher, R. S. Suicide by vehicular crash. Am. J. Psychiatry 134:175–178, 1977.

701. Boglioli, L. R., Taff, M. L., Green, A. S., Lukash, L. I., Lane, R. A bizarre case of vehicular suicide. Am. J. Forensic Med. Pathol. 9:169–178, 1988.

702. von Bremen, A. The comparison of brake and accelerator pedals with marks on shoe soles. J. Forensic Sci. 35:14–24, 1990.

703. Prichard, P. D. A suicide by self–decapitation. J. Forensic Sci. 38:981–984, 1993.

704. Murphy, G. K. Suicide by gunshot while driving an automobile. Am. J. Forensic Med. Pathol. 10:285–288, 1989.

705. Durso, S., Del Vecchio, S., Ciallella, C. Hanging in an automobile: a report on a unique case history. Am. J. Forensic Med. Pathol. 16:352–354, 1995.

706. Zugibe, F. T., Costello, J. T. The jigsaw puzzle identification of a hit–and–run automobile. J. Forensic Sci. 31:329–332, 1986.

707. Drummond, F. C., Pizzola, P. A. An unusual case involving the individualization of a clothing impression on a motor vehicle. J. Forensic Sci. 35:746–752, 1990.

708. Murphy, G. K. Death on the railway. J. Forensic Sci. 21:218–226, 1976.

709. Romero Palanco, J. L., Gamero Lucas, J. J., Vizcaya Rojas, M. A., Arufe Martinez, M. I. An unusual case of railway suicide. J. Forensic Sci. 44:444–446, 1999.

710. Davis, G. G., Alexander, C. B., Brissie, R. M. A 15-year review of railway-related deaths in Jefferson County, Alabama. Am. J. Forensic Med. Pathol. 18:363–368, 1997.
711. Lerer, L. B., Matzopoulos, R. G. Fatal railway injuries in Cape Town, South Africa. Am. J. Forensic Med. Pathol. 18:144–147, 1997.
712. Copeland, A. R. Accidental railway-related fatalities. The Metro Dade County experience, 1980–1984. Am. J. Forensic Med. Pathol. 10:196–199, 1989.
713. Driever, F., Schmidt, P., Madea, B. About morphological findings in fatal railway collisions. Forensic Sci. Int. 126:123–128, 2002.
714. Shapiro, M. J., Luchtefeld, W. B., Durham, R. M., Mazuski, J. E. Traumatic train injuries. Am. J. Emerg. Med. 12:92–93, 1994.
715. Pelletier, A. Deaths among railroad trespassers. The role of alcohol in fatal injuries. JAMA 277:1064–1066, 1997.
716. Cina, S. J., Koelpin, J. L., Nichols, C. A., Conradi, S. E. A decade of train-pedestrian fatalities: the Charleston experience. J. Forensic Sci. 39:668–673, 1994.
717. Kligman, M. D., Knotts, F. B., Buderer, N. M., Kerwin, A. J., Rodgers, J. F. Railway train versus motor vehicle collisions: a comparative study of injury severity and patterns. J. Trauma 47:928–931, 1999.
718. Shkrum, M. J., Hurlbut, D. J., Young, J. G. Fatal light aircraft accidents in Ontario: a five year study. J. Forensic Sci. 41:252–263, 1996.
719. Ast, F. W., Kernbach-Wighton, G., Kampmann, H., et al. Fatal aviation accidents in Lower Saxony from 1979 to 1996. Forensic Sci. Int. 119:68–71, 2001.
720. Li, G., Baker, S. P. Injury patterns in aviation-related fatalities. Implications for preventive strategies. Am. J. Forensic Med. Pathol. 18:265–270, 1997.
721. Wiegmann, D. A., Taneja, N. Analysis of injuries among pilots involved in fatal general aviation airplane accidents. Accid. Anal. Prev. 35:571–577, 2003.
722. Hellerich, U., Pollak, S. Airplane crash. Traumatologic findings in cases of extreme body disintegration. Am. J. Forensic Med. Pathol. 16:320–324, 1995.
723. Reals, W. J., Davidson, W. H., Karnitsching, H. H. Pathology of light-aircraft accidents. Aerosp. Med. 35:133–135, 1964.
724. Stevens, P. J. The pathology of fatal public transport aviation accidents. Med. Sci. Law 8:41–48, 1968.
725. Krefft, S. Estimation of pilot control at the time of crash. In: Mason, J. K., Reals, W. J., eds. Aerospace Pathology. College of American Pathologists, Chicago, pp. 96–104, 1973.

第9章
颅脑损伤及脊柱损伤

概述

　　头部及脊柱常产生局灶性或弥漫性损伤,伤及颅骨及脑组织("颅脑损伤")或脊椎及脊髓("脊柱损伤")。局灶性损伤包括:骨折、硬脑膜两侧的血肿(硬脑膜外血肿及硬脑膜下血肿)、蛛网膜下腔出血、脑内或脊髓内血肿、脑室内出血、中枢神经系统组织撕裂及破碎(脑挫伤、脑挫裂伤)、脑梗死。弥漫性脑损伤包括:脑肿胀、弥散性或创伤性轴索损伤、缺氧－缺血性脑病、广泛性血管损伤。在大多数案例中,不同类型的颅脑损伤及脊柱损伤同时存在,损伤特征能反映颅脑损伤、脊柱损伤的类型。患者可因颅脑损伤和脊柱损伤出现特征性的临床症状,使法医能在尸体解剖之前对可能的神经损伤类型进行预判。这些症状包括以下患者状态:"死于现场"、在损伤与死亡之间有一段神志清醒期、损伤后即昏迷、植物人状态、重度残疾、中度残疾、轻度残疾、伤后完全康复、孤立性四肢麻痹或截瘫。

　　关键词: 脑损伤;脑水肿;缺氧－缺血,脑;颅脑损伤;弥散性轴索损伤;颅内出血,外伤性;脑垂体损伤;摇晃婴儿综合征;颅骨骨折;脊髓损伤;脊柱骨折

1 前言

　　颅脑创伤是常见的死亡原因[美国每年每10万人中就有18人死于颅脑创伤(1)],主要由交通事故、高坠及不同类型的打击所致。因此,常需对头部、脊柱及中枢神经系统损伤案例进行尸体解剖。在解剖中枢神经系统、相应的骨骼及周围软组织时应密切关注异常改变,这些异常改变能够提示、确认及证实中枢神经系统曾发生暴力性损伤。任何总体和微观的异常改变特征,包括头部及脊柱周围的皮肤及软组织,都将用于解释外力的作用方式、外力大小以及外力对中枢神经系统功能的破坏程度。这些推论及概述将有助于对损伤与死亡原因的关系作出如下结论:偶然的、辅助的、因果的或意义未明的。

中枢神经系统损伤常常由以下一个或多个因素造成：
- 直接碰撞头部。
- 在碰撞或非碰撞情况下头部运动速度或轨迹的迅速改变。
- 寰枕关节或椎体形变超出"正常"或生理极限。
- 物体刺入（即进入而未穿出）或贯穿（即穿过）颅腔或脊髓腔。

外力对中枢神经系统的影响相比于对身体其他部位的影响更加复杂，原因如下：
- 小损伤造成巨大的中枢神经功能损害，与损伤程度不成比例。
- 创伤所致的中枢神经系统病理改变会导致机体衰弱甚至死亡，但当这些病理改变发生在其他器官时则很容易自愈或治愈。
- 由于大脑悬浮在脑膜和脑脊液中，当脑组织相对于颅骨运动时，可在短时间内独立运动或保持相对静止，此时由于颅骨、硬脑膜及脑组织间的相对运动会产生脑损伤。
- 寰枕关节和颈椎椎体的解剖结构允许头部在冠状面、水平面和矢状面作复杂的运动，因此，脑的不同部位之间也会产生相对位移。
- 受损的神经细胞及轴突会表现出独特的生化或形态学改变。

颅骨和脑损伤（即颅脑损伤）以及椎体和脊髓损伤（即脊椎脊髓损伤）可以是原发性损伤，由外力直接造成（如组织破坏、撕裂及牵拉、轴浆运输障碍、震荡所致的功能性影响）；也可以是继发性损伤，由原发性损伤引起（如出血、缺血性损伤、炎症、水肿）。有的继发性损伤几乎瞬时发生（如组织撕裂导致出血），有的则需要数小时至数天进展（如迟发性出血、炎症、脑水肿、轴浆运输障碍或轴突断裂所致的轴突水肿）。根据损伤的分布情况，中枢神经系统原发性和继发性损伤又可分为"局灶性"或"弥漫性"（后者通常指多灶性分布，并非真正意义上的弥漫性分布）。

尽管所产生的功能性损害后果不同，机械性外力对中枢神经系统及其覆盖物的作用与其对身体其他部位的作用没有差别。检查疑似中枢神经系统损伤案例时，有必要记住损伤可发生于神经系统的多个部位，能量在这些部位会以某种形式被吸收并或多或少地产生耗散效应，而耗散效应可能会造成多种神经病理学改变。例如，摔跌时头部后仰撞击较硬的物体表面，可即刻或在几小时内出现不同类型的损伤，包括枕骨骨折、额部挫伤、胼胝体局灶创伤性轴索损伤、脑水肿。此外，脑水肿还可继发脑挫伤区或其周围脑实质神经元缺血缺氧性损伤，其覆盖的区域多变复杂，难以通过脑动脉或穿支动脉供血区解释。

颅脑损伤和脊椎脊髓损伤包括以下几种：
- 头皮挫、裂伤。
- 椎骨周围软组织挫伤。
- 颅骨骨折。
- 脊椎脱位和骨折。

- 脑膜周围（硬脑膜外、硬脑膜下、蛛网膜下腔）出血。
- 脑和脊髓挫伤、裂伤、撕裂伤和出血。
- 脑室出血。
- 弥散性脑损伤（脑水肿、轴索损伤、缺血缺氧性损伤、血管损伤）。

损伤类型大致反映了能量作用于中枢神经系统的机制。两大类型如下：

- 头部接触性损伤：冲击力接触部位的头皮擦伤、挫裂创，头皮下颅骨骨折，冲击部位周围及一定距离的脑膜和脑组织撕裂、出血。
- "惯性"（加速性或减速性）损伤：深部脑组织广泛性撕裂、不同程度的出血和弥散性轴索损伤（DAI），而不伴有头皮损伤和颅骨骨折。

接触性和惯性颅脑损伤常有重叠。

创伤案例中对中枢神经系统的检查还可能发现非创伤性中枢神经系统疾病，这可用于解释引起致死性中枢神经损伤的令人费解的意外事件。例如，位于视觉通路上的脑部肿瘤引起同侧偏盲，这或许可解释司机患者自主转向迎面而来的车辆的怪异行为。此外，先天性疾病可能引起其他典型的创伤性损伤，特别是没有明显创伤史的硬脑膜外血肿［如破裂的浆果样动脉瘤（颅内小动脉瘤）可能引起孤立的硬脑膜下出血，脊髓周围常自发出血（2）］。

2 中枢神经系统损伤解剖实践中的注意事项

虽然尸体解剖中应用于头皮、颅骨、脑检查的很多技术都很常规，但对疑有神经系统损伤的案例进行解剖时，还应注意以下事项：

- 解释中枢神经系统肉眼及组织病理学改变时，应同时参考患者死前的神经影像学检查结果。与案情介绍一起提交神经影像学检查报告的副本（在检查中枢神经系统病变时常用的神经系统影像学检查包括X线成像、CT、MRI、血管造影、超声检查）。毫无疑问，死后神经影像学检查在中枢神经系统解剖中起重要作用（3,4；参阅第1章标题6.2）。
- 对比确认颅骨和颅底骨折的检查方法，虽然肉眼观察比颅骨影像学检查更为敏感，但开颅之前的颅脑影像学检查结果显示颅腔内可能存在空气，是颅骨骨折的有效标志，但需要排除诊断性腰椎穿刺将空气引入蛛网膜下腔的可能。
- 常规开颅方法可能导致人为颅骨骨折或加重原有的骨折（5），如果采取以下预防措施则可将上述风险最小化：
  - 应该用开颅锯完全锯透颅骨（相较于区分细小的人为骨折和先前存在的骨折，判断大脑表面的锯片割伤更为容易）。
  - 只能用杠杆轻柔地分离颅骨的切割边缘。
  - 不可使用锤子和凿子开颅。
- 在怀疑硬脑膜下或硬脑膜外出血时，应在头下放置一器皿盛血并测量体积。开颅时会从硬脑膜窦流出大量血液（尤其在常规尸体解剖中没有打开上腔静脉时），此时应注意不应该将这种出血和急性硬脑膜外出血相混淆(5)，因为后一种出血通常会部分凝固，并部分黏附于蛛网膜或硬脑膜上。

- 形成时间达数小时的硬脑膜外血肿中，可卡因代谢物和乙醇的血液浓度反映了受伤时这些物质在血液循环中的水平(6–8)。
- 取出大脑后，应尽量剥离颅顶和颅底硬脑膜以寻找骨折线。对于颅底，应尽量剥离硬脑膜，并仔细检查细微的骨折线。颅骨上的血管压迹走行较为缓和，而骨折线较细，在延伸方向上有成角变化。
- 应记录单处骨折或多处骨折与头皮损伤之间所有的空间对应关系，该信息可用于推断着力部位。
- 尸检发现的所有损伤（包括脑各切面的损伤）都应记录在图表中［模板可以从美国武装部队病理学研究所获取(9)］。相较于尸检照片，这些记录对损伤的回顾更有价值、更加准确。与死因有联系的或具有辅助作用的"有意义"的损伤，均应拍摄照片作为图表的补充。对于细微的骨折线，在擦干、用标记笔描绘骨折线走行后，可拍照以有效记录。对于粉碎性骨折中的凹陷性骨折，因其大小可能与撞击或打击颅骨的物体吻合，可在用绳子描绘出骨折轮廓后再用相机拍照记录（参阅标题3.4）。
- 取出大脑时需仔细检查脑神经。
    - 嗅球是否存在和（或）完整？（头部损伤中，由于嗅神经穿过筛板时被撕扯，可导致嗅球断裂、出血。）
    - 颈内动脉是否正常？（颅底骨折时可能发生堵塞或撕裂。）
    - 垂体柄是否完整？（头部外伤时可能被撕断。）
    - 观察颞叶内侧（海马旁回钩）和小脑幕之间的关系，是否形成海马钩回疝？
    - 颅底是否存在原因不明的蛛网膜下腔出血？（尝试不同的解剖方法找到出血来源；参阅第10章标题4.2。）
    - 延髓和脊髓的连接是否完整可见？（在寰枕关节脱位或高位颈椎骨折的情况下，是出血、扭曲还是压扁。）
    - 椎动脉大体检查是否正常？（头颈部外伤时可发生撕裂或离断。）
    - 在尸体内留下一小段椎体动脉，如果怀疑动脉夹层还可鉴别和追溯。
    - 最后取脑时沿脊髓头侧切断，使延髓暴露比较清楚。
    - 识别和分离小脑幕附着缘、延髓脊髓连接缘和椎动脉附着缘，是否困难？一定程度上可能是牵引造成大脑脚或他处的人为撕裂(10)。
- 在所有颅脑外伤涉及脑水肿的或必需排除脊椎脊髓损伤的案例中，应取出脊髓。缺血缺氧性损伤可以引起脑水肿。若存在脊髓运动神经元缺血性坏死，则表明机体是由于系统性原因（即呼吸、心搏停止或严重低血压）引起的缺血缺氧性损伤，这与外伤性局部大脑血流中断引起的缺血缺氧性损伤不同。
- 关于尸体解剖后是否保留脑和其他器官（11），目前争论较多，特别是在英国。只要负责尸体解剖的法医就尸体解剖结果、案件过程或这两点综合考虑，认为存在神经病理异常"与法医学相关（或其鉴定结果）有助于确定自然或非自然因素在死亡过程中的参与程度"（11），即法医认为存在"合理和可靠"的理由，大脑组织就应该被保留和固定。
- 对已固定的大脑应系统切片，并将所有切片放置后进行观察和分析。我们将大脑半球沿冠状面切成厚1厘米的切面，将脑干沿水平面切成厚0.5厘米的切面，将小脑切成厚约0.5厘米的切面。小脑切片时应先在小脑蚓部做一矢状切面，而后继续以倾斜或与矢状面平行的角度直角切开，并垂直于小脑小叶。脑干和小脑也可以整体切成厚0.5厘米的水平切面。后一种方法对于婴儿的大脑更有效，因为婴儿的大脑较小，在弥散性轴索损伤的情况下，该方法可清楚地显示脑桥背外侧和小脑中上脚相邻部分的出血性撕裂。如果在大脑切片之前将小脑从脑干上取出，可能会错失上述发现。
- 如果怀疑或确认存在特定性异常，应调整大脑切开的方向。例如通过脑桥延髓连接的矢状切法是证实脑桥延髓撕裂的最佳方式，沿着子弹射入方向冠状切开脑组织可观察到完整的弹道轨迹。
- 被血液重度浸染的大脑各切面应在检查前进行冲洗并铺开，从而避免掩盖异常的发现。

其他特殊情况在脊椎脊髓损伤（参阅标题8.1）、颅脑枪弹创（参阅第6章标题19）和外伤性颅底蛛网膜下腔出血（参阅第10章标题4.2）章节中有相应描述。

3 颅骨骨折

3.1 发生率

在临床人群研究中，颅骨骨折的发生率为每年每十万人中有44例，多数（53%）是简单骨折（即线性或粉碎性），颅底骨折、凹陷性骨折和复合性骨折分别占19%、16%和12%（12）。机动车交通事故（38%）和摔跌（36%）是颅骨骨折最常见的原因，头部打击占10%（12）。简单骨折常与摔跌有关，多发生于婴幼儿和老年人，而颅底骨折、多发性骨折和凹陷性骨折则多发生于机动车交通事故和头部打击后（12）。不同于临床数据，致命性头部损伤案例中骨折的发生率缺乏基于人群的统计数据，但约一半的致命性机动车交通事故案例中存在颅骨骨折（13），其中大部分是颅底骨折或颅盖骨复合性凹陷性骨折。

3.2 机械作用

对颅骨的打击可以引起颅骨弹性变形，包括冲击部位的颅骨"内陷"和距冲击部位一定距离的局部、不对称、可变的颅骨"外凸"（14,15）。当超过颅骨弹性形变时，颅骨变形的部位便发生骨折。一般而言,如果力施加的颅骨面积较小(如来自武器的冲击),则颅骨向内屈曲发生骨折,若力作用在较大面积的颅骨上则可导致颅骨的外凸性骨折(14,15)。由于颅盖骨占据了颅骨的大部,因此颅骨穹隆的形状可有效分散外力的能量;多数情况下,线性骨折线沿颅盖骨骨缝延伸形成分离性骨折。相比之下,由于颅底存在众多孔隙和含气的窦腔,所以通过颅底的能量引起的骨折线可以传导至颅骨薄弱区域,并汇聚于或穿过蝶鞍(16)。

导致颅骨骨折所需要力的大小的变化幅度是很大的,并且与颅骨覆盖物[包括可以减少30%冲击力的头皮(15)和头部覆盖物]、颅骨的厚度及发生冲击的部位有关。法医对引起颅骨骨折的作用力类型应作一般性的评论和解释。从广义上说,与引起颅盖骨线性骨折的头部外伤暴力相比,产生粉碎性颅骨骨折的头部外伤暴力更强,凹陷性骨折则提示外力对头部的局部作用,如槌击、摔跌至凸起物上或机动车交通事故中部分车架侵入撞击头部。杂乱排列的粉碎性骨折表明头部与钝性大平面之间有撞击,这与摔跌和机动车交通事故相关的颅骨骨折特征相吻合,但并不仅限于此。一旦颅骨被破坏,即使额外施加极小的外力也可产生更多骨折或使既有的骨折线扩展(15)。

大部分颅骨骨折由头部动态运动引起(如头部运动或碰撞后停止运动)。这意味着产生骨折的撞击与头部运动有关,"脑震荡"经常发生,但其并不总与颅骨骨折相关联。脑震荡被定义为一过性的脑功能改变,表现为定向障碍、对相关事件的遗忘和(或)意识丧失。引起脑震荡的结构基础仍然是假设性的,对其功能基础的解释也是推测性的(17,18)。

单纯的颅骨骨折不会引起死亡,但颅骨骨折表明外力已经施加到头部,且暴力的能量可影响大脑,或产生与骨折相关的其他并发症,这些均可以引起死亡。

3.3 骨折的外部表现

尸表检查结果可作为反映颅底骨折的间接证据,这些外部表现包括眶周皮肤出血["熊猫眼"(19)]、巩膜出血、耳后皮肤出血(Battle征象 – 乳突出血)和耳道出血(图9-1)。

3.4 分类和形状

颅骨骨折的表现形式多种多样。颅骨线性骨折是指贯穿颅盖骨(图9-2)或颅底(图9-3)的单一裂缝。颅骨分离性骨折是指骨缝哆开(图9-4A)。颅骨粉碎性骨折由多条骨折线组成,这些骨折线排列杂乱或呈同心圆形,或者从撞击部位辐射而呈放射形。粉碎性骨折(图9-4)可包含游离的骨折碎片,如果其向内移位,就形成凹陷性骨折(图8-4B);如果其向外移位,则形成崩裂性骨折(图8-4C)。颅骨开放性骨折指颅腔和颅外连通,比较典型的是伴头皮裂创的颅骨骨折(图8-4C);筛板骨折时颅腔和鼻腔连通,或者颞骨岩部骨折时颅腔和中耳道连通(参阅标题3.7)。

第 9 章 | 颅脑损伤及脊柱损伤

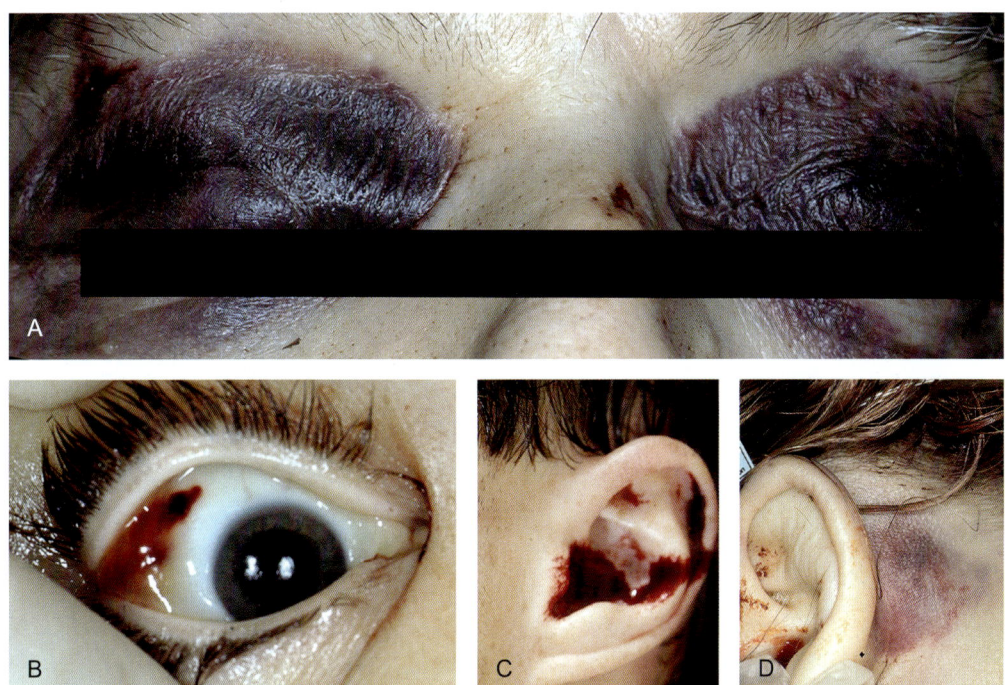

图 9-1 颅底骨折的外部表现。(A) 显著的眶周皮肤出血("熊猫眼")。(B) 巩膜出血(检查者戴手套用手指翻开眼睑)。(C) 耳道出血。(D) 耳后皮肤出血(Battle 征象 – 乳突出血)。

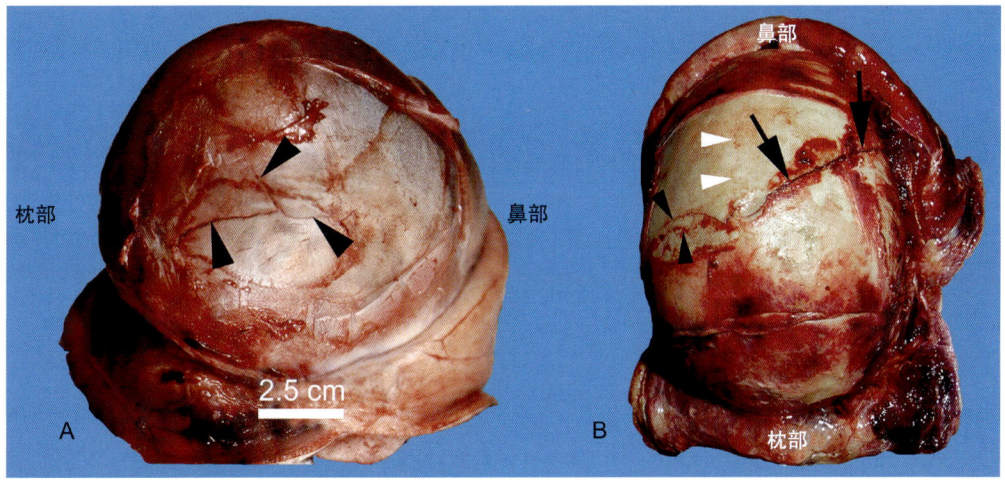

图 9-2 颅骨线性骨折。(A) 婴儿颅顶骨折的右侧观。具有分支、细窄的线性骨折(三角箭头)。(B) 成人颅顶骨的右斜位观。通过矢状缝(白色三角箭头)的线性骨折(箭头),并在终点处分叉(黑色三角箭头)(加拿大安大略省伦敦市伦敦健康科学中心 L. C. Ang 博士供图)。

对冲性骨折[不可与冲击伤和对冲伤相混淆(参阅标题 5.4)]是枕骨、顶骨或颞骨受撞击后发生在颅前窝涉及眶骨或筛板等薄弱部位的骨折(20,21)(图 9-5),经常但不总是与撞击部位的骨折有关(20)。对冲性骨折可表现为单条极细的裂

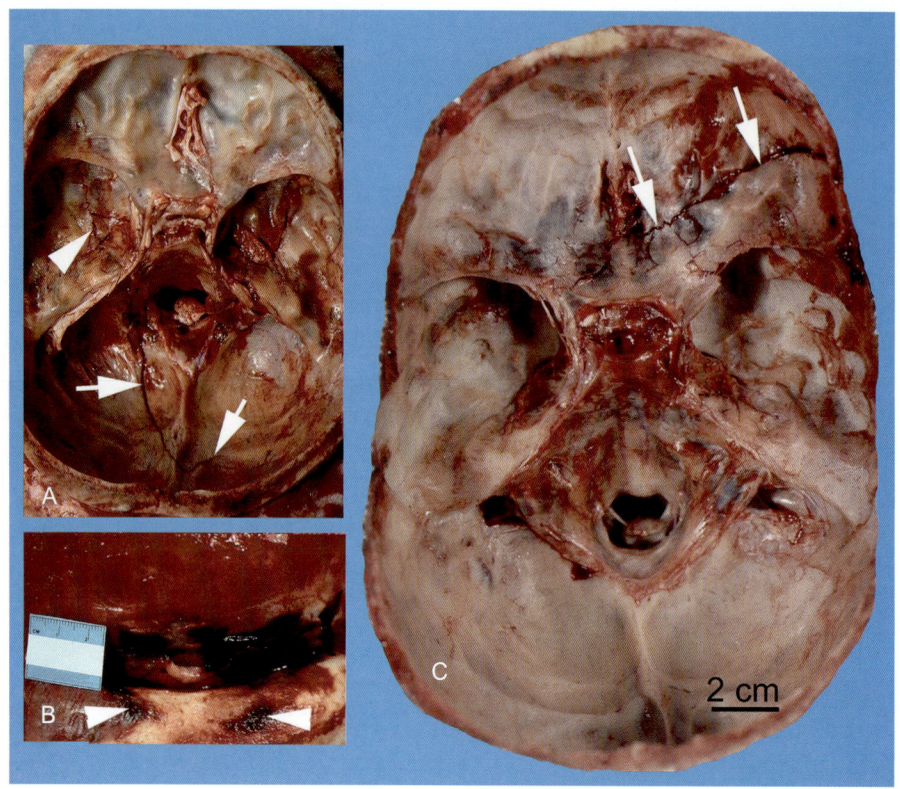

图 9-3 颅底线性骨折。(A) 颅底。枕骨分支骨折(白色箭头)延伸至左侧颅中窝(三角箭头)。(B) 枕部头皮。与 (A) 相对应的头皮挫伤(三角箭头),表明受力部位。(C) 颅底。右前额撞击所致的颅底线性骨折(白色箭头)。

纹,也可以是更复杂多样、弯曲和多角度的骨折线。对冲性骨折常与眶周血肿有关,当存在枕部挫伤或裂创时,在检查头外部时可能产生头部遭受多次外力作用的错误判断。

概括如下(16):
- 骨折线的方向大致与引起骨折的暴力方向对应。
- 骨折线的起始部位接近但不一定在受撞击部位。
- 骨折线可穿过受撞击部位。

虽然头皮局部损伤(可以很小;图 9-6)可用于推断头部的撞击部位,但在很多情况下,头皮损伤,尤其是头皮下深层组织出血,由于损伤太广泛,无法准确判断引起颅骨骨折的撞击位置。在这种情况下,若尝试确定受力部位,应谨慎分析颅骨骨折的分布特征(凹陷性颅骨骨折除外)。

3.5 颅底骨折

1912 年学者 Rawling 对颅底骨折加以概述:"在很多方面,颅底是颅骨最薄弱的部分。颅底有许多孔道,这些孔道有的和鼻窦相连,有的成为听觉器官的一部分。此

第 9 章 | 颅脑损伤及脊柱损伤

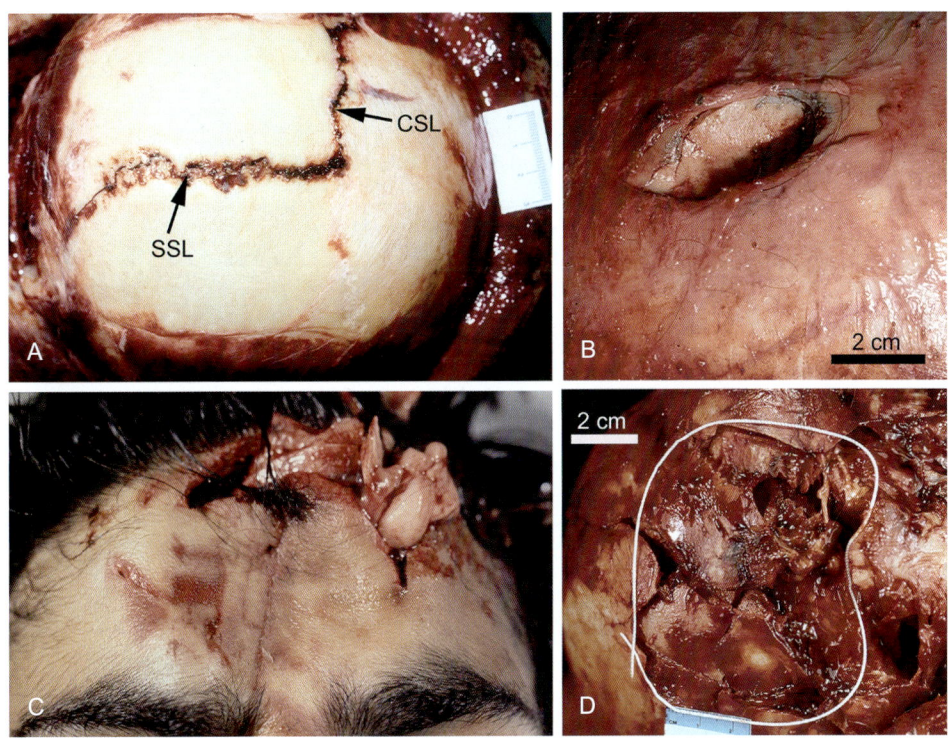

图 9-4 不同类型的颅骨骨折。（A）涉及冠状缝（CSL）和矢状缝（SSL）的分离性骨折。（B）凹陷性颅骨骨折。（C）崩裂性颅骨骨折伴脑组织溢出。（D）粉碎性凹陷性颅骨骨折。用白线标记颅骨凹陷区域的边缘，其尺寸和形状与损伤工具的接触面相吻合。

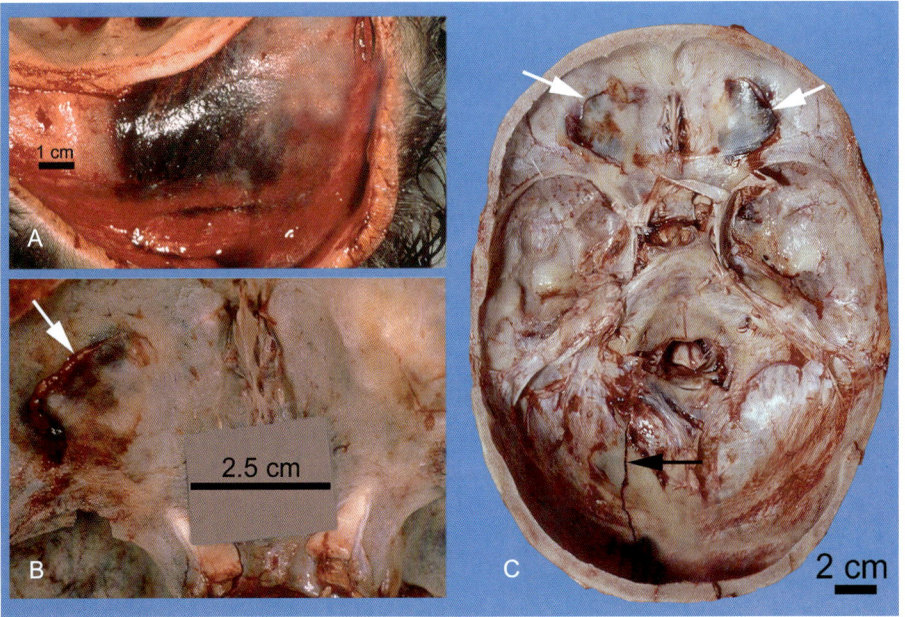

图 9-5 对冲性颅骨骨折（2 个案例）。（A）枕部头皮挫伤伴 B 图中的骨折。（B）左侧眶板（箭头）对冲性骨折。（C）第二个案例中枕骨骨折（黑色箭头）和其对面双侧眶板的对冲性骨折（白色箭头）。

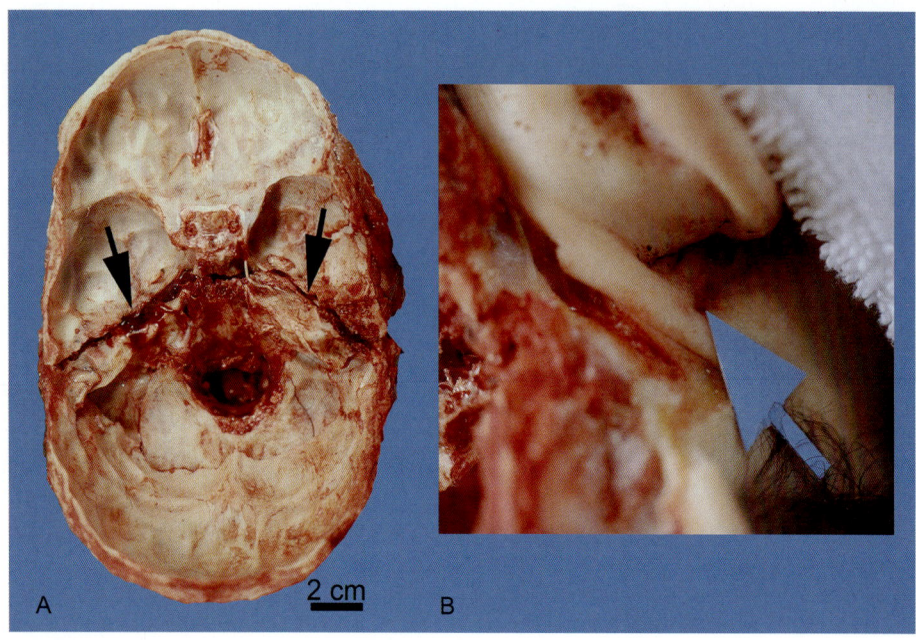

图 9-6 颅底("铰链")骨折。(A)颅底横断("铰链")骨折(黑色箭头)。(B)显示撞击部位的耳后轻微皮肤挫伤(箭头)。

外,颅底还存在一些参差不齐的平面,这些平面在各方面都不同于颅盖骨显著的凸面。因此,颅底受到的暴力不像在颅盖骨上那样会扩散,颅底难以承受直接或传导的暴力作用。但从另一个角度来看,大自然已充分考虑到这一点,并能合理充分地预防引起颅底损伤的危险事件。"(16)

大部分颅底骨折由与颅底大致相同平面(即额隆突、眶上嵴、额骨颧突、颞骨下方、乳突区、枕骨,以及由上、下项线围成的区域)的撞击所致,且可预测颅底骨折线的走行(图9-7)。某些案例中的骨折线是不连续的。铰链型骨折指颅底横断骨折,在取出大脑后颅底分离的两部分骨骼可以活动(图9-6)。

3.5.1 环形骨折

虽然大量案例中颅底骨折的骨折线都遵循从撞击部位向外辐射的原则(22),但在远离暴力作用部位的扩散型骨折,则与额部、枕部及下颌骨的撞击有关(22,23)。这些骨折可以局限于颞骨岩部,也可进一步穿过枕骨和颞鳞部进行不同程度的特征性延伸,围绕枕骨大孔形成不同距离的"环形骨折"(23)。高坠时臀部着地或头顶部被击打后发生靠近枕骨大孔的环形骨折产生于颈椎和颅底的碰撞(23)。波及颞骨岩部的环形骨折与颞叶对冲伤、脑干前侧挫伤或脑桥延髓撕裂有关(22)。

3.6. 颅骨挤压性骨折

静止的头部被两个重物挤压造成颅骨的静态负载。由于缺乏大脑和颅骨间相

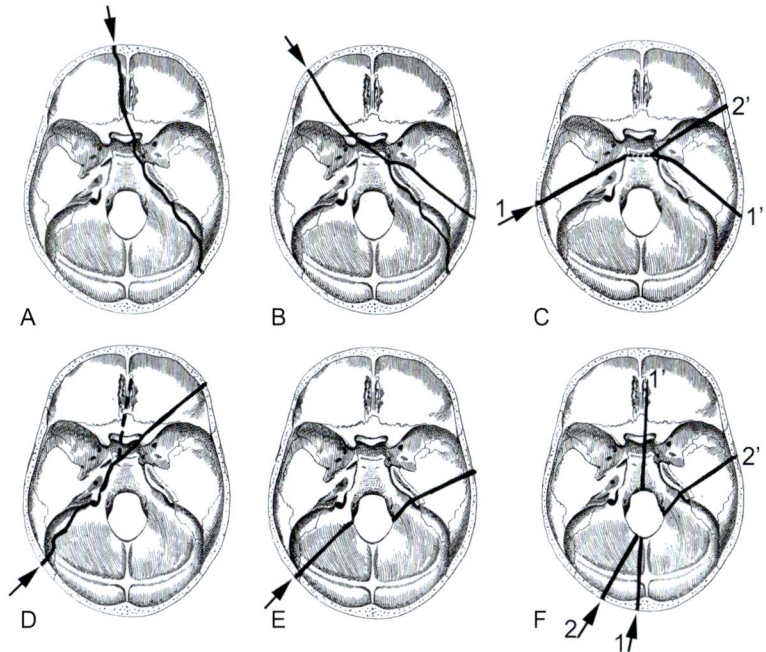

图9-7 箭头指示与碰撞部位相关的颅底骨折在通过颅底时近似的路径。注意,骨折是否完全贯穿颅底,取决于暴力的特征和遇到的阻力,对于颅底和颅盖骨,其受力强度的变化幅度很大。任何规律都有例外情况,实践中的骨折似乎不遵循任何规律,或者由于暴力过强可以贯穿颅底,而不服从一般规律(16)。(A)暴力作用于额部中央。(B)暴力作用于额部侧面(图9-3C)。(C)暴力作用于外耳部。1-1'线是最常见的骨折线,有时也可见1-2'线(图9-6和图9-8)。(D)暴力作用于乳突部。(E)暴力作用于枕部侧面。(F)暴力作用于枕部(图9-3A和图9-5C)。暴力作用的方向决定了是1-1'骨折线还是2-2'骨折线(经牛津大学出版社许可改编自文献[16])。

对运动及引起脑震荡的外力,伤者神志意识较少改变(参阅标题3.2.)。颅底骨折通常呈双侧分布,骨折线向垂直于受力部位的方向延伸,并使颞骨岩部与蝶骨大翼和颞鳞部分离(24)。

3.7 颅骨骨折的并发症

跨越血管的骨折可导致血管撕裂,引发颅内出血,通常为硬脑膜外出血。当颅底骨折撕裂海绵窦内的颈内动脉时,可引起致命性的耳道(25)及鼻腔(26)出血(图9-8)。在这一部位也会发生外伤性颈动脉瘤的迟发性致死性出血(27)。通常,临床中少数(10%)的颅底骨折病例中会出现颈动脉相关的症状,以鼻出血、颈动脉海绵窦瘘、假性动脉瘤或血管外血凝块压迫动脉为症状特征(26)。在斜坡纵向骨折的裂缝中,基底动脉或椎动脉的陷入("嵌顿")会导致脑干梗死(28)。多发性骨折中窦壁广泛性撕裂使空气进入静脉系统可形成肺栓塞(29,30),当骨折所致的广泛性脑挫伤位于撕裂的静脉窦部位时,可发生肺内脑组织栓塞(参阅第7章标题12.1;第8

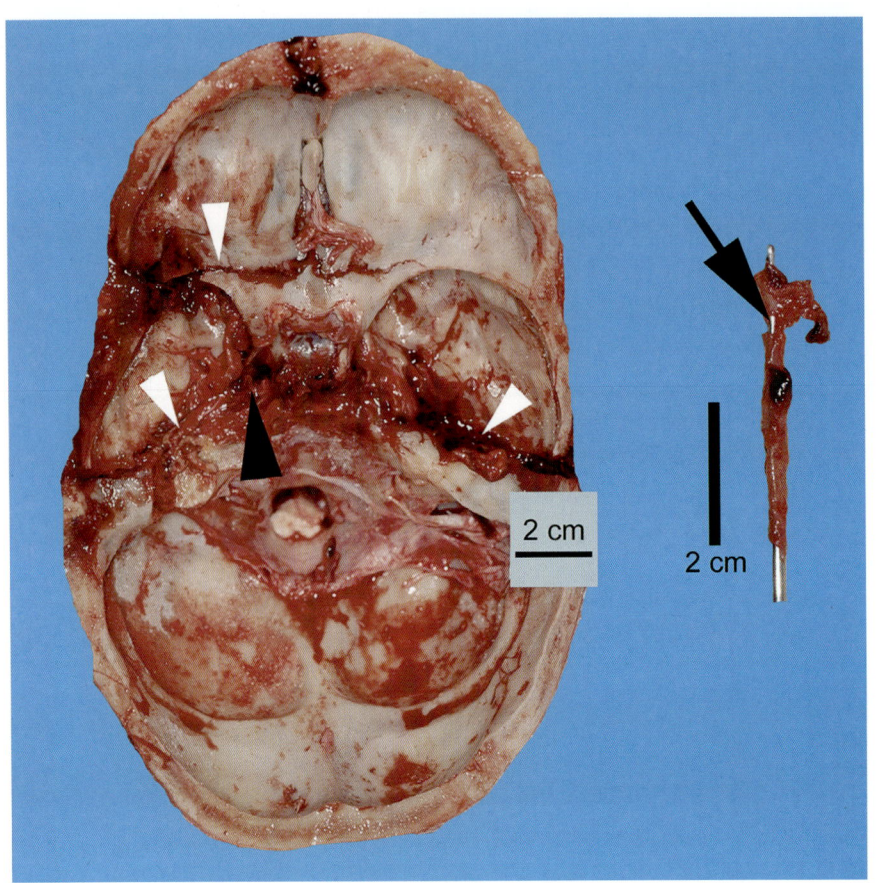

图 9-8 颅底骨折和颈动脉撕裂。颅底粉碎性骨折（白色三角箭头）通过左侧破裂孔（黑色三角箭头），引起颈动脉撕裂（黑色箭头）。

章标题 12.4）(31)。筛板和颞骨岩部的多发性骨折可分别形成脑脊液鼻漏和耳漏；在多发性骨折中，感染有产生急性细菌性脑膜炎或硬脑膜外脓肿的风险（图 9-9）。当儿童颅盖骨的骨折线被硬脑膜外水囊瘤[即硬脑膜外局部聚集的清亮淡黄色液体(32,33)]分离时，该线性骨折会逐渐扩大（"生长性骨折"）。若骨折的边缘移向大脑，会导致大脑表面线状的挫伤，即"骨折断端挫伤"（图 9-10）。

3.8 枕骨髁骨折

枕骨髁骨折比较少见，轻者引起颈部疼痛(34)，重者导致多种脑神经麻痹症状(35)，甚至死亡(36)。如果支撑的韧带完整，骨折相就对稳定；若韧带断裂，则可引起致命性的寰枕关节脱位，2%-4% 的致命性道路交通事故会发生这种情况(36,38)。

3.9 烧伤受害者和枪弹伤后的颅骨骨折及中枢神经系统损伤

与热损伤有关的颅骨骨折和中枢神经系统损伤主要在第 4 章标题 3.1、3.3、4.3、7.3 和 7.4 中讲述。与枪弹创有关的在第 6 章标题 18 和 19 中有所描述。

第 9 章 | 颅脑损伤及脊柱损伤

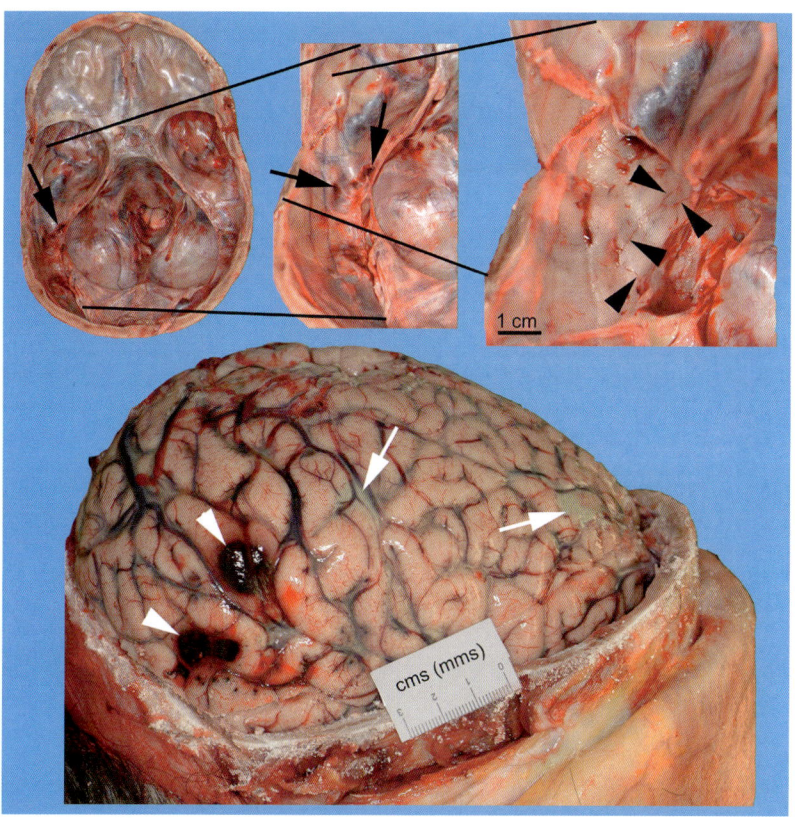

图 9-9 颅底骨折伴急性细菌性脑膜炎。直线表示骨折部位的视图逐级放大。硬脑膜出血（黑色箭头-硬脑膜存在）覆盖在颞骨岩部（黑色三角箭头-硬脑膜剥离）极细的骨折线上。位于头部撞击部位下面的大脑表面存在脓性渗出物（白色箭头）、局部模糊的脑沟和小挫伤（白色三角箭头）。

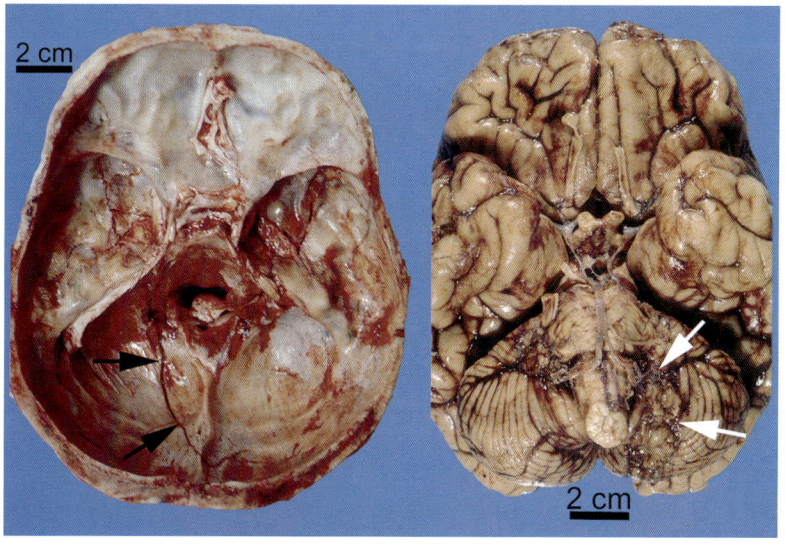

图 9-10 骨折致出血。枕部线性骨折（黑色箭头）及与之相对应的小脑基底部表面轻微线性撕裂出血（白色箭头）（同样的例子在图 9-3A、B 中说明）。

4 外伤性颅内出血

出血可以不同的形式显示组织和血管撕裂的部位,同时也显示出能量传递的区域。外伤性颅内中枢神经系统出血发生在以下部位:
- 硬脑膜外出血。
- 硬脑膜下出血。
- 蛛网膜下腔出血。
- 脑组织出血(即脑内出血)。
- 脑室系统出血。

4.1 外伤性硬脑膜外血肿

硬脑膜外血肿指在硬脑膜外层和颅骨内板之间的出血。碰撞导致硬脑膜外出血与出现颅内出血临床症状的间隔时间通常短至几小时,但少数患者也可能延迟到数天之后才出现出血症状(39,40)。慢性进展性硬脑膜外血肿则较罕见,提示可能存在陈旧性硬膜下血肿(41)。硬脑膜外血肿的范围和程度取决于出血是源自静脉还是动脉,也取决于硬脑膜外层和颅骨内板之间黏附的紧密程度。不同个体黏附的紧密程度存在差异,而且随年龄增长黏附也会更加紧密。在向上抬颅盖骨取大脑的过程中,可从硬脑膜与颅顶骨分离的难易程度加以判断。

硬脑膜外血肿由头部创伤撕裂动脉或静脉窦引起[尽管很少有例外(42)],这些血管撕裂通常由骨折引起,但并不总是如此。极少数硬脑膜外血肿不是因骨折所致,其出血可因板障静脉撕扯、破裂或窦壁拉伸、裂开所致。硬脑膜外血肿通常发生在颞部或顶部,暴力作用引起颞部比较薄弱的颞鳞部骨折,骨折断端边缘可引起其下潜在的脑膜中动脉撕裂出血。

颅顶很少出现硬脑膜外血肿,多见为双侧出血,与骨折及继发的上矢状窦撕裂有关(43,44)。颅后窝的硬脑膜外血肿多由枕骨骨折及横窦或矢状窦壁撕裂引起(45,46)。多部位硬脑膜外血肿较少见,但发生时静脉比动脉出血更常见,某些血肿没有伴随骨折,且中线处的撞击比外侧更常见(47–49)。也有案例报道硬脑膜外血肿发生在撞击部位的对侧,也就是对冲性硬脑膜外血肿(50)。

硬脑膜外血肿的伤者在送到医院时可具有进行性神经系统症状,可能已经死亡或濒临死亡。在几个小时前,这些伤者可能有轻微的或其他形式的高坠外伤史。如果硬脑膜外血肿大到压迫大脑,就可使颅内压增加并阻断脑部血液循环;如果出现临床症状和清除血肿的间隔时间过长,就可导致不可逆的缺血缺氧性脑损伤。以上情况的伤者在神经外科手术后会死亡。因此,血肿一侧的脑半球术后出现进行性、致命性的脑肿胀,似乎比未经手术治疗观察到的脑肿胀更严重,因为清除血肿为损伤的大脑提供了更多的肿胀空间。

4.1.1 病理基础

未经治疗的硬脑膜外血肿的尸检结果比较明确(图9-11)。血肿对应的颞部头皮存在挫伤,当掀起颅盖骨时,在硬脑膜外易发现大血肿,血肿表面的颞骨骨折穿过脑膜中动脉或其主要分支,且脑膜中动脉表面的小血凝块提示血管撕裂的部位。尸检中很可能发现严重的弥漫性脑肿胀,法医可观察到由血肿引起的颅内"空间占位"效

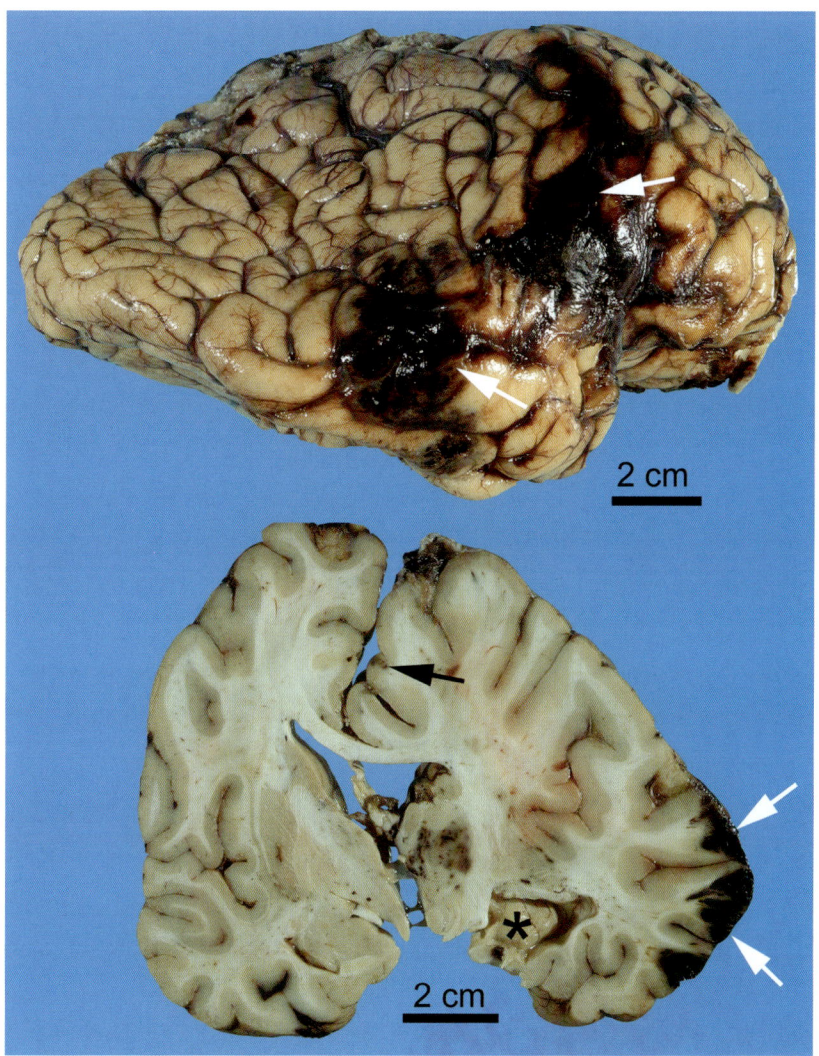

图9-11 急性硬脑膜外血肿的影响。图中的大脑来源于一名酒精中毒患者,晚上摔跌致头部左侧撞击沙发边缘,无意识丧失,后被发现死于床上。尸检时发现急性硬脑膜外血肿(500毫升)。急性硬脑膜外血肿侧的大脑半球明显扁平,与撞击后的脑挫伤有关(白色箭头)。在从右至左的大脑镰下疝的上方是一个近中线偏右侧的微小脑出血(黑色箭头),其发生可由脑水肿继发脑组织压迫性坏死所致,或是摔跌过程中脑组织和大脑镰边缘碰撞所致(疝性挫伤)。右侧颞中叶的广泛性挫伤由钩回疝造成用星号标记。硬脑膜外血肿的脑表面光滑,与急性硬膜下血肿的脑回形态存在差异(图9-12),对侧大脑半球受压。

应,包括从血肿一侧延伸至另一侧的大脑镰下疝和小脑幕疝,后者通常在血肿部位更显著。血肿会引起大脑半球肿胀,并导致脑沟变浅(沟的抹平)和脑回增宽,有这种改变的大脑外观上看起来比较平滑。能观察到扁桃体疝,但较少见,可见于硬脑膜外血肿,也可见于其他引起颅内压升高的情况(51)。有时可观察到局部创伤性脑损伤,尤其是大脑挫伤。

4.2 外伤性硬脑膜下血肿

外伤性硬脑膜下血肿在临床分为急性、亚急性、慢性及慢急性,取决于受伤时间的长短、神经影像学检查结果及血肿引流出的血液性质。急性血肿引流出的血液是凝固的(即损伤时间在受伤后48小时内);亚急性血肿的血液部分凝固,部分为液体(即2天至3周时间);慢性血肿的血液具有流动性(即超过3周时间)(52)。"慢急性"硬脑膜下血肿是指慢性硬脑膜下血肿的伤者先前没有临床症状或症状轻微,近期再次出血并出现新的神经系统症状。

病理学家面对的硬脑膜下血肿主要有以下几类:

- 小而薄的近期出血(涂片型)硬脑膜下血肿,可能与其他的颅脑创伤,尤其是弥漫性颅脑损伤有关。
- 近期几小时至几天(急性硬脑膜下血肿)的大量出血,可能还未被手术清除。
- 陈旧性硬脑膜下出血大小可变,其周围可形成不同程度的假膜。
- 局部硬脑膜下不均匀增厚的硬脑膜见含铁血黄素染色,表明小范围的愈合性出血。

就死亡原因而言,大面积急性硬脑膜下血肿和慢性硬脑膜下血肿的阐述和解释是法医在硬脑膜下血肿方面面临的最常见问题。

4.2.1 急性硬脑膜下血肿

急性硬脑膜下血肿既可以是单一的(或"单纯的"),意指不伴有明显的脑损伤,也可以是复杂的,或多或少伴有广泛性颅脑损伤。急性硬脑膜下血肿或快速或缓慢地进展,一些复杂的急性硬脑膜下血肿也反映了共存的脑损伤症状。小范围、未治疗的急性硬脑膜下血肿可自发吸收,很少发展成慢性硬脑膜下血肿(53)。由于脑肿胀的填塞效应,部分伤者的急性硬脑膜下血肿在影像学检查结果中可快速自我消散(54)。

4.2.1.1 单一性急性硬脑膜下血肿

单一性急性硬脑膜下血肿占外伤性急性硬脑膜下血肿的比例为13%—30%,包括原发性出血[自发性出血(56,57)]、外伤性出血[发生于头部外伤后(55)]或继发性出血[浆果样动脉瘤或血管畸形破裂出血、脑内出血破入硬脑膜下腔、硬脑膜下肿瘤并发出血、获得性或医源性凝血功能障碍(57,58)]。

4.2.1.2 复杂性急性硬脑膜下血肿

30%—50%的严重头部损伤的住院患者存在复杂性急性硬脑膜下血肿(59,60),由于通常伴随着弥漫性脑损伤,所以往往致命(61)[虽然文献报道的单一性急

第9章 | 颅脑损伤及脊柱损伤

性硬脑膜下血肿的预后差异性较大(62,56),其致死率随出血范围和损伤持续时间增加而增加。但可以预见的是,在出血范围、持续时间和治疗方法相当的情况下,单一性性硬膜下血肿的预后往往好于复杂性硬脑膜下血肿,因为后者常伴随着其他脑损伤]。

4.2.1.3 急性硬脑膜下血肿的发生机制

急性硬脑膜下血肿多由摔跌或受击打引起,道路交通事故中比较少见(59)。这与动物实验结果相对应,急性硬脑膜下血肿发生于碰撞过程中脑－颅骨瞬时的相对加速,是摔跌伤的特征,损伤程度随加速度的增加而加重(52,59)。其出血源可变,出血位置通常与受力部位无关。急性硬脑膜下血肿由位于大脑皮质表面和硬脑膜窦间的桥静脉撕裂引起(图9-12E),脑皮质表面细动脉或小动脉撕裂也可形成(55,63);来自于小动脉撕裂的急性硬脑膜下血肿往往发生在外侧裂区域(55,62)。其他导致急性硬脑膜下出血的原因包括大面积挫裂创中走行的血管撕裂,如果硬脑膜的动脉被骨折撕裂且血液流入硬脑膜下腔,会快速形成急性硬脑膜下血肿。急性硬脑膜下血肿常伴弥漫性脑水肿(52),其形成原因尚不明确(61)。然而,脑水肿可提示弥漫性外伤性缺血性损伤,也可提示复杂性急性硬脑膜下血肿引起的弥漫性脑水肿,但靠近血肿部位的脑水肿更加明显,这表明急性硬脑膜血肿具有递增和可能的协同效应[与单纯性急性硬脑膜下血肿的临床观察结果一致,大脑半球可能严重肿胀(55,

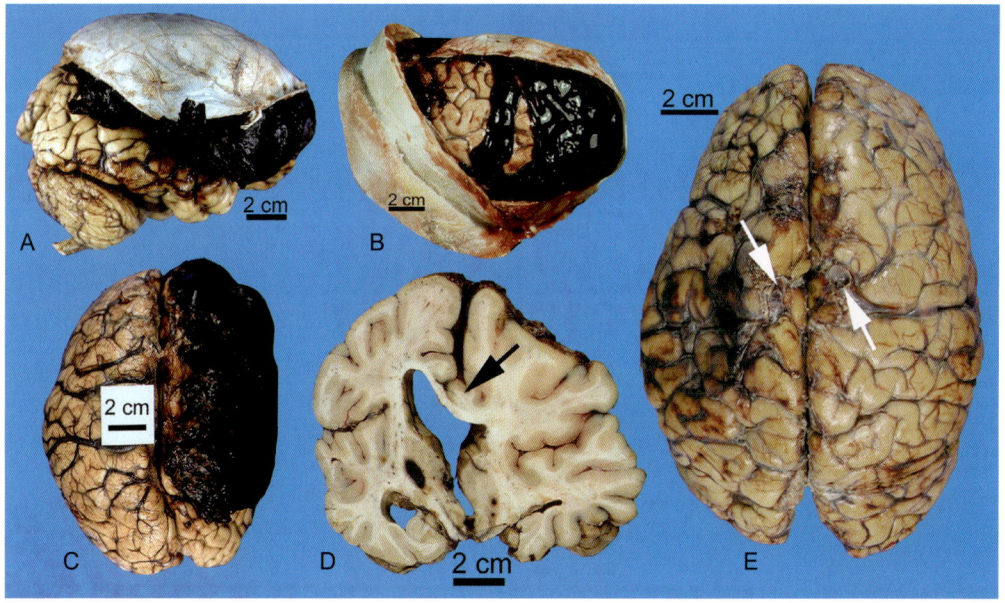

图9-12 急性硬脑膜下出血。(A)、(B)两例致命性急性硬脑膜下出血。(C)A图上面观中的硬脑膜剥离后。(D)A图的冠状面观。脑回上的血肿轮廓被保留,与对侧光滑的大脑半球形成明显对比。从右至左形成大脑镰下疝(箭头),血肿对侧的侧脑室"反常性"扩张,透明隔被撕裂。(E)第3例急性硬膜下出血的部位,以左侧大脑半球的血染压迹为特征。硬脑膜桥静脉由白色箭头标记(图A、C和D由加拿大安大略省伦敦市伦敦健康科学中心 Dr. R. Hammond 提供)。

56)],血肿的局部压迫效应导致毛细血管闭塞,随后出现缺血性脑损伤,进而出现脑水肿,正如上文中关于硬脑膜外血肿所述。

4.2.1.4 大体改变

急性硬脑膜下血肿的外观检查可反映致伤原因(图9-12)。对于多数单纯性急性硬脑膜下血肿案例,无论是受击打还是摔跌所致,都有钝器损伤的外部证据,且更常见于面部而非头部(55)。颅骨骨折最常见。在未经手术治疗的情况下,由于硬脑膜边界层的脆性,血凝块或部分液化的血肿可在硬脑膜下延伸一定的距离(参阅标题4.2.2.2),尽管大多数急性硬脑膜下血肿发生在大脑半球凸面,但也可延伸至大脑镰(64)或局限于颅后窝(46)。硬脑膜下血肿没有封闭的膜。血肿镶嵌在大脑表面,所以即使在发生严重弥漫性脑水肿的情况下也可保留脑皮质凹凸不平的外观(与硬脑膜外血肿下光滑的脑表面正好相反,参阅标题4.1.1)。对侧半球脑回平坦,并且邻近的脑沟变浅,提示血肿的空间占位效应及继发性脑水肿。小脑幕裂孔疝(通常在血肿的同侧更明显)和扁桃体疝比较常见。通常存在远离血肿一侧的大脑镰下疝,可能与相应侧脑室狭窄有关。严重的大脑镰下疝使得对侧的室间孔闭塞,从而出现对侧侧脑室反常性扩张。即使血肿被清除、引流,脑组织仍会出现严重脑水肿,尤其是位于血肿同侧的大脑半球,同时脑肿胀还会引发脑疝。复杂性硬脑膜下出血可以伴发各种颅脑损伤。在严重情况下,尤其是发生于额颞部的损伤,急性硬脑膜下血肿可能伴有大面积的脑挫碎改变(出血呈果酱样)或脑实质出血,这些损伤呈现出组织"崩裂"的征象(52)。

4.2.1.5 镜下所见

急性及慢性硬脑膜下出血的组织病理学表现常作为推断伤后存活时间的基础(65,66)。然而,由于存在个体差异、不同部位凝血块在镜下异常改变的演化率不同以及陈旧性硬脑膜下出血可能存在多次出血,这些镜下所见(及凝血块的大体改变)只能用来初步推断伤后存活时间。在硬脑膜下出血区域边缘的组织反应中,由铁染色显示的含铁血黄素沉积是急性出血最可靠的证据,如果发现存在含铁血黄素,说明至少在死亡前2-3天发生了硬脑膜下出血。还需要检查同侧和对侧硬脑膜,以排除陈旧性出血导致的含铁血黄素沉积。毫无疑问,急性硬脑膜下出血与弥散性轴索损伤可同时发生(67),但弥散性轴索损伤更可能在没有急性硬脑膜下出血的情况下发生,反之急性硬脑膜下出血也往往不伴有弥散性轴索损伤,这些结果表明,不同的加速度和持续时间可产生不同类型的损伤(59)。

4.2.2 慢性硬脑膜下出血

慢性硬脑膜下出血有多种表现(68)。大部分为"经典"类型,即具有特征性的内膜[91%,Ⅰ型(68)];少数表现为硬脑膜上多见含铁血黄素的肉芽组织,表面无包膜形成,可能是未诊断或未治疗的急性硬脑膜下出血处于愈合期[6%,Ⅱ型(68)];最罕见的类型是硬膜下水囊瘤,通常为含稻草色液体的血液[3%,Ⅲ型(68)]。

大部分经典的慢性硬脑膜下出血有临床症状,液体逐渐渗透、积聚或反复的血肿内细毛细血管出血,引起缓慢的颅内空间占位效应。

4.2.2.1 流行病学(69,70)

慢性硬脑膜下出血在所有年龄段的年发生率为十万分之一,70岁以上年龄段的年发生率为十万分之七。患者大部分为男性,但在老年人中并不明显倾向于男性(71)。大部分案例发生于60－70岁老人。老年患者的症状和体征无特异性,包括跌倒、精神状态改变或进行性局灶性神经损伤。在因慢性硬脑膜下出血引起神经症状而去普通内科门诊就诊的老年患者中,约有三分之一需要神经外科治疗。与老年患者相比,年轻患者的症状常表现为颅内压升高(72),这或许说明年轻患者的脑组织萎缩较少,颅内允许脑肿胀和血肿扩张的"余地"较小。硬脑膜下出血案例中约有13%[50岁和更年轻的患者(72)]至25%[老年患者(70)]发生双侧血肿。50%－70%的案例有头部外伤史(年轻患者中更常见)。1%－2%的年轻患者及6%的老年患者直接因血肿死亡。多种因素增加了慢性硬脑膜下出血的风险,包括脑萎缩、酒精滥用(10%案例有病史)、癫痫、凝血功能异常(获得性和医源性)、硬脑膜下结构异常(包括脑膜瘤和转移瘤),以及引起颅内低压的病情(颅内分流术、脑脊液漏、腰椎穿刺)和脱水。

4.2.2.2 发病机制

硬脑膜－蛛网膜间隙不是"虚拟"或"潜在"的空间,它是从硬脑膜内表面到蛛网膜外表面连续分布的细胞,其外侧硬脑膜边界层黏附松散、支持细胞贫乏、缺乏细胞间连接、胶原蛋白和网状纤维最少,内侧蛛网膜边界层更加牢靠,指突状细胞通过大量细胞桥粒和其他类型的细胞间彼此交联(73,74)。硬脑膜下出血常发生在较脆弱的硬脑膜边界细胞层。

尽管引起硬脑膜下腔出血的原因还不确定,但通常认为由于外层膜有反复小出血,轻微的无症状急性硬脑膜下出血逐步加重形成慢性硬脑膜下出血(75)。然而,出血发生的顺序与某些观察结果并不一致,包括无包膜形成的Ⅱ型慢性硬脑膜下出血(参阅标题4.2.2)(68)、易发生于脑萎缩个体的慢性硬脑膜下出血(通常的解释是脑萎缩牵拉桥静脉,致使其易于撕裂)以及低颅压,也包括未经治疗的急性硬脑膜下出血患者的自发性愈合倾向(53)。另一种替代性(或附加性)解释是,脆弱的外层硬脑膜边界层在轻微的头部外伤中更容易撕裂,特别是脑萎缩患者脑组织对硬脑膜的支撑或固定不充分。硬脑膜边界层撕裂后,脑脊液渗透进入硬脑膜下腔(即产生小型硬脑膜下水瘤)并刺激瘤腔周围形成包膜。瘤外膜小血管形成,导致反复少量出血并逐渐扩张形成硬脑膜下血肿(76)。无出血的硬脑膜下腔扩张导致大型硬脑膜下水瘤,被内外膜包裹,内部有稻草色或澄清液体。出现澄清液体表明硬脑膜下腔和蛛网膜下腔存在交通,从而证明了蛛网膜囊肿和硬脑膜下水瘤有联系(77)。

4.2.2.3 大体改变

慢性硬脑膜下出血的外观多样,与血肿大小及形成时间有关。一般来说,血肿腔宽窄不一，含有血液或各色血性液体。血肿由薄的内膜和厚的外膜包绕。外膜看起来色泽不一，由近期出血、色泽暗淡的陈旧性出血、含铁血黄素、灰白色的胶原蛋白和其他纤维组织组成。如果血肿是导致死亡的原因，则空间占位效应所致大脑镰下疝、海马钩回疝、小脑扁桃体疝比较明显，类似于急性硬脑膜下出血对脑组织的影响。一般情况下，尽管慢性硬脑膜下血肿是偶然发现，但老年患者即使血肿很大，对大脑解剖结构的影响却可能很小（图 9-13）。在一些案例中，慢性硬脑膜下血肿与局灶性或弥漫性大脑浅层皮质含铁血黄素沉积症密切相关（图 9-14）。

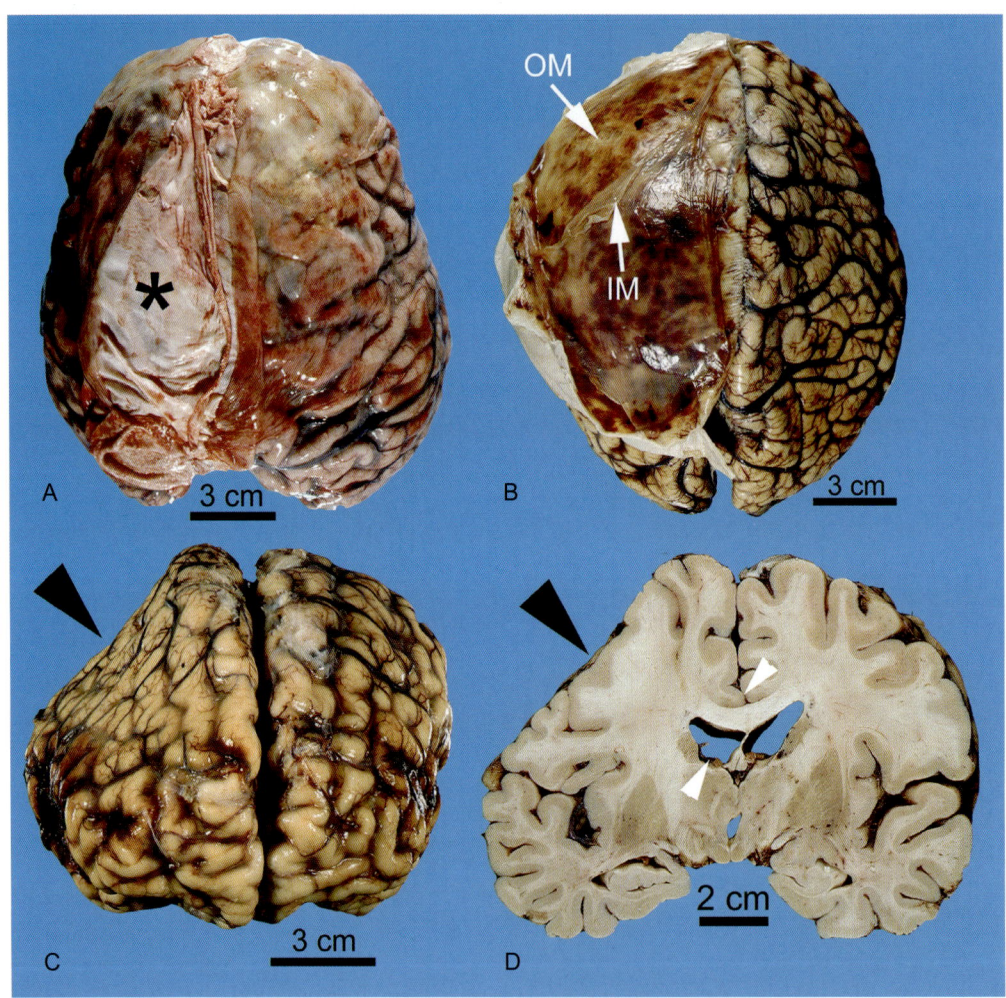

图 9-13 慢性硬脑膜下出血（SDH）。(A)、(B) 2 例慢性硬脑膜下出血病例显示不同程度的内膜（IM）和外膜（OM）。2 例中右侧凸面的脑膜已被反转到左侧（A 图中星号）。(C) 硬脑膜下血肿在右侧大脑半球表面形成明显的压迹（三角箭头所示，和 B 图同样的案例）。(D) B 图中的冠状切面。尽管右侧大脑半球轮廓受压（黑色三角箭头），右侧侧脑室只有轻度狭窄（靠下的白色三角箭头），从右至左的大脑镰下疝的微小而明显的证据（靠上的白色三角箭头），缺乏对侧大脑半球肿胀的证据（与图 9-11 和图 9-12 展示的急性硬脑膜外血肿比较）。

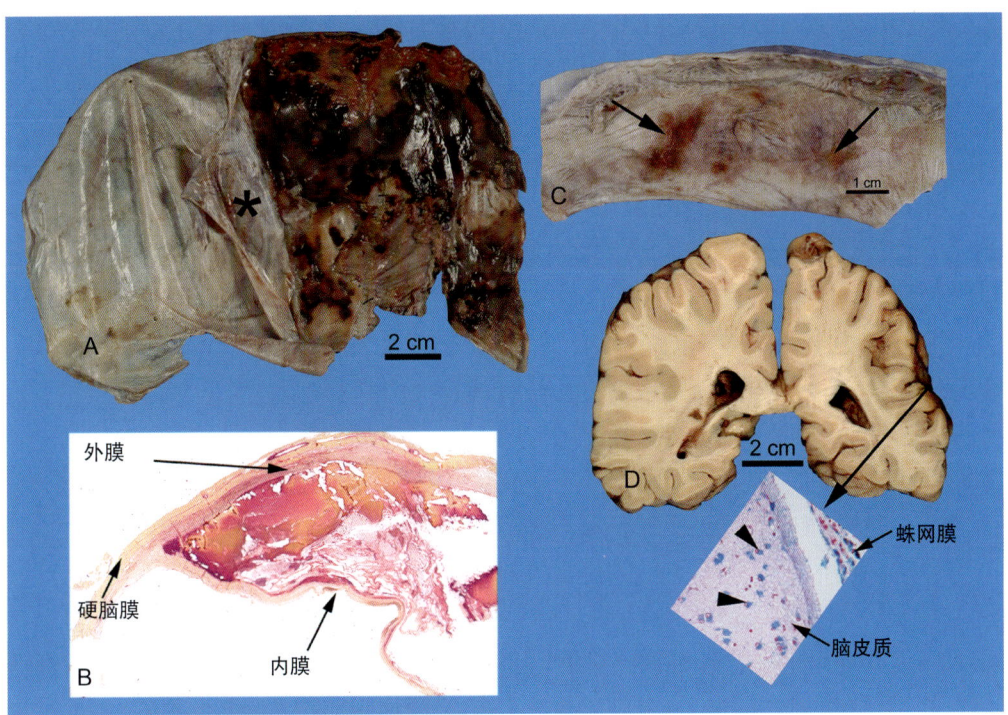

图 9-14 来自慢性硬脑膜下血肿病例的硬脑膜,继发性软脑膜和脑皮质含铁血黄素沉积。(A) 硬脑膜下血肿的外观色泽不一(星号标记大脑镰)。(B)全组织包埋处理,HPS 染色,展示了硬脑膜和慢性硬脑膜下血肿周围的内膜、外膜。(C)大脑镰下"涂片型"陈旧性硬脑膜下出血(黑色箭头)。(D)右侧大脑半球由硬脑膜下血肿引起的凹面区域显示大脑表面轻微变色(黄色),若用 Perl 法对铁染色的显微照片观察(×25 物镜),显示是由于含铁血黄素沉积在蛛网膜下腔和皮质浅层的星形胶质细胞所致(三角箭头)。

4.2.2.4 镜下所见

慢性硬脑膜下血肿的内膜很薄,近乎透明,呈黄褐色,厚 30-300 微米,易与大脑表面分离。内膜由杂乱无章的胶原纤维、弹性纤维及类似于硬脑膜边界层细胞的细胞构成。与血肿相邻的细胞排列紧密,靠近蛛网膜的细胞则排列疏松,还存在数量不等的巨噬细胞、嗜酸性粒细胞和红细胞(78)。与之相反,直接位于硬脑膜下的外膜则较厚,由平滑肌、成纤维细胞、胶原纤维和弹性纤维组成(79)。嗜酸性粒细胞可能较明显(80),提示髓外造血的有核红细胞也较常见。薄壁的血管丛(有时是大血管)是外膜的典型特征,这些血管非常脆弱,加上外膜内及其周围纤维蛋白的溶解活性增高,解释了慢性硬脑膜血肿中频繁发现的新鲜小出血和病变随时间增大的趋势。

4.3 死亡原因与硬脑膜外出血、急性硬脑膜下出血量

对疑有头部外伤的死者,检查仅发现头皮挫伤、急性硬脑膜外出血(伴或不伴颅骨骨折)和不同程度的大脑镰下疝的情况较为少见。尽管当案件是绝对偶然发生(根据可靠目击证人的证据)且缺乏其他任何发现的情况下,可以合理地推断硬脑膜外出

血是死亡的原因,但当死因可疑或存在他杀可能时,需要经过仔细审查以排除其他死亡原因后再作诊断。虽然有知名的法医教科书指出硬脑膜下快速积血50毫升足以威胁生命(81),但文献中几乎没有信息可以明确解决这一潜在争议的问题。

有一项临床研究基于CT对42例到达医院时存活的硬脑膜外出血患者的出血量进行了分析,发现在6例因血肿死亡的致命性案例中有5例出血量大于50毫升,另一例中虽然出血量小于20毫升,但患者于伤后20小时才到医院治疗(82)。在35位幸存者中,硬脑膜外出血量为50－100毫升和大于100毫升的患者分别有13人和4人。这项研究中,102例急性硬脑膜下出血患者中有57%死亡,其中急性硬脑膜下出血量大于120毫升的8人全部死亡(82)。另一项关于98例硬脑膜外出血和91例急性硬脑膜下出血患者的临床研究得到了类似数据,虽然其中出血量超过110毫升的急性硬脑膜下出血的患者都没有存活,但"不利"后果组(即重度残疾、持续性植物状态或死亡)与"有利"后果组(即中度或轻度残疾、完全康复)患者的出血量没有明显的统计学差异(83)。

这些观察结果尽管有一定的启发性,但对病理学家而言作用有限,因为大部分血肿已被手术清除,如果任由病情发展,很可能随着血肿的不断增大导致更多患者死亡。然而还是可以合理地作出推断:任何情况的硬脑膜外血肿可能会、也可能不会导致死亡(可能性随血肿的增大、损伤持续时间增长、脑疝出现而增加);急性硬脑膜下出血超过120毫升必定致命,出血在50－120毫升可能致死(特别是存在显著和有意义的大脑镰下疝和海马钩回疝),出血少于50毫升则不会致死。对这一谨慎的说明还要加以补充:当复杂的急性硬脑膜下出血伴有其他潜在致死性颅脑损伤时,如果损伤和死亡的间隔时间短暂,可能还没有足够时间呈现损伤的结构特征。此外,无论硬脑膜外出血量如何,都表明头部受到暴力损伤,因此可能出现脊髓功能障碍,这与"脊髓震荡"(参阅第10章标题4.3)类似,可能是引起死亡的另一个原因或参与因素。

4.4 创伤性蛛网膜下腔出血

与颅脑创伤相关的蛛网膜下腔出血通常分布广泛,因为脑脊液和未凝固的血液在蛛网膜下腔内可自由流动。蛛网膜下腔出血量与损伤－死亡间隔时间成正比(当颅脑损伤即刻或不久后患者死亡,出血量可能最少),和出血源大小也成正比,尽管蛛网膜下腔出血范围可能广泛分布,但通常在出血源附近更明显。

创伤性蛛网膜下腔出血可能有以下不同类型(图9－15):
- 头部损伤的情况下,大脑表面局部蛛网膜下腔少量(涂片)出血几乎不变,无论创伤多少,都认为其反映了蛛网膜下腔血管有轻微撕裂。
- 蛛网膜下腔出血可能被分割成孤立的血肿,特别在脑沟和外侧裂深处。
- 发生颅脑损伤时,以下情况可能出现广泛性蛛网膜下腔出血:
  - 挫伤和裂创处蛛网膜下腔出血范围反映了脑损伤的大小和损伤－死亡间隔时间。

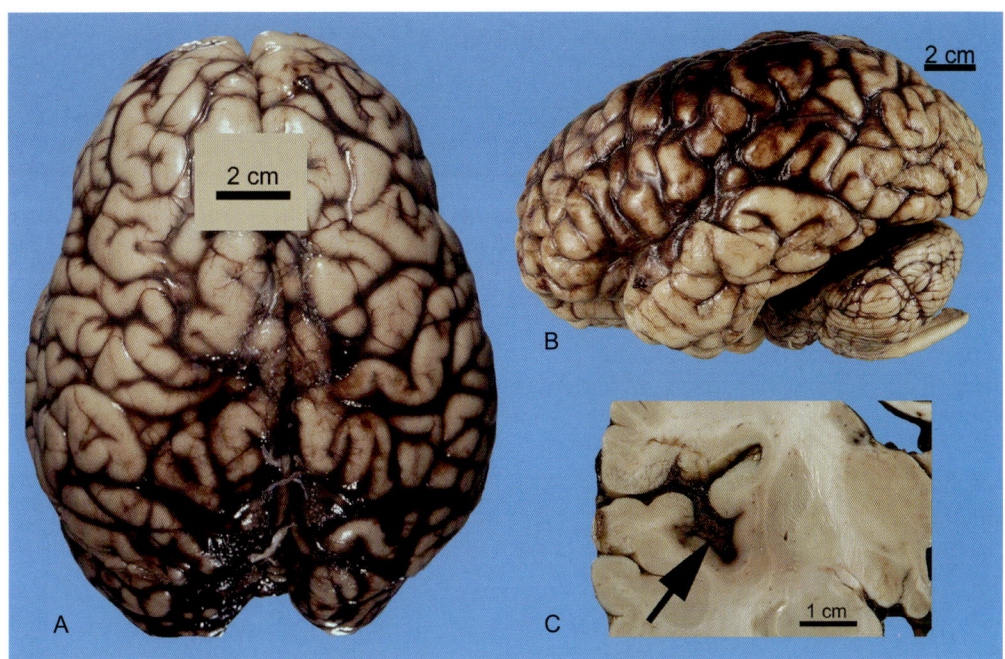

图 9-15 创伤性蛛网膜下腔出血（SAH）。(A) 弥散性轴索损伤案例中枕部软脑膜（依附于）少量的蛛网膜下腔出血。(B) 左额、顶部局部涂片型蛛网膜下腔出血。(C) 大脑外侧裂中少量孤立型蛛网膜下腔出血（箭头）（同样见于图 9-19 中与挫伤相关的蛛网膜下腔出血）。

- 由于创伤性颅内出血破入蛛网膜下腔或脑室，随后血流通过 Magendie 孔（正中孔）和 Luschka 孔（外侧孔）进入蛛网膜下腔。
- 与非创伤性颅内出血相关。最常见的原因是浆果样动脉瘤破裂，可自发突然破裂，也可由造成颅脑损伤的事故造成；但非创伤性颅内血肿也可破入蛛网膜下腔，特别是分布于大脑半球边缘时（通常与大脑淀粉样血管病有关）。

正如第 10 章标题 4.2 的概述所述，对所有广泛性蛛网膜下腔出血的案例，无论是否有明显的外伤表现，在尸体解剖未检见明显出血来源的情况下，都应在尸体移送到殡仪馆前彻底检查蛛网膜下腔出血的来源。

4.5 创伤性脑内出血

创伤性脑内出血表现为以下形式：

- 挫伤 – 血肿（参阅标题 5）。
- 小脑幕裂孔疝导致脑干出血（参阅标题 6.4）。
- 远离大脑半球凸面的脑内深部血肿，即孤立性创伤性脑内血肿（"孤立"指无论是从血肿位置还是发病机制来考虑，血肿与伴随脑肿胀的脑挫伤、出血都是分离或分开的）。孤立性创伤性脑内血肿包括以下情况：
  - 发生于灰质与白质交界处、灰质深处（图 9-16），或者位于脑不同部位存在"撕开"（即牵拉）或剪切作用的部位（通常是胼胝体、小脑脚或"颞柄"——

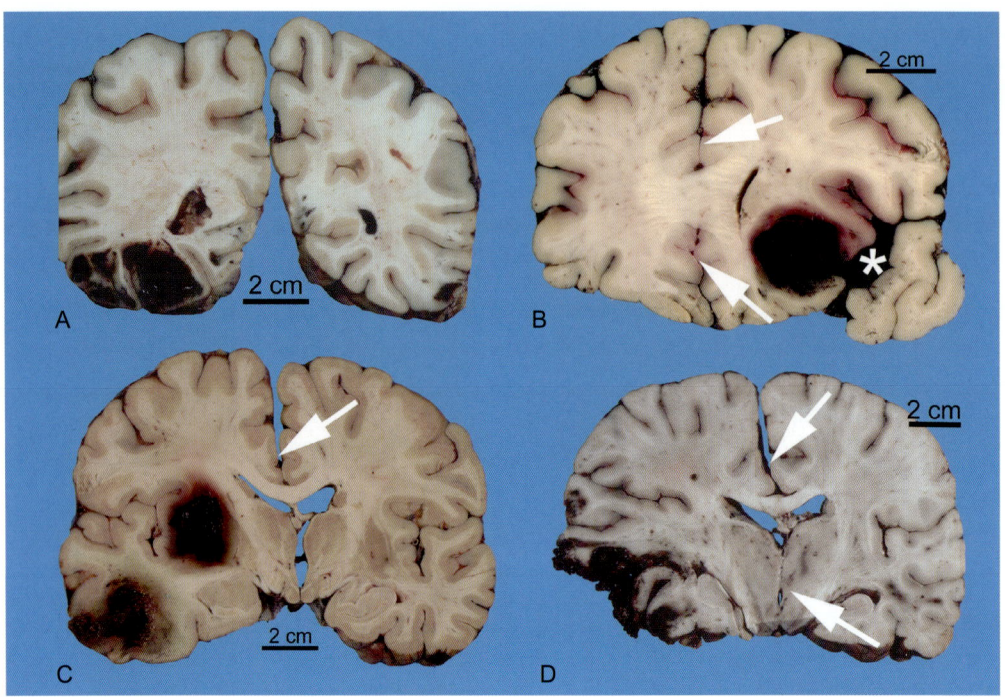

图 9-16 急性创伤性脑内血肿。(A) 枕叶脑挫伤、出血。(B) 额眶部脑挫伤伴蛛网膜下腔出血扩张（白色星号）。(C) 左侧大脑内基底核外侧孤立性外伤性血肿，颞叶巨大的脑挫伤、出血。(D) 颞叶被广泛性出血破坏（"脑叶爆炸"）。B、C 和 D 图中出血的形成与不同程度的大脑镰下疝相关（白色箭头）。

一个位于脑白质头腹侧的独立区域，连接颞叶前部与深部的灰质结构）的多发性小型或中型出血。
- 这类出血经常与 DAI 相关，但也并非始终相关（参阅标题 6.1；参考文献 84，85）。
○ 孤立性中到大型神经节外或脑叶内血肿。
- 此类出血原因有时并不确定，很难排除巧合性的高血压性出血或脑淀粉样血管病变所致出血的可能性。
- 排除高血压性脑出血的推定依据是缺乏高血压病史及高血压的大体改变（即心脏肥大和颗粒性固缩肾）和镜下病理学特征（基底核和齿状核血管的高血压血管病变，包括血管壁的透明样变和玻璃样变性）。
- 当刚果红染色的血管在显微镜下无淀粉样蛋白时，可排除脑淀粉样血管病变所致的脑出血。
○ 孤立性小脑血肿（参阅标题 5.4.7）。
○ 当胼胝体背外侧和扣带回间发生撕裂时会发生罕见性脑内出血，并导致血液进入脑室。血肿形成会撕裂胼胝体外侧和扣带回间的脑白质（图 9-17）。

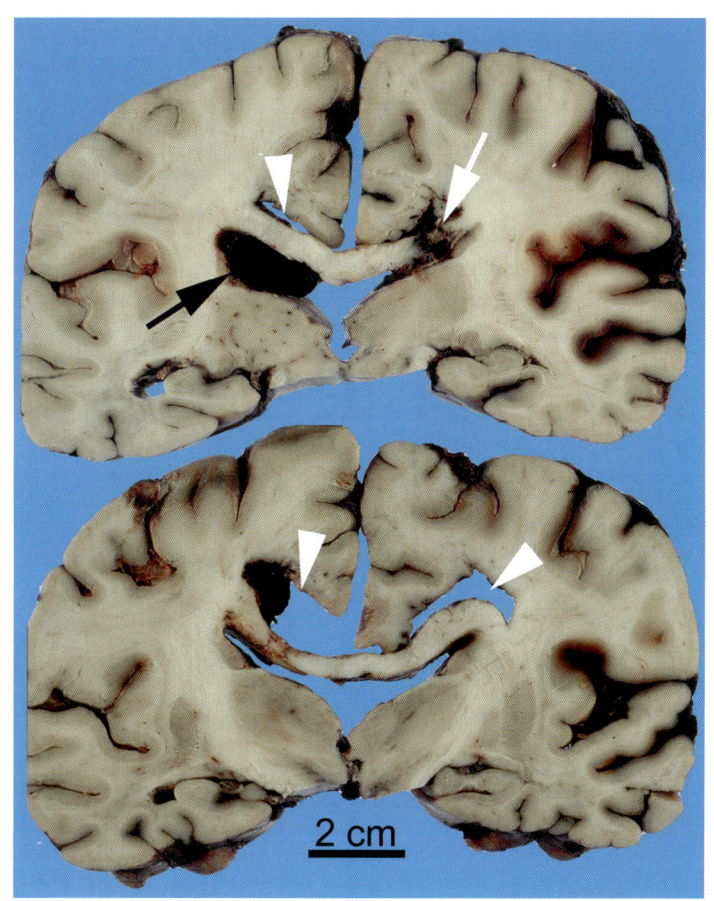

图 9-17 急性胼胝体周围与扣带回下血肿。脑组织来自一位下楼时摔倒致头部损伤的老年患者。右侧胼胝体脚撕裂（白色箭头）与脑室积血（黑色箭头）和双侧血肿密切相关，血肿在胼胝体和扣带回之间形成间隙（白色三角箭头）。没有证据表明存在外伤性轴索损伤。

4.5.1 迟发性创伤性血肿

创伤性脑内出血的时间可能延迟（这意味着通常在数小时到一天的稳定期后随着出血的进展会引发新的神经系统症状）。在可能发生延迟出血的情况下，可根据连续的神经影像学研究对外伤性脑内出血进行分类：尺寸缩小的血肿（Ⅰ型）、尺寸增加的小型或中型血肿（Ⅱ型）、原本正常部位形成的血肿（Ⅲ型），以及与脑挫伤相关的血肿[Ⅳ型(86)]。

4.6 创伤性脑室内积血

在脑切片之前，通过 Luschka（外侧孔）和 Magendie 孔（正中孔）可观察到第四脑室的大量出血，这在尸体解剖脑切片前可作为脑室内出血的间接证据。创伤性脑室内出血既可以原发也可以继发。

4.6.1 原发性脑室内出血

虽然有症状的原发性创伤性脑室内出血很少见，但会在机动车交通事故和受击打

(87-91)后出现,包括相对轻微的头部创伤导致的出血(92)。虽然可能是广泛性出血,但在神经影像学研究中却有不同的模式,包括Munro孔(室间孔)周围出血、单侧侧脑室体部和后角血肿、单个或两侧侧脑室后角中的独立性出血[这种情况下,由于患者处于仰卧位,经常出现脑脊液-血液分层(91)]。尽管多数情况下难以确定出血来源,但可能是多来源的出血,如脉络丛撕裂(65)、脉络组织撕裂(87)或脑室壁撕裂致室管膜下静脉血管破裂。

当透明隔或胼胝体和穹隆的连接部位撕裂时,会频繁发生多变但少量的脑室内出血(参阅标题7)。

同时也应考虑非创伤性脑室内出血的可能性。原发性非创伤性脑室内出血起源于颅内小动脉瘤或血管畸形的破裂,也可能与多种情况相关,包括高血压、抗凝治疗、甲基苯丙胺滥用、纤维肌性发育不良、烟雾病和脑瘤(93-95)。但在大量非创伤性案例中无法明确脑室内出血来源。

4.6.2 继发性脑室内出血

常见的继发性脑室内出血类型是创伤性脑室内出血(96,97),当对脑切片后发现脑内出血与脑室内出血是连续的时候,其出血机制就显而易见了(图9-38B;参阅标题6.4)。

4.7 人为的或微小的创伤性颅内出血

在大脑或其覆盖物中通常会发现人为的或无关紧要的出血。这种情况多数发生于死亡前右心室压力升高(急性心力衰竭或肺栓塞的后果)或颈静脉阻塞(如勒颈或悬吊)导致脑静脉压升高的尸体。这种情况下,脑血管淤血较明显,有时比大脑的其他部位(脑发绀)更明显(参阅第2章标题5.2)。淤血的血管破裂导致显微镜下局灶性稀疏性蛛网膜下腔出血和脑内出血点(在第三脑室腹侧壁更常见),或在硬脑膜下和蛛网膜下腔见到非常薄的血膜(参阅第2章标题5.2)。尽管存在争议,但这可解释婴幼儿镜下微小可见的硬脑膜内出血、向硬脑膜外和硬脑膜下轻微延伸的出血,否则就没有其他合理的依据怀疑是非意外性损伤所致(98)。尸检时颈髓背部和胸髓硬脊膜外区域也可能发现出血(相对于后者,脊柱最依赖的部分),特别是婴儿,组织病理学检查显示急性出血和毛细血管破裂(99,100)。

5 挫伤和裂创

导致头部外伤的外力通常会造成中枢神经系统局部出血性破坏或撕裂。

5.1 术语

脑或脊髓周边组织的出血性破坏(撕裂伤)区域,若软脑(脊)膜完整,通常称为挫伤,若软脑(脊)膜被撕裂,则称为裂创(52)。但对病理学家而言,除非在镜下检查了切片的每一处挫伤,否则很难确定软脑(脊)膜是否已经撕裂,因此没有必要这样做,因为实践中区分软脑(脊)膜完整的挫伤和镜下软脑(脊)膜撕裂的挫伤是没有意义的。此外，一般来说，尤其在颅脑损伤的神经影像描述中，法医倾向于将非血肿性的脑出血性破坏或脑撕裂损伤简单描述为挫伤。实际上在检查固定的脑组织时，可识别出创伤性出血破坏或中枢神经系统组织撕裂的几种损伤类型，包括以下内容（在本文的其余部分将使用这些术语）：

- 局灶性散在分布的小瘀点状或线状出血（单纯性挫伤）。
- 比单纯性挫伤分布更广泛的组织破坏、出血，且包括明显的大体软脑（脊）膜撕裂或破坏（挫裂创）。
- 出血区组织的破坏，通常位于单纯性挫伤和挫裂创的特征性分布中，其大小不一，与出血或血肿（挫伤 – 血肿）的大小相关。很难准确定义哪一阶段的挫裂创应归类为挫伤 – 血肿。
- 肉眼可见的巨大裂创，与最小或轻微的损伤周围的出血、组织破坏（撕裂）相关。脑裂创由凹陷性颅骨骨折、头部贯穿或穿孔样损伤引起。

尽管有以上特定的术语，但在下文中若无特别说明，"挫伤"一词统一指代单纯性挫伤、挫裂创和挫伤 – 血肿。

也可检见位于脑深部的出血性撕裂，有时被称为中间性挫伤（图 9-18B）或深部挫伤，通常提示存在 DAI。这些损伤与多个中小型孤立性创伤性脑内出血相关（参阅标题 4.5）。

5.2 发病机制

虽然挫伤的病理生理学机制复杂且受多种因素影响，但一般来说，挫伤通常是大脑与颅骨间相对运动引起的组织撕裂。因此，挫伤指示了脑与颅骨及硬脑膜间作用的部位、脑与硬脑膜暴力分离的部位、脑与硬脑膜及脑毗邻组织间差异运动的部位。

头部撞击常造成大脑与其遮盖物间的相对运动，随之造成挫伤，运动开始或中断时脑组织相对于硬脑膜和颅骨的滞后效应是惯性损伤的一种形式，即撞击惯性损伤。然而，当头部处于加速或减速运动中但没有碰撞时，外力作用很少能达到引起特征性的冲击性惯性损伤的量级（参阅标题 6.1.）。

就挫伤的大小和程度而言，颅骨骨折后造成的挫伤比颅骨完整时更严重，接触性损伤比撞击惯性损伤更易形成挫伤（101）。挫伤程度与枕部撞击的外力直接相关，但与侧面撞击没有相关性（102）。与枕部撞击导致的挫伤相比，颅骨侧面撞击产生脑挫伤时的加速度更小（102）。无论撞击的部位如何，脑挫伤多发生于额极、眶板上额叶、颞叶外侧和基底部以及大脑外侧裂壁（101-103）。相较于颅顶部光滑的内表面，眶板表面更加粗糙，更易造成眶额部脑皮质挫伤（65, 102），蝶骨嵴与吻侧颞叶之间复杂的机械性作用导致颞叶和外侧裂周围组织挫伤。顶部和枕部脑挫伤通常较轻，但与毗邻的颅骨骨折或冲击性挫伤有关的挫伤一般较严重（参阅标题 5.4.2）。尽管挫伤在损伤发生时立即形成，但随着时间的进展或出现影响血液凝固的因素时，其出血性外观会更加明显。当有明显坏死或涉及大血管损伤时，挫伤的出血更加显著。

乙醇中毒与严重的脑挫伤密切相关,因为醉酒者往往容易摔跌,而且由于保护性运动反射迟钝,醉酒者的挫伤比清醒者更加严重。此外,伴有肝脏疾病和急性乙醇中毒可能也不利于止血。

5.3 病理学
5.3.1 急性挫伤

脑表面急性挫伤的宏观改变较多,从脑表面轻微变色(单纯性脑挫伤;图9-18)到大面积出血和坏死(挫裂创;图9-19)都有。外力作用于脑回表面造成挫伤,但根据损伤严重程度的不同,这些损伤可仅局限于灰质,也可延伸至邻近的脑白质,其损伤程度及类型各不相同。蛛网膜下腔出血与挫伤相关(图9-19)。在脑切片中,小挫伤或损伤至死亡时间间隔短暂的脑挫伤都表现为垂直于软脑膜的线性出血,反映出与脑皮质血管类似的走行路径,说明了这些血管撕裂是如何形成挫伤的(图9-18和图9-20)。广泛的脑挫裂创表现为形状破碎且不规则的出血区域(图9-19和图9-20)。冲击性脑挫伤呈楔形,其基底位于软脑膜表面(参阅图6-51)。挫伤周围局部的脑肿胀与挫伤大小呈正比。

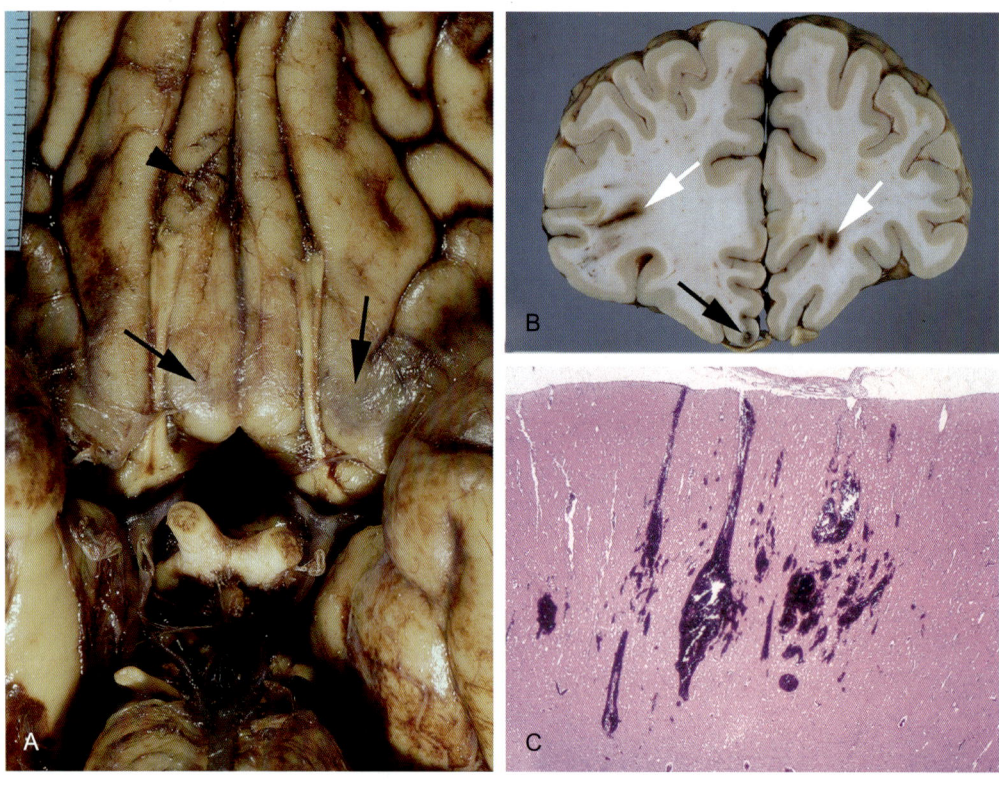

图9-18 单纯性急性脑挫伤。(A)眶额叶尾部皮质表面昏暗变色是小型单纯性脑挫伤的典型表现(箭头)(小挫裂创由三角所示)。(B)单纯性脑挫伤存在于左侧直回(黑色箭头)。白质有小血肿(白色箭头)。(C)低倍镜下大脑皮质,展示了单纯性脑挫伤的线性特征,反映了垂直于皮质表面的小血管撕裂路径(H-E 染色;×1.6 倍物镜)。

第9章 | 颅脑损伤及脊柱损伤

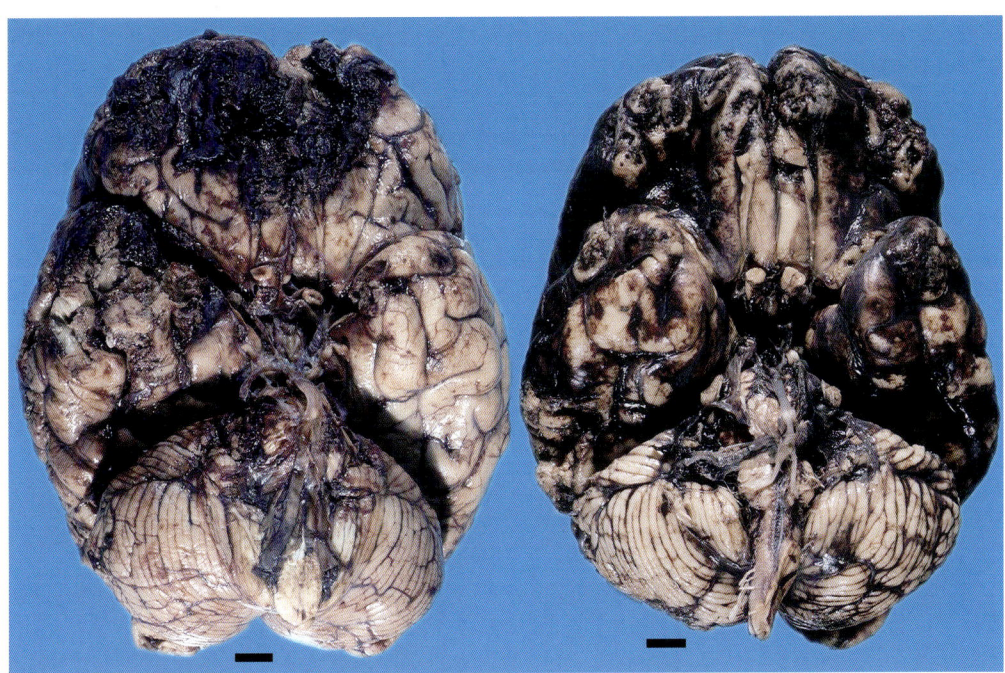

图9-19 急性脑挫伤的大体外观（比例尺＝1厘米）。急性额颞叶广泛的非对称性（左图）和对称性（右图）脑挫裂创，并引起明显的继发性蛛网膜下腔出血。

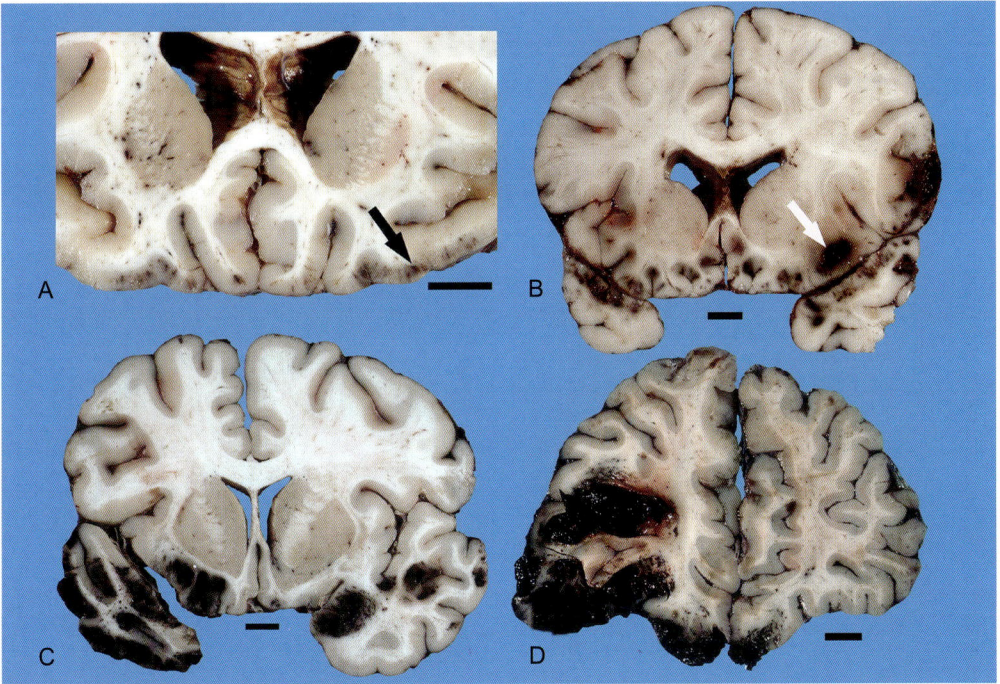

图9-20 急性脑挫伤的脑组织切面（比例尺＝1厘米）。（A）细小线性的单纯性脑挫伤（黑色箭头）。（B）单纯性脑挫伤，挫伤－血肿（白色箭头）。（C）多发挫伤－血肿和单纯性脑挫伤。（D）广泛挫伤－血肿及挫裂创。

急性挫伤的镜下改变包括血管周围出血及不同程度的融合性出血。损伤周围的神经元在损伤后几乎即刻出现非特异性改变,包括细胞变色暗淡、细胞扭曲,这些改变可反映机械性损伤或早期神经缺血性改变(参阅标题 6.3)。3-5 小时后,挫伤中心部位显示明显苍白的小空泡化分界区,这是大脑灌注不足继发性坏死的早期征象(104)。存活 6-24 小时后,相同区域的一些神经元形成明确的缺血性损伤特征,包括细胞质嗜酸性样变和细胞核固缩。尽管脑挫伤时发生相当程度的神经元损伤是不可避免的,但并不会坏死。

炎症对挫伤的反应程度及其在损伤后出现的时间多种多样(105, 106)。一般规律是损伤 3 小时内可见中性粒细胞着边,血管外中性粒细胞 6 小时后出现在损伤组织并持续至损伤后 3 天左右,吞噬细胞、激活的小胶质细胞和淋巴细胞的混合浸润大约出现在损伤后 3-4 天。损伤后大 2-3 天吞噬细胞的胞质内出现含铁血黄素。反应性星形胶质细胞在损伤后 5-7 天中较为明显。损伤后大约 24 小时可在脑白质挫伤边缘发现轴索肿胀。

5.3.2 陈旧性脑挫伤

损伤后数周至数月,血液和坏死组织逐渐被吸收,形成与挫伤、出血相对应的界限清晰的分界空腔,以及与较大的单纯性脑挫伤和脑挫裂创相对应的囊性结构或具有脑回顶部扇形特征的脑软化区域(图 9-21 和图 9-22)。不同的陈旧性脑挫伤的含铁

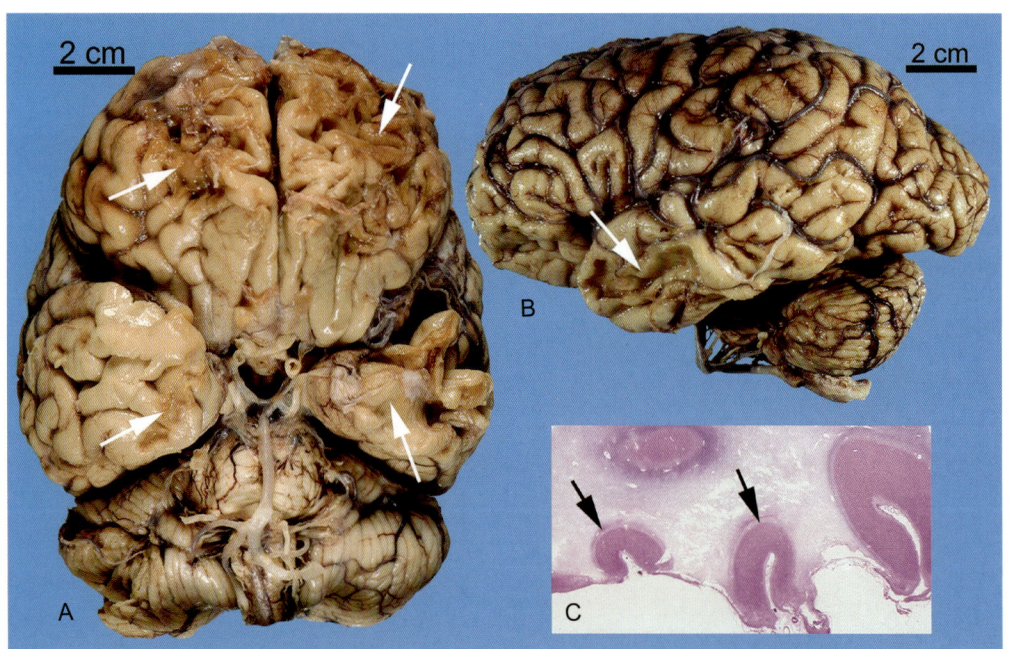

图 9-21 陈旧性脑挫伤。两份标本展示了(A)陈旧性额颞叶和(B)颞叶挫裂伤(白色箭头),表现为脑表面的凹点和凹槽。(C)两脑沟深处完整的皮质(箭头)及脑回顶部的撕裂。白质苍白区延伸至右侧完整脑回下面。

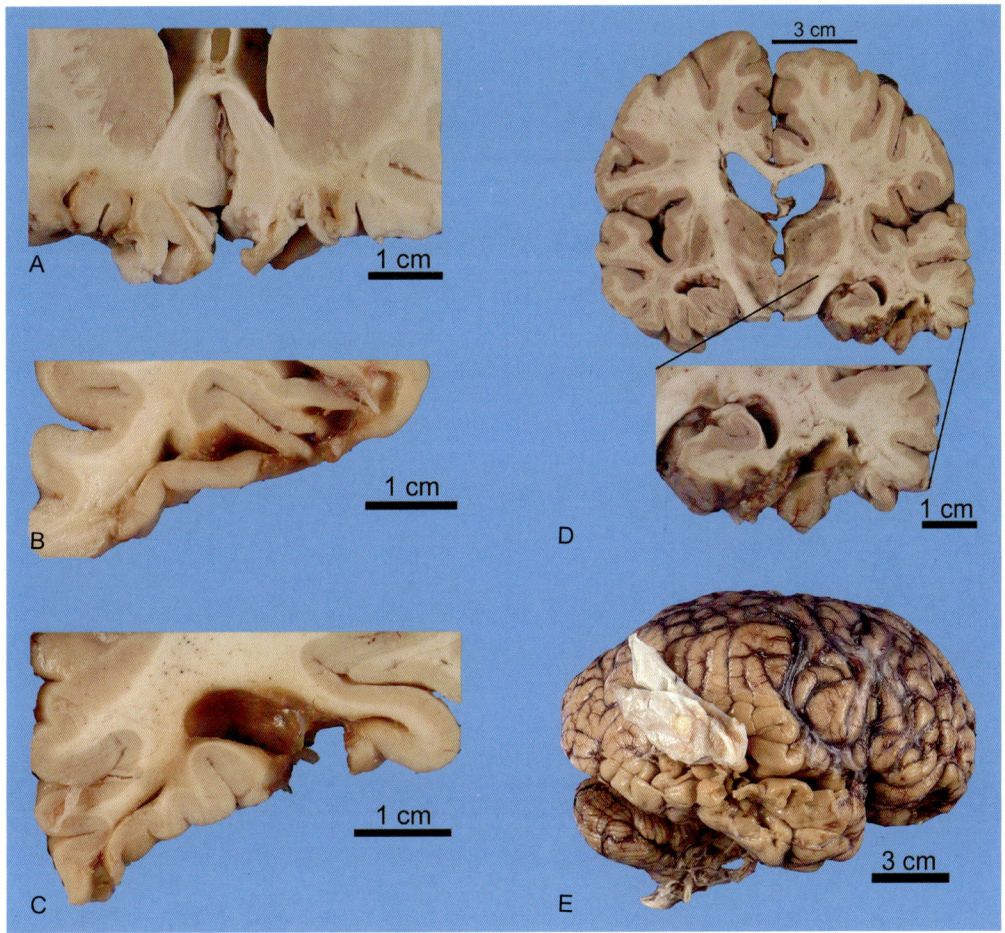

图 9-22 陈旧性脑挫伤。(A)陈旧性额眶部挫裂创。(B)、(C)额眶部陈旧性脑挫伤-血肿。(D)颞叶陈旧性脑挫裂创(画线局限了特写的来源)。(E)右颞叶挫裂创伴随硬脑膜黏附。

血黄素沉积(表现为相应的黄色)各不相同,从无到少量再到显著存在,大体反映原始的出血量及个体对损伤的炎症反应的快慢差异。挫伤区和毗邻正常皮质的脑白质呈苍白色,这是由有髓轴突缺失(及可能的脱髓鞘)、局部继发性缺血性损伤和水肿所致(图 9-21C)。硬脑膜可黏附于陈旧性脑挫伤表面(图 9-22E)。镜下可见轻微的单纯性脑挫伤,表现为神经元缺失部位的星形胶质细胞和含铁血黄素细胞呈垂直线性分布。

5.4 脑挫伤类型

以下几种常见类型的脑挫伤可用于初步推断头部损伤机制。

5.4.1 对冲性脑挫伤

发生在颅骨撞击部位对侧的脑挫伤习惯上称为对冲性脑挫伤。在颅骨已经停止运动而脑继续运动,或者撞击时颅骨运动而脑仍保持静止等情况下,会发生对冲性脑挫伤。颅脑间相对运动引起组织牵拉(拉伸)或滑动(剪切),作用力超过血管的弹性强度,超过脑-覆盖物间分离或撞击部位组织的弹性强度,换言之,脑及其覆盖物间的相对运动导致外力作用点对侧的脑组织发生撕裂、扭曲或负压抽吸。典型的对冲性脑挫伤是后仰摔倒致枕部撞击坚硬平面引起的额颞部脑挫伤。

然而,从头皮损伤或骨折部位推断出在其他部位(而不是精确诊断到的头部受碰撞部位的对侧)发现脑挫伤也非常多见(101,102)。加速度较低的暴力更趋向于引起对冲性脑挫伤,而加速度较高的暴力引起的脑挫伤则分布更加广泛(102)。相对于头部外力作用的部位,脑挫伤部位的多变性提示引起颅脑损伤的外力非常复杂且难以预测,也证实了对冲性脑挫伤不仅只发生在撞击点对侧,而是"一个不即刻出现于撞击部位之下的地方,而无论其确切位置在何处"(52)。

5.4.2 冲击性脑挫伤

即刻发生在颅骨撞击部位之下的挫伤称为冲击性脑挫伤(图9-9、图9-11和图9-23;参阅图6-51),由撞击时颅骨局部的凹陷变形对其下脑组织的直接压迫,以及变形颅骨的回弹对脑组织的牵拉(抽吸)引起。冲击性脑挫伤伴或不伴有颅骨骨折。撞击外力被颅骨耗散,所以头部运动的加速度较小,脑由于惯性保持相对稳定。

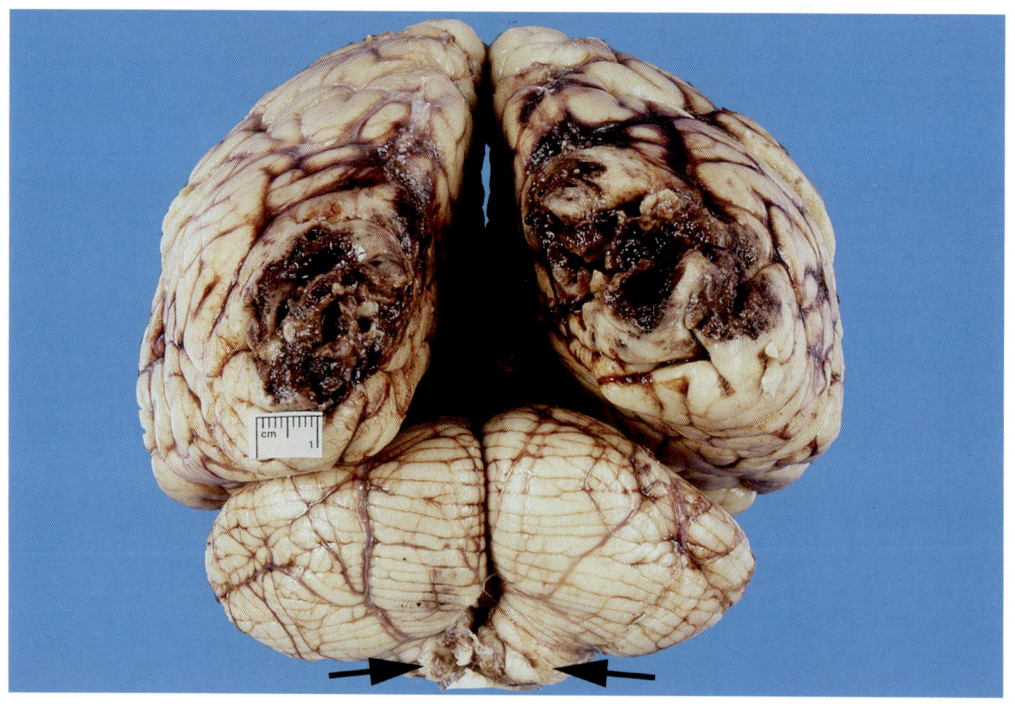

图9-23 冲击性脑挫伤。划船事故中被划水牵引杆击中枕部导致双侧枕部冲击性脑挫伤。继发于脑水肿的严重小脑扁桃体疝(箭头)(由枪弹创、击打及摔跌至凸起物体上引起的冲击伤分别在第6章图6-51和本章图9-9和图9-11中说明)。

5.4.3 冲击性脑挫伤和对冲性脑挫伤的意义

一般而言,对冲性脑挫伤是由头与具有较大平面、较大物体间的碰撞引起的损伤,头部因骤然减速停止运动或因较快的加速运动而导致损伤。冲击性脑挫伤是静止的头部与具有相对较小平面的物体间碰撞导致的脑接触性损伤。在实践中,对冲性脑挫伤由摔跌引起,冲击性脑挫伤则是撞击的结果。然而,对于具体的个案,因为存在例外情况,在缺乏其他可靠信息时应慎重使用这种一般化的结论。尤其是头部在摔跌时撞击小平面物体的凸出部位,就可产生冲击性脑挫伤(图9-11)(65),在预期应形成对冲性脑挫伤的部位可能会发现小范围冲击性脑挫伤伴随更严重的对冲性脑挫伤(图9-24)。对冲性脑挫伤也可发生于殴打后,但冲击性脑挫伤也可在此类案例中出现,且严重程度通常超过对冲性脑挫伤(65,81,107)。经典的法医教科书中提到,殴打可形成对冲性脑挫伤而无冲击性脑挫伤(65,81),这可能是由于殴打后摔跌所致(81),但目前缺乏足够的信息以了解这些观察结果所依据的具体案例,因而难以评估其可靠性。小脑冲击性脑挫伤比较特殊,因为其通常由枕骨摔跌形成(参阅标题5.4.7)。

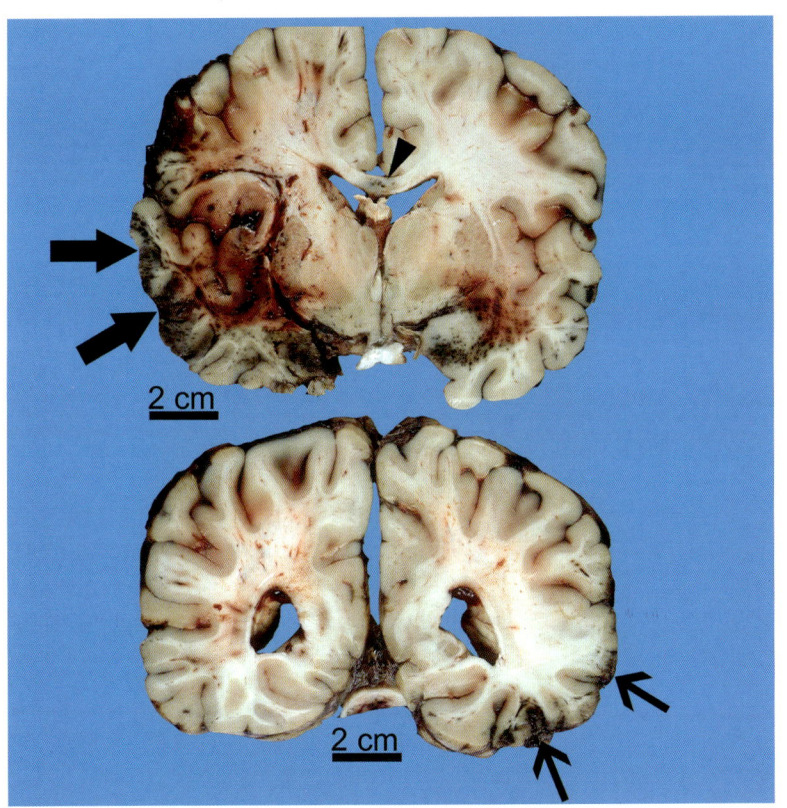

图9-24 冲击性和对冲性脑挫伤。脑标本源于一位因交通事故死亡患者。右侧枕骨明显骨折,提示该区域的钝性外力损伤。小箭头指示轻微的冲击性脑挫伤,大箭头则指示广泛性对冲性脑挫伤。胼胝体局部的出血性撕裂(三角)提示交通事故中大脑半球突发性从右至左的运动。

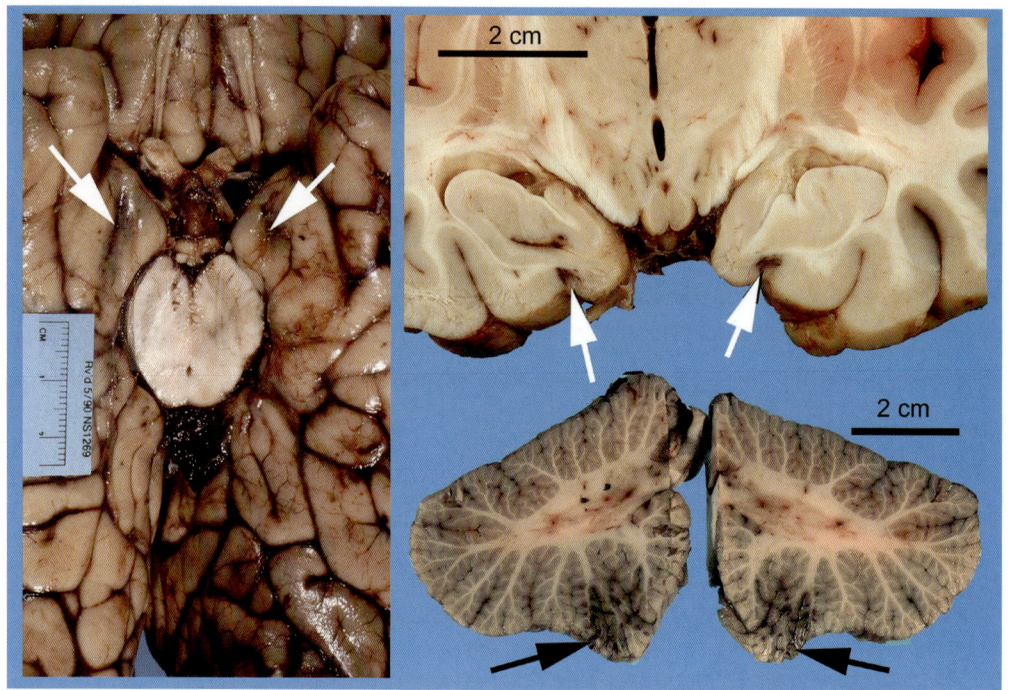

图 9-25 疝性脑挫伤。轻微的海马钩回（白色箭头）和小脑扁桃体（黑色箭头）疝性脑挫伤。

5.4.4 疝性脑挫伤

当海马钩回和小脑扁桃体分别疝入小脑幕切迹和枕骨大孔边缘时，会形成疝性脑挫伤（图 9-25）。此类脑挫伤发生于严重的头部外伤之后，尤其是高坠物体撞击头顶部、打击头顶部、头部高坠着地或头部枪弹伤（参阅第 6 章图 6-44）。疝性脑挫伤与创伤性脑肿胀继发的海马钩回疝和扁桃体疝引起的出血性坏死很难甚至无法区分。

5.4.5 滑动性（与矢状面平行）脑挫伤

相较于摔跌，滑动性脑挫伤在机动车交通事故中更常见，患者一般既无清醒期（参阅标题 11.2），也无颅骨骨折。脑挫伤发生于脑半球白质和背侧正中区域（背侧角）的灰质，特别额叶、顶叶区域，且往往双侧损伤。典型的滑动性脑挫伤是离散分布的单纯性脑挫伤或脑挫裂创，但是引起该挫伤的外力也可导致严重的脑挫伤、血肿（图 9-26）、出血点或不明确的出血变色区域（107）。"滑动性脑挫伤"有时也用于描述脑底部挫伤，用于强调说明脑在不平坦的颅底"滑动"时发生挫伤（65，108）。然而，这一术语的扩大化应用存在误导性，因为其掩盖了背侧角挫伤（即"真正"的滑动性脑挫伤）和弥散性轴索损伤（107，109）之间重要、常见但并非一成不变的关联性，而脑底部挫伤不存在这种关联性。

形成滑动性脑挫伤的原因在于脑和硬脑膜之间的相对运动，相对运动会牵拉及撕裂穿行于大脑皮质和上矢状窦的副矢状窦桥静脉的主干及分支，引起大脑皮质和皮质

第 9 章 | 颅脑损伤及脊柱损伤

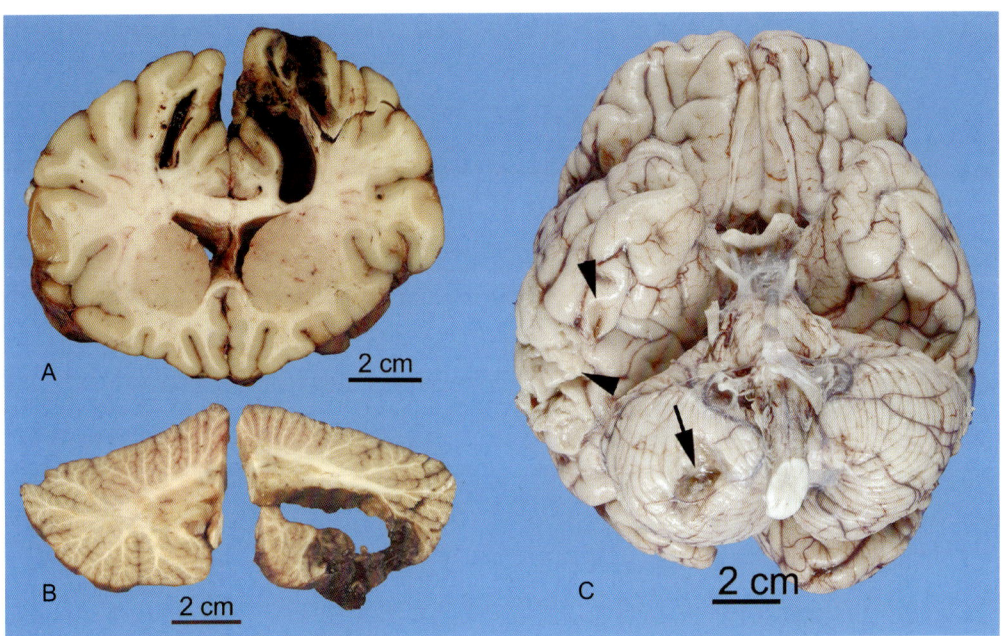

图 9-26 小脑挫伤与出血。A 图和 B 图中的脑切面来自向后摔倒致枕部受撞击的患者,枕骨发生骨折。(A)大片双侧额叶出血和脑挫伤、血肿。与滑动性脑挫伤的位置相对应(但没有出现弥散性轴索损伤)。(B)大片小脑挫裂创。小脑切片时血肿从挫伤部位掉出。(C)陈旧性小脑挫裂创(箭头)和与 A 图和 B 图中相似来源的轻微同侧颞叶挫裂创(三角)。

下白质间的差异性运动。副矢状窦桥静脉跨脑膜干的撕裂说明急性蛛网膜下腔出血与滑动性脑挫伤间有关联性。

5.4.6 骨折性脑挫伤

骨折性脑挫伤是线性的脑挫裂创,位于未移位骨折或凹陷性骨折线下方,或与之靠近(图 9-10;参阅标题 3.7)。无论在事实上,还是在重要性上,都不应该将其误认为冲击性脑挫伤。

5.4.7 小脑挫伤与出血

在排除与弥散性轴索损伤或脑肿胀相关的脑干出血后,单纯的外伤性颅后窝出血很罕见。临床实践中,在入院且通过 CT 或 MRI 扫描的头部损伤患者中约 3% 会发生颅后窝出血,致死率为 40%(46)。外伤性颅后窝出血包括硬膜外出血(由于横窦或乙状窦撕裂)、硬膜下出血,以及小脑挫伤或出血,发生比例大致相同。小脑挫伤的发生率稍低,可能与枕骨平滑的轮廓以及小脑固定于枕骨内表面与小脑幕包围的空间内有关。小脑挫伤、出血与摔跌或头后部受打击及枕骨骨折有关(110),但也存在罕见的例外情况,如可能由额部受撞击引起(111)。小脑挫伤可单纯发生于小脑中,也可与大脑半球损伤相关,后者在致命性小脑挫伤、出血案例中更为常见(46,112,113)。血肿可能由脑挫伤进展而来,在这种情况下血肿位于小脑旁;但在某些案例中,血肿可出现在小脑中线深部,远离挫伤的部位(114)。头部受撞击后平均12小时才会出现血肿(46)。

尸检中的小脑挫伤和创伤性小脑出血可能引发疑惑,因为其位置紧靠打击部位(也就是撞击部位)之下,提示损伤源自武器的打击而非高坠所致,同时伴发的额、颞叶脑挫伤会让人错误地怀疑头部遭受多次打击(图9-26)。此外,如果小脑损伤主要表现为出血,则引起出血的自然原因(尤其是高血压)可能会被用于解释高坠所致的小脑幕上损伤。在这种情况下,很难排除高血压性脑出血。但当死者缺乏高血压病的临床病理学特征时(参阅标题4.5)应考虑为创伤所致。外科手术清除小脑幕上的硬脑膜下血肿可能造成非创伤性小脑出血,使得解释小脑出血的原因更加复杂(115,116),可能导致误判为III型迟发性创伤性血肿(参阅标题4.5.1)。

5.5 脑挫伤的记录及量化

不同创伤性脑损伤案例中脑挫伤的分布与发病率差异显著,使得脑挫伤难以记录。最简单的记录方法是在脑切面简图[如美国军事病理研究所提供的简图(9)]上标记挫伤位置,这样更易理解其分布位置及严重程度。具有代表性的脑切面(或可疑死亡案件中的全部脑切面)应拍照留存。诊断时应说明挫伤的大小和严重程度。以一例向后摔跌至坚硬平面致急性创伤性脑损伤的案件为例,以下材料列举了一种神经病理学发现的记录方法:

- 急性严重颅脑创伤:
  - 巨大的枕部左侧挫裂创。
  - 枕骨左侧线性骨折。
  - 双侧大脑半球弥漫性"涂片型"蛛网膜下腔出血。
  - 广泛性脑挫伤:
    - 额-眶部(右侧>左侧,多发性,中等大小)
    - 右额叶凸面(多发性,中等大小)
    - 右颞叶(多发性,巨大,伴随挫伤性出血)
    - 右顶叶(多发性,中等大小,伴随巨大的挫伤性出血)
    - 枕叶(双侧,少,小)

已有文献描述了脑挫伤的量化方法(101-103),虽然其对于脑挫伤的研究有效,但对于常规检查仍过于复杂。此外还有一种简化的方案,在法医学常规实践中可能更易被法医所接受(117)。

5.6 脑挫伤的鉴别诊断

如果熟悉脑前部的额颞叶和外侧裂周区及脑后部常规的血管分布,就不会将脑挫伤与出血性脑梗死混淆。脑皮质小的毛细血管动脉瘤、显著的局灶性小血管或毛细血管扩张可能类似于小灶脑挫伤,镜下可明确区分。陈旧性脑梗死和陈旧性脑挫伤均以局灶性组织坏死为特征,有时很难区分。然而,相较于脑梗死,脑挫伤的界限更清晰、边缘更光滑,更易发生在脑回表面,具有能让蜘蛛网般的胶质血管束相对自由穿通的空腔,并能跨越大脑血管分布区域(106)。此外,陈旧性脑梗死中软脑膜边缘及皮质第一层都是完整的,而陈旧性脑挫伤的这些区域是被撕裂的。

6 弥漫性脑损伤

弥漫性(或多发性)脑损伤有4种类型:弥散性轴索损伤、弥漫性血管损伤、缺血缺氧性脑病和弥漫性脑肿胀。这些类型相互之间存在重叠且常伴有各种类型的局灶性脑损伤。

6.1 弥散性轴索损伤和创伤性轴索损伤

弥散性轴索损伤具有典型的临床表现,表现为受害者受伤当时即丧失意识,之后呈持续昏迷或进入"植物人"状态(118—121)。弥散性轴索损伤最常发生在道路交通事故中,有时也发生在打击(122)或高坠后(123)。"创伤性轴索损伤"是一个更常用的术语,指临床病史与弥散性轴索损伤不符时的广泛性轴索肿胀。

弥散性轴索损伤已在灵长类动物实验中得到验证,实验中头部在成角平面中运动,尤其是冠状面(即头部的横向运动)运动时,可引起轴突损伤。研究证明,与高坠过程中头部撞击坚硬平面时的作用力相比,导致弥散性轴索损伤的作用力持续时间更长,加速度或减速度的变化率更小。车辆碰撞过程中车体与人体相对缓慢挤压时,系安全带的驾驶员头部受到的作用力相对较小,而高坠时头部撞击硬物表面的作用力的变化更快(59,124,125)。这些外力作用导致大脑各部分间彼此牵拉(剪切)。因此,弥散性轴索损伤是广泛性的大脑相邻组织间相对运动(剪切)的结果,可导致运动部位的轴索损伤和轴索功能障碍。

弥散性轴索损伤的动物实验表明,轴索损伤部位的轴浆运输会产生局部堵塞,并引起神经元内化学物质堆积,导致该处轴索肿胀、破裂(126,127)。在严重的弥散性轴索损伤中,大脑不同部位的不同步运动会撕裂轴索(即"轴索离断")和小血管,小血管撕裂可引起局灶性出血或血肿(126,127)。

6.1.1 弥散性轴索损伤病理学改变

弥散性轴索损伤常缺乏头皮和颅骨的接触性损伤,但如果存在接触性头皮损伤,则常提示接触性损伤和弥散性轴索损伤的病理学改变同时存在。脑表面此类发现较少,有时局限于急性少量蛛网膜下腔出血的案例中(图9-15A)。弥散性轴索损伤的脑切面肉眼观无明显改变,或在胼胝体,大脑半球背侧角和邻近小脑上、中脚的延髓脑干背外侧出现不同程度的出血性撕裂(图9-27和图9-28)。滑动性脑挫伤较常见(参阅标题5.4.5),丘脑和基底节出血也常见(图9-27;参阅标题4.5;参考文献84)。

存活数周到数月的弥散性轴索损伤患者,其损伤的肉眼改变比较轻微,不仔细检查可能很难发现(图9-28和图9-29)。脑干的出血性撕裂会继发胼胝体萎缩,

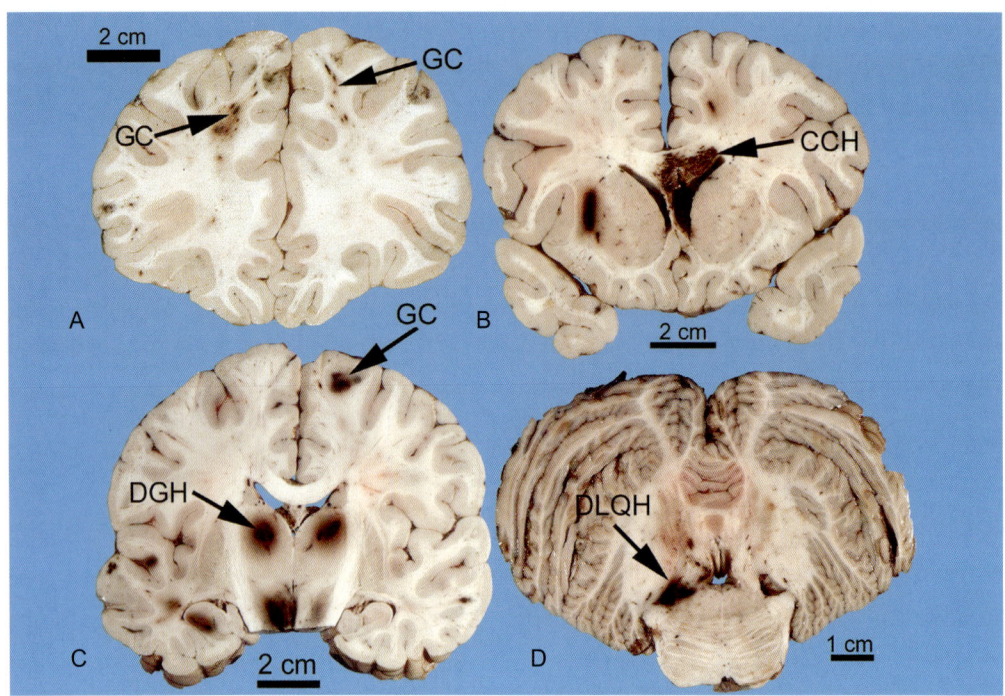

图9-27 与弥散性轴索损伤相关的出血性撕裂。(A) 矢状窦旁滑动性脑挫伤 (GC)。(B) 胼胝体出血性撕裂 (CCH)。(C) 矢状窦旁滑动性脑挫伤和深部灰质血肿 (DGH)。(D) 脑桥背外侧血肿 (DLQH)。

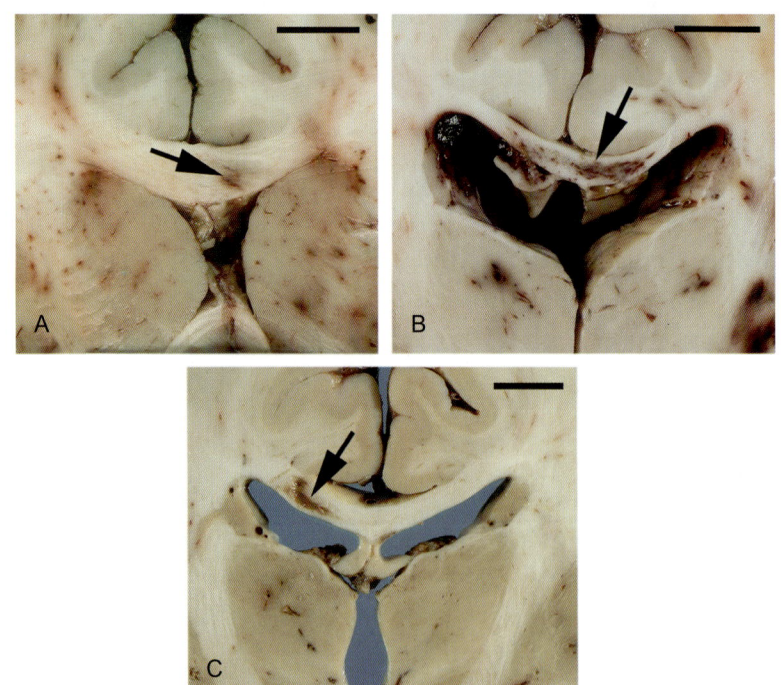

图9-28 弥散性轴索损伤中的胼胝体损伤 (比例尺 = 1厘米)。(A) 急性胼胝体出血点 (箭头)。(B) 中等大小急性出血性撕裂 (箭头)。(C) 淡黄色改变的微小陈旧性囊性病变。

第9章 | 颅脑损伤及脊柱损伤

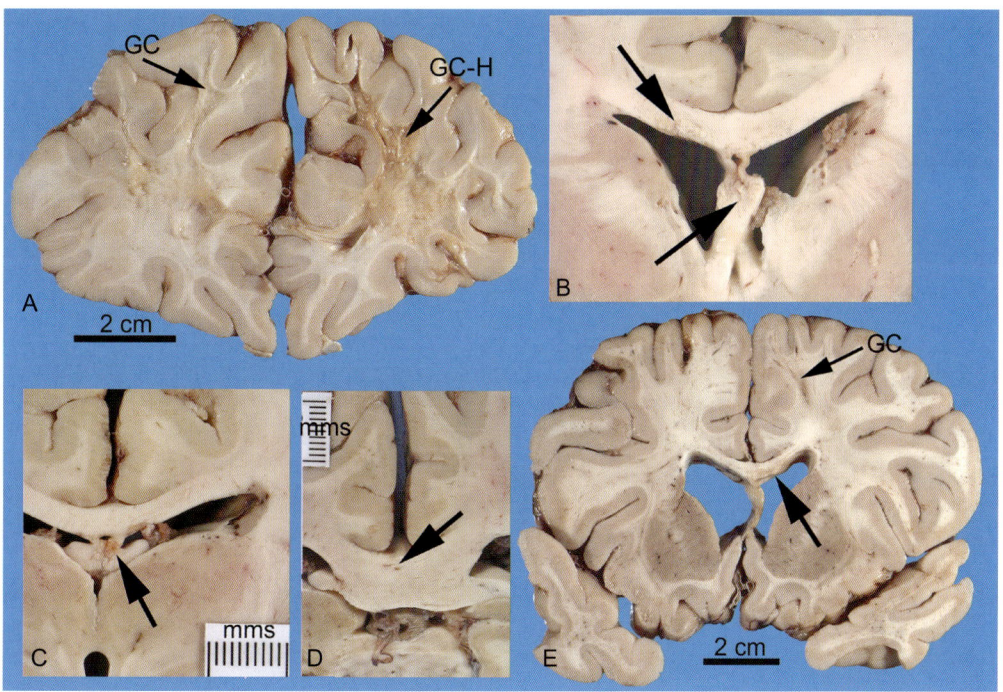

图 9-29 陈旧性弥散性轴索损伤的肉眼改变。(A)陈旧性滑动性脑挫伤(GC)或额部白质滑动性脑挫伤-血肿(GC-H)。(B)胼胝体体部(上方箭头)和穹隆降部(下方箭头)软化区的颗粒样变。(C)穹隆根部灶性黄色变(箭头)。(D)胼胝体压部小囊性病变(箭头)。(E)胼胝体体部萎缩,伴局灶颗粒样变(箭头),侧脑室不对称扩张和背内侧额叶白质的陈旧性滑动性脑挫伤。

尤其是胼胝体压部和尾部萎缩,以及中脑导水管扩张。急性出血性撕裂部位可检见散在分布的病灶,或镜检发现点状的含铁血黄素。脑萎缩部位呈颗粒状外观,质地较软。

急性弥散性轴索损伤的镜下特征包括皮质下的白质、内囊、胼胝体、大脑脚和桥脑基底部的广泛性轴索肿胀(图 9-30)。在走行于同一方向的神经束中可见大量的轴索肿胀,而在相邻的呈直角穿行的神经束中却很少见或没见轴索肿胀,这种现象在桥脑基底部最明显。坏死和血管周围性出血的区域与轴索肿胀的分布区域基本相似。5 天内可在轴索球周围发现小胶质细胞聚集;损伤后 10-11 天可首次检测到小胶质细胞簇,几天后更加容易检测到。损伤后约 9 天用胶质纤维酸性蛋白的免疫组化法可检见星形胶质细胞(128)。损伤后 1 个月内,星形胶质细胞和小胶质细胞的增生灶较明显,这与泡沫状巨噬细胞的出现有关(129)。在生存数月至数年后,这些损伤部位会逐渐演变成萎缩的微囊状区域,并散在分布含铁血黄素细胞(129)。轴索继发性变性可开始于连合束(包括胼胝体未受累的其他区域)和脑干的长束上星形胶质细胞和小胶质细胞的出现(130)。

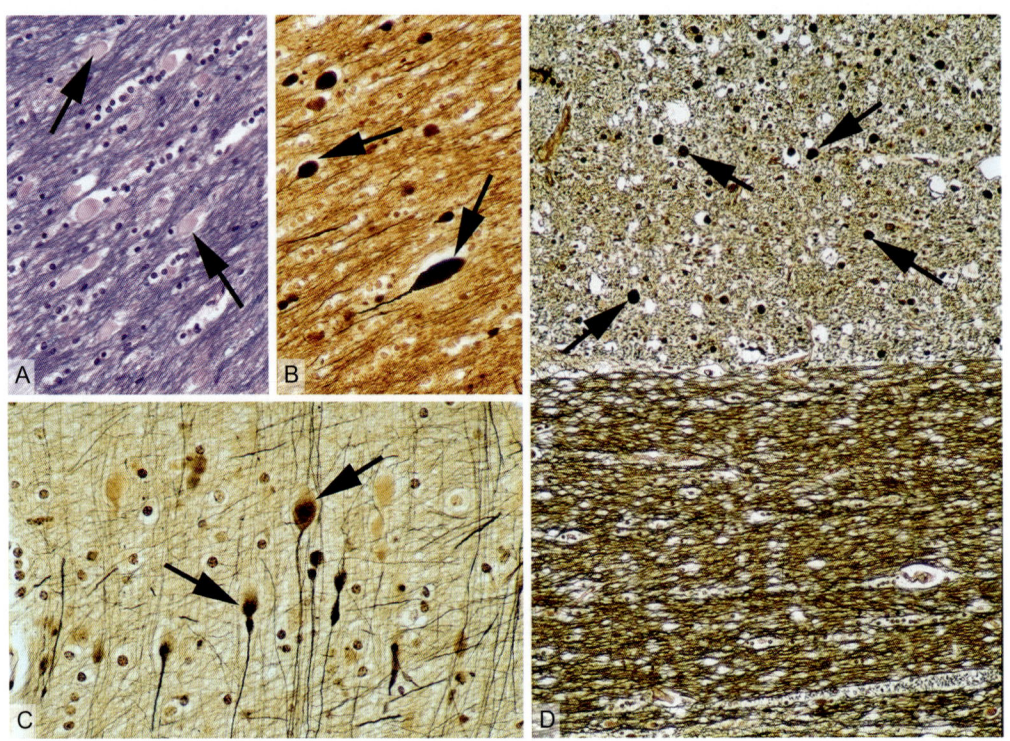

图9-30 急性弥散性轴索损伤的镜下表现。(A)胼胝体轴索肿胀(箭头)(HE and Luxol fast blue 染色,神经髓鞘染色,用于观察白质损伤:×40倍物镜)。(B)胼胝体轴索肿胀(箭头;比尔朔夫斯基法,神经镀银染色法:×40倍物镜)。(C)额叶皮质下白质轴索肿胀(箭头;Bielschowsky 法、神经镀银法染色:×40倍物镜)。(D)桥脑基底部轴索肿胀(箭头),下行神经纤维比交叉神经纤维的轴索肿胀量更多(Bielschowsky 法、神经镀银法染色:×10倍物镜)。

6.1.2 弥散性轴索损伤和创伤性轴索损伤的脑组织取材

对疑似弥散性轴索损伤的脑组织进行显微镜检查时,需对可能遭剪切力或牵拉力作用区域的脑白质全面取样(126)。这些区域包括胼胝体和额叶尾部白质、胼胝体压部、深部灰质(包括内囊后支)、小脑半球白质、中脑尾部(小脑上脚交叉的水平)、脑桥前侧(包括基底节和小脑上、中脚)。为证明弥散性轴索损伤,不能在局灶性脑损伤周围(如出血和梗塞区)的组织取材,因为此类损伤周围的轴索断裂常会引起轴索肿胀。

如未在组织块内发现轴索肿胀,则可排除弥散性轴索损伤和外伤性轴索损伤。然而,对头部受伤后持续昏迷的患者,可通过胼胝体、额叶白质和基底节区大量轴索肿胀的表现来诊断弥散性轴索损伤。

6.1.3 弥散性轴索损伤和创伤性轴索损伤的特殊染色和免疫组化染色

尽管 H-E 染色或髓鞘染色(如罗可沙尔坚牢蓝染色)的切片在损伤后约 24-36 小时后可检见轴索肿胀,但也有必要对组织切片进行银染[如比尔朔夫斯基法或神经镀银染色法,可检测损伤后 12–18 小时的轴索肿胀(131,132)]。神经纤维的免疫组化染色,如 β 淀粉样前体蛋白(B–APP)的免疫组化染色[可检见损伤 2 小时后的轴索异常(132,133)和损伤后 3 小时的轴索肿胀(132,134),大面积的轴索肿胀可在损伤后约 85 小时检见(134)]。尽管在损伤 2 周后一些轴索肿胀数量减少,B–APP 免疫阳性表达变弱(126),但损伤几周后仍可检测到轴索肿胀(131,135)。常规 H-E 染色切片可见小胶质细胞结节,但若对切片作 CD68 免疫组化染色则更容易识别。镜下局部损伤也可通过铁染色检测含铁血黄素来证实。

6.1.4 弥散性轴索损伤分级

根据病理特征严重程度,弥散性轴索损伤可分为三级(136)。一级弥散性轴索损伤仅限于多个典型部位的轴索肿胀,如前所述。二级和三级弥散性轴索损伤指除了广泛分布的轴索肿胀外,还存在胼胝体(二级)和胼胝体以及脑干前部背外侧区域(三级)局灶性出血或坏死性改变。这些局灶性损伤(包括坏死或出血)或肉眼可见,或显微镜下才可见。

6.1.5 创伤性轴索损伤(轻度弥散性轴索损伤)

大量观察结果表明,包括弥散性轴索损伤在内的大部分脑损伤或多或少都存在轴索肿胀(137)。不同损伤程度的创伤性轴索损伤的表现也有不同(126),依损伤严重程度的递减次序,损伤表现包括以下几点:
- 典型的弥散性轴索损伤[严重的创伤性轴索损伤(126)]。
  - 受害者从一开始就失去意识。
- 创伤性轴索损伤。
  - 受害者表现为间断清醒,然后死亡(参阅标题 11.2);或未丧失意识,以中度或轻度神经功能障碍状态存活(123,130,136,138);或具有最轻度的神经功能异常(131,133,135,139)。
  - 相比于弥散性轴索损伤,致死性案例中的轴索肿胀分布范围小、数量少。死亡是由于局灶性脑损伤、脑肿胀、缺血缺氧性脑病或颅外损伤所致。
  - 注意:在这些案例中可发现小的胼胝体出血。
- 磁共振检查所示创伤性脑白质病。
  - 头部轻微外伤,神经功能完全恢复。分布式的 MRI 脑信号改变的观察结果提示弥散性轴索损伤所致的轴索肿胀(140)。

根据临床和病理学结果,已证实轴索损伤的严重程度对应于动物实验中的创伤性损伤的等级强度,也包括可逆性轴索功能障碍这一较轻的分级结果(126,127,141)。

6.1.6 非创伤性轴索损伤

已证明 β 淀粉样前体蛋白的免疫染色是检测轴索异常的敏感、特异性方法,典型的轴索肿胀("收缩球")仅是其中的一种。轴索运输发生局部延缓或中止时,任何轴索内均会积聚 β 淀粉样前体蛋白。β 淀粉样前体蛋白的弥漫分布(或至少是广泛、多

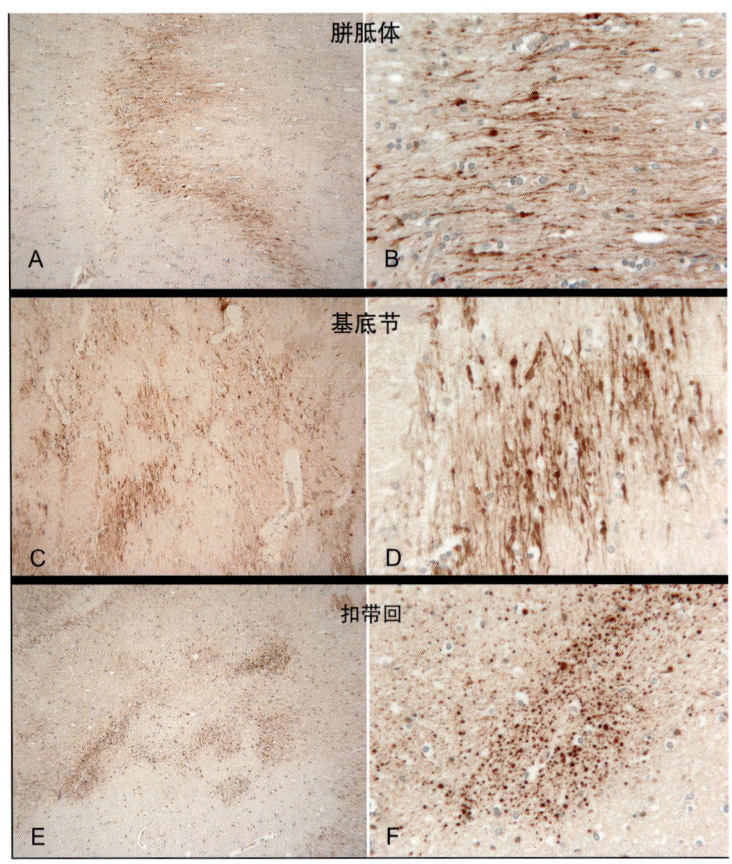

图9-31 β淀粉样前体蛋白免疫组织化学染色结果。受害人头部遭受打击倒地后就医治疗,临床诊断为广泛性硬膜下血肿。尽管对血肿进行了手术清除,但受害人仍因严重的脑水肿于伤后几小时死亡。该案例无法通过β淀粉样前体蛋白解释轴索损伤的性质。对死者包括胼胝体(A)、(B)、基底节(C、D)及扣带回(E、F)的多部位脑组织进行β淀粉样前体蛋白免疫组化染色。结果显示大量阳性表达的轴索呈带状和颗粒状分布,病变分界不清。尽管未见明显的轴索肿胀,但这些阳性表达仍提示轴索可能存在"微肿胀"。

灶性)异常也发现于非创伤性疾病中,包括低血糖、缺氧性脑损伤、癫痫发作、一氧化碳中毒(参阅第3章标题24)和Creutzfeldt-Jakob病等(139, 142-144)。虽然难以确定某些非创伤性轴索损伤引起轴突肿胀的原因,但脑肿胀确实会引起脑组织(及轴索)形变,尤其在缺血缺氧性脑病中(139)。由于"弥散性轴索损伤"这一术语与创伤明确相关,因此不能用于描述这些情况下的轴索异常改变用导致轴索损伤的原因表述会更好,如"低血糖性轴索损伤""缺血缺氧性轴索损伤",甚至"不明原因的轴索损伤"亦可,从而避免了混淆的风险,尤其在将创伤作为轴索病变的可能病因时(128)。

6.1.7 β淀粉样前体蛋白在关于鉴别轴索损伤性质上的局限性

对于大多数非创伤性轴突损伤,由于非创伤性因素有其自身的组织病理学特征,所以轴突异常的原因较为明确(145)。然而,在疾病演变的早期,仅依据β淀粉样前

体蛋白免疫组化染色检验的结果则难以进行准确诊断,其原因如下:
- 尽管β淀粉样前体蛋白可在其他诊断指标显现前就用于识别轴索损伤,但因缺乏特异性,使得法医在此时缺乏足够的诊断疾病的依据。
- 在疾病早期,病变轴索仅表现为局灶性β淀粉样前体蛋白强阳性表达,相比于创伤性轴索损伤的病理学改变(即散在规则的轴索肿胀)缺乏明显的形态学改变。

外力直接作用或脑外伤后的继发性改变(如脑水肿、缺血性脑损伤)均可导致轴索损伤。然而,在两者兼有的情况下,β淀粉样前体蛋白难以加以甄别和解释。

在缺氧性轴索损伤中,β淀粉样前体蛋白阳性表达往往呈片状、带状(特别易见于脑桥中线部位)以及散在零星状分布(128,133),而创伤性轴索损伤的病理学特征则以轴索肿胀为主,即病变轴索呈蝌蚪样改变。然而,在某些特殊情况下,如疾病发作后存活时间较短的案例,β淀粉样前体蛋白检测几乎不能区分因脑缺氧、脑肿胀及外伤导致的轴索损伤(图9-31)。

综上可知,β淀粉样前体蛋白免疫组化染色能较敏感地识别各种原因导致的轴索损伤,甚至在轴索功能障碍后数小时内即可进行识别,但对涉及某一特定机制的轴索损伤缺乏足够的特异性。因此,就β淀粉样前体蛋白在法医病理学诊断中的地位和作用尚未达成共识,尤其是死因可疑的案例。鉴于不确定因素较多,法医还可结合银染或髓鞘染色对损伤的轴索进行识别。发现脑组织出现多部位轴索肿胀时方可针对弥散性轴索损伤或一般的创伤性轴索损伤进行明确诊断。

6.2 弥漫性血管损伤

弥漫性血管损伤(图9-32)始终具有致命性,伤者或在受伤时当即死亡,或仅能存活几个小时。接触性头部损伤可能不明显。检查脑组织时能发现弥漫性蛛网膜下腔出血和散在点状出血。后者或许仅能在显微镜下发现(146,147)。室管膜下(第三脑室、中脑导水管和第四脑室)、中脑和脑桥外侧、下丘脑中线及延髓脑干出血较为明显,而延髓出血不显著(147)。丘脑和额、颞叶白质也可出血,但不会同弥散性轴索损伤并发出血一样显著(52,146,147),这可能是由于出血的进展时间不够。出血源于毛细血管、静脉或动脉(147)。引起弥漫性血管损伤的外力可能与弥散性轴索损伤的外力类型一致,但外力强度更大,引起的神经元功能的破坏更广泛,导致在轴突肿胀发生前即死亡。

6.2.1 多发性点状脑出血的鉴别诊断

不应将弥漫性血管损伤的出血点与血管淤血相混淆,致死性头部损伤往往出现脑血管淤血。脑血管淤血在脑组织中存在好发区域,如第三脑室室壁,而在脑干中往往不易发生或不明显。

广泛性点状出血也可发生于非外伤性案例中,包括弥散性血管内凝血、血栓性血小板减少性紫癜、空气栓塞、脂肪栓塞和脑疟疾(参阅第7章标题12.1;第8章标题

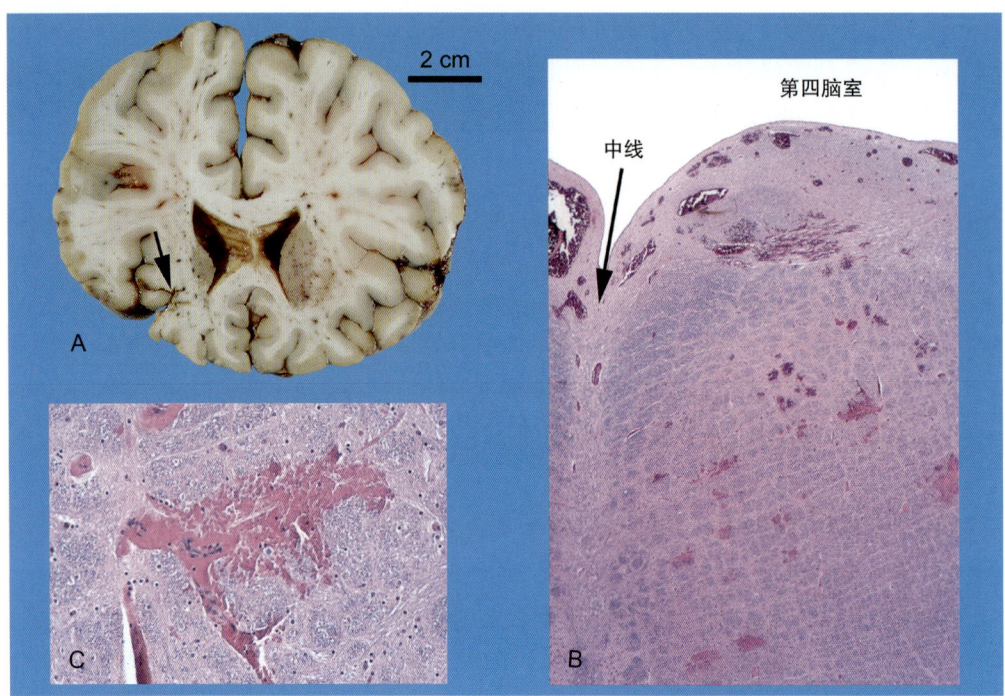

图 9-32 弥漫性血管损伤。样本来自交通事故死者的脑组织。死者的车被卡车追尾,存在轻微的头皮挫伤和枕骨骨折。(A)散在、不明显的白质点状出血,左额叶挫伤(箭头)。(B)脑桥多处点状出血(H-E 染色和 Luxol Fast Blue 染色: ×1.6 倍物镜)。(C)血管周围出血。脑干广泛分布(HE 染色和 Luxol Fast Blue 染色: ×25 倍物镜)。

12.1、12.4)。参考案情和病史有助于判断外伤性和非外伤性中枢神经系统的点状出血。

6.3 创伤性缺氧缺血性脑损伤

缺氧具有危害性,因为组织中氧含量过低会引起细胞能量代谢障碍并最终导致细胞死亡。缺血也具有危害性,因为组织所需代谢物(包括氧气)的运输和代谢产物的排出会因缺血而受到影响。尽管存在许多学术争议,目前仍使用"缺氧缺血"来描述低氧浓度和低血流量的损害(148),但这不能解释缺氧及缺血对组织损伤的影响程度。

致命性创伤性轴索损伤案例中缺氧缺血比较常见(149,150),但因为头部损伤过程及损伤后机体变化较复杂,故其缺氧缺血的原因并不明确。充足的全脑/局部脑灌注和氧合作用与脑灌注压(即平均动脉压减去颅内压)、血红蛋白氧合程度及血液携氧能力有关。由于低血压(或心肺衰竭)、脑肿胀、呼吸功能不全及失血等因素,外伤案例中的脑灌注压、血红蛋白氧合程度及血液携氧能力均会受影响。

缺氧缺血程度与其持续时间成正比。此外,不同细胞类型和脑部区域对缺氧缺血损害的反应程度也存在差异(神经元对缺氧缺血更敏感,小脑、海马及丘脑核更脆弱)。实际上,缺氧缺血会导致神经元坏死(选择性神经元坏死)和所有组织坏死(广泛性坏死)。

创伤性缺氧缺血脑损伤呈弥漫性（通常为选择性神经元坏死）或局灶/多灶性分布（组织学特征为选择性神经元坏死、广泛性坏死，或两者兼有）。

6.3.1 弥漫性创伤性缺氧缺血性神经元损伤

心搏、呼吸停止或严重低血压的颅脑损伤患者，治疗期间更易出现弥漫性缺氧缺血性神经元坏死。受伤时已经昏迷且只有散在局灶性损伤的患者，也能观察到弥漫性缺氧缺血性神经元坏死。这类现象至少存在两种解释。首先，脑血流量的神经影像学检查结果表明许多患者在缺氧缺血性脑损伤后最初几个小时内存在全脑血流量灌注不足，而受伤 24 小时后脑血流量得到改善（151, 152）。其次，头部受撞击时可能发生自限性心搏、呼吸骤停，造成全脑血流灌注不足（心脏停搏性脑病）。脑损伤引起的心搏、呼吸骤停导致脊髓神经元缺血，局部创伤性脑灌注不足则难以造成脊髓血流量改变。自限性外伤性心搏、呼吸骤停可能与"脊髓震荡"有关（参阅第 10 章标题 4.3）。

6.3.2 局灶性/多发性创伤性缺氧缺血性神经元损伤

不同脑动脉供血区交界处的局灶性缺血性神经元损伤提示低血压为其发病原因。杂乱分布的缺血性坏死区是局部脑肿胀继发局部灌注不足的结果。脑挫伤及其周围、脑内血肿边缘及硬脑膜外血肿下的神经元均会表现出早期脑缺血的病理改变（153, 154）。肿胀脑组织中，钩回或颞叶内侧、小脑幕切迹边缘间的大脑后动脉及其分支受压，或扣带回与大脑镰游离缘间的大脑前动脉分支受压，可分别引起颞叶内侧（大脑后动脉区域）和大脑半球间（大脑前动脉区域）的出血性梗死（参阅标题 6.4）。严重外伤性蛛网膜下腔出血以及涉及椎动脉、颈内动脉的骨折可继发动脉血管痉挛，从而产生局灶性脑缺血（155）。

6.3.3 缺氧缺血性脑损伤的病理改变

6.3.3.1 选择性神经元坏死

选择性神经元坏死脑组织的肉眼观较为正常，或仅有局部或弥漫性非特异性脑肿胀或颜色改变。选择性神经元坏死需通过显微镜观察神经元胞质改变，即细胞核收缩、深染（缺血性神经元坏死，细胞均质化改变；图 9-33 和图 9-34）。损伤后 6—12 小时内难以发现缺血性神经元坏死的特异性改变，如果在此期间伤者因脑肿胀造成血流灌注停止，仅能通过机械通气维持生命，其特异性病理改变可能会被掩盖或延迟出现。因此，遭受严重缺血性损伤的脑组织可能没有明显的病理学改变，因为损伤至脑血流停止之间缺乏足够的时间来呈现脑缺氧缺血性损伤的病理学改变。

尽管缺血性神经元坏死在脑和脊髓中的分布变化较多，但有两种模式非常明确：弥漫性或广泛性缺血性神经元坏死（提示全脑灌注停止并被归类为缺氧缺血性脑病），或者局部/多灶性缺血性神经元坏死（由脑损伤或损伤并发症所致）。

老年性选择性神经元坏死的大脑肉眼观为正常或略有萎缩，胼胝体可能由于有髓纤维的减少而变窄，在显微镜下可通过星形胶质细胞增生和神经元缺乏来识别神经元坏死部位。

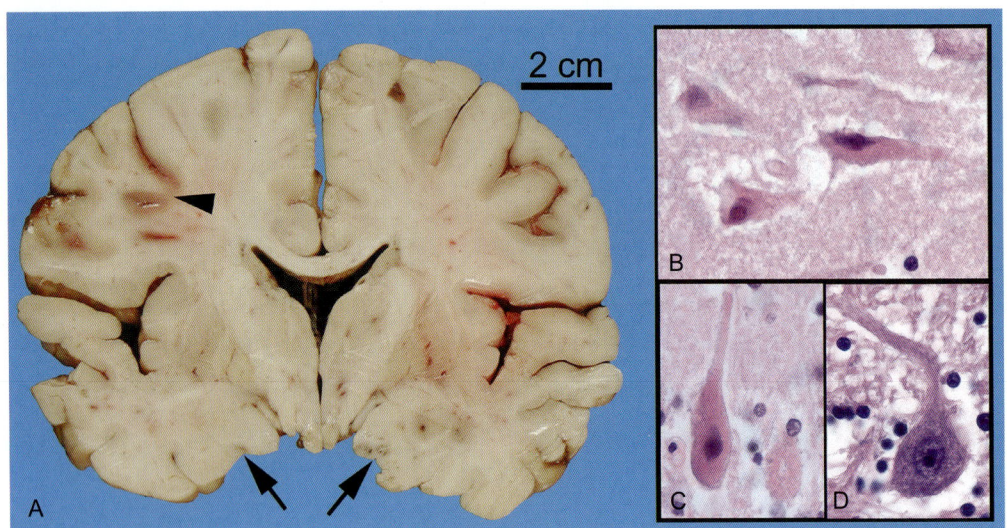

图 9-33 创伤性缺氧缺血性脑病。(A) 脑冠状切面轮廓平滑,是缺氧缺血性脑损伤继发脑肿胀的典型表现。左侧大脑前动脉与大脑中动脉的"分水岭"区脑皮质呈暗褐色变(三角)。两侧钩回形成明显凹槽(箭头),右侧钩回点状出血是脑肿胀挤压形成的疝性脑挫伤。透明隔被撕裂。(B) 海马锥体神经元缺血性坏死。神经元萎缩,胞质均匀(嗜酸性),核深染、缩小、形态不规则(H-E 染色: ×40 倍物镜)。(C) 浦肯野细胞显示出与 B 图类似的改变(H-E 染色: ×40 倍物镜)。(D) 正常的浦肯野细胞,细胞核圆形,尼氏小体颗粒样物质(蓝色)(H-E 染色: ×40 倍物镜)。

6.3.3.2 致密或暗色神经元及海马下托部位的暗红色神经元

致密或暗淡细胞质的神经元("致密"或"暗色"神经元)是脑损伤中常见的非特异性改变,可能是神经细胞遭受机械外力作用的结果[由死后对大脑的处理或巨大的机械外力(如高坠)引起],不应与缺血性神经元坏死相混淆(图 9-34)。引起这些神经元改变的原因仍不清楚,但动物研究表明并非总是人为所致,即使在损伤后即刻发生,也不表示必然是致命性神经元损伤所致(156-158)。

另一个引起混淆的潜在原因是拉长的暗红色嗜酸性(暗红色)神经元簇,具有开放性泡状细胞核,在粗略检查中类似于缺血性神经元坏死,这种神经元簇位于因各种原因突然死亡患者(包括突然、意外和不明原因死亡的"健康"人)的海马 CA1 段与海马区下托间的连接处,以及海马区下托处(图 9-35)。这可能与致密性神经元的发病机制相似,无论是何种致损原因,相似的位置反映出海马下托部位是"选择性易损区"。

6.3.3.3 缺氧缺血性神经元广泛性坏死

广泛性神经元坏死与选择性神经元坏死的机制相似。广泛性坏死主要的大体改变是局部肿胀和变色。损伤后 18-24 小时内坏死区域发生软化,损伤后 2-3 天内大脑在坏死和正常组织交界处产生裂隙。数周至数月内坏死组织逐渐吸收,并出现一个复杂的胶质增生和囊肿区域。显微镜下,损伤后 12-18 小时后组织明显坏死,随后的病理学改变与挫伤相似(参阅标题 5.3)。

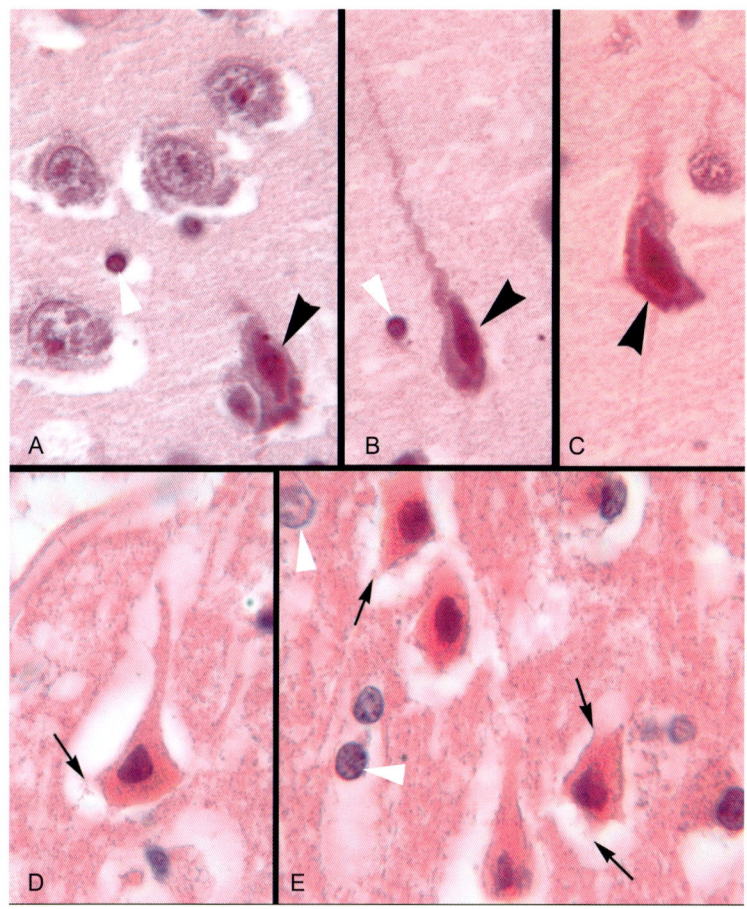

图 9-34 非缺血性神经元可呈现出致密("暗色")状。(A)-(C) 三角指示致密的神经元。A 图左上方有 4 个正常的神经元。致密神经元的特点是明显暗淡或暗黑的胞质和核。其细胞核被拉长,比正常核更致密。在某些情况下,皮质锥体神经元顶端的树突具有螺旋形外观(B)(H-E 染色:×100 倍物镜)。(D)、(E) 神经元缺氧缺血性坏死的典型改变,与 A-C 图中的致密神经元相比呈现胞质更均匀、颜色更明亮的嗜酸性改变。神经元内空泡性坏死(由星形胶质细胞胞浆肿胀引起)比致密神经元更明显,而且神经元周围液泡内包含被肿胀的星形胶质细胞(黑色箭头)吞噬了的破碎神经元胞质(结构)。另外要注意神经胶质细胞的细胞核比相邻的致密神经元拥有更多的空泡(白色三角)。其他有助于从致密神经元中区分出坏死缺血性神经元(图 9-35)的线索包括神经纤维的微空泡形成,神经元细胞核扭曲、固缩或崩解,以及毛细血管内皮细胞胞浆肿胀(H-E 染色:×100 倍物镜)。

6.4 创伤性脑肿胀

创伤性脑损伤中脑肿胀很常见。脑肿胀发生于损伤区域,尤其在伴发缺氧缺血性损伤的脑挫伤及脑内血肿周围。广泛且无明显脑组织结构破坏的脑肿胀常发生于硬脑膜外血肿同侧的大脑半球,特别好发于儿童和青少年一侧或两侧大脑半球,有时也在相对轻微的撞击且无其他脑损伤的情况下发生(159-161)。硬脑膜下血肿下的脑肿胀在血肿清除后尤为明显,可能导致脑组织从开颅区疝出。

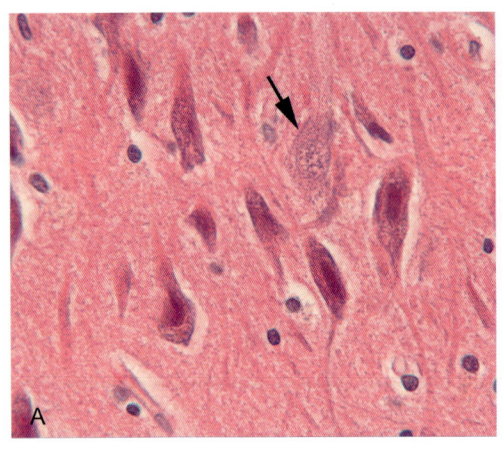 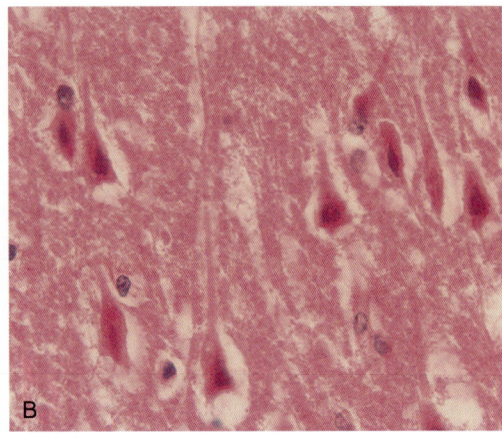

图 9-35 海马下托"暗红色"神经元。(A) 不确定起源的暗红色神经元,此类神经元常出现在海马 CA1 段和海马下托部位连接处以及各种原因(包括不明原因)导致的突然和意外死亡者的海马下托。箭头所示为正常神经元的斜切面(H-E 染色:×40 倍物镜)。(B) 来自海马下托的显微镜下照片,显示缺血性神经元坏死的特征。对比 A 图中海马下托暗红色的神经元,该切面下的神经元收缩得更明显,胞质嗜酸性更均匀、更透亮,胞核更致密,神经元内空泡化程度更高,背景脑组织显示细小的微空泡化改变(H-E 染色:×40 倍物镜)。

不同类型的创伤性脑肿胀的发病机制尚未明确,尤其无法确定是因缺乏脑血流自我调节导致脑血管扩张(如充血性脑肿胀)引起的,还是由脑内水含量增加(如脑水肿)造成的,或两者兼有(52)。损伤后数分钟至数小时内快速产生的脑肿胀很可能是充血性肿胀(51,159),损伤后几小时至一两天形成的肿胀在没有脑组织破坏或严重缺氧缺血性脑损伤的情况下,则很可能由脑水肿引起。

6.4.1 病理学改变

脑肿胀早期的病理学特征是脑回增宽及脑沟变窄或消失。脑肿胀挤压大脑表面正常的沟回,形成光滑、平坦的轮廓,在脑切面上尤其明显,大脑半球的脑切面轮廓就像是光滑的安全帽外边缘(图 9-33)。青壮年的脑组织在颅腔内一般比较充盈("满"),因此有时很难确定是否存在脑肿胀。

脑肿胀也能引起脑室狭窄,当出现局部脑肿胀时,肿胀区域可挤进邻近的颅腔(形成疝)。相应地,如果大脑半球肿胀,钩回内侧缘、海马旁回、颅底的颞叶和枕叶都会被推向小脑幕切迹,挤压在小脑幕边缘上,在脑组织和脑幕边缘间挤压形成凹槽。这一过程早期表现为双侧钩回上明显的凹槽(图 9-33)。显微镜检查示神经元扭曲、缺血性改变或压痕处脑坏死,是颅内压明显升高的敏感性指标(51)。由于缺乏组织病理学改变的钩回压痕比较常见,这些病理改变至关重要。

进展型的脑肿胀将颞叶内侧区域挤向颅后窝(钩回疝或小脑幕疝),大脑后动脉分支被挤压在肿胀的大脑半球及小脑幕切迹边缘之间(图 9-36A)。血管闭塞导致大脑后动脉供血区域梗死,形成出血性梗死。梗死区出血由脑损伤区域的断续供血

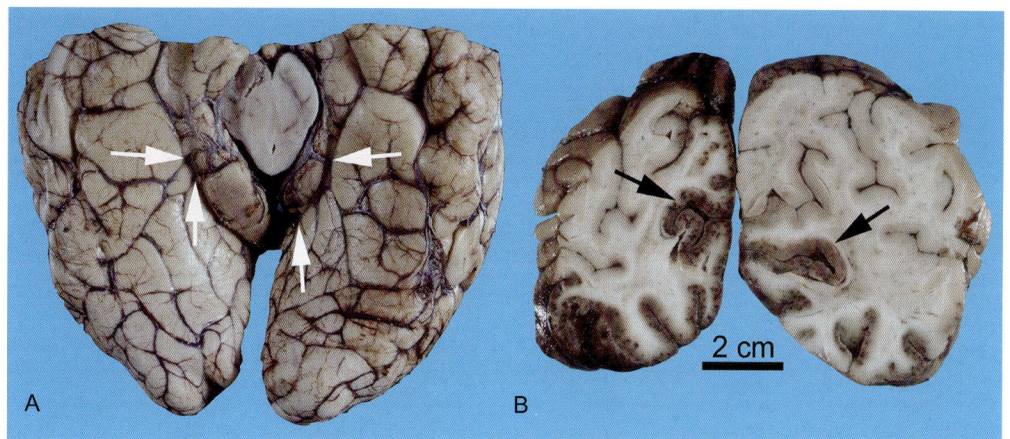

图 9-36 脑肿胀引起的小脑幕疝。(A)双侧凹槽，脑组织在小脑幕边缘受压，以及由于内侧颞叶大脑后动脉不同分支在多个点受压形成（大脑后动脉；白色箭头）。(B)枕部脑后动脉区域双侧急性出血性梗死（黑色箭头），由小脑幕疝及脑后动脉分支闭塞引起。

引起，少部分是临床减轻脑肿胀的治疗行为所致（图 9-36B）。在对固定后的大脑进行切片前应先移除脑干及小脑，充分暴露颞叶基底部及枕叶，是有效找到被小脑掩盖的小脑幕疝的方法。

由脑肿胀引起的大脑半球尾部的移位也可导致脑中线结构拉伸和扭曲，包括丘脑及脑干。在冠状位脑切片上，丘脑的位置比正常位置低（中央型脑疝）；对于脑干，因颅后窝空间局限，外观检查时可见脑桥髓质成角或"屈曲"变形。屈曲变形导致脑后动脉及基底动脉被挤压在小脑幕边缘，引起脑干上基底动脉分出的小穿通动脉发生牵拉、撕裂，随后发生脑干出血（有时发生梗死）。这些继发性（Duret）出血在脑桥前端中线或整个脑桥及中脑被盖部尤其典型、明显（图 9-37 和图 9-38）(147)，严重的出血可延伸至第四脑室（图 9-38）。

大脑半球持续下降、颅后窝内组织肿胀挤压，迫使小脑内后侧区域穿过枕骨大孔（扁桃体疝），引起小脑扁桃体铸模成枕骨大孔的形状，随着该过程的持续，受压部位发生坏死（图 9-37 和图 9-23）。在确定的扁桃体疝案例中，坏死的小脑扁桃体可能破碎并掉入脊髓的蛛网膜下腔内，最远可达腰大池。如果小脑扁桃体没有可辨识的大体坏死改变，但其凸出程度表明与疝的铸模相关，则应对显著凸起的小脑扁桃体进行显微镜检查，以证实神经元损伤及邻近部位的出血点，因为明显的小脑扁桃体凸起就像钩回凹槽一样，在正常人中非常常见。

假如一侧大脑半球肿胀（如硬脑膜外血肿或巨大单侧脑挫伤），肿胀的大脑半球内侧面在大脑镰的游离缘下受压（镰下疝或扣带回疝），可在大脑组织切片检查前观察到纵裂。检查大脑组织切面可比较容易地证实大脑镰下疝（图 9-11 和图 9-12）。与大脑镰下疝相伴随的还有肿胀侧大脑半球的侧脑室狭窄。

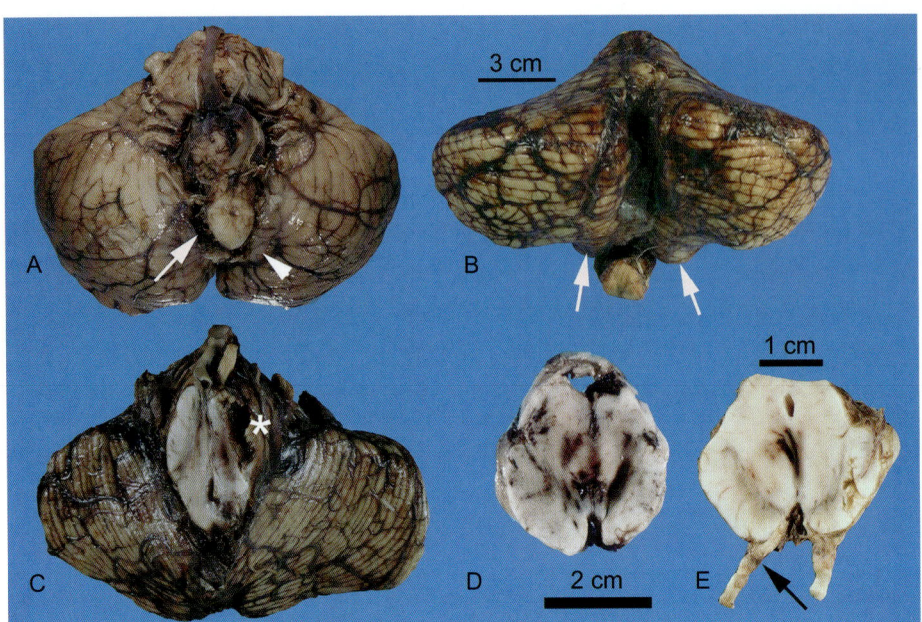

图 9-37 脑肿胀对脑干及小脑的影响。(A) 小脑底面观示小脑扁桃体显著的隆起(箭头)和扁桃体坏死(三角箭头)。(B) 白色箭头显示明显的小脑扁桃体隆起,背侧观。(C) 白色星号显示了大脑脚坏死区域(Kernohan 压迹/颞叶疝压迹),发生在肿胀大脑半球的对侧,在肿胀半球侧造成假性定位体征。(D) 继发性(Duret 出血)脑干出血。(E) 动眼神经挫伤(箭头),此神经穿越小脑幕边缘,小脑幕裂孔疝能引起同侧瞳孔散大。在中线部位还可见线性的继发性出血。

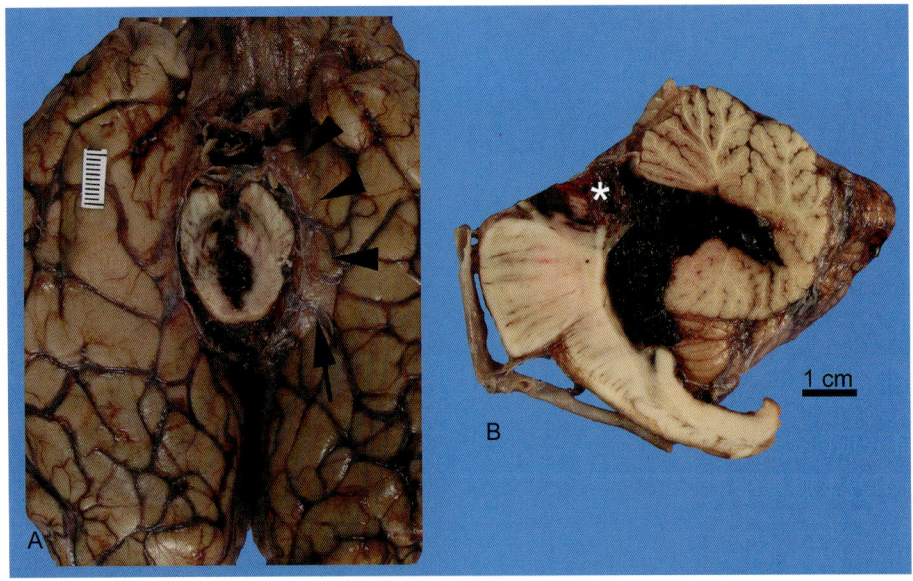

图 9-38 继发于脑干出血伴脑室内扩张的脑肿胀。(A) 明显的中线继发性脑干出血(继发于急性左硬膜下大出血),以及小脑幕切迹边缘挤压形成的单侧小脑幕切迹疝(箭头)和后脑动脉分支(箭头)穿过凹槽。(B) 与 A 图同一案例中,经脑干和小脑蚓部的矢状切面显示继发性脑干出血(星号)扩展到第四脑室。

在极少数情况下，颅后窝巨大的小脑内血肿可迫使小脑头部穿过小脑幕切迹（小脑幕切迹上疝），如果脑室内插入引流管以控制小脑出血引起的继发性脑积水，则发生小脑幕切迹上疝的风险更大。

7 其他的局灶性创伤性颅脑损伤

穹隆根部及透明隔的撕裂常见于多种类型的颅脑外伤中，这些损伤被认为反映了此类局部易损区域与上胼胝体的小范围分离（图9-39A、B）。在因全身性损伤致死的死者身上可发现此类损伤，而局灶性创伤患者只有很少甚至没有相应的神经系统症状。上述损伤通常与仰卧位患者侧脑室后角池的小脑室内出血相关。法医往往意外发现陈旧性透明隔撕裂，尤其是在脑萎缩及陈旧性脑挫伤患者中，无论此人是否具有颅脑外伤病史。

延髓小脑连接处腹侧的撕裂出现在颈部过伸及颅底撞击案例中，尤其是因摩托车交通事故受伤者（图9-39C、D）（10, 23, 162, 163）。近4%的致命性道路交通事故案例可发生此类损伤，大部分伤者在送医前即死亡，部分伤者存活数周至数月。大

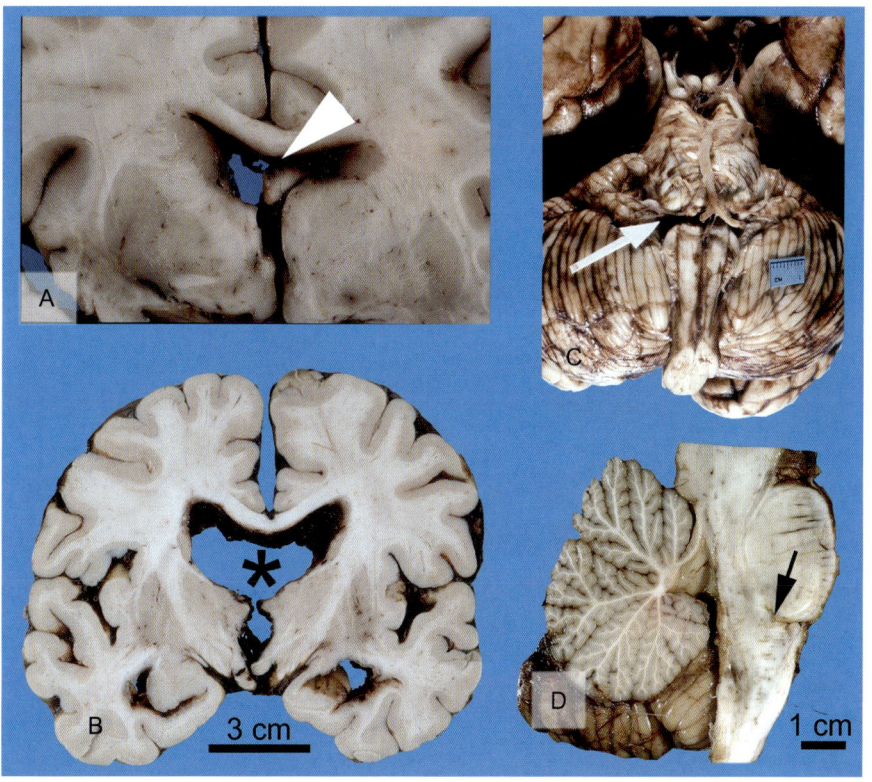

图9-39 其他局灶性创伤性颅脑损伤。（A）穹隆与胼胝体连接部位撕裂（三角）。（B）透明隔完全撕裂与移位，造成单个巨大的中央型脑室（星号）。（C）脑桥延髓连接处撕裂并伴少量出血（箭头）。（D）经脑干及小脑蚓部的矢状切面（C图部位）显示不完全的脑桥延髓连接处撕裂（箭头）。

部分案例中存在面部碰撞,小脑挫裂伤也比较常见,有 50% 的案例出现创伤性大脑半球功能障碍。高位颈椎损伤较少见,经常表现为寰枕关节脱位或第 1 颈椎(C1)与第 2 颈椎(C2)间的骨折脱位。

8 脊椎及脊髓损伤

8.1 脊椎脊髓损伤的实践研究

脊椎及脊髓的尸体检查是一项棘手而漫长的过程。以下是解剖室对脊柱检查的一般指导意见[已有各种复杂和详细的脊髓取材及切片方法,但对常规的法医病理学实践缺乏实用价值(165、166)]:

- 脊椎原位大体检查不是证实脊椎骨折及脊柱韧带损伤的敏感方法。
- 生前 CT 扫描是检查脊椎骨折最敏感的方法。生前 MRI 扫描是检测韧带及其他软组织损伤的敏感方法,可用于显示相邻椎体间骨折的可能性。随着技术的进步,MRI 扫描在测定脊髓损伤性质及程度方面将越来越精确,而且在脊髓的尸体检查中也发挥重要作用(参阅第 1 章 6.2;参考文献 4)。因此对法医而言,生前的 CT 及 MRI 检查结果应该作为可疑脊椎脊髓损伤案例的重要评估手段。
- 如果缺乏详实的生前神经影像学检查结果,应对所有可疑的颈部损伤拍摄颈部伸展和屈曲视角的 X 线片(168)。但 X 线片无法反映大部分的脊椎骨折情况(166、169)。
- 当可能存在脊髓损伤时,应打开项背部取出脊髓。如果怀疑颈部上段损伤,应该在摘除大脑前解剖脊髓。将尸体头部放置在解剖台末端,使颈部向前屈曲从而矫直颈部生理弯曲,有利于脊髓的暴露。
- 椎体周围的软组织出血提示可能存在脊椎和韧带损伤以及损伤位置。
- 其他提示颈椎损伤的指征包括:发现颈椎前肌肉不明原因出血,在脊髓解剖前摘除脑组织时椎管内排出大量血性脑脊液。
- 如果在脊髓解剖前摘除脑组织,一般可通过检查枕骨大孔确定颈椎上段骨折,通过检查可确定枕骨髁与 C1、C2 椎体是否对齐,将手指放入枕骨大孔内晃动头部以检查椎体骨折的粗糙边缘、骨擦感及椎管狭窄等。
- 通过计算从延髓脊髓连接处向下的神经根数来确定脊髓损伤的节段水平。另外,颈膨大很容易被发现,可用于定位 C5—T1 椎体的水平线(在极少数情况下臂丛比正常位置低一个节段或高一个节段穿出)。
- 在怀疑椎动脉破裂或撕裂的情况下,必须暴露椎动脉,特别是与 C1、C2 椎体相关时(参阅第 10 章 4.2;170-172)。

8.2 脊椎骨折的发病机制及分类

作用于脊椎上的外力分为旋转性力(包括屈曲、伸展、侧方弯曲及扭转)和线性力[压在一起(压缩)、拉开分离(拉伸)、脊柱不同部分间的滑动(剪切)]。这些外伤既可作用于单个椎体,大部分情况下也可作用于所有椎体;既可有生理性载荷,也可在超过各解剖结构的生理极限时造成病理性结果。病理性外力作用于脊柱上可造成椎骨周围软组织撕裂、椎体半脱位、椎体骨折及脊髓损伤(SCI)。考虑致死性脊椎脊髓损伤时应牢记以下原则:

- 脊椎骨折并不一定与脊髓损伤及神经根损伤相关联。
- 脊椎骨折伴有韧带撕裂,引起不稳定骨折并导致骨折脱位和继发性脊髓损伤。
- 无脊椎骨折的韧带撕裂,并伴有致命性脊髓损伤。
- 非对称性脊椎骨折提示旋转或侧屈时发生损伤。
- 与其他椎骨相比,寰枕关节和寰枢关节的独特解剖结构会引起特有的椎骨损伤。
- 特定的骨折形态可提示但无法直接证明损伤机制。
- 简单来说,不论考虑损伤部位和成因,脊椎脊髓损伤分为以下几类(174):
  - 椎体或后部结构骨折,无半脱位。
  - 半脱位骨折。
  - 半脱位,无骨折。
  - 脊髓损伤,影像学证据显示无骨折或半脱位。
- 对脊椎骨折有大量的分类方案,但都严重依赖于神经影像学的发现(173,175–178)。这些分类方案能够反映脊椎骨折的复杂性和多样性,其中大量的分类方案是由骨科医生和神经外科医生所开发,以用于确定应手术固定的骨折类型和应保守治疗的骨折类型。
- 经常发生的损伤类型包括:
- 屈曲损伤
  - 单纯的屈曲损伤会导致椎体腹侧部分受压(压缩性骨折)和背侧部分的牵拉(导致棘间韧带和后纵韧带撕裂、关节突脱位或骨折)。
  - 在不稳定脊椎骨折中,撕裂软组织上方的椎骨会在下方椎骨上向腹侧移动(骨折–脱位),导致脊髓被挤压于前方椎骨椎板与后方椎体后部结构之间。
  - 如果损伤还包括旋转分量,则可能发生一侧关节突关节完整的不对称性脊椎骨折脱位。
  - 在某些情况下,椎骨的双侧椎弓根骨折可避免脊髓受压,因为相当于仅椎体向前移动而避免了脊髓的受压。
- 伸展损伤
  - 强行伸展可导致前纵韧带撕裂、椎间盘撕脱(可能从撕裂处上方椎体上撕脱小块碎片)、后纵韧带撕裂、关节突关节面骨折或脱位和椎弓根骨折(导致骨折脱位)(图40)。
- 挤压损伤
  - 通过椎体的轴向载荷施加纯压缩力,例如在高坠头顶或臀部着地时,导致椎体压缩性骨折、椎体粉碎性骨折和椎弓根骨折（爆裂性骨折），其骨折严重程度依次升高。
- 当椎体强度因骨质疏松或癌转移而变弱时，骨折风险增加。
- 这些骨折引起的骨碎片移位可能会压迫脊髓。
- 对于寰椎，相似的力可引起前后弓同时骨折（Jefferson 骨折）。
- 压缩力通常与屈曲力同时出现。

8.3 解剖中常见的脊柱损伤类型

解剖中常见的脊椎脊髓损伤分为以下三类：
- 致命性寰椎 – 枕骨和颈部上段损伤。
- 患者死于脊髓损伤并发症或其他原因的颈椎、胸椎及腰椎损伤。
- 脊椎脊髓损伤作为严重的多发性创伤中的一种损伤。

一般来说，不论何种原因的脊椎脊髓损伤，发生在颈部和腰部的损伤较胸部损伤更为常见，因为胸腔具有额外的支撑作用（179）。

8.4 颈椎骨折

在 34 069 例钝性损伤的急诊伤者中，通过影像学检查证实颈椎损伤患者占 2.4%（180），在这 818 例患者中：
- 三分之一患者的损伤轻微。
- 最常见的骨折部位是 C2 椎体（其中 32% 是齿状突骨折）。
- C3 椎体最不容易骨折。
- 39% 的骨折发生于 C6 和 C7 椎体。
- 颈椎椎体是最常见的骨折部位。
- 骨折移位最可能发生在 C5 和 C6 及 C6 和 C7 椎体间，最不容易发生在寰枕交界处以及 C7 和 T1 椎体间。

所有入院的儿科创伤病例中，约 2% 的患儿存在颈椎损伤，其中 30% 致命，这些死亡事故大多数由机动车辆事故引起，并与其他颅脑损伤相关联（181）。

因道路交通事故当场死亡或在到达医院后死亡的死者中至少有 25% 存在颈部损伤（168，182，183）。大部分颈部损伤是由机动车交通事故引起，包括行人被机动车碰撞。与系安全带的司机相比，未系安全带的司机更易发生颈部损伤。颈部损伤大多发生于头颈结合部或 C1、C2 椎体上（图 9-40）。常见的致命性颈部上段损伤包括：
- 寰枕移位（过伸性损伤，很少伴随 C1 颈椎骨折，其特征在于不同程度的翼状韧带撕裂和颅骨的向前移位；图 9-40A；184 和 185）。
- 寰枢椎移位，包括：
  - 屈曲型损伤引起的齿状突韧带断裂（186）或齿状突基底部骨折，使头和寰椎向相对于轴的前侧移位（图 9-40B）。

第 9 章 | 颅脑损伤及脊柱损伤

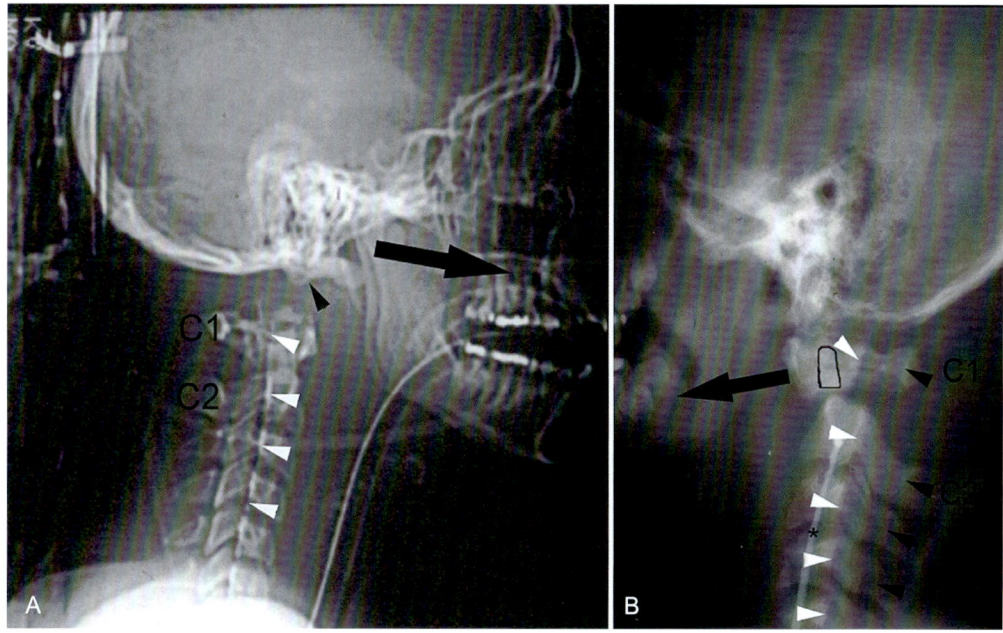

图 9-40 高颈椎损伤。(A) 寰枕脱位(外侧平片)。白色三角指示椎管腹侧边缘,该边缘应与枕骨髁中心对齐(黑色三角)。大箭头指示头部在寰椎(C1)上向前方移动,导致脊髓被压在错位的上方大孔背缘和下方的椎管腹缘间。还要注意寰椎和颅底间隙扩大(加拿大安大略省伦敦市伦敦健康科学中心 D. Lee 博士供图)。(B) 寰枢椎脱位(CT 外侧"定位"胶片)。齿状突(画圈处)发生 2 型骨折,向前移动并倾斜。寰椎已沿大箭头指示方向前移,使脊髓被压在上方寰椎弓和下方轴椎体背缘间。白色和黑色三角分别指示脊髓腹缘和背缘。注意在颈椎腹缘线 C1 和 C2 间明显的阶梯变形。星号指示血管内导管[齿状突骨折:发生在齿状突体部为(1 型),发生在齿状突基部为(2 型),发生在基部轴体中为(3 型)](加拿大安大略省伦敦市伦敦健康科学中心 D. Lee 博士供图)。

- 过伸型损伤引起的齿状突骨折以及寰椎相对于轴的后侧移位、C2 椎体骨折(最常见的是"hangman 骨折",即 C2 椎体(枢椎)椎弓根骨折,又称创伤性枢椎滑脱。由 C2 椎体椎弓根或椎体峡部的双侧骨折引起,使 C2 椎体相对于 C3 椎体移位(参阅图 3-36)(168,182,183 和 187)。

这些损伤大部分都伴有严重的咽后壁出血和肿胀。

颈部上段损伤常伴有颅骨和脑损伤[包括颅骨骨折、脑挫伤和各种颅内出血(181,182,185,188-190)],虽然头部碰撞对颈髓损伤的产生并非必要,但是颈部突发伸展性运动(挥鞭样)会产生严重的颈部损伤(参阅图 8-81)。高位颈部损伤有时也伴有下颌部钝性损伤(183,189,191,192),但至少在某些情况下,这可能是多重创伤下的巧合(193,194)。如果个体太靠近气囊,则安全气囊弹出会导致高位颈椎骨折(参阅第 8 章标题 14.2;图 8-64;参考文献 195 和 196)。

如上所述,与高位颈部损伤相比,临床实践中低位颈髓损伤更常见,但死亡案例较少,这是因为后者部分或完全避开了来自 C3、C4、C5 颈髓控制的膈肌运动,而且并发的脑损伤较高位颈椎损伤少见(190)。因此,法医遇到的低位损伤远远少于高位损伤,但遇到的该类案例大多发生于损伤后至少几天到几周内。中位和低位颈椎损伤通常不是死亡的直接原因,但是作用显而易见(如由制动引起的肺栓塞以及继发于尿毒症的败血症)。尽管常发生于机动车交通事故中,但在摔跌、遭殴打及运动意外中也较为常见。前面所述,枕骨和高位颈椎骨折与下颌部损伤间可能存在关联,但也有研究认为低位颈椎过度伸展损伤可能与脸上半部分遭钝性外力作用有关(192)。

8.5 胸椎骨折

胸椎骨折和胸脊髓损伤较腰部及颈部损伤少见,因为与该水平的脊髓相比,胸椎椎管相对较宽,而且肋软骨关节和肋骨提供了机械支撑。因此,需要相当大的暴力才能产生胸椎骨折,若暴力较大,由于胸廓的旋转受到限制,屈曲或轴向负荷作用会导致胸椎压缩性骨折(197)。上位胸椎的负荷可能引起间接的胸骨骨折,其特征是上胸骨节段相对于下胸骨节段后向移位(与方向盘对胸骨冲击的影响相反,它引起骨折端相反方向移位;参阅第8章标题6.1、14.1)。相比于腰椎及颈椎骨折,胸椎骨折更具多发性[因此也相应地与多个部位的脊髓损伤相关(参阅标题8.8)],并可伴后外侧和后内侧肋骨骨折,而且在对前侧椎旁软组织出血的患者治疗期间,会因胸部平片可见纵隔增宽而被误诊为主动脉破裂(198)。

8.6 腰椎骨折

腰椎骨折包括楔形骨折(临床实践中最常见)、爆裂性骨折(两种类型都由于过度屈曲和挤压暴力引起)、安全带骨折(发生在道路交通事故中,因没有系对角线肩带,腰椎在安全带前方位置支点处周围过度屈曲)以及骨折移位(胸、腰段最常见)(参阅第8章标题14.2)。楔形骨折的特点是腰椎腹侧椎体压缩、棘突韧带完整,从而防止脊椎后凸。爆裂性骨折影响椎体背侧及脊椎后韧带,且有时涉及椎弓根部分。汽车安全带损伤的案例中,运动支点的前部位置可引起复杂的损伤模式,包括腰椎后侧分离或牵拉、韧带断裂,以及一个或多个腰椎不同部分骨折。腰椎骨折脱位特征性地发生于胸腰椎结合部,并可出现T12椎体相对于L1椎体的腹侧移位(173,178,198)。

8.7 无脊椎骨折的创伤性脊髓损伤

与创伤相关的脊髓损伤可发生于没有神经影像学证实的骨折或软组织损伤案例中(脊髓损伤无影像学异常),尤其在先天性椎管狭窄或因椎关节僵硬、后纵韧带骨化导致的椎管狭窄的成人中(199)。过伸更易发生此类损伤,因为过伸产生的椎管狭窄程度较屈曲程度更大。儿童在脊柱屈曲、伸展及拉伸过程中都会出现类似现象,由于儿童软组织弹性较大,在大多数案例中,伤后4天出现严重创伤性脊髓损伤的唯一迹象是创伤时轻微的神经系统症状(参阅第10章标题8;参考文献200和201)。长期昏迷患者的颈部处于屈曲位也会发展为创伤性脊髓病,但无软组织损伤或脊椎骨折(202)。

8.8 创伤性脊髓损伤

8.8.1 发病机制

骨折脱位所致的脊髓机械性压迫是引起脊髓损伤的主要原因。其结果是脊髓被夹在椎体背侧与相邻椎板腹侧间。椎管内原有的疾病,如先天性狭窄、老年性改变、骨关节炎及其他退行性脊椎疾病,会加重椎管侵入的后果。在某些情况下,特别是无法证实的不稳定骨折或韧带撕裂时,脊髓拉伸或震荡性损伤则是脊髓损伤的另一种解释。

无论何种原因所致的脊髓损伤,其继发性改变,包括炎症和缺血性损伤,都会加重原发性损伤,因此临床上使用多种治疗策略以减轻继发性损伤的危害(203)。少数情况下,脊髓损伤后不久发生的脊髓功能恶化由治疗操作期间不稳定骨折的进一步移位所致(通常在损伤后 24 小时内),低血压继发于脊髓损伤或其他创伤引起的神经源性血压不稳(伤后 24 小时至 7 天),或因椎动脉颈段受椎骨损伤影响而发生的椎动脉闭塞(204)。伤后数周、数月至数年出现的脊髓功能恶化(与痉挛状态进展无关)由脊髓囊性扩张(位于脊髓损伤部位且囊腔向头侧或尾侧延伸,也就是"瘘管")、椎骨骨折后的椎管渐进性变形或椎骨退行性病变叠加所致(205)。

8.8.2 病理特征

无论损伤的发病机制和部位如何,损伤脊髓中的大体和显微表现都相似。

8.8.2.1 大体改变

椎体脊髓损伤时硬脊膜通常不会被撕裂,脊髓损伤在急性案例中表现为硬脊膜外出血,而在慢性案例中表现为局部硬脊膜狭窄或松弛。受损脊髓的大体和显微镜下改变与损伤时间、程度及软脊膜是否完整有关。当软脊膜完整时,如果受伤时或伤后几分钟内死亡,则无大体异常。此时需依赖脊椎和脊髓周围损伤粗略判断脊髓损伤部位。这类问题常在无脊髓横断的寰枕或寰枢椎体脱位时遇到。

伤后短时间内(最长几小时)脊髓会肿胀、变色、出血,之后损伤组织的再吸收会引起脊髓软化和萎缩。由于其柔软性,触摸检查较肉眼观察更容易发现不严重的陈旧性损伤。如果软脊膜已被撕裂,则会存在脊髓断端痕迹,这些断端多少存在残余的中枢神经系统组织黏附,在检查此处脊髓时很容易断裂。

在水平切面上,脊髓断端两侧的大体异常改变与软脑膜完整的损伤改变相似。在急性案例中主要表现为出血性破坏和损伤组织撕裂(图 9-41－图 9-43),在陈旧性损伤中则主要表现为不同程度的囊性变。异常改变由病变中心向两侧延伸一或两个节段,因此将异常最明显的区域简单定义为病变中心。病变中心与椎骨或椎旁软组织损伤位置大致对应(但不是节段水平,由于脊髓节段相对于脊椎节段较高,所以骶脊髓位于 L1 或 L2 椎体水平)。因为脊髓－椎骨间相对运动,脊髓和椎骨损伤的空间关系并不确切,特别是在脊柱活动较多的部位。

8.8.2.2 镜下改变

如果脊髓损伤后几分钟内患者死亡,那么特征性改变仅包括血管扩张、瘀点性出

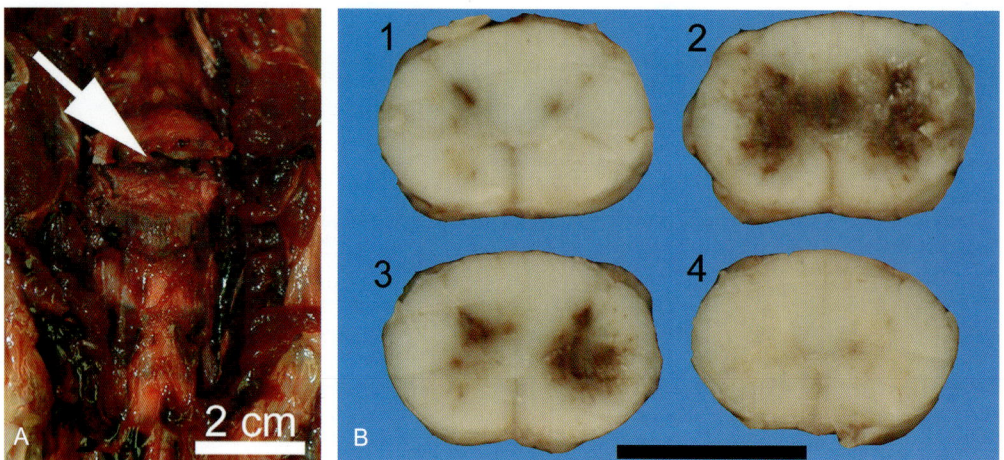

图 9-41 颈椎骨折移位,创伤性脊髓损伤(中央灰质坏死类型)。(A)通过 C4 低位椎体的骨折移位,伴 C4-C5 椎间盘撕裂(箭头)(加拿大安大略省伦敦市伦敦健康科学中心 E. Tweedie 博士供图)。(B)与 A 图同一个案例,将脊髓经由 C4 椎体水平按从上至下的顺序水平切面(比例尺 = 1 厘米)。中央灰质局灶性坏死比较明显(加拿大安大略省伦敦市伦敦健康科学中心 L. C. Ang 博士供图)。

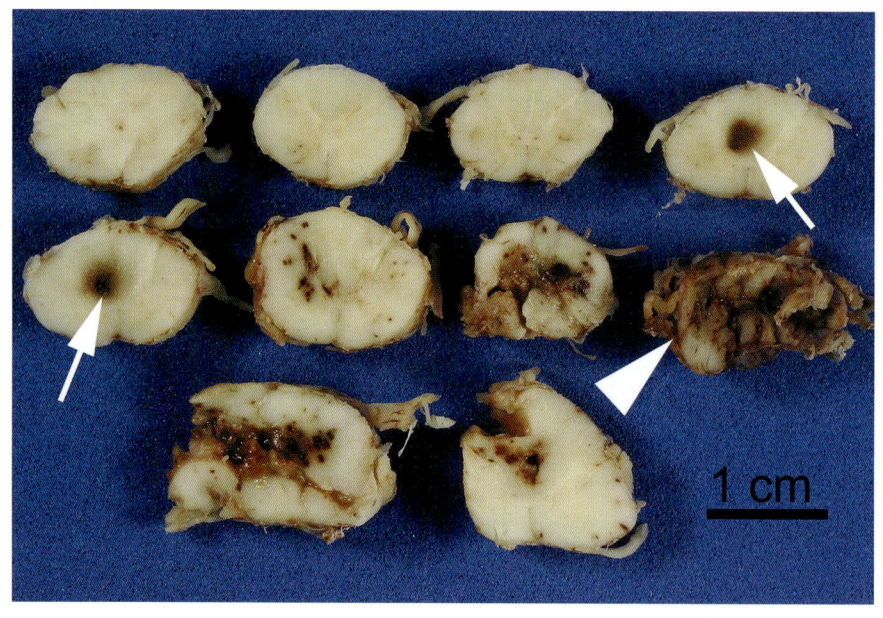

图 9-42 创伤性脊髓病变(浸软)。横向出血性撕裂显示出病变的中心(三角)。铅笔样坏死出现在延髓的两个切面中(箭头)。

血(特别是灰质),以及局部白质神经纤维束改变。几小时后瘀点性出血更加明显、广泛,脊髓运动神经元表现为缺血性神经元坏死(参阅标题 6.3.3.1)或细胞质溶解(表现为尼氏小体消失、细胞质嗜酸性增强及细胞核移向细胞一侧)。中性粒细胞损伤后 24-36 小时、巨噬细胞损伤后约 5 天浸润损伤组织(206)。在 CD68 免疫标记组织

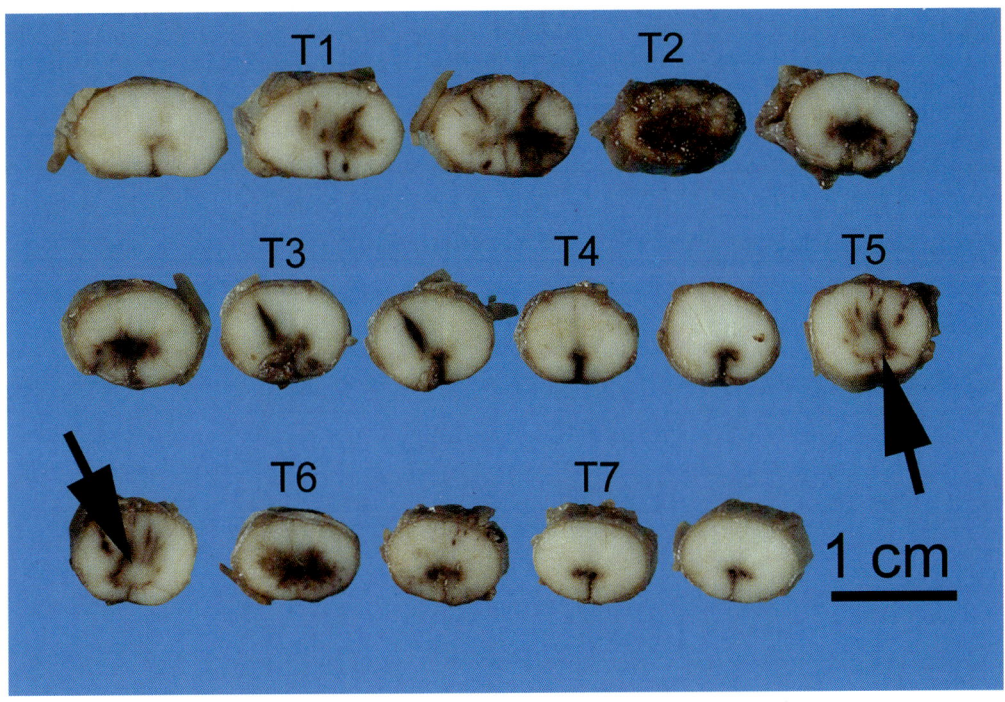

图 9-43 多灶性胸髓创伤性病变。T2（浸软）横向出血性撕裂以及 T6 中心灰质坏死是胸椎多发骨折的后果。线性单侧出血性坏死位于 T3 和 T4 后角之间。铅笔样坏死出现在 T5 和 T6 之间（箭头）。

切片中容易观察到"活化"的小胶质细胞，其胞体呈圆形，外观不同于细长的"静息"小胶质细胞。

激活小胶质细胞和巨噬细胞的出现标志着组织吸收开始，进而逐渐出现更加明显的囊性变。包含碎屑的巨噬细胞可长期存在。尽管吞噬细胞常出现在坏死组织边缘，但急、慢性炎症细胞几乎总是混杂分布。淋巴细胞稀疏且不明显。轴索肿胀随时间的进展与脑损伤进展过程相似，损伤后一周内可检测到星形胶质细胞活化。离脊髓损伤一定距离处也可发现 β 淀粉样前体蛋白免疫阳性的轴索异常(162)，其意义尚不明确，但类似于创伤对脑轴突的弥漫性影响，或许代表脊髓弥漫性创伤性轴索损伤或原发的进展性创伤性跨神经元束变性病变。

随着脊髓组织的严重损伤以及伤者生存期的延长，损伤部位发生纤维化，尤其是软脑膜的破坏，伴随施万细胞的生长及轴突的再生，在损伤部位形成类似创伤性神经瘤的改变。

损伤后几周至数月，在距脊髓损伤一定距离的部位可以检见损伤以下的皮质脊髓束及损伤以上的脊髓丘脑束、后束纤维退行性变。主要标志是在神经束中检见散落分布的含碎屑的吞噬细胞。随后有髓轴突进行性脱落，导致神经纤维束切面亚甲蓝染色呈现苍白色。

8.8.3 创伤性脊髓损伤分类

由于脊髓横断面上最严重的脊髓损伤分布具有很大差异,因此就损伤外观而言,有理由认为每一种脊髓损伤均具有独特性。一般而言,最严重的损伤表现为中枢神经组织连续性中断(207)。然而在很多案例中,坏死组织周围可检见广泛性的狭窄且常无完整边缘的软脊膜下组织,包括有髓神经纤维(急性案例),或检见复杂的胶质血管囊肿(慢性案例)(208)。较小的损伤表现为偶发和不对称性分布的坏死或囊性退行性变。以白质轴突损伤为主是局灶性创伤性脊髓轴索损伤的一种形式,出现于"急性颈中央脊髓损伤综合征"案例中,其临床特征为颈部损伤后上肢相较于下肢不成比例的肌力减弱,此类伤者事先已存在因骨退行性变或椎间盘疾病引起的椎管狭窄,且通常无颈椎骨折的明显证据(207,209-211)。

尽管损伤外观存在差异性,创伤性脊髓损伤可大体分为(207)挫伤/囊肿(冲击性损伤或短暂的压迫性损伤,软脊膜完整)、浸软(骨折脱位案例中因脊髓的广泛性撕裂引起的损伤;图9-42和图9-43)、挫裂创(局限于穿透及贯穿性脊柱损伤,通常由枪弹创引起)及脊髓实质损伤(与急性颈中央脊髓损伤综合征相关)。此外,某些情况下浸软坏死主要出现于中央灰质(中央灰质坏死),这是较典型的脊髓低血压性血管损伤特征(图9-41)。脊髓腹侧中线挫伤,有时与脑桥延髓牵拉相关,可能是颈部过伸或屈曲损伤的表现(尤其是儿童)(图9-44)。完整的轴突髓鞘早期选择性脱落(脱髓鞘)及随后髓鞘再生(理论上具有改善脊髓功能的可能性)也是脊髓损伤的特征(207,208)。

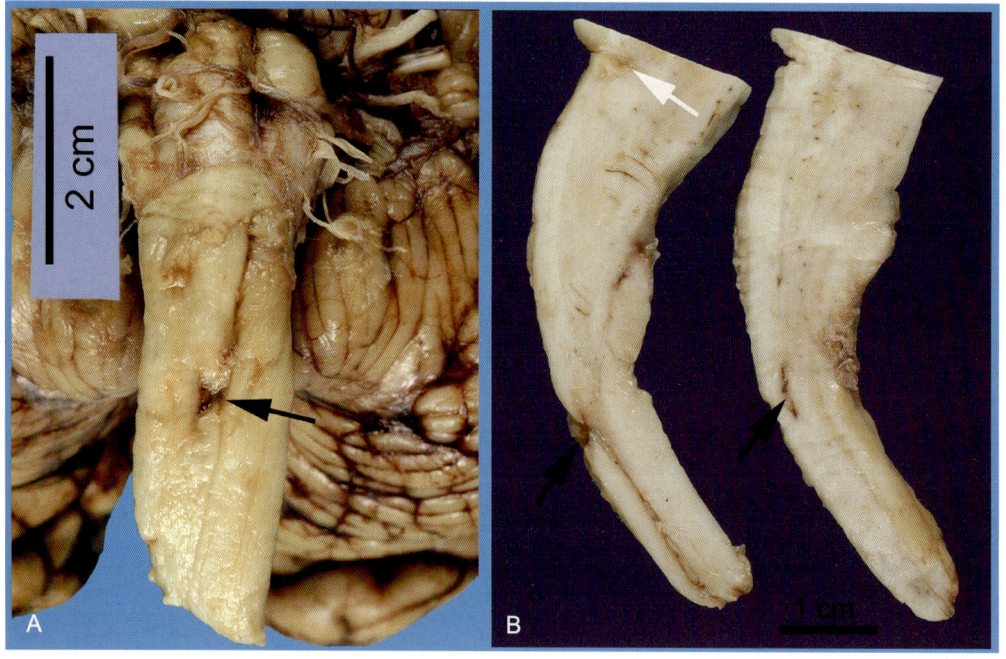

图9-44 儿童脑桥延髓撕裂及脊髓挫伤。(A)高位颈髓腹侧中线挫裂创(箭头)。(B)脑干和脊髓矢状面和旁矢状面。脊髓腹侧挫裂伤(黑色箭头),脑桥延髓灶性撕裂(白色箭头)。

8.8.4 铅笔样坏死（纵行扩展损伤）

创伤性胸髓和低位颈髓损伤中常见坏死组织中心，且在横断面上有椭圆或圆形轮廓（"铅笔样坏死"或"纵行扩展损伤"），通常位于脊髓损伤上方并与损伤部位连续（图 9-42 和图 9-43）。它常发生在后索腹侧或单侧后角，也可延伸数个脊髓节段。邻近的白质无细胞反应，但在坏死组织边缘可见一圈巨噬细胞浸润。铅笔样坏死的发病机制及法医学意义还不清楚，但这一坏死是脊椎脊髓创伤的直接后果，非人为所致（212, 213），且可通过实验再现（214）。铅笔样坏死和由于脊髓误操作所形成的人为"挤牙膏"式的损伤形态相似，有时较难区分（215, 216）。

9 儿童颅脑损伤

儿童颅脑－脊髓损伤机制与成人类似（160）。10 岁以下儿童寰枕复合体易于受损（167），影像学解剖结构异常时脊髓损伤的风险更高（174, 217）。分娩时损伤、摔跌或机动车交通事故会引起婴幼儿颅顶骨局部凹陷["乒乓"骨折（218）]，特别是在非意外性的伤害案例中（219），5 个月以下的婴幼儿遭受各种头部损伤均会发生白质撕裂，颅顶骨单一线性骨折后会引起"延长性骨折"（32, 33）。即使相对轻微的头部损伤也存在严重暴发性脑肿胀的风险（159-161）。

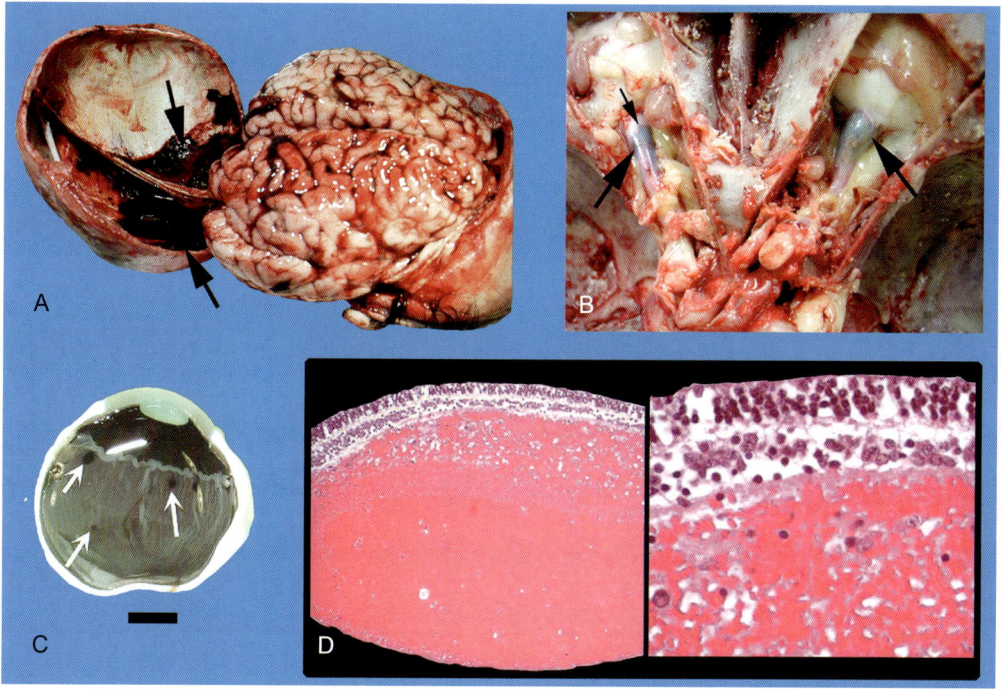

图 9-45 婴幼儿非意外损伤三联征。（A）枕骨硬脑膜下血肿（箭头）。（B）眶板破坏使眼球和视神经外露，存在双侧球后眼周硬脑膜下血肿（大箭头）。小箭头为血肿（下）与视神经可见段（上）间的边界。（C）眼球断层（角膜最上层），视网膜前的两个小血肿都接近于锯状缘（箭头，比例尺＝0.5 厘米）。（D）显微镜检查显示的视网膜下的血肿（H-E 染色：左＝×10 倍物镜，右＝×40 倍物镜）。

9.1 婴儿非意外性损伤

根据法庭接受的医疗证据和证人证词，婴儿摇晃损伤或头部直接钝性损伤，或两者兼有[即非意外性损伤（NAI）]，常具有三个异常的损伤指标，也称婴幼儿非意外损伤"三联征"（图9-45），即：

- 视网膜内和视网膜周出血，特别是在视网膜周边。
- 视神经周围硬脑膜下或硬脑膜内出血（眶后周围硬脑膜外及硬脑膜下出血）。
- 颅内硬脑膜下出血通常较小，常为双侧，多分布在枕叶以及大脑镰周围。

这种三联征与缺氧缺血性脑病（其病因未被证实）、β淀粉样前体蛋白免疫阳性轴索变化（其起源有争议，但有时可能与创伤性轴索损伤相同）及脑肿胀的关系并不完全一致。脑肿胀通常是这些案例死亡的最终原因，但其病因可能不确定，或由多种因素所造成。通常还存在其他的身体损伤，包括不同部位不同类型的皮肤挫伤、软组织损伤及肋骨和四肢骨骨折。因此，当发现婴儿急性硬膜下出血时，应积极检查和排除眼睛和视神经症状，并考虑婴幼儿故意伤害的可能。

表9-1　疑似非意外性损伤案例中法医确定死因的方法

是否存在三联征	致命性脑肿胀	非意外性损伤的非致命性颅外损伤	广泛性组织学改变[a]	死亡原因	可能与死因有关或无关的因素
是	否	否	否	未明确[b]	颅脑损伤
是	是	否	是或否	颅脑损伤	无
是	否	是	是	颅脑损伤	颅外钝性暴力损伤
是	否	是	否	未明确[b]	颅脑损伤，颅外钝性暴力损伤
是	是	是	是或否	颅脑损伤	颅外钝性暴力损伤
否	否	是	否	未明确[b]	颅外钝性暴力损伤

注：a 病理学改变是缺氧损伤和轴索损伤的组织学特征（无论其本质是缺氧还是损伤）。病理学改变广泛且严重，常认为它们是致命性神经功能障碍的结构基础。

b 对于存在"特征性三联征"的案例，虽然三联征本身不是致命的损伤，但可推断存在重大的或危险性暴力作用于中枢神经系统，虽然缺乏脑肿胀以及广泛性组织学改变即不支持也不反对这一观点。这种危险性暴力如果破坏脑干和延髓的重要中枢，则可能致命。假设三联征与婴幼儿死亡之间存在因果关系，那么缺乏神经组织结构破坏的证据可表明死亡发生在中枢神经系统损伤组织学病理证据形成前[即死亡发生在损伤后2小时内（依赖于β淀粉样前体蛋白免疫组织化学证据，参阅标题6.1.7）；或6—12小时内损伤（依赖于用各种组织学技术证实轴突或缺血性神经元损伤，参阅标题6.1.3和6.3.3），也可表明产生三联征的暴力以及其他作用是致命的，但没能形成结构性破坏。虽然三联征的存在与儿童的死亡是事实，但是三联征指明了致命性暴力在中枢神经系统中的传导通路，以及将颅脑损伤作为死因的结论具有假设性。无论这种假设及其所依据的理论是否合理，法院最终都应对所有与案件有关的证据进行权衡和分析并作出决定。

法医实践中，可以发现一系列疑似婴幼儿故意伤害的案例，这些案例会检见三联征、严重脑肿胀，以及皮肤、软组织和骨损伤，或者只有三联征表现。部分专家把三联征作为婴幼儿非意外伤害的明确证据，认为即使没有颅外损伤或脑肿胀，也足以解释患儿的死亡。然而在这种情况下，特别是如果尸检结果仅有三联征时，必须维持法医鉴定的基本原则：经过完整的尸体解剖及毒化检测后，是否有足够的证据来形成一个完整明确的结构性、代谢性或毒理学死因？

如果没有足够的证据能肯定地回答这个问题，那么就法医而言，死亡原因可能不确定。表9-1提供了对这些案例中死因进行分类的方法。

9.2 婴幼儿孤立性硬脑膜下出血

在没有其他创伤证据的情况下，如果肉眼和显微镜下均检见婴儿孤立、散在的急性或陈旧性脑硬膜下出血，就表明已发生出血，只是没有直接导致死亡。尽管不能排除是否与婴幼儿故意伤害相关，但硬膜外出血是分娩常见的并发症，来源于此的组织小血肿即可作为解释。

10 颅脑损伤与脑垂体

脑损伤中的腺垂体及其覆盖物表现出不同的异常。59%的案例出现囊性出血(220)，尽管也与不同原因所致的蛛网膜下腔出血有关(220)。瘀点性出血或少见的较大出血灶可能由牵拉（拉伸）性损伤所致，在45%-48%的颅脑损伤案例中发生于垂体柄及神经垂体中[比例为1:7(220)]，但腺垂体的创伤性出血比较少见(221)。外伤后腺垂体会出现局灶性、多灶性或缺血性坏死，尤其见于外伤后存活超过12小时的案例[35%的案例(220)]，这是垂体细胞死亡后出现能够呈现组织学特征的最小间隔时间(220,222)。小范围脑垂体坏死的机制尚不明确。广泛性脑垂体坏死的机制有多种解释，其中以腺垂体的血供中断最为可信；腺垂体血供位于垂体柄的长垂体门脉系统中，因垂体柄受压[由严重的脑肿胀引起(221,223,224)]或创伤性垂体柄横断(221)而导致血供中断。

任何原因引起的广泛性腺垂体坏死的表现都极具特征(220-225)。约90%的腺垂体发生坏死(221)，而神经垂体得以幸免(221,225)，坏死的腺垂体细胞常被一圈狭窄的垂体细胞包裹（血供源于囊状毛细血管），垂体前叶和后叶交界面可见完整的垂体细胞，此处血供来源于蝶鞍内的短垂体门脉系统(223)。腺垂体坏死也可能由其他原因所致，包括脑肿胀（不论其成因）、糖尿病和产后恢复期(222-226)。

神经垂体坏死而腺垂体完好可能是术中低血压的并发症(227)。

11 创伤性中枢神经系统损伤相关的临床症状

尽管外伤可以造成脑、脊髓及其覆盖物等多种组织结构的破坏及各种临床表现，但在尸体解剖之前，受害者的病史可体现出特有的临床症状，这些症状经常与特定的神经病理学结果有关。将待检案件进行归类对于指导尸体检验非常有用。这些临床症状总结于表9-2中。

表9-2 创伤性中枢神经系统症状及相关的神经病理学诊断

临床症状	神经病理学诊断
"死于现场"	• 广泛性颅脑外伤 • 弥漫性血管损伤 • 脑桥延髓撕裂 • 高位颈髓损伤 • "延髓震荡"（参阅第10章标题4.3） • 创伤性基底部蛛网膜下腔出血（参阅第10章标题4.2）
"交谈后死亡"的患者（228, 229）	• 硬脑膜外出血 • 脑挫伤/脑内血肿 • 脑肿胀 • 颅骨骨折并发症（参阅标题3.7）
昏迷和植物人状态（129）	• 2-3级DAI • 包含丘脑的弥漫性缺氧缺血性损伤
重度残疾（235）	• 2-3级DAI • 含丘脑或不含丘脑的弥漫性缺氧缺血性损伤 • 多发性脑损伤（缺血性损伤、脑挫伤） • 既往颅内压增高的证据 • 手术清除颅内血肿的病史 • 1级DAI
中度残疾（130）	• 轻到中度脑挫伤 • 手术清除颅内血肿的病史 • 1级DAI • 外伤性癫痫猝死（参阅第10章标题5）
脑损伤后轻微残疾或完全恢复	• 额-眶部挫伤 • 陈旧性涂片型硬脑膜下出血 • 镜检所见局灶性散在分布的硬脑膜下含铁血黄素沉积 • 镜下散在分布的小囊肿或局灶性胶质细胞增多 • 无神经病理学异常改变
孤立的四肢瘫痪或截瘫	• 脊髓损伤

11.1 死于现场

大多数创伤性中枢神经系统损伤后即刻死亡者的神经病理学异常非常明显（图9-46），包括严重的粉碎性骨折，伴随继发性脑挫裂伤或颈部脊柱头端损伤。其他原因包括弥漫性血管损伤、创伤性基底部蛛网膜下腔出血（参阅第10章标题4.2）、脑受撞击的特殊反应、"延髓震荡"[排除性诊断（参阅第10章标题4.3）]。

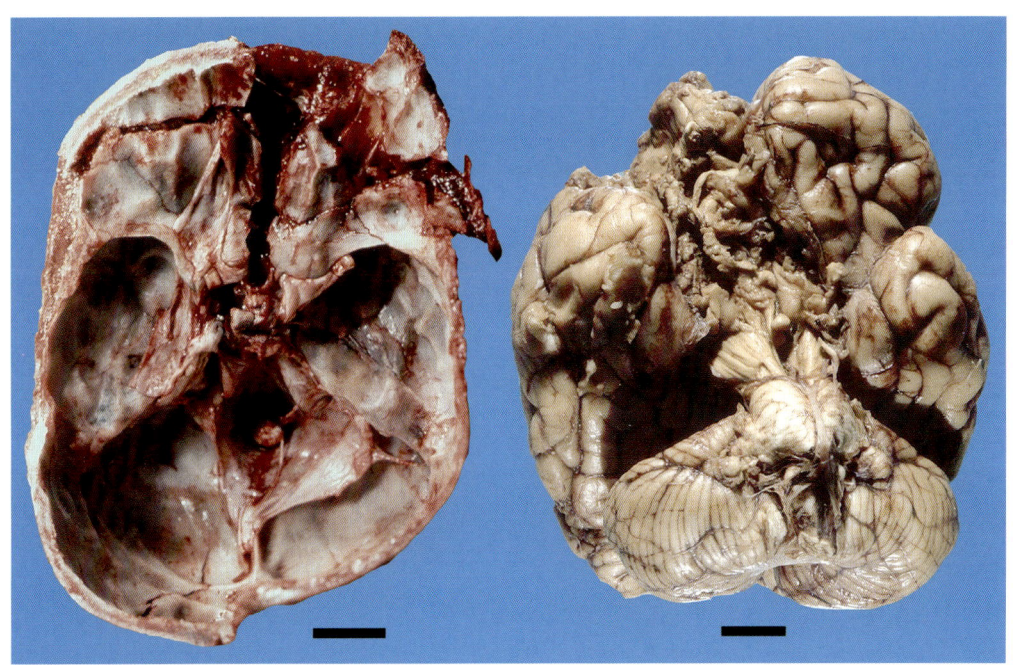

图 9-46 死于现场。死者从一辆全地形越野车内被抛出,其未受保护的头部与树发生碰撞,导致右额骨及颅底粉碎性多发性骨折和严重的脑挫裂伤。此类案例的死亡原因毫无疑问是广泛性颅脑损伤。

11.2 "交谈后死亡"的伤者:神志清醒期

"交谈后死亡"的伤者存在一段神志清醒期,即伤者头部损伤后尚能交谈,因此也可推测伤者在当时不存在致命性原发性脑损伤,而随后死于治疗延误以及由此产生的外伤并发症(228,229),6%—10%"严重"头部损伤后能够说话的伤者死于迟发性创伤性颅脑损伤。与存活下来的伤者相比,致命性案例中死者更加年长、颅外损伤更严重、Glasgow 昏迷量表(GCS 评分)中的运动及睁眼部分评分更低(229)。此类伤者致命性神经病学的恶化主要由以下因素引起(229):

- 硬脑膜周围血肿(50% 的案例),常常是急性硬脑膜下出血。
- 脑挫伤及脑内血肿(40% 案例)。
  - 明显的双侧额叶挫伤,尤其易于引起迟发性恶化(230)。
- 脑肿胀(10% 案例)。

基于相同原因,许多头部损伤后清醒的患者病情也会发生恶化,但会以植物人状态或重度残疾状态存活下来。

颅骨骨折后的各种并发症(参阅标题 3.7),特别是急性细菌性脑膜炎,可导致患者在清醒期后死亡,一般持续数天甚至数周。

11.3 植物人状态

植物人状态被定义为"持续性意识不清,没有意识存在或认知反应,即使患者存在可睁眼的觉醒周期"(231)。处于植物人状态的伤者存在微弱的复苏机会，但损伤4周后当患者被分类为"持续"性植物人状态时，复苏的机会就越来越小。当伤者存活达12个月，已进入"永久"性植物人状态时，在任何情况下都没有复苏的机会(232)。植物人状态常与创伤性颅脑损伤或心脏停搏所致的缺氧缺血性脑损伤相关。大部分创伤性植物人状态由2-3级的弥散性轴索损伤(DAI)或弥漫性创伤性缺氧缺血性损伤(全脑灌注失败)所致，或由两者同时引起(129)。即使没有弥散性轴索损伤的依据，丘脑的缺血性损伤在植物人状态伤者中也存在，与之相反，不管其损伤成因如何，大脑皮质缺血性损伤不会引起植物人状态，除非已经发生丘脑缺血性损伤。

11.4 重度残疾

头部损伤所致的重度残疾会影响个人日常生活行为，并且生活上需要获得他人帮助［Glasgow结果量表(234)］。严重残疾的程度范围从患者可移动到最低意识状态(235)。约50%严重残疾的神经病理学异常类似于植物人状态，但其余案例既没有丘脑损伤，也无2级或3级的弥散性轴索损伤。不同类型的局灶性脑损伤似乎会促进严重残疾发生，包括脑挫伤、脑内血肿(已手术清除)的多种残余效应、局灶性缺血性脑损伤、脑干损伤(通常为缺血性损伤和出血)。在极少数案例中，1级弥散性轴索损伤是唯一的异常。可自主活动、卧床不起及严重意识障碍的伤者在血肿发生率、既往颅内压升高证据、缺血性损伤等方面均无明显差异。

11.5 中度残疾

创伤性颅脑损伤后由Glasgow预后分级(GOS)评定为中度残疾的伤者可独立自主生活，但在身体或精神功能方面长期存在部分损害(234)。高坠是引起创伤性颅脑损伤的常见原因，会引起颅骨骨折。此类伤者大部分存在外伤后癫痫，超过70%的患者需行颅内血肿清除术。此类案例的神经病理学改变包括：大部分存在脑表层挫伤(缺乏广泛性损伤)，30%的案例为1级弥散性轴索损伤，少数案例为局灶性缺血性脑损伤，显著脑肿胀的案例较少(130)。

11.6 脑损伤后轻微残疾或完全康复

缺乏或仅有轻微中枢神经功能障碍的脑外伤患者，也会死于与脑损伤无关的其他原因，尸体解剖中这种情况较常见。本书中的轻微中枢神经功能障碍是指头部受伤所致的轻微认知功能障碍。大部分案例中没有发现神经病理学异常，但部分案例中也可检见小灶性陈旧性脑挫伤(多分布于额颞叶区域)或者继发性局灶性及弥漫性硬脑膜下含铁血黄素浸染。脑挫伤引起轻微的创伤后症状的意义不够明确，因为尸检中常偶然发现无症状的陈旧性脑挫伤。在某些情况下，轻微创伤性颅脑损伤后可能表现为小的结构相关的脑MRI信号异常［参阅标题6.1.5(140)］，或者稀疏分布的微小或镜下所见的白质囊性损伤(常伴少量嗜含铁血黄素的巨噬细胞)，或者观察到灰质和白质中轻微的小胶质细胞增生。

11.7 孤立的四肢瘫痪或截瘫

大部分案例中四肢瘫痪和截瘫由脊髓损伤引起,但在某些情况下可由脑干损伤引起。

11.8 未在现场死亡的颅脑损伤者的死亡原因

大部分脑损伤后昏迷的伤者依靠呼吸机维持生命,一旦关闭呼吸机则会死亡。中枢神经系统损伤会导致呼吸中枢衰竭,这是引起死亡的直接死因。其他昏迷患者,无论是否依赖呼吸机维持或重度残疾,其直接死因通常为感染或中枢神经系统损伤后血管并发症。但在某些情况下,尽管存在严重脑损伤,也难以明确"正式"的直接死因,因为此类伤者的死因是中枢性循环、呼吸功能障碍。程度较轻的重、中度残疾患者的死亡原因一般与中枢神经系统损伤无关。如果伤者存在创伤后癫痫表现,则应根据癫痫的猝死标准进行鉴定(参阅第10章标题5)。

12 急性神经源性肺水肿

神经源性肺水肿(neurogenic pulmonary edema, NPE)是指与神经系统疾病相关的肺水肿。患者并无导致肺水肿的心肺疾病(236,237),神经源性肺水肿有时可能是头部损伤患者的直接死因。神经源性肺水肿与严重的急性神经系统疾病相关,包括一般的自发性颅内出血(238)与动脉瘤破裂所致的蛛网膜下腔出血(239)、癫痫性猝死(240)和各种颅脑创伤(241-243)。推断为非意外头部损伤的婴儿案例中也有神经源性肺水肿的报道(244)。

神经源性肺水肿常在神经系统症状出现后数小时内就发生或表现出来。全面的临床数据也表明肺水肿能够在头部损伤后即刻或数分钟内发生,以下观察结果证实了上述观点:

- 41例死于现场的头部损伤患者,双肺总重量平均值为997克(标准差359克)(241)。
- 20例在越南战争中因火器伤或高坠致头部损伤后数分钟内死亡的伤员,其中2例肺重量小于800克,18例肺重量为800-1 500克,1例肺重量为1 501-2 000克(242)。
- 23例"创伤性脑内出血"伤者的"存活时间为半小时或更短",其双肺总重量超过900克(238)。

创伤性颅脑损伤后数分钟内发生的肺水肿在动物实验中也得以重复(245-248)。

神经源性肺水肿的病理机制尚不明确。主要理论认为脑损伤引发神经介导的肺血管阻力交感神经调节的变化,此过程中肺毛细血管通透性增加与血管张力变化无关。如果肺水肿延迟数小时发生,则可能与创伤后体液介导的高浓度儿茶酚胺有关。

13 痴呆症与创伤性颅脑损伤

当考虑因痴呆症行为障碍引起的致命性事件或头部受伤后一段时间出现痴呆症状时，就会出现痴呆症与创伤性颅脑损伤间因果关系的问题，并应考虑颅脑创伤是否会引起认知障碍。

13.1 痴呆症作为致命性事件的原因

如果死者具有痴呆症病史，法医应该固定并保留脑组织。目前有测验算法用于痴呆症的组织病理学研究(249)，但如果条件可能，痴呆患者的脑组织应由神经病理科医生进行评价和诊断，尤其是具有退行性疾病经验的神经病理科医生。因为痴呆症分类复杂，脑组织需要广泛取材，以用于显微镜检查及免疫组化检查，从而明确诊断。然而，阿尔茨海默病[Alzheimer病，构成痴呆症的50%—70%(250)]和弥散性包涵体病[构成痴呆症的10%—25%(250)]的诊断相对比较明确(250,251)。

阿尔茨海默病的诊断依赖于银染和免疫组化方法，在大脑皮质和海马区可发现神经炎症斑块和神经原纤维结节(neurofibrillary tangles, NFT)。可应用评估神经炎症斑块和神经原纤维结节发生率的半定量方法对该类病变作出诊断(252,253)，但患者即使出现严重的阿尔茨海默病的病理学改变，也未必会表现出痴呆(254)。

弥散性包涵体病可在脑皮质神经元中检见嗜酸性、泛素蛋白阳性、突触核蛋白阳性的包涵体。在脑干黑质中可观察到残存神经元的色素消退、神经元缺失及包涵体存在。脑皮质包涵体的发生率与认知和运动功能障碍间的相关性很小(255,256)，但简单可重复的组织病理学分期方法具有可行性(255,257)。

在尸检中，如果考虑因痴呆症引起头部损伤时，应注意以下事项：

- 无痴呆症病史
    - 法医应确认是否存在阿尔茨海默病或包涵体病的病理学改变。
    - 如果两类疾病同时存在，法医应详细记录(如"阿尔茨海默病样改变"或"弥散性包涵体样改变")，并声明难以明确患者是否存在精神错乱的临床症状。
- 有明确的痴呆症病史
    - 法医应明确死者可能的病因是阿尔茨海默病还是弥散性包涵体病，或两者均有(因为这两种疾病经常共存)。
    - 法医不应对伤者行为功能障碍是否引起头部损伤的原因进行评价，这应由患者的精神病主治医生来判断。
    - 如果没有发现阿尔茨海默病或弥散性包涵体病的病理学特征，法医应安排神经病理科医生寻找其他引起痴呆症的原因(249,250)。

13.2 创伤性颅脑损伤作为痴呆症的病因

有证据表明头部损伤与痴呆症之间存在因果关系(258,259)。分析和解释该问题已超出本书的内容范围。但综合而言，痴呆症和头部损伤常存在以下联系：

- 脑损伤的程度，包括继发于头部损伤的缺血性损伤，可能就足以单独解释伤者伤后即刻出现认知功能障碍以及伤后严重残疾者出现类似痴呆症状的原因。只要排除了引起痴呆症的其他因素，头部损伤后数月内海马神经元的进行性退化可用于解释认知功能的逐渐恶化（260）。
- 老年性痴呆是一种众所周知的退行性病变，特征性病变是位于脑皮质及脑干神经元中广泛分布的神经原纤维结节，以及稀疏分布的神经炎症斑块（261）。长期对头部重复性、冲击性的打击容易发生老年性痴呆，这在拳击手身上经常发生。
- 既往的头部损伤是引起阿尔茨海默病进展的重要危险因素（262）。以下三种观察结果表明这不仅仅是偶然的联系：
  - 携带 Apo E 基因、ε4 等位基因的患者是阿尔茨海默病的高发人群（52）。
  - 与拥有其他 Apo E 等位基因的患者相比，拥有 ε4 等位基因的患者，其头部损伤预后结果较差（52）。
  - 参与了阿尔茨海默病发病机制的 β 淀粉样蛋白沉积在单纯性头部损伤后死亡者中增加了 30%，常由高坠所致，大部分死者为老年人（263）。

这些观察结果能否表明头部损伤与阿尔茨海默病有因果关系或共同缺陷，还有待进一步明确。

在实践中，法医只能说明由创伤性颅脑损伤引起的结构性改变可能导致认知功能障碍，而且没有确切的证据表明既往的头部损伤完全是由于阿尔茨海默病的进展所致。

李正东　董贺文　张慧　译

参考文献

1. Langlois, J. A., Rutland-Brown, W., Thomas, K. E. Traumatic Brain Injury in the United States: Emergency Department Visits, Hospitalizations, and Deaths. Centers for Disease Control and Prevention, National Center for Injury Prevention and Control, Atlanta, GA, 2004.

2. Kreppel, D., Antoniadis, G., Seeling, W. Spinal hematoma: a literature survey with meta-analysis of 613 patients. Neurosurg. Rev. 26:1-49, 2003.

3. Rutty, G.N.Editorial: Are invasive autopsies necessary?Forensic Sci.Med.Pathol. 1:71-73, 2005.

4. Croul, S. E., Flanders, A. E. Neuropathology of human spinal cord injury. Adv. Neurol. 72:317-323, 1997.

5. Moritz, A. R. Classical mistakes in forensic pathology. Am. J. Clin. Pathol. 26:1382-1397, 1956.

6. Cassin, B. J., Spitz, W. U. Concentration of alcohol in delayed subdural hematoma. J.Forensic Sci. 28:1013-1015, 1983.

7. Smialek, J. E., Spitz, W. U., Wolfe, J. A. Ethanol in intracerebral clot. Report of two homici- dal cases with prolonged survival after injury. Am. J. Forensic Med. Pathol. 1:149–150, 1980.
8. McIntyre, I. M., Hamm, C. E., Sherrard, J. L., Gary, R. D., Riley, A. C., Lucas, J. R. The analysis of an intracerebral hematoma for drugs of abuse. J. Forensic Sci. 48:680–682, 2003.
9. Armed Forces Institute of Pathology. Armed Forces Medical Examiner–Autopsy Diagrams. http://www.afip.org/Departments/oafme/diagrams.html, 2005.
10. Ezzat, W., Ang, L. C., Nyssen, J. Pontomedullary rent. A specific type of primary brain- stem traumatic injury. Am. J. Forensic Med. Pathol. 16:336–339, 1995.
11. Royal College of Pathologists. Guidance for Retention of Brain and Spinal Cord Following Post–Mortem Examination and Where Criminal Proceedings are in Prospect: Available at http://www.rcpath.org/resources/pdf/GUIDELINESBRAIN–ARNedited.pdf. Royal College of Pathologists, London, 2002.
12. Nelson, E. L., Melton, J., Annegers, J. F., Laws, E. R., Offord, K. P. Incidence of skull frac- tures in Olmsted County, Minnesota. Neurosurgery 15:318–324, 1984.
13. Shkrum, M. J., Green, R. N., McClafferty, K. J., Nowak, E. S. Skull fractures in fatalities due to motor vehicle collisions. J. Forensic Sci. 39:107–122, 1994.
14. Gurdjian, E. S., Gurdjian, E. S. Acute head injury: a review. Surg. Annu. 12:223–241, 1980.
15. Gurdjian, E. S. Impact head injury: Mechanistic, clinical and preventive correlations. Charles C. Thomas, Springfield, IL, 1975.
16. Rawling, L. B. The Surgery of the Skull and Brain. Oxford Medical Publications, London, 1912.
17. McCrory, P. R., Berkovic, S. F. Concussion: the history of clinical and pathophysiological concepts and misconceptions. Neurology 57:2283–2289, 2001.
18. Shaw, N. A. The neurophysiology of concussion. Prog. Neurobiol. 67:281–344, 2002.
19. Herbella, F. A., Mudo, M., Delmonti, C., Braga, F. M., Del Grande, J. C. "Raccoon eyes" (periorbital haematoma) as a sign of skull base fracture. Injury 32:745–747, 2001.
20. Hirsch, C. S., Kaufman, B. Contrecoup skull fractures. J. Neurosurg. 42:530–534, 1975.
21. Hein, P. M., Schulz, E. Contrecoup fractures of the anterior cranial fossae as a consequence of blunt force caused by a fall. Acta Neurochir. (Wien) 105:24–29, 1990.
22. Harvey, F. H., Jones, A. M. "Typical" basal skull fracture of both petrous bones: an unre- liable indicator of head impact site. J. Forensic Sci. 25:280–286, 1980.
23. Voigt, G. E., Skold, G. Ring fractures of the base of the skull. J. Trauma 14:494–505,

1974.

24. Russell, W. R., Schiller, F. Crushing injuries to the skull: Clinical and experimental observations. J Neurol. Neurosurg. Psychiat. 12:52–60, 1949.
25. Pollanen, M. S., Deck, J. H., Blenkinsop, B., Farkas, E. M. Fracture of temporal bone with exsanguination:pathology and mechanism. Can. J. Neurol. Sci. 19:196–200, 1992.
26. Resnick, D. K., Subach, B. R., Marion, D. W. The significance of carotid canal involvement in basilar cranial fracture. Neurosurgery 40:1177–1181, 1997.
27. Ildan, F., Uzuneyupoglu, Z., Boyar, B., Bagdatoglu, H., Cetinalp, E., Karadayi, A. Traumatic giant aneurysm of the intracavernous internal carotid artery causing fatal epis-taxis: case report. J. Trauma 36:565–567, 1994.
28. Sato, S., Iida, H., Hirayama, H., Endo, M., Ohwada, T., Fujii, K. Traumatic basilar artery occlusion caused by a fracture of the clivus—case report. Neurol. Med. Chir. (Tokyo) 41:541–544, 2001.
29. Adams, V. I., Hirsch, C. S. Venous air embolism from head and neck wounds. Arch. Pathol. Lab. Med. 113:498–502, 1989.
30. Adams, V., Guidi, C. Venous air embolism in homicidal blunt impact head trauma. Case reports. Am. J. Forensic Med. Pathol. 22:322–326, 2001.
31. Ogilvy, C. S., McKee, A. C., Newman, N. J., Donnelly, S. M., Kiwak, K. J. Embolism of cerebral tissue to lungs: report of two cases and review of the literature. Neurosurgery23:511–516, 1988.
32. Ersahin, Y., Gulmen, V., Palali, I., Mutluer, S. Growing skull fractures (craniocerebral erosion). Neurosurg. Rev. 23:139–144, 2000.
33. Sugiultzoglu, M. K., Souweidane, M. M. Early management of craniocerebral injury with avoidance of post-traumatic leptomeningeal cyst formation. Report of two cases. Pediatr. Neurosurg. 35:329–333, 2001.
34. Tuli, S., Tator, C. H., Fehlings, M. G., Mackay, M. Occipital condyle fractures. Neurosurgery 41:368–376, 1997.
35. Legros, B., Fournier, P., Chiaroni, P., Ritz, O., Fusciardi, J. Basal fracture of the skull and lower (Ⅸ, Ⅹ, Ⅺ, Ⅻ) cranial nerves palsy: four case reports including two fractures of the occipital condyle—a literature review. J. Trauma 48:342–48, 2000.
36. Bucholz, R. W., Burkhead, W. Z., Graham, W., Petty, C. Occult cervical spine injuries in fatal traffic accidents. J. Trauma 19:768–771, 1979.
37. Anderson, P. A., Montesano, P. X. Morphology and treatment of occipital condyle fractures. Spine 13:731–736, 1988.
38. Miltner, E., Kallieris, D., Schmidt, G., Muller, M. Injuries of the occipital condyles in fatal

traffic accidents. J. Legal Med. 103:523−528, 1990.
39. Bonilha, L., Mattos, J. P., Borges, W. A., Fernandes, Y. B., Andrioli, M. S., Borges, G. Chronic epidural hematoma of the vertex. Clin. Neurol. Neurosurg. 106:69−73, 2003.
40. Domenicucci, M., Signorini, P., Strzelecki, J., Delfini, R. Delayed post−traumatic epidural hematoma. A review. Neurosurg. Rev. 18:109−122, 1995.
41. Watanabe, T., Nakahara, K., Miki, Y., Shibui, S., Takakura, K., Nomura, K. Chronic expanding epidural haematoma. Case report. Acta Neurochir.（Wien）. 132:150−153, 1995.
42. Ng, W. H., Yeo, T. T., Seow, W. T. Non−traumatic spontaneous acute epidural haematoma—report of two cases and review of the literature. J. Clin. Neurosci. 11:791−794, 2004.
43. Kett−White, R., Martin, J. L. Bilateral frontal extradural haematomas caused by rupture of the superior sagittal sinus: case report. Br J. Neurosurg. 13:77−78, 1999.
44. Miller, D. J., Steinmetz, M., McCutcheon, I. E. Vertex epidural hematoma: surgical versus conservative management: two case reports and review of the literature. Neurosurgery45:621−624, 1999.
45. Gelabert, M., Prieto, A., Allut, A. G. Acute bilateral extradural haematoma of the posterior cranial fossa. Br. J. Neurosurg. 11:573−575, 1997.
46. d'Avella, D., Servadei, F., Scerrati, M., et al. Traumatic acute subdural haematomas of the posterior fossa: clinicoradiological analysis of 24 patients. Acta Neurochir.（Wien）. 145:1037−1044, 2003.
47. Gupta, S. K., Tandon, S. C., Mohanty, S., Asthana, S., Sharma, S. Bilateral traumatic extradural haematomas: report of 12 cases with a review of the literature. Clin. Neurol. Neurosurg. 94:127−131, 1992.
48. Franck, E., Berger, S., Tew, J. Bilateral epidural hematomas. Surg. Neurol. 17:218−222, 1982.
49. Huda, M. F., Mohanty, S., Sharma, V., Tiwari, Y., Choudhary, A., Singh, V. P. Double extradural hematoma: an analysis of 46 cases. Neurol. India 52:450−452, 2004.
50. Mishra, A., Mohanty, S. Contre−coup extradural haematoma: a short report. Neurol. India 49:94−95, 2001.
51. Graham, D. I., Lawrence, A. E., Adams, J. H., Doyle, D., McLellan, D. R. Brain damage in non−missile head injury secondary to high intracranial pressure. Neuropathol. Appl. Neurobiol. 13:209−217, 1987.
52. Graham, D. I., Gennarelli, T. A., McIntosh, T. K. Trauma. In: Graham, D. I., Lantos, E. R., eds. Greenfield's Neuropathology, Seventh Edition, Volume 1. Arnold, London, pp.

823–898, 2002.

53. Croce, M. A., Dent, D. L., Menke, P. G., et al. Acute subdural hematoma: nonsurgical man‑agement of selected patients. J. Trauma 36:820–826, 1994.
54. Edwards, R. J., Britz, G. W., Critchley, G. R. Spontaneous resolution of an acute subdural haematoma. Br. J. Neurosurg. 16:609–610, 2002.
55. Maxeiner, H., Wolff, M. Pure subdural hematomas: a postmortem analysis of their form and bleeding points. Neurosurgery 50:503–508, 2002.
56. Missori, P., Fenga, L., Maraglino, C., et al. Spontaneous acute subdural hematomas. A clin‑ical comparison with traumatic acute subdural hematomas. Acta Neurochir. (Wien). 142:697–701, 2000.
57. Depreitere, B., Van Calenbergh, F., van Loon, J. A clinical comparison of non‑traumatic acute subdural haematomas either related to coagulopathy or of arterial origin without coagulopathy. Acta Neurochir. (Wien) 145:541–546, 2003.
58. Avis, S. P. Nontraumatic acute subdural hematoma. A case report and review of the litera‑ture. Am. J. Forensic Med. Pathol. 14:130–134, 1993.
59. Gennarelli, T. A. Head injury in man and experimental animals: clinical aspects. Acta Neurochir. Suppl. (Wien) 32:1–13, 1983.
60. Zygun, D. A., Laupland, K. B., Hader, W. J., et al. Severe traumatic brain injury in a large Canadian health region. Can. J. Neurol. Sci. 32:87–92, 2005.
61. Tandon, P. N. Acute subdural haematoma : a reappraisal. Neurol. India 49:3–10, 2001.
62. Matsuyama, T., Shimomura, T., Okumura, Y., Sakaki, T. Acute subdural hematomas due to rupture of cortical arteries: a study of the points of rupture in 19 cases. Surg. Neurol. 47:423–427, 1997.
63. Koc, R. K., Pasaoglu, A., Kurtsoy, A., Oktem, I. S., Kavuncu, I. Acute spontaneous subdural hematoma of arterial origin: a report of five cases. Surg. Neurol. 47:9–11, 1997.
64. Senel, A., Cokluk, C., Onder, A., Iyigun, O., Incesu, L. Acute interhemispheric subdural hematomas. Report of nine cases. J. Neurosurg. Sci. 45:97–102, 2001.
65. Leestma, J. E., Grcevic, N. Impact injuries to the brain and head. In: Leesma, J. E., ed. Forensic Neuropathology. Raven Press, New York, pp. 184–275, 1988.
66. Munro, D., Merritt, H. H. Surgical pathology of subdural hematoma. Based on a study of one hundred and five cases. Arch. Neurol. Psychiatry 35:64–78, 1936.
67. Sahuquillo‑Barris, J., Lamarca‑Ciuro, J., Vilalta‑Castan, J., Rubio‑Garcia, E., RodriguezPazos, M. Acute subdural hematoma and diffuse axonal injury after severe head trauma. J. Neurosurg. 68:894–900, 1988.
68. Yamashima, T., Yamamoto, S. Clinicopathological classification of chronic subdural

hematoma. Zentralbl. Neurochir. 46:304–314, 1985.
69. Iantosca, M. R., Simon, R. H. Chronic subdural hematoma in adult and elderly patients. Neurosurg. Clin. N. Am. 11:447–454, 2000.
70. Adhiyaman, V., Asghar, M., Ganeshram, K. N., Bhowmick, B. K. Chronic subdural haematoma in the elderly. Postgrad. Med. J. 78:71–75, 2002.
71. Jones, S., Kafetz, K. A prospective study of chronic subdural haematomas in elderly patients. Age Ageing 28:519–521, 1999.
72. Missori, P., Maraglino, C., Tarantino, R., et al. Chronic subdural haematomas in patients aged under 50. Clin. Neurol. Neurosurg. 102:199–202, 2000.
73. Friede, R. L., Schachenmayr, W. The origin of subdural neomembranes. II. Fine structural of neomembranes. Am. J. Pathol. 92:69–84, 1978.
74. Schachenmayr, W., Friede, R. L. The origin of subdural neomembranes. I. Fine structure of the dura–arachnoid interface in man. Am. J. Pathol. 92:53–68, 1978.
75. Munro, D. The diagnosis and treatment of subdural hematomas. N. Engl. J. Med. 210:1145–1160, 1934.
76. Lee, K. S. Natural history of chronic subdural haematoma. Brain Inj. 18:351–358, 2004.
77. Albuquerque, F. C., Giannotta, S. L. Arachnoid cyst rupture producing subdural hygroma and intracranial hypertension: case reports. Neurosurgery 41:951–955, 1997.
78. Yamashima, T. The inner membrane of chronic subdural hematomas: pathology and pathophysiology. Neurosurg. Clin. N. Am. 11:413–424, 2000.
79. Killeffer, J. A., Killeffer, F. A., Schochet, S. S. The outer neomembrane of chronic subdural hematoma. Neurosurg. Clin. N. Am. 11:407–412, 2000.
80. Sarkar, C., Lakhtakia, R., Gill, S. S., Sharma, M. C., Mahapatra, A. K., Mehta, V. S. Chronic subdural haematoma and the enigmatic eosinophil. Acta Neurochir. (Wien) 144:983–988, 2002.
81. DiMaio, V. J., DiMaio, D. Forensic Pathology. Second Edition. CRC Press, Boca Raton, FL, 2001.
82. Firsching, R., Heimann, M., Frowein, R. A. Early dynamics of acute extradural and subdural hematomas. Neurol. Res. 19:257–260, 1997.
83. van den Brink, W. A., Zwienenberg, M., Zandee, S. M., van der Meer L., Maas, A. I., Avezaat, C. J. The prognostic importance of the volume of traumatic epidural and subdural haematomas revisited. Acta Neurochir. (Wien) 141:509–514, 1999.
84. Adams, J. H., Doyle, D., Graham, D. I., Lawrence, A. E., McLellan, D. R. Deep intracerebral (basal ganglia) haematomas in fatal non–missile head injury in man. J. Neurol. Neurosurg. Psychiatry 49:1039–1043, 1986.

85. Lee, J. P., Wang, A. D. Post–traumatic basal ganglia hemorrhage: analysis of 52 patients with emphasis on the final outcome. J. Trauma 31:376–380, 1991.
86. Fukamachi, A., Nagaseki, Y., Kohno, K., Wakao, T. The incidence and developmental process of delayed traumatic intracerebral hematomas. Acta Neurochir.（Wien）74:35–39, 1985.
87. Berry, K., Rice, J. Traumatic tear of tela choroidea resulting in fatal intraventricular hemor– rhage. Am. J. Forensic Med. Pathol. 15:132–137, 1994.
88. Chapman, R. C., Rossi, M. L. Cerebral intraventricular haemorrhage in a young adult. Int. J. Legal Med. 105:243–245, 1993.
89. Karavelis, A., Sirmos, C. Primary post–traumatic intraventricular hemorrhage. J.Neurosurg. Sci. 39:253–256, 1995.
90. Christie, M., Marks, P., Liddington, M. Post–traumatic intraventricular haemorrhage: a reappraisal. Br. J. Neurosurg. 2:343–349, 1988.
91. Sato, M., Tanaka, S., Kohama, A., Fujii, C. Traumatic intraventricular haemorrhage. Acta Neurochir.（Wien）88:95–103, 1987.
92. Kim, C. H., Tanaka, R., Kawakami, K., Ito, J. Traumatic primary intraventricular hemorrhage. Surg. Neurol. 16:415–417, 1981.
93. Moriya, F., Hashimoto, Y. A case of fatal hemorrhage in the cerebral ventricles following intravenous use of methamphetamine. Forensic Sci. Int. 129:104–109, 2002.
94. Passero, S., Ulivelli, M., Reale, F. Primary intraventricular haemorrhage in adults. Acta Neurol. Scand. 105:115–119, 2002.
95. Bakshi, R., Kamran, S., Kinkel, P. R., et al. MRI in cerebral intraventricular hemorrhage:analysis of 50 consecutive cases. Neuroradiology 41:401–409, 1999.
96. Lee, J.P., Lui, T. N., Chang, C. N. Acute post–traumatic intraventricular hemorrhage analysis of 25 patients with emphasis on final outcome. Acta Neurol. Scand. 84:85–90, 1991.
97. Zuccarello, M., Iavicoli, R., Pardatscher, K., et al. Posttraumatic intraventricular haemorrhages. Acta Neurochir.（Wien）55:283–293, 1981.
98. Geddes, J. F., Tasker, R. C., Hackshaw, A. K., et al. Dural haemorrhage in non–traumatic infant deaths: does it explain the bleeding in "shaken baby syndrome"? Neuropathol. Appl. Neurobiol. 29:14–22, 2003.
99. Harris, L. S., Adelson, L. "Spinal injury" and sudden infant death. A second look. Am. J.Clin. Pathol. 52:289–295, 1969.
100. Rutty, G. N., Squier, W. M., Padfield, C. J. Epidural haemorrhage of the cervical spinal cord: a post–mortem artefact? Neuropathol. Appl.Neurobiol. 31:247–257, 2005.

101. Adams, J. H., Scott, G., Parker, L. S., Graham, D. I., Doyle, D. The contusion index: a quantitative approach to cerebral contusions in head injury. Neuropathol. Appl. Neurobiol. 6:319–324, 1980.
102. Ryan, G. A., McLean, A. J., Vilenius, A. T., et al. Brain injury patterns in fatally injured pedestrians. J. Trauma 36:469–476, 1994.
103. Adams, J. H., Doyle, D., Graham, D. I., et al. The contusion index: a reappraisal in human and experimental non-missile head injury. Neuropathol. Appl. Neurobiol. 11:299–308, 1985.
104. Chieregato, A., Fainardi, E., Servadei, F., et al. Centrifugal distribution of regional cerebral blood flow and its time course in traumatic intracerebral hematomas. J. Neurotrauma 21:655–666, 2004.
105. Oehmichen, M., Raff, G. Timing of cortical contusion. Correlation between histomorphologic alterations and post-traumatic interval. Z. Rechtsmed. 84:79–94, 1980.
106. Lindenberg, R., Freytag, E. Morphology of cortical contusions. AMA Arch. Pathol. 63:23–42, 1957.
107. Lindenberg, R. The mechanism of cerebral contusions. A pathologic-anatomic study. Arch. Pathol. 69:440–469, 1960.
108. Leestma, J. E. Forensic neuropathology. In: Duckett, S., de la Torre, J. C., eds. Pathology of the Aging Human Nervous System. Second Edition. Oxford University Press, Oxford, pp. 572–586, 2001.
109. Adams, J. H., Doyle, D., Graham, D. I., Lawrence, A. E., McLellan, D. R. Gliding contusions in nonmissile head injury in humans. Arch. Pathol. Lab. Med. 110:485–488, 1986.
110. Vrankovic, D., Splavski. B., Hecimovic, H, et al. Anatomical cerebellar protection of contrecoup hematoma development. Analysis of the mechanism of 30 posterior fossa coup hematomas. Neurosurg. Rev. 23:156–160, 2000.
111. Olin, M. S., Young, H. A., Schmidek, H. H. Contrecoup intracerebellar hemorrhage: Report of a case. Neurosurgery 7:271–273, 1980.
112. Martin, A. J., Thomas, N. W. N. Evolving traumatic cerebellar hematoma. Neurology 57:1565, 2001.
113. Pozzati, E., Grossi, C., Padovani, R. Traumatic intracerebellar hematomas. J. Neurosurg. 56:691–694, 1982.
114. Nagata, K., Ishikawa, T., Ishikawa, T., et al. Delayed traumatic intracerebellar hematoma: Correlation between the location of the hematoma and the pre-existing cerebellar contusion—case report. Neurol. Med. Chir. (Tokyo) 31:792–796, 1991.

115. Kaplan, S. S., Lauryssen, C. Cerebellar haemorrhage after evacuation of an acute supratentorial subdural haematoma. Br. J. Neurosurg. 13:329–331, 1999.
116. Honegger, J., Zentner, J., Spreer, J., Carmona, H., Schulze–Bonhage, A. Cerebellar hemorrhage arising postoperatively as a complication of supratentorial surgery: A retrospective study. J. Neurosurg. 96:248–254, 2002.
117. Omalu, B. I., Nnebe–Agumadu, U. H., Shakir, A. M., Rozin, L., Wecht, C. H. Postmortem grading of cerebral contusions. A proposed modification of the Adams' contusion index with re–definition of anatomic markers. Forensic Sci. Med. Pathol. 1:105–112, 2005.
118. Adams, J. H., Graham, D. I., Murray, L. S., Scott, G. Diffuse axonal injury due to nonmissile head injury in humans: an analysis of 45 cases. Ann. Neurol. 12:557–563, 1982.
119. Pilz, P. Axonal injury in head injury. Acta Neurochir. Suppl. (Wien) 32:119–123, 1983.
120. Strich, S. J. Shearing of nerve fibres as a cause of brain damage due to head injury: a pathological study of twenty cases. Lancet ii:443–448, 1961.
121. Peerless, S. J., Rewcastle, N. B. Shear injuries of the brain. Can. Med. Assoc. J. 96:577–582, 1967.
122. Graham, D. I., Clark, J. C., Adams, J. H., Gennarelli, T. A. Diffuse axonal injury caused by assault. J. Clin. Pathol. 45:840–841, 1992.
123. Adams, J. H., Doyle, D., Graham, D. I., Lawrence, A. E., McLellan, D. R. Diffuse axonal injury in head injuries caused by a fall. Lancet 2:1420–1422, 1984.
124. Adams, J.H., Graham, D. I., Gennarelli, T. A. Head injury in man and experimental animals: neuropathology. Acta Neurochir. Suppl. (Wien) 32:15–30, 1983.
125. Gennarelli, T. A., Thibault, L. E., Adams, J. H., Graham, D. I., Thompson, C. J., Marcincin, R.P. Diffuse axonal injury and traumatic coma in the primate. Ann. Neurol. 12:564–574, 1982.
126. Geddes, J. F., Whitwell, H. L., Graham, D. I. Traumatic axonal injury: practical issues for diagnosis in medicolegal cases. Neuropathol. Appl. Neurobiol. 26:105–116, 2000.
127. Povlishock, J. T. Traumatically induced axonal injury: pathogenesis and pathobiological implications. Brain Pathol. 2:1–12, 1992.
128. Geddes, J. F., Vowles, G. H., Beer, T. W., Ellison, D. W. The diagnosis of diffuse axonal injury:implications for forensic practice. Neuropathol. Appl. Neurobiol. 23:339–347, 1997.
129. Adams, J. H., Jennett, B., McLellan, D. R., Murray, L. S., Graham, D. I. The neuropathology of the vegetative state after head injury. J. Clin. Pathol. 52:804–806, 1999.

130. Adams, J. H., Graham, D. I., Jennett, B. The structural basis of moderate disability after traumatic brain damage. J. Neurol. Neurosurg. Psychiatry 71:521–524, 2001.
131. Blumbergs, P. C., Jones, N. R., North, J. B. Diffuse axonal injury in head trauma. J. Neurol. Neurosurg. Psychiatry 52:838–841, 1989.
132. McKenzie, K. J., McLellan, D. R., Gentleman, S. M., Maxwell, W. L., Gennarelli, T. A., Graham, D. I. Is beta–APP a marker of axonal damage in short–surviving head injury? Acta Neuropathol. (Berl) 92:608–613, 1996.
133. Blumbergs, P. C., Scott, G., Manavis, J., Wainwright, H., Simpson, D. A., McLean, A. J.Topography of axonal injury as defined by amyloid precursor protein and the sector scoring method in mild and severe closed head injury. J. Neurotrauma 12:565–572, 1995.
134. Wilkinson, A. E., Bridges, L. R., Sivaloganathan, S. Correlation of survival time with size of axonal swellings in diffuse axonal injury. Acta Neuropathol. (Berl) 98:197–202, 1999.
135. Blumbergs, P. C., Scott, G., Manavis, J., Wainwright, H., Simpson, D. A., McLean, A. J.Staining of amyloid precursor protein to study axonal damage in mild head injury. Lancet344:1055–1056, 1994.
136. Adams, J. H., Doyle, D., Ford, I., Gennarelli, T. A., Graham, D. I., McLellan, D. R. Diffuse axonal injury in head injury: definition, diagnosis and grading. Histopathology 15:49–59, 1989.
137. Gennarelli, TA. The spectrum of traumatic axonal injury. Neuropathol. Appl. Neurobiol. 22:509–513, 1996.
138. Adams, J. H., Doyle, D., Graham, D. I., Lawrence, A. E., McLellan, D. R. Microscopic diffuse axonal injury in cases of head injury. Med. Sci. Law 25:265–269, 1985.
139. Dolinak, D., Smith, C., Graham, D. I. Global hypoxia per se is an unusual cause of axonal injury. Acta Neuropathol. (Berl) 100:553–560, 2000.
140. Mittl, R. L., Grossman, R. I., Hiehle, J. F., et al. Prevalence of MR evidence of diffuse axonal injury in patients with mild head injury and normal head CT findings. AJNR Am. J. Neuroradiol. 15:1583–1589, 1994.
141. Povlishock, J. T., Becker, D. P., Cheng, C. L., Vaughan, G. W. Axonal change in minor head injury. J. Neuropathol. Exp. Neurol. 42:225–242, 1983.
142. Dolinak, D., Smith, C., Graham, D. I.Hypoglycaemia is a cause of axonal injury. Neuropathol. Appl. Neurobiol. 26:448–453, 2000.
143. Liberski, P. P., Budka, H. Neuroaxonal pathology in Creutzfeldt–Jakob disease. ActaNeuropathol. (Berl) 97:329–334, 1999.
144. Oehmichen, M., Meissner, C., Schmidt, V., Pedal, I., Konig, H. G., Saternus, K. S. Axonal injury—a diagnostic tool in forensic neuropathology? A review. Forensic Sci. Int. 95:67–

83, 1998.

145. Reichard, R. R., Smith, C., Graham, D. I. The significance of beta-APP immunoreactivity in forensic practice. Neuropathol. Appl. Neurobiol. 31:304–313, 2005.

146. Pittella, J. E., Gusmao, S. N. Diffuse vascular injury in fatal road traffic accident victims:its relationship to diffuse axonal injury. J. Forensic Sci. 48:626–630, 2003.

147. Tomlinson, B. E. Brain-stem lesions after head injury. J. Clin. Pathol. Suppl. (R. Coll. Pathol.) 4:154–165, 1970.

148. Auer, R. N., Sutherland, G. R. Hypoxia and related conditions. In: Graham, D. I., Lantos, E. R., eds. Greenfield's Neuropathology, Seventh Edition, Volume 1. Arnold, London, pp. 233–280, 2002.

149. Graham, D. I., Adams, J. H., Doyle, D. Ischaemic brain damage in fatal non-missile head injuries. J. Neurol. Sci. 39:213–234, 1978.

150. Graham, D. I., Ford, I., Adams, J. H., et al. Ischaemic brain damage is still common in fatal non-missile head injury. J. Neurol. Neurosurg. Psychiatry 52:346–350, 1989.

151. Marion, D. W., Darby, J., Yonas, H. Acute regional cerebral blood flow changes caused by severe head injuries. J. Neurosurg. 74:407–414, 1991.

152. Bouma, G. J., Muizelaar, J. P. Evaluation of regional cerebral blood flow in acute head injury by stable xenon-enhanced computerized tomography. Acta Neurochir. Suppl. (Wien) 59:34–40, 1993.

153. Schroder, M. L., Muizelaar, J. P., Bullock, M. R., Salvant, J. B., Povlishock, J. T. Focal ischemia due to traumatic contusions documented by stable xenon-CT and ultrastructural studies. J. Neurosurg. 82:966–971, 1995.

154. Schroder, M. L., Muizelaar, J. P., Kuta, A. J. Documented reversal of global ischemia immediately after removal of an acute subdural hematoma. Report of two cases. J. Neurosurg. 80:324–327, 1994.

155. Mirvis, S. E., Wolf, A. L., Numaguchi, Y., Corradino, G., Joslyn, J. N. Posttraumatic cere- bral infarction diagnosed by CT: Prevalence, origin, and outcome. AJNR Am. J. Neuroradiol. 11:355–360, 1990.

156. Csordas, A., Mazlo, M., Gallyas, F. Recovery versus death of "dark" compacted. neurons in non-impaired parenchymal environment: light and electron microscopic observations. Acta Neuropathol. (Berl.) 106:37–49, 2003.

157. Ishida, K., Shimizu, H., Hida, H., Urakawa, S., Ida, K., Nishino, H. Argyrophilic dark neurons represent various states of neuronal damage in brain insults: some come to die and others survive. Neuroscience 125:633–644, 2004.

158. Zsombok, A., Toth, Z., Gallyas, F. Basophilia, acidophilia and argyrophilia of "dark"

(compacted) neurons during their formation, recovery or death in an otherwise undamaged environment. J. Neurosci. Methods 142:145–152, 2005.

159. Bruce, D. A., Alavi, A., Bilaniuk, L., Dolinskas, C., Obrist, W., Uzzell, B. Diffuse cerebral swelling following head injuries in children: the syndrome of "malignant brain edema". J. Neurosurg. 54:170–178, 1981.

160. Graham, D. I., Ford, I., Adams, J. H., et al. Fatal head injury in children. J. Clin. Pathol. 42:18–22, 1989.

161. Kazan, S., Tuncer, R., Karasoy, M., Rahat, O., Saveren, M. Post-traumatic bilateral diffuse cerebral swelling. Acta Neurochir. (Wien) 139:295–301, 1997.

162. Cornish, R., Blumbergs, P. C., Manavis, J., Scott, G., Jones, N. R., Reilly, P. L. Topography and severity of axonal injury in human spinal cord trauma using amyloid precursor protein as a marker of axonal injury. Spine 25:1227–1233, 2000.

163. Lindenberg, R., Freytag, E. Brainstem lesions characteristic of traumatic hyperextension of the head. Arch. Pathol. 90:509–515, 1970.

164. Pilz, P., Strohecker, J., Grobovschek, M. Survival after traumatic ponto-medullary tear. J. Neurol. Neurosurg. Psychiatry 45:422–427, 1982.

165. Hooper, A. D. A new approach to upper cervical injuries. J. Forensic Sci. 24:39–45, 1979.

166. Jonsson, H., Jr., Bring, G., Rauschning, W., Sahlstedt, B. Hidden cervical spine injuries in traffic accident victims with skull fractures. J. Spinal Disord. 4:251–263, 1991.

167. Sun, P. P., Poffenbarger, G. J., Durham, S., Zimmerman, R. A. Spectrum of occipito-atlantoaxial injury in young children. J. Neurosurg. 93:28–39, 2000.

168. Alker, G. J., Jr., Oh, Y. S., Leslie, E. V. High cervical spine and craniocervical junction injuries in fatal traffic accidents: a radiological study. Orthop. Clin. N. Am. 9:1003–1010, 1978.

169. Leditschke, J., Anderson, R. M., Hare, W. S. The cervical spine in fatal motor vehicle accidents. Clin. Exp. Neurol. 29:263–271, 1992.

170. Bromilow, A., Burns, J. Technique for removal of the vertebral arteries. J. Clin. Pathol. 38:1400–1402, 1985.

171. Ludwig, J. Handbook of Autopsy Practice, Third Edition. Humana Press, Totowa, NJ, 2002.

172. Vanezis, P. Techniques used in the evaluation of vertebral artery trauma at post-mortem. Forensic Sci. Int. 13:159–165, 1979.

173. Vollmer, D. G., Gegg, C. Classification and acute management of thoracolumbar fractures. Neurosurg. Clin. N. Am. 8:499–507, 1997.

174. Hadley, M. N., Zabramski, J. M., Browner, C. M., Rekate, H., Sonntag, V. K. Pediatric

spinal trauma. Review of 122 cases of spinal cord and vertebral column injuries. J. Neurosurg. 68:18–24, 1988.

175. Argenson, C., De Peretti, F., Ghabris, A., Eude, P., Lovet, J., Hovorka, I. A scheme for the classification of lower cervical spine injuries. http://www.maitrise-orthop.com/corpus0maitri/orthopaedic/mo61_spine_injury_class/spine_injury.shtml, 2005.

176. Allen, B. L., Jr., Ferguson, R. L., Lehmann, T. R., O'Brien, R. P. A mechanistic classification of closed, indirect fractures and dislocations of the lower cervical spine. Spine 7:1–27, 1982.

177. Harris, J. H., Jr., Edeiken-Monroe, B., Kopaniky, D. R. A practical classification of acute cervical spine injuries. Orthop Clin. N. Am. 17:15–30, 1986.

178. Mirza, S. K., Mirza, A. J., Chapman, J. R., Anderson, P. A. Classifications of thoracic and lumbar fractures: rationale and supporting data. J. Am. Acad. Orthop. Surg. 10:364–377, 2002.

179. Fife, D., Kraus, J. Anatomic location of spinal cord injury. Relationship to the cause of injury. Spine 11:2–5, 1986.

180. Goldberg, W., Mueller, C., Panacek, E., Tigges, S., Hoffman, J.R., Mower, W. R. Distribution and patterns of blunt traumatic cervical spine injury. Ann. Emerg. Med. 38:17–21, 2001.

181. Brown, R. L., Brunn, M. A., Garcia, V. F. Cervical spine injuries in children: a review of 103 patients treated consecutively at a level 1 pediatric trauma center. J. Pediatr. Surg. 36:1107–1114, 2001.

182. Alker, G. J., Oh, Y. S., Leslie, E. V., Lehotay, J, Panaro, V.A., Eschner, E. G. Postmortem radiology of head neck injuries in fatal traffic accidents. Radiology 114:611–617, 1975.

183. Bucholz, R.W., Burkhead, W.Z. The pathological anatomy of fatal atlanto–occipital dislocations. J. Bone Joint Surg. Am. 61:248–250, 1979.

184. Adams, V. I. Neck injuries: I. Occipitoatlantal dislocation—a pathologic study of twelve traffic fatalities. J. Forensic Sci. 37:556–564, 1992.

185. Tepper, S. L., Fligner, C. L., Reay, D. T. Atlanto–occipital disarticulation: Accident characteristics. Am. J. Forensic Med. Pathol. 11:193–197, 2005.

186. Adams, V. I. Neck injuries: II. Atlanto–axial dislocation—a pathologic study of 14 traffic fatalities. J. Forensic Sci. 37:565–573, 1992.

187. Shkrum, M. J., Green, R. N., Nowak, E. S. Upper cervical trauma in motor vehicle collisions. J. Forensic Sci. 34:381–390, 1989.

188. Silver, J. R., Morris, W. R., Otfinowski, J. S. Associated injuries in patients with spinal injury. Injury 12:291–324, 1980.

189. Imaizumi, T., Sohma, T., Hotta, H., Teto, I., Imaizumi, H., Kaneko, M. Associated injuries

and mechanism of atlanto-occipital dislocation caused by trauma. Neurol. Med. Chir. (Tokyo) 35:385-391, 1995.

190. Iida, H., Tachibana, S., Kitahara, T., Horiike, S., Ohwada, T., Fujii, K. Association of head trauma with cervical spine injury, spinal cord injury, or both. J. Trauma 46:450-452, 1999.

191. Ardekian, L., Gaspar, R., Peled, M., Manor, R., Laufer, D. Incidence and type of cervical spine injuries associated with mandibular fractures. J. Craniomaxillofac. Trauma 3:18-21, 1997.

192. Lewis, V. L., Jr., Manson, P. N., Morgan, R. F., Cerullo, L. J., Meyer, P. R., Jr. Facial injuries associated with cervical fractures: recognition, patterns, and management. J. Trauma 25:90-93, 1985.

193. Oller, D. W., Meredith, J. W., Rutledge, R., et al. The relationship between face or skull fractures and cervical spine and spinal cord injuries: a review of 13, 834 patients. Accid. Anal. Prev. 24:187-192, 1992.

194. Sinclair, D., Schwartz, M., Gruss, J., McLellan, B. A retrospective review of the relationship between facial fractures, head injuries, and cervical spine injuries. J. Emerg. Med. 6:109-112, 1988.

195. Shkrum, M. J., McClafferty, K. J., Nowak, E. S., German, A. Driver and front seat passenger fatalities associated with air bag deployment. Part 1: A Canadian study. J. Forensic Sci. 47:1028-1034, 2002.

196. Shkrum, M. J., McClafferty, K. J., Nowak, E. S., German, A. Driver and front seat passenger fatalities associated with air bag deployment. Part 2: A review of injury patterns and investigative issues. J. Forensic Sci. 47:1035-1040, 2002.

197. Kinoshita, H. Pathology of spinal cord injuries due to fracture-dislocations of the thoracic and lumbar spine. Paraplegia 34:1-7, 1996.

198. Brandser, E. A., el Khoury, G. Y. Thoracic and lumbar spine trauma. Radiol. Clin. N. Am. 35:533-557, 1997.

199. Koyanagi, I., Iwasaki, Y., Hida, K., Akino, M., Imamura, H., Abe, H. Acute cervical cord injury without fracture or dislocation of the spinal column. J. Neurosurg. 93:15-20, 2000.

200. Pang, D., Wilberger, J. E. Spinal cord without radiographic abnormalities in children. J. Neurosurg. 57:114-129, 1982.

201. American College of Neurological Surgeons. Spinal cord injury without radiographic abnormality. Neurosurgery 50 (Suppl.) .:S100-S104, 2002.

202. Kaye, K. L., Ramsay, D. A., Young, B. Y. Cervical flexion myelopathy after valproic acid overdose. Spine 26:E459-E462, 2001.

203. Tator, C. H. Update on the pathophysiology and pathology of acute spinal cord injury. Brain Pathol. 5:407-413, 1995.

204. Harrop, J. S., Sharan, A. D., Vaccaro, A. R., Przybylski, G. J. The cause of neurologic deterioration after acute cervical spinal cord injury. Spine 26:340–346, 2001.
205. Kochan, J. P., Quencer, R. M. Imaging of cystic and cavitary lesions of the spinal cord and canal. The value of MR and intraoperative sonography. Radiol. Clin. N. Am. 29:867–911, 1991.
206. Fleming, J. C., Norenberg, M. D., Ramsay, D. A., et al. The acute cellular inflammatory response after human spinal cord injury. J. Neurotrauma 22:1170 (Abstract), 2005.
207. Bunge, R. P., Puckett, W.R., Becerra, J.L., Marcillo, A., Quencer, R.M. Observations on the pathology of human spinal cord injury. A review and classification of 22 new cases with details from a case of chronic cord compression with extensive focal demyelination. Adv. Neurol. 59:75–89, 1993.
208. Kakulas, B. A. A review of the neuropathology of human spinal cord injury with emphasis on special features. J. Spinal Cord Med. 22:119–124, 1999.
209. Jimenez, O., Marcillo, A., Levi, A. D. A histopathological analysis of the human cervical spinal cord in patients with acute traumatic central cord syndrome. Spinal Cord38:532–537, 2000.
210. Martin, D., Schoenen, J., Lenelle, J., Reznik, M., Moonen, G. MRI–pathological correlations in acute traumatic central cord syndrome: case report. Neuroradiology 34:262–266, 1992.
211. Quencer, R. M., Bunge, R. P., Egnor, M., et al. Acute traumatic central cord syndrome: MRI–pathological correlations. Neuroradiology 34:85–94, 1992.
212. Ito, T., Oyanagi, K., Wakabayashi, K., Ikuta, F. Traumatic spinal cord injury: a neuropathological study on the longitudinal spreading of the lesions. Acta Neuropathol. (Berl.) 93:13–18, 1997.
213. Hashizume, Y., Iljima, S., Kishimoto, H., Hirano, A. Pencil–shaped softening of the spinal cord. Pathologic study in 12 autopsy cases. Acta Neuropathol. (Berl.) 61:219–224, 1983.
214. Balentine, J. D. Pathology of experimental spinal cord trauma. I. The necrotic lesion as a function of vascular injury. Lab. Invest. 39:236–253, 1978.
215. Hirano, A., Iwata, M., llena, J. F., Matsui, T. Color Atlas of Pathology of the Nervous System. Igaku–Shoin, New York, 1980.
216. Hirano, A. A Guide to Neuropathology. Igaku–Shoin, New York, 1981.
217. Ghatan, S., Newell, D.W., Grady, M. S., et al. Severe posttraumatic craniocervical instability in the very young patient. Report of three cases. J.Neurosurg. 101:102–107, 2004.
218. Ersahin, Y., Mutluer, S., Mirzai, H., Palali, I. Pediatric depressed skull fractures: analysis of 530 cases. Childs Nerv. Syst. 12:323–331, 1996.

219. Lindenberg, R., Freytag, E. Morphology of brain lesions from blunt trauma in early infancy. Arch. Pathol. 87:298–305, 1969.
220. Kornblum, R. N., Fisher, R. S. Pituitary lesions in craniocerebral injuries. Arch. Pathol. 88:242–248, 1969.
221. Treip, C. S. Hypothalamic and pituitary injury. J. Clin. Pathol. Suppl. (R. Coll. Pathol.) 4:178–186, 1970.
222. Kovacs, K. Necrosis of anterior pituitary in humans. II. Neuroendocrinology 4:201–241, 1969.
223. Daniel, P. M., Spicer, E. J., Treip, C. S. Pituitary necrosis in patients maintained on mechanical respirators. J. Pathol. 111:135–138, 1973.
224. Kovacs, K., Bilbao, J. M. Adenohypophysial necrosis in respirator–maintained patients. Pathol. Microbiol. (Basel) 41:275–282, 1974.
225. Kovacs, K. Adenohypophysial necrosis in routine autopsies. Endokrinologie 60:309–316. 1972.
226. Kovacs, K. Necrosis of anterior pituitary in humans. I. Neuroendocrinology 4:170–199, 1969.
227. Mooney, E. E., Toner, M., Farrell, M. A. Selective necrosis of the posterior pituitary gland—case report. Clin. Neuropathol. 14:42–44, 1995.
228. Reilly, P. L., Graham, D. I., Adams, J. H., Jennett, B. Patients with head injury who talk and die. Lancet 2:375–377, 1975.
229. Dunn, L. T., Fitzpatrick, M. O., Beard, D., Henry, J. M. Patients with a head injury who "talk and die" in the 1990s. J. Trauma 54:497–502, 2003.
230. Statham, P. F., Johnston, R. A., Macpherson, P. Delayed deterioration in patients with trau- matic frontal contusions. J. Neurol. Neurosurg. Psychiatry 52:351–354, 1989.
231. Jennett, B., Plum, F. Persistent vegetative state after brain damage. A syndrome in search of a name. Lancet 1:734–737, 1972.
232. Working Group of the Royal College of Physicians of the United Kingdom. The permanent vegetative state. Review by a working group convened by the Royal College of Physicians and endorsed by the Conference of Medical Royal Colleges and their faculties of the United Kingdom. J. R. Coll. Physicians. Lond. 30:119–121, 1996.
233. Adams, J. H., Graham, D. I., Jennet, t B. The neuropathology of the vegetative state after an acute brain insult. Brain 123:1327–1338, 2000.
234. Jennett, B., Bond, M. Assessment of outcome after severe brain damage. Lancet1:480–484, 1975.
235. Jennett, B., Adams, J. H., Murray, L. S., Graham, D. I. Neuropathology in vegetative and

severely disabled patients after head injury. Neurology 56:486–490, 2001.

236. Baigelman, W., O'Brien, J. C. Pulmonary effects of head trauma. Neurosurgery 9:729–740, 1981.

237. Fontes, R. B., Aguiar, P. H., Zanetti, M. V., Andrade, F., Mandel, M., Teixeira, M. J. Acute neurogenic pulmonary edema: case reports and literature review. J. Neurosurg. Anesthesiol. 15:144–150, 2003.

238. Weisman, S. J. Edema and congestion of the lungs resulting from intracranial hemorrhage. Surgery 6:722–729, 1939.

239. Weir, B. K. Pulmonary edema following fatal aneurysm rupture. J. Neurosurg. 49:502–507, 1978.

240. Terrence, C. F., Rao, G. R., Perper, J. A. Neurogenic pulmonary edema in unexpected, unexplained death of epileptic patients. Ann. Neurol. 9:458–464, 1981.

241. Rogers, F. B., Shackford, S. R., Trevisani, G. T., Davis, J. W., Mackersie, R. C., Hoyt, D. B.Neurogenic pulmonary edema in fatal and nonfatal head injuries. J. Trauma 39:860–866, 1995.

242. Simmons, R. L., Martin, A. M., Jr., Heisterkamp, C. A., III, Ducker, T. B. Respiratory insufficiency in combat casualties. II. Pulmonary edema following head injury. Ann. Surg. 170:39–44, 1969.

243. Ducker, T. B. Increased intracranial pressure and pulmonary edema. 1. Clinical study of 11 patients. J. Neurosurg. 28:112–117, 1968.

244. Rubin, D. M., McMillan, C. O., Helfaer, M. A., Christian, C. W. Pulmonary edema associ- ated with child abuse: case reports and review of the literature. Pediatrics 108:769–775, 2001.

245. Beckman, D. L., Bean, J. W. Pulmonary damage and head injury. Proc. Soc. Exp. Biol. Med. 130:5–9, 1969.

246. Hucker, H., Frenzel, H., Kremer, B., Richter, I. E. Time sequence and site of fluid accumu- lation in experimental neurogenic pulmonary edema. Res. Exp. Med. (Berl.) 168:219–227, 1976.

247. Ducker, T. B., Simmons, R. L. Increased intracranial pressure and pulmonary edema. 2. The hemodynamic response of dogs and monkeys to increased intracranial pressure. J. Neurosurg. 28:118–123, 1968.

248. Simmons, R. L., Ducker, T. B., Anderson, R. W. Pathogenesis of pulmonary edema following head trauma. An experimental study. J. Trauma 8:800–811, 1968.

249. Lowe, J. Establishing a pathological diagnosis in degenerative dementias. Brain Pathol. 8:403–406, 1998.

250. Stewart, W., Black, M., Kalimo, H., Graham, D. I. Non-traumatic forensic neuropathology. Forensic Sci. Int. 146:125–147, 2004.
251. Ellison, D., Love, S., Chimelli, L., Harding, B., Lowe, J. S., Vinters, H. Neuropathology, Second Edition—A Reference Text of CNS Pathology. Mosby, Edinburgh, 2004.
252. Braak, H., Braak, E. Neuropathological stageing of Alzheimer-related changes. Acta Neuropathol. (Berl.) 82:239–259, 1991.
253. Mirra, S. S., Heyman, A., McKeel, D., et al. The Consortium to Establish a Registry for Alzheimer's Disease (CERAD). Part II. Standardization of the neuropathologic assessment of Alzheimer's disease. Neurology 41:479–486, 1991.
254. Davis, D. G., Schmitt, F. A., Wekstein, D. R., Markesbery, W. R. Alzheimer neuropathologic alterations in aged cognitively normal subjects. J. Neuropathol. Exp. Neurol. 58:376–388, 1999.
255. Muller, C. M., de Vos, R. A., Maurage, C. A., Thal, D. R., Tolnay, M., Braak, H. Staging of sporadic Parkinson disease-related alpha-synuclein pathology: inter- and intra-rater reliability. J. Neuropathol. Exp. Neurol. 64:623–628, 2005.
256. McKeith, I. G., Galasko, D., Kosaka, K., et al. Consensus guidelines for the clinical and pathologic diagnosis of dementia with Lewy bodies (DLB): report of the consortium on DLB international workshop. Neurology 47:1113–1124, 1996.
257. Braak, H., Del Tredici, K., Rub, U., de Vos, R. A., Jansen Steur, E. N., Braak, E. Staging of brain pathology related to sporadic Parkinson's disease. Neurobiol. Aging 24:197–211, 2003.
258. Jellinger, K. A. Head injury and dementia. Curr. Opin. Neurol. 17:719–723, 2004.
259. Szczygielski, J., Mautes, A., Steudel, W. I., Falkai, P., Bayer, T. A., Wirths, O. Traumatic brain injury:cause or risk of Alzheimer's disease?A review of experimental studies. J. Neural Transm. 112:1147–1164, 2005.
260. Maxwell, W. L., Dhillon, K., Harper, L., et al. There is differential loss of pyramidal cells from the human hippocampus with survival after blunt head injury. J. Neuropathol. Exp. Neurol. 62:272–279, 2003.
261. Jordan, B. D. Chronic traumatic brain injury associated with boxing. Semin. Neurol. 20:179–185, 2000.
262. de la Torre, J. C. Brain trauma and the elderly. In: Duckett, S., de la Torre, J. C., eds. Pathology of the Aging Human Nervous System, Second Edition. Oxford University Press, Oxford, pp. 458–473, 2001.
263. Graham, D. I., Gentleman, S. M., Nicoll, J. A., et al. Altered beta-APP metabolism after head injury and its relationship to the aetiology of Alzheimer's disease. Acta Neurochir. Suppl. 66:96–102, 1996.

第 10 章
神经源性猝死

概述

虽然神经系统疾病是常见的死亡原因之一,在发病后不久患者即可死亡,但它是一个相对不常见的猝死原因,明确诊断通常需要较长时间。与创伤相关的突发神经源性死亡的原因包括:大面积颅脑损伤、高位颈髓损伤、创伤后癫痫导致难以解释的癫痫发作中猝死、急性创伤性脑干功能障碍("髓质震荡")、与创伤性椎动脉和基底动脉撕裂相关的蛛网膜下腔出血,以及创伤引起的椎动脉血栓所致的脑干梗死。

关键词: 脑干梗死;脑血管损伤;颅脑损伤;癫痫,创伤后;猝死;脊髓损伤;蛛网膜下腔出血,创伤性;难以解释的癫痫发作中猝死

1 前言与术语定义

猝死鉴定是法医病理学实践的核心工作之一。严重冠状动脉疾病的尸检显示,心源性死亡不一定与冠状动脉早期血栓栓塞或急性心肌坏死有关,如果没有发现其他器质性、代谢性或中毒性的死亡因素,则死亡符合致命性心律失常所致的特征,因为心脏的电生理紊乱具有致命性。大脑也是一个带电器官,也会定期被"异常不良情况"干扰,通常表现为癫痫发作,但如果存在各种神经功能障碍,脑干功能会受到干扰并影响控制心肺功能的神经区域,从而发生致命性衰竭(1,2)。在某些情况下,颅脑损伤和脊椎损伤通过损害脑电平衡而导致脑干致命性衰竭。本章旨在讨论引起突发和意外的神经源性死亡的中枢神经系统(sudden neurological death, CNS)创伤性疾病。

神经源性死亡分为两类:意外性神经源性死亡(出于章节的完整性考虑,本章仅简要提及)和突发性神经源性死亡(sudden neurological death, SND)。

1.1 意外性神经源性死亡

意外性神经源性死亡分为两类。第一类急性神经系统性疾病通常在死亡前至少

一天左右才有症状（如胶质囊肿引起的位置相关性前驱头痛）；第二类急性神经系统疾病如能被及时发现就可确定其先兆症状和体征，而且疾病发展较缓慢，可在死亡前有充足的时间加以诊断。因此，第二类意外性神经源性死亡会在睡眠期间发生，或在无法或不愿意寻求帮助的社会性孤立个体中发生。

意外性神经源性死亡的原因众多，常见原因如下：
- 急性细菌性脑膜炎。
- 各种脑血管疾病，包括：
  ○ 脑梗死。
  ○ 无创性脑内出血。
  ○ 导致蛛网膜下腔出血（subarachnoid hemorrhage, SAH）的浆果状动脉瘤破裂。
- 颅脑外伤：
  ○ 硬脑膜外血肿。
  ○ 急性硬脑膜下血肿。

1.2 突发性神经源性死亡（SND）

突发性神经源性死亡被定义为神经系统疾病或神经系统症状发生后的快速死亡或脑死亡。其实践意义重大，有助于法医解释死亡原因。

1.2.1 突发性神经源性死亡的分类

突发性神经源性死亡分为以下几类：
- 在发现临床症状和体征前便已死亡。有些案例致死原因的条件较为明显，也有些案例只有在尸检后才能确认是神经性原因致死，这对法医来说非常重要。
- 神经系统疾病突然发作会导致心搏、呼吸停止，患者接受心肺复苏后常会引发不可逆的脑损伤；患者虽然可通过仪器维持生命，但在临床上已属于"脑死亡"；心脏停搏的原因无法通过临床和神经影像学检查揭示，通过尸体解剖才能证明是神经系统性原因。随着神经成像技术敏感度的日益提高，这一种类也将越来越少。
- 癫痫患者在有目击者或没有目击者的情况下猝死。

2 突发性神经源性的死因

大多数情况下，突发性神经源性死亡是由脑干或高位颈髓急性功能障碍导致心肺功能衰竭所致的。在概念上，由于其发生速度快且破坏脑电平衡，突发性神经源性死亡与心脏猝死也密切相关。突发性神经源性死亡通常有以下3种机制：
- 急性脑积水，引起脑灌注受损或脑干压迫。
- 明显的脑干或颈髓结构破坏。
- 脑干活动的功能性损伤，通过标准尸体解剖也未发现器质性病变。

2.1 可能与突发性神经源性死亡相关的非创伤性神经系统性疾病

很多案例报告和分析显示，突发性神经源性死亡与各种中枢神经系统疾病有明显联系，包括中枢神经系统疾病如下：

- 原发性中枢神经系统肿瘤［法医尸检率为 0.17%（3）］：
  - 脑膜瘤（3）。
  - 垂体腺瘤（3）。
  - 胶体囊肿（3,4）。
  - 脑半球神经胶质瘤（3,5）。
  - 脑干胶质瘤（6-8）。
  - 小脑胶质瘤（7）。
  - 髓母细胞瘤（3）。
  - 松果体囊肿（9）。
  - 表皮囊肿（10）。
- 隐匿性原发性或继发性脑瘤出血（11）。
- 中枢神经系统感染：
  - 急性化脓性脑膜炎（11）。
  - 急性淋巴细胞性脑膜炎（12）。
  - 病毒性小脑炎（13）。
  - 神经性肉芽肿病（14）。
- 多发性硬化症（15）。
- Chiari 1 畸形（小脑扁桃体下疝畸形）（16）伴有或不伴有慢性脑积水。
- 血管疾病，通常是破裂的浆果状动脉瘤和急性蛛网膜下腔出血（17）。

以上案例中，可根据既往病史将死因归类为意外性神经源性死亡。

2.2 创伤造成的突发性神经源性死亡

突发性神经源性死亡与创伤的关系可在以下案例中发现：

- 损伤明显。
- 颅脑损伤和椎板外伤直接造成死亡，外伤不明显。
- 创伤并发症导致突发性神经源性死亡（通常为癫痫）。
- 疑似神经系统性疾病引起突发性神经源性死亡，并导致颅脑损伤（如浆果状动脉瘤破裂导致机动车驾驶人员急性呼吸衰竭后发生交通事故）。

本章将讨论以下情况及其与创伤和突发性神经源性死亡的关系：

- 明显因素所致的创伤性突发性神经源性死亡。
- 不明显因素所致的创伤性突发性神经源性死亡。
- 创伤后癫痫发作突然意外死亡。
- 浆果状动脉瘤破裂、急性蛛网膜下腔出血、卒中。

- "缺乏影像学异常的脊髓损伤"。

3 明显因素所致的创伤性突发性神经源性死亡

此类情况在第9章中已有描述,包括严重的颅脑损伤、高位颈髓损伤、弥漫性血管损伤和脑桥延髓撕裂。

4 不明显因素所致的创伤性突发性神经源性死亡

4.1 轻微头部损伤与突发性神经源性死亡

与摔跌和机动车辆碰撞引起的严重头部受伤相比,这种情况的头部损伤程度较"轻微"。轻度头部损伤和突发性神经源性死亡具有以下临床特征:

- 受害人(常见为酗酒者)在打斗过程中(或有时头部与其他物体发生轻、中强度碰撞)死亡。
- 受害者头部或颈部受轻微外力,可通过证人描述或尸检结果推断出该轻微外力。
- 在常规死后检查中未发现器质性、中毒性、代谢性或感染性疾病死亡因素的证据。
- 神经病理学检查显示任意下列情况:
  - 急性蛛网膜下腔出血集中在脑底部(创伤性基底部蛛网膜下腔出血)。
  - 未受伤或轻微损伤:
    - 在这种情况下,有证据表明死亡由延髓功能障碍引起,将在标题4.3中加以讨论。
    - 为便于参考,这种情况被称为"脊髓震荡",类推自心脏震荡猝死综合征(心前区受到外力导致致命性心脏停搏)(参阅第8章标题6.4)。

4.2 创伤性基底部蛛网膜下腔出血

在轻度头部损伤的情况下,孤立性脑基底部蛛网膜下出血由浆果状动脉瘤破裂引起(图10-1;标题6)或与脑血管壁撕裂有关,但在某些情况下仍无法确定出血来源(18,19)。

外伤性动脉撕裂患者的耳后颈部常有皮肤瘀斑(20)。椎动脉是颅内(19-24)或颅外段(19,20,25)最常见的受损血管,也会发生小脑后下动脉(19,26)和基底动脉撕裂(19,24)。在某些情况下,C1椎体横突骨折(19,20)或发育性颈椎异常(27)与动脉撕裂有关,但在许多案例中,除了撕裂与创伤的时间关联之外并没有其他解释(21,28,29)。

目前已有很多方法确定出血源,但并非所有的方法都符合法医实践要求。这些方法包括椎动脉原位解剖,死后椎动脉血管造影(20,30),脑基底部、脑干、颈髓和脊椎部位解剖后脱钙和其他检查处理(21,27,31)。虽然大多数法医尸检中心均有各

第 10 章 | 神经源性猝死

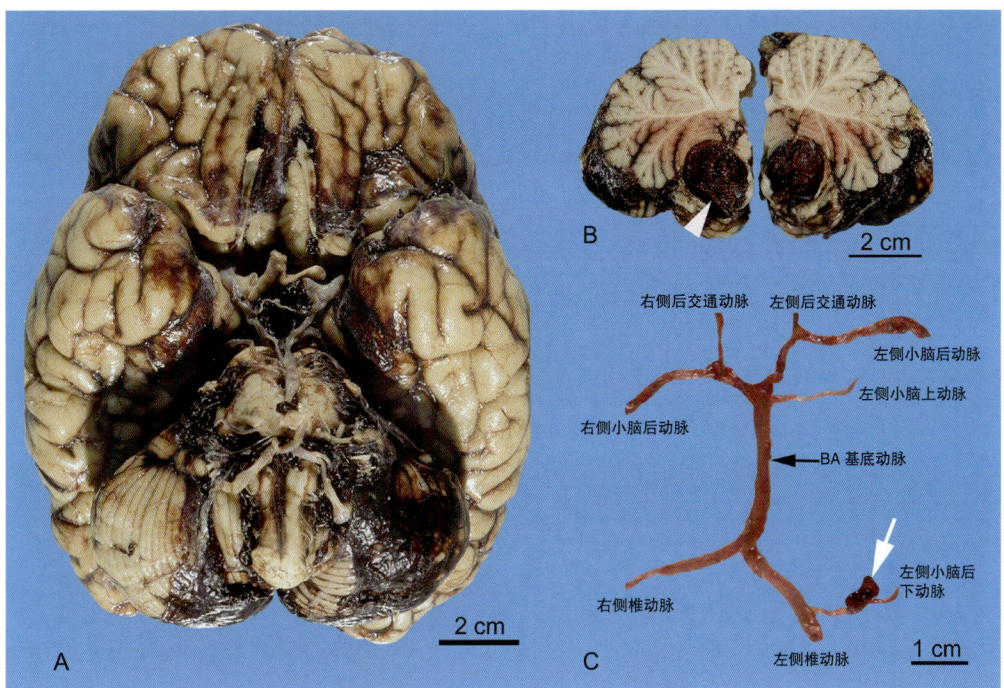

图 10-1 基底部蛛网膜下腔出血。(A)脑底。小脑左侧尾部表面轻、中度蛛网膜下腔出血,小脑右侧半球轻度蛛网膜下腔出血。大脑固定切开后才能发现出血源。(B)通过小脑蚓部的 A 图中大脑矢状切面。可检见动脉瘤破裂,起源于右下后脑小动脉远端分支,埋在尾部小脑中线内(白色三角)。(C)Willis 环。年轻女性尸检发现基底部蛛网膜下腔出血,系醉酒后与丈夫争吵时死亡,嫌疑人不记得受害人自己是摔倒的还是他推倒的。白色箭头所指为左侧后下小脑动脉动脉瘤破裂。

自熟悉可靠的检验方法解剖病变的椎动脉和基底动脉,但这一处理过程不但耗时而且困难。在技术力量较弱的尸检中心,法医遇到创伤性基底部蛛网膜下腔出血这类复杂疑难案件时会面临以下困难:

- 是否将该类案件提交上级法医部门处理(这在一些地域辽阔的国家可能不切实际)?
- 对极少数遇到该类复杂疑难案件的基层法医中心,是否值得学习该类案件的处理程序[基层法医中心每 1000 例尸体解剖可以遇到 0.5-1 例复杂疑难案件(19,20,27)]?
- 殴打过程中死亡的受害者基底部蛛网膜下腔出血是否由创伤所致(需要提供颅内椎动脉的肉眼和组织学检查,排除是否存在动脉疾病)?
- 如果通过不规范的血管造影检查和解剖得出异常检验结果,如何确定出血性质?

无论如何,当尸体解剖时发现基底部蛛网膜下腔出血时,需仔细寻找出血来源。如果没有特殊设施,以下方法较为切实可行:

- 用生理盐水冲洗,用棉签轻轻去除脑表面蛛网膜下腔的血块。

- 暴露脑底 Willis 环及其分支,包括大脑前、中、后动脉,小脑上动脉,小脑后下动脉和椎动脉。
- 剥离 Willis 环及其分支,用放大镜或解剖显微镜检查:
  - 对附有血栓的任何区域进行显微镜检查,并分别检查两侧椎动脉。
  - 椎动脉在石蜡包埋之前应该垂直于血管纵轴修剪成短段。
  - 应保留 Willis 环的剩余部分。
- 从颈动脉处暴露眼动脉起点,排查此处的动脉瘤。
- 全面检查颅腔内近端椎动脉,尤其是穿透硬脑膜的位置。打开硬脑膜,探查侧面颅外动脉路径直至寰椎横突。如果此区域没有出血,则动脉不存在病变,但是仍需去除暴露的椎动脉并进行显微镜检查。
- 如果远端颅外椎动脉周围出血,需进行以下步骤:
  - 完整的椎动脉解剖探查(32–34)。
  - 切除椎动脉。
  - 对动脉中任何出血区域进行显微镜检查。
  - 寻找寰椎横突的骨折。
  - 如果当地的葬礼习俗允许,可考虑去除 C1 和 C2 椎体进行体外影像学检查。

虽然突发性创伤性死亡的发生和急性基底部蛛网膜下腔出血及动脉局部撕裂的因果关联似乎非常明显,但关于动脉撕裂的作用仍存在较大争议(31,35,36),特别是当它可能是人为因素或继发现象时,猝死的原因是创伤引起的延髓功能障碍而非出血本身。

4.2.1 颈动脉和椎动脉的自发性夹层

对颈动脉和椎动脉夹层的解剖发现,卒中(特别是年轻患者)的一个比较常见的原因是血液通过损伤的血管内膜进入血管壁,在数小时至几天后引起大脑缺氧缺血症状和疼痛(37)。血管内膜下血肿导致管腔狭窄,外膜下血肿导致假性动脉瘤形成。"自发"性动脉夹层与颈部的快速运动(如打喷嚏)、更极端的颈部运动(如在汽车转向或练习瑜伽时)、颈部轻度创伤甚至正常运动都可能有关。实际上,对于颅脑和脊髓创伤综合征,自发性动脉夹层与以下情况有关(37):

- 自发性动脉夹层很少引起动脉破裂,发病机制也不同于创伤性基底部蛛网膜下腔出血综合征。
- 自发性动脉夹层不被认为是导致突发性神经源性死亡的原因(参阅标题 7 中的讨论部分)。
- 颈部运动或轻度颈部创伤与动脉夹层间是否存在因果关系,目前仍存有争议。
- 对特殊案件中夹层的因果关系,仍难以明确出现症状和颈部运动或轻微创伤的时间关联是巧合性的、促进性的(存在主要动脉疾病),还是因果性的。
- 在许多自发性动脉夹层案例中会发现动脉病变(应排除创伤性基底部蛛网膜

下腔出血案例),包括:
- 纤维肌瘤发育不良。
- 囊性中央坏死。
- 遗传性结缔组织疾病(1%—5% 的病例)。
  - Ehlers-Danlos 综合征Ⅳ型。
  - 马方综合征。
  - 常染色体显性多囊肾病。
  - Ⅰ型成骨发育不全。

4.3 髓质震荡

髓质震荡这种死亡形式,从严格意义上说,通常没有明显的常见原因,符合 Di Maio 所描述的综合征:"急性醉酒者,面部受到严重殴打后倒在现场,随后被发现死亡"(38),之后进行了更为详细的描述(图 10-2;39,40)。确诊这种综合征较为简单,只需确定其本质、排除其他因素。然而其死亡机制尚未完全明确,有动物实验和个别临床研究为以下有关该综合征的主要问题提供了参考:

- 轻度至中度头部受伤如何导致死亡?
- 乙醇中毒如何使症状恶化?

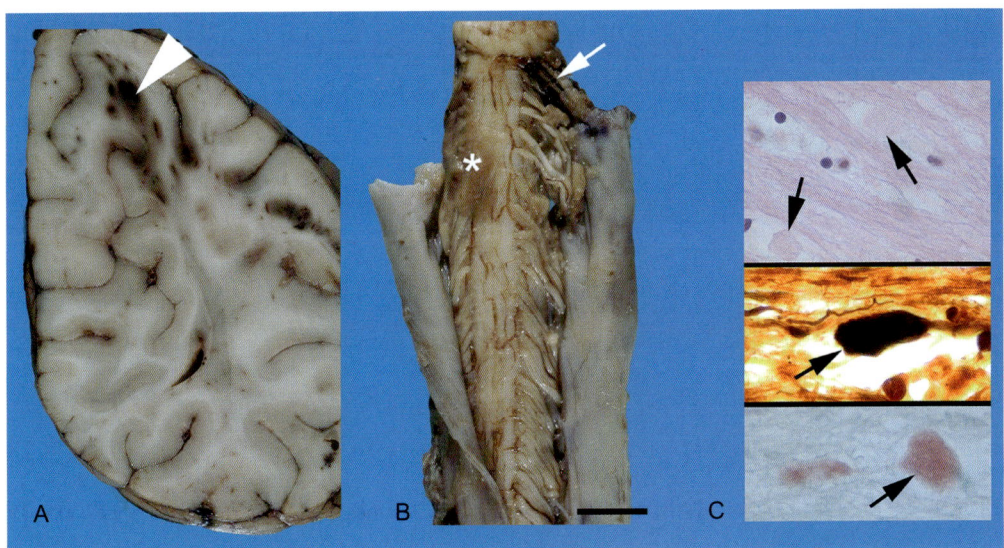

图 10-2 髓质震荡。标本来自男性醉酒青年案例,被他人用拳头击打,头面部遭受脚踢,随即发生呼吸停止,复苏推迟 20 分钟。复苏后脑死亡,但仍维持人工机械通气 3 天。(A)右枕叶冠状面切片中线旁的脑挫伤(白色三角)。(B)颈部脊髓与硬脊膜后表面。少量出血存在于 C1 右后神经根处(白色箭头)。严重的脑肿胀引起小脑扁桃体疝,坏死的小脑组织疝入脊髓蛛网膜下腔(星号)(比例尺 = 1 厘米)。(C)孤束核附近的显微照片。图中显示轴索肿胀(顶部图片,H-E 染色;中间图片,Bielschowsky 染色;底部图片,神经纤维丝免疫组织化学染色:所有图片均为 ×100 油浸物镜观察)(经 Lippincott Williams 和 Wilkins 许可引自文献 40)。

4.3.1 头部损伤后的心肺改变

神经介导的呼吸暂停和循环变化在实验性头部损伤模型中有相关报道。火器性、接触性、加速性头部受伤后均可立即发生呼吸暂停，如轻度或中度震荡损伤后的呼吸暂停可呈自限性(41-43)。呼吸暂停的持续时间通常小于30秒，与伤害程度成正比(41,44)。持续性呼吸停止仅发生于严重性头部损伤中(41,45)。各类头部受伤几乎均伴有高血压和心动过缓，程度与创伤严重程度成正比(42,46,47)。轻度头部损伤即会引起心肺功能改变，重度脑损伤则会导致意识障碍(42)。轻度和中度头部损伤的动物研究表明，损伤后血压升高是通过交感神经介导的，心动过缓则由交感神经系统引发(44,47)。

人体头部受伤时心肺功能瞬时变化的原因还不明确，但有研究表明，持续原发性呼吸暂停会使轻度头部损伤复杂化，如果不及时辅助通气，可能会导致死亡(48)。如果质疑持续原发性呼吸暂停是死因，应首先排除体位性窒息死亡的可能性(参阅第3章标题3.7)。

轻度或中度头部受伤引起心肺改变的机制尚未明确。在个案中可以检见轴索肿胀，支持髓质震荡是外伤性轴突损伤的临床表现(图10-2)(40)。但另一种解释是，头部突然运动脑干被拉伸可能会破坏髓质功能(41)，上颈部区域的神经根断裂便是有效证据(图10-2)(40)。无论何种情况，该综合征的解释均涉及"髓质"，故使用"髓质震荡"这一术语更准确。

4.3.2 乙醇中毒对头部损伤所致心肺功能改变的影响

动物实验表明，乙醇会干扰脑干循环、呼吸中枢的功能。因为乙醇可能通过与巴比妥酸盐(49)所共有的相对选择能力来加强L-氨基丁酸诱导氯离子(提高L-氨基丁酸的抑制作用)并抑制N-甲基-D-天冬氨酸受体介导的L-谷氨酸的兴奋作用(49-51)。交感神经活动压力感受性反射抑制增强，引起髓内血管运动中枢上的净效应(49)。因此，乙醇中毒可以阻碍循环、呼吸中枢反射，以纠正头部受伤后循环、呼吸功能的过度紊乱。动物实验表明，适量乙醇可延长中度脑震荡引起的呼吸暂停(52)。另外两项实验结果也支持了乙醇作为中枢神经系统抑制剂，会加重轻度或中度头部损伤程度：轻度麻醉动物头部损伤后不久注射小剂量的巴比妥类药物可导致致命性急性循环衰竭(53,54)，头部受伤之前服用硫喷妥也会增加创伤后死亡率(55)。

对于醉酒的伤者，酒后与脑损伤无关的猝死率也会增加(56-58)，需全面分析髓质震荡机制。死亡风险增加常见于长期重度乙醇摄入的中年人(59,60)，但往往可能缺乏缺血性心脏病的临床和心电图证据(58)。因此，对存在明显髓质震荡伤者，单纯性乙醇中毒就可能导致猝死，尤其对有过量饮酒史和近期纵酒过度的中年人["假日心脏综合征"(56,57)]，但如果存在明显冠状动脉粥样硬化，则需考虑心肌缺血猝死。

4.3.3 髓质震荡病理机制

轻度至中度的震荡性脑损伤会影响循环、呼吸功能，但通常不会引起呼吸暂停或心脏停搏。但也有例外，清醒个体损伤后循环、呼吸功能的反应也会特异性增强，或乙醇对醉酒者延髓循环、呼吸中枢产生影响引起的增强反应导致神经源性猝死。循环、呼吸变化可能是外伤性轴索损伤的结果，也可能因为头部受伤引起突发性颈部运动，造成髓质局部拉伸和压缩变形。

髓质震荡可为头部损伤案件的死亡原因提供合理解释（通过可靠证人的案情描述或头皮挫伤、颅骨骨折证实）。有些创伤性脑损伤案件（通常表现为蛛网膜下腔出血和小挫伤）的损伤程度轻微，难以导致患者死亡，或者大脑结构是正常的。这种情况下，受害者通常在现场死亡，乙醇中毒不一定是死亡原因，也没有发现其他器质性、代谢性或中毒性的死亡原因。在这种情况下的死亡原因被归为脑震荡（38）或"心脏神经放电"（74）。

5 癫痫猝死

癫痫猝死是癫痫发作导致的非损伤非溺水突发性意外死亡，可有目击者也可无目击者，案件中有或没有证据证明癫痫是否发作和癫痫发作持续的状态，尸检亦未发现毒理学或解剖学上的死亡原因（61）。对法医而言，认识癫痫猝死极为重要，因为这是一种比较常见的猝死原因，可影响到颅脑外伤中有中度残疾的患者（参阅第 9 章标题 11.5）。癫痫猝死在所有猝死中占 1%－1.5%（62），在 30% 的癫痫猝死案例中发现死者有陈旧性颅脑损伤（62,63）。

虽然对癫痫猝死发生率的估计因数据不同而有所变化，但一般癫痫患者的死亡发生率约每年（1－2）/1 000（64,65），青年和早期中年人群中的年发生率最高。与正常人群相比，这意味着猝死风险的大大增加（66）。癫痫猝死主要与广泛性强直阵挛性癫痫发作、癫痫发作控制不当及抗惊厥药物依从性差有关（64,67），其他风险因素也有报道（64）。大多数癫痫猝死患者被发现死于床上或家中（64,65）。死亡常发生在癫痫发作期，较少在癫痫发作后死亡（64,65）。死亡机制可能是癫痫发作引起心律失常或呼吸暂停（65,68－70）。某些情况下癫痫发作会导致致命性肺水肿（71）。

癫痫猝死的尸检中可发现肺淤血，部分会发现舌头被咬伤（参阅第 5 章图 5－16）。某些情况下，存在组织学上的心脏异常病变，包括不明原因的血管周围和间质性心肌纤维化和心肌细胞空泡化改变（72）（可能与缺氧缺血性损伤有关）。癫痫猝死者常能检见陈旧性脑挫伤（62,63,73）。癫痫患者的大脑可能解剖结构正常，癫痫发作不是创伤后并发症。在少数案例中观察到非创伤性癫痫患者也存在脑病变，包括神经胶质瘤、发育性皮质异常和血管畸形（参阅图 5－17）（62,63）。在某些情况下，癫痫活动对脑结构的影响表现为多灶性神经元损失和神经胶质增生（特别是海马）、继发于脑内缺血和兴奋性毒素损伤、颞叶内侧硬化(62)。

对于没有癫痫病史的猝死个体,即使存在理论上引起癫痫的脑损伤(包括陈旧性损伤),也不应将其作为癫痫猝死的原因。

6 浆果状动脉瘤(颅内小动脉瘤)破裂和突发性神经源性死亡

法医有时会遇到因争吵或轻度颅脑损伤引起的颅内动脉瘤破裂,导致突发性神经源性死亡。还有更少见的情况,引起颅内小动脉瘤破裂的急性脑功能障碍,可能导致伴或不伴头部或身体其他部位损伤的事故。对于这两种情况,都会有以下两个问题:
- 创伤本身是否会导致动脉瘤破裂?
- 颅内小动脉瘤破裂是否导致突发性神经源性死亡?

6.1 轻度头部损伤是否会导致颅内动脉瘤破裂

这一问题难以回答,特别是对于法医而言。通常而言,动脉瘤体积越大,发生破裂的风险就越大。由于在运动过程中会有血压的生理性波动,动脉瘤容易发生破裂,但患者在休息或睡眠时也同样会发生动脉瘤破裂(17)。换言之,颅内动脉瘤可在任何时候破裂;就某一单独案例而言,无法确定患者发生动脉瘤破裂导致蛛网膜下腔出血时参与的活动是否是其原因,尽管人们往往认为事件之间的时间关联存在因果关系的证据。

6.2 颅内动脉瘤破裂是否导致突发性神经源性死亡

尽管颅内小动脉瘤破裂继发急性蛛网膜下腔出血在直觉上是导致突发性神经源性死亡的重要原因,但如前所述,这种死亡情况较为罕见。1991—1996年,在加拿大安大略省伦敦市维多利亚医院所做的1 592例尸体解剖中,有28名死者伴有颅内小动脉瘤破裂,其中仅有4例(14%)引起突发性神经源性死亡,这与大样本群体研究显示的结果一致(约10%的患者在症状发作后24小时内死亡)(17)。在这些情况下,颅内小动脉瘤似乎并不偏好大脑前或后循环的某一特定区域(11)。正如Leestma所总结的:"伴动脉瘤破裂的急性蛛网膜下腔出血很少在几分钟内引发死亡,但死亡往往会在几小时内发生"(74)。

急性蛛网膜下腔出血猝死的机制仍然只是推测,但可能与低压脑脊液填充的蛛网膜下腔突然暴露于高动脉压对脑干的冲击作用有关,或与主要脑动脉瞬时血管痉挛有关。

7 脑卒中、神经源性猝死和颅脑损伤

卒中是由脑梗死(缺血性卒中)或脑内出血(出血性卒中)引起的急性神经功能障碍;蛛网膜下腔出血有时也被认为是卒中。前文已讨论动脉瘤破裂、蛛网膜下腔出血和神经源性猝死之间的关系。脑出血是神经源性猝死的罕见原因(尽管以前曾被认为是意外性神经源性死亡的常见原因;11),由于易于检见明显出血,多年来该

类型的出血和神经源性猝死的关系一直被忽视。缺血性卒中与梗死发作时死亡之间的因果关系难以证实,主要原因如下:

- 梗死的肉眼和显微镜下组织改变需要若干小时,这意味着患者在此期间死亡时,大脑可能无法检出器质性改变。
- 在猝死案件中几乎难以发现 Willis 环的分支堵塞。
- 颈动脉分叉或椎动脉发生堵塞的表现不明显,这些动脉发生梗死时常无症状或症状非常轻微。
- 大多数被怀疑有急性脑梗猝死的患者同时也患有缺血性心脏病,而心脏病常被用作解释死亡原因。

鉴于以上困难,我们尸检的印象仍然是大脑半球梗死不太可能在发病时突然导致死亡(并引发致命事故)。然而,致命性心律失常可能发生在大脑半球梗死(75)或脑干梗死的进展后期,在后一种情况下,孤束核的参与可能引发了致命性心脏事件(76—79)。也有罕见的情况,在头部或颈部受伤期间,颈部突然运动会加重预先存在的椎动脉异常,导致脑干梗死,进而引起突发性神经源性死亡,如图 10-3 所示的案

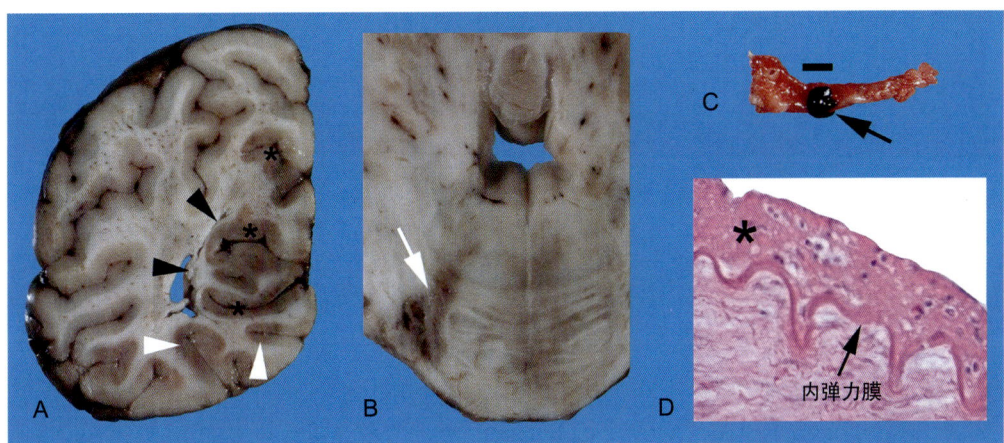

图 10-3 脑干梗死后创伤性神经源性猝死。样本来自男性青少年,在操场上与人争吵时被人从后面推倒,随即失去生命体征。心肺复苏被拖延,2 天后停用呼吸机。死前 3 周曾跌倒并造成斜颈。大脑检查显示(A)左枕叶、(B)右脑桥梗死和(C)右侧椎动脉外膜局灶性急性出血梗死,(D)新近形成的血栓附着于基底内膜,无动脉夹层的证据。这些发现(结果)证明:跌倒引起局部椎动脉损伤,动脉损伤部位形成血栓,推倒引起的突然性颈部运动导致动脉外膜出血和血栓移位,血栓在包括髓质在内的大脑后循环多部位引发栓塞,随后发生心搏、呼吸骤停。在梗死区域附近未发现血栓,可能因为血栓被纤维溶解系统溶解。(A)经左枕叶的冠状切片。尽管在整个脑半球中,由于心搏、呼吸停止后的复苏延迟,存在广泛的缺血缺氧性损伤的微观证据,但左脑后脑区域(星号)也存在局部软化和坏死(即梗死),分离的坏死组织来自相邻的完整白质(黑色三角),并且在梗死边缘,脑回深处的皮质中存在更大程度的缺血性损伤。(B)经脑桥的水平切片。白色箭头指示三角形梗死区。(C)右侧椎动脉。外膜中存在近期出血(黑色箭头)(比例尺 = 0.5 厘米)。(D)右侧椎动脉。新近形成的血栓附在内膜上(H-E 染色 ×40 倍物镜)。

例。总体而言，各类创伤均不太可能导致卒中相关的突发性神经源性死亡。

8 突发性神经源性死亡和无影像学检查异常的脊髓损伤

第9章（标题8.7）描述了无影像学检查异常的脊髓损伤，也特别注意到在脊柱弹性比成年人更好的儿童中，此类情况发生的风险会增加（80，81）。高位颈椎，无影像学检查异常的脊髓严重损伤从而导致突发性神经源性死亡。文献中还有一些证据显示，婴儿期非意外性损伤中会发生脊髓性颈椎损伤（82–86）。识别这种情况的标准如下：

- 无其他解释原因的死亡。
- 有目击者描述的造成极端颈部运动的创伤。
- 渗入到颈部肌肉的出血。
- 在高位颈椎区域，沿颈部韧带有局部线性出血的证据。
- 硬脊膜外出血。
- 颈髓白质中的点状出血和有髓纤维变形。

李成志　王磊　杨明真　译

参考文献

1. Natelson, B. H. Neurocardiology. An interdisciplinary area for the 80s. Arch. Neurol. 42:178–184, 1985.

2. Natelson, B. H., Chang, Q. Sudden death. A neurocardiologic phenomenon. Neurol. Clin. 11:293–308, 1993.

3. DiMaio, S. M., DiMaio, V. J., Kirkpatrick, J. B. Sudden, unexpected deaths due to primary intracranial neoplasms. Am. J. Forensic Med. Pathol. 1:29–45, 1980.

4. Aronica, P. A., Ahdab–Barmada, M., Rozin, L., Wecht, C. H. Sudden death in an adolescent boy due to a colloid cyst of the third ventricle. Am. J. Forensic Med. Pathol. 19:119–122, 1998.

5. Lindboe, C. F., Svenes, K. B., Slordal, L. Sudden, unexpected death in subjects with undiagnosed gliomas. Am. J. Forensic Med. Pathol. 18:271–275, 1997.

6. Dolinak, D., Matshes, E., Waghray, R. Sudden unexpected death due to a brainstem glioma in an adult. J. Forensic Sci. 49:128–130, 2004.

7. Gleckman, A. M., Smith, T. W. Sudden unexpected death from primary posterior fossa tumors. Am. J. Forensic Med. Pathol. 19:303–308, 1998.

8. Ortiz–Reyes, R., Dragovic, L., Eriksson, A. Sudden unexpected death resulting from previ– ously nonsymptomatic subependymoma. Am. J. Forensic Med. Pathol. 23:63–67, 2002.

9. Milroy, C. M., Smith, C. L. Sudden death due to a glial cyst of the pineal gland. J. Clin. Pathol. 49:267–269, 1996.
10. Matschke, J., Stavrou, D., Puschel, K. Sudden death resulting from epidermoid cyst of the brain. Am. J. Forensic Med. Pathol. 23:368–370, 2002.
11. Black, M., Graham, D. I. Sudden unexplained death in adults caused by intracranial pathol– ogy. J. Clin. Pathol. 55:44–50, 2002.
12. Matschke, J., Makrigeorgi–Butera, M., Stavrou, D. Sudden death in a 35–year–old man with occult malformation of the brain and aseptic meningitis. Am. J. Forensic Med. Pathol. 24:83–86, 2003.
13. Levy, E. I., Harris, A. E., Omalu, B. I., Hamilton, R. L., Branstetter, B. F., Pollack, I. F. Sudden death from fulminant acute cerebellitis. Pediatr. Neurosurg. 35:24–28, 2001.
14. Maisel, J. A., Lynam, T. Unexpected sudden death in a young pregnant woman: unusual presentation of neurosarcoidosis. Ann. Emerg. Med. 28:94–97, 1996.
15. Barnett, M. H., Prineas, J. W. Relapsing and remitting multiple sclerosis: pathology of the newly forming lesion. Ann. Neurol. 55:458–468, 2004.
16. Wolf, D. A., Veasey, S. P., III, Wilson, S. K., Adame, J., Korndorffer, W. E. Death following minor head trauma in two adult individuals with the Chiari I deformity. J. Forensic Sci. 43:1241–1243, 1998.
17. Locksley, H. B. Natural history of subarachnoid haemorrhage, intracranial aneurysms and arteriovenous malformations. In: Sahs, A. L., ed. Intracranial Aneurysms and Subarachnoid Haemorrhage: A Co–operative Study. Lippinicott, Philadelphia, pp. 35–108, 1969.
18. Dymock, R. B. Traumatic basal subarachnoid haemorrhage. Med. J. Aust. 2:216–218, 1977.
19. Simonsen, J. Fatal subarachnoid haemorrhages in relation to minor injuries in Denmark from 1967 to 1981. Forensic Sci. Int. 24:57–63, 1984.
20. Opeskin, K., Burke, M. P. Vertebral artery trauma. Am. J. Forensic Med. Pathol. 19:206–217, 1998.
21. Coast, G. C., Gee, D. J. Traumatic subarachnoid haemorrhage: an alternative source. J. Clin. Pathol. 37:1245–1248, 1984.
22. Deck, J. H., Jagadha, V. Fatal subarachnoid hemorrhage due to traumatic rupture of the vertebral artery. Arch. Pathol. Lab. Med. 110:489–493, 1986.
23. Miyazaki, T., Kojima, T., Chikasue, F., Yashiki, M., Ito, H. Traumatic rupture of intracranial vertebral artery due to hyperextension of the head: reports on three cases. Forensic Sci. Int. 47:91–98, 1990.
24. Takahara, T., Terai, C., Okada, Y., Mimura, K., Mukaida, M. Fatal traumatic subarachnoid

hemorrhage due to rupture of the vertebral artery. Intensive Care Med. 19:172–173, 1993.

25. Johnson, P., Burns, J. Extracranial vertebral artery injury—evolution of a pathological illusion? Forensic Sci. Int. 73:75–78, 1995.

26. Dolman CL. Rupture of posterior inferior cerebellar artery by single blow to head. Arch. Pathol. Lab. Med. 110:494–496, 1986.

27. Gross, A. Traumatic basal subarachnoid hemorrhages: autopsy material analysis. Forensic Sci. Int. 45:53–61, 1990.

28. Farag, A. M., Franks, A., Gee, D. J. Simple laboratory experiments to replicate some of the stresses on vertebro–basilar arterial walls. An investigation of possible mechanisms of trau– matic subarachnoid haemorrhage. Forensic Sci. Int. 38:275–284, 1988.

29. Pollanen, M. S., Deck, J. H., Boutilier, L., Davidson, G. Lesions of the tunica media in trau– matic rupture of vertebral arteries: histologic and biochemical studies. Can. J. Neurol. Sci. 19:53–56, 1992.

30. Dowling, G., Curry, B. Traumatic basal subarachnoid hemorrhage. Report of six cases and review of the literature. Am. J. Forensic Med. Pathol. 9:23–31, 1988.

31. Leadbeatter, S. Extracranial vertebral artery injury—evolution of a pathological illusion? Forensic Sci. Int. 67:33–40, 1994.

32. Bromilow, A., Burns, J. Technique for removal of the vertebral arteries. J. Clin. Pathol. 38:1400–1402, 1985.

33. Ludwig, J. Handbook of Autopsy Practice, Third Edition. Humana Press, Totowa, NJ, 2002.

34. Vanezis, P. Techniques used in the evaluation of vertebral artery trauma at postmortem. Forensic Sci. Int. 13:159–165, 1979.

35. Johnson, P., Burns J. Letter to the Editor. Forensic Sci. Int. 73:75–76, 1995.

36. Leadbeatter, S. Letter to the Editor: Reply to Johnson and Burns. Forensic Sci. Int. 73:77–78, 1995.

37. Schievink, W. I. Spontaneous dissection of the carotid and vertebral arteries. N. Engl. J. Med. 344:898–906, 2001.

38. DiMaio, V. J., DiMaio, D. Forensic Pathology. Second ed. CRC Press, Boca Raton, FL, 2001.

39. Milovanovic, A. V., DiMaio, V. J. Death due to concussion and alcohol. Am. J. Forensic Med. Pathol. 20:6–9, 1999.

40. Ramsay, D. A., Shkrum, M. J. Homicidal blunt head trauma, diffuse axonal injury, alcoholic intoxication, and cardiorespiratory arrest: a case report of a forensic syndrome of acute brainstem dysfunction. Am. J. Forensic Med. Pathol. 16:107–114, 1995.

41. Gennarelli, T., Segawa, H., Wald, U., Czernicki, Z., Marsh, K., Thompson, C. Physiological

response to angular acceleration of the head. In: Grossman, R. G., Gildenberg, P. L., eds. Head Injury: Basic and Clinical Aspects (Seminars in Neurological Surgery). Raven Press, New York, pp. 129–140, 1982.

42. Miller, J. D. Physiology of trauma. Clin. Neurosurg. 29:103–130, 1982.
43. Nilsson, B., Ponten, U., Voigt, G. Experimental head injury in the rat. Part 1: Mechanics, pathophysiology, and morphology in an impact acceleration trauma model. J. Neurosurg. 47:241–251, 1977.
44. Brown, F. D., Jafar, J. J., Krieger, K., Johns, L., Leipzig, T. J., Mullan, S. Cardiac and cerebral changes following experimental head injury. In: Grossman, R. G., Gildenberg, P. L., eds. Head Injury: Basic and Clinical Aspects (Seminars in Neurological Surgery). Raven Press, New York, pp. 151–157, 1982.
45. Millen, J. E., Glauser, F. L., Zimmerman, M. Physiological effects of controlled concussive brain trauma. J. Appl. Physiol. 49:856–862, 1980.
46. Hilton, D. L., Jr., Einhaus, S. L., Meric, A. L., III, et al. Early assessment of neurological deficits in the fluid percussion model of brain injury. J. Neurotrauma 10:121–133, 1993.
47. Rosner, M. J. Systemic response to experimental brain injury. In: Becker, D. P., Povlishock, J. T., eds. Central Nervous System Trauma Status Report. National Institute of Neurological and Communicative Disorders and Stroke, Washington, DC, pp. 404–415, 1985.
48. Levine, J. E., Becker, D., Chun, T. Reversal of incipient brain death from head–injury apnea at the scene of accidents. N. Engl. J. Med. 301:109, 1979.
49. Sun, M. K., Reis, D. J. Effects of systemic ethanol on medullary vasomotor neurons and baroreflexes. Neurosci. Lett. 137:232–236, 1992.
50. Carlen, P. L., Zhang, L. A., Cullen, N. Cellular electrophysiological actions of ethanol on mammalian neurons in brain slices. Ann. N. Y. Acad. Sci. 625:17–25, 1991.
51. Engberg, G., Hajos, M. Ethanol attenuates the response of locus coeruleus neurons to excita– tory amino acid agonists in vivo. Naunyn Schmiedebergs Arch. Pharmacol. 345:222–226, 1992.
52. Zink, B. J., Feustel, P. J. Effects of ethanol on respiratory function in traumatic brain injury. J. Neurosurg. 82:822–828, 1995.
53. Crockard,, H. A., Brown, F. D., Calica, A. B., Johns, L. M., Mullan, S. Physiological con– sequences of experimental cerebral missile injury and use of data analysis to predict sur– vival. J. Neurosurg. 46:784–794, 1977.
54. Crockard, H. A., Brown, F. D., Johns, L. M., Mullan, S. An experimental cerebral missile injury model in primates. J. Neurosurg. 46:776–783, 1977.
55. Bean, J. W., Beckman, D. L. Centrogenic pulmonary pathology in mechanical head injury. J.

Appl. Physiol. 27:807–812, 1969.

56. Ettinger, P. O., Wu, C. F., De La Cruz, C., Jr., Weisse, A. B., Ahmed, S. S., Regan, T. J. Arrhythmias and the "Holiday Heart": alcohol–associated cardiac rhythm disorders. Am. Heart J. 95:555–562, 1978.

57. Greenspon, A. J., Schaal, S. F. The "holiday heart": electrophysiologic studies of alcohol effects in alcoholics. Ann. Intern. Med. 98:135–139, 1983.

58. Wannamethee, G., Shaper, A. G. Alcohol and sudden cardiac death. Br. Heart J. 68:443–448, 1992.

59. Gordon, T., Kannel, W. B. Drinking habits and cardiovascular disease: the Framingham Study. Am. Heart J. 105:667–673, 1983.

60. Lithell, H., Aberg, H., Selinus, I., Hedstrand, H. Alcohol intemperance and sudden death. Br. Med. J. (Clin. Res. Ed.) 294:1456–1458, 1987.

61. Nashef, L., Brown, S. Epilepsy and sudden death. Lancet 348:1324–1325, 1996.

62. Leestma, J. E., Hughes, J. R., Teas, S. S., Kalelkar, M. B. Sudden epilepsy deaths and the forensic pathologist. Am. J. Forensic Med. Pathol. 6:215–218, 1985.

63. Leestma, J. E., Kalelkar, M. B., Teas, S. S., Jay, G. W., Hughes, J. R. Sudden unexpected death associated with seizures: analysis of 66 cases. Epilepsia 25:84–88, 1984.

64. Opeskin, K., Berkovic, S. F. Risk factors for sudden unexpected death in epilepsy: a controlled prospective study based on coroners cases. Seizure 12:456–464, 2003.

65. Langan, Y., Nashef, L., Sander, J. W. A. S. Sudden unexpected death in epilepsy: a series of witnessed deaths. J. Neurol. Neurosurg. Psychiat. 68:211–213, 2000.

66. Ficker, D. M. Sudden unexplained death and injury in epilepsy. Epilepsia 41 Suppl. 2:S7–S12, 2000.

67. Langan, Y. Sudden unexpected death in epilepsy (SUDEP): risk factors and case control studies. Seizure 9:179–183, 2000.

68. Dasheiff, R. M., Dickinson, L. J. Sudden unexpected death of epileptic patient due to cardiac arrhythmia after seizure. Arch. Neurol. 43:194–196, 1986.

69. Fincham, R. W., Shivapour, E. T., Leis, A. A., Martins, J. B. Ictal bradycardia with syncope: a case report. Neurology 42:2222–2223, 1992.

70. Nashef, L., Walker, F., Allen, P., Sander, J. W., Shorvon, S. D., Fish, D. R. Apnoea and bradycardia during epileptic seizures: relation to sudden death in epilepsy. J. Neurol. Neurosurg. Psychiatry 60:297–300, 1996.

71. Terrence, C. F., Rao, G. R., Perper, J. A. Neurogenic pulmonary edema in unexpected, unexplained death of epileptic patients. Ann. Neurol. 9:458–464, 1981.

72. Natelson, B. H., Suarez, R. V., Terrence, C. F., Turizo, R. Patients with epilepsy who die

suddenly have cardiac disease. Arch. Neurol. 55:857–860, 1998.

73. Leestma, J. E., Walczak, T., Hughes, J. R., Kalelkar, M. B., Teas, S. S. A prospective study on sudden unexpected death in epilepsy. Ann. Neurol. 26:195–203, 1989.

74. Leestma, J. E. Forensic aspects of general neuropathology. In: Leestma, J. E., ed. Forensic Neuropathology. Raven Press, New York, pp. 24–156, 1988.

75. Abboud, H., Berroir, S., Labreuche, J., Orjuela, K., Amarenco, P. Insular involvement in brain infarction increases risk for cardiac arrythmia and death. Ann. Neurol. 59:691–699, 2006.

76. Jaster, J. H., Smith, T. W. Arrhythmia mechanism of unexpected sudden death following lateral medullary infarction. Tenn. Med. 91:284, 1998.

77. Jaster, J. H., Porterfield, L. M., Bertorini, T. E., Dohan, F. C., Jr., Becske, T. Cardiac arrest following vertebrobasilar stroke. J. Tenn. Med. Assoc. 88:309, 1995.

78. Jaster, J. H., Porterfield, L. M., Bertorini, T. E., Dohan, F. C., Jr., Becske, T. Stroke and cardiac arrest. Neurology 47:1357, 1996.

79. De Caro, R., Parenti, A., Montisci, M., Guidolin, D., Macchi, V. Solitary tract nuclei in acute heart failure. Stroke 31:1187–1193, 2000.

80. Hadley, M. N., Zabramski, J. M., Browner, C. M., Rekate, H., Sonntag, V. K. Pediatric spinal trauma. Review of 122 cases of spinal cord and vertebral column injuries. J. Neurosurg. 68:18–24, 1988.

81. Pang, D., Wilberger, J. E. Spinal cord without radiographic abnormalities in children. J. Neurosurg. 57:114–129, 1982.

82. Geddes, J. F., Hackshaw, A. K., Vowles, G. H., Nickols, C. D., Whitwell, H. L. Neuropathology of inflicted head injury in children. I. Patterns of brain damage. Brain 124:1290–1298, 2001.

83. Geddes, J. F., Vowles, G. H., Hackshaw, A. K., Nickols, C. D., Scott, I. S., Whitwell, H. L. Neuropathology of inflicted head injury in children. II. Microscopic brain injury in infants. Brain 124:1299–1306, 2001.

84. Ghatan, S., Ellenbogen, R. G. Pediatric spine and spinal cord injury after inflicted trauma. Neurosurg. Clin. N. Am. 13:227–233, 2002.

85. Hadley, M. N., Sonntag, V. K., Rekate, H. L., Murphy, A. The infant whiplash–shake injury syndrome: a clinical and pathological study. Neurosurgery 24:536–540, 1989.

86. Piatt, J. H., Jr., Steinberg, M. Isolated spinal cord injury as a presentation of child abuse. Pediatrics 96:780–782, 1995.

图书在版编目（CIP）数据

法医损伤病理学 /（加）迈克尔·J. 史克朗姆,（加）大卫·A. 拉姆齐著；陈忆九，黄平主译 . 一上海：上海科学技术文献出版社，2022

ISBN 978-7-5439-8218-5

Ⅰ. 法… Ⅱ. ①迈… ②大… ③陈… ④黄… Ⅲ. ①法医损伤学—病理学 Ⅳ. ① D919.4

中国版本图书馆 CIP 数据核字 (2021) 第 212556 号

Forensic Pathology of Trauma
First published in English under the title
Forensic Pathology of Trauma
by Michael J. Shkrum and David A. Ramsay
Copyright © Humana Press, 2007
This edition has been translated and published under licence from
Springer Science+Business Media, LLC, part of Springer Nature.

Copyright in the Chinese language translation (simplified character rights only) © 2021
Shanghai Scientific and Technological Literature Press

版权所有，翻印必究

图字：09-2019-282

责任编辑：王　珺
装帧设计：方　明

法医损伤病理学

FAYI SUNSHANG BINGLIXUE

[加] 迈克尔·J. 史克朗姆　大卫·A. 拉姆齐 著　陈忆九　黄　平 主译

出版发行：上海科学技术文献出版社
地　　址：上海市长乐路 746 号
邮政编码：200040
经　　销：全国新华书店
印　　刷：上海新开宝商务印刷有限公司
开　　本：787mm×1092mm　1/16
印　　张：41.75
版　　次：2022 年 1 月第 1 版　2022 年 1 月第 1 次印刷
书　　号：ISBN 978-7-5439-8218-5
定　　价：298.00 元
http://www.sstlp.com